THE GUINNESS
TELEVISION
ENCYCLOPEDIA

JEFF EVANS

GUINNESS PUBLISHING

Project Editor: Tina Persaud
Page make up: Sallie Collins
Adviser: P. R. Jackson
Cover illustrations: Front – Trevor McDonald (ITN News), BAFTA logo
(The British Academy Award is based on a design by Mitzi Cunliffe),
BBC TV test card (© BBC. Licenced by BBC Worldwide Limited),
The Big Breakfast's Zig and Zag (Channel 4), Grant and Sharon of
EastEnders (Syndication International), Maddie and David of
Moonlighting (Courtesy of ABC Cable and International Broadcast, Inc.),
Alexandra Palace mast (BBC 1935). Back – BBC TV production booth
(reproduced by the kind permission of BBC Television Centre Studios).

Published in Great Britain by Guinness Publishing Ltd
33 London Road, Enfield, Middlesex EN2 6DJ

'GUINNESS' is a registered trademark of Guinness Publishing Ltd

First published in 1995
Reprint 10 9 8 7 6 5 4 3 2 1 0

Printed and bound in Great Britain by Bath Press

ISBN 0-85112-744-4

A catalogue record for this book is available from the British Library

INTRODUCTION

Mountaineers claim to climb peaks 'because they're there'. Conversely, this book was written precisely because such a volume did not exist. You can't move in bookshops these days for the number of film guides which pack the shelves. But, until now, if you tried looking for one book which comprehensively and factually covered the world of television you would have been sadly disappointed.

That is not to say that no-one has published books on TV matters. There have been scores of titles on specific genres like science fiction, children's programmes, classic drama, police series, comedies and soap opera. There have also been 'overview' books that have chronologically traced the development of British television, and books tied into individual series like *Coronation Street*, *The Bill*, *The Avengers*, *Inspector Morse* and *Neighbours*. However, there hasn't been a work that, in one single volume, has provided in-depth details about historic TV programmes and the people who made them. At a time when classic television is big business, with repeats now revered rather than reviled, satellite channels specialising in archive material and videotapes of past treasures topping the sales charts, such a book is surely overdue.

The Guinness TV Encyclopedia, therefore, aims to give the facts – 'Just the facts', as Sgt Joe Friday of *Dragnet* would have put it. This book has been written not by a professional critic or a TV insider. It has been written by a viewer for the viewer, with the goal of providing the sort of details the viewer will want to know. There are no attempts to rate or criticize programmes or performers. Instead, priority has been given to hard information, both important and trivial. Anyone seeking that odd fact will, hopefully, find it here and anyone casually browsing through is likely to find themselves drawn nostalgically back into the golden days of television.

There are over 1000 programmes featured in this book. They are listed with their country of origin, production company, UK transmission channel and transmission dates (where available). Cast lists of the regular characters follow, then major production credits, centring on creators, writers and the most prominent producers of programmes (these being the main creative forces). Each programme's description covers the general concept, the main storylines, character details and a good dose of trivia. There are also around 1400 entries for TV stars and behind the scenes contributors. Each person's major television work has been highlighted, although film and theatre credits (falling outside the brief) have been largely ignored. Real names and dates of birth have been

provided where obtainable, although some performers are famously shy about their ages and others, understandably, prefer their privacy respected in such matters.

So what is and isn't included? One thing I have learned while compiling this book is that any attempt to lay down hard and fast ground rules is sure to end in dissatisfaction. It is possible, for instance, to restrict programme entries to those that have attracted the most viewers, based on the ratings charts. Except that this instantly precludes programmes on the 'minority' channels BBC 2 and Channel 4. Would the book be complete without *M*A*S*H*, *GBH* or *Cheers*? Based on the ratings charts, it would also rule out children's programmes and other daytime offerings. Another option would have been to consider including only award-winning programmes, peak-hour programming or only UK-produced programmes, but these formats would fall down in similar ways. Consequently, I have adopted a loose set of criteria for the programmes featured in this book. These involve general acclaim, historical significance, biggest audiences, cult status and nostalgia value. The programmes cover nearly all fields: dramas, documentaries, situation comedies, variety shows, current affairs series, children's favourites, quiz shows, panel games, sports programmes, soap opera, mini-series and important one-off plays. TV movies, however, have not been included. As a result, the following pages are a tribute to the good, the bad and the sometimes very ugly moments in TV's past. You will find everything from the most critically acclaimed to the most cruelly derided, and even some programmes you may just have forgotten.

The entries for people are similarly based on those who have contributed most, or enjoyed most success, in television's first 60 years. They include actors, comedians, comediennes, presenters, writers, producers and executives. To complete the picture, there are also entries for television companies and explanations of some of the technical terms that confront the viewer on a day-to-day basis as programme credits roll by.

Researching this book has been great fun. It has also proved rather frustrating at times. For instance, whilst there has been no shortage of information about American programmes, vintage British television is shrouded in obscurity. The main reason for this is that many US programmes (pre-videotape) were captured on film and have, therefore, been preserved. British programmes in the 1940s and 1950s mostly went out live and any primitive recordings which were made, together with episodes of 1960s classics like *Doctor Who* and *Steptoe and Son*, were famously wiped as an economy and space-saving measure by the BBC in the 1970s. Thankfully, written sources like *Radio Times* and *TV Times* have survived to help steer the confused researcher along his way. Inevitably, however, the detail unearthed about early British programmes is rather thinner than for American contemporaries.

Transmission dates have proved to be another thorny area. Some overseas programmes screened on ITV have not been fully networked, for instance, and have only been seen in some areas. The regions have also transmitted episodes out of sequence, sometimes years apart. It does not follow that the region offering the first ever transmission of a programme will also be the first to show the last episode. Consequently, while I have attempted to give the earliest date such a programme was screened in the UK, I have thought it wiser to omit the last transmission date, where it is unclear, to avoid confusion. Otherwise, programmes are listed with their first and last transmission dates. Where a break of more than one year has occurred during the programme's run, this has been indicated with separate sets of dates. Only the original transmissions (not repeats) have been charted. Programmes shown on BBC Television before the advent of BBC 2 (and therefore BBC 1) in 1964 have the channel listing 'BBC' only. Those beginning before, and continuing after, the BBC was split into two channels have the listing 'BBC 1' or 'BBC 2',

depending on which channel they were subsequently allocated. TV programmes that have an entry of their own are indicated by bold italics in the text.

As well as the two listings magazines and the specialist programme publications mentioned earlier, the author would like to acknowledge the assistance of the BBC Written Archives Centre (Neil Somerville in particular), the staff of the ITC library and numerous press officers and agents for the help they have willingly given during the last four years of research. A big thank you to my wife Jacquie, and son, Christopher, for their endless support and for allowing me this huge indulgence. There are so many facts and figures in this book that it would be a miracle if all were totally correct, and, if you know better, your comments will be more than welcome. Television archaeology is still a relatively new art and all encouragement will be gratefully received. As already stated, the book has been fun to compile. I hope it will provide as much pleasure to the reader – be they historian, media analyst, nostalgia freak, quiz buff, couch potato, or, like me, a mixture of all five.

Happy viewing!

Jeff Evans

A FOR ANDROMEDA/ANDROMEDA BREAKTHROUGH, THE

UK (BBC) Science Fiction. BBC 1961/1962

John Fleming ....Peter Halliday
Professor Reinhart ....Esmond Knight
Dr Geers...Geoffrey Lewis
Dr Madeleine Dawnay ....Mary Morris
Christine/Andromeda
  (A for Andromeda) ....Julie Christie
  (Breakthrough) ....Susan Hampshire
Dennis Bridger......................................Frank Windsor
Dr Hunter..Peter Ducrow
Harvey ....John Murray-Scott
Judy Adamson.....................................Patricia Kneale
Major Quadring ....Jack May
Harries ....John Nettleton
J.M. Osborne ....Noel Johnson
General Vandenberg ....Donald Stewart
Minister of Science ....Ernest Hare
Prime Minister ....Maurice Hedley
Defence Minister ....David King
Kaufman...John Hollis
Egon ....Peter Henchie
Professor Neilson (Breakthrough) ....Walter Gotell
Mlle Gamboule (Breakthrough) ....Claude Farell
Colonel Salim (Breakthrough) ....Barry Linehan
Dr Abu Zeki (Breakthrough) ....David Saire
President of Azaran
  (Breakthrough)..................................Arnold Yarrow

Writers: Fred Hoyle, John Elliot. Producers: Michael Hayes, Norman Jones (*A for Andromeda*), John Elliot (*Breakthrough*)

A beautiful girl is created by a sinister alien computer.

In 1970 (nine years into the future), a radio telescope in the Yorkshire Dales, managed by Professor Reinhart, picked up a series of signals from the direction of the constellation Andromeda. Working through the messages, brilliant scientist John Fleming concluded that they formed plans for a highly sophisticated computer. In a top secret project, sponsored by the government and hidden away on a remote Scottish island, he followed the alien instructions and built the machine. A battle then began for the use of its powers between good and bad scientists, government agencies and the Swiss business cartel Intel, headed by the evil Kaufman.

Through collaboration with amoral biologist Madeleine Dawnay, the computer succeeded in developing an embryo, based on the biological blueprint of Christine, a lab assistant it had electrocuted. The embryo rapidly blossomed into a replica of the girl (though blonde not brunette, as Christine had been) and was given the name of Andromeda. Unfortunately, the replica girl was mentally linked to the corrupt machine and became its agent. It wasn't until the conscientious Fleming drew her warmer, more human emo-

tions to the fore that she was able to break free from her computer master.

In a sequel series, *The Andromeda Breakthrough*, shown a year later, Fleming and Andromeda – now enjoying a more romantic relationship – were kidnapped by Intel and imprisoned in the Middle Eastern country of Azaran, Intel with the help of Dawnay, were still trying to create their own computer. Another threat came from a toxic enzyme, which had been released by the original machine and was slowly suffocating the Earth. In this follow-up, the part of Andromeda was taken over by Susan Hampshire.

Now recognized as classic TV science fiction, *A for Andromeda* and *The Andromeda Breakthrough* were created by BBC producer John Elliot from a storyline by Cambridge astronomer and novelist Fred Hoyle. *A for Andromeda* was the BBC's first attempt at adult science fiction since the **Quatermass** serials and is well remembered for giving young drama school student Julie Christie her first starring role.

A.J. WENTWORTH, BA

UK (Thames) Situation Comedy. ITV 1982

A.J. Wentworth.......................................Arthur Lowe
Matron...Marion Mathie
Reverend R.G. Saunders
  ('Headmaster') ....Harry Andrews
Rawlinson ....Ronnie Stevens
Gilbert ....Michael Bevis
Miss Coombes.......................................Debbie Davies

Writer: Basil Boothroyd. Producer: Michael Mills

The exploits of an absent-minded schoolteacher.

In his last TV series, recorded just weeks before he died, Arthur Lowe played a maths teacher in a 1940s prep school who was obsessed with old-fashioned school virtues. Fighting internal battles with his arch-enemy, Matron, the disaster-prone teacher (who was weak on discipline but strong on dignity) was constantly preoccupied by such trivial matters as the high cost of pen nibs. The snobbish cleric Reverend R.G. Saunders was the school's headmaster. The series was based on stories by H.F. Ellis, although just six episodes were made.

A-TEAM, THE

US (Universal/Stephen J. Cannell) Adventure. ITV 1983–8

Colonel John 'Hannibal' Smith ....George Peppard
Sgt Bosco 'BA' Baracus........Mr T (Lawrence Tureaud)
Lt Templeton Peck ('Faceman') ....Dirk Benedict

Captain HM 'Howling Mad'
Murdock ....Dwight Schultz
Amy Amanda Allen ('Triple A') ....Melinda Culea
Colonel Lynch ....William Lucking
Colonel Roderick Decker ....Lance LeGault
Tawnia Baker ....Maria Heasley
General Hunt Stockwell ....Robert Vaughn
'Dishpan' Frankie Sanchez ....Eddie Velez
Carla ....Judy Ledford

Creators/Executive Producers: Stephen J. Cannell, Frank Lupo

Four soldiers of fortune, all Vietnam veterans, use their diverse skills to help citizens in trouble.

The A-Team, an unlikely group of heroic renegades, had worked together as commandos in the Vietnam War, only to be captured behind enemy lines and accused of raiding the Bank of Hanoi four days after the war had ended. They maintained they were under orders to do so, but, with no proof, the gang were imprisoned by their own country. Following their escape, the series told how they evaded attempts to recapture them, firstly by Colonel Lynch, then Colonel Decker, and their mercenary-style righting of wrongs along the way.

Each member of the Team was a specialist. The cigar-chewing leader, Hannibal Smith, was a master of disguise; Howling Mad Murdock was a brilliant but crazy pilot, who had to be sprung from a psychiatric hospital to join the Team on their missions; the gold-swathed BA ('Bad Attitude') was the inventive mechanic, a Mohican-haired giant of a man who, none the less, dreaded flying with Murdock, while Faceman (played by Tim Dunigan in the pilot episode) was the smooth talker and procurer of their material needs. Together they travelled the world in a heavily-armed transit van, initially accompanied by attractive journalist Amy Allen.

Although their escapades were often violent, they were never gory. This was comic-book action, with plenty of crashes and explosions but little blood. A few years into the programme's run, the guys were eventually caught by General Stockwell, but they evaded the firing squad by becoming undercover Government agents. At this time, a new addition, Dishpan, a special effects expert, joined the squad.

ABBOT, RUSS (RUSS ROBERTS; 1948–)

Tall, twinkly eyed comedian and impressionist who entered showbiz as a member of the Black Abbots cabaret group. His big TV break came from appearances in *Bruce Forsyth's Big Night* in 1980 and led directly to a series he shared with Freddie Starr, *Variety Madhouse*. With Starr's

departure, the show became *Russ Abbot's Saturday Madhouse* (later just *Russ Abbot's Madhouse*) and featured farcical creations such as inept superhero Cooperman (an exaggerated impersonation of Tommy Cooper), secret agent Basildon Bond, air ace Boggles, Irish crooner Val Hooligan, rock 'n' roller Vince Prince and C.U. Jimmy, the indecipherable, kilted Scotsman. The same format was applied when the show switched to BBC 1 in 1986 and became *The Russ Abbot Show*. Back on ITV in 1994, Abbot pioneered some new creations, including the Noisy Family, Clueless Cleric and the good folk of Pimpletown, such as Percy Pervert and Mrs Verruca. In his comedy work he has been well supported by the likes of Bella Emberg, Les Dennis, Dustin Gee, Michael Barrymore and Jeffrey Holland, but Abbot has also enjoyed success in serious roles, most notably as Ted Fenwick in two series of *September Song*, alongside Michael Williams.

ABC

Early ITV franchise holder covering the Midlands and the North of England at weekends only. An offshoot of the ABC (Associated British Cinemas) theatre chain, the company was mostly owned by ABPC (Associated British Picture Corporation), although Warners also held shares in the 1950s. ABC went on air on 18 February 1956 in the Midlands and on 5 May 1956 in the North. Its network programming successes included *Armchair Theatre*, *Opportunity Knocks* and *The Avengers*. At the behest of the ITA, during the 1968 franchise reassessments, the company merged with Associated-Rediffusion to create Thames Television. ABC then gave up its Midlands and North of England franchises, but, as Thames, took over London's Monday to Friday coverage.

ABC (AMERICAN BROADCASTING COMPANY)

American television network, for years the least successful of the three national networks. It was founded in 1943 by Edward J. Noble, the maker of Life Savers confectionery, when he purchased a radio network from NBC. In 1953 the company merged with United Paramount Theaters. Despite struggling against its competitors CBS and NBC from its earliest days (largely because it owned fewer affiliate stations), ABC has nevertheless made its mark on US television history. It was the first company to bring Hollywood studios into TV production, thereby accelerating the move from live to filmed broadcasts. It notched numerous sports firsts in the USA and amongst its programming successes have been *The Wonderful World of Disney*, *Batman* and three of the biggest ever mini-series: *Roots*, *The Thorn Birds* and *The Winds of War*. By the end of the 1970s, ABC had elevated itself into the top bracket of US TV, becoming a very serious competitor to the two big networks. The company was bought by Capital Cities Communications in 1986.

ABOUT THE HOME

UK (BBC) Magazine. BBC 1951–8

Presenter: Joan Gilbert

Producer: S.E. Reynolds

Practical tips for housewives.

This long-running afternoon programme was designed to help housewives improve their domestic skills, such as cookery and needlework, although other items covered included shopping, deportment and even puppy training. Home improvement tips from Barry Bucknell proved so popular that he gained his own series, *Do It Yourself*, in 1957.

ABSOLUTELY

UK (Absolutely) Comedy. Channel 4 1989–93

Gordon Kennedy
Jack Docherty
Moray Hunter
Morwenna Banks
Peter Baikie
John Sparkes

Producers: Alan Nixon, David Tyler

Eccentric comedy sketch show with a Scottish accent.

Absolutely drew together some of Scotland's new breed of comics and gave them a licence for creativity. The result was a collection of surreal and silly sketches. Morwenna Banks perfected the 'Yes, it's twue', worldly wise junior schoolgirl, Moray Hunter became the anoraky Calum Gilhooley, and the Welsh member of the team, John Sparkes, created accident prone DIY expert Denzil and the lavatorial Frank Hovis. The parish council of the fictitious village of Stoneybridge was also featured on a regular basis, and with Jack Docherty portrayed as rabid nationalist McGlashen. Docherty and Hunter (both formerly of *Friday Night Live*) took their creations Donald McDiarmid and George McDiarmid – 'two friends with but a single surname' – into a spin-off series, *Mr Don and Mr George*, in 1993. Gordon Kennedy has since enjoyed prime-time exposure as co-host of *The National Lottery Live*.

ABSOLUTELY FABULOUS

UK (French & Saunders/BBC) Situation Comedy. BBC 2/BBC 1 1992–5

Edina Monsoon ....Jennifer Saunders
Patsy Stone ....Joanna Lumley
Saffron Monsoon ....Julia Sawalha
Bubble ....Jane Horrocks
Mother ....June Whitfield

Creators: Jennifer Saunders, Dawn French. Writer: Jennifer Saunders. Producer: Jon Plowman

The drink- and drug-laden world of a neurotic PR agent and her fashion editor friend.

Edina Monsoon, a single mother of two children, by different fathers, was head of her own public relations agency. Her long-time friend, Patsy Stone, was editor of a fashion magazine. Work for both of them, however, was one long lunchbreak at a trendy restaurant, a spell of shopping at Harvey Nicks or an evening's clubbing. Striving to be seen in all the right places, rubbing shoulders with every celebrity they could find, they ladled out the 'darlings' and 'sweeties' as they struggled to reclaim their late 1960s youth.

Edina shared her three-storey, expensively appointed home in Holland Park with her teenage daughter, Saffron (her son was away at university). However, theirs was not the usual mother–teenager relationship, but quite the reverse. Edina was the disruptive influence staying out late, getting drunk, throwing tantrums and selfishly spoiling all her daughter's fun. Saffy was simply far too sensible to be corrupted by her mother, a plain Jane who preferred science to sex and books to booze. Their incompatibility was highlighted whenever Patsy arrived to drag Edina off to a fashion shoot or some wild party, much to the disapproval of both Saffron and Edina's mother. The archetypal society slag, Patsy lived on a diet of cigarettes, drink, drugs and younger men. She wasn't happy unless she was smoking, slurping, sniffing or sleeping with someone. Also seen was Bubble, Edina's chirpy but brainless northern secretary.

Derived from a sketch in *French and Saunders*, in which Dawn French played the swotty daughter, *Absolutely Fabulous* emerged from its first season clutching a handful of awards, with Joanna Lumley singled out for her successful first stab at comedy and the way in which she gleefully debunked her traditional, aristocratic roles. The second and third seasons earned itself a BBC 1 time slot. The theme song, Bob Dylan's 'This Wheel's on Fire', was sung by Jennifer Saunders's husband, Adrian Edmondson, with Julie Driscoll, vocalist on the original 1968 hit version by the Brian Auger Trinity.

ACCESS TELEVISION

Programmes produced by members of the public or by pressure groups, who are given editorial control of the project but are also offered the assistance of a professional crew. It is otherwise known as public access. The BBC's *Open Door*, beginning in 1973, is one of the most famous British examples, while the wacky *Manhattan Cable* compilations revealed just how much further public access is taken in the USA's cable industry.

ACE OF WANDS

UK (Thames) Children's Adventure. ITV 1970–2

Tarot	Michael MacKenzie
Sam Maxstead	Tony Selby
Lillian ('Lulli') Palmer	Judy Loe
Mr Sweet	Donald Layne-Smith
Mikki	Petra Markham
Chas	Roy Holder

Creator: Trevor Preston. Producers: Pamela Lonsdale, John Russell

A young stage magician tackles crime and evil in his spare time.

Tarot was a magical entertainer, a combination of conjurer and escapologist, whose youthful appearance concealed a mysterious background and a resourceful mind. Billed as 'a 20th-century Robin Hood, with a pinch of Merlin and a dash of Houdini', he was assisted in his adventures by Sam and Lulli. Sam, a reformed ex-convict, shared Tarot's luxury apartment and built many of his stage props, while Lulli, an orphan and fellow telepath, was Tarot's stage partner. Mr Sweet, an eccentric, tweed-suited man who ran an antique bookshop and rode a motorbike, also lent a hand, chipping in with his expert knowledge of the insect world. In the background perched Ozymandias, a Malayan fishing owl.

The so-called 'Ace of Wands' and his companions ran into a host of weird and wonderful, *Batman*-esque supercriminals, with names like Madame Midnight, Mr Stabs and Ceribraun. But perhaps the most sinister was Mama Doc, who turned people into dolls which bled when broken. In the final season, Sam and Lulli were replaced by Mikki and Chas. Mikki, another telepath, worked as a reporter, and Chas was her photographer brother. Mr Sweet, now based at a university, was also seen again.

ACKLAND, JOSS (1928–)

Solid British actor regularly seen in guest star roles. He supported Alec Guinness in *Tinker, Tailor, Soldier, Spy* and also appeared in the ITV George Smiley dramatization, *A Murder of Quality*, as well as playing the spymaster Cumming in Somerset Maugham's *Ashenden*. He was newspaper editor William Stevens in *Kipling*

in 1964, D'Artagnan in the 1967 series *The Further Adventures of the Musketeers*, widower Joseph Lockwood in the sitcom *Thicker Than Water* and for a while took the part of Inspector Todd in *Z Cars*. Other credits have included *Blackmail*, **The Gold Robbers**, **Country Matters**, **The Crezz**, **Enemy at the Door** and *Shadowlands*, plus numerous single dramas.

ADAM ADAMANT LIVES!

UK (BBC) Science Fiction. BBC 1 1966–7

Adam Adamant	Gerald Harper
Georgina Jones	Juliet Harmer
William E. Simms	Jack May
The Face	Peter Ducrow

Creators: Donald Cotton, Richard Harris. Producer: Verity Lambert

An Edwardian adventurer, trapped in ice, thaws out in the swinging Sixties.

Adam Llewellyn De Vere Adamant was a legend in his own lifetime – a smooth, dashing man of action who countered crooks and defended the weak in turn-of- the-century England. However, in 1902, he was ensnared by his arch-enemy, a megalomaniac in a leather mask known only as 'The Face'. Injected with a preservative drug, Adamant was encased in a block of ice and left to posterity. In 1966, a group of London workmen discovered his body and thawed it out. Adam Adamant, now aged 99, but still with the body of a 35-year-old, was back in action.

However, swinging London, buzzing with loud noise, bright lights and the permissive society, confused the revitalized adventurer. To his rescue rode Georgina Jones, a trendy young nightclub DJ and an Adam Adamant fan (having learned from her grandfather about the great man's exploits). Together with Georgie and William E. Simms, a former music hall artist who became his manservant, our hero (still sporting Edwardian clothing) again turned his attentions to the criminal fraternity. They embarked on a series of *Avengers*-style, off-beat adventures, in which Adamant's keen intellect, athletic abilities and adeptness with weapons (especially his sword) were put to excellent use. In the second series, his old enemy, The Face, returned to instigate yet more trouble.

Alive with the colour of Carnaby Street (despite being taped in black and white), *Adam Adamant Lives!* was firmly set in the era of mini-skirts, mods and early psychedelia, with much interest derived from the jarring juxtaposition of Edwardian morals with the liberal society of the 1960s. It provided Gerald Harper with a chance to develop his suave toff image, which reached its pinnacle in **Hadleigh** three years later. It also opened doors for behind-the-scenes crew-members such as Ridley Scott, who went on to direct films like *Alien* and *Blade Runner*. The James Bond-like theme music was sung by Kathy Kirby.

ADAM DALGLIESH see *P.D. James*.

ADAMS, TOM (1938–)

British actor making his TV debut as a crook in *Dixon of Dock Green* and moving on to other supporting, as well as leading, roles, which have generally been of a stern and serious nature. He was Major Sullivan in *Spy Trap*, Dr Wallman in *General Hospital*, DCI Nick Lewis in *The Enigma Files*, Daniel Fogarty in *The Onedin Line* and Mal Bates in *Emmerdale Farm*. Other credits have included *Remington Steele*, *Villains*, *West Country Tales* and *Emergency – Ward 10*.

ADAMSON, PETER (1930–)

Burly, gruffly spoken actor who is remembered by all as Len Fairclough, *Coronation Street*'s 1960s/70s he-man. In the 1950s Adamson enjoyed small parts in Granada series like *Knight Errant* and *Skyport*, before joining the *Street* in 1961. He filled the role of heavy-drinking, womanizing builder Fairclough for 22 years, until alleged off-screen indiscretions led to his dismissal by Granada. The writers had the two-timing Fairclough killed in a car crash on the way home from visiting a mistress. Adamson has since failed to secure another notable TV role and has emigrated to Canada.

ADDAMS FAMILY, THE

US (Filmways) Situation Comedy. ITV 1965–

Morticia Addams	Carolyn Jones
Gomez Addams	John Astin
Uncle Fester Frump	Jackie Coogan
Lurch	Ted Cassidy
Grandmama Addams	Blossom Rock
Pugsley Addams	Ken Weatherwax
Wednesday Thursday Addams	Lisa Loring
Cousin Itt	Felix Silla
Thing	Ted Cassidy

Creator: David Levy

The misadventures of a macabre family, based on the cartoon strip by Charles Addams.

The weird and wonderful Addams Family was headed by Gomez, a lawyer and man of independent wealth, with his sultry, slinky wife, Morticia. They lived in a musty, spooky Victorian mansion, in a street appropriately called Cemetery Ridge, with Morticia's bald, habit-wearing Uncle Fester, Gomez's mother, Grandmama (a witch), their son Pugsley, daughter Wednesday, and a high-pitched, gobbledegook-speaking mass of hair

called Cousin Itt. Their servants were a disembodied hand in a box known as Thing and a 6 ft 9 in butler named Lurch, who groaned the question 'You rang?' when summoned by a gong which shook the whole house.

In line with their strange, but pleasure-filled lifestyle, the family had unusual pets. Gomez took delight in his octopus, Aristotle, Morticia was comforted by her man-eating African Strangler called Cleopatra, and Homer, Wednesday's pet, was a Black Widow spider. For toys, Pugsley had an electric chair and a gallows, while Wednesday played with a headless doll. Gomez, on the other hand, indulged his violent instincts by blowing up toy trains or sword swallowing, if he wasn't fencing his wife or devouring her with kisses at the slightest hint of a French word. Fester lit light bulbs in his mouth, Grandmama practised knife throwing and Lurch was often called upon to play the harpsichord. Cousin Itt was easily pleased: it hung upside down in the chimney. And yet, for all their eccentricities, the Addams Family believed that they were normal and that it was the world around them that was bizarre. As a result, whenever contact was made with neighbours, or other 'ordinary' folk, misunderstanding was rife. The same premise was used in *The Munsters*, which reached TV screens at about the same time. Another memorable feature of the series was its finger-clicking theme song.

The cast had a good pedigree. Carolyn Jones was already a Hollywood name, Astin had previously starred in *I'm Dickens, He's Fenster*, Jackie Coogan had appeared with Chaplin in *The Kid*, at the age of four, and Blossom Rock was the sister of singer Jeanette McDonald. A couple of Addams Family movies followed in the early 1990s, with Anjelica Huston as Morticia and Raul Julia as Gomez.

ADIE, KATE, OBE (1945–)

British news reporter, the BBC's Chief News Correspondent since 1989. Adie joined the BBC in 1969, as a producer in local radio, having spent three years with the National Youth Theatre. She moved to BBC South as a reporter in 1977 and then joined the BBC national news set-up in 1979. In 1980 she covered the seige of the Iranian Embassy in London and went on to make her name as an on-the-spot reporter in the most hazardous situations, in places as diverse as Libya, Tiananmen Square and the Gulf.

ADMAGS

Short for advertising magazines, admags are programmes that are used to promote commercial products, generally employing less than subtle techniques. The practice was commonplace in Britain following the advent of ITV in 1955 but was outlawed by Parliament in 1963. Probably the best remembered admag is *Jim's Inn*, a pub-orientated programme set in the fictitious village of Wembleham, hosted by 'landlords' Jimmy and Maggie Hanley. Customers used to wander in and discuss their latest bargains over a pint or two. Other notable admags in the UK were Noele Gordon's *Homes and Gardens* (1956), Peter Butterworth and Janet Brown's *Where Shall We Go?* (also 1956) and John Slater's *Slater's Bazaar* (from 1957).

ADVENTURER, THE

UK (ITC) Secret Agent Drama. ITV 1972–3

Gene Bradley	Gene Barry
Mr Parminter	Barry Morse
Diane Marsh	Catherine Schell
Gavin Jones	Garrick Hagon
Vince	Stuart Damon

Producer: Monty Berman

A US secret agent operates under the cover of an international film star.

Gene Bradley was a wealthy, jet-setting movie celebrity who indulged himself in business ventures of all kinds, but whose real job involved secret assignments for US intelligence. Employing his acting skills to the full and taking on various disguises, Bradley was an international knight who came to the rescue of threatened women, defecting scientists and others in need of assistance. His assignments were given to him by his 'manager', Mr Parminter, and he was accompanied by fellow agent Gavin Jones. Diane was his contact with the agency. John Barry provided the theme music.

ADVENTURES OF BLACK BEAUTY, THE

UK (LWT/Talbot/Freemantle) Children's Adventure. ITV 1972–74

Dr James Gordon	William Lucas
Victoria Gordon	Judi Bowker
Kevin Gordon	Roderick Shaw
Jenny Gordon	Stacy Dorning
Amy Winthrop	Charlotte Mitchell
Albert	Tom Maidea
Squire Armstrong	Michael Culver

Executive Producer: Paul Knight. Producer: Sidney Cole

A black stallion is the pride and joy of a young Victorian girl.

This series, based on Anna Sewell's classic children's novel, was set in 1877 on a spacious English country estate. Vicky Gordon was the young owner of a thoroughbred, Black Beauty, who had been badly treated by a succession of cruel owners before Vicky and her family took him in and nursed him back to health. Brother Kevin and sister Jenny lent a hand and their dad, a doctor, and Amy, his housekeeper, were also drawn into the horsy goings-on. Most stories had little to do with the original book.

ADVENTURES OF CHAMPION, The see *Champion the Wonder Horse*.

ADVENTURES OF LONG JOHN SILVER, THE

Australia (Isola dell'Oro) Adventure. ITV 1957

Long John Silver	Robert Newton
Jim Hawkins	Kit Taylor
Purity Pinker	Connie Gilchrist
Israel Hands	Rodney Taylor
Billy Bowledge	Henry Gilbert
Mendoza	Lloyd Berrell
Patch	Grant Taylor
Governor Strong	Harvey Adams

Producers: Mark Evans, Joseph Kaufman

The further adventures of *Treasure Island*'s scurrilous, one-legged ship's cook.

In this TV follow-up to successful cinema films, Silver and his cabin-boy friend, Jim Hawkins, were based on Portobello, an island in the Spanish Main in the 1700s. Here they worked on behalf of Governor Strong, thwarting the advances of the Spanish fleet and preserving the island for the British Crown, with a dash of treasure hunting thrown in for good measure. Off-duty, the rolling-eyed, bearded grog-swiller could be found in Purity Pinker's pub. Sadly, Robert Newton died not long after this series was made.

ADVENTURES OF RIN-TIN-TIN, THE

US (Herbert B. Leonard/Screen Gems) Children's Adventure. ITV 1956–61

Corporal Rusty 'B' Company	Lee Aaker
Lt Ripley 'Rip' Masters	James L. Brown
Sgt Aloysius 'Biff' O'Hara	Joe Sawyer
Corporal Randy Boone	Rand Brooks
Colonel Barker	John Hoyt

Producer: Herbert B. Leonard

An orphan and his talented Alsatian become members of a US Cavalry troop.

Discovered as the two survivors of a wagon train raid sometime in the 1880s, 11-year-old Rusty and his pet German Shepherd dog, Rin-Tin-Tin, were rescued by 'B' Company of the 101st Cavalry unit 'The Fighting Blue Devils'. Taken back to the Fort Apache camp, somewhere near the fictional town of Mesa Grande in Arizona, they were adopted by Lt Rip Masters and Sgt Biff O'Hara and became members of the troop. Fearing discovery, Rusty and 'Rinty' hid themselves away when an important officer, Colonel Barker, arrived for an inspection. While hiding, however, they unearthed a plot against the Colonel's life. Saving the day, Rusty was awarded corporal stripes and invited to live on the base with 'Private' Rinty (Rin Tin Tin) for as long as he wished.

So began *The Adventures of Rin-Tin-Tin*. The action dog, a great rival of the collie Lassie, was quickly at the forefront of Cavalry activity, leading charges against Apache Indians (spurred on by a 'Yo ho, Rinty'), sniffing out danger and wresting weapons from enemy hands. Two of the dogs that played the lead were actually descendants of the former German army dog whose movie debut came in 1923 in the film *Where the North Begins*. He was such a box-office hit in those silent days that he saved Warner Brothers from bankruptcy. In this 1950s series, he generated a new legion of young fans.

ADVENTURES OF ROBIN HOOD, THE

UK (ITC/Sapphire) Adventure. ITV 1955–9

Robin Hood ....Richard Greene
Maid Marian ....Bernadette O'Farrell
                                                  Patricia Driscoll
Friar Tuck...Alexander Gauge
Little John ....Archie Duncan
                                                  Rufus Cruikshank
Sheriff of Nottingham ....Alan Wheatley
Prince John ....Hubert Gregg
                                                  Brian Haines
                                                  Donald Pleasence
Will Scarlett ....Ronald Howard
                                                  Paul Eddington
Alan-a-Dale ....Richard Coleman
Derwent ....Victor Woolf
Deputy Sheriff ....John Arnatt
Joan ....Simone Lovell
Prince Arthur ....Peter Asher
                                                  Richard O'Sullivan
                                                  Jonathan Bailey

Executive Producer: Hannah Weinstein.
Producer: Sidney Cole

Dashing tales of the 12th-century hero.

Robbing the rich and saving the poor in this early costume drama was Richard Greene, a man forever identified thereafter with the man in Lincoln green from Sherwood Forest. The series was broadly based on the Robin Hood legend, with Robin of Locksley, the Earl of Huntingdon, forced to rebel against the cruel Regent Prince John and his local henchman, the Sheriff of Nottingham. All the traditional clan were there, from Friar Tuck to Little John, plus Lady Marian Fitzwalter, known to the Merrie Men as Maid Marian.

The Adventures of Robin Hood was one of the pioneers of British television in America. Thoroughly popular with younger viewers, it inspired a host of other rousing costume dramas, such as *The Adventures of William Tell*, *The Buccaneers* and *The Adventures of Sir Lancelot*. The theme song, sung by Dick James, was a hit single in 1956. Note the famous names in the cast list, especially Paul Eddington, Richard O'Sullivan and ***Picture Book*** presenter Patricia Driscoll.

ADVENTURES OF SHERLOCK HOLMES, THE

UK (Granada) Detective Drama. ITV 1984–

Sherlock Holmes ....Jeremy Brett
Dr John Watson..David Burke
                                                  Edward Hardwicke
Mrs Hudson ....Rosalie Williams
Inspector Lestrade ....Colin Jeavons
Mycroft Holmes..Charles Gray

Executive Producer: Michael Cox. Producers: Michael Cox, June Wyndham Davies

Conan Doyle's celebrated sleuth, depicted in all his original colour.

After 90 years of trying, and with some 70 actors attempting the title role on film and TV, it wasn't until 1984 that fans found the celluloid Sherlock Holmes they really liked. Generally accepted as being the closest in detail, style and mood to the author's original tales (published in the Victorian *Strand Magazine*), Granada's treatment pitched Jeremy Brett into the famous role, a part with which he has now become indelibly linked. Quite different to the stereotyped Basil Rathbone version, Brett's Holmes was a man of intelligence and courage, but also a reflective, tactful man with a dark side; a man seen wide-eyed and moody under the influence of cocaine; and a man with respect, not just tolerance, for his trusty (and surprisingly spritely) companion, Watson. The settings were realistic, too, and had been well researched, re-creating Sidney Paget's original *Strand* illustrations.

Two series of Holmes tales were initially revived, culminating in *The Final Problem,* in which our hero was seen to meet his end in a confrontation with the evil Moriarty at Reichenbach Falls. But the pipe-smoking, violin-playing detective resurfaced in two further series, entitled *The Return of Sherlock Holmes* (in 1986), in which Watson was played by Edward Hardwicke. Hardwicke also kept the role for the two-hour versions of *The Sign of Four* and *The Hound of the Baskervilles*, as well as all subsequent adventures, some of which went out under the title of *The Casebook of Sherlock Holmes* (in 1991). The specially constructed Baker Street set can be visited as part of the Granada TV Studios Tour in Manchester. It stands next to Coronation Street.

ADVENTURES OF SIR LANCELOT, THE

UK (ITC/Sapphire) Adventure. ITV 1956–7

Sir Lancelot du Lac ....William Russell
Queen Guinevere.....................................Jane Hylton
King Arthur ....Bruce Seaton
....Ronald Leigh-Hunt
Merlin ....Cyril Smith
Leonides ....Peter Bennett
Brian ....Bobby Scroggins

Executive Producer: Hannah Weinstein.
Producers: Sidney Cole, Dallas Bower, Bernard Knowles

Stories of the celebrated Knight of the Round Table, arguably misplaced in the 14th century.

Sir Lancelot du Lac was the Queen's Champion – 'the bravest knight the world has ever seen', according to the theme song – and the man who warded off all threats to her court at Camelot. In the background was King Arthur, his famous sword Excalibur, the revered sorcerer Merlin, plus Lancelot's squire, former kitchen-boy Brian. The authenticity of the settings was researched at Oxford University, but the era was moved from Sir Lancelot's alleged time of the 6th century up to the 1300s. No mention was made of his dalliance with Queen Guinevere, or the conception of Sir Galahad behind the King's back.

William Russell became one of TV's first heart-throbs through this role. He later played Ian Chesterton, a *Doctor Who* assistant, before arousing fond memories in middle-aged female viewers when he returned as Ted Sullivan in *Coronation Street* in the early 1990s.

ADVENTURES OF SUPERMAN, The see *Superman.*

ADVENTURES OF TUGBOAT ANNIE, THE

Canada (Normandie) Situation Comedy. ITV 1957–

'Tugboat' Annie Brennan....................Minerva Urecal
Captain Horatio Bullwinkle ....Walter Sande
Whitey...Don Baker
Pinto ....Don Orlando
Jake ....James Barron

Rivalry and excitement at sea with two tugboat captains.

Widow Annie Brennan was the stocky, booming-voiced skipper of the *Narcissus*, a tug based in a harbour on the north-west coast of America. Her main aim in life was to get the better of fellow skipper Horatio Bullwinkle, but, though the pair fought keenly for the best jobs and traded generously in insults, they also shared many an ocean adventure. Whitey and Pinto were Annie's deck-hands, and Jake was Bullwinkle's crewman. The series was based on a cartoon strip by Norman Reilly Raine, following on from a 1933 film starring Marie Dressler and Wallace Beery.

ADVENTURES OF TWIZZLE, THE

UK (AP Films/Associated-Rediffusion). Children's Entertainment. ITV 1957–8

Twizzle (voice only)................................Denise Bryer

Creator/Writer: Roberta Leigh

Puppet tales of a toy with elastic arms and legs.

Notable for being Gerry Anderson's first contribution (as director) to British television, *The Adventures of Twizzle* concerned a toy with a Wee Willy Winkie hat and stretchable arms and legs who ran away from a toy shop and ended up in all sorts of scrapes. At Twizzle's side was a large, nauseating cat named Footso (after his enormous paws). Twizzle and Footso built a haven for stray toys, a sort of refuge from naughty children. They called it Stray Town and that was where most of the adventures took place. Amongst the mistreated and neglected toys were Chawky (a white-faced golliwog), Jiffy the Broomstick Man, Polly Moppet, Candy Floss (a 'Mamma doll' which couldn't say 'Mamma') and Bouncy (a ball which had lost its bounce).

The brains behind Twizzle was Roberta Leigh, later noted for *Torchy* and *Space Patrol*. However, it is largely for Anderson's direction that the series is remembered today, even though he only contributed to the first 26 episodes.

ADVENTURES OF WILLIAM TELL, THE

UK (ITC/National Telefilm) Adventure. ITV 1958–9

William Tell ....Conrad Phillips
Hedda Tell ....Jennifer Jayne
Walter Tell ....Richard Rogers
Landburgher Gessler ....Willoughby Goddard
Fertog ('The Bear') ....Nigel Greene

Executive Producer: Ralph Smart.
Producer: Leslie Arliss

A 14th-century freedom fighter helps the poor people of Switzerland.

Loosely based on the original story by Johann von Schiller, this series told the legend of William Tell, an alpine hero from the settlement of Berglan, who fought at the side of the oppressed people of Altdorf against the occupying Austrians. The first episode saw Tell challenged by Gessler (the hated Austrian leader) to display his celebrated markmanship with the crossbow by shooting an apple off his own son's head. This

Tell duly did, but with a second arrow tucked away for Gessler in case his aim had failed. Discovering this subterfuge, the tyrant ordered Tell's arrest and William fled to the mountains with his son, Walter, and his wife, Hedda. From here, assisted by a small band of followers, he set about disrupting Austrian activities with clever and cunning forays, taking on the mantle of a Swiss Robin Hood. Gessler never got his man, and as solace ate vast amounts of food. Scene after scene saw him stuffing his face with meat.

The series (filmed partly in Snowdonia) was punctuated by the appearance of numerous aspiring actors, including Michael Caine and Frazer Hines, and other notable guests such as Christopher Lee, John Le Mesurier, Patrick Troughton and Wilfrid Brambell. Many years later, star Conrad Phillips resurfaced in **Emmerdale Farm**, playing Christopher Meadows, MD of NY Estates. Later still (1989), an Anglo-French revamp of William Tell was made. This starred Will Lyman as Jen and Jeremy Clyde as Gessler. Conrad Phillips appeared as a guest star.

AFFILIATE STATION

An independent TV station that links up with one of the large networks to take a proportion of the latter's programming in exchange for a fee, but still leaving gaps in its schedule for its own local output. Affiliate stations are commonplace in the USA and are used by ABC, NBC and CBS to extend their audiences. The smaller stations gain from being able to offer first-run, highly rated programmes, at no expense to themselves.

AFRICAN PATROL

UK (ME/Kenya) Adventure. ITV 1958–9

Inspector Paul Derek ....John Bentley

Producer: Michael Sadler

Law and order with a jungle policeman.

British Patrol Inspector Paul Derek worked in the African bush, using his expert knowledge of East African safari country to keep the peace. It was his duty to thwart poachers and other criminals who disturbed the natural balance of the environment. The series was filmed entirely on location in Africa. Star John Bentley re-emerged in the 1960s and 1970s as Hugh Mortimer in *Crossroads*.

AFTER HENRY

UK (Thames) Situation Comedy. ITV 1988–92

Sarah France ....Prunella Scales

Eleanor Prescott..................................Joan Sanderson
Clare France ....Janine Wood
Russell Bryant ....Jonathan Newth
Vera Poling ....Peggy Ann Wood

Producers: Peter Frazer-Jones, Bill Shepherd

A widow shares her home with her demanding mother and her obstinate daughter.

This gentle comedy, contrasting the lives of three generations of women, focused chiefly on the one in the middle. Sarah France was the fortysomething widow of the late Dr Henry France, a man who had been much loved and was now greatly missed. She shared her home in Stipton with her young, headstrong daughter, Clare, and suffered intrusions from her domineering mother, Eleanor, who lived in an adjoining granny flat. Much of the humour arose from Sarah's attempts to reconcile the various generations, which was not without pain and anguish. Sarah's confidant was Russell, her boss at the Bygone Books antiquarian bookshop. Vera Poling was Eleanor's geriatric rival.

After Henry transferred to television after three successful years on BBC Radio. Prunella Scales reprised her radio role, as did Joan Sanderson, although Russell was played by Benjamin Whitrow and Clare by Gerry Cowper in the sound version.

AFTON, RICHARD (1913–)

BBC light entertainment producer in the 1950s who went on to become a Fleet Street TV critic in the 1970s. Amongst his major contributions were *Café Continental* and *Television Dancing Club*.

AGATHA CHRISTIE HOUR, THE

UK (Thames) Thriller. ITV 1982

Executive Producer: John Frankau. Producer: Pat Sandys

An anthology of the Mistress of Crime's lesser-known tales.

This series did not feature the mighty Hercule Poirot. Nor did Miss Marple steal the limelight. For once, Agatha Christie's earlier characters were introduced to television in these ten 1920s dramas, which were generally lighthearted, unassuming period adventures, with the cast changing each week.

AGE OF KINGS, AN

UK (BBC) Drama Anthology. BBC 1960

Producer: Peter Dews

The ambitious dramatization of five Shakespearean plays as an historical project.

In *An Age of Kings*, the kings in question were Richard II, Henry IV, Henry V, Henry VI and Richard III, as portrayed by William Shakespeare in his plays of the same title. Spread over 15 episodes, a fortnight apart, the plays were dramatized in sequence to give the overall effect of depicting a continuous stretch (86 years) of British history. Always as a backdrop was the lust for the throne and the burdens of wearing the crown. Michael Hayes directed the plays and the theme music was composed by Sir Arthur Bliss. Featured actors included Robert Hardy, Paul Daneman, David William, Sean Connery and Eileen Atkins.

AGONY

UK (LWT) Situation Comedy. ITV 1979–81

Jane Lucas	Maureen Lipman
Laurence Lucas	Simon Williams
Bea	Maria Charles
Andy Evol	Peter Blake
Val	Diana Weston
Diana	Jan Holden
Rob	Jeremy Bulloch
Michael	Peter Denyer
Mr Mince	Robert Gillespie
Vincent Fish	Bill Nighy
Junior Truscombe	Robert Austin

Creators: Anna Raeburn, Len Richmond. Writers: Anna Raeburn, Len Richmond, Stan Hey, Andrew Nickolds. Producer: John Reardon

A successful agony aunt's own life is a mess.

Jane Lucas was the popular problem-page editor for *Person* magazine and also ran her own radio phone-in. However, for all the sound advice she gave to distressed readers and listeners, her personal life was far from straightforward and she was surrounded by people liable to make things worse. There was her psychiatrist husband, Laurence, who didn't understand people (and from whom she eventually parted), her typically Jewish mother, Bea, who dispensed advice and worried over her, and a couple of homosexual friends (Rob and Michael) who were always quarrelling – all this on top of 'friends' at work who sought her professional advice for their own little worries. These included her dragon-like editor, Diana, her virtuous secretary, Val, and radio DJ Andy Evol.

The series was created by (and based on the real life of) agony aunt Anna Raeburn. A sanitized American version, *The Lucy Arnaz Show*, starred Lucille Ball's daughter in the lead role.

AIRD, HOLLY (1969–)

British actress coming to the fore in her formative years in programmes like *The History of Mr Polly* and ***The Flame Trees of Thika*** (as Elspeth Grant), before securing lead status in the seaside comedy *Hope It Rains* (as Jace) and the light military drama ***Soldier, Soldier*** (as Corporal Nancy Thorpe). Other credits have included the sitcom *Double First*.

AIRLINE

UK (Yorkshire) Drama. ITV 1982

Jack Ruskin	Roy Marsden
Peter Witney	Richard Heffer
McEvoy	Sean Scanlan
Jennie Shaw	Polly Hemingway
Ernie Cade	Terence Rigby

Creator: Wilfred Greatorex. Executive Producer: David Cunliffe. Producer: Michael Ferguson

An RAF pilot starts his own airline in the immediate postwar years.

Jack Ruskin, demobbed after World War II but with flying still in his blood, struggled to find work with civilian airlines and so chanced his arm by founding his own. His partner in the new Ruskin Air Services was forces colleague Peter Witney. Operating with an old aircraft Ruskin had bought, they aimed to cut themselves a slice of the world cargo market. However, the business had difficulty getting off the ground, in more ways than one.

Ensnared by shady business deals and hampered by bad weather, Ruskin Air Services offered its staff and management an uncomfortable ride, as Jack lurched from one financial crisis to another. But his entrepreneurial spirit was not to be denied. He raised his sights, took on passenger transport and later became involved in the Berlin Airlift. Ernie Cade was the company's dodgy backer, McEvoy was the company engineer and Jennie Shaw was Jack's girlfriend.

Roy Marsden, Polly Hemingway and the whole *Airline* ethos was borrowed for a British Airports Authority commercial several years later, a move which brought an unsuccessful law suit from the show's creator, William Greatorex.

AIRWOLF

US (CBS) Adventure. ITV 1984–6

Stringfellow Hawke	Jan-Michael Vincent
Dominic Santini	Ernest Borgnine
Michael Archangel	Alex Cord
Marella	Deborah Pratt
Caitlin O'Shannessy	Jean Bruce Scott
St John Hawke	Barry Van Dyke
Jason Lock	Anthony Sherwood
Jo Santini	Michele Scarabelli
Major Mike Rivers	Geraint Wyn Davies

Creator: Donald Bellisario. Executive Producers: Bernard Kowalski, Donald Bellisario

Thrills and spills with a high-tech helicopter.

When Airwolf, a new breed of super helicopter, was spirited away to Libya by its designer, the US Government called on the services of ace pilot Stringfellow Hawke to retrieve it for Uncle Sam. Hawke, a cello-playing mountain recluse, fulfilled his mission, but refused to hand the aircraft back until the US found his brother, who was still missing in Vietnam. In the meantime, Hawke flew secret and spectacular assignments with the super chopper for a Government agency known as The Firm. His contact at The Firm was Archangel, who wore a white suit and an eye patch, and carried a stick. Hawke's accomplice on his missions was middle-aged co-pilot Dominic Santini, and he was also joined by female pilot Caitlin O'Shannessy in later episodes. Marella, Archangel's attractive assistant, sometimes represented The Firm.

The series left American network television in 1986 and was acquired by a cable company. For subsequent episodes the cast changed. Dominic had been killed and Hawke himself seriously injured when a sabotaged helicopter exploded. Replacements Mike Rivers, Jo (Dominic's niece) and Jason Locke, the new contact man for The Company (no longer 'The Firm'), took Airwolf to rescue Hawke's brother, St John, who then assumed command of the helicopter, continuing to use it for secret missions.

Airwolf itself was a pretty impressive piece of machinery. An attack helicopter, it had a massive array of weapons and was capable of supersonic flight. It was not unique, however. At the same time, another high-tech chopper, *Blue Thunder*, also began its own series.

ALAN, RAY (1930–)

Ventriloquist/comedian ubiquitous in the 1950s and 1960s with his Mikki the Martian, Lord Charles, Tich and Quackers and Ali Cat dummies. In the 1970s and 1980s, Alan branched out into panel games, compering shows like *Three Little Words* and *Where in the World* for HTV. He also holds the record for the number of appearances on **The Good Old Days**, calling on the experience he gained in variety theatre before TV beckoned (he was allegedly taught the ukelele by George Formby while working as a call boy at Lewisham Hippodrome, aged 13). As a writer, Alan has contributed scripts for **The Two Ronnies** and Dave Allen, as well as penning 26 episodes of **Bootsie and Snudge** (under the pseudonym Ray Whyberd).

ALAS SMITH AND JONES/ SMITH AND JONES

UK (BBC/Talkback) Comedy. BBC 2/BBC 1 1984–92

Mel Smith
Griff Rhys-Jones

Producers: Martin Shardlow, Jimmy Mulville, John Kilby, Graham C. Williams, Chris Bould, Jon Plowman

Comedy sketches with two members of the *Not the Nine O'Clock News* team.

Cleverly mimicking the title of the 1970s Western series starring Pete Duel and Ben Murphy, this vehicle for Mel and Griff's talents is best remembered for the 'head-to-head' scenes, where the idiotic Smith attempted to explain something straightforward to the even dimmer Jones (these were largely scripted by Clive Anderson). Another notable feature was the spoof home video slot, years before Jeremy Beadle picked up a camcorder. After several seasons, the first word was dropped and the show, taken into independent production, was retitled simply *Smith and Jones*, with the series switching to BBC 1 at the same time.

ALBERT see *Dear Mother – Love Albert*.

ALBION MARKET

UK (Granada) Drama. ITV 1985–6

Derek Owen	David Hargreaves
Tony Fraser	John Michie
Lynne Harrison	Noreen Kershaw
Roy Harrison	Jonathan Barlow
Lisa O'Shea	Sally Baxter
Morris Ransome	Bernard Spear
Miriam Ransome	Carol Kaye
Duane Rigg	Alistair Walker
Larry Rigg	Peter Benson
Brenda Rigg	Valerie Lilley
Phil Smith	Burt Caesar
Raju Sharma	Dev Sagoo
Jaz Sharma	Paul Bhattacharjee
Lam Quoc Hoa	Philip Tan
Ly Nhu Chan	Pik-Sen Lim
Ted Pilkington	Anthony Booth

Viv Harker ....Helen Shapiro
Geoff Travis...Geoffrey Leesley
Keith Naylor ....Derek Hicks

Executive Producer: Bill Podmore

**Day to day ups and downs in a
Manchester market.**

Contrived as a sister programme to *Coronation
Street*, with the aim of lifting ITV's weekend
schedules (it went out on Fridays and Sundays),
Albion Market arrived with a bang and left with a
whimper. Much was made of the launch of this
ambitious new series, but its poor audience ratings (beaten by *Wogan* and *Open All Hours*)
resulted in some ITV regions moving it to even
less advantageous time slots and *Albion Market*
eventually shut up shop a year after it began, after
exactly 100 half-hour episodes.

Set in a covered Manchester market (actually a
converted Salford warehouse), the series monitored the complex lives of an ethnically mixed
group of stall holders. At the forefront of the
action were the likes of hunky, cake-selling wide
boy Tony Fraser, his 19-year-old girlfriend Lisa
O'Shea, her mum Lynne Harrison, who ran a
domestic goods stall, and Lynne's two-timing,
no-good husband, Roy. Lam Quoc Hoa and Ly
Nhu Chan were Vietnamese refugee cousins,
Raju and Jaz Sharma were expelled Ugandan
denim merchants and Morris and Miriam
Ransome were the Jewish couple who ran the
pottery stall. Derek Owen was the harassed market supervisor, Phil, the West Indian, worked in
the café and Duane Rigg was the market's
teenage delinquent. Towards the end of its run,
two new personalities were introduced in an
attempt to give the show a lift. Sixties pop singer
Helen Shapiro played Viv, a hairdresser, and former *Till Death Us Do Part* 'Scouse git' Tony
Booth was seen as Ted Pilkington, licensee of the
market's local, The Waterman's Arms.

ALDA, ALAN (1936–)

Slick actor/comedian/writer/director who shot
to fame as Hawkeye Pierce in *M*A*S*H*. An
ever-present in the series' 11-year run (though he
did not appear in the original film), he gradually
became one of the programme's creative controllers and picked up Emmys for acting, writing
and directing on the show. Earlier Alda had filled
a satirist's chair on the US version of *That Was
The Week That Was* and made one appearance in
The Phil Silvers Show. Branching out into cinema, his TV work has been thin since *M*A*S*H*
ended, but that one series – and in particular his
portrayal of the sarcastic, wisecracking, humanitarian surgeon – has marked Alda down as one of
TV's all-time greats. He is the son of actor
Robert Alda.

ALDERTON, JOHN (1940–)

Popular British comedy actor first seen in
Emergency – Ward 10 as Dr Richard Moone
(alongside his first wife, Jill Browne), but best
remembered as the hapless, naive school teacher,
Bernard Hedges, in *Please Sir!*. It was this series
that launched Alderton into a succession of other
sitcoms, most notably *My Wife Next Door*, *The
Upchat Line* and *Wodehouse Playhouse*. Straight
parts have still been accepted, however. Alderton
played chauffeur Thomas Watkins in *Upstairs,
Downstairs* (opposite his second wife, Pauline
Collins), and this led to a spin-off series, *Thomas
and Sarah*. The duo have also starred together in
the 1970s comedy *No Honestly* and the
1980s/90s rustic drama *Forever Green*.

ALDRIDGE, MICHAEL (1920–94)

Distinguished British actor, a 1960s star as
Dimmock in *The Man In Room 17* who resur-
faced in 1985 as Seymour Utterthwaite, Foggy
Dewhurst's replacement in *Last of the Summer
Wine*, and the inquisitive old buffer Caldicott, in
Charters and Caldicott. He was also seen in
Tinker, Tailor, Soldier, Spy.

ALEXANDER, JEAN (1926–)

British actress forever known to viewers as
Coronation Street's Hilda Ogden, one of TV's
most celebrated characterizations. After appearances in *Jacks and Knaves*, *Top Secret* and *Z Cars*,
Jean Alexander joined the Street in 1964, donning Hilda's curlers and pinny and moving into
number 13 with Bernard Youens as her layabout
husband, Stan. When she decided to retire 23
years later, she had made Hilda a national institution. Her finest hour came in 1984 with the
death of Youens and the passing of Stan, when
she turned in one of the most acclaimed and
moving pieces of acting in TV history. Since
leaving the **Street**, Alexander has struggled to
shake off the Ogden persona, despite appearing as
Granny Trellis in her own sitcom, *Rich Tea and
Sympathy*, and providing cameo performances as
Auntie Wainwright in *Last of the Summer Wine*.

ALEXANDER, TERENCE (1923–)

Long-serving, all-purpose supporting actor who
achieved semi-star status as Charlie Hungerford
in *Bergerac*. His earlier credits ranged from the
1950s aviation adventure series *Garry Halliday*,
The Forsyte Saga and *The Pallisers* to the comedies *All Aboard*, *Hancock's Half-Hour*, *The Dick
Emery Show*, *Terry and June*, *The Fall and Rise of
Reginald Perrin*, *Just Liz*, *Devenish* and *The New
Statesman*, plus single dramas.

ALF

US (Lorimar) Situation Comedy. ITV 1987–89

ALF (voice only) ....Paul Fusco
Willie Tanner ....Max Wright
Kate Tanner ....Anne Schedeen
Lynn Tanner ....Andrea Elson
Brian Tanner ....Benji Gregory
Raquel Ochmonek ....Liz Sheridan
Trevor Ochmonek ....John LaMotta

Creators: Paul Fusco, Tom Patchett. Executive
Producers: Bernie Brillstein, Tom Patchett

**An Alien Life Form (ALF) is looked after
by a suburban American family.**

When ALF crash-landed his spacecraft on the
Tanner family's garage roof, they took him into
their kitchen and their care. Just like ET, ALF
instantly won over his adoptive family. Unable to
return home, as his planet (Melmac) had blown
up and his spacecraft was beyond repair, he settled
into a domestic lifestyle, to the bemusement of
the Tanners' slow-witted neighbours, the
Ochmoneks. Although warm-hearted, this furry,
wisecracking alien was also somewhat mischievous, with a penchant for watching TV and over-
eating. His favourite food was cat, sadly for the
Tanners' own pet, Lucky. He was said to have
been 229 years old and, on his own planet, went
by the name of Gordon Shumway. Like Mork in
Mork and Mindy, he presented viewers with a
cynical view of the way of life on Earth. In the
first series Michu Meszaros, a midget, wore ALF's
furry suit, while ALF's gravelly voice belonged to
Paul Fusco, one of the show's creators.

ALFRED HITCHCOCK PRESENTS

US (Universal/Shamley) Suspense Anthology.
ITV 1957–

Host: Alfred Hitchcock

Executive Producer: Joan Harrison. Producer:
Norman Lloyd

**An anthology of murder mysteries with a
sting in the tale, introduced by the 'Master
of Suspense'.**

Alfred Hitchcock himself directed only about 20
of the 300-plus episodes in this series, but was
very involved in selecting stories and plots (often
from the work of authors such as Roald Dahl,
Ray Bradbury and H.G. Wells). Other directors
who worked on the programmes included
Robert Altman, Sydney Pollack and William
Friedkin, while famous actors such as Robert
Redford, Burt Reynolds, Walter Matthau,
Charles Bronson, Steve McQueen and William
Shatner occasionally starred.

Each programme was introduced by Hitchcock
with a creaky 'Good Evening' and wrapped up

with his postscript, glibly explaining how the
perpetrator of what seemed a perfect crime had
been found out. Very often these deadpan intros
and tailpieces had nothing at all to do with the
actual tale being told, but were just a device
allowing Hitchcock to appear in a bizarre and
macabre setting – sitting in an electric chair or
impaled on a pole like a scarecrow, for instance –
highlighting his renowned black humour. No
allusion was ever made to these weird props and
he delivered his piece to camera as if all was perfectly normal. The stories themselves were cleverly crafted and centred on crimes such as murder and blackmail, but each had a surprising twist
in the tail. The series primarily consisted of 30-
minute dramas, but over 90 stories were made in
a 60-minute format and went out as *The Alfred
Hitchcock Hour*. The doodled caricature used as
the show's logo was drawn by the man himself,
while the jaunty but sinister theme music was
based on Gounod's *Funeral March of a Marionette*.

The concept was intriguingly revived in the
1980s, using new stories or reworking old tales,
but with the original Hitchcock segments
repainted in colour by computer technology. The
producer of the original series was Norman
Lloyd, who also acted and went on to become Dr
Daniel Auschlander in *St Elsewhere*.

ALIAS SMITH AND JONES

US (Universal) Western. BBC 2 1971–4

Hannibal Heyes (Joshua Smith) ....Pete Duel
                                                  Roger Davis
Jed 'Kid' Curry (Thaddeus Jones) ....Ben Murphy
Clementine Hale ....Sally Field
Harry Briscoe ....J.D. Cannon
Narrator ....Roger Davis
                                                  Ralph Story

Executive Producer: Roy Huggins.
Creator/Producer: Glen A. Larson

**Jaunty exploits of a pair of likeable ex-
bank robbers on the run in the Wild West.**

Hannibal Heyes and Kid Curry were two members of the Devil Hole Gang, wanted for a series
of bank robberies. Having given themselves up,
they agreed a deal with the Governor of Kansas
that if they stayed out of trouble for a year they
would be granted a pardon. The only snag was
that virtually every lawman thought the pair were
still on the run, and plenty of other outlaws still
held a grudge against them or were keen to tempt
them off the straight and narrow. Under their
new identities of Joshua Smith and Thaddeus
Jones, they roamed the West, trying desperately
to keep their heads down. But by the time the
series closed they still hadn't received their pardon. Clementine Hale, a friend of Curry's, was
introduced to provide some female interest in
later episodes.

The series was devised as a TV cash-in on the huge success of the film *Butch Cassidy and the Sundance Kid*, but was rocked at the end of 1971 by the suicide of Pete Duel. Roger Davis, the narrator of the series, was recast as Hannibal Heyes, and Ralph Story brought in to do the voice-overs.

ALL CREATURES GREAT AND SMALL

UK (BBC) Drama. BBC 1 1978–90

James Herriot ....Christopher Timothy
Siegfried Farnon ....Robert Hardy
Tristan Farnon ....Peter Davison
Helen Alderson/Herriot...................Carol Drinkwater
                                                        Lynda Bellingham
Calum Buchanan ....John McGlynn
Mrs Hall ....Mary Hignett
Mrs Pumphrey ....Margaretta Scott
Deirdre McEwan.....................................Andrea Gibb
Mrs Greenlaw..Judy Wilson
Mrs Alton ....Jean Heywood

Producer: Bill Sellars

Tales from a vet's life in the Yorkshire Dales.

Based on the celebrated autobiographical novels of James Herriot, *All Creatures Great and Small* proved to be an enormous success as a TV series, inspired by a 1974 cinema version featuring Simon Ward, and its 1976 sequel, *It Shouldn't Happen to a Vet*, starring John Alderton. With Christopher Timothy now pulling on the vet's wellies, the TV adaptation (with its echoes of *Dr Finlay's Casebook*) took viewers back to the 1930s as Herriot arrived at Skeldale House, home of the veterinary practice in the North Riding town of Darrowby (the real-life Askrigg). There he joined senior partner Siegfried Farnon, his easy-going brother, Tristan, and housekeeper Mrs Hall, helping to build up the practice and dealing with all manner of agricultural and domestic animal ailments. If James was not preventing foot and mouth or groping around up a cow's posterior, he was treating the likes of Tricki-Woo, villager Mrs Pumphrey's pampered Pekinese.

James met and married Helen Alderson (later to bear him a son, Jimmy, and a daughter, Rosie), before the series 'ended' after three years when James and Tristan headed off to join the war effort (Herriot's original novels had run out). A couple of Christmas specials kept the concept alive during the early 1980s, before public clamour was answered with a new series in 1988.

With Peter Davison largely tied up elsewhere and his appearances restricted to a minimum, a new vet was added to the cast. The naive, badger-keeping idealist Calum Buchanan joined the practice. The part of Helen was taken over by

'Oxo mum' Lynda Bellingham, and the time had moved on to the postwar years. Some unpublished Herriot memoirs were used for plots and the writers were given the freedom to invent new situations, but the cosy, country air, the slow pace of village life and the warm, gentle humour were maintained. The series ran for three more seasons, plus another Christmas special.

ALL GAS AND GAITERS

UK (BBC) Situation Comedy. BBC 1 1967–71

Rev. Mervyn Noote ....Derek Nimmo
Bishop..William Mervyn
Archdeacon ....Robertson Hare
Dean ....Ernest Clark
....John Barron

Writers: Edwin Apps, Pauline Devaney.
Producers: Stuart Allen, John Howard Davies

Fun and games in the cloisters of a cathedral.

Gently poking fun at the clergy (one of the first comedies to do so), *All Gas and Gaiters* centred on the farcical team at St Ogg's Cathedral, namely its bishop, archdeacon and, particularly, its bumbling, ultra-sincere, plummy chaplain, Rev. Mervyn Noote. Their adversary was the rather sober Dean. Nimmo later took his dithery clerical creation on to **Oh Brother** and its sequel, *Oh Father*, playing Brother/Father Dominic. *All Gas and Gaiters* began life as a **Comedy Playhouse** presentation in 1966, with the subsequent five series scripted by husband and wife writers Edwin Apps and Pauline Devaney.

ALL IN THE FAMILY

US (Yorkin-Lear) Situation Comedy. BBC 1/BBC 2 1971–5

Archie Bunker ....Carroll O'Connor
Edith Bunker ....Jean Stapleton
Gloria Stivic..Sally Struthers
Mike Stivic ....Rob Reiner
Lionel Jefferson...Mike Evans
Louise Jefferson ....Isabel Sanford
Henry Jefferson ....Mel Stewart
George Jefferson ....Sherman Hemsley
Irene Lorenzo ....Betty Garrett
Frank Lorenzo ....Vincent Gardenia

Writer/Producer: Norman Lear.
Creators: Norman Lear, Bud Yorkin

Innovative American sitcom centring on an arrogant, bigoted labourer and his loudmouthed prejudices, unashamedly based on Johnny Speight's **Till Death Us Do Part**.

Archie Bunker was America's Alf Garnett and his family, too, bore a strong resemblance to members of the Garnett household. Archie's wife,

Edith, affectionately known as 'Dingbat', was somewhat dim, and his sales assistant daughter, Gloria, had disappointed her father by marrying Mike, an antagonizingly liberal sociology student of Polish extraction, whom Archie called 'Meathead'. They lived with the Bunkers and added to the domestic friction.

Outside characters were more prominent than in the British equivalent. Early victims of Archie's pigheadedness were his mixed race colleagues at the Prendergast Tool and Die Company, and then there were the Bunkers' ethnic neighbours in Queens, NYC, the Jeffersons (black), and the Lorenzos (Italian). The Jeffersons were eventually given their own series and another spin-off was *Maude*, based around Edith's cousin, Maude Findlay (played by Bea Arthur).

The series ran until 1983 in the USA, but towards the end of the 1970s the programme format was drastically restructured. Archie bought shares in a bar and Gloria, Mike and their son, Joey, moved to California. A little niece, Stephanie Mills (played by Danielle Brisebois), filled the gap by moving in with Archie and Edith, but actress Jean Stapleton eventually tired of the series and was written out. Edith, it was revealed, died of a stroke. During these changes, the series was renamed *Archie Bunker's Place*.

All in the Family became a landmark in US television comedy and was the top show for five years. This was a programme that dared to raise such issues as race, politics and sex. No one had dared to speak like that on American TV before and, after Archie Bunker, the twee, 'Honey I'm home' domestic sitcom was dead. Like Alf Garnett in the UK, he became part of American society.

ALL OUR YESTERDAYS

UK (Granada) Documentary. ITV 1960–73; 1987–9

Presenters: James Cameron, Brian Inglis, Bernard Braden (1987)

Producers: Tim Hewat, Douglas Terry, Jeremy Isaacs, David Plowright, Bill Grundy, Mike Murphy (1987)

Nostalgic documentary series looking back 25 years in time.

Using old theatrical newsreels, *All Our Yesterdays* reflected on events taking place in the world in the same week 25 years earlier. Consequently, the first programme looked back to a week in the year 1935. Foreign correspondent James Cameron added footnotes to the film coverage before he was replaced as frontman by Brian Inglis after one year. When the series was resur-

rected in 1987, Bernard Braden was the new host and television archives were raided for footage. Over 600 editions were produced.

ALL SQUARE see *It's a Square World*.

ALL YOU NEED IS LOVE

UK (LWT/Theatre Projects) Documentary. ITV 1977

Producers: Richard Pilbrow, Neville C. Thompson

A history of 20th-century popular music.

Researched in depth, this 13-part documentary traced the development of popular music in all its strands, from jazz and blues to chart pop and progressive rock. Much obscure footage was retrieved and interviews with music legends were wrapped around the narrative. The brains behind the project was Tony Palmer, one of the first heavyweight rock critics and the producer of the controversial 1968 **Omnibus** film *All My Loving*, which interwove music and musicians with horrifying scenes of war and war crimes.

ALL YOUR OWN

UK (BBC) Children's Entertainment. BBC 1952–61

Presenter: Huw Wheldon

Editors: Cliff Michelmore, Joanne Symons. Producers: Michael Westmore, Tony Arnold

Showcase for young talents and children's hobbies.

Hosted for the most part by future BBC Television Managing Director Huw Wheldon, and edited by a young Cliff Michelmore from 1952, *All Your Own* invited youngsters from all over the UK to show off their skills and talents or discuss their hobbies and pastimes. Guitarist John Williams was featured on one programme and used it as a stepping stone to greater things. Led Zeppelin's Jimmy Page was, reputedly, another youthful guest. Jimmy Logan, Brian Johnston and Cliff Morgan also appeared as hosts.

ALLEN, DAVE (DAVID TYNAN O'MAHONY; 1936–)

Suave Irish comedian, a former journalist and Red Coat, famed for monologues casually delivered from a high stool with a drink and cigarette at hand. His favourite hunting grounds are sex and religion (also parodied in short sketches and echoed in his closing catchphrase 'May your god go with you'). After initially appearing on *The Val Doonican Show* in 1965 and compering

Sunday Night at the London Palladium, Allen's first solo series was *Tonight With Dave Allen* in 1967, which was followed by *The Dave Allen Show* (both for ITV). However, it was through numerous series of *Dave Allen at Large* for the BBC in the 1970s that he became a household name. Later 1970s contributions included *Dave Allen and Friends*, *Dave Allen* and the documentary *Dave Allen in Search of the Great English Eccentric*. He returned to television in the 1990s with a new (somewhat controversial) series of frank monologues.

ALLEN, GRACIE (1906–64)

The scatterbrained TV and real-life wife of George Burns. Together they worked their way from vaudeville, through radio to TV, where, in 1950, they created one of America's earliest comedy hits, *The Burns and Allen Show*, in which they played themselves in a sitcom environment. Gracie's trademarks were a confused logic and a flair for malapropisms. After eight years, Gracie retired, leaving George to continue alone. She died in 1964 after a long illness.

ALLEN, IRWIN (1916–91)

American producer/director responsible for some of the most extravagant science-fiction series of the 1960s, all created on the tightest of budgets. Much use was made of stock film footage and cinema cast-offs to add depth to his studio-bound dramas. His first major TV offering was *Voyage to the Bottom of the Sea* in 1964, inspired by his 1962 film release with the same title (and most of the same props). Then came *Lost in Space*, *Time Tunnel* and *Land of the Giants*, as well as the less memorable *The Swiss Family Robinson*.

ALLEN, JIM (1926–)

Former miner and socialist-minded playwright, often in collaboration with director Ken Loach, who moved on from scripting for *Coronation Street* to creating some particularly poignant – and controversial – dramas for the BBC, most notably *The Lump* in 1967, *The Rank and File* in 1971 and *Days of Hope* in 1976. The last enraged pillars of the Establishment, who claimed it crossed the boundary between fiction and propaganda in its story of two young pacifist lovers in the era of the Great War and General Strike. Later works included *The Spongers* (1978), *United Kingdom* (1981) and *The Gathering Seed* (1983).

ALLEN, PATRICK (1927–)

Square-jawed, bass-voiced actor and voice-over specialist, perhaps best remembered as the man in the helicopter in the Barratt homes commercial, though also star of several series, including *Crane*, *Brett* and *Hard Times*. His other TV credits have included *Glencannon* (as Bosun Hughes), *The Dick Emery Show*, *The Winds of War* and numerous single plays. He is married to actress Sarah Lawson (the third governor in *Within These Walls*).

ALLEN, RONALD (1930–91)

Although Ronald Allen is clearly best recalled as the lugubrious David Hunter in *Crossroads*, his career began well before that famous motel opened its doors. His matinee idol looks could well have seen him in Hollywood in the 1950s, but the several small film roles he gained failed to take him to the top. However, his TV break came in 1962, when he was cast as editor Ian Harman in the woman's magazine drama *Compact*, a part which he followed in 1966 with that of Mark Wilson, one of Brentwich United's managers, in the soccer drama *United!*. He joined *Crossroads* in 1969 and remained with the programme for 16 years, until he was surprisingly axed by a new regime in 1985, together with his screen (and later real-life) wife, Sue Lloyd. Later, the suave but rather starchy Allen was seen to 'loosen up', taking a cameo role as the gay Uncle Quentin in the *Comic Strip*'s *Five Go Mad In Dorset*. He died of lung cancer in 1991.

'ALLO 'ALLO

UK (BBC) Situation Comedy. BBC 1 1984–92

René Artois	Gorden Kaye
Edith Artois	Carmen Silvera
Yvette	Vicki Michelle
Maria	Francesca Gonshaw
Michelle	Kirsten Cooke
Colonel Von Strohm	Richard Marner
Captain Hans Geering	Sam Kelly
Lt Gruber	Guy Siner
Helga Geerhart	Kim Hartman
Herr Otto Flick	Richard Gibson
	David Janson
Von Smallhausen	John Louis Mansi
Officer Crabtree	Arthur Bostrom
General Von Klinkerhoffen	Hilary Minster
Mimi La Bonc	Sue Hodge
Monsieur Leclerc	Jack Haig
	Derek Royle
	Robin Parkinson
Monsieur Alfonse	Kenneth Connor
Fanny	Rose Hill
Flying Officer Fairfax	John D. Collins
Flying Officer Carstairs	Nicholas Frankau
Captain Alberto Bertorelli	Gavin Richards
	Roger Kitter

Creators: Jeremy Lloyd, David Croft. Producers: David Croft, John B. Hobbs

A wartime French café-owner is in demand with both the Germans and the Résistance.

René Artois was the proprietor of a café in the northern French town of Nouvion. He ran the bar with his wife, Edith, and a couple of shapely waitresses, Yvette and Maria. At least, that was until the Germans occupied the town. He soon found himself having to pander to the local Nazis, headed by Colonel Von Strohm, the clumsy Captain Geering and the gay Lt Gruber. At the same time, his bar was taken over as a French Résistance safehouse, primarily to house two gormless British airmen, Fairfax and Carstairs. In this way, this man's war became rather more trying than others'.

Introducing each episode by speaking to camera, René updated viewers on earlier happenings (the show was run as a kind of serial farce). Usually, the highly exaggerated plots centred on René's reluctant attempts to help the airmen escape, or to sabotage the Germans' efforts to steal a priceless painting, the so-called *Fallen Madonna with the Big Boobies* by Van Clomp. Instigator of most of the action was the local Résistance leader, Michelle, comandeerer of René's bar and supplier of the show's prime catchphrase: 'Listen very carefully. I shall say this only once.' She was aided by Officer Crabtree, an inept British agent disguised as a gendarme, spouting appalling French which translated into warped English phrases like 'Good moaning'. Indeed, the use of stereotypical accents to convey different languages was one of *'Allo 'Allo*'s success stories. Also influencing affairs was the cruel Herr Flick, the limping local Gestapo chief who demanded kinky affection from his adjutant, Helga, and abused his incompetent sidekick, Von Smallhausen.

Around the central action there were plenty of subplots: René's steamy affairs with both Yvette and Maria (later replaced by Mimi), the marriage of Edith's bedridden mother, Fanny, to ageing Résistance operative Leclerc, and René's alleged death which allowed Edith to court Monsieur Alphonse, the local undertaker with a 'dicky ticker' and a 'small 'earse with a small 'orse'. But the programme also had some well-rehearsed running jokes: Edith's excruciating singing, for instance, which forced the bar's customers to stuff their ears with cheese, Lt Gruber's advances to René, and René's (codename Nighthawk) laboured attempts to get the wireless to work from its secret hiding place beneath Fanny's chamber pot.

Rich in innuendo and slapstick, *'Allo 'Allo* was much criticized for its 'bad taste', though it always claimed to be poking fun at over-the-top wartime dramas and not at the cruelty of war itself. *Secret Army* was its main target. When it ended, after nearly nine years, the war had finished and Nouvion was liberated. Viewers were treated to a 'flashforward' to the present day and introduced to René's son (still played by Gorden Kaye), who explained what had happened to the locals in the postwar years to a visiting Gruber, who had, surprisingly, married Helga. A West End stage version, with original cast members, was also produced.

AMERICA

UK (BBC) Documentary. BBC 2 1972-3

Presenter: Alistair Cooke

Writer: Alistair Cooke. Producer: Michael Gill

Thoughtful retrospective on the growth of the USA.

'A personal history of the United States,' was the subtitle to this well-considered account of the birth and development of a nation, presented from the viewpoint of Alistair Cooke, a top British correspondent and an American citizen. Cooke's dual nationality allowed him to portray the USA from both internal and external viewpoints, fashioning a TV history designed for consumption on both sides of the Atlantic. In 13 weekly episodes, he charted the hopes, experiences and achievements of the men who shaped the most powerful country in the world, tracing developments from before Columbus right up to the Nixon era.

His compassionate, gentle narration and poignant anecdotes allowed Cooke to convey the enormity of the problems facing the earliest settlers, and he incisively analysed the political movements and the agricultural and industrial changes that moulded the country over the centuries, winning wide acclaim for his understanding and perception. His conclusion centred on the fact that America at the turn of the 1970s fell a long way short of the dreams of its founding fathers.

Alistair Cooke was for many years *The Guardian*'s Chief America Correspondent. His *Letter from America* is the longest-running single radio programme (since 1946) and can be heard weekly on Radio 4.

AMERICAN BROADCASTING COMPANY see *ABC*.

AMOS BURKE – SECRET AGENT see *Burke's Law*.

AMY PRENTISS

US (Universal) Police Drama. ITV 1976

Amy Prentiss ....Jessica Walter

Detective Tony Russell	Steve Sandor
Detective Rod Pena	Arthur Metrano
Detective Contreras	Johnny Seven
Jill Prentiss	Helen Hunt
Joan Carter	Gwenn Mitchell

Executive Producer: Cy Chermak

A 35-year-old widow becomes San Francisco's first female Chief of Detectives.

When her boss died suddenly, Amy Prentiss found her name on top of the list to succeed him. She took on the role, but there had never been a female Chief of Detectives in the SFPD before and, for her colleagues, that took a bit of getting used to. Fighting prejudice, this was one lady cop who was determined to make the grade. Jill was her young daughter. *Amy Prentiss* aired as part of the *Mystery Movie* sequence, but didn't last more than three outings. The pilot had been an episode of *A Man Called Ironside*.

ANCHOR/ANCHORMAN

The person who presents a news, current affairs, sports or magazine programme, linking contributions from other reporters or cueing in pre-recorded inserts. In some instances, the anchor is instrumental in setting the tone or style of the programme. The term has also been employed for the questionmaster in a game show. It was allegedly first used in 1952 by Sig Mickelson, President of CBS News, when describing the fundamental role played by celebrated news frontman Walter Cronkite in CBS bulletins.

AND MOTHER MAKES THREE/AND MOTHER MAKES FIVE

UK (Thames) Situation Comedy. ITV 1971–6

Sally Harrison/Redway	Wendy Craig
Simon Harrison	Robin Davies
Peter Harrison	David Parfitt
Auntie Flo	Valerie Lush
Mr Campbell	George Selway
David Redway	Richard Coleman
Jane Redway	Miriam Mann *(Makes Three)*
	Maxine Gordon *(Makes Five)*
Joss Spencer	Tony Britton *(Makes Five)*
Monica Spencer	Charlotte Mitchell *(Makes Five)*

Creator/Writer: Richard Waring. Producer: Peter Frazer-Jones

A young widow struggles to cope with her two young sons.

Left with her two young boys, Simon and Peter, when her husband died, scatty housewife Sally Harrison took a job at a vet's surgery. Working for Mr Campbell, she struggled along in traditional sitcom fashion with the help of her Auntie Flo whom she persuaded to join the household. Further assistance came eventually from the new man in her life, David Redway (Mr Campbell's replacement), a widower with a young daughter named Jane. Sally later worked in David's antiquarian bookshop, a marriage ensued and the series turned into *And Mother Makes Five*, in 1974, when they all moved in together. Auntie was rehoused in the flat above the shop and the Spencers became their next door neighbours.

ANDERSON, CLIVE (1953–)

British presenter and humourist, coming to the fore as chairman of the improvization show *Whose Line Is It Anyway?* Anderson, a practising barrister, was President of the Cambridge Footlights club in the early 1970s and performed stand-up routines at The Comedy Store and other clubs before breaking into television as a writer on programmes such as *Not the Nine O'Clock News* and *Alas Smith and Jones*. After *Whose Line Is It Anyway?*, he graduated to his own Channel 4 chat show, *Clive Anderson Talks Back*, and also stood in on *Wogan* and *Points of View*. Then came the BBC 2 information programme *Notes and Queries With Clive Anderson*. In 1995 Anderson appeared in *Our Man In . . .* , a series of light-hearted documentaries from exotic locales around the world.

ANDERSON, GERRY (1929–)

British television's puppet master, Gerry Anderson, actually began his TV career working as director for Roberta Leigh, creator of *The Adventures of Twizzle* and *Torchy*. However, Anderson had already set up his own film company with colleague Arthur Povis (Anderson/Povis films – APF), and, seeing the potential of such animation, launched his own series, *Four Feather Falls*, in 1960. This story of a courageous, crooning Western lawman with magic feathers to protect him was sold to Granada and Anderson was up and running.

It wasn't until 1962, when he created *Supercar*, that Anderson embarked on science fiction. These dashing tales of a vehicle that could go anywhere and do anything heralded a new era for TV sci-fi, although it also proved a little too expensive for Granada. Thankfully Lew Grade stepped in and ITC became Anderson's new backers. *Supercar's* more adventurous follow-up, *Fireball XL5*, concerning the exploits of Steve Zodiac and his crew, proved very popular, so popular in fact that Anderson decided to go for colour on his next project. This was *Stingray*, the adventures of a supersub and its fearless commander, Troy Tempest. All the while, Anderson's new

'Supermarionation' was reaching maturity, the puppets' strings becoming ever finer and their mouths synchronized with the dialogue for added realism. Working closely with Anderson were Barry Gray (who supplied all the rousing theme tracks), and co-producer Reg Hill. Involved in the scripting, and supplying some of the female voices, was Gerry's wife, Sylvia Anderson.

Their next opus proved to be their masterpiece. *Thunderbirds*, filmed in 50-minute episodes, focused on the agents of International Rescue, an anonymous world protection force with a fleet of super aircraft. After *Thunderbirds*, Anderson's puppetry was perfected in *Captain Scarlet and the Mysterons*, produced by Century 21 Productions (as APF had now become). Gone were awkward, bulbous-headed puppets, in came perfectly proportioned, beautifully characterized human models, as the indestructible Spectrum agent and his colleagues fought off the vengeful raiders from Mars. Following these last two successes was always going to be difficult and the Anderson team disappointed fans with two very tame offerings, namely *Joe 90* and *The Secret Service*. This led Anderson to look more seriously at live action as the way forward, spawning *UFO* as the next project. Sci-fi was subsequently abandoned when he turned his attention to *The Protectors*, starring Robert Vaughn, Nyree Dawn Porter and Tony Anholt as a trio of international crime fighters, but it was back on the table when *Space: 1999*, with Martin Landau and Barbara Bain, arrived in 1975. The major 1980s offering was *Terrahawks*, a return to puppetry featuring the grizzly alien Zelda.

None of the post-*Captain Scarlet* series has fared particularly well and little has been seen of Anderson's creativity in recent years. A collection of short detective spoofs, *Dick Spanner PI*, arrived on Channel 4 in 1985, but fans everywhere are still waiting for another *Thunderbirds* to take them well and truly into Century 21. Whether or not his new combination of animation and live action, Space Precinct, will fit the bill in the long term remains to be seen.

ANDERSON, JEAN (1908–)

British actress specializing in crusty, upper-class roles and most familiar as the scheming mother in *The Brothers*. Her other lead credits include *Tenko* (as Joss Holbrook) and there have been plenty of supporting roles, from *Dr Finlay's Casebook* to *The Good Guys*.

ANDREWS, ANTHONY (1948–)

Suave English leading man, coming to the fore as the Earl of Silverbridge in *The Pallisers* and as Lt

Brian Ash in Thames TV's *Danger UXB*. *Brideshead Revisited* followed (playing Sebastian Flyte), for which he picked up a BAFTA award as Best Actor on TV. Other notable credits have included *Upstairs, Downstairs*, *The Duchess of Duke Street*, *Ivanhoe*, *Z for Zachariah*, *Suspicion*, *The Woman He Loved* and the elaborate miniseries *AD (Anno Domini)*, in which he played Nero. Trivia buffs will recall that Andrews was originally cast as Bodie in *The Professionals* but lost the part because he looked too much like Martin Shaw in screen tests.

ANDREWS, EAMONN, CBE (1922–87)

Former boxer (the All Ireland Juvenile Champion) and sports commentator who became one of TV's most durable comperes. Having built a successful career in radio, in both Ireland and Britain, Andrews's first TV break came in 1951 when he was selected as host of *What's My Line?*, the BBC's new panel game. In 1955, he became presenter of *This Is Your Life*, a light-hearted, biographical tribute show imported from the USA. Ironically, Andrews was surprised in the first show by American compere Ralph Edwards and became the programme's first victim. *What's My Line* and *This Is Your Life* were to become stalwarts of Andrews's TV career, although he also dabbled in children's television through *Playbox* and, most notably, *Crackerjack*. When his BBC contract elapsed in 1964 (*This Is Your Life* was cancelled), he moved to ITV to host *World of Sport* and his own late-night celebrity series, *The Eamonn Andrews Show* (echoing the title of a 1956 BBC comedy show Eamonn had presented). *This Is Your Life* was revived by Thames in 1969 and *What's My Line* returned in 1984 (again courtesy of Thames, for whom Andrews presented the nightly news magazine *Today* for ten years). His other credits included *Time for Business* and the ambitious satellite quiz *Top of the World* (linking contestants on three continents). Eamonn Andrews died in 1987 from heart disease. In his career, he had been voted Television Personality of the Year four times and had helped to set up RTE, the Irish television corporation.

ANDROMEDA BREAKTHROUGH, The

see *A for Andromeda*.

ANDY PANDY

UK (BBC) Children's Entertainment. BBC 1950–7; 1970

Creators: Freda Lingstrom, Maria Bird.
Writer/Narrator: Maria Bird. Producers: Peter Thompson, David Boisseau

The tame adventures of a puppet and his toy friends.

Dressed in a fetching blue-and-white-striped suit, with a matching floppy hat, Andy Pandy was one of the pioneers of children's TV in the early 1950s. In fact, he remained a source of fun for infants right through the 1960s, too. Taking up the King of the Kids' Show baton from Muffin the Mule, Andy was a cherub-faced toddler who lived in a picnic basket. He first appeared solo, but then was joined by the moth-eaten Teddy and, later, a rag doll named Looby Loo.

Andy and Teddy's adventures were remarkably uninspiring, stretching no further than a ride on a swing or a turn on the see saw, accompanied by a rather patronizing commentary from co-creator/ writer/narrator Maria Bird and shrill, jingly songs, voiced by Gladys Whitbred and Julia Williams. The greatest excitement came when their backs were turned and Looby Loo sprang to life. With her simple features, yellow plaits and polka dot dress, Looby played, danced and then skipped to the ditty 'Here We Go Looby Loo'. At the end of each show, Andy and Teddy popped back in the basket to the strains of the closing song, which declared it was 'Time to go home' (later 'Time to stop play').

Andy Pandy was jointly the brainchild of Maria Bird and Freda Lingstrom, later Head of the BBC's Children's Department, and first aired in 1950, marking an expansion in programmes for younger viewers. Its first slot was Tuesday at 3.45pm and it was soon joined by similar programmes on other days, making up the **Watch with Mother** strand. Only 26 original programmes were made, but they were repeated endlessly until 1969. Thirteen new, colour episodes were written and produced by Freda Lingstrom in 1970, to replace the fading black and white films. The puppets' chunky strings (a world away from the micro-wires used by Gerry Anderson) were pulled by Audrey Atterbury and Molly Gibson.

ANGELIS, MICHAEL

Liverpudlian actor, often in comic roles like that of Lucien, the rabbit-loving brother of Carol Boswell in **The Liver Birds**. More recently, he appeared in **GBH** and starred as Harold Craven in **Luv**, as well as playing gay bartender Arnie in **September Song** and taking over as narrator of **Thomas the Tank Engine and Friends** from Ringo Starr. Other credits have included **Rock Follies**, **Boys from the Black Stuff**, **Reilly – Ace of Spies**, **Bread**, **Boon**, **Between the Lines**, **Lovejoy** and **Casualty**. He is married to **Coronation Street** actress Helen Worth.

ANGELS

UK (BBC) Drama. BBC 1 1975–83

Patricia Rutherford	Fiona Fullerton
Jo Longhurst	Julie Dawn Cole
Sita Patel	Karan David
Ruth Fullman	Lesley Dunlop
Shirley Brent	Clare Clifford
Maureen Morahan	Erin Geraghty
Miss Windrup	Faith Brook
Linda Hollis	Janina Faye
Elaine Fitzgerald	Taiwo Ajai
Sarah Regan	Debbie Ash
Jennifer Sorrell	Marsha Miller
Kathy Betts	Shirley Cheriton
Rose Butchins	Kathryn Apanowicz
Vicky Smith	Pauline Quirke
Beverley Slater	Judith Jacob
Ron Frost	Martin Barrass
Alison Streeter	Juliet Waley
Tracey Willoughby	Julia Williams
Linda Mo	Sarah Lam
Dave Nowell	Neil West
Janet Dickens	Michelle Martin

Creator: Paula Milne. Producers: Ron Craddock, Julia Smith, Ben Rea

Student nurses struggle to make a success of their lives and careers.

Beginning as a 50-minute drama series, then in 1979 switching to two half-hour episodes a week, *Angels* told the stories of student nurses of St Angela's Hospital, Battersea. It showed them at work and at play, and, shot in semi-documentary style, it exposed their long hours and thankless chores. Although they were angels, these nurses were no saints, which came as a shock to some viewers expecting another dose of **Emergency – Ward 10**'s soppy romance. In many ways, *Angels*, with its grittiness, can be seen as a forerunner of **EastEnders**. Producer Julia Smith went on to create the latter and perhaps used *Angels* as a dress rehearsal for the East End drama (even though *Angels* was only seen in 13-week blocks and not all year round). Some of the stars, too – Shirley Cheriton, Kathryn Apanowicz and Judith Jacobs – moved to Albert Square, while others, like Pauline Quirke (**Birds of a Feather**), Fiona Fullerton (**The Charmer**) and Lesley Dunlop (**May to December**), found different avenues to success.

ANGLIA TELEVISION

The independent television company serving East Anglia since 27 October 1959 from a headquarters in Norwich and a handful of smaller studios around the region. Inheriting a predominantly agricultural and rural area, the company at first pitched its regional programmes accordingly, although with the gradual expansion into the industrial centres of the East Midlands, its style has become more cosmopolitan. In the early 1970s it relinquished coverage of Lincolnshire and Humberside to Yorkshire Television (thanks to an IBA transmitter swap) and nearly joined Yorkshire and Tyne Tees in a joint holding company, Trident Television. Although the other two companies went ahead, the IBA refused Anglia permission to become Trident's 'third prong'.

Nationally, Anglia did very well in the quiz show line in the 1970s, thanks to *Sale of the Century* and Gambit, in particular. The company has also built up a reputation for very competent drama, with the likes of *P.D. James*'s Adam Dalgliesh mysteries, *The Chief* and Jilly Cooper's Riders all recent contributions to the network. Probably its best known series, however, was *Tales of the Unexpected*, which notched up huge international sales. Yet Anglia's name for drama has been dwarfed by its worldwide status as a maker of natural history films, thanks to the acclaim showered on *Survival* since it began in 1961. This programme is now looked after by a subsidiary company, Survival Anglia Ltd.

Anglia, successfully retaining its franchise in the 1991 ITV auctions, was taken over by the MAI group (owners of Meridian Television) in 1994. Film-maker Sir David Puttnam is a member of the Anglia board.

ANHOLT, TONY (1941–)

One of TV's smoothies, Singapore-born Tony Anholt's first starring role came as Paul Buchet in *The Protectors*, alongside Robert Vaughn and Nyree Dawn Porter. In 1975 he popped up in *Coronation Street* playing David Law, the crooked boss of a model agency, but it was not until the 1980s that his career really revived, when he was cast as tycoon Charles Frere in *Howards' Way*. His other TV credits have included *The Strauss Family* (as Eduard), *Space: 1999* (as First Officer Tony Verdeschi), *A Family at War*, plus numerous guest spots in the likes of *Minder*, *Bulman* and *Only Fools and Horses*.

ANIMAL MAGIC

UK (BBC) Natural History. BBC 1 1962–83

Presenters: Johnny Morris, Terry Nutkins

Producers: Winwood Reade, Jeffrey Boswell, Douglas Thomas, George Inger

A whimsical look at the world of animals for younger viewers.

Hosted by the inimitable Johnny Morris, the man who talked *for* animals, *Animal Magic* was a stalwart of the BBC's children's output for 21 years. As well as welcoming guest animals into the studio (always a hazardous practice), Morris went out and about to see creatures at work and play. A favourite stomping ground was Bristol Zoo and Morris later over-dubbed the films he made, putting humorous words in the animals' mouths. Camels were his favourite beasts because they always looked as if they were talking. Also seen in the early days were film-maker Tony Soper and naturalist Gerald Durrell. Terry Nutkins joined Morris in the 1980s.

ANIMAL, VEGETABLE, MINERAL?

UK (BBC) Panel Game. BBC 1952–9

Chairman: Glyn Daniel. Producer: David Attenborough

Erudite, name the item quiz.

Unusually popular, considering its learned tone, *Animal, Vegetable, Mineral?* was one of the BBC's first major panel games. A team of three experts tried once a fortnight to identify a succession of objects taken from Britain's museums and to explain how they worked out the answer. Britain's great 'national inheritance' received a plug in the process. The first chairman was Lionel Hale, but, from the second programme, Cambridge University Fellow Glyn Daniel hosted proceedings. Among the numerous experts taking part were archaeologist Sir Mortimer Wheeler, Adrian Digby, Norman Cook, Dr W.E. Swinton, Dr Julian Huxley, Jacquetta Hawkes, Professor Thomas Bodkin and other cerebral folk. David Attenborough was the programme's chief producer. A short-lived revival followed in 1971.

ANNIS, FRANCESCA (1944–)

British leading actress, best remembered on TV for her acclaimed portrayal of Lillie Langtry in *Lillie*, reprising a role she had played in some episodes of *Edward the Seventh*. The earlier *Madame Bovary* for BBC 2, plus the later Agatha Christie dramas *Why Didn't They Ask Evans* and *The Secret Adversary*, leading to the series *Partners In Crime* (in which she played Tuppence Beresford), consolidated her appeal in sophisticated roles. Some of her first TV appearances came in episodes of *Danger Man* and *Dr Finlay's Casebook*.

ANNOUNCER

The person who, either in vision or simply by voice-over, links programmes, reads trails and provides important additional information to viewers. He/she is also known as a continuity announcer. The BBC has long abandoned on-screen announcers, though its early broadcasts were characterized by the presence on camera of personalities such as Jasmine Bligh, Elizabeth Cowell, Leslie Mitchell, Mary Malcolm, McDonald Hobley and Sylvia Peters. ITV stations have held on to in-vision announcers longer, but most now rely on off-screen links.

ANTHOLOGY

A collection of dramatic works, generally by various authors, with no continuous characters or plots, even though the stories may share a common theme or style. Examples include *Out of the Unknown*, *Thriller* and *The Wonderful World of Disney*. Sometimes one character or actor is employed as the host of each programme, to hold the concept together, as exemplified by Alfred Hitchcock in *Alfred Hitchcock Presents* or Rod Serling in *The Twilight Zone*.

ANTIQUES ROADSHOW

UK (BBC) Antiques. BBC 1 1979–

Presenters: Angela Rippon, Bruce Parker, Arthur Negus, Hugh Scully

Producers: Robin Drake, Christopher Lewis

A team of experts values the treasured possessions of ordinary citizens.

Antiques Roadshow has travelled the length and breadth of the United Kingdom, inviting viewers to drop by and have their family heirlooms valued. Since the first broadcast, from Newbury in 1979, there has been much raiding of attics and basements across the land, in the hope of discovering something of value. Punters have queued up, cherished items in hand, awaiting the verdict of one of the experts, who have all been drawn from leading auction houses and dealerships.

Participants have explained how the items came into their family's possession and the specialists have then provided more background information, explaining where, when and by whom it was probably made and winding up with a financial valuation. One piece a week has usually proved to be a real find – a magnificent specimen of furniture, a long-lost work by a distinguished artist, etc. – much to the delight of both the excited connoisseur and the gasping proprietor. Hugh Scully has hosted proceedings in recent years and the programme has become a Sunday afternoon favourite.

APPLEYARDS, THE

UK (BBC) Children's Drama. BBC 1952–7

Mr Appleyard .... Frederick Piper
Douglas Muir

Mrs Appleyard .... Constance Fraser
John Appleyard .... David Edwards
Janet Appleyard .... Tessa Clarke
Tommy Appleyard .... Derek Rowe
Margaret Appleyard .... Pat Fryer

Writer: Philip Burton

Major moments in the life of a suburban, middle-class family.

The Appleyards was an early children's soap opera, transmitted once a fortnight as part of the *Children's Television* slot (around 4.30–5pm). It featured the Appleyard family – mum, dad, teenagers John and Janet, and younger siblings Tommy and Margaret – and picked up a number of awards during its five-year run. A reunion special, entitled *Christmas with the Appleyards*, was shown in 1960.

AQUARIUS

UK (LWT) Arts. ITV 1970–7

Presenters: Humphrey Burton, Russell Harty, Peter Hall

Editor: Humphrey Burton

Late-night arts magazine.

Produced fortnightly, on Saturday or Sunday nights, *Aquarius* was originally hosted by its editor, Humphrey Burton, though Russell Harty and Peter Hall took over in later years, when the programme was screened weekly. A rival to the BBC's *Omnibus*, *Aquarius* incorporated reports on all aspects of the artistic and cultural world. During its seven years, the series included items on the likes of Salvador Dali, Arthur Rubinstein, Pablo Casals and Stanley Spencer. When it ended in 1977 it was succeeded by *The South Bank Show*.

ARCHIE BUNKER'S PLACE see *All in the Family*.

ARE YOU BEING SERVED?

UK (BBC) Situation Comedy. BBC 1 1973–85

Mrs Betty Slocombe .... Mollie Sugden
Mr Humphries .... John Inman
Captain Stephen Peacock .... Frank Thornton
Mr Cuthbert Rumbold .... Nicholas Smith
Miss Brahms .... Wendy Richard
Mr Grainger .... Arthur Brough
Mr Lucas .... Trevor Bannister
Mr Harman .... Arthur English
Mr Tebbs .... James Hayter
Mr Spooner .... Mike Berry
Young Mr Grace .... Harold Bennett
Mr Goldberg .... Alfie Bass

Creators/Writers: Jeremy Lloyd, David Croft. Executive Producer: David Croft. Producers: David Croft, Bob Spiers, Michael Shardlow

Fun and games with the staff of a traditional department store.

Chock-full of nudge-nudge, wink-wink innuendo, this long-running farce centred on the members of staff in the clothing department on the first floor of Grace Brothers. Clearly divided into male and female sections, supervised by department manager Mr Rumbold and floor walker Captain Peacock, the clothing section employed some well-defined comedy stereotypes. On the men's side there was the swishy homosexual Mr Humphries, declaring 'I'm free' whenever a customer needed attention and always poised to take that inside leg measurement. He worked alongside grouchy old Mr Grainger and the department junior, Mr Lucas, who was later replaced by Mr Spooner. In charge of the ladies' cash desks, amidst the intimate apparel, was billowing Mrs Slocombe, a superficially dignified mistress of the unfortunate phrase, who brought howls of laughter from the studio audience with her fluorescent rinses and her constant worries about her pussy. She was ably supported in the battle of the sexes by the buxom, young Miss Brahms. Overseeing the whole operation, and telling everyone that they'd 'all done very well', was the store's owner, doddery Young Mr Grace, a failing geriatric with a dolly bird on each arm. Mr Harman was the cantankerous caretaker.

Though plots were thin and obvious, the in-jokes kept coming – for 12 years. Even then the characters refused to die, with Messrs Peacock, Humphries and Rumbold, Mrs Slocombe and Miss Brahms resurfacing in a 1992 revival, set at a country hotel. Now under the banner of *Grace and Favour*, the team had been made redundant at Grace Brothers, following the death of Young Mr Grace, and discovered that the firm's pension fund had been invested in the run-down Millstone Manor, where Mr Rumbold was the struggling manager. With nothing to lose, the others decided to join him in an attempt to turn the business around, hoping the country air might do them good. Two series were made.

The pilot for *Are You Being Served?* was an episode of **Comedy Playhouse** seen in September 1972. John Inman had a minor hit with a novelty spin-off record, *Are You Being Served Sir,* in 1975, and a feature film version was released in 1977.

ARENA

UK (BBC) Arts. BBC 2 1975–

Editors: Alan Yentob, Nigel Finch, Anthony Wall

All-embracing, popular arts series.

The umbrella title of *Arena* has encompassed documentary features on many subjects. Indeed, in its early days each edition was categorized by a subtitle – *Arena: Theatre, Arena: Art and Design, Arena: Cinema, Arena: Television* or *Arena: Rock.* The categories alternated weekly. Some contributions have been seriously arty, others more trivial and populist.

ARLOTT, JOHN (1914–91)

Hugely respected cricket commentator and wine expert whose rich Hampshire burr is now badly missed in cricketing circles. He joined the BBC in 1945 as a poetry specialist, after 11 years in the police force, and, though he did plenty of TV work in the 1960s, his later contracts were once again with BBC Radio. He pulled stumps on a 33-year commentating career at the Centenary Test in 1980, taking retirement in the Channel Islands.

ARMCHAIR THEATRE

UK (ABC/Thames) Drama Anthology. ITV 1956–74

Producers: Sydney Newman, Leonard White, Lloyd Shirley

Influential, long-running series of single dramas.

Although initiated in 1956 (with the play *The Outsider,* starring David Kossoff and Adrienne Corri), *Armchair Theatre* only really began to gain authority in 1958, with the arrival of Canadian producer Sydney Newman. In his five years in charge (before leaving for the BBC, where he created **Doctor Who** amongst other offerings), Newman focused on contemporary themes and 'real' issues, and such grubby realism earned the series the unfortunate nickname of 'Armpit Theatre'.

Newman assembled around him some of the top dramatic talents of the day, including such directors as Philip Saville, George More O'Ferrall and William T. Kotcheff, story editors Irene Shubik and Peter Luke, and young playwrights such as Harold Pinter, Alun Owen, Robert Muller and Ray Rigby. Pinter's first TV play, *A Night Out,* was a 1960 *Armchair Theatre* production and Owen's *Lena, O My Lena* was another of that year's contributions. There were quality performers in front of the camera, too. These included Tyrone Power, Flora Robson, Gracie Fields, Joan Greenwood, Billie Whitelaw, Donald Pleasence, Tom Courtenay and a young Diana Rigg. Some early plays were transmitted live and the perils of such practice were cruelly highlighted in 1958, when actor Gareth Jones collapsed and died during a rendition of a play entitled *Underground*.

The series produced some notable spin-offs. A 1962 version of John Wyndham's *Dumb Martian* was used as a taster for the new *Out of this World* science-fiction anthology which began the following week, while James Mitchell's *A Magnum for Schneider*, in 1967, resulted in the hugely popular Callan series. *Armchair Theatre* survived the ITV franchise swap of 1968, with production switching from ABC to the newly formed Thames Television. Thames later tinkered with the format, introducing *Armchair Cinema*, a film-based equivalent, which included *Regan*, the pilot for *The Sweeney*, amongst its successes.

Armchair Theatre became compulsive Sunday night entertainment for many viewers, particularly during its heyday at the turn of the 1960s. The alternative title of *Armchair Summer Theatre* was occasionally used for seasonal episodes, whilst *Armchair Mystery Theatre* was a variation on the theme by the same production team, airing between 1960 and 1965.

ARMSTRONG, ALUN (1946–)

A familiar face on TV, Alun Armstrong is one of those character actors still waiting for a lasting vehicle of his own. He has played prominent roles and supported the leads in such programmes as *Villains*, *The Stars Look Down*, **Days of Hope**, *A Sharp Intake of Breath*, *Inspector Morse*, **Bulman** and *Stanley and the Women*, usually taking on gruff working-class parts. He was also Squeers in *The Life and Adventures of Nicholas Nickleby*, played Roy Grade in *Goodbye Cruel World*, the hated stepfather in *Goggle Eyes*, Uncle Teddy in *The Life and Times of Henry Pratt* and has been seen in numerous plays, including Alan Plater's *Get Lost!*, an early version of *The Beiderbecke Affair*.

ARMY GAME, THE

UK (Granada) Situation Comedy. ITV 1957–61

Major Upshot-Bagley	Geoffrey Sumner
	Jack Allen
CSM Bullimore	William Hartnell
Sgt Claude Snudge	Bill Fraser
Corporal Springer	Michael Medwin
Pte 'Excused Boots' Bisley	Alfie Bass
Pte 'Cupcake' Cook	Norman Rossington
	Keith Banks
Pte 'Popeye' Popplewell	Bernard Bresslaw
Pte 'Prof' Hatchett	Charles Hawtrey
	Keith Smith
Captain Pilsworthy	Bernard Hunter
Major Geoffrey Gervaise Duckworth	C.B. Poultney
Pte Bone	Ted Lune
Corporal 'Flogger' Hoskins	Harry Fowler
Captain Pocket	Frank Williams
Pte Dooley	Harry Towb
Lance Corporal Ernest 'Moosh' Merryweather	Mario Fabrizi
Pte Billy Baker	Robert Desmond
Pte 'Chubby' Catchpole	Dick Emery

Creator: Sid Colin. Producers: Peter Eton, Eric Fawcett

The schemes and scams of a gang of National Service soldiers.

This extremely popular early comedy was set in Hut 29 of the Surplus Ordnance Depot at Nether Hopping, somewhere in remotest Staffordshire, and featured the exploits of a mixed bag of army conscripts. At the forefront were Pte 'Bootsie' Bisley, so named because he was allowed to wear plimsolls instead of boots, Pte Hatchett, who knitted to pass the time and was known as 'The Professor', Liverpudlian Pte 'Cupcake' Cook, taking his name from the many food parcels his mother sent him, gormless Pte 'Popeye' Popplewell and their Cockney spiv ring leader, Corporal Springer. Trying to knock them into shape were the bellowing Sgt Major Bullimore and then (when future **Doctor Who** Bill Hartnell left to star in the very similar *Carry On Sergeant*) the pompous Sgt Claude Snudge (whose catchphrase became 'I'll be leaving you now, Sah!'). Toffee-nosed dimwit Major Upshot-Bagley was nominal head of the camp.

There were many personnel changes in the series' four-year run. Upshot-Bagley was replaced by other commandants (Pilsworthy, Duckworth and Pocket) and new conscripts were brought in. Popeye was succeeded by the equally dense Pte Bone, Springer by another chirpy Londoner, 'Flogger' Hoskins, and other new arrivals included 'Chubby' Catchpole, Lance Corporal Ernie Merryweather and Privates Dooley and Baker. Of the characters that remained, some changed actors. Barry Took and Marty Feldman were amongst the numerous writers involved.

The Army Game was originally transmitted live once a fortnight, though when its popularity increased, it switched to once a week. In 1958, the series engendered a spin-off film, *I Only Arsked* (based on Popeye's catchphrase). In the same year the Signature tune of the *Army Game* was a top five hit for Michael Medwin, Bernard Bresslaw, Alfie Bass and Leslie Fyson, and, in 1960, a sequel series, **Bootsie and Snudge**, was produced.

ARNAZ, DESI

(Desiderio Alberto Arnaz y de Acha; 1917–86) Cuban-born musician and band leader, who, as

Lucille Ball's real and on-screen husband, became one of TV's earliest superstars. Arnaz grew up in a wealthy Cuban family, but, in 1933, with the installation of the Battista regime, he fled penniless to Miami with his mother. His Latin looks and musical abilities secured him work with bands like Xavier Cugat's and saw him arrive in Hollywood. There he met the up-and-coming Lucille Ball and they married in 1940. Ten years later, to save their turbulent marriage, they agreed to work together on a new TV comedy, *I Love Lucy* – the mother of all sitcoms – playing husband and wife duo Lucy and Ricky Ricardo. To produce the show, Arnaz founded their own production company, Desilu (later responsible for shows such as **The Untouchables** and **Mannix**). However, their marriage was not to last and they divorced in 1960. Lucy persevered with her scatterbrained TV characterizations, while Desi turned more to production. He was seen only rarely on screen in later years.

ARNESS, JAMES (JAMES AURNESS; 1923–)

The brother of **Mission Impossible**'s Peter Graves, a strapping giant of an actor who became synonymous with the Western lawman, thanks to his long-running portrayal of Marshal Matt Dillon in **Gunsmoke**. Arness, a veteran of the Anzio campaign in World War II, entered the movie business in the 1940s, winning parts in assorted B-movies, most memorably *The Thing* and *Them!* In 1955 he was recommended for the *Gunsmoke* role by his friend John Wayne and reluctantly accepted, fearing a flopped TV series would jeopardize his cinema career. To help things along and guarantee a big audience, Wayne offered to introduce the very first *Gunsmoke* episode. Arness need not have worried. The series ran for 20 years on US TV and during that time he had no cause to look for other TV work. Indeed, by the close, he was also part owner of the production. Following the cancellation of *Gunsmoke* in 1975, Arness returned to the screen as Zeb Macahan in *How The West Was Won* and then took on the role of veteran cop Jim McClain in **McClain's Law**.

ARNOLD, ROSEANNE (1953–)

Outspoken, stand-up comedienne who quickly took control of the TV series named after her. In *Roseanne*, she has portrayed a shirty, sarcastic working mum (Roseanne Conner) and led the programme to the top of the US ratings. Her name changed from Barr to Arnold after her marriage to comic Tom Arnold, who also worked on the show. However, she now prefers to be billed simply as Roseanne.

AROUND THE WORLD IN 80 DAYS

UK (BBC) Documentary. BBC 1 1989

Presenter: Michael Palin

Producer: Clem Vallence

Light-hearted attempt to emulate the voyage of Phileas Fogg.

Initially earmarked as a vehicle for Alan Whicker, this humorous travelogue found its modern-day Phileas Fogg in the form of ex-*Python* Michael Palin. The aim of the venture was to follow closely the journey made by Jules Verne's hero, travelling around the world in 80 days using just land and sea transport (the only methods available 115 years earlier, when Fogg's journey took place). However, Palin discovered that Fogg's network of passenger liners had long disappeared, and he was forced to rely on unpredictable merchant vessels for large sections of his journey. Delays at customs points, narrowly missed departures and uncooperative locals added to the tension as Palin sought to return to London's Reform Club within the imposed time limit. His voyage took him on the Orient Express, on numerous ferries and by land across Saudi Arabia and the United Arab Emirates. Most dramatically, he boarded a primitive dhow for the crossing of the Arabian Sea. He then crossed India, China and the USA by train, before steaming into Felixstowe for the last leg into London. The circumnavigation took place in 1988.

Supporting Palin on his travels were his 'Passepartout', an openly acknowledged production team of producer/director Clem Vallence, director Roger Mills and crew of Nigel Meakin, Nigel Walters, Ron Brown, Simon Maggs, Julian Charrington, Dave Jewitt, Angela Elbourne and Ann Holland. Half the team followed Palin as far as Hong Kong and the others completed the trip home. They shot film on 77 of the 80 days and their recordings were edited into seven intriguing episodes. An accompanying book, written by Michael Palin, was a massive success, selling over half a million copies.

An even more ambitious venture followed in 1991. In *Pole to Pole*, Palin and his team (including several *80 Days* veterans) attempted to travel from the North to the South Pole, using only public transport where available. The exhausting 141-day voyage took them through the Soviet Union just days before its collapse and then down through civil war-ravaged Africa. Again, a book accompanied the series, which was screened in 1992.

ARREST AND TRIAL

US (Revue/Universal) Detective Drama. BBC 1
1964

Detective Sgt Nick Anderson	Ben Gazzara
Attorney John Egan	Chuck Connors
Deputy DA Jerry Miller	John Larch
Assistant Deputy DA Barry Pine	John Kerr
Detective Sgt Dan Kirby	Roger Perry
Detective Lt Bone	Noah Keen
Jake Shakespeare	Joe Higgins
Mitchell Harris	Don Galloway
Janet Okada	Jo Anne Miya

Producer: Frank P. Rosenberg

**Innovative drama series, comprising
programmes of two separate halves: the
first showing a criminal investigation, the
second the subsequent trial.**

Setting the pattern for a host of crime movies
many years later, *Arrest and Trial* depicted the
exploits of Detective Sgt Nick Anderson of the
LAPD and local defence lawyer John Egan. The
first 45-minute segment of each programme concerned itself with the execution of a crime and
the efforts of Anderson and his colleagues to find
the culprit. The second 45 minutes were then
devoted to the trial, giving Egan and his legal
eagles the chance to negate Anderson's good
work by getting the defendant off the hook.

ARTHUR, BEATRICE (BERNICE FRANKEL; 1926–)

Tall, deep-voiced, forceful stalwart of American
sitcoms, who gained international recognition
later in life as Dorothy in **The Golden Girls**.
Earlier, Arthur had played Archie Bunker's
cousin, Maude Findlay, in **All in the Family** and
in her own spin-off, *Maude*. She also starred in
Amanda's, the US version of **Fawlty Towers**.

ARTHUR C. CLARKE'S MYSTERIOUS WORLD

UK (Yorkshire) Documentary. ITV 1980

Host: Arthur C. Clarke
Narrator: Gordon Honeycombe

Executive Producer: John Fairley. Producer:
Simon Welfare

**The Earth's strange phenomena investigat-
ed by the celebrated science-fiction writer.**

Hosting this documentary series from his Sri
Lankan home, novelist Arthur C. Clarke turned
his attention away from fiction and towards the
weird and wonderful, unexplained real-life phenomena to be witnessed around the world.
Looking at the strange moving rocks of America's

Death Valley and discussing how it can rain frogs
were just two of the topics covered as Clarke
focused on mysteries of the world that challenge
modern-day thinking. Former ITN newscaster
Gordon Honeycombe handled the narration of
this half-hour series.

ARTHUR OF THE BRITONS

UK (HTV) Adventure. ITV 1972–3

Arthur	Oliver Tobias
Llud	Jack Watson
Kai	Michael Gothard
Mark of Cornwall	Brian Blessed
Cerdig	Rupert Davies

Executive Producer: Patrick Dromgoole.
Producer: Peter Miller

**A dashing young Celtic leader takes on
the Saxon invaders.**

With no Camelot, no Guinevere and no Merlin,
this series dispelled the myth of round tables,
chivalrous knights and mystic sorcery, bringing
Arthur back down to earth with a bump. Here,
young and ruggedly good-looking, the legendary
king was depicted as a 6th-century Welsh ruler
who fronted a tough, swashbuckling army of
Celts against intruders from the East led by
Cerdig. Supported by the pagan Llud the Silver
Hand and Kai, a Saxon orphan, Arthur's aim was
to unite the native tribes of Britain against the
invading Saxon forces. Tough battles ensued and
there were woodland skirmishes aplenty. The
Saxons apart, Arthur's other great rival was the
powerful Mark of Cornwall. Many guest artists
featured in the series, including Michael
Gambon, Tom Baker and Catherine Schell, and
Oliver Tobias made the most of his first starring
role.

AS TIME GOES BY

UK (Theatre of Comedy) Situation Comedy.
BBC 1 1992–

Jean Pargetter	Judi Dench
Lionel Hardcastle	Geoffrey Palmer
Judith Pargetter	Moira Brooker
Alistair Deacon	Philip Bretherton
Sandy	Jenny Funnell
Rocky Hardcastle	Frank Middlemass
Madge Hardcastle	Joan Sims

Creator/Writer: Bob Larbey. Producer: Sydney
Lotterby

**Two middle-aged former lovers rekindle
their romance.**

Taking its inspiration from the 1931 song, voiced
by Joe Fagin over the credits, *As Time Goes By*
was a will-they, won't-they gentle comedy about
two young lovers who had gone their separate

ways only to rediscover each other in middle age. Jean Pargetter and Lionel Hardcastle had each mistakenly believed the other had broken off their youthful romance and both had drifted off to marry someone else. Jean, a nurse, and Lionel, a second lieutenant in the Middlesex Regiment, had met in Hyde Park, but when Lionel was posted to Korea a vital letter from Jean never reached him. After 38 years, fate brought them together again, when Lionel, now divorced, employed Jean's secretarial agency (Type For You) to type up his book *My Life in Kenya*, which described his career as a coffee planter in East Africa. Jean's husband, David, had died and she lived with her daughter Judith, who one evening brought Lionel home after dinner, with obvious consequences. Jean and Lionel were married in the 1995 series. Also seen were Jean's efficient secretary, Sandy, and Lionel's pushy publisher, Alistair (Judith's boyfriend). The series was created by Bob Larbey from an original idea by Colin Bostock Smith.

ASCENT OF MAN, THE

UK (BBC/Time-Life) Documentary. BBC 2 1973

Writer/Presenter: Dr Jacob Bronowski

Producer: Adrian Malone

An inspirational account of man's scientific and philosophical progress.

Through the eyes of Polish-born, California-based historian and philosopher Dr Jacob Bronowski, this 13-part series reflected on the development of man through his technological achievements, considering how the introduction of new inventions and the appreciation of new discoveries changed social and moral patterns. In short, it revealed how man became the shaper of his own environment. From the use of primitive tools to the effects of the Industrial Revolution and beyond, vivid examples and illustrations sug-ared the pill for less scientifically minded viewers, as did the charisma and enthusiasm of the curi-ous, hunched presenter. Bronowski travelled the world for the series and worked so hard in the four years of production that he collapsed from exhaustion at its completion and died the following year. He was an unlikely TV star but his series was widely acclaimed.

ASH, LESLIE

British actress, formerly a model. One of her first leading roles was as computer whizkid Fred Smith in *C.A.T.S. Eyes*, although there had been plenty of minor parts in series like *Seconds Out*, **Shelley** and *The Two Ronnies*. Ash was also co-presenter of Channel 4's rock show *The*

Tube for a while, replacing Paula Yates. More recently, as well as appearances in *Perfect Scoundrels*, *Love Hurts* and *Haggard*, she has starred as Nancy Gray in *The Happy Apple*, Deborah in *Men Behaving Badly* and Jo in *Stay Lucky*. She is married to footballer Lee Chapman.

ASHCROFT, DAME PEGGY (EDITH MARGARET EMILY ASHCROFT; 1907–91)

Notable British stage and, occasionally, film actress who added television credits to her name in her later years. Most memorably, Dame Peggy appeared as Queen Mary in *Edward and Mrs Simpson* and Barbie, the missionary, in Granada's lavish *The Jewel in the Crown*.

ASK ASPEL

UK (BBC) Children's Entertainment. BBC 1 1970–81

Presenter: Michael Aspel

Producers: Iain Johnstone, Will Wyatt, Frances Whitaker, Granville Jenkins

Long-running children's request show.

Taking over from *Junior Points of View* as the kiddies' feedback series, *Ask Aspel* encouraged youngsters to write in with their views on the BBC's latest offerings. Host Michael Aspel also played requested snippets, and interviews with star guests filled out the programme.

ASK THE FAMILY

UK (BBC) Quiz. BBC 1 1967–84

Presenter: Robert Robinson

Producers: Cecil Korer, Linda McCarthy

Mind-bending quiz for cerebral families.

Open to families of four (invariably teachers and their egg-headed offspring), *Ask The Family* was a surprisingly durable early evening intellectual quiz. Host Robert Robinson fired off a succession of riddles, mental posers and general knowledge questions, some directed to 'children only', 'mother and younger child', 'father and elder child' or other combinations of contestants. The winning family then progressed through the annual knock-out tournament.

ASKEY, ARTHUR, CBE (1900–82)

Indefatigable, diminutive music hall veteran who became one of postwar TV's biggest names, appearing in assorted variety spectaculars and his own series, *Before Your Very Eyes* (based on one of his catchphrases, with Dickie Henderson, Diana

Decker and the busty Sabrina) from 1953. Two years later, Askey's Blackpool summer show was recorded and shown in five parts by ITV as *Love and Kisses*. In 1958, Askey appeared with his former partner Richard Murdoch in *Living It Up*, a re-creation of their popular 1930s radio show *Band Waggon*, and then, in 1961, he starred in a sitcom, *The Arthur Askey Show*. The following year, back with the BBC, he shared the limelight with Alan Melville in *Raise Your Glasses*. Always popular, Askey was on our screens till the end. In the 1970s he was one of the regular (and kindest) expert panellists on the talent show *New Faces*, never failing to shower the contestants with praise, however dire their act.

ASNER, ED (1929–)

American actor who shot to fame as grouchy news editor Lou Grant in *The Mary Tyler Moore Show* (a performance which won him three Emmys). When the sitcom ended, he made a rather unusual move, staying in the same role when Grant was shipped to the West Coast to become editor of the *Los Angeles Tribune* in a straight drama sequel. Another Emmy followed. After several successful seasons, *Lou Grant* was cancelled amidst rumours of a rift between the producers and the star, revolving around his outspoken political views. Asner's earliest TV credits included guest spots in programmes like *The FBI*, *The Defenders*, *A Man Called Ironside* and *The Fugitive*, as well as a continuous role in a series called *Slattery's People*. He also starred as Axel Jordache in *Rich Man, Poor Man* and the slave ship captain in *Roots* (earning two more Emmys).

ASPEL, MICHAEL, OBE (1933–)

Highly relaxed presenter and chat show host, initially seen on BBC TV news programmes in the 1950s, after working as an actor on BBC Wales radio. Since then he has presented *Crackerjack*, *Come Dancing*, *Miss World*, the long-running kids' request show *Ask Aspel*, *Child's Play*, *Star Games*, *Give Us A Clue*, *The Six O'Clock Show* (London), *Aspel and Company* and the paranormal series *Strange But True*, as well as taking over from Eamonn Andrews as holder of the big red book in *This Is Your Life*. He is married to, though separated from, actress Elizabeth Power (Mrs Hewitt in *EastEnders*).

ASSOCIATED-REDIFFUSION

Company formed by Broadcast Relay Services and Associated Newspapers to operate the very first ITV franchise. A-R (as it became known) went on air on 22 September 1955 and covered London on weekdays. The company shortened its name to Rediffusion in the mid-1960s and was forced by the ITA to merge with ABC in 1968. The resulting company, Thames Television, retained the London weekday franchise. Amongst A-R's successes were **Take Your Pick**, **Double Your Money**, **Do Not Adjust Your Set** and **Ready, Steady, Go!**

ASSOCIATED TELEVISION see ATV.

ASTIN, JOHN (1930–)

Tall, moustached American comic actor chiefly remembered as Gomez in *The Addams Family*. Previously, he had scored a success as Harry Dickens in the sitcom *I'm Dickens, He's Fenster*, alongside Marty Ingels, and was later one of the actors to play The Riddler in *Batman*. His attention then switched to directing, working on programmes like *CHiPS* and *Holmes and Yoyo*. He was at one time married to former child actress Patty Duke (Astin).

ASTRA

Broadcast satellite independently owned by the Luxembourg company SES (Société Européene des Satellites) and launched into orbit in December 1988. Three additional satellites (1B, 1C and 1D) have since been located alongside to extend the number of channels available from an initial 16 to 64, and more are planned. Sky was one of Astra's first customers, taking four channels from February 1989. German, Spanish and Scandinavian broadcasters also make use of Astra's services.

AT LAST THE 1948 SHOW

UK (Rediffusion) Comedy. ITV 1967

John Cleese
Tim Brooke-Taylor
Graham Chapman
Marty Feldman
Aimi Macdonald

Writers: John Cleese, Tim Brooke-Taylor, Graham Chapman, Marty Feldman. Executive Producer: David Frost

Manic comedy sketch series.

Emerging from the funny side of *The Frost Report* and masterminded by David Frost himself, *At Last the 1948 Show* was one of the stepping stone programmes which led to *Monty Python's Flying Circus* and a whole new generation of British comedy. Although essentially a sketch show, its skits were unrelated, in the manner perfected later by *Python*. The humour was visual, wacky and verging on the surreal, and there was also a heavy dose of slapstick (foreshadowing Tim Brooke-Taylor's days in *The Goodies*). Aimi Macdonald supported the show's writer-performers, linking events in her trademark whiny voice.

ATKINSON, ROWAN (1955–)

Rubber-faced comedian of various talents, first surfacing on *Not the Nine O'Clock News*, having begun performing while a post-graduate at Oxford. He is equally at home with both of his major roles since *Not The Nine O'Clock News*, namely the weasely historical blackguard Edmund *Blackadder* and the gormless mute *Mr Bean*. Atkinson runs his own production company, Tiger Television.

ATTENBOROUGH, DAVID, SIR, CBE (1926–)

Television's leading naturalist, David Attenborough, brother of Sir Richard, studied zoology at Cambridge. Joining the BBC as a trainee in 1952, he went on to host and produce the long-running *Zoo Quest*, before being made Controller of BBC 2 in 1965 (overseeing amongst other things the commissioning of *The World About Us*) and the BBC's Director of Programmes in 1969. Although he never totally abandoned wildlife to concentrate on administration, it was not until 1979 that he returned to television in a big way, when he launched his mammoth production *Life on Earth*. This seminal work was followed by *The Living Planet* in 1984, *Trials of Life* in 1990 and *The Private Life of Plants* in 1995. He has also contributed to *Wildlife on One* and *Life in the Freezer*. His whispering, authoritative delivery has been much mimicked by impressionists.

ATV (ASSOCIATED TELEVISION)

The ITV franchise holder for London at weekends and the Midlands on weekdays from 1956 to 1968, and then the seven-day contractor for the Midlands from 1968 to 1981. ATV began life as ABC (Associated Broadcasting Company) but was forced to change its name to avoid confusion with Associated British Cinemas who ran the early franchises for the Midlands and the North on weekends. The company was a merger of interests between Lew Grade and Prince Littler's ITC (which initially owned 50 per cent) and a consortium headed by Norman Collins and Sir Robert Renwick which had originally been awarded the franchise but which seemed to be having difficulties starting up. ATV went on air on 24 September 1955 in London and on 17 February 1956 in the Midlands. ITC (see separate entry) was swallowed up by ATV in 1957, and ATV was itself reconstituted as Central Independent Television to meet the requirements of the IBA's 1981 franchise changes. Central subsequently took over ATV's Midlands area. Amongst ATV's many programming successes were *Sunday Night at the London Palladium*, *Danger Man*, *The Saint*, *Crossroads* and *The Muppet Show*, plus the Gerry Anderson futuristic puppet dramas.

AUF WIEDERSEHEN, PET

UK (Witzend/Central) Comedy Drama. ITV 1983–6

Denis Patterson	Tim Healy
'Oz' Osbourne	Jimmy Nail
Neville Hope	Kevin Whately
Wayne	Gary Holton
Bomber	Pat Roach
Barry Taylor	Timothy Spall
Moxey	Christopher Fairbank
Ally Fraser	Bill Paterson

Creators: Dick Clement, Ian La Frenais, Franc Roddam. Executive Producer: Allan McKeown. Producer: Martin McKeand

The misadventures of a gang of building labourers on secondment overseas.

With jobs scarce in the recession-ridden UK of the early 1980s, the Geordie trio of Denis, Neville and Oz decided to leave their wives and girlfriends in search of employment overseas. Denis was the most mature of the three, philosophical and reasonably level-headed. Neville was the drippy one, emotionally strained at having to leave his new wife, whilst Oz was the archetypal slob, big, fat, bigoted and dense. They were taken on as labourers on a Düsseldorf building site where they shared a hut with four other expatriots. These were girl-crazy Cockney carpenter Wayne, boring Brummie electrician Barry, down-to-earth Bristolian wrestler Bomber and Scouse petty crook Moxey. The 'magnificent seven' formed quite a team. Sharing each others' joys, despairs, hopes and worries, they wined, womanized and sang through their tour of duty, edging from scrape to scrape and scam to scam.

In the second season, shown two years later, the boys were reunited to renovate the Derbyshire mansion of Newcastle gangster Ally Fraser, for whom Denis had been forced to work after amassing gambling debts. When that ended in the usual chaos, the lads headed off to the Costa del Crime for a few episodes' labour under the Spanish sun. One sad aspect of this last series was the death of actor Gary Holton, who was, nevertheless, still seen in all episodes, thanks to early location filming and the subtle use of a double.

Since *Auf Wiedersehen, Pet* most of the cast have progressed to bigger and better things. The closing theme song, 'That's Living Alright', by Joe Fagin was a top three hit in 1984.

AUTOCUE

Trade name for a means of projecting a script on to the front of a camera lens to allow the presenter to read his lines. The words remain unseen by viewers. The system is universally used for news bulletins and other programmes using set scripts. Other trade names include Teleprompt.

AUTRY, GENE (1907–)

Texan singing cowboy of the 1930s and 1940s who quickly clambered aboard the TV bandwagon when it began rolling in the 1950s. His *Gene Autry Show*, popular with American kiddies, was a small-screen version of his cinema antics and radio series, with bumbling sidekick Pat Buttram still in tow. He later developed his own business empire. Apart from owning the Challenge record label, a baseball team, a host of radio and TV stations across the States and assorted hotels, he also founded Flying A Productions. This was the company responsible for such hits as **The Range Rider** and **Champion the Wonder Horse** (Champion was Autry's own trusty steed).

AVENGERS, THE

UK (ABC) Secret Agent Drama. ITV 1961–9

John Steed	Patrick MacNee
Dr David Keel	Ian Hendry
Carol Wilson	Ingrid Hafner
Catherine Gale	Honor Blackman
Venus Smith	Julie Stevens
Dr Martin King	Jon Rollason
One-Ten	Douglas Muir
One-Twelve	Arthur Hewlett
Emma Peel	Diana Rigg
Tara King	Linda Thorson
'Mother'	Patrick Newell
Rhonda	Rhonda Parker

Creators: Sydney Newman, Leonard White. Executive Producers: Albert Fennell, Julian Wintle, Gordon L.T. Scott. Producers: Leonard White, John Bryce, Julian Wintle, Albert Fennell, Brian Clemens

Very British crime/science fiction series involving a suave, gentlemanly agent and his athletic female partners.

The Avengers began life as a spin-off from a programme called *Police Surgeon*, which starred Ian Hendry as Dr Geoffrey Brent. In *The Avengers* Hendry played Dr David Keel, who, when his girlfriend was murdered by a drugs gang, went to British Intelligence and an agent called John Steed for help in 'avenging' her death – hence the title. The early episodes, with Steed acting as a foil for the amateur sleuth, were essentially cops and robbers fare; also seen at this time were Carol Wilson, Keel's secretary, and Steed's bosses, One-Ten and One-Twelve. Following Hendry's departure during a technician's strike, Steed was temporarily partnered by Dr Martin King, night club singer Venus Smith and then one Avenger who stayed, Cathy Gale.

Immaculately turned-out in a three-piece suit, Steed oozed class. He lived in a select London district, drove a vintage Bentley and, amongst other idiosyncrasies, insisted on his coffee being stirred anticlockwise. His manners were impeccable at all times. He could defend himself from attack (often with a sword drawn from his umbrella) and still exhibit the utmost courtesy to his adversary. The versatile umbrella (which also performed other remarkable functions), together with Steed's protective bowler hat, became the show's trademark. With Cathy Gale, a widowed anthropologist and judo expert, Steed's career moved from mundane detection and basic counter-intelligence into the world of futuristic international intrigue. Dressed in tight-fitting leather and the now infamous kinky boots, Gale brought a new raciness to the series. However, after two series, Honor Blackman left to play Pussy Galore in *Goldfinger*. She was replaced by Patrick MacNee's most celebrated colleague, Diana Rigg.

The karate-chopping, kung fu kicking, ultra-fashionable Mrs Peel (widow of test pilot Peter Peel) lived in the fast lane, speeding around in a white Porsche. Her name, it is said, was taken from the British film industry expression 'M-Appeal', meaning 'man appeal'. With her arrival *The Avengers* was aimed more at the US market and played up the picture postcard English village stereotype in its settings. Viewed today, these episodes appear very British and redolent of the Swinging Sixties. It was also during this period that arty programme titles were introduced and Johnny Dankworth's original theme music replaced by the dramatic Laurie Johnson score.

When Rigg left after three seasons to return to the stage (Peter Peel was, it seemed, found alive), another accomplice was required. Unknown actress Linda Thorson was introduced as farm girl Tara King and, for the first time, a romantic liaison for Steed was suggested. Unlike her predecessors, King was not a martial arts expert, but she was just as aggressive when necessary, laying out opponents with a swipe of her brick-laden handbag or simply with a bunch of fives. In the 1970s the programme was revived under the title **The New Avengers**, with Steed (now in his 50s) having the benefit of two rather more active assistants, weapons expert Mike Gambit and Purdey, a high-kicking ex-ballet dancer.

The Avengers' plots were always far-fetched but highly inventive, usually focusing on zany attempts to take over the world. They echoed the exploits of James Bond, in a less extravagant way, but still with gadgets and gimmicks galore. Steed and Tara were even given their own version of Bond's boss 'M', in the form of the wheelchair-bound 'Mother', with his Amazonian secretary Rhonda. Best remembered among the baddies are the cybernauts (not to be confused with *Doctor Who*'s cybermen).

AWEFUL MR GOODALL, THE

UK (LWT) Spy Drama. ITV 1974

Mr Jack Goodall	Robert Urquhart
Millbrook	Donald Churchill
Alexandra Winfield	Isobel Dean

Producer: Richard Bates

A retired civil servant still works for the intelligence services.

After more than 15 years as a lieutenant-colonel in M15 and D15, 55-year-old widower Jack Goodall had hung up his spy-catching equipment and happily retired to Eastbourne. However, he found the intelligence game hard to give up, especially as he was endowed with a kind of sixth sense, a nose for intrigue which made him invaluable to his former employers. These were fronted by Millbrook, Head of Section at an unspecified British security department. Six episodes were produced.

AYCKBOURN, ALAN (1939–)

British playwright responsible for light dramas often concerning the middle classes. His TV credits have included *Bedroom Farce* and the trilogy *The Norman Conquests* (consisting of *Table Manners*, *Living Together* and *Round and Round the Garden*), which viewed the relationship between three couples from three individual vantage points.

AYRES, PAM (1947–)

British colloquial poet with a yokel accent who came to fame after winning appearances on *Opportunity Knocks* in 1975. There followed several TV series and assorted guest appearances on the likes of *The Black and White Minstrel Show*. She has made a modest comeback to showbiz after taking time out to raise a family.

BACHELOR FATHER

UK (BBC) Situation Comedy. BBC 1 1970–1

Peter Lamb	Ian Carmichael
Anna	Briony Roberts
Ben	Ian Johnson
Donald	Roland Pickering
Jane	Beverley Simons
Mandy	Angela Ryder

Writer: Richard Waring. Producers: Graeme Muir

A wealthy bachelor decides he still wants a family, despite not having a wife.

Peter Lamb loved children but his romantic liaisons had never amounted to much and he still wasn't married. Undaunted, he made himself available as a foster parent, taking in five children, who caused him plenty of concern. The series was based on the real-life story of Peter Lloyd Jeffcock, bachelor foster parent of 12 children.

BAFTA

The British Academy of Film and Television Arts was formed in 1959 as the Society of Film and Television Arts by the amalgamation of the British Film Academy and the Guild of Television Producers and Directors. It was reorganized and given its current name in 1975. Membership comprises senior creative workers in the film and television industries and the aim of the Academy is to raise production standards in both media. The BAFTA Awards, announced annually since 1975, with trophies modelled on classical drama masks, have become a highlight of the TV calendar. These began as The British Film Academy Awards in 1947, developing into The Society of Film and Television Arts Awards in 1969. Achievement in film and television is recognized in various categories: single play/drama, drama series, factual series, light entertainment programme, comedy series, best actor, best actress.

BAGPUSS

UK (Smallfilms) Children's Entertainment. BBC 1 1974

Narrator: Oliver Postgate
Creators: Peter Firmin, Oliver Postgate. Writer: Oliver Postgate

A fat, baggy, cloth cat lives on a cushion in a shop window.

Bagpuss was the story of a magic lost-and-found shop, owned by a Victorian girl named Emily. Emily would bring to the shop interesting items she had discovered, with the aim of repairing them and returning them to the owner. To do so, she relied on the help of her fat, pink-and-white-striped cloth cat, Bagpuss, and his industrious little friends. Reciting her magical spell, Emily awoke Bagpuss from sleep (the picture turned from sepia into colour) and he and the other inhabitants of the shop then set about repairing what Emily had found. Down from a shelf came Professor Yaffle, a wooden woodpecker bookend with a German accent. He provided the brains for the task ahead and led the investigation into the identity and usefulness of the object. Up popped Madeleine the rag doll, Gabriel the toad began to strum his banjo and the mice fired up their Marvellous Mechanical Mouse Organ with bellows. Head mouse Charlie kept his crew ahead of the game and the whole team chanted and sang their way through their chores. Once the item had been mended, it was placed in the window in the hope that its owner would call and, at this point, Bagpuss crawled gratefully back to sleep.

Only 13 episodes of *Bagpuss* were ever produced, but re-runs abounded.

BAILEY, ROBIN (1919–)

`Upright British actor fond of crusty codger parts, perhaps best remembered as the cynical Uncle Mort in the Brandon saga *I Didn't Know You Cared*. Previously, however, he had compered *The $64,000 Question* in the 1950s and appeared in a host of major series, including *The Pallisers*, *The Newcomers* and *Upstairs, Downstairs*. In 1983 he took over the role of Redvers *Potter* from the late Arthur Lowe and, two years later, he was cast as Charters alongside Michael Aldridge's Caldicott in the BBC's revival of the two snoopy old public school duffers *Charters and Caldicott*. Among his other credits have been *Sorry I'm A Stranger Here Myself* (as hen-pecked librarian Henry Nunn), *Tales from a Long Room*, *Rumpole of the Bailey* (as Judge Graves) and *Tinniswood Country*.

BAIN, BARBARA (1931–)

American actress, the wife and co-star of Martin Landau (in *Mission Impossible* and *Space: 1999*). Earlier appearances came in *Richard Diamond, Private Detective* (as Karen Wells, opposite David Janssen) and series such as *Hawaiian Eye*, *Perry Mason*, *The Dick Van Dyke Show* and *Wagon Train*.

BAIRD, JOHN LOGIE (1888–1946)

Scottish inventor, widely acknowledged as the father of television, although not the first to experiment in the field. In 1925 Baird

demonstrated a mechanical scanning television system, which produced a rudimentary picture. A year later, he had improved its efficiency so that human faces became recognizable. After much badgering, the BBC picked up Baird's invention and placed it central to their television experiments in 1929. However, rival systems, using electronic rather than mechanical scanning, quickly proved more effective and the Corporation switched to EMI-Marconi's cathode ray tube version a year after regular broadcasts began in 1936. Undaunted, Baird continued to progress his brainchild, experimenting with colour images. Earlier he had also devised a primitive form of video disc, using wax records, and even managed to transmit a TV signal across the Atlantic in 1928, years before satellite relays became a possibility. Just before his death, he had successfully worked on stereoscopic television images.

BAKER, BOB (1939–)

British scriptwriter, usually in collaboration with Dave Martin, who specializes in children's science fiction. Their biggest successes have been for HTV, with series such as *Sky* and *King of the Castle*. Other credits include the TV movie *Thick As Thieves*, *Murder at the Wedding* and episodes of *Z Cars*, *Doctor Who*, *Bergerac* and *Shoestring*.

BAKER, COLIN (1943–)

British actor favoured in pompous, confident roles. He first came to light in *The Brothers*, playing the unscrupulous whiz-kid Paul Merroney, although his most prominent role was as the sixth *Doctor Who* (albeit quite shortlived). He has also been seen in episodes of *The Edwardians*, *Blake's 7* and *Casualty*.

BAKER, DANNY (1957–)

Garrulous Londoner who specializes in pop culture nostalgia. Formerly a *New Musical Express* journalist, he joined LWT's *Six O'Clock Show* and then moved on to the daytime cartoon quiz *Win Lose or Draw*. However, greater prominence came after he took over the Radio 5 breakfast show Morning Edition, which led to his hosting assorted panel games, ranging from *Bygones* to *Pets Win Prizes*, as well as his own Saturday night chat show. He is also much seen in TV commercials and presented the series of humorous\nostalgic shorts, *TV Heroes*.

BAKER, GEORGE (1931–)

Dignified and versatile TV actor most closely associated with the rural detective Inspector

Wexford in *The Ruth Rendell Mysteries* (for which he also scripted some episodes). His other major credits have included *Tiberius* in *I, Claudius*, Stanley Bowler in *Bowler* (a spin-off from *The Fenn Street Gang*) and the smarmy Tory Godfrey Eagan in *No Job for a Lady*, opposite Penelope Keith. Over the years, there have been plenty of other notable appearances, in the likes of *Undermind*, *The Prisoner* (as one of the Number Twos), *Doctor Who*, *Up Pompeii* (as Jamesus Bondus), Room at the Bottom, *Hart to Hart*, *A Woman of Substance*, *Dead Head* and single dramas such as Dennis Potter's *Alice* (playing Charles Lutwidge Dodgson, aka Lewis Carroll).

BAKER, HYLDA (1908–86)

Distinctive northern comedienne, forever identified as Nellie Pledge, one of the squabbling siblings (with Jimmy Jewel) who ran the pickle factory in *Nearest and Dearest*. However, Hylda Baker's career began in music hall and she toured with many of the big names in the 1940s. In the 1950s, she branched out on her own, hitting the limelight in an episode of *The Good Old Days* in 1955. In those days it was her act with Cynthia (a man in drag) which brought most laughs. 'She knows you know' became her catchphrase. TV series followed: *Our House* (as Henrietta), *Best of Friends* (as Nellie, café proprietress) and subsequently *Nearest and Dearest* in 1968. Baker also starred as pub landlady Nellie Pickersgill in another northern sitcom, *Not On Your Nellie*. Although she was equally adept at straight drama (for instance in David Mercer's 1961 play *Where The Difference Begins* and in a couple of episodes of *Z Cars*), her comic timing, jerky mannerisms and flair for the double entendre and malapropism made her one of TV's most distinctive comic stars in the 1960s and 1970s.

BAKER, RICHARD, OBE (1925–)

Eloquent TV and radio host who, in 1954, became BBC Television's first newsreader, having joined the BBC as an announcer on the Third Programme in 1950. Although initially only supplying the voice behind the pictures in *BBC Television Newsreel*, Baker was later chosen as one of the main three 'in-vision' newsreaders, along with Kenneth Kendall and Robert Dougall. He presented the news until 1982 and has subsequently concentrated on his first love, classical music, appearing on such programmes as *Omnibus*, *The Proms* and *Face the Music*. In contrast, he also provided the narration for the *Watch with Mother* cartoon *Mary, Mungo and Midge*.

BAKER, ROBERT S. (1916–)

British producer heavily involved with ITC adventure series of the 1960s, often in collaboration with Monty Berman. Among his efforts were *The Saint* (and, in the 1970s, *The Return of the Saint*), *The Baron*, *Gideon's Way* and *The Persuaders!*.Z

BAKER, TOM (1935–)

Popular British actor, known for eccentric characters and famous as the fourth *Doctor Who*, the one with the curly hair and long scarf. In the 1980s he was the decadent priest in *The Life and Loves of a She Devil*, donned the deerstalker of Sherlock Holmes in *The Hound of the Baskervilles* and guest-starred in *Blackadder*. In recent years, he has filled the role of Professor Geoffrey Hoyt in *Medics*. He hosted the kids' literature programme *The Book Tower* in the 1970s.

BAKEWELL, JOAN (1933–)

Intellectual presenter, one of the early stars of BBC 2 as an interviewer on *Late Night Line-Up*. In subsequent years she struggled to shake off the tag of 'the thinking man's crumpet', bestowed on her by Frank Muir. Other TV credits have included *Reports Action*, *On the Town* and *Holiday 76*, and, more recently, she has been seen as presenter of the Sunday late-night morality programme *Heart of the Matter*.

BALL, BOBBY (Robert Harper 1944–) see Cannon, Tommy.

BALL, JOHNNY (1938–)

Quirky presenter of intelligent programmes for children. A former Red Coat and clubland comedian, his TV break came with *Play School*, on which he was a regular for a number of years. Moving on to *Play Away*, he then progressed to the likes of *Star Turn* and *Secret's Out* before his biggest success, *Think of a Number*.

BALL, LUCILLE (1911–89)

The doyenne of TV comediennes, Lucille Ball came to television after 20 years' experience on stage and screen. Although considered to be 'the new Harlow' by some, Ball never quite made it to the top in pre-war Hollywood and switched her attention instead to radio in 1948. When she took on the role of a scatterbrained housewife in the series *My Favorite Husband*, her card was marked for the rest of her career. This series was soon translated to television as *I Love Lucy*, co-starring her real-life husband, Desi Arnaz, and produced by their own company, Desilu. The show went on to set standards for other sitcoms to follow. As Lucy Ricardo, Ball became one of TV's earliest superstars and, when her marriage to Arnaz irretrievably broke down, she persevered alone, still as the hapless housewife (albeit in various guises) in the follow-up series, *The Lucy Show* and *Here's Lucy*. Although a late attempt to return to television in the 1980s with *Life With Lucy* was not a success, viewers have always had plenty of opportunity to enjoy her pioneering comic talents, as re-runs of *I Love Lucy* are never far from the screen.

BALL, NICHOLAS (1946–)

British actor who came to light in *The Crezz* and progressed to his own series, *Hazell*, playing a cynical London private eye. Among his later credits was the part of film director Alan Hunter in *Colin's Sandwich*. He was the first husband of Pamela Stephenson.

BANACEK

US (Universal) Detective Drama. ITV 1975–7

Thomas Banacek .... George Peppard
Jay Drury .... Ralph Manza
Felix Mulholland .... Murray Matheson
Carlie Kirkland .... Christine Belford

Creator: Anthony Wilson. Executive Producer: George Eckstein. Producer: Howie Horowitz

Tales of a modern-day bounty hunter.

Cool, calm and sophisticated Thomas Banacek was a wealthy man. He lived in a mansion in Boston's prosperous Beacon Hill area and was driven around by a chauffeur, Jay Drury. The reason for his wealth? He was good at collecting rewards from insurance companies. He specialized in retrieving stolen valuables and, on a 10 per cent rake off, the greater the prize, the richer he became. The loot may have been gold bullion, or perhaps a prize racehorse. On one occasion it was even a professional footballer. Felix Mulholland, proprietor of Mulholland's Rare Book and Print Shop, was his best friend, and Carlie Kirkland, another insurance agent, became Banacek's rival and romantic interest.

Banacek made George Peppard popular with Polish-Americans. These people had long been the butt of everyday humour and at last here was a TV hero to show the world that they really could be clever. Plenty of Polish sayings found their way into the script. The series was shown as part of the *Mystery Movie* anthology.

BANANA SPLITS, THE

US (Hanna-Barbera) Children's Comedy. BBC 1 1970

Voices:
Fleegle .... Paul Winchell
Bingo .... Daws Butler
Drooper .... Allan Melvin
Snorky .... Don Messick

Executive Producers: William Hanna, Joseph Barbera

Zany comedy featuring four animal pop stars.

The Banana Splits were an animal pop group, a sort of zoological *Monkees*, miming to pre-recorded tracks and dashing around in fast-action sequences. Played by men in outsize costumes, the four were Fleegle, a guitar-strumming lisping bassett hound, Bingo, a bongo-playing gorilla, Drooper, a lion, and Snorky, an elephant. At *Laugh-In* pace, these wacky creatures were used to link various cartoon inserts such as *The Arabian Knights*, *The Micro Ventures*, *The Hillbilly Bears* and *The Three Musketeers*. There was also a live-action adventure entitled *Danger Island* (starring Frank Aletter as Professor Irwin Haydn). Wisecracks and slapstick scenes were the order of the day. Drooper unsuccessfully tried to take out the trash (the bin refused to accept rubbish), Fleegle wrestled with the mailbox for the mail, and the stroppy cuckoo clock made time telling less than easy. Seldom did an episode pass without someone yelling 'Hold the bus!'. Regular features were Banana Buggie races, song and dance from the rival Sour Grape Girls gang and an 'information' spot called Dear Drooper, where the smart-alec lion attempted to answer viewers' queries. The show is probably best remembered today for its catchy 'One banana, two banana' theme song. Episodes were shown again as part of *The Big Breakfast* on Channel 4.

BANNISTER, TREVOR (1936–)

Familiar character and comic actor, starring in the 1967 trilogy *The War of Darkie Pilbeam*, and the sitcoms *The Dustbinmen* (as Heavy Breathing) and *Are You Being Served?* (as Mr Lucas). Amongst other series, Bannister was also seen in *Wyatt's Watchdogs* (playing Peter Pitt).

BARBER, GLYNIS

Striking South African leading lady who arrived on TV as Soolin, the blonde gunslinger in *Blake's 7*, before stripping down to her underwear in the title roles of *Jane* and *Jane in the Desert*, BBC 2's revivals of the *Daily Mirror's* wartime cartoon heroine. From there, Barber switched to detective work when cast as the plummy Harriet Makepeace in **Dempsey and Makepeace**, alongside Michael Brandon. Her other credits have included **The Sandbaggers** and **Tales of the Unexpected**.

BARCLAY, HUMPHREY

Former Cambridge Footlights graduate and mastermind of the 1963 revue Cambridge Circus, which featured such up and coming performers as John Cleese, Tim Brooke-Taylor, Bill Oddie, Graham Chapman, Jonathan Lynn, Graeme Garden and future head of BBC Radio Comedy David Hatch. Barclay then moved into television, working as a comedy producer with Rediffusion and then LWT. His many credits have included **Do Not Adjust Your Set** (for which he discovered David Jason), **Hark at Barker, Doctor in the House** (and its sequels), **No, Honestly, Two's Company, Whoops! Apocalypse** and **Hot Metal**. In the 1980s Barclay set up his own production company, Humphrey Barclay Productions, which contributed series such as **Desmond's** and **Surgical Spirit**.

BARKER, RONNIE, OBE (1929–)

Comedian and comic actor, universally recognized as one of television's finest. From his earliest appearances in **It's A Square World** (with Michael Bentine), **Six More Faces of Jim** (with Jimmy Edwards) and **The Frost Report** (alongside John Cleese and Ronnie Corbett), Barker has enjoyed a reputation second to none for comic timing and verbal dexterity. He was given a showcase in 1968, **The Ronnie Barker Playhouse**, in which he introduced the character of Lord Rustless, who was then spun-off into two series of his own, **Hark at Barker**, and **His Lordship Entertains**. In 1971 Barker was paired again with Ronnie Corbett for **The Two Ronnies**, a mixture of monologues, soliloquies and humorous sketches which ran for 15 years, with some material written by Barker himself under the pen name of Gerald Wiley. **Six Dates with Barker**, aired in 1971, and another anthology series, **Seven of One** in 1973, yielded two major sitcoms and two of TV's brightest creations. The first, Dick Clement and Ian La Frenais's **Porridge**, saw Barker's classic portrayal of the old lag Fletcher (later set free in **Going Straight**). The second, Roy Clarke's **Open All Hours**, featured the stuttering, penny-pinching grocer Arkwright. Some of his other efforts have been understandably less memorable, namely the short-sighted removal man **Clarence** and the flamboyant, lecherous Welsh photographer **The Magnificent Evans**. Barker's other credits over the years have included parts in lesser comedies like **The TV Lark, Bold as Brass** and **Foreign**

Affairs. He retired from showbiz in 1988.

BARKWORTH, PETER (1929–)

Avuncular English character actor, generally in upper middle-class parts, probably best recalled as the retiring bank manager Mark Telford in **Telford's Change**. Previously Barkworth had appeared as Kenneth Bligh in **The Power Game**, starred as Vincent in the wartime drama **Manhunt**, played detective Arthur Hewitt in **The Rivals of Sherlock Holmes** and added a series of guest appearances to his portfolio. He also took on the role of Eustace Morrow in **Good Girl**, Stanley Baldwin in **Winston Churchill – The Wilderness Years**, and that of computer executive Geoffrey Carr in the kidnap drama **The Price**. In 1977 Barkworth picked up a BAFTA award for his performance in Tom Stoppard's **Play of the Week Professional Foul**.

BARLOW AT LARGE/BARLOW

UK (BBC) Police Drama. BBC 1 1971–3/1974–5

Detective Chief Supt
  Charlie Barlow ....Stratford Johns
A.G. Fenton ....Neil Stacy
Detective Sgt David Rees..................Norman Comer
Detective Inspector Tucker (*Barlow*)....Derek Newark

Creator: Elwyn Jones. Executive Producer: Leonard Lewis. Producer: Keith Williams

An aggressive police detective is assigned to the Home Office.

In this, the third part of the Charlie Barlow story, the former **Z Cars** and **Softly, Softly** bully boy was somewhat uncomfortably installed in Whitehall, working with a rather smarmy superior, A.G. Fenton, with whom he didn't always see eye to eye. As part of the Police Research Services Branch, his job was to help regional police forces with any difficult cases they encountered. Though he was accompanied by Detective. Sgt Rees, he always seemed a little lost without his old mucker John Watt. The series evolved into another sequel, simply entitled Barlow, in which he was joined by Detective Insp. Tucker.

BARNABY JONES

US (Quinn Martin) Detective Drama. ITV 1974–80

Barnaby Jones..Buddy Ebsen
Betty Jones..Lee Meriwether
Jedediah Romano (J.R.) Jones ....Mark Shera
Lt Joe Taylor ....Vince Howard
Lt John Biddle..John Carter

Executive Producer: Quinn Martin. Producers: Gene Levitt, Philip Salzman, Robert Sherman

A Los Angeles private eye comes out of retirement to find the killer of his son.

Barnaby Jones, after an impressive career as a private eye, had relaxed into horsebreeding retirement. But when his son, Hal, the new proprietor of the Jones Detective Agency, was murdered on a case, he set about tracking down the killer. After nailing his man, Barnaby turned his back on retirement and took over control of the firm once more, assisted by his widowed daughter-in-law, Betty (played by Lee Meriwether, Miss America 1955). Barnaby's young cousin, law student J.R. Jones, was recruited to the team in the fifth series, after the murder of his father.

Like most TV private eyes in the 1970s, Barnaby was unconventional. The softly spoken, milk-drinking gumshoe used his vague, totally unassuming appearance to trick criminals into a false sense of security and then pounced when they least expected. He backed this up by being thoroughly methodical, working on cases in a special crime lab he had constructed at home.

Through this role, star Buddy Ebsen quickly dispelled any fears of typecasting that may have existed following his years as millionaire bumpkin Jed Clampett in *The Beverly Hillbillies*.

Elegant, intelligent panellist of *What's My Line?*. Born in Scotland, and a medical student at Glasgow, Isobel Barnett worked as a GP for a number of years before becoming a Justice of the Peace. It was in 1953 that she joined the new game show *What's My Line?* as a resident panellist and her graceful manner and shrewd questioning quickly endeared her to viewers. She later appeared in various other panel games, on radio as well as TV, but her life ended on a sad note when she committed suicide in 1980 a week after being found guilty of petty shoplifting. She was the wife of a former Lord Mayor of Leicester, Sir Geoffrey Barnett.

BARNEY MILLER

US (Four D) Situation Comedy. ITV 1979–

Captain Barney Miller	Hal Linden
Detective Phil Fish	Abe Vigoda
Detective Sgt Chano Amenguale	Gregory Sierra
Detective Stanley Wojohowicz ('Wojo')	Maxwell Gail
Detecive Nick Yemana	Jack Soo
Detective Ron Harris	Ron Glass
Elizabeth Miller	Barbara Barrie
Rachael Miller	Anne Wyndham
David Miller	Michael Tessier
Bernice Fish	Florence Stanley
Detective Janice Wentworth	Linda Lavin
Inspector Frank Luger	James Gregory
Officer Carl Levitt	Ron Carey
Detective Baptista	June Gable
Detective Arthur Dietrich	Steve Landesberg
Lt Scanlon	George Murdock

Creators: Danny Arnold, Theodore J. Flicker. Executive Producer: Danny Arnold. Producers: Chris Hayward, Arne Sultan

The ups and downs of life in a Greenwich Village police station under its genial Jewish captain.

Barney Miller was set in New York's 12th Precinct police station. Although Barney's family life featured prominently in the early episodes, it was quickly pushed into the background and all the subsequent action took place in the old precinct house. This soon became home to all kinds of weird and wonderful callers, as well as a motley crew of police officers.

Barney was very much the father figure of the station. He was compassionate and a good listener. His office even had a leather couch for those who needed to pour their hearts out. His colleagues included the decrepit Fish, grumbling his way through his last years on the force and always in need of a bathroom. On retirement, he was given his own spin-off series, *Fish*. There were also the naive, people-loving Wojo, the philosophical Yemana (who made awful coffee and followed horse racing) and the fast-talking Puerto Rican Amenguale, who was later replaced by Dietrich, a walking encyclopedia. Black jokester Ron Harris eventually had a book published (*Blood on the Badge*), Levitt was the 5 ft 3 in officer who longed to be a detective but was 'too short', and Inspector Luger was Barney's boss.

Barney Miller was a police show that relied on talk not action. There were no car chases, no explosions and none of the fast talk seen in TV's other cop dramas. Instead, the humane side of policing was revealed through the inter-personal relationships of the multi-ethnic officers and the social misfits they brought in. As a result, the programme was much appreciated by real-life police officers for its authenticity and the stars were made honorary members of the New York Police Department. The series ended when the police station was declared a historic site, after the discovery that it had been used by Teddy Roosevelt when he was President of the New York Police Board in the 1890s. Barney and Levitt were promoted, but the gang was dispersed across the city. The pilot for the show was a segment in a comedy anthology *Just For Laughs* called *The Life and Times of Captain Barney Miller*.

BARON, THE

UK (ATV/ITC) Secret Agent Drama. ITV 1966–7

John Mannering ('The Baron')	Steve Forrest

Cordelia Winfield..Sue Lloyd
John Alexander Templeton-Green ....Colin Gordon
David Marlowe ....Paul Ferris

Producer: Monty Berman

An international art dealer works as an undercover agent in his spare time.

In this series, very loosely based on the British Intelligence agent created by John Creasey, Steve Forrest starred as John Mannering, a suave American antiques expert who helped the Secret Service whenever a crime involved the theft of valuable pieces. His nickname, the title of the programme, was taken from his family's ranch in Texas (although in Creasey's stories Mannering was British not American).

Millionaire Mannering drove a Jensen (registration BAR 1) and owned exclusive antique shops in London, Washington and Paris, from which he planned his secret missions. In his assignments for John Templeton-Green of British Intelligence, he was joined by attractive Cordelia Winfield of the Special Branch Diplomatic Service. David Marlowe was sometimes seen as Mannering's business associate.

BARR, ROBERT (1910–)

British writer and producer with many successes for the BBC. His work has included episodes of *Maigret*, *Z Cars*, *Softly, Softly*, *Parkin's Patch* and *Secret Army*, although even earlier credits were *Germany Under Control* in 1946, *Saturday Night Stories* (as producer in 1948), a 1949 adaptation of H.G. Wells's *The Time Machine* and the police drama *Pilgrim Street* (again as producer in 1952). The 1959 series *Spycatcher* and the 1963 series *Moonstrike* were the peaks of his writing career, but he also created *Gazette*, from which **Hadleigh** was derived.

BARR, ROSEANNE see *Arnold, Roseanne*.

BARRACLOUGH, ROY (1935–)

Northern character actor and comedian, partner to Les Dawson on numerous occasions (particularly as Cissie and Ada, the two gossipy women), but better known in the 1980s as Alec Gilroy, landlord of the Rovers Return in **Coronation Street**, a character he had played on and off since 1972 (in addition to four other *Street* visitors). Earlier appearances included contributions to various dramas and sitcoms from *The War of Darkie Pilbeam* and **Nearest and Dearest** to **Never Mind the Quality, Feel the Width** and *Love Thy Neighbour*, as well as one of the leads in the comedy *The More We Are Together* (Frank Wilgoose) and major parts in the children's

comedies *Pardon My Genie* (Mr Cobbledick) and *T-Bag Strikes Again*. His most recent starring role was as Leslie Flitcroft, the 50-year-old bachelor still under his mother's thumb, in the comedy *Mother's Ruin*.

BARRETT, RAY (1927–)

Australian-born, rugged-looking actor whose first starring role was as Dr Don Nolan in *Emergency – Ward 10*. As well as making guest appearances in series like **Z Cars** and **Doctor Who**, he starred as Peter Clarke in the **Ghost Squad** sequel, *GS5* before taking his best remembered part, in 1965, that of oil executive Peter Thornton in **Mogul** and **The Troubleshooters**. From then on Barrett was a regular face in British TV drama and his voice was familiar, too. Amongst other voice-overs, he provided the dialogue for **Stingray**'s Commander Shore and **Thunderbirds'** John Tracy in Gerry Anderson's puppet classics. In 1976 he returned to Australia and continued to win plaudits for his performances in film and television Down Under.

BARRIE, AMANDA (SHIRLEY ANN BROADBENT; 1939–)

Although known today as Alma Sedgewick/Baldwin in **Coronation Street**, Amanda Barrie's TV credits have been numerous and varied, ranging from hostessing on **Double Your Money** to comedy support to Morecambe and Wise in their first TV outing, *Running Wild* (1954), and then in the likes of *Bulldog Breed* (as Sandra Prentiss with Donald Churchill), *The Reluctant Romeo* (as Geraldine Woods with Leslie Crowther), *Time of My Life* (as Jean Archer with Mark Kingston) and *L for Lester* (as Sally Small with Brian Murphy). She has also been seen in **Are You Being Served?** and **Spooner's Patch**. She joined the *Street* briefly in 1981 and became a member of the regular cast in 1988. Outside television she has danced with Lionel Blair and appeared in several films, playing the title role in *Carry On Cleo*.

BARRIE, CHRIS (1960–)

British comedian, impressionist and comic actor, whose most memorable roles have been as the obnoxious Arnold Rimmer in **Red Dwarf** and as the incompetent Gordon Brittas in The Brittas Empire. Barrie has also contributed to satire shows such as **Carrott's Lib** and **Spitting Image**, where his impressionist talents have been put to good use. Other credits have included **The Young Ones**.

BARRON, JOHN (1920–)

Tall, booming actor generally cast in eccentric roles. He is best known for his C.J. in *The Fall and Rise of Reginald Perrin* ('I didn't get where I am today . . . '), but he first came to viewers' attention in *Emergency – Ward 10* and *All Gas and Gaiters* (as the Dean), before playing the warped scientist Devereaux in the kids' sci-fi serial *Timeslip*, the Minister in *Doomwatch*, the Vicar in *Potter* (opposite Arthur Lowe and Robin Bailey), US security adviser The Deacon in *Whoops! Apocalypse* and assorted supporting roles in comedy and drama series.

BARRON, KEITH (1934–)

Busy northern actor whose TV work has swung between drama and comedy, with varying degrees of success. In the 1960s he made his name as an angry young man in the title role of Dennis Potter's *Vote, Vote, Vote For Nigel Barton* and its prequel, *Stand Up, Nigel Barton*. In the 1980s he starred as David Pearce in Eric Chappell's *Duty Free* and, in contrast, the love-lorn taxi driver Tom in the drama *Take Me Home*. He played Guy Lofthouse in *The Good Guys* and one of his most recent offerings has been the burglar-turned-baker Bill Chivers in *All Night Long*. Other credits have included *The Odd Man* and *It's Dark Outside* (as Sgt Swift), *The Further Adventures of Lucky Jim* (the 1967 version, in the title role of Jim Dixon), *My Good Woman* (neighbour Philip Broadmore), *No Strings* (Derek), *Telford's Change* (Tim Hart), *Late Expectations* (Ted Jackson), *Leaving* (Daniel Ford), *Room at the Bottom* (TV boss Kevin Hughes) and *Haggard* (title role). He was also seen in the dramas *A Family at War* and *Upstairs, Downstairs*. Keith is the father of actor James Barron.

BARRY, GENE (EUGENE KLASS; 1921–)

American supporting actor of the 1950s, who flourished in the 1960s, winning glamorous title roles in Bat Masterson, *Burke's Law* and *The Adventurer* (as Steve Bradley). In the 1970s and 1980s he concentrated on more lavish productions, particularly TV movies, but, in 1994, he returned to our screens as Amos Burke, the millionaire head of Los Angeles Police's homicide department. In this new series, the debonaire detective was joined by his son, Peter, played by Peter Barton.

BARRY, MICHAEL (1910–)

Head of BBC Drama in the pioneering days of the 1950s, responsible for commissioning such classics as *Quatermass* and *1984*. Previously, as producer, Barry had introduced the BBC's limited audience to such dramas as Edgar Wallace's *The Case of the Frightened Lady* and *Smoky Cell* (both 1938), *Toad of Toad Hall* (1946) and *Boys in Brown* (1947). In 1965 he produced a Royal Shakespeare Company trilogy of plays under the banner of *The Wars of the Roses*.

BARRYMORE, MICHAEL (1952–)

Tall, energetic comedian and quiz show host. After appearing in support of stars like Russ Abbot, Michael Barrymore found a niche of his own in the late 1980s and early 1990s, in such shows as *Michael Barrymore's Saturday Night Out*, *Live From Her Majesty's*, *Barrymore* (a chance for the public to show off their party pieces) and the 'strike the screen' quiz for couples *Strike It Lucky*. His humour is based on physically exhausting, almost acrobatic routines and gentle mimicry of his programme participants, with his catchphrase 'Awight!' well to the fore.

BASEHART, RICHARD (1914–84)

American character actor chiefly remembered by TV viewers as Admiral Harriman Nelson in *Voyage to the Bottom of the Sea*. Other credits (as guest stars) included *Ben Casey*, *The Twilight Zone*, *Gunsmoke*, *Marcus Welby, MD*, and *The Love Boat*, plus a catalogue of TV movies. Basehart also provided narration for *Knight Rider*.

BASIL BRUSH

Puppet fox created and voiced by Ivan Owen (formerly the operator of Yoo-Hoo the Cuckoo in the 1950s' *Billy Bean and His Funny Machine* and dog Fred Barker in *Tuesday Rendezvous*, *Five O'Clock Club*, etc.). His gap-toothed grin, effervescent character and posh voice (more than reminiscent of Terry-Thomas), not to mention his trademark 'boom boom' and roaring laugh, made Brush a favourite of both children and adults. He first appeared in *The Three Scampis* in 1962 (alongside Howard Williams and a Scottish hedgehog called Spike McPike voiced by Wally Whyton), and then guest starred with David Nixon, before hiring a succession of straight men to read stories to him on his own Saturday teatime series from 1968 to 1980. Rodney Bewes was first into the role, then came Derek Fowlds, Roy North, Billy Boyle and Howard Williams (again).

BASS, ALFIE (1921–87)

Cheeky cockney comedian who enjoyed a long film and TV career. One of his earliest small screen appearances was in the drama *The Bespoke Overcoat* in 1954, although it was as the pessimistic Private 'Excused Boots' Bisley – 'Bootsie' for short – in *The Army Game* that he shot to fame in 1957. This national service comedy ran for four years and led to a sequel, ***Bootsie and Snudge***, in which Bass and his co-star Bill Fraser took their characters into civvy street, working together at a seedy gentlemen's club. It was through Bootsie that Bass picked up his catchphrase: 'Never mind, eh?'. The characters were drafted into a third sitcom, *Foreign Affairs*, and then Bass and Fraser explored new ground in *Vacant Lot* (with Bass as Alf Grimble). His later TV work included the sitcoms ***Till Death Us Do Part*** (as Bert), ***Are You Being Served?*** (Mr Goldberg) and *A Roof Over My Head* (Flamewell), the adventure series ***Dick Turpin*** (Isaac Rag) and a 1974 revival of ***Bootsie and Snudge***.

BATES, MICHAEL (1920–78)

Versatile character actor who was part of the original trio of childish old men in ***Last of the Summer Wine*** (playing Blamire) and starred (blacked up) as the lead wallah, Rangi Ram, in ***It Ain't Half Hot Mum***. His earlier credits included several one-off dramas, such as a 1965 version of *A Passage To India* (again blacked up). The Indian connections should not have been surprising: Bates was born in the subcontinent and spoke Urdu.

BATES, RALPH (1940–91)

Hammer horror actor who showed his versatility in two diverse TV roles, namely the mean, moody George Warleggan in ***Poldark*** and the wimpish lonely heart John Lacey in ***Dear John***. Other TV credits included the parts of Caligula in ***The Caesars*** and Michel Lebrun in Moonbase 3, an appearance in ***Crime of Passion*** with Cyd Hayman and a short-lived sitcom about divorce, *Second Chance* (as Chris Hurst, alongside Susannah York). Bates, a descendant of French scientist Louis Pasteur, died of cancer in 1991. His two wives were both actresses, Joanna Van Gyseghem and Virginia Wetherall, and he has left two acting children. His daughter Daisy was seen in ***Forever Green*** and his son William appeared as his son in ***Dear John***.

BATMAN

US (20th Century-Fox/Greenway) Science Fiction. ITV 1966–

Bruce Wayne (Batman)	Adam West
Dick Grayson (Robin)	Burt Ward
Alfred Pennyworth	Alan Napier
Aunt Harriet Cooper	Madge Blake
Police Commissioner Gordon	Neil Hamilton
Chief O'Hara	Stafford Repp
Barbara Gordon (Batgirl)	Yvonne Craig
The Joker	Cesar Romero
The Riddler	Frank Gorshin
	John Astin
The Penguin	Burgess Meredith
Catwoman	Julie Newmar
	Eartha Kitt
	Lee Ann Meriwether
Narrator	William Dozier

Executive Producer: William Dozier. Producer: Howie Horowitz

Camp TV version of the popular comic strip created by Bob Kane in 1939.

Batman was renowned for its purposeful overacting, corny quips and far-fetched storylines. It made a star out of Adam West, albeit a very typecast star, and featured a host of celebrities anxious to grab a piece of what was a very successful series. It played the story very close to the comic book in style and substance, with the addition of Aunt Harriet to detract from the suspicious nature of three men sharing a house. The three were millionaire playboy Bruce Wayne, his 15-year-old ward, Dick Grayson, and their gaunt English butler, Alfred. Only he knew that these two were really the famous Batman and Robin, crime fighters extraordinaire.

The 'Dynamic Duo' lived at Wayne Manor, 14 miles from Gotham City, beneath which was concealed Batman's headquarters, the Batcave. A flick of a switch hidden in a bust of Shakespeare revealed firemen's poles (the 'Batpoles') behind a bookcase which allowed them to descend to the cave. Remarkably, on reaching the bottom, they were already clothed in their famous crime-fighting gear and masks. In this high-tech den they puzzled and pondered over the amazing crimes which time and again afflicted the city, before setting out to wreak vengeance on the underworld, a vengeance promised by Wayne when he had been criminally orphaned in his teens.

Their enemies (or 'arch-enemies') were most frequently the Joker, adorned with a sick painted smile, the Riddler, in his question-marked cat suit, the waddling Penguin, with his cigarette holder, and the leather-clad Catwoman, although the series also introduced some baddies not known in the comic strip. These included Egghead (Vincent Price), King Tut, Mr Freeze (Otto Preminger) and the Bookworm (Roddy McDowell).

Batman and Robin rocketed into action in the Batmobile, a converted 17 ft-long Lincoln Continental, but this was just one of their many gadgets and ingenious devices. Adam West played the lead very dryly, while Burt Ward's Robin was dramatically excitable and prone to 'Holy' expressions of farcical topicality like 'Holy sewer pipe', as the Riddler emerged from a manhole, and 'Holy fork in the road'. The villains were ridiculously twisted: the Joker loved to play nasty tricks, while the Riddler always gave the heroes a seemingly unfathomable clue. The action was laughably violent and partially obscured by exclamations like 'Pow!', 'Zap!' and 'Thud' writ large on the screen, and each episode closed with a cliff-hanger in the style of the old movie serials.

Our heroes were usually summoned into action by the desperate Commissioner Gordon over the Batphone, or by the Batsignal in the sky. However, if Commissioner Gordon was helpless, his librarian daughter certainly was not. She joined the series late in its run as Batgirl, aboard the Batcycle, with her true identity unknown even to her crime-busting colleagues.

BATTLESTAR GALACTICA/ GALACTICA 1980

US (Universal/Glen A. Larson) Science Fiction. ITV 1980– /1984–

Battlestar Galactica:
Commander Adama ....Lorne Greene
Captain Apollo ....Richard Hatch
Lt Starbuck...Dirk Benedict
Lt Boomer ....Herb Jefferson, Jnr
Athena..Maren Jensen
Flt Sgt Jolly...Tony Swartz
Boxey ....Noah Hathaway
Colonel Tigh ....Terry Carter
Cassiopeia ....Laurette Spang
Count Baltar ....John Colicos

Galactica 1980:
Sheba ....Anne Lockhart
Captain Troy ....Kent McCord
Lt Dillon ....Barry Van Dyke
Jamie Hamilton ....Robyn Douglass
Dr Zee ....Robbie Risk
....Patrick Stuart
Colonel Sydell ....Allan Miller
Xavier...Richard Lynch

Executive Producer: Glen A. Larson. Producers: John Dykstra, Leslie Stevens

Much-hyped, expensive imitation of *Star Wars*, a cross between the *Book of Exodus* and *Wagon Train*.

In the seventh millennium, 12 of the 13 humanoid civilizations had been wiped out by the treacherous Cylons, enemies of humanoids for a thousand years. A motley convoy of 220 small ships joined the battlestar spaceship *Galactica* in making a break for the last remaining refuge, the mythical 'Golden Planet' (Earth). However, as it meandered through the universe, it was stalked by the Cylons and prone to regular attacks.

Adama was the commander of the ship, a Moses figure aided by his son, Apollo, head of the Viper fighter squadron. Starbuck was the impetuous top gun pilot, roguishly appealing, especially to Adama's daughter, Athena, the communications officer. Other members of the crew included second-in-command Colonel Tigh, Cassiopeia, the medic, and Boomer, another pilot. Villain of the piece was Count Baltar, who had betrayed the humanoids to the Cylons. The players were not clothed in futuristic garments, but in gowns and tunics reminiscent of Earth's early civilizations. The evil, robotic Cylons, on the other hand, had a chrome appearance and peered sinisterly through two red light-beam 'eyes'. The malign nature of the enemy was further emphasized by the batlike wings of its spacecraft, whereas Galactica was more of a comfortable city in space, one mile wide.

The special effects, with lasers and colourful explosions aplenty, were spectacular and magnificently handled by producer John Dykstra, who had previously worked on *Star Wars*, but the storylines found plenty of critics. As a result the programme was halted and revamped in a new form known as *Galactica 1980*. This moved the time on 30 years and saw the ship arriving on Earth only to find the Cylons plotting its destruction. Lorne Greene as Adama was the sole survivor of the original cast. He was now assisted by Captain Troy, a grown-up version of Adama's adopted son Boxey, a star of the original series.

The pilot episode of *Battlestar Galactica* received a cinema release in the UK, in an attempt to recoup money lost after the flop of the series in the USA.

BAVERSTOCK, DONALD (1924–95)

Influential BBC current affairs producer of the 1950s and 1960s, responsible to no small degree for such programmes as *Highlight*, *Tonight* and *That Was The Week That Was*. He later became head of BBC 1 before moving on to the fledgling Yorkshire Television, where he was programme director from 1968 to 1973.

BAXTER, RAYMOND (1922–)

Veteran, distinguished BBC presenter, heard to best effect in coverage of air shows (he was a World War II RAF pilot), royal occasions and motor sports events. He presented the weekly science programme *Tomorrow's World* for 12 years and his other credits have included *Eye On Research* and *The Energy File*.

BAXTER, STANLEY (1926–)

Scottish comedian and impersonator, fond of mimicking TV's grandes dames and Hollywood idols. Following his breakthrough in 1950s' series like **Chelsea at Nine** and *On The Bright Side*, Baxter appeared in his own fortnightly comedy in 1964, *Baxter On . . .* , which included programmes on travel, television, law, theatre and sex. His major TV work was yet to come, however. In 1968 he starred in *The Stanley Baxter Show* for the BBC before switching channels in 1972 to present *The Stanley Baxter Picture Show*, the first in a series of specials which continued with the award-winning Stanley Baxter Big Picture Show, *The Stanley Baxter Moving Picture Show, Stanley Baxter On Television* and *The Stanley Baxter Series*. His Christmas shows proved particularly popular and he also appeared in the lead role in the children's comedy *Mr Majeika*.

BAYLDON, GEOFFREY (1924–)

British actor fondly remembered as Catweazle, the 11th-century sorcerer trapped in the 20th century. Among his other TV credits have been **Z Cars, The Avengers, The Saint,** *The Victorians,* **Edward the Seventh, All Creatures Great and Small, Bergerac, Worzel Gummidge** (as The Crowman), **Star Cops** and **Casualty,** plus numerous single dramas.

BAYWATCH

US (Tower 12) Drama. ITV 1990–

Lt Mitch Bucannon	David Hasselhoff
Jill Riley	Shawn Weatherly
Craig Pomeroy	Parker Stevenson
Eddie Kramer	Billy Warlock
Shauni McLain	Erika Eleniak
Trevor Cole	Peter Phelps
Gina Pomeroy	Holly Gagnier
Hobie Bucannon	Brandon Call
	Jeremy Jackson
Gayle Bucannon	Wendie Malok
John D. Cort	John Allen Nelson
Lt Garner Ellerbee	Gregory Alan-Williams
Captain Don Thorpe	Monte Markham
Harvey Miller	Tom McTigue
Lt Ben Edwards	Richard Jaeckel
Matt Brody	David Charvet
C.J. Parker	Pamela Denise Anderson
Lt Stephanie Holden	Alexandra Paul
Summer Quinn	Nicole Eggert
Jimmy Slade	Kelly Slater
Jackie Quinn	Susan Anton
Caroline Holden	Yasmine Bleeth
Logan Fowler	Jaason Simmons

Thrills and spills with scantily clad LA lifeguards.

The Los Angeles County lifeguards have been the stars of this all-action seaside romp, known variously as 'Barewatch' and 'Boobwatch' because of its acres of tanned flesh. Chief hunk and programme mastermind has been David Hasselhoff in the guise of Mitch Bucannon, at the outset a

newly installed lieutenant in the seaside patrol force. Working alongside Mitch in the early days were his lawyer friend Parker Stevenson and Jill Riley, sadly killed by a shark during the first season. Thorpe was Bucannon's officious captain and assorted rookie lifeguards milled around the team's Malibu Beach headquarters. These included Shauni McLain, Trevor Cole and Eddie Kramer. Part of the fabric was Mitch's son, Hobie, who lived with his dad following Mitch's marriage break-up, and officers from the LAPD beach patrol squad, particularly Garner Ellerbee, were also seen. John D. Cort ran the local beach shop, Sam's Surf and Dive.

Despite success outside the USA, *Baywatch* was cancelled after just one season. Hasselhoff and a consortium of three others pooled resources to finance the production of more episodes, which they sold into syndication and to networks overseas. The almost cult following the series enjoyed in the UK no doubt swayed their decision. With the fresh set-up, new characters appeared, including Ben Edwards, a weather-beaten but good-natured lifeguard, and young joker Harvey Miller. Matt Brody, C.J. Parker and Stephanie Holden have been among the even more recent recruits.

BBC (BRITISH BROADCASTING CORPORATION)

Britain's major broadcasting organization was founded as the British Broadcasting Company in 1922, with executives drawn from the ranks of radio receiver manufacturers, who had been invited to provide a broadcasting service by the Postmaster General. Then, as today, funding was provided by a licence fee, payable by all users of radio (now TV) sets, at a rate set by Parliament. To this day, neither the BBC's radio nor television service has accepted paid advertising. The company was reconstituted as the British Broadcasting Corporation (a public corporation, working 'as a trustee for the national interest') on 1 January 1927, and since that time has derived its authority from a Royal Charter. The Charter has been considered for renewal on several occasions, each time instigating a heated debate about the role of the BBC and its funding.

Organizationally, the BBC is headed by a board of Governors, all appointed by the Queen on the advice of the Government, for a five-year term. Day-to-day control is assumed by the Director-General and his executives. The BBC's first Director-General, and effectively the father of public service broadcasting in the UK, was John (later Lord) Reith, who instilled in programme makers his belief in the need to 'Educate, Inform, Entertain'.

The BBC began television experiments in 1932, from a studio in Broadcasting House, Portland Place, London. On 2 November 1936 the Corporation inaugurated the world's first regular high-definition television service, but this was suspended on 1 September 1939 for defence reasons, with war imminent. It resumed on 7 June 1946, with the same Mickey Mouse cartoon that had closed the station down seven years earlier. A major milestone in the development of the television service was the Coronation of Queen Elizabeth in 1953. The BBC covered the proceedings live and sales of television sets rocketed. However, its monopoly position as the UK's only television broadcaster was broken with the launch of ITV in 1955.

On 29 June 1960 the BBC opened its new Television Centre in Shepherd's Bush, West London, having previously broadcast from Alexandra Palace and the old film studios at Lime Grove. On 20 April 1964 the Corporation's second channel, BBC 2, was launched (although a power cut curtailed its opening night). Its focus, from the beginning, has been on minority interest programmes, innovation and education. Colour broadcasts began on BBC 2 on 1 July 1967 (initially only five hours a week). The colour service was officially inaugurated on 2 December the same year and spread to BBC1 (and ITV) on 15 November 1969. Both BBC channels have allowed for regional opt-out programmes, to cover local news, current affairs, sports and entertainments. These are prepared by a network of BBC studios around the country. In 1991 BBC World Service Television was launched. This largely satellite channel beams BBC news and entertainment programmes around much of the world, 24 hours a day.

In technical terms and also programme-wise, the BBC has a reputation second to none in world broadcasting. Its news coverage has been viewed as authoritative and its drama output, particularly its period classics, is legendary. However, recent years have witnessed a degree of turmoil within the organization. Under the 1989 Broadcasting Bill, 25 per cent of all programmes now have to be supplied by independent contractors. This has inevitably led to a loss of BBC jobs. Another consequence has been 'Producer Choice'. This system of allocating cash to BBC programme makers to buy technical and other services, from either within the BBC or without, was introduced by the new Director-General, John Birt, the man charged with leading the Corporation through its next Royal Charter renewal, in 1996. It has not proved popular with BBC employees.

BBC TELEVISION NEWSREEL, THE
UK (BBC) News. BBC 1948–54

Editor: D.A. Smith. Producer: Harold Cox

News events from around the world.

Hardly topical, and consisting largely of fading news items, *The BBC Television Newsreel* was BBC TV's first attempt at presenting news footage. Previously, the news had been conveyed in sound only, radio fashion, and up-to-date, in-vision news bulletins were still six years away (they began in 1954). This programme filled the gap, using the style of cinema newsreels, but running for 15 minutes instead of ten and including fewer stories. International items were incorporated thanks to an exchange deal with America's NBC network. The same programme was initially transmitted four times a week, on Mondays, Wednesdays and twice on Saturdays.

BBC TELEVISION SHAKESPEARE, THE
UK (BBC) Drama Anthology. BBC 2 1978–85

Producers: Cedric Messina, Jonathan Miller, Shaun Sutton

Ambitious staging of all 37 Shakespeare plays.

Creating the definitive television version of Shakespeare's oeuvre proved even more difficult than imagined when the BBC launched the project in 1978. Some productions ran into 'technical' troubles and the numerous styles applied by directors resulted in a rather piecemeal effect for the series as a whole. Some plays, for instance, were totally studio-bound, while others were shot on location. Cedric Messina was the brains behind the concept and took charge of production for the first two years. Jonathan Miller was drafted in to continue the project and Shaun Sutton completed affairs.

The first plays to be covered were *Richard II, Romeo and Juliet, Julius Caesar, As You Like It, Measure for Measure* and *Henry VIII*. Among the stars appearing over the seven years were Anthony Hopkins, Helen Mirren, Derek Jacobi, John Gielgud, Wendy Hiller, James Bolam, Virginia McKenna, Timothy West and Anthony Quayle. Perhaps the most unusual casting was John Cleese as *The Taming of the Shrew*'s Petruchio. Desmond Davis, Herbert Wise, Basil Coleman and David Giles were among the directors employed.

BBC 3
UK (BBC) Comedy. BBC 1 1965–6

John Bird
Robert Robinson
Lynda Baron

Producer: Ned Sherrin

Controversial programme of topical humour and debate.

Son of *That Was The Week That Was*, by way of *Not So Much A Programme, More a Way of Life*, this late-night satire show is chiefly remembered today for allowing the first known use of the 'F' word on national television. It came in 1965 during an interview with Kenneth Tynan about theatre censorship. Such frank discussions mingled with sketches, filmed inserts and music in the programme plan, but the show never achieved the heights of *TW3*, despite employing writers like David Frost, Christopher Booker, John Mortimer and Keith Waterhouse. Supporting the principals on screen were the likes of Malcolm Muggeridge, Patrick Campbell, John Fortune, Roy Dotrice, Denis Norden, Leonard Rossiter and Bill Oddie.

BEACHAM, STEPHANIE (1949–)

Glamorous British actress often seen in the determined female role. Her most prominent part has been as Sable Colby in *Dynasty* and *The Colbys*, transatlantic success arriving after several notable performances on British television. Amongst these were the parts of Rose Millar in *Tenko* and Connie in the series of the same name. Her earlier credits included guest appearances in *The Saint*, *Armchair Theatre*, *Callan*, *Jason King*, *UFO*, *The Protectors*, *Marked Personal* and *Hadleigh*.

BEADLE, JEREMY (1948–)

Bearded British presenter of audience participation shows, especially those involving pranks, stunts and hidden cameras. Breaking into television as one of the four original presenters of *Game for a Laugh*, Beadle has since hosted *Beadle's About*, *Beadle's Box of Tricks*, *People Do The Funniest Things* and the video howler show *You've Been Framed*. He has also worked as a writer and consultant on other programmes and was the brains behind the successful publications *The Book of Lists* and *Today's The Day*.

BEAN, SEAN

British actor with a Shakespearean stage background. On television he starred as Lovelace in *Clarissa*, Mellors in *Lady Chatterley* and Richard Sharpe in the various *Sharpe* dramas. Other credits include *Inspector Morse*. Bean is married to actress Melanie Hill.

BEATON, NORMAN (1934–94)

Actor of West Indian origin, star of the barber shop series *Desmond's* (as Desmond Ambrose). His earlier work took in leading roles in *Empire*

Road (Everton Bennett) and *The Fosters* (Samuel Foster) and he was also seen in *Dead Head*, amongst other dramas.

BEAUTY AND THE BEAST

US (Republic Pictures) Adventure. ITV 1988–

Assistant DA Catherine Chandler	Linda Hamilton
Vincent	Ron Perlman
Father	Roy Dotrice
Deputy DA Joe Maxwell	Jay Acavone
Edie	Ren Woods
Kipper	Cory Danziger
Mouse	David Greenlee
Diana Bennett	Jo Anderson
Gabriel	Stephen McHattie
Elliott Burch	Edward Albert

Creator: Ron Koslow. Executive Producers: Ron Koslow, Paul Junger Witt, Tony Thomas, Stephen Kurzfeld

A beautiful girl's life is saved by a deformed man, who then protects her in her fight against crime.

This adventure series had links with both the fairytale world and *The Phantom of the Opera*. When attractive attorney Catherine Chandler was attacked and left for dead in Central Park, New York, her life was saved by the strangely deformed Vincent (his face was marked like a lion), who took her to his underground refuge and nursed her back to health. When she returned to civilization, the love and the strong telepathic bond which had grown between them allowed Vincent to spring to her assistance whenever she fell into danger.

Vincent, for all his grotesque looks, was a compassionate, gentle soul and a lover of poetry. But he lived among the shadows, hitching rides on top of tube trains. Abandoned as a child, he had been taken in by the people who lived in the catacombs beneath Manhattan ('Tunnel World'), where he had been raised by a reclusive genius known as Father. Kipper and Mouse were Father's helpers.

After an initially platonic relationship, Catherine and Vincent fell in love and the fairytale continued until Catherine was kidnapped and murdered by Gabriel, head of a criminal organization, but not before she had given birth to Vincent's son. Diana Bennett was brought in by Catherine's boss to investigate the case and she became Vincent's new friend. Assisted by businessman Elliott Burch, they tracked down and captured Gabriel, leaving Vincent and his son to retreat to the peace and tranquillity of the underworld.

BECKINSALE, RICHARD (1947–79)

Affable comedy actor whose tragic early death cut short a TV career that had already produced some classic roles. He is probably best recalled as

Ronnie Barker's cellmate, Godber, in **Porridge** and *Going Straight*, although he was just as popular as the sex-starved Geoffrey opposite Paula Wilcox in **The Lovers** and Rigsby's medical student tenant, Alan Moore, in **Rising Damp**. His last series was *Bloomers*, in which he played Stan, a resting actor who became a partner in a florist's. His daughter, Samantha, from his first marriage, has appeared in **London's Burning**, while his second wife, actress Judy Loe, is still occasionally seen on TV.

BED-SIT GIRL, THE

UK (BBC) Situation Comedy. BBC 1 1965–6

Sheila Ross	Sheila Hancock
Dilys	Dilys Laye
David	Derek Nimmo
Liz	Hy Hazell

Writers: Ronald Chesney, Ronald Wolfe. Producers: Duncan Wood, Graeme Muir

A single girl dreams of a more glamorous life.

Living in a bed-sit and working as a typist didn't amount to much for dreamy, disorganized Sheila Ross. She envied the exotic lifestyle of her air stewardess neighbour Dilys, with whom she fought for eligible bachelors with little success. When Dilys moved on after the first season, Sheila gained a boyfriend in the form of David, her next-door neighbour, but her girly chats continued with the worldly wise Liz, who also lived in the house.

BEENY, CHRISTOPHER (1941–)

Chirpy British character actor whose first TV outing was as Lenny (aged 12) in **The Grove Family**, the grandmother of all UK soaps, way back in 1954. However, most viewers remember him as Edward, the footman in **Upstairs, Downstairs**, or as Thora Hird's hapless nephew Billy in the funereal sitcom **In Loving Memory**. He briefly played Geoffrey, Paula Wilcox's neighbour/friend in **Miss Jones and Son**, and was also seen as Tony in the 1970s revival of **The Rag Trade**, taking on the foreman role vacated by Reg Varney. Other appearances have included **Dixon of Dock Green**, **Emergency – Ward 10**, **Armchair Theatre**, **Z Cars**, **The Plane Makers** and the kids' programme **Play Away**.

BEGGAR MY NEIGHBOUR

UK (BBC) Situation Comedy. BBC 1 1967–8

Gerald Garvey	Peter Jones
	Desmond Walter-Ellis
Rose Garvey	June Whitfield
Harry Butt	Reg Varney
Lana Butt	Pat Coombs

Writers: Ken Hoare, Mike Sharland. Producers: David Croft, Eric Fawcett

Neighbour and family conflict in the London suburbs.

Gerald Garvey lived with his wife, Rose, in Muswell Hill. Rose's sister, Lana Butt, and her husband, Harry, lived next door, but things were far from cosy because of their unequal prosperity. Harry was an overpaid fitter, while Gerald was an underpaid junior executive, which made the flashy Butts the haves and the impoverished Garveys the have-nots. The Garveys' attempts to keep up with the Joneses (or Butts) provided most of the humour. The programme stemmed from a 1966 **Comedy Playhouse** pilot and ran for three series.

BEGGARMAN, THIEF see *Rich Man, Poor Man.*

BEIDERBECKE AFFAIR, THE/THE BEIDERBECKE TAPES/THE BEIDERBECKE CONNECTION

UK (Yorkshire) Drama. ITV 1985/1987/1988

Trevor Chaplin (All)	James Bolam
Jill Swinburne (All)	Barbara Flynn
Detective Sgt/Detective	
Insp. Hobson (*Affair/Connection*)	Dominic Jephcott
Mr Carter (All)	Dudley Sutton
Mr Wheeler (All)	Keith Smith
Big Al (*Affair/Connection*)	Terence Rigby
Little Norm (*Affair/Connection*)	Danny Schiller
Chief Supt Forrest (*Affair*)	Colin Blakely
Sylvia (*Tapes*)	Beryl Reid
Peterson (*Tapes*)	Malcolm Storry
John (*Tapes*)	David Battley
Bella Atkinson (*Tapes*)	Maggie Jones
Ivan (*Connection*)	Patrick Drury

Writer: Alan Plater. Executive Producers: David Cunliffe (*Affair/Tapes*), Keith Richardson (*Connection*). Producers: Anne W. Gibbons (*Affair*), Michael Glynn (*Tapes/Connection*)

Two schoolteachers unravel a web of corruption, against a background of classic jazz.

In *The Beiderbecke Affair*, Leeds comprehensive woodwork master Trevor Chaplin and his English teacher girlfriend Jill Swinburne had really rather modest ambitions. He was looking for a set of Bix Beiderbecke records, following a mix-up in his mail order, and she was seeking election to the local council on a conservation ticket. However, fate took a hand to lead them into a murky world of underhand dealing, bureaucracy and corruption, bringing their relationship into crisis and themselves into conflict with the police.

Such was the success of this quirky, light-hearted six-parter that a sequel, *The Beiderbecke Tapes*, appeared two years later. In this two-episode tale, Trevor bought some jazz tapes from the barman of an empty pub only to find that one contained a recording of plans to dump nuclear waste in the Yorkshire Dales. Having survived that escapade, he and Jill resurfaced for a third and final time in the four-part *The Beiderbecke Connection*, which brought them into contact with a Russian refugee and saw them attract suspicion from the authorities.

Music played a sizeable part in these genial tales of intrigue in which the hero and heroine travelled around in a beaten-up old motor, reluctantly playing detective and running into all kinds of odd characters. They were accompanied by the sounds of jazz great Bix Beiderbecke, re-created for the series by Kenny Baker, with new music by Frank Ricotti. Writer Alan Plater had earlier contributed a similar series under the title of *Get Lost!* Screened in 1981, this four-parter saw two teachers, played by Alun Armstrong and Bridget Turner, investigating missing persons.

BELL, ANN (1940–)

British actress, well versed in upper-class, but well-meaning and kindly roles. She played Marion Jefferson, the British group leader, in *Tenko* and later Gracie Ellis, the finishing school headmistress, in the rock 'n' roll retrospective *Head Over Heels*, with plenty of other credits before and in between. These have included the parts of Maria in the 1965 adaptation of *For Whom the Bell Tolls* and Mary Webster in the 1988 sitcom *Double First*, as well as appearances in *The Saint*, *Mr Rose*, *Callan*, *Danger Man*, *The Baron*, *War and Peace*, *Tumbledown* and *Christabel*. She is married to actor Robert Lang.

BELL, TOM (1932–)

British actor, often seen in dry, unsmiling roles. His credits have included *Armchair Theatre*, *Play For Today*, *Holocaust*, *Reilly – Ace of Spies*, *Angels*, *The Rainbow*, *Chancer*, *King's Royal* and *Prime Suspect*. His other major roles have varied from menacing hero/villain Frank Ross in *Out* to Walter Morel in *Sons and Lovers* and waxworks owner Harry Nash in the sitcom *Hope It Rains*.

BELLAMY, DAVID, OBE (1933–)

Enthusiastic, bearded naturalist, much mimicked by TV impressionists. After a few early programmes like *Bellamy on Botany* and *Bellamy's Britain* for the BBC, and then prime-time

exposure on ITV's *Don't Ask Me*, he launched into a run of successful, light-hearted documentary series, which included *Bellamy's Europe*, the award-winning *Botanic Man*, *Up a Gumtree*, *Bellamy's Backyard Safari* (in which he was shrunk by special effects to explore the wilderness of a typical garden), *Bellamy's New World*, *Bellamy's Bugle*, *Bellamy on Top of the World*, *Bellamy's Bird's Eye View* and *Bellamy Rides Again*.

BELLINGHAM, LYNDA (1948–)

British actress, the mum in the Oxo commercials, but already familiar to TV viewers from series such as *General Hospital*, *Don't Forget to Write*, *Angels*, *Z Cars* and *The Fuzz*. She also guested in *Doctor Who* and replaced Carol Drinkwater as Helen Herriot in *All Creatures Great and Small*, before becoming Faith Grayshot in the comedy *Second Thoughts* (on both radio and TV).

BELLISARIO, DONALD P.

The creator and executive producer of *Magnum, PI* and *Airwolf* and later founder of his own production company, Bellisarius, responsible for such hits as *Quantum Leap*. His earlier work took in *Kojak* (as writer) and *Battlestar Galactica* (as writer/producer).

BEN CASEY

US (Bing Crosby) Medical Drama. ITV 1961–

Dr Ben Casey	Vince Edwards
Dr David Zorba	Sam Jaffe
Dr Maggie Graham	Bettye Ackerman
Dr Ted Hoffman	Harry Landers
Nick Kanavaras	Nick Dennis
Nurse Wills	Jeanne Bates
Jane Hancock	Stella Stevens
Dr Mike Rogers	Ben Piazza
Dr Daniel Niles Freeland	Franchot Tone
Dr Terry McDaniel	Jim McMullan
Sally Welden	Marlyn Mason

Creator: James Moser. Producer: Matthew Rapf

A gifted but brooding young surgeon works at a large hospital.

Unlike the baby-faced Dr Kildare, his screen rival in the early 1960s, Ben Casey was surly, tough and determined. He worked as a neurosurgeon at the County General Hospital and was very much a rebel who would happily flaunt the rules if it was in his patient's interest. His stabilizing influence, however, was the venerable Dr Zorba, a white-haired, mad scientist type, whom Casey respected enormously. It was Zorba who spoke the dramatic words which opened each programme and summed up the extremes of hospital life: 'Man; Woman; Birth; Death; Infinity'. When Zorba left, the Chief of Surgery role was assumed by Dr Freeland. Other familiar faces were Nick Kanavaras, the hospital orderly, Dr Ted Hoffman and Nurse Wills.

Ben Casey was a bold series which was never afraid to tackle difficult subjects like abortion. It was also shot in such a way (extreme close-ups, etc.) that the true tension of critical medicine was effectively conveyed. Romance was kept to the sidelines and, for all his macho appeal, Casey was only rarely linked with a woman. His relationship with anaesthetist Maggie Graham was softly alluded to, but his most dramatic entanglement came with beautiful Jane Hancock, a 13-year coma victim, for whose attentions he fought with Dr Mike Rogers.

Ben Casey became less convincing and 'soapier' towards the end of its run and finally drew to a close in the USA in 1966, five months before *Dr Kildare*. During its five years on air it had made a sex symbol out of the profusely hairy Vince Edwards, a handsome young actor discovered by Bing Crosby, whose company produced the series.

BENEDICT, DIRK (DIRK NIEWOEHNER; 1944–)

Known in the 1980s as Faceman in *The A-Team*, Dirk Benedict had earlier appeared on the small screen in the short-lived cop series *Chopper One*, before taking on the mantle of Lt Starbuck in the sci-fi spectacular *Battlestar Galactica*. He has also starred in various TV movies.

BENNETT, ALAN (1934–)

Bespectacled, gently spoken northern playwright, actor and narrator, a former Beyond The Fringe star, also seen in the satire show *BBC 3* and Jonathan Miller's TV version of *Alice In Wonderland* when starting out in television. However, it has been for his collection of TV dramas that he has won plaudits since. Most notable have been A *Day Out* (1972), *Sunset Across the Bay* (1975), *One Fine Day* (1979), *Objects of Affection* (1982), *A Little Outing* (1977), *The Insurance Man* (1986), *A Question of Attribution* (1991) and *An Englishman Abroad* (1983; the tale of a chance meeting between spy Guy Burgess and actress Coral Browne). He has also written a series of comedy sketches, *On The Margin* (1966), an anthology series, *By Alan Bennett – Six Plays* (1978), and received much acclaim for *Talking Heads* (1988). This season of monologues epitomized Bennett's flair for character observation and realistic dialogue, as well as offering performers like Thora Hird (delivering A *Cream Cracker Under the Settee*) and Bennett himself the chance to shine. He was also seen in

the 1991 drama *Selling Hitler*, playing historian Hugh Trevor-Roper.

BENNETT, HARVE (HARVE FISCHMAN; 1930–)

Prolific US producer of action series like *The Six Million Dollar Man*, *The Bionic Woman* and *The Invisible Man*, as well as the mini-series *Rich Man, Poor Man*.

BENNETT, HYWEL (1944–)

Welsh juvenile actor, very popular in British films of the 1960s, whose most durable television role was as the unemployed graduate *James Shelley*. One of his earliest TV appearances was in a 1960s *Doctor Who* story and he has also played memorable parts in *Malice Aforethought* (as Dr Bickleigh), *Pennies from Heaven* (as Tom), *Tinker, Tailor, Soldier, Spy*, *Frank Stubbs Promotes* and various plays and films, including the sci-fi fantasy *Artemis 81*. He was formerly married to *Ready, Steady, Go!* presenter Cathy McGowan and is the brother of *Emmerdale* actor Alun Lewis.

BENNETT, LENNIE (MICHAEL BERRY; 1938–)

Northern comedian and game show host, formerly one half of Lennie and Jerry (with Jerry Stevens). He first appeared on *The Good Old Days* in 1966 after working for a while as a journalist, and his later credits have included *The Lennie and Jerry Show*, *The Comedians*, *London Night Out*, *Starburst*, *Bennett Bites Back* and *All Star Secrets*. He also hosted *Punchlines* and *Lucky Ladders*.

BENNY, JACK (BENJAMIN KUBELSKY; 1894–1974)

One of TV's earliest celebrities, Jack Benny's career began in music in the 1920s. As a vaudeville violinist, he billed himself as Ben K. Benny, soon adding humour to his routine and becoming Jack Benny. Although he made a number of films, his greatest success pre-TV came on American radio, where he finely tuned the character traits that were to become so popular later. Playing himself in the long-running *Jack Benny Show* (with announcer Don Wilson and Eddie 'Rochester' Anderson, his valet, in support), he quickly gained a reputation for his stinginess, his lied-about age (always 39) and appalling violin playing. He was married to his sometime co-star Mary Livingstone.

BENTINE, MICHAEL, CBE (1922–)

Part-Peruvian comedian and one-time Goon, the deviser and presenter of some of TV's most bizarre comedy shows. These have included *The Bumblies* (a 1954 animation for kids, featuring pear-shaped creatures from the planet Bumble), *Yes, It's The Cathode-Ray Tube Show!* (1957, with Peter Sellers), the influential *It's a Square World* (1960), All Square (1966) and *Michael Bentine's Potty Time* (with puppets, 1973).

BENTLEY, JOHN (1916–)

British film actor who re-emerged in the 1970s as Hugh Mortimer, Meg Richardson's ill-fated new husband in **Crossroads**. Playing the millionaire businessman, he had attempted to win Meg's hand as far back as 1965, but received the brush-off. Reconciled, their 1975 wedding was one of the TV events of the year. Previously, Bentley had starred as Patrol Inspector Paul Derek in the 1950s jungle adventure series **African Patrol**. His TV portfolio also includes *Strictly Personal* and **Armchair Theatre**.

BERGERAC

UK/Australia (BBC/The Seven Network) Police Drama. BBC 1 1981–91

Detective Sgt Jim Bergerac	John Nettles
Charlie Hungerford	Terence Alexander
Chief Inspector Barney Crozier	Sean Arnold
Francine	Cecile Paoli
Deborah Bergerac	Deborah Grant
Marianne Bellshade	Celia Imrie
Susan Young	Louise Jameson
Philippa Vale	Liza Goddard
DC Terry Wilson	Geoffrey Leesley
Danielle Aubry	Therese Liotard
Inspector Victor Deffand	Roger Sloman
DC Willy Pettit	John Telfer
DC Ben Lomas	David Kershaw
Diamante Lil	Mela White
Charlotte	Annette Badland
Peggy Masters	Nancy Mansfield
Dr Lejeune	Jonathan Adams

Creator: Robert Banks Stewart. Producers: Robert Banks Stewart, Jonathan Alwyn, George Gallaccio, Juliet Grimm

A single-minded copper roots out smugglers and swindlers in Jersey.

Jim Bergerac did not have the best credentials to be a policeman, physically or mentally – a gammy leg caused him to limp, and he had once been a drunk. His life had been in ruins, with his wife, Deborah, leaving him and his career in the balance. Turning over a new leaf, he became the Channel Islands' most successful detective, displaying genuine determination to get to the bottom of cases.

Working for the Bureau des Etrangers (which dealt with crimes involving non-island folk), and tearing around in a 1947 Triumph TR1 sports car, his gaze fell upon visitors and tourists up to no good, and he was never afraid of getting physical in the search for justice. His superiors and colleagues (like Barney Crozier) regularly questioned his methods, but always supportive was his amiable ex-father-in-law, Charlie Hungerford, a businessman constantly on the fringe of dodgy deals.

Despite his new dedication to the job, Bergerac was never far from the temptation of the bottle, especially when there was trouble in his personal life, as the girls came and went. First there was Francine, and then lawyer Marianne Bellshade, before estate agent Susan Young provided some stability for a while. Their relationship ended with her murder. There was even more spark in his occasional encounters with Philippa Vale, a glamorous jewel thief. It was Bergerac's obsession with a woman which eventually brought the series to a close. Jim's relationship with French girl Danielle Aubry resulted in his leaving Jersey to work as a private investigator in Provence. Though the final series saw Jim return to the island on several assignments, it was only a matter of time before the programme finally called it a day.

Bergerac employed a number of semi-regulars, who ensured continuity during the programme's ten-year run. These included assorted constables, pathologist Dr Lejeune, the Bureau's secretaries, Charlotte and Peggy, and Diamante Lil, proprietress of the bar Lil's Place. Such longevity was not anticipated when the series began. It was intended as a short filler and was only developed because Trevor Eve had refused to continue with **Shoestring**. *Bergerac* was also good for Jersey. It gave the island's tourist trade an enormous lift. John Nettles, who had become to Jersey what Steve McGarrett had been to Hawaii and Inspector Morse was to become to Oxford, also made it his home.

BERLE, MILTON (MENDEL BERLINGER; 1908–)

Although his name means little to British viewers, Milton Berle was 'Mr Television' to US audiences in the 1950s. A former silent movie star as a child and later an established vaudevillian, he broke into television in 1948 as host of the variety show *The Texaco Star Theatre* (later *The Milton Berle Show*). So popular were his brash comic sketches, buffoonery, outrageous costumes and awful puns that NBC quickly signed him up on a 30-year contract. His best years were in the early 1950s and his humour soon dated, but he continued to appear sporadically until the 1980s. British viewers may have caught 'Uncle Miltie' as guest star in **The Defenders**, **F Troop** (Wise Owl), **Batman** (Louie the Lilac), in some episodes of **The Love Boat**, or in one of his TV movies.

BERLUSCONI, SILVIO (1936–)

Italian media magnate and owner of the AC Milan football club who became his country's Prime Minister for a while in 1994. Berlusconi's television interests began almost by chance when he established a small closed circuit station in the Milan suburb that he was developing as part of his real estate business. This grew into TeleMilano which evolved into the national network Canale 5, following the deregulation of television in Italy. He has subsequently added two more commercial channels to his empire, Retequattro and Italia 1 (giving himself three national networks to match the three controlled by the state-owned RAI corporation), as well as pioneering pay TV in Italy via his shareholding in Telepiù. Berlusconi has also had interests in Spanish television, through Tele 5, and France, via La Cinq. His TV and publishing businesses are handled by his company, Fininvest.

BERMAN, MONTY (1913–)

British TV producer of action series for ITC, working closely with Robert S. Baker in developing programmes like **The Saint**, **The Baron** and **Gideon's Way**, and with Dennis Spooner on **Randall and Hopkirk (Deceased)**, **Department S** and **The Champions**.

BERNSTEIN, LORD SIDNEY (1899–1993)

British film and television executive who, after building up his father's cinema chain (and introducing the idea of a Saturday matinee for kids), worked as a consultant for the Ministry of Information in World War II. Later he produced three films for Alfred Hitchcock and went on to found **Granada Television** (and the whole Granada group) with his brother, Cecil. Granada (the name was inspired by a walking holiday in Spain) introduced commercial television to the North of England in 1956 and Bernstein succeeded in running it as almost a family business for many years. He was made a life peer in 1969.

BERRY, NICK (1963–)

Former child actor whose best-known television work has been as Simon 'Wicksy' Wicks in **EastEnders** and PC Nick Rowan in **Heartbeat**.

Other credits have included **The Gentle Touch**, **Box of Delights** and **Cluedo**.

BERYL'S LOT

UK (Yorkshire) Comedy Drama. ITV 1973–7

Beryl Humphries	Carmel McSharry
Tom Humphries	Mark Kingston
	George Selway
Rosie Humphries	Verna Harvey
Jack Humphries	Brian Capron
Babs Humphries	Anita Carey
Trevor Tonks	Tony Caunter
Vi Tonks	Barbara Mitchell
Horace Harris	Robert Keegan
Wully Harris	Annie Leake
Charlie Mills	Norman Mitchell
Wacky Waters	Johnny Shannon
Fred Pickering	Robin Askwith
Freda	Queenie Watts

Writers: Kevin Laffan, Bill MacIlwraith. Executive Producers: Peter Willes, David Cunliffe. Producers: John Frankau, Jacky Stoller, Derek Bennett

A milkman's wife tries to better herself in middle age.

One morning, at the age of 40, charlady Beryl Humphries woke up and decided she hadn't done enough with her life. Married to Tom, a milkman, she realized she wanted to be more than a cleaner and, to the surprise of her children, Rosie, Jack and Babs, and that of her many friends and neighbours, set about improving her lot, signing up for evening classes.

The series was based on the life of cook Margaret Powell, also a milkman's wife, who passed 'O' and 'A levels while in her 50s and at the age of 61 had her first book published.

BETAMAX see VHS

BETWEEN THE LINES

UK (BBC/Island World) Police Drama. BBC 1 1992–4

Detective Supt Tony Clark	Neil Pearson
Detective Inspector Harry Naylor	Tom Georgeson
Detective Sgt Maureen Connell	Siobhan Redmond
Chief Supt John Deakin	Tony Doyle
Commander Huxtable	David Lyon
Sue Clark	Lynda Steadman
Jenny Dean	Lesley Vickerage
Chief Supt Graves	Robin Lermite
Commander Sullivan	Hugh Ross
Angela Berridge	Francesca Annis
Joyce Naylor	Elaine Donnelly
Kate Roberts	Barbara Wilshere
Sarah Teale	Sylvestra le Touzel

Creator: J.C. Wilsher. Executive Producer: Tony Garnett. Producers: Peter Norris, Joy Lale

The professional and private lives of a police internal investigator.

Between The Lines revolved around the somewhat complex life of Detective Supt Tony Clark, an ambitious, but headstrong member of the Complaints Investigation Bureau (CIB), a division of the Metropolitan Police. As the head of a team of two detectives, it was Clark's job to root out bent coppers – at all levels in the force. Unfortunately, the hard-drinking, emotionally immature Clark was also a pawn in political games played by his superiors and his job was further complicated by his own turbulent private life. His biggest problem, it seemed, was keeping his trousers on. Indeed, the series was cruelly nicknamed 'Between the Sheets' and even 'Between the Loins'. His marriage broke up because of an affair with WPC Jenny Dean, and other women, such as Home Office official Angela Berridge and TV producer Sarah Teale, also drifted into his bed during the programme's three-series run.

Clark's sidekicks were Harry Naylor and Mo Connell. Harry, the chain-smoking dependable copper type, became increasingly more reckless and violent in his work as his wife's terminal illness developed, while Mo's own personal affairs (of the gay variety) began to infiltrate her working world, too. Above Clark initially were Commander Huxtable and Chief Supt John Deakin. Clark managed to nail the menacing Deakin for corruption at the end of the first series but Deakin wriggled off the hook and remained a powerful influence in Clark's life, particularly in the third series when Clark, Naylor and Connell found themselves outside the force and Deakin controlled their work as security advisors.

Between The Lines was a unexpected hit, picking up many awards and opening new doors for its star, Neil Pearson, previously seen as randy Dave Charnley in the Channel 4 comedy **Drop the Dead Donkey**. The executive producer of the series was Tony Garnett, responsible for striking plays like *Up the Junction* and **Cathy Come Home** in the 1960s and the controversial series **Days of Hope** and **Law and Order** in 1976 and 1978 respectively.

BEVERLY HILLBILLIES, THE

US (Filmways) Situation Comedy. ITV 1964–

Jed Clampett	Buddy Ebsen
Daisy Moses (Granny)	Irene Ryan
Elly May Clampett	Donna Douglas
Jethro Bodine	Max Baer, Jnr
Milburn Drysdale	Raymond Bailey
Jane Hathaway	Nancy Kulp
Cousin Pearl Bodine	Bea Benaderet
Mrs Margaret Drysdale	Harriet MacGibbon
Jethrene Bodine	Max Baer, Jnr
John Brewster	Frank Wilcox
Ravenswood	Arthur Gould Porter
Janet Trego	Sharon Tate
Lawrence Chapman	Milton Frome
John Cushing	Roy Roberts
Dash Riprock (né Homer Noodleman)	Larry Pennell
Homer Cratchit	Percy Helton
Shorty Kellems	George 'Shug' Fisher
Shifty Shafer	Phil Silvers
Flo Shafer	Kathleen Freeman
Mark Templeton	Roger Torrey

Creator/Producer: Paul Henning. Executive Producer: Al Simon

A family of country bumpkins strikes oil, becomes rich and moves to Beverly Hills.

When Jed Clampett went out hunting on his land he found more than he bargained for. Stumbling across a bubbling oil reservoir meant that life in Bug Tussle in the Ozark mountains was about to end for Jed and his family. They sold the drilling rights to John Brewster of the OK Oil Company and, with their new-found wealth, packed their bags on to their rickety old boneshaker and headed for the city, taking up residence among the rich and famous of Beverly Hills. And that's where the comedy began, for this family was not designed to live in an urban mansion. They were used to the rough and ready wild outdoors and thought smog was a small hog. It was their inability to adapt to modern conveniences and day-to-day life in a prosperous neighbourhood that provided the laughs.

Although Jed himself was fairly level-headed, the same couldn't be said for the other members of the Clampett family. Granny, his wrinkly, irritable mother-in-law, fought manfully against modern-day comforts and still tried to buy such items as possum innards for her many potions and recipes. Elly May provided the glamour as Jed's animal-loving daughter whom Granny was always trying to marry off, while brawny Cousin Jethro (played by the son of former World Boxing Champion Max Baer) was a dim, clumsy womanizer.

The Clampetts were chaperoned by Milburn Drysdale, President of the Commerce Bank, which held their money. Assisted by the starchy Jane Hathaway, Drysdale moved the family into the house next to his own, in order to keep an eye on them and to keep out poachers, including his rival John Cushing of the Merchant's Bank. Snooty Mrs Drysdale, however, was not so pleased to have the Clampetts as neighbours. They hardly allowed her to keep up appearances and she hated her husband's grovelling.

Max Baer, Jnr also took the part of Jethro's sister, Jethrene, in the early days, and another original character was Cousin Pearl Bodine, mother of Jethro and Jethrene. But, as the series developed, so the storyline moved along. Jethro finally graduated from school and, in his quest for true playboy status, began investing in flawed business ventures. The Clampetts purchased the majority holding in Mammoth Studios, run by Lawrence Chapman, which led to Elly May's romance with film star Dash Riprock. Before the series closed (after nine years on US TV), she at last found her Mr Right, in the shape of navy frogman Mark Templeton. By that time the Clampetts' fortune had risen from a comfortable $25 million to a mighty $95 million.

Occasional visitors to the show throughout its run were musicians Lester Flatt and Earl Scruggs, banjo-picking performers of the memorable theme song, 'The Ballad of Jed Clampett'.

BEVERLY HILLS 90210

US (Twentieth Century-Fox/Torand/Spelling Entertainment) Drama. ITV 1991–2

Brenda Walsh	Shannen Doherty
Brandon Walsh	Jason Priestley
Jim Walsh	James Eckhouse
Cindy Walsh	Carol Potter
Kelly Taylor	Jennie Garth
Steve Sanders	Ian Ziering
Dylan McKay	Luke Perry
David Silver	Brian Austin Green
Andrea Zuckerman	Gabrielle Carteris
Donna Martin	Tori Spelling
Scott Scanlon	Douglas Emerson
Chris Suiter	Michael St. Gerard
Nat	Joe E. Tata
Henry Thomas	James Pickens Jnr
Emily Valentine	Christine Elise

Creator: Darren Star. Executive Producer: Charles Rosin. Producers: Aaron Spelling, Darren Star, Sigurjon Sighvatsson

Teenage years in America's most select residential neighbourhood.

Beverly Hills 90210 was a zip code to die for, the zip code of the most fashionable residential area on the West Coast, a place where film stars and hugely successful business folk mingled in an atmosphere of gaudy prosperity. Into this glamorous setting stepped the Walshes, an altogether unassuming new family in town. Arriving from Minneapolis, they were comfortably well off but strangely content with their lot, unlike their showy, ambitious neighbours, who lived for designer clothes, nose jobs and flash cars. They were unusual, too, in being a family in a town where most other homes were run by single parents. What's more dad, Jim, an accountant, and his wife, Cindy, actually *cared* for their children, 16-year-old twins Brandon and Brenda, who,

with their new high-school friends, provided the real focus of the series.

Dealing with realistic 1990s teen troubles like safe sex and drugs, as well as traditional adolescent woes such as peer pressure and school grades, *Beverly Hills 90210* quickly gathered a cult following among younger viewers. Apart from the Walsh family, the main protagonists were Brenda's new friend Kelly, the snooty brat-pack leader whose mother was an alcoholic; Steve, Kelly's ex-boyfriend and son of Samantha Sanders, star of a TV show called *Hartley House*; Brandon's surfing buddy Dylan (Brenda's boyfriend); Andrea, the poor-girl editor of the school newspaper, who gave her grandmother's address in Beverly Hills so she could go to the top school (West Beverly Hills High); insecure freshman David Silver; David's pal Scott, and Donna, another of Brenda's friends (played by the daughter of TV executive Aaron Spelling).

So much did the series involve itself in teenage troubles that, in the USA, *Beverly Hills 90210* was followed each week by a list of special help lines, encouraging kids to call if they had experienced the problems highlighted in that particular episode. More recent series have been run on the Sky One satellite channel.

BEWES, RODNEY (1938–)

Northern comedy actor, one of TV's *Likely Lads* (Bob Ferris) in the 1960s and 1970s. He also starred as Albert Courtnay in *Dear Mother . . . Love Albert* (which he wrote and co-produced) and its follow-up, *Albert*, and as Reg Last in I, as well as playing the straight man to *Basil Brush* in the late 1960s. Numerous guest appearances have included parts in *Doctor Who* and *Z Cars*.

BEWITCHED

US (Screen Gems) Situation Comedy. BBC 1 1964–76

Samantha Stephens	Elizabeth Montgomery
Darrin Stephens	Dick York
	Dick Sargent
Endora	Agnes Moorhead
Maurice	Maurice Evans
Larry Tate	David White
Louise Tate	Irene Vernon
	Kasey Rogers
Tabitha Stephens	Erin and Diane Murphy
Adam Stephens	David and Greg Lawrence
Abner Kravitz	George Tobias
Gladys Kravitz	Alice Pearce
	Sandra Gould
Aunt Clara	Marion Lorne
Uncle Arthur	Paul Lynde
Esmerelda	Alice Ghostley
Dr Bombay	Bernard Fox

Creator: Sol Saks. Executive Producer: Harry Ackerman. Producer: William Asher

An attractive young witch marries a human and tries to settle down. However, she cannot resist using her magical powers, much to her husband's dismay.

Darrin Stephens was given a big surprise on his wedding day: he learned that his beautiful blonde bride, Samantha, was actually a witch, who had been around for hundreds if not thousands of years. She was, however, tired of the supernatural life and wanted to become part of normal society. Promising Darrin that she would rein back her magic, the newlyweds set up home deep in Connecticut suburbia.

However, all did not go to plan, largely because of Endora, Samantha's mother, who fiercely opposed this 'mixed' marriage and used every opportunity to cast spells on her unfortunate son-in-law, changing him into chimps and frogs at will. She made no effort to learn his name, calling him variously Darwin, Donald, Durwood or something equally wrong. All of this was rather irritating for the hapless Darrin, an ambitious advertising executive with McMann and Tate. Whenever he managed to worm his way into boss Larry Tate's good books, there was Endora to foul things up. Fortunately, Samantha was always on hand to put things straight.

Samantha herself was very content in her domesticated life. She and Darrin were happy in their marriage, but she could never quite resist the temptation to twiddle her nose and let magic do the housework. Occasional visitors to the bizarre Stephens home were Samantha's confused Aunt Clara, a clumsy witch who forgot how to undo her spells, Maurice, Samantha's father, and practical joker Uncle Arthur. And then there were Abner and Gladys Kravitz, the neighbours. Witnessing the amazing events in the house next door from behind her twitching curtains, Gladys always failed to attract her husband's attention in time. Not surprisingly, he thought she was barmy.

The Stephenses soon began a family, with Tabitha the first born. She inherited her mother's special powers and the gift was also passed on to her brother, Adam, born a few years later. Later additions to the cast were Esmerelda, a bungling, failing sorceress who was taken on as housekeeper, and the ineffective Dr Bombay.

Bewitched saw many personnel changes in its run and caused much confusion when, unannounced, Dick York was suddenly replaced by Dick Sargent (York suffered continually from back trouble and eventually could not go on). Alice Pearce, who originally played Gladys Kravitz,

died in 1966, and the part of Louise Tate, Larry's wife, was also played by two actresses. A convention in American TV production was to use twins to play young children, to circumvent the limited hours minors were allowed to work. As a result, both Tabitha and Adam were played by twins, Tabitha by three sets before one of the last pair, Erin Murphy, took on the role full-time. When Tabitha grew up, she was given her own spin-off series, *Tabitha*, in which, played by Lisa Hartman, she worked for a Los Angeles TV station.

Bewitched was based on the 1942 film *I Married a Witch*, which, in turn, was taken from Thorne Smith's 1941 novel, *The Passionate Witch*.

BIG BREADWINNER HOG

UK (Granada) Crime Drama. ITV 1969

Hog	Peter Egan
Ackerman	Donald Churchill
Edgeworth	Rosemary McHale
Grange	David Leland
Lennox	Timothy West
Raspery	Peter Thomas
Izzard	Alan Browning
Singleton	Tony Steedman
Ryan	Godfrey Quigley

Producer: Robin Chapman

A vicious underworld mobster strives to be Mr Big.

Young, handsome Hog was a villain. A nasty villain. The sort of villain you didn't want to cross. He was also ambitious, aiming to be London's gangland king, and would stop at nothing to achieve that goal. But, with the established city mobsters resisting his rise to power, the scene was set for some particularly violent action. In one episode, acid was thrown in someone's face. In others, beatings were commonplace. Indeed the violence was so heavy that an apology had to be made to viewers. It seems the public were not yet ready for the criminal fraternity to be shown in all their gory colours.

BIG BREAKFAST, THE

UK (Planet 24) Entertainment. Channel 4 1992–

Presenters:
Chris Evans
Gaby Roslin
Paula Yates
Bob Geldof
Mark Lamarr
Keith Chegwin
Mark Little
Paul Ross
Richard Orford

Executive Producer: Charlie Parsons. Editor: Sebastian Scott

Fast-moving, weekday morning (7–9 am) entertainment mix.

Departing from the established news- and magazine-based format of other breakfast TV shows, *The Big Breakfast* placed the emphasis on fun from the start. Its all-action combination of competitions, interviews and music videos was designed to appeal to the younger end of the audience spectrum, with news items restrained to brief headlines every 20 minutes (supplied by ITN and read by Peter Smith). A real house (three converted lock-keepers' cottages) in East London – and not a typical TV studio – has been used for production, adding a cramped, chaotic atmosphere.

In the early programmes Bob Geldof (director of the production company Planet 24) conducted a series of pre-recorded interviews with major figures on the world stage, although these have since been abandoned in favour of more trivial items. His wife, Paula Yates, is still involved, however, welcoming celebrities into her boudoir and discussing fashion and other issues on her bed. A real family has joined the programme each week, and Keith Chegwin has spent most mornings interviewing motorists in traffic jams and knocking up families in 'Down Your Doorstep'. Other features have included 'Cupid's Arrow' (real-life tales of romance), American imports like *The Banana Splits*, sketches with puppets Zig and Zag, and 'Snap, Cackle and Pop' (entertainment news). However, the real success story of the programme to date has been host Chris Evans, whose relaxed approach and distinctive humour made him TV's hottest property in the mid-1990s and lured him away to programmes such as *Don't Forget Your Toothbrush*.

BIG DEAL

UK (BBC) Drama. BBC 1 1984–5

Robby Box	Ray Brooks
Jan Oliver	Sharon Duce
Debby Oliver	Lisa Geoghan
Tommy	James Ottaway
Henry Diamond	Tony Caunter
Joan	Deirdre Costello
Geordie	Andy Mulligan
Irish	Alan Mason
Vi Box	Pamela Cundell
Ferret	Kenneth Waller
Dick Mayer	Stephen Tate
Kipper	Roger Walker
Black George	Alex Tetteh-Lartey
Alison Diamond	Marion Bailey

Creator/Writer: Geoff McQueen. Producer: Terence Williams

A middle-aged gambler attempts to kick the habit.

At the age of 40 Londoner Robby Box had not done a day's work since leaving school. Instead, he made a living playing poker and betting on horses and dogs. The sudden realization, however, that his life was passing him by and that he had nothing to show for his misspent youth made Box decide to 'go straight', calling on the help of his blonde girlfriend, Jan, and her teenage daughter, Debby. Things didn't always go to plan, though, especially with the taxman on Robby's tail and Jan always likely to walk out on him. Jan, too, had her problems. She wanted Robby to change, but loved him just the way he was. In the second season Robby's efforts to become respectable led to him taking over The Dragon Club, but life didn't get any easier.

BIG TIME, THE

UK (BBC) Documentary. BBC 1 1976–7; 1980

Presenter/Producer: Esther Rantzen

Magic wand programme allowing amateurs to become professionals for a day.

Esther Rantzen was responsible for this series, which enabled ordinary viewers to achieve life-long ambitions. Amongst those featured were a housewife who was given the chance to prepare a banquet at a swish hotel, a vicar who wrote a newspaper gossip column and a sales assistant who joined a circus. However, the real success story concerned Scottish teacher Sheena Easton, who, from singing part-time in clubs, not only cut a record but went on to become an international star in her own right. Two series were produced, with a three-year gap in between.

BIG VALLEY, THE

US (Four Star) Western. ITV 1965–

Victoria Barkley	Barbara Stanwyck
Jarrod Barkley	Richard Long
Nick Barkley	Peter Breck
Heath Barkley	Lee Majors
Audra Barkley	Linda Evans
Eugene Barkley	Charles Briles
Silas	Napoleon Whiting

Producers: Jules Levy, Arthur Gardner, Arnold Laven

Life with a cattle-ranching family in California's San Joaquin Valley in the 1870s.

The Big Valley told the story of hard-headed widow Victoria Barkley and her ranching family in the Old West. Her sons ranged from the refined lawyer Jarrod, to the brawny Nick, the foreman on the 30,000-acre holding. Heath was the good-looking one, although he was not Victoria's own (being the illegitimate son of her late husband, Tom, and an Indian squaw), and the youngest son was Eugene, a bashful youth only seen in the earliest episodes. Victoria also had a beautiful but impetuous daughter named Audra. Silas was the family's black servant. Storylines followed the usual Western pattern, revolving around constant battles with rustlers, criminals and con men.

Future **Six Million Dollar Man** Lee Majors made his TV debut in this series, and Linda Evans also went on to bigger and better things (as Krystle in **Dynasty**).

BIGGINS, CHRISTOPHER (1948–)

Cheerful, bespectacled actor/comedian/presenter, initially finding favour as the effeminate Lukewarm in **Porridge**, the Rev. Ossie Whitworth in **Poldark** and Nero in **I, Claudius**. He was also Adam Painting in **Rentaghost** and co-host of **Surprise, Surprise** with Cilla Black. His other TV credits have included **The Likely Lads**, **Paul Temple**, **Upstairs, Downstairs**, **Shoestring**, **Watch This Space** and **On Safari**.

BIGGLES

UK (Granada) Children's Adventure. ITV 1960

Inspector 'Biggles' Bigglesworth........Neville Whiting
Ginger..John Leyton
Bertie..................................David Drummond
Von Stalheim................................Carl Duering

Producers: Harry Elton, Kitty Black

The adventures of a celebrated flying ace.

In this action-packed series, Biggles, Captain WE Johns's daredevil pilot, had left the Air Force with his chums Ginger and Bertie and was attached to Scotland Yard. Now a Detective Air Inspector, the intrepid air ace turned his sights away from enemy aircraft and on to airborne villains, ensuring each episode had a thrilling flying sequence and cliff-hanger ending. Among the show's writers was a young man called Tony Warren, who went on to devise **Coronation Street**, while John Leyton, who played Ginger, became more famous as a pop singer, topping the charts with 'Johnny Remember Me' a year after *Biggles* was screened.

THE BILL

UK (Thames) Police Drama. ITV 1984–

Detective Inspector Roy Galloway......John Salthouse
Sgt Bob Cryer ....Eric Richard
PC Francis 'Taffy' Edwards ....Colin Blumenau
PC Dave Litten ....Gary Olsen
PC/DC Jim Carver ....Mark Wingett
WPC June Ackland ....Trudie Goodwin
WPC/WDC Viv Martella ....Nula Conwell
PC Timothy Able ....Mark Haddigan
Detective Sgt Ted Roach ....Tony Scannell
WPC Claire Brind..........................Kelly Lawrence
PC Reg Hollis ....Jeff Stewart
PC Tony 'Yorkie' Smith ....Robert Hudson
PC Robin Frank ....Ashley Gunstock
PC Lyttleton ....Ronny Cush
Chief Supt Charles Brownlow ....Peter Ellis
PC Abe Lyttleton ....Ronnie Cush
PC Richard Turnham ....Chris Humphreys
PC Pete Muswell...........................Ralph Brown
Inspector Kite ....Simon Slater
Sgt Tom Penny ....Roger Leach
Sgt Alec Peters..........................Larry Dann
PC Nick Shaw.............................Chris Walker
PC Ken Melvin ....Mark Powley
PC Patel ....Sonesh Sira
Inspector Christine Frazer ....Barbara Thorn
PC Pete Ramsey ....Nick Reding
Det. Chief Insp. Gordon Wray ....Clive Wood
PC Malcolm Haynes.......................Eamonn Walker
PC Phil Young...........................Colin Aldridge
Chief Inspector Derek Conway ....Ben Roberts
Inspector Andrew Monroe ....Colin Tarrant
Detective Chief Inspector Kim Reid ....Carolyn Pickles
Detective Inspector Frank Burnside ....Christopher Ellison
Detective Sgt Alistair Greig........Andrew Mackintosh
DC Alfred 'Tosh' Lines ....Kevin Lloyd
DC Mike Dashwood.........................Jon Iles
Sgt John Maitland ....Sam Miller
PC Tony Stamp ....Graham Cole
PC Dave Quinnan ....Andrew Paul
WPC Cathy Marshall ....Lynne Miller
PC Steven Loxton ....Tom Butcher
WPC Norika Datta ....Seeta Indrani
WPC Delia French ....Natasha Williams
WPC Suzanne Ford ....Vikki Gee-Dare
PC George Garfield ....Huw Higginson
PC Ron Smollett ....Nick Stringer
Sgt Matthew Boyden ....Tony O'Callaghan
Detective Inspector Jack Meadows ....Simon Rouse
PC Barry Stringer ....Jonathan Dow
DC Woods ....Tom Cotcher
Detective Sgt/Detective
 Inspector Harry Haines ....Gary Whelan
Detective Sgt/Detective
 Inspector. Chris Deakin ....Shaun Scott
WPC/WDC Suzi Croft......................Kerry Peers
Detective Sgt Danny Pearce.............Martin Marquez
PC Jarvis..............................Stephen Beckett
Sgt Steele ....Robert Perkins
Detective Inspector Sally Johnson ....Jaye Griffiths
WPC Harris ....Louise Harrison
DC Rod Skase...........................Iain Fletcher
PC Gary McCann ....Clive Wedderburn
Chief Inspector Cato ....Philip Whitchurch
Woman Detective. Sgt Morgan ....Mary Jo Randle
WPC Polly Page ....Lisa Geoghan
Detective Sgt Don Beech.................Billy Murray
PC Nick Slater ....Alan Westaway
WPC Debbie Keane ....Andrea Mason
Chief Inspector Paul Stritch ....Mark Spalding

Creator: Geoff McQueen. Executive Producers: Lloyd Shirley, Peter Cregeen, Michael Chapman. Producers: Michael Chapman, Peter Cregeen, Richard Bramall, Brenda Ennis, Michael Ferguson, Geraint Morris, Pat Sandys, Michael Simpson, Tony Virgo, Peter Wolfes, Richard Handford, Mike Dormer

The rigours of day-to-day inner-city policing.

The Bill focused on life at the Sun Hill police station, somewhere in London's East End. It showed the local law enforcers in their everyday work, catching crooks, keeping the peace and dealing with the general public. For once, personal lives were pushed well into the background.

Criticized by real police for its portrayal of policing methods, *The Bill* was also attacked for suggesting that racism was a facet of today's force. Nevertheless, the series continued to show just how policemen cope with the realities of the modern world, showing officers of the law as people with a job to do, however unpleasant that job may be.

Head of the station was Chief Supt Charles Brownlow, a man mostly concerned with the image of his force, and beneath him worked an ever-changing squad of inspectors, sergeants, detectives and constables. Most notable were Bob Cryer, the paternal station officer, the hot-headed Detective Chief Inspector Galloway (who was never afraid to bend the rules) and his devious successor Detective Chief Inspector Burnside. Young PCs 'Taffy' Edwards and Jim Carver, the hypochondriac Reg Hollis, ambitious Dave Litton, impetuous Ted Roach, well-groomed Mike Dashwood, scruffy 'Tosh' Lines and dependable WPCs Ackland and Martella were also prominent.

The Bill began in 1983 as an episode of Thames TV's **Storyboard** series, entitled '*Woodentop*' (a CID nickname for uniformed officers). After four years as an hour-long drama, it 'turned tabloid', splitting into two self-contained, half-hour episodes each week. A new rule was added: there had to be a police person in every scene. Hand-held camera work was introduced to provide a touch of on-the-streets realism and it certainly helped with the pace of the programme, although characterization and plot development were victims of the truncated format. At the time of writing, it had become one of TV's longest-running cop shows. Those famous plodding feet in the title sequence must now be rather tired.

UK (Thames) Drama. ITV 1976

Bill Brand ....Jack Shepherd

Creator/Writer: Trevor Griffiths. Producer: Stuart Burge

Problems in the life of a left-wing MP.

Somewhat autobiographical in tone, Trevor Griffith's Bill Brand focused on a young, idealistic lecturer who climbed his way up the socialist ladder to become a Member of Parliament. Courting controversy all the way, he earned himself many enemies. Eleven episodes were made and, although applauded by the critics, viewers remained unimpressed.

UK (BBC) Situation Comedy. BBC 1952–61

Billy Bunter ....Gerald Campion

Creator/Writer: Frank Richards. Producers: Joy Harington, David Goddard, Pharic Maclaren, Shaun Sutton, Clive Parkhurst

Jolly japes and wizard wheezes with a plump boarding school pupil.

Performed live twice on a Friday night (at 5.25 pm for children and at 8 pm for grown-ups) in the days before videotape, *Billy Bunter of Greyfriars School* was one of the BBC's earliest long-running comedies. Scripted by Frank Richards and based on his *Magnet* comic stories, it told tales of the ever-hungry William George Bunter, the Fat Owl of the Remove. Twenty-nine-year-old Gerald Campion filled out for the part and let loose a barrage of Crikeys and Yaroos in raiding tuck shops, avoiding canings and waiting for postal orders from Bunter Court. Mocking Bunter was the beastly schoolboy posse of Harry Wharton, Frank Nugent, Bob Cherry, Hurree Jamset Ram Singh and Johnny Bull (played by a host of young performers), all avoiding the clutches of arch-enemy form-master Mr Quelch (played initially by Kynaston Reeves). Guesting among the boys were aspiring actors like Anthony Valentine, Michael Crawford, Melvyn Hayes and David Hemmings.

US (Universal/Harve Bennett) Science Fiction. ITV 1976–

Jaime Sommers	Lindsay Wagner
Oscar Goldman	Richard Anderson
Dr Rudy Wells	Martin E. Brooks
Jim Elgin	Ford Rainey
Helen Elgin	Martha Scott
Peggy Callahan	Jennifer Darling

Creator: Kenneth Johnson. Executive Producer: Harve Bennett

A girl with superhuman abilities works for a counter-espionage agency.

In this spin-off from *The Six Million Dollar Man*, Steve Austin's one-time girlfriend, Jaime Sommers, took centre stage. In the original series, Jaime broke up with Steve when he became an astronaut, but they were temporarily reunited after she was crippled in a sky-diving accident. Jaime was then given the same bionic treatment as her boyfriend, endowing her with special abilities.

She now had bionic legs which allowed her to run fast, a bionic ear for long-distance hearing and the strength of a bionic right arm. With these new skills, and in her own series, she settled down to life as a schoolteacher at the Ventura Air Force base in Ojai, California, although, in repayment for her futuristic medical treatment, she also worked for the anti-espionage agency OSI (Office of Scientific Information). Steve, too, undertook secret missions for OSI and, inevitably, the two were drawn together yet again. Sadly, the damage to Jaime's memory had wiped out her love for him, but this didn't affect their working relationship. Jaime even took up residence in an apartment at the farm owned by Steve's mother and stepfather (Helen and Jim Elgin).

The series also introduced Max, the bionic German shepherd dog, as a companion for Jaime, and the Bionic Boy (played by Vincent Van Patten). But more often seen were OSI executive Oscar Goldman and Dr Rudy Wells, the pioneer of bionic medicine. These characters, and that of Peggy Callahan, Oscar's secretary, also appeared in *The Six Million Dollar Man*.

BIRD The slang term for a communications satellite.

BIRD, JOHN (1936–)

British comedian, actor, writer and director, a graduate of the Cambridge Footlights troupe. His earliest TV credits included *That Was The Week That Was*, *Not So Much A Programme, More a Way of Life*, *BBC 3*, Jonathan Miller's *Alice In Wonderland* and *The Late Show*, although he has more recently enjoyed success as support to Rory Bremner (with long-time partner John Fortune) and as Douglas Bromley in *El C.I.D.* As well as notable appearances in *Blue Remembered Hills*, *Oxbridge Blues*, *Travelling Man* and *A Very Peculiar Practice*, he has starred in a couple of comedies of his own, namely *A Series of Bird's* and *With Bird Will Travel*, *Well Anyway* (a shared venture with Fortune), and the sitcoms *If It Moves – File It* (as civil servant Quick), *Joint Account* (as Ned Race) and *Educating Marmalade* (as Mr Atkins).

BIRD OF PREY

UK (BBC) Drama. BBC 1 1982

Henry Jay	Richard Griffiths
Anne Jay	Carole Nimmons
Tony Hendersly	Jeremy Child
Charles Bridgnorth	Nigel Davenport
Harry Tompkins	Roger Sloman
Rochelle Halliday	Ann Pennington
Mario	Guido Adorni
Dino	Eddie Mineo
Hugo Jardine	Christopher Logue

Writer: Ron Hutchinson. Producer: Michael Wearing

A Government employee stumbles into international intrigue.

Henry Jay, a civil servant in his mid-30s, was working on a case of computer fraud when he unearthed by chance a massive financial conspiracy. He decided to investigate further and, despite the close attentions of a shadowy agency known as Le Pouvoir and various bureaucratic attempts to silence him, Jay proved to be a determined detective, discovering clues that pointed to the involvement of a Euro MP by the name of Hugo Jardine.

Following the success of this four-part drama, dubbed 'a thriller for the electronic age', a sequel, entitled *Bird of Prey 2*, was made in 1984. In this, Henry, on the run with his wife, Anne, continued to expose the murky activities of Le Pouvoir.

BIRDS OF A FEATHER

UK (Alomo) Situation Comedy. BBC 1 1989–

Sharon Theodopolopoudos	Pauline Quirke
Tracey Stubbs	Linda Robson
Dorien Green	Lesley Joseph
Chris Theodopolopoudos	David Cardy
	Peter Polycarpou
Darryl Stubbs	Alun Lewis
Garth Stubbs	Simon Nash
	Matthew Savage
Marcus Green	Nickolas Grace
	Stephen Greif
Melanie Fishman	Jan Goodman

Creators: Laurence Marks, Maurice Gran. Producers: Esta Charkham, Nic Phillips, Candida Julian-Jones, Charlie Hanson

Two sisters live together after their husbands are sent to jail.

Tracey and Sharon were two adopted sisters from North London. Of the two, Tracey had patently done better for herself. She had a nice neo-Georgian home in the Essex suburb of Chigwell, whereas Sharon still lived in Camelot House, a council tower block in Edmonton. Furthermore, Tracey's son, Garth, now attended a public school. What she didn't realize was that her husband, Darryl, was paying for all this on the proceeds of crime. All was revealed when he and Sharon's dim Greek husband, Chris, were arrested for armed robbery and earned themselves 12-year prison sentences. At that point Sharon moved in with Tracey and set about finding a new man in her life. Indeed, sex – or at least talk of it – became their main obsession, even though they still visited their partners in Maidstone prison. Money problems formed their other pre-occupation, as Darryl's ill-gotten cash began to run out, and Sharon opened up a café to earn a living.

The girls' lives were regularly spiced up by Dorien Green, their snooty, man-eating, next-door neighbour, who enjoyed a succession of toy boys in the absence of her accountant husband, Marcus. Dorien's great rival on the local social scene was Melanie Fishman.

BIRT, JOHN (1944–)

Controversial Director-General of the BBC, whose internal reforms caused much unease in the early 1990s. The streamlining of staff and the introduction of the 'Producer Choice' internal market system proved the most inflammatory, as Birt was charged with leading the BBC through a particularly difficult period in a new multi-channel environment and with the BBC's Charter due for renewal in 1996. Birt's career took off at Granada, where he was responsible in 1968 for the *Nice Time*, the innovative comedy show starring Jonathan Routh, Kenny Everett and Germaine Greer. He later moved to LWT, where his input into current affairs television proved equally influential (amongst other projects he was executive producer of **Weekend World**). Through famous articles in *The Times*, Birt openly questioned the 'bias against understanding' in TV current affairs. He eventually took over as head of Features and Current Affairs before rising to Programme Controller in 1981. He joined the BBC as Deputy Director-General in 1987, brought in by the then Director-General Michael Checkland to reappraise the BBC's journalistic operations. He was somewhat controversially named as the next Director-General in 1991, while Checkland still had two years of his contract to run.

BIT OF A DO, A

UK (Yorkshire) Comedy Drama. ITV 1989

Ted Simcock	David Jason
Rita Simcock	Gwen Taylor
Elvis Simcock	Wayne Foskett
Paul Simcock	David Thewlis
Laurence Rodenhurst	Paul Chapman
Liz Rodenhurst/Badger	Nicola Pagett
Simon Rodenhurst	Nigel Hastings
Jenny Rodenhurst/Simcock	Sarah-Jane Holm
Neville Badger	Michael Jayston
Rodney Sillitoe	Tim Wylton
Betty Sillitoe	Stephanie Cole
Carol Fordingbridge	Karen Drury
Gerry Lansdown	David Yelland
Corinna Price-Rodgerson	Diana Weston
Geoffrey Ellsworth-Smythe	Malcolm Tierney
Lucinda Snellmarsh	Amanda Wenban
Eric	Malcolm Hebden
Sandra	Tracy Brabin

Creator/Writer: David Nobbs. Executive Producer: Vernon Lawrence. Producer: David Reynolds

Social rivalry between two families who regularly meet at local functions.

Set in a small Yorkshire town, where everyone knew each other's business, *A Bit of a Do* focused on the relationships between members of the Rodenhurst and Simcock families. Laurence Rodenhurst was a dentist, while the socially inferior Ted Simcock ran an iron foundry. The first 'do' which brought them together was the marriage of Laurence's daughter Jenny to scruffy Paul, Ted's son. During the reception, Ted enjoyed some extra-marital exercise with Laurence's wife, Liz, which resulted in an unplanned offspring and the break up of Ted's marriage to Rita. That set the tone for the series.

Other 'dos' the families attended included the Angling Club Christmas party, the Dentists' dance and the crowning of Miss Frozen Chicken UK at the Cock-a-Doodle Chickens event. As the series progressed, Laurence died, Liz picked up with widower Neville Badger, Ted's business hit hard times and Jenny married her brother-in-law, Elvis. Rodney and Betty Sillitoe were boozy regulars at every function and also seen were barman Eric and waitress Sandra. The episodes were dramatized by David Nobbs from his own novels.

BIXBY, BILL (1934–93)

American actor famous as the mild-mannered Dr David Banner in **The Incredible Hulk**, with earlier starring roles as Anthony Blake in **The Magician** (as part for which he learned conjuring tricks) and Tim O'Hara in **My Favorite Martian**. His other major TV credit was in a comedy series not seen in the UK, **The Courtship of Eddie's Father**. Bixby also turned his hand to directing, calling the shots on some episodes of **Rich Man, Poor Man**, as well as appearing in front of the camera as Willie Abbott in that mini-series.

BLACK, CILLA (PRISCILLA WHITE; 1943–)

Liverpudlian singer turned presenter whose career break came while working as a cloakroom attendant and occasional vocalist at The Cavern club, famous for The Beatles' early performances. Spotted by Brian Epstein, Black secured a recording contract and entered the charts with a Lennon and McCartney song, 'Loved of the Loved', in 1963, before notching up two number ones with 'Anyone Who Had a Heart' and 'You're My World'. She ventured into television in 1968, gaining her own Saturday night series, *Cilla*, on BBC 1, which ran for several years. In these live programmes she sent an outside broadcast team to surprise unsuspecting residents somewhere in the UK. She also gave viewers the chance to choose the Song for Europe. Black later tried her hand at sitcom in *Cilla's Comedy Six* and *Cilla's World of Comedy* and, after a quiet period during the 1970s, she resurfaced as host of ***Surprise, Surprise*** (in 1984) and ***Blind Date*** (in 1985).

BLACK AND WHITE MINSTREL SHOW, THE

UK (BBC) Variety. BBC 1 1958–78

Creator: George Inns. Producers: George Inns, Ernest Maxin, Brian Whitehouse

Sing-along variety show featuring the Mitchell Minstrels and guests.

Stemming from a one-off special entitled *The 1957 Television Minstrels*, this old-fashioned, fast-moving series was a showcase for conductor George Mitchell's Mitchell Minstrels and especially lead vocalists Dai Francis, John Boulter and Tony Mercer. Other long-serving Al Jolson look alikes were Benny Garcia, Les Rawlings, Andy Cole and Les Want, and female contributions came from Margo Henderson, Margaret Savage, Penny Jewkes, Delia Wicks and others. In the background the Television Toppers dancers (previously stars of *Toppers About Town*) provided the glamour. Adding light relief were comedians like Leslie Crowther, George Chisholm and Stan Stennet.

The Minstrels specialized in schmaltzy medleys in the sing-along vein, some originating from America's deep South (like the 19th-century minstrel concept itself). Other tunes were of Country and Western origin, or were derived from foreign folk cultures. The programme was a Saturday night favourite, but, by the end of the 1970s, the political incorrectness of men with blacked-up faces and broad white smiles resulted in its cancellation after over 20 years on air.

BLACK BEAUTY See *Adventures of Black Beauty, The.*

BLACKADDER

UK (BBC) Situation Comedy. BBC 1 1983–9

The Black Adder (1983)
Edmund, Duke of Edinburgh
('The Black Adder') ....Rowan Atkinson
Baldrick ....Tony Robinson
Lord Percy ....Tim McInnerny
Richard IV ....Brian Blessed
Queen ....Elspet Gray
Prince Harry..Robert East

Blackadder II (1986)
Lord Edmund Blackadder ....Rowan Atkinson
Baldrick ....Tony Robinson
Queen Elizabeth I.......................Miranda Richardson
Lord Melchett...Stephen Fry
Lord Percy ....Tim McInnerny
Nursie..Patsy Byrne

Blackadder the Third (1987)
Edmund Blackadder ....Rowan Atkinson
Baldrick ....Tony Robinson
George, Prince of Wales ....Hugh Laurie
Mrs Miggins.............................Helen Atkinson-Wood

Blackadder Goes Forth (1989)
Captain Edmund Blackadder............Rowan Atkinson
Pte Baldrick ....Tony Robinson
Lt George Colthurst St Barleigh ....Hugh Laurie
General Hogmanay Melchett ....Stephen Fry
Captain Darling....................................Tim McInnerny

Semi-regulars:
Lord Flashheart (*II/Goes Forth*) ....Rik Mayall
Kate/Bob (*II*)/Driver
 Parkhurst (*Goes Forth*) ....Gabrielle Glaister
Princess Maria (*The Black
 Adder*)/Lady Whiteadder (*II*) ....Miriam Margolyes
Amy Hardwood (*The Third*)/
 Nurse Mary (*Goes Forth*)...........Miranda Richardson

Creators: Rowan Atkinson, Richard Curtis. Writers: Rowan Atkinson, Richard Curtis, Ben Elton. Producer: John Lloyd

Historical double-dealing with various generations of a cowardly family.

Blackadder was a collection of comedies which, although running into four eras, splits neatly into two clear parts: the first series and the rest. Viewers who later came to love the devious, treacherous, selfish rogue of *Blackadder II*, *Blackadder the Third* and *Blackadder Goes Forth*, were not over-enamoured of the character portrayed in the first series, which was simply entitled *The Black Adder*. This series was written by Rowan Atkinson and Richard Curtis. By the second generation, Ben Elton had replaced Atkinson as co-writer and the scripts were graced with more rounded plots and filled with choice one-liners.

The Blackadder saga began with Edmund, Duke of Edinburgh. Crudely based on supposedly true historical accounts, the comedy came from the feeblemindedness of the cringing duke and his sly, cowardly ways. Filmed around Alnwick Castle in Northumberland, at great expense, it was set during the Wars of the

Roses, as the houses of Lancaster and York battled for the English throne, with Edmund allegedly the son of Richard IV, one of the Princes in the Tower.

By the second series (the concept having just survived cancellation) Edmund Blackadder, great-great-grandson of the original Black Adder and a courtier of Queen Elizabeth I, had added buoyant confidence to his ancestor's repertoire of deceit and cruelty. He was admirably complemented in his Tudor treachery by an overgrown schoolgirl version of the Virgin Queen, as well as his pompous rival, Lord Melchett, and his foppish hanger-on, Lord Percy. But the best support came from the rodent-like manservant, Baldrick, like Lord Percy an even stupider descendant of a character first seen in *The Black Adder*.

For *Blackadder the Third*, time had moved on two centuries to the Georgian Age, and the Blackadder in question was butler to the idiotic George, Prince of Wales. In between frequenting Mrs Miggins's coffee shop and cuffing Baldrick about the ear, Blackadder schemed his way in and out of the society groups who surrounded the Prince, meeting the likes of Dr Johnson (Robbie Coltrane) and the Duke of Wellington (Stephen Fry).

The last incarnation came in the World War I trenches of *Blackadder Goes Forth*. Here the weaselly Captain Edmund Blackadder worked every ruse in the book to try to flee the impending carnage, but was inhibited by his imbecile lieutenant, George, and, of course, Private Baldrick. Then there was the arrogant, insensitive General Melchett, booming out orders to his subservient adjutant, Captain Darling, yet another object of contempt for our hero. The tragedy and futility of the Great War were never ridiculed and the series concluded in rich pathos. As all the 'ordinary men' (not the General, of course) were forced 'over the top' to certain death, the slow motion action faded silently into a field of swaying poppies.

Series two to four were essentially performed by what amounted to a high-class repertory company. Joining Atkinson and Robinson in their roles as Blackadder and Baldrick were Stephen Fry, Hugh Laurie, Miranda Richardson, Tim McInnerny and Rik Mayall, each reprising parts played in earlier series. There was also a Christmas special set in various time zones, including the future, and depicting Blackadder as Ebenezer Scrooge in reverse – he began the story a kind and generous patrician, winding up as the Blackadder we had all grown to know, love and hate. A short insert (*Blackadder: The Cavalier Years*)

was produced for *Comic Relief* in 1988, placing the troupe in the Civil War era, with Stephen Fry as King Charles I.

BLACKMAN, HONOR (1926–)

Blonde British leading lady, a graduate of the Rank charm school who sprang to fame as the athletic Cathy Gale in *The Avengers*, having already appeared in the series *Probation Officer*. After two years as Gale, Blackman headed for Hollywood, winning the part of Pussy Galore in *Goldfinger*. Recently, her most prominent role has been as Laura West in *The Upper Hand*, although she has also been seen in other comedy series like *Robin's Nest* (as Marion Nicholls) and *Never The Twain* (as Veronica Barton). Additional credits over the years have ranged from *The Four Just Men*, *The Invisible Man* and *Ghost Squad* to *Top Secret*, the mini-series *Lace* and *Doctor Who*.

BLAIR, LIONEL (1934–)

Elegant British dancer and TV personality, one of the team captains on *Give Us A Clue* and later host of *Name That Tune*.

BLAKE'S 7

UK (BBC) Science Fiction. BBC 1 1978–81

Roj Blake	Gareth Thomas
Kerr Avon	Paul Darrow
Jenna Stannis	Sally Knyvette
Vila Restal	Michael Keating
Cally	Jan Chappell
Zen (voice only)	Peter Tuddenham
Gan Olag	David Jackson
Orac (voice only)	Peter Tuddenham
Dayna Mellanby	Josette Simon
Captain Del Tarrant	Steven Pacey
Soolin	Glynis Barber
Supreme Commander Servalan	Jacqueline Pearce
Commander Travis	Stephen Greif
	Brian Croucher
Slave (voice only)	Peter Tuddenham

Creator: Terry Nation. Producers: David Maloney, Vere Lorrimer

In the distant future, a band of escaped criminals fights back against an oppressive government.

Sometime in the 3rd century of the second calendar, the populated worlds of our galaxy found themselves at the mercy of a cruel, remorseless dictatorship known as The Federation. This ruthless regime tolerated no opposition. Petty criminals, by way of pay-offs, were allowed to exist and make life a misery for the population, but no political dissent was tolerated. There were, however, small bands of resistance. One such band was comprised of escaped prisoners, led by the falsely convicted Roj Blake. On their way to exile on the penal colony of Cygnus Alpha, they had made their burst for freedom in an abandoned spacecraft renamed *Liberator* and now they wandered the galaxy avoiding recapture, hell bent on sabotaging the activities of The Federation.

Blake, a natural-born leader, became a genuine freedom fighter, a hero in a corrupt universe. But even if he was a Robin Hood figure, his followers were far from merry men. His number two, computer genius Kerr Avon, was an ambitious, arrogant man given only to preserving his own skin, while the safe-cracker, Vila, suffered from a broad yellow streak. There were also smuggler/pilot Jenna Stannis, Cally, a combative, telepathic native of the planet Auron, and the brawny Gan, who had an electronic limiter fitted to his brain to prevent him killing. Although their well being depended on mutual assistance, this was never a team, rather a collection of squabbling, selfish renegades thrown together by outside pressures.

The seventh member of the group was the *Liberator*'s master computer, Zen, but characters came and went during the course of the programme's run and the composition of the Seven changed. Gone were Gan and Jenna when mercenary Del Tarrant and weapons expert Dayna Mellanby were added to the cast, with the beautiful blonde Soolin, a crack shot, joining later. Not even Blake was a fixture. He disappeared at the end of the second series, to be replaced as leader by the stony faced Avon. There were also new computers, Orac and, in *Scorpio* (a new spacecraft which replaced the destroyed *Liberator*), Slave. In pursuit of the rebels were Supreme Commander Servalan, icy and calculating, and her vicious henchman, Travis. Blake returned briefly, just long enough to be killed by Avon in the very last episode.

For all their efforts, the Seven only ever succeeded in causing minor problems for The Federation. Their cause was a hopeless one and a sense of futility pervaded the series. Its creator, Terry Nation, also instilled it with fascist allegory, in line with the rather gloomy views of the future he conveyed in works such as *Doctor Who* and *Survivors*. Despite a lacklustre final season, when the budget had clearly been slashed, *Blake's 7* achieved cult status, not just in the UK but in America, too, even though it was never fully networked in the USA.

BLAKELY, COLIN (1930–87)

Northern Irish classical actor whose TV roles were usually in the quietly determined vein. His most prominent part was Jesus Christ in Dennis Potter's controversial play *Son of Man* in 1969, although he also starred as Lew Burnett in *The Hanged Man* and was very nearly cast as the lead in *Target*, the BBC's answer to *The Sweeney*. Other TV credits included the Alun Owen plays *Lena, O My Lena* and *Shelter*, and the dramas *The Breaking of Colonel Keyser*, *Peer Gynt*, *The Birthday Party*, *Drums Along Balmoral Drive*, *Operation Julie* (as Detective Inspector Richard Lee), *Cousin Bette* (as Steinbock), *The Beiderbecke Affair* (as Chief Supt Forrest) and *Paradise Postponed* (as Dr Salter).

BLANC, MEL (1908–89)

Hollywood's most celebrated cartoon voicer, famous for the likes of Bugs Bunny, Daffy Duck, Sylvester and Tweety Pie, Woody Woodpecker, Porky Pig and Speedy Gonzales. His television voices included Barney Rubble and Dino in *The Flintstones*, Cosmo C. Spacely in *The Jetsons* and Twiki the robot in *Buck Rogers in the 25th Century*. He actually appeared in vision with Jack Benny in the 1950s, playing Benny's violin teacher, Professor LeBlanc.

BLANKETY BLANK

UK (BBC) Game Show. BBC 1 1979–89

Presenters: Terry Wogan, Les Dawson.

Producers: Alan Boyd, Marcus Plantin, Stanley Appel

Contrived comic guessing game.

Considering its dire prizes and contrived format, *Blankety Blank* proved remarkably durable. It was undoubtedly established by the appeal of first host Terry Wogan (with his unusual, magic wand-like microphone), but it remained popular when Les Dawson took charge in 1984. What the four contestants (two sets of two) had to do was guess the missing word in a somewhat risqué statement read out by Wogan or Dawson. To edge towards the prizes, their word had to match the guesses made by a panel of six celebrities. The more matches made, the more points (circles or triangles) were accrued. With celebrity help (or hindrance), the winning contestant then had to complete a short, final phrase, hopefully matching it to a word selected in a public survey to win one of the prizes, which were staggeringly modest (Dawson once quipped 'Some prizes are so bad, they're left in the foyer'). Losing contestants walked away with a *Blankety Blank* cheque book and pen. Of more interest to the viewer were the exchanges between the host and the celebrity panel, which generally overshadowed the main contest.

BLEASDALE, ALAN (1946–)

Liverpudlian playwright whose work has emphasized social injustice through wry humour and
sharp characterizations. His first TV play was
Early to Bed in 1975, but it was his drama *The
Black Stuff*, screened in 1980, which attracted
more interest. With unemployment poised to
soar in Britain, Bleasdale's skilful observation of a
band of Scouse tarmac layers, working away from
home and hovering on the brink of the dole, gave
more than a hint of his work to come. It ultimately led to a complete series **Boys from the
Blackstuff**, a 1982 five-part sequel which
explored the stresses life on the dole brought to
its main protagonists, including the celebrated
Yosser ('Gissa job') Hughes, played by Bernard
Hill. Earlier, Bleasdale had rewritten the intended first episode of the series as the one-off play
The Muscle Market. In 1984 he developed his own
Scully novels (as first seen in a 1978 **Play For
Today**) for Channel 4, creating a 'real world'
teenage drama, before embarking on another
controversial series for the BBC. This time it was
The Monocled Mutineer, the four-part story of
Percy Toplis, the World War I army rebel who
was executed by the Secret Service. It was loosely based on a true story, although the BBC unfortunately claimed full authenticity. The Tory press
was outraged. In 1991, back on Channel 4,
Bleasdale turned his attention once more to
Liverpool and the contrasting lifestyles of rising
political star Michael Murray (Robert Lindsay)
and gentle schoolteacher Jim Nelson (Michael
Palin) in the much acclaimed **GBH**. For the same
channel he switched to production, offering a
helping hand to aspiring writers in the four-part
anthology *Alan Bleasdale Presents* in 1994.

BLESS THIS HOUSE

UK (Thames) Situation Comedy. ITV 1971–6

Sid Abbott	Sidney James
Jean Abbott	Diana Coupland
Mike Abbott	Robin Stewart
Sally Abbott	Sally Geeson
Trevor	Anthony Jackson
Betty	Patsy Rowlands

Creators: Vince Powell, Harry Driver. Producer:
William G. Stewart

**Generation gap comedy with a suburban
family.**

Cheery Londoner Sid Abbott, a middle-aged sta-
tionery salesman, was fond of booze, women and
football. He still considered himself one of the
lads, but had little chance to prove it, as his long-
suffering wife, Jean, was always around to keep
him in check. They lived in Birch Avenue,
Putney, with their two teenage children, and that
was where their real problems began. Mike
(trendily garbed in beads and Afghan coat) had
just left art college and was far too busy protest-
ing about this and that to find himself a job, and
with-it Sally, apple of her dad's eye, was in the
final year of grammar school. Sadly their 1970s
morals and vices were a touch too daring for their
rather staid parents, who were constantly
bemused at the permissive society and seldom
failed to jump to wrong conclusions. Trevor was
Sid's next door neighbour and drinking pal at the
Hare and Hounds, with Betty his nagging wife.

A big ratings success, *Bless This House* numbered
amongst its writers Carla Lane and its creators
Vince Powell and Harry Driver. Produced by
future **Fifteen to One** host William G. Stewart, it
was Sid James's last major television series. Geoff
Love wrote the theme music. A feature film version was issued in 1972.

BLESSED, BRIAN (1937–)

Big, booming northern character actor, whose
full-blooded performances have earned gentle
mimicry. He first came to light in **Z Cars**, in
which, as PC Fancy Smith, he was one of the
original stars. Then, in 1966, he played Porthos
in the BBC's adaptation of *The Three Musketeers*.
In the 1970s and 1980s he was Augustus in **I,
Claudius**, Mark of Cornwall in **Arthur of the
Britons** and another 'historical' character, King
Richard IV, in the first series of **Blackadder**.
Blessed then proved to be a well-cast successor
to Robert Newton in *John Silver's Return to
Treasure Island*. Amongst his other TV credits
have been episodes of *Justice*, *Hadleigh*, *Public
Eye*, *Churchill's People*, **Space: 1999**, *The
Sweeney*, *Minder* and *War and Remembrance*. In
the footsteps of Hilary and Tensing, he fulfilled
a long-held ambition by climbing Mount
Everest in the early 1990s. He is married to
actress Hildegard Neil.

BLIGH, JASMINE (1913–91)

One of television's first personalities, Jasmine
Bligh joined the BBC in 1935, becoming,
together with Elizabeth Cowell and Leslie
Mitchell, one of the three host-announcers for
the Corporation's TV test transmissions. Her earlier experience as an actress stood her in good
stead in those days before autocues, as she had to
learn all her announcements word for word.
Although television was suspended during World
War II, Bligh returned to our screens to open up
the new postwar service in 1946. Abandoning
television work for a while, she returned to the
BBC to narrate the Noddy series and resurfaced
yet again in the 1970s as presenter of Thames

TV's daytime magazine *Good Afternoon.* Jasmine Bligh was a descendant of Captain Bligh, of *Bounty* fame.

BLIND DATE

UK (LWT) Game Show. ITV 1985–

Presenter: Cilla Black

Producers: Gill Stribling-Wright, Kevin Roast, Michael Longmire

Girls and guys select unseen partners for a prize trip.

In this dating service of the air, young men and women selected a member of the opposite sex to join them on a 'blind date' excursion. Three unseen contestants delivered rehearsed answers to three scripted questions posed by a boy or girl looking for a date. On the strength of their answers, one was chosen to accompany the questioner on a special trip. This may have involved anything from a week on the Mediterranean to a day at a safari park, depending on their luck in drawing envelopes. The following week the blind daters returned to tell all about their experience and to give honest opinions about their unfortunate partners. Cilla Black egged them on.

The first couple to marry as a result of meeting on the programme were Sue Middleton and Alex Tatham. Their 1991 wedding was captured in a special programme entitled *Blind Date Wedding of the Year.*

BLOCKBUSTERS

UK (Central) Quiz. ITV 1983–

Presenter: Bob Holness

Producers: Graham C. Williams, Tony Wolfe, Terry Steel, Bob Cousins

Daily general knowledge quiz for sixth-formers.

In this easy-going contest, Bob Holness asked the questions and three 16–18-year-old students (two played one) provided answers to light up hexagonal blocks on an electronic board. The team of two had to score a line of five blocks across a board to win a game, while the single contestant needed four in a row down the board. Each block selected bore the initial letter of the answer and much fun was had when contestants asked: 'Can I have a P please Bob?'. Money was awarded for every correct answer and matches consisted of three games (the winner won two of the three). The winning pupil (or one of the twosome) was then put on the 'hot spot'. He or she, by answering more questions, had to light up a path across the board in 60 seconds to win a prize. The hot spot prizes increased in value the more wins that were achieved, but five wins

were the maximum for any contestant(s).

Blockbusters gained a cult following among schoolkids and adults alike, and the studio audience enthusiastically showed their support by hand-jiving to the rousing theme music. In addition to a lengthy run on ITV, *Blockbusters* has also been seen on Sky One.

BLOCKER, DAN (1929–72)

Massive American actor, fondly remembered as the gentle giant, Hoss Cartwright, in *Bonanza*, although he appearing in other earlier TV Westerns, including *Gunsmoke* and *Cimarron City. Bonanza* lasted only one series after Blocker's untimely death.

BLOTT ON THE LANDSCAPE

UK (BBC) Comedy Drama. BBC 2 1985

Sir Giles Lynchwood MP	George Cole
Lady Maud Lynchwood	Geraldine James
Blott	David Suchet
Mrs Forthby	Julia McKenzie
Dundridge	Simon Cadell
Ganglion	Geoffrey Bayldon
Hoskins	Paul Brooke
Densher	Jeremy Clyde

Writer: Malcolm Bradbury. Producer: Evgeny Gridneff

An unscrupulous MP attempts to build a motorway through his wife's ancestral home.

Sir Giles Lynchwood was the Member of Parliament for South Worfordshire, a man with weird fetishes (which were indulged in extrovert sex sessions down in London) and a greedy desire to make more money. One of his plans was to direct a new motorway through the grounds of his wife's stately home, Handyman Hall, which was picturesquely set in Cleene Gorge. Rallying to its defence, the eccentric Lady Maud (a devotee of country sports) fought tooth and nail to preserve her home, assisted by her surreptitious gardener Blott. Mrs Forthby was the housekeeper and Dundridge the hapless man from the ministry who found himself immersed in the murky goings-on.

This six-part series was an adaptation by Malcolm Bradbury of Tom Sharpe's black comic novel of the same name. Filming took place at Stanage Park, near Ludlow.

BLUE PETER

UK (BBC) Children's Magazine. BBC 1 1958–

Presenters:
Leila Williams
Christopher Trace
Valerie Singleton

John Noakes
Peter Purves
Lesley Judd
Simon Groom
Christopher Wenner
Tina Heath
Sarah Greene
Peter Duncan
Janet Ellis
Michael Sundin
Mark Curry
Caron Keating
Yvette Fielding
John Leslie
Diane-Louise Jordan
Anthea Turner
Tim Vincent
Stuart Miles

Creator: John Hunter Blair. Editors: Biddy Baxter, Lewis Bronze

Long-running, squeaky-clean children's magazine.

Blue Peter is one programme most of Britain's thirtysomethings grew up with. It began as an idea of BBC producer John Hunter Blair in 1958 and was scheduled for a mere seven-week run, with each programme lasting just 15 minutes. Actor Christopher Trace and former Miss Great Britain Leila Williams were the first hosts and helped set the safe, middle-class tone which was to characterize the programme for years to come. However, the golden age of *Blue Peter* was undoubtedly the mid-1960s, when, with the programme extended to a half-hour in length, and well entrenched in its Monday and Thursday teatime slots, its best-known trio of presenters were Valerie Singleton, John Noakes and Peter Purves.

Over the years, the programme's trademarks have been its unwhistlable hornpipe theme tune (entitled *Barnacle Bill*), its *Blue Peter* badges (bearing the ship logo) for contributors and its spacious, sparsely furnished studio set, with just a few freestanding shelves and ornaments for decoration. The running order has mixed together interviews with guests, chats to precocious kids with unusual hobbies, assorted competitions (design the Christmas stamps was one), the daredevil exploits of the intrepid John Noakes and later Peter Duncan (both went on to star in their own spinoffs, *Go with Noakes* and *Duncan Dares*), and educational and historical inserts. In the early days the illustrated tales of *Packi* (an elephant drawn by Tony Hart) and space travellers *Bleep and Booster* were occasional features, and, for years, Percy Thrower looked after the *Blue Peter* garden. Chris Trace diligently cared for the elaborate *Blue Peter* train set, and rides on the programme's namesake steam engine, the 532 *Blue Peter*, have also been scheduled. A new-born baby became a regular

visitor to the show in 1968. Daniel Scott became the *Blue Peter* Baby, allowing Noakes and Purvis to make a complete hash of changing his nappy.

The programme's animals have shared equal billing with its human hosts. Amongst the most famous *Blue Peter* pets have been Petra, Patch, Shep, Bonny and Goldie, the dogs; Jason, the Siamese cat, and fellow felines Jack, Jill and Willow; Joey, the parrot; Honey, the guide dog, and Fred (later discovered to be Freda), the tortoise. Guest animals have proved particularly troublesome (especially as the show has always gone out live), with the chaos caused by Lulu, the defecating elephant, almost matched by a troupe of feuding St Bernards some years later.

Each year the pets have been packed off to the country for the summer while their masters and mistresses have headed for exotic climes in the annual *Blue Peter* expedition. Places visited have included Ceylon (now Sri Lanka) and the USA. Each Christmas has been heralded by the lighting of the advent crown (made from two tinsellagged coat hangers) and a blast from the Chalk Farm Salvation Army Band. Indeed, *Blue Peter's* Heath Robinson creations like the advent crown have gone into folklore, primarily because of the imaginative use of egg cartons, used toilet rolls, detergent bottles ('Sqeezy' was never mentioned) and sticky backed plastic (nor was 'Fablon'). For many years, these were largely the ideas of Margaret Parnell. 'Here's one I made earlier' became a catchphrase.

Another annual feature has been the *Blue Peter* Appeal, raising funds for international causes, although not by asking for money. Instead, used stamps, milk bottle tops, paperback books, old wool, aluminium cans and other such recyclables have been collected and sold in bulk to bring in cash. Among the best remembered appeals have been for Guide Dogs for the Blind, inshore lifeboats, Biafran war victims, horse-riding centres for handicapped children and equipment for children's hospitals and Romanian orphanages.

As well as the spin-off series mentioned above, another extra was the *Blue Peter Royal Safari to Africa* in 1971, in which Val accompanied HRH Princess Anne (the Princess Royal) into the Kenyan outback. It led to other *Blue Peter Special Assignments* for Val and allowed her to retire from the twice-weekly programme with grace.

Nearly 40 years after making its debut, *Blue Peter* is still going strong. Although long-serving programme editor Biddy Baxter retired in 1988, it shows no sign of running out of steam. Indeed, a third weekly programme was added from April 1995.

BOCHCO, STEVEN (1943–)

After a chequered career writing and producing shows like **Columbo**, **McMillan and Wife**, **The Six Million Dollar Man**, **Griff** and *Delvecchio*, Steven Bochco's career took a sharp upturn when he created **Hill Street Blues** and then **LA Law**. Setting a new style for TV drama (ensemble casts, continuing storylines, awkward topics, etc.), he earned himself a prestigious contract with ABC, for whom he went on to develop *Hooperman* and the less successful *Doogie Howser, MD* and *Cop Rock*, which attempted to combine pop songs with police action. Unfortunately, the public didn't take to miming murderers and jiving juries.

BOHT, JEAN (1936–)

Although synonymous now with the long-suffering Nellie Boswell in the dole sitcom **Bread**, Jean Boht's television career has stretched over programmes like **Juliet Bravo**, *Spyship* and the Alan Bleasdale dramas **Boys from the Blackstuff** and *Scully*. She also starred in *The Cloning of Joanna May* and the unsuccessful *Brighton Belles*, the UK translation of **The Golden Girls** (as Josephine, the equivalent of Sophia).

BOLAM, JAMES (1938–)

Geordie actor/comedian, one of TV's **Likely Lads** (Terry Collier) in the 1960s and 1970s, but enjoying a varied TV career since those days. He gained a new following as Jack Ford in **When the Boat Comes In**, appeared in the BBC Television Shakespeare production of *As You Like It* and played nosy schoolteacher Trevor Chaplin in **The Beiderbecke Affair** and its sequels. Not abandoning comedy, he has taken the roles of Roy Figgis in **Only When I Laugh**, Nesbitt Gunn in *Room at the Bottom*, Father Matthew in *Father Matthew's Daughter* and Bill MacGregor in **Second Thoughts** (on both TV and radio). He also played the lead in *Andy Capp* and over the years has been seen in series like **Take Three Girls**, **The Protectors**, *Executive Stress* and *Sticky Wickets*. He is married to actress Susan Jameson.

BONANZA

US (NBC) Western. ITV 1960–

Ben Cartwright	Lorne Greene
Little Joe Cartwright	Michael Landon
Eric 'Hoss' Cartwright	Dan Blocker
Adam Cartwright	Pernell Roberts
Hop Sing	Victor Sen Yung
Sheriff Roy Coffee	Ray Teal
Mr Canaday ('Candy')	David Canary
Dusty Rhoades	Lou Frizzel
Jamie Hunter	Mitch Vogel
Griff King	Tim Matheson

Creator/Producer: David Dortort

The adventures of an all-male ranching family in the 1860s.

This hugely successful Western opened with a pounding theme song and a map which burst into flames. It was the story of the Cartwright family, owners of the 1000-square mile Ponderosa ranch, set on the edge of Virginia City, Nevada. Head of the family was father Ben and he was ably supported by his three sons, all from different, deceased mothers. The pensive (and eldest) one was Adam, then came the slow-witted, 21-stone Hoss, who, for all his bulk, could be as meek as a kitten. (The name 'Hoss' means 'good luck' in Norwegian and was a tribute to his Scandinavian mother, who had been killed by Indians.) The third son was Little Joe, an impetuous lad with an eye for the girls. The Cartwrights' kitchen was looked after by Chinese cook Hop Sing.

The series revolved around the family's encounters with the dregs of society, their own self-preservation and the help they gave to others. There were many guest stars throughout its run, but also a few cast changes. Pernell Roberts left the show after six years and was not replaced for a couple of seasons. Then along came Candy, to work as a ranch hand. One of Ben's friends, Dusty Rhoades, was taken on when Candy temporarily moved away, and also seen was orphaned teenager Jamie Hunter. But the series was dealt a mortal blow by the sudden death of actor Dan Blocker in 1972, and, when Lorne Greene suffered a mild heart attack a few months later, the end of the series was in sight. By then *Bonanza* had been a Sunday night favourite in the USA for 14 years.

BOND, ALAN (1938–)

British-born Australian media mogul and real estate millionaire whose wealth and influence rose and fell very quickly in the 1980s. At one point Bond owned Australia's Nine Network (purchased from Kerry Packer), TVB in Hong Kong and a share in the fledgling British Satellite Broadcasting (BSB). With Australian TV companies bidding high prices for imported programmes, Nine Network's profits fell and the company returned to Packer's hands in 1990. BSB, meanwhile, quickly lost out in the UK satellite battle to Rupert Murdoch's Sky thanks to problems with its squarial.

BOND, JULIAN (1930–)

British dramatist and producer, contributor to **The Saint** and **Upstairs, Downstairs**, and creator of **Police Surgeon** (the series that led to **The Avengers**). His later TV successes included *A*

Man of Our Times, *The Ferryman* (for the Haunted anthology), ***Wings***, ***Dick Barton – Special Agent*** (with Clive Exton), *Love for Lydia* and the Channel 4 adaptation of ***The Far Pavilions***.

BOND, WARD (1903–60)

American actor chiefly remembered as the trailmaster Major Seth Adams in ***Wagon Train***. He died at the height of the series' success and was replaced by John McIntire as Christopher Hale.

BONEHEAD

UK (BBC) Children's Comedy. BBC 1960–2

Bonehead ....Colin Douglas
Boss...Paul Whitsun-Jones
Happy ....Douglas Blackwell

Creator/Writer/Producer: Shaun Sutton

Three inept crooks prove crime doesn't pay.

Bonehead introduced kids to three of the most incompetent villains ever seen on television. Head of the trio was the bulky, gangster-like Boss, deviser of great plans which always ended in failure; also in the team was the ironically named Happy. However, it was the dim-witted Bonehead, a lovable imbecile, who was the show's nominal star. Two seasons were made before actor Colin Douglas moved on to more sensible dramas, like *A Family at War*.

BONEY

Australia (Norfolk International) Police Drama. ITV 1975–

Detective Inspector Napoleon
  Bonaparte ('Boney') ....James Laurenson

Executive Producers: Bob Austin, Lee Robinson. Producer: John McCallum

The cases of an Aborigine detective.

Although, a white man 'coloured up', New Zealander James Laurenson took the lead in this popular series about an Aborigine police detective whose beat was the Australian bush. It shouldn't have been the busiest patch for crime, but Boney found plenty to keep him occupied among the farmers, prospectors and drifters of the outback. The series was based on the novels by Arthur Upfield and received only sporadic screenings in the UK.

BOOM

An extendible, manoeuvrable arm holding a microphone which may be positioned, out of shot, over actors' and presenters' heads to pick up voices.

BOON

UK (Central) Comedy Drama. ITV 1986–92

Ken Boon ....Michael Elphick
Harry Crawford ....David Dakar
Doreen Evans...Rachel Davies
Ethel Allard ....Joan Scott
Rocky Cassidy ....Neil Morrissey
Debbie Yates ....Lesley-Anne Sharpe
Laura Marsh.................................Elizabeth Carling
Alex Wilton ....Saskia Wickham

Creators: Jim Hill, Bill Stair. Executive Producers: Ted Childs, William Smethurst. Producers: Kenny McBain, Esta Charkham, Michele Buck, Simon Lewis

A kind-hearted, retired fireman becomes a freelance troubleshooter.

When Ken Boon was forced to leave the fire service on grounds of ill-health (he had damaged his lungs in a heroic rescue), he struggled to make ends meet. After a succession of failed money-making schemes, including a disastrous market gardening venture, he placed an ad in the local press. It read: 'Ex-fireman seeks interesting work – anything legal considered.' In response he was offered a variety of strange jobs, from child-minding to private detective work, not all of them, as he had hoped, legal. But the stocky, lugubrious Boon, with his heart of gold, was a soft touch, committed to his work and unhappy about letting down employers. His early associates were Doreen Evans and Ethel Allard.

Boon thought of himself as an urban cowboy, cruising the streets of the Midlands on his silver charger, a 650cc BSA Norton motorbike, which he called 'White Lightning'. He soon made his hobby his business by opening a courier agency, The Texas Rangers, and employing a dopy biker by the name of Rocky Cassidy as his sidekick, and teenager Debbie Yates as his secretary. Ken's best friend was fireman-turned-hotelier Harry Crawford, a businessman of little brain who moved from premises to premises, trading up, until he finally went bust as owner of a country house hotel. Ken, who was then working as a private eye with Rocky and a new secretary, Laura Marsh, agreed to join Harry in a new venture, Crawford Boon Security. Laura was later replaced by the resourceful Alex Wilton.

Although the series ended in 1992, one episode remained untransmitted until 1995. The show's theme song, 'Hi Ho Silver', by Jim Diamond, was a UK top five hit in 1986.

BOONE, RICHARD (1917–81)

American actor, a hit in the roles of hired gun Paladin in ***Have Gun, Will Travel*** and Wild West detective **Hec Ramsey**. His lesser successes included *Medic* and an anthology, *The Richard Boone Show*, both largely confined to US TV. Like singer Pat Boone, Richard Boone was a descendant of frontiersman Daniel Boone.

BOOTS AND SADDLES

US (California National) Western.
BBC 1958–60

Capain Shank Adams	Jack Pickard
Lt Colonel Hayes	Patrick McVey
Lt Kelly	Gardner McKay
Lt Binning	David Willock
Sgt Bullock	John Alderson
Luke Cummings	Michael Hinn

Cavalry patrols in the Wild West.

Subtitled *The Story of the Fifth Cavalry*, *Boots and Saddles* told of brave uniformed men tackling Indians and other 'baddies' in the American West of the 1870s. Shank Adams was the Captain in charge of the troop, supported by Lt Colonel Hayes and Lts Kelly and Binning. Luke Cummings was the scout. Thirty-nine half-hour episodes were made and appeared to be more popular in the UK than in their native USA.

BOOTSIE AND SNUDGE

UK (Granada) Situation Comedy. ITV 1960–4; 1974

Bootsie Bisley	Alfie Bass
Claude Snudge	Bill Fraser
Hesketh Pendleton	Robert Dorning
Henry Beerbohm 'Old' Johnson	Clive Dunn

Producers: Peter Eton, Milo Lewis, Eric Fawcett, Bill Podmore (1974)

Two National Service veterans find themselves back in Civvy Street.

Initially titled *Bootsie and Snudge in Civvy Life*, this spin-off from **The Army Game** focused on two of its most popular characters, Pte 'Excused Boots' Bisley and the bullying Sgt Claude Snudge. It related how the old sparring partners took up positions in a seedy gentlemen's club called The Imperial. Bootsie appropriately became boot boy, while Snudge was the new major-domo. The club was run by its Right Honourable Secretary, Hesketh Pendleton, and Clive Dunn gave one of his first 'old man' performances as the decrepit 83-year-old waiter Old Johnson.

In 1964 Bootsie and Snudge were seen in diplomatic circles in the series *Foreign Affairs* (they were given jobs at the British Embassy in the city of Bosnik), and Alfie Bass and Bill Fraser went on to play similar characters (this time known as Alf Grimble and William Bendlove, respectively) in

the 1967 series *Vacant Lot. Bootsie and Snudge* was resurrected in 1974, but the characters' relationship was reversed, with Bootsie now the powerful force, having won the football pools, and Snudge the lowly man from the pools company. The revival was short-lived.

BORDER TELEVISION

Based in Carlisle, Border is the ITV contractor for the extreme north-west of England, the Scottish borders and the Isle of Man, taking to the air on 1 September 1961 (Isle of Man from 26 March 1965). One of the UK's smallest broadcasters, Border numbers amongst its board members the arts critic Melvyn Bragg. It has successfully retained its franchise on every occasion but has not contributed significantly to the national ITV network. Perhaps the best-known offering has been the married couples quiz **Mr and Mrs**, hosted by Derek Batey (who has also been a Border director).

BORGIAS, THE

UK (BBC) Historical Drama. BBC 2 1981

Rodrigo Borgia	Adolfo Celi
Cesare Borgia	Oliver Cotton
Giuliano della Rovere	Alfred Burke
Lucrezia Borgia	Anne Louise Lambert
Juan Borgia	George Camiller

Creator/Producer: Mark Shivas. Writers: John Prebble, Ken Taylor

Much ridiculed attempt at dramatizing the tyranny of the infamous Borgia family.

Set in the 15th century, *The Borgias* aimed to expose the excesses and vices of late-Renaissance Italy. At the heart of the action was the hideous Rodrigo Borgia, a man who had bribed his way to the title of Pope Alexander VI. A wonderfully impious man, Rodrigo's cruelty and greed were only surpassed by the barbarity of his son, Cesare, and his treacherous daughter, Lucrezia, mistress of poison. They murdered, debased, plundered, raped and violated their way to power, becoming the most hated, but the most potent, family in Italy.

Unhappily, because of star Adolfo Celi's fractured English, the series became rather difficult to follow and collapsed into an unintentional parody of historical drama. Pitched in the same vein as *I, Claudius* and other BBC epics, *The Borgias* failed magnificently to reach the same heights. What should have been the most shocking moments were rendered laughable by over-the-top performances and poor scripting. Critics were not impressed, nor was the Vatican, which issued a note of censure.

BOSANQUET, REGINALD (1932–84)

Popular ITN newsreader of the 1960s and 1970s, whose lively private life became regular tabloid fare. Bosanquet, the son of Middlesex and England cricketer B.J.T. Bosanquet (the man who invented the 'googly', still known as the 'Bosie' Down Under), joined ITN at its inception in 1955, as a trainee. From there he developed into one of its leading reporters, eventually becoming diplomatic correspondent and presenting programmes like **Roving Report** and *Dateline*. In 1967 he was chosen as one of the newscasters to launch the revolutionary *News at Ten*, and his on-air partnerships with Andrew Gardner and Anna Ford proved particularly popular with viewers, who enjoyed the sense of unpredictability he brought to newsreading. However, his rather stilted delivery and lop-sided smirk were the result of a medical condition and nothing more sinister like drink, as some columnists had it. Bosanquet resigned from ITN in a blaze of publicity in 1979, during a lengthy technicians' strike and presented a few reports for **Nationwide** before his death in 1984.

BOSLEY, TOM (1927–)

American actor, familiar as the sympathetic father, Howard Cunningham, in the nostalgic sitcom **Happy Days**, which ran for 11 years in the USA from 1974. His 'pop' roles had begun a couple of years earlier, when he provided the voice for harrassed Harry Boyle in *Wait Till Your Father Gets Home*, although more recently Bosley has switched from dad to detective, playing Sheriff Amos Tupper **in Murder, She Wrote** and the title role in **Father Dowling Investigates**. His TV career began in 1964 in the US version of **That Was The Week That Was** and continued through the likes of *The Debbie Reynolds Show*, in which he played Debbie's brother-in-law, Bob Landers. He was also narrator for the showbiz restrospective *That's Hollywood* and has appeared as guest star in many other series.

BOSS CAT

US (Hanna-Barbera) Cartoon. BBC 1962–3

Voices:
Top Cat ('TC') ....Arnold Stang
Benny the Ball ....Maurice Gosfield
Choo Choo...Marvin Kaplan
Spook ....Leo De Lyon
The Brain ....Leo De Lyon
Fancy-Fancy ....John Stephenson
Officer Dibble...Allen Jenkins
Pierre ....John Stephenson
Goldie...Jean Vander Pyl
Honey Dew ....Sallie Jones

Creator: Joseph Barbera. Executive Producers: William Hanna, Joseph Barbera

A scheming tom is leader of a scrounging squad of alley cats.

Boss Cat, or *Top Cat* as it was known outside Britain (the UK already had a cat food of that name), was a feline version of *Sgt Bilko*. Fort Baxter gave way to a Manhattan alleyway, and uniforms were swapped for fur coats, but otherwise the guys were all there, from the sweet-talking con cat leader to the dimmest of the dim fall guy. The gang was headed by Top Cat, commonly known as TC, who lived in a luxurious dustbin, ate scraps from the local deli, drank milk from nearby doorsteps and used the local police phone to make his calls, much to the consternation of the neighbourhood copper, Officer Dibble. Like Bilko, TC always had an eye for a fast buck, or the equivalent in cat terms. His dense henchmen, the equivalent of Bilko's platoon, were Brain, Fancy-Fancy, Spook, Choo Choo and Benny the Ball, the last voiced by Maurice Gosfield, Pte Doberman in **The Phil Silvers Show**. Pierre, Goldie and Honey Dew were other moggies seen.

BOTTOM

UK (BBC) Situation Comedy. BBC 2 1991–

Richie Richard ....Rik Mayall
Eddie Hitler ....Adrian Edmondson

Creators/Writers: Rik Mayall, Adrian Edmondson. Producer: Ed Bye

Two no-hopers share a derelict flat.

Bottom – or *Your Bottom*, as its stars had considered calling it (hoping viewers would declare 'I saw *Your Bottom* on the telly last night') – focused on the directionless lives of a pair of obnoxious flatmates. Richie and Eddie were characters straight out of the Mayall and Edmondson stock repertoire and bore more than a resemblance to their roles in **The Young Ones**. Richie, cringingly self-centred, dreamed of having sex – with anyone; Eddie, graphically violent and purposefully direct, fouled up his flatmate's best-laid plans. Constantly bickering and endlessly battering each other, they lived in squalor above a Hammersmith shop but virtually destroyed their putrid flat in every episode, amidst an avalanche of juvenile jokes about smells, vomiting and other disgusting habits. They really were at the *Bottom* of life's pile.

BOUGH, FRANK (1933–)

Avuncular presenter who has been one of TV's most relaxed performers. As host of **Grandstand** from 1968, then *Nationwide*, *Holiday* and *Breakfast Time*, Bough became a household name, although things took a turn for the worse in the late 1980s when indiscretions in his private life hit the headlines. He has since returned to the screen on lower-key programmes for Sky and regional companies (including LWT and Meridian) and has presented a talk show for LBC and London Radio in London.

BOUNDER, THE

UK (Yorkshire) Situation Comedy. ITV 1982–3

Howard ....Peter Bowles
Trevor Mountjoy ....George Cole
Mary Mountjoy ....Rosalind Ayres
Laura ....Isla Blair

Creator/Writer: Eric Chappell. Producer: Vernon Lawrence

A conman becomes a cuckoo in his sister and brother-in-law's nest.

Fresh out of jail after serving time for embezzlement, the suave and untrustworthy Howard found a roof over his head courtesy of his sister, Mary, but much to the dismay of her dependable estate agent husband, Trevor. They hoped he would turn over a new leaf but then he met Laura, the young, attractive and *rich* widow living next door.

BOUQUET OF BARBED WIRE

UK (LWT) Drama. ITV 1976

Peter Manson..Frank Finlay
Prue Manson/Sorenson ....Susan Penhaligon
Gavin Sorenson......................................James Aubrey
Cassie Manson ....Sheila Allen
Sarah Francis ....Deborah Grant

Writer: Andrea Newman. Executive Producer: Rex Firkin. Producer: Tony Wharmby

A father's incestuous love for his daughter wrecks the family.

Publisher Peter Manson, his wife, Cassie, and daughter, Prue, lived in middle-class harmony in Surrey. Then in stepped American Gavin Sorenson and their lives began to crumble. Gavin married Prue and a wave of lust, infidelity and incest swept over the family. Peter's obsession with his pouting daughter finally tore the family apart. *Bouquet of Barbed Wire*, written by Andrea Newman from her own novel, graphically revealed the turmoil such steamy, forbidden passions can provoke and fully enjoyed the attentions of the tabloid press. Although Prue died after childbirth at the end of the serial, a sequel, *Another Bouquet*, followed a year later. It saw Cassie resuming a relationship with Gavin, and

Peter falling for Gavin's new girlfriend. Clearly, lessons had not been learned.

BOWEN, JIM (JAMES WHITTAKER; 1937–)

Northern comic and game show presenter, a former schoolteacher and night club comedian, unearthed by *The Comedians*. As host of the darts quiz *Bullseye* he has attracted much criticism (and acclaim) for his forthright, down-to-earth treatment of contestants and his fumbling presentation. 'Great', 'smashing' and 'super' have become his catchphrases. He has also acted in *Muck and Brass* and *El C.I.D.* (playing himself).

BOWLER, NORMAN (1932–)

A familiar face on British television, Norman Bowler has meandered from one successful series to another. Among his best known roles are David Martin in *Park Ranger*, Detective Inspector Harry Hawkins in *Softly, Softly*, Sam Benson in *Crossroads* and, most recently, Frank Tate in *Emmerdale*. His other appearances range from *Harpers West One* and *The Ratcatchers* to *Jesus of Nazareth* and *Deadline Midnight*.

BOWLES, PETER (1936–)

Prolific, suave English actor, star of numerous series, often in a slightly untrustworthy role. His major credits include Toby Meres in the pilot for *Callan* (the **Armchair Theatre** presentation *A Magnum for Schneider*), Guthrie Featherstone in *Rumpole of the Bailey*, Richard De Vere in *To The Manor Born*, Archie Glover in *Only When I Laugh*, Howard in *The Bounder*, Neville Lytton in *Lytton's Diary* (which he also created), Major Sinclair Yeates in *The Irish RM* and the conman Guy Buchanan in *Perfect Scoundrels*. Other appearances have included episodes of *Doctor Knock* (some of his first TV, back in 1961), *The Saint*, *The Avengers*, *The Baron*, *The Prisoner*, *Survivors*, *Good Girl*, *Churchill's People*, *Space: 1999*, *I, Claudius* (as Caractacus), *The Crezz*, and *Executive Stress*, as well as Ken Russell's 1966 film *Isadora* and the mini-series *Shadow on the Sun*.

BOYD QC

UK (Associated-Rediffusion) Legal Drama. ITV 1956–64

Richard Boyd QC ....Michael Denison
Jack ....Charles Leno

Writer: Jack Roffey. Producer: Caryl Doncaster

The ups and downs of a barrister's life.

Suave, elegant Richard Boyd QC was the gentle hero of this series of courtroom dramas. Ably supported by his clerk, Jack (who also acted as narrator), he prosecuted at times, but usually defended, generally turning up the right result. Filmed in semi-documentary style, the series was one of the first programmes to explore the world of the British judiciary, becoming a major hit, particularly towards the end of its long run. All scripts were penned by real-life assizes official Jack Roffey.

BOYD, WILLIAM (1895–72)

Silver-haired American actor forever remembered as *Hopalong Cassidy*, a role he literally made his own, buying the TV rights to the character. However, Cassidy had only hopped along when Boyd's career seemed just about over, in 1934, with his days as a leading man in dramatic films of the 1920s fading fast. Boyd, despite his dislike of horses, learned to ride and never looked back. The character made him a millionaire.

BOYLE, KATIE (KATERINA IMPERIALI DI FRANCABILLA; 1928–)

Dignified international presenter who graced several *Eurovision Song Contests* and some editions of *It's a Knockout*, putting her multilingual skills to full use. Born into an aristocratic Italian family, Boyle nevertheless has always seemed eminently English. A former Vogue fashion model, she was a familiar face on 1950s' and 1960s' panel games and variety shows (like *Quite Contrary* and *Juke Box Jury* and has written an agony aunt column for *TV Times*.

BOYS FROM THE BLACKSTUFF

UK (BBC) Drama. BBC 2 1982

Chrissie Todd	Michael Angelis
Yosser Hughes	Bernard Hill
Dixie Dean	Tom Georgeson
George Malone	Peter Kerrigan
Loggo Logmond	Alan Igbon
Kevin Dean	Gary Bleasdale
Angie Todd	Julie Walters
Miss Sutcliffe	Jean Boht
The Wino	James Ellis

Writer: Alan Bleasdale. Producer: Michael Wearing

A gang of tarmac layers face life on the dole.

In 1980 Alan Bleasdale's single drama *The Black Stuff* was shown. It focused on a tarmac gang working away from their home city of Liverpool. It proved so magnetic that the BBC asked Bleasdale to write a series of connected plays, one for each of the main characters. The first of the follow-ups was reworked into a drama called *The*

Muscle Market but the remaining five scripts were put together as a black comedy-drama called *Boys from the Blackstuff*.

In the series the lads were back home. Out of work and signing on in a desolate city riddled with unemployment, their future was bleak and reflected the prospects of millions like them around the country at the time. Undoubtedly the best remembered of the gang was Yosser Hughes, a man so desperate for work to keep his family afloat that he begged people to 'Gissa job', claiming 'I can do dat'.

In these poignant episodes Yosser and his contemporaries became standard-bearers for men who were willing to work but who were having to suffer the indignities of life on the 1980s' scrapheap.

BOYS FROM THE BUSH, THE

UK (Cinema Verity/Entertainment Media/BBC) Comedy Drama. BBC 1 1991–2

Reg Toomer	Tim Healy
Dennis Tontine	Chris Haywood
Leslie	Mark Haddigan
Arlene Toomer	Nadine Garner
Doris Toomer	Pat Thomson
Delilah	Kris McQuade
Corrie	Kirsty Child
Stuart Stranks	Rob Steele
Stevie Stranks	Russell Fletcher

Creator: Douglas Livingstone. Producers: Verity Lambert, David Shanks

Life with an ex-pat detective and his Australian partner.

Although Reg Toomer had lived in Australia for over 20 years, there was only one Bush for him and that was Shepherd's Bush. However, while pining for his long-lost football team, Queens Park Rangers, he still had a business to look after in Melbourne. Melbourne Confidential was part-marriage consultancy and part-detective agency, but, as long as it paid, any job was considered. Reg's unlikely partner was Aussie Dennis Tontine, a man obsessed with women, but who was on the run from both middle age and his former wife. Also involved was Reg's daydreaming missus, Doris, and their man-hungry, starry-eyed daughter, Arlene. Les was Reg's second cousin and Arlene's on-off lover, who became one of the company's private eyes. Dodgy tycoon Stuart Stranks and his amorous son, Stevie, were added to the cast in the second series.

BRADBURY, MALCOLM CBE (1932–)

Novelist and one-time Professor of American Studies at the University of East Anglia who often reflects his academic background in his writing and has become one of TV's most controversial playwrights. Some of his earliest work was for *That Was The Week That Was*, leading to plays like *The After Dinner Game* in 1975 and *Standing In for Henry* in 1980, although his greatest successes were in adapting Tom Sharpe's *Blott on the Landscape* and *Porterhouse Blue* for television in 1985 and 1987. His own novel, *The History Man*, had itself been adapted (by Christopher Hamilton) in 1981 and drew criticism for its raunchy sexual content. Bradbury's later work has included *Anything More Would Be Greedy* (1989), *The Gravy Train* (1990) and *The Gravy Train Goes East* (1991), and a version of Kingsley Amis's *The Green Man* (also 1991).

BRADEN, BERNARD (1916–93)

Canadian actor and presenter, one of TV's first consumers' champions. He moved to the UK in 1949 after working in Canadian radio and embarked on a theatre and radio career. On television, he began by presenting schools' programmes, was one of the BBC's team covering the Coronation and was then chairman of *The Brains Trust* (1957) and host of the sports magazine *Let's Go* (1959). Very often he was seen in tandem with his wife, Barbara Kelly, in sitcoms like *The Rolling Stones* (as Sandy Stone) and *B and B* (as himself). *Early to Braden*, *On the Braden Beat* and *Braden's Week* were other contributions, the last (beginning in 1968) introducing a young researcher by the name of Esther Rantzen. *Braden's Week*, with its consumer content, proved to be the inspiration for Esther's *That's Life*. Sacked by the BBC for promoting Stork margarine on ITV, Braden returned to Canadian television before resurfacing on programmes such as *After Noon Plus* and a revamped *All Our Yesterdays* in 1987. Among his three children was actress Kim Braden (star of the BBC's version of *Anne of Green Gables*).

BRADEN'S WEEK

UK (BBC) Entertainment. BBC 1 1968–72

Presenter: Bernard Braden

Editors: Desmond Wilcox, Bill Morton. Producers: John Lloyd, Adam Clapham, Tom Conway

Saturday evening slice of light entertainment and consumer affairs.

The clear ancestor of *That's Life*, *Braden's Week* not only humorously reviewed the week's events but was also an early consumers' champion, tackling thorny subjects with a light touch. Bernard Braden fronted affairs supported by a team of

reporter/researchers who included John Pitman, Esther Rantzen and Harold Williamson. Williamson specialized in interviewing children. Rantzen and producer John Lloyd headed off to *That's Life* once *Braden's Week* came to a controversial end in 1972. The BBC were unhappy that Braden had decided to advertise Stork margarine on ITV and dismissed him, claiming it was not viable for the host of a consumer programme to be seen endorsing goods commercially.

BRADY, TERENCE (1939–)

British writer and actor, the husband of writing partner Charlotte Bingham. Together they have penned a number of successful sitcoms, including *No, Honestly*, *Take Three Girls* and *Pig in the Middle* (in which Brady also starred), as well as episodes of dramas like *Upstairs, Downstairs*, *Nanny* and *Riders*.

BRAGG, MELVYN (1939–)

Presenter, novelist and playwright, widely acknowledged as TV's Mr Arts after his work as editor and host of *The South Bank Show* and the paperback review *Read All About It*. Earlier he worked as a producer and writer on the influential *Monitor* series, for which he worked closely with Ken Russell. He joined Russell again in 1978 to script *Clouds of Glory*, two films about the Lakeland poets. Bragg has also edited various other arts programmes, and has been Head of Arts at LWT as well as chairman of Border Television. One of his most recent offerings, the play *A Time to Dance*, dramatized from his own novel, drew criticism for its bold sex scenes.

BRAINS TRUST, THE

UK (BBC) Panel Game. BBC 1955–61

Chairmen: Hugh Ross Williamson, Michael Flanders. Creator: Howard Thomas. Producers: John Furness, Peter Brook

A panel of unprimed intellectuals answer questions from listeners.

This completely unscripted discussion programme began on BBC Radio in 1941, at the height of the Blitz, and became a valuable morale-lifter during the hostilities. Its popularity stemmed as much from the badinage amongst its three main participants (Professor C.E.M. Joad, Commander A.B. Campbell and Dr Julian Huxley) as from the knowledge it imparted. When this television version began 14 years later, a more sober tone prevailed, with the intimacy of the cramped radio studio replaced by a TV set filled with armchairs and coffee tables. The first host was Hugh Ross Williamson and the panel changed on a regular basis. Guests included such diverse personalities as Julian Huxley, Egon Ronay and the Archbishop of Cape Town, but one of the stalwarts was Dr Jacob Bronowski (later to compile *The Ascent of Man*). Viewers' contributions varied from the sublime to the ridiculous, taking in factual queries, philosophical posers and, at times, almost rhetorical questions, and the panellists (unaware of what was going to be asked) made every effort to provide a coherent and accurate response.

BRAMBELL, WILFRID (1912–85)

Diminutive actor forever cherished by viewers as grubby old Albert Steptoe in *Steptoe and Son*, a role he played, off and on, for 12 years from 1962. Born in Dublin, Brambell's first television appearances were a mixture of comedy parts (in shows that included *Life with the Lyons*) and serious drama. He appeared as a drunk in the science fiction milestone *The Quatermass Experiment* and also popped up in *1984*, as an old tortured prisoner. Typecast as old man Steptoe, Brambell's subsequent TV work was thin on the ground, although he did take up a few film roles, playing Paul's grandfather, for instance, in The Beatles' *A Hard Day's Night*, and was also seen in Jonathan Miller's *Alice In Wonderland*. He was another Albert, one of the patients, in Peter Tinniswood's 1970 sitcom *Never Say Die* and one of his last television appearances was as a guest in an episode of *Citizen Smith*.

BRAND, JOSHUA

Writer/producer whose highly successful work with partner John Falsey has included *St Elsewhere*, *Northern Exposure* and *I'll Fly Away*. Together they run Falahey-Austin Street Productions.

BRANDED

US (Goodson-Todman) Western. ITV 1965–6

Jason McCord ....Chuck Connors

The wanderings of an ex-soldier, dismissed from the army on a charge of cowardice.

It was the 1880s and Jason McCord, once a star pupil at West Point, had been dishonourably discharged from the rank of captain in the US Army, accused of cowardice. The only survivor of an Indian massacre at the Battle of Bitter Creek in Wyoming, he had lost consciousness and somehow had been spared. However, the top brass believed he had run away and kicked him out of the force.

In an effort to clear his name, McCord meandered across the Wild West, using his skills as an engineer and a mapmaker in a variety of jobs but predominantly aiming to prove to the world that he was no chicken. He also hoped to gather some clues about what really happened on that fateful day. But, by the end of the series' short run, despite unearthing occasional evidence in his favour, viewers were no nearer to knowing the truth about poor McCord.

BRANDRETH, GYLES, MP (1948–)

Professional game show panellist and TV trivialist, wearer of bold sweaters and deviser of various quizzes and puzzles. His work has included *Call My Bluff*, *Tell the Truth*, *Catchword*, *Babble*, *The Railway Carriage Game*, *Countdown* (consulting the dictionary), *Dear Ladies* (as writer) and various pieces for breakfast television. A prolific author and Scrabbler, he became Conservative MP for Chester in 1992.

BRASS

UK (Granada) Situation Comedy. ITV/Channel 4 1983–4/1990

Bradley Hardacre	...............................Timothy West
Patience Hardacre	.........................Caroline Blakiston
George Fairchild	...............................Geoffrey Hinsliff
	Geoffrey Hutchings
Agnes Fairchild	....................................Barbara Ewing
Austin Hardacre	...............................Robert Reynolds
	Patrick Pearson
Morris Hardacre	.....................................James Saxon
Charlotte Hardacre	.............................Emily Morgan
Isobel Hardacre	......................................Gail Harrison
Dr Macduff	....David Ashton
Lord Mountfast	...................................John Nettleton
Jack Fairchild	....Shaun Scott
Matthew Fairchild	......................................Gary Cady

Creators/Writers: John Stevenson, Julian Roach. Producers: Bill Podmore, Mark Robson (1990)

Social injustice, family rivalries and red hot passion in a 1930s northern industrial town.

Set in the fictitious town of Utterley, *Brass* exposed the open animosity between two rival families, one rich and powerful, the other poor and subservient, which resulted in much 'trouble at mill'. At the heart of the action was cruel, power-crazed Bradley Hardacre, a self-made man with interests in mining, munitions and especially cotton milling. His loopy, bitter wife, Patience, though confined to a wheelchair, was a chronic alcoholic and his children, too, all had their quirks. Austin was ambitious and wanted to take over the Empire, Morris was intelligent but immoral, Charlotte was the innocent do-gooder with feminist tendencies and Isobel was a temptress who later married into nobility.

Working for the Hardacres were the Fairchilds, headed by 'Red' Agnes, who, as well as stoking conflict in the workplace, was also Bradley's mistress. Her sons, Jack and Matthew, were openly hostile to their betters, but her husband, George (played by Geoff Hinsliff, later Don Brennan in **Coronation Street**), was just happy to be in their employ.

This tongue-in-cheek parody of TV's gritty, northern industrial dramas was briefly revived by Channel 4 in 1990, with many of the actors resuming their original roles. For the new series the action was set in 1939 at the outset of war.

BRAVO

Bravo Launched in 1980 as an American cable station specializing in foreign films and the performing arts, Bravo has since undergone a major conversion. Now available in Europe as part of Sky's Multi-Channels package, the channel focuses on cult (mostly American) TV programmes from bygone days (under the umbrella title of *Timewarp Television*) weepy old movies and weird science fiction films. The channel is on air 12 hours a day, from midday to midnight.

BREAD

UK (BBC) Situation Comedy. BBC 1 1986–91

Nellie Boswell	Jean Boht
Freddie Boswell	Ronald Forfar
Joey Boswell	Peter Howitt
	Graham Bickley
Jack Boswell	Victor McGuire
Aveline Boswell	Gilly Coman
	Melanie Hill
Adrian Boswell	Jonathan Morris
Billy Boswell	Nick Conway
Grandad	Kenneth Waller
Lilo Lil	Eileen Pollock
Shifty	Bryan Murray
Martina	Pamela Power
Julie	Caroline Milmoe
	Hilary Crowson
Oswald	Giles Watling
Derek	Peter Byrne
Celia Higgins	Rita Tushingham
Leonora Campbell	Deborah Grant

Creator/Writer: Carla Lane. Producers: Robin Nash, John B. Hobbs

The trials of a Liverpool family confidently living life on the dole.

The Boswells were the scourge of the DHSS. Although they attempted to make their own way in the world, like many families in the 1980s they were forced to rely on state handouts. But they did so with pride. They knew their entitlements and exploited all the loopholes. Head of their claustrophobic terraced household at 30 Kelsall

Street was Nellie Boswell, a devout Catholic housewife who demanded the presence of her loyal family at mealtimes, which is when most of the squabbling took place. Her husband, Freddie, was a waster who spent most of his time in an allotment shed with the local strumpet Lilo Lil, so Nellie relied more on her eldest son, the leather-clad Joey, to bring his siblings into line. Squeaky-voiced daughter Aveline was a tasteless dresser who longed to be a model but ended up marrying a vicar named Oswald. Dry, philosophical Jack was the soft-hearted son, Adrian was a poetic, easily hurt, gentle soul, who changed his name from Jimmy to something more appropriate, and the youngest son, Billy, was his antithesis, tactless, big-mouthed and impulsive. Replacing Jack (who had disappeared to America) in some episodes was their cousin Shifty, an appropriately named Irish jailbird. Completing the line-up were the Boswells' impatient and intolerant Grandad, who lived next door and constantly yelled for his dinner, their dog Mongy and the exasperated DHSS counter clerk Marina. Also in the action were assorted friends, lovers, wives and neighbours.

BREAKFAST NEWS see *Breakfast Time*.

BREAKFAST TIME

UK (BBC) News Magazine. BBC 1 1983–9

Presenters:
Frank Bough
Selina Scott
Nick Ross
Mike Smith
Debbie Greenwood
John Mountford
Sue Cook
Sally Magnusson
Jeremy Paxman

Editor: Ron Neil

Britain's first national breakfast television programme.

Airing at 6.30 am on 17 January 1983, *Breakfast Time* raced past its commercial rival, *Good Morning Britain*, to be the first breakfast television programme seen nationally across the UK. Its bright 'sun' logo and cosy studio set reflected the programme's intention to offer a relaxed and informal introduction to the day. Avuncular Frank Bough and Selina Scott were the main hosts, supported by specialist presenters like Francis Wilson (weather), Diana Moran – the 'Green Goddess' (fitness), Russell Grant (horoscopes), Glynn Christian (cookery) and Chris Wilson (gossip column). The news was read by Debbie Rix, and later Fern Britton and Sue Carpenter, while sport was handled by David Icke and then Bob Wilson. Nick Ross, Mike

Smith, Debbie Greenwood, John Mountford, Sue Cook, Sally Magnusson and Jeremy Paxman also took their places on the red leather sofa at various times.

In 1989 the magazine element of the programme was dropped in favour of in-depth news coverage. The programme title was changed to *Breakfast News* and newsreaders such as Nicholas Witchell and Jill Dando replaced the jovial, casual presenters.

BREMNER, RORY (1961–)

Scots-born impressionist, majoring in topical satire. As well as having his own series for the BBC (*Rory Bremner*) and Channel 4 (*Rory Bremner . . . Who Else?*), Bremner has also contributed to *Spitting Image*. From beginnings as a cabaret performer while studying at London University, he has become the UK's leading exponent of the impressionist's art. His speciality take-offs include Richie Benaud, Desmond Lynam, Derek Jameson and Denis Norden.

BRETT, JEREMY (JEREMY HUGGINS; 1938–)

English Shakespearean and character actor now associated with Conan Doyle's Sherlock Holmes, having given his moody portrayal of the celebrated detective for more than ten years. He played D'Artagnan in the BBC's 1966 version of *The Three Musketeers* and Maxim de Winter in its 1979 adaptation of *Rebecca*. He was William Pitt the Younger in *No. 10* and has taken parts in many series, such as *The Champions*, *Country Matters*, *Affairs of the Heart*, *Supernatural*, *Haunted* and *Mother Love*. Brett's first wife was actress Anna Massey.

BRIDESHEAD REVISITED

UK (Granada) Drama. ITV 1981

Charles Ryder	Jeremy Irons
Lord Sebastian Flyte	Anthony Andrews
Lord Marchmain	Laurence Olivier
Edward Ryder	John Gielgud
Lady Julia Flyte	Diana Quick
Lady Marchmain	Claire Bloom
Lady Cordelia Flyte	Phoebe Nicholls
Lord Brideshead	Simon Jones
Anthony Blanche	Nickolas Grace
Mr Samgrass	John Grillo
Rex Mottram	Charles Keating
Celia Mulcaster	Jane Asher
Cara	Stephane Audran

Writer: John Mortimer. Producer: Derek Granger

Aristocratic decadence in the inter-war years.

Brideshead Revisited told the story of Army Captain Charles Ryder, whose unit was stationed in the grounds of Brideshead Castle in Wiltshire in the closing days of World War II. But Ryder himself had been there before and during this of this 11-part drama he recounted events in his earlier life, reflecting on the passing of an era.

Charles's connections with Brideshead had begun with Sebastian Flyte, the teddy-bear ('Aloysius') carrying son of Lord Marchmain, proprietor of the estate. They had met at Oxford in the 1920s and Charles had fallen in with Sebastian's drunkenly decadent troupe of gay young blades. He became a house guest at Brideshead and Sebastian's lover, although he later also fell for Julia, Sebastian's sister. With the family Charles (a painter) travelled extensively, and life in this aristocratic household opened his eyes to many things. He was fascinated by their behaviour, their mannerisms, their conversations. The beautiful Marchmain estate, with its gardens, fountains and private chapel, held him in awe. Indeed, he was absorbed by their closed, extravagant world and a style of living that belonged to an age rapidly drawing to a close. But it was the overwhelming power that Catholicism held over the family which proved most intriguing.

Brideshead Revisited, closely adapted by John Mortimer from Evelyn Waugh's passionate novel, very nearly became one of television's great disaster stories. Soon after production had begun (using Castle Howard in Yorkshire as the fictitious Brideshead) filming was halted by an ITV technician's dispute. By the time the strike ended, many of the cast and crew had other commitments, contracts had run out and it seemed that the work would never be finished. But to scrap the project would have been almost as costly as continuing, so the decision was made by Granada to press on. Director Michael Lindsay-Hogg had to be replaced by young Charles Sturridge and Jeremy Irons was dragged away for three months to make *The French Lieutenant's Woman*. But, at more than twice the original cost, *Brideshead Revisited* did eventually reach the TV screen. For viewers and critics alike, it was well worth the wait. The beauty of the photography and easy pace of the rich narrative won many fans. Awards were showered on the production and sales around the world were enormous.

BRIERS, RICHARD OBE (1934–)

Extremely popular, chummy British sitcom star, often in whimsical, slightly eccentric roles. Richard Briers first found TV fame in the early 1960s, starring as Roger Thursby in *Brothers in Law* and alongside Prunella Scales as newly wed George Starling in Richard Waring's *The*

Marriage Lines. However, it was more than ten years later, after numerous other comedy roles in series like *Ben Travers Farces* and the sitcom *Birds on the Wing* (as Charles Jackson), that he became a household name. His portrayal of Tom Good, with Felicity Kendal as his spirited wife, in *The Good Life*, inspired some viewers to leave the rat race and give self-sufficiency a go. After an appearance in *The Norman Conquests* and lesser success in the sitcoms *The Other One* (as Ralph) and *Goodbye Mr Kent* (as Travis Kent), Briers bounced back in *Ever Decreasing Circles*, as the pedantic Martin Brice opposite an exasperated Penelope Wilton. In 1985 he took on the role of vicar Philip Lambe in Thames TV's *All In Good Faith*. After time on the stage with Kenneth Branagh's Renaissance Theatre, he returned to the small screen in 1993 in *If You See God, Tell Him*, playing Godfrey Spry, a man with an attention span of only 30 seconds. In 1995 he starred as ex-diplomat Tony Fairfax in another sitcom, *Down to Earth*. Briers is also a voice-over specialist – he narrated the anarchic cartoon series *Roobarb and Custard*, for instance – and has also won plaudits for his classical roles, which have included Malvolio in *Twelfth Night* and a stage version of *King Lear*. He is married to actress Ann Davies.

<h2>BRIGGS, JOHNNY (1935–)</h2>

Short, chirpy Cockney actor, earlier in his career often seen on the wrong side of the law. His television break came when he switched sides to become Detective Sgt. Russell in *No Hiding Place*, progressing into soap opera in 1973 with *Crossroads* (as Clifford Leyton) and ultimately assuming his present day alter-ego, that of devious businessman Mike Baldwin in *Coronation Street*, in 1976. In the 1960s and 1970s, Briggs also appeared in programmes as diverse as *The Plane Makers*, *The Saint*, *Z Cars*, *Mogul*, *The Avengers*, *Love Thy Neighbour*, *My Wife Next Door*, *No, Honestly* and *Yus My Dear*.

BRITISH ACADEMY OF FILM AND TELEVISION ARTS see BAFTA.

BRITISH BROADCASTING CORPORATION see BBC.

BRITISH SATELLITE BROADCASTING see BSkyB.

BRITISH SKY BROADCASTING see BSkyB.

<h2>BRITTAS EMPIRE, THE</h2>

UK (BBC) Situation Comedy. BBC 1 1991–4

Gordon Brittas ....Chris Barrie

Helen Brittas ....Pippa Heywood
Laura Lancing ....Julia St John
Carole ....Harriet Thorpe
Colin Wetherby....................................Michael Burns
Tim Whistler...Russell Porter
Gavin Featherly......................................Tim Marriott
Julie ....Judy Flynn
Linda..Jill Greenacre

Creators/Writers: Richard Fegen, Andrew Norriss. Producer: Mike Stephens

An over-zealous manager brings daily chaos to a modern sports centre.

Insufferable, pedantic, patronizing, incompetent and accident-prone were all inadequate ways of describing Gordon Brittas, manager of the Whitbury Newtown leisure centre. Whatever he attempted inevitably ended in failure and near loss of life. Brittas ran his little kingdom with a firm hand, planning events meticulously and laying down the law to his unfortunate staff. With disaster always lurking around the corner, it was left to his level-headed number two, Laura, to pick up the pieces and restore calm. Julie, his secretary, simply despaired and the only member of staff who looked up to Brittas was the loyal Colin, the dim, Geordie maintenance man. Other team members were tearful, often homeless receptionist Carol (who kept her children in a cupboard behind her desk), ambitious coaches Tim and Gavin, and blonde assistant Linda. Gordon's wife, Helen (later mother of twins Matthew and Mark), popped tranquillizers to keep herself sane. The series ended when the sanctimonious Brittas was appointed a European Commissioner.

<h2>BRITTON, TONY (1924–)</h2>

British character actor, familiar in snooty upper-class parts. His most successful TV roles have been as James Nicholls in *Robin's Nest*, Dr Toby Latimer in *Don't Wait Up* and Vivian Bancroft in *Don't Tell Father*, although other credits have included *Father, Dear, Father*, *And Mother Makes Five* and *Strangers and Brothers*, plus *Armchair Theatre* presentations and plays like *The Nearly Man* (1974) and *The Dame of Sark* (1976). He is the father of presenter Fern Britton.

<h2>BROADCASTING</h2>

The transmission of radio or TV signals to be received by the general public, as opposed to narrowcasting, cable or closed circuit systems that supply signals only to a limited audience.

<h2>BRONCO</h2>

US (Warner Brothers) Western. BBC 1959–

Bronco Layne ....Ty Hardin

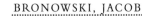

A former Confederate Army captain drifts across the Wild West.

Bronco was a series that evolved out of *Cheyenne* and a star-versus-studio squabble. The star was Clint Walker, of *Cheyenne*, and the studio was Warner Brothers. Failing to resolve the dispute, Warners recast *Cheyenne* with a new lead character, pitching Ty Hardin into the role of Bronco Layne. Eventually Walker returned to the fold, but Bronco continued in his own series. To add to the confusion, some *Bronco* episodes were then screened in the USA under the umbrella title of *Cheyenne*, as part of a rotating trilogy which also included *Sugarfoot*, starring Will Hutchins (shown in the UK as *Tenderfoot*).

The character of Bronco was very much a loner. With the end of the Civil War, he headed west, where he met up with the likes of Billy the Kid and Jesse James, but he was never given a regular supporting cast.

BRONOWSKI, JACOB (1902–74)

Polish-born scientist Jacob Bronowski became an unlikely TV hero in 1973 when his ambitious TV series *The Ascent of Man* was screened on BBC 2. His raw enthusiasm, curious hunched poses and evident erudition produced a winning combination for viewers, many of whom would never have watched such an academic series without him. Sadly, he had little time to enjoy his new fame, dying a year later at the age of 72, exhausted by his efforts on the series. Bronowski had been educated at Cambridge and settled with his family in Britain. As well as writing various scientific tomes he had also presented several programmes in the same vein on television and was a member of *The Brains Trust*. Since 1964 he had worked as a Senior Fellow at the Salk Institute for Biological Studies in San Diego, California.

BROOKE-TAYLOR, TIM (1940–)

British comic actor and writer, a product of the Cambridge Footlights Revue. Emerging from innovative 1960s comedy shows like *On the Braden Beat*, *The Frost Report* (writing with Eric Idle), *At Last the 1948 Show* (which he also produced), *Twice a Fortnight* (largely as writer), *Broaden Your Mind* and *Marty* (as straight man to Marty Feldman), Brooke-Taylor hit the big time as one of *The Goodies*, playing the feeble, patriotic one. From there he moved into sitcom with less success, appearing in *His and Hers* (as Toby Burgess), *The Rough with the Smooth* (as Richard Woodville and also as co-writer), *Me and My Girl* (as Derek Yates) and *You Must Be the Husband* (as Tom Hammond). He also has plenty of radio work to his name.

BROOKS, JAMES L. (1940–)

American writer/producer whose first success came with *The Mary Tyler Moore Show*, followed by one of its spin-offs, *Rhoda* (both with his partner, Allen Burns). Brooks moved on to *Taxi*, *The Associates* and *Lou Grant*, before branching out into movies (*Terms of Endearment*, *Broadcast News*, *Big*, *The Wars of the Roses*), then returning to TV with *The Tracey Ullman Show* and *The Simpsons* (as executive producer).

BROOKS, RAY (1939–)

English character actor whose TV break came in the harrowing 1966 play *Cathy Come Home*, opposite Carol White. After appearances in programmes such as *Gideon's Way*, *Coronation Street*, *Randall and Hopkirk (Deceased)* and *Taxi* (the UK version), Brooks narrated the *Watch with Mother* animation *Mr Benn* and then starred as Robbie Box in *Big Deal* in 1984. Subsequently, he has appeared in *Running Wild* and *The World of Eddie Weary* (in the title role), as well as *Growing Pains* (as Tom Hollingsworth).

BROOKSIDE

UK (Mersey) Drama. Channel 4 1982–

Roger Huntington	Rob Spendlove
Heather Huntington/ Haversham/Black	Amanda Burton
Sheila Grant/Corkhill	Sue Johnston
Bobby Grant	Ricky Tomlinson
Barry Grant	Paul Usher
Damon Grant	Simon O'Brien
Karen Grant	Shelagh O'Hara
Paul Collins	Jim Wiggins
Annabelle Collins	Doreen Sloane
Lucy Collins	Katrin Cartlidge
	Maggie Saunders
Gordon Collins	Nigel Crowley
	Mark Burgess
Gavin Taylor	Daniel Webb
Petra Taylor	Alexandra Pigg
Matty Nolan	Tony Scoggo
Ducksie Brown	Mark Birch
Gizzmo Hawkins	Robert Smith
Sizzler	Renny Krupinski
Alan Partridge	Dicken Ashworth
Samantha Partridge	Dinah May
Harry Cross	Bill Dean
Edna Cross	Betty Alberge
Pat Hancock	David Easter
Kate Moses	Sharon Rosita
Sandra Maghie	Sheila Grier
Tommy McArdle	Malcolm Tierney
Mona Harvey/Fallon	Margaret Clifton
Michelle Jones	Tracey Jay
Vicki Cleary	Cheryl Leigh
Terry Sullivan	Brian Regan
Kirsty Brown	Joanne Black

Ralph Hardwick	Ray Dunbobbin
Madge Richmond	Shirley Stelfox
Jonathan Gordon-Davies	Steven Pinner
Laura Wright/Gordon-Davies	Jane Cunliffe
Cheryl Boyanowsky	Jennifer Calvert
Billy Corkhill	John McArdle
Doreen Corkhill	Kate Fitzgerald
Rod Corkhill	Jason Hope
Tracy Corkhill	Justine Kerrigan
Jimmy Corkhill	Dean Sullivan
Jackie Corkhill	Sue Jenkins
George Jackson	Cliff Howells
Marie Jackson	Anna Keaveney
Gary Jackson	Allan Patterson
Michael Choi	David Yip
Caroline Choi	Sarah Lam
Jessica Choi	Anna Sung
Christopher Duncan	Stifyn Parri
Kathy Roach	Noreen Kershaw
Sean Roach	Derek Hicks
Nicholas Black	Alan Rothwell
Debbie McGrath	Gillian Kearney
Jamie Henderson	Sean McKee
Nikki White	Michelle Byatt
Thomas 'Sinbad' Sweeney	Michael Starke
Sue Harper/Sullivan	Annie Miles
Teresa Nolan	Ann Haydn Edwards
Jack Sullivan	William Maxwell
Marcia Barrett	Cheryl Maiker
Graeme Curtis	David Banks
Fran Pearson	Julie Peasgood
Mick Johnson	Louis Emerick
Josie Johnson	Suzanne Packer
Ellis Johnson	Francis Johnson
Gemma Johnson	Naomi Kamanga
Leo Johnson	Leeon Sawyer
Frank Rogers	Peter Christian
Chrissy Rogers	Eithne Browne
Sammy Rogers/Daniels	Rachael Lindsay
Geoff Rogers	Kevin Carson
	Stephen Walters
Katie Rogers	Debbie Reynolds
	Diane Burke
Leanne Powell	Vickie Gates
Owen Daniels	Danny McCall
Diana Spence/Corkhill	Paula Frances
Julia Brogan	Gladys Ambrose
John Harrison	Geoffrey Leesley
Barbara Harrison	Angela Morant
Peter Harrison	Robert Beck
Margaret Clemence	Nicola Stephenson
Derek O'Farrell	Clive Moore
D-D Dixon	Irene Marot
Ron Dixon	Vince Earl
Cyril Dixon	Allan Surtees
Jacqui Dixon	Alexandra Fletcher
Mike Dixon	Paul Byatt
Tony Dixon	Gerard Bostock
	Mark Lennock
Keith Rooney	Kirk Smith
Max Farnham	Steven Pinder
Patricia Farnham	Gabrielle Glaister
David 'Bing' Crosbie	John Burgess
Jean Crosbie	Marcia Ashton
Penny Crosbie	Mary Tamm
Ruth Sweeney	Mary Healey
Audrey Manners	Judith Barker

Anna Wolska	Kazia Pelka
Bev McLoughlin	Sarah White
Lyn Matthews/Rogers	Sharon Power
Mandy Jordache	Sandra Maitland
Trevor Jordache	Brian Murray
Beth Jordache	Anna Friel
Rachel Jordache	Tiffany Chapman
Marianne Dwyer	Jodie Hanson
Eddie Banks	Paul Broughton
Rosie Banks	Susan Twist
Carl Banks	Stephen Donald
Sarah Banks	Andrea Marshall
Lee Banks	Matthew Lewney
Joe Halsall	Susie Ann Watkins
Brian Kennedy	Jonathan Caplan
Simon Howe	Lee Hartney
Emma Piper	Paula Bell
Mo McGee	Tina Malone

Creator/Executive Producer: Phil Redmond.
Producers: Nicholas Prosser, Mal Young

Innovative Channel 4 soap opera.

Brookside was the series that changed the concept of soap opera in Britain. Taking to the air on Channel 4's opening night, it aimed to make realism the key to its success. Creator Phil Redmond (formerly of **Grange Hill**) went out and bought a new housing estate in Liverpool, using the various homes as permanent, 'live-in' sets and shunning the wobbly walls of studio mock-ups. Lightweight, hand-held cameras provided a newsy, ever-moving image of life in Brookside Close. Redmond also went for realism in his characters. They spoke dialectally in heavy, guttural, Merseyside accents, the kids in particular using real swear words not transparent euphemisms. Their lives were purposefully down to earth and unromantic, and storylines revolved around the bleakness of life on the dole and the salvation provided by the black economy. Other normally 'taboo' subjects such as homosexuality, suicide, AIDS, religious fanaticism, rape and drug abuse have all since been given an airing in *Brookside*.

The first residents of the Close included the working-class Grants, the snooty Collinses and young couples Roger and Heather Huntingdon and Gavin and Petra Taylor. Some characters like Barry Grant have remained with the series for years, but plenty of new faces have moved in and out of the cul-de-sac. Major contributors have included crotchety old Harry Cross, the Corkhills, the Rogers, the Dixons, the Johnsons, the Farnhams, the Crosbies, the Jordaches and window cleaner Sinbad.

Redmond's initial frankness went unrewarded. Audiences dwindled and a change of tact was required. Out went some of the grimmer characters, and in came one or two comic creations, to bring some levity. Bad language was toned down and a few more sensationalist elements were introduced. Storylines like the 'Free George Jackson' campaign (revolving around a jailed, innocent fireman) garnered media attention and a drawn-out siege, ending in a double death, also brought in the viewers. Things have largely settled down again at *Brookside*, although every now and again the hype is turned up for moments like the death of Terry Sullivan's wife and son, the lesbian kiss between Beth Jordache and Margaret Clemence, or the discovery of wife-batterer Trevor Jordache's body beneath a patio and the subsequent murder trial.

Brookside (the working title was *Meadowcroft* until Redmond stumbled across the real Brookside Close) was originally screened twice a week with a Saturday omnibus, but was expanded to three weekly episodes in 1990. It has also produced two spin-offs. The three-part *Damon and Debbie* (1987) focused on the dispirited son of the Grant family and his school girlfriend as they went on the run from the police in York, while Tracy Corkhill and her boyfriend, Jamie, were seen in a two-part schools programme *South* (part of Channel 4's *The English Programme* in 1988).

BROSNAN, PIERCE (1952–)

Irish actor, TV's *Remington Steele* but now cast as James Bond, a role earmarked for him for a number of years. Contractual obligations to *Steele* meant that he missed out on the Bond role when Timothy Dalton took over and it seemed his chance had gone. However, when Dalton stepped aside in 1993, Brosnan was once again first choice to play the suave secret agent. His other TV credits have included *Nancy Astor*, *The Manions of America* and *Noble House*.

BROTHERS, THE

UK (BBC) Drama. BBC 1 1972–6

Mary Hammond	Jean Anderson
Edward Hammond	Glyn Owen
	Patrick O'Connell
Brian Hammond	Richard Easton
David Hammond	Robin Chadwick
Jennifer Kingsley/Hammond	Jennifer Wilson
Ann Hammond	Hilary Tindall
Carol Hammond	Nicola Moloney
Jill Hammond	Gabrielle Drake
Paul Merroney	Colin Baker
Bill Riley	Derek Benfield
Gwen Riley	Margaret Ashcroft
April Merroney	Liza Goddard
Jane Maxwell	Kate O'Mara
Barbara Trent	Julia Goodman

Creators: Gerard Glaister, N.J. Crisp. Producers: Gerard Glaister, Ken Riddington, Bill Sellars.

Three brothers fight for control of the family haulage business.

When Robert Hammond died, his eldest son, Edward, braced himself to take over the family's long-distance lorry business, Hammond Transport Services. After all, he had helped to build up the company. However, with the reading of the will, he learned that his two younger brothers had inherited equal shares and his hard-nosed mother, Mary, was just as reluctant to give up her influence. To make matters worse, Robert's mistress, Jennifer Kingsley, had also been handed a slice of the cake.

For over four years *The Brothers* played out the boardroom and bedroom battles of this squabbling family and became a firm Sunday night favourite. Keeping the trucks conveniently in the background, it followed Edward's attempts to assert his authority over his brothers (David, a restless young graduate, and Brian, a boring accountant), and the whole family's concern over the involvement of the prim Jennifer. The truckers were represented by the working-class Bill Riley and his wife, Margaret.

Later additions to the cast were future **Doctor Who** Colin Baker as obnoxious financial whizz-kid Paul Merroney (an early J.R. Ewing), and Kate O'Mara as air-freight baroness Jane Maxwell.

BROTHERS IN LAW

UK (BBC) Situation Comedy. BBC 1962

Roger Thursby	Richard Briers
Henry Blagrove	Richard Waring
Kendall Grimes	John Glyn-Jones
Sally Mannering	June Barry
Judge	Walter Hudd

Writers: Denis Norden, Frank Muir

A trainee barrister fumbles his way through his early cases.

Roger Thursby was an enthusiastic pupil barrister undertaking his first year in chambers. Although he was chaperoned by the more experienced Henry Blagrove and the veteran Kendall Grimes, his courtroom experiences descended into farce as he struggled with the vagaries of legal life. Sally Mannering was his supportive girlfriend.

The series was based on a novel of the same name by Henry Cecil which had been filmed by the Boulting Brothers in 1956. Cecil also contributed to Denis Norden and Frank Muir's TV scripts. *Brothers in Law* gave Richard Briers his first leading role and led to **Marriage Lines** and greater things. A judge who appeared in the final episode was given his own spin-off series in 1963. Named *Mr Justice Duncannon*, it pitched **Dr Finlay's Casebook** star Andrew Cruickshank into the title role.

BROWN, JUNE

British Shakespearean and character actress much seen in films and television before achieving star status as the resident gossip and hypochondriac Dot Cotton in *EastEnders*, a role she played for eight years. Viewers may recall her in episodes of *The Duchess of Duke Street*, *The Sweeney*, *Churchill's People*, *South Riding*, *The Prince and the Pauper*, *Shadows*, *The Bill*, *Lace* and *Minder*. Her second husband, Robert Arnold, played PC Swain in *Dixon of Dock Green*.

BROWNE, JILL (1937–91)

One of TV's earliest sweethearts, playing trainee nurse (later Sister) Carole Young in *Emergency – Ward 10*, Jill Browne found herself inundated with fan mail from male viewers. In 1964, having just been dropped from the hospital soap, she married former co-star John Alderton, although the marriage ended in 1970. Her other major TV role – in the pub variety show *The New Stars and Garters* – was not a success and she eventually left the business, marrying theatre producer Brian Wolfe in 1971.

BRUNSON, MICHAEL (1940–)

ITN's Political Editor, Michael Brunson began his broadcasting career with BBC External Services in 1964 as a writer/producer. He moved to BBC Radio South-East the same year, before becoming an assistant producer on *24 Hours* in 1966. He joined ITN in 1968, was its US correspondent 1972–7 and then European correspondent 1979–80. Brunson was also seen as a newscaster between 1977 and 1981. In 1980 he took over as Diplomatic Editor, a post he held until becoming Political Editor in 1986.

BRUSH STROKES

UK (BBC) Situation Comedy. BBC 1 1986–91

Jacko	Karl Howman
Eric	Mike Walling
Jean	Nicky Croydon
Sandra	Jackie Lye
Elmo Putney	Howard Lew Lewis
Lionel Bainbridge	Gary Waldhorn
Veronica Bainbridge	Elizabeth Counsell
Lesley Bainbridge	Kim Thomson
	Erika Hoffman

Creators/Writers: John Esmonde, Bob Larbey. Producers: Sydney Lotterby, Mandie Fletcher, Harold Snoad, John B. Hobbs

A chirpy London decorator has an eye for the ladies, but also a heart of gold.

This gentle comedy focused on the life of Jacko, an appropriately named Cockney Jack the lad who lived in Motspur Park and worked for Bainbridge's, a small family painting and decorating company. His work colleague (and landlord) was his down-to-earth brother-in-law, Eric (complete with NHS specs), and his boss was the intolerant Lionel. Lionel's wife, Veronica, took over when Lionel died and one of the girls Jacko dated was Lionel's snooty daughter, Lesley. However, Jacko's soft spot was really reserved for Sandra, Bainbridge's Geordie secretary. Also seen was Jean, Eric's wife and Jacko's sensible sister, and bulky Elmo Putney, gormless landlord of the local boozer, The White Hart. Elmo briefly emigrated to Australia, found opals with the aid of his pet dingo and returned in style to London to open a ghastly pink wine bar (imaginatively dubbed Elmo Putney's Wine Bar), where Lesley took a job waitressing.

The programme's credits showed Jacko working his way along a wall with a paint roller and featured a theme song by Dexy's Midnight Runners. Entitled 'Because of You', it entered the Top Twenty in 1986.

BSKYB (BRITISH SKY BROADCASTING)

The major DBS (Direct Broadcasting by Satellites) station in the UK, formed by a merger of Sky Television and British Satellite Broadcasting (BSB) in 1990. The two companies had previously been rivals.

BSB was the company selected by the IBA to provide satellite television to the UK. In accordance with IBA advice, it opted for a technically advanced system using novel 'squarial' dishes, which were designed to receive signals from the specially constructed Marco Polo satellite. However, development problems ensued and BSB was beaten into the marketplace by Sky, an 'unofficial' company, which used larger, round dishes and transmitted from the Astra satellite. Being independently owned, and operating out of Luxembourg, Astra was beyond the control of UK broadcasting regulators. Sky developed from a primitive satellite channel known as Satellite TV, which broadcast to cable stations (for onward transmission) around Europe from 1982, using existing telecom satellites. Satellite TV was bought by Rupert Murdoch's News International and, with a change of name to Sky, began satellite/cable experiments in the UK, using Swindon as its testing ground. By the time the Astra satellite went into orbit in December 1988, Sky was well established and able to launch four satellite channels direct to homes in February the following year.

The Marco Polo and Astra systems, however, were incompatible and this meant that viewers had to gamble on which to purchase (in much the same way as the incompatible VHS and Betamax home video systems clashed head to head, with the result that Betamax soon became obsolete). Although Sky continued to lose money, the fact that it was already up and running by the time BSB finally went on air in 1990 proved terminal for BSB and the latter company was forced into a merger (resembling more of a take-over) with its rival later that year. Only the Astra system is now in use. BSkyB is now the official company name, but only the name Sky is used for the various channels operated by the company.

Sky now offers nine channels: Sky One (a general entertainments channel), Sky News, Sky Sports and Sky Sports 2, Sky Travel, Sky Soap and three film channels, Sky Movies, The Movie Channel and Sky Movies Gold. The company has also marketed a range of other channels in its Sky Multi-Channels package since September 1993. For one fee, viewers can subscribe to the Sky channels: Bravo, The Children's Channel, UK Gold, UK Living, The Discovery Channel, CMT, QVC (the shopping channel), The Family Channel, VH-1, Nickelodeon, TLC and Cartoon Network.

BSB see BSkyB.

BUCCANEERS, THE

UK (ITC/Sapphire) Adventure. ITV 1956–7

Dan Tempest	Robert Shaw
Lt Beamish	Peter Hammond
Governor Woodes Rogers	Alec Clunes
Blackbeard	George Margo
	Terence Cooper
Benjy	Hugh David
Armando	Edwin Richfield
Taffy	Paul Hansard
Dickon	Wilfrid Downing
Gaff	Brian Rawlinson
Van Brugh	Alec Mango
Estaban	Roger Delgado

Executive Producer: Hannah Weinstein. Producer: Sidney Cole

A pirate swears loyalty to the King, receives a pardon and defends the colonies from the Spanish.

In the 1720s pirate Dan Tempest had been the leader of a band of freebooters in the British Caribbean province of New Providence. However, he was persuaded by Lt Beamish, the new deputy governor, to switch sides and fight on behalf of the Crown against the advancing Spanish, and to help counter the disruptive influence of other pirates, such as the famous Blackbeard. Benjy, Armando, Taffy, Gaff and Van Brugh were all loyal members of Tempest's

swashbuckling crew on the brig *Sultana*, with Dickon, a stowaway-turned-cabin boy, and Captain Morgan, Tempest's pet monkey, also seen. Estaban (played by Roger Delgado, the future Master in **Doctor Who**) was one of the Spanish principals.

The Buccaneers was reputedly TV's first pirate series and was also unusual in that its lead character did not appear until the third episode, the first two being devoted to setting the scene. The sea sequences were filmed off Falmouth and the ship featured was a showbusiness veteran, having already played the part of the *Hispaniola* in Disney's *Treasure Island* and the *Peaquod* in John Huston's *Moby Dick*.

BUCK ROGERS IN THE 25TH CENTURY

US (Universal/Glen A. Larson) Science Fiction. ITV 1980–2

Captain William 'Buck' Rogers	Gil Gerard
Colonel Wilma Deering	Erin Gray
Dr Elias Huer	Tim O'Connor
Twiki	Felix Silla
Twiki (voice)	Mel Blanc
	Bob Elyea
Dr Theopolis (voice only)	Eric Server
Princess Ardala	Pamela Hensley
Kane	Henry Silva
	Michael Ansara
Hawk	Thom Christopher
Dr Goodfellow	Wilfred Hyde-White
Admiral Asimov	Jay Garner
Crichton (voice only)	Jeff David
Lt Devlin	Paul Carr
Narrator	William Conrad

Executive Producers: Glen A. Larson, John Mantley. Producers: Richard Caffey, John Gaynor, David J. O'Connell, Leslie Stevens, Bruce Lansbury, John G. Stevens, Calvin Clements

An astronaut is rocketed 500 years into the future.

The comic-strip character Buck Rogers was given a second bite of the TV cherry in this series, following an earlier dramatization seen in the USA in 1950. On this occasion, the space hero found himself in the 25th century, in the year 2491 to be precise. His space capsule (Ranger 3), launched in 1987, had gone missing for 504 years, but, being in suspended animation, Rogers survived the experience, awaking aboard a Draconian spaceship on its way to a peace conference on Earth. The planet, devastated by nuclear war, had forged a new civilization based in a futuristic city (New Chicago) in the Mid West. Outside the city was Anarchia, a wilderness housing the dregs of a mutilated society. The Draconians aimed to take control. Rogers, although initially viewed with suspicion by the Earth Defense Directorate, became the planet's ally in fighting off the aliens, who were led by the glamorous Princess Ardala and her sidekick, Kane. Rogers found romance with attractive defence commander Wilma Deering, and teamed up with top scientist Dr Huer, who supplied a new robot chum, Twiki, and also the computer Dr Theopolis, seen mostly as a disc around Twiki's neck.

In its second season the series changed considerably. Buck and Twiki were no longer on Earth but on the spaceship *The Searcher*, seeking out Earthlings who had fled the holocaust. They were now supported by Admiral Asimov (supposedly a descendent of the science-fiction writer Isaac Asimov), Lt Devlin and old, inquisitive scientist Dr Goodfellow. Also aboard were Hawk (a half-man, half-bird from the planet Throm) and a pompous robot named Crichton.

While the series was not without its critics, its tongue-in-cheek presentation and elaborate special effects proved to be its saving graces. The pilot, explaining Rogers's arrival in the future, was initially released in cinemas.

BUCKNELL, BARRY

TV 'home improvement' expert whose programmes in the 1950s and early 1960s included *Do It Yourself* and *Bucknell's House*, in which he refitted a derelict Victorian house in Ealing. A former motor engineer, he first appeared as part of the magazine *About the Home*.

BUDGIE

UK (LWT) Comedy Drama. ITV 1971–2

Budgie Bird ....Adam Faith
Charlie Endell ....Iain Cuthbertson
Hazel ....Lynn Dalby
Jean..Georgina Hale
Mrs Endell..June Lewis
Jack Bird ....George Tovey
Laughing Spam Fritter ....John Rhys-Davies
Grogan ....Rio Fanning

Writers: Keith Waterhouse, Willis Hall.
Executive Producer: Rex Firkin. Producer: Verity Lambert

A chirpy London spiv keeps hoping things will turn up.

Budgie Bird was a born loser. Always down on his luck, he nevertheless believed that life was about to change. For him Easy Street was just around the corner, but everyone knew that the yellow brick road was leading only to one place – jail. Shunning regular employment, he clung to the fringes of the Soho underworld, filled with

ambitious plans and ideas for his personal betterment, all doomed to instant failure. The best he could manage was a job as a runner for Glaswegian gangster Charlie Endell, proprietor of a dodgy book shop. Endell was a local 'Mr Big' who was always happy to let Budgie take the rap for his illegal activities. But, despite being used and pushed around, the long-haired delinquent remained an eternal optimist, meandering through life, dreaming up worthless ways of making his fortune, ducking and diving and incurring the wrath of the local heavies. Jean was his estranged wife and Hazel his long-suffering girlfriend. Laughing Spam Fritter and Grogan were two other members of the Soho low-life.

The series brought a new direction to the career of 1960s pop star Adam Faith, who returned to TV 20 years later in *Love Hurts* after remarkable interim success as a city wheeler-dealer. A short-lived *Budgie* spin-off, *Charles Endell Esquire*, set in Glasgow and featuring Iain Cuthbertson but not Adam Faith, was seen in 1979.

BULLSEYE

UK (ATV/Central) Game Show. ITV 1981–

Presenter: Jim Bowen

Creator: Norman Vaughan. Producers: Peter Holmans, Bob Cousins

Quiz based around the game of darts.

A good throwing action and a fair level of general knowledge were what was required in this long-running game show in which comic Jim Bowen welcomed three pairs of contestants to throw darts and answer questions to win cash and prizes. The first segment of the game involved a standard dartboard. One team member aimed three darts and the other collected cash to the value of the score achieved by answering a question correctly. After three rounds of darts the team with the lowest aggregate score was eliminated. The consolation prize was a 'bendy Bully' (a rubber dummy of the show's bull mascot). The two remaining pairs then moved on to the category dartboard, where the thrower aimed for a specialist subject and the partner, again, answered to win cash. Once more the lower scorers were eliminated. The final game saw both partners in the remaining team throwing darts at a prize dartboard (six for the main thrower, three for the non-darter), hoping to hit numbers which corresponded to washing machines, colour TVs, etc. When all the prizes won by the top duo had been totalled up, they were offered the chance to gamble them for a star prize, hidden behind screens. With three darts each, if they scored a total of 101 or more the star prize was theirs. Any less and the prizes were forfeited. Cruelly, Bowen always invited losing contestants to 'Look what you would have won', whipping back the screen to reveal a speedboat, a new car or a foreign holiday for four people. An additional element of the programme involved a guest professional player throwing nine darts for charity. Darts commentator Tony Green kept score throughout.

It is fair to say that *Bullseye* (devised by comic Norman Vaughan) was one of the most unlikely TV successes produced by Central Television. Host Jim Bowen became notorious for his insensitive handling of contestants ('What do you do for a living?' 'I'm unemployed, Jim.' 'Super.') and his various gaffes. Some recorded programmes were allegedly binned, being judged too poor to transmit, but the series quickly built up a cult following, particularly amongst the young.

BULMAN

UK (Granada) Detective Drama. ITV 1985–7

George Bulman	Don Henderson
Lucy McGinty	Siobhan Redmond
William Dugdale	Thorley Walters

Creator: Kenneth Royce. Writer: Murray Smith
Executive Producer: Richard Everitt. Producers: Steve Hawes, Sita Williams

An ex-policeman retires to the world of antiques but is coaxed back into private detection.

Sgt George Bulman first appeared in *The XYY Man*, pursuing the aggressive chromosome freak Spider Scott. The character then re-emerged in the series *Strangers*, but his personality and character traits had changed dramatically. Although still uncompromising, he had become rather eccentric and less conventional, wearing fingerless grey gloves on duty and sporting gold-rimmed reading spectacles. In this follow-up series of his own the character became quirkier still.

Bulman had retired from the force to open an antique shop and repair clocks in the Shanghai Road, south-west London. But his knowledge of the criminal world and his powers of detection were too great to lay to waste and he found himself dragged back into action. Egging him on was Lucy McGinty, the daughter of a former colleague. A Medieval Studies student, she had thrown it all in to work with George and learn his criminology skills. An academic secret serviceman named William Dugdale, a throwback to *Strangers* days, was also seen.

The softly spoken Bulman's trademarks included his 2CV car, a knowledge of the classics and the use of a nasal inhaler. He always carried a plastic bag, too. Several of these gimmicks were intro-duced by accident. For instance, actor Don Henderson first used an inhaler because he really did have a cold and the gloves were employed to cover up a stubborn wedding ring which couldn't be removed (Bulman was not married). The scarf covered Henderson's throat cancer surgery scars and the fact he sometimes talked in a whisper was also connected to this ailment. After two seasons, the series' chief writer, Murray Smith, went on to create **The Paradise Club** for the BBC, taking Henderson with him. A few TV movies and guest spots in **The Love Boat** and **Fantasy Island**.

BURKE, ALFRED (1918–)

British actor and writer, remembered for his long-running portrayal of the down-at-heel private detective Frank Marker in **Public Eye**. Among his later roles were Reverend Patrick Brontë in *The Brontës of Haworth*, the Nazi Major Richter in **Enemy at the Door**, Long John Silver in *Treasure Island*, Giuliano della Rovere in **The Borgias** and a guest spot in **Bergerac** (as Jim's old headmaster).

BURKE, JAMES (1936–)

Talkative, excitable, bespectacled presenter particularly adept at explaining complex scientific issues in layman's terms on programmes like **Tomorrow's World** and his own series, **Connections**. He was also part of the BBC's team covering the Apollo moon missions and was scientific adviser on the drama series *Moonbase 3*.

BURKE'S LAW/AMOS BURKE – SECRET AGENT

US (Four Star) Detective Drama. ITV 1963–

Captain Amos Burke	Gene Barry
Detective Tim Tilson	Gary Conway
Detective Sgt Lester Hart	Regis Toomey
Henry	Leon Lontoc
Sgt Ames	Eileen O'Neill
'The Man'	Carl Benton Reid (*Amos Burke*
	– Secret Agent)

Creators: Ivan Goff, Ben Roberts. Producer: Aaron Spelling

The cases of the head of the Los Angeles homicide squad, a multi-millionaire.

This glossy series focused on Captain Amos Burke, the obscenely wealthy boss of the LAPD's murder squad, who was dragged away from society functions and expensive wining and dining to head up all manner of homicide investigations. Burke cruised to the scene of crime in the back of a Rolls-Royce, driven by his chauffeur, Henry. There he was assisted by young detective Tim

Tilson and wise veteran sergeant Lester Hart. Policewoman Ames was added to Burke's staff later. As unlikely as it seems, the debonair bachelor was evidently the right man for this particular job, as most of the victims appeared to come from the elite end of society. Each programme was subtitled *Who killed . . . ?*, with the name of that week's unfortunate victim filling the gap.

Burke eventually quit the police force to become an undercover agent, and set out on the trail of criminals all over the world. His contact was known only as 'The Man' and was the sole supporting actor in the new-look series. With this change of tack (a response to the success of *The Man from UNCLE*), the programme was renamed *Amos Burke – Secret Agent*.

Burke's Law, littered with famous guest stars (sometimes more than half a dozen in one episode) was originally planned as a vehicle for Dick Powell, who had played the character in an American anthology series a year or two earlier. It was revived in 1994, with Gene Barry again in the title role. Taking things somewhat easier, in accordance with his age, he now relied on the help of his son, Peter (played by Peter Barton). The role of Henry was taken over by Danny Kamekona.

BURNET, SIR ALASTAIR (1928–)

British news and current affairs presenter who joined ITN as political editor in 1963. Despite taking over as editor of *The Economist*, Burnet preserved his ITN career and became one of the first two newscasters on *News at Ten* in 1967 (with Andrew Gardner). Although he left for the BBC and *Panorama* in 1972, and went on to edit the *Daily Express*, he later returned to ITN to launch *News at 5.45*. Subsequently he anchored *News at Ten* for many years. His other television work included *This Week*, as well as numerous election programmes, Budgets, royal interviews and commentaries on State occasions. He was knighted in 1984 and retired in 1990.

BURNETT, HUGH (1924–)

British producer and reporter in the 1950s and 1960s whose work centred largely on current affairs and religion, taking in programmes like *Panorama*, *Face to Face* and *The Late Show* along the way.

BURNS AND ALLEN SHOW, THE

US (CBS) Situation Comedy. BBC 1955–61

George Burns	Himself
Gracie Allen	Herself
Blanche Morton	Bea Benaderet
Harry Morton	Fred Clark
	Larry Keating
Harry Von Zell	Himself
Ronnie Burns	Himself

Producer: Ralph Levy

Television vehicle for a vaudeville act that had been running for 30 years.

Real-life husband and wife George Burns and Gracie Allen had long been stage and radio partners. As television began to take off, they moved into this unexplored medium and, in doing so, laid down benchmarks for other comedians to follow. Their series was essentially a sitcom, although extended dialogues between the two stars offered more than an echo of their variety days. In the style of *I Love Lucy* and other contemporary US comedies, this one was domestic-based, with the pair playing a husband and wife living in Beverly Hills. Like Lucy, Gracie's confidante was her next-door neighbour, in this case Blanche Morton. Her husband, Harry, had a short fuse which contrasted sharply with the relaxed approach of the philosophical Burns. However, Burns did have an advantage. It was his show and he was able to step out of the action and talk to the audience, pondering what to do next or how the plot should develop. He even had a TV set to watch scenes involving the others and could drag the show's announcer, Harry Von Zell, into the action. It's easy to see where Gary Shandling's inspiration came from. (see *It's Gary Shandling's Show*.)

Gracie's character was a real scatterbrain, but what drove many guest stars to despair was her alternative logic and strange, convoluted reasoning with which they couldn't argue. Thankfully, tolerant George understood her. Why else would he fall for the same ending each week: 'Say Goodnight Gracie'; 'Goodnight Gracie'? (an ending copied by Rowan and Martin in *Laugh-In*). The Burns' son, Ronnie, also appeared, but the show ended in America in 1958, when Gracie announced her retirement from the business. Co-star Bea Benaderet went on to provide the voice for Betty Rubble in *The Flintstones* and the irrepressible George soldiered on alone.

BURNS, GEORGE (1896–)

New York-born, cigar-puffing vaudeville comic (born Nathan Birnbaum) whose partnership with his scatterbrained wife Gracie Allen proved successful on stage, radio and ultimately television. *The George Burns and Gracie Allen Show* revolutionized TV comedy in the 1950s (with debunking of television conventions), and was a hit on both sides of the Atlantic. With Gracie's retirement and subsequent death, George's career seemed to fade out, but he bounced back in the mid-1970s with a run of cinema successes (such as *The Sunshine Boys* and *Oh God!*) and even began a new US TV series, *The George Burns Comedy Week*, in 1985. He still performs, despite heading for his 100th birthday.

BURNS, GORDON (1942–)

Presenter, narrator and quiz show host, and since 1977 questionmaster on *The Krypton Factor*. Born in Belfast, Burns began his career with Ulster Television (as sports editor and news presenter). From there he moved to Granada, working on *World In Action* and *Granada Reports*. He has also presented *Surprise, Surprise* with Cilla Black and various regional programmes.

BURR, RAYMOND (1917–93)

Canadian actor, star of two of the 1950s and 1960s best-loved series, *Perry Mason* and *A Man Called Ironside*. As Mason, Burr played a defence lawyer who never lost a case; as Ironside, he was a crippled detective confined to a wheelchair. Between them, Perry Mason and Ironside notched up 18 years of continuous success for their star, leaving him little time to play other roles. Burr did take up the offer of a few TV movies and mini-series (including *79 Park Avenue*), but it wasn't until he revived the old legal-eagle Mason in 1986 that he was prominent on our screens again. Earlier in his career Burr had appeared in around 90 movies, Hitchcock's *Rear Window* among them.

BURTON, HUMPHREY (1931–)

British arts presenter and producer, associated with such programmes as *Monitor*, *Omnibus* and *Aquarius*.

BUSMAN'S HOLIDAY

UK (Granada/Action Time) Quiz.
ITV 1985–93

Presenters:
Julian Pettifer
Sarah Kennedy
Elton Welsby

Executive Producers: Stephen Leahy, Dianne Nelmes. Producers: Stephen Leahy, Patricia Pearson, Richard Bradley, Jenny Dodd, Kieran Roberts

Teams compete for a chance to see how their own jobs are done in other corners of the world.

In this occupational quiz, three teams of workers from various professions were cross-examined about each other's jobs and answered questions about their own specialities. A general knowledge

element was also thrown in. The three teams were whittled down to one which then collected a European or worldwide 'Busman's Holiday'. This saw the three members whisked away to an exotic location to see how their jobs were carried out in that part of the world. A film was made of their experience and shown as an insert in the following week's programme. Contestants included the likes of seaside landladies, hovercraft pilots, antiques dealers, osteopaths and wardens of stately homes. Julian Pettifer was the original host, succeeded by Sarah Kennedy and then Elton Welsby.

BUTLER, DAWS (1916–88)

American cartoon voicer, the voice of Yogi Bear, Huckleberry Hound and scores of Hanna-Barbera characters, including Elroy Jetson, Lambsy in *It's the Wolf* and Peter Perfect and others in *Wacky Races*.

BUTTERFLIES

UK (BBC) Situation Comedy. BBC 2 1978–82

Ria Parkinson	Wendy Craig
Ben Parkinson	Geoffrey Palmer
Russell Parkinson	Andrew Hall
Adam Parkinson	Nicholas Lyndhurst
Leonard Dunn	Bruce Montague
Ruby	Joyce Windsor
Thomas	Michael Ripper

Creator/Writer: Carla Lane. Producers: Gareth Gwenlan, Sydney Lotterby

The frustrations of an overlooked suburban housewife.

It seemed as if Ria Parkinson's role in life was already over, after 19 years of marriage. Her two slightly wayward sons, Russell and Adam, had grown up and now had lives of their own. Her dentist husband, Ben, a manic depressive, was too wrapped up in his work and his hobby (butterfly collecting) and so Ria found herself entering a mini-midlife crisis. What was worse, even her housekeeping skills were subject to criticism, particularly her cooking, with anything more complicated than corn flakes becoming a game of chance. To ease the pain, she contemplated an extra-marital affair with the recently divorced Leonard Dunn, a smooth, wealthy businessman she met in a restaurant, although it barely amounted to more than words. Ruby was the Parkinsons' rough and ready daily, often bemused at the strange goings-on in the household, with Thomas Leonard's chauffeur.

The series proved to be a useful stepping stone for actor Nicholas Lyndhurst, taking him out of the realm of child stars and into adult performances.

Before *Butterflies* had ended **Only Fools and Horses** had begun. A reworking of Dolly Parton's 'Love Is Like a Butterfly' was used for the theme tune.

BUTTERWORTH, PETER (1919–79)

Carry On actor whose television work stretched from the 1950s through to his death in 1979. Credits included the sitcoms *Meet the Champ* (as a boxing trainer), *Bulldog Breed* (as Henry Broadbent), *Kindly Leave the Kerb* (as busker Ernest Tanner), *A Class By Himself* (as the valet Clutton) and *Odd Man Out* (as Wilf), plus straight drama roles in **Doctor Who** (as the Time Meddler), **Emergency – Ward 10, Danger Man, The Odd Man** and **Public Eye**. He was married to impressionist Janet Brown and was father of actor Tyler Butterworth. With Janet he hosted the *Where Shall We Go?* admag in 1956.

BY THE SWORD DIVIDED

UK (BBC) Drama. BBC 1 1983–5

Anne Lacey/Fletcher	Sharon Mughan
Sir Thomas Lacey	Timothy Bentinck
John Fletcher	Rob Edwards
Lucinda Lacey/Ferrar	Lucy Aston
Sir Martin Lacey	Julian Glover
Major General Horton	Gareth Thomas
Susan Protheroe	Judy Buxton
Captain Hannibal Marsh	Malcolm Stoddard
King Charles I	Jeremy Clyde
Sir Henry Parkin	Charles Kay
Nathaniel Cropper	Andrew Maclauchlan
Goodwife Margaret	Rosalie Crutchley
Will Saltmarsh	Simon Dutton
Walter Jackman	Edward Peel
Captain Charles Pike	Mark Burns
Rachel	Debbie Goodman
Emma Bowen/Skinner	Janet Lees Price
Hannah Jackman	Joanna Myers
Dick Skinner	Peter Guinness
Hugh Brandon	Simon Butteriss
Mrs Dumfry	Claire Davenport
Sir Ralph Winter	Robert Stephens
Sir Austin Fletcher	Bert Parnaby
Oliver Cromwell	Peter Jeffrey
Frances Neville/Lacey	Joanna McCallum
King Charles II/Will Jones	Simon Treves
Minty	Eileen Way
John Thurloe	David Collings

Creator: John Hawkesworth. Producers: Brian Spiby, Jonathan Alwyn

A family is torn apart by the English Civil War.

Beginning in May 1640, *By the Sword Divided* told the story of a noble English family as Civil War loomed. Head of the family was Sir Martin Lacey, a staunch Royalist who found his relatives siding with his Parliamentarian opponents and his own daughters marrying into 'the other side'. In the course of the first series Sir Martin fought at Edgehill, the Laceys' home at Arnescote Castle fell under siege from Cromwell's troops and the family silver was smuggled to the King at Oxford, all this taking events up to summer 1647. The second series, which aired in 1985, covered the period 1648–1660 and picked up with Arnescote Castle firmly in the hands of Sir Martin's daughter Anne and her Parliamentarian husband, John Fletcher. It continued through the execution of Charles I, a visit from Cromwell, assorted witch hunts, the arrival of Charles II, Royalist attempts to regain Arnescote and the eventual restoration of the monarchy, with family turmoil, as always, competing fiercely with the outside hostilities.

BYGRAVES, MAX (WALTER BYGRAVES; 1922–)

London-born entertainer who earned the nickname 'Max' after an impression he performed of Max Miller whilst in the RAF. Although training as a carpenter, Bygraves was able to turn professional as a singer and comedian soon after the war, working on stage, radio, records and film, eventually arriving on television with his *Singalongamax* nostalgic music shows and numerous Royal Variety Performances. His hosting of **Family Fortunes** proved less successful and the series was cancelled, only to be brought back a few years later with Les Dennis in charge. 'I wanna tell you a story' became his catchphrase.

BYRNE, JOHN (1940–)

Scottish painter and playwright whose **Tutti Frutti** was one of the most highly acclaimed drama serials of the late 1980s. Starring Robbie Coltrane and Emma Thompson, it focused on ageing rock 'n' roll band The Majestics' eventful tour of Scotland. He followed it up with *Your Cheatin' Heart*.

BYRNE, PETER (1928–)

For years Jack Warner's son-in-law, Andy Crawford, in **Dixon of Dock Green**, Peter Byrne pleased his female admirers by turning out again in the 1980s, playing the part of Nellie Boswell's fancy man in **Bread**. Over the years his other appearances have included parts in *The New Canadians*, **Blake's 7** and his earliest programme, *The Pattern of Marriage*, in 1953.

BYRNES, EDD (EDWARD BREITENBERGER; 1933–)

Short-lived cult figure of the late 1950s and early 1960s, otherwise known as Kookie, the jive-talking car-park attendant in **77 Sunset Strip**. Since that role ended in 1963 the blond-haired Byrnes has found work difficult to come by, meandering in and out of minor series and spaghetti Westerns. He had a hit single (with Connie Stevens) in 1960, entitled 'Kookie, Kookie (Lend Me Your Comb)', based on his excessive grooming in the series.

CABLE

A system involving the relay of television programmes via a network of cables, using one central reception/transmission centre. Initially cable was introduced to provide TV pictures to parts of the country where aerial reception was poor or nonexistent. Rediffusion was one such supplier in the UK. However, with the new generation of cabling, and the introduction of optical fibre (allowing many more channels to be carried), a host of new cable companies has sprung up across the UK. These provide dedicated national cable stations (like Wire TV and Super Channel), alongside satellite channels and locally made community programmes. Some of the most advanced cable networks serve towns such as Swindon, Aberdeen, Windsor and Slough, Croydon, Coventry and parts of London. The systems are regulated in the UK by the ITC's Cable and Satellite Division.

CABLE NEWS NETWORK see CNN.

CADE'S COUNTY

US (Twentieth Century-Fox) Police Drama.
ITV 1972

Sam Cade	Glenn Ford
J.J. Jackson	Edgar Buchanan
Arlo Pritchard	Taylor Lacher
Rudy Davillo	Victor Campos
Pete	Peter Ford
Joannie Little Bird	Sandra Ego
Betty Ann Sundown	Betty Ann Carr

Executive Producer: David Gerber. Producer: Charles Larson

Exciting moments in the life of a chief lawman.

This modern Western focused on Sheriff Sam Cade, leading crimebuster of Madrid County, California. Cade himself was mostly rooted to his Madrid town base, but his deputies out and about, keeping the peace around the sprawling county, were J.J. Jackson, an experienced veteran, and younger colleagues Arlo, Rudy and Pete (played by Glenn Ford's son). Two real-life American Indian girls, Sandra Ego and Betty Ann Carr, played police dispatchers Joannie Little Bird and Betty Ann Sundown.

CADELL, SIMON (1950–)

British comedy actor accomplished in straight-laced, nervous roles such as entertainments manager Jeffrey Fairbrother in **Hi-De-Hi!**, the hapless civil servant Dundridge in **Blott on the Landscape**, estate agent Larry Wade in **Life Without George** and actor Dennis Duval in **Singles**. His earlier TV credits included **Hadleigh**, **Hine**, **The Glittering Prizes**, **Wings**, **Space: 1999**, William Douglas-Home's 1976 play The Dame of Sark, the similar in content **Enemy at the Door**, and **Edward and Mrs Simpson**.

CAESARS, THE

UK (Granada) Drama.
ITV 1968

Augustus	Ronald Culver
Germanicus	Eric Flynn
Tiberius	André)Morell
Sejanus	Barrie Ingham
Caligula	Ralph Bates
Claudius	Freddie Jones
Livia	Sonia Dresdel

Writer/Producer: Philip Mackie

Power and corruption in ancient Rome.

Pre-dating the celebrated **I, Claudius** by eight years, The Caesars tackled the same subject, namely the political dog-fighting of Imperial Rome and the craven pastimes of its foremost citizens. Written and produced by Granada's Head of Drama, Philip Mackie, and directed by Derek Bennett, it was, in critics' eyes, no less successful. The six episodes focused chiefly on the six emperors and generals Augustus, Germanicus, Tiberius, Sejanus, Claigula and Claudius, with the scheming matriarch Livia also immersed in the action. Overall, a compact study of Rome's decline and fall was compiled.

CAFE CONTINENTAL

UK (BBC) Variety. BBC 1947–53

Creator/Producer: Henry Caldwell

International cabaret presented from a fake night club.

This initially 45-minute, later one-hour, variety show took the form of a Saturday night visit to a sophisticated international cabaret and dining club, complete with presiding maître d'hôtel and master/mistress of ceremonies. Claude Frederic and Pier Auguste were two of the artists to take the roles of the former; Al Burnett and Hélène Cordet two to take the latter. Sydney Jerome was the orchestra leader. Probably the biggest name to appear behind the Café's smart swing doors was Folies Bergères star Josephine Baker (in 1948).

CAGNEY AND LACEY

US (Orion) Police Drama.
BBC 1 1982–8

Detective Mary Beth Lacey ....Tyne Daly
Detective Christine Cagney ....Meg Foster
....Sharon Gless
Lt Bert Samuels..Al Waxman
Detective Mark Petrie ....Carl Lumbly
Detective Victor Isbecki ....Martin Kove
Detective Paul La Guardia ....Sidney Clute
Deputy Inspector Marquette...............Jason Bernard
Desk Sgt Ronald Coleman ....Harvey Atkin
Harvey Lacey ....John Karlen
Harvey Lacey, Jnr ....Tony La Torre
Michael Lacey ....Troy Slaten
Alice Lacey.........................Dana and Paige Bardolph
....Michelle Sepe
Sgt Dory McKenna ....Barry Primus
Inspector Knelman ....Michael Fairman
Detective Jonah Newman ....Dan Shor
David Keeler ....Stephen Macht
Detective Manny Esposito...................Robert Hegyes
Detective Al Corassa ....Paul Mantee
Josie ....Jo Corday
Tom Basil ....Barry Laws
Charlie Cagney ....Dick O'Neill
Detective Verna Dee Jordan ....Merry Clayton
Nick Amatucci......................................Carl Weintraub

Creators: Barney Rosenzweig, Barbara Avedon, Barbara Corday. Executive Producer: Barney Rosenzweig. Producer: Richard A. Rosenbloom

Two female cops win through in a man's world, despite the pressures of their personal lives.

Cagney and Lacey was a pioneer among TV cop series. It broke new ground in that it allowed women to be seen in the buddy-buddy context epitomized by series like **Starsky and Hutch**. It was based on two girls, Mary Beth Lacey and Chris Cagney, cops paired together as a team on the New York streets, and it struck a firm feminist stance in rejecting all the established preconceptions of women on television. The girls were seen holding their own in a tough, tough world, where the conflict and male prejudice they met within the police force was sometimes as great as the violence outside.

Cagney and Lacey was not the usual cops and robbers fare. It showed the grimier side of police work, the ups *and* the downs, and the girls were more than partners. In the sanctuary of the ladies' room at the police station, they poured their hearts out to each other, discussing the strains of work and their personal worries. Mary Beth was married (to construction worker Harvey Lacey) with young sons (Harvey Jnr and Michael) and

later a daughter (Alice). She had come from a broken home, had been through an abortion at 19 and had battled her way through a breast cancer scare. Chris was ambitious and single, but, dreading being alone all her life, she was continually drawn into unsuccessful relationships, such as with attorney David Keeler.

The programme never shirked heavy issues, such as Chris's occasional alcohol-dependency and the drug addiction of her one-time boyfriend, fellow cop Dory McKenna. In one episode she was even raped. Her alcoholic father, Charlie, also once on the force, appeared from time to time until he died, ironically just before she won her promotion to sergeant.

The series was not an instant hit in the States. After a pilot starring Loretta Swit of **M*A*S*H** in the part of Cagney, a short first series was produced, with Meg Foster cast alongside Tyne Daly. However, it was criticized for being too hard and too unfeminine, and so, when the next episodes were made, the producers softened it up, replacing Foster with Sharon Gless. Even then the studio was not impressed with the ratings and they cancelled the show, only for it to be brought back by huge public demand. It seems that the public were right.

CAINE, MARTI (LYNNE SHEPHERD; 1945–)

Slim northern comedienne and singer, a former model who came to fame via the *New Faces* talent-spotting show (she won the 1975 series), a programme she hosted for three series on its revival in 1986. In between, she starred in her own comedy/variety shows and attempted sitcom with *Hilary*, in which she played an accident-prone TV researcher.

CALDER, GILCHRIST (1918–)

Influential early BBC producer and director, working on drama-documentaries in the 1950s. Among his best remembered works were Colin Morris's 1957 and 1959 plays *The Wharf Road Mob* (as producer) and *Who, Me?* (as producer and director), Morris's 1961 mini-series *Jacks and Knaves* (as producer) and Nigel Kneale's 1970 Wednesday Play *Wine of India* (as director). He also directed episodes of **Detective**, **The Onedin Line** and **When the Boat Comes In** amongst other BBC fare.

CALL MY BLUFF

UK (BBC) Panel Game. BBC 2 1965–88

Chairmen: Robin Ray, Joe Melia, Peter Wheeler, Robert Robinson. Team Captains: Robert Morley, Frank Muir, Patrick Campbell, Arthur Marshall

Creators: Mark Goodson, Bill Todman.
Producers: T. Leslie Jackson, Bryan Sears,
Johnny Downes

Panel game based on the true meaning of obscure words.

Despite lasting just one year in its native USA, *Call My Bluff* was a stalwart of the BBC 2 schedule almost from the channel's inception. In keeping with the more erudite nature of the BBC's second channel, this programme looked at strange words, with two teams of three celebrities attempting to mislead each other as to the true meaning of arcane dictionary entries. Each panellist gave a lengthy, humorous definition of the word offered up by the chairman and the other team had to decide which description was genuine. Success or failure was denoted by the turning over of the description cards to reveal, in big letters, TRUE or BLUFF.

The programme's first chairman was Robin Ray, although the longest-serving and best known was Robert Robinson (from 1967). Joe Melia and Peter Wheeler also hosted proceedings in the early days. Frank Muir and Robert Morley were the first team captains, Patrick Campbell later replaced Morley and Arthur Marshall took over from the late Campbell in the 1980s. However, numerous other celebrities also stood in as team captains. They included Kenneth Horne, Alan Melville and Kenneth Williams.

A one-off programme was shown in 1994 with Joanna Lumley opposing Frank Muir and Robert Robinson in the chair.

CALLAN

UK (ABC/Thames) Secret Agent Drama. ITV
1967–72

David Callan..................................Edward Woodward
Lonely ....Russell Hunter
Hunter ....Ronald Radd
                           Michael Goodliffe
                           Derek Bond
                           William Squire
Toby Meres ....Anthony Valentine
Cross ....Patrick Mower
Hunter's secretary ....Lisa Langdon

Creator: James Mitchell. Executive Producer:
Lloyd Shirley. Producers: Reginald Collin

The assignments of a notoriously tough British Secret Intelligence agent.

Callan was a far cry from the glamorous world of James Bond. The hero was a hard man, edgy and friendless. He worked for the intelligence service, bluntly snuffing out enemies and others who represented a danger to British security. But he was also a rebel and a thinker who brought his own version of justice into play, rather than just killing willy-nilly as instructed. Callan, as a consequence, was constantly in trouble with his superiors.

In his first appearance, in a 1967 episode of ABC's *Armchair Theatre* called *A Magnum for Schneider*, Callan himself was the target. He had been given the chance to retrieve his dodgy reputation within British intelligence by bumping off an enemy agent, but this was merely a ruse to nail him for murder and so dispose of him. Turning the tables, Callan won through and public interest in the character led to a fully fledged series later the same year.

In the series the star was assisted by a dirty, smelly petty crook called Lonely, who supplied him with under-the-counter firearms and useful information. Callan treated Lonely, one of life's perpetual losers, with complete disdain. At the same time, though, he protected his little accomplice, finding him a job as driver of the communications car, a taxi filled with high-tech listening devices. Within the intelligence service, Callan's immediate boss was Hunter, not a specific person but a codename for the various heads of department supervising him. There was also Meres (played by Peter Bowles in the *Armchair Theatre* play), a fellow agent who resented Callan's position and contrived to dislodge him. Another agent seen later, the trigger-happy Cross, shared the same sentiments.

Nine years after the series ended, Callan was brought back in a one-off 90-minute play for ATV entitled *Wet Job*. Now retired and running a militaria shop under the alias of David Tucker, he was re-enlisted by the security services for one last mission. Hunter was played by Hugh Walters and Lonely resurfaced, too, in the unlikely position of a bathroom store proprietor.

Callan, with its distinctive 'swinging light bulb' opening sequences, was created by writer James Mitchell, who was later responsible for *When the Boat Comes In*. One series (the second) went out under the title of *The Callan Saga*. A cinema version was released in 1974.

CAMBERWICK GREEN/TRUMPTON/CHIGLEY

UK (Gordon Murray) Children's
Entertainment. BBC 1 1966/1967/1969

Narrator: Brian Cant

Creator/Producer: Gordon Murray. Writers:
Gordon Murray, Alison Prince (Trumpton)

Rural puppet soap operas for kids.

Animated by Bob Bura and John Hardwick, Gordon Murray's rustic puppet trilogy began in

1966, when *Camberwick Green* took over the Monday **Watch with Mother** slot. It gave children an insight into the lives of the folk of Camberwick Green, a small village deep in the English countryside. Each episode opened and ended with a shot of a musical box, 'wound up and ready to play', from which one of the villagers slowly emerged, allowing viewers to follow them as they went about their typical day. Sadly, a minor tragedy always struck at some point and the gallant lads at Pippin Fort, under the command of Captain Snort and Sgt Major Grout, were usually called in to restore order. The good people of Camberwick Green were: the famous Windy Miller of Colley's Mill; Roger Varley, the chimney sweep; Mr Carraway, the fishmonger; gossipy Mrs Honeyman, the chemist's wife (and her baby boy); Dr Mopp with his boneshaker car; farmer Jonathan Bell; Mr Crockett, the garage owner; Mickey Murphy, the baker (with children Paddy and Mary); salesman Mr Dagenham; Thomas Tripp, the milkman; Peter Hazel, the postman; Mrs Dingle, the postmistress (and Packet, the Post Office puppy), and, of course, PC McGarry (number 452). A pierrot puppet turned over the opening and closing titles.

A few *Camberwick Green* characters appeared in the spin-off series, *Trumpton*, a year later, dropping in on an occasional basis. This time the action had moved to the larger town of Trumpton, where the role played earlier by the soldiers of Pippin Fort was taken over by Capt. Flack's courageous local firemen: Hugh, Pugh, Barney McGrew, Cuthbert, Dibble and Grubb. Mrs Honeyman gave way to the blethering Miss Lovelace and her yapping dogs, and also featured were the Mayor; the Town Clerk, Mr Troop; Mrs Cobbit, and Mr Platt. The start of each episode focused on the Trumpton clock, 'telling the time for Trumpton', and all programmes ended with a fire brigade band concert in the park.

The third instalment of this puppet melodrama came from Chigley, a hamlet described as being 'near Camberwick Green, Trumptonshire'. This was an altogether more modest little settlement, chiefly consisting of a biscuit factory, a canalside wharf, a pottery and a stately home, Wingstead Hall. The last belonged to Lord Belborough, a charitable aristocrat who, with his loyal butler, Mr Brackett, ran a steam train known as Bessie for the benefit of the local people. Goods were ferried in and out at Treadles Wharf, where the bargees and dockers were watched over by Mr Swallow. The biscuit factory, meanwhile, was in the hands of Mr Cresswell and his employees held a dance after the six o'clock whistle at the end of each episode. Also seen were Mr Clamp, the greengrocer; Harry Farthing, the potter, and his daughter, Winnie; Mr Clutterbuck, the builder;

carpenter Chippy Minton and his son, Nibbs; Mr Bilton, Belborough's gardener, and assorted cross-over characters from both *Camberwick Green* and *Trumpton*.

Despite only 13 episodes being made of each series, repeat showings continued for many years. While the storylines were always very limited and the songs (by Freddie Phillips) crushingly repetitive, Brian Cant's whimsical delivery and the quality of the animation and characterization have made this little trilogy into children's television classics.

CAMCORDER

A video camera and recorder in one smallish unit, much more flexible than separate camera and recording machines.

CAMERON, JAMES OBE (1911–85)

British current affairs reporter of the 1960s and 1970s. He was the first commentator on the retrospective series *All Our Yesterdays* and later turned to drama writing. The 1979 *Screenplay* presentation *The Sound of the Guns* was his first offering.

CAMPBELLS, THE

UK (Scottish) Adventure. ITV 1986

Dr James Campbell	Malcolm Stoddard
Emma Campbell	Amber-Lea Weston
Neil Campbell	John Wildman
John Campbell	Eric Richards
Captain Thomas Simms	Cedric Smith
Rebecca Simms	Wendy Lyon
Gabriel Leger	Julien Poulin

Producers: Leonard White, John Delmage

The trials of life for a Scottish family in a new land.

The Campbells, like many of their contemporaries, had left their native country in the 1830s in search of a better life. Emigrating to an unknown territory of Canada, they soon discovered this was no easy option. The series tracked their day-to-day struggles in a hard and forbidding land. Head of the household was widower James Campbell and his family consisted of a daughter, Emma, and two sons, Neil and John. The Simms were their neighbours.

CAMPION

UK (BBC/WGBH Boston) Detective Drama. BBC 1 1989–90

Albert Campion	Peter Davison
Magersfontein Lugg	Brian Glover
Chief Inspector Stanislaus Oates	Andrew Burt

Producers: Ken Riddington, Jonathan Alwyn

Murder investigations in the 1930s with an unassuming, bespectacled detective.

Albert Campion, the creation of novelist Margery Allingham and star of 26 books, first reached the TV screen in 1959 in the BBC serial *Dancers in Mourning*. In this and the follow-up, *Death of a Ghost*, a year later, he was played by Bernard Horsfall. Campion reappeared later in the 1960s in the anthology series **Detective**. On that occasion he was played by Brian Smith. However, it was the 1989–90 series, starring Peter Davison, which really brought him to the attention of the viewing public.

Practising his skills in the 1930s, in the same genteel circles as Lord Peter Wimsey and Hercule Poirot, the aristocratic Campion was a determined and shrewd amateur sleuth, with strong moral principles – even if his mild-mannered appearance conveyed quite the opposite. Sporting large, horn-rimmed glasses and with his amiable and unassuming personality pushed well to the fore, villains thought it easy to shrug off Campion's enquiries. They soon learned better, as our hero doggedly pieced together the relevant clues. Also at hand was Campion's brawny, down-to-earth manservant, a reformed burglar named Lugg, whose duties ranged from taking care of the baggage to obtaining information his master couldn't reach by mixing with the lower classes. The duo rode around the East Anglia countryside in a splendid vintage Lagonda, wrapping up crimes before their Scotland Yard associate, Stanislaus Oates, could move in.

CAMPION, GERALD (1921–)

British actor, TV's Billy Bunter in the 1950s (even though aged 29 at the time). No other starring roles followed and Campion turned instead (somewhat fittingly) to the restaurant business.

CANDID CAMERA

UK (ABC) Comedy. ITV 1960–7

Presenters: Bob Monkhouse, Jonathan Routh

Creator: Allen Funt

Hidden camera stunts at the expense of the general public.

Candid Camera was imported into the UK from the USA, where it had been devised by archprankster Allen Funt. Funt began gauging the public's reaction to unusual, not to say bizarre, situations in his radio show, *Candid Microphone*. It transferred to television in 1949 with the same title, before becoming *Candid Camera* in 1953. ABC produced the UK version, installing Bob Monkhouse as its host and sending Jonathan Routh out and about in search of gullible citizens. Hidden cameras surreptitiously witnessed their reactions to impossible situations – a man selling £5 notes for £4 10s, garage mechanics asked to discover why a car wouldn't start and finding it had no engine, etc. Eventually, the poor punters were put out of their misery with the words 'Smile, you're on *Candid Camera*'. The series was revived by LWT in 1974, when it was produced and presented by Peter Dulay.

CANNELL, STEPHEN J. (1941–)

American producer and writer of all-action series in the 1970s and 1980s, whose first major success was **The Rockford Files.** His production company was also responsible for **The A-Team** and **Hardcastle and McCormick**, amongst other racy series.

CANNON

US (Quinn Martin) Detective Drama. BBC 1 1972–8

Frank Cannon ....William Conrad

Executive Producer: Quinn Martin. Producer: Anthony Spinner

An overweight, middle-aged private detective puffs and pants after crooks in Los Angeles.

William Conrad was the only star of this successful series, which had been tailor-made for him. After 11 years of providing the voice of Matt Dillon in the American radio version of **Gunsmoke**, he was denied the TV role because of his physical appearance (James Arness got the job). *Cannon*, at last, was his overdue reward.

Frank Cannon was an unlikely detective. He loved the good life and his body bore the scars. His hefty frame meant that every case was a real effort, particularly when it came to a sweaty chase after a fleeing murderer, because, having no sidekick, Cannon had to do all the legwork himself. Still, he was well reimbursed for his work, charging enough to keep up his bon viveur lifestyle and to repair the big Lincoln Continental he pranged around the LA streets. Cannon was one of the first gimmicky cops. After him came Kojak, McCloud and Columbo. The series first aired in the UK under the umbrella title of *The Detectives*, in sequence with **The Rockford Files**, **Harry O** and **A Man Called Ironside**.

CANNON, TOMMY (THOMAS DERBYSHIRE; 1938–)

The partner of diminutive northern comic Bobby Ball. After a long apprenticeship as the

Shirell Brothers and then the Harper Brothers, Cannon and Ball arrived on television courtesy of a not so promising debut on **Opportunity Knocks** in 1968 and did not secure their own show until 1979 (following guest appearances with Bruce Forsyth). As well as their own peak-time variety shows (mostly scripted by Sid Green), the duo have also attempted a quiz, *Cannon and Ball's Casino*, and a sitcom, *Plaza Patrol*, playing shopping-centre security men Bernard Cooney (Cannon) and Trevor Purvis (Ball).

CAPTAIN PUGWASH

UK (John Ryan) Children's Entertainment. BBC 1 1957–66; 1974–5

Narrator: Peter Hawkins

Creator/Writer: John Ryan. Producers: Gordon Murray, John Ryan

The maritime adventures of a blustery pirate and his crew.

Animated by John Ryan in the most basic fashion, with crudely drawn characters making the simplest of movements against a static background, *Captain Pugwash* was a remarkably cheap series to produce. All the same, it became a perennial favourite and a great filler programme for the BBC. First appearing in 1957, and updated in colour in the 1970s, it related tales of the pirate Captain Horatio Pugwash, podgy skipper of the *Black Pig*. His hapless crew were workshy and rather dense, and included able seamen Barnabas and Willy, the dubiously named Master Bate and a loyal cabin boy named Tom, clearly the brightest of the bunch. Most of the time they sought to avoid the clutches of the barbarous Cut Throat Jake, a black-bearded pirate of the worst order, and the five-minute episodes ran in serial form, each ending with a cliffhanger finish. The distinctive accordian sea shanty theme music, 'The Hornblower', was performed by Tommy Edmondson and the many voices belonged to Bill and Ben vocalist Peter Hawkins.

Such was the success of *Captain Pugwash* that it spawned a *Radio Times* cartoon strip and a successor series in 1972, *The Adventures of Sir Prancelot*, which revolved around a fearless knight in shining armour.

CAPTAIN SCARLET AND THE MYSTERONS

UK (Century 21/ITC) Children's Science Fiction. ITV 1967–8

Voices:
Captain Scarlet (Paul Metcalfe) ......Francis Matthews
Colonel White (Charles Gray)................Donald Gray
Captain Blue (Adam Svenson) ....Ed Bishop
Captain Grey (Bradley Holden).............Paul Maxwell
Captain Magenta (Patrick Donaghue) ....Gary Files
Captain Ochre (Richard Frazier) ....Jeremy Wilkin
Lt Green (Seymour Griffiths) ....Cy Grant
Dr Fawn (Edward Wilkie).................Charles Tingwell
Melody Angel (Magnolia Jones) ......Sylvia Anderson
Harmony Angel (Chan Kwan) ....Lian-Shin
Symphony Angel (Karen Wainwright)........Janna Hill
Rhapsody Angel (Diane Sims) ....Liz Morgan
Destiny Angel (Juliette Pointon) ....Liz Morgan
Captain Black (Conrad Turner)...............Donald Gray
The Voice of the Mysterons ....Donald Gray
World President.....................................Paul Maxwell

Creators: Gerry Anderson, Sylvia Anderson. Producer: Reg Hill

An indestructible puppet super-agent takes on a vengeful alien force.

In the year 2068, Spectrum, the world's security command, undertook a mission to Mars, a mission which turned to disaster. When the native Mysterons locked their antennae on to the landing party, they were mistaken for guns and the order was given for a Mysteron city to be destroyed. In response, the Mysterons slaughtered the Spectrum envoys, including their leader, Captain Black, vowing to wreak vengeance on the people of Earth.

The Mysterons possessed the remarkable power of retro-metabolism – the re-creation of destroyed matter, which rendered it indestructible at the same time. The first thing they did was to reconstruct their destroyed city and piece together Captain Black, formerly Spectrum's top agent, for use against his former allies. The Mysterons also tried to destroy and re-create another Spectrum officer, Captain Scarlet, but this time their plan failed, and, although Scarlet became indestructible, he nevertheless remained loyal to Spectrum and proved time and again crucial in the defence of the Earth.

Spectrum, operating from a floating control centre called Cloudbase, was run by Colonel White. The other agents and officers were also code-named after colours, with uniforms to reflect their identities, and they were ably supported by the five female pilots of Angel Interceptor aircraft: Melody, Harmony, Symphony, Destiny and Rhapsody. All operatives raced into action on the command SIG (Spectrum Is Green).

In each episode the Mysterons threatened the Earth's security by attacking key command centres or personnel, sabotaging world conferences or simply gunning for Spectrum. The aliens themselves were never seen, but the introduction to each programme featured the gravelly 'Voice of the Mysterons', reiterating their avowed intention to gain revenge. As the voice boomed out, two rings of light played over a dead body or wrecked aircraft, indicating that the regeneration process was under way. Spectrum needed to be well equipped to handle the Mysteron threat, but, despite its Spectrum Pursuit Vehicles (SPVs), Maximum Security Vehicles (MSVs) and other high-tech wizardry, it still relied heavily on one man – the indestructible (if rather humourless) Captain Scarlet.

The producers' attention to detail in this series was remarkable. For the first time Gerry Anderson puppets were perfect in proportion, with the electronic circuitry that made his earlier marionettes 'big-headed' transferred into the puppets' bodies. The puppets were also made to look like the actors who supplied their voices. Scarlet, for instance, was a model of Francis Matthews. The characterization, too, was more detailed than in previous efforts. The agents were given private lives and real identities (Scarlet was really Paul Metcalfe), and were furnished with other biographical data. It was revealed, for instance, that the Trinidadian communications specialist, Lt Green, and the American Captain Grey had both previously been assigned to WASP on the **Stingray** project, and that Diane Sims (Rhapsody Angel) had once worked with Lady Penelope of **Thunderbirds** fame.

The series was re-run on BBC 2 in 1993–4.

CAPTION ROLLER

Mechanical system of running continuous captions that can be superimposed over another shot or filmed independently. It has traditionally been used for a programme's closing credits, although computer-generated graphics are now taking over.

CAR 54, WHERE ARE YOU?

US (Euopolis) Situation Comedy. ITV 1964–

Officer Gunther Toody...............................Joe E. Ross
Officer Francis Muldoon ....Fred Gwynne
Lucille Toody ....Bea Pons
Captain Martin Block ....Paul Reed
Officer O'Hara ....Albert Henderson
Officer Anderson ....Nipsey Russell
Officer Antonnucci ....Jerome Guardino
Officer Steinmetz ....Joe Warren
Officer Riley ....Duke Farley
Officer Murdock ....Shelley Burton
Officer Leo Schnauser ....Al Lewis
Sylvia Schnauser ....Charlotte Rae
Officer Kissel ....Bruce Kirby
Officer Ed Nicholson ....Hank Garrett

Creator/Producer: Nat Hiken

The slapstick escapades of an inept team of New York City cops.

Hot on the heels of his success with **The Phil Silvers Show**, producer Nat Hiken introduced viewers to **Car 54, Where Are You?** and the ropiest bunch of cops yet seen on TV. At the forefront were Toody and Muldoon, the former short, podgy and amiable, the latter tall and sullen. Not only did they look odd together, they were also pretty hopeless in action. Their beat was in the 53rd Precinct, the troubled Bronx, although you really wouldn't have known it as the series only played on the lighter side of police work. Much of the fun came from within the police station itself.

Hiken brought Joe E. Ross with him from '**Bilko**' (he had played Sgt Rupert Ritzik, where Bea Pons played his nagging wife, as here), while Fred Gwynne was to go on to greater fame as Herman in **The Munsters**. Al Lewis joined him as Grandpa in that series. **Car 54, Where Are You?** was re-run on Channel 4 in 1983.

CARGILL, PATRICK (1918–)

Although gaining a reputation as Britain's leading farceur in the 1970s, thanks to series like **Father, Dear, Father** (as novelist Patrick Glover), **The Many Wives of Patrick** (as antiques dealer Patrick Woodford) and the anthology **Ooh La La**, Patrick Cargill's earlier television roles had been in quite a different vein. After appearing as a baddie in **The Adventures of Robin Hood**, Cargill was cast as mysterious agent Miguel Garetta (who worked under the identity of an Argentinian businessman) in **Top Secret**, and later played one of the Number Twos in **The Prisoner**. He also guest starred in action series like **The Avengers** and **Man in a Suitcase**. However, his flair for comedy was already apparent. He played the doctor in the famous **Hancock's Half Hour** sketch 'The Blood Donor', for instance, and also appeared in the follow-up series **Hancock** (playing Tony's department store boss Mr Stone). Since his television heyday, Cargill has returned to the stage, starring in numerous West End plays.

CARLTON TELEVISION

The contractor for the London weekday ITV franchise, Carlton is part of Carlton Communications, which also owns Central Television, 20 per cent of Meridian Television, 20 per cent of GMTV and 36 per cent of ITN. Carlton surprisingly ousted the successful Thames Television from the London area in the 1991 franchise auctions, taking to the air on 1 January 1993. Carlton's policy has been to commission most of its network proposals from external suppliers.

CARMICHAEL, IAN (1920–)

Well-groomed, rather aristocratic English actor whose TV high spot was as Lord Peter Wimsey, the toff detective created by Dorothy L. Sayers. In similar style, he had earlier perfected the silly ass comic character, playing Bertie in *The World of Wooster* (1965), before becoming the harassed dad, Peter Lamb, in *Bachelor Father* (from 1970). His other TV credits have included *All for Love*, *Just A Nimmo*, **Survival** (as narrator) and, more recently, the part of Sir James Menzies in *Strathblair*, although he first appeared on television way back in the 1940s, guesting in variety shows.

CARPENTER, HARRY, OBE (1925–)

Durable BBC sports presenter and boxing commentator (over four decades), who retired from **Grandstand**, **Sportsnight**, Wimbledon, the Olympics, the Boat Race and Open Golf coverage in the early 1990s, before finally counting himself out of the boxing game at the 1994 Commonwealth Games. His friendship with heavyweight Frank Bruno marked the later years of his career – 'Know what I mean, 'Arry?'

CARPENTER, RICHARD

Former actor (Peter Parker in **Knight Errant**) turned writer of juvenile adventures whose major contributions have been **Catweazle** (allegedly inspired by a word scratched on a gate), *The Ghosts of Motley Hall*, **Dick Turpin**, *Smuggler* and **Robin of Sherwood**. He has also contributed to series like *The Adventures of Black Beauty*.

CARRADINE, DAVID (JOHN ARTHUR CARRADINE; 1936–)

American actor whose TV fame is owed chiefly to the part of Kwai Chang Caine in the 1970s martial arts Western **Kung Fu**, a role he revived in the 1990s. If he appeared at home in the character, it was because Caine's philosophical approach to life was not, it has been reported, that far removed from Carradine's own thoughtful disposition. His sad, gaunt features were also put to good use in the 1960s cowboy series *Shane*, in which he played the title role, and shows like **Alfred Hitchcock Presents** and **Ironside**. In the 1980s he resurfaced in the miniseries *North and South*. David is a member of the famous Hollywood acting family, son of John Carradine and half-brother to Keith and Robert.

CARROLL, LEO G. (1892–1972)

Distinguished British actor, a star in his seventies as the sober Mr Waverly in **The Man** (and *The Girl*) *from UNCLE*. Earlier, playing men of authority, Carroll featured in numerous Hollywood movies, including several Hitchcock classics. He arrived on TV in the ghostly 1950s sitcom *Topper*, playing the title role, Cosmo Topper, and also starred in a short-lived version of Bing Crosby's film *Going My Way* in 1962. Other television credits included **Ironside**. However, it is as the boss of Napoleon Solo, Illya Kuryakin and April Dancer in the mid-1960s that he is best remembered.

CARROTT, JASPER (ROBERT DAVIES; 1945–)

Broad Brummie comic, a sharp observer of public failings who hosted his own series on BBC 1 throughout most of the 1980s. His earlier work came on BBC regional television and he gained a cult following which took him into the record charts in 1975 with 'Funky Moped'/'Magic Roundabout'. There followed a series of *The Jasper Carrott Show* for LWT, along with a few one-off shows and spoof documentaries, such as *Carrott Del Sol*. However, it was in *Carrott's Lib*, *Carrott Confidential* and *Canned Carrott* that he established himself in the mainstream of British comedy, combining long satirical, often ranting monologues (about Reliant Robins, Birmingham City FC, Sun readers, etc.) with assorted sketches (assisted at various times by the likes of Emma Thompson, Chris Barrie, Steve Punt and Hugh Dennis). One segment of *Canned Carrott*, **The Detectives**, a send up of ITV cop shows like **Special Branch** and **The Sweeney**, and co-starring Robert Powell, was spun-off into its own half-hour series.

CARSON, FRANK (1926–)

Irrepressible, Ulster-born, bespectacled stand-up comedian, fond of laughing at his own jokes because 'It's the way I tell 'em'. After coming to light on **Opportunity Knocks** and as one of **The Comedians**, he popped up to spout his juvenile gags on the raucous **Tiswas** programme. He has also contributed to *The Good Old Days*.

CARSON, JOHNNY (1925–)

An American institution, Johnny Carson hosted *The Tonight Show* for 30 years, garnering huge audiences with his boyish looks, cheeky grin and quick wit. Carson did little else on TV after his run as host of the show began in 1962, save a few guest appearances and the occasional piece of emceeing. In 1981 he attempted to bring his show to Britain but it didn't catch on. On his retirement in 1992, NBC named comedian Jay Leno as Carson's *Tonight* successor.

CARSON, VIOLET, OBE (1898–1983)

In the shape of **Coronation Street** battleaxe Ena Sharples, Violet Carson brought us one of television's unforgettable characterizations. An original member of the cast in 1960 (at the age of 62), she stayed with the show until 1980, enjoying some glorious spats with the Street's vixen Elsie Tanner and some classic moments in the snug of the Rovers with Minnie Caldwell and Martha Longhurst. But beneath Ena's hairnet, Violet Carson's natural talent lay in music. She played piano for Wilfrid Pickles in the radio quiz *Have A Go*, and in her later years was a regular guest on **Stars on Sunday**, singing and playing the organ. Once *Coronation Street* had taken off, Carson had few other opportunities to show off her acting skills, however, although some viewers still recalled her as Auntie Vi on radio's *Children's Hour* and as an early contributor to *Woman's Hour*.

CARTER, LYNDA (1951–)

Statuesque former Miss USA (1973), understandably cast as TV's **Wonder Woman**, given her Amazonian figure. She has since appeared in assorted TV movies, as well as an unsuccessful detective series with Loni Anderson, *Partners In Crime*.

CARTIER, RUDOLPH (1908-94)

Viennese director/producer who arrived in the UK in the late 1930s, joining the BBC in 1952. He stayed with the Corporation for 25 years, bringing with him the influences of continental cinema and directing some of its most influential plays and serials. His treatment of Nigel Kneale's **The Quatermass Experiment** (and its sequels) shocked the country, his *1984* was a milestone, and both helped to establish him as a seminal figure in TV drama. His work also covered TV opera (*Otello* in 1959 and *Carmen* in 1962, for instance) as he demonstrated his love of the spectacular and his adventurous, extravagant approach to studio drama. Among his other major contributions were Sunday-Night Theatre offerings like *The White Falcon* (1956), plus *Arrow to the Heart* (1952), *Wuthering Heights* (1953), *Thunder Rock* (1955), *Captain of Koepenick* (1958), *Mother Courage and Her Children* (1959), *Anna Karenina*, *Rashomon* (both 1961), *Dr Korczak and The Children* (1962), *Stalingrad* (1963, for the Festival anthology), *The July Plot* (a 1964 Wednesday Play) and *Lee Oswald – Assassin* (a 1966 Play of the Month). He also directed more mundane BBC efforts like episodes of **Maigret**, **Out of the Unknown** and **Z Cars**.

CARTOON NETWORK

The world's first 24-hour all-cartoon channel was launched by Turner Broadcasting on cable in the USA in 1992. In Europe, since September 1993, the service has been available 14 hours a day, from 6 am to 8 pm, courtesy of the Astra 1C satellite, where it shares the same channel as its sister network, TNT. It provides a showcase for Hanna-Barbera, Warner Brothers and MGM animations and is available in six languages. Like TNT and Turner's other Astra channel, CNN, the signal is unscrambled and free to owners of satellite receivers.

CARTY, TODD (1963–)

Irish-born actor whose earliest TV appearances came in **Z Cars**, *Our Mutual Friend* and other juvenile parts, although it was as Tucker Jenkins in the school drama **Grange Hill** that he gained his first lasting role. Indeed, out of this came his own spin-off, *Tucker's Luck*, which followed Jenkins as he left school. When actor David Scarboro, who played Mark Fowler in **EastEnders**, died in 1988, Carty was drafted in (two years later) to join numerous other former **Grange Hill** stars in Albert Square.

CASANOVA

UK (BBC) Drama. BBC 2 1971

Giovanni Casanova	Frank Finlay
Lorenzo	Norman Rossington
Christina	Zienia Merton
Barbarina	Christine Noonan
Carlo	Patrick Newell
Senator Bragadin	Geoffrey Wincott
Senior Inquisitor	Ronald Adam

Writer: Dennis Potter. Producer: Mark Shivas

The famed 18th-century Italian poet and lover reflects on his life.

In this six-part drama, Giovanni Casanova from his prison cell, cast his mind back over the events of his life, evaluating whether his actions had been just and his deeds honourable. He questioned the dogmas of the time and attempted to find escape, physical and mental, from his incarceration at the hands of the Spanish Inquisition. The flashback sequences, taking the romantic writer from the age of 30 to his death at 73, majored on bold language, nudity and sexual antics, leading Mrs Whitehouse to accuse the series of gross indecency. Writer Dennis Potter hit back, claiming his work was, on the contrary, very moral.

CASE HISTORIES OF SCOTLAND YARD

UK (Anglo Amalgamated Films) Police Drama Anthology. ITV 1955

Inspector Duggan	Russell Napier

Inspector Ross	Ken Henry
Sgt Mason	Arthur Mason

Host: Edgar Lustgarten. Producer: Jack Greenwood

Drama series based on actual Scotland Yard case files.

Introduced by noted journalist and criminologist Edgar Lustgarten, this early half-hour film series was particularly popular in the USA (where it was known simply as *Scotland Yard*). It offered dramatized accounts of real-life crimes which had been investigated by the men of the Metropolitan Police. Although casts changed every week, a few characters like Inspector Duggan appeared on a semi-regular basis.

CASEBOOK OF SHERLOCK HOLMES, The see *Adventures of Sherlock Holmes, The*

CASES OF SHERLOCK HOLMES, THE

UK (BBC) Detective Drama. BBC 1 1968

Sherlock Holmes	Peter Cushing
Dr Watson	Nigel Stock
Inspector Lestrade	William Lucas
Mrs Hudson	Grace Arnold
Mycroft Holmes	Ronald Adam

Producer: William Sterling

Baker Street's cerebral sleuth, played by one of Britain's masters of horror.

Taking his lead from the rather bastardized perception of the great detective as a thorough do-gooder and an essentially kind man, Peter Cushing donned the deerstalker, picked up the hooked pipe and became the late 1960s TV Holmes. There was no cocaine, no violent mood swings and none of the rudeness which Conan Doyle had perceived and which Jeremy Brett reintroduced in the 1980s. Fifteen stories comprised this rendition, including all the favourites, from *A Study in Scarlet* to *The Hound of the Baskervilles*, with Nigel Stock cast as the inept Dr Watson. Only two years earlier Stock had played the same role alongside Douglas Wilmer (see *Sherlock Holmes*). Cushing, too, was familiar with his character, having already portrayed Sherlock Holmes in the 1959 Hammer version of *The Hound of the Baskervilles*.

CASEY JONES

US (Columbia/Briskin) Children's Western. BBC 1958–

John Luther 'Casey' Jones	Alan Hale Jnr
Casey Jones Jnr	Bobby Clark
Alice Jones	Mary Lawrence
Wallie Simms	Dub Taylor

Red Rock	Eddy Waller
Sam Peachpit	Pat Hogan

Excitement on a Midwestern railroad in the 1890s.

Based on the mournful ballad in which the hero is tragically killed, this series for youngsters was much more perky. Casey Jones (steamin' and a rollin') was an engineer for the Illinois Central Railroad, the man behind the throttle of the celebrated Cannonball Express. Living with his wife, Alice, his young son, Casey Jnr, and dog, Cinders, in Jackson, Tennessee, and loyally supported by his railroad colleagues Wallie Simms, the fireman, and Red Rock, the conductor, Casey somehow always managed to fulfil his missions, in the face of the greatest adversity. This was one Casey Jones who wouldn't die.

CASSIDY, DAVID (1950–)

Actor/singer heart-throb of the 1970s, soaring to international fame as Keith Partridge in *The Partridge Family*, in which he starred with his own stepmother, Shirley Jones. On the back of the series he topped the record charts on both sides of the Atlantic with songs like 'How Can I Be Sure' and 'Daydreamer', as well as having Partridge Family hits that included 'I Think I Love You' and 'Breaking Up Is Hard To' Do. Since those heady days TV work has been thin for Cassidy, except for an unusual detective series created specifically for him in 1978, *David Cassidy – Man Undercover*, in which he played Officer Dan Shay. His earliest work consisted of minor roles in series like *Bonanza*. Cassidy married actress Kay Lenz in 1977. His father was actor Jack Cassidy and his brother, Shaun, has also made showbiz his career.

CASSIDY, TED (1932–79)

Giant American actor, chiefly remembered in his guise of Lurch, the groaning butler in *The Addams Family*. (He also played the hand, Thing, unless Lurch was also in shot.) Later Cassidy appeared as Injun Joe in *The New Adventures of Huck Finn* and provided the voice for numerous Hanna-Barbera characters, including *Frankenstein Jnr*. He died following heart surgery in 1979.

CASTLE, ROY, OBE (1933–94)

Very popular and extremely versatile entertainer whose talents stretched from singing and dancing to playing obscure musical instruments. Early in his career he acted as straight man to Jimmy James and then appeared in numerous films, ranging from *Dr Who and The Daleks* to *Carry On Up the*

Khyber. From 1972 he hosted the superlatives show **Record Breakers** (holding some world records himself) and his other TV offerings included *Castle Beats Time* and *The Roy Castle Show*. The last years of his life were dedicated to fighting (and raising the profile of) lung cancer, a disease he claimed he had contracted from passive smoking, having spent years playing the trumpet in smoky club rooms.

CASUALTY

UK (BBC) Medical Drama. BBC 1 1986–

Charlie Fairhead	Derek Thompson
Lisa 'Duffy' Duffin	Catherine Shipton
Megan Roach	Brenda Fricker
Dr Ewart Plimmer	Bernard Gallagher
Clive King	George Harris
Kuba Trzcinski	Christopher Rozycki
Susie Mercier	Debbie Roza
Dr Barbara 'Baz' Samuels Hayes	Julia Watson
Elizabeth Straker	Maureen O'Brien
Katie Hardie	Karen O'Malley
Dr Mary Tomkinson	Helena Little
Cyril James	Eddie Nestor
Dr David Rowe	Paul Lacoux
Susan Franklyn	Valerie Sinclair
Keith Cotterill	Geoffrey Leesley
Sadie Tomkins	Carol Leader
Dr Lucy Perry	Tam Hoskyns
Alex Spencer	Belinda Davison
Dr Beth Ramanee	Mamta Kaash
Dr Julian Chapman	Nigel Le Vaillant
Jimmy Powell	Robson Green
Tony Walker	Eamon Boland
Andrew Bower	William Gaminara
Martin Ashford	Patrick Robinson
Helen Green	Maggie McCarthy
Norma Sullivan	Anne Kristen
Kelly Liddle	Adie Allen
Patricia Baynes	Maria Friedman
Dr Rob Khalefa	Jason Riddington
Kate Miller	Joanna Foster
Sandra Nicholl	Maureen Beattie
Maxine Price	Emma Bird
Simon Eastman	Robert Daws
Dr Mike Barratt	Clive Mantle
Brian Crawford	Brendan O'Hea
Jane Scott	Caroline Webster
Mark Calder	Oliver Parker
Mie Nishi-Kawa	Naoko Mori
Frankie Drummer	Steven O'Donnell
Dave Masters	Martin Ball
Rachel Longworth	Jane Gurnett
Dr Karen Goodliffe	Suzanna Hamilton
Adele Beckford	Doña Croll
Kenneth Hodges	Christopher Guard
Helen Chatsworth	Samantha Edmonds
Mary Skillett	Tara Moran
Lucy Cooper	Jo Unwin
Kate Wilson	Sorcha Cusack
Eddie Gordon	Joan Oliver
Matt Hawley	Jason Merrells
Adam Cooke	Steven Brand
Jude Kocarnik	Lisa Coleman
Liz Harker	Sue Devaney

Creators: Jeremy Brock, Paul Unwin. Producers: Geraint Morris, Peter Norris, Michael Ferguson, Corinne Hollingworth

A hectic night's work in a city's accident and emergency unit.

Set at nighttime in the casualty department of Holby (a thinly disguised Bristol) City Hospital, this extremely popular series has echoed American imports like **Hill Street Blues** and **St Elsewhere** in its construction, with one disturbing lead story merged with one or two more light-hearted sub-plots to ease the tension and add contrast. While the 'stars' of each show have been the various patients, of the regular cast the main man has been Charlie Fairhead, the avuncular charge nurse who to all intents and purposes runs the night shift. In the early years he shared the limelight with mother-figure Megan Roach and the explosive, single-mother senior nurse Lisa 'Duffy' Duffin. Among the other notable cast members have been former surgeon Ewart Plimmer, heartthrob Dr Julian Chapman, Geordie porter Jimmy Powell and dependable Martin 'Ash' Ashford. However, new supporting casts have come with each season, and only a few characters have lasted any great length of time. This is possibly because the action in *Casualty* has traditionally come more from events in the wards than from the personal lives of its protagonists, although the characters have increasingly come through over the years. Charlie, for example, has suffered from alcohol addiction, a nervous break-down and numerous romantic upheavals, but life goes on at Holby.

The series has never been afraid to court controversy. The status of the NHS has always been an issue, much to the dismay of some politicians, and touchy medical matters have bravely been covered, including AIDS and anorexia. Other social menaces like terrorism, rioting, arson and plane crashes have been given equal prominence and drawn similar venom from sensitive critics. Production-wise, too, *Casualty* has been daring. The 1994–5 season was initially shot on film to add greater depth and slickness. However, viewers preferred the tamer atmosphere of video-tape and later episodes were electronically recorded as before.

CATCHPHRASE

UK (TVS/Action Time) Game Show. ITV 1986–

Presenter: Roy Walker

Executive Producers: John Kaye Cooper, Stephen Leahy. Producers: Graham C. Williams, Frank Hayes, Liddy Oldroyd, Patricia Mordecai, Royston Mayoh

Spot-the-saying quiz involving complex computer graphics.

'See what you say and say what you see' has become the *Catchphrase* catchphrase. This undemanding game show has asked two contestants to solve a series of computer-generated visual puzzles representing well-known phrases or sayings. Wrong guesses have been generously rejected by host Roy Walker with his own trademark quips like 'It's good, but it's not right'. Cash and travel prizes have been awarded to successful contestants.

CATHODE RAY TUBE

The electron tube invented by Karl Ferdinand Braun in 1897 which was modified by Philo T. Farnsworth and Vladimir Zworykin in the 1920s to display television pictures. The device includes a gun that fires a stream of electrons at a phosphor-coated screen, causing it to glow and so display the TV image. Familiarly known as the 'tube', early versions were expensive and not known for their longevity. A common gripe with viewers in the 1950s and 1960s was that their 'tube had gone'.

CATHY COME HOME

UK (BBC) Drama. BBC 1 1966

Cathy Ward ....Carol White
Reg Ward ....Ray Brooks
Mrs Ward ....Winnifred Dennis

Writer: Jeremy Sandford. Producer: Tony Garnett

Documentary-style drama focusing on the plight of a homeless mother and her children.

Cathy Come Home was possibly the most important contribution made by *The Wednesday Play*. It told of Cathy, a young northern lass who made her way to the bright lights of London, met and married a local lad (Reg) and found herself mother of three young children (Sean, Stephen and Marlene). It revealed how the family was torn apart by the fact that they soon had no permanent roof over their heads, following Reg's accident at work and his subsequent struggle for employment. It showed how they lurched steadily downmarket, from a comfortable maisonette to Reg's mum's overcrowded, squalid tenement, to run-down lodgings, to a pokey caravan on an unhealthy site, to a derelict house and finally to a hostel for the homeless, where the father was separated from his wife and children. Physically torn apart, Cathy and Reg grew increasingly distant emotionally until he stopped paying for the family's keep and they were thrown onto the streets. The despair and helplessness experienced by Cathy as her kids were taken into care touched the hearts of viewers and led to angry calls for action to prevent such tragic circumstances. Shelter, the homeless charity, was able to capitalize on the furore and become an important voice in housing matters.

The play was directed by Ken Loach who used documentary, news-style camera angles and hand-held cameras in the search for realism. The soundtrack was punctuated with urban noise and scenes were kept short and snappy to avoid over-dramatization. Housing facts and figures were quoted throughout the play, adding a political commentary to the events in view.

C.A.T.S. EYES

UK (TVS) Detective Drama. ITV 1985–7

Maggie Forbes ....Jill Gascoine
Pru Standfast ....Rosalyn Landor
Frederica 'Fred' Smith ....Leslie Ash
Nigel Beaumont ....Don Warrington
Tessa Robinson.............................Tracy-Louise Ward

Creator: Terence Feely. Executive Producer: Rex Firkin. Producers: Dickie Bamber, Frank Cox, Raymond Menmuir

A female detective agency is really a front for a Home Office security team.

This was the story of three intrepid girl agents – a sort of British *Charlie's Angels*. Head of the team was Pru Standfast, a tall Oxford graduate with a War Office background, renowned for her organizational abilities. Her colleagues were ex-policewoman Maggie Forbes and young computer buff Fred Smith. Forbes had 18 years of police experience behind her (see *The Gentle Touch*) and brought formal detection skills to the team. Smith, in addition to her computer wizardry, was an ace driver. Together they operated as the Eyes Enquiry Agency, a front for a Home Office investigation team known as Covert Activities Thames Section (C.A.T.S.). Their missions took them into the areas of international espionage, corruption, terrorism and organized crime, and supporting their efforts and keeping an eye on their work was Ministry man Nigel Beaumont. When the show returned for a second season, changes had been made. Most notably, Pru Standfast had gone, Forbes had taken over as leader and a new recruit, Tessa Robinson, had been added.

CATWEAZLE

UK (LWT) Children's Science Fiction. ITV 1970–1

Catweazle ....Geoffrey Bayldon
Carrot Bennett ....Robin Davis

Mr Bennett	Charles Tingwell
Sam	Neil McCarthy
Cedric Collingford	Gary Warren
Lord Collingford	Moray Watson
Lady Collingford	Elspet Gray
Groome	Peter Butterworth

Creator/Writer: Richard Carpenter. Executive Producer: Joy Whitby. Producers: Quentin Lawrence, Carl Mannin

An 11th-century wizard becomes stranded in the 20th century.

Catweazle, an alchemist in Norman times, was attempting to harness the power of flight when his magic failed him and he found himself transported 900 years into the future. In an age when man really could fly, this scrawny, rag-bag of a wizard was astounded and absorbed by simple, everyday objects. Items like the light bulb ('electrickery' as he called it) or the telephone ('telling bone') were simply beyond his comprehension. As he strove to find a way back to his own time, Catweazle was befriended by Carrot, a farmer's son, who soon discovered that life wasn't easy with an ancient magician in tow.

Despite, at last, finding a way home at the end of the first series, Catweazle promptly returned to our time for a second run, on this occasion arriving in the village of King's Farthing and finding a new ally in Cedric, son of Lord and Lady Collingford. Still struggling to master the art of flight, he now also sought the mystic 13th sign of the zodiac, which would enable him to return to his own age. Finally achieving his objective, Catweazle disappeared back into the past for good.

CAZENOVE, CHRISTOPHER (1945–)

Aristocratic British actor who, after success as Richard Gaunt in *The Regiment*, George Cornwallis-West in *Jennie, Lady Randolph Churchill* and as the Honourable Charles Tyrrell in *The Duchess of Duke Street*, flew to the USA to star as Ben Carrington in *Dynasty*. Among his other credits have been *The Rivals of Sherlock Holmes*, *Affairs of the Heart*, *Ladykillers*, *Jenny's War*, *Lou Grant* and *Kane and Abel*. Cazenove has been married to actress Angharad Rees.

CBS

CBS was, for many years, America's number-one network. Founded in 1927 as United Independent Broadcasters by Arthur Judson, the company quickly took on a partner, the Columbia Phonograph and Records Company, at the same time renaming itself Columbia Phonograph Broadcasting System. When the phonograph company withdrew because of mounting losses, the name was shortened to Columbia Broadcasting System (CBS). In 1929 William S. Paley bought control of the company and became its most influential executive. He remained on the board until 1983, leading CBS into television, aggressively signing up affiliate stations and making the network America's number one. In 1974 the company name was changed from Columbia Broadcasting System to CBS Inc. and various internal power struggles in the 1970s and 1980s ensued, reflecting CBS's fall from the top spot. The company diversified into publishing, toys and other interests and was finally taken over by the Tisch family, owners of the Loews Corporation. In its heyday CBS boasted the biggest stars and the top shows: *I Love Lucy*, *The Honeymooners*, *The Dick Van Dyke Show*, *All in the Family* and *M*A*S*H* all aired on CBS, and the station was also home to revered news journalists Ed Murrow and Walter Cronkite.

CELEBRITY SQUARES

UK (ATV/Central) Quiz. ITV 1975–9/1993–

Presenter: Bob Monkhouse

Producer: Paul Stewart Laing, Glyn Edwards, Peter Harris (1993)

Noughts and crosses quiz featuring show-business personalities.

In this light-hearted game show nine celebrities inhabited the squares of a giant (18 ft) noughts and crosses board. Two contestants took turns to nominate celebrities to answer general knowledge questions and then tried to work out if the celebrity's answer was right or wrong. If they guessed correctly, they won an X or an O for that space on the board and a line of three noughts or three crosses earned cash and prizes. Quick-fire gags and contrived answers abounded as the quiz element played second fiddle to comedy. Kenny Everett provided the wacky voice-overs. The celebrities taking part in the first show were Diana Dors, Leslie Crowther, Aimi McDonald, Alfred Marks, Vincent Price, Hermione Gingold, Terry Wogan, Arthur Mullard and William Rushton.

One segment of the programme saw the tables turned on host Bob Monkhouse. Each celebrity fired a question at him and his correct answers collected money for charity. *Celebrity Squares*, which was revived in 1993 after a 14-year absence, was a copy of the popular American game show *Hollywood Squares*.

CENTRAL INDEPENDENT TELEVISION

The ITV contractor for the Midlands, Central Independent Television came into being as a restructured version of ATV, which previously held the Midlands franchise. It went on air on 1 January 1982 and retained its franchise in 1991 with a bid of just £2000 (there were no challengers). Central has since been taken over by Carlton Communications, the franchise holder for London weekdays, which already had a minority holding in Central. Central's two studio bases are in Birmingham and Nottingham, and among the company's many programming successes have been **Auf Wiedersehen, Pet**, **Crossroads**, **Blockbusters**, **The Price Is Right** and **Spitting Image**.

CHALMERS, JUDITH (1935–)

British presenter and announcer, host of ITV's travelogue **Wish You Were Here?** since 1974. Chalmers began her career as a child actor at the age of 13, working on BBC Radio's *Children's Hour*, and her later radio credits have included *Family Favourites*, *Woman's Hour* and her own Radio 2 morning show. On TV she has been seen on **Come Dancing**, *After Noon Plus* and various beauty contests, including **Miss World**.

CHAMBERLAIN, RICHARD (1935–)

1960s heart-throb actor with boyish looks, gaining international fame as the dedicated young **Dr Kildare**. Although initially typecast after playing Kildare for five years, Chamberlain has since managed to break into other starring roles in film and on TV, often in mini-series and most notably in *The Count of Monte Cristo*, *The Man in the Iron Mask*, as Alexander McKeag in *Centennial*, as the English captain John Blackthorne (or Anjin) in **Shogun** and as the troubled Australian priest Ralph de Bricassart in **The Thorn Birds**.

CHAMPION THE WONDER HORSE

US (Flying A) Children's Adventure. BBC 1956–7

Ricky North	Barry Curtis
Sandy North	Jim Bannon
Will Calhoun	Francis McDonald
Sheriff Powers	Ewing Mitchell

Executive Producer: Armand Schaefer.
Producer: Louis Gray

A 12-year-old boy and his multi-talented horse find adventure in the Wild West.

Ricky North lived on his Uncle Sandy's North Ranch, somewhere in Texas in the 1880s. His pride and joy was Champion, once leader of a herd of wild horses and now domesticated to the point where Ricky (but noone else) could safely ride him. From the very first episode, when Champion hauled Ricky to safety with a rope looped around his neck, it was clear that this was no ordinary nag. Indeed, the haughty stallion continued to earn his keep, constantly foiling criminals, alerting his owner to freak natural disasters and generally keeping the young boy out of trouble. Rebel, Ricky's German Shepherd dog, also lent a paw from time to time.

The series (known in America, and sometimes billed in the UK, as *The Adventures of Champion*) was created by Gene Autrey in celebration of Champion, who was his own horse. Only 26 episodes were ever made.

CHAMPIONS, THE

UK (ITC) Science Fiction. ITV 1968–9

Craig Stirling	Stuart Damon
Sharon McCready	Alexandra Bastedo
Richard Barrett	William Gaunt
Comander W.L. Tremayne	Anthony Nicholls

Creators: Monty Berman, Dennis Spooner.
Producer: Monty Berman

Three superhumans help maintain peace in the world.

In this '**Six Million Dollar Man** meets *Lost Horizon*' caper, American Craig Stirling and Britons Sharon McCready and Richard Barrett worked for the international peace agency Nemesis. But these were no ordinary secret agents. Having suffered a plane crash in the Himalayas on a mission to China, they had been saved and healed by an old man from a reclusive Tibetan civilization. Endowed with superhuman powers, they found that their senses had been fine-tuned so that they could hear, see and smell acutely. They also had enhanced strength and stamina, and special mental powers like telepathy.

Promising to preserve the lost city's anonymity, the trio returned to the West and began to use their remarkable talents on behalf of Nemesis. Their boss, Tremayne (who was based in Geneva), issued them with assignments aimed at diffusing international flashpoints and potential sources of world tension. The aim was to maintain the existing balance of power between nations. The agents' special attributes, however, always remained a secret and they were certainly not infallible or invincible, needing to work very much as a team. Although they were as mortal as any other human, they became 'Champions of law, order and justice'.

The series was re-run on BBC 2 in 1995.

CHANNEL

The frequency allocated to a TV service.

CHANNEL 4

Britain finally received its fourth channel in 1982, after years of debate. Channel 4 was set up as a wholly owned subsidiary of the IBA, with the brief to serve minority interests and encourage innovation through programming supplied by outside independent producers. Its first chief executive was Jeremy Isaacs and he 'sugared the pill' of minority programming by buying in popular overseas series like *Cheers* and *The Paul Hogan Show*. The channel – first airing on 2 November 1982 – proved more successful than doubters had predicted. Some felt that its narrow target audience would not generate sufficient advertising revenue. However, it did so well that the basis of its advertising sales was changed in 1993. Whereas sales were originally the responsibility of the other ITV companies, who then paid for the upkeep of Channel 4 through a levy on their incomes, since 1993 Channel 4 has sold its own advertising.

Channel 4 has always courted controversy and provided a valuable mouthpiece for minority groups but it has also excelled at commissioning award-winning films. *My Beautiful Launderette* and *Room With a View* are just two examples. The first programme seen on Channel 4 was *Countdown*, which is still being screened today. Equally durable has been the revolutionary soap *Brookside*, and other Channel 4 successes have included *The Tube*, *GBH*, *The Far Pavilions* and *Channel 4 News*. Michael Grade has been chief executive since 1989, following Jeremy Isaacs's departure to become Director of the Royal Opera House, at Covent Garden.

Channel 4 does not cover Wales, which is served by a bilingual channel, **S4C**.

CHANNEL TELEVISION

The smallest of the ITV contractors, Channel Television went on air on 1 September 1962 to serve the various Channel Islands (which were represented in the company's first logo of six linked hexagons). Early on there were serious doubts as to whether such a small audience would generate enough advertising income to keep an independent television service alive, but Channel is still afloat after over 30 years. (A reflection of the size of the area was the fact that the company retained its franchise in the 1991 auctions with a bid of just £1000.) To make ends meet, at various times Channel has been forced to link up with Westward, TSW, TVS and Meridian for advertising sales and administration. These companies have also been the suppliers of ITV national output to Channel, beaming programmes over the English Channel for relay by local transmitters.

Another consequence of low advertising turnover has been the almost negligible contribution Channel has been able to make to network programming (the most prominent examples have been editions of *About Britain* and **Highway**), although Channel – or CTV, as it has become known – has won many fans for its local news and regional documentary service, including some programmes in French and Portuguese. The station mascot, Oscar Puffin, has enjoyed his own children's series, *Puffin's Pla(i)ce*, for many years.

CHANNEL 3 (ITV)

Independent television arrived in the UK in 1955 after years of debate. There were widespread fears that commercial television would turn out to be a vulgar and gimmicky concept, fears which were stimulated by the American experience where sponsors and game shows ruled the airwaves. Nevertheless, the Television Act of 1954 bravely opened up the television market to an advertising-led channel.

This channel was controlled and regulated by a public body, the Independent Television Authority (ITA), who owned the transmitters, oversaw programme standards and monitored advertising. A federal system was conceived for broadcasters. For coverage, each part of the UK was carved up into regions. Independent companies then applied for sole transmission rights, selling advertising to generate revenue and paying a levy to the ITA for their licences. The first ITV region to go on air was London, where the franchise was split into weekdays and weekends. Associated-Rediffusion was awarded the Monday to Friday contract, with ATV handling Saturday and Sunday. The first transmission was on 22 September 1955, when Associated-Rediffusion and ATV jointly held a Gala Opening Night, beginning with a formal inauguration ceremony at London's Guildhall. The new channel was known by a number of names, the most common being CTV, Channel 9 or ITA.

Piecemeal, the other elements of the ITV network fell into place until, by 1962, nearly all of the UK, including the Channel Islands, was covered (the one exception, the Isle of Man, followed in 1965). The ITV companies were closely monitored for performance and over the years several franchise reviews were held. In 1964 all the companies passed muster (except for Wales West and North, which had gone out of business). In 1967 there were several changes. ATV was given the Midlands on a seven-day-a-week basis, and Associated-Rediffusion and ABC (the contractor for the Midlands and the north at weekends) were asked to merge to take on the London weekday franchise. This they did under the name of Thames Television. London at weekends was given to London Weekend Television (LWT). In Wales and the west, TWW lost its licence to Harlech Television and in the north, Granada was allowed to extend its transmission times from five to seven days a week, but had to relinquish the area east of the Pennines to a new franchisee (ultimately Yorkshire Television). In 1980 there were more changes. Out went Westward Television (the contractor for the south-west) and Southern (southern England), to be replaced by TSW and TVS respectively. At the same time ATV was obliged to reconstitute itself as Central Independent Television to hang on to the Midlands area.

For the next round of franchise renewals a new system was brought into play by the Conservative Government. Instead of merely applying for the licence to broadcast, prospective ITV companies were asked to bid for the franchise. This was designed to extract more money from ITV companies, which the Government felt were operating advertising monopolies in their individual areas. Under the new system, the highest bidder would get the franchise, provided that the new regulatory body, the ITC, was happy with the business plan and the commitment to programme quality. In highly controversial circumstances, Thames was outbid by Carlton Communications and lost its franchise. However, Granada was outbid by Mersey Television but retained its franchise. Other losers were TVS and TSW (both deemed to have overbid) and these gave way to Meridian and Westcountry respectively. TV-am, the breakfast-time contractor appointed in 1980, lost out to Sunrise Television (soon to be renamed GMTV). The farcicality of the situation was further outlined when it was revealed that Central (unopposed in its application) secured the profitable Midlands area with a bid of just £2000. Since this restructuring, ITV has been known as Channel 3.

CHAPPELL, ERIC (1933–)

British comedy writer, responsible for some of ITV's most popular sitcoms. These have included *Rising Damp*, *The Squirrels*, *The Bounder*, *Only When I Laugh*, *Singles* and *Duty Free* (the last two in collaboration with Jean Warr).

CHAPMAN, GRAHAM (1941–89)

Tall, satirical comedian, a qualified doctor and stalwart of the *Monty Python* team, for whom his speciality was the starchy but slightly silly army colonel. Previously Chapman had been seen with John Cleese and others in *At Last the 1948 Show* and he was also a prolific writer for other series (usually in conjunction with Cleese). His script credits included *The Frost Report*, *Marty* and the *Doctor in the House* sequence of sitcoms, as well as the Ronnie Corbett series *No – That's Me Over Here*, *Now Look Here . . .* and *The Prince of Denmark* (with Barry Cryer).

CHARACTER GENERATOR

A device for superimposing text (captions, names, etc.) on to the TV picture. Also known as a caption generator or by tradenames like Anchor and Aston.

CHARLIE CHAN see *New Adventures of Charlie Chan, The.*

CHARLIE'S ANGELS

US (Spelling-Goldberg) Detective Drama. ITV 1977–82

Sabrina Duncan	Kate Jackson
Jill Munroe	Farrah Fawcett-Majors
Kelly Garrett	Jaclyn Smith
Kris Munroe	Cheryl Ladd
Tiffany Welles	Shelley Hack
Julie Rogers	Tanya Roberts
John Bosley	David Doyle
Charlie Townsend (voice only)	John Forsythe

Executive Producers: Aaron Spelling, Leonard Goldberg. Producer: Rick Husky, David Levinson, Barney Rosenzweig

Three beautiful ex-policewomen work undercover for a mysterious detective agency boss.

'Once upon a time there were three girls who went to the police academy and they were each assigned very hazardous duties. But I took them away from all that and now they work for me. My name is Charlie.' So stated the opening titles of this glitzy detective series in which Sabrina Duncan, Kelly Garrett and Jill Monroe were the original team of Angels. Sabrina, nominal leader of the trio, was a multilinguist, Kelly was a former showgirl, while Jill was an athletic blonde. Together they had been hired by Charlie Townsend of Townsend Investigations, a Los Angeles detective agency. Charlie himself was never seen, only heard on the telephone (and in the intro), leaving the avuncular John Bosley to act as the girls' personal contact.

The Angels were able to take on missions that were out of bounds for most other investigators. Their stunning looks allowed them to work undercover (often with little cover), as night club singers, models, strippers and even army recruits. Although their assignments were rough and dangerous, the girls' appearance was never less than immaculate, and their skimpy outfits (often without bras) led to *Charlie's Angels* being labelled the doyen of 'jiggly' TV.

The first changes in the series came with the departure of Farrah Fawcett-Majors (later just Fawcett after her divorce from Lee Majors) to pursue a film career. She did agree to make occasional guest appearances but her permanent replacement was Alan Ladd's daughter-in-law, Cheryl, as Jill's younger sister, Kris. Two more Angels were also brought in. Tiffany Welles, daughter of a Connecticut police chief, took over from Sabrina, then she, in turn, was replaced by Julie Rogers. The voice of the enigmatic Charlie was actually provided by John Forsythe, later Blake Carrington in *Dynasty*.

CHARLTON, MICHAEL (1927–)

Australian-born journalist who became one of *Panorama*'s most prominent presenters after arriving in the UK as a cricket commentator in the 1950s. He also reported on NASA's Apollo missions.

CHARMER, THE

UK (LWT) Drama. ITV 1987

Ralph Ernest Gorse	Nigel Havers
Donald Stimpson	Bernard Hepton
Joan Plumleigh-Bruce	Rosemary Leach
Clarice Mannors	Fiona Fullerton
Alison Warren	Judy Parfitt
Pamela Bennett	Abigail McKern

Writer: Allan Prior. Executive Producer: Nick Elliott. Producer: Philip Hinchcliffe

A suave, young con merchant wins the hearts of wealthy ladies.

Ralph Gorse was a cad. Exercising his skill at smooth talk, he worked his way around the seaside resorts of 1930s Britain preying on rich, gullible ladies who could not resist his good looks and gentle manner. No sooner had they taken him to their hearts than he was away with the family silver or at least a wallet full of 'borrowed' notes. It all worked very well until he deceived the delightfully tweedy Joan Plumleigh-Bruce, whose estate agent friend Donald Stimpson took exception and promised revenge. The series was based on the books by Patrick Hamilton.

CHARTERS AND CALDICOTT

UK (BBC/Network Seven) Detective Drama. BBC 1 1985

Charters	Robin Bailey
Caldicott	Michael Aldridge

Writer: Keith Waterhouse. Producer: Ron Craddock

Two retired old buffers immerse themselves in murder.

Appearing initially as bit characters in Hitchcock's *The Lady Vanishes* in 1938, Charters and Caldicott were portrayed by actors Basil Radford and Naunton Wayne as a couple of well-meaning, upper-class twits with no grasp of reality. Their eccentric, Englishmen abroad roles simply brought a touch of comic relief to an otherwise spooky and melodramatic tale. Soon afterwards, however, they resurfaced in another cameo role in *Night Train to Munich*, before gaining top billing in their own vehicle, *Crooks' Tour* in 1940. Over 40 years later they became stars of their own BBC series.

Now in retirement, the two perpetual schoolboys were played by Robin Bailey and Michael aldridge. They enjoyed regular monthly lunches at their Pall Mall club, where they discussed the inadequacies of women, the wonders of cricket and how things simply weren't as they used to be. Strictly public school, they pitied people who didn't share their backgrounds and interests, and voiced prejudiced concerns about the state of the world. Charters, a widower, lived in a country cottage near Reigate and religiously hailed a Green Line bus on the first Friday of every month to meet his chum Caldicott at his residence in Viceroy Court, Kensington. However, when a girl's body was discovered at Caldicott's flats, the old buffers found themselves embarking on the trail of a murderer.

CHAT SHOW see talk show.

CHATAWAY, CHRISTOPHER (1931–)

Middle-distance athlete turned broadcaster who read the news for ITN in its early days. He later joined the BBC's *Panorama* before switching to politics and becoming a Conservative MP and subsequently Postmaster General. He was the BBC's first *Sports Personality of the Year*, in 1954.

CHEATERS, THE

UK (Danziger) Detective Drama. ITV 1960–2

John Hunter	John Ireland
Walter Allen	Robert Ayres

Producers: Edward J. Danziger, Harry Lee Danziger

The investigations of an insurance inspector.

The door-to-door enquiries of claims inspector John Hunter formed the basis of this series. Diligent and honest, Hunter and his assistant, Walter Allen, were relentless in their pursuit of nasty people who were swindling his company, the Eastern Insurance Company, at the ultimate expense of decent policy holders. Those who attempted crafty frauds and fiddles were quickly sussed out. Star John Ireland went on to play Jed Colby in *Rawhide*.

CHECKLAND, MICHAEL, SIR (1936–)

BBC Director-General from 1987 to 1993, when he was succeeded in rather controversial circumstances by his former deputy, John Birt. Checkland had previously been Deputy Director-General himself (from 1985) and was an expert in the financial affairs of the Corporation, joining the BBC in 1964 as an accountant and working his way up to chief accountant status. In 1977 he became controller of planning and resource management for the television division. The announcement (surprisingly well in advance) of John Birt's promotion to the Director-General position made Checkland's last two years in the position somewhat uncomfortable and led some commentators to label him a lame duck controller.

CHEERS

US (Paramount) Situation Comedy. Channel 4
1982–93

Sam Malone	Ted Danson
Diane Chambers	Shelley Long
Carla Tortelli/LeBec	Rhea Perlman
Ernie Pantusso ('Coach')	Nicholas Colasanto
Norm Peterson	George Wendt
Cliff Clavin	John Ratzenberger
Dr Frasier Crane	Kelsey Grammar
Woody Boyd	Woody Harrelson
Rebecca Howe	Kirstie Alley
Dr Lilith Sternin/Crane	Bebe Neuwirth
Janet Eldridge	Kate Mulgrew
Evan Drake	Tom Skerritt
Eddie LeBec	Jay Thomas
Robin Colcord	Roger Rees
Kelly Gaines/Boyd	Jackie Swanson
John Hill	Keene Curtis
Paul	Paul Willson

Creators/Producers: Glen Charles, Les Charles, James Burrows

Award-winning comedy centring around the staff and regulars at a Boston bar.

Cheers bar (established 1895) was owned by former Boston Red Sox pitcher Sam 'Mayday' Malone, a reformed alcoholic and a successful womanizer. But he met his match in the first episode of this cult comedy with the arrival of Diane Chambers, an over-educated academic researcher. Ditched by her husband-to-be, she accepted Sam's offer of a job as a waitress, a move which led to years of good-natured sparring and on-off relationships with her boss.

Revolving around Sam and Diane's intermittent romance were the lives of the other staff and bar regulars. Carla Tortelli, a sharp-tongued, streetwise mother of many, was the perfect antidote to the sophisticated Diane, and Ernie Pantusso, the mild-mannered ex-Red Sox coach, was another leading character in the show's early years. His naivety and absent-mindedness were much missed when actor Nicholas Colasanto died in 1985, but the gap was soon filled with the arrival of Woody Boyd, a young farmboy from the backwaters of Hanover, Indiana. He came to Boston to meet Coach, his pen-pal, took a job behind the bar and eventually married the extremely wealthy but rather dizzy Kelly Gaines.

Woody's innocence and gullibility were genially abused by regulars Norm, Cliff and Frasier. Norm, an accountant, spent most of his waking life in Cheers savouring freedom from his wife, Vera, while know-all Cliff, the mailman, was the butt of all the jokes. The third regular was Frasier Crane, an insecure psychiatrist who was introduced as Diane's new fiancé. However, their relationship broke up and the pompous, emotional shrink joined Cliff and Norm as one of the losers hugging the bar. He eventually found his perfect partner in a severe, intellectual colleague, Dr Lilith Sternin, and they had a son, Frederick.

Four years into its run *Cheers* was forced into a major recast. Not only had Coach died but Diane, too, said goodbye to the bar – and to Sam – taking herself away for six months to write a book. Sam knew that she would not return, so he sold the bar to a leisure conglomerate, bought a boat and planned to sail around the world. When the next series opened, Sam's boat had sunk and he had returned to Cheers to talk his way into a job. Only this time he was just a member of staff, responsible to sultry new manageress Rebecca Howe. Another love-hate relationship began.

Frigid and sycophantic, Rebecca was a real career-chaser. For a while she pursued company bigwig Evan Drake, then her attention turned to smarmy English businessman Robin Colcord. When Colcord used her to gain inside knowledge of her company in order to launch a takeover bid, Sam shopped him and was given his bar back for only $1. Rebecca stayed on as manageress and later as a partner.

In the extended final episode of *Cheers*, Diane walked back into Sammy's life. Her book had been published and had picked up a major award, but she and Sam could still not make their relationship work and she left once more. This time, it was clearly for good.

Although the inside shots of the bar were studio produced, the exterior of Cheers was a real

Boston bar, The Bull and Finch, which now does a roaring tourist trade. After 11 years one element of *Cheers* was allowed to live on as Frasier, now separated from Lilith, was given his own spin-off series, *Frasier*.

CHEF!

UK (APC/Crucial) Situation Comedy. BBC 1
1993–

Gareth Blackstock	Lenny Henry
Janice Blackstock	Caroline Lee Johnson
Everton	Roger Griffiths
Lucinda	Claire Skinner
Piers	Gary Parker
Otto	Erkan Mustafa
Lola	Elizabeth Bennett
Gustave	Ian McNeice
Donald	Gary Bakewell
Crispin	Tim Matthews
Alice	Hilary Lyon
Debra	Pui Fan Lee
Alphonse	Jean Luc Rebaliati

Creator: Lenny Henry. Writer: Peter Tilbury. Executive Producer: Polly McDonald. Producer: Charlie Hanson

An ambitious but egocentric chef strives to succeed in his own restaurant.

Gareth Blackstock was the gifted chef de cuisine at Le Château Anglais, a stately French restaurant deep in the Oxfordshire Cotswolds. When the Château fell into financial difficulties, he and his wife, Janice, sold Linden Cottage, their picture-postcard home, and bought control themselves. Keen to build on his Michelin two-star status, Blackstock found his ambitions hindered by his inept kitchen hands, especially the accident-prone soul food specialist Everton. No one escaped the chef's fits of pique, as he lambasted staff and customers alike with pearls of sarcastic abuse. But, although he ruled with a rod of iron, Gareth, deep-down, nursed a fragile ego.

Well supported by a team of top chef advisors, particularly John Burton-Race, Lenny Henry and writer Peter Tilbury brought viewers a revealing insight into the world of a top kitchen, with its exacting standards and finest attention to detail, gently parodying the celebrity status of Britain's leading chefs.

CHEGWIN, KEITH (1957–)

Former child actor and pop musician (in the band Kenny), whose earliest appearances were in pro-grammes like *Junior Showtime*, *The Liver Birds*, *The Tomorrow People*, *The Wackers* (as Raymond Clarkson) and *Open All Hours*. In 1976 his big break came with *Multi-Coloured Swap Shop*, for which he was roving reporter/entertainer. He

stayed with the Saturday morning show when it evolved into *Saturday Superstore*, marrying one of his co-presenters, Maggie Philbin (they have since separated). His own kids' music show, *Cheggers Plays Pop*, followed, as well as a couple of investigative series, *Cheggers' Action Reports* and *Cheggers Checks It Out*. Most recently he has con-centrated on writing theme music and commer-cial scores, though still appearing on Sky and *The Big Breakfast* (once again out and about, knock-ing on doors). Chegwin is the brother of radio presenter Janice Long.

CHELSEA AT NINE

UK (Granada) Variety. ITV 1957–60

Producer: Denis Forman

International cabaret direct from a London theatre.

Chelsea at Nine was Monday night's big variety offering, presented by Granada Television from its Chelsea Palace theatre. It showcased top transatlantic stars (the likes of Billie Holliday, Alan Young and Ferrante and Teicher appeared), with American directors employed to give the show an international sheen. As well as major entertain-ment names of the day the programme included regular comedy skits from the team of Mai Zetterling, Dennis Price and Irene Handl, while The Granadiers were the house song- and-dance troupe. With a timing change, the series became *Chelsea at Eight* in 1958 and, in the same year, adopted the title of *Chelsea Summertime* for its sea-sonal programmes.

CHESNEY, RONALD

British comedy writer, usually in tandem with Ronald Wolfe. Together they penned *The Rag Trade*, *Meet the Wife*, *The Bed-Sit Girl*, *Sorry I'm Single*, *Wild, Wild Women*, *On the Buses* and episodes of *'Allo 'Allo*. Chesney also collaborated with Marty Feldman on the 1950s series *Educating Archie*.

CHEYENNE

US (Warner Brothers) Western. ITV 1958–

Cheyenne Bodie	Clint Walker
Bronco Layne	Ty Hardin
Smitty	L.Q. Jones

A wanderer works his way across the American West.

Based on the 1947 film of the same name starring Dennis Morgan, *Cheyenne* related the adventures of Cheyenne Bodie, a drifter who travelled the Wild West in the years following the Civil War. The hero was a frontier scout, a strapping giant of a man who had learnt Indian skills and who now strayed from town to town, from job to job and from girl to girl. Constantly falling foul of outlaws and villains, Bodie was often on the receiving end of a severe beating. He did, however, enjoy some friendly company during the first series in the shape of Smitty, a mapmaker.

Of as much interest as the programme itself were the behind the scenes wrangles. When Clint Walker walked out after a legal dispute with Warner Brothers, he was temporarily replaced in the lead by Ty Hardin as Bronco Layne. When Walker was reinstated, Hardin was not dropped but given his own spin-off series, **Bronco**.

CHIEF, THE

UK (Anglia Films) Police Drama. ITV 1990–

Chief Constable John Stafford	Tim Pigott-Smith
Assistant Chief Constable Anne Stewart	Karen Archer
Dr Elizabeth Stafford	Judy Loe
Detective Chief Supt Jim Gray	Eamon Boland
Emma Stafford	Sara Griffiths
Tim Stafford	Ross Livingstone
Martin Stewart	David Cardy
Assistant Chief Constable/ Chief Constable Alan Cade	Martin Shaw
Detective Chief Supt Sean McCloud	Stuart McGugan
Nigel Crimmond	Michael Cochrane
Colin Fowler	T.P. McKenna
Alison Dell	Ingrid Lacey
Andrew Blake	Julian Glover
Doc Wes Morton	Bosco Hogan
Detective Supt Rose Penfold	Gillian Bevan
Sam Lester	Davyd Harries
PC Charlie Webb	Brian Bovell

Creator: Jeffrey Caine. Executive Producer: Brenda Reid. Producers: Ruth Boswell, John Davies

The problems facing the Chief Constable of a regional police force.

When John Stafford gained promotion to the rank of Chief Constable of Eastland, an East Anglian police force, he quickly made himself a number of enemies. Bringing with him Anne Stewart, his CID supremo from Nottinghamshire, and promoting her to Head of Crime and Operations was not a good start, and immediately triggered resentment among Eastland's long-serving officers. But when the outspoken Chief began to lay down the law on police drinking and aggressive police driving, and then refused to ban a student protest against a visiting Government minister, he was made very aware of the disillusionment all around him, including from those who had appointed him. However, *The Chief* was also a personal drama, revealing how Stafford coped with the pressures of office,

how he and his doctor wife, Elizabeth, struggled to keep their teenage kids in check, and how Anne's marriage foundered when her husband, Martin, began to resent her devotion to work.

After two seasons a major cast change was enforced. Stafford moved to a job with Europol in Brussels and the race to replace him was won by the smart, ambitious Metropolitan Police officer Alan Cade, another man set to ruffle feathers in Eastland. First to take umbrage was Anne, who had been overlooked for the job. Some biting home truths from Alison Dell, Cade's PR consultant, helped him sharpen up his act.

This was not a standard cops and robbers series. Instead of dwelling on day-to-day routine police work, it focused on the principles and policies of crime prevention, homing in on the crucial decisions that an officer at the top of the ladder has to make. For authenticity, John Alderson, former Chief Constable of Devon and Cornwall, acted as advisor.

CHIGLEY see *Camberwick Green*.

CHILDREN IN NEED

UK (BBC) Telethon. BBC 1 1980–

Presenters:
Terry Wogan
Esther Rantzen
Sue Cook

Star-studded annual appeal marathon.

From humble origins on radio on Christmas Day 1927, *Children in Need* has progressed to become one of the highlights of the British TV year, taking over BBC 1's entire evening schedule (apart from the news) on the third Friday in November. The first major TV appeal was held in 1980, when the now established format was launched, involving seven hours of live television. Terry Wogan and Esther Rantzen (later replaced by Sue Cook) were the first hosts, with the assistance of Andi Peters in recent years and numerous celebrity guests. Esther Rantzen has also welcomed the year's Children of Courage, and BBC regional presenters have taken charge of the numerous opt-out segments, which have covered fund-raising events locally. Throughout the evening, appeals for cash donations to help deprived children have been made, with running totals announced on a regular basis. Family-orientated stunts have filled the early part of the programme, with a more mellow atmosphere prevailing towards the closedown at around 2 am. After midnight, stars of West End shows have tended to drop in with buckets of cash collected from their own audiences. The 1980 appeal raised £1.2 million, but in the years around the turn of the 1990s more than £20 million was the norm. Reports on how the money has been spent have been shown in the following year's programme. The appeal's mascot has been Pudsey, a forlorn-looking, bandaged teddy bear.

CHILDREN'S CHANNEL,

The (TCC) Satellite and cable channel specifically aimed at the younger end of the market (largely the under-tens, but also early teens). It began life on cable on 1 September 1984 and became part of the Sky Multi-Channels package on the Astra 1C satellite in September 1993. It is also beamed from the Thor satellite. The 11-hours-a-day (6 am to 5 pm) schedule is filled with a mixture of newly commissioned programmes and bought-in old and new material (including pre-school programmes like **Sesame Street** and *The Adventures of Rosie and Jim*, and the Australian drama *Heartbreak High*). The Children's Channel is jointly owned by Flextech (75 per cent) and TCI (25 per cent).

CHINESE DETECTIVE, THE

UK (BBC) Police Drama. BBC 1 1981–2

Detective Sgt Johnny Ho ....David Yip
Detective Chief Inspector Berwick ....Derek Martin
Detective Sgt Donald Chegwyn ....Arthur Kelly
Joe Ho ....Robert Lee

Creator: Ian Kennedy Martin. Producer: Terence Williams

Life on the beat for an ethnic copper.

Britain's first Chinese police hero was Detective Sgt Johnny Ho. He had joined the police partly as a means of clearing his father's name, but had been refused entry to the Metropolitan Police on grounds of height. Finding a way in elsewhere, Ho managed to work his way back to London's Limehouse district, where he found the going tough and his colleagues unsupportive. A natural loner, he encountered plenty of harassment, not least from his rigid boss, DCI Berwick, who hated his scruffy appearance and sloppy behaviour. To bring Ho back into line, he paired him with experienced sergeant Donald Chegwyn.

The Chinese Detective came from the pen of *The Sweeney* creator Ian Kennedy Martin. Not surprisingly the real police did not appreciate the suggestion that racism existed in the ranks, whether intentional or not.

CHIPS

US (MGM) Police Drama. ITV 1979–

Officer Francis 'Ponch' Poncherello ....Erik Estrada
Officer Jonathan Baker............................Larry Wilcox

Sgt Joe Getraer..Robert Pine
Officer Gene Fritz ....Lew Saunders
Officer Baricza ....Brodie Greer
Officer Sindy Cahill ....Brianne Leary
Harlan..Lou Wagner
Officer Grossman ....Paul Linke
Officer Bonnie Clark ....Randi Oakes
Officer Turner ....Michael Dorn
Officer Steve McLeish..............................Bruce Jenner
Officer Bobby 'Hot Dog' Nelson ....Tom Reilly
Officer Kathy Linahan ....Tina Gayle
Cadet Bruce Nelson................................Bruce Penhall
Officer Webster ....Clarence Gilyard, Jnr

Creator: Rick Rosner. Producers: Rick Rosner, Cy Chermak, Ric Randall

The adventures of two hunky police motorcyclists in and around Los Angeles.

Baker and Ponch worked as a team for the California Highway Patrol (CHiPS): the fair-haired Baker was the sensible, serious one, the swarthy Ponch was his devil-may-care partner, often falling foul of their boss, Sgt Getraer. They were both single and their private lives mingled with their crime fighting in every action-packed episode. The supporting cast included a mechanic, Harlan, and a sequence of female cops, beginning with Sindy Cahill (later replaced by Bonnie Clark and then Kathy Linahan).

At one point Erik Estrada fell into dispute with the programme's makers and was replaced by Olympic decathlon champion Bruce Jenner, who duly made way for Estrada when the matter was resolved. Larry Wilcox was the first to make a permanent break and Baker was written out before the final season. Ponch then gained a new partner, Bobby Nelson, and Nelson's brother, Bruce, was also seen, played by another sports star, speedway rider Bruce Penhall.

CHROMA KEY

Another term for colour separation overlay, i.e. the electronic technique that allows one colour in the picture (usually blue) to be filled with another image. It has been used over the years for studio backdrops and also for crude special effects. Blue is the most popular choice as it is least common in human skin colourings.

CHRONICLE

UK (BBC) Historical Documentary. BBC 2 1966–

Presenters: Glyn Daniel, Magnus Magnusson

Producer: Paul Johnstone

New developments in the world of history and archaeology.

This monthly educational series looked at the latest findings of the world's leading archaeologists and historians. Cambridge archaeologist (and former **Animal, Vegetable, Mineral?** chairman) Glyn Daniel was the first host, with a pre-**Mastermind** Magnus Magnusson taking over later.

CHRONICLES OF NARNIA, THE

UK (BBC) Children's Drama. BBC 1 1988–90

Peter Pevensie ....Richard Dempsey
Susan Pevensie ....Sophie Cook
Edmund Pevensie ....Jonathan R. Scott
Lucy Pevensie ....Sophie Wilcox
The White Witch............................Barbara Kellerman
Aslan (voice only).................................Ronald Pickup

Writer: Alan Seymour. Producer: Paul Stone

Adaptations of the classic children's fantasies by C.S. Lewis.

Employing a plethora of animal costumes and extensive special effects, the BBC set out to dramatize C.S. Lewis's epic stories of the fictitious world of Narnia. In the end, four of his seven books were covered, beginning with the first, *The Lion, the Witch and the Wardrobe* (cast as above). *Prince Caspian/ Voyage of the Dawn Treader* and *The Silver Chair* followed, with various changes in cast. A particular feature was the complicated human and mechanical operation of the giant lion, which represented Aslan, the awesome Narnia deity.

CHURCHILL, DONALD (1930–91)

British actor and playwright whose speciality was seedy middle-aged romantics. His writing credits included *Never a Cross Word* (with Michael Pertwee), *Moody and Pegg* (with Julia Jones), Charlie Drake's comedy *Who Is Sylvia?* (co-written with Drake) and an adaptation of Dickens's *Our Mutual Friend*. He also wrote for series like *Armchair Theatre* and *The Sweeney*. On screen, he starred in the 1958 sitcom *Trouble for Two* (as a cleaner), *Bulldog Breed* (as the hapless Tom Bowler), *Spooner's Patch* (as Inspector Spooner, succeeding Ronald Fraser), *The Awful Mr Goodall* (as spymaster Millbrook) and *Goodnight and God Bless* (as Ronnie Kemp, a game show host; also as co-writer with Joe McGrath). Among his other appearances were bits in *El C.I.D* (as Metcalf), *C.A.T.S. Eyes*, *Don't Wait Up*, *Bergerac* and *Stanley and the Women*. Churchill was married to actress Pauline Yates.

CINEMA

UK (Granada) Film Review. ITV 1964–75

Presenters:
Bamber Gascoigne
Derek Granger
Michael Scott
Mark Shivas
Michael Parkinson
Clive James
Brian Trueman

Producers: Derek Granger, John Hamp, Peter Wildeblood, Mark Shivas

Long-running weekly film magazine.

Eight years before Barry Norman began reviewing films in *Film 72*, Granada launched its own half-hour series revolving around the world of the silver screen. *Cinema* ran for 11 years and over 500 episodes, mixing critiques of the latest releases, interviews with film celebrities and some retrospective material. A common theme or a personality linked most items. Its first host, Bamber Gascoigne, occupied the presenter's chair for just three months, and the best-remembered frontmen have been later incumbents Mike Scott and Michael Parkinson. The programme's natural 'successor' was the junior film magazine *Clapperboard* (also from Granada), hosted by Chris Kelly, which began in 1972 and ran for ten years.

CIRCUS BOY

US (Herbert B. Leonard/Screen Gems) Children's Adventure. BBC 1957–8

Corky ....Mickey Braddock
Joey...Noah Beery, Jnr
Big Tim Champion..............................Robert Lowery
Hank Miller..Leo Gordon
Little Tom...Billy Barty
Swifty ....Olin Howlin
Barker...Eddie Marr
Pete ....Guinn Williams
Col Jack ....Andy Clyde
Elmer Purdy ....Sterling Holloway

Producers: Herbert B. Leonard, Norman Blackburn

The turn-of-the-century adventures of a 12-year-old orphan taken in by a colourful travelling circus.

When little Corky's parents had been killed in a high-wire act, he was adopted by Big Tim Champion, proprietor of the Champion Circus. Earning his keep by acting as water boy for Bimbo, the baby elephant, Corky was surrounded by a giant, colourful family, including Little Tom, the midget, Joey, the clown, and animals like Sultan, the Tiger, and Nuba, the Lion. As the circus moved from town to town, so each story unfolded.

Mickey Braddock later achieved considerably more fame, under his real name of Dolenz, as drummer in The Monkees pop group.

CISCO KID, THE

US (The Cisco Company/Ziv) Children's
Western. BBC 1954

The Cisco Kid ....Duncan Renaldo
Pancho...Leo Carrillo

Producer: Philip N. Krasne

**The exploits of a Mexican Robin Hood
and his fat, smiling sidekick.**

In the late 19th century, the Cisco Kid and his
partner, Pancho, travelled around the south-west-
ern United States, helping the oppressed, thwarting bandits and steering clear of sheriffs and
deputies who thought that they were outlaws.
They kept violence to a minimum, with Cisco
confining himself to shooting guns from his
opponents' hands, sometimes aided by the totally
unathletic Pancho, who was an expert with the
whip.

Cisco was a ladies' man, a bit of a dandy, dressed
up in finely embroidered shirts and silver spurs.
He sported a giant sombrero and was quite a
charmer. Pancho's only affair, however, was with
his food. Cisco's horse was Diablo (with whom
star Duncan Renaldo continued to make personal appearances long after the show had ended),
while Pancho rode Loco, but they were two very
unlikely cowboys. Their adventures were largely
played for laughs and Pancho's abysmal grip of
the English language was milked to the full.

The Cisco Kid was created by writer O. Henry
and the character appeared in the cinema as early
as the 1920s. Duncan Renaldo had already played
the part in the movies before the TV series was
conceived and was in his 50s by the time it was
made. Leo Carrillo was even older, in his 70s.
Unusually for TV series of this period, it was
filmed in colour.

CITIZEN JAMES

UK (BBC) Situation Comedy. BBC 1960–2

Sidney Balmoral James ....Sid James
William 'Bill' Kerr ....Bill Kerr
Liz Fraser..Liz Fraser
Charlie ....Sydney Tafler

Writers: Ray Galton, Alan Simpson, Sid Green,
Dick Hills. Producers: Duncan Wood, John
Street, Ronald Marsh

**A London sponger takes on society and
usually gets beaten.**

Resuming his role as a Cockney layabout with
contempt for authority, Sid James branched out
from *Hancock's Half Hour* and into this series of
his own. His new sparring partners were Bill Kerr
and girlfriend Liz Fraser, the owner of a club.

Charlie, a bookie's sidekick, was added later in
the series when James set himself up as a champion of the underdog and fighter of lost causes
(usually with the wrong result).

CITIZEN SMITH

UK (BBC) Situation Comedy. BBC 1 1977–80

Walter Henry 'Wolfie' Smith ....Robert Lindsay
Ken Mills ....Mike Grady
Tucker ....Tony Millan
Anthony 'Speed' King ....George Sweeney
Shirley Johnson ....Cheryl Hall
Charlie Johnson................................Peter Vaughan
                                                          Tony Steedman
Florence Johnson...Hilda Braid
Harry Fenning ....Stephen Greif
Ronnie Lynch ....David Garfield

Creator/Writer: John Sullivan. Producers:
Dennis Main Wilson, Ray Butt

**The farcical exploits of a workshy Tooting
revolutionary.**

'Power to the People!' Wolfie Smith was the Che
Guevara of south-east London – or so he
believed. Sporting an Afghan coat and a commando beret, he was the guitar-strumming figurehead of the Tooting Popular Front (TPF), a
team of hapless Marxist freedom fighters whose
members totalled six in number. His right-hand
man was Ken, a weedy, vegetarian pacifist-cum-
Buddhist with whom he shared a flat above the
home of Charlie and Florence Johnson, the parents of Wolfie's girlfriend, Shirley. (Played by
Robert Lindsay's real wife, Cheryl Hall, Shirley
only appeared in the first three seasons, when she
worked in the Sounds Cool record shop.) Her
dad, a security guard at Haydon Electronics, was
an irascible social climbing Yorkshireman who
had no time for 'that bloody yeti', as he branded
Wolfie. (Peter Vaughan also left the series after
three years, handing the role to Tony Steedman.)
His dopy wife, on the other hand, was genuinely
fond of the lodger she mistakenly knew as 'Foxy'.

The other main characters in the TPF were
Tucker and Speed. Tucker, a nervous family man
with a formidable wife (June) and nine kids,
owned the van the gang used for their 'manoeuvres'. Speed was the team's hard man, a brainless,
violent thug who drifted in and out of jail.
Lurking in the background was the manor's Mr
Big, Harry Fenning, who was owner of Wolfie's
local, The Vigilante. Fenning was replaced in the
last series by the just as nasty, but cruelly hen-
pecked, Welsh gangster Ronnie Lynch.

Wolfie's cack-handed attempts at liberating the
proletariat, in between shirking jobs and cadging
pints, provided the focus for the series. 'Come
the glorious day,' he threatened, his enemies

would be lined up against the wall for a 'last fag,' then 'bop, bop, bop,' the struggle would be over. But with such inept ideas and such gormless allies, capitalism was never in any danger. After all, who was going to take notice of a revolutionary who rode a scooter?

Citizen Smith was John Sullivan's big break. The writer of **Only Fools and Horses**, **Just Good Friends**, **Dear John** and **Sitting Pretty** was working as a scene shifter at the BBC at the time. Convinced he could produce something better than the humourless sitcoms he was watching, he created the character of an ageing hippy turned working-class hero, whose support for Fulham was yet another lost cause. The script was taken up for an episode of **Comedy Playhouse** in 1977 and a full series was commissioned the same year.

CIVILISATION

UK (BBC) Documentary. BBC 2 1969

Presenter: Kenneth Clark

Producers: Michael Gill, Peter Montagnon

A chronicle of man's cultural development and the benefits and comforts it has brought to the world.

This documentary looked at history not from a perspective of dates and battles but through the ideas and values that shaped man over the centuries. Charting developments since the Dark Ages, Kenneth Clark's aim was to show viewers, through examples of art and architecture, how man had risen above the common beast, how he had discovered 'Civilisation'. The work was inspired by a fear that man was slipping back into moral chaos, and, by profiling men of genius – painters, thinkers, poets and musicians, people who had brought order to our lives – Clark sought to prove that we really were above all the hassles of the modern-day industrial society. Presented in an old-fashioned, simple style, shunning clever TV gimmickry and relying on good prose over well-framed images, the series was a remarkable success, especially considering the contemporary climate in which Andy Warhol, Jackson Pollock, The Beatles and Flower Power had asserted their heavy influence. Clark, a highbrow, learned art historian and former Chairman of the Independent Television Authority, became an unlikely TV hero, a status he did not in the least relish.

CLANGERS, THE

UK (Smallfilms) Children's Entertainment. BBC 1 1969–74

Creators/Writers/Producers: Oliver Postgate, Peter Firmin

The moral adventures of the mousey inhabitants of a blue planet.

Strange, pink and woolly, the Clangers were mouse-like creatures with pronounced noses and perky ears who lived inside a small blue planet. They wore personal suits of armour for protection from the many meteorites that broke through the thin atmosphere, and they took their name from the sound made when they battened down their dustbin-lid hatches and retreated underground. The Clangers spoke only in musical whistles – to each other and to the other inhabitants of their planet, the Soup Dragon and the Froglets. The Soup Dragon lived in the soup wells, where the Clangers' staple diet was obtained (they also ate Blue String Pudding), while the Froglets were small orange amphibians who lived in a deep pond and travelled around in a top hat. Also seen was the Iron Chicken, a metal bird that nested a little way out in space. The Clangers themselves were Major and Mother Clanger, Grandmother, Small and Tiny.

The Clangers' world was a little haven of peace and happiness. Apart from minor concerns like how to pick notes from music trees for Major Clanger's Music Boat, their only worries were occasional disturbances from aliens or stray alien inventions. These instances were used to moral effect, revealing just how happy uncluttered, modest lives could be. When, for instance, gold coins began to fall on the planet, the Clangers each built up their own secret hoard and avarice began to erode their harmonious existence. Thankfully, the coins were discovered to be chocolate and all was well again.

This five-minute, pre-evening news animation came from the Smallfilms duo of Oliver Postgate and Peter Firmin, who were also responsible for **Noggin the Nog**, **Pogles' Wood**, **Bagpuss** and **Ivor the Engine**.

CLAPPERBOARD see Cinema.

CLAPPERBOARD

A hinged marker board used during filming to indicate the title of the programme, the scene and the take. The board is hinged to allow its two parts to be 'clapped' together at the start of the take, the noise of the clap then being used to synchronize sound and vision tracks in editing. New electronic systems have gradually undermined the clapperboard's usefulness.

CLARENCE

UK (BBC) Situation Comedy. BBC 1 1988

Clarence Sale ....Ronnie Barker
Jane Travers ....Josephine Tewson

Writer: Bob Ferris. Producer: Mike Stephens

A short-sighted removals man sets up home in the country with an out-of-work parlour maid.

Londoner Clarence Sale, a middle-aged, self-employed removals man with his own company (Get A Move On), was clumsy and short-sighted. Not that this did anything to dampen his confidence. Meeting up with Jane Travers, an unemployed parlour maid to the rich, on Coronation Day 1937, he took her back to his Peckham flat for some fish and chips. There they began a gentle romance that developed when they moved out to the Oxfordshire countryside, taking up residence in a run-down cottage Travers had inherited from her aunt. The ensuing episodes revolved around Clarence's attempts to bed Travers, their acclimatization in the country and Clarence's abysmal eyesight.

CLARK, LORD KENNETH (1903–83)

British art historian whose 13-part *Civilisation* in 1969 became feted as a television masterpiece. The spin-off book proved equally as profitable for the BBC and was one of the first successful 'TV tie-ins'. Earlier in his life Clark had been Director of the National Gallery, worked for the Ministry of Information in World War II, assumed the chairmanship of the Arts Council and then became first Chairman of the Independent Television Authority (1954–7). In 1964 he presented the series *Great Temples of the World* and among his other contributions were talks on Rembrandt and series like *Landscape Into Art*, *Discovering Japanese Art*, *Pioneers of Modern Painting* and *Romantic v. Classic Art*. He was made a life peer in 1969 and one of his sons was former Conservative minister Alan Clark.

CLARKE, CECIL (1917–)

British television producer, working largely for ATV in the 1960s and 1970s, becoming Head of Drama and handling special projects such as the TV film *Brief Encounter* (1976). Among his credits have been *Crime of Passion*, *Edward the Seventh*, *Disraeli*, *Will Shakespeare* and the mini-series *I Remember Nelson*.

CLARKE, MARGI (1954–)

Blonde Liverpudlian actress, a former Granada presenter (*What's On*), mostly seen in coarse, down-to-earth roles such as Queenie in *Making Out*. The first series of her *Good Sex Guide* for Carlton in 1993 caused quite a stir. She is the sister of scriptwriter/director Frank Clarke.

CLARKE, ROY (1930–)

British comedy writer, a former policeman, responsible for such hits as *The Misfit*, *Last of the Summer Wine*, *Open All Hours*, *Rosie*, *Flickers*, *Pulaski*, *Potter*, *Keeping Up Appearances* and *Ain't Misbehavin'*. His humour is of the gentle nature, relying on shrewd observance of character, and most of his work has been set in his native Yorkshire. Clarke has also contributed to drama series like *Mr Rose* and *The Troubleshooters*.

CLARKE, WARREN

British actor, seen in a variety of roles (including comic) and most notably in the series *Shelley*, *The Jewel in the Crown*, *The Onedin Line*, *The Manageress*, *Nice Work*, *Gone to the Dogs*, *Gone to Seed* and *Moving Story*. His guest appearances have been many.

CLEESE, JOHN (1939–)

Tall British actor/comedian/writer, a Cambridge Footlights graduate who was already a TV legend thanks to *Monty Python's Flying Circus* when achieving even greater acclaim for his manic *Fawlty Towers* (as star and co-writer with wife Connie Booth). Pre-Python, Cleese had appeared with Ronnies Barker and Corbett in *The Frost Report*, and with Graham Chapman et al in *At Last the 1948 Show*. He had also written (mostly in collaboration with Chapman) for David Frost, *That Was The Week That Was*, *Marty* and the *Doctor in the House* series. His numerous guest appearances have taken in shows as diverse as *Whoops! Apocalypse*, *Cheers*, *The Avengers*, *The Goodies*, *Doctor Who* and *The Muppet Show*, although in recent years film work has taken over, with the most notable contributions being *Clockwise* and the enormously successful *A Fish Called Wanda*.

CLEMENS, BRIAN (1931–)

British producer and scriptwriter whose work for ITC in the 1960s has earned him a real following among fans of TV adventure. By far his greatest impact was in *The Avengers*, although he also contributed to *The Invisible Man*, *Danger Man*, *Adam Adamant Lives!*, *The Champions*, *The Persuaders!*, *The Protectors* and *Bergerac*, as well as creating *The Professionals* and the suspense anthology *Thriller*, and co-creating the sitcom *My Wife Next Door* (with Richard Waring). In 1995 Clemens was series consultant on the high-tech action drama *Bugs*.

CLEMENT, DICK (1937–)

British writer and producer, partner of Ian La Frenais and creator of some of British television's classic comedies. After working as a producer on shows like *Not Only . . . But Also . . .*, Clement teamed up with Geordie insurance salesman La Frenais and scripted a series about two young pals from Newcastle, *The Likely Lads*, which became one of BBC 2's first hits and was successfully revived in the 1970s as *Whatever Happened to the Likely Lads?* The duo went on to create *Porridge* and their success continued into the 1980s with *Auf Wiedersehen, Pet*. Among their other offerings over the years have been *The Further Adventures of Lucky Jim* (two versions), *Mr Aitch*, *Thick as Thieves*, *Mog* and the *Porridge* sequel, *Going Straight*. In the 1990s they penned the limousine-for-hire drama *Full Stretch* and the sitcoms *Freddie and Max*, *Old Boy Network* and *Over the Rainbow*, the last inspired by their own screenplay for the film *The Commitments*. La Frenais (without Clement) has also adapted Jonathan Gash's *Lovejoy* novels for television, co-created *Spender* with Jimmy Nail and contributed to the 1972 sitcom *The Train Now Standing*.

CLEOPATRAS, THE

UK (BBC) Drama. BBC 2 1983

Cleopatra	Michelle Newell
Pot Belly	Richard Griffiths
Cleopatra II	Elizabeth Shepherd
Cleopatra Thea	Caroline Mortimer
Cleopatra IV	Sue Holderness
Cleopatra Tryphaena	Amanda Boxer
Cleopatra Selene	Prue Clarke
Cleopatra Berenike	Pauline Moran
Fluter	Adam Bareham
Mark Antony	Christopher Neame
Chickpea	David Horovitch
Alexander	Ian McNeice
Julius Caesar	Robert Hardy
Theodotus	Graham Crowden
Criton	Jack May
Charmian	Shirin Taylor
Arsinoe	Francesca Gonshaw
Iras	Carole Harrison

Writer: Philip Mackie. Producer: Guy Slater

The history of Greek rule in ancient Egypt.

This wry, 'horror-comic' look at the unscrupulous, incestuous dynasty of Greek women that ruled Egypt from 145 BC to 35 BC was played rather deadpan. The aim was to avoid flippancy but also to skip over the more grotesque incidents. In eight parts, the story of the Cleopatras was told by the last Cleo (played by Michelle Newell, who also played her great-grandmother),

and flashbacked to her six ruthless ancestors of the same name. Also involved in the sordid goings on was the flabby Potbelly. Dozens of brave girls with little hair and even less clothing wobbled around in the background. Actress Amanda Boxer even shaved her head for her role. Sadly, the series failed to achieve respect and suffered the ridicule of both critics and viewers.

CLIVE JAMES – FAME IN THE TWENTIETH CENTURY

UK (BBC) Documentary. BBC 1 1993

Writer/Presenter: Clive James. Producer: Beatrice Ballard

An eight-part, decade-by-decade look at the famous and infamous in the 20th century.

In this nostalgic series, Clive James, with his usual wry observation, looked back over the 20th century, the first century to experience the power of mass media and all its fame-creating potential. He scrutinized the people who had made the news and gained celebrity status in each decade, examining how and why they came to the fore. He then scratched away the veneer to reveal the truth behind the headlines. Archive footage traced the lives of leading politicians, film stars, criminals and pioneers, from Charlie Chaplin and Mahatma Ghandi to Madonna and Norman Schwarzkopf.

CLOCHEMERLE

UK (BBC/Bavaria Atelier) Comedy. BBC 2 1972

Mayor Barthelemy Piechut	Cyril Cusack
Curé Ponosse	Roy Dotrice
Ernest Tafardel	Kenneth Griffith
Justine Putet	Wendy Hiller
Adèle Torbayon	Cyd Hayman
The Baroness Courtebiche	Micheline Presle
Alexandre Bourdillat	Hugh Griffith
Nicholas the Beadle	Bernard Bresslaw
Hortense Girodot	Madeline Smith
Monsieur Girodot	Wolfe Morris
Rose Bivaque	Georgina Moon
Narrator	Peter Ustinov

Writers: Ray Galton, Alan Simpson. Producer: Michael Mills

Plans to install a new pissoir in a French village result in civil unrest.

Gabriel Chevallier's 1934 comedy was adapted by Ray Galton and Alan Simpson in nine parts to create this gentle farce. It concerned the good people of Clochemerle who found themselves divided over plans to open a new pissoir in the centre of the small French village. Reaction from the snootier members of society, and especially the prim lady folk, reached such a peak that the army was called in to quell the unrest. Filmed in France, in the village of Marchampt in Beaujolais, the series attracted a celebrated cast of both British and French performers.

CLOSE DOWN

In the days before 24-hour television, the final announcement of the TV day, often involving a look at the clock, a preview of the next day's fare and a rendition of the national anthem and the station signature tune.

CLOSE-UP

A detailed shot of an object or, more commonly, a head-and-shoulders shot of the presenter or actor.

CLOSED CIRCUIT

A television system that is not broadcast but transmitted via a sequence of cables or by microwaves to a restricted number of receivers. It is generally in use in educational establishments, but has been used for showing major sporting or entertainment events to a limited audience in theatres or stadia.

CLOSING TITLES

The roll call of performers' and technicians' credits seen at the end of a television programme or film.

CLUEDO

UK (Granada/Action Time) Game Show. ITV 1990–3

Season One:

Host	James Bellini
Mrs Peacock	Stephanie Beacham
Mrs White	June Whitfield
Colonel Mustard	Robin Ellis
Miss Scarlett	Tracy-Louise Ward
Reverend Green	Robin Nedwell
Professor Plum	Kristoffer Tabori

Season Two:

Host	Chris Tarrant
Mrs Peacock	Rula Lenska
Mrs White	Mollie Sugden
Colonel Mustard	Michael Jayston
Miss Scarlett	Koo Stark
Reverend Green	Richard Wilson
Professor Plum	David McCallum

Season Three:

Host	Richard Madeley
Mrs Peacock	Susan George
Mrs White	Pam Ferris
Colonel Mustard	Lewis Collins
Miss Scarlett	Lysette Anthony
Reverend Green	Christopher Biggins
Professor Plum	Tom Baker

Season Four:

Host	Richard Madeley
Mrs Peacock	Joanna Lumley
Mrs White	Liz Smith
Colonel Mustard	Leslie Grantham
Ms Scarlett	Jerry Hall
Reverend Green	Nicholas Parsons
Professor Plum	John Bird

Executive Producer: Dianne Nelmes. Producers: Stephen Leahy, Brian Park, Kieran Roberts, Mark Gorton

Celebrity whodunnit based on the enormously successful board game invented by Anthony Pratt in 1944.

In this light-hearted, studio-bound mystery, a murder was committed each week at Arlington Grange (not at Tudor Close, as in the board game), a house owned by society widow Mrs Peacock. What the two teams of two celebrities had to do was work out whodunnit, where in the house and with what weapon, having viewed the video evidence and closely questioned the suspects. Apart from Mrs Peacock, there was also the flighty Miss Scarlet, housekeeper Mrs White, retired military man Colonel Mustard, decidedly dodgy vicar Reverend Green and eccentric Professor Plum. The cast changed every season, including for a 1990 Christmas special, which saw Kate O'Mara as Mrs Peacock, Joan Sims as Mrs White, Toyah Wilcox as Miss Scarlett, David Robb as Colonel Mustard, Derek Nimmo as Reverend Green and Ian Lavender in the role of Professor Plum. James Bellini hosted this one-off. The series was not entirely dissimilar to the earlier *Whodunnit?*.

CLUFF

UK (BBC) Police Drama. BBC 1 1964–5

Detective Sgt Caleb Cluff	Leslie Sands
Inspector Mole	Eric Barker
	Michael Bates
DC Barker	John Rolfe
PC Harry Bullock	John McKelvey
Annie Croft	Olive Milbourne

Creator: Gil North. Producer: Terence Dudley

Easy-paced policing with an old-fashioned Yorkshire detective.

Caleb Cluff was a traditional sort of copper. Not for him the exhausting business of tearing around after criminals, largely because there weren't that many where he lived (fictional Gunnarshaw) at that time (the early 1960s). No, this detective was painfully slow about his business, much to the annoyance of his superior, Inspector Mole, but he was also good at his job, probably because he was so thorough and took time to get to know everyone. His young sidekick, DC Barker, certainly benefited from his methodical approach.

The tweed-suited Cluff's idea of fun was a good walk, with a pipe in his mouth, chestnut-walking stick in his hand and Clive, his loyal black and tan dog, at his side. He lived alone, and was looked after by a daily housekeeper, Annie Croft. Created by Gil North, the character had first appeared as part of the *Detective* anthology series.

CMT see Country Music Television.

CNN (CABLE NEWS NETWORK)

CNN was founded in Atlanta by Ted Turner in 1980, against the advice of experts of the day who believed that a dedicated, round-the-clock news channel could not survive in the limited world of cable. Indeed, the first few years in the company's history were unremarkable and it was not until 1985 that it enjoyed its first year in profit. In 1982 a second channel, majoring on continuous 30-minute news summaries and known initially as CNN-2, was launched. It is now called CNN Headline News. In 1985 a third channel, with a global rather than American bias, was opened up. Called CNN International, it is this channel that can be seen all around the planet and has led the field in international news gathering and dissemination. Its uniqueness was underscored by the outbreak of the Gulf War in 1991, when CNN became the channel to watch for 'as it happens' reports on air raids and other unfolding events. CNN International has been supplied to hotels and other broadcasting stations since its earliest days and became available to European homes via Astra 1B in April 1992. Its signal is not scrambled, making it free to anyone who possesses a satellite system.

COLBOURNE, MAURICE (ROGER MIDDLETON; 1939–89)

Determined-looking British actor whose big TV break came as John Kline in the violent **Gangsters** series. However, it is as Tom Howard in the maritime soap **Howards' Way** that he is best remembered and it was while working on the fifth series of the show that he died of a heart attack. Among his other credits were The Day of the Triffids, the part of Charles Marston in **The Onedin Line** and guest spots in **Shoestring**, **Doctor Who**, **Van Der Valk** and **The Return of the Saint**.

COLBYS, THE

US (Aaron Spelling) Drama. BBC 1 1986–7

Jason Colby	Charlton Heston
Sable Scott Colby	Stephanie Beacham
Francesca Scott Colby/Langdon	Katherine Ross
Jeff Colby	John James
Fallon Carrington/Colby	Emma Samms
Monica Colby	Tracy Scoggins
Miles Colby	Maxwell Caulfield
Bliss Colby	Claire Yarlett
Zachary Powers	Ricardo Montalban
Constance Colby	Barbara Stanwyck
Lord Roger Langdon	David Hedison
Garrett Boydston	Ken Howard
Hutch Corrigan	Joseph Campanella
Sean McAllister	Charles Van Eman
Channing Carter/Colby	Kim Morgan Greene
Senator Cash Cassidy	James Houghton
Adrienne Cassidy	Shanna Reed
Hoyt Parker/Phillip Colby	Michael Parks

Creator: Aaron Spelling. Writers: Robert Pollock, Eileen Pollock. Producers: Richard Shapiro, Esther Shapiro

Glamorous spin-off from *Dynasty*, initially entitled *Dynasty II – The Colbys*.

This soap was set in Los Angeles, around the wealthy Colby family, who had been introduced in a few episodes of *Dynasty* before being left to their own devices. The central character was Jason Colby, head of Colby Enterprises, a company with a finger in more than one pie. Oil, real estate, shipping and aerospace all contributed to its success. Similar to *Dynasty*'s Blake Carrington in many respects, Jason was proud, ruthless and exceptionally rich, not that that made him or his family particularly happy. His wife, Sable, was usually in the thick of the action, fighting with her sister, Frankie, and attempting to murder Constance, Jason's sister, who was the matriarch of Belvedere, the family's estate. The younger generation were represented by Miles (Jason and Sable's son), Monica (their elder daughter), and Bliss (their younger daughter). The link with *Dynasty* came through the character of Jeff Colby, who was Frankie's son and Jason's nephew (though later revealed to be his son, too).

The Colbys ran the gamut of the usual soap stories – illicit affairs, divorce, terminal illness, inheritance disputes, acts of vengeance and commercial wrangles – and introduced a host of temporary characters. But it also took the genre to higher plains (or lower depths, depending on the point of view) when Fallon, Jeff's love from *Dynasty* (who had already been resurrected from a fatal plane crash and had married Miles in a fit of amnesia), witnessed the landing of a UFO and was whisked away to galaxies new. This was meant to be an end of season cliffhanger, but *The Colbys* never came back. Despite the enormous sums of money spent on performers, clothes and sets, the ratings were disastrous. It was left to *Dynasty* to bring Fallon back down to Earth.

COLDITZ

UK (BBC/Universal) Drama. BBC 1 1972–4

Lt Colonel John Preston............................Jack Hedley
Captain Pat Grant...........................Edward Hardwicke
Flt Lt/Major Phil Carrington ....Robert Wagner
Flt Lt Simon Carter ....David McCallum
Kommandant ....Bernard Hepton
Lt Dick Player ....Christopher Neame
Captain George Brent ....Paul Chapman
Hauptmann Ulmann ....Hans Meyer
Captain Tim Downing ....Richard Heffer
Major Horst Mohn ....Anthony Valentine
Lt Colonel Max Dodd ....Dan O'Herlihy

Creators: Brian Degas, Gerard Glaister.
Producer: Gerard Glaister

Prisoners of war attempt to flee an escape-proof German castle.

Based on the book by Major Pat Reid, a genuine survivor of Colditz who acted as technical advisor, this series followed the adventurous bids for freedom of a group of high-level Allied POWs, most of whom had already succeeded in escaping from other prison camps. After an initial three episodes which showed how all the main characters had arrived at Castle Colditz (a supposedly impregnable fortress, known as Oflag IV C, perched high on sheer cliffs in eastern Germany), the series settled down into a portrayal of the rivalry and suspicions that existed among the various Allied nationalities. Their relationship with their German captors was also in focus. Although a mutual respect grew between the POWs, led by the British Lt Colonel Preston, and the camp's tolerant Kommandant, friction increased when the SS threatened to take over the castle and when, in the second series, the sadistic Major Mohn was introduced.

The desperate escape plans included launching home-made gliders off the castle roof, as well as the more conventional guard impersonations and wall scalings. One inmate, Wing Commander Marsh, worked on insanity as a means of getting out. He succeeded, but, when finally freed, the stress of acting mad had actually warped his mind. Guest stars came and went (Patrick Troughton, Peter Barkworth and Nigel Stock among them), and the progress of the war outside the castle walls was used as a backdrop to events in the closed world of Colditz itself. The series concluded with liberation in 1945.

Colditz revived the flagging career of Robert Wagner, who played Canadian airman Phil Carrington. The series also led to a variety of spin-off ventures, ranging from bizarre holidays at the real castle to a children's board game. The inspiration had been the 1955 film *The Colditz Story*, starring John Mills and Eric Portman.

COLE, GEORGE, OBE (1925–)

For most viewers George Cole is, and always will be, Arthur Daley. Though his TV work has been prolific and varied, his portrayal of *Minder*'s Cockney spiv with a lock-up full of dodgy goods and a fine line in persuasive banter has dwarfed all his other contributions to the small screen. Cole came to television after a successful stage, radio and film career in which he worked closely with Alastair Sim, and his profile as a rather unreliable, Jack the Lad figure, was established by the St Trinians films, in which he played Flash Harry. In 1960, his radio role of David Bliss, in the comedy *A Life of Bliss*, moved to television and Cole never looked back. He went on to star in *A Man of our Times* (as Max Osborne), *Don't Forget to Write* (as Gordon Maple), *The Bounder* (as Trevor), *Blott on the Landscape* (as Sir Giles Lynchwood), Comrade Dad (as Reg Dudgeon) and *Root Into Europe* (as Henry Root), as well as appearing in series as diverse as *The Gold Robbers*, *UFO*, The Voyage of Charles Darwin and *Natural Causes*, and numerous single dramas.

COLE, JOHN (1927–)

Northern Ireland-born BBC political editor 1981–92. Cole began his journalistic career with the *Belfast Telegraph*, before joining the *Guardian* in 1956 and moving on to the *Observer* in 1975. In the 1980s he was one of the most familiar faces (and voices) on British television, earning great respect from both viewers and politicians. Cole has also been seen on *What The Papers Say* and has compiled some reports for *Holiday*. His TV memoirs, *A Progress Through Politics*, were shown in 1995.

COLE, STEPHANIE (1941–)

British actress, usually seen as a hard-headed female, as exemplified by the roles of Dr Beatrice Mason in *Tenko* and Diana Trent in *Waiting for God*. She was also Mrs Featherstone, a grouchy customer in *Open all Hours*, Sarah Mincing in the children's series Return of the Antelope and Betty Sillitoe in *A Bit of a Do*. Cole also performed one of Alan Bennett's Talking Heads monlogues.

COLEMAN, DAVID, OBE (1926–)

Former journalist and Cheshire mile champion who has been one of the BBC's most prominent sports commentators and presenters since the 1950s. Previously editor of the *Cheshire County Express* and a radio presenter, Coleman established himself as a BBC political reporter then contributor to *Sports Special*, main host of

Grandstand and one of *Match of the Day's* commentary team, before taking on his own mid-week sports magazine *Sportsnight With Coleman* (which is still running today as *Sportsnight*). Over the years he has become known for his detailed background research (put to good use when ad libbing on *Grandstand* during the teleprinter results spot, for instance) and for the rather unfortunate turn of phrase which has given rise to the neologism 'Colemanballs' (thanks to *Private Eye*). Among the classics was 'Juantorena opens his legs and shows his class'. He currently specializes in athletics commentary and has been the chairman of *A Question of Sport* since 1980.

COLIN'S SANDWICH

UK (BBC) Situation Comedy. BBC 2 1988–90

Colin Watkins	Mel Smith
Jenny Anderson	Louisa Rix
Des	Mike Grady
Mr Travers	Andrew Robertson
Sarah	Jane Booker
John Langley	Michael Medwin
Alan Hunter	Nicholas Ball

Writers: Paul Smith, Terry Kyan. Producer: John Kilby

An under-achieving British Rail clerk lacks the conviction to build a new career as a writer.

Described by some as 'Hancock for the 1980s', *Colin's Sandwich* revolved around the efforts of terminal worryguts Colin Watkins to balance his daytime job in the British Rail complaints department with a fledgling career as a writer of thriller stories. The acceptance of one of his tales for the *Langley Book of Horror* did nothing to ease the pressure as Colin toyed with the idea of becoming a professional scribe. Later episodes saw Colin still holding down his BR position whilestruggling to pen a screenplay for pig ignorant, cult film director Alan Hunter. Colin's girlfriend, Jenny, bore the brunt of his neurotic, self-questioning rants, while his anoraky pal, Des, and other yuppie acquaintances, like the love-lorn Sarah, just got in the way. At work, his moronic colleagues and his delegating boss, Mr Travers, helped drive Watkins round the bend.

COLLINS, JOAN (1936–)

British movie actress of the 1950s and 1960s who hit the big time through raunchy films and glossy television in the 1970s. Her most prominent role has been as the vicious Alexis Carrington/Colby in *Dynasty*, making her Queen of the soap bitches. Amongst her other TV credits (most as a guest) have been *The Human Jungle*, *The Virginian*, *The Man from UNCLE*, *Batman*, *Star Trek*, *Mission: Impossible*, Orson Welles Great Mysteries, *Space: 1999*, *The Persuaders!*, *Starsky and Hutch*, *Fantasy Island*, *Tales of the Unexpected*, *Monte Carlo* and *Sins* (a mini-series produced by her own company). She is the sister of novelist Jackie Collins and was once married to entertainer Anthony Newley (one of four husbands).

COLLINS, LEWIS (1946–)

British actor whose television break came alongside Diane Keen and David Roper in *The Cuckoo Waltz*, playing the unwanted lodger, Gavin Rumsey. After this came *The Professionals*, in which he was teamed up as Bodie with Martin Shaw's Doyle to work for Gordon Jackson's Cowley and CI5 in tackling terrorists. His other appearances have included parts in *Warship*, *The New Avengers*, *Robin of Sherwood* and *Jack the Ripper*.

COLLINS, PAULINE (1940–)

British actress who shot to fame as Sarah, the pert parlour maid in *Upstairs, Downstairs*. So popular was her character that a spin-off, *Thomas and Sarah,* was produced for her and her real-life husband, John Alderton. Collins's TV break had come with *Emergency – Ward 10* and was followed by her first starring role as Dawn in *The Liver Birds*, alongside Polly James. However, after a short first series, Nerys Hughes joined as James's new flatmate and Collins left. Post-*Upstairs, Downstairs*, she has starred with hubby Alderton on three further occasions – as Clara Danby in the sitcom *No, Honestly*, as various characters in *Wodehouse Playhouse* and as Harriet Boult in *Forever Green*.

COLONEL MARCH OF SCOTLAND YARD

UK (Sapphire) Police Drama. ITV 1956–7

Colonel Perceval March	Boris Karloff
Inspector Ames	Ewan Roberts
Inspector Gordon	Eric Pohlmann

Producer: Hannah Weinstein

The strange cases of a specialist detective.

One-eyed Colonel March worked for D-3, the Department of Queer Complaints at Scotland Yard, a position that led to his involvement in seemingly unsolvable cases. Sometimes it appeared the supernatural had played a hand in murder. On other occasions, supposedly impossible crimes landed on his desk (including a murder in a sealed compression chamber where no one could have reached the victim). March even confronted the Abominable Snowman in one episode. Nevertheless, the dogged detective, who sported a black patch over his left eye, always found the answer. The stories were based on stories by Carter Dickson (John Dickson Carr).

COLOUR TELEVISION

Although initially earmarked for 1956–7, colour television did not officially begin in the UK until 2 December 1967, some 13 years after the USA had begun regular colour broadcasts (although, it is true to say, significant colour viewing figures in the USA were not established until around 1965). The factors that inhibited the development of colour in the UK were varied. They included the need for the Government to approve a suitable system, preferably in conjunction with its European neighbours so that standard technology was achieved. The American NTSC system was initially employed by the BBC for test transmissions, which began in 1962, but was quickly dropped in favour of the French SECAM technology. Eventually it was the German-originated PAL system, a 625-line variant of the 525-line NTSC system, that was adopted in the UK.

COLTRANE, ROBBIE (ANTHONY McMILLAN; 1950–)

Scottish comic actor whose early television work took in *A Kick Up The Eighties*, *Laugh? I Nearly Paid My Licence Fee*, *Alfresco* and various *Comic Strip* plays, including *The Professionals* send-up, *The Bullshitters*, and *GLC* (as Charles Bronson playing Ken Livingstone). He also appeared in *The Young Ones*, *Girls on Top*, *Blackadder* and *Saturday Live* before starring as Danny McGlone in John Byrne's rock 'n' roll comedy drama *Tutti Frutti*. He has since had his own show, appeared with Emma Thompson and turned to serious acting to play Fitz in the acclaimed crime drama *Cracker*. In 1993 he made a light-hearted American road film documentary for Meridian, *Coltrane in a Cadillac*.

COLUMBO

US (Universal) Detective Drama. ITV 1972–9; 1991-

Lt Columbo ....Peter Falk

Creators: Richard Levinson, William Link.
Executive Producers: Roland Kibbee, Dean Hargrove, Richard Alan Simmons . Producers: Edward K. Dodds, Everett Chambers, Richard Alan Simmons, Stanley Kallis

The investigations of a grubby, seemingly ineffective police detective.

Each episode of *Columbo* opened in the thick of the action. A murder was committed and the cul-

prits quickly covered their tracks, pulling off an apparently perfect crime. However, soon on the scene was America's most unlikely policeman, Lt Columbo, and, by piecing together even the most minute fragments of evidence, the LA-based detective always got his man. Of course, viewers came to expect Columbo to be successful, but the same couldn't be said for the murderers. Lulled into a false sense of security by his tramp's raincoat, battered old car, well-chewed cigar and excessively polite manner, they never believed that this scruffy old cop could nail them. But, by throwing his suspects off-guard, Columbo knew he could catch them unawares. From the outset he seemed to know who the murderer was, and viewers were able to watch the battle of wills that developed between the culprit manoeuvring to allay suspicion and the detective homing in on his prey. Much mentioned, but never seen, was his wife, but she did appear in her own spin-off series, *Mrs Columbo*, played by Kate Mulgrew. Columbo's lone companion seemed to be his bassett hound, Fang.

The character of Columbo was allegedly modelled on Petrovich, an inspector in Dostoevski's *Crime and Punishment*, and first reached the screen in a segment of USA's *Sunday Mystery Hour* way back in 1961. Then the character was played by Bert Freed. When Columbo was looked at again in the late 1960s, Bing Crosby and Lee J. Cobb were the two names touted for the role. Both were unavailable, so in stepped Peter Falk to appear in two TV movies, *Prescription: Murder* in 1968 (in which we learned Columbo's christian name was Philip) and *Ransom for a Dead Man* in 1971. When in full production, with feature-length episodes, the show aired as part of the *Mystery Movie* anthology, although it has also been billed simply under its own title. Guest stars abounded, from Dick Van Dyke and William Shatner to Patrick McGoohan and Donald Pleasence. The detective returned in the 1990s in a new series of two-hour adventures.

COMBAT

US (Selmur) War Drama. ITV

Lt Gil Hanley	Rick Jason
Sgt Chip Saunders	Vic Morrow
PFC Paul 'Caje' Lemay	Pierre Jalbert
Pte William G. 'Wildman' Kirby	Jack Hogan
Littlejohn	Dick Peabody
Doc Walton	Steven Rogers
Doc	Conlan Carter
Pte Braddock	Shecky Greene
Pte Billy Nelson	Tom Lowell

Producer: Gene Levitt

A US Army platoon fights its way across Europe in the wake of D-Day.

Filmed for most of its run in black and white, and interspersed with some actual war footage, *Combat* was the most successful of the new breed of 1960s war sagas. It featured K Company, Second Platoon of the US Army, which was headed by Lt Gil Hanley. With Hanley were Sgt Chip Saunders and a varied company of men, most notably the wisecracking Braddock, a Cajun known simply as 'Caje' and an impressionable young medic, Doc Walton. While the war was hard to avoid, other aspects of platoon life were also handled, and realism was the bedrock of the series. Robert Altman directed many of the episodes, which aired on US TV from 1962 and which were seen sporadically around the ITV network.

COME BACK MRS NOAH

UK (BBC) Situation Comedy. BBC 1 1978

Mrs Noah	Mollie Sugden
Clive Cunliffe	Ian Lavender
Carstairs	Donald Hewlett
Fanshaw	Michael Knowles
Garstang	Joe Black
Garfield Hawk	Tim Barrett
Scarth Dare	Ann Michelle
TV presenter	Gorden Kaye
Technician	Jennifer Lonsdale

Writers: Jeremy Lloyd, David Croft. Producer: David Croft

A housewife is lost in space.

When, in the 21st century, housewife Mrs Noah won herself a trip around Britain's newest space station, little did she know that her voyage would be so adventurous. Accidentally blasted into orbit, she and a hotchpotch crew found themselves floating around the world at 56,325 kmh (35,000 mph), as Mission Control fought desperately to retrieve their spaceship. Among those alongside Mrs Noah was roving TV reporter Clive Cunliffe.

Despite coming from the pen of the creators of *'Allo 'Allo* and featuring the usual Croft/Perry/Lloyd repertory company actors, with Mollie Sugden in full sail, this sitcom failed to take and survived only one short season.

COME DANCING

UK (BBC) Entertainment. BBC 1 1950–

Creator: Eric Morley. Producers: Barrie Edgar, Ray Lakeland, Philip Lewis, Simon Betts

Perennial ballroom dancing contests.

Now one of television's longest running programmes, *Come Dancing* has proved remarkably durable. Initially conceived as a showcase for

events from regional ballrooms, with professionals Syd Perkins and Edna Duffield offering instruction for viewers at home, it assumed the more familiar dance contest format in 1953. The competition has since taken the form of an inter-regional knock-out, pitting teams from areas such as Home Counties North against the South-West, or another part of the UK. Swathed in a sea of sequins, the athletic, mostly amateur, enthusiasts have competed in various formal dance categories, from the tango to the paso doble. There has also been a section for formation dancing, and newer crazes like rock 'n' roll have been incorporated over the years. The deviser of the programme, Mecca's Eric Morley, has also emceed proceedings, although the programme's presenters and on-the-floor comperes have been many. The most notable have included McDonald Hobley, Peter Dimmock, Sylvia Peters, Peter West, Brian Johnston, Pete Murray, Don Moss, Keith Fordyce, Michael Aspel, Judith Chalmers, Terry Wogan, Noel Edmonds, Peter Marshall, Angela Rippon, David Jacobs and Rosemarie Ford.

COMEDIANS, THE

UK (Granada) Comedy. ITV 1971–3; 1979; 1985; 1992

Frank Carson
Bernard Manning
Colin Crompton
Ken Goodwin
Mike Reid
Jim Bowen
Charlie Williams
Duggie Brown
Mike Burton
George Roper
Tom O'Connor
Russ Abbot
Lennie Bennett
Stan Boardman (1979)
Roy Walker (1979)
Vince Earl (1979)
Charlie Daze (1979)
George King (1979)
Brian Carroll (1979)
Harry Scott (1979)
Lee Wilson (1979)
Mick Miller (1979)
Tom Pepper (1992)
Pauline Daniels (1992)
Jimmy Bright (1992)

Producers: John Hamp, Ian Hamilton

Wall-to-wall gags from leading club comics.

With musical interludes from Shep's Banjo Boys, *The Comedians* was a showcase for the top talent from the northern clubs. Producer John Hamp brought the country's fastest wise-crackers into the studio, recorded their (somewhat cleaned-up) routines before a live audience, then inter-cut their gags with those from other contributors to create a non-stop barrage of quick-fire jokes. Snappy editing ensured a lively pace and a joke a minute, at the very least, was guaranteed.

The Comedians launched the television careers of a number of funny men. These included abrasive Bernard Manning, weedy Colin Crompton (the pair came together again later in **Wheeltappers' and Shunters' Social Club**), Ken 'Settle down now' Goodwin, Mike 'Terr-i-fic' Reid, Frank 'It's the way I tell 'em' Carson and Jim 'Smashing, super' Bowen. Lennie Bennett, Tom O'Connor and Russ Abbot were three other performers who carved out new careers after appearances on the show, Duggie Brown (brother of **Coronation Street**'s Lynne Perrie) has since turned to acting (with appearances in **Brookside**), but Charlie Williams, a black comic with a thick Yorkshire accent, unfortunately failed to make the grade when given charge of **The Golden Shot** and has been seldom seen since.

The Comedians was revived in 1979, with a new intake of stand-up comics that included Roy Walker and Stan Boardman. A third revival in 1985, mixing old faces with new talent, proved less memorable, as did a fourth in 1992.

COMEDY PLAYHOUSE

UK (BBC/Carlton) Situation Comedy Anthology. BBC 1961–74; ITV 1993

Creator: Tom Sloan

Sporadic collections of sitcom pilots.

Comedy Playhouse was an umbrella title given to occasional series of single comedies. Each comedy acted as a pilot and, if successful, stood a fair chance of being extended into a series of its own. Ray Galton and Alan Simpson wrote the first collection, but many other writers (including Johnny Speight, Roy Clarke and Richard Waring) made contributions later. The most famous of *Comedy Playhouse*'s protegés have been **Steptoe and Son** (piloted as **The Offer** in 1962), **Till Death Us Do Part** and **The Liver Birds**. Others have included **All Gas and Gaiters**, **Not in Front of the Children**, **Me Mammy**, **Last of the Summer Wine**, **Happy Ever After** and **Open All Hours**.

Similar in concept was *Comedy Special* in 1977, which introduced **Citizen Smith**, and the 1973 Ronnie Barker showcase *Seven of One*, which included *Prisoner and Escort*, the pilot for **Porridge**. Carlton resurrected *Comedy Playhouse* in 1993, giving birth to two series, **Brighton Belles** (the UK version of **The Golden Girls**) and **The 10%ers**.

COMIC RELIEF

UK (BBC) Telethon. BBC 1 1988–

Comedy charity marathon.

Exploiting the talents of comedians and comic actors from various generations and backgrounds, *Comic Relief* has been described as **Children In Need** with gags. Hosted by Griff Rhys Jones and Lenny Henry, with the assistance of the likes of Jonathan Ross, Angus Deayton and, latterly, Chris Evans, it began in 1988 as an extension to the Live Aid projects of the mid-1980s, with proceeds (over £15 million initially, rising over the years to over £26 million) going to help famine victims in Africa. The second *Comic Relief* came in 1989, but the appeal has since settled into a biannual routine, taking place on a date in February/March which has been dubbed 'Red Nose Day' (clowns' red noses of assorted designs have been sold to raise money).

Appeals for cash have been made throughout the evening's live programming, with running totals announced at regular intervals. Reports on how funds have been spent have punctuated each appeal. Viewers have been invited to bid for their favourite clips from old comedy series and among the many comedians giving their time to the show have been Jasper Carrott, Rowan Atkinson, Tony Robinson, Ken Dodd, Stephen Fry, Richard Wilson, Ben Elton, Frank Carson, Jo Brand, Julian Clary, French and Saunders, Harry Enfield, Ernie Wise, Paul Merton, Ian Hislop, Hale and Pace, Rory Bremner, Victoria Wood and the Spitting Image team, as well as other stars like Joanna Lumley, Cilla Black, Chris Tarrant, Bill Wyman, Barry Norman and Tom Jones.

COMIC STRIP PRESENTS, THE

UK (Filmworks/Comic Strip) Comedy. Channel 4/BBC 2 1982–92

Peter Richardson
Dawn French
Jennifer Saunders
Adrian Edmondson
Rik Mayall
Daniel Peacock
Robbie Coltrane
Nigel Planer
Alexei Sayle
Keith Allen

Producer: Michael White (Channel 4), Lolli Kimpton (BBC 2)

Spoof and satire with a new generation of comedians.

The Comic Strip, a comedy club opened by writer Peter Richardson in 1980 above the Raymond Revue Bar in Soho, was the venue that gave early opportunities to many of the 1980s most successful young comedians. Its compere was Alexei Sayle and prominent amongst its performers were French and Saunders, Nigel Planer, Rik Mayall and Adrian Edmondson. *The Comic Strip Presents* was its television manifestation, but instead of focusing on stand-up routines it centred on satire and send-up. The premiere was an Enid Blyton spoof, *Five Go Mad in Dorset*, which rounded off Channel 4's first night in 1982. A half-hour parody of the snooty, class themes of Blyton's books, it cast French and Saunders as George and Anne, with Adrian Edmondson as Dick and Peter Richardson as Julian. Memorably, it also featured serious-looking **Crossroads** star Ronald Allen as Uncle Quentin, proudly declaring 'I'm a screaming homosexual, you little prigs', before being carted off by Inspector Lockhart of **No Hiding Place** fame.

Five Go Mad in Dorset led to five series of Comic Strip productions, plus occasional specials, all drawing their humour more from atmosphere and characterization than from jokes and one-liners. Titles were as varied as *War*, *The Beat Generation*, *A Fistful of Travellers' Cheques* and *The Bad News Tour* (featuring an inept heavy metal band). One notable episode, entitled *Strike*, explored the miners' dispute through the eyes of Hollywood, with Peter Richardson as Robert De Niro playing Arthur Scargill and Jennifer Saunders as Meryl Streep playing Scargill's wife. The same theme was extended to a later production, *GLC*, in which Robbie Coltrane was Charles Bronson playing Ken Livingstone. *The Bullshitters* (a parody of **The Professionals**) was not officially a Comic Strip production, but did feature several members of the team. With its stars now name performers, *The Comic Strip Presents* moved to BBC 2 in 1990 for its later episodes.

COMMENTATOR

A person who expresses a view on news and current affairs or reports direct from sporting events, usually describing the action as it happens.

COMMERCIAL

A television advertisement that may vary in length from a few seconds to a few minutes. In the UK these are grouped together in commercial breaks lasting several minutes, which are screened between and also during programmes. In other countries and on some satellite networks commercials are seen between programmes only. In the USA breaks are more frequent and have traditionally been more rigidly enforced, causing much concern when programmes have been halted to accommodate a break. Commercial television (aka ITV) arrived in the UK on 22 September 1955 and the first advert in the first 'natural break' (as it was then termed) was for Gibbs SR toothpaste. Then, as now, there were strict rules regarding advertising. Today the ITC monitors commercials, with the main concerns being that they do not mislead, do not encourage or condone harmful behaviour and do not cause widespread or exceptional offence. Certain products, in line with Government legislation, are prohibited (tobacco, etc.), and controversial subjects like alcohol, financial services, children's goods, medical products and religious and charitable concerns are subject to more detailed regulation. An average of seven minutes per hour of advertising are now allowed on ITV and Channel 4, with an extra half-minute permitted during peak hours. Satellite stations can offer nine minutes' worth per hour, although shopping channels are not restricted in the same way. The timing of commercials is also controlled. No advertising is allowed during religious services, for example.

COMO, PERRY (PIERINO COMO; 1912–)

Laid back Italian-American crooner whose variety shows in the 1950s (and extravagant Christmas specials since) were hits on both sides of the Atlantic.

COMPACT

UK (BBC) Drama. BBC 1 1962–5

Joanne Minster	Jean Harvey
Jimmy	Nicholas Selby
Richard	Moray Watson
Mark Viccars	Gareth Davies
Alison Gray/Morley	Betty Cooper
Alec	Leo Maguire
Sally	Monica Evans
Edmund Bruce	Robert Flemyng
Mary Augusta 'Gussie' Brown	Frances Bennett
Iris Alcott	Louise Dunn
Stan Millett	Johnny Wade
Ian Harmon	Ronald Allen
Lois	Dawn Beret
Lily	Marcia Ashton
Camilla Hope	Carmen Silvera
Maggie	Sonia Graham
Ruth	Anna Castaldini
Adrian Coombs	Robert Desmond
David Rome	Vincent Ball
Doug Beatty	Lawrence James
Alan Drew	Basil Moss
Anthea Keen	Julia Lockwood
Tessa	Bridget Armstrong
Sir Charles Harmon	Newton Blick
Babbage	Donald Morley

Creators: Hazel Adair, Peter Ling. Producers: Alan Bromly, Douglas Allen, Morris Barry, Bernard Hepton, Joan Craft, Harold Clayton, William Sterling

The lives and loves of the staff at a women's magazine.

Compact was the BBC's first soap opera since the demise of *The Grove Family* in 1957, it took place in the offices of *Compact*, a glossy magazine that majored in schmaltzy fiction and other matters of female interest, and, as the programme blurb declared, focused on 'the talented and temperamental people who worked on a topical magazine for the busy woman'.

The magazine's first editor was Edmund Bruce, but he soon gave way to Joanne Minster. Also part of the team were fiction editor Mark Viccars, photographer Alec, features editor Gussie Brown, art editor Adrian Coombs, showbiz correspondent David Rome, librarian Alan Drew, Babbage the accountant and assorted writers and secretaries. The problem page editor was Alison Morley. Her name was originally given as Alison Gray, until the producers realized there was already a contributor to *Reader's Digest* with that name.

Action centred around the hassle of getting the magazine on to the presses each week, with staff squabbles promoted to the realms of high drama. Personal relationships bloomed and died, and there was much sparring for position in the office. When Minster left, a new editor was appointed. Ian Harmon, son of Sir Charles Harmon (the chairman of Harmon Enterprises, the magazine's proprietor), took over her chair, bringing with him suave looks and gentlemanly behaviour. Before long he married Sally, his secretary, and they left for America.

Compact followed *Tonight* on to the screens every Tuesday and Thursday night. It was criticized for being too wholesome and goody-goody (despite touching on one or two controversial items, like unmarried mothers and drug abuse), but was very successful in the ratings. All the same, the BBC bosses were less than satisfied. They pulled the plug on the series in July 1965, after just three years on air – ironically assigning *Compact* the same fate that had befallen *The Grove Family*.

CONNECTIONS

UK (BBC/Time-Life) Documentary. BBC 1 1978

Presenter: James Burke

How scientific progress has changed the world.

This ambitious series attempted to explain the relationship between technological achievement and the course of world history. The case was argued in a lively, but highly informative manner by ex-*Tomorrow's World* presenter James Burke.

CONNOLLY, BILLY (1942–)

Glasgowegian comedian, familiarly known as 'The Big Yin'. Connolly was once a member of the Humblebums folk duo with Gerry Rafferty, before turning to stand-up comedy. His TV successes have come on both sides of the Atlantic. He starred in the US series *Head of the Class* and *Billy*, and in the UK has made appearances on *Not the Nine O'Clock News*, *The Comic Strip Presents*, *The Kenny Everett Video Show* and *Minder*. He has starred in his own comedy specials and in 1994 went on *Billy Connolly's World Tour of Scotland*. He is married to comic actress Pamela Stephenson.

CONNORS, CHUCK (KEVIN CONNORS; 1921–92)

Athletic American actor, a former professional baseball player who turned to film and television and starred in various action series, particularly as Lucas McCain in *The Rifleman*, Jason McCord in *Branded* and Jim Sinclair in Cowboy in Africa. He also played defence attorney John Egan in *Arrest and Trial* and, in the 1970s, resurfaced in *Roots*, taking the part of Tom Moore. Other TV credits include episodes of *Fantasy Island*, *The Six Million Dollar Man* and *Murder, She Wrote*.

CONRAD, WILLIAM (1920–94)

Gravel-voiced American actor, a fighter pilot in World War II but forever remembered by viewers as the huffing and puffing, overweight private eye Frank Cannon. It was a starring role at last for Conrad, who had missed out on several previous occasions. His resonant voice had made him a prolific radio actor and announcer, and he had been seen in numerous films in the 1940s and 1950s, but his portly frame always spoiled his chances of on-screen TV success. *Gunsmoke* was a point in question. Although he had voiced the part of Matt Dillon for years on US radio, there was no way the producers could cast Conrad as the strapping marshal of Dodge City and the role went instead to James Arness. Conrad, consequently, concentrated on work behind the camera. He produced/directed episodes of series like *Naked City*, *77 Sunset Strip* and, ironically, *Gunsmoke*. He also provided narration for such programmes as *The Fugitive* and *The Invaders*, but it wasn't until Frank Cannon was born that his screen success was assured. He followed it with two more detective romps, *Nero Wolfe* and *Jake and the Fatman*, but he still continued to dabble in voice-overs, speaking the lines of the Lone Ranger in the 1980s cartoon revival, for instance.

CONTI, TOM (1941–)

Latin-looking Scottish actor, popular on stage and film but also prominent on TV thanks to dramas like *Madame Bovary*, **The Glittering Prizes**, *The Norman Conquests*, *Voices Within* and Dennis Potter's *Blade on the Feather*.

CONTINUITY ANNOUNCER see announcer.

CONTRAST

The relationship between the lightest and darkest elements of a TV picture.

CONTROL DESK

Found in the controlroom or gallery, the control desk houses the vision mixer and other technical apparatus used by the director, his production assistant and other technicians as they monitor recordings or live transmissions.

CONWAY, GARY (GARETH CARMODY; 1936–)

American light actor best remembered as Captain Steve Burton in **Land of the Giants** and, previously, Detective Tim Tilson in **Burke's Law**.

CONWAY, RUSS (TREVOR STANFORD; 1924–)

British piano-playing celebrity of the late 1950s and early 1960s, a stalwart of variety spectaculars and series like *The Billy Cotton Band Show*. Self-taught, he sold millions of copies of records like 'Sidesaddle' and 'Roulette' before his career took a downturn and he faded off UK TV screens.

COOK, PETER (1937–95)

Dry, satirical comedian, a Cambridge Footlights graduate whose celebrated two-year partnership with Dudley Moore in **Not Only . . . But Also . . .** in the mid-1960s followed a couple of years of success with the Beyond The Fringe revue. Cook's collaborators in those early days included Moore, Jonathan Miller and Alan Bennett and it was during that time that he developed his philosophical E.L. Wisty character, complete with grubby mac and flat cap, which he brought to TV in *On the Braden Beat* in 1964. In 1966 he also played the Mad Hatter in Miller's adaptation of *Alice In Wonderland*. After moving into film, Cook returned to television in the late 1970s, appearing as a seedy dance hall manager in Granada's late-night rock show *Revolver*, and in 1981 he switched to sitcom, starring with Mimi Kennedy in *The Two of Us*, the American version of *Two's Company*. Among his other credits has

been the 1992 series *Gone to Seed* (in which he played unscrupulous property developer Wesley Willis), the first series of **Blackadder** (as King Richard III) and assorted cameo performances. Cook was co-founder of London's Establishment Club in 1960 and became a major shareholder in the fledgling *Private Eye* magazine in the same year.

COOK, ROGER (1943–)

New Zealand-born, Australia-raised investigative reporter, formerly on radio (*The World At One* and *Checkpoint*). Through his ITV series *The Cook Report*, Cook has exposed any number of fraudsters and con men, as well as upbraiding the authorities on behalf of the consumer. Cook has bravely tackled the most risqué of subjects and the most violent of characters, from child pornographers and badger baiters to terrorists and racketeers. His foot-in-the-door, camera-in-the-face method of confronting his targets has been much mimicked by comics.

COOK, SUE (1949–)

Former radio broadcaster and TV news and current affairs presenter (**Nationwide**) who has become a fixture on the annual **Children In Need** appeals. She has also presented **Breakfast Time**, worked on various magazine programmes and has hosted **Crimewatch UK** with Nick Ross since its inception. She was once married to classical guitarist John Williams.

COOKE, ALISTAIR, KBE (HON) (1908–)

Manchester-born journalist now an American citizen who has presented Radio 4's *Letter From America* since 1946. A one-time BBC film critic, for many years Cooke was *The Guardian's* chief US correspondent and also worked for American radio stations as a specialist in British affairs. He first appeared on British television in the 1930s, presenting a short programme, *Accent In America*, although his TV masterpiece was undoubtedly *America*, a 13-week personal analysis of the birth and development of a nation, delivered in his customary modest but incisively knowledgeable style and filled with feeling and affection for his adopted homeland. In the USA he has been the host of *Masterpiece Theatre*, a PBS anthology series of top British drama programmes like **Upstairs, Downstairs**, **The Six Wives of Henry VIII** and **Poldark**.

COOKE, BRIAN see Mortimer, Johnnie.

COOL FOR CATS

UK (Associated-Rediffusion) Pop Music. ITV 1956–61

Hosts: Ker Robertson, Kent Walton

Creator: Joan Kemp-Welch

Britain's first pop music show.

Cool for Cats was British TV's first pop music showcase, airing the latest single releases. Given its minuscule budget, the programme was forced to rely on artists miming and the talents of a resident dance group (led by Douglas Squires), which, to ring the changes, used the stairs and passageways of Associated-Rediffusion's offices as well as its studios. All the same, it proved particularly popular and was screened three times a week, on Mondays, Wednesdays and Fridays. Journalist Ker Robertson, the first host, was succeeded after a month by Kent Walton, later better known for his ITV wrestling commentaries.

COOMBS, PAT (1930–)

Wiry Cockney comedy actress, typically in dithery or distressed parts, or as a timid soul dominated by a female dragon. She appeared in just such a role with Peggy Mount in the 1977 retirement home comedy *You're Only Young Twice*, playing Cissie Lupin, having previously played Violet, Mount's sister-in-law, in *Lollipop Loves Mr Mole*. Her comedy career began, however, with Arthur Askey (she was Nola in the radio show *Hello Playmates*), and some of her earliest TV appearances were with Tony Hancock. Coombs then starred in the 1967 sitcom *Beggar My Neighbour* as Reg Varney's wife, Lana Butt. She later joined Stephen Lewis (playing his sister, Dorothy) in the *On the Buses* spin-off *Don't Drink the Water* and over the years has also appeared in programmes like *Marty*, *The Dick Emery Show*, *Till Death Us Do Part*, *Wild, Wild Women*, *The Lady is A Tramp* and the kids' series *Hogg's Back*, *Ragdolly Anna* and *Mr Majeika*. Coombes also spent some time in *EastEnders*, as Marge Green, the Girl Guide leader.

COOPER, TOMMY (1922–84)

Tall, Welsh comedian, notorious as the fez-wearing magician with the bad gags and bemused look whose tricks always failed. Tommy Cooper's hugely successful career began in the army and continued after the war on the London variety circuit. In the 1950s he branched out into television, appearing in series like *It's Magic* and winning a run of his own series, including *Cooper – Life with Tommy*, *Cooper's Capers*, *Cooperama*, *Life With Cooper*, *Cooper At Large*, *The Tommy Cooper Hour*, *Cooper King Size* and *Cooper – Just Like That!* (after his catchphrase). He became a cult comedian and enjoyed great respect among his fellow artistes. It was actually on television that he died, suffering a heart attack while appearing on *Live from Her Majesty's* in 1984.

COPE, KENNETH (1931–)

British character actor/scriptwriter with a few prominent roles to his name and plenty of guest appearances. Cope came to the fore as one of the presenters of *That Was The Week That Was* before joining *Coronation Street* as a semi-regular in the mid-1960s, turning up from time to time as Scouser Jed Stone, the petty crook Minnie Caldwell adored and knew as Sonny Jim. However, it was as the deceased part of *Randall and Hopkirk (Deceased)* that he is best remembered by fans of cult TV, playing the white-suited ghost detective, Marty Hopkirk, for 26 episodes. Other credits have included *Whack-O!* (as schoolmaster Price Whittaker), *Dixon of Dock Green*, *Z Cars*, *The Avengers*, *Bergerac*, *Shelley* (as DHSS clerk Forsyth), *Minder*, *Strangers* and *Doctor Who*. Among his writing successes have been the kids' soccer series Striker, the sitcom *Thingumybob* and episodes of the comedies *The Squirrels* and *A Sharp Intake of Breath*.

CO-PRODUCTION

A programme made jointly by two or more companies, sometimes from more than one country, in an effort to disperse the financial risk.

CORBETT, HARRY, OBE (1918–89)

'Bye bye, everybody, bye, bye.' These were the weary, resigned closing words of each show which became the catchphrase of Harry Corbett, a genial northern entertainer, the man who gave the world Sooty and Sweep. Beginning his working life as an electrical engineer, Corbett, an amateur pianist and magician, transformed his life in 1948 when he purchased a bear glove puppet on Blackpool's North Pier for 7/6d. He built the bear into his magic act, which led to an appearance on the BBC's *Talent Night* in 1952. The bear was simply known as Teddy at the time, but after applying some chimney soot to his ears and nose, in order to add more character, he was re-christened Sooty. Five years later, Sweep, a squeaky, rather dim dog with a lust for sausages, joined Sooty, making Corbett's life a misery as they spoiled his magic tricks, sprayed him with water and smashed him around the head with a balsa wood hammer. Corbett then introduced other characters to the show, including Kipper the cat, Butch the dog and Ramsbottom the snake, but most controversial was its first female star, Soo, a cute panda who did all the housework. In 1968 Corbett switched channels, taking his puppets to ITV, where he stayed until he suffered a heart attack in 1975. His son, Matthew, has since taken over as Sooty and Sweep's harassed straight man.

CORBETT, HARRY H. OBE (1925–82)

Although he subsequently appeared in a range of TV shows, Harry H. Corbett will forever be remembered as Harold Steptoe, the seedy rag and bone man with artistic pretensions whose dreams were constantly shattered by his vulgar old dad. Corbett came to television via film and the Shakespearean and classical stage, having served in the Marines in the war and then training as a radiographer. **Steptoe and Son** arrived in 1962 as an episode of **Comedy Playhouse**, before spinning off into a series of its own. It ran – off and on – for 12 years and left Corbett heavily typecast, despite numerous appearances in programmes like **The Goodies**, **Tales of the Unexpected** and **Shoestring**, his own three sitcoms – as the status-seeking Mr Aitch in 1967, the determined bachelor Alfred Wilcox in **The Best Things in Life** in 1969, and newsagent Grundy in 1980 – and a prominent role in the comedy **Potter**, as local gangster Harry Tooms. Corbett, whose first wife had been comedienne Sheila Steafel, died of a heart attack in 1982, ironically three years before his TV father, Wilfrid Brambell. The unusual 'H' in his name stood, allegedly, for 'Hanything' and was included to avoid confusion with Harry Corbett of Sooty fame.

CORBETT, RONNIE (1930–)

Tiny, bespectacled Scots-born comedian and comic actor, one half of the celebrated **Two Ronnies** partnership. Ronnie Corbett's TV career actually began on **Crackerjack** in the 1950s and progressed via series like **The Dickie Henderson Show** to **The Frost Report** (on which he worked with John Cleese and Ronnie Barker). His own sitcom, **No – That's Me Over Here**, followed in 1967, then, in 1971, he was teamed once again with Barker for **The Two Ronnies**. One of the show's highlights were Corbett's drawn-out monologues delivered from an outsize armchair. During the programme's lengthy run, Corbett moved back into situation comedy with the series **Now Look Here . . .**, **The Prince of Denmark** and **Sorry!**, with the part of mummy's boy Timothy Lumsden in the last tailor-made for him. Since 1994 he has hosted **Small Talk**, a humorous quiz game based on children's views of the world. Corbett also has plenty of variety performances and guest appearances to his name.

CORONATION STREET

UK (Granada) Drama. ITV 1960

Original Cast:
Ena Sharples...Violet Carson
Annie Walker ....Doris Speed

Jack Walker..Arthur Leslie
Elsie Tanner/Howard ....Pat Phoenix
Dennis Tanner ....Philip Lowrie
Frank Barlow.....................................Frank Pemberton
Ida Barlow ....Noel Dyson
Ken Barlow...William Roache
David Barlow ....Alan Rothwell
Martha Longhurst ....Lynne Carol
Minnie Caldwell ....Margot Bryant
Elsie Lappin ....Maudie Edwards
Ivan Cheveski ....Ernst Walder
Linda Cheveski ....Anne Cunningham
Harry Hewitt ....Ivan Beavis
Christine Hardman/Appleby ......Christine Hargreaves
May Hardman ....Joan Heath
Susan Cunningham ....Patricia Shakesby
Albert Tatlock ....Jack Howarth
Florrie Lindley ....Betty Alberge
Esther Hayes..................................Daphne Oxenford
Leonard Swindley ....Arthur Lowe
Concepta Riley/Hewitt/Regan ....Doreen Keogh
Lucille Hewitt ....Jennifer Moss
Valerie Tatlock/Barlow ....Anne Reid

Prominent later cast members:
Emily Nugent/Bishop ....Eileen Derbyshire
Billy Walker...................................Kenneth Farrington
Len Fairclough ....Peter Adamson
Bill Gregory ....Jack Watson
Jerry Booth....................................Graham Haberfield
Myra Dickinson/Booth ....Susan Jameson
Esther Hayes..................................Daphne Oxenford
Jed Stone ....Kenneth Cope
Sheila Birtles/Crossley ....Eileen Mayers
Doreen Lostock ....Angela Crow
Charlie Moffitt ....Gordon Rollings
Dave Smith...Reginald Marsh
Hilda Ogden ....Jean Alexander
Stan Ogden ....Bernard Youens
Irma Ogden/Barlow ....Sandra Gough
Lionel Petty ....Edward Evans
Sandra Petty ....Heather Moore
Ray Langton ....Neville Buswell
Steve Tanner ....Paul Maxwell
Susan Barlow/Baldwin ....Wendy Jane Walker
                              Katie Heanus (*Barlow* only)
                       Susan Patterson (*Barlow* only)
Peter Barlow ....John Heanus
                                                        Mark Duncan
                                                        Chris Dormes
                                                        Linus Roache
                                                        Joseph McKenna
                                                        David Lonsdale
Alf Roberts..Bryan Mosley
Audrey /Bright Fleming ....Gillian McCann
Dickie Fleming ....Nigel Humphries
Maggie Clegg/Cooke ....Irene Sutcliffe
Les Clegg ....John Sharp
Gordon Clegg.....................................Bill Kenwright
Betty Turpin ....Betty Driver
Cyril Turpin ....William Moore
Alice Pickens ....Doris Hare
Janet Reid/Barlow ....Judith Barker
Ernest Bishop.................................Stephen Hancock
Alan Howard..................................Alan Browning
Frank Bradley...Tommy Boyle
Bet Lynch/Gilroy ....Julie Goodyear

Rita Bates/Littlewood/Fairclough/Sullivan ....Barbara Mullaney/Knox
Norma Ford..Diana Davies
Jacko Ford ....Robert Keegan
Mavis Riley/Wilton ....Thelma Barlow
Deirdre Hunt/Langton/Barlow/RachidAnne Kirkbride
Blanche Hunt..Maggie Jones
Ron Cooke ....Eric Lander
Idris Hopkins ....Richard Davies
Vera Hopkins ....Kathy Staff
Granny Hopkins ....Jessie Evans
Tricia Hopkins..Kathy Jones
Eddie Yeats...Geoffrey Hughes
Fred Gee ....Fred Feast
Derek Wilton ....Peter Baldwin
Gail Potter/Tilsley/Platt.........................Helen Worth
Mike Baldwin ....Johnny Briggs
Suzie Birchall ....Cheryl Murray
Renee Bradshaw/Roberts.....................Madge Hindle
Tracy Langton/Barlow ....Christabel Finch
                                                        Holly Chamarette
                                                              Dawn Acton
Steve Fisher ....Lawrence Mullen
Ivy Tilsley/Brennan.....................................Lynne Perrie
Bert Tilsley...Peter Dudley
Brian Tilsley ....Christopher Quinten
Audrey Potter/Roberts............................Sue Nicholls
Arnold Swain ....George Waring
Martin Cheveski .... Jonathon Caplan
Eunice Nuttall/Gee.................................Meg Johnson
Nicky Tilsley/Platt ....Warren Jackson
Nellie Harvey ....Mollie Sugden
Marion Willis/Yeats ....Veronica Doran
Sharon Gaskell ....Tracie Bennett
Maggie Dunlop/Redman...........................Jill Kerman
Tom 'Chalkie' Whiteley ....Teddy Turner
Craig Whiteley ....Mark Price
Phyllis Pearce ....Jill Summers
Victor Pendlebury ....Christopher Coll
Percy Sugden ....Bill Waddington
Vera Duckworth..................................Elizabeth Dawn
Jack Duckworth ....William Tarmey
Terry Duckworth ....Nigel Pivaro
Norman 'Curly' Watts ....Kevin Kennedy
Shirley Armitage ....Lisa Lewis
Kevin Webster.....................................Michael Le Vell
Bill Webster..Peter Armitage
Debbie Webster ....Sue Devaney
Harry Clayton...Johnny Leeze
Connie Clayton..Susan Brown
Andrea Clayton ....Caroline O'Neill
Sue Clayton......................................Jane Hazlegrove
Sam Tindall ....Tom Mennard
Jenny Bradley ....Sally Ann Matthews
Alan Bradley...Mark Eden
George Wardle ....Ron Davies
Sally Seddon/Webster.........................Sally Whittaker
Gloria Todd ....Sue Jenkins
Martin Platt ....Sean Wilson
Alma Sedgewick/Baldwin.....................Amanda Barrie
Sarah Louise Tilsley ....Lynsay King
Alec Gilroy ....Roy Barraclough
Don Brennan ....Geoff Hinsliff
Tina Fowler...................................Michelle Holmes
Dawn Prescott ....Louise Harrison
Liz McDonald ....Beverley Callard
Jim McDonald......................................Charles Lawson

Andy McDonald ....Nicholas Cochrane
Steve McDonald ....Simon Gregory
Wendy Crozier ....Roberta Kerr
Des Barnes......................................Philip Middlemiss
Steph Barnes ....Amelia Bullmore
Vicky Arden.....................................Chloe Newsome
Felicity 'Flick' Khan.....................................Rita Wolf
Kimberley Taylor ....Suzanne Hall
Angie Freeman...........................Deborah McAndrew
Phil Jennings ....Tommy Boyle
Reg Holdsworth ....Ken Morley
Raquel Wolstenhulme ....Sarah Lancashire
Lisa Horten/Duckworth ....Caroline Milmoe
Ted Sullivan ....William Russell
Brendan Scott..Milton Johns
Denise Osbourne....................................Denise Black
Maureen Naylor/Holdsworth ....Sherrie Hewson
Maud Grimes............................Elizabeth Bradley
Fiona Middleton ....Angela Griffin
Tanya Pooley...Eva Pope
Charlie Whelan......................................John St Ryan

Creator: Tony Warren

Working-class life in a northern backstreet.

Coronation Street is a British institution. However, after the first episode went out at 7 pm on 9 December 1960 one critic famously declared that it had no future, being all doom and gloom. Like the Decca records executive who turned down The Beatles, he couldn't have been more wrong. The '*Street*' is now surging towards its 40th anniversary and is still at the top of the ratings. That said, anyone viewing early recordings will immediately recognize how the series has changed over the years. It began in an age of industrial grime and sweat, but has progressed to reflect the many changes that have taken place in British life. The smoking chimney pots and leaden skies of the early programme credits echoed a dour but vibrant society, and creator Tony Warren (a 23-year-old Granada staff writer, tired of adapting **Biggles** stories) initially produced scripts similar to the kitchen-sink dramas seen on **Armchair Theatre**. But the programme quickly mellowed, introducing more humour and occasional farcical elements. Indeed, the programme wandered so far from Warren's original goals that he disowned it at one time. These days *Coronation Street* plays almost like a situation comedy, although shocks, tragedy and moments of high drama are liberally dispersed throughout its episodes. Warren himself has now conceded that with society growing 'softer', *Coronation Street* has had to follow suit.

The programme is set in the fictional Manchester suburb of Weatherfield, Coronation Street (the working name was Florizel Street but, allegedly, sounded too much like a lavatory cleaner) being a typical northern back-street terrace with a pub on one corner and a shop on the other. The first ever scene took place in the shop on the day that Florrie Lindley arrived to take over the business from the retiring Elsie Lappin. Also in that historic original cast were Annie and Jack Walker, landlords of the pub, the Rovers Return. The genial Jack (and actor Arthur Leslie) died in 1970, but Annie, the *Street's* duchess and mistress of the withering look, held the licence until 1983, when she retired and left the series. Ena Sharples was the local hair-netted battleaxe, caretaker of the Glad Tidings Mission. Her OAP friends in the pub's snug were meek and mild Minnie Caldwell and Martha Longhurst, who was sensationally killed off in 1964, slumping dead over her milk stout. Another veteran was pensioner Albert Tatlock, proud of his war medals but never too proud to cadge a free rum if one was offered. Elsie Tanner was the fiery brunette whose promiscuity nettled the local puritans (especially Ena), and Dennis was her layabout son. And then there were the Barlows, hard-working, salt of the earth dad, Frank, his loyal wife, Ida (soon to be crushed by a bus), and two sons, Ken and David. David, a one-time professional footballer, was subsequently killed in a car accident in Australia, while Ken, always the *Street's* intellectual (thrice-married: to Albert Tatlock's niece Valerie, to suicide victim Janet Reid and to Deirdre Langton), is today the only remaining original cast member.

Over the years the series has introduced plenty of other memorable characters. Leonard Swindley was the teetotal, lay-preaching draper who was jilted at the altar by the mousey Emily Nugent. Swindley later starred in the only *Coronation Street* spin-off series, **Pardon the Expression**. Nugent, another long-serving member of the cast, went on to marry photographer Ernie Bishop and, after he was shot dead in a wages snatch, wed bigamist Arnold Swain. Lucille Hewitt was the troublesome teeager who lived with the Walkers after her father, Harry, and barmaid step-mother, Concepta, left for Ireland, while Len Fairclough was the *Street's* he-man, a hard-drinking, roughly hewn builder who eventually signed away his bachelorhood (after years of flirtation with Elsie Tanner) in a marriage to red-headed singer Rita Littlewood. After 23 years in the series, he was killed off in a car crash in 1983, following a visit to his mistress. Lovable Jerry Booth was Len's stuttering assistant at the builder's yard. His place was taken later by the untrustworthy Ray Langton.

Stan and Hilda Ogden moved into number 13 in 1964 and forged one of TV's great double acts, a partnership that was only broken by actor Bernard Youens's illness and subsequent death in 1984. A combination of a workshy boozer and a tittle-tattling skivvy, the Ogdens were the

unluckiest couple on television, although their misfortune was usually self-inflicted. For many, Hilda's grief when Stan died provided moments of unsurpassable drama and actress Jean Alexander's performances won universal acclaim. The Ogdens' wayward daughter, Irma (she of the rasping voice), became David Barlow's wife, while their lodger, chortling jailbird dustman Eddie Yeats, was one of the show's most popular stars of the 1970s.

With the retirement of Annie Walker, the Rovers Return eventually passed into the hands of brassy, buxom Bet Lynch, the tarty, blonde barmaid who first arrived in the series in 1966 and became a fixture in 1970. Bet has since taken over as the *Street's* mother confessor, although her own problems (notably with men – including her failed marriage to entertainments agent Alec Gilroy) have been far from trivial. One of her liaisons was with rag trade wide boy Mike Baldwin, arch-enemy of Ken Barlow (having tried to steal Ken's wife, Deirdre, and then marrying his daughter, Susan). Rita Fairclough's harrowing ordeal at the hands of vicious Alan Bradley was another *Coronation Street* highlight, ending with Bradley's death beneath the wheels of a Blackpool tram. Twittering away behind Rita has been Mavis, her dithery colleague in The Kabin newsagent's shop, and regular interruptions have come from Mavis's wimpy suitors, Derek Wilton and Victor Pendlebury.

The younger element has also been well represented. In the 1970s action focused around flighty shop assistant Suzie Birchall, corner shop girl Tricia Hopkins and insecure Gail Potter. Gail has since matured into a mother of three – and wife of two. Her first husband was the brawny Brian Tilsley (son of Ivy, arch-nagger, devout Catholic and one-time factory shop steward), while her second husband was trainee nurse Martin Platt, one of the 1980s intake of teenagers. Along with Martin, the 1980s brought in star-gazing binman (later supermarket manager) Curly Watts, bookie Des Barnes and mechanic Kevin Webster and his pretty blonde wife, Sally. Occasionally on the scene was sneering Terry Duckworth, the ne'er-do-well son of shiftless Jack and loud-mouthed Vera, who have assumed the Ogdens' crown as the *Street's* perpetual losers.

Shopkeeper Alf Roberts has been one of the series' senior figures ever since becoming a permanent cast member in 1968, no doubt helped by the fact that he has been Weatherfield's mayor on two occasions. His wife Renee was killed in a car accident and Alf has since suffered at the hands of his spendthrift second wife, Audrey, Gail's unreliable mother. Among the other senior characters have been policeman's widow Betty

Turpin (the pub's homely barmaid and ace hot-pot cook), gravel-voiced blue-rinser Phyllis Pearce and the apple of her eye, war cook Percy Sugden, Emily's interfering, insensitive lodger. One of the series' latest cult characters has been Reg Holdsworth, the pompous, vain retail executive.

Coronation Street's writers have been many, with the most notable including John Finch, Jack Rosenthal, Harry Driver, Harry (H.V.) Kershaw, Adele Rose, Jim Allen and John Stevenson. Stuart Latham, Tim Aspinall, Bill Podmore and Mervyn Watson, as well as Finch, Rosenthal and Kershaw, have been among the most influential producers. The series' melancholic, solo cornet theme tune was written by Eric Spear. In addition to the cast list above, the roll call of 'guesting' actors and actresses is impressive to say the least. Among those cutting their teeth in the series have been singers Peter Noone of Herman's Hermits (Len Fairclough's son, Stanley), Monkee Davy Jones (Ena Sharples's grandson, Colin Lomax) and Michael Ball (Malcolm Nuttall, Kevin Webster's one-time rival in love), as well as the likes of Joanna Lumley (Ken Barlow's girlfriend, Elaine Perkins), Prunella Scales (bus conductress Eileen Hughes), Martin Shaw (hippie Robert Croft), Ray Brooks (Norman Phillips), Michael Elphick (Douglas Wormald, who wanted to buy The Kabin), Paula Wilcox (Ray Langton's sister, Janice), Peter Dean (lorry driver Fangio Bateman), Stan Stennett (Norman Crabtree, Hilda Ogden's chip shop-owning brother), Richard Beckinsale (a policeman), *The Good Old Days* compere Leonard Sachs (Sir Julius Berlin), Paul Shane (post office worker Frank Draper), Bill Maynard (music agent Mickey Malone), Ben Kingsley (a Jack the lad who chatted up Irma Ogden and Valerie Barlow), Max Wall (Elsie Tanner's friend, Harry Payne) and a very young Joanne Whalley-Kilmer (Pamela Graham). Singer Chris Sandford appeared as binman Walter Potts, aka pop hopeful Brett Falcon, who recorded the song 'Not Too Little Not Too Much', a real-life Top Twenty hit in 1963.

Originally screened live on Wednesdays and Fridays, *Coronation Street* switched to Monday and Wednesday evenings in 1961 and was, for the first time, fully networked (the earliest episodes were not seen in the Midlands or in the Tyne-Tees area). Since 1989 a third helping has been served up on Fridays in a bid to win the soap war with BBC rival *EastEnders*. *Coronation Street* has also been viewed with much pleasure all around the world, although one of the few places it has yet to catch on is the USA. America did produce its own copycat soap, however, in the shape of

Peyton Place. Outliving its glamorous American clone by many years, *Coronation Street* is now the world's longest running fictitious television series.

COSBY, BILL (1937–)

Hugely successful black American comedian/actor/producer, a former night club comic whose TV career began with *I Spy* alongside Robert Culp in 1965. In playing the part of Alexander Scott, Cosby became the first black actor to co-star in a US prime time drama series. He followed *I Spy* with a succession of comedy, variety and children's programmes, most of which were not aired in the UK. After spending eight years out of television, in which he gained a doctorate in education, he was tempted back by the offer of a sitcom over which he had complete creative control. The result was *The Cosby Show* and his portrayal of caring dad Cliff Huxtable enabled Cosby to give vent to his own philosophies of how to raise and educate children. The show picked up numerous awards and was a massive ratings success. More recently Cosby has filled Groucho Marx's shoes in the revival of the 1950s US quiz show *You Bet Your Life*, which has been screened on Channel 4.

COSBY SHOW, THE

US (Carsey-Werner) Situation Comedy.
Channel 4 1985–94

Dr Heathcliff (Cliff) Huxtable	Bill Cosby
Clair Huxtable	Phylicia Ayres-Allen/Rashad
Denise Huxtable Kendall	Lisa Bonet
Theodore Huxtable	Malcolm-Jamal Warner
Vanessa Huxtable	Tempestt Bledsoe
Rudy Huxtable	Keshia Knight Pulliam
Sondra Huxtable/Tibideaux	Sabrina Le Beauf
Peter Chiara	Peter Costa
Anna Huxtable	Clarice Taylor
Russell Huxtable	Earle Hyman
Elvin Tibideaux	Geoffrey Owens
Kenny ('Bud')	Deon Richmond
Cockroach	Carl Anthony Payne
Denny	Troy Winbush
Lt Martin Kendall	Joseph C. Phillips
Olivia Kendall	Raven Symone
Pam Turner	Erika Alexander

Creators: Bill Cosby, Ed Weinberger, Michael Leeson. Producer: Bill Cosby

Family life in a caring New York household.

After a chequered TV past, Bill Cosby created this gentle sitcom and turned it into one of US TV's biggest ever moneyspinners. *The Cosby Show* followed developments in the life of a black middle-class family, showing the children growing up, leaving school and college, eventually getting married and having children of their own. The parents were the charming Cliff Huxtable, an obstetrician, and his confident lawyer wife, Clair. Their children ranged in age from Sondra, a Princetown student, to five-year-old Rudy, with, in between, teenagers Denise and Theo and eight-year-old Vanessa. The children's friends were also included. Cockroach was a pal of Theo's, while Peter, Bud and Denny were a few of Rudy's classmates. Anna and Russell, Cliff's parents, made occasional appearances and, later, the Huxtables took in Pam Tucker, the teenage daughter of a distant cousin from the Brooklyn slums. The family lived in a New York terraced house, from where Cliff also practised his medicine.

Bill Cosby wasn't just the show's creator, his control was evident throughout. He was involved in many aspects of the production and the series became a personal statement about how he felt children should be brought up, i.e. with firmness and love, a philosophy he had developed while taking an education degree in the 1970s.

COTTON, BILL, CBE (1928–)

The son of bandleader Billy Cotton, Bill Cotton's showbusiness career began in Tin Pan Alley as a record plugger. He was joint MD of Michael Reine Music Co., 1952–6, before joining the BBC as a light entertainment producer. He became Assistant Head of Light Entertainment in 1962, moving up to Head of Variety in 1967. From 1970 he was Head of Light Entertainment and progressed to Controller of BBC 1 in 1977, and then Deputy Managing Director of BBC Television in 1981. After time chairing BBC Enterprises, Cotton was installed as Managing Director of BBC Television in 1984. In 1988 he left to join the Noel Gay Organization. Among his other interests has been the deputy chairmanship of Meridian (since 1991).

COTTON, BILLY (1899–1969)

'Wakey, wakey!' With a yell like this, and a rousing rendition of his theme tune, 'Somebody Stole My Girl', jovial bandleader Billy Cotton ensured viewers never missed the start of his weekly variety revue. With its emphasis on comedy and music, *The Billy Cotton Band Show* was a stalwart of the BBC's programming for 12 years from 1956 and he also had success with *Wakey Wakey Tavern* and *Billy Cotton's Music Hall*, as well as being seen in variety programmes like *Saturday Showtime* and *The Tin Pan Alley Show*. Cotton arrived on television via BBC radio. He first broadcast in 1924 and his Band Show was a Sunday lunchtime favourite for 19 years from

1949. He was also a keen sportsman, despite his 17-stone frame. His son, Bill Cotton Jnr (who also produced some of his dad's programmes), later became Controller of BBC 1 and Managing Director of BBC Television.

COUNT OF MONTE CRISTO, THE

UK (ITP) Adventure. ITV 1956

Edmund Dantes	George Dolenz
Jacopo	Nick Cravat
Rico	Robert Cawdron
Princess Anne	Faith Domergue

Producers: Sidney Marshall, Dennis Vance

A falsely imprisoned man learns of lost treasure from a fellow prisoner and escapes to claim it.

In 18th-century France, Edmund Dantes had been wrongly convicted of crimes against the state and incarcerated in the infamous Château d'If. There, a dying prisoner told of the treasure to be found on the island of Monte Cristo and Dantes broke free to take it for his own, setting himself up as a nobleman on the proceeds. The original story came from the novel of the same name by Alexandre Dumas, although the TV series expanded on Dantes's swashbuckling adventures on Monte Cristo, making the Frenchman a kind of Robin Hood battling for fairness and justice for all. Star George Dolenz was the father of future Monkee Mickey.

COUNTDOWN

UK (Yorkshire) Game Show. Channel 4 1982–

Presenters: Richard Whiteley, Carol Vorderman. Creator: Armand Jammot. Executive Producers: Frank Smith, John Meade

Daily afternoon words and numbers game.

The aim for the two *Countdown* contestants has been, to construct in 30 seconds, the longest word they can from nine letters chosen at random. Whoever has used up the most letters in forming a word has earned the same number of points as letters used. Between word rounds a couple of numbers games have been introduced. For these, the contestants have needed to add, subtract, multiply and divide randomly selected numbers to arrive at a given total (or as close to it as possible). The contestant with the sum nearest the total has gained ten more points. The final round has been the *Countdown* conundrum, an anagram worth ten points for first correct solution. The higher scoring contestant has then met a new challenger on the following day and the series' best participants have taken part in an end of term knockout to find the overall champion.

Richard Whiteley has hosted proceedings from day one, Carol Vorderman has been the numbers and letters girl and Beverley Isherwood and Kathy Hynter acted as hostesses in the early programmes. A guest celebrity has helped verify the words, and those gleefully undertaking this chore have included Ted Moult, Kenneth Williams, Sylvia Sims, Richard Stilgoe and Gyles Brandreth. *Countdown* was the first programme to be seen on Channel 4 and was based on a French concept. From the late 1980s its twice-yearly runs have alternated with series of the quiz *Fifteen to One* in the 4.30 pm time slot.

COUNTRY MATTERS

UK (Granada) Drama Anthology. ITV 1972–3

Producer: Derek Granger

Dramatization of assorted rustic stories.

This anthology of 13 attractively framed rustic tales was adapted from the works of H.E. Bates and A.E. Coppard. It featured stars like Ian McKellan, Joss Ackland, Pauline Collins, Jane Lapotaire, Michael Elphick, Jeremy Brett and Gareth Thomas, and the plays revolved around love, rivalry and times of adversity in beautiful country locations.

COUNTRY MUSIC TELEVISION

(CMT) Broadcasting 13 hours a day from the Astra 1B satellite (and piped 24 hours a day on cable), CMT is a country music-based channel, making much use of pre-recorded videos. CMT Europe – launched in October 1992 – is programmed separately from the parent operation in the USA to include the big names in European country, and is available as part of the Sky Multi-Channels package. The company is jointly owned by Gaylord Entertainment Company and Group W Satellite Communications (GWSC).

COURT MARTIAL

UK/US (Roncom/ITC) Legal Drama. ITV 1965–7

Captain David Young ....Bradford Dillman
Major Frank Whittaker............................Peter Graves
Master Sgt John MacCaskey ....Kenneth J. Warren
Sgt Wendy...Diane Clare

Producers: Robert Douglas, Bill Hill

A team of military lawyers investigates crimes committed during the war.

Based in England during World War II, the industrious legal beagles of the US Army Judge Advocate General's Office were assigned to the continent of Europe. Their mission: to track down perpetrators of war crimes and bring them

to justice. Each episode devoted much time to their excursions into war-torn Europe, winding up with the court martial proceedings themselves. Major Frank Whittaker was senior officer and chief prosecutor, Captain David Young the defending barrister. Sgt John MacCaskey was their aide and Sgt Wendy their secretary. The series was spun off a two-part story entitled *The Case Against Paul Ryker*, which aired as part of the *Kraft Suspense Theater* anthology in the USA.

COUSTEAU, JACQUES (1910–)

French marine expert and a former Navy officer who, during the war, was largely responsible for the development of the aqualung (and the new freedom it gave divers) during World War II. In the postwar years he branched out into cinematic documentaries that charted his scientific explorations beneath the waves. Working from his converted minesweeper, *Calypso*, Cousteau later revealed the mysteries of the deep to TV viewers, in series like *Under the Sea*, **The World About Us**, the internationally successful *Undersea World of Jacques Cousteau* (which ran for eight years) and *The Cousteau Odyssey*. His entertaining, authoritative, rather nasal delivery opened up the complexities of marine biology to an enthralled general public and won him numerous awards and commendations. In recent years he has become a vociferous environmental campaigner.

CRACKER

UK (Granada) Drama. ITV 1993–

Eddie 'Fitz' Fitzgerald.......................Robbie Coltrane
Judith Fitzgerald....................................Barbara Flynn
Detective Sgt
 Jane Penhaligon........................Geraldine Somerville
Detective Chief Inspector
 David Bilborough ....Christopher Eccleston
Detective Sgt Jimmy Beck ....Lorcan Cranitch
Mark Fitzgerald ....Kieran O'Brien
Detective Chief Inspector Wise ....Ricky Tomlinson
DC Harriman...Colin Tierney

Creator: Jimmy McGovern. Producers: Gub Neal, Paul Abbott

A larger-than-life police psychologist cracks complicated crimes but fails to keep his life in order.

'Fitz' Fitzgerald was an outstanding but totally unconventional criminal psychologist, working freelance for the Greater Manchester Police. His speciality was reading a criminal's mind, drawing up character profiles and helping the police break down a suspect's outer shell, although his approach was often crude, insensitive and far from gentle. Bilborough (and later Wise) was the DCI who called on Fitz's services, and

'Panhandle' Penhaligon was the sergeant usually despatched to chaperon him. As brilliant as Fitz was at his job, his own personal life was in a mess. Grossly overweight, a heavy drinker, a compulsive gambler and a chain smoker, Fitz could 'spot a guilty cough in a football crowd but not know if World War III was breaking out in his living room', according to Panhandle. And when Fitz's long-suffering wife, Judith, walked out on him, he only made matters worse by embarking on a stormy affair with his attractive police associate.

Intense, shocking and riddled with unexpected twists and turns, *Cracker* won universal acclaim, with Robbie Coltrane collecting the BAFTA Best Actor award for his efforts. It was also graphically and realistically violent, although such excesses were presented in a defiantly unglorified manner.

CRACKERJACK

UK (BBC) Children's Entertainment. BBC 1955–84

Presenters:
Eamonn Andrews
Leslie Crowther
Michael Aspel
Ed Stewart
Stu Francis

Other regulars:
Jack Douglas
Ronnie Corbett
Peter Glaze
Jillian Comber
Pip Hinton
Christine Holmes
Frances Barlow
Rod McLennan
Don Maclean
Little and Large
Jan Hunt
Bernie Clifton

Producers: Johnny Downes, Peter Whitmore, Brian Jones, Robin Nash, Paul Ciani

Live music and comedy show for kids.

In the USA, *Crackerjack* is a brand of popcorn – an appropriate name really for this variety show, which leaned heavily on top pop stars and corny jokes to carry the day. But carry the day it did – on Fridays, at five to five (or thereabouts), for no less than 29 years. With its trademark '*Crackerjack*' echo from the studio audience every time the programme's name was mentioned, it offered slapstick sketches (most memorably featuring a young Leslie Crowther and former Crazy Gang extra Peter Glaze), the latest pop hits (big names appearing included Roy Orbison, Tom Jones and Cliff Richard) and a sing-along, grand finale, usually comprising a medley of chart records with

'funny' new words added. In between, competitions held sway. These were strictly divided into boys' and girls' games in the show's formative years, and best remembered is *Double or Drop* (which was devised by the programme's first host, Eamonn Andrews, and ran until 1964). In *Double or Drop*, kids answered questions and were then loaded up with prizes which, if dropped, were confiscated. Wrong answers led to armfuls of booby prize cabbages. But all contestants, win or lose, walked away with a coveted *Crackerjack* pencil.

Ronnie Corbett and Jack Douglas cut their TV teeth on *Crackerjack* and Leslie Crowther's career was done no harm by an eight-year stretch as comic and then compere. Richard Hearne's Mr Pastry was also a regular guest in the 1950s. Eamonn Andrews and Michael Aspel moved on to bigger and better things, whilst later hosts Ed 'Stewpot' Stewart and Stu 'I could crush a grape' Francis were established children's entertainers who found their niche with the programme. Reassuring female hostesses like Jillian Comber, Pip Hinton and Christine Holmes became almost as popular as the male stars.

CRADOCK, FANNY (PHYLLIS CRADOCK; 1909–94)

Fanny Cradock was one of the small screen's first cooks and an unlikely star of TV's golden age. Shunning the apron in favour of impractical evening gowns and pearls, she epitomised the rather starchy attitude prevalent in the BBC in the 1950s. She and her third husband, Major John Cradock, were published gourmets, writing the Bon Viveur column in the *Daily Telegraph*, for instance. They joined the BBC in 1955 to present Kitchen Magic but were soon snapped up by the new, less pompous ITV, where, instead of being Phyllis and John, they became Fanny and Johnny and hosted Fanny's Kitchen, Chez Bon Viveur and The Cradocks. They also chipped in with the Happy Cooking sequence in the kids' series Lucky Dip. Although they were mostly billed as a twosome, it was Fanny who was clearly in charge, leaving the monocled Johnny hovering in the background as she thrashed a few eggs around or whipped up a pudding. Her rather brusque, demanding style made her and Johnny (often jokingly portrayed as a kitchen boozer) easy targets for comedians like Benny Hill. They rejoined the BBC in the 1960s, presenting programmes like Giving A Dinner Party, Fanny Cradock Invites and Fanny Cradock Cooks for Christmas, carrying on until retirement in the 1970s. Johnny died in 1987.

CRAIG, MICHAEL (MICHAEL GREGSON; 1929–)

Silver-haired, rugged British actor, born in India. A Rank movie star of the 1950s and 1960s, his starring TV roles have included Johann in the steamy Husbands and Lovers, 50-year-old Harry who fell in love with a girl half his age in the sitcom *Second Time Around*, William Parker, the dad of the Australia-bound family in *The Emigrants*, and ship's officer John Anderson in *Triangle*. Other credits have included *Emergency – Ward 10* and *Doctor Who*.

CRAIG, WENDY (1934–)

British actress strongly associated with daffy, harassed mother roles, evidenced in such series as *Not in Front of the Children* (as Jennifer Corner), *And Mother Makes Three/Five* (Sally Harrison/Redway) and *Butterflies* (Ria Parkinson). She branched out into serious drama in her own creation *Nanny* (playing 1930s nanny Barbara Gray), but returned to sitcom with the short-lived *Laura and Disorder*, a series that she co-wrote (under her pen name of Jonathan Marr) and in which she played accident-prone divorcée Laura Kingsley arriving back in the UK after ten years in America. Craig has also been seen in recent years in *The Golden Girls* clone *Brighton Belles* (as Annie, the Rose character), although her earliest credits include the 1964 sitcom *Room at the Bottom* and various single dramas.

CRANE

UK (Associated-Rediffusion) Adventure. ITV 1963–5

Richard Crane	Patrick Allen
Orlando O'Connor	Sam Kydd
Colonel Mahmoud	Gerald Flood
Halima	Laya Raki

Creators: Patrick Alexander, Jordan Lawrence
Producer: Jordan Lawrence

The adventures of a city businessman turned contrabrand dealer in North Africa.

Bored of the routine of city life, Richard Crane took himself off to sunny Morocco, bought a boat and opened a beachfront bar near Casablanca. To pass the time, he indulged himself in petty smuggling – minor items like tobacco and booze. Keeping an eye on his activities was elegant local police chief Colonel Mahmoud, although he and Crane sometimes worked together against 'serious' criminals. Crane's well-worn friend and accomplice was Orlando O'Connor, a former member of the French Foreign Legion. He later appeared in his own spin-off series for children, *Orlando*. Halima was the café's sultry young bartender. Star Patrick

Allen, an actor with the booming, authoritative voice, went on to more success off-camera, cornering the market in advert voice-overs.

CRANHAM, KENNETH (1944–)

Scottish-born actor well versed in rough diamond roles with a host of one-off dramas and guest appearances to his name. Among his starring roles have been Harvey Moon, the demobbed RAF corporal in *Shine On Harvey Moon*, the over-zealous Pastor Finch in *Oranges Are Not the Only Fruit* and villain Gus Mercer in *El C.I.D.*. Other credits have included *A Sort of Innocence*, *Coronation Street*, *Danger UXB*, *Thérèse Raquin*, *Reilly – Ace of Spies* (as Lenin), *Inspector Morse*, *Boon*, *Rules of Engagement*, *Van Der Valk*, *Bergerac*, *Murder Most Horrid* and *Chimera*.

CRAVEN, JOHN (1940–)

Leeds-born presenter whose first TV appearances came at the age of 16 on *Sunday Break*. Later he was seen on regional news magazines; including *Look North* and *Points West*, and the kids' show *Search*, before he secured the job of children's news presenter on his own *John Craven's Newsround*. From this came *Multi-Coloured Swap Shop* (encouraging a 'News Swap') and its successor *Saturday Superstore*. Most recently he has been host of *Country File*.

CRAWFORD, BRODERICK (WILLIAM BRODERICK CRAWFORD; 1911–86)

The man who gave the world the catchphrase 'Ten-Four'. Brawny Broderick Crawford's career began in 1930s gangster movies, in the sort of shady role he was initially to take into television. However, it was on the other side of the law that he made his name, playing Chief Dan Matthews in the hugely successful *Highway Patrol*. His bulky frame leaning against a car window, hollering 'Ten-Four' down the radio, is fondly remembered by viewers. Although he did secure lead roles in a couple of other American series (*King of Diamonds* and *The Interns*) after *Highway Patrol* ended in 1959, he was mostly seen by British viewers in guest appearances in TV movies and shows such as *Get Smart, Burke's Law* and *Fantasy Island*. The son of comedienne Helen Broderick, he won the Oscar for Best Actor in 1949 for his performance in *All the King's Men*.

CRAWFORD, MICHAEL, OBE (MICHAEL DUMBLE SMITH; 1942–)

Popular British comic actor whose starring role in *Some Mothers Do 'Ave 'Em* came after years of supporting parts in early ITC adventures like **Sir Francis Drake** (playing Drake's nephew, John), comedies such as **Billy Bunter of Greyfriars School** and such dramas as **Police Surgeon**, **Probation Officer** and **Emergency – Ward 10**. However, it was as the accident-prone Frank Spencer that he made his name, winning huge acclaim for his comic performances and exhausting stunt routines. From this base, Crawford moved on to the less successful *Chalk and Cheese* (as Dave Finn, a Cockney among posher neighbours) and then more into theatre, although still finding time to pop up as a guest star and singer on numerous variety shows.

CREDITS

The roll call of programme participants (both in front of and behind the cameras), usually seen at the end of the programme. Occasionally credits are given during the opening titles, but usually these are confined to the major stars and the writers.

CREW

The technical team working on a programme, essentially the operators of sound, lighting and camera equipment but, in wider terms, associated staff involved in make-up, wardrobe, set construction, etc.

CREZZ, THE

UK (Thames) Drama. ITV 1976

Charles Bronte	Joss Ackland
Emma Antrobus	Isla Blair
Ken Green	Peter Bowles
Dr Balfour-Harvey	Hugh Burden
Brenda Pitman	Janet Key
Jackie Bronte	Elspet Gray

Creator: Clive Exton. Producer: Paul Knight

Tales of the residents of a London crescent.

Set in fictitious Carlisle Crescent, a middle-class London residential street, this series delivered 12 soapy, hour-long plays about the people who lived in *The Crezz*. It analysed their personal lives and monitored their inter-relationships, with one household assuming centre stage in each episode.

CRIBB

UK (Granada) Police Drama. ITV 1980–1

Sgt Cribb	Alan Dobie
Constable Thackeray	William Simons
Inspector Jowett	David Waller

Executive Producer: Peter Eckersley. Producer: June Wyndham-Davies

Victorian crime detection with a persistent CID officer.

Sgt Cribb, a dry, stubborn detective, worked for the newly formed Criminal Investigation Department, inaugurated to clean up the grimy streets of London in the time of Jack the Ripper. Cribb, a tough and determined officer with an eye for the ladies, outwitted the city's cleverest crooks (and his smartest colleagues) to bring to book all who crossed his path. He was assisted in his investigations by loyal Constable Thackeray, with Inspector Jowett, the commanding officer, often getting in the way.

The series, based on the novels of Peter Lovesey, involved its hero in all manner of crimes from blackmail to murder, usually set against the backdrop of the Victorians at leisure, with prize-fighting, the music hall and a six-day walking marathon among the featured activities. The detail was well researched and genuine events like the publication of Jerome K. Jerome's *Three Men in a Boat* and the purchase of London Zoo's elephant, Jumbo, by Barnum and Bailey's Circus, were woven into the plots. The series was spun off a 90-minute pilot episode, seen as part of Granada's *Screenplay* anthology in 1979.

CRIBBINS, BERNARD (1928–)

Whimsical British actor/comedian, a familiar voice as well as face on television. The milestones of his long TV career have been his own show, *Cribbins*, **The Wombles** (for which he provided the narration), *Cuffy* (as the eponymous tinker, spun off from **The Shillingbury Tales**) and *High and Dry* (as Ron Archer, owner of a seaside pier). These accompany numerous contributions to **The Good Old Days** and **Jackanory**, various guest spots (in series as varied as **The Avengers** and **Fawlty Towers**) and assorted panel game appearances, including as host of *Star Turn*. Cribbins also has many stage and film credits to his name and was the voice of Buzby, the chatty bird in the BT commercials.

CRIME OF PASSION

UK (ATV) Legal Drama Anthology. ITV 1970–3

President of the Court	Anthony Newlands
Maître Savel	Daniel Moynihan
Maître Lacan	John Phillips
Maître Dubois	Bernard Archer

Creator: Ted Willis. Producers: Cecil Clarke, Robert D. Cardona, Ian Fordyce

French barristers do battle over crimes of the heart.

Created by Ted Willis, using authentic French court cases (Crime of Passion is a legitimate defence in France), this series featured Maître Lacan for the prosecution and Maître Savel for the defence. Another lawyer, Maître Dubois, was seen in the last series. Each episode opened showing the crime in question, before moving on to the trial and finally the verdict of the Judge, the President of the Court. Among the guest stars were Felicity Kendall, Johnny Briggs, Ralph Bates and Tessa Wyatt.

CRIME SHEET

UK (Associated-Rediffusion) Police Drama. ITV 1959

Detective Chief Supt
  Tom Lockhart ....Raymond Francis

Creator: Glyn Davies. Producer: Barry Baker

The second part of the Supt Lockhart trilogy.

In this series, the sharp-witted, snuff-taking Supt Lockhart of **Murder Bag** had been promoted to detective chief superintendent and now cast his net farther afield than mere murder investigations. His talents were employed on crime of all sorts, but he remained so diligent and infallible in his pursuit of villains that he was quickly transferred to Scotland Yard and **No Hiding Place**. Two years later, Associated-Rediffusion revived the title *Crime Sheet* for a play starring Gerald Case as Chief Supt Carr.

CRIMEWATCH UK

UK (BBC) Factual. BBC 1 1984–

Presenters: Nick Ross, Sue Cook

Editor: Peter Chafer

Crime recontruction series inviting viewer assistance in catching villains.

Based on the German series *File XY Unsolved*, and originally scheduled for just three editions, *Crimewatch UK* has combined dramatic re-enactments of unsolved crimes with a plea to the general public to ring in with further information. Tips on crime prevention have also been included and 'treasure trove' spots have allowed burgled viewers to reclaim stolen property. Two resident police officers, David Hatcher and Helen Phelps, plus visiting detectives, initially helped give the police side of each story. Phelps later left the force and joined the programme's production team. Her place alongside Hatcher has since been taken by Jacqui Hames. The programme has been aired monthly and occasional review programmes have also been made, bringing viewers up to date with past stories. The series' clear-up rate has been impressive, with nearly 400 arrests made as a result of new information given by viewers.

CRISS CROSS QUIZ

UK (Granada) Quiz. ITV 1957–67

Presenter: Jeremy Hawk

Long-running noughts and crosses quiz.

This popular game show took the form of noughts and crosses with questions. One contestant scored crosses, the other scored noughts and, by giving correct answers, both sought to make a line of three, either vertically, diagonally or horizontally. For each correct answer cash was forthcoming and large totals were possible. Jeremy Hawk (father of actress Belinda Lang) was the original questionmaster of this thrice-weekly show and he also hosted a children's version, *Junior Criss Cross Quiz*, which ran for the same number of years. Chris Kelly was another presenter of the youth version, as were (at various times) Bob Holness, Mike Sarne, Chris Howland, Gordon Luck, Peter Wheeler, Bill Grundy and soccer star Danny Blanchflower. *Criss Cross Quiz* was derived from the American game show *Tic Tac Dough*.

CROFT, DAVID, OBE (1922–)

British comedy writer and producer, particularly in collaboration with Jimmy Perry and Jeremy Lloyd. With Perry, Croft created the doyen of British sitcoms, **Dad's Army**, and went on to script (and produce) comedy favourites **It Ain't Half Hot, Mum** and **Hi-De-Hi!** These reflected Croft's experiences as an ARP warden, a military entertainments officer in India and a producer of stage shows at Butlins. Croft and Perry also contributed **You Rang, M'Lord?** With Lloyd, Croft wrote **Oh Happy Band!, Are You Being Served?** and **'Allo 'Allo**. Croft's production credits have also included **Hugh and I, Beggar My Neigbour** and **Up Pompeii!**.

CRONKITE, WALTER (1916–)

An American institution, Walter Cronkite was the USA's foremost newsreader and commentator for some 20 years. Joining CBS as a reporter in 1950, he moved up to newsreader and news editor on the network's *Evening News* in 1962, quickly establishing himself as the country's most trusted anchorman. His avuncular, cosy, sometimes emotional style and his 'That's the way it is' sign-off became his trademarks.

CROSBIE, ANNETTE (1934–)

Busy Scottish actress most recently seen as Margaret, the long-suffering wife of Victor Meldrew, in **One Foot in the Grave**. Her television career, however, has spanned over three decades and has included the role of Catherine of Aragon in the acclaimed historical drama *The Six Wives of Henry VIII* and a BAFTA award-winning portrayal of Queen Victoria in *Edward the Seventh*. In addition to assorted one-off dramas, Crosbie's other notable performances have included a Résistance worker in *The White Rabbit*, Liz, Keith Barron's frumpy wife, in *Take Me Home*, and Joyce, Mel Smith's mother, in *Colin's Sandwich*. She was also seen in John Mortimer's *Paradise Postponed* and played Janet in the 1993 revival of *Doctor Finlay*.

CROSBY, BING (HARRY LILLIS CROSBY; 1903–77)

Internationally renowned crooner and light actor whose television work was largely confined to guest appearances and variety shows, with an attempt at sitcom in *The Bing Crosby Show* proving less rewarding. However, his behind the scenes credits were important and his film company, Bing Crosby Productions, was responsible for several US hit series, including *Ben Casey*. Trivia buffs will note that Crosby was the first choice for the role of *Columbo* but turned it down, allegedly because it would have interfered with his golf.

CROSSROADS

UK (ATV/Central) Drama. ITV 1964–88

Meg Richardson/Ryder/Mortimer	Noele Gordon
Jill Richardson/Harvey/Chance	Jane Rossington
Sandy Richardson	Roger Tonge
Kitty Jarvis	Beryl Johnstone
Dick Jarvis	Brian Kent
Brian Jarvis	David Fennell
Penny Richardson	Diane Grayson
Janice Gifford/Jarvis	Carolyn Lyster
Carlos Raphael	Anthony Morton
Diane Lawton/Parker/Hunter	Susan Hanson
Vince Parker	Peter Brookes
Andy Fraser	Ian Paterson
Ruth Fraser	Pamela Greenall
Marilyn Gates/Hope	Sue Nicholls
	Nadine Hanwell
Benny Willmott	Deke Arlen
Amy Turtle	Ann George
Miss Tatum	Elisabeth Croft
Mr Lovejoy	William Avenell
Malcolm Ryder	David Davenport
Ted Hope	Charles Stapley
Tish Hope	Joy Andrews
Wilf Harvey	Morris Parsons
Stan Harvey	Edward Clayton
Sheila Harvey/Mollison	Sonia Fox
David Hunter	Ronald Allen
Rosemary Hunter	Janet Hargreaves
Chris Hunter	Freddie Foot
	Stephen Hoye
Sandra Gould	Diane Keen
Paul Stevens	Paul Greenwood
Josephine Raphael	Gillian Betts
Myrtle Cavendish	Gretchen Franklin
Clifford Leyton	Johnny Briggs
Sharon Metcalfe	Carolyn Jones
Archie Gibbs	Jack Haig
Vera Downend	Zeph Gladstone
Shughie McFee	Angus Lennie
Hugh Mortimer	John Bentley
Anthony Mortimer	Jeremy Sinden
Paul Ross	Sandor Elès
Carney	Jack Woolgar
Jim Baines	John Forgeham
Benny Hawkins	Paul Henry
Ed Lawton	Thomas Heathcote
Doris Luke	Kathy Staff
Marian Owen	Margaret John
Iris Scott	Angela Webb
Kath Brownlow	Pamela Vezey
Arthur Brownlow	Peter Hill
Glenda Brownlow/Banks	Lynette McMorrough
Kevin Banks	David Moran
Joe McDonald	Carl Andrews
Adam Chance	Tony Adams
Barbara Brady/Hunter	Sue Lloyd
Sid Hooper	Stan Stennett
Mavis Hooper	Charmian Eyre
Anne-Marie Wade	Dee Hepburn
Roy Lambert	Steven Pinder
J. Henry Pollard	Michael Turner
Miranda Pollard	Claire Faulkenbridge
Valerie Pollard	Heather Chasen
Nicola Freeman	Gabrielle Drake
Tommy 'Bomber' Lancaster	Terence Rigby
Charlie Mycroft	Graham Seed
Daniel Freeman	Philip Goodhew
John Maddington	Jeremy Nicholas

Creators: Hazel Adair, Peter Ling. Producers: Reg Watson, Jack Barton, Philip Bowman, Marian Nelson, William Smethurst, Michele Buck

The day-to-day events at a Midlands motel.

Few programmes have endured as much ridicule as *Crossroads*. At the same time, few programmes have won the hearts of so many viewers. From its earliest days, *Crossroads* was taunted with criticisms of its wobbly sets and often wobblier performers. Lines were fluffed or simply forgotten, scripts were wooden and plots transparent, but much of this could be put down to the demands of a hectic recording schedule, given that *Crossroads* began as a five-times-a-week early evening serial. Despite this and the constraints of a small budget, its popularity was such that it ran and ran – for 24 years in all.

The programme's queen bee was Meg Richardson, widowed owner of the Crossroads Motel, set in the fictitious village of King's Oak somewhere in the West Midlands. Around her buzzed her next of kin: daughter Jill, son Sandy and sister Kitty, with Kitty's husband, Dick, and architect son, Brian. Meg's extended family were the motel staff, most of them dyed-in-the-wool Brummies, with the notable exception of Spanish chef Carlos Raphael. The most popular employees over the years included Diane Lawton, the blonde waitress who steadily worked her way up the motel ladder, singing waitress Marilyn Gates, gossipy little Amy Turtle, pompous chef Mr Lovejoy, hairstylist Vera Downend (who lived on a houseboat), coffee bar worker Benny Wilmott, gardener Archie Gibbs, gruff nightwatchman Carney, spinster Doris Luke, oily restaurant manager Paul Ross, Scots chef Shughie McFee and receptionist Anne-Marie Wade. At the Crossroads garage worked Jim Baines, Sid Hooper and Joe McDonald and the good folk of King's Oak also had a look in, especially miserable old Wilf Harvey (whose electrician son, Stan, married Jill), post-mistress Miss Tatum, antique dealers Tish and Ted Hope and shopkeeper Roy Lambert. Probably the best loved of all *Crossroads* characters, however, was the slow-witted, woolly-hatted Benny Hawkins, first seen as a labourer at Diane's uncle's farm. He followed 'Miss Diane' back to King's Oak, although continued to suffer more than his fair share of misfortune, including the death of his gypsy girlfriend, Maureen Flynn, on their wedding day.

But tragedy and romance were the name of the game at Crossroads. Young Sandy was crippled in a car accident and spent most of his time afterwards in a wheelchair (actor Roger Tonge was later confined to a wheelchair himself, before dying prematurely in 1981). Jill married three times (once bigamously) and Meg herself married twice. Her first new husband, Malcolm Ryder, tried to poison her and she later fell for old flame Hugh Mortimer, a millionaire businessman who then died of a heart attack while being held as a terrorists' hostage. This may sound rather far-fetched but such extravagant storylines were always possible. In 1967, a re-discovered wartime bomb blew up the motel. In 1981 it was destroyed by fire, but rose again, phoenix-like, from the ashes. However, *Crossroads* was also a brave serial and could be stonily earnest at times. It tackled issues other soaps happily shirked, these ranging from teenage runaways, abortion and test tube babies to racism, rape and physical handicaps.

Power struggles contributed to much of the action, too. Suave David Hunter was brought in as partner in 1969 and shared Meg's limelight until she was written out in 1981 (she sailed away on the QEII to a new life). Four years later, David and his novelist wife Barbara were also despatched to pastures new. In their place, fighting for control of the motel, were Jill, Adam Chance (her smoothie husband), tycoon J. Henry Pollard, new leading lady Nicola Freeman and businessman Tommy Lancaster. It was when Daniel Freeman, Nicola's stepson, assumed control in 1988 that the series finally ended. Jill, who had spoken the first ever words on the series – 'Crossroads Motel. Can I help you?' – also spoke the last, as she drove away with the new man in her life, John Maddington, to open up a small hotel in the west.

Crossroads also focused on the motel guests, some of whom were celebrities indulging a fancy to appear in the show. These included Bob Monkhouse, Ken Dodd and Larry Grayson, who in one of his appearances acted as chauffeur to Meg and Hugh Mortimer on their wedding day. Some big names were given their break on the series. Malcolm McDowell played PR man Crispin Ryder, Diane Keen was waitress Sandra Gould and Elaine Paige was seen in the guise of Caroline Winthrop. Another guest was singer Harriet Blair, played by Stephanie de Sykes, who then took her song in the programme, 'Born With A Smile On My Face', to number two in the 1974 charts. It wasn't the first *Crossroads* hit: Sue Nicholls (later Audrey Roberts in **Coronation Street**) made the Top Twenty with 'Where Will You Be' in 1968. Nor was it the last: Simon May recorded a vocal version of his 'Summer Of My Life' tune in 1976, Paul Henry spoke the words of 'Benny's Theme' (played by the Mason Glen Orchestra) in 1978 and Kate Robbins (in the series as Kate Loring) succeeded with 'More Than In Love' in 1982. Paul McCartney and Wings' reworking of Tony Hatch's thumpingly catchy theme tune was used on some episodes (particularly those with sad or soppy endings), but when the series changed its title to *Crossroads, King's Oak* under producer William Smethurst in 1987, a new theme tune by Max Early and Raf Ravenscroft was introduced.

Devised by former **Compact** writers Hazel Adair and Peter Ling, from an idea by producer Reg Watson (later of **Prisoner: Cell Block H** and **Neighbours** fame), *Crossroads'* working title was *The Midland Road*. Adopting the snappier name, the series began in 1964 but, despite gaining a cult following, was not fully networked by ITV until 1972. Its heavy workload was cut to four episodes a week in 1967, and then, on the instructions of the IBA, which was concerned about its quality, three episodes a week in 1980. When the plug was pulled altogether in 1988, after over 4500 programmes, there was a huge outcry, but the bosses at Central Television were adamant that *Crossroads'* day was done and refused to reconsider. In its place fans have had to make do with Victoria Wood's cheeky send up, *Acorn Antiques*.

CROWN COURT

UK (Granada) Drama. ITV 1972–84

Long-running afternoon courtroom drama.

Presenting a different case each week, over three half-hour episodes, *Crown Court* was a stalwart of ITV's first afternoon schedules. Viewers were treated to hearings on a variety of subjects, from drug pushing to murder, and then awaited the deliberations of the jury (a panel of viewers) which were revealed at the close of the last episode. Many distinguished actors graced this popular series, including the likes of John Le Mesurier, Juliet Stevenson, Vivien Merchant, Michael Elphick, Liz Fraser, Michael Gough, Anthony Bate and Connie Booth. Richard Wilson was a regular, playing barrister Jeremy Parsons QC. The setting was the fictitious Fulchester Crown Court.

CROWTHER, LESLIE, CBE (1933-)

English funny man – the son of stage actor Leslie Crowther Snr – who sprang to fame as resident clown on the kids' show *Crackerjack* in 1960 and stayed with the series for eight years, finally acting as compere. As well as regular appearances in variety programmes like *The Black and White Minstrel Show*, Hi Summer, *The Saturday Crowd* and *Starburst*, Crowther has also dabbled in sitcom. He starred as bachelor Thomas Jones in *The Reluctant Romeo*, Clive Gibbons, a husband beholden to a charity-obsessed wife (Sylvia Sims), in **My Good Woman**, and mummy's boy Tony Marchant in *Big Boy Now*. He also ventured into game shows, hosting the 'Come on down' shopping quiz **The Price Is Right** and also presented *Whose Baby?* and the look-alike talent show **Stars in their Eyes**. Over the years he has had various showcases of his own, including *Crowther's In Town*, *The Crowther Collection* and *Leslie Crowther's Scrapbook*, but his career was abruptly halted by a serious car accident in 1992. Leslie is the father of actress Liz Crowther.

CRUICKSHANK, ANDREW, MBE (1907–88)

Distinguished Scottish stage and screen actor who arrived on television in the 1930s in early productions like *Bleak House*. In 1962 he was cast as the grouchy Dr Cameron in **Dr Finlay's Casebook**, a role he filled until the series ended in 1971. His other TV work included *Mr Justice Duncannon*, the satire *The Old Men at the Zoo* (as Mr Sanderson) and the part of eccentric old Mr Hodinett in *King and Castle*.

CRYER, BARRY (1935-)

Long-serving Leeds-born comedian and sketch writer, at times providing scripts for some of the world's finest, including Bob Hope and George Burns. As well as behind-the-scenes work on the sitcoms **No – That's Me Over Here!**, **Doctor in the House**, Now Look Here . . . , *The Prince of Denmark* and *Langley Bottom* (in collaboration with such writers as Graham Chapman and John Junkin), and series like **The Two Ronnies**, *The Morecambe and Wise Show*, *Marty Back Together Again*, *Carrot Confidential*, *Mike Yarwood In Persons* and *The Kenny Everett Television Show*, Cryer has also been a familiar face in front of the camera, particularly on panel games. He hosted the quick-fire gag show *Jokers Wild* in the 1970s and was one of the team of impressionists on **Who Do You Do?**

CRYSTAL MAZE, THE

UK (Chatsworth) Game Show. Channel 4 1990–

Presenters: Richard O'Brien, Edward Tudor-Pole

Producers: Malcolm Heyworth, David G. Croft

Prizes await contestants skilled at physical and mental puzzles.

In this cross between *The Krypton Factor* and Indiana Jones, impish Mazemaster Richard O'Brien invited a team of contestants (all strictly aged under 40) to tackle a series of mental and physical games with the aim of winning time crystals. The more crystals collected, the longer the team were given in the finale to gather floating strips of gold foil which then translated into prizes. If a contestant ran out of time in any of the games, he or she was sealed into the room housing the game and a crystal was forfeited. All the games were thematically linked to four fantasy zones similar to those seen in computer games, and the quality of the imaginative sets ensured a good 'Dungeons and Dragons' atmosphere. The programme quickly earned itself a cult following and a children's edition was shown at Christmas 1991. In 1994 O'Brien left and was replaced by Ed Tudor-Pole.

CRYSTAL TIPPS AND ALISTAIR

UK (BBC) Animation. BBC 1 1972–

Creator: Hilary Hayton. Writers: Hilary Hayton, Graham McCallum. Producer: Michael Grafton-Robinson

Quirky, psychedelic animation about a girl and her dog.

Crystal Tipps and Alistair was a product of the BBC's animation department, a unit that barely got off the ground in the early 1970s. Employing just one illustrator and one animator, it was soon disbanded and this series was subsequently made by outside contractors. It featured the adventures of a girl with a very bushy, violet-coloured hair-do (Crystal Tipps) and her large, square-headed dog (Alistair). The 25 five-minute programmes were screened in the '*Magic Roundabout* slot' just before the early evening news.

CTV see Channel.

CUCKOO WALTZ, THE

UK (Granada) Situation Comedy. ITV 1975–7; 1980

Chris Hawthorne	David Roper
Felicity 'Fliss' Hawthorne	Diane Keen
Gavin Rumsey	Lewis Collins
Connie Wagstaffe	Clare Kelly
Austen Tweedale	John McKelvey
Adrian Lockett	Ian Saynor

Writers: Geoffrey Lancashire, John G. Temple. Producers: Bill Gilmour, Brian Armstrong, John G. Temple

Two hard-up newlyweds take in a lodger and live to regret it.

Chris and Fliss Hawthorne were young, recently married and in love. However, their cashflow was virtually nonexistent and they were as poor as the proverbial church mice. Their living-room furniture consisted of a deckchair marked 'Property of Prestatyn UDC' and they had no room for the luxuries of life, a fact which made Chris rather doleful. Fliss generally cheered him up with a murmur of 'Chris-Fliss-Kiss', followed by a quick snog. To ease their financial problems, the Hawthornes took in Chris's friend Gavin Rumsey, a refugee from a broken marriage, as their lodger. Unlike his hosts, sporty Gavin always had cash to burn. He brought with him a van load of expensive furniture and a flashy car. He also tended to flirt with his pretty landlady, who always remainded loyal to her lacklustre journalist husband. When Fliss gave birth to twins, further demands were placed on the Hawthorne's meagre resources and, as a result, Gavin remained the 'cuckoo' for three seasons. However, when the series returned after a three-year hiatus, he had given way to another lodger, Adrian Lockett, who, to complicate matters, quickly became besotted with Fliss.

CUE

The signal (usually visual) given to a presenter or actor to start speaking or moving. Camera operators and other technicians also have to be 'cued', although their cues are usually vocal and given via their headphones.

CUE CARD see idiot board.

CUNLIFFE, DAVID (1935–)

British TV executive, for a number of years Controller of Drama at Yorkshire Television, although previously working as producer/director for Granada, LWT and the BBC. Among his credits have been *Saturday Night Theatre*, **The Onedin Line**, **Harry's Game**, **Hadleigh**, **The Main Chance** and **Emmerdale Farm**.

CURRAN, SIR CHARLES (1921–80)

BBC Director-General 1969–77, Dublin-born Charles Curran joined the BBC as a radio producer in 1947, before leaving for a career in newspapers. He rejoined the Corporation in 1951 and worked his way up the administrative ladder, eventually succeeding Hugh Greene as Director-General. Curran was also President of the European Broadcasting Union and chief executive of the Visnews news agency.

CURRY AND CHIPS

UK (LWT) Situation Comedy. ITV 1969

The Foreman	Eric Sykes
Kevin O'Grady ('Paki-Paddy')	Spike Milligan

Creator/Writer: Johnny Speight. Producer: Keith Beckett

A Pakistani immigrant starts work at a factory and suffers the expected racial abuse.

There have been few comedy series more controversial than *Curry and Chips*. Penned by **Till Death Us Do Part** creator Johnny Speight, it looked at life in the factory of Lillicrap Ltd. Newly arrived was Kevin O'Grady, an Asian with an Irish father, a genetic combination that resulted in his nickname of Paki-Paddy. Played by a blacked-up Spike Milligan, Paki-Paddy suffered the racist taunts of his workmates, even though Eric Sykes's foreman was rather more liberal in his outlook. Speight's intention was to turn such bigotry and narrow-mindedness into ridiculous caricatures, but viewers and critics found the crude 'factory' language too much to swallow and only one series was made. Actors like Kenny Lynch, Sam Kydd, Geoffrey Hughes and Norman Rossington provided support for the principals.

CURTIS, RICHARD, MBE

British comedy writer, best known these days for his screenplay for the award-winning film *Four Weddings and a Funeral*. His earlier writing was in collaboration with former Oxford colleague Rowan Atkinson and then Ben Elton (**Not the Nine O'Clock News** and the **Blackadder** series in particular). Curtis now works on scripts with his girlfriend, radio presenter Emma Freud.

CURTIS, TONY (BERNARD SCHWARZ; 1925–)

Hollywood film name whose television experience has been confined to action adventures such as *The Persuaders!* (playing millionaire Danny Wilde alongside Roger Moore's Lord Brett Sinclair), *McCoy* (as a confidence trickster) and *Vega$* (as casino boss Phil Roth).

CUSHING, PETER, OBE (1913–94)

Hammer horror master Peter Cushing was also a prolific TV performer, even if you just take into account the number of times he appeared on *The Morecambe and Wise Show* requesting a cheque. He played Winston Smith in the controversial 1954 adaptation of George Orwell's *1984*, Sherlock Holmes for the BBC in 1968 and cropped up in many other single dramas and series as a guest performer, from *The Avengers* to *Space: 1999* and, of course, *Hammer House of Horror*.

CUTHBERTSON, IAIN (1930–)

Bold Scottish actor, chiefly remembered as seedy spiv Charlie Endell in *Budgie* and its sequel, *Charles Endell Esquire*, and the Scottish lawyer John Sutherland in *Sutherland's Law*. His other starring performances have included roles in *The Borderers*, *Diamond Crack Diamond* (as lawyer Mark Terson), *Scotch on the Rocks*, *Tom Brown's Schooldays* (as Dr Arnold), *Children of the Stones* (as psychic megalomaniac Hendrick), *The Voyage of Charles Darwin*, *Rep* (as theatre troupe manager J.C. Benton) and *Supergran* (as the nasty Scunner Campbell). Cuthbertson has also enjoyed many guest appearances in series as varied as *Z Cars*, *The Duchess of Duke Street*, *Survivors*, *Danger UXB*, *Doctor Who*, *Return of the Antelope*, *Rab C. Nesbitt*, *Minder* and *Inspector Morse*. He is married to actress Anne Kirsten.

DAD'S ARMY

UK (BBC) Situation Comedy. BBC 1 1968–77

Captain George Mainwaring	Arthur Lowe
Sgt Arthur Wilson	John Le Mesurier
L/Corporal Jack Jones	Clive Dunn
Private James Fraser	John Laurie
Private James Walker	James Beck
Private Frank Pike	Ian Lavender
Private Charles Godfrey	Arnold Ridley
Chief ARP Warden William Hodges	Bill Pertwee
The Vicar	Frank Williams
Mr Yeatman	Edward Sinclair
Mrs Mavis Pike	Janet Davies
Mr Cheeseman	Talfryn Thomas
Mrs Mildred Fox	Pamela Cundell
Private Sponge	Colin Bean

Creators/Writers: Jimmy Perry, David Croft. Producer: David Croft

The bumbling exploits of a World War II Home Guard platoon in an English coastal town.

Drawing nostalgically on 1940s Britain, this long-running farce has been described as *the* classic British sitcom. It focused on the misadventures of the Local Defence Volunteers of fictional Walmington-on-Sea (supposedly Bexhill). In true Home Guard tradition, the platoon was comprised of men too old, too young or too weak to take their place on the front line (hence, 'Dad's Army').

Self-appointed head of the unit was Captain George Mainwaring, the town's pompous, incompetent bank manager with a tragically misplaced sense of his own importance. His much-maligned second in command, in the bank as well as in uniform, was Arthur Wilson. Public school educated and polite to the point of asking the platoon if they 'would mind awfully falling in', he was far more level-headed than Mainwaring, and never failed to unwittingly undermine his CO. Next in line was the town's butcher, fading Boer War veteran Jack Jones, master of the long-winded, far from pertinent tale, but a man with the heart of a lion and always the first to volunteer for the most dangerous tasks.

The other key members of the platoon were just as distinctive. Pte Fraser was a rolling-eyed, penny-pinching Scottish undertaker, and Godfrey was the company's doddery first-aider, who lived in a picture-postcard cottage with his sisters, Dolly and Cissy. Private Walker and movie-mad teenager Frank Pike were the other two principals, Walker a black market spiv and Pike a bank clerk and mummy's boy whose mother conducted a semi-covert affair with Sgt Wilson, his 'Uncle Arthur'.

Valiantly failing to patrol the resort or to fulfil demanding military exercises, the platoon were constantly nettled by the local ARP warden, Mr Hodges, the greengrocer. He and 'Napoleon' (as he labelled Mainwaring) jostled for military command in the town and disputes over the use of the church hall for parade nights led to the interference of the whinging Vicar and his loyal verger, Mr Yeatman. Other characters who popped up from time to time included toothy Welsh reporter Mr Cheeseman and Jones's rotund lady friend, Mrs Fox.

Bound together with 1940s tunes vocalized by Bud Flanagan, the series threw up some of the most memorable lines in TV comedy. Mainwaring's 'Stupid Boy' (to Pike), Wilson's ominous 'Do you think that's wise, Sir', Jones's 'Permission to speak, Sir' and 'Don't panic', and Fraser's 'We're doomed' all became catchphrases. With the exception of young Ian Lavender, the cast had all done their time on stage and screen, and Arnold Ridley was also the author of *The Ghost Train*, a much-adapted stage play. The death of James Beck in 1973 (ironically one of the youngest cast members) was not allowed to stop the series. The cast was full and talented enough to continue, and lesser characters like Pte Sponge were given more prominence in support. A film version of *Dad's Army* was released in 1971.

DBS

Direct Broadcasting by Satellites (DBS) was first conceived in the 1970s as a means of relaying TV signals to homes without the need for terrestrial transmitters or masts. At an international conference in 1977, Britain was allocated five channels, and the BBC was charged with setting up the first two, with a proposed air date of 1986. Unfortunately, numerous difficulties (not least lack of Government financial support) resulted in the concept, as it stood, being scrapped. The IBA took over the idea instead, eventually issuing a licence to a consortium known as British Satellite Broadcasting (BSB). BSB, in turn, ran into problems of its own. Although its Marco Polo satellite was soon in position, delays resulted from technical difficulties (particularly with the revolutionary smaller reception dish, the 'squarial'). BSB eventually went on air in spring 1990, but Rupert Murdoch's company, Sky, had stolen a march and was already broadcasting from the Luxembourg-owned Astra satellite, enjoying over a million viewers. In November the same year, with both companies operating at a loss, BSB was forced to merge with Sky, creating British Sky Broadcasting (BSkyB). See also BSkyB.

DAKTARI

US (MGM/Ivan Tors) Adventure. BBC 1 1966–9

Dr Marsh Tracy	Marshall Thompson
Paula Tracy	Cheryl Miller
Jack Dane	Yale Summers
District Officer Hedley	Hedley Mattingly
Mike	Hari Rhodes
Bart Jason	Ross Hagen
Jenny Jones	Erin Moran

Creators: Ivan Tors, Art Arthur. Executive Producer: Ivan Tors. Producer: Leonard Kaufman

The adventures of an American vet based at an African wildlife compound.

'Daktari' means 'doctor' in an African language, and this series revolved around Marsh Tracy, respected animal doctor and head of the Wameru Study Centre for Animal Behaviour. He was assisted by his daughter, Paula, American conservationist Jack Dane, and Mike, a native African. Hedley, a British game warden, called upon Tracy for advice and help from time to time. Later arrivals were hunter-turned-guide Bart Jason and a seven-year-old orphan, Jenny Jones, who the Tracys adopted. Together they found themselves dealing with conservation issues, tackling the iniquitous hunting trade and riding to the rescue of stranded cubs and badly injured beasts.

The animals were the real stars of *Daktari*, especially Judy, the chimpanzee, and Clarence, who had already appeared in his own film, *Clarence the Cross-Eyed Lion* (also featuring Marshall Thompson and Cheryl Miller). It was this cinema release which inspired the TV series, which was filmed at producer Ivan Tors's Africa, USA wildlife park near Los Angeles. Child actress Erin Moran went on to greater success as Joanie in *Happy Days*.

DALLAS

US (Lorimar) Drama. BBC 1 1978–91

John Ross (JR) Ewing, Jnr	Larry Hagman
Eleanor Southworth (Miss Ellie) Ewing/Farlow	Barbara Bel Geddes
	Donna Reed
John Ross (Jock) Ewing	Jim Davis
Bobby Ewing	Patrick Duffy
Pamela Barnes/Ewing	Victoria Principal
Lucy Ewing/Cooper	Charlene Tilton
Sue Ellen Ewing	Linda Gray
Ray Krebbs	Steve Kanaly
Cliff Barnes	Ken Kercheval
Willard 'Digger' Barnes	David Wayne
	Keenan Wynn
Gary Ewing	David Ackroyd
	Ted Shackelford
Valene Ewing	Joan Van Ark
Liz Craig	Barbara Babcock
Jenna Wade	Morgan Fairchild
	Francine Tacker
	Priscilla Presley
Kristin Shepard	Colleen Camp
	Mary Crosby
'Dusty Farlow'	Jared Martin
Dr Ellby	Jeff Cooper
Donna Culver/Krebbs	Susan Howard
Dave Culver	Tom Fuccello
Harve Smithfield	George O. Petrie
Vaughn Leland	Dennis Patrick
Connie	Jeanna Michaels
Louella	Meg Gallagher
Jordan Lee	Don Starr
Mitch Cooper	Leigh McCloskey
John Ross Ewing III	Tyler Banks
	Omri Katz
Punk Anderson	Morgan Woodward

Mavis Anderson ....Alice Hirson
Marilee Stone ....Fern Fitzgerald
Afton Cooper....................................Audrey Landers
Rebecca Wentworth...........................Priscilla Pointer
Jeremy Wendell ....William Smithers
Clayton Farlow.......................................Howard Keel
Katherine Wentworth ....Morgan Brittany
Mickey Trotter ....Timothy Patrick Murphy
Holly Harwood ....Lois Chiles
Mark Graison...John Beck
Peter Richards ....Christopher Atkins
Serena Wald ....Stephanie Blackmore
Paul Morgan...Glenn Corbett
Charlie Wade ....Shalane McCall
Sly ....Deborah Rennard
Phyllis ....Deborah Tranelli
Jessica Montford ....Alexis Smith
Mandy Winger.................................Deborah Shelton
Jamie Ewing/Barnes ....Jenilee Harrison
Christopher Ewing ....Joshua Harris
Jack Ewing...Dack Rambo
Angelica Nero ....Barbara Carrera
April Stevens ....Sheree J. Wilson
Ben Stivers/Wes Parmalee ....Steve Forrest
Bruce Harvey ....Jonathan Goldsmith
Casey Denault ....Andrew Stevens
Carter McKay ....George Kennedy
Rose McKay ....Jeri Gaile
Don Lockwood ....Ian McShane
Cally Harper/Ewing ....Cathy Podewell
Tracy Lawton ....Beth Toussaint
James Richard Beaumont ....Sasha Mitchell
Michelle Stevens ....Kimberly Foster
Jackie Dugan...............................Sherril Lynn Rettino
Kendall ....Danone Simpson
Vanessa Beaumont...........................Gayle Hunnicut
Stephanie Rogers ....Lesley-Anne Down
Liz Adams ....Barbara Stock
Sheila Foley/Hillary Taylor........................Susan Lucci
Breslin ....Peter White
LeeAnn De La Vega..............................Barbara Eden

Creator: David Jacobs. Producer: Leonard
Katzman

**A wealthy Texan oil family indulge in
sexual and commercial intrigue, in a bid
to unsettle their rivals and each other.**

This prime-time American soap was based
around the life and affairs (business and personal)
of the Texan Ewing family and their associates
and introduced one of television's all-time great
bad guys, the legendary JR Ewing. The Ewings'
wealth flowed from the oil industry, thanks to the
manoeuvring of John Ross ('Jock') Ewing, the
head of the clan, who had cheated his great rival,
Digger Barnes, out of the proceeds of a giant oil
strike some 40 years earlier. Jock also stole
Digger's girl, Eleanor Southworth ('Miss Ellie'),
leaving the two families the bitterest enemies
since the Capulets and Montagues.

Jock and Ellie's three sons were John Ross Jnr
('JR'), the rarely seen Gary, and Bobby. They
lived on the Southfork ranch in Braddock

County, just outside Dallas. Gary moved away
and into his own spin-off series, *Knots Landing*,
leaving JR and Bobby prime heirs to the Ewing
fortune. Whereas JR was ruthless and bad and
never happy unless he was hurting someone,
Bobby was honest and good, almost his brother's
missing conscience. Their relationship was always
uneasy and JR resented Bobby's involvement in
Ewing Oil. Another leading character was ranch
foreman Ray Krebbs, who turned out to be
Jock's illegitimate son, and therefore a Ewing.

The Ewing–Barnes rivalry passed down a generation from Jock and Digger to JR and Cliff
Barnes, who, as an Assistant District Attorney,
explored every avenue for exposing Ewing corruption, in the hope of gaining revenge for his
father's humiliation. Cliff eventually became head
of his own family's oil enterprise, Barnes-
Wentworth. The Ewings and the Barneses were
forced together in the first episode of *Dallas* when
Bobby controversially married Cliff's sister, Pam.
It was a sign of things to come, with marriage and
divorce commonplace among these excessively
wealthy, beautiful people. JR was married (twice)
to Sue Ellen, a former Miss Texas but a helpless
drunk, whom he cheated on unmercifully. Bobby
had his girlfriends, too. Jenna was one, April
another. And when Jock was killed in a helicopter accident in South America, Miss Ellie was
re-married, to Clayton Farlow.

Amidst all the marriages, ex-marital alliances and
underhand wheeling and dealing, the series was
punctuated by two key storylines. In the first, JR
received his come-uppance when he was victim
of an attempted assassination. The whole world
spent months between series agonizing over
'Who shot JR?', and it wasn't an easy question to
answer, so many were his enemies. In order to
hold the suspense, the studio filmed several possible conclusions, so that not even the cast knew
who had pulled the trigger. It turned out to be
Kristin, Sue Ellen's pregnant (by JR) sister. JR
recovered, Kristin left town and the baby,
Christopher, was adopted by Bobby and Pam.

The other storyline on which the series turned
was the death and resurrection of Bobby. In one
of TV's greatest comebacks, he was first murdered
in a hit and run accident after saving Pam's life,
and then, when the series began slipping in the
ratings, he was miraculously reintroduced. This
was achieved, quite unashamedly, by waking Pam
from a dream to find Bobby lathering himself in
the shower, turning all that had happened in the
previous series into just a nightmare. During the
'dream sequence' Pam had married Mark
Graison.

Other highlights in the series' long run were JR's loss of control of Ewing Oil to Bobby when his criminal dealings were discovered; his fight to regain his power; his attempts to get Sue Ellen institutionalized for her alcoholism; Bobby being shot by his wife's half-sister, Katherine Wentworth, and the arrival of the suspicious Wes Parmalee, who claimed to be Jock back from the dead and very nearly convincing Miss Ellie in the process. JR floated in and out of prisons and mental asylums, as his manoeuvring was matched by those around him. The marriages, divorces, illicit affairs, sneaky business deals and overwhelming duplicity continued throughout the show's run.

By the series' close, JR's world had collapsed around him. His various ex-wives and children had all left home, Bobby had been given Southfork by Miss Ellie, who had gone to Europe with Clayton, and, worst of all, Cliff Barnes now owned Ewing Oil. In the final episode, inspired by the film *It's A Wonderful Life*, JR sat, drank and reflected on his life. An angel (or was it a devil?) popped up to show him just how others might have lived had JR never been born. Some had a much happier life, others were worse off, but it all seemed a bit much for JR to take. As he pulled out a revolver, viewers heard a shot. Only Bobby, who dashed into the room, saw exactly what had happened.

As evidenced by its cast list, *Dallas* was never afraid to introduce new characters and situations. Nor did it ever shy from switching actors and actresses when pressed into it. When Barbara Bel Geddes became ill, a far from convincing replacement was found in Donna Reed. There were two Garys, two John Rosses (JR and Sue Ellen's son), two Diggers and two Kristins, including Mary Crosby (Bing's daughter). There were actually three Jennas, with Morgan Fairchild and Francine Tacker both making the odd appearance before Priscilla Presley (wife of Elvis) made the part her own.

DALY, TYNE (1946–)

Born to an acting family, Tyne Daly's first TV appearance came in an episode of *The Virginian*, which she followed up with a stint in the US daytime soap *General Hospital*. After numerous TV and cinema movies, she finally gained stardom as Mary Beth Lacey in the detective series *Cagney and Lacey*. She first played the woman cop with family responsibilities working in a man's force, in the series' pilot, in which her partner, Christine Cagney, was played by Loretta Swit. When the series proper began, she was initially accompanied by Meg Foster before Sharon Gless became her regular co-star. Emmy awards followed.

DAN AUGUST

US (Quinn Martin) Police Drama. ITV 1976–

Detective Lt Dan August	Burt Reynolds
Sgt Charles Wilentz	Norman Fell
Sgt Joe Rivera	Ned Romero
Chief George Untermeyer	Richard Anderson
Katy Grant	Ena Hartmann

Executive Producer: Quinn Martin. Producer: Adrian Samish

A home-town cop uses his local knowledge to track down criminals.

In this short-lived series, Detective Lt Dan August patrolled his home town beat in Santa Luisa, California. Having grown up with many of the area's offenders and their victims, the tough young cop took a deep personal interest in his investigations, an interest which earned him respect and brought him results. Made before Burt Reynolds hit the box office big time, the series lasted only one year. But, capitalizing on the star's success, it fared much better on its re-runs and was being shown on satellite TV in the UK in the 1990s.

DANCE, CHARLES (1946–)

British heart-throb actor seen to best light in dramas like *The Jewel in the Crown*, in which he played Guy Perron, the thriller series *The Secret Servant* and the sci-fi drama *First Born* (as Edward Forester). He also played the title role in the mini-series version of *Phantom of the Opera*, with other credits including *Edward the Seventh* and *Nancy Astor*.

DANDO, JILL (1961–)

British news and travel presenter, seen on most of the BBC's news bulletins but particularly on *Breakfast News*. In 1993 she became host of *Holiday* and amongst her other credits have been *Safari UK* and *Songs of Praise*.

DANGER MAN

UK (ATV) Secret Agent Drama. ITV 1960–1; 1964–7

John Drake	Patrick McGoohan
Hobbs	Peter Madden

Creator: Ralph Smart. Executive Producer: Ralph Smart. Producers: Sidney Cole, Aida Young

The adventures of a sophisticated, globe-trotting intelligence agent.

John Drake worked for NATO, covertly assisting governments wherever security breaches were suspected. His aim was to preserve world peace and he risked life and limb to achieve it. He was highly competent, athletic, cool and sharp-witted. He was a man of few words who intensely disliked violence but often needed to tackle his enemies head on. His missions took him to all parts of the world.

Three years after the initial half-hour episodes had ended, the producers were spurred back into action by the success of the first James Bond movies. Drake was re-cast in a new, hour-long series, as a member of the British Secret Service, a Special Security Agent working for M19. This time he also had an immediate boss, Hobbs, and, inspired by Bond, his array of electronic gadgetry had increased. This series was screened under the title of *Secret Agent* in the USA.

DANGER UXB

UK (Thames/Euston Films) Drama. ITV 1979

Lt Brian Ash	Anthony Andrews
Sgt James	Maurice Roëves
Susan Gillespie/Ash	Judy Geeson
Captain Mould	Norman Chappell
Wilkins	George Innes
Norma Baker	Deborah Watling
Corporal Horrocks	Ken Kitson
Ivor Rogers	Jeremy Sinden

Creator/Producer: John Hawkesworth.
Executive Producer: Johnny Goodman

High drama series charting the bravery of a World War II bomb disposal squad.

These stories were drawn from the memoirs of real-life sapper Major A.P. Hartley and followed the progress of 97 Bomb Disposal Company (UXB standing for unexploded bomb) from the Blitz to D-Day. Hero of the piece was young Lt Brian Ash, like many of his colleagues new to the profession and learning the ropes as he went along. There was no room for trial and error, however, as they were playing with lives – other people's and their own. Each mission placed the sappers in impossible positions, a hair's breadth away from oblivion. Some did not make it, dragging emotion into the plots; others like Brian Ash survived to dispose of other bombs. Yet Ash himself was to become a victim of this perilous trade when he was killed in action, attempting to make safe a bomb on a seaside pier in the final episode. Susan Gillespie provided Ash's romantic interest.

DANGERMOUSE

UK (Cosgrove Hall/Thames) Cartoon. ITV 1981–7; 1991–2

Voices:

Dangermouse	David Jason
Penfold	Terry Scott
Baron Greenback	Edward Kelsey
Nero	David Jason
Colonel K	David Jason
Stiletto Mafioso	Brian Trueman
Narrator	David Jason

Creators: Mike Harding, Brian Trueman.
Writers: Brian Trueman, Angus Allen.
Executive Producer: John Hambley. Producers: Brian Cosgrove, Mark Hall

The all-action adventures of a mouse secret agent and his timid sidekick.

Working for the British Secret Service from a base in a Baker Street postbox, Dangermouse – 'the greatest secret agent the world has ever known' – was the saviour of civilization on more than one occasion. This eye patch-wearing, white-suited, daring hero was usually called into action by his whiskery boss, Colonel K, to deal with the fiendishly inventive plans of megalomaniac toad Baron Greenback. At the cool-headed Dangermouse's side was the loyal, if cowardly, Penfold (prone to fretful exclamations like 'Crikey'), while Greenback's chief henchman was the caterpillar Nero, supported by a group of gangster crows headed by Stiletto Mafioso (Italian in the UK, Stiletto became a Cockney when the series was sold to the USA). Another adversary, Count Duckula, a vegetarian vampire (also voiced by David Jason), was later spun off into his own series.

Narrated in breathless *Dick Barton* fashion and littered with puns and parodies of James Bond and other superhero stories (not to mention plays on adult literature), *Dangermouse* proved a hit with all ages. Co-creator Mike Harding supplied the musical content.

DANIEL BOONE

US (Arcola-Fesspar/ Twentieth Century-Fox) Western. ITV

Daniel Boone	Fess Parker
Yadkin	Albert Salmi
Mingo	Ed Ames
Rebecca Boone	Patricia Blair
Jemima Boone	Veronica Cartwright
Israel Boone	Darby Hinton
Cincinnatus	Dal McKennon
Jericho Jones	Robert Logan
Gideon	Don Pedro Colley
Gabe Cooper	Roosevelt Grier
Josh Clements	Jimmy Dean

Executive Producers: Aaron Rosenberg, Aaron Spelling. Producers: George Sherman, Barney Rosenzweig, Joseph Silver

Tales of one of America's great folk heroes.

In this series, created to capitalize on Fess Parker's earlier success as Davy Crockett, the actor played the lead in much the same way, even to the point of wearing the same racoon-skin cap. It was, of course, somewhat of an exaggeration of the life of the real Daniel Boone, who was one of America's great frontiersmen.

Boone lived during the American Wars of Independence, in the area bordering North Carolina, Kentucky and Tennessee. As played by Parker, he was one of the pioneers; a calm, peaceful, strong hero who carved new paths into the vast unknown continent, surveying and mapping the landscape, hunting wild animals, and befriending or fighting off Indians. Larger than life, he was seen in the title sequence splitting a tree with a single throw of an axe.

With his wife, Rebecca, and children, Jemima and Israel, Boone was based in the town of Boonesborough, where among his associates were the town barkeeper, Cincinnatus, and an Oxford-educated Cherokee Indian named Mingo. Yadkin, a friend from the backwoods, travelled with him on his early forays and another pioneer, Jericho Jones, joined Boone later in the series. Also seen were Josh Clements, a fur trapper, Gideon, a black Indian, and the escaped slave Gabe Cooper.

The series was first screened in its native USA in 1964 and received sporadic showings around the ITV network.

DANIEL, GLYN (1914–86)

British archaeologist who became a prominent TV personality in the 1950s and 1960s, thanks to his appearances as host of *Animal, Vegetable, Mineral?* and *Chronicle*. He was a don at Cambridge.

DANIELS, PAUL (1938–)

Northern comedian and illusionist, latterly a host of quiz shows and panel games. Before gaining his own BBC magic show, Daniels took his nightclub act in and out of TV variety programmes, appearing on *Opportunity Knocks* and *Wheeltappers' and Shunters' Social Club* amongst other series, and briefly presenting his own variety showcase for Granada, *Paul Daniels' Blackpool Bonanza*. In the 1980s he became TV's most popular magician and used his success to branch out into ame shows, hosting *Odd One Out*, *Every Second Counts* and *Wipeout*. He is married to his glamorous assistant Debbie McGee and his son (and former assistant) Martin is now an entertainer in his own right, a one-time presenter of *Game for a Laugh*.

DANSON, TED (1947–)

Square-jawed American leading man whose huge success as romeo bartender Sam Malone in the sitcom *Cheers* won him a run of Hollywood starring roles. His earlier appearances included a couple of years in the US daytime soap *Somerset* and a small part in *Magnum, PI*.

DARREN, JAMES (JAMES ERCOLANI; 1936–)

American leading man whose TV highspots have included *The Time Tunnel* (as lost scientist Dr Tony Newman) and *T.J. Hooker* (as Officer Jim Corrigan). He has also appeared as a guest star on *Fantasy Island* and *Vega$*, among many other series. Small-screen success came after movie fame in the 1950s, when he was cast as a teenage heart-throb figure. He even branched out into singing, hitting the UK charts in the early 1960s with 'Goodbye Cruel World' and three other discs.

DARLING BUDS OF MAY, THE

UK (Yorkshire/Excelsior Group) Comedy Drama. ITV 1991–3

Sidney Charles 'Pop' Larkin	David Jason
Ma Larkin	Pam Ferris
Mariette Larkin/Charlton	Catherine Zeta Jones
Cedric 'Charley' Charlton	Philip Franks
Primrose Larkin	Julie Davies
	Abigail Romison
Montgomery Larkin	Ian Tucker
Petunia Larkin	Christina Giles
Zinnia Larkin	Katherine Giles
Victoria Larkin	Stephanie Ralph
Edith Pilchester	Rachel Bell
Ernest Bristow	Michael Jayston
The Brigadier	Moray Watson

Writers: Bob Larbey, Richard Harris, Paul Wheeler. Executive Producers: Richard Bates, Vernon Lawrence. Producers: Robert Banks Stewart, Peter Norris, Simon Lewis

Tales of a happy-go-lucky rural Kent family in the 1950s.

Based on H.E. Bates's five Larkin books (which began with a novel entitled *The Darling Buds of May*), this hugely popular, wholesome series engendered a 'feel good' factor in viewers. Here was a family which chortled its way through life, enjoying the simple pleasures of the countryside and having little time for the stresses of the real world. Head of the clan was the boisterous Pop Larkin, a man of independent means who ran a 22-acre smallholding and earned a bob or two wherever he could. Larkin by name and larking by nature, Pop was seldom flustered and usually had an answer for every problem. His irrepressible common-law wife (they had skipped the formality of marriage), known to all as Ma, was a roly-poly, laugh-a-minute character, always at work in the kitchen preparing gigantic feasts for breakfast, lunch and dinner (which Pop liberally doused with ketchup), and snacks for moments in between. Their six children began with their beautiful eldest daughter Mariette and were generally named after assorted flowers. In the first episode, Cedric Charlton, a naive young poetry-loving Inland Revenue official, called to investigate Pop's affairs. Befuddled by Pop's anti-tax logic, 'Charley' stayed for lunch, fell in love with Mariette and never left. They married and Mariette gave birth to a son, John Blenheim. 'Perfick', as Pop would have put it.

Working as executive producer on the series was Richard Bates, son of the Larkins' creator, who had originally sold the rights of the novels to an American company, but bought them back when their adaptation was slow to get off the ground. He took the idea to Yorkshire Television and gave the company one of their greatest hits. Bob Larbey wrote the first series, with other writers employed for later episodes. A less subtle American film version of *Darling Buds*, entitled *The Mating Game*, starring Debbie Reynolds and Tony Randall, was released in 1959.

DAVENPORT, NIGEL (1928–)

Prolific English character actor, much seen on television. He is particularly associated today with tetchy businessman roles, thanks to appearances as Sir Edward Frere in **Howards' Way** and James Brant in **Trainer**. Among his career highspots have been the parts of Councillor Robert Carne in **South Riding**, Jack Hoxton in the sitcom *Don't Rock the Boat*, King George III in *Prince Regent* and the South African police chief in the drama-documentary *The Biko Inquest*. He also starred in *Oil Strike North* and has had credits in such series as *Travelling Man*, *Madame Bovary* and **Bird of Prey**. His wife is actress Maria Aitken.

DAVIDSON, JIM (1953–)

Chirpy, Cockney comedian, fond of dirty jokes but somewhat toned down for television appeal. He came to light on the talent show **New Faces** and has subsequently appeared in assorted variety specials, his own sitcoms, *Up the Elephant and Round the Castle* and *Home James* (as Jim London in both), and his own quiz show, *Big Break*, based around the game of snooker. His third wife was presenter Alison Holloway.

DAVIES, ANDREW (1936–)

Former university lecturer and one of British TV's foremost dramatists. Davies began his script-ing career with one-off adaptations and plays like *The Signalman* (starring Denholm Elliott) in 1976 and *Fearless Frank* (starring Leonard Rossiter) in 1978, although his first series successes were *The Legend of King Arthur* and the kids' comedy *Educating Marmalade* and its sequel, *Danger – Marmalade At Work*. He adapted R.F. Delderfield's *To Serve Them All My Days* and *Diana* for the BBC and went on to deliver the surreal **A Very Peculiar Practice**, set in the quirky world of Lowlands University and starring Peter Davison. Following two series of *Practice*, Davies adapted *Pride and Prejudice*, chipped in with *Mother Love* and then reworked Michael Dobbs's **House of Cards** and *To Play the King*, with great success. The most recent acclaim has come from his adaptation of *Middlemarch* and in quite a different vein, he co-wrote the flat share sitcom *Game On* with Bernadette Davis in 1995. Over the years, there have also been several other notable pieces, such as *The Old Devils* and *Anglo-Saxon Attitudes*, as well as numerous one-off plays and Screen One/Two productions, such as *Bavarian Night*, *Ball Trap on the Côte d'Azur* and *A Very Polish Practice* (picking up where the earlier series left off).

DAVIES, DIANA (1936–)

Northern actress first coming to light as Freda Ashton's friend Doris in **A Family at War** but familiar to soap fans as Norma Ford in **Coronation Street** in the 1970s and, more recently, Caroline Bates in **Emmerdale**. However, she has enjoyed many other roles over the years in series like **The Liver Birds**, *Send in the Girls*, **Juliet Bravo**, *Enemy at the Door*, **Shoestring**, *All Creatures Great and Small* and **Medics**.

DAVIES, DICKIE (1933–)

ITV sports presenter, initially with Southern Television but host of **World of Sport** from 1968. Davies, with his trademark 'badger' streak in his hair, has also hosted other sporting events, including boxing, snooker and the Olympic Games, as well as the quiz show *Sportsmasters* (which he produced for HTV).

DAVIES, FREDDIE (1937–)

British comedian known for his 'Parrotface' routine and his spluttering pronunciation. He found his way into television via **Opportunity Knocks** and was a variety show regular in the 1960s and 1970s, becoming particularly popular with younger viewers. He went on to star in his own kids' sitcom, *The Small World of Samuel Tweet* (as Tweet), but, more recently, Davies was seen in a cameo role in *All Quiet on the Preston Front*.

DAVIES, JOHN HOWARD (1939–)

Former child actor, star of such classics as *Oliver Twist* and *Tom Brown's Schooldays*, who became a BBC producer/director, working largely on comedy shows. Among his contributions have been *Steptoe and Son*, *All Gas and Gaiters*, *Misleading Cases*, *The Goodies*, As Good *Cooks Go*, *No Strings*, *Whoops Baghdad!*, *The Fall and Rise of Reginald Perrin*, *The Good Life*, *Fawlty Towers*, *The Other One*, *Andy Capp*, *We'll Think of Something*, *Executive Stress*, *No Job for a Lady*, *Hope It Rains* (the last five for Thames), *Law and Disorder* (for Central) and, most significantly, *Monty Python's Flying Circus*.

DAVIES, RICHARD

Overtly Welsh character and comic actor, usually sporting National Health glasses and with plenty to say. Although remembered by many as the couldn't-give-a-damn sports teacher, Pricey, in *Please Sir!*, Davies has popped up in all manner of programmes over the years, especially those needing a strong Welsh presence, including the drama *The Citadel* (as Mr Watkins), the sitcom *Rule Britannia* (as Taffy Evans) and the short-lived HTV soap *Taff Acre* (as Max Johnson). For a while in the mid-1970s, as Idris Hopkins (married to Kathy Staff's Vera), he ran the corner shop in *Coronation Street*. Davies has also been seen in the comedies *Oh No! It's Selwyn Froggitt* (as Clive), *Bottle Boys* (as Stan Evans) and *Whoops! Apocalypse* (as the Chancellor of the Exchequer), plus the 1970s children's series *Robert's Robots* (as Grimble).

DAVIES, RUPERT (1916–76)

With the strike of a match and a puff on his pipe at the start of each episode, Rupert Davies instantly became the French detective *Maigret*, a character he played for three years from 1960 and remained heavily associated with for the rest of his life. As Maigret, he also introduced the BBC's *Detective* anthology series. It is said that the sleuth's creator, Georges Simenon, considered Davies to be perfect for the part, although it wasn't his first TV detective role; that was as Inspector Duff in the late-1950s production of *The New Adventures of Charlie Chan*. Earlier, Davies had taken the part of Vincent Broadhead in *Quatermass II* and played Seamus in *Sailor of Fortune* (alongside Lorne Greene) after moving into TV and films from the stage and radio. He also made guest appearances in programmes like *The Invisible Man*. In 1968 he provided the voice for Professor McClaine in *Joe 90*, and a few years later was Cerdig in *Arthur of the Britons* and Count Rostov in *War and Peace*, but his subse-

quent work was thin on the ground, as the millstone of Maigret hung ever heavier.

DAVIES, WINDSOR (1930–)

Welsh comic actor, the bawling, intolerant Sgt Major Williams in *It Ain't Half Hot Mum*. Davies's other major TV role has been as Oliver Smallbridge alongside Donald Sinden's Simon Peel in the antique trade sitcom *Never the Twain*, although his TV appearances have been plentiful, regular and have also included the part of George Vance in a 1985 sitcom called *The New Statesman* (no connection with the Rik Mayall series). Where his face hasn't appeared, his voice has been heard, as in the Gerry Anderson puppet series *Terrahawks* (speaking the lines of Sgt Major Zero). 'Whispering Grass', his recording with *It Ain't Half Hot Mum* co-star Don Estelle, topped the charts in 1975.

DAVISON, PETER (1951–)

Popular British light actor, Tristan Farnon in *All Creatures Great and Small*, Dr Stephen Daker in *A Very Peculiar Practice*, the 1930s detective Albert *Campion* and TV's fifth *Doctor Who*. Added to this notable list of starring roles are a handful of sitcoms, of varying success: *Sink or Swim* (as Brian Webber), *Holding the Fort* (as Russell Milburn), *Fiddlers Three* (as Ralph Fiddler) and *Ain't Misbehavin'* (as Clive Quigley). Guest appearances in programmes such as *The Tomorrow People*, *Love for Lydia*, *Miss Marple* and *The Hitch-hiker's Guide to the Galaxy*, and a theme music credit for the sitcom *Mixed Blessings*, add yet more to his portfolio. He is married to actress Sandra Dickinson.

DAVRO, BOBBY (ROBERT NANKEVILLE; 1959–)

English comedian and impressionist, coming to the fore via *Copycats* and much seen on variety and game shows. He has hosted several series of his own, including *Bobby Davro on the Box*, *Bobby Davro's Television Weekly*, *Davro's Sketch Pad* and *Davro*.

DAVY CROCKETT

US (Disney) Adventure. ITV 1956

Davy Crockett	Fess Parker
Georgie Russell	Buddy Ebsen

Executive Producer: Walt Disney. Producer: Bill Walsh

Tales of the great American frontiersman.

'Born on a mountain top in Tennessee', according to the enormously successful theme song,

Davy Crockett in reality was a one-time militia scout and a US Congressman who died in the legendary siege of the Alamo. For this action series, Crockett became an all-American hero, helping to tame the Wild West and thwarting the advances of the Mexicans with the aid of his trusty rifle, Old Betsy, and his loyal sidekick, Georgie Russell. His raccoon-skin cap became his trademark and was adopted by addicted children on both sides of the Atlantic as the merchandising spin-offs took hold. The series originally aired in the USA as part of the anthology series *Disneyland*.

Fess Parker took on a similar part in the 1960s, when he again donned a furry hat for the role of another American hero, **Daniel Boone**. Buddy Ebsen, meanwhile, went on to play a different sort of backwoodsman, Jed Clampett, in **The Beverly Hillbillies**.

DAWN, ELIZABETH (SYLVIA BUTTERFIELD; 1939–)

Coronation Street's formidable Vera Duckworth who arrived in Weatherfield in 1976 as one of the girls in Mike Baldwin's sweat shop. Elizabeth Dawn's working life had begun in a real factory, before progressing via a stint in Woolworth's to singing in nightclubs. *Street* stardom eventually came after TV commercials, waitressing on **Wheeltappers' and Shunters' Social Club**, guesting with Larry Grayson, minor roles in series like **Z Cars** and **Country Matters** and notable one-off plays like *Kisses at Fifty*, *Leeds United* and *The Greenhill Pals*.

DAWSON, LES (1934–93)

Highly respected northern comedian, a former jazz pianist who used his keyboard skills to great effect in his useless pianist routine. Otherwise, Dawson was noted for his dry, pessimistic delivery and his catalogue of mother-in-law and wife jokes. Discovered on **Opportunity Knocks!**, he quickly moved on to star in his own YTV series *Sez Les*, in which he developed characters like the seedy Cosmo Smallpiece, and perfected a gossipy housewife double act (Cissie and Ada) with Roy Barraclough. Taking over **Blankety Blank** from Terry Wogan, he maintained the show's high ratings and, still with the BBC, he also hosted *The Les Dawson Show*. His career came full circle in 1990, when he became compère of **Opportunity Knocks!**, succeeding Bob Monkhouse. One of his most unusual roles was that of a 100-year-old woman in the straight drama *Nona*, but his last appearance came in the comedy-drama *Demob* in which he took the role of comic Morton Stanley.

DAY, SIR ROBIN (1923–)

The doyen of British political interviewers, Robin Day was a barrister who joined the BBC as a radio producer in 1955. With the start of ITV, he moved to ITN to become one of its first two newscasters (along with Chris Chataway), also presenting the company's **Roving Report** and *Tell the People*. In 1959 he left in order to stand as Liberal parliamentary candidate for Hereford, but, failing to win the seat, he returned to television as a reporter/presenter on **Panorama**, staying with the programme until 1972. In later years he hosted *Newsday*, all the BBC's main political events (as well as Radio 4's *The World at One*) and initiated **Question Time** in 1979. One famous interview for Nationwide during the Falklands conflict was rudely interrupted when his interviewee, Defence Secretary John Nott, stormed out after being dubbed a 'here today, gone tomorrow politician'. Retiring in 1989, Day has since taken his brusque, breathy, yet dogged interviewing style – and his famous spotted bow tie – to satellite and regional television.

DAY TODAY, THE

UK (Talkback) Comedy. BBC 2 1994

Christopher Morris
Steve Coogan
Rebecca Front
Doon MacKichan
Patrick Marber
David Schneider

Creators/Writers: Christopher Morris, Armando Iannucci. Executive Producer: Peter Fincham. Producer: Armando Iannucci

Award-winning spoof news and current affairs programme.

A sort of **Monty Python** meets **Newsnight**, *The Day Today* was the television manifestation of Radio 4's *On the Hour*. It took the form of a TV news magazine, anchored by Christopher Morris, an argumentative, disdainful, Jeremy Paxman-like interviewer and reader of sensational but obscure headlines. Doon MacKichan presented business news in the guise of Collaterlie Sisters and Steve Coogan's cringingly awful sports correspondent, Alan Partridge, was later given his own chat show, *Knowing Me, Knowing You with Alan Partridge*. Typically quirky reports from the USA were provided by CBN's Barbara Wintergreen, Sylvester Stuart was the decapitated weatherman with the innovative graphics, Peter O'Hanraha'hanrahan dealt with economic issues, Valerie Sinatra warned of traffic chaos from her mile-high travel tower and Speak Your Brains was the weekly vox pop spot. The voice of Michael Alexander St John was also heard.

DAYS OF HOPE

UK (BBC) Drama. BBC 1 1975

Ben Matthews ....Paul Copley
Sarah Hargreaves............................Pamela Brighton
Philip Hargreaves...........................Nikolas Simmonds

Writer: Jim Allen. Producer: Tony Garnett

Young idealism during the turbulent days of World War I and the General Strike.

Much acclaimed but highly controversial, *Days of Hope*, set in the years 1916 to 1924, was the four-part story of three young northern Christians: farmer Ben Matthews, his sister, Sarah, and her husband, Philip. As well as being pacifists they were also socialists, working towards the election of a Labour Government, their lives touched by the dramatic events of the time and the poverty and injustice which surrounded them. Applauded for its courageous stance and undeniably impressive production, the mini-series was viciously slated by Conservative-minded critics for its subversive tone, historical inaccuracy and socialist sentiments. Ken Loach directed all four parts: *1916: Joining Up, 1921: Black Friday, 1924: The First Labour Government* and *1926: The General Strike*.

DE LA TOUR, FRANCES (1944-)

British Shakespearean actress finding a comedy niche as the plain Jane Miss Jones in *Rising Damp*. Among her other credits have been the anthologies *Crime of Passion* and *Cottage To Let, Flickers, A Kind of Living* and, more recently, the greasy spoon comedy *Every Silver Lining* (as Shirley Silver).

DEADLINE MIDNIGHT

UK (ATV) Drama. ITV 1960–1

Joe Dunn ....Peter Vaughan
Neville Crane ....Jeremy Young
Matt Stewart ....Bruce Beeby
Tom Douglas.......................................James Culliford
Peggy Simpson..Mary Law
Mike Grieves ....Glyn Houston
Mark Byron ....Olaf Pooley

Producers: Hugh Rennie, Rex Firkin

Action and adventure with the reporters of a fictitious daily newspaper.

Focusing on the investigations of the journalists of the *Daily Globe*, *Deadline Midnight* took its inspiration from the intrepid reporters of Fleet Street. Former *Daily Express* editor Arthur Christiansen acted as programme consultant to ensure authenticity, although many Fleet Street hacks were not impressed with proceedings. Peter Vaughan starred as the *Globe*'s news editor, Joe

Dunn (replaced later by Glyn Houston as Mike Grieves), and the ever-changing cast was filled with relatively unknown actors in a quest for a realistic atmosphere.

DEAR JOHN

UK (BBC) Situation Comedy. BBC 1 1986–7

John Lacey ....Ralph Bates
Kate...Belinda Lang
Kirk St Moritz ....Peter Blake
Ralph Dring ....Peter Denyer
Louise Williams ....Rachel Bell
Mrs Arnott ....Jean Challis
Mrs Lemenski...Irène Prador
Sylvia Watkins.......................................Lucinda Curtis
Ricky Fortune ....Kevin Lloyd
Wendy ....Wendy Allnutt

Creator/Writer: John Sullivan. Producer: Ray Butt

A wimpy divorcé finds solace in an encounter group.

Language teacher John Lacey had a shock on returning home from work one day. He found a note from his wife, Wendy, revealing that she had left him for his best friend, taking Toby, their eight-year-old son, with her. In the subsequent divorce proceedings, John lost his house and was forced to move into a crummy bedsit. Among his new neighbours was the elderly Mrs Lemenski, a foreign immigrant who was sure John was crazy.

His social life in tatters, John spotted an advert in a newspaper for The 1-2-1 Club, a divorced persons' encounter group, and decided to give it a go. The class was run by officious beauty consultant Louise Williams, whose chief interest was in her members' sexual problems and fetishes. Joining John in the group was Ralph Dring, one of life's great bores and the proud driver of a motorcycle combination. His Polish wife had married him to avoid extradition and had left him during their wedding reception. Also seen was Kate, an attractive but uptight girl whose three marriages had broken down because of her frigidity. This also seemed to prevent her warming to John. While other minor characters hovered in the background (including the virtually silent Mrs Arnott, Sylvia with the silly laugh and faded rock star Ricky Fortune – of Ricky Fortune and the Fortunates), the other main protagonist was Kirk St Moritz, a John Travolta lookalike, who had not even been married, let alone divorced, and attended simply to pick up 'frustrated chicks'. This spinner of exotic yarns, who claimed to be a spy, turned out to be a dowdy mummy's boy whose real name was Eric Morris.

Writer John Sullivan sold the idea to an American company and spent some time as a consultant and writer on their version of the series. This aired in the UK as *Dear John: USA* and starred Judd Hirsch.

DEAR MOTHER – LOVE ALBERT

UK (Thames/Yorkshire) Situation Comedy. ITV 1969–72

Albert Courtnay	Rodney Bewes
Mr A.C. Strain	Garfield Morgan
Vivian McKewan	Sheila White
Mrs McKewan	Geraldine Newman
Frances Ross	Mary Land
Leslie Willis	Luan Peters
Doreen Bissel	Liz Gebhardt
	Cheryl Hall (*Albert*)
Mrs Ada Bissel	Amelia Bayntun

Creators/Writers/Producers: Rodney Bewes, Derrick Goodwin

A young man's letters home to his mother exaggerate his success in the big city.

When naive North Country lad Albert Courtnay moved to the bright lights of London he had high hopes. Unfortunately, life turned out to be rather more mundane than anticipated, not that he told his mother this in his weekly letters home. Albert worked for Mr A.C. Strain as a sales and marketing consultant in a confectionery factory. Vivian McKewan was the girl in his life and her mother was also seen. Later Albert moved into a flat with two girls, Frances and Leslie, to the disapproval of his new fiancée, Doreen Bissel, and his prospective mother-in-law. After three seasons, the title was shortened to *Albert*.

DEATH OF A PRINCESS

UK (ATV) Drama Documentary. ITV 1980

Princess Misha'al	Suzanne Abou Taleb
Ryder	Paul Freeman

Writer: Antony Thomas. Producers: Antony Thomas, Martin McKeand

Highly controversial simulated documentary about the execution of an Islamic princess.

Death of a Princess, a two-hour special, sparked off one of the mightiest rows ever caused by a television programme. It reconstructed the investigations made by writer/co-producer Antony Thomas into the case of a 19-year-old Arab princess who had wavered from strict adherence of the Islamic religion and committed adultery. The price she paid for this capital crime was public execution. No country was named in evidence, but Saudi Arabia was so offended with the programme and its open criticism of Islamic culture that it cut diplomatic ties with the United Kingdom. Arguments raged over the accuracy of the information, although Thomas claimed to have travelled widely and talked to various witnesses in the course of his research. Normality was only restored once Foreign Secretary Lord Carrington had openly condemned the film.

DEATH OF AN EXPERT WITNESS see P.D. James.

DEAYTON, ANGUS (1956–)

British writer, comedian and comic actor, an Oxford graduate and one-time collaborator with Rowan Atkinson. However, Deayton is best known as Patrick, Victor Meldrew's frustrated neighbour, in **One Foot in the Grave** and as the chairman of the topical satire show **Have I Got News For You**. His other major credits have included **KYTV** (as Mike Channel), **Who Dares Wins**, **Mr Bean**, *Chelmsford 123*, *Alexei Sayle's Stuff*, **Tiswas**, *Doctor at the Top* and *Bad Company* (as Paul Foot). He has also written for *Aspel & Co.* and is a popular choice for commercial voice-overs.

DEE, SIMON (NICHOLAS HENTY DODD; 1935–)

Controversial DJ and talk show presenter, at one time all the rage but quickly fading out of view. His heyday came with the trendy tea-time pop and chat show Dee Time in 1967, the year in which he also compered **Miss World**. Previously, he had been the first voice on the pirate radio station Radio Caroline when it opened in 1964 and remained on the high seas until the following year. He then joined the BBC, presenting programmes like *Housewives' Choice* and *Midday Spin*, as well as contributing to Radio Luxembourg. Although he made a small comeback with LWT in the early 1970s, hosting *The Simon Dee Show*, little has been seen of him in recent years.

DEF II

UK (BBC) Youth Magazine. BBC 2 1988–94

Executive Producer: Janet Street-Porter

Early evening youth programming strand.

The *DEF II* slot (roughly between 6 and 7.30 pm on Mondays and Wednesdays) was aimed at the 16- to 25-year-old market and emulated Channel 4's *Network 7* (also once in the care of Janet Street-Porter). Among the programmes airing under the *DEF II* umbrella were the *Rough Guides* series with Magenta De Vine and Sankha Guha, *Rapido* with Antoine de Caunes, the US comedies *Wayne's World* and *The Fresh Prince of Bel-Air*, *Dance Energy* (later *D Energy*) with

Normski, *Job Bank* (career profiles), *Liquid Television* (animations), the football magazine *Standing Room Only*, *Cyberzone* (a virtual reality game show), *Behind the Beat* (a black music show), *Reportage* (news and views from around the world) and *Open to Question*, in which youngsters interviewed celebrities.

DEFENDERS, THE

US (Plautus) Legal Drama. BBC 1962–7

Lawrence Preston....................................E.G. Marshall
Kenneth Preston ....Robert Reed
Helen Donaldson.....................................Polly Rowles
Joan Miller ....Joan Hackett

Creator: Reginald Rose. Producers: Herbert Brodkin, Robert Markell

Father and son lawyers defend clients accused of socially 'difficult' crimes.

In this very well-respected courtroom series, two generations of a legally minded family were brought together in the conscientious partnership of Preston and Preston. Lawrence Preston was the father and the old hand, educating his rookie son, Kenneth, who was fresh from law school and full of worthy ideas. Together they undertook a variety of cases, often dealing with subjects that pricked the public's conscience, such as civil rights, abortion and mercy killing, but, unusually for TV advocates, they didn't always win. In early episodes the pair were supported by secretary Helen Donaldson, and Kenneth's girlfriend, Joan Miller, a social worker, was also seen.

Ralph Bellamy and William Shatner were the stars of the pilot episode, which was shown in 1957, four years before *The Defenders* became a series in the USA. In that pilot, the pair acted on behalf of a client played by Steve McQueen. Many famous guest stars embellished the show over the years, from the likes of Gene Hackman and Jon Voight to Robert Redford and Dustin Hoffman.

DEFINITION

The clarity and sharpness of the TV screen picture.

DEMPSEY AND MAKEPEACE

UK (LWT/Golden Eagle) Police Drama. ITV 1985–6

Lt James Dempsey ....Michael Brandon
Detective Sgt Harriet
  Makepeace (Harry) ....Glynis Barber
Chief Supt Gordon Spikings ....Ray Smith
Detective Sgt Charles Jarvis (Chas) ....Tony Osoba

Creator/Producer: Tony Wharmby. Executive

Producer: Nick Elliott

A streetwise Yank and a plummy member of the British aristocracy form an unlikely police partnership.

James Dempsey was a New York cop from Manhatten's Ninth Precinct, who, having uncovered corruption in his own force and shot dead his own partner, was transferred to Britain for safety. There he was teamed with Lady Harriet Makepeace, a stunning, blonde Cambridge science graduate with distant claims to the throne, who, for some reason, had decided to pursue a police career. The two formed an uneasy partnership, working for SI 10, a covert division of Scotland Yard.

Dempsey was the typical brash American, a Vietnam veteran, hasty in his actions and fast on the trigger. Makepeace was a crack shot, a former archery champion, who, rather more subtly, achieved results by using her contacts in high places. In charge of the pair was vociferous Liverpudlian Gordon Spikings, with Chas, another detective, occasionally joining them in their investigations.

In all, *Dempsey and Makepeace* was a rather violent series, offering car chases aplenty and dragging in all sorts of criminals, from terrorists to drug pushers. Stars Michael Brandon and Glynis Barber took their partnership on to a new footing when they were later married in real life.

DENCH, DAME JUDI, OBE (1934–)

Busy, award-winning British actress, in straight drama and classical roles as well as situation comedy. While the 1980s and 1990s have seen her star in two cosy domestic sitcoms – as Laura in *A Fine Romance* (opposite her real-life husband Michael Williams) and Jean in *As Time Goes By*, Dench's TV career stretches back to the mid-1960s, with appearances in *Z Cars*, *Mogul* and assorted Shakespearean adaptations. Other notable performances have come in *Love In a Cold Climate* (again with Williams), *Saigon, Year of the Cat*, *Going Gently*, *Behaving Badly*, Harold Pinter's *Langrishe, Go Down*, Rodney Ackland's *Absolute Hell* (part of BBC 2's *Performance* season) and John Hopkins's *Theatre 625* quartet *Talking to a Stranger*.

DENIS, ARMAND (1897–1971) AND MICHAELA (1914–)

A cross between David Attenborough and Fanny and Johnny Cradock, Armand and Michaela Denis were UK TV's first wildlife specialists. Through his interest in photography, Armand, a Belgian-born but Oxford-educated chemist, branched out into filming wildlife and met London-born Michaela in New York and again while filming in South America. They married and also teamed up professionally to bring the great outdoors to BBC viewers. Their distinctive presentation – he with his Belgian accent and she with her blonde, pin-up looks – brought them instant fame. Their series *Filming Wild Animals* and *Filming In Africa* in 1954 and 1955 were followed by *Michaela and Armand Denis* for ITV, before they returned to the BBC in 1957 to present *On Safari*, a series that ran for many years. On leaving television they retired to their home in Kenya, where Armand died in 1971. After a tragically short second marriage to Sir William O'Brien Lindsay, the last English Chief Justice of Sudan (he died weeks after the ceremony), Michaela turned to spritual healing, setting up a centre in Nairobi.

DENISON, MICHAEL, CBE (1915–)

Distinguished, Doncaster-born, Harrow- and Oxford-educated actor, first seen on TV in the 1930s in plays like Eugene O'Neill's *Marco Millions*. For eight years Denison was the suave Richard Boyd in ITV's *Boyd QC* (1956–64), Britain's answer to *Perry Mason*, although his later television appearances have been less prominent, but have included *Crown Court*, *Private Schultz*, *The Agatha Christie Hour*, *Rumpole of the Bailey*, the controversial *Blood Money*, *Howards' Way* (as Admiral Redfern) and one-off plays, including Joe Orton's *Funeral Games*. He is married to actress Dulcie Gray.

DENNIS, LES (LESLIE HESELTINE; 1954–)

Liverpudlian light comedian and impressionist, for a few years partner of the late Dustin Gee. His TV break came when winning *New Faces*, from which he progressed to *Who Do You Do?*, *The Comedians*, *Russ Abbot's Madhouse*, assorted variety shows and his own vehicle (originally with Gee), *The Laughter Show*. In 1987 he took over as host of the quiz game *Family Fortunes*.

DEPARTMENT S

UK (ITC) Detective Drama. ITV 1969–70

Jason King	Peter Wyngarde
Stewart Sullivan	Joel Fabiani
Annabelle Hurst	Rosemary Nicols
Sir Curtis Seretse	Dennis Alaba Peters

Creators: Monty Berman, Dennis Spooner. Producer: Monty Berman

A trio of special agents solve impossible cases for a division of Interpol.

Department S was the Paris-based secret wing of Interpol, the international police force, undertaking assignments that baffled regular detectives and government agents alike. The team's figurehead was the rakish Jason King, a thriller novelist who grappled with the facts of each case by putting himself in the shoes of his detective creation, Mark Caine. He was joined by the equally perceptive American action man Stewart Sullivan (who loved to shoot down King's extravagant theories), and Annabelle Hurst, an attractive computer buff with an eye for detail. Their head of section was Oxbridge-educated black African Sir Curtis Seretse.

The trio's cases ranged from investigating what had happened to an airliner strangely lost for six days to discovering how a tailor's dummy managed to crash a car. The enquiries called more for lateral thinking than pure detection, but the unorthodox team always achieved results, despite striving to outdo each other along the way. The undoubted star, the flamboyant, womanizing King – wearer of the magnificently pyschedelic shirts and kipper ties – was soon given his own spin-off series, *Jason King*.

DEPUTY DAWG

US (Terrytoons) Cartoon. BBC 1 1963–4

Voices: Dayton Allen

Creator: Larz Bourne. Executive Producer: Bill Weiss

The misadventures of an inept and accident-prone lawkeeper.

Hounded by pesky pranksters like the short-sighted Vince (Vincent Van Gopher), the dickie-bowed racoon Ty Coon, Muskie the muskrat and Pig Newton, Deputy Dawg strove in vain to maintain law and order in sleepy Mississippi. With frustrated yells of 'Just a cotton-picking moment' and 'Dagnabit Muskie', the drawling canine in the wide black hat tried desperately to defend a hen house from would-be invaders. He answered to the show's only human, The Sheriff, for the succession of disasters and mishaps that befell him, and from which he was only rescued by a stroke of good luck. Dayton Allen voiced Deputy Dawg, plus most of his adversaries. Ralph Bakshi, one of the show's directors, later enjoyed success with the controversial adult cartoon film *Fritz the Cat*.

DERBYSHIRE, EILEEN (1930–)

Coronation Street's perennial do-gooder Emily Nugent/Bishop, one of the programme's longest serving stars. Derbyshire joined the *Street* in January 1961.

DESMOND'S

UK (Humphrey Barclay) Situation Comedy.
Channel 4 1989–94

Desmond Ambrose	Norman Beaton
Shirley Ambrose	Carmen Munroe
Matthew	Gyearbuor Asante
Pork Pie	Ram John Holder
Lee	Robbie Gee
Tony	Dominic Keating
Sean Ambrose	Justin Pickett
Michael Ambrose	Geff Francis
Gloria Ambrose	Kim Walker
Louise	Lisa Geoghan
Beverley	Joan Ann Maynard
Mandy	Matilda Thorpe

Creator: Trix Worrell. Writers: Trix Worrell,
Joan Hooley. Producer: Humphrey Barclay

**A Peckham barber's shop in the hub of
the local West Indian community.**

Grumpy Desmond Ambrose was the proprietor
of Desmond's barber shop in southeast London.
He ran it with his wife, Shirley, with whom he
had three children, Michael, Sean and Gloria. He
also had many friends and acquaintances who
used the shop as a meeting place. There they
chewed the fat, enjoyed Shirley's refreshments,
indulged in various social events and occasionally
had their hair cut as well. Mixing various generations of black Londoners, *Desmond's* drew its
humour from London street life and West Indian
generation gap conflicts, contrasting the ways and
attitudes of the older, immigrant members with
those of the youngsters, who had been born and
bred locally.

DESTINATION DOWNING STREET

UK (TV Scripts/Associated-Rediffusion) Spy
Drama. ITV 1957

Mike Anson	John Stone
Jacques	Donald Morley
Sylva	Sylva Langova
Colin	Graham Crowden
Phoebe	Diana Lambert

Creator/Writer: St John Curzon. Producer: Eric
Maschwitz

**The adventures of a select team of secret
agents, responsible directly to the Prime
Minister.**

When Britain was threatened by ruthless foreign
saboteurs, there was only one person to call:
Major Mike Anson. Anson, a former commando,
was one of TV's first secret agents, ably assisted in
his counter-espionage by two former resistance
fighters, the Frenchman Jacques and Sylva, a
beautiful Czech girl. Colin, a university don-
cum-explosives expert, and Phoebe, a WAAF

officer who worked as the team's organizer, completed the line-up.

The quintet were brought together after a trio of
uncanny disasters had all struck at one time – an
atomic scientist went missing, a ship sank and an
African village disappeared – the work, it seemed,
of the evil spy syndicate, ARKAB. Other similarly bizarre encounters followed. Such was the
prestige of this hand-picked squad that they were
answerable only to the PM himself (hence the
title).

DETECTIVE

UK (BBC) Detective Drama Anthology. BBC 1
1964; 1968–9

Chief Inspector Maigret	Rupert Davies

Producers: David Goddard, Verity Lambert,
Jordan Lawrence

**Anthology series giving air time to some
of literature's finest detectives, as well as
some novel TV sleuths.**

This intriguing collection of detective tales
appears just as interesting in retrospect as when it
first reached the screens. For among the selected
sleuths were characters who would soon gain
their own series, albeit sometimes in the hands of
other actors. *Detective* introduced viewers to
Margery Allingham's Albert Campion, for
instance, played here by Brian Smith, as well as
G.K. Chesterton's Father Brown, as portrayed by
Mervyn Johns, and Ngaio Marsh's Inspector
Roderick Alleyne, depicted by Michael Allinson.
Cluff and Sherlock Holmes, with their stars Leslie
Sands and Douglas Wilmer, were launched into
full series virtually straight away.

The other characters (some of whom appeared
more than once) were Carter Dickson's Sir
Henry Merrivale (David Horne and Martin
Wyldeck), E.C. Bentley's Philip Trent (Michael
Gwynn), Edmund Crispin's Professor Gervase
Fen (Richard Wordsworth), Nicholas Blake's
Nigel Strangeways (Glyn Houston and Bernard
Horsfall), John Trench's Martin Cotterell (Alan
Dobie) and Roy Vickers's Inspector Rason
(Michael Hordern and John Welsh). Jeffery
Farnol's Jasper Shrig (Patrick Troughton and
Colin Blakely) was another featured investigator,
as were Douglas Sanderson's Bob Race (Frank
Lieberman), Selwyn Jepson's Eve Gill (Jane
Merrow and Penelope Horner), Austin Freeman's
Dr Thorndyke (Peter Copley), Delano Ames's
Jane and Dogobert Brown (Joan Reynolds and
Leslie Randall), H.C. Bailey's Reggie Fortune
(Denholm Elliott), Joyce Porter's Detective Chief
Inspector Dover (Paul Dawkins), Colin Morris's
Detective Chief Inspector Dew (Glynn Edwards),

Ethel Lina White's Miss Pye (Angela Baddeley), Francis Didelot's Commissaire Bignon (Edward Woodward) and Edgar Allen Poe's Auguste Dupin (Edward Woodward, again).

The series was introduced for the first season by Rupert Davies in his famous guise of **Maigret**, although no Maigret tales were actually included. A gap of four years lapsed before the series resumed in 1968, continuing through to 1969.

DETECTIVES, THE

UK (Celador) Situation Comedy. BBC 1 1993–

Bob Louis...Jasper Carrott
Dave Briggs...Robert Powell
Supt Frank Cottam...............................George Sewell

Writers: Steve Knight, Mike Whitehill.
Producer: Ed Bye

Spin-off series from *Canned Carrott*, featuring the two incompetent detectives, Briggs and Louis.

Bob Louis and Dave Briggs were two gormless, plain-clothes detectives who achieved results despite their best efforts. Paired on undercover investigations by their no-nonsense boss, Supt Cottam, their bumbling and bickering, petty rivalry and hair-brained schemes usually spelt disaster for themselves, but, somehow, success for the force. Star names from other BBC series cropped up from time to time: Jim Bergerac and Charlie Hungerford in an episode set on Jersey, and Danny Kane from *The Paradise Club* in an East London gang story. Jerry Hall, Jimmy Tarbuck, Tony Jacklin, Frank Windsor, Noel Edmonds and Tony Head all made cameo appearances.

DIAL 999

UK (Towers of London/ZIV) Police Drama. ITV 1958–9

Detective Inspector Mike Maguire ......Robert Beatty
Detective Inspector Winter...............Duncan Lamont
Detective Sgt West ....John Witty

Producer: Harry Alan Towers

A Canadian Mountie is seconded to the Metropolitan Police.

Inspector Mike Maguire was sent to London by the Royal Canadian Mounted Police to study advanced crime detection techniques. Operating on a sort of 'work experience' basis, he was given an acting rank of detective inspector and assisted in his investigations by Detective Inspector Winter and Detective Sgt West. The series was made in conjunction with Scotland Yard and involved much location filming.

DIAMOND, ANNE (1954–)

Birmingham-born journalist and presenter whose work on ATV and Central's regional news programmes and then *Nationwide* eventually led to her appointment as co-host of the TV-am breakfast show *Good Morning Britain,* as the company sought to brighten up its act. Alongside Nick Owen, she helped reconstruct the ailing station's viewing figures. After leaving the breakfast sofa she moved into quiz shows (*The Birthday Show*, with Benny Green) and daytime TV, hosting *The Time, The Place, This Morning* and *TV Weekly* before teaming up with Nick Owen again for the BBC's *Good Morning With Anne and Nick.* Married to producer Mike Hollingsworth, Diamond has been outspoken in campaigns about cot deaths, following the loss of one of her own children.

DICK BARTON – SPECIAL AGENT

UK (Southern) Secret Agent Drama. ITV 1979

Dick Barton ....Tony Vogel
Snowey White ....Anthony Heaton
Jock Anderson ....James Cosmo
Sir Richard Marley ....John Gantrel
Melganik..John G. Heller

Writers: Clive Exton, Julian Bond. Executive Producers: Terence Baker, Lewis Rudd. Producer: Jon Scofield

Light-hearted television revival of a legendary radio hero.

Fearless, dependable Dick Barton, demobbed after six years in the Army, found civilian life a touch too mundane for his liking. So, when he received a call from an old friend, Sir Richard Marley, asking him to find his missing son and daughter, he willingly dashed once more into the fray, in the company of his former colleagues Snowey and Jock. The trio then stumbled into other enquiries, and more than once confronted their evil adversary, Melganik.

Unfortunately, this twice-weekly, 15-minute serial failed to capture the public's imagination in the same way as the original radio series, which went out between 1946 and 1951 and drew audiences of 15 million. Radio's Barton, Noel Johnson, reputedly received 2000 letters a week. Perhaps it was his very clean cut, wholesome portrayal of the dashing former commando who shunned hard drink and loose women which endeared him to listeners. On TV, Tony Vogel's Barton was considerably more earthy.

DICK TURPIN

UK (Gatetarn/Seacastle/LWT) Adventure. ITV 1979–82

Dick Turpin......................................Richard O'Sullivan

Nick Smith ('Swiftnick') ....Michael Deeks
Sir John Glutton........................Christopher Benjamin
Captain Nathan Spiker ....David Dakar

Creator/Writer: Richard Carpenter. Producers: Paul Knight, Sidney Cole

Tales of the famous 18th-century highwayman.

Dick Turpin, cheated out of his wealth while on military service in Flanders, decided to flout the law to regain his prosperity. His chief adversaries were the corrupt (and appropriately named) Sir John Glutton and Glutton's sneering, ambitious steward, Spiker. Assisted by Swiftnick, a young tearaway who became his closest companion, Turpin soon became a folk hero and rode to the aid of many a troubled countryman. These swashbuckling adventures saw the pair in and out of prison before Turpin's final capture and sentencing to death by hanging.

DICK VAN DYKE SHOW, THE

US (Calvada/T&L) Situation Comedy. BBC 1963–

Rob Petrie...Dick Van Dyke
Laura Petrie ....Mary Tyler Moore
Sally Rogers ....Rose Marie
Maurice 'Buddy' Sorrell ....Morey Amsterdam
Ritchie Petrie ....Larry Mathews
Melvin Cooley ....Richard Deacon
Dr Jerry Helper ....Jerry Paris
Millie Helper ....Ann Morgan Guilbert
Alan Brady ....Carl Reiner

Creator: Carl Reiner. Executive Producer: Sheldon Leonard. Producers: Carl Reiner, Sam Denoff

Gentle mishaps in the life of a TV scriptwriter.

Rob Petrie was head writer for *The Alan Brady Show*, a TV comedy programme. With his wife, Laura (a former dancer), and son, Ritchie, he lived in the suburbia of New Rochelle, where dentist Jerry Helper and his wife, Millie, were their next-door neighbours. Rob's life also extended to the TV studio in New York where he worked. His 'family' there included the man-hungry Sally Rogers and the wisecracking, loud-mouthed Buddy Sorrell. As a trio, they were constantly harrassed by the arrogant Mel Cooley, the show's bald producer who was also the brother-in-law of the star, Alan Brady. Carl Reiner, who played the neurotic Brady, was, in fact, the show's creator and was not seen, only heard, for the first few seasons, before eventually making a visual appearance. Reiner had developed the series with himself in mind for the Dick Van Dyke role, but the networks were not impressed.

Many of the stars went on to further success: Jerry Paris became a successful producer and director, working on *Happy Days* amongst other programmes, while Mary Tyler Moore became a TV superstar, having her own series, *The Mary Tyler Moore Show*, and setting up the MTM production company.

DICKENS OF LONDON

UK (YTV) Drama. ITV 1976

Charles Dickens (as a boy) ....Simon Bell	
(as an old man)	Roy Dotrice
(as a young man)	Gene Foad
John Dickens...Roy Dotrice	
Catherine Dickens.............................Diana Coupland	
Catherine Hogarth/Dickens (as a child) ..Patsy Kensit	
(as a woman) ....Adrienne Burgess	
Georgiana Hogarth ....Christine McKenna	
Fanny Dickens (as a child)...............Pheona McLellan	
(as a woman)	Henrietta Baynes
Maria Beadnell ....Karen Dotrice	
Mr Hogarth ....Richard Leech	

Executive Producer: David Cunliffe. Producer: Marc Miller

The great writer looks back on his formative years.

This biopic focused on an ageing, failing Charles Dickens as he recalled scenes from his early life. It followed his development up to the age of 32 and offered ample opportunity for viewers to identify people and events that were to shape his writings. Roy Dotrice played Dickens as an old man and also the young Dickens's father.

DICKINSON, ANGIE (ANGELINE BROWN; 1931–)

TV fame came quite late to former beauty queen Angie Dickinson, who had appeared with John Wayne in the film *Rio Bravo* (amongst other movies) way back in the 1950s. Although she won herself a selection of interesting guest spots in programmes like *Perry Mason*, *The Fugitive*, *Alfred Hitchcock Presents* and *Dr Kildare*, it wasn't until 1974 that she was cast in a lead role, that of Sgt Pepper Anderson in *Police Woman*. The series ran for four years and she followed it up with a couple of other drama series in the USA, neither of which made inroads on the other side of the Atlantic. Dickinson does, however, have plenty of TV movies to her name.

DICKINSON, SANDRA

Squeaky-voiced, blonde-haired, mostly comedy actress, the wife of actor Peter Davison. Although born in Washington DC, Dickinson's television work has been concentrated in the UK, taking in series as varied as **The Tomorrow People**, *What's On Next?*, **Triangle** and **The Two Ronnies**. She also appeared with Roy Kinnear in *The Clairvoyant* (as Lily) and **The Hitch hiker's Guide to the Galaxy** (as Trillion).

DID YOU SEE . . . ?

UK (BBC) TV Review. BBC 2 1980–7; 1991–3

Presenters: Ludovic Kennedy, Jeremy Paxman

Producers/Editors: John Archer, Sue Mallinson, Chris Mohr, Anne Tyerman

Intellectual reviews of the week's television programming.

Chaired initially by Ludovic Kennedy, but from 1991 by Jeremy Paxman, *Did You See . . . ?* invited guests (usually writers, producers and politicians, rather than professional critics) to examine three of the previous week's TV offerings. Each guest was assigned one programme for close study and gave a full appraisal, with the others chipping in with their views in due course. Before the debate began, a brief overview of the week's TV happenings was provided by the host.

DIMBLEBY, DAVID (1938–)

Son of Richard and brother of Jonathan, David Dimbleby has long been one of the BBC's foremost political commentators and interviewers, working on programmes like **Panorama**, **Nationwide**, *This Week, Next Week, The Dimbleby Talk-In* and most election coverages. In 1971 he ran into controversy when his **24 Hours** programme *Yesterday's Men* provoked anger among Labour politicians for an unfair and biased (they claimed) interview with deposed premier Harold Wilson. He has also presented **Top of the Form** and, more notably, such documentaries as the award-winning The White Tribe Of Africa and the analytical series *An Ocean Apart,* which looked at how the UK and the USA had developed in different cultural directions. He is the current chairman of **Question Time.**

DIMBLEBY, JONATHAN (1944–)

Following his father, Richard, and elder brother, David, into the current affairs side of television (and radio), Jonathan Dimbleby's progress came largely thanks to the independent sector. Beginning as a reporter with the BBC in Bristol, Dimbleby switched to ITV to present **This Week**, *TV Eye* and some prominent individual documentaries. Then came **First Tuesday** (also as associate editor), before he joined the BBC to host the lunchtime political analysis show *On the Record*. In 1994 his interview with the Prince of Wales hit the headlines, Prince Charles conced-

ing, at Dimbleby's prompt, that he had been unfaithful to Princess Diana. Dimbleby is married to writer Bel Mooney.

DIMBLEBY, RICHARD, CBE (1913–65)

Celebrated as one of Britain's finest broadcasters, Richard Dimbleby's radio work veered between light-hearted items like *Down Your Way* and *Twenty Questions* and sombre, graphic reporting. Joining the Corporation's news department in 1936, he became its first war correspondent and was the reporter who brought British listeners on-the-spot coverage of events like El Alamein and D-Day, even commentating from an active RAF bomber over Germany. In doing so, he revealed a remarkable flair for conveying the awesome nature and true horror of such campaigns. Moving into television, he became synonymous with state occasions (the 1953 Coronation was one of the highspots of his career), technical innovations (such as presenting new Eurovision and satellite links) and political debates. Once installed as anchorman of *★Panorama★* in 1955, the programme soon took off and Dimbleby earned himself a unique position of trust in the country, almost becoming a father figure and recognized internationally as the voice of the BBC. He died in 1965, not long after presenting the BBC's coverage of the state funeral of Sir Winston Churchill. His two sons, David and Richard, have both followed him into current affairs broadcasting.

DIMMOCK, PETER, CVO, OBE (1920–)

Former RAF pilot who became one of BBC Television's first outside broadcast producers and sports commentators, joining the Corporation in 1946. He hosted **Come Dancing** and **Sportsview**, and was in the chair for the first edition of **Grandstand** in 1958. Dimmock was sports advisor to the European Broadcasting Union 1959-72, as well as being the liaison executive between the BBC and the royal family 1963-77. In the 1970s he was General Manager of BBC Enterprises and then became an executive with America's ABC network.

DIRECTOR

The creative/artistic executive in a production team. The director is the one who takes charge of the performances of the actors and camera crew, and who also supervises the post-production stages.

DIRECTOR-GENERAL

The title given to the chief executive of the BBC.

DISAPPEARING WORLD

UK (Granada) Natural History. ITV 1970–

Creator/Editor: Brian Moser

Long-running, intermittently screened documentary series looking at civilizations in the far corners of the world.

Former **World in Action** producer Brian Moser was the brains behind this award-winning collection of films on 'lost' tribes hidden away in the remotest parts of the planet. His reports on the customs and ways of life of such peoples as the Cuiva in Colombia, the Meo in Laos, the Mursi in Ethiopia and the Mehinacu in Brazil brought anthropology in to the living room and revealed how ancient lifestyles were being threatened by the advance of the modern world. No commentators were used. The subjects spoke for themselves, in their own languages, and subtitles provided an English translation.

DISCOVERY CHANNEL, THE

Using the slogan 'Make the voyage', The Discovery Channel (founded in 1985 by John S. Hendricks) has broadcast eight hours each evening from the Astra 1C satellite since September 1993 and has been available on cable in the UK since April 1989. The service is provided by The Discovery Channel Europe, which is programmed separately from the original American channel to take account of European interests. Through documentaries and other factual programmes, Discovery covers a very wide range of subjects in five programme genres: adventure, travel, nature, history and technology. It does not feature current affairs or the arts. The channel commissions many programmes of its own, some in conjunction with other broadcasters, but also carries suitable material first seen on terrestrial channels. The parent company, Discovery Communications Inc., also owns The Learning Channel (TLC).

DISH A

Round aerial for receiving satellite transmissions. Attempts by the ill-fated British Satellite Broadcasting (BSB) to introduce a smaller, more angular 'squarial' for domestic use met with initial technical difficulties, although some versions have since been made available.

DISNEY, WALT (WALTER ELIAS DISNEY; 1901–66)

Alhough Walt Disney's contributions to television are small beer when compared to his influence in the cinema, nevertheless the man and his organization have been responsible for some notable achievements on the box. His Disneyland anthology, first shown to US audiences in 1954, was instrumental in bringing Hollywood studios into the mainstream of television production. The series continued right into the 1990s, under various names, including *Walt Disney's Wonderful World of Color* and **The Wonderful World of Disney**, and has been given credit for raising the standards of children's TV entertainment and education. Out of Disneyland came **Davy Crockett**, an adventure series loosely based around the legendary frontiersman, and, a year after Disneyland started, *The Mickey Mouse Club* was launched, proving a huge hit with young mousketeers (ears and all) all across the States. Also popular in the 1950s was another Disney series, **Zorro**. Although Disney himself refused to release his movie classics for TV consumption, believing that there would always be a new market for his theatrical cartoons, his company did instigate The Disney Channel in 1983, allowing this cable station to benefit from the organization's treasure trove of films and past programmes.

DISSOLVE

The merging of one shot into another, by fading one out at the same time as fading another in. It is also known as a mix.

DISTRICT NURSE, THE

UK (BBC) Drama. BBC 1 1984; 1987

Megan Roberts	Nerys Hughes
David Price	John Ogwen
Gwen Harries	Margaret John
Hugh Morris	Philip Raymond
Dr O'Casey	Rio Fanning
Nesta Mogg	Deborah Manship
Teg	Ken Morgan
Bryn Morris	Gareth Potter
Dylan Roderick	Ian Saynor
Sarah Hopkin	Elen Roger Jones
Will Hopkin	Ernest Evans
Evelina Williams	Beth Morris
Mrs Prosser-Davies	Elizabeth Morgan
Nora	Nathalie Price
Dr Charles Barclay	Philip Hurdwood
Reverend Geraint Rhys	Ifan Huw Dafydd
Dr Emlyn Isaacs	Freddie Jones

Creators: Julia Smith, Tony Holland. Producer: Julia Smith

A nurse fights for respect in the poverty-ridden South Wales valleys of the 1920s.

Megan Roberts was the new 'Queen's Nurse' in the mining village of Pencwm. Typically conservative (with a small 'c'), the local residents treated their new arrival with suspicion. Perhaps it was her sit-up-and-beg pushbike and hideous hat that frightened the miners. More probably it was because she came from *North* Wales and, what's more, was a walking symbol of uniformed authority. The fact that she was a woman, taking control in a man's world, only made matters worse. Battling prejudice and ignorance at every turn, the determined and bossy Megan finally won acceptance and was able to improve medical practice in the village. For the second series, shown three years later and set in the 1930s, Megan had moved to a seaside town where she lived in the busy household of Dr Emlyn Isaacs.

DIVING TO ADVENTURE see *Hass, Hans and Lotte.*

DIXON OF DOCK GREEN

UK (BBC) Police Drama. BBC 1 1955–76

PC/Sgt George Dixon................................Jack Warner
PC/Detective Sgt Andy Crawford.............Peter Byrne
Mary Crawford ....Billie Whitelaw
                                                     Jeanette Hutchinson
                                                     Anna Dawson
Inspector Cherry ....Stanley Beard
                                                     Robert Crawdon
PC 'Laudy' Lauderdale ....Geoffrey Adams
Sgt Flint..Arthur Rigby
PC Johnny Wills ....Nicholas Donnelly
PC 'Tubb' Barrell ....Neil Wilson
Sgt Grace Millard...............................Moira Mannion
Cadet Jamie MacPherson ....David Webster
PC Bob Penney.....................................Anthony Parker
WPC Kay Shaw/Lauderdale.............. Jocelyne Rhodes
PC Swain ....Robert Arnold
WPC Liz Harris ....Zeph Gladstone
PC Newton ....Michael Osborne

Creator: Ted Willis. Producers: Douglas Moodie, Ronald Marsh, Philip Barker, Joe Waters

The cases of a traditional London bobby.

George Dixon was a policeman of the old school, the sort of dependable copper who helped old ladies across the road and whose idea of justice for young tearaways was a clip around the ear. Perhaps that was not surprising given that the series began in the mid-1950s. But, when you consider that it was still on our screens 21 years later, at a time when Jack Regan (*The Sweeney*) was dishing out knuckle sandwiches on the same London streets, it is easy to see just how dated this series had become. Indeed, even by 1962, the series was beginning to show its age, with the all-action men of *Z Cars* vying for viewers' attentions. But *Dixon of Dock Green* soldiered on, plodding its own beat, unashamedly unspectacular in style and content, and almost turning a blind eye to the rapidly rising crime rate.

George Dixon first saw the light of day in the 1949 Rank film *The Blue Lamp*, in which the genial veteran was gunned down by armed robber Dirk Bogarde. His creator, Ted Willis, exhumed the character six years later when the BBC were looking for a replacement for **Fabian of the Yard**. He placed PC Dixon at London's Dock Green police station, where he became a source of inspiration and comfort not only to the community but also to his younger colleagues. One such colleague was PC Andy Crawford, who went on to marry George's daughter, Mary (played by Billie Whitelaw in the first year), and provide him with twin grandchildren.

It was Crawford and his more spritely pals who took over the running around as Dixon grew older and was promoted (amidst almost national celebrations) in 1964 to the rank of Desk Sgt, replacing the icy Sgt Flint. Other familiar faces at the Dock Green nick in the early days were PCs 'Laudy' Lauderdale and 'Tubb' Barrell, and Sgt Grace Millard, but many other officers came and went over the years. With his promotion, Dixon rarely strayed beyond the station counter, as Warner's advancing years began to take their toll. By the time the series ended in 1976, he was aged 80, and the last two seasons had shown him coming to terms with retirement.

Although it became atypical of a London policeman's lot (despite Ted Willis's thorough initial research and regular story feeds from active force members), cosy *Dixon of Dock Green* remains one of British TV's most fondly remembered series. George's opening and closing monologues beneath the famous blue lamp, whistling 'Maybe It's Because I'm a Londoner' as he drifted into shot from the shadowy night, are classic TV memories, as is the lilting theme music, 'An Ordinary Copper', that wafted into living rooms every Saturday teatime, hot on the heels of *Juke Box Jury* or *Doctor Who*.

Jack Warner, brother of musichall stars Elsie and Doris Waters, died five years after the series ended and his funeral turned into a tribute from fans and policemen alike. His coffin was borne by officers from the police station at Paddington Green, where Willis had carried out much of his early research. At the ripe old age of 85, George had bidden viewers his final 'Evening All'.

DO NOT ADJUST YOUR SET

UK (Rediffusion/Thames) Children's Comedy. ITV 1967–8/1968–9

Eric Idle
Michael Palin
Terry Jones
David Jason
Denise Coffey
Terry Gilliam
The Bonzo Dog Doo-Dah Band

Writers: Eric Idle, Michael Palin, Terry Jones.
Producers: Humphrey Barclay, Ian Davidson

Silly sketches and goofy gags for younger viewers.

Although aimed at the children's hour audience, this wacky series was a direct predecessor of *Monty Python's Flying Circus* and all that programme was to achieve. Corralling together for the first time the talents of Eric Idle, Michael Palin, Terry Jones and animator Terry Gilliam, plus comic actress Denise Coffey and promising newcomer David Jason, producer Humphrey Barclay offered a madcap, 25-minute show of sketches and sight gags. One element featured the zany adventures of superhero Captain Fantastic (Jason), who was hounded by his nemesis, Mrs Black (Coffey). Fantastic was also seen in *Magpie*. The Bonzo Dog Doo-Dah Band provided musical relief.

DOBIE, ALAN (1932–)

British actor most highly acclaimed for his performance as the Victorian Detective Sgt *Cribb* in the 1980 series of the same name. He played David Corbett in *The Plane Makers* in the mid-1960s, John Diamond in *Diamond Crack Diamond* in 1970, Prince Dmitri in Tolstoy's *Resurrection* in 1971 and Prince Andrei Bolkonsky in his *War and Peace* in 1973. Other credits have included *The Troubleshooters*, *Hard Times*, *Kessler*, *Master of the Game* and numerous single dramas. His first wife was actress Rachel Roberts.

DOBSON, ANITA (1949–)

London-born actress who has so far failed to find a role to match her portrayal of boozy pub landlady Angie Watts in *EastEnders*. She arrived in Albert Square at the programme's inception, taking advantage of the show's popularity to have a top five hit with a vocal version of its theme song, 'Anyone Can Fall In Love', in 1986. Her other TV appearances have ranged from *Play Away* and *Nanny* to *Partners In Crime*, *Up the Elephant and Round the Castle* and *The World of Eddie Weary*. She also played Cath in the short-lived hairdresser's sitcom *Split Ends*.

DOCTOR FINLAY

UK (Scottish) Medical Drama. ITV 1993–

Dr John Finlay	David Rintoul
Dr Cameron	Ian Bannen
Dr Neil	Jason Flemyng
Janet MacPherson/Livingstone	Annette Crosbie
Brenda Maitland	Margo Gunn
Dr Gilmore	Ralph Riach
Angus Livingstone	Gordon Reid
Rhona Swanson	Jackie Morrison
Dr Napier	Jessica Turner

Producers: Peter Wolfes, Bernard Krichefski

In 1946 John Finlay returns to Tannochbrae after wartime service and finds things have changed.

Moving on two decades from the classic 1960s series (*Dr Finlay's Casebook*), this *Doctor Finlay* was set amidst the struggles of postwar revival. The old Arden House practice was now run down. Dr Cameron had grown tired and was troubled by the changes being enforced by the new National Health Service. Janet was no longer the gentle, inconspicuous housekeeper of the 1920s, but a woman of the 1940s, hardened to the stresses, crises and inadequacies of wartime life. Into this background ambled Dr John Finlay, fresh from service as a major in the Royal Army Medical Corps, and, with some uncertainty, now reaching a crossroads in his career. He was not overpleased to be joined as partner by the young, impulsive Dr Neil, who was taken on to help with Dr Cameron's workload.

With the arrival of the third series, in 1995, the year had progressed to 1949. Janet had married Angus Livingstone, abdicating her place as housekeeper to young Rhona Swanson, but still keeping an eye on Arden House in her new role of practice receptionist. Dr Neil had moved on to pastures new and his replacement was, somewhat provocatively, a woman, Dr Napier.

Although the village of Callander had served admirably as a setting for the original series, a new location had to be sought for the Tannochbrae of the 1940s. It was discovered in the Fife town of Auchtermuchty.

DR FINLAY'S CASEBOOK

UK (BBC) Medical Drama. BBC 1962–71

Dr Alan Finlay	Bill Simpson
Dr Angus Cameron	Andrew Cruickshank
Janet	Barbara Mullen
Dr Snoddie	Eric Woodburn
Mistress Niven	Effie Morrison

Producers: Campbell Logan, Andrew Osborn, Gerard Glaister, Douglas Allen, Royston Morley, John Henderson

Young and old doctors share a Scottish village practice.

Set in and around the settlement of Tannochbrae (real-life Callander) in the late 1920s, *Dr Finlay's Casebook* related the ups and downs in the life of young, ambitious Dr Alan Finlay and his crusty, ex-surgeon partner, Dr Angus Cameron. In the best tradition of medical dramas, the whippersnapper with the new-fangled ideas did not always see eye to eye with the stick-in-the-mud old hand, but all the same Tannochbrae was well served by its two dedicated GPs, who mutually benefited from their working arrangement. Watching over proceedings at their base, Arden House, was their trusty housekeeper, Janet, and also seen from time to time were the odious Dr Snoddie and the gossipy midwife Mistress Niven.

The series, which ran for nine years, despite keen competition from the likes of *Dr Kildare* and *Ben Casey*, was based on stories published as *The Adventures of a Black Bag* by doctor-novelist A.J. Cronin. The series was revived by ITV in 1993 (see *Doctor Finlay*).

DOCTOR IN THE HOUSE

UK (LWT) Situation Comedy. ITV 1969–70

Michael Upton	Barry Evans
Duncan Waring	Robin Nedwell
Dick Stuart-Clark	Geoffrey Davies
Paul Collier	George Layton
Huw Evans	Martin Shaw
Dave Briddock	Simon Cuff
Professor Geoffrey Loftus	Ernest Clark
The Dean	Ralph Michael
Danny Hooley	Jonathan Lynn

Producer: Humphrey Barclay

Medical students at London's St Swithin's Teaching Hospital run riot.

Loosely based on the *Doctor* books by Richard Gordon, which had been filmed in the 1950s with Dirk Bogarde in the lead role, this TV version led to a run of spin-off series: *Doctor at Large* (1971), *Doctor in Charge* (1972–3), *Doctor at Sea* (1974) and *Doctor on the Go* (1975–7). There was also an Australian version, *Doctor Down Under* (1981). The central character was initially naive, young student Michael Upton, but when Barry Evans left the show in 1972, Robin Nedwell as Duncan Waring, one of Upton's friends, took over centre stage. Amongst the other hell-raisers were the upper-crust, workshy Dick Stuart-Clark, Welshman Huw Evans, genial Paul Collier and crazy Irishman Danny Hooley. Prim spoilsport Laurence Bingham (Richard O'Sullivan) was seen in the *Doctor at Large* and *Doctor in Charge* series. Haughty Professor Loftus cast a disapproving eye on the goings on as the red-blooded students chased nurses, played childish pranks and generally caused chaos. The characters were revived in 1991 in a new BBC series, *Doctors in Charge*, which viewed the lads 20 years on in their respective practices.

Doctor in the House was a decisive step forward in the careers of several actors who played a major part in British sitcoms of the 1970s and 1980s. Richard O'Sullivan went on to his own series, *Man about the House*, Barry Evans to *Mind Your*

Language, George Layton to *It Ain't Half Hot Mum* and behind the scenes scriptwriting on a host of comedy shows, and Jonathan Lynn teamed up with Anthony Jay to create the hugely successful *Yes Minister*. Writers on the *Doctor* series themselves included *The Goodies* duo of Bill Oddie and Graeme Garden, as well as *Python*s Graham Chapman and John Cleese. Cleese allegedly based his *Fawlty Towers* on a hotel-keeper he had created for one of the *Doctor* episodes.

DR KILDARE

US (Arena/MGM) Medical Drama. BBC 1 1962–6

Dr James Kildare	Richard Chamberlain
Dr Leonard Gillespie	Raymond Massey
Dr Simon Agurski	Eddie Ryder
Dr Thomas Gerson	Jud Taylor
Susan Deigh	Joan Patrick
Nurse Zoe Lawton	Lee Kurty
Dr Lowry	Steven Bell
Nurse Fain	Jean Inness

Executive Producer: Norman Felton

A sensitive young doctor learns the ropes from an experienced senior physician.

Baby-faced James Kildare worked at the Blair General Hospital under the watchful eye of wise old Leonard Gillespie. The series began with Kildare and two other doctors, Agurski and Gerson, taking up new posts at the hospital. The others left after one season but the dedicated Kildare stayed on, battling with medical matters, furthering his knowledge and education, and striving to meet the standards set by his mentor, Gillespie.

The programme kept fairly true to life, exposing the moral and ethical dilemmas experienced by the medical fraternity and the suffering endured by patients and their families, although the initial hour-long dramas later gave way to a half-hour serial format. Its big TV rival was always *Ben Casey*, which ran for about the same length of time.

Dr Kildare made Richard Chamberlain into a household name. He even hit the charts with a vocal version of the theme song, 'Three Stars Will Shine Tonight', in 1962, and found it difficult to shake off the persona of the heart-throb doctor he portrayed so effectively. The character, which was created by Max Brand, had already appeared in several films in the 1930s and 1940s, mostly played by Lew Ayres, with Lionel Barrymore in the role of Gillespie.

DOCTOR WHO

UK (BBC) Science Fiction. BBC 1 1963–89

Doctor Who ....William Hartnell
.....................Patrick Troughton
Jon Pertwee
Tom Baker
Peter Davison
Colin Baker
Sylvester McCoy

The Doctor's Assistants:
Susan Foreman (*Hartnell*) ....Carole Ann Ford
Ian Chesterton (*Hartnell*) ....William Russell
Barbara Wright (*Hartnell*) ....Jacqueline Hill
Vicki (*Hartnell*) ....Maureen O'Brien
Steven Taylor (*Hartnell*) ....Peter Purves
Dodo Chaplet (*Hartnell*) ....Jackie Lane
Polly (*Hartnell/Troughton*) ....Anneke Wills
Ben (*Hartnell/Troughton*) ....Michael Craze
Jamie McCrimmon (*Troughton*) ....Frazer Hines
Victoria Waterfield (*Troughton*) ....Deborah Watling
Zoe Herriot (*Troughton*) ....Wendy Padbury
Liz Shaw (*Pertwee*) ....Caroline John
Jo Grant (*Pertwee*)................................Katy Manning
Sarah Jane Smith (*Pertwee/*
 Tom Baker)..Elisabeth Sladen
Harry Sullivan (*Tom Baker*) ....Ian Marter
Leela (*Tom Baker*) ....Louise Jameson
K9 (voice only: *Tom Baker*) ....John Leeson
David Brierley
Romana (*Tom Baker*) ....Mary Tamm
Lalla Ward
Adric (*Tom Baker/Davison*) ......Matthew Waterhouse
Nyssa (*Tom Baker/Davison*) ....Sarah Sutton
Tegan Jovanka (*Tom Baker/Davison*)...Janet Fielding
Turlough (*Davison*) ....Mark Strickson
Perpugillian ('Peri') Brown (*Davison/*
 Colin Baker) ....Nicola Bryant
Melanie Bush (*Colin Baker/McCoy*) Bonnie Langford
Ace (*McCoy*) ....Sophie Aldred

Others:
Colonel Brigadier Lethbridge Stewart (Troughton/
 Pertwee/Tom Baker/Davison/McCoy)
 ....Nicholas Courtney
Sgt RSM Benton (Pertwee/Tom Baker) ..John Levene
Captain Mike Yates (Pertwee) ....Richard Franklin
The Master ....(Pertwee/Tom Baker/Davison/
 ....Colin Baker/McCoy)
Roger Delgado.....................................Anthony Ainley
Davros (Tom Baker/Davison/Colin Baker/McCoy)
 ....Michael Wisher
 ....David Gooderson
 ....Terry Molloy
The Black Guardian (Tom Baker/Davison)
 ....Valentine Dyall
The White Guardian (Tom Baker/Davison)
 ....Cyril Luckham
The Valeyard (Colin Baker)................Michael Jayston
The Inquisitor (Colin Baker) ....Lynda Bellingham
The Rani (Colin Baker/McCoy) ....Kate O'Mara

Creator: Sydney Newman. Producers: Verity
Lambert, Innes Lloyd, Peter Bryant, Barry Letts,
Philip Hinchliffe, Graham Williams, John
Nathan-Turner

**Classic BBC science-fiction series
concerning an eccentric time traveller.**

Doctor Who first reached the TV screens on the
day after President Kennedy was assassinated,
transmitted live at first, it quickly lodged itself into
the Saturday teatime slot and gained a wonderful
reputation for frightening children and entertaining adults. From behind the sofa, kids of all ages
wallowed in the concept of a galactic do-gooder
with unusual habits working his way around the
dimensions of time and space, protecting the
innocent and thwarting the oppressive.

Initially, *Doctor Who* had an educational thrust,
with creator Sydney Newman intending to
involve The Doctor in real historical events,
showing viewers just how things had actually
happened. But, although there were instances
when our hero found himself at the Gunfight at
the OK Corral or the Great Fire of Rome, for
example, the idea was quickly dropped in favour
of more popular scary monsters and superbeasts.

The Doctor was first encountered in the then
today of 1963 in the episode *An Unearthly Child*.
The child in question was his alleged granddaughter, Susan, a hyper-intelligent pupil at a
London school. Her snooping teachers, Ian
Chesterton and Barbara Wright, discovered her
home was an old police box, parked in a junk
yard, where she lived with her grandfather, a
mysterious, white-haired, tetchy old man dressed
in Edwardian clothing. They sneaked into the
police box only to find it was larger inside than
out and was, in fact, a kind of spaceship. Fearing
his secret would be made public, The Doctor
activated the ship, took off (dematerialized) and
landed (materialized) on a prehistoric Earth
inhabited by primitive tribesmen. The first *Doctor
Who* adventure had begun.

It was at this point that we learned more about
The Doctor's spaceship. It was known as the
TARDIS, standing for Time And Relative
Dimensions In Space, and, as implied, it could
travel through time as well as space. Sadly, The
Doctor had little control over it, and as one adventure ended, so another began, with the TARDIS
depositing its reluctant crew in yet another perilous situation. The cliffhangers at the end of the
programme were always worth waiting for.

As the series progressed, The Doctor's companions changed frequently. Susan left her grandfather to stay with anti-Dalek freedom fighters
(see below) in the year 2167, and Ian and Barbara
eventually returned to their own time. In their
places, The Doctor picked up Vicki (a stranded
Earth girl), Steven Taylor (a space pilot, played by
future *Blue Peter* presenter Peter Purves) and
Dodo, from 16th-century France. Then came

Polly, a scientist's secretary, and Ben, a Cockney merchant seaman, before The Doctor himself changed. In an episode called *The Tenth Planet*, something happened that was to prove vital to the longevity of the series: The Doctor regenerated. Viewers learned that he had the power to revitalize himself when close to death, and, by the time the series ended, there had, in fact, been six regenerations. On this occasion, the grey locks and craggy features of William Hartnell gave way to the pudding basin haircut and elfish grin of Patrick Troughton. Along with his appearance, The Doctor's character also changed. His dour snappiness was replaced by spritely joie de vivre, as Troughton turned The Doctor into a kind of scientific clown, a cosmic hobo in baggy checked trousers, who passed the time piping up tunes on a recorder. With Doctor No. 2 travelled Polly, Ben and then some of his best-remembered assistants, the Scots Highlander Jamie (a pre-*Emmerdale* Frazer Hines), Victoria, the orphaned daughter of an antique shop owner, and a super-intelligent alien, Zoe. They also encountered some of the most fearsome enemies, including the Cybermen (first seen in *The Tenth Planet*) and the Yeti.

When Troughton decided to bow out, it was easy to drop in a replacement, given that the regeneration idea had been comfortably established, and, with his departure, another of The Doctor's many secrets was revealed. Viewers learned that The Doctor was actually one of the Time Lords, a race which lived on the planet Gallifrey and acted as guardians of the time concept. In fact, he had been a bit of a rebel, a runaway who had stolen a TARDIS, albeit not a very good one. Not only was its navigation control hopelessly flawed, but its chameleon circuits were also defunct. Consequently, instead of being able to change appearance to blend in with the background (as it had done in 1963), it was now stuck in its police box guise. All the same, the Time Lords were not forgiving. Finally catching up with The Doctor, they put him on trial and exiled him to Earth.

Troughton's successor, Jon Pertwee, played the role as a brilliant scientist with martial arts skills, a dandy in a frilly shirt and a velvet jacket, who drove a yellow vintage car named Bessie (registration WHO 1). He worked as a consultant at UNIT (United Nations Intelligence Taskforce), commanded by Brigadier Lethbridge Stewart, a by-the-book, traditional army man who had first appeared as a Colonel in the Troughton days and who appeared with all The Doctors except William Hartnell and Colin Baker. Earth was suddenly under threat from all quarters, as malevolent aliens cast their eyes on the planet, and it was during this period that The Doctor's arch-rival, The Master, a scheming, mesmeric, rene-

gade Time Lord with a goatee beard and a sinister smirk, made his debut. Working with The Doctor at UNIT to counter such adversaries were scientist Liz Shaw, headstrong agent Jo Grant and the tomboyish journalist Sarah Jane Smith.

Sarah Jane continued with the next Doctor, a madcap, mop-haired adventurer played by Tom Baker. Sporting a floppy hat, a flowing scarf and an inane grin, chewing jelly babies in times of danger, Baker's Doctor was once again airborne, the Pertwee version having regained his freedom late in the day. Baker's reign as The Doctor proved to be the longest (seven years) and spanned no less than eight assistants, most notably alien warrior girl Leela, Time Lady Romana (or Romanadvoratrelundar, who regenerated, like The Doctor, into a new body), the artful Adric, the aristocratic Nyssa and, briefly, the mouthy Australian air stewardess Tegan. One companion most fans now wish to forget is the robot dog K9.

Baker was succeeded by the gentler, conscientious, cricket-loving Peter Davison depiction, who was admirably supported by Nyssa, Tegan and the schoolboy/alien Turlough. On Davison's departure, a Baker returned, but this time Colin, not Tom. Adding a touch more whimsy and a hefty dose of arrogance to the part, this plumper, curly-headed Doctor's time was short-lived, and he was not generally liked (he even squabbled with his American companion, Peri). He was briefly joined by the red-haired Mel before Sylvester McCoy was drafted in for the seventh and last portrayal of The Doctor. On this occasion, our hero was a dashing but dotty man of action, carrying a question-mark-shaped umbrella that mirrored his studious but quirky temperament. His best-remembered travelling chum was the aggressive Ace.

Over the years, The Doctor's enemies were easily as important as his assistants. Amongst the most menacing were the aforementioned Cybermen, inhabitants of Earth's twin planet, Telos, who had replaced their decaying organs with artificial ones and had gradually turned into aggressive robot men. The Yeti were furry little robots sent to conquer the Earth, and other memorable invaders included the Ice Warriors (from Mars), the Sea Devils (prehistoric creatures reclaiming their planet from beneath the waves), the Silurians (the Sea Devils' reptile cousins) and The Rani, another rebel Time Lord. The giant ants called Zarbi were some viewers' favourite aliens, but top of the list for most had to be the Daleks, a ruthless race of metal megalomaniacs.

The Daleks were first encountered in the second *Doctor Who* story, *The Dead Planet*. Set on the planet Skaro, it revealed how the Daleks, a dying race, had developed special transporter machines, armed with deadly ray guns, to overcome the Thals, their peace-loving rivals. These transporters (with the seldom seen squidgy Dalek mutants inside), skated around on castors, operating controls with a long suction arm (or occasionally a claw), and viewing the world out of one Cyclops-style eye stick. Their grating electronic voices provided one of the show's most frightening catchphrases: 'Exterminate!' In later, retrospective episodes, it was revealed that the Daleks had been the mutated remains of the Kaled race, saved by a power-crazed scientist, Davros. Sadly, he had refused to programme the Daleks with compassion and they had turned on him, too, in their relentless quest for domination.

Although often mocked for its primitive special effects and ridiculous soundtracks (particularly in the Pertwee era), few programmes have earned more respect than *Doctor Who*. Two feature film copies were made in the early days – *Doctor Who and the Daleks* and *Daleks: Invasion Earth 2150 ad*, both starring Peter Cushing in the title role. The various incarnations of The Doctor have actually appeared together on more than one occasion. The first was in 1972 in a story entitled *The Three Doctors*, in which the incumbent, Pertwee, was given the help of his two predecessors to combat a threat to the Time Lords. By the time of the next reunion, *The Five Doctors*, in 1983, William Hartnell had died and his portrayal was given by Richard Hurndall. Tom Baker declined to appear and footage from a never-finished production, *Shada*, was used to bring him into the action. Troughton and Colin Baker met up in *The Two Doctors* in 1985, and all except Hartnell/Hurndall and the late Troughton resurfaced for a short and extremely confusing 3-D TV experiment for 1993's *Children In Need*, in which they fought a collection of old enemies (particularly The Rani) in and around *EastEnders*' Albert Square.

Doctor Who trivia is available in abundance. Allegedly he was around 750 years old and, being a Time Lord, had two hearts and was allowed 13 regenerations. Among his favourite gadgets was the sonic screwdriver, used for anything from opening electronic doors to detonating unexploded bombs. He was never called 'Doctor Who', but simply 'The Doctor' (or, somewhat confusingly, 'The Professor' by Ace), and the atmospheric original theme music (modernized by later producers) was composed by Ron Grainer of the BBC's Radiophonic Workshop.

DOCTORS, THE

UK (BBC) Drama. BBC 1 1969–71

Dr John Somers	John Barrie
Dr Roger Hayman	Richard Leech
Dr Elizabeth McNeal	Justine Lord
Tom Durham	Paul Massie
Dr Thomas Owen	Nigel Stock
Nella Somers	Alexander Dane
Jo Hayman	Elaine Mileham
Molly	Lynda Marchal
Mrs Baynes	Maureen O'Reilly
Mrs Groom	Pamela Duncan
Bob Gilmore	David Savile
Edna Gilmore	Alison Fiske
Nurse Norman	Doreen Aris

Creator: Donald Bull. Producers: Colin Morris, Bill Sellars

Visits to a fictitious NHS practice.

The first twice-weekly BBC serial to be recorded in colour, *The Doctors* was another attempt by the Corporation to crack the soap opera market, having had only limited success with *Compact*, *United!* and *The Newcomers*. This time the setting was a general practice in North London, which was headed by serious, pipe-smoking Dr John Somers. He was ably supported by weary Dr Roger Hayman and industrious Dr Liz McNeal, as well as Welsh veteran Dr Thomas Owen (later of the spin-off *Owen, MD*) from the second series. With limited resources, they aimed to care for 9000 patients.

The idea was to portray events with due realism, avoiding the schmaltz of American doctors series and skipping the romantic liaisons which characterized *Emergency – Ward 10* and similar UK offerings. However, despite the efforts of writers like Elaine Morgan and Fay Weldon, the net result was worthy BBC drama and not the hoped-for grittiness seen in *EastEnders*, which was still 14 years away.

DOCUMENTARY

A programme focusing on facts – factual people, objects, instances or circumstances – for the purpose of reporting truth or educating the viewer. Inevitably, the maker's viewpoint is incorporated in to the programme (whether directly in the narration or through the camera techniques and editing) and comment is made (sometimes purposefully, at other times unintentionally) on the matter in hand. This led 1930s documentary supremo John Grierson to describe the medium as 'the creative treatment of reality'. Documentary techniques have sometimes been borrowed by drama producers to bring an extra degree of realism or objectivity to their work.

DODD, KEN, OBE (1927–)

Merseyside comic, a stalwart of variety shows and his own comedy programmes during the 1960s and 1970s. As well as stand-up routines in the classic music hall style (complete with tickling stick), Dodd has been known to burst into sentimental song (he had a string of hits in the 1960s, including the chart-topping 'Tears'). He also introduced us to the Diddymen – Dicky Mint, Mick the Marmalizer, Evan, Hamish McDiddy, Nigel Ponsonby-Smallpiece, et al – who worked the jam butty mines of Knotty Ash. They were either presented as kids in costume or in animated puppet sketches, with Dodd providing the voices. His programme titles have included *The Ken Dodd Show, Doddy's Music Box, Funny You Should Say That, Ken Dodd's World of Laughter, The Ken Dodd Laughter Show* and *Ken Dodd's Showbiz,* and other appearances have come in **The Good Old Days**, **Stars On Sunday** and *A Question of Entertainment* (as team captain), with more intriguing 'straight' guest spots in **Crossroads** and **Doctor Who**.

DOGTANIAN AND THE THREE MUSKEHOUNDS

Spain (BRB) Cartoon. BBC 1 1985

Creator/Writer/Executive Producer: Claudio Biern Boyd

The adventures of a heroic puppy and his dashing colleagues.

In this canine version of Alexandre Dumas's *The Three Musketeers,* the lead figure was Dogtanian, a puppy from Gascony who became a French national hero when teaming up with a trio of dogfighters, Athos, Porthos and Aramis (the Three Muskehounds). Under their motto of 'one for all and all for one', they championed the underdog throughout the country. Dogtanian's love interest was Juliette, a Crufts winner if ever there was.

DOLLY

A mounting for a camera, usually on wheels or rails to allow camera movement.

DONAHUE, PHIL (1935–)

Silver-haired American talk show host, the presenter of a long-running national daytime programme (*Donahue*) in which the audience reveal their views on political and social topics, not to mention sexual matters. His programmes have been aired late at night in the UK. He is married to actress Marlo Thomas.

DONOVAN, JASON (1968–)

Boyish blond actor who shot to fame as Scott Robinson in **Neighbours**, using the series to launch a successful singing career. He was the second actor to take the part (following Darius Perkins) and came to Erinsborough via shows like *The Henderson Kids.* Outside of Ramsay Street, Donovan also starred in the wartime drama *The Heroes,* playing a nervous young sailor. His father, Terence Donovan, is a veteran of Australian TV and has since joined the *Neighbours* cast as Doug Willis.

DON'T ASK ME

UK (Yorkshire) Science. ITV 1974–8

Presenters:
Derek Griffiths
Miriam Stoppard
Magnus Pyke
David Bellamy
Robert Buckman
Austin Mitchell
Brian Glover

Producer: Duncan Dallas

The hows, whys and wherefores of science explained in everyday terms.

Prompted by questions from a studio audience, Dr Magnus Pyke, Dr Miriam Stoppard and David Bellamy took the wonders of science, medicine and technology into Britain's living rooms. 'Why do golf balls have dimples?' and 'Do crocodiles shed tears?' were two typical queries, with one question always coming from a celebrity guest. Derek Griffiths hosted proceedings in the early days, before he was succeeded (briefly) by Adrienne Posta and then Brian Glover. Dr Rob Buckman and future Labour MP Austin Mitchell also became part of the team. A follow-up series, *Don't Just Sit There,* featured the same pundits.

DON'T FORGET TO WRITE!

UK (BBC) Situation Comedy. BBC 1 1977–9

Gordon Maple	George Cole
Mabel Maple	Gwen Watford
Tom Lawrence	Francis Matthews

Creator/Writer: Charles Wood. Producer: Joe Waters

A dramatist encounters problems in his personal and professional life.

Gordon Maple was a moody, struggling screenwriter, supplying scripts for feature films that were never actually made, dealing with awkward movie producers who made his life difficult with their niggly demands. Maple was also prone to bouts of writers' block and, to compound the agony, his writer friend Tom Lawrence was altogether more successful. Mabel was Gordon's long-suffering wife.

Don't Forget To Write! had its origins in two plays which, like this series, were written by Charles

Wood and starred George Cole and Gwen Watford. The first, entitled *A Bit of a Holiday*, was screened by Yorkshire Television as part of its 1968 anthology *The Root of All Evil*. The second, *A Bit of a Family Feeling*, aired in 1971 as part of Yorkshire's *The Ten Commandments* season.

DON'T WAIT UP

UK (BBC) Situation Comedy. BBC 1 1983–90

Dr Tom Latimer	Nigel Havers
Dr Toby Latimer	Tony Britton
Helen Latimer	Jane How
Angela Latimer	Dinah Sheridan
Madeleine Forbes/Latimer	Susan Skipper
Dr Charles Cartwright	Richard Heffer
	Simon Williams
Susan Cartwright	Tricia George
Felicity Spicer-Gibbs	Jane Booker

Creator/Writer: George Layton. Producer: Harold Snoad

Father and son doctors are brought together by divorce.

Hard-working GP Tom Latimer, newly divorced from Helen, lost his home and his surgery in the ensuing settlement. He managed to rent back the surgery but was forced to share a flat with his pompous dad, Toby, a Harley Street dermatologist who had just seen the break-up of his own marriage to Tom's mother, Angela. Playing on the generation gap, and also on the conflict between NHS and private medicine, the series saw the two men at each other's throats as they tried to rebuild their lives, with Tom working for a reconciliation between his parents. Madeleine was Toby's secretary and Tom's new girlfriend (later wife). Charles Cartwright was Tom's practice partner.

DOOMWATCH

UK (BBC) Science Fiction. BBC 1 1970–2

Dr Spencer Quist	John Paul
Dr John Ridge	Simon Oates
Tobias 'Toby' Wren	Robert Powell
Colin Bradley	Joby Blanshard
Pat Hunisett	Wendy Hall
Barbara Mason	Vivien Sherrard
Geoff Hardcastle	John Nolan
Dr Fay Chantry	Jean Trend
Dr Anne Tarrant	Elizabeth Weaver
Commander Neil Stafford	John Bown
Minister	John Barron

Creators: Gerry Davis, Kit Pedler. Producer: Terence Dudley

A special government department monitors dangers to society from scientific 'progress'.

Standing for the Department for the Observation and Measurement of Science, Doomwatch was a governmental agency dedicated to preserving the world from the dangers of unprincipled scientific research. The Government's intention in setting up the agency had been to stifle protest and secure votes, and it believed it was establishing a quango with little power. However, its principal activists, the incorruptible Dr Spencer Quist and the heroic pairing of Dr John Ridge and Toby Wren, soon gave Doomwatch some real bite.

Quist had worked on the development of the atomic bomb but had then seen his wife die of radiation poisoning. Ridge was an all-action, women-chasing, secret agent type, and Wren (making the unknown Robert Powell the heart-throb of the series) was a conscientious researcher. Together they took ecology into viewers' living rooms, questioning the real value of certain scientific discoveries in a series of dramas which, in many respects, were years ahead of their time. Among the problems they tackled were embryo research, subliminal messages, so-called 'wonder drugs', the dumping of toxic waste, noise pollution, nuclear weaponry, man-made viruses, genetic manipulation and animal exploitation. Consequently, Doomwatch has been described as the first 'green' TV drama series. It was novel in another TV sense, too, taking the drastic and risky step of killing off one of its lead characters at the end of the first season: Wren was blown up defusing a bomb on a seaside pier. Among his replacements was Dr Fay Chantry, who was introduced to strengthen the female profile of the programme.

Radical, unusual and controversial, *Doomwatch* was the brainchild of former **Doctor Who** collaborators Gerry Davis and Kit Pedler. However, they became increasingly disillusioned with the series as mundane drama elements took hold. By the third and final season, they had severed their link completely and were openly voicing criticisms of storylines. A feature film of the same title was released in 1972, starring Ian Bannen, but Ridge, Quist and their Yorkshireman lab assistant, Colin Bradley, made only fleeting appearances in it.

DOONICAN, VAL (1929–)

Relaxed Irish singer whose Saturday night variety shows became a staple of the BBC (and briefly ITV) diet in the late 1960s and 1970s. Mixing sentimental ballads with novelty songs like 'O'Rafferty's Motor Car', 'Delaney's Donkey' and 'Paddy McGinty's Goat', Doonican was a firm favourite with both old and young viewers, and his distinctive sweaters and cosy rocking chair established themselves as his trademarks. Comedian Dave Allen was 'discovered' thanks to the weekly slot Doonican gave him.

DORS, DIANA (DIANA FLUCK; 1931–84)

Bold, blonde British leading lady, a product of the Rank Charm School whose film career never quite reached the heights it promised. Later in life she found herself more in demand on television. She starred as Queenie Shepherd in the 1970 sitcom **Queenie's Castle**, as rugby league manageress Di Dorkins in the 1973 comedy *All Our Saturdays*, played the commandant in **The Two Ronnies** saga *The Worm That Turned* and also appeared as Mrs Bott in *Just William*. Her numerous guest spots included **Hammer House of Horror**, **Thriller** and villainous roles in both **Shoestring** and **The Sweeney**. She also briefly presented an afternoon chat show for Southern TV. Never short of personal problems, Diana Dors died in 1984 after major surgery. One of her last TV roles was as slimming presenter on TV-am's *Good Morning Britain*.

DOTTO

UK (ATV) Quiz. ITV 1958–60

Presenters: Robert Gladwell, Jimmy Hanley, Shaw Taylor

Producer: John Irwin

Join-the-dots based game show.

In *Dotto*, a quiz show brought over to the UK from the USA, two contestants, by answering questions, joined dots to reveal a celebrity's face. The first contestant to guess the mystery person received a cash sum for every unjoined dot left on the board. There were 50 dots at the start of each round. Robert Gladwell was the show's original host and he was succeeded by Jimmy Hanley and then future **Police Five** presenter Shaw Taylor during the programme's two-year run.

The original American version was forced off the screen after being implicated in the so-called 'Quiz Show Scandal' which rocked US game shows in the late 1950s. It was alleged that certain 'interesting' contestants (those viewers liked and who generated good audiences) were favoured by programme sponsors and given the answers to questions in advance so they could continue as reigning champions from programme to programme.

DOUBLE DECKERS, The see *Here Come The Double Deckers*.

DOUBLE YOUR MONEY

UK (Associated-Rediffusion/Arlington) Quiz. ITV 1955–68

Host: Hughie Green
Hostesses: Valerie Drew, Jean Clarke, Alice Earrey, Nancy Roberts, Julie de Marco, Monica Rose

Creator: John Beard

Extremely popular double-or-quit quiz show.

Airing first on Radio Luxembourg, *Double Your Money* was brought to television by Associated-Rediffusion, with its Canadian compere, Hughie Green, once again in charge of events. Participants had the chance to win up to £1000 by answering questions on specialized subjects. Beginning with a lowly £1 question, the contestants selected from 42 available topics and then 'doubled or quit' with each answer to a total of £32. They were then eligible to enter the Treasure Trail, which led to the jackpot prize. For the nail-biting £1000 question, contestants were isolated in a sound-proofed booth.

As much a part of the programme as the quiz itself was Hughie Green's over-the-top showmanship, as he clowned around telling corny jokes and poking fun at his contestants. The show's hostesses were also part of the act. The most prominent are listed above and included 77-year-old Alice Earrey, a former charlady who, having appeared as a contestant, was brought back by popular demand. The same public warmth was felt for chirpy Cockney teenager Monica Rose, who became Hughie's sidekick for most of the 1960s. Robin Richmond was the programme's resident organist.

Along with **Take Your Pick**, *Double Your Money* was a stalwart of ITV's earliest programme schedules and ran until Associated-Rediffusion lost its franchise in 1968. One edition, in 1966, was recorded in Moscow and, because the Communist Party banned cash prizes, the winner picked up a television set instead. In 1971 the concept was revived by Yorkshire Television as *The Sky's the Limit*, in which air miles (up to 21,000) and spending money (£600) replaced pure cash as prizes. Monica Rose was again seen at Hughie Green's side.

Double Your Money was based on the American show *The $64,000 Question*, which, somewhat confusingly, also aired in the UK in 1956–8 as *The 64,000 Question*, hosted by Jerry Desmonde and, for a while, Robin Bailey. Impoverished Britain offered only multiples of sixpence a question instead of dollars, with the top prize fixed at £1600 (later doubled). Nevertheless, matters were taken extremely seriously and retired copper Detective Supt Robert Fabian was employed as custodian of the questions. With its original title of *The $64,000 Question*, it was revived in 1990 with Bob Monkhouse asking the questions.

DOUGALL, ROBERT, MBE (1913–)

Distinguished and genial BBC newsreader, one of the Corporation's first TV news presenters.

Dougall joined the BBC via its accounts department before moving to the Empire Service as an announcer in the early 1930s. After spending the war with the Royal Naval Volunteer Reserve, he returned to the BBC in 1946, working as a reporter for its European and Far Eastern services, before switching to the Light Programme, again as announcer. When TV news began in 1954, he (like his early colleagues Richard Baker and Kenneth Kendall) was kept out of sight, only reaching the limelight when ITN pushed their newscasters into the picture. Dougall read the news until 1973 and subsequently made programmes about bird watching (he was at one time President of the RSPB). He also hosted **Stars on Sunday** and Channel 4's senior citizens' magazine **Years Ahead**.

DOUGLAS, COLIN (1912–91)

Familiar northern character actor whose most prominent roles were as dim-witted crook **Bonehead** in the children's series of the same name and as Edwin Ashton, the father of **A Family at War**. Among his other credits were parts in the 1955 version of **The Children of the New Forest**, **Fire Crackers**, **Love Story**, **Follyfoot**, **Telford's Change**, **The Sweeney**, **Dick Barton – Special Agent** and **Nanny**, with his last performance coming in Alan Bleasdale's **GBH**, as troubled Labour Party veteran Frank Twist.

DOUGLAS FAIRBANKS PRESENTS

UK (Douglas Fairbanks) Drama Anthology. ITV 1955–9

Host/Executive Producer: Douglas Fairbanks Jnr

Popular, filmed collection of single stories.

Hollywood leading man Douglas Fairbanks Jnr introduced, produced and occasionally starred in this anthology of dramas, which ranged from murders to farces. Guest stars included Buster Keaton and Christopher Lee. Production took place at the British National Studios in Elstree and around 120 half-hour episodes were made.

DOUGLAS, JACK (1927–)

British comedian and stooge whose Alf Ippititimus act (complete with nervous tics) was much played to TV audiences in the 1960s, especially on **The Des O'Connor Show**. He was also at one time the resident comic on **Crackerjack** and was seen in **Not on Your Nellie** (as Stanley Pickersgill) and **The Shillingbury Tales** and its sequel, **Cuffy** (as Jake).

DOUGLAS, MICHAEL (1944–)

The son of Kirk Douglas and now a Hollywood giant in his own right. Michael Douglas came to the fore as Inspector Steve Keller, Mike Stone's (Karl Malden) partner in **The Streets of San Francisco**. While working on the series, he was busy furthering his film executive career, producing **One Flew Over the Cuckoo's Nest**, and television has since played a poor second fiddle.

DRAGNET

US (MCA/Mark VII) Police Drama. ITV 1955–

Sgt Joe Friday	Jack Webb
Sgt Ben Romero	Barton Yarborough
Sgt Ed Jacobs	Barney Phillips
Officer Frank Smith	Herb Ellis
	Ben Alexander
Officer Bill Gannon	Harry Morgan
Announcers	George Fenneman
	Hal Gibney

Creator/Producer: Jack Webb

Documentary-style police series relating the cases of a no-nonsense, straight-laced cop.

'Ladies and Gentlemen, the story you are about to see is true. Only the names have been changed to protect the innocent.' So began every episode of this highly successful police drama, which was the first to realistically portray a policeman's lot, including the pressures of his private life. It centred on plodding bachelor cop Sgt Joe Friday, badge number 714 in the Los Angeles Police Department. His earliest colleague was Ben Romero, but when actor Barton Yarborough died after only three episodes, Friday was briefly accompanied by Ed Jacobs and then through the show's glory years by Officer Frank Smith (mostly played by the chubby Ben Alexander). When the programme was relaunched in 1967, after seven years off the air, Harry Morgan (later Colonel Potter in **M*A*S*H**) joined Friday on the beat as the hypochondriac Bill Gannon. This series was entitled **Dragnet '67** and brought the 1950s series bang up to date, dealing with topical issues like drug pushing and student protest.

Dragnet had previously been a hit on US radio and was the brainchild of actor Jack Webb, who also directed the series and researched the concept tirelessly. His contacts in the real-life police department allowed him access to genuine case files, from which the programme's storylines were adapted. Right from the show's characteristic 'dum-de-dum-dum' opening bars, music was skilfully used to heighten the tension. Documentary-style camera angles were often employed, and Webb himself provided a clinical, ultra-serious narration throughout each episode, incorporating dates and times as a policeman would when relating the facts to a courtroom. An announcer wound up the show, explaining the fate of the captured criminals.

Friday became known for his frank dialogues. He demanded 'Just the facts, ma'am', and matter-of-factly explained 'My name's Friday, I'm a cop'. Towards the end of the first run of the series, he was promoted to lieutenant, although, strangely, when the show was revived in 1967 he was a sergeant again. Harry Morgan paid tribute to his time in *Dragnet* (which was the first American police drama to be seen on British television) by appearing in a 1987 film parody, which starred Dan Ackroyd and Tom Hanks.

DRAKE, CHARLIE (CHARLES SPRINGALL; 1925-)

Short, ginger, cherubic comedian, fond of slapstick routines and mispronunciations. It was as **The Worker** that he became a 1960s TV favourite, turning up at the labour exchange to make Henry McGee's life (as Mr Pugh – or, rather, Mr Pooh) a misery. Drake's TV break came in the 1950s, when he appeared with Bob Monkhouse and Dennis Goodwin in *Fast and Loose* (in which Monkhouse blew off his left ear with a blank bullet). He also starred in several children's shows (one being *Mick and Montmorency* as part of an unlikely double act with lanky comedian Jack Edwardes) and with Irene Handl in *Laughter in Store*. His own series, *Drake's Progress*, *Charlie Drake* and *The Charlie Drake Show*, followed. In one episode of the last (entitled Bingo Madness), Drake was knocked unconscious when a stunt went wrong during a live transmission. After a period of 'retirement', the jaunty Londoner bounced back and *The Worker* arrived in 1965. Drake also appeared in the marriage agency sitcom *Who Is Sylvia?* (which he co-wrote with Donald Churchill) and the vaudeville series *Slapstick and Old Lace*, before switching to straight roles in dramas like *Crime and Punishment*, *Endgame*, *Bleak House* and *Filipina Dreamgirls*. However, he did revive *The Worker* in 1978 as a segment of *Bruce Forsyth's Big Night* and also popped up in Eric Sykes's silent film *Mr H Is Late* in 1988. At the peak of his comedy career, Drake ventured into films, with limited success, and even into the pop charts, notching up a run of novelty hits. 'Hallo my dahlings' became his catchphrase.

DRAKE, GABRIELLE

British actress born in Pakistan and much seen on television from the late 1960s onwards. Having appeared in series like **The Saint** and **The Champions**, Drake was cast as Lt Gay Ellis in another ITC romp, **UFO**, and then appeared as Jill Hammond in the road haulage saga **The Brothers**. However, it was as motel supremo Nicola Freeman in **Crossroads** that she made a

name for herself in the world of soap, staying with the series for a couple of years and rejoining it again very briefly just before the programme was cancelled. Among her other credits have been *Kelly Monteith* (playing his wife), *No. 10* and *The Importance of Being Earnest*.

DRAMA '61

UK (ATV) Drama Anthology. ITV 1961–7

Popular Sunday evening collection of plays.

Seen every other week, in rotation with **Armchair Theatre**, *Drama* was ATV's Sunday night theatrical contribution to the ITV network. An anthology of one-off plays, the series reflected the year of transmission in its title, with *Drama '61* eventually progressing to *Drama '67*. The first offering was *The Cruel Day*, by Reginald Rose, which was produced and directed by Herbert Wise. Other dramatists contributing to the series included Frederic Raphael, Philip Levene and Harold Swanton.

DRAMA-DOC

Short for dramatized documentary, the style of programming that reconstructs historical events using actors working from a script built around a number of known facts. It is a style of programming that has brought much confusion in the past, with facts sometimes embroidered or assumptions introduced. Consequently, some viewers have been unsure of the real or fictional nature of the programme. Genuinely fictional dramas made using documentary camera techniques and editing, in a search for extra realism, have clouded the issue even further, although this convention is now widely accepted and acknowledged.

DREAM ON

US (HBO) Situation Comedy. Channel 4 1991

Martin Tupper	Brian Benben
Judith Tupper/Stone	Wendie Malick
Toby Pedalbee	Denny Dillon
Jeremy Tupper	Chris Demetral
Eddie Charles	Jeffrey Joseph

Creators/Writers: David Crane, Marta Kauffman
Executive Producers: John Landis, Kevin Bright.
Producers: Ribb Idels, David Crane, Marta Kauffman

A hapless American's life is dominated by old TV programmes.

Martin Tupper was a 36-year-old New York publishing executive recently divorced from Judith, the psychiatrist mother of his 11-year-old son, Jeremy. Martin, however, found it difficult to adapt to his re-found bachelorhood. Stumbling from one-night stand to one-night stand, and always keeping an eye on Judith's new relationship with 'Mr Perfect', Richard Stone, Martin sought guidance in the ways of the single man from his friend Eddie Charles, a local talk show host. There was little comfort, at work, however, from his bulldog secretary, Toby.

Martin, a neurotic type, rode an emotional rollercoaster, and for every emotion there was a TV clip from his youth. Having been sat in front of the television as a child in the 1950s, Martin's mind now worked overtime, dredging up moments from classic black and white series that encapsulated his prevailing moods and feelings. For viewers, the clips (usually just one-liners) acted as Martin's thought bubbles.

Dream On was created to make use of a library of old material that could no longer find a market in syndication. The writers viewed hundreds of classic programmes in the search for snappy lines around which they could build a story. Sometimes the story came first and the lines followed. Among the vintage cuttings were pieces by Ronald Reagan, Lee Marvin, Jack Benny, Groucho Marx, Bette Davis, George Burns and Vincent Price. The series was not networked in the USA but aired on the HBO cable channel, giving the producers greater freedom with sexual content. Its executive producer, John Landis, is better known for feature films like *The Blues Brothers*, *Trading Places* and *An American Werewolf in London*.

DRISCOLL, PATRICIA (1930–)

A familiar face with younger viewers in the 1950s, it was Cork-born Patricia Driscoll who originally related the contents of *Picture Book* for Monday's *Watch with Mother*. However, in 1957, she left to replace Bernadette O'Farrell as Maid Marian in *The Adventures of Robin Hood*, allowing Vera McKechnie to take over as page turner for the toddlers. Despite continuing with her acting career, Driscoll never gained another major TV role after she left Sherwood Forest.

DRIVER, BETTY (1920–)

Although universally known today as Betty Turpin, homely barmaid and queen of the hotpot, Betty Driver's TV career pre-dates even *Coronation Street* by a number of years. As a child star, she took over from Gracie Fields on a stage tour and later spent seven years as singer with Henry Hall's band, entertaining the troops in World War II. After appearing in a number of stage plays and Ealing comedies, Driver was given her own variety programme, *The Betty Driver*

Show, by the BBC in 1952. She later turned to drama and appeared as the bossy canteen manageress Mrs Edgeley in the *Coronation Street* spin-off *Pardon the Expression* (with Arthur Lowe), and then in Granada's *Love on the Dole*, before being signed by the company in 1969 to appear in the *Street* proper as policeman Cyril Turpin's wife. She has been in Weatherfield ever since.

DRIVER, HARRY

British scriptwriter and producer, one-time partner of Jack Rosenthal and later in collaboration with Vince Powell on sitcoms. As well as contributing to *Coronation Street*, Driver also penned (with Rosenthal) a few episodes of the crime drama *The Odd Man* and some scripts for *Taxi*. He worked with Powell on the comedies *Bulldog Breed*, *Bootsie and Snudge* and *Here's Harry*, and produced *Pardon the Expression*, although his straight drama work continued through series like *Adam Adamant Lives!* in 1966. Driver and Powell's best remembered contributions were still to come, however. Among their later creations were *George and the Dragon*, *Two In Clover*, *Never Mind the Quality, Feel the Width*, *For the Love of Ada*, *Nearest and Dearest*, *Spring and Autumn*, and *Mike and Bernie*, with certainly the most controversial of all being the racist comedy *Love Thy Neighbour*. The duo also created and wrote several episodes of *Bless this House*.

DROP THE DEAD DONKEY

UK (Hat Trick) Situation Comedy. Channel 4 1990–

Gus Hedges	Robert Duncan
George Dent	Jeff Rawle
Alex Pates	Haydn Gwynne
Henry Davenport	David Swift
Sally Smedley	Victoria Wicks
Damien Day	Stephen Tomkinson
Dave Charnley	Neil Pearson
Joy Merryweather	Susannah Doyle
Jenny	Sara Stewart
Helen Cooper	Ingrid Lacey

Creators/Writers/Producers: Gus Jenkin, Andy Hamilton. Executive Producer: Denise O'Donoghue

Topical satire based around the staff of a TV newsroom.

It would be difficult to make comedy more up to date than *Drop the Dead Donkey*. By recording each episode the night before transmission and editing it on the day, with voice-overs on the closing credits for up-to-the-minute comment on breaking news, this was a situation comedy with a difference. However, considering the 'situation' was a TV newsroom, it needed to be hypertopical to succeed.

The newsroom in question was that of Globelink News, owned by the unseen Sir Royston Merchant but run by his responsibility shirking, yuppie yes-man Gus Hedges. Editor of the news team was George Dent, a hypochondriac divorcé and father of a rebellious teenager. His assistant in the first two series was the wily Alex Pates, whose mum was seldom off the phone. The rest of the team consisted of a cynical production secretary (the inappropriately named Joy Merryweather), an alcoholic, toupee-wearing news anchor Henry Davenport and his sanctimonious on-air colleague Sally Smedley, plus reporters Dave Charnley (the office romeo and compulsive gambler) and unscrupulous Damien Day (known to fabricate tragedy to enliven a story). Helen Cooper later joined the news team as Alex's replacement.

Drop the Dead Donkey was an instant hit and quickly picked up a cult following, with the result that celebrities and politicians queued up for cameo roles. However, as the characterizations became more defined, reliance on real-life news for humour decreased, and the programme focused more on its protagonists, using topical stories more as fillers.

DRURY, JAMES (1934–)

As the classic strong, silent cowboy, James Drury was TV's *The Virginian*, the eastern ranch foreman who travelled west to bring new ideas to the Shiloh ranch in Wyoming. Drury first played the role in 1958, when he starred in the pilot. But, in that seldom seen episode, *The Virginian* was a dandy, dressed in fancy clothes and sporting short pistols, and it took four years before the series was revamped and accepted by the network. Drury's TV fame arrived after some teenage theatre work and films like *Forbidden Planet*, *Love Me Tender* and *Pollyanna*. His other television performances included episodes of **Gunsmoke** and **The Rifleman**, but little was seen of him after *The Virginian* ended its nine-year run. He did star in *Firehouse*, a short-lived adventure series, but his later employment has been confined to TV movies (including the pilot for **Alias Smith and Jones**) and guest spots.

DRY RUN

A rehearsal in which the crew merely observe the script and the movement of the performers, without the equipment running.

DUBBING MIXER

The technician responsible for mixing the soundtracks on a programme.

DUCE, SHARON (1950–)

British actress much seen on TV as the star of series like *Big Deal* (as Jan Oliver), *Growing Pains* (as Pat Hollingsworth, both opposite Ray Brooks) and *Coming Home* (as Sheila Maddocks). She also appeared as Carole, the other woman in *Helen – A Woman of Today*, was WPC Cameron in *Z Cars* and has also been seen in *Minder*, among several other offerings.

DUCHESS OF DUKE STREET, THE

UK (BBC/Time-Life) Drama. BBC 1 1976–7

Louisa Trotter	Gemma Jones
Charles Tyrrell	Christopher Cazenove
Mary	Victoria Plucknett
Merriman	John Welsh
Starr	John Cater
Major Toby Smith-Barton	Richard Vernon
Lizzie	Maureen O'Brien
Irene Baker	Jan Francis
Augustus Trotter	Donald Burton
Mrs Leyton	June Brown
Mr Leyton	John Rapley
Mrs Cochran	Mary Healey
Violet	Holly De Jong
Lottie	Lalla Ward

Creator/Producer: John Hawkesworth

A cook in Edwardian London works her way out of the kitchen to become the owner of a select hotel.

Loosely based on the life story of Rosa Lewis, a kitchen maid who became manageress of the fashionable Cavendish Hotel in Jermyn Street, this series introduced viewers to Louisa Trotter, a gruff, hard-working, Cockney girl determined to better herself. Arriving at the Bentinck Hotel in Duke Street, she adjusted quickly to the world of service, becoming one of the capital's top cooks. Amidst mouthwatering displays of traditional English food (created by chef Michael Smith), Louisa bustled around barking out orders to her pretty Welsh helper, Mary, as she catered for the highest social circles.

Louisa soon attracted the attentions of both royalty and aristocracy (in the form of the Honourable Charles Tyrrell, Lord Haslemere), although her humble roots continued to show through in her rough and ready mannerisms and, more poignantly, in recurring echoes of her earlier, less salubrious days. The arrival of her illegitimate daughter, Lottie, was one such blast from the past. By this point, however, Louisa was well integrated into upstairs circles and, with a little outside help, she had been able to purchase the hotel, which she ran with great style. Assisting her were Starr, the porter, with his fox terrier companion, Fred, cook Mrs Cochran, maid

Violet and Major Smith-Barton, a retired military man who had seen better days and now paid for his keep by lending a hand.

If the programme had more than an echo of *Upstairs, Downstairs* about it, that wasn't coincidental. It was also created by John Hawkesworth.

DUEL, PETE (PETER DEUEL; 1940–71)

Popular and handsome leading American actor of the 1960s, whose TV highspot (and, sadly, last role) was as Hannibal Heyes in *Alias Smith and Jones*. Originally using his real name, Deuel, he appeared in shows like *Combat*, *The Big Valley* and *The Fugitive*, and then gained more fame as a regular in the popular US sitcom *Gidget*. His own comedy, *Love on a Rooftop*, followed, as well as a handful of movie roles. During the first season of *Alias Smith and Jones*, Duel, always highly ambitious and politically sensitive, was found dead of a bullet wound to his head. That was on New Year's Eve 1971, and, although some contend that it was an accident, or even murder, it was judged that he was a suicide victim. His role as Heyes was taken over by the show's narrator, Roger Davis.

DUFFY, PATRICK (1949–)

A 1970s and 1980s heart-throb, Patrick Duffy's most celebrated role was as Bobby Ewing, JR's sincere brother, in *Dallas*. Such was his importance to the series that, after leaving the show in 1985 (and being killed off in a car accident), he was coaxed back to boost the viewing figures, his death (and the whole of one season) being bizarrely explained away as just a dream experienced by his screen wife Pam (Victoria Principal). Previously, Duffy had starred as the amphibious hero (Mark Harris) of *The Man from Atlantis*.

DUKES OF HAZZARD, THE

US (Warner Brothers/Piggy) Adventure.
BBC 1 1979–85

Luke Duke	Tom Wopat
Bo Duke	John Schneider
Daisy Duke	Catherine Bach
Uncle Jesse Duke	Denver Pyle
Sheriff Roscoe P. Coltrane	James Best
Jefferson Davis 'Boss' Hogg	Sorrell Booke
Deputy Enos Strate	Sonny Shroyer
Cooter	Ben Jones
Deputy Cletus	Rick Hurst
Lulu Hogg	Peggy Rea
Miz Emma Tisdale	Nedra Volz
Sheriff Little	Don Pedro Colley
Laverne	Lila Kent
Emery Potter	Charlie Dell
Coy Duke	Byron Cherry
Vance Duke	Christopher Mayer
The Balladeer (voice only)	Waylon Jennings

Creator: Guy Waldron. Producers: Joseph Gantman, Paul Picard

High-speed, slapstick action with two modern-day Robin Hoods.

The Dukes of Hazzard were cousins Luke and Bo Duke, who lived with third cousin, the scantily clad Daisy, and their wise old Uncle Jesse somewhere east of the Mississippi and south of the Ohio. Avoiding traps set by their corrupt adversaries, the fat, white-suited Boss Hogg (a local politician) and his incompetent brother-in-law, Sheriff Coltrane, the Dukes rode to the rescue of the good folk of Hazzard County. They raced around in a souped-up, red and white, 1969 Dodge Charger, known as 'General Lee', often getting involved in spectacular chases and crashes, and becoming extremely popular with younger viewers.

After a year or so, Sonny Shroyer, who played Coltrane's grinning deputy, Enos Strate, was given his own spin-off series on US TV, temporarily making way for Rick Hurst in the new role of Deputy Cletus. However, more substantial cast changes were required when stars Tom Wopat and John Schneider fell out with producers over merchandising royalties. For a while they were replaced by Byron Cherry and Christopher Mayer as two other Duke cousins (the storyline had it that Luke and Bo had gone to try their luck in a motor-racing circuit), but they were brought back when ratings fell, the two new boys leaving at the same time. Banjo-picking country music accompanied all the action and Waylon Jennings, who acted as narrator, also performed the show's theme song.

DUMONT, ALLEN B. (1901–65)

American TV pioneer, largely responsible for the development of the cathode ray tube. He founded the DuMont network in 1946 but the channel struggled to survive and, when comprehensively beaten by CBS for status as America's third network, DuMont closed in 1955. In its short time it had specialized in sports events, political coverage and quiz and variety shows.

DUNCAN, LINDSAY

British actress best remembered for her roles in *Traffik* (Helen), *GBH* (Barbara Douglas), *A Year in Provence* (Annie Mayle) and *The Rector's Wife* (Anna). Other credits include *The Kit Curran Radio Show*, *TECX*, *Reilly – Ace of Spies* and numerous single dramas.

DUNLOP, LESLEY (1956–)

Newcastle-born actress with an extensive television portfolio. Although best known today as Zoe Callendar in *May to December* (the second actress to play the part, taking over from Eve Matheson), Dunlop also appeared as Ruth Fullman in *Angels* and as Sara in *Capstick's Law*. Among her other credits have been *South Riding*, *Penmarric*, *The Adventures of Black Beauty*, *Our Mutual Friend*, *Smuggler* and *Doctor Who*. She is married to actor Christopher Guard.

DUNN, CLIVE, OBE (1922–)

Now at last in his seventies, Clive Dunn has been playing old men for four decades. Principally he will always be remembered fondly as the senile butcher Jack Jones, panicky veteran of Boer War conflicts, in *Dad's Army*, but he also brought his doddery charms to kids' TV as Charlie Quick, aka Grandad in the series of the same name in the late 1970s. Earlier, Dunn had come to light as Old Johnson in *Bootsie and Snudge*, as well as joining Michael Bentine in *It's a Square World* and Spike Milligan in *The World of Beachcomber*. In 1974 he starred as Sam Cobbett in the YTV sitcom *My Old Man*, with his real-life wife Priscilla Morgan taking the role of his daughter, Doris.

DURBRIDGE, FRANCIS (1912–)

British writer of suspense serials, working for the BBC from the early 1950s. Among his most prominent contributions were *The Broken Horseshoe*, *Operation Diplomat* (both 1952), *Portrait of Alison* (1955), *The World of Tim Frazer* (1960, starring Jack Hedley), *The Desperate People* (1963), *Melissa* (1964), *A Man Called Harry Brent* (1965), *A Game of Murder* (1966), *Bat Out of Hell* (1966), *The Passenger* (1971), *The Doll* (1975) and *Breakaway* (1980) – many packaged under the umbrella title *Francis Durbridge Presents*. Durbridge was also the creator of wealthy sleuth *Paul Temple*.

DUSTBINMEN, THE

UK (Granada) Situation Comedy. ITV 1969–70

Bloody Delilah ....John Woodvine
                                                        Brian Wilde
Cheese and Egg ....Bryan Pringle
Winston Platt ....Graham Haberfield
'Smellie' Ibbotson ....John Barrett
Heavy Breathing ....Trevor Bannister
Eric..Tim Wylton

Creator: Jack Rosenthal. Producers: Jack Rosenthal, Richard Everitt

The misadventures of a team of refuse collectors.

Based on a 1968 play by Jack Rosenthal, entitled *There's a Hole in Your Dustbin, Delilah*, *The Dustbinmen* was Rosenthal's series about a gang of northern binmen, viewing their progress as they set about their rounds, shirking work and lusting after housewives. Leader of the team was Cheese and Egg (his initials were C.E.), and riding with him on their bin lorry (affectionately dubbed Thunderbird Three) were Manchester City fanatic Winston, slow-witted Eric, ladies' man Heavy Breathing and the unfortunately nicknamed Smellie. Their boss at the corporation depot was the so-called Bloody Delilah.

Despite its vulgarity and coarse language, *The Dustbinmen* was a big hit with viewers and all six first series episodes topped the ratings. Rosenthal opted out after the first two seasons, leaving the scriptwriting to others, having already passed the producer's chair over to Richard Everitt. The original one-off play had three cast differences: Frank Windsor played Bloody Delilah, Jack MacGowran played Cheese and Egg and Harold Innocent was Heavy Breathing.

DUTY FREE

UK (Yorkshire) Situation Comedy. ITV 1984–6

David Pearce ....Keith Barron
Amy Pearce ....Gwen Taylor
Robert Cochran ....Neil Stacy
Linda Cochran ....Joanna Van Gyseghem
Carlos ....Carlos Douglas

Writers: Eric Chappell, Jean Warr. Producer: Vernon Lawrence

Two couples toy with adultery in the Spanish sun.

When David Pearce was made redundant, he and his wife, Amy, used some of the payoff for a holiday in Spain, where they palled up with Robert and Linda Cochran. Through various compromising and farcical situations, including much hiding in wardrobes and under beds, the series focused on David and Linda's attempts at adultery, with Robert and Amy remaining rather straight-laced throughout. Carlos was the bemused waiter who witnessed the bizarre goings on. Their package holiday lasted seven weeks on screen and indeed was not completed until a second series ended a year later. A third season saw the foursome reunited on a winter holiday in the same hotel, and there was also a Christmas special in the same location.

DYKSTRA, JOHN (1947–)

American special effects producer, the man behind the *Star Wars* stunts who has also been in demand for television sci-fi offerings like *Battlestar Galactica*.

DYNASTY

US (Aaron Spelling/Fox-Cat) Drama. BBC 1
1982–9

Blake Carrington.....................................John Forsythe
Krystle Jennings/Carrington ....Linda Evans
Alexis Carrington/Colby/Dexter...............Joan Collins
Fallon Carrington/Colby...............Pamela Sue Martin
                                                        Emma Samms
Steven Carrington...Al Corley
                                                        Jack Coleman
Adam Carrington/Michael Torrance
....Gordon Thomson
Cecil Colby ....Lloyd Bochner
Jeff Colby...John James
Claudia Blaisdel...............................Pamela Bellwood
Matthew Blaisdel ....Bo Hopkins
Lindsay Blaisdel.....................................Katy Kurtzman
Walter Lankershim.............................Dale Robertson
Joseph Anders ....Lee Bergere
Kirby Anders/Colby ....Kathleen Beller
Andrew Laird ....Peter Mark Richman
Sammy Jo Dean/Carrington/Fallmont
....Heather Locklear
Michael Culhane ....Wayne Northrop
Dr Nick Toscanni ....James Farentino
Mark Jennings ....Geoffrey Scott
Congressman Neal McVane......................Paul Burke
Farnsworth 'Dex' Dexter ....Michael Nader
Amanda Carrington...................Catherine Oxenberg
                                                        Karen Cellini
Dominique Deveraux ....Diahann Carroll
Gerard ....William Beckley
Gordon Wales ....James Sutorius
Daniel Reece..Rock Hudson
Lady Ashley Mitchell ....Ali MacGraw
Danny Carrington..........................Jameson Sampley
Joel Abrigore....................................George Hamilton
King Galen ....Joel Fabiani
Prince Michael ....Michael Praed
Clay Fallmont...Ted McGinley
Ben Carrington ....Christopher Cazenove
Caress Morell ....Kate O'Mara
Dana Waring/Carrington ....Leann Hunley
Krystina Carrington ....Jessica Player
Sable Colby ....Stephanie Beacham
Sgt Johnny Zorelli.....................................Ray Abruzzo
Virginia Metheny ....Liza Morrow
Captain William Handler ....John Brandon
Rudy Richards ....Lou Beatty, Jnr
Joanna Clauss/Sills ....Kim Terry-Costin
Monica Colby ....Tracy Scoggins

Creators: Richard Shapiro, Esther Shapiro.
Executive Producer: Aaron Spelling. Producer:
Douglas Cramer

**Oil, money and family rivalries in a Denver
setting.**

Closely modelled on *Dallas*, *Dynasty* almost
bettered it in the ratings. As with the saga of the
Ewings, the wealth came from oil (indeed, the

programme's working title was *Oil*), with the
beneficiaries this time the Carrington family and
the setting Denver, Colorado. Head of the family was Blake Carrington, who married his blonde
secretary, Krystle Jennings, in the first episode.
His children by previous marriages were a man-
hungry, precocious daughter named Fallon and a
bisexual son, Steve. Other original cast members
included geologist Matthew Blaisdel, once a lover
of Krystle, Claudia, his disturbed wife, and their
attractive young daughter, Lindsay.

From the start Krystle's unhappiness in her marriage was clear, as Blake devoted most of his time
to keeping his empire intact. Her problems were
only beginning, however, for at the end of the
first season, Blake's vindictive ex-wife, Alexis,
arrived, seeking to regain her share of the family
fortune. From this point on, the programme
hinged around this female JR's attempts to
remove Krystle or unseat Blake himself. Alexis
married Blake's great rival, Cecil Colby, and,
though he died of a heart-attack soon after, she
inherited the power of his oil company, Colbyco,
and became even more formidable. Meanwhile,
daughter Fallon continued her promiscuous ways,
having affairs with all and sundry, including Jeff
Colby, whom she married, producing LB ('Little
Blake'). Steve married Sammy Jo Dean and conceived a son, Danny. He also became involved
with Claudia, endured a period of exile in
Indonesia and underwent plastic surgery following an explosion (actor Al Corley left the series).
This clumsy switch of actors was later repeated
with Fallon, who strangely lost three inches in
height, became 14 years younger and began to
speak with an English accent.

As in **Dallas**, new characters were constantly
introduced, some of them members of the
Carrington clan, keen to get their hands on the
family silver. These included Adam Carrington,
Blake's illegitimate son (it was later proven that
this was not so), who arrived using the name
Mark Torrance, black singer Dominique
Deveraux, one of Tom, Blake's dad's, unplanned
offspring, and Blake's younger brother, Ben.
Alexis was far from pleased to see the arrival of
her sister, Caress, who tried to publish a damag-
ing book about her called *Sister Dearest*. Alexis
bought the publishers to prevent her doing so.

Always keen to better its mentor, *Dynasty* took
the high road, introducing world statesmen and
royalty into its plots. Ex-President Gerald Ford
and his wife, Betty, were joined in one episode by
former Secretary of State Henry Kissinger. The
royalty came in the form of the fictitious Prince
Michael of Moldavia, who planned to wed
Alexis's daughter, Amanda. But, in a sensational
cliffhanger, the Carringtons were 'massacred' at

the European wedding reception by gun-toting revolutionaries. However, it turned out that only two guests had died and the action returned once more to Denver.

Other highlights of the show's run were the conviction of Alexis for murdering Mark Jennings (Krystle's former husband), although the deed was actually done by Congressman Neal McVane in an Alexis disguise; the birth of Blake and Krystle's daughter, Krystina; Krystle's affair with Daniel Reece (Rock Hudson's last role); the abduction of Krystle and her replacement by a lookalike actress, so good she even fooled Blake; Alexis finally wresting power from Blake, before kicking him and Krystle out of the 48-room Carrington mansion; and the destruction in a fire of Blake's hotel, La Mirage, in which Claudia, who had started it, was killed. Marriages came and went, Blake lost his memory and thought he was still married to Alexis, little Krystina needed a heart transplant and was then abducted, and Blake finally regained his company.

Sensational to the end, the last season saw a mummified body dragged from the Carringtons' lake (it turned out to be one of Alexis's old flames, but who had killed him?). Cousin Sable arrived from Los Angeles to sort out Alexis, Krystle fell into a coma in a Swiss hospital, Blake and a bent policeman shot each other, Alexis and her husband, Dex, were pushed off a balcony by Adam, and Fallon and little Krystina found themselves trapped down an old mineshaft with a Nazi art collection! A two-hour special, *Dynasty: The Reunion*, seen in 1992, aimed to conclude matters. This revealed that Alexis had survived, somehow, and explained how Fallon and Krystina were pulled free, how Krystle returned from her sanitorium, and how Blake both lost and won back his business empire, going to prison for murder inbetween.

In the pilot for *Dynasty*, the role of Blake was filled by George Peppard but, for the series proper, he was replaced by John Forsythe, the man who had earlier provided the voice for Charlie in **Charlie's Angels**. *Dynasty* was also responsible for the spin-off, **The Colbys**, which temporarily took Jeff and Fallon away from the original series.

EASTENDERS

UK (BBC) Drama. BBC 1 1985–

Arthur Fowler	Bill Treacher
Pauline Fowler	Wendy Richard
Michelle Fowler/Holloway	Susan Tully
Mark Fowler	David Scarboro
	Todd Carty
Lou Beale	Anna Wing
Pete Beale	Peter Dean
Kathy Beale/Mitchell	Gillian Taylforth
Ian Beale	Adam Woodyatt
Dennis Watts	Leslie Grantham
Angie Watts	Anita Dobson
Sharon Watts/Mitchell	Letitia Dean
Dot Cotton	June Brown
Nick Cotton	John Altman
Charlie Cotton	Christopher Hancock
Ethel Skinner	Gretchen Franklin
Simon Wicks	Nick Berry
Pat Wicks/Butcher	Pam St Clement
George 'Lofty' Holloway	Tom Watt
Mary Smith	Linda Davidson
Dr Harold Legg	Leonard Fenton
Ali Osman	Nejdet Salih
Sue Osman	Sandy Ratcliff
Mehmet Osman	Haluk Bilginer
Guizin Osman	Ishia Bennison
Tony Carpenter	Oscar James
Cassie Carpenter	Delanie Forbes
Hannah Carpenter	Sally Sagoe
Kelvin Carpenter	Paul J Medford
Andy O'Brien	Ross Davidson
Debbie Wilkins	Shirley Cheriton
Naima Jeffery	Shreela Ghosh
Saeed Jeffery	Andrew Johnson
Martin Fowler	Jon Peyton Price
Vicki Fowler	Samantha Leigh Martin
James Willmott-Brown	William Boyde
Cindy Williams/Beale	Michelle Collins
Tom Clements	Donald Tandy
Donna Ludlow	Matilda Ziegler
Colin Russell	Michael Cashman
Barry Clark	Gary Hailes
Duncan Boyd	David Gillespie
Jan Hammond	Jane How
Danny Whiting	Saul Jephcott
Rod Norman	Christopher McHallem
Carmel Roberts/Jackson	Judith Jacob
Matthew Jackson	Steven Hartley
Darren Roberts	Gary MacDonald
Junior Roberts	Aaron Carrington
Aisha Roberts	Aisha Jacob
Ashraf Karim	Aftab Sachak
Sufia Karim	Rani Singh
Shireen Karim	Nisha Kapur
Sohail Karim	Ronnie Jhutti
Dr David Samuels	Christopher Reich
Magda 'Mags' Czajkowski	Kathryn Apanowicz
Frank Butcher	Mike Reid
Mo Butcher	Edna Doré
Diane Butcher	Sophie Lawrence
Ricky Butcher	Sid Owen
Sam Mitchell/Butcher	Danniella Westbrook
Janine Butcher	Rebecca Michael
	Alexia Demetriou
Paul Priestley	Mark Thrippleton
Trevor Short	Phil McDermott
Disa O'Brian	Jan Graveson
Marge Green	Pat Coombs
Julie Cooper	Louise Plowright
Eddie Royle	Michael Melia
Grant Mitchell	Ross Kemp
Phil Mitchell	Steve McFadden
Peggy Mitchell	Jo Warne
	Barbara Windsor
Rachel Kominsky	Jacquetta May

Jules Tavernier	Tommy Eytle
Celestine Tavernier	Leroy Golding
Etta Tavernier	Jacqui Gordon-Lawrence
Clyde Tavernier	Steven Woodcock
Hattie Tavernier	Michelle Gayle
Lloyd Tavernier	Garey Bridges
Kofi Tavernier	Marcel Smith
Christine Hewitt	Elizabeth Power
Mandy Salter	Nicola Stapleton
Aidan Brosnan	Sean Maguire
Steve Elliot	Mark Monero
Richard 'Tricky Dicky' Cole	Ian Reddington
Nigel Bates	Paul Bradley
Debbie Tyler/Bates	Nicola Duffett
Clare Tyler/Bates	Gemma Bissix
Gill Fowler	Susannah Dawson
Shelley	Nicole Arumugam
Sanjay Kapoor	Deepak Verma
Gita Kapoor	Shobu Kapoor
Carol Jackson	Lindsey Coulson
Alan Jackson	Howard Antony
Bianca Jackson	Patsy Palmer
Robbie Jackson	Dean Gaffney
Sonia Jackson	Natalie Cassidy
Blossom Jackson	Mona Hammond
Natalie Price	Lucy Speed
Nellie Ellis	Elizabeth Kelly
David Wicks	Michael French
Geoff Barnes	David Roper
Ruth Aitken/Fowler	Caroline Paterson
Della Alexander	Michelle Joseph
Binnie Roberts	Sophie Langham
Big Ron	Ron Tarr
Ray Evans	Tony Caunter

Creators: Julia Smith, Tony Holland. Producers: Julia Smith, Mike Gibbon, Corinne Hollingworth, Richard Bramall, Michael Ferguson, Pat Sandys, Helen Greaves, Leonard Lewis, Barbara Emile, Mike Hudson, Jane Fallon, Diana Kyle, Nicholas Hicks-Beach

The continuing story of working-class East End folk.

EastEnders has succeeded where **Compact**, **United!** and **The Newcomers** all failed, namely in providing a serious, lasting, 52-weeks-a-year challenger to **Coronation Street** in the great soap opera war. Set in the fictitious London borough of Walford E20, the series has focused on life in and around grimy Albert Square, a decaying Victorian residential area with a market tagged on the side. A greasy-spoon café and a downbeat pub, The Queen Victoria, have seen as much of the action as any of the houses. The major characters at the start were the related Beale and Fowler families. Head of the clan was crotchety Lou Beale, who lived with her daughter, Pauline Fowler, Pauline's husband, Arthur, and children, Michelle and Mark. New baby, Martin, arrived soon after Pauline's twin brother, Pete Beale, ran the market fruit and veg stall, occasionally assisted by his blonde wife, Kathy, and schoolboy son, Ian. Den and Angie Watts were the squabbling pub landlords, fighting for the attentions of their adopted daughter, Sharon. Café Osman was run by Turk Ali Osman and his English wife, Sue, and other major characters in the early days included gossipy hypochondriac Dot Cotton, her villainous son, Nick, daffy old Ethel Skinner, barman Simon 'Wicksy' Wicks, dopey Lofty Holloway, yuppie boy- and girlfriend Andy O'Brien and Debbie Wilkins, Naima and Saeed Jeffery, two Asian grocers, and the Carpenters, a West Indian family. As the cast list above shows, many other characters have taken up residence in Albert Square over the years.

EastEnders has always kept up a good pace, bustling along twice a week, with an omnibus edition on Sundays. A third weekly episode was added in April 1994. The best-remembered storylines have included Michelle's pregnancy by 'Dirty' Den and her subsequent jilting of Lofty. Arthur's endless unemployment and eventual nervous breakdown was a long-running saga, and Kathy's rape at the hands of smoothie Willmot-Brown was another pot-boiler. The break-up of Den and Angie's marriage, Den's disappearance (murder?) and Nick's attempts to poison his mother were further highspots.

Never afraid to court controversy, *EastEnders* has bravely tackled touchy issues such as prostitution (through unmarried mum Mary), homosexuality (with lovers Colin and Barry), homelessness (of teenagers Mandy and Aidan), abortion (Michelle's unborn child by Lofty), Alzheimer's Disease (the mental deterioration of Mo Butcher) and AIDS (the HIV infection of Mark Fowler). Murder was the first subject on the programme's lips and the series raced to a flying start with the death of resident Reg Cox in episode one (killed, it was revealed later, by Nick Cotton). But through all the doom and gloom that has dominated *EastEnders*, there have been many lighter and funnier moments, too.

The series was the brainchild of producer Julia Smith and script editor Tony Holland, who had worked together on dramas like **Angels** and **District Nurse**. Legend has it that the idea was concocted in 45 minutes in a Shepherd's Bush wine bar. The execution of the idea was far more thorough, however, and saw the flimsy working titles of *East 8* and *London Pride* quickly dropped. With its enormous initial publicity push, *EastEnders* was a hit from day one. It has gained more than its share of moral critics but the audience figures have spoken for themselves. Not only matching *Coronation Street*, *EastEnders* has regularly knocked its northern rival off the top of the ratings.

EastEnders trivia is boundless. Fans can reveal that the beer served at The Vic has been brewed by Luxford & Copley, that the pub poodle was Roly and Ethel's dog was named Willy. They'll tell you the name of Willmott-Brown's pub (The Dagmar) and the man who owns the grotty launderette (Mr Opidopoulous), as well as the numbers of the houses where the characters live: the Fowlers at number 45 and Dr Legg at number 1, for instance. And they'll recall the spin-off records that made the UK charts: 'Anyone Can Fall In Love' (a vocal version of the theme music) by Anita Dobson, 'Every Loser Wins' by Nick Berry and 'Something Outa Nothing' by Letitia Dean and Paul Medford (known as The Banned in the series). All were hits in 1986. There was also an *EastEnders* spin-off programme. *Civvy Street*, a one-hour special screened in 1988, looked back to the Albert Square of 1942, and featured a young Lou Beale played by Karen Meagher and her friend, Ethel, played by Alison Bettles.

EASTWOOD, CLINT (1930–)

Legendary movie cowboy-turned-award-winning director, whose rise to fame was greatly assisted by his seven-year portrayal of Rowdy Yates in *Rawhide*. Previously, Eastwood had gained only parts in B-movies and guest spots in minor TV series. As such an unknown, he was cast as the trail rider Yates in 1959, growing with the series into a major TV star and securing, as a result, the lead in the spaghetti Western trilogy that began with *A Fistful of Dollars* in 1964.

EBSEN, BUDDY (CHRISTIAN RUDOLF EBSEN; 1908–)

Versatile American actor who appeared to be typecast when his marathon stint as country bumpkin Jed Clampett in *The Beverly Hillbillies* came to an end, but who branched out effectively into detective work as the ageing private eye *Barnaby Jones* and returned yet again in the 1980s as retired investigator Roy Houston in *Matt Houston*. In his pre-TV days (which effectively comprised most of his career), Ebsen had been a Hollywood song and dance man, appearing in lavish stage and movie musicals in the 1930s and 1940s. His first foray on to the small screen came in Walt Disney's *Davy Crockett*, playing Crockett's sidekick Georgie Russell, and this led to parts in western series such as *Maverick*, *Have Gun, Will Travel*, *Bonanza*, *Rawhide* and *Gunsmoke*, as well as the adventure series *Northwest Passage*. When *The Beverly Hillbillies* beckoned, Ebsen was already in his mid-fifties, but he stayed with the show until its close, nine years later. Among his other TV appearances have been guest spots in *Hawaii*

Five-O, *Hardcastle and McCormick* and *Alias Smith and Jones*. He is also a published song writer.

ECHO FOUR-TWO

UK (Associated-Rediffusion) Police Drama. ITV 1961

Detective Insector Harry Baxter	Eric Lander
Detective Sgt Joe York	Geoffrey Russell
Acting Supt Dean	Geoffrey Chater

Producer: Richard Matthews

No Hiding Place spin-off, which gave bright young detective Harry Baxter more of the limelight.

Promoted from sergeant to inspector, Harry Baxter, Chief Detective Supt Lockhart's sidekick in *No Hiding Place*, became the star of this short-lived series. He was now placed in charge of E Division's Q-cars, a squad of unmarked vehicles used for surveillance, and, with his assistant, Joe York, tackled various assignments from an office in Bow Street. A strong female following for Eric Lander instigated this series, but an actors' strike hastened its downfall before all 13 planned episodes were produced. Lander then returned to the mother series.

EDDINGTON, PAUL, CBE (1927–)

Refined British character actor whose TV work stretches way back to the 1950s when he played Will Scarlett in *The Adventures of Robin Hood*. A plethora of other ITC adventures followed, and Eddington was easily spotted in the likes of *The Avengers*, *The Prisoner* and *The Champions*. He also popped up as a bent copper in *Dixon of Dock Green*, played Brutus in *The Spread of the Eagle* presentation of Julius Caesar, was a reporter in the Raj series *Frontier* and played the civil servant Strand in *Special Branch*. However, it was as Jerry Leadbeatter, wife of Margo and neighbour of the Goods, in *The Good Life* that he at last achieved top billing. This was followed by the enormously successful *Yes Minister* and *Yes Prime Minister* (in which he starred as the bamboozled MP and PM Jim Hacker), the sitcom *Let There Be Love* (as bachelor Timothy Love, opposite Nanette Newman) and numerous other high-profile performances. These have included *Outside Edge*, *Miss Marple* and Channel 4's controversial *The Camomile Lawn*.

EDEN, MARK

Shakespearean stage and film actor whose most dramatic television role came with the character of Alan Bradley in *Coronation Street*. Moving in with Rita Fairclough, Bradley's persona gradually changed from gentle man-friend to psychotic misogynist, making him one of the *Street's* most evil creations. Fittingly, he was mown down by a Blackpool tram. Eden's earlier TV appearances had been as crusading sports writer Ray Saxon in the 1968 series *Crimebuster*, Detective Inspector Parker in **Lord Peter Wimsey**, parts in the Victorian copper caper **Cribb** and **Jesus of Nazareth**, plus a pre-Bradley incarnation in *Coronation Street* as one of Elsie Tanner's boyfriends, Wally Randle. He lives with *Street* star Sue Nicholls.

EDGE OF DARKNESS

UK (BBC) Drama. BBC 2 1985

Ronald Craven	Bob Peck
Emma Craven	Joanne Whalley
Darius Jedburgh	Joe Don Baker
James Godbolt	Jack Watson
Grogan	Kenneth Nelson
Bennett	Hugh Fraser
Pendleton	Charles Kay
Detective Chief Supt Ross	John Woodvine
Harcourt	Ian McNeice
Terry Shields	Tim McInnerny
Clemmy	Zoe Wanamaker
Chilwell	Alan Cuthbertson
Childs	Trevor Bowen

Writer: Troy Kennedy Martin. Producer: Michael Wearing

A Yorkshire policeman, following up the murder of his daughter, is drawn into nuclear subterfuge.

When Detective Inspector Ronald Craven's scientist daughter, Emma, was gunned down at his side by a shotgun-wielding Irishman, he initially believed the murder was a botched attempt to kill him. After all, he had been involved with terrorist informers in Northern Ireland. However, the more he considered the case, and the more he discovered about his daughter's links with an environmental action group called Gaia, the less certain he became. Branching out into some lone detective work, Craven found himself immersed in political intrigue, egged on by two devious civil servants, Pendleton and Harcourt, and drawing in interested parties from around the globe. The trail led to Northmoor, a disused coal mine, which was revealed to be a secret nuclear waste dump that had been infiltrated by Gaia activists, including Emma, shortly before her death. With the assistance of Darius Jedburgh, an abrasive Texan CIA agent, Craven penetrated the site. Both were fatally contaminated and the whole affair was eventually swept under the carpet by the authorities. The only hope of exposing the scandal then rested with Gaia, with whom Craven filed a report.

Edge of Darkness was one of the BBC's most successful drama series of all time. Screened initially to great acclaim on BBC 2, it earned itself a repeat showing on BBC 1 just a few weeks later, before picking up various awards the following year. Its dark, gloomy imagery enhanced the gravity of its subject matter, the ghostly appearances of Craven's dead daughter, supplying him with snippets of information, added to the 'out of our hands' atmosphere, and Eric Clapton's bluesy electric guitar provided powerful incidental music. The series also courted controversy. Gaia, the name given to the action group, had been plucked from Greek mythology by writer Troy Kennedy Martin (Gaia, or Gaea, was the Goddess of the Earth), but had already been adopted by an environmental publishing house with connections to Prince Philip. They were not pleased to be linked with this contentious project.

EDITOR

The creative technician who cuts and arranges the recorded material into the finished form. The term is also applied to the ultimate decision-maker or chief producer of a current affairs, news, sport or magazine programme.

EDMONDS, NOEL (1948–)

Chummy, bearded disc jockey turned TV presenter, fond of gentle pranks and hidden camera routines. A Radio Luxembourg DJ as a teenager, Edmonds quickly moved to Radio 1, where his breakfast show was a huge success in the years 1972 to 1977. His TV breaks came with **Top of the Pops**, *Z-Shed* and then, more significantly, with a new-style Saturday morning programme for kids, **Multi-Coloured Swap Shop**. Moving on from *Swap Shop*, Edmonds has dominated Saturday teatimes with (mostly live) programmes like *Lucky Numbers*, **The Late, Late Breakfast Show**, *The Saturday Roadshow* and, most recently, **Noel's House Party**. Over the years, he has also presented **Top Gear** (reflecting his interest in motor sports), a revival of **Juke Box Jury**, **Come Dancing**, the nostalgic *Time of your Life*, the guessing game *Whatever Next?* and the perennial TV quiz **Telly Addicts**. His dazzling shirts and sweaters have become a trademark. Despite his enormous success in the UK, an attempt at a talk show in the USA in 1986 failed to work out.

EDMONDSON, ADRIAN

English 'alternative' comedian and comic actor, with a distinctively aggressive style, once part of an act known as 20th Century Coyote with Rik Mayall. As Vyvyan in **The Young Ones** he perfected his violent moron character, which he carried through into **Filthy, Rich and Catflap** (as Eddie Catflap) and **Bottom** (as Eddie Hitler). He is married to Jennifer Saunders, with whom he appeared in **Happy Families** (as idiot Guy Fuddle), **Girls on Top**, *French and Saunders* and assorted *Comic Strip* satires. He has also appeared in **Blackadder** (as Baron Von Richthoven), *Saturday Live* (with Rik Mayall, as the Dangerous Brothers), the futuristic comedy *Snakes and Ladders* (as Giles) and the Richard Briers comedy-drama *If You See God, Tell Him* (playing Gordon Spry). In addition, Edmondson sang the theme song, 'This Wheel's on Fire', for **Absolutely Fabulous**.

EDWARD AND MRS SIMPSON

UK (Thames) Historical Drama. ITV 1978

Edward	Edward Fox
Mrs Wallis Warfield Simpson	Cynthia Harris
Queen Mary	Peggy Ashcroft
Stanley Baldwin	David Waller
George, Duke of York	Andrew Ray
King George V	Marius Goring
Walter Monckton	Nigel Hawthorne
Aunt Bessie	Jessie Matthews

Writer: Simon Raven. Producer: Allan Cameron

The story of the last abdication.

This expensive seven-part drama related events leading up to the abdication crisis of 1936, with particular focus on the controversial affair between Prince Edward (later King Edward VIII) and American divorcée Wallis Simpson. Based on the biography by Frances Donaldson, the series portrayed Mrs Simpson as a calculating schemer, something which distressed the real Duchess of Windsor, who was still alive and residing in France. Edward Fox won much acclaim for his performance as the emotionally torn king.

EDWARD THE SEVENTH

UK (ATV) Historical Drama. ITV 1975

Edward (as an adult)	Timothy West
(as a teenager)	Charles Sturridge
Queen Victoria	Annette Crosbie
Prince Albert	Robert Hardy
Princess Alexandra	Deborah Grant
	Helen Ryan
Princess Vicky	Felicity Kendall
Duchess of Kent	Alison Leggatt
Colonel Bruce	Harry Andrews
Lord Palmerston	André Morell
Benjamin Disraeli	John Gielgud
William Gladstone	Michael Hordern
Princess Dagmar	Jane Lapotaire
Lillie Langtry	Francesca Annis
Lord Salisbury	Richard Vernon
Lord Coventry	Robert Flemyng
Lady Brooke	Carolyn Seymour
Kaiser Wilhelm	Christopher Neame
Prince Eddy	Charles Dance
Herbert Asquith	Basil Dignam
Sir Henry Campbell-Bannerman	Geoffrey Bayldon

Writer: David Butler. Producer: Cecil Clarke

A detailed dramatization of the life of King Edward VII.

Edward was 60 years of age when he succeeded his long-reigning mother, Queen Victoria, to the throne, which meant that his better years were behind him. This 13-part biopic looked closely at the life and loves of the Prince and also focused on the personality of the great Queen herself and other members of the royal family. With scenes filmed within Osborne House, Sandringham and other royal properties, by permission of the present Queen, the series was much applauded for its attention to detail, production techniques and the performances of the lead actors. Based on a biography by Philip Magnus, it was mostly written by David Butler, formerly Dr Nick Williams in **Emergency – Ward 10**. Butler went on to co-write **Lillie** for LWT in 1978, in which Francesca Annis reprised her Lillie Langtry role. *Edward the Seventh* was retitled *Edward the King* when shown in the USA.

EDWARDIANS, THE

UK (BBC) Drama. BBC 2 1972–3

Producer: Mark Shivas

Eight dramatizations of the lives of turn-of-the-century British pioneers.

This series of drama-documentaries looked closely at nine early 20th-century figures of note: Messrs Charles Rolls and Frederick Royce (played by Michael Jayston and Robert Powell), writers E. Nesbit and Arthur Conan Doyle, Daisy (mistress of Edward VII), scout-founder Robert Baden-Powell, music-hall star Marie Lloyd, journalist and MP Horatio Bottomley (played by Timothy West) and Prime Minister David Lloyd-George (Anthony Hopkins).

EDWARDS, JIMMY, DFC (1920–88)

English comedian whose handlebar moustache became a trademark. Awarded the DFC for his wartime RAF efforts, Edwards broke into radio in the late 1940s, where, as Pa Glum, he appeared in Navy Mixture and its spin-off *Take It From Here*. This ran for 12 years and The Glums were revived on TV as part of *Bruce Forsyth's Big Night* in 1978. However, it is as Professor Jimmy Edwards, the corrupt principal of Chislebury School in **Whack-O!**, that he will always be remembered, and, after playing the role for four years, 1956–60, he donned his gown and picked up his cane once more for a revival in 1971. His other TV starring roles were in **Seven Faces of Jim** in 1961, *Six More Faces of Jim* in 1962, *More Faces of Jim* in 1963, *Bold as Brass* in 1964 (as musician Ernie Briggs), *Mr John Jorrocks* in 1966 (as Jorrocks, Master of Foxhounds), *Blandings Castle* in 1967 (as Sir Gregory Parsloe-Parsloe), *The Fossett Saga* in 1969 (as Victorian writer James Fossett) and as the cowardly knight Sir Yellow in 1973. The famous moustache was apparently grown to obscure facial injuries received when one of his aircraft crashed in the war.

EDWARDS, VINCE (VINCENTO EDUARDO ZOINE; 1928–)

American leading man of the 1960s, an international heart-throb thanks to his star status in **Ben Casey**. He has generally only been seen in the UK in guest spots and TV movies (including the pilot for **Knight Rider**) since the series ended in 1966, although he has popped up in a couple of lesser dramas in the USA (notably *Matt Lincoln*). His earliest TV performances came in shows such as **Alfred Hitchcock Presents** and **The Untouchables**.

EGAN, PETER (1946–)

Suave English actor whose many roles have varied between drama and comedy. Following his performance as a violent gangster in 1969's **Big Breadwinner Hog** and the somewhat different part of the Earl of Southampton in **Elizabeth R** in 1971, Egan remained in period costume for *Prince Regent* in 1979. In the 1980s he charmed sitcom viewers as the super-smooth and successful Paul Ryman in **Ever Decreasing Circles**, before becoming Hannah Gordon's house husband, David Braithwaite, in the banking comedy *Joint Account*. He still found time to win acclaim as Magnum Pym in the BBC's adaptation of Le Carré's *A Perfect Spy* and as a war cripple in the one-off play *A Day in Summer* for YTV. Amongst his other credits have been Oscar Wilde in **Lillie**, *Mother Love*, **Reilly – Ace of Spies**, *The Dark Side of the Sun*, **Tales of the Unexpected**, *Thriller*, *Paradise Postponed*, **The Ruth Rendell Mysteries** and the glossy mini-series **A Woman of Substance**.

EL C.I.D.

UK (Granada) Comedy Drama. ITV 1990–2

Douglas Bromley	John Bird
Bernard Blake	Alfred Molina
Frank	Tony Haygarth
Metcalf	Donald Churchill
Delgado	Simon Andreu
Mercedes	Viviane Vives
Stevie Blake	Robert Reynolds
Rosie Bromley	Amanda Redman
Gus Mercer	Kenneth Cranham
Graham	Niven Boyd
Señora Sanchez	Maria Isbert

Creators: Chris Kelly, Iain Roy. Executive Producer: Sally Head. Producer: Matthew Bird

Two former Scotland Yard officers take up residence on the Costa del Crime.

When police clerk Douglas Bromley was told he was being relocated to Derbyshire, the idea didn't greatly appeal. So, he encouraged his beefy CID colleague Bernard Blake to join him in early retirement and a voyage of adventure to Spain. Setting out in a motorized yacht, aptly named El C.I.D., they moored up on the Costa del Sol, near Marbella, where they quickly immersed themselves in the area's dodgy goings on. The bar they intended to open was criminally destroyed and the hapless duo joined forces with Delgado and Mercedes, father and daughter detectives, in a long-running battle with the local underworld (and, in particular, nasty Gus Mercer and his henchman Graham). Metcalf was the bombastic owner of the marina where their boat was berthed and Frank was the ex-pat proprietor of the snappily named Chez Frank restaurant. Blake's troublesome brother, Stevie, turned up in the second season, before Blake himself left in the third series, to be replaced by Rosie, Bromley's long-lost daughter. She arrived in Marbella after being dumped by her boyfriend and joined her dad as an accomplice in Delgado and Partners.

ELDORADO

UK (Cinema Verity/J Dy T) Drama. BBC 1 1992–3

Gwen Lockhead	Patricia Brake
Drew Lockhead	Campbell Morrison
Blair Lockhead	Josh Nathan
Nessa Lockhead	Julie Fernandez
Trish Valentine	Polly Perkins
Dieter Schultz	Kai Maurer
Joy Slater	Leslee Udwin
Snowy White	Patch Connolly
Roberto Fernandez	Franco Rey
Rosario Fernandez	Stella Maris
Maria Fernandez	Maria Sanchez
Abuela Fernandez	Maria Vega
Javier Fernandez	Iker Ibanez
Ingrid Olsson	Bo Corre
Marcus Tandy	Jesse Birdsall
Pilar Moreno	Sandra Sandri
Olive King	Faith Kent
Isabelle Leduc	Framboise Gommendy
Philippe Leduc	Daniel Lombart
Arnaud Leduc	Mikael Philippe
Lene Svendsen	Nanna Moller

Per Svendsen	Kim Romer
Trine Svendsen	Marchell Betak
	Clare Wilkie
Gavin Hindle	Darren Newton
Allan Hindle	Jon Morrey
Gerry Peters-Smith	Buki Armstrong
Bunny Charlson	Roger Walker
Freddie Martin	Roland Curram
Fizz Charlson	Kathy Pitkin
Stanley Webb	William Lucas
Rosemary Webb	Hilary Crane
Tracy	Hayley Bromley
Antonio	Jose Antonio Navarro
'Razor' Sharpe	Kevin Hay
Sergio Munoz D'Avila	Alexander Torriglia
Alex Morris	Derek Martin

Creators: Julia Smith, Tony Holland. Executive Producers: Verity Lambert, John Dark. Producers: Julia Smith, Corinne Hollingworth

Drama with an ex-patriot community in Spain.

In 1992, the year of falling European barriers, the BBC did its bit for the cause by launching a thrice-weekly 'soap for Europe'. Trailed in the tabloids as 'sex, sun and sangria', *Eldorado* was set in the Spanish fishing village of Los Barcos and focused on its community of ex-patriot Brits, Frenchmen and Danes, all 'living their dream' of a home in the sun but discovering that their new life was not one long holiday after all.

The community's mother figure was Gwen Lockhead, a teacher who ran the English language newspaper. Gwen's husband, Drew, was a lazy, hard-drinking Glaswegian, her son, Blair, was a typically troublesome teenager and her daughter, Nessa, although wheelchair bound, was determinedly independent. The Lockheads' neighbours were retired military man Stanley Webb, who lived with his young at heart wife, Rosemary, Olive King, the local nosy parker, and another ex-army man, Bunny Charlson, who was shacked up with Fizz, a 17-year-old runaway. Charmer Marcus Tandy was the 'Costa del Crime' villain in hiding, gay Freddie Martin knocked about with the rebellious Gerry (a girl), and Snowy White was the Los Barcos handyman. Brothers Gavin and Allan Hindle ran the beach bar, Joy Slater owned the wine bar and Trish Valentine was the ageing nightclub singer who enjoyed a stormy relationship with Dieter Schultz, a 19-year-old German windsurfing teacher. The French were represented by tennis coach Philippe Leduc, his flirty wife, Isabelle, and their 16-year-old romantic son, Arnaud. The Svendsen family offered the Danish input. Dad Per ran a chandlery business, mum Lene was a beautician and their 14-year-old daughter was called Trine. Completing the line up of Los Barcos principals were Swedish tour guide Ingrid

Olssen and a handful of local Spaniards, mostly from the Fernandez family: Roberto, the town doctor, his wife, Rosario, and two teenage children, Maria and Javier. Abuella was Roberto's traditionally minded mother. Pilar Moreno was the other native and she worked at Marcus Tandy's stables, eventually becoming his girlfriend. The interaction of this motley band of retirees, escapees from the rat race, old bigots and young new Europeans was the source of the series' drama.

Eldorado was the biggest and most ambitious series yet awarded to an independent production company (Cinema Verity) by the BBC. A whole village was especially constructed in Spanish woodland for filming and the cast and crew took up residence locally. Sadly, *Eldorado* did not capture the public's imagination in the way Julia Smith and Tony Holland's earlier creation, **EastEnders**, did, and critics piled on the agony. Although viewing figures were on the mend, it was cancelled by new BBC 1 boss, Alan Yentob, just a year after it had begun.

ELECTRONIC NEWS GATHERING see ENG.

ELIZABETH R

UK (BBC) Historical Drama. BBC 2 1971

Elizabeth I	Glenda Jackson
Robert Dudley	Robert Hardy
William Cecil	Ronald Hines
Mary Tudor	Daphne Slater
Thomas Cranmer	Bernard Hepton
Kat Ashley	Rachel Kempson
Edward VI	Jason Kemp
Catherine Parr	Rosalie Crutchley
Count de Feria	Leonard Sachs
Bishop de Quadra	Esmond Knight
Sir James Melville	John Cairney
Mary, Queen of Scots	Vivian Pickles
Sir Francis Walsingham	Stephen Murray
Duke of Alençon	Michael Williams
Catherine de Medici	Margareta Scott
Earl of Essex	Robin Ellis
Sir Anthony Babington	David Collings
Phillip II of Spain	Peter Jeffrey
Sir Francis Drake	John Woodvine
Sir Walter Raleigh	Nicholas Selby
Francis Bacon	John Nettleton
Father Robert Parsons	Paul Hardwick
O'Neill, Earl of Tyrone	Patrick O'Connell
Sir Robert Cecil	Hugh Dickson
Earl of Southampton	Peter Egan

Producer: Roderick Graham

The troubled life of England's Virgin Queen.

In six self-contained episodes of 90 minutes' length, *Elizabeth R* dramatized the tortuous life of the famous 16th-century monarch, beginning with her difficult road to the throne and ending with her lonely death. In doing so, it also afforded viewers an insight into court life in Tudor times.

Following hot on the heels of the enormously successful *The Six Wives of Henry VIII*, *Elizabeth R* had much to achieve but, thanks to its large (for the time) budget of £237,000, close attention to detail and excellent cast (some reprising the roles they had taken in *Six Wives*), it enjoyed similar acclaim. For her role as Elizabeth, Glenda Jackson shaved her forehead, donned eccentric hairpieces and wore a false nose. Courtesy of hours in the make-up room, she was seen to age from a youthful, determined 15 to a grotesque, pallid 70-year-old over the course of the series.

ELLIOT, JOHN (1918–)

Early BBC documentary maker, writer, producer and director (1954's *War in the Air* was his greatest achievement) who went on to script some influential dramas, including *A for Andromeda* and *The Andromeda Breakthrough* (both with Fred Hoyle, the latter also as producer). Elliot also created *Mogul* and penned some episodes for *Z Cars*, as well as producing the drama anthology *The Sunday Play* in 1963. He later became a BBC executive.

ELLIOTT, DENHOLM, CBE (1922–92)

Actor readily cast as a distinguished, but slightly dodgy or sinister Englishman in many films and TV dramas. His major television performances were in *The Man in Room 17* (as Imlac Defraits, succeeding Michael Aldridge's Dimmock), *Mystery and Imagination* (as Count Dracula), *Clayhanger*, *The Signalman*, *Blade on the Feather*, *Hôtel du Lac*, *Bleak House*, *Scoop*, *Codename Kyril* and the mini-series *Marco Polo* (as Niccolò Polo). He also played George Smiley in Thames TV's *A Murder of Quality*. His first wife was Virginia McKenna.

ELPHICK, MICHAEL (1946–)

British actor and comedy star, headlining in a range of 1970s and 1980s programmes. In *Private Schulz* he portrayed a cowardly German orderly wrapped up in a scheme to flood Britain with dud fivers; in *Boon*, he played former fireman turned adventurer Ken Boon; and in *Three Up, Two Down* he gave us the working-class Sam Tyler longing for the attentions of his snooty flatmate Daphne (Angela Thorne). Among his many other credits have been the comedy *Pull the Other One* (as Sidney Mundy), *Auf Wiedersehen, Pet*

(as Magowan, the Irish labourer), *Coronation Street*, *Crown Court*, *Blue Remembered Hills*, *This Year, Next Year*, *The Sweeney*, *Shoestring*, *Roger Doesn't Live Here Anymore*, *Supergran*, *Jenny's War*, *Stanley and the Women*, *The One and Only Phyllis Dixey* and *Harry* (as news agency boss Harry Salter).

ELTON, BEN (1959–)

Lively British stand-up comic and comedy scriptwriter, never afraid to shock. Among his writing credits have been *The Young Ones* (with Rik Mayall and Lise Mayer), *Happy Families*, *Filthy, Rich and Catflap*, *Lenny Henry Tonite* and, with Richard Curtis, *Blackadder* (apart from the first series). In front of the camera (complete with sparkling jacket), he has hosted *South of Watford* and *Saturday Live*, appeared in Granada's *Alfresco* and once stood in for Wogan. More recently, Elton has been *The Man from Auntie* in a monologue and sketch show that has given a thorough airing to his sharp, sometimes embarrassing (for the viewer) social and political observations. Outside of television, Elton has had a couple of novels published (including *Stark*, in which he appeared on its adaptation for BBC 2) and has scripted two West End plays.

EMERGENCY – WARD 10

UK (ATV) Drama. ITV 1957–67

Nurse Pat Roberts	Rosemary Miller
Nurse Carole Young	Jill Browne
Sister Cowley	Elizabeth Kentish
Nurse Stevenson	Iris Russell
Dr Alan Dawson	Charles Tingwell
Dr Patrick O'Meara	Glyn Owen
Potter	Douglas Ives
Dr Simon Forrester	Frederick Bartman
Dr Peter Harrison	Peter Howell
Dr Brook	William Wilde
Nurse Wilde	Tricia Money
Dr Richmond	Noel Coleman
Dr Chris Anderson	Desmond Carrington
Mr Lester Large	John Carlisle
Dr Don Nolan	Ray Barrett
Dr John Rennie	Richard Thorp
Dr Louise Mahler	Joan Hooley
Dr Giles Farmer	John White
Nurse Kate Ford	Jane Rossington
Dr Nick Williams	David Butler
Dr Richard Moone	John Alderton
Nurse Kwei	Pik-Sen Lim
Mr Verity	Paul Darrow

Creator: Tessa Diamond. Producers: Anthony Kearey, John Cooper, Cecil Petty, Josephine Douglas

Britain's first twice-weekly, long-running drama series, focusing on the staff and patients in a large general hospital.

Emergency – Ward 10 was the brainchild of ATV staff writer Tessa Diamond, who created a six-week filler entitled Calling Nurse Roberts. It proved so popular that under its racier new title it was kept on, running for ten years and drawing huge audiences. Its cancellation in 1967 was, according to Lew Grade, boss of ATV, one of his biggest mistakes. The trainee Nurse Roberts in the original title was quickly joined in the limelight by a host of budding stars. Jill Browne as Nurse (later Sister) Carole Young won most male admirers, although some of her male colleagues also became heart-throbs for female viewers. These included Charles Tingwell as surgeon Alan Dawson, Desmond Carrington as Dr Chris Anderson, Ray Barrett as Dr Don Nolan and Dr John Rennie played by a youngster by the name of Richard Thorp, now better known as Emmerdale's Alan Turner. John Alderton joined the cast in 1963 as youthful Dr Richard Moone (he was later to marry his co-star Jill Browne).

The action took place at Oxbridge General Hospital, and, although drama was high, tragedy was scarce; of more concern were the lives and loves of the hospital staff. Patient deaths were strictly limited to five per year and this was later reduced to just two. That was good news for emerging names like Ian Hendry, Albert Finney and Joanna Lumley, who all signed up for treatment. Emergency – Ward 10's success spawned a feature film, Life in Emergency Ward 10, in 1958, and also one spin-off series, Call Oxbridge 2000. This saw Dr Rennie heading off into private practice and itself led to another series entitled 24-Hour Call. Emergency – Ward 10, for all intents and purposes, was resurrected by ATV in the 1970s in the guise of General Hospital.

EMERY, DICK (1917–83)

British comedian, fond of outrageous characterizations and drag sketches. His Dick Emery Show, which began in 1963 and ran for nearly two decades, saw him adopting the guises of a sex-starved spinster (always 'Miss' not 'Madam'), an effeminate swinger ('Hello Honky Tonk'), a toothy vicar, a dim bovver boy, Farmer Finch, a classy tramp, the conniving, chortling old codger Lampwick, and Mandy, the brassy blonde who always misunderstood the interviewer, so providing Emery with his catchphrase 'Ooh, you are awful, but I like you!'. Earlier, after radio success on Educating Archie, Emery had appeared with Libby Morris in Two's Company, supported Michael Bentine on It's a Square World, played Chubby Catchpole in the last series of The Army Game and also turned up in Hancock's Half Hour. In 1964 he took the role of Mr Hughes in the early version of the TV station comedy Room

at the Bottom. Emery hosted The Dick Emery Hour for Thames in 1979, but returned to the BBC in 1982 to star in a comedy-thriller series entitled simply Emery, playing the part of investigator Bernie Weinstock (and several of his suspects) in cases entitled Legacy of Murder and Jack of Diamonds.

EMMERDALE FARM/EMMERDALE

UK (Yorkshire) Drama. ITV 1972–

Annie Sugden/Kempinski	Sheila Mercier
Jack Sugden	Andrew Burt
	Clive Hornby
Joe Sugden	Frazer Hines
Sam Pearson	Toke Townley
Peggy Skilbeck	Jo Kendall
Matt Skilbeck	Frederick Pyne
Amos Brearly	Ronald Magill
Henry Wilks	Arthur Pentelow
Marian Wilks	Gail Harrison
Rosemary Kendall	Lesley Manville
Dolly Arcaster/Skilbeck	Katherine Barker
	Jean Rogers
Ruth Merrick	Lynn Dalby
Tom Merrick	Edward Peel
	Jack Carr
Pat Merrick/Sugden	Helen Weir
Jackie Merrick	Ian Sharrock
Sandie Merrick	Jane Hutcheson
Reverend Donald Hinton	Hugh Manning
Seth Armstrong	Stan Richards
Alan Turner	Richard Thorp
Caroline Bates	Diana Davies
Kathy Bates/Merrick/Tate	Malandra Burrows
Phil Pearce	Peter Alexander
Nick Bates	Cy Chadwick
Archie Brooks	Tony Pitts
Bill Middleton	Johnny Caesar
Eric Pollard	Christopher Chittell
Mark Hughes	Craig McKay
Rachel Hughes	Glenda McKay
Sarah Connolly/Sugden	Madeleine Howard
	Alyson Spiro
Stephen Fuller	Gregory Floy
Karen Moore	Annie Hulley
Elsa Feldmann	Naomi Lewis
Michael Feldmann	Matthew Vaughan
Elizabeth Feldmann/Pollard	Kate Dove
Frank Tate	Norman Bowler
Christopher Tate	Peter Amory
Kim Tate/Barker	Claire King
Zoe Tate	Leah Bracknell
Reverend Tony Charlton	Stephen Rashbrook
Richard Anstey	Carl Rigg
Sita Sharma	Mamta Kash
Kate Hughes/Sugden	Sally Knyvette
Lynn Whiteley	Fionnuala Ellwood
Carol Nelson	Philomena McDonagh
Leonard Kempinski	Bernard Archard
Vic Windsor	Alun Lewis
Viv Windsor	Deena Payne
Scott Windsor	Toby Cockerell
Kelly Windsor	Adele Silva
Donna Windsor	Sophie Jeffrey

Shirley Foster/Turner	Rachel Davies
Bernard McAllister	Brendan Price
Angharad McAllister	Amanda Wenban
Jessica McAllister	Camilla Power
Luke McAllister	Noah Huntley
Betty Eagleton	Paula Tilbrook
Britt Woods	Michelle Holmes
Terry Woods	Billy Hartman
Robert Sugden	Christopher Smith
Nellie Dingle	Sandra Gongh
Butch Dingle	Paul Loughran
Sam Dingle	James Hooton
Tina Dingle	Jacqueline Pirie
Zak Dingle	Steve Halliwell
Ned Glover	Johnny Leeze
Jan Glover	Roberta Kerr
Roy Glover	Nicky Evans
David Glover	Ian Kelsey
Linda Glover	Tonicha Jeronimo
Biff Fowler	Stuart Wade
Emma Nightingale	Rachel Ambler

Creator: Kevin Laffan. Executive Producers: Peter Holmans, David Cunliffe, Michael Glynn, Keith Richardson. Producers: David Goddard, Robert D. Cardona, Michael Glynn, Anne W. Gibbons, Richard Handford, Michael Russell, Stuart Doughty, Morag Bain, Nicholas Prosser, Mervyn Watson

Long-running saga of Yorkshire farming folk.

Airing twice a week, *Emmerdale Farm* began life as one of the dramas commissioned by ITV to fill its afternoon schedules. It quickly attracted sizeable audiences and was moved to an early evening slot in 1977, becoming fully networked the following year. Since then the series has developed into one of the UK's major soaps.

The focus of the series has been the Sugden family, inhabitants of Emmerdale Farm itself, set on the fringes of the fictitious rural village of Beckindale. The first ever episode saw the funeral of Jacob Sugden, the family's wastrel father, leaving level-headed wife Annie to take charge of farm affairs. Annie, a wholesome farmer's wife in the old tradition, was supported by her sons, Jack and Joe, daughter Peggy, and crusty old Sam Pearson, Annie's dad, who was known to all as Grandad. Also on hand was Peggy's husband, shepherd Matt Skilbeck. Down in the village, the local hostelry (purveyor of Ephraim Monk ales) was The Woolpack, jointly owned and managed by stroppy Amos Brearly (a part-time columnist for the *Hotten Courier*) and kindly, pipe-smoking Henry Wilks, whose daughter Marian was also seen. The parish vicar was Mr Hinton. Storylines generally followed the farming calendar, with worries over crop yield, river pollution or lamb sickness merging with the usual stresses and strains of family life.

Unavoidable in such soap marathons, cast changes followed aplenty. Peggy was killed off, leaving Matt to marry Dolly Acaster. Jack disappeared to Rome and became a writer, only to return played by a different actor several years later. And Joe spent some time in France. New characters came and went. Among the most durable have been poacher-turned-gamekeeper Seth Armstrong, and Alan Turner, once-hated manager of NY Estates who has displayed more geniality as The Woolpack's new landlord. The Emmerdale farmhouse resounded to the bickering of several new families, as the Sugden boys brought home their latest wives and step-offspring. But, through it all, Annie remained the matriarchal figure, barking words of advice to her wayward children between cooking meals and doing the ironing. However, major changes were afoot.

In the mid-1980s the programme was taken by the neck and given a good shake. In came grittier plots and meaner characters. Now the lads not only baled the hay, but rolled in it, too. Extramarital liaisons became a speciality, much to the dismay of the programme's creator, Kevin Laffan. Finally, in recognition of the changes that had swept through the series, the name was shortened to the snappier *Emmerdale* in November 1989. Even since then, there have been new brooms at work and, in an effort to boost viewing figures, increasingly sensational storylines have been introduced. The Christmas 1993 plot involving a plane crashing on the village provoked much controversy, but enabled the producers to clear out the dead wood and bring in some fresh faces. This 'coming of age' of *Emmerdale* has been much lamented by those viewers who enjoyed the slow-paced, pastoral pleasures of the early years.

For the record, the screen Beckindale is actually the Yorkshire village of Esholt, near Bradford, although initially another village, Arncliffe, was used. The Woolpack's exterior is really that of Esholt's Commercial Inn.

EMPIRE ROAD

UK (BBC) Drama. BBC 2 1978–9

Everton Bennett	Norman Beaton
Walter Issacs	Joseph Marcell
Hortense Bennett	Corinne Skinner-Carter
Marcus Bennett	Wayne Laryea
Ranjanaa Kapoor	Nalini Moonasar
Miss May	Rosa Roberts
Desmond	Trevor Butler
Royston	Vincent Taylor
Sebastian Moses	Rudolph Walker

Writer: Michael Abbensetts. Producer: Peter Ansorge

Life in a racially mixed Midlands street.

Filmed in the Handsworth area of Birmingham, *Empire Road* focused on the relationship between the West Indian and Asian inhabitants of a residential street. At the centre of the action were Guyanan grocer Everton Bennett, owner of four of the houses, and his stuttering brother-in-law, Walter Issacs. Through the romance of Everton's son, Marcus, and their Asian neighbour, Ranjanaa, the series exposed inter-racial friction. It also revealed the different outlooks and mentalities of the various generations.

Empire Road broke new ground in being the first drama to be written, performed and directed entirely by black artists. Its writer was Guyanan Michael Abbensetts. The 1978 first season consisted of only five episodes, but ten more episodes followed a year later. In that second series, two white women were added to provide balance and former **Love Thy Neighbour** star Rudolph Walker was introduced as Sebastian Moses, a new menacing landlord. The final episode focused on Marcus and Ranjanaa's wedding and the hopes it brought for racial harmony in Empire Road.

ENCRYPTION

The scrambling of a TV signal allowing it to be decoded only by those who have paid the relevant subscription and have the appropriate equipment or viewing card. It is the everyday working basis for most satellite and cable channels.

ENEMY AT THE DOOR

UK (LWT) Drama. ITV 1978–80

Major Richter	Alfred Burke
Clare Martel	Emily Richard
Olive Martel	Antonia Pemberton
Dr Philip Martel	Bernard Horsfall
Oberleutnant Kluge	John Malcolm
Hauptmann Reinicke	Simon Cadell
Major Freidel	Simon Lack
Peter Porteous	Richard Heffer

Creator/Writer: Michael Chapman. Producers: Michael Chapman, Jonathan Alwyn. Executive Producer: Tony Wharmby

Life in the Channel Islands during the German occupation.

The Channel Islands were the only part of the United Kingdom to be occupied by the Germans during World War II. This 13-part drama analysed the effect the occupation had on the day to day life of the local residents, looking particularly at the Guernsey-based Martel family and especially their 20-year-old daughter, Clare. The action began in June 1940, with the islanders awaiting with trepidation the impending invasion, and continued through the darkest days of the war itself.

ENFIELD, HARRY (1961–)

English comedian coming to the fore on *Saturday Live* with his characterization of Stavros, the Greek kebab-shop owner. On the back of Stavros he created the brash plasterer Loadsamoney and his antithesis, hard-up Geordie Buggerallmoney. Enfield then gained his own BBC series, *The Harry Enfield Show*, in which a host of new characters were introduced (some in collaboration with Paul Whitehouse and Kathy Burke), most notably the sadistic Old Gits, Tim Nice-but-Dim, Wayne and Waynetta Slob, the constantly surprised Double-Take Brothers, mechanics Lee and Lance, and Miles Cholmondely-Warner, whose cracked and jumpy bits of old documentary inspired Enfield's commercials for Mercury. There were also The Scousers (a send-up of **Brookside**), sensational DJs Mike Smash and Dave Nice from Radio Fab FM and the constantly interfering father-in-law ('Only me.You don't want to do that'). Once bored with his creations, Enfield has tended to drop them and introduce new characters. His 1994 series, *Harry Enfield and Chums*, gave birth to the Lovely Wobbly Randy Old Ladies, the Self-Righteous Brothers, Brian Bewildered, Hampstead writer Martin Bollinger, Kevin the sulky teenager and others. Enfield has also provided voices for **Spitting Image** and starred as Little Jim Morley in *Gone to the Dogs* and Dermot in the first series of **Men Behaving Badly**. He also presented in the old thespian send-up *Norbert Smith – A Life*.

ENG (ELECTRONIC NEWS GATHERING)

Traditionally, news departments have relied on filmed reports from correspondents, which are slow to process and require a large crew to produce. With the development of videotape technology, including smaller, lighter cameras and camcorders, and the use of microwave or satellite links back to the studio (collectively known as ENG), news coverage has become more immediate and much more flexible.

ENGLISH, ARTHUR (1919–95)

Veteran British entertainer who arrived in television after years on the music hall boards, playing wide boy characters. In the early 1970s, he took on the part of Slugger in the horsy series **Follyfoot**, which led to roles in series like *Copper's End* and **Crown Court**. He played Ted Cropper in *How's Your Father*, Bodkin in *The Ghosts of Motley Hall*, caretaker Mr Harman in **Are You Being Served?** and became Arthur, one of Alf Garnett's new sparring partners, in **In Sickness and In Health**. English was also seen in the drama *Funny Man* and played Sid in Channel 4's 1987 retirement home sitcom *Never Say Die*.

EPILOGUE

A tailpiece to the day's viewing (now seldom seen, thanks to 24-hour TV), in which usually some religious or moral reflection was delivered by a guest speaker.

EQUALIZER, THE

US (Universal) Detective Drama. ITV 1986–

Robert McCall ....Edward Woodward
Control......................................Robert Lansing
Lt Burnett.................................Steven Williams
Lt Isadore Smalls ....Ron O'Neal
Scott McCall ....William Zabka
Mickey Kostmayer ....Keith Szarabajka
Sgt Alice Shepherd....................Maureen Anderman
Pete O'Phelan ....Chad Redding
Harley Gage................................Richard Jordan

Creators: Michael Sloan, Richard Lindheim. Executive Producer: James McAdams. Producer: Alan Barnette

A former secret agent hires himself out to those seeking justice.

Robert McCall had retired from the world of US Government espionage in which he had been given the name 'The Equalizer'. Now, somewhat ashamed of his duplicitous past, he hired himself out, via newspaper classified ads, to clients in big trouble. Weeding out the callers on his answerphone, he then set out to adjust the balance of good and evil on their behalf, acting as a private eye, or simply as a bodyguard, but often bringing his gun into play. His fee was small, if he ever charged one.

Despite his tough, streetwise exterior, McCall was really compassionate, intelligent and articulate. Always immaculately turned-out, he lived in a stylish Manhattan apartment, loved music and drove a swish black Jaguar. In his work he was supported by Mickey Kostmayer (who did much of the running around), and, from time to time, he linked up with Control, his former agency boss. His son, Scott, a music student, also appeared, as did Pete O'Phelan, an old friend from his spying days, who ran the bistro where McCall went to relax. Stewart Copeland of The Police rock group composed the theme music.

ESMONDE, JOHN

British comedy writer, usually in collaboration with Bob Larbey. Their joint successes have included *Room at the Bottom*, *Please Sir!*, *Get Some In*, *The Good Life*, *Don't Rock the Boat*, *The Other One*, *Double First*, *Now and Then*, *Ever Decreasing Circles*, *Brush Strokes* and *Mulberry*. Larbey, singly, has also penned *A Fine Romance*, *As Time Goes By*, *On the Up* and episodes of *The Darling Buds of May*.

ESPIONAGE

UK (ATV/Plautus) Spy Drama Anthology. ITV 1963–4

Executive Producer: Herbert Hirschman. Producer: George Justin

Collection of spy dramas based on true stories.

This series, filmed throughout Europe, treated the subject of espionage much more somberly than its spoofy successors like *The Man from UNCLE*, especially as it gleaned its facts from real events (some newsreel footage was used in production). The gloom was lightened somewhat by the appearances of talented guest stars like Patrick Troughton, Jim Backus and Bernard Lee ('M' from the James Bond films).

EUROSPORT

Trans-continental sports channel operated by the French network TF1. It broadcasts unscrambled and free of charge from the Astra satellites, offering a variety of sports from soccer to basketball. Viewers can select the language of the commentaries.

EUROVISION

The international network of cable and satellite links established by the European Broadcasting Union in 1954 to facilitate the transfer of programmes, news items and sports events between countries and to allow simultaneous broadcasts across the Continent.

EUROVISION SONG CONTEST

Europe (including BBC) Entertainment. BBC 1 1956–

Annual Europe-wide song competition.

Much ridiculed but nevertheless a big crowd puller (if only for the voting at the end), the *Eurovision Song Contest* has been a fixture of the television calendar for some 40 years. Originally devised as a showcase for the new Eurovision network, which linked broadcasters across the Continent, its popularity has now increased to the point where over 40 nations wish to compete and countries such as Israel, Turkey and the former Eastern Bloc have joined the fray. To accommodate allcomers, the lowest-scoring countries now have to sit out the following year's event.

The format involves each country presenting an original song in turn and then voting (via the Eurovision link) on each other's contributions to find the winner, allocating marks from 12 points down to one. The winning country stages the next year's *Contest*. Scores are conveyed multilingually by the show's compere (Katie Boyle is one of the best-remembered hostesses), with individual, voice-only commentaries provided for each country (Terry Wogan has become associated with this role for the UK, although the likes of David Jacobs, Rolf Harris, David Gell, Dave Lee Travis, Pete Murray, Michael Aspel and John Dunn have also performed this task). Technical hiccups, unavoidable in a live, pan-European link-up of this magnitude, have become part of the attraction for viewers.

The United Kingdom did not participate in the inaugural *Contest* in 1956, but soon initiated its own monthly competition, known as the *Festival of Popular Songs*. The 1956 *Festival* winner, 'All', sung by Patricia Bredin, went on to represent the UK (and finish seventh) in the 1957 *Contest*. In recent year, the British entry has been selected through an annual *Song for Europe* showdown.

The UK has won the competition on four occasions, with the *Contest's* whipping boys traditionally the Norwegians, thanks to their glorious nil score one year. *Eurovision* music has been roundly condemned for not moving with the times and for rewarding countries who regurgitate the established 'Boom-bang-a-puppet-in-a-box' catchy song formula. Only on rare occasions has the real music world peeped through – Abba's 1974 victory with 'Waterloo', for instance, Ireland's brave entry with Hothouse Flowers' 'Don't Go' in 1988; and Love City Groove's rap contribution for the UK in 1995.

EVANS, BARRY (1945–)

Fresh-faced British actor whose major roles have been in situation comedy. He starred in *Doctor in the House* and *Doctor at Large* as naive young Michael Upton, although he didn't stay with the series' sequels, relinquishing the lead to Robin Nedwell. He also played Jeremy Brown, the hapless night-school teacher in the controversial *Mind Your Language*, and was seen in the Emery comedy-thriller *Legacy of Murder*, amongst other programmes.

EVANS, CHRIS (1966–)

Red-haired, bespectacled DJ and presenter of light entertainment shows such as *Don't Forget Your Toothbrush* and *Comic Relief*. Evans began in radio with Piccadilly in Manchester before moving to GLR in London and then Radio 1. His television work commenced with the satellite channel The Power Station, before he moved to Channel 4's *The Big Breakfast*, where he quickly established himself as one of TV's

most adaptable live programme presenters. He also presents Radio 1's breakfast show and runs his own TV production company, Ginger Productions.

EVANS, LINDA (1942–)

Glamorous blonde American actress who endured a 12-year wait between her starring roles. Her TV career began with bit parts in popular US series like *Bachelor Father* (incidentally with John Forsythe, her subsequent TV husband) and *My Favorite Martian*, but her big break finally arrived with *The Big Valley*, in which she was cast as Audra Barkley, the family's beautiful daughter. *The Big Valley* ended in 1969 and the 1970s proved more difficult for Evans. She appeared for a while in a spy series called *Hunter* (with James Franciscus) and made a few TV movies, but it wasn't until *Dynasty* arrived in 1981 that she regained a high profile, starring as Krystle Jennings/Carrington. Ironically, she had originally been earmarked for an undefined role which turned out to be that of Pam in *Dallas*, but the concept took too long to reach the studio, plans changed and Evans was released from her contract. Her first husband was director John Derek.

EVE, TREVOR

British actor, largely seen in the theatre but coming to television prominence in the role of the radio detective *Shoestring*. Eve's subsequent TV work has included *Jamaica Inn*, *Lace*, *The Corsican Brothers*, *Shadow Chasers* and the steamy drama *A Sense of Guilt*, in which he played the irresponsible writer Felix Cramer, and *The Politician's Wife* (as MP Duncan Matlock).

EVER DECREASING CIRCLES

UK (BBC) Situation Comedy. BBC 1 1984–9

Martin Brice	Richard Briers
Ann Brice	Penelope Wilton
Paul Ryman	Peter Egan
Howard Hughes	Stanley Lebor
Hilda Hughes	Geraldine Newman

Creators/Writers: John Esmonde, Bob Larbey.
Producers: Sydney Lotterby, Harold Snoad

A pedantic neighbourhood do-gooder is continually upstaged by the smoothie next door.

Martin Brice, employee of Mole Valley Valves and driver of a Dormobile, liked things done properly. And because no one else could be trusted, he liked to do them himself. By immersing himself in the well-being of his local community, endlessly chairing meetings, organizing functions, tackling bureaucracy and generally leading from the front, Martin would have severely tested the patience of Job, let alone his long-suffering wife, Ann. For Martin, bedtime meant only one thing – drawing up rotas. Next door to the Brices moved Paul Ryman, the suave proprietor of a beauty salon, for whom things seemed to fall very nicely. Without the slightest effort, he always managed to unintentionally steal the limelight and rob Martin of all the credit. From the way he flirted with Ann, it was clear that he could have stolen Martin's wife, too, but Paul was too nice for that, and Ann too loyal. Friends to all were their childlike neighbours, Howard and Hilda Hughes, who usually dressed in matching sweaters.

EVERETT, KENNY (MAURICE COLE; 1944–95)

Zany, controversial DJ turned TV comedian. After working for the pirate radio station Radio London and Radio Luxembourg, Kenny Everett became one of Radio 1's first presenters and quickly moved into television. In 1968 he was one of the presenters of *Nice Time* (with Germaine Greer and Jonathan Routh), was given his own series, *The Kenny Everett Explosion,* in 1970 and subsequently became a familiar face on panel games, also announcing the prizes on *Celebrity Squares*. In 1978 came the comedy series *The Kenny Everett Video Show,* which he hosted in front of a bank of TV monitors. Sketches involved his own character-izations like Cupid Stunt (the buxom movie star who did everything 'in the best possible taste'), Sid Snot (the greaser), Gizzard Puke (the punk), Marcel Wave and the space anima-tion Captain Kremmen. Arlene Phillips's Hot Gossip writhed around between sketches and Everett was also supported by Miss Whiplash, Cleo Rocas. In 1982, after numerous guest appearances on *Blankety Blank,* Everett returned to the BBC and his show was renamed *The Kenny Everett Television Show.* Among his other series were *Making Whoopee, Ev* and the quiz *Brainstorm.* Everett died of an AIDS-related illness in 1995.

EVERY SECOND COUNTS

UK (BBC) Quiz. BBC 1 1986–9

Presenter: Paul Daniels

Producers: David Taylor, Stanley Appel

Light-hearted quiz for married couples.

Hosted by Paul Daniels, *Every Second Counts* invited three married couples to answer questions which earned them vital seconds on a clock. The highest scoring couple then progressed to the final, in which they used the seconds they had gained to answer yet more questions and win progressively better prizes. Each set of questions related to a subject and in the 'true or false' fashion, contestants had to state whether Daniels was reading a correct answer. Red herrings and contrived gags abounded. For the final stage, the couple needed to extinguish a series of triangular lamps with quick and accurate responses to tricky little posers.

EXECUTIVE PRODUCER

The chief overseer of a programme or a series of programmes, usually responsible for the control of budgets. Sometimes the executive producer is the head of the department in a television company.

EXPERT, THE

UK (BBC) Detective. BBC 2/BBC 1 1968–71; 1976

Dr John Hardy	Marius Goring
Dr Jo Hardy	Ann Morrish
Detective Chief Inspector Fleming	Victor Winding
Jane Carter	Sally Nesbitt

Creators: Gerard Glaister, N.J. Crisp. Producer: Gerard Glaister

A pathologist digs deep to help police with their investigations.

Dr John Hardy was a Warwickshire pathologist who, with the help of his somewhat younger wife, Jo (also a doctor), and his secretary, Jane Carter, turned up the vital evidence needed by police to secure tricky convictions. Detective Chief Inspector Fleming was his police ally, and the two men enjoyed a strong mutual respect and a close friendship.

Meticulously researched by actor Marius Goring (formerly TV's *Scarlet Pimpernel*), the character was the invention of producer Gerard Glaister, whose own uncle had been Professor of Forensic Science at Glasgow University. *The Expert* ran from 1968 to 1971, initially on BBC 2, before returning for one more run in 1976, on BBC 1. With its modest, thoughtful tone, it contrasted sharply with TV's other major pathologist series, *Quincy*.

FABIAN OF THE YARD

UK (BBC) Police Drama. BBC 1954–6

Detective Inspector Robert Fabian ....Bruce Seton

Producers: John Larkin, Anthony Beauchamp

The cases of a po-faced London detective.

Screaming around the streets of the capital in a heavy, black Humber Hawk squad car, pipe-smoking Detective Inspector Robert Fabian was one of TV's first police heroes. Based on the life of a real Detective Inspector Fabian (a Flying Squad officer who, on retirement from the force, went on to be 'Guardian of the Questions' on ITV's big money quiz show, *The 64,000 Question*), this was straight-laced, by-the-book, 1950s detective work, dramatizing cases from the files of Scotland Yard.

Fabian's success was largely down to his innovative detection methods, as he dragged the police force into the 1950s with all its forensic advances. The series, made on film and heavily laden with plummy accents, was screened in the USA as *Fabian of Scotland Yard* or *Patrol Car*, and included brief tourism guides for American viewers, explaining where and what were Hampton Court or Somerset House, for instance, if the plot required Fabian to visit them. The real Inspector Fabian popped up at the end of each programme to deliver some personal homilies on the events taking place. Some episodes were re-edited into feature films for cinema release. These went out as *Fabian of the Yard* (1954) and *Handcuffs, London* (1955).

FACE THE MUSIC

UK (BBC) Quiz. BBC 2 1967–84

Presenter: Joseph Cooper

Producer: Walter Todds

High-brow music quiz.

Hosted at the piano by the jovial Joseph Cooper, *Face The Music* was BBC 2's long-running music quiz for celebrities, focusing mainly on the classical world but also drawing on other musical styles. Regular panel members who attempted to identify snippets of tunes included Joyce Grenfell, Richard Baker and Robin Ray.

FACE TO FACE

UK (BBC) Interview Programme. BBC 1959–62

Presenter: John Freeman

Producer: Hugh Burnett

Series of incisive interviews with famous people, probing their personalities and lifestyles.

Face to Face broke new ground in TV interviewing. Although celebrities had faced the camera before, the public had never seen them so exposed by what was essentially a cross-examination. The interrogator was *Panorama* presenter John Freeman. As he probed he never wavered from the courteous and polite, but his assault on the interviewee was relentless and seldom failed to open up the real person behind the famous front. Strangely, the victims seemed quite happy to bear their souls.

Each programme began with caricature sketches of the week's guest by Felix Topolski, which faded into the real image to the lilting strains of a Berlioz overture. The set was stark – simply two uncomfortable chairs a yard apart – and the whole atmosphere one of interrogation. Seldom was Freeman himself seen, and then usually only from the back of his head. The focus was always on the interviewee as he or she was dissected. Over 30 guests appeared in all, although only a couple of them were women. They included Martin Luther King, Adam Faith, Stirling Moss, Bertrand Russell, Dame Edith Sitwell, King Hussein of Jordan, Tony Hancock, John Osborne, Evelyn Waugh, Carl Jung and Henry Moore, but by far the most controversial appearance was by Gilbert Harding. The *What's My Line* panellist was notorious for being gruff, rude and intolerant, but Freeman exposed a gentler, more humane, side. During the interview, Harding was even reduced to tears when questioned about his mother, who, unknown to Freeman, had just died.

The highlights of the series were repeated in 1988 with introductions by Joan Bakewell, and, in a special episode, Freeman himself was quizzed by Dr Anthony Clare. In the interim years he had been Editor of the *New Statesman*, Ambassador to the USA and head of London Weekend Television. *Face to Face* resurfaced as an occasional segment of *The Late Show*, with Jeremy Isaacs as interrogator.

FAIRBANKS, DOUGLAS, JNR (1909–)

American actor, the son of silent film star Douglas Fairbanks. In the mid-1950s he hosted and sometimes acted in an anthology series of half-hour dramas entitled **Douglas Fairbanks Presents**, which was made in the UK (where he lived for a number of years) but seen around the world. The stories generally had the theme of people caught up in unusual circumstances. His more recent TV performances have included a guest spot on **The Love Boat**.

FAIRLY SECRET ARMY

UK (Video Arts) Situation Comedy. Channel 4 1984–6

Major Harry Kitchener Wellington Truscott
....Geoffrey Palmer

Nancy	Diane Fletcher
Beamish	Jeremy Child
Sgt Major Throttle	Michael Robbins
Doris Entwistle	Liz Fraser
Stubby Collins	Ray Winstone
Crazy Colin Carstairs	James Cosmo
Jill	Diana Weston
Peg Leg Pogson	Paul Chapman
Ron Boat	Richard Ridings

Writer: David Nobbs. Producer: Peter Robinson

An inept retired military man sets up his own right-wing army to keep moral standards high.

With the influence of left-wing sympathizers, anarchists and feminists increasing in Britain, or so he perceived, Major Harry Kitchener Wellington Truscott, a quite unemployable old army bigot, decided to combat growing subversion by forming a private army of sympathizers. He called his force the Queen's Own West Mercian Lowlanders and rallying to his cause were a motley crew of half-wits, National Front supporters, ex-military colleagues and people with nothing better to do. To take on the loony left, Truscott assembled the raving right and, as he tried to whip them into shape, sounded not unlike a latter-day Alf Garnett.

FAITH, ADAM (TERENCE NELHAMS; 1940–)

Chirpy Cockney teen singer of the late 1950s/early 1960s, much seen on pop shows of the day, including *Oh Boy!* and *Boy Meets Girls*. He later branched out into acting, appearing in the anthology series *Seven Deadly Sins* in 1966 and earning his own series, *Budgie*, in 1971. After a couple of years as Soho's perennial loser, Budgie Bird, Faith didn't return to the small screen, apart from the odd guest appearance, until *Love Hurts* arrived in 1991. As Frank Carver opposite Zoe Wanamaker's Tessa Piggott he found himself with yet another hit on his hands.

FALCON CREST

US (Lorimar) Drama. ITV 1982–

Angela Channing/Stavros	Jane Wyman
Chase Gioberti	Robert Foxworth
Maggie Gioberti/Channing	Susan Sullivan
Lance Cumson	Lorenzo Lamas
Tony Cumson	John Saxon
Cole Gioberti	William R. Moses
Victoria Gioberti/Hogan/Stavros	Jamie Rose
	Dana Sparks
Julia Cumson	Abby Dalton
Gus Nunouz	Nick Ramus
Phillip Erikson	Mel Ferrer
Emma Channing	Margaret Ladd
Douglas Channing	Stephen Elliott
Sheriff Turk Tobias	Robert Sampson
Mario Nunouz	Mario Marcelino
Chau-Li	Chau-Li Chi
Melissa Agretti/Cumson/Gioberti	Ana Alicia
Carlo Agretti	Carlos Romero
Richard Channing	David Selby
John Costello	Roger Perry
Diana Hunter	Shannon Tweed
Jacqueline Perrault	Lana Turner
Nick Hogan	Roy Thinnes
Darryl Clayton	Bradford Dillman
Lori Stevens	Maggie Cooper
Sheriff Robbins	Joe Lambie
Linda Caproni/Gioberti	Mary Kate McGeehan
Vince Caproni	Harry Basch
Dr Michael Ranson	Cliff Robertson
Pamela Lynch	Sarah Douglas
Terry Hartford/Ranson	Laura Johnson
Joseph Gioberti	Jason Goldberg
Norton Crane	Jordan Charney
Francesca Gioberti	Gina Lollobrigida
Greg Reardon	Simon MacCorkindale
Lorraine Prescott	Kate Vernon
Joel McCarthy	Parker Stevenson
Gustav Riebmann	J. Paul Freeman
Father Bob	Bob Curtis
Jordan Roberts	Morgan Fairchild
Father Christopher	Ken Olin
Cassandra Wilder	Anne Archer
Robin Agretti	Barbara Howard
Apollonia	Patricia 'Apollonia' Kotero
Peter Stavros	Cesar Romero
Eric Stavros	John Callahan
Erin Jones	Jill Jacobson
Kit Marlowe	Kim Novak
Dan Fixx	Brett Cullen
Meredith Braxton	Jane Badler
Dina Wells	Robin Greer
Guy Stafford	Jeff Kober
Mrs Whitaker	Laurel Schaefer
Carly Fixx	Mariska Hartigay
Garth	Carl Heid
Frank Agretti	Rod Taylor
Pilar Ortega/Cumson	Kristian Alfonso
Nick Agretti	David Beecroft
Ben Agretti	Brandon Douglas
Tommy Ortega	Dan Ferro
Cesar Ortega	Castulo Guerra
Gabriel Ortega	Danny Nucci
R.D. Young	Allan Royal
Michael Channing	Robert Gorman
Michael Sharpe	Gregory Harrison
Julius Karnow	Norman Parker
Ed Meyers	Philip Baker Hall
Brian	Thom Adcox
Lauren Daniels	Wendy Phillips
Walker Daniels	Robert Ginty
Jace Sampson	Stuart Pankin
Genele Ericson	Andrea Thompson

Creator: Earl Hamner. Executive Producers: Earl Hamner, Michael Filerman

Family and business rivalries in Californian wine country.

Hot on the heels of *Dallas* and *Dynasty* came *Falcon Crest*, an American soap born of the same stock as its predecessors. The setting this time was California's Napa Valley ('Tuscany Valley' in the series), the industry providing the opulence was wine production and the central character was ruthless Angela Channing. Angela's rival was Chase Gioberti, who had moved from New York to take up his share of the Falcon Crest vineyard fortune. He was the son of her late brother, Jason, and the two sparred, fought and tussled over power and prestige. The difference between them was that where Angela was hard and cruel, Chase was essentially good, caring for his employees and the people of the valley. Other principals included Chase's wife, Maggie, his son, Cole, and daughter, Victoria, as well as Angela's family, consisting of daughters Julia and Emma (the former mentally deranged, the latter a man-eater), Julia's son, Lance Cumson, and his wife, Melissa Agretti, daughter of another big wine family. As the series progressed, Angela's tyranny was challenged by a new rival, newspaper magnate Richard Channing, the son of her former husband, Douglas. Richard had inherited half of *The Globe* newspaper in San Francisco (Julia and Emma each had 25 per cent) and fought unscrupulously for yet more power, including control of the vineyards (which he eventually achieved).

The series became more and more violent as the years went by, stretching credulity as it did so. First a sinister business co-operative called 'The Cartel', led by Gustav Riebmann, was introduced. Then another treacherous institution, an underworld gang known as 'The Thirteen', made its bow. Like *Dallas* and *Dynasty*, *Falcon Crest* was well endowed with shootings, framings, trials, stormy marriages, unknown heirs, disputed fathers, amnesiacs, schizophrenics, bombings, plane crashes, white slave rings and numerous skeletons which popped out of cupboards. It did, however, allow its cast a happy ending.

In the final episode, after years of wrangling, attempted murders and the like, the family were reunited and reconciled. Richard (who had turned out to be Angela's son after all) married newcomer Lauren Daniel and sold the vineyard back to Angela, whom he recognized at last as its 'rightful owner'. Plans were made for Falcon Crest to be handed down after her death, hopefully without recrimination.

Falcon Crest was the brainchild of **The Waltons** creator Earl Hamner. Interestingly, it made a point of casting famous film stars who seldom appeared on television, and the likes of Rod Taylor, Gina Lollobrigida, Kim Novak and Lana Turner all made appearances.

FALK, PETER (1927–)

New York-born actor who arrived on US television in the early 1960s, playing gangster roles in series like *The Untouchables* and *Naked City*. He picked up an Emmy for a performance on *The Dick Powell Show* and was given his first star billing in the legal drama series *The Trials of O'Brien*. However, in 1968, Falk won the part of a very odd character that was to change his life. In the TV movie *Prescription: Murder* he donned the grubby mac and picked up the stubby cigar of offbeat Los Angeles detective Lt. Columbo, after Bing Crosby had turned down the part. *Columbo* proved popular and returned in another movie in 1971 before steady production began and the series became part of the *Mystery Movie* anthology. With his grouchy voice, scruffy appearance and sad squint (Falk had lost an eye as a child), Columbo became one of TV's classic creations, resurfacing again in the 1980s. Falk has had little need to seek TV work elsewhere.

FALL AND RISE OF REGINALD PERRIN, THE

UK (BBC) Situation Comedy. BBC 1
1976–9

Reginald Perrin	Leonard Rossiter
Elizabeth Perrin	Pauline Yates
CJ	John Barron
Joan Greengross	Sue Nicholls
David Harris-Jones	Bruce Bould
Tony Webster	Trevor Adams
Jimmy	Geoffrey Palmer
Peter Cartwright	Terence Conoley
Linda	Sally-Jane Spencer
Tom	Tim Preece
	Leslie Schofield
Doc Morrissey	John Horsley
Prue Harris-Jones	Theresa Watson
McBlane	Joseph Brady

Creator/Writer: David Nobbs. Producers: John Howard Davies, Gareth Gwenlan.

When a mid-life crisis strikes, a suburban commuter decides to fake his death and seek new horizons under another identity.

Reggie Iolanthe Perrin worked for Sunshine Desserts in a boring office job. He travelled to work each morning from his Norbiton home on the same crowded commuter train, always arriving eleven minutes late for a variety of wacky British Rail reasons (including dead dog on the line). There, despite the attentions of his loyal secretary, Joan Greengross, his career was going nowhere (perhaps symbolized by the crumbling letters on the company sign) and he was constantly browbeaten by his bumptious boss, CJ, who regaled him with advice beginning 'I didn't get where I am today . . . '. Home life had become rather mundane, too, with his wife's day revolving around waving him off in the morning and greeting him in the evening, and the thought of visiting his mother-in-law inexplicably filled him with images of a waddling hippopotamus.

It all became too much and Reggie planned a way out. He took himself off to the seaside, abandoned his clothes on the beach to fake drowning and branched out into a new life. After a period wandering Britain's country lanes he resurfaced back in suburbia, courting his wife, Elizabeth, under the new identity of Martin Wellbourne. He soon reassumed his true name, although by now he had developed an anarchic streak.

Perrin set up his own chain of shops, Grot, which specialized in selling useless objects – cruet sets without holes, square footballs, etc. – and employed his former colleagues from the defunct Sunshine Desserts. Joan once again became his secretary, tempting him with her womanly wiles, and he took delight in taking on CJ as a minor executive. There was also room for his two syco-phantic juniors from the old company, Tony 'Great' Webster and David 'Super' Harris-Jones, as well as Elizabeth. But things went too well for Grot and, resenting the success, Reggie set out to bring the company to its knees before, once again, embarking on a new existence. This time the whole cast joined him in the mock seaside suicide. When they resurfaced in a third season, Reggie had opened Perrins, a rehabilitation com-mune for stressed executives, finding room for all the usual cronies, including his military-minded brother-in-law, Jimmy (who was always apologiz-ing for something, claiming there had been a 'bit of a cock-up'), and an indecipherable Scottish cook, McBlane.

The role was a marvellous vehicle for Leonard Rossiter, who won acclaim for his portrayal of the highly agitated, stuttering eccentric. Filled with memorable catchphrases, it was scripted by David Nobbs from his original novel *The Death of Reginald Perrin*, which, some claim, inspired MP John Stonehouse to fake his death in the same way.

FALL GUY, THE

US (Twentieth Century-Fox) Adventure. ITV 1982–

Colt Seavers	Lee Majors
Howie Munson	Douglas Barr
Jody Banks	Heather Thomas
Samantha 'Big Jack' Jack	Jo Ann Pflug
Terri Shannon/Michaels	Markie Post
Pearl Sperling	Nedra Volz

Creator/Producer: Glen A. Larson

A movie stuntman doubles up as a modern-day bounty hunter.

Colt Seavers was the Fall Guy, a courageous, dar-ing movie stunt double who topped up his income by acting as a bounty hunter, tracking down bail jumpers and other fugitives who had a price on their heads. The spectacular stunts he had perfected in films often came in handy when apprehending the runaways. Seavers was assisted by beautiful stuntwoman Jody Banks, as well as his cousin, Howie Munson, who acted as his business manager. Big Jack, the bail bondswoman, handed out the orders, until she was replaced by Terri Shannon (her surname was later changed to Michaels), who then gave way to a grumpy old lady named Pearl Sperling. Star Lee Majors also sang the theme song.

FALSEY, JOHN (1951–) see Brand, Joshua.

FAME

US (MGM/United Artists) Drama. BBC 1 1982

Lydia Grant	Debbie Allen
Coco Hernandez	Erica Gimpel
Danny Amatullo	Carlo Imperato
Leroy Johnson	Gene Anthony Ray
Bruno Martelli	Lee Curreri
Doris Schwartz	Valerie Landsburg
Julie Miller	Lori Singer
Montgomery MacNeil	P.R. Paul
Mr Benjamin Shorofsky	Albert Hague
Elizabeth Sherwood	Carol Mayo Jenkins
Mr Greg Crandall	Michael Thoma
Mrs Charlotte Miller	Judy Farrell
Angelo Martelli	Carmine Caridi
Dwight	David Greenlee
David Reardon	Morgan Stevens
Mrs Gertrude Berg	Ann Nelson
Holly Laird	Cynthia Gibb
Christopher Donlon	Billy Hufsey
Quentin Morloch	Ken Swofford
Cleo Hewitt	Janet Jackson
Jesse Valesquez	Jesse Borrego
Nicole Chapman	Nia Peeples
Mr Lou Mackie	Dick Miller
Laura Mackie	Carolyn J. Silas
Dusty Tyler	Loretta Chandler
Mr Bob Dyrenforth	Graham Jarvis
Reggie Higgins	Carrie Hamilton
Jillian Beckett	Elisa Heinsohn
Kate Riley	Page Hannah
Ian Ware	Michael Cerveris
Mr Paul Seeger	Eric Pierpoint
Maxie	Olivia Barash
Miltie Horowitz	Robert Romanus

Producer: Stanley C. Rogow

Energetic musical drama following the lives of students and staff at a performing arts college.

Based on Alan Parker's film of the same name, *Fame* was set in the New York High School for the Performing Arts and focused on a group of talented youngsters learning how to take their place in the world of show business. The empha-sis was on sweat, the only way to the top being through dedication and hard work, and the series traced the students' ambitions, their progress, their personal crises and their hard-earned successes, beginning with their arrival as freshers and running through to graduation.

The teachers and instructors were led by sultry Lydia Grant, the demanding dance teacher. She was supported by the much-revered, white-bearded Mr Shorofsky, the music teacher, no-nonsense English tutor Elizabeth Sherwood and drama instructor Mr Crandall, who was later replaced by David Reardon and then Paul Seeger. Quentin Morlach was the Principal who was forced to realize that his precocious students could not be treated like normal pupils, and the scatty school secretary was Mrs Berg.

The real stars, however, were the kids themselves: Leroy, an agile, creative dancer from Harlem, who later joined the teaching staff; Coco an over-ambitious, impetuous singer and dancer; Bruno, a keyboard genius who was too cocky for his own good; Doris, a talented comedienne, actress and writer, and Danny, another comic. Julie was a brilliant cellist from the backwoods of Grand Rapids, Michigan, who struggled to come to terms with life in the city, while Montgomery was the son of a successful actress and longed to emulate her achievements.

Characters introduced later included new Head Bob Dyrenforth, and a second influx of students. These included dancers Jesse and Christopher, Holly, who concentrated on drama, Dwight, a chubby tuba player, and Ian, an English rock guitarist. There was also the beautiful Nicole, a singer and dancer, who was tragically killed in a car accident. Most of the action took place in the classrooms, but, as the series progressed, so the students took to frequenting Lou's bowling alley.

Four of the original film's stars reprised their roles in this TV version, namely Gene Anthony Ray, Lee Curreri, Albert Hague and Debbie Allen (who also took charge of the show's choreography). The theme song from the film had been a number one hit for Irene Cara in 1982, but Erica Gimpel, her successor as Coco, provided the vocals on the TV version. The programme also spun-off several British chart hits, performed by The Kids from Fame, with 'Hi-Fidelity' and 'Starmaker' being the most successful. There were no hits in the States, but Fame was always more successful in the UK than in its native USA.

FAMILY, THE

UK (BBC) Documentary. BBC 1 1974

Producer: Paul Watson

Fly-on-the-wall documentary series about a working-class Reading family.

The Wilkins family from Reading enjoyed temporary stardom through this warts-and-all, 12-part look at their turbulent domestic life. Terry Wilkins was a bus conductor and his outspoken wife, Margaret, sons, Gary and Christopher, daughters, Marion and Heather, plus Gary's wife, Karen, and Marion's live-in boyfriend, Tom, completed the crowded family group housed in a maisonette above a greengrocer's shop. A camera crew virtually lived with the family for three months and recorded their high spots and their lowest ebbs. Blazing rows made colourful viewing and the Wilkinses' flair for letting family skeletons out of the cupboard added to the drama. Later, one-off retrospectives revealed how the family had gradually drifted apart once the series had ended.

Producer Paul Watson repeated the experiment nearly 20 years later, although in rather sunnier climes, in his Australian documentary series *Sylvania Waters*.

FAMILY AT WAR, A

UK (Granada) Drama. ITV 1970–2

Edwin Ashton	Colin Douglas
Jean Ashton	Shelagh Fraser
Margaret Ashton/Porter	Lesley Nunnerley
Freda Ashton	Barbara Flynn
Philip Ashton	Keith Drinkel
Sheila Ashton	Coral Atkins
David Ashton	Colin Campbell
Sefton Briggs	John McKelvey
Tony Briggs	Trevor Bowen
John Porter	Ian Thompson
Mrs Porter	Margery Mason
Ian McKenzie	John Nettles

Creator: John Finch. Producers: Richard Doubleday, James Brabazon, Michael Cox

Glum portrayal of 1930s and 1940s hardships, seen through the lives of a Liverpool family.

Granada's most expensive-ever serial at the time, *A Family at War* focused on the middle-class Ashton family as they struggled through the lean years between 1938 and 1945. It saw them emerge from the decay of the Depression to face the even more bitter realities of World War II, and witnessed family and romantic relationships disintegrate along the way. Never a day passed without a new worry for the Ashtons, headed by morose dad Edwin. The programme's symbolic titles sequence, showing a demolished sandcastle, is as well remembered as the series itself.

FAMILY CHANNEL, THE

Established in the USA in 1977 as CBN Satellite Service, providing religious programmes for the non-profit-making Christian Broadcasting Network, The Family Channel changed its name and philosophy in 1981, when it became CBN Cable Network and focused instead on 'wholesome', morally sound entertainment. The Channel's Christian roots were further distanced by the change to the current name in 1988. The Family Channel UK was launched in September 1993, the same year that its parent company, International Family Entertainment (IFE), bought the disenfranchised TVS and its Maidstone studios for £58 million. The Family Channel now broadcasts 12 hours a day (5 pm to 5 am) from the Astra 1C satellite (as part of the Sky Multi-Channels package) and also via cable. Its programming is organized around material which is suitable for viewing by the entire family, mixing heart-warming drama series like *Road to Avonlea* and **The Darling Buds of May** with comedy and quiz shows. The channel has access to the 1300-title MTM library of programmes such as **Hill Street Blues**, **Lou Grant** and *St Elsewhere* and also the back catalogue of TVS, which includes such contributions as **The Ruth Rendell Mysteries** and **C.A.T.S. Eyes**.

FAMILY FORTUNES

UK (Central) Game Show. ITV 1980–5; 1987–

Presenters:
Bob Monkhouse
Max Bygraves
Les Dennis

Producers: William G. Stewart, Graham C. Williams, Tony Wolfe, Dennis Liddington

Game show in which families guess what the public thinks.

Based on the American quiz *Family Feud*, *Family Fortunes* used a giant computer (initially known as Mr Babbage – after the inventor of the first computer) to display the findings of a public survey. One hundred members of the public were asked to name various items – a song you sing at parties, things you find at the seaside, etc. – and the two competing families (each consisting of five contestants) tried to work out which answers had been given. The most popular answers provided the most points. There were cash prizes and other valuables to be won. Bob Monkhouse was the first host, succeeded in 1983 by Max Bygraves. After a two-year gap in production, the series returned with Les Dennis as host.

FANTASY ISLAND

US (Spelling-Goldberg) Drama. ITV 1978–

Mr Roarke	Ricardo Montalban
Tattoo	Herve Villechaize
Julie	Wendy Schaal
Lawrence	Christopher Hewett

Executive Producers: Aaron Spelling, Leonard Goldberg

Dreams come true for visitors to a mysterious tropical island.

Fantasy Island, owned and run by the enigmatic Mr Roarke, was the place where, temporarily at least, dreams really could come true. By paying a mere $10,000 for their trip, each visitor could have one wish fulfilled, provided it wasn't *too* fanciful. Whether it was to date attractive women or to make lots of money, this was the chance of a lifetime, and the customers were not short-changed. Things always worked out and endings tended to be happy, even if a few problems or hiccups had been encountered along the way. What's more, all the guests went away having learned some valuable lessons about themselves.

Helping Mr Roarke to keep the customer satisfied were his assistants, initially the midget, Tattoo, and then Lawrence. Roarke's goddaughter, Julie, was also featured for a while. Rourke himself became increasingly mysterious as the series progressed. It was ultimately revealed that it was his sorcery which lay behind the fantasy factory and he was seen to face up to the Devil in one episode. Each hour-long programme was built around two or three separate fantasies and the series was modelled on **The Love Boat**, also a hit for the Aaron-Spelling production team.

FAR PAVILIONS, THE

UK (Geoff Reeve and Assoc./Goldcrest) Drama. Channel 4 1984

Ashton Pelham-Martyn	Ben Cross
Princess Anjuli	Amy Irving
Kaka-Ji Rao	Christopher Lee
Koda Dad	Omar Sharif
Cavagnari	John Gielgud
Wally	Benedict Taylor
The Rana of Bhithor	Rossano Brazzi
Biju Ram	Saeed Jaffrey
The Commandant	Robert Hardy
Princess Shushila	Sneh Gupta
Mrs Viccary	Jennifer Kendal

Writer: Julian Bond. Producer: Geoffrey Reeve

Sumptuous story from the days of the Raj.

Costing some £8 million to make, *The Far Pavilions*, like **The Jewel in the Crown**, capitalized on the interest in Raj India generated by Richard Attenborough's film *Gandhi*. In three two-hour episodes, it told of a young British army officer, Ash Pelham-Martyn, in service with the elite Corps of Guards. Because of his Indian upbringing, Ash found himself torn between the British and Indian cultures, and his forbidden love for former childhood playmate Princess Anjuli added to the torment. On a wider stage, political intrigue and civil unrest led to battles galore. The series was adapted by Julian Bond from the novel by M.M. Kaye.

FARROW, MIA (MARIA FARROW; 1945–)

The daughter of actress Maureen O'Sullivan, Mia Farrow owes much of her movie fame to her single prime time TV role, that of Allison McKenzie in *Peyton Place*. Even though she only stayed two years with the series, it allowed her to gain important exposure and led to a succession of film roles. However, once she had left the series her character was not forgotten, and the mysterious whereabouts of Allison continued to pervade the storylines of *Peyton Place* right through to its end. Her two husbands were Frank Sinatra and André Previn, and she has also lived with Woody Allen.

FARSON, DANIEL (1930–)

Effective Anglo-American interviewer of the 1950s when, for ITV, he presented some of the channel's more revealing documentaries. His credits included *This Week* and *People in Trouble*, plus a film on pub entertainers entitled *Time, Gentlemen, Please!* He also introduced *SMS*, a series of adaptations of stories by Somerset Maugham, in 1960.

FATHER BROWN

UK (ATV) Detective Drama. ITV 1974

Father Brown	Kenneth More
Flambeau	Dennis Burgess

Writer: Hugh Leonard. Producer: Ian Fordyce

The cases of a clerical detective in the 1920s.

Based on the novels of G.K. Chesterton, 15 years before Father Dowling began investigating, this quaint, period series featured Father Brown, TV's first detective in holy orders. Wily and perceptive, Brown was a mild-mannered, easy-going criminologist who solved cases using a mixture of human understanding and conventional detection. Whether it was identifying a decapitated corpse at a garden party, or helping a young girl to avoid blackmail, the saintly sleuth came through. His motto was, 'Have Bible, will travel.' Flambeau was his close friend.

FATHER, DEAR, FATHER

UK (Thames) Situation Comedy. ITV 1968–73

Patrick Glover	Patrick Cargill
Anna Glover	Natasha Pyne
Karen Glover	Ann Holloway
Matilda 'Nanny' Harris	Noel Dyson
Barbara Mossman	Ursula Howells
Mrs Glover	Joyce Carey
Georgie	Sally Bazely
	Dawn Addams
Bill Mossman	Patrick Holt
	Tony Britton

Creators/Writers: Johnny Mortimer, Brian Cooke. Producer: William G.Stewart

A womanizing novelist struggles to keep his family and friends in check.

Patrick Glover, writer of spy novels, was divorced and a free spirit – in principle. However, plagued by his dotty mother, his agent (Georgie), his ex-wife (Barbara), her new, scrap-metal merchant husband (Bill), a fussy nanny and two trendy daughters (Anna and Karen), his life was never his own. Although he drove a swish sports car and lived in a spacious, well-appointed house in Hampstead, complete with a cuddly St Bernard named H.G. Wells, his peace and privacy were constantly shattered by the household entourage. This archetypal TV farce was produced by future *Fifteen-To-One* host William G. Stewart. An Australian version (with only Patrick Cargill and Noel Dyson from the original cast) was made in 1977. A spin-off feature film was released in 1973.

FATHER DOWLING INVESTIGATES

US (Viacom) Detective Drama. ITV 1990–94

Father Frank Dowling	Tom Bosley
Sister Stephanie ('Sister Steve')	Tracy Nelson
Marie Brody	Mary Wickes
Father Philip Prestwick	James Stephens
Sgt Clancy	Regina Krueger

Creators: Ralph McInerny, Dean Hargrove, Joel Steiger. Executive Producers: Fred Silverman, Dean Hargrove. Producer: Barry Steinberg

A Catholic priest has a nose for crime.

Amiable Father Frank Dowling was the parish priest of St Michael's in Chicago, but he found his true vocation in amateur detective work. Joined in his investigations by a nun, Sister Stephanie (or Sister Steve as she preferred to be known), the detective in the dog collar found himself drawn into the most complicated murder mysteries, which he unravelled with great aplomb. Steve, a street kid-turned-nun, was a more than useful ally. She still knew all the tricks of the trade, from picking locks to gathering information. She even dropped her nun's habit, on occasions, to go incognito. The unlikely duo drove around in Dowling's rundown old station wagon and, using their cleric appearances, were able to go where normal detectives feared to tread. In the background were the bumbling

Father Prestwick, a junior priest dispatched by the Bishop to keep an eye on the wayward Dowling, and Marie, the loyal housekeeper at the St Michael's vicarage. Sgt Clancy acted as Dowling's police contact.

The character was created by novelist Ralph McInerny and the series – known as *The Father Dowling Mysteries* in the USA – gave Tom Bosley his first starring role since *Happy Days*.

FAWCETT, FARRAH (1946–)

Glamorous American leading lady with shaggy blonde hair, the face of 1977 after starring as one of *Charlie's Angels* (sporty Jill Munroe). On a wave of lookalike dolls and merchandising, Fawcett left the series after just one season, but was forced to make occasional return appearances (to avoid contractual difficulties). Previously, she had gained bit parts in series like *The Flying Nun*, *Marcus Welby, MD* and *The Six Million Dollar Man*, and had also appeared as David Janssen's neighbour in *Harry-O*. Little television came her way after leaving *Charlie's Angels*, but she did win a fair amount of film work. She was at one time married to actor Lee Majors and was known as Farrah Fawcett-Majors when *Charlie's Angels* began.

FAWLTY TOWERS

UK (BBC) Situation Comedy. BBC 2 1975; 1979

Basil Fawlty	John Cleese
Sybil Fawlty	Prunella Scales
Manuel	Andrew Sachs
Polly Sherman	Connie Booth
Major Gowen	Ballard Berkeley
Miss Tibbs	Gilly Flower
Miss Gatsby	Renee Roberts
Terry	Brian Hall

Writers: John Cleese and Connie Booth.
Producers: John Howard Davies, Douglas Argent

Chaos in a seaside hotel, courtesy of its manic owner.

Fawlty Towers, a modest little Torquay hotel, was run by husband and wife Basil and Sybil Fawlty. Modest the hotel may have been, but Basil had ambitious plans for his small empire and ran it with great enthusiasm. Sadly, the guests tended to get in the way. Inhibited also by his nagging, droning, gossiping wife and Manuel, a useless Spanish waiter from Barcelona who understood little English ('I know nathing'), Fawlty's best-laid plans always ended in disaster.

Fawlty was a master at turning the simplest procedures – like serving dinner to late guests – into complete chaos, and his patronizing air, biting sarcasm and bouts of rage all contrived to make matters worse. When practising a fire drill, he refused to allow a real kitchen fire to interrupt the flow of proceedings; when entertaining German guests, a blow on the head encouraged the already unbalanced hotelier to goosestep around the dining room, magnificently failing not to 'mention the war'. When an undercover hotel inspector came to town, Fawlty unctuously fawned over every guest except the right one, and on a planned gourmet evening, Terry, his chef, got blind drunk.

Hovering on the fringe at all times were the hotel's permanent guests, two doddery old ladies (Miss Tibbs and Miss Gatsby) and the senile and deaf Major Gowen. But, thankfully, there was also Polly, the chambermaid, who attempted to bring some order back to the hotel. Hers was generally only a limited success, with her lanky, hot-headed boss screwing things up time and again. He couldn't even keep control of the hotel's name plate, which was constantly tampered with by meddling hands to offer Fatty Owls, Farty Towels, Watery Fowls or other anagramatic names.

The series combined the best aspect of farce – miscontrued conversations, well-timed exits and entrances, etc. — with some classic one-liners and insults. Very few series have managed to imbue the viewers with so much tension, frustration and exasperation, but *Fawlty Towers* has been generally accepted as one of the gems of British TV comedy. It was allegedly inspired by a visit by the **Monty Python** team to a Torquay hotel and their discovery of a rude hotelier who threw Eric Idle's briefcase into the street, thinking it was a bomb. The character was written into one of John Cleese and Graham Chapman's **Doctor at Large** scripts, before finally achieving greatness in his own right in this sitcom several years later. After the acclaim of the first six *Fawlty Towers* episodes, the second series took four years to arrive (partly because Cleese and his co-writer wife, Connie Booth, had split up), but most people thought it well worth the wait.

FBI, THE

US (Warner Brothers/Quinn Martin) Police Drama. ITV 1965–

Inspector Lewis Erskine	Efrem Zimbalist, Jnr
Agent Arthur Ward	Philip Abbott
Barbara Erskine	Lynn Loring
Special Agent Jim Rhodes	Stephen Brooks
Special Agent Tom Colby	William Reynolds
Agent Chris Daniels	Shelly Novack
Narrator	Marvin Miller

Executive Producer: Quinn Martin. Producer: Charles Lawton

Successful series highlighting the cases of a fictitious FBI agent.

Inspector Lew Erskine worked for the Federal Bureau of Investigation and travelled the length and breadth of the USA, seeking out criminals and fraudsters and unearthing political subversives and other enemies of the state. During the course of the programme's run he was assisted by a number of different colleagues. One of these, Jim Rhodes, was romantically entwined with Barbara, Erskine's daughter, in the first series, but she was then dropped from the cast. This was a deliberate ploy by the producers, who wanted to isolate the cold, methodical Erskine even further (his wife had already been killed in a shoot-out). Not that Erskine, a dedicated, businesslike operator, appeared to mind. He insisted his work *always* took precedence over his private life. A career detective, he had been with the Bureau for 30 years, right from the turbulent days of the 1930s, when he had helped round up gangsters. Now he reported to Arthur Ward, assistant to the Bureau's Director.

The series won the approval of the real FBI chief, J. Edgar Hoover, who permitted filming at their Washington headquarters. Many of the stories were allegedly based on true cases and, in America, appeals for assistance in tracking down real villains were sometimes made at the end of the show.

FELDMAN, MARTY (1933–82)

Mop-haired, wide-eyed English comedian, a companion of Mel Brooks and Gene Wilder in the cinema but, before his movie days, a success on the small screen. Feldman's career began in writing. His collaborator was Barry Took and between them they penned scores of scripts for radio series like *Round the Horne* and *Educating Archie*, and TV sitcoms such as *The Army Game*, *Bootsie and Snudge*, *Scott On . . .*, *The Walrus and the Carpenter* and *Barney Is My Darling*. They also wrote for comics like Frankie Howerd, and Feldman (with John Law) also provided the famous 'class' sketch, featuring Barker, Corbett and Cleese, for *The Frost Report*. With Bill Hitchcock, he co-produced Corbett's comedy *No – That's Me Over Here!* Moving in front of the camera, he starred in the manic *At Last the 1948 Show*, alongside Cleese, Graham Chapman, Tim Brooke-Taylor and Aimi MacDonald, and out of this gained his own BBC 2 series, Marty (co-written by Took and also featuring Brooke-Taylor), which developed the zany visual humour that was to characterize his later movie work. Other series followed, such as *The Marty Feldman Comedy Machine* and *Marty Back Together Again*. Feldman died of a heart attack while filming in Mexico in December 1982.

FELLOWS, THE

UK (Granada) Detective Drama. ITV 1967

Oldenshaw ....Richard Vernon
Dimmock ....Michael Aldridge
Mrs Hollinsczech ....Jill Booty
Thomas Anthem ....James Ottaway
Alec Spindoe ....Ray McAnally

Creator: Robin Chapman. Producers: Robin Chapman, Peter Plummer

Two academic criminologists solve crimes from a Cambridge college.

A follow-up series to *The Man in Room 17* (and indeed subtitled *Late of Room 17*), *The Fellows* focused on two Government-financed crime-crackers, Oldenshaw and Dimmock, who had, at last, left the famous Room 17 to take up residence at All Saints' College, Cambridge. Appointed by the Home Office to the Peel Research Fellowship, their role now was to study how the nature of crime changed as society evolved. However, they soon re-established themselves as formidable detectives, calling on the assistance of number cruncher Mrs Hollinsczech and servant Thomas Anthem. Alec Spindoe, a gangster convicted during the series, was later given his own TV spin-off series, *Spindoe*.

FELTON, NORMAN (1922–)

American producer responsible for such hits as *Dr Kildare* and *The Man from UNCLE* (also as co-creator).

FENN STREET GANG, The see *Please Sir!*

FENNELL, ALBERT (1920–)

British producer, closely associated with *The Avengers* and later *The Professionals*, both in collaboration with Brian Clemens.

FIFTEEN TO ONE

UK (Regent) Quiz. Channel 4 1988–

Presenter/Producer: William G. Stewart.
Creator: John M. Lewis

Fast-moving daily general knowledge quiz involving 15 contestants.

Dryly compered by experienced producer William G. Stewart (formerly of *Father, Dear, Father*, *Bless this House* and *The Price Is Right*, amongst other popular series), *Fifteen To One*'s aim has been to whittle down 15 hopefuls into one daily winner. Arranged in an arc around Stewart, the contestants are asked two questions in turn. Those failing to get at least one right are eliminated. For the next stage, the contestants defend what has remained of their initial three lives by nominating each other to answer questions. The last three contestants, with a life intact, have progress to the last round. In this, they battle head to head, trying to eliminate each other through nomination and also looking to notch a high score for themselves. The last surviving contestant is the day's winner. The 15 highest-scoring daily winners compete in the grand final at the end of the series. As on **Mastermind**, no flashy prizes have been on offer, just a simple but tasteful commemorative trophy and the prestige of being a *Fifteen To One* champion. Two series have been made each year and have shared the 4.30 pm Channel 4 time slot with the words and numbers game **Countdown**.

FILM 71

UK (BBC) Film Review. BBC 1 1971–

Presenter: Barry Norman

Producers: Iain Johnstone, Patricia Ingram, Barry Brown, Jane Lush, Bruce Thompson

Topical review of the cinema world.

Beginning in 1971 as a programme for the southeast only, the *Film* series has since established itself as the most valuable cinema review on television, incorporating appraisals of the latest releases, interviews with major stars about their forthcoming films and details of the current box-office hits. In its early days the presenter was Jacky Gillott. However, Barry Norman took over in 1972 and quickly made the series his own. When he stood down briefly in 1982 to take over as frontman for **Omnibus**, a succession of temporary stand-ins (including producer Iain Johnstone) held the fort pending his return. The programme's title has changed with each year, becoming *Film 72*, etc.

FILTHY, RICH AND CATFLAP

UK (BBC) Situation Comedy. BBC 2 1987

Filthy Ralph ....Nigel Planer
Richard Rich ....Rik Mayall
Eddie Catflap ....Adrian Edmondson

Writer: Ben Elton. Producer: Paul Jackson

Aggression and anarchy dominate the lives of a TV performer, his minder and his agent.

This send-up of television celebrity saw comedian and 'TV star' Richie Rich striving to keep in with his peers (the likes of 'Brucie' and 'Tarby'), but continually hampered by his useless agent, Filthy Ralph, who could never get him any work, and his mindless minder, Eddie Catflap.

Penned by Ben Elton, the series offered more than an echo of **The Young Ones**.

FINE ROMANCE, A

UK (LWT) Situation Comedy. ITV 1981–4

Laura..Judi Dench
Mike ....Michael Williams
Helen..Susan Penhaligon
Phil ....Richard Warwick
Harry ....Geoffrey Rose

Creator: Bob Larbey. Producers: James Cellan Jones, Don Leaver

A middle-aged couple fumble their way through a relationship.

Laura and Mike were perfect for each other, or so it seemed to their friends and relations. They themselves were unsure, though, which led to much humming and ha-ing and an on-off romance. Middle-aged and each set in their ways, they were incapable of grasping the nettle (even though Mike's business was landscape gardening), and despite much prompting from Laura's daughter, Helen, and her husband, Phil, it took them three years to make the right decision. Things have proved simpler in real life, however, for stars Judi Dench and Michael Williams. They are husband and wife.

FINCH, JOHN

Scriptwriter whose work has generally focused on northern working-class situations. Amongst his credits have been **A Family At War**, **Sam**, *This Year, Next Year, Flesh and Blood, Nightingale's Boys, Spoils of War* and numerous episodes of **Coronation Street**.

FINLAY, FRANK, CBE (1926–)

British character actor, prone to controversial roles. His portrayal of Casanova in Dennis Potter's 1971 series enraged Mrs Whitehouse and he followed it up with performances as publisher Peter Manson in the equally sensational **Bouquet of Barbed Wire** and *Another Bouquet*. He was the Führer in the drama *The Death of Adolf Hitler* and among his many other appearances have been parts in plays and series like *Target Luna, Doctor Knock, This Happy Breed, Candide, The Adventures of Don Quixote* (as Sancho Panza), *84 Charing Cross Road, Count Dracula* (as Van Helsing), *Saturday, Sunday, Monday, The Last Campaign,* **Tales of the Unexpected**, **Blackadder**, *Aspects of Love* and *The Other Side*, as well as assorted Shakespearean roles. He also starred in the **Armchair Theatre** pilot for the comedy **Never Mind the Quality, Feel the Width** (as Patrick Kelly).

FINNIGAN, JUDY (1948–)

Daytime TV presenter, co-host of ITV's *This Morning* with her husband Richard Madeley. Finnigan's career began as a researcher with Granada and progressed via the company's regional news magazines. *Classic Coronation Street* saw her introduce epic moments from the long-running soap.

FIREBALL XL5

UK (AP Films/ATV/ITC) Children's Science Fiction. ITV 1962–3

Voices:
Colonel Steve Zodiac.............................Paul Maxwell
Professor Matthew Matic ....David Graham
Venus ....Sylvia Anderson
Commander Zero ....John Bluthal
Lt 90 ....David Graham
Zoonie..David Graham
Robert the Robot................................Gerry Anderson

Creators: Gerry Anderson, Sylvia Anderson.
Producer: Gerry Anderson

The crew of a state-of-the-art spacecraft protects Earth from invaders.

This was Gerry Anderson's second venture into Supermarionation (high-tech puppetry) and centred on the exploits of dashing Steve Zodiac, the handsome, blond, dare-devil commander of the spacecraft Fireball XL5, one of the XL series of faster-than-light rockets. Working for World Space Patrol in the year 2063, the ship was assigned to Sector 25 of the Solar System to counter the aggressive advances and cunning subterfuge of extra-terrestrials like Mr and Mrs Spacespy. Zodiac was ably supported by Venus, his French girlfriend, who was also a Doctor of Space Medicine, and Professor Matt Matic, the navigator, technical genius and designer of XL5. Robert, a transparent robot, was the co-pilot and a 'Lazoon' named Zoonie was also aboard. Missions were co-ordinated by Commander Zero and his junior, Lt 90, from Space City.

The adventures took Zodiac and his crew all across the galaxy. If a planet landing was in order, the rocket's nose cone ('Fireball Junior') detached itself and took the team to the surface. On the planet, they travelled on souped-up scooters known as jet-mobiles. *Fireball XL5* was the only Gerry Anderson series to be fully networked in the USA. Its theme song, 'Fireball', by Don Spencer, narrowly missed the UK Top 30 in 1963.

FIRE CRACKERS

UK (ATV) Situation Comedy. ITV 1964–5

Charlie..Alfred Marks
Jumbo..Joe Baker
Weary Willie ....Sidney Bromley
Loverboy...Ronnie Brady
Hairpin...Cardew Robinson
Tadpole ....Clive Elliott
Rosie ....Maureen Toal
George...Colin Douglas
Station Officer Blazer ....John Arnatt
Leading Fireman Piggott ....Norman Chappell

Producer: Alan Tarrant

The slapstick adventures of an incompetent village fire brigade.

Set in the fictitious settlement of Cropper's End (population 70), *Fire Crackers* concerned the inept local firemen and their decrepit 1907 engine, which was known as Bessie. Somehow this particular band of fire-fighters had been forgotten by the powers that be, so, even though they happily drew their salary, they didn't need to man the pumps. Instead, in times of trouble, they called out Station Officer Blazer and his crew from the neighbouring town, which meant that Charlie, the fire chief, and his workshy team could spend more time cadging pints in The Cropper's Arms. It was just as well, as their token attempts at fire drills usually ended in disaster anyway.

FIRST BORN

UK (BBC/Australian Broadcasting Corporation/Television New Zealand) Science Fiction. BBC 1 1988

Edward Forester ....Charles Dance
Ann Forester ....Julie Peasgood
Lancing ....Philip Madoc
Chris Knott ....Peter Tilbury
Nancy Knott ....Rosemary McHale
Dr Graham ....Roshan Seth
Marais ....Marc de Jonge
Jessop..Niven Boyd
Emily Jessop ....Sharon Duce
Gor ....Jamie Foster
Young Gor..Peter Wiggins
Gerry ....Nina Zuckerman
Nell Forester ....Gabrielle Anwar
Young Nell ....Beth Pearce

Writer: Ted Whitehead. Producer: Sally Head

A scientist creates a man/gorilla hybrid, with dangerous consequences.

It was genetics specialist Edward Forester's God-like desire to create a new breed of creature, one endowed with all man's intelligence but without the aggressive instincts associated with mankind. To this end, he began experimenting with female gorilla cells and his own sperm. The result was the birth of a man-gorilla, which he named Gordon, or Gor. After losing his infantile ape hair, Gor matured into a model son, but, eventually confronted with facts about his birth, demanded to see his mother, a gorilla named Mary, who beat him to death in a violent rage. The consequences of Forester's genetic tamperings were not at an end, however, as his daughter, Nell, then gave birth to Gor's child, a baby clearly of mixed species.

This three-part series was an adaptation of the novel *Gorsaga* by Maureen Duffy.

FIRST CHURCHILLS, THE

UK (BBC) Historical Drama. BBC 2 1969

John Churchill ....John Neville
Sarah Churchill ....Susan Hampshire
Sidney Godolphin ....John Standing
Charles II...James Villiers
York ....John Westbrook
Princess Mary ....Lisa Daniely
Princess Anne ....Margaret Tyzack
Shaftesbury.......................................Frederick Peisley

Writer/Producer: Donald Wilson

Period drama charting the distant ancestry of the famous 20th-century prime minister.

Long before Sir Winston was even a twinkle in his father's eye, his family was heavily entwined with British politics – as far back as Stewart times, when John Churchill wrestled for power in the court of King Charles II. Putting his military skills to good use in assorted European battles, Churchill won from the sovereign the title of the first Duke of Marlborough and, with his wife, Sarah (a lady-in-waiting to the future Queen Anne), instigated the famous line of statesmen bearing his name. Written, directed and produced by Donald Wilson, the series ran to 12 episodes.

FIRST OF THE SUMMER WINE see *Last of the Summer Wine.*

FIRST TUESDAY

UK (Yorkshire) Documentary. ITV 1983–93

Presenters: Jonathan Dimbleby, Olivia O'Leary

Powerful series of documentaries on wide-ranging subjects of contemporary significance.

Shown in a post-*News at Ten* slot, *First Tuesday* offered a collection of influential documentaries on subjects as diverse as housewife strippers, joy riders, radioactive pollution and Siamese twins. One notable programme followed a Geordie living and working in China and another investigated the man who shot John Lennon. Using pictures to tell their own story, the series also exposed the abuse dished out in old people's homes, went behind the scenes of the

Hillsborough disaster and looked again at the case of the Guildford Four. Jonathan Dimbleby was the first presenter, succeeded by Olivia O'Leary in later years. The name was derived from the fact that the programme was screened on the first Tuesday of the month.

FISH, MICHAEL (1944–)

Long-serving BBC weatherman (since 1974), the presenter who unfortunately assured viewers that there were no hurricanes on the way in 1987. He has also made guest appearances on other shows.

FISHER, GREGOR

Scottish comic actor, best known as the string-vested philosopher Rab C. Nesbitt, a spin-off character from *Naked Video*. Another *Naked Video* product which Fisher took into its own offshoot was *The Baldy Man*. Fisher also starred as Para Handy in the revival of the old 1950s comedy, and earlier appearances came in such series as *Foxy Lady* (as Hector Ross), *City Lights*, *The Bill* and *Boon*.

FIVE O'CLOCK CLUB

UK (Associated-Rediffusion) Children's Entertainment. ITV 1963–6

Presenters: Muriel Young, Howard Williams, Wally Whyton

Twice-weekly light magazine for younger viewers.

Taking its cue from the earlier series *Small Time*, *Lucky Dip* and *Tuesday Rendezvous*, all very much in the same vein, *Five O'Clock Club* was a popular Tuesday and Friday offering for the under-12s. Its hosts, Muriel Young, Howard Williams and, later, Wally Whyton, presented a mixed bag of pop singers and other guests, and gently sparred with their puppet co-stars, Fred Barker and Ollie Beak. Additional items included guitar tips from Bert Weedon, hobbies with Jimmy Hanley and animals with Graham Dangerfield. The programme became *Ollie and Fred's Five O'Clock Club* in 1965. The same year, the cheeky puppets popped up alongside presenter Marjorie Sigley in *Five O'Clock Funfair.*

FLAMBARDS

UK (YTV) Drama. ITV 1979

Christina Parsons ....Christine McKenna
Uncle Russell..Edward Judd
Mark Russell...Steven Grives
William Russell.......................................Alan Parnaby
Dick ....Sebastian Abineri
Sandy ....Peter Sethelen

Executive Producer: David Cunliffe. Producer: Leonard Lewis

A teenage orphan is terrorized by her uncle and cousin.

During World War I, Christina Parsons, a young orphan girl, was taken under the wing of her tyrannical Uncle Russell at Flambards, his decaying estate in the Essex countryside. There her life was made a misery by her cousin, Mark, a sadistic bully who wanted her for his wife. His gentler brother, William, sympathized with Christina but found a more important interest in the new craze of aviation. The series followed her wretched life through the difficulties of the war years. Based on a trilogy of romantic novels by K.M. Peyton, the 12-part series was adapted by various writers, including Alan Plater.

FLAMINGO ROAD

US (Lorimar/MF) Drama. BBC 1 1981–

Sheriff Titus Semple	Howard Duff
Sam Curtis	John Beck
Claude Weldon	Kevin McCarthy
Eudora Weldon	Barbara Rush
Skipper Weldon	Woody Brown
Constance Weldon/Carlyle	Morgan Fairchild
Fielding Carlyle	Mark Harmon
Lane Ballou	Cristina Raines
Lute-Mae Sanders	Stella Stevens
Sande Swanson	Cynthia Sikes
Elmo Tyson	Peter Donat
Michael Tyrone	David Selby

Greed, corruption and scandal in a sleepy Southern town.

Based on the 1949 film starring Joan Crawford, *Flamingo Road* was another of the *Dallas/Dynasty* clones that attempted to secure a permanent prime-time slot. In the event, the series was short-lived, lasting only two seasons.

It was set in the small town of Truro, Florida, where the wealthiest street was Flamingo Road. On Flamingo Road lived Claude Weldon, proprietor of the local paper mill, together with his wife, Eudora, son, Skipper (who ran the mill) and spoiled adopted daughter, Constance. Constance married Fielding Carlyle, a local politician, whose advancement was owed in no small measure to the manipulative sheriff of Truro, Titus Semple. Semple knew the ins and outs of the whole neighbourhood, including the sort of secrets that made him all-powerful. Fielding had really loved Lane Ballou, singer at Lute-Mae's casino-cum-brothel, but was badgered into the marriage that would best suit his, or rather Semple's, plans. Lane was now romantically entwined with construction developer Sam Curtis.

Also featured was Elmo Tyson, the owner of the town's newspaper, *The Clarion*, although a major new character arrived in the next season in the shape of Michael Tyrone, an angry tycoon out to avenge the execution of his innocent father. His schemes introduced murder and voodoo to the dozy old town, spicing up the family jealousies, business rivalries and political intrigue that dominated the sleazy storylines.

FLETCHER, CYRIL (1913–)

That's Life's 'odd ode' performer, Cyril Fletcher's TV career stretches way back to the medium's earliest days. It was in 1936 that he appeared on the fledgling BBC service, reciting his novel poems and participating in the Corporation's first pantomime, Dick Whittington. He also appeared in revues like *Tele-Ho!* After the war, his seaside pier show, *Saturday Night Attraction* was screened in 1949 and he went on to join the panel of *What's My Line?* and take part in the religious series *Sunday Story*. He joined *That's Life* in the 1970s, composing his odd odes and selecting bizarre newspaper clippings. He has also presented gardening programmes.

FLINTSTONES, THE

US (Hanna-Barbera) Cartoon. ITV 1961–6

Voices:

Fred Flintstone	Alan Reed
Wilma Flintstone	Jean Vander Pyl
Barney Rubble	Mel Blanc
Betty Rubble	Bea Benaderet
	Gerry Johnson
Dino	Mel Blanc
Pebbles Flintstone	Jean Vander Pyl
Bamm Bamm Rubble	Don Messick

Creators/Executive Producers: William Hanna, Joseph Barbera

Comic animation which imaginatively placed 1960s lifestyles in a Stone Age setting.

The Flintstones were Fred and Wilma, with little daughter Pebbles an addition to the family in later years. They lived (with their pet dinosaur, Dino) in the city of Bedrock sometime around one million years bc. Loud-mouthed, hapless Fred worked as a crane operator at the Bedrock Construction Co., alongside his next-door neighbour and best buddy, Barney Rubble. Barney's wife, Betty, was a close friend of Wilma's and the Rubbles soon extended their family, too, when they adopted a baby boy, Bamm Bamm.

The cartoon's humour was largely due to the fanciful idea of presenting prehistoric man with 20th-century mod cons. The cave-dwelling inhabitants of Bedrock had the lot, if in a very primitive form. Fred's hi-fi system, for example, consisted of a bird with a large beak scratching out sounds from a stone disc, and the Flintstones' car, complete with tail fins, ran only when they ran (it was feet-powered). The household waste disposal system was a gluttonous buzzard hidden under the sink, a baby elephant on roller skates acted as Wilma's vacuum cleaner, while Fred's crane at work was dinosaur-powered. Their newspaper, The Daily Slate, arrived on heavy stone slabs, and, of course, they owned a Stoneway piano. Several famous 'guest stars' made appearances, including Perry Masonry, the crack barrister, actor Stony Curtis and TV host Ed Sullystone. Meanwhile, Fred's yell of 'Yabba Dabba Do!' became one of TV's best-remembered catchphrases.

The Flintstones (originally planned as The Flagstones) had the honour of being the first animation to be made specifically for US TV's prime time, and is still being run on TV stations across the world. The Stone Age setting apart, it borrowed much from the hit American series The Honeymooners (seldom seen in the UK), which starred Jackie Gleason and revolved around pal-neighbours who were constantly in hot water. A feature film, A Man Called Flintstone, reached the cinema in 1966 and a spin-off series, Pebbles and Bamm Bamm, premiered in 1971. In 1994 John Goodman starred in a live-action film version. The Flintstones concept was reworked in another Hanna-Barbera production, The Jetsons. This time the 20th-century way of life was applied to the space age.

FLIP SIDE OF DOMINICK HIDE, THE/ANOTHER FLIP FOR DOMINICK

UK (BBC) Science Fiction. BBC 1 1980/1982

Dominick Hide ....Peter Firth
Jane ....Caroline Langrishe
Ava ....Pippa Guard
Caleb Line...Patrick Magee
Great Aunt Mavis ....Sylvia Coleridge
Helda ....Jean Trend

Writers: Alan Gibson, Jeremy Paul. Producer: Chris Cherry

A time traveller from the future is bewildered by 1980s London.

This Play for Today achieved almost cult status with its tale of a friendly but naive lad from 150 years in the future who visited Britain in the 1980s. By sending his flying saucer through a time warp, Dominick Hide left the year 2130 and returned to London in 1980 to do some historical research. He discovered a city far removed from the one he had just left. In his time, the world was a hygienic place of order and calm, and Hide was bemused and confused by the hustle and bustle he now encountered. Happily, he was befriended by a girl named Jane, who became his lover and, in a quirk of fate, gave birth to Dominick's own great-great-grandfather.

Hide resurfaced in a second Play for Today two years later entitled Another Flip for Dominick, in which his boss, Caleb Line, sent him back to 1982 to find a missing researcher. Once again Dominick met up with Jane (and his two-year-old son/great-great-grandfather), before returning to his wife, Ava, in his own time.

FLIPPER

US (MGM/Ivan Tors) Adventure. ITV 1966

Porter 'Po' Ricks ....Brian Kelly
Sandy Ricks...Luke Halpin
Bud Ricks...Tommy Norden
Hap Gorman ....Andy Devine
Ulla Norstrand ....Ulla Stromstedt

Creator/Executive Producer: Ivan Tors.
Producer: Stanley Colbert

The adventures of two young boys and their pet dolphin at a Florida marine park – a kind of underwater Lassie.

Fifteen-year-old Sandy Ricks and his ten-year-old brother, Bud, lived at the Coral Key Park in Florida, where their widower father, Po Ricks, was Chief Ranger. In the early episodes, carpenter Hap Gorman, an old sea dog, also hung around, regaling the boys with tall stories in a gravelly voice, but he was replaced by glamorous Scandinavian oceanographer Ulla Norstrand. The family had a pet labrador, Spray, and even a pet pelican, Pete, but it was with Flipper, their tame dolphin, that they had the most fun. This incredibly intelligent sea mammal led Bud and Sandy into a host of maritime adventures and was often at hand to help them out of awkward or dangerous situations. Together they flushed out crooks, averted disasters and swam to the rescue of struggling sailors.

The bottle-nosed dolphin was mostly played by an animal named Suzy and the series was based on the 1963 film of the same name, which starred Chuck Connors as dad alongside son Luke Halpin.

FLOOR MANAGER

The person who takes charge on the studio floor during production, passing on instructions given through headphones by the director in the control room. It is the floor manager who cues the presenters, etc. The term is often abbreviated to FM.

FLOWERPOT MEN, THE

UK (BBC) Children's Entertainment. BBC
1952–4; 1957–8

Voices: Peter Hawkins

Creators: Freda Lingstrom, Maria Bird. Writer:
Maria Bird

**The secret adventures of two flowerpot
dwellers who lived at the bottom of a
garden.**

Airing in Wednesday's *Watch with Mother* slot,
The Flowerpot Men exposed the covert activities of
identical puppets Bill and Ben. Made out of pots
themselves, their hands covered in big gardening
gloves and feet in hobnail boots, Bill and Ben
lived in two giant (normal size to humans)
flowerpots down by a potting shed. Whenever
the gardener popped home for a spot of lunch,
the two rascals would slowly raise their heads out
of the pots to see if the coast was clear, before
leaping out to play. Games generally centred
around whatever object they could find but a
constant guessing game for viewers was which of
the twin puppets had done this or that in the programme. 'Was it Bill or was it Ben?', toddlers
were asked, and the truth came out when the
culprit turned around to reveal his name on his
back. (Older viewers knew instantly as Bill's voice
was about an octave higher than his pal's.) When
the man who worked in the garden had finished
his lunch and was on his way down the garden
path, the Flowerpot Men, in the nick of time,
scrambled back into their pots. Keeping counsel
was their neighbour, Weed, who kindly alerted
them to signs of danger. Also in on the boys'
secret was the little house, which probably 'knew
something about it, too', if its smile was anything
to go by.

The Flowerpot Men was *Watch with Mother's* second
offering, hot on the heels of *Andy Pandy*.
Behind the project were *Andy Pandy's* creators
Freda Lingstrom and Maria Bird, with Audrey
Atterbury and Molly Gibson once again pulling
the strings and Gladys Whitred and Julia Williams
adding the songs. Bill and Ben's 'flobbalot' gibberish was provided by master voicer Peter
Hawkins, later to add his talents to *The
Woodentops* and *Captain Pugwash*, amongst
other animations.

FLOYD, KEITH (1943–)

Restaurateur turned TV celebrity, Keith Floyd
made his name in a series of programmes for the
BBC which dissected the culinary traditions of
various corners of the world. These included
*Floyd On France, Floyd On Spain, Floyd On Italy,
Floyd On Britain and Ireland, Floyd's American Pie,*

Floyd On Oz and *Far Flung Floyd.* Other series
were *Floyd On Food* and *Floyd On Fish.*
Establishing himself as a popular, if garrulous
frontman, he barked out orders to his camera
crew while clutching his trademark glass of wine.
Floyd was also chosen to succeed Clive James in
what became *Floyd On TV,* before himself making way for Chris Tarrant.

FLYING DOCTOR, THE

UK (ABC) Adventure. ITV 1959–

Dr Greg Graham	Richard Denning
Mary Meredith	Jill Adams
Dr Jim Harrison	Peter Madden
Charley Wood	Alan White

Producer: David Macdonald

**Adventures in the bush with an American
doctor.**

Nearly 30 years before *The Flying Doctors* took off
from Cooper's Crossing, tall, handsome
American doctor Greg Graham, his blind assistant, Dr Harrison, and his trusty nurse, Mary,
were life-savers in the Australian outback.
Responding to urgent radio messages, they
winged their way (always in the nick of time) to
remote patients in a small plane piloted by their
friend, Charley. Graham had arrived in Australia
on leave from a research institute in San
Francisco. The series was filmed partly at Elstree
and partly on location in Australia.

FLYNN, BARBARA (BARBARA McMURRAY; 1948–)

English character actress whose most memorabale
performances have been as Freda Ashton in
Granada's *A Family at War*, schoolteacher Jill
Swinburne in the *Beiderbecke* trilogy and the
feminist Dr Rose Marie in *A Very Peculiar
Practice*, although she has many other pro-
gramme credits to her name. These include *Keep
It in the Family, Open All Hours, Second Chance,
Maybury, Barchester Towers, Day To Remember* and
Inspector Morse. She also played Mme Maigret in
the 1990s revival of *Maigret* and has been seen as
Judith, Fitz's wife, in *Cracker* and private investi-
gator Dee Tate in *Chandler and Co.*

FOLLYFOOT

UK (Yorkshire) Children's Drama. ITV 1971–3

Dora	Gillian Blake
Steve	Steve Hodson
Slugger	Arthur English
The Colonel	Desmond Llewellyn
Ron Stryker	Christian Rodska
Lewis Hammond	Paul Guess

Executive Producer: Tony Essex. Producer: Audley Southcott

Eventful days at a home for neglected horses in Yorkshire.

Follyfoot Farm was a retirement home for old and unwanted horses. It was owned by a patrician former army man known as The Colonel and run by his niece, Dora, and Steve, a formerly wayward youth turned reliable stable hand. The farm kitchen was run by a rough and ready old boxer named Slugger (once The Colonel's batman) and also in the action was daily hand Ron Stryker, a layabout biker with a heart of gold beneath an abrasive exterior. Lewis Hammond, son of the proprietors of the rival Pinecrest Riding Hotel, and a thoroughly bad egg, was Ron's pal.

Adventures at Follyfoot revolved around the rehabilitation of distressed and neglected horses and were broadly based on the novels by Monica Dickens (particularly the first one, *Cobbler's Dream*, published in 1963). In the farmyard stood a burnt out tree, victim of a lightning bolt. The Colonel reckoned it would bloom again if given enough attention so everyone who passed by was required to throw a bucket of water onto its roots. The tree became a good luck charm to the farm folk (and a symbol of hope for worn out horses) and was featured in the programme's theme song, 'The Lightning Tree', performed by The Settlers, which was a minor chart hit in 1971.

FOOD AND DRINK

UK (BBC/Bazal) Food Magazine. BBC 2 1982

Presenters:
Henry Kelly
Susan Grossman
Jilly Goolden
Chris Kelly
Michael Barry
Oz Clarke
Paul Heiney

Producer: Peter Bazalgette

Eating and drinking magazine.

Crafty recipes, drink reviews and the latest news from the catering world have formed the basis of this popular BBC 2 programme. The main line-up (since 1984) has been Chris Kelly as anchor, Michael Barry in charge of cooking and Jilly Goolden judging various drinks from wines to teas, conveying her findings in an avalanche of over-the-top adjectives. Where wines and beers have been concerned, she has been increasingly joined by wine writer Oz Clarke. Paul Heiney hosted one series while Chris Kelly was working on another project. Every Christmas a *Food and Drink Christmas Quiz* has pitted the experts, joined by celebrity guests, against each other in a series of blind tastings and quick cookery.

FOOTPRINT

The area of the Earth that a satellite's transmissions reach. If you live outside the footprint area, you can't pick up the signals.

FOR THE CHILDREN

UK (BBC) Children's Entertainment. BBC 1946–51

Producers: Mary Adams, Andrew Miller Jones

Early entertainment for school-age children.

Among the items offered under this umbrella title were features on stamp collecting and other wholesome pursuits, classic stories and tales and, from August 1946, music and fun with Muffin the Mule and his piano-playing escort, Annette Mills. Muffin was originally just one of the puppets Annette (and her puppeteer Ann Hogarth) worked with, but he quickly outshone the likes of Peregrine the Penguin, Sally the Sea Lion, Oswald the Ostrich and Louise the Lamb, to the point where he was given his own series (see *Muffin the Mule*). Only Prudence and Primrose Kitten came close to equalling his popularity, also appearing in their own series in the 1950s. *For the Children*, meanwhile, gave way to **Andy Pandy** and the **Watch with Mother** crew.

FOR THE LOVE OF ADA

UK (Thames) Situation Comedy. ITV 1970–1

Ada Cresswell	Irene Handl
Walter Bingley	Wilfred Pickles
Leslie Pollitt	Jack Smethurst
Ruth Pollitt	Barbara Mitchell

Creators/Writers: Vince Powell, Harry Driver. Producer: Ronnie Baxter

Romance in the twilight years with two game pensioners.

When Ada Cresswell buried her late husband, little did she know that the man who had dug the grave would be her next spouse. Beginning a gentle love affair with fellow senior citizen Walter Bingley, Ada moved in to his home at Cemetery Lodge, much to the surprise of her daughter, Ruth, and Manchester Utd fanatic son-in-law, Leslie. The spritely 70-year-olds were eventually married. A feature film version was released in 1972.

FORD, ANNA (1943–)

English newsreader and presenter, one of TV-am's Famous Five. Prior to her short stint on breakfast television, Ford had been an ITN newscaster (on *News at Ten*), **Tomorrow's World** presenter and a reporter on **Man Alive** and *Reports Action*, arriving on TV after a time as an Open University tutor. She is now one of the BBC's senior newsreaders, working on the *Six O'Clock News* in particular.

FORDYCE, KEITH (1928–)

Former Radio Luxembourg and Light Programme disc jockey, a Cambridge law graduate who presented some of the early 1960s pop shows, especially *Wham!!*, **Thank Your Lucky Stars** and **Ready, Steady, Go!** He also hosted **Come Dancing**, a few gardening programmes and Westward's regional quiz *Treasure Hunt*.

FOREVER GREEN

UK (LWT/Picture Partnership) Drama. ITV 1989; 1992

Jack Boult ....John Alderton
Harriet Boult ....Pauline Collins
Freddy Boult ....Daisy Bates
Tom Boult ....Nimer Rashed
Lady Patricia Broughall ....Paola Dionisotti
Hilly ....Wendy Van Der Plank

Executive Producer: Nick Elliott. Producer: Brian Eastman

A town family moves to the country and discovers rural life is tougher than it looks.

Jack and Harriet Boult, concerned for the health of their asthmatic daughter, Freddy, decided to up sticks from London and head for the country. Taking up residence at the run-down Meadows Green Farm, somewhere in deepest Gloucestershire, the townies soon discovered that country life had its downs as well as its ups. They found themselves immersed in protests against toxic waste, battling against horse rustlers and protecting barn owls in danger. Tom was their son and also seen were cranky aristocrat Lady Pat and animal-loving local girl Hilly. Two series of this slow-moving, sentimental drama were made, three years apart.

FORREST, STEVE (WILLIAM FORREST ANDREWS; 1924–)

The brother of actor Dana Andrews, Steve Forrest was one of TV's action men in the 1960s, taking the part of Texas antiques dealer-cum-investigator John Mannering, aka **The Baron**. He followed this up with the role of Lt. Hondo Harrelson in *SWAT* in the mid-1970s and resurfaced in the 1980s as Ben Stivers in **Dallas**. He also has plenty of TV movies to his name.

FORSYTE SAGA, THE

UK (BBC/MGM) Drama. BBC 2 1967

Jolyon 'Jo' Forsyte ....Kenneth More
Soames Forsyte ....Eric Porter
Irene Heron/Forsyte ....Nyree Dawn Porter
Jolyon 'Old Jolyon' Forsyte ....Joseph O'Conor
James Forsyte ....John Welsh
Winifred Forsyte..............................Margaret Tyzack
Michael Mont ....Nicholas Pennell
Ann Forsyte ....Fay Compton
Montague Dartie ....Terence Alexander
Helene Hilmer ....Lana Morris
Philip Bosinney ....John Bennett
Frances Forsyte ....Ursula Howells
Swithin ....George Woodbridge
Mrs Heron ....Jenny Laird
Fleur Forsyte ....Susan Hampshire
Annette Forsyte ....Dallia Penn
Jolyon 'Jon' Forsyte ....Martin Jarvis
June Forsyte ....Susan Pennick
....June Barry
Jolyon 'Jolly' Forsyte ....Michael York

Producer: Donald Wilson

Family squabbles and scandals in the Victorian and Edwardian ages.

The Forsyte Saga was the BBC's last major serial to be produced in black and white, which probably explains why it has not been repeated in recent years, despite its enormous worldwide success. It was the serial which put BBC 2 on the map, attracting six million viewers on Sunday evenings, disrupting church services and emptying pubs. A year later, it was repeated on BBC 1, gaining an audience of 18 million. It was the first serial the BBC ever sold to the Soviet Union and was purchased by stations all over America. And yet *The Forsyte Saga* almost never happened. Producer Donald Wilson had longed to televise John Galsworthy's novels for years, but a combination of problems over rights and stubborness at the BBC had thwarted him. However, putting together a star cast, Wilson got his way and the series was produced in 26 episodes, each presented as a separate act but with a cliffhanger ending to draw viewers back the following week.

The television script extended the time-scale of Galsworthy's novels, using historic references made in the text to begin the story somewhat earlier. The time covered ran from 1879 to 1926 and the story charted the feuding and fighting of the Forsytes, a London merchant family headed by Jolyon (Jo) and his cousin, Soames. Other notable family members included Old Jolyon, the ageing patriarch, and Irene, Soames's wife in a loveless marriage, who was cruelly raped by her husband in one memorably shocking scene. Irene later married Jo and gave birth to Jon, who became illicitly entwined with Fleur, Soames's daughter by a second marriage.

The series confirmed the BBC's reputation for costume dramas and spawned a host of lookalikes, such as *The First Churchills* and *The Pallisers*. Its influence was also seen in the glossy American soaps of the next decade (like *Dallas*). More immediately, it revived the flagging career of Kenneth More and made a star out of Susan Hampshire. Eric Porter reaped the accolades, too.

FORSYTH, BRIGIT

Scottish actress much seen in supporting roles, such as Bob's bossy wife, Thelma, in *Whatever Happened to the Likely Lads?* However, she has enjoyed lead roles of her own, particularly in the sitcoms *Tom, Dick and Harriet* (Harriet Maddison) and *Sharon and Elsie* (Elsie Bancroft) and the drama *Holly*. She also played Veronica Haslett in *The Glamour Girls*, Dr Judith Vincent in *The Practice* and among her other appearances have been parts in *The Master of Ballantrae*, *Boon*, Agatha Christie's *Poirot* and assorted plays.

FORSYTH, BRUCE (BRUCE FORSYTH-JOHNSON; 1928-)

Highly popular British entertainer whose career stretches back to stage variety performances as Boy Bruce, The Mighty Atom. He broke into television in the 1950s and became the main compere of *Sunday Night at the London Palladium* in 1958, where he demonstrated his unique and gently aggressive style of handling live audiences and nervous amateur contestants, gaining one of his many catchphrases, 'I'm in charge'. Becoming one of TV's top entertainers, he was given his own variety series, *The Bruce Forsyth Show*, by ATV and proceeded to develop a one-man cabaret routine, singing, dancing, playing the piano and cracking jokes along the way. 'Nice to see you, to see you nice' became another of his catchphrases. In the 1970s he hosted *The Generation Game* (picking up yet more gimmicks: 'Didn't he do well!', 'Good game. Good game.', etc.) and then, moving to ITV, presented *Bruce Forsyth's Big Night*, *Play Your Cards Right* (revived in 1994), *Hollywood or Bust* and *You Bet!* Back with the BBC, he hosted the game show *Takeover Bid* and a relaunched *Generation Game*. He has also tried his hand at situation comedy, replacing the late Leonard Rossiter in the supermarket farce *Tripper's Day* (as Cecil Slinger in the renamed *Slinger's Day*), and drama, in a 1960s version of Oscar Wilde's *The Canterville Ghost*. His second wife was *Generation Game* hostess Anthea Redfern and his daughter Julie was once a singer with the Guys and Dolls pop group. His third wife is Miss World 1975, Wilnelia Merced.

FORSYTHE, JOHN (JOHN FREUND; 1918-)

American actor well versed in father-figure roles, from the 1950s to the 1980s. A one-time baseball commentator, Forsythe switched to acting, appearing on stage, radio and film, before – on Alfred Hitchcock's advice – concentrating on television. He appeared as a guest on *Alfred Hitchcock Presents* and other anthology series, before headlining in *Bachelor Father* from 1957 to 1962. *The John Forsythe Show* followed and then another comedy, *To Rome with Love*. Neither of these made it on to British screens. A quiet spell as narrator and voice-over actor resulted in the role of Charlie in *Charlie's Angels*, a part in which he was never seen, only heard. In 1981 he was enticed back in front of the camera as distinguished tycoon Blake Carrington in *Dynasty* and became an international celebrity.

FORTUNES OF WAR

UK (BBC) Drama. BBC 1 1987

Guy Pringle	Kenneth Branagh
Harriet Pringle	Emma Thompson
Prince Yakimov	Ronald Pickup
Dobson	Charles Kay
Inchcape	James Villiers
Simon	Robert Graves
Edwina	Diana Hardcastle

Writer: Alan Plater. Producer: Betty Willingale

A young couple's life and relationship are thrown into turmoil by global conflict.

Opening in Bucharest at the outset of World War II, *Fortunes of War* was the story of newly weds Guy and Harriet Pringle. Naive, outgoing Guy worked as a lecturer for the British Council and with his sensible, more reserved wife lived in a cosy little academic community, seemingly oblivious to the unfolding events outside. However, as the conflict deepened and the Pringles were separated from home (in Romania, in Greece and in Egypt, behind the German front), they found themselves inconvenienced by friends like Prince Yakimov. More importantly, parted from each other, their love was put to the test and their characters and personalities forced to change.

Costing £6 million, *Fortunes of War* was the BBC's response to Granada's success with lavish dramas like *Brideshead Revisited* and *The Jewel in the Crown*. It was adapted in seven parts by Alan Plater from Olivia Manning's two trilogies, comprising the novels *The Great Fortune*, *The Spoilt City*, *Friends and Heroes* (*The Balkan Trilogy*), *The Danger Tree*, *The Battle Lost* and *The Sum of Things* (*The Levant Trilogy*).

FORTY MINUTES

UK (BBC) Documentary. BBC 2 1981–94

Editors: Roger Mills, Edward Mirzoeff, Caroline Pick, Paul Watson

Acclaimed documentary series tackling a variety of offbeat subjects.

With each programme lasting, as expected, 40 minutes, this collection of documentaries looked at subjects as varied as child prostitution, lavatories, gifted children, homing pigeons, battered husbands, amateur dramatics and prize-winning leeks. A well-remembered 1986 contribution was entitled *The Fishing Party* and focused on four well-bred men having a laugh on an angling trip, whilst another, *Away the Lads* in 1994, followed boisterous English youths on holiday in Benidorm.

FOSTER, BARRY (1931–)

Fair, curly haired actor whose TV highspot was the *Van Der Valk* series of the early 1970s, in which he played the lead character, a Dutch police detective. The series was briefly revived in 1991. Amongst his other credits have been parts in *Skyport*, *Mogul* (as Robert Driscoll), *Divorce His, Divorce Hers*, *The Fall of Eagles* (as Kaiser Wilhelm), *The Three Hostages* (as Richard Hannay), *Smiley's People*, *A Woman Called Golda*, **Death of an Expert Witness**, *Hôtel Du Lac*, **Bergerac** and **Inspector Morse**.

FOSTER, JULIA (1941–)

Popular, fair-haired British character actress. She appeared in **Emergency – Ward 10**, starred as Angie Botley in *Good Girl*, played Amy Wilde opposite John Stride in **The Wilde Alliance** and took the title role in a version of *Moll Flanders*. She was also Janet in the domestic sitcom *The Cabbage Patch* and Doris Doyle, the mum, in the kids' fantasy *News at Twelve*. Among her other credits have been numerous single dramas, some in anthologies like **Love Story** and *Play for Tomorrow*.

FOSTERS, THE

UK (LWT) Situation Comedy. ITV 1976–7

Samuel Foster	Norman Beaton
Pearl Foster	Isabelle Lucas
Vilma	Carmen Munro
Sonny Foster	Lenny Henry
Shirley Foster	Sharon Rosita
Benjamin Foster	Lawrie Mark

Producer: Stuart Allen

Fun and games with a black family in south London.

Breaking new ground as the first British series to feature an all-black cast, *The Fosters* was based on an American sitcom entitled *Good Times* (a spin-off from *Maude*, itself a spin-off from **All in the Family**). It featured an immigrant family living in a south London tower block. The Fosters were harassed dad Samuel, coping mum Pearl, artistic eldest son Sonny, 16-year-old Shirley and young Benjamin. In the same block lived Vilma, Pearl's friend and confidante. The programme was also notable for giving Lenny Henry (then aged 17) his first series role, but was attacked by some critics for reinforcing racial stereotypes.

FOUR FEATHER FALLS

UK (AP Films/Granada) Children's Western. ITV 1960

Voices:

Tex Tucker	Nicholas Parsons
Rocky	Kenneth Connor
Dusty	Kenneth Connor
Pedro	Kenneth Connor
Grandpa Twink	David Graham
Fernando	David Graham
Ma Jones	Denise Bryer
Little Jake	Denise Bryer

Producer: Gerry Anderson

Cowboy puppetry; Gerry Anderson's second TV venture.

Tex Tucker was the sheriff of the Western town of Four Feather Falls, but he was no ordinary lawman. His job was made considerably more comfortable by four magical feathers that he wore in his stetson. The feathers, given to Tex by Indian Chief Kalamakooya for rescuing his injured son, each had a function: one feather enabled Tex's dog, Dusty, to speak; another gave the power of speech to his horse, Rocky. The last two feathers controlled his two pistols, which swivelled and fired accurately whenever the Sheriff was in danger.

Ably supported by Rocky and Dusty, his unofficial deputies, Tex was a true Western hero, standing for no nonsense in a typical cowboy town. Among the villains were Fernando, Big Bad Ben and Pedro the Bandit, and the townsfolk who relied on their hero included Doc Haggerty, Ma Jones the storekeeper, Grandpa Twink and his grandson, Little Jake. Short on killing and big on songs (Michael Holliday provided Tex's singing voice), the 15-minute series ran to 39 episodes.

FOUR JUST MEN, THE

UK (Sapphire/ATV) Adventure. ITV 1959–60

Ben Manfred MP	Jack Hawkins
Tim Collier	Dan Dailey
Jeff Ryder	Richard Conte

Ricco Poccari	Vittorio De Sica
Nicole	Honor Blackman
Vicky	June Thorburn
Giulia	Lisa Gastoni

Executive Producer: Hannah Weinstein.
Producers: Sidney Cole, Jud Kinberg

Four wartime colleagues reunite to combat crime.

The Four Just Men, as they styled themselves, were MP and amateur detective Ben Manfred, American reporter Tim Collier, who was based in Paris, New York lawyer Jeff Ryder and wealthy Roman hotelier Ricco Poccari. They had all been members of the same Allied unit during the war and were brought together again by Manfred at the dying request of their wartime leader, Colonel Bacon, to tackle injustice around the world. The men generally worked alone (with each episode featuring only one star), although Manfred's men were also supported by their personal assistants: Nicole for Collier, Vicky for Ryder and Giulia for Poccari. The series was based on the 1906 novel by Edgar Wallace, and the 1939 film, which cast the men in a more sinister light.

FOWLDS, DEREK (1937–)

British actor whose career has veered between reading stories to an animal puppet, manoeuvring a confused politician and supervising a sincere young policeman. It was as Basil Brush's straight man that Fowlds first became known, a role he followed up with appearances in dramas such as **Edward the Seventh**, Clayhanger, **Strangers**, **Cribb**, **Triangle**, Affairs of the Heart (starring as heart-attack victim Peter Bonamy), **My Son, My Son**, Rules of Engagement, **Boon** and Chancer, as well as comedies such as **Miss Jones and Son**, **Robin's Nest** and **Rings on their Fingers**. As private secretary Bernard Wooley in **Yes Minister** and its sequel, Yes Prime Minister, he helped keep Paul Eddington's Jim Hacker on the straight and narrow, and in **Heartbeat**, as the fatherly, if set-in-his-ways, Sgt Blaketon, he has maintained a keen eye on Nick Berry's PC Nick Rowan.

FOWLER, HARRY, MBE (HENRY FOWLER; 1926–)

Cheeky, chirpy Cockney actor and presenter, a star of **The Army Game** (as Corporal Flogger Hoskins) and **Our Man at St Mark's** (as Harry the Yo Yo, the verger and reformed crook) before branching out into children's programmes, hosting Going a Bundle with Kenny Lynch and Get This with James Villiers. He has also appeared in series like **Spooner's Patch** (as Jimmy the Con), Dead Ernest (as Cherub Fred), Dramarama, Scarecrow and Mrs King, Supergran, Davro's Sketch Pad, **The Bill**, Casualty, **In Sickness and in Health**, World's End and **Love Hurts**, as well as around 80 films.

FOX

UK (Thames/Euston Films) Drama. ITV 1980

Billy Fox	Peter Vaughan
Connie Fox	Elizabeth Spriggs
Kenny Fox	Ray Winstone
Joey Fox	Larry Lamb
Vin Fox	Bernard Hill
Ray Fox	Derrick O'Connor
Phil Fox	Eamon Boland
Renie Fox	Rosemary Martin
Andy Fox	Richard Weinbaum
Nan	Cindy O'Callaghan

Writer: Trevor Preston. Executive Producer: Verity Lambert. Producer: Graham Benson

The singular and collective lives of a south London family with shady connections.

This 13-part filmed drama revolved around the Fox family, headed by local Mr Big, Billy Fox, who celebrated his 70th birthday in the opening episode. The same episode introduced his clan, made up of his second wife, Connie, his five sons and their respective wives, mistresses and offspring. The boys were Vin, working in the construction industry, Kenny, an aspiring welterweight boxer, Joey, a womanizing taxi driver, Phil, a student, and finally Ray. Also prominent were Vin's wife, Renie, and their deaf son, Andy (Billy's pride and joy). The drama unfolded in two phases: before and after 'King' Billy's death, showing how the family struggled to deal with the loss of this larger-than-life figure, who terrified other villains but was kind to the ordinary folk on his manor.

FOX BROADCASTING COMPANY

America's new fourth network, making inroads where others (particularly DuMont in the 1940s and 1950s) failed. The company is headed by Rupert Murdoch and former Paramount executive Barry Diller, and takes its name from the old 20th Century-Fox studios, which are now part of the company. Fox went on air in November 1986 and soon began to eat into the market share of America's big three networks (CBS, NBC and ABC), cleverly launching new programmes in August when the other stations have traditionally scheduled re-runs. While Fox is still not in the same league as the established networks, it is having its successes and amongst its innovative programmes have been The Simpsons, The Joan Rivers Show and Married . . . with Children.

FOX, EDWARD (1937–)

Upright British actor, star of *Edward and Mrs Simpson*. Among his other credits have been parts in *The Avengers, Man in a Suitcase, Journey to the Unknown*, *Hard Times* and the mini-series *Shaka Zulu*, although he has been more prolific in the cinema. He is the brother of actor James Fox.

FOX, SIR PAUL, CBE (1925–)

Former paratrooper and journalist, Paul Fox joined the BBC in 1950 as holiday relief writer on *BBC Television Newsreel*, but he quickly set down roots. He was influential in the setting up of the *Sportsview* unit and was the programme's editor from 1953. Fox went on to edit *Panorama* and then progressed up the ladder to the position of Controller of BBC 1 in 1967. He was lured away to Yorkshire Television in 1973, to succeed Donald Baverstock as programme controller, becoming the company's managing director in 1977. He also chaired ITN for two years. In 1988 Fox returned to the BBC on a three-year contract as Managing Director of BBC Television. He has since left broadcasting to work with the Race Courses Association.

FOXY LADY

UK (Granada) Situation Comedy. ITV 1982–4

Daisy Jackson	Diane Keen
Joe Prince	Geoffrey Burridge
J.P. Schofield	Patrick Troughton
Ben Marsh	Milton Johns
Tancred Taylor	Alan David
Hector Ross	Gregor Fisher
Owen Buckley	Steven Pinder
Acorn Henshaw	Tom Mennard

Writer: Geoffrey Lancashire. Producer: John G. Temple.

A new female editor rides to the rescue of an ailing northern newspaper.

Set in 1959, *Foxy Lady* related how Daisy Jackson gamely took on the editorship of the *Ramsden Reminder*, a weekly local rag tottering on the brink of bankruptcy following the death of the previous incumbent. Her all-male team consisted of accountant Joe Prince, feature writer J.P. Schofield, gambling sports writer Ben Marsh, women's page editor Hector Ross, arts editor Tancred Taylor, print trainee Owen Buckley and odd-job man Acorn Henshaw. Circulation initially picked up, but life was never easy for Daisy.

The cast list makes interesting reading today. Not only did it feature veterans like former *Doctor Who* Patrick Troughton and Tom Mennard (*Coronation Street*'s Sam Tindall), but also a pre-

Crossroads and *Brookside* Steven Pinder, and Gregor Fisher before he donned the string vest of **Rab C. Nesbitt**.

FRANCIS, CLIVE (1946–)

The son of *No Hiding Place* star Raymond Francis, Clive Francis has enjoyed a successful TV career of his own. Among his major roles has been Francis Poldark in *Poldark*, Detective Sgt Dexter in *New Scotland Yard*, Major Maurice Drummond in *The Piglet Files* and Dominic Eden in *The 10%ers*. He has also been seen in *Bulman, The Far Pavilions, David Copperfield, May to December, Yes Prime Minister* and *Old Flames*.

FRANCIS, JAN (1951–)

Dark-haired English actress, seen in both dramatic and comedy roles. Her most prominent performance was as Penny Warrender in the sitcom *Just Good Friends*, opposite Paul Nicholas's Vince Pinner. However, she has enjoyed several other starring roles, as resistance worker Lisa Colbert in *Secret Army* and newly widowed Sally Hardcastle in *Stay Lucky*, for instance. Her ballet training came in useful for her part in *A Chance to Sit Down*, and among the many other programmes she has contributed to have been *Jackanory, Sutherland's Law*, *Looking for Clancy, Rooms, The Duchess of Duke Street, Raffles, A Play for Love, The Racing Game, Target, Ripping Yarns, The Good Companions, Tales of the Unexpected* and Alan Plater's Premiere offering *Give Us A Kiss, Christabel*.

FRANCIS, RAYMOND (1911–87)

One of British television's earliest coppers, Raymond Francis played the snuff-taking Supt. Tom Lockhart in three different series. He arrived on our screens in *Murder Bag* in 1957, branched out into other investigations in *Crime Sheet* in 1959, and finally settled down in *No Hiding Place*, which ran for eight years up to 1967. He had previously appeared in a handful of TV plays and starred as Dr Watson in a 1951 BBC version of *Sherlock Holmes*. Not long before he died he returned to make a cameo appearance in the *Comic Strip*'s *Five Go Mad in Dorset*, popping up to arrest Ronald Allen's gay Uncle Quentin. In addition, he appeared in such series as *Thomas and Sarah, Edward and Mrs Simpson, Miss Marple* and *Me and My Girl*. He was the father of actor Clive Francis.

FRANCISCUS, JAMES (1934–91)

American leading man who guested in various 1950s series like *Have Gun, Will Travel* and *The*

Twilight Zone before winning a lead role in *Naked City*. As Detective Jim Halloran, he stayed with the series for just one year. Throughout the 1960s and 1970s, he was never short of work. US dramas, including *The Investigators* and *Mr Novak*, plus smaller parts in programmes like *The FBI*, kept him busy for most of the time. In 1971 he played the blind private detective *Longstreet* and later starred in a couple of other series, *Doc Elliott* and *Hunter*. He had several TV movies to his name, too.

FRANK STUBBS PROMOTES/ FRANK STUBBS

UK (Carlton/Noel Gay) Comedy Drama. ITV 1993–

Frank Stubbs	Timothy Spall
Petra Dillon	Lesley Sharp
Dawn Dillon	Danniella Westbrook
Archie Nash	Trevor Cooper
Dave Giddings	Nick Reding
Karen Lai	Choy-Ling Man
Diane Stubbs	Hazel Ellerby
Blick	Roy Marsden

Creator: Simon Nye. Producer: Hilary Bevan Jones

An aspiring showbiz promoter never quite makes it big.

Ticket-tout Frank Stubbs was tired of pacing the West End streets hawking overpriced tickets for the top shows. He was even more tired of being nicked and having to spend the night in the cells. Inspired by the success of smooth, young Dave Giddings, he decided that promotion was to be the name of the game from then on. His first break came with an Australian country and western singer, whom he staged despite the best efforts of his more established rivals. Predictably, she then left him for a real professional. After that, the ever-optimistic Frank and his colleague, Archie, found themselves ducking and diving in and out of schemes to promote kit cars, Russian skaters, graffiti artists, hopeful actresses, ambitious film directors, a low-profile politician and an American evangelist. Frank had just as many troubles in his personal life, too. He lived with his recently widowed (and virtually bankrupted) sister, Petra, and her daughter, Dawn, in a flat above a betting shop. His own wife, Diane, had kicked him out after his much-regretted fling with a teenager. In the second series, shown in 1994, Stubbs had moved to a swish new office block, owned by a character named Blick.

Borrowing heavily from the Arthur Daley school of wheeling and dealing, the series was based on Simon Nye's novel *Wideboy*. Nye also wrote some of the episodes.

FRANKENSTEIN JR AND THE IMPOSSIBLES

US (Hanna-Barbera) Cartoon. BBC 1 1967

Voices:

Frankenstein Jr	Ted Cassidy
Buzz Conroy	Dick Beals
Professor Conroy	John Stephenson
Multi Man	Don Messick
Fluid Man	Paul Frees
Coil Man	Hal Smith

Executive Producers: William Hanna, Joseph Barbera

Cartoon package featuring two helpings of superheroes – a giant Frankenstein robot and a vigilante pop group.

Frankenstein Jr was the invention of red-headed boy scientist Buzz Conroy, son of the eminent Professor Conroy. A 50-feet tall, talking, thinking, rocket-powered robot, Frankenstein Jr looked just like his horror movie namesake but was used entirely for good causes, defeating supervillains like Dr Shock and Birdman. Buzz controlled Jr with a special radar ring and also joined the robot on his missions. Clambering up on his back, Buzz uttered the magic command 'Allakazoom!', which blasted them off from the Professor's mountain lab. Once in action, Buzz donned his rocket belt, which enabled him to fly, and Jr employed an armoury of ingenious weapons that ranged from a freezing mist (used for stiffening up their opponents) to a magnetic ray.

The Impossibles were a three-man, touring pop group, whose performances were constantly interrupted by their boss, Big D, who spoke to them from a video screen hidden in a guitar. With the cry of 'Rally-Ho!', the trio bounded into action against crooks like the Satanic Surfer, the Terrible Twister and the Fiendish Fiddler, making full use of their incredible abilities. Coil Man had spring-loaded, extending limbs, Fluid Man had the power to become any kind of liquid (allowing him to trickle under doors, for example) and Multi Man could make instant and unlimited copies of himself. The 'Impossicar' took them from gig to gig.

Any actors worried about typecasting ought to consider Ted Cassidy's role in this series. Fresh from playing Lurch in *The Addams Family*, he now found himself voicing a Frankenstein robot. The giant robot idea was derived from a Japanese series called *Gigantor*.

FRANKLIN, GRETCHEN (1911–)

London-born actress familiar in down-to-earth, dithery female roles, most notably as Ethel

Skinner in *EastEnders*. She played Alf Garnett's wife in the *Comedy Playhouse* pilot of *Till Death Us Do Part*, but didn't continue with the series when it began. Those programmes she has appeared in, in a varied career, have included *Quatermass*, *The Artful Dodger*, *The Dick Emery Show*, *George and Mildred*, *Bowler*, *Churchill's People*, plus various dramas. She was also Myrtle Cavendish in *Crossroads*, Auntie Lil in *I Didn't Know You Cared* and Alice in *Dead Ernest*.

FRANKLYN, WILLIAM (1926–)

For all his TV work, smoothie William Franklyn will always be remembered as the 'Schh! You know who' man, after his commercials for Schweppes soft drinks. However, he entered television in the mid-1950s, taking roles in series like *Douglas Fairbanks Presents*, *The Count of Monte Cristo* and *International Detective*, before securing star billing in the 1961 adventure series *Top Secret*, in which he played undercover agent Peter Dallas, working in South America alongside Patrick Cargill. He was a familiar face in the 1960s and 1970s, cropping up in action series like *The Avengers* and *The Baron*, detective stories like *Maigret* and *Public Eye*, the sketch show *What's On Next?* and the sitcom *Paradise Island* (as ship's entertainment officer Cuthbert Fullworthy). He hosted the panel game *Masterspy* and, more recently, has been seen in *Moon and Son*, *The Upper Hand* and *GBH*. His daughter Sabina is also in the acting game.

FRASER, BILL (1908–87)

Busy British character actor, best remembered as Sgt Claude Snudge in *The Army Game* and its sequels, *Bootsie and Snudge* and *Foreign Affairs*, as well as the slightly different *Vacant Lot* (as builder William Bendlove). His other performances included Barney Pank in *Barney Is My Darling*, a defrocked priest in Joe Orton's play *Funeral Games*, undertaker Basil Bulstrode in *That's Your Funeral* and station master Hedley Green in *The Train Now Standing*. Fraser was also seen as one of Alf Garnett's buddies in *Till Death Us Do Part*, and played Mr Micawber in a BBC version of *David Copperfield*, Bert Baxter in *The Secret Diary of Adrian Mole, Aged 13¾*, Dr Fellows-Smith in *Doctors' Daughters* and Mr Justice Bullingham in *Rumpole of the Bailey*, although his TV credits, in fact, dated way back to the 1940s. His wife was actress Pamela Cundell.

FRASER, RONALD (1930–)

British character and comic actor, star of the 1970 sitcom *The Misfit*, in which he played Basil

'Badger' Allenby-Johnson, an expatriate who returned to London to discover that the Swinging Sixties had happened and then struggled to come to terms with the new liberalism of the day. Fraser also took the part of Inspector Spooner in the first series of *Spooner's Patch* and has enjoyed plenty of other TV roles, popping up in drama anthologies like *Rogues' Gallery* and *Conceptions of Murder*, and comedies such as *Life Without George* (as senile pianist Mr Chambers).

FRAUD SQUAD

UK (ATV) Police Drama. ITV 1969–70

Detective Inspector Gamble	Patrick O'Connell
Detective Sgt Vicky Hicks	Joanna Van Gyseghem
Helen Gamble	Elizabeth Weaver
Lucy Gamble	Katherine O'Connell
Supt Proud	Ralph Nossek

Creator: Ivor Jay. Producer: Nicholas Palmer

The enquiries of Scotland Yard's Fraudulent Crimes Squad.

The featured members of the Fraud Squad were Detective Inspector Gamble and his assistant, Detective Sgt Hicks (one of TV's first prominent female detectives). Together they tackled fraud in all areas, from the activities of con-men to the dubious financial status of a religious sect. Problems within Gamble's own family also came to the fore. The series was created by Ivor Jay, a former *Dixon of Dock Green* and *Crossroads* scriptwriter.

FRED BARKER

TV puppet dog of the 1960s and 1970s, voiced by Ivan Owen (better known as Basil Brush). He appeared with Wally Whyton and Muriel Young on shows like *Tuesday Rendezvous* and *Five O'Clock Club*, alongside fellow puppets Pussy Cat Willum and Ollie Beak, and later resurfaced on *Lift Off with Ayshea*.

FREEMAN, RIGHT HON. JOHN, MBE (1915–)

Serious, determined British interviewer (almost interrogator) of the late 1950s/early 1960s, mostly on *Face to Face*. A former *Panorama* contributor and Labour MP for Watford, he went on to edit *New Statesman*, become British High Commissioner in India and Ambassador to the USA and chairman of both London Weekend Television and ITN.

FRENCH, DAWN (1957–)

British comedienne and comic actress, long time partner of Jennifer Saunders and wife of Lenny

Henry. After a spell as a teacher and some club work with Saunders, she broke into television as part of the *Comic Strip* team, appearing in all their irreverent films. With Saunders, Ruby Wax and Tracey Ullman, she starred as Amanda, the feminist, in **Girls On Top** (also as co-writer) and then appeared in the comic mystery plays *Murder Most Horrid*. She was Geraldine Granger, *The Vicar of Dibley*, and has hosted the programmes *Scoff* and *Swank*, as well as taking roles in **The Young Ones**, **The Storyteller**, **Happy Families** (the cook) and, of course, **French and Saunders**.

FRENCH FIELDS see Fresh Fields.

FRESH FIELDS/FRENCH FIELDS

UK (Thames) Situation Comedy. ITV 1984–6/1989–91

Hester Fields	Julia McKenzie
William Fields	Anton Rodgers
Sonia Barratt	Ann Beach
Nancy Penrose	Fanny Rowe
Guy Penrose	Ballard Berkeley
Peter Richardson	Philip Bird
Emma Richardson	Debbie Cumming
	Sally Baxter (*French Fields*)
	Karen Ascoe (*French Fields*)
Monsieur Dax	Olivier Pierre (*French fFelds*)
Marie-Christine	Victoria Baker (*French Fields*)
Madame Romoleux	Valerie Lush (*French Fields*)
Chantal Moriac	Pamela Salem (*French Fields*)
Jill Trendle	Liz Crowther (*French Fields*)
Hugh Trendle	Robin Kermode (*French Fields*)

Creators/Writers: John Chapman (*Fresh Fields/French Fields*), Ian Davidson (*French Fields*). Producers: Peter Frazer-Jones (*Fresh Fields*), James Gilbert (*French Fields*)

A middle-aged couple spice up their life after the kids leave home.

With the children having flown the nest, Hester and William Fields needed new challenges and new zest in their life. They embarked on a rejuvenated relationship, enjoying each other's company and bouncing along in their new-found freedom, trying out new hobbies and pastimes. They lived in Barnes, west London. The slightly scatty Hester worked one day a week as a cook in Lucy's Kitchen and William was an accountant in the City, but their lives were playfully entwined, even if interrupted (especially at mealtimes) by nosy neighbour Sonia and Nancy, Hester's mum, who lived in the granny flat in the garden. Nancy's former husband, Guy, was also seen from time to time. In 1989 the programme was revived after a three-year hiatus, but with its format and title changed. William was headhunted for a job in France, so the Fields jumped on the foreign property bandwagon and grappled with the language across the Channel.

FREUD, SIR CLEMENT (1924–)

TV personality, writer, humorist and gourmet, much seen on dog food adverts. For many years Freud was a Liberal MP. He is the father of radio and TV presenter Emma Freud.

FRONT MAN

The main presenter of a news, sports or magazine programme, the link between the various items that make up the programme. Also known as anchor.

FROST REPORT, THE

UK (BBC) Comedy. BBC 1 1966–7

David Frost
Ronnie Barker
Ronnie Corbett
John Cleese
Julie Felix
Nicholas Smith
Tom Lehrer
Nicky Henson
Sheila Steafel

Producers: Duncan Wood, James Gilbert

Topical satire show, debunking a different subject every week.

Whereas David Frost's 1968 offering *The Frost Programme* focused on in-depth interviews and exposés, the earlier *Frost Report* was a light-hearted affair. It took a different topic each week – holidays, Parliament, sin, etc. – and reviewed it satirically through sketches performed by the likes of John Cleese and Ronnies Barker and Corbett, complemented by a suitable song from Julie Felix. Offerings included the famous 'class' sketch in which the tall, upper-class Cleese looked down on the shorter, middle-class Barker who in turn looked down on the diminutive, working-class Corbett. The programme's writers included the **Monty Python** team of Eric Idle, John Cleese, Graham Chapman, Michael Palin and Terry Jones (in tandem for the first time), as well as Tim Brooke-Taylor, John Law and Marty Feldman. A compilation of the best moments, *Frost Over England*, won the Golden Rose at the Montreux Festival in 1967.

FROST, SIR DAVID, OBE (1939–)

British broadcaster who became an overnight success (or 'rose without trace', as Malcolm Muggeridge's wife is alleged to have put it) on the revolutionary satire show **That Was The Week That Was** in 1962. Having presented a few low-key programmes about the Twist dance craze for ITV, Frost, the Cambridge graduate son of a Beccles minister, was thrust into the TW3 host's chair when both John Bird and Brian Redhead pulled out. His unflappability shone through and he also took the show to the USA, where it established itself but failed to win the same acclaim. Back in the UK, with TW3 off the air, Frost compered its less successful offspring, *Not So Much a Programme, More a Way of Life*, and then married comedy with hard-hitting interviews, hosting *The Frost Report* (complete with sketches from Messrs Barker, Corbett and Cleese) on the BBC and *The Frost Programme* (instigating 'trials by television') on ITV. He was executive producer of *At Last the 1948 Show* (a clear forerunner of *Monty Python*), *No – That's Me Over Here!* and *The Ronnie Barker Playhouse*, and starred in his own *Frost On Friday*, *Frost On Saturday* and *Frost On Sunday* (while commuting across to the USA), before he seemed to suffer from over-exposure and remained off our screens for a number of years. In 1976 he secured a series of exclusive interviews with disgraced President Nixon, which were screened on both sides of the Atlantic and offered some important revelations and disclosures. In 1982 he formed part of TV-am's Famous Five as they launched commercial breakfast television in the UK. With the company's problems spilling over into the public domain, he soon found himself the last of the five still at the station. However, his Sunday morning show established itself as an important weekly focal point for the political world and he was enticed to take it across to the BBC. However, he did return to ITV in a regional late night discussion show for Carlton, again called *The Frost Programme*, in 1993. To reinforce his versatility, Frost has also produced a couple of TV movies, hosted the panel game *Through the Keyhole* and presented superlative facts and feats in special editions of *The Guinness Book of Records*. As an executive, Frost has been a member of the LWT and TV-am boards and owns his own company, David Paradine Productions (using his middle name). 'Hello, good evening and welcome' has been his much mimicked catchphrase. His first wife was actress Lynne Frederick.

FRY, STEPHEN (1957–)

British comedian and actor, the partner of Hugh Laurie on *Saturday Live*, *A Bit of Fry and Laurie* and *Jeeves and Wooster* (as Jeeves). He played the conniving Lord Melchett in *Blackadder II* and his descendent, the booming General Melchett, in *Blackadder Goes Forth*, and his other contributions have come in *Alfresco*, *The Young Ones*, *Filthy, Rich and Catflap*, *Happy Families* (as Dr De Quick), *Alas Smith and Jones*, *Old Flames* and the investigative reporter spoof *This Is David Lander*. While still a student at Cambridge, Fry reworked the musical *Me and My Girl*, which was

taken to the West End with great success. He has also written some best-selling novels.

F TROOP
US (Warner Brothers) Situation Comedy. ITV

Captain Wilton Parmenter	Ken Berry
Sgt Morgan O'Rourke	Forrest Tucker
Corporal Randolph Agarn	Larry Storch
Wrangler Jane	Melody Patterson
Chief Wild Eagle	Frank deKova
Crazy Cat	Don Diamond
Bugler Hannibal Dobbs	James Hampton
Trooper Duffy	Bob Steele
Trooper Vanderbilt	Joe Brooks
Trooper Hoffenmuller	John Mitchum
Roaring Chicken	Edward Everett Horton

Creator: Richard M. Bluel. Producers: Richard M. Bluel, Hy Averback

The farcical exploits of a cavalry troop on the Indian front line.

Fort Courage, a cavalry outpost somewhere in deepest Kansas, was commanded by Captain Wilton Parmenter. Well that's what he thought. Parmenter had been a laundry orderly in the Union army at the end of the Civil War, but one day a simple sneeze changed his life. The loud snort, apparently, sounded just like 'Charge!' to his own side's cavalry, which sped into action just in time to thwart an attack by the Confederacy. Parmenter was commended for his initiative, promoted to captain and given the posting at Fort Courage. Unfortunately, he was not the real boss of the outfit. That honour was usurped by his sergeant, Morgan O'Rourke, a kind of Wild West Bilko figure who ran the show with his sidekick, Corporal Agarn but always gave the credit to his nominal camp commander. O'Rourke had even agreed a secret pact with the supposedly hostile Hekawi Indians, headed by the canny Chief Wild Eagle. Between them, O'Rourke and Wild Eagle ran an Indian souvenir racket and protected their business interests by staging fake attacks on the fort whenever the top brass came for an inspection.

O'Rourke's workshy soldiers were as incompetent as the fort's captain. The bugler, Dobbs, always played a bum note, one private, Hoffenmuller, was a German who spoke no English and Vanderbilt, the look-out, was officially blind. Little wonder the Indians couldn't be bothered to fight them. Also on the scene was Wrangler Jane, a sharp-shooting cowgirl who ran the post office and chased after the boyish Parmenter.

The series, airing first in the USA in 1965, was shown at various times around the ITV network.

FUGITIVE, THE

US (QM) Drama. ITV 1964–7

Dr Richard Kimble................................David Janssen
Lt Philip Gerard ....Barry Morse
Donna Taft ....Jacqueline Scott
Fred Johnson ('The One-Armed Man') ......Bill Raisch
Helen Kimble ....Diane Brewster
Narrator ....William Conrad

Executive Producer: Quinn Martin

A doctor wrongly convicted of the murder of his wife goes on the run, trying to find her killer before he himself is apprehended.

Dr Richard Kimble had returned home one evening to find his wife dead and a mysterious one-armed man running from the direction of the house. Kimble was arrested for murder and convicted on circumstantial evidence – no one else had seen the one-armed man, but the neighbours had heard the Kimbles quarrelling. Fortunately for Kimble, the train taking him to prison for execution was derailed and he took the chance to slip his unconscious guard, Lt Gerard, and make a break. Realizing his only chance of redemption lay in finding the real culprit, he began to comb the entire United States for the one-armed man, all the while knowing that Gerard was always only one step behind him.

Plagued by Gerard's relentless pursuit, Kimble was forced to shift from town to town, from low-paid job to low-paid job and from identity to identity, only occasionally making contact with his sister, Donna Taft. His tense life on the run even took him to Mexico and Canada, and the different setting for each episode kept the show fresh, giving producers the scope to try out new ideas and to bring in guest stars.

Unlike most suspense series, *The Fugitive* was allowed a proper conclusion in its final episode, which drew massive audiences all around the world. Kimble at last quarried the one-armed man in a deserted amusement park. As the two men struggled, Gerard arrived to shoot the man he now realized was the real murderer. This day, August 29, 1967, was, as narrator William Conrad affirmed, 'The day the running stopped'. (The episode was shown a day later in the UK.)

The Fugitive was inspired by Victor Hugo's 19th-century French classic, *Les Miserables*, and the concept was just as appealing in 1993, when Harrison Ford starred in a new cinema version of the Kimble story. The series was re-run on BBC 2 in 1994.

FULLERTON, FIONA (1956–)

Fair-haired British actress, progressing from youthful roles in the 1970s to star in series like *Angels* (as Patricia Rutherford), *The Charmer* (as Clarice Mannors) and various other dramas.

FUNT, ALLEN (1914–)

The grandfather of today's TV pranksters like Jeremy Beadle and Noel Edmonds, Funt was the man who devised *Candid Camera*, a series which evolved from his forces radio series *Candid Microphone*, which captured people unawares, with humorous results.

FURTHER ADVENTURES OF LUCKY JIM, The see *New Adventures of Lucky Jim, The*.

GAFFER

The chief electrician in a team.

GALL, SANDY, CBE (1927–)

Former ITN newscaster and foreign correspondent, joining the organization from Reuters in 1963. In his 29 years with ITN, he gained a reputation for venturing behind the lines and into trouble spots like Uganda, Vietnam and Afghanistan, presenting his findings in a series of important documentaries. He is also a well-published author.

GALLERY

The control room; home of the director, production assistant, vision mixer and other technicians during recording or live transmission.

GALTON, RAY (1930–)

British comedy scriptwriter, usually in collaboration with Alan Simpson. After meeting while both were convalescing from TB, Galton and Simpson were jointly responsible for Tony Hancock's scripts on *Hancock's Half Hour* on radio and television, later moving on to pen *Citizen James* for Sid James and then, in 1962, an episode of *Comedy Playhouse* entitled *The Offer*. This proved to be the pilot for *Steptoe and Son*, a series they wrote for 12 years (with a five-year hiatus in the middle). Their later work (efforts like *Casanova '73*), by common consent, was not in the same league, although they did win fans with their 1972 adaptation of Gabriel Chevalier's *Clochemerle*. Galton, without Simpson, joined forces with Johnny Speight to write the police comedy *Spooner's Patch* in 1979, and John Antrobus to script *Room at the Bottom* in 1986.

GAMBON, MICHAEL (1940–)

Distinguished Irish stage actor who reached new heights with his award-winning portrayal of Philip Marlow in Dennis Potter's *The Singing*

Detective. Subsequently, he has starred in the revival of *Maigret*. Most of his other television work has been of a heavy nature, in dramas like *The Seagull*, *Eyeless In Gaza*, *Oscar Wilde* and *The Heat of the Day*, although he has also been spotted in *Minder*, *Bergerac* and *The Storyteller*, and starred in the 1968 adventure series *The Borderers*.

GAME FOR A LAUGH

UK (LWT) Comedy. ITV 1981–5

Presenters: Jeremy Beadle, Henry Kelly, Matthew Kelly, Sarah Kennedy, Rustie Lee, Martin Daniels, Lee Peck, Debbie Rix

Executive Producer: Alan Boyd. Producers: Phil Bishop, Keith Stewart, Brian Wesley, Bob Merrilees

Practical jokes and silly stunts designed to make a fool out of the public.

In the vein of *Candid Camera*, *Game for a Laugh* was a combination of pre-filmed hidden camera pranks and studio-based stunts, all aimed at catching out Joe Public. Victims' embarrassment was glossed over by shrieks of laughter from the studio audience. Each week the hosts – perched on four high stools – signed off with a contrived 'Watching us, watching you' farewell. Rustie Lee, Lee Peck, Debbie Rix and Martin Daniels later joined the team and Jeremy Beadle moved on to even greater practical joking in *Beadle's About*. *Game for a Laugh* was based on the 1950s US game show *People Are Funny*.

GAME, SET AND MATCH

UK (Granada) Spy Drama. ITV 1988

Bernard Samson	Ian Holm
Fiona Samson	Mel Martin
Erich Stinnes	Gottfried John
Werner Volkmann	Michael Degen
Dicky Cruyer	Michael Culver
Gloria Kent	Amanda Donohoe
Bret Rensselaer	Anthony Bate
Frank Harrington	Frederick Treves
Silas Gaunt	Michael Aldridge
Julian MacKenzie	John Wheatley
Morgan	Struan Rodger
Zena Volkmann	Brigitte Karner
David Kimber-Hutchinson	Peter Vaughan
Henry Tiptree	Jeremy Child

Writer: John Howlett. Producer: Brian Armstrong

A desk-bound intelligence agent is sent back into action.

After allegedly bungling a counter-espionage mission in Poland and losing his nerve, loner Bernard Samson had been retired to desk duty.

Earlier, he had formed a secret agency known as the Brahms Network, and, when this was infiltrated by an enemy activist, Samson was called back into the front line to sort it out. He found himself in East Berlin, confronting his long-time friend, Werner Volkmann, and his own KGB agent wife, Fiona, who headed an underground intelligence unit called Yellow Submarine.

The 13-part series was based on a trilogy of books by Len Deighton, *Berlin Game*, *Mexico Set* and *London Match*, and was filmed in all three locations.

GANGSTERS

UK (BBC) Crime Drama. BBC 1 1975–8

John Kline	Maurice Colbourne
Khan	Ahmed Khalil
Ann Darracott	Elizabeth Cassidy
Dermot Macavoy	Paul Antrim
Malleson	Paul Barber
Sarah Gant	Alibe Parsons
Rafiq	Saeed Jaffrey
Rawlinson	Philip Martin
Lily Li Tang	Chai Lee
Mr Tang	Robert Lee

Writer: Philip Martin. Producer: David Rose

The violent face of the underworld in 1970s Birmingham.

Gangsters focused on former SAS man John Kline, freed from prison to work for D16 agent Khan in monitoring and manipulating events in the Birmingham underworld. Installed as the manager of The Maverick nightclub, Kline found himself mixing with all manner of evil characters, including Chinese triads, pimps, whores, extortionists, terrorists, drug pushers and illegal immigrant rings.

Shot on video using a roving camera, *Gangsters* won acclaim for effectively conveying the tension in the city's underworld and the menace of its low life. However, its graphic violence was heavily criticized. The 12-part series resulted from a one-off *Play for Today* of the same title, also written by Philip Martin. Chris Farlowe sang the theme song and Dave Greenslade composed the music.

GARDEN, GRAEME (1943–)

Cambridge medical student (now qualified doctor) who began writing for television in the mid-1960s, eventually appearing on screen in a sketch show entitled *Twice a Fortnight* (with Tim Brooke-Taylor, Bill Oddie, et al). This was followed by a short-lived series called *Broaden Your Mind*, before Garden and Oddie set about preparing scripts for LWT's *Doctor in the House* and

Doctor At Large sitcoms. In 1970 Garden, Brooke-Taylor and Oddie were offered their own series, based around three crazy do-gooders. The working title was Super-Chaps Three but everyone now knows it as **The Goodies**. Playing an over-the-top version of himself, Garden was the trio's mad scientist and the series ran for ten years on the BBC, before they switched to ITV for a season in 1982. Since then, Garden has continued writing (for shows such as **Alas Smith and Jones**, and Smith and Jones in Small Doses, **Surgical Spirit** and, with Oddie, the sci-fi spoof *Astronauts*), straight acting (among his appearances was an episode of **Strangers**), panel gaming (*Tell the Truth*) and presenting TV pop science programmes (he was one of the hosts of *Bodymatters*).

GARDENING CLUB

UK (BBC) Gardening. BBC 1 1955–67

Host: Percy Thrower

Producers: John Furness, Paul Morby

Gardening tips and news.

Gardening Club, the forerunner of today's many gardening programmes, was originally screened from a rooftop garden at the BBC's Lime Grove, where Percy Thrower offered useful advice to growers nationwide. Each week he was joined by specialist guests and enthusiastic amateurs. With the arrival of colour television, *Gardening Club* gave way to *Gardeners' World*, again hosted by Percy Thrower.

GARDNER, ANDREW (1932–)

Respected ITN newscaster, one of the first two presenters of *News At Ten* (with Alastair Burnet), having anchored ITN's earlier offerings: *Reporting '66* and *Reporting '67*. After leaving the company, he worked for Thames, presenting regional news magazines.

GARNER, JAMES (JAMES BAUMGARNER; 1928–)

American actor who entered television in the mid-1950s, playing small roles in series like **Cheyenne** while under contract to Warner Brothers. Warners then gave him his own vehicle, the Western spoof **Maverick**, which more and more began to reflect Garner's own understated sense of humour. However, tied to a limiting contract, Garner fell into conflict with the studio and walked out in 1960. He remained out of major TV work for 11 years, until he was cast as lead in another *Maverick*-like series entitled *Nichols*, made by his own Cherokee Productions. Three years later he achieved greater success as

Jim Rockford, the ex-con private investigator in **The Rockford Files**, before he returned to *Maverick* in a TV movie and a short-lived revamp, which went out under the name of *Bret Maverick*.

GARNETT, TONY (1936–)

British producer and one-time actor whose political sympathies have manifested themselves in plays like *Up the Junction*, **Cathy Come Home**, *The Gangster Show* and *The Gamekeeper*, and the series **Days of Hope** and *Law and Order*. In the 1990s he has been chairman of World Productions, an independent company which has made **Between the Lines**, a programme Garnett co-created and produced.

GASCOIGNE, BAMBER (1935–)

The doyen of British quizmasters, erudite Bamber Gascoigne was host of **University Challenge** for 25 years (1962-87), during which time he established catchphrases like 'Starter for ten'. He has also presented **Cinema**, his own 13-part history of Christianity, *The Christians*, the cultural quiz *Connoisseur*, and various other highbrow documentaries.

GASCOINE, JILL (1937–)

British leading lady, much seen on TV in series like **The Gentle Touch** and **C.A.T.S. Eyes** (both as female copper Maggie Forbes) and **The Onedin Line** (as Letty Gaunt). Among her other credits have been parts in **Dixon of Dock Green**, *Dr Finlay's Casebook*, **General Hospital**, *Raffles*, **Z Cars**, **Softly, Softly**, **Within These Walls**, *Beryl's Lot*, *Justice*, *Boon*, *Taggart* and *El C.I.D.*

GAUNT, WILLIAM (1937–)

British actor whose baby-faced looks made him popular in the late 1950s and 1960s, giving him parts in *Colonel Trumper's Private War* (as Lt Hastings), **Sergeant Cork** (as Sgt Bob Marriott), **Harpers West One**, **Probation Officer**, *The Avengers*, *The Saint* and *Softly, Softly*, culminating in the role of Richard Barrett in the supernatural spy series **The Champions**. In the 1980s he resurfaced as foster parent Tony Hunter in *Claire*, harassed dad Arthur Crabtree in the sitcom **No Place Like Home**, solicitor Edward Capstick in *Capstick's Law*, old buffer Aubrey in *A Gentlemen's Club* and grandfather Andrew in *Next of Kin*. Also in his portfolio are performances in **Crown Court**, *Cottage to Let*, *Holly*, *The Foundation* and *Love and Marriage*.

GBH

GBH Films) Drama. Channel 4 1991

Michael Murray ....Robert Lindsay

Jim Nelson	Michael Palin
Barbara Douglas	Lindsay Duncan
Mrs Murray	Julie Walters
Laura Nelson	Dearbhla Molloy
Franky Murray	Philip Whitchurch
Peter	Andrew Schofield
Martin Niarchos	Michael Angelis
Diane Niarchos	Julia St John
Mr Weller	David Ross
Lou Barnes	Tom Georgeson
Mervyn Sloan	Paul Daneman
Bubbles	Peter-Hugo Daly
Geoff	Bill Stewart
Teddy	Alan Igbon
Frank Twist	Colin Douglas
Researcher	Jimmy Mulville

Writer: Alan Bleasdale. Executive Producer: Verity Lambert. Producers: Alan Bleasdale, David Jones

An ambitious council leader and a gentle schoolteacher cross swords against a backdrop of political subversion.

Michael Murray was the newly installed leader of Liverpool City Council. Power, fame and women were the keystones of his life and militancy his watchword. Jim Nelson, in contrast, was the caring headteacher of a school for children with special needs, a family man whose ambitions were modest. When Nelson's school defied a Murray strike call, the two men became bitter enemies, to the detriment of Murray's career and Nelson's sanity. However, *GBH* was far more complicated than that. This seven-part drama had various subplots and undercurrents. It revealed how the two men became pawns in a sinister political game, and Murray's murky past come back to haunt him in the form of the beautiful but mysterious Barbara Douglas. The *GBH* of the title did not stand, as many initially believed, for Grievous Bodily Harm, but for Great British Holiday, referring to a sequence when Nelson – his mental health breaking up – headed off on vacation, returning to find the family home ransacked.

GBH was a labour of love for Alan Bleasdale. He had already abandoned attempts to script the idea as a film and as a novel. As a tense piece of television drama it won many plaudits, although, in established Bleasdale fashion, it ruffled a few feathers at the same time. Former Liverpool Council Deputy Leader Derek Hatton sought legal advice over what he saw as a fictionalization of his time in power, but Bleasdale denied that Michael Murray had been based on anyone in particular. Rather, as star Robert Lindsay explained, *GBH* was a reminder to the public that our lives are manipulated by activists from both left and right. Bleasdale, in the *Radio Times*, described the drama as 'one caring, liberal madman's odyssey through the appalling farce of life

in Britain today; trying to make some sense of the place'.

GEE, DUSTIN (GERALD HARRISON; 1942–86)

British comedian and impersonator, for some time partner of Les Dennis, with whom he starred in *Go For It* and *The Laughter Show*. His TV break came with **Who Do You Do?** in the mid-1970s and he followed it up with regular appearances in *Russ Abbot's Madhouse*. Among his best remembered take-offs were Larry Grayson and *Coronation Street*'s Vera Duckworth. He died of a heart attack in 1986.

GEMINI MAN

US (Universal) Adventure. BBC 1 1976

Sam Casey	Ben Murphy
Leonard Driscoll	William Sylvester
Dr Abby Lawrence	Katherine Crawford

Executive Producer: Harve Bennett. Producer: Leslie Stevens

An invisible man works as a secret agent for a Government think tank.

When NBC's *Invisible Man* series, starring David McCallum, was not a success, the company reworked the formula with a new cast and some subtle changes. The result was *Gemini Man*, which fared even worse in the US ratings war. It centred on Sam Casey, an agent for INTERSECT, who had been exposed to underwater radiation and rendered invisible. Thanks to the efforts of his superior, Leonard Driscoll (played by Richard Dysart in the pilot episode), and computer specialist Abby Lawrence, Casey was able to restore his appearance using a special watch-like device. He could, when required, turn the device off and return to invisibility – a very useful ploy for a secret agent, but if he did this for more than 15 minutes in one day, he would die.

GENERAL HOSPITAL

UK (ATV) Drama. ITV 1972–79

Dr Matthew Armstrong	David Garth
Dr William Parker-Brown	Lewis Jones
Dr Martin Baxter	James Kerry
Sister Edwards	Monica Grey
Dr Peter Ridge	Ian White
Arnold Capper	John Halstead
Dr Robert Thorne	Ronald Leigh-Hunt
Dr Neville Bywaters	Tony Adams
Sister Ellen Chapman	Peggy Sinclair
Dr Joanna Whitworth	Patricia Maynard
Nurse Hilda Price	Lynda Bellingham
Dr Richard Kirby	Eric Lander
Nurse Katy Shaw	Judy Buxton
Dr Knight	Carl Rigg

Dr Guy Wallman ....Tom Adams
Dr Chipapo ....Jason Rowe
Sister Washington ....Carmen Munroe
Staff Nurse Sister Holland ....Pippa Rowe
Nurse Stevens ....Amber Thomas

Producers: Ian Fordyce, Royston Morley

The day-to-day dramas involving staff and patients at a major hospital.

Although sharing its name with a long-running American soap, *General Hospital* was effectively *Emergency – Ward 10* revisited, albeit with a new cast and setting. Having cancelled *Ward 10* in 1967, and living to regret it, Lew Grade and his ATV associates decided to revamp the idea. They wanted an afternoon series to fill space newly made available after restrictions on broadcasting hours had been lifted. The result was a drama set in Midland General Hospital.

While not quite achieving the cult following *Ward 10* had enjoyed, the series still picked up a sizeable audience, enough to earn a transfer to an evening time slot three years into its run. Episode length increased from a half-hour to a full hour at the same time, and two programmes a week became one. As in its predecessor, it was the lives and loves of the *General Hospital* staff which took centre stage, as well as internal power struggles. Housewives were offered a new generation of heartthrob doctors, most notably Martin Baxter and Neville Bywaters (the latter played by Tony Adams, later Adam Chance in *Crossroads*), while veterans like Drs Armstrong and Parker-Brown seldom saw eye to eye and added sparks of tension and excitement.

GENERATION GAME, THE

UK (BBC) Game Show. BBC 1 1971–82; 1990–

Presenters: Bruce Forsyth, Larry Grayson
Hostesses: Anthea Redfern, Isla St Clair, Rosemarie Ford.

Producers: Alan Tarrant, Terry Heneberry, James Moir, Robin Nash, Alan Boyd, Marcus Plantin, David Taylor (1990)

Family couples compete in silly games and challenges.

The Generation Game has become the number-one game show in British TV history, enjoying two lengthy prime time runs. Simple in format, it has involved four couples (each composed of an elder and a younger member of a family – father and daughter, aunt and nephew, etc.) competing in two heats and a semi-final. The heats have consisted of two games based on little quizzes and challenges – guessing film themes and miming the answer to a partner, spotting personalities in disguise, etc. Demonstrations by experts (making pots, icing cakes, spinning plates, performing a dance, etc.), which the contestants have had to copy, have proved particularly popular. Points have been awarded for performance and the two heat-winning couples have then competed in a semi-final. This has often taken the form of a comic playlet, with celebrity judges allocating marks for performances. The winning duo have progressed to a final 'conveyor belt' round, in which a succession of household goodies (always including a cuddly toy) has passed before their eyes. Everything that they can recall in a set time has been taken home as prizes.

The Generation Game was devised by a Dutch housewife, who was inspired by game shows like *Beat the Clock* (see **Sunday Night at the London Palladium**), and when it was televized in Holland as *Een Van De Aacht* (*One From Eight*), it topped the ratings. Former *Beat the Clock* host Bruce Forsyth was the obvious choice to take charge of the UK version and he quickly established the programme as an integral part of Saturday evening viewing. Forsyth revelled in the party game format. With a twinkle in his eye, he bullied and coerced the hapless contestants through each show, combining words of encouragement with false anger and gentle mockery. The contestants loved it. Assisting Bruce was the leggy Anthea Redfern, who was soon to be his second wife. When Bruce was lured away to ITV in 1978, it seemed that *The Generation Game*'s heyday was over. Camp comedian Larry Grayson was not an obvious replacement, yet he made the show an even bigger hit. Sensibly avoiding Forsyth's aggressive approach, Grayson instead brought his own effete style to proceedings, in which he was assisted by Scottish folk singer Isla St Clair. *The Generation Game* was cancelled in 1982 but was brought back with Bruce Forsyth again at the helm in 1990. Once more, his skilful manipulation of the studio audience and his ease with contestants ensured the programme was as popular as ever. Dancer Rosemarie Ford became his girl Friday.

The Generation Game has aired under several titles. In the early days it was known as *Bruce Forsyth and the Generation Game*. It then became *Larry Grayson's Generation Game* and the latest incarnation has been called *Bruce Forsyth's Generation Game*. It has also given us catchphrases galore – from 'Let's meet the eight who are going to generate' and 'Let's see the scores on the doors' to 'Good game, good game' and 'What's on the board, Miss Ford?'. King of the catchphrases, however, has been 'Didn't he do well?' – just like the programme itself.

GENTLE TOUCH, THE

UK (LWT) Police Drama. ITV 1980–4

Detective Inspector Maggie Forbes ....Jill Gascoine

Detective Chief Inspector Russell....William Marlowe
Detective Sgt Jake Barratt ....Paul Moriarty
Detective Sgt Jimmy Fenton...........Derek Thompson
Detective Inspector Bob Croft ....Brian Gwaspari
Detective Sgt Peter Phillips...................Kevin O'Shea
Detective Inspector Jack Slater
....Michael Graham Cox
Steve Forbes.......................................Nigel Rathbone
Detective Inspector Mike Turnbull ....Bernard Holley
Sgt Sid Bryant ....Michael Cronin

Executive Producers: Tony Wharmby, Nick
Elliott. Producers: Kim Mills, Jack Williams,
Michael Verney-Elliott

**Softly, softly crime-busting with a female
police officer.**

Maggie Forbes was a former police cadet who
had worked her way up through the ranks and
was now posted to London's Seven Dials police
station, covering the areas of Soho and Covent
Garden. As the series began she found herself
almost simultaneously promoted to the rank of
detective inspector and widowed by the murder
of her PC husband (Leslie Schofield), Ray.
Despite being ordered to take time off, she
dragged herself back into action to pursue her
husband's killers but then resigned from the force.
Persuaded to rejoin, she found the subsequent
months difficult, as problems with Steve, her
teenage son, interfered with her progress at the
station. Eventually, she and the series settled
down into a catalogue of routine crime stories,
with the 'gentle touch' of the title always evident
in Maggie's investigations.

Maggie Forbes held the distinction of being
British TV's first female detective in a starring
role. Her colleagues at Seven Dials were
Detective Inspector Bob Croft, Det. Sgt Jake
Barratt, Detective Sgt Jimmy Fenton and, later,
Detective Sgt Peter Philips. Their grouchy boss
was DCI Russell. After four years, Maggie left
Seven Dials, only to resurface in *C.A.T.S. Eyes*.

GEORGE AND MILDRED

UK (Thames) Situation Comedy. ITV 1976–9

George Roper ....Brian Murphy
Mildred Roper ....Yootha Joyce
Jeffrey Fourmile ....Norman Eshley
Ann Fourmile ....Sheila Fearn
Tristram Fourmile ....Nicholas Bond-Owen
Ethel ....Avril Elgar
Humphrey..Reginald Marsh
Jerry ....Roy Kinnear

Writers: Johnnie Mortimer, Brian Cooke.
Producer: Peter Frazer-Jones

**The further adventures of the feuding
landlord and landlady from *Man about the
House*.**

In this spin-off, George and Mildred Roper had
moved from their ground-floor flat to a middle-
class housing development (46 Peacock Crescent,
Hampton Wick). There, the pushy, man-hungry
Mildred strived to be upwardly mobile and the
weedy, shiftless George – with his motorcycle and
sidecar – defiantly proclaimed his working-class
roots. Next door lived the Fourmiles: snotty
Jeffrey, his likeable wife, Ann, and their bespectacled young son, Tristram, who was constantly
corrupted by George. The Fourmiles later added
baby Tarquin to their family. Regular visitors,
much to Mildred's embarassment, were her mate-
rialistic sister, Ethel, and brother-in-law,
Humphrey. Jerry was George's layabout pal and
Truffles Mildred's pampered Yorkshire terrier.

Like *Man about the House*, which became *Three's
Company* in the USA, this series was also translated into an American version, *The Ropers*, starring Norman Fell and Audra Lindley.

GEORGE AND THE DRAGON

UK (ATV) Situation Comedy. ITV 1966–8

George Russell ....Sid James
Gabrielle Dragon..................................Peggy Mount
Colonel Maynard...........................John Le Mesurier
Ralph ....Keith Marsh

Creators/Writers: Vince Powell, Harry Driver.
Producers: Alan Tarrant, Shaun O'Riordan

**A lecherous chauffeur has his style cramped
by a formidable new housekeeper.**

Randy George Russell was driver and general
handyman to the distinguished Colonel Maynard
and enjoyed his privileged position in the stately
household. That all changed, however, when a
new housekeeper was appointed. George's wandering hands had already seen off 16 domestics,
but when Miss Gabrielle Dragon arrived, recommended by the Premier Domestic Agency, there
was little chance of George making unwanted
advances to *her*. A bellowing, battleaxe of a
widow, Gabrielle had reverted to her (appropriate) maiden name on the death of her husband,
and now battle duly commenced between
George and the Dragon. Also seen was Ralph,
the smelly, sloppy gardener.

**GEORGE BURNS AND GRACIE ALLEN
SHOW, The** see *Burns and Allen Show, The*.

GEORGESON, TOM (1941–)

Prolific, Liverpudlian actor, best known today as
Inspector Harry Naylor in *Between the Lines* but
previously one of the stars of *Boys from the
Blackstuff* (as Dixie Dean). Georgeson's other
credits have been many, with the major offerings

being *The Manageress* (as Eddie), *When the Boat Comes In*, *The Bill*, *Turtle's Progress*, *Maybury*, *Les Girls*, *Scully*, *Dempsey and Makepeace*, *Stay Lucky*, *Resnick*, *The Last Place on Earth* and *GBH* (as Lou Barnes).

GERBER, DAVID (1925–)

Prolific and successful American producer of the 1970s, working on shows like *Cade's County*, *Nanny and The Professor*, *The Ghost and Mrs Muir*, *Born Free*, *Police Story*, *Police Woman*, *Gibbsville* and *The Quest*. In 1986 he joined the newly merged MGM and United Artists, introducing new blood and building up the company's prime-time share through such series as like *thirtysomething* and *In the Heat of the Night*. He went on to become head of the MGM Worldwide Television Group.

GET SMART

US (Talent Associates/Heyday) Situation Comedy. BBC 1 1965–9

Maxwell Smart	Don Adams
Agent 99	Barbara Feldon
Thaddeus ('The Chief')	Edward Platt
Agent 13	Dave Ketchum
Professor Carlson	Stacy Keach
Conrad Siegfried	Bernie Kopell
Starker	King Moody
Hymie, the robot	Dick Gautier
Agent 44	Victor French
Agent Larrabee	Robert Karvelas
Charlie Watkins	Angelique Pettyjohn
99's mother	Jane Dulo

Creators: Mel Brooks, Buck Henry. Producer: Leonard Stern

Spoof on the James Bond/*Man from UNCLE* espionage capers, featuring an incompetent secret agent and his ineffective colleagues.

Maxwell Smart was Agent 86 for CONTROL, an intelligence service with headquarters ten storeys beneath Main Street in Washington DC. The offices were entered through the bottom of a telephone kiosk. Disaster-prone, but always enthusiastic, Smart operated undercover as a salesman for the Pontiac Greeting Card Company and wound up in the most embarrassing predicaments for a spy. He usually blundered his way through, but not before saying 'Sorry about that Chief' umpteen times to Thaddeus, his long-suffering boss.

CONTROL's adversaries were KAOS, run by the megalomaniac Siegfried and his sidekick, Starker. Against them, Smart worked closely with his attractive and intelligent partner, Agent 99 (her real name was never revealed), who later became

his wife and bore him twins. Another colleague was Agent 13, who took his undercover role rather too seriously, hiding in the most unusual places, like mailboxes and vending machines. There were also Agent Larrabee, who was even dimmer than Smart, Charlie Watkins, a spy in drag (but that was some make-up!), and Fang, a dog, code-numbered Agent K13.

Smart was generously supplied with gadgetry to help him perform his duties, although these devices (such as a telephone hidden in his shoe) never functioned quite as intended. For top secret discussions, CONTROL used an anti-bugging device known as the Cone of Silence, a clear dome which descended from the ceiling. Whilst the intention was that people *outside* the dome would not hear the conversation, unfortunately those *inside* were similarly excluded. In addition, CONTROL had an intelligent robot, Hymie, which took every command literally, with disastrous results.

GET SOME IN

UK (Thames) Situation Comedy. ITV 1975–8

Corporal Percy Marsh	Tony Selby
Jakey Smith	Robert Lindsay
	Karl Howman
Ken Richardson	David Janson
Bruce Leckie	Brian Pettifer
Matthew Lilley	Gerard Ryder
Alice Marsh	Lori Wells
Min	Madge Hindle
Corporal Wendy Williams	Jenny Cryst

Creators/Writers: John Esmonde, Bob Larbey. Producer: Michael Mills

Four young lads are drafted into the RAF, where they are bullied by a brainless corporal.

Like *The Army Game* before it, *Get Some In* focused on the National Service years, when thousands of unwilling and often unsuitable young men were conscripted into the forces. This time the action took place in 1955, at RAF Skelton, where the motley draftees included teddy boy Jakey Smith, dim Scotsman Bruce Leckie, wet vicar's son Matthew Lilley and clean-living, level-headed, grammar school boy Ken Richardson. On arrival at the camp, their worst nightmare was realized when they were assigned to the care of Corporal Marsh, a vindictive, cowardly bully-boy. Marsh made his intentions clear from the start – 'My name is Marsh: B.A.S.T.A.R.D. Marsh' – and, treating his charges like lackies, he made their training period a misery. However, it was usually Marsh who suffered in the end, as the lads, led by 'Poof House' Richardson, easily outwitted their thick NCO.

After subsequent training as nursing assistants at RAF Midham (again alongside Marsh), the lads were posted to Malta but were immediately recalled to RAF Hospital Druidswater. There, they found themselves intimidated yet again by Marsh, who now enjoyed hero status having allegedly carried a superior officer 84 miles to safety in the snows of Labrador. Marsh's demanding wife, Alice, was also seen, as was NAAFI serving girl Min and Leckie's butch girlfriend and later wife, Corporal Wendy.

GHOST

A distortion or double image on a TV picture, generally caused by signals bouncing off another building, or badly positioned aerials.

GHOST SQUAD/GS5

UK (Rank/ATV) Police Drama. ITV 1961–4

Nick Craig...Michael Quinn
Sir Andrew Wilson ....Donald Wolfit
Helen Winters ....Angela Browne
Tony Miller ....Neil Hallett
Geoffrey Stock...................................Anthony Marlowe
Jean Carter ....Claire Nielson
Peter Clarke.......................................Ray Barrett

Producers: Connery Chappell, Anthony Kearey, Dennis Vance

The dangerous adventures of a team of undercover policemen.

The 'Ghost Squad', an elite division of Scotland Yard, operated in total secrecy. Their job was to infiltrate underworld gangs, spy rings or other secret societies, lying low for possibly months at a time and using an alias which only they and their direct superior knew about. They could not rely on the regular police force or other governmental agencies for their salvation: their lives were on the line and this contributed to the suspense of each episode. Number one agent was American Nick Craig, a master of disguise. Tony Miller was his friend and colleague, and their superior was Sir Andrew Wilson, supported by his secretary, Helen Winters. When Wilson and Winters were posted to another department, they were succeeded by Geoffrey Stock and his secretary, Jean Carter, who also became an agent.

The dangers of the job were poignantly illustrated at the end of the second season, when Craig was killed by a bomb. When the programme returned, he had been replaced by the meek and more methodical Peter Clarke, who offered quite a contrast to Miller, his tough and physical partner. The programme title also changed, to GS5. The series was based on the book The Ghost Squad, an account of real police undercover activity, by former detective John Gosling.

GIDEON'S WAY

UK (ATV) Police Drama. ITV 1965–6

Commander George Gideon ....John Gregson
Chief Inspector David Keen...........Alexander Davion
Kate Gideon..................................Daphne Anderson

Producers: Robert S. Baker, Monty Berman

Determined detection with a talented Scotland Yard sleuth.

Filmed in documentary fashion, with much location shooting, the gritty, somewhat violent Gideon's Way told of the CID investigations of Commander George Gideon and his partner, Chief Inspector David Keen, two men who had worked their way up through the force. The series, transmitted in the USA under the title Gideon CID, and based on the novels by John Creasey, aka J.J. Marric, followed a 1958 film version, Gideon's Day, starring Jack Hawkins.

GILBERT, JAMES (1923–)

British producer, with the BBC from the early 1960s, although latterly in the independent sector, responsible for comedies like **It's a Square World**, **The Seven Faces of Jim**, The Big Noise (with Joe McGrath), Barney Is My Darling, **Not Only . . . But Also . . .** , The Walrus and the Carpenter, **The Frost Report**, The Old Campaigner, **Me Mammy**, **Whatever Happened to the Likely Lads?**, **The Two Ronnies**, **Last of the Summer Wine**, **French Fields** and The Labours of Erica.

GILES, BILL, OBE (1939–)

Devon-born meteorologist, a BBC weather presenter since 1975 and head of the BBC Weather Centre since 1983. He closes his forecasts with a trademark wink to the camera.

GILL, MICHAEL (1923–)

British producer/director of documentaries, in charge of Kenneth Clark's **Civilisation** and Alistair Cooke's **America**.

GILLIGAN'S ISLAND

US (Gladasaya/United Artists) Situation Comedy. ITV 1965–

Gilligan ....Bob Denver
Jonas Grumby ('The Skipper') ....Alan Hale, Jnr
Thurston Howell III ....Jim Backus
Mrs Lovey Howell ....Natalie Schafer
Roy Hinkley ('The Professor') ....Russell Johnson
Ginger Grant ....Tina Louise
Mary Ann Summers ....Dawn Wells

Creator/Executive Producer: Sherwood Schwartz

A group of castaways tries to escape from a tropical island.

A rough time was in store for the motley band of tourists on board the good ship *Minnow*. During their three-hour charter cruise from Honolulu, a storm blew up, the boat was lost and they were shipwrecked on a desolate South Pacific island. Their futile attempts to escape and return home provided this sitcom's storylines.

The castaways included two members of the boat's crew, the genial, chubby Skipper and the incompetent first mate, Gilligan, who was usually responsible for the failure of escape bids. Other members of the party were obnoxious millionaire Thurston Howell III and his dim wife, Lovey; 'The Professor', a science teacher and the group's escape planner; Mary Ann Summers, a simple country girl from Horners Corners, Kansas; and glamorous movie starlet Ginger Grant. However, realism was not *Gilligan's Island*'s strong point. Numerous guest stars turned up to help the party to get off the island, but how these visitors came and went was never explained, nor was the cast's changes of clothes or the presence of a reference library used by The Professor. If the cruise was only meant to be three hours long, how come they were now so far from civilization?

Gilligan's Island only enjoyed a sporadic screening in the UK. As a result, star Alan Hale, Jnr has always been better known in Britain as *Casey Jones*. Two or three revivals were made for American audiences in the late 1970s and early 1980s.

GILMORE, PETER (1931–)

German-born, Yorkshire-raised actor, a hit in the 1970s as handsome sea captain James Onedin. Previously, Gilmore had been a singer with the George Mitchell singers and, in addition to stage and film work, had appeared in the TV series *Hugh and I*, as well as having his own song and dance act. When *The Onedin Line* ended, Gilmore's work became less obvious, though he did play safari park supremo Ben Bishop in *One By One* and starred in the drama *A Man Called Intrepid*. His two marriages have both been to actresses, to Una Stubbs and Jan Waters.

GIRL FROM UNCLE, THE

US (Arena/MGM) Spy. BBC 1 1966–7

April Dancer	Stefanie Powers
Mark Slate	Noel Harrison
Alexander Waverly	Leo G. Carroll
Randy Kovacs	Randy Kirby

Producer: Douglas Benton

A female secret agent and her British partner fight an anarchic global crime syndicate.

In this spin-off from *The Man from UNCLE*, The Girl from UNCLE was April Dancer, paired on assignments with British agent Mark Slate (played by Rex Harrison's son, Noel). Like their counterparts in the original series, they took their orders from agency supremo Mr Waverly and worked to combat the efforts of THRUSH to take over the world. Robert Vaughn, as Napoleon Solo, made the odd cross-over appearance, but this series, coming hot on the heels of the campy *Batman*, was even more far-fetched than the original UNCLE adventures and quickly died a death.

Dancer and Slate first appeared in a *Man from UNCLE* episode entitled *The Moonglow Affair*, but the roles were filled at the time by former Miss America Mary Ann Mobley and veteran actor Norman Fell. In the UK, *The Girl from UNCLE* and *The Man from UNCLE* shared the same BBC 1 time slot, appearing on alternate weeks.

GIRLS ABOUT TOWN

UK (ATV) Situation Comedy. ITV 1970–1

Rosemary Pilgrim	Julie Stevens
Brenda Liversedge	Denise Coffey
George Pilgrim	Robin Parkinson
Harold Liversedge	Peter Baldwin
Mrs Pilgrim	Dorothy Reynolds

Creator/Writer: Adele Rose. Producer: Shaun O'Riordan

Two bored housewives try to spice up their lives.

Suffering from a severe case of marriage tedium, housewife friends Rosemary Pilgrim and Brenda Liversedge decided to add some zest to their lives by getting out and about. They hoped to make their husbands sit up and take notice, but with little success. Adding to Rosemary's frustration was her interfering, true blue mother-in-law.

The series sprang from a 1969 single drama starring Anna Quayle and Barbara Mullaney (later *Coronation Street*'s Rita Fairclough), in which Rosemary and Brenda joined an escort agency. When the series began, another future *Street* name, Peter Baldwin (Derek Wilton), was added to the cast, and the roles of Rosemary were filled by former *Play School* presenter Julie Stevens and *Do Not Adjust Your Set* star Denise Coffey.

GIRLS ON TOP

UK (Central) Situation Comedy. ITV 1985–6

Candice	Tracey Ullman
Amanda	Dawn French
Jennifer	Jennifer Saunders
Shelley	Ruby Wax

Lady Carlton ....Joan Greenwood

Writers: Dawn French, Jennifer Saunders, Ruby Wax. Producers: Paul Jackson, Trevor Walton

Four zany, but incompatible, girls share a London flat.

Described by some as a female equivalent of *The Young Ones*, *Girls on Top* concerned four wacky girls who shared a comfortably appointed Chelsea flat, owned by Lady Carlton, a batty romantic novelist who lived downstairs. The four were the mendacious Candice (a blonde hypochondriac), domineering feminist Amanda (who worked for a magazine called *Spare Cheeks*), slouchy, slow-witted Jennifer and rich, brash American Shelley (who had come to London to be an actress). When the second season began, Candice had left for the USA (actress Tracey Ullman also headed in that direction).

GIVE US A BREAK

UK (BBC) Comedy Drama. BBC 1 1983

Mickey Noades ....Robert Lindsay
Mo Morris..Paul McGann
Tina Morris..Shirin Taylor
Ron Palmer ....David Daker

Creator/Writer: Geoff McQueen. Producer: Terence Williams

An East End wide boy takes a snooker prodigy under his wing.

Mickey Noades was a 36-year-old waster who had never made anything of his life. For a living, he gambled and wheeled and dealed, spending much of his time in Ron Palmer's pub, The Crown & Sceptre, where his girlfriend, Tina, was a barmaid. When Tina's young brother, Mo, arrived from jobless Liverpool, Mickey made him less than welcome, until he realized that Mo was an exceptional snooker player. With plenty of money to be made from hustling in London's snooker halls, Mickey saw his life open up before him and his 'big break' just around the corner.

The series was the first drama written by former carpenter Geoff McQueen, who later went on to create *The Bill*. A Christmas special was produced in 1984. Snooker coaching for the series was provided by professional Geoff Foulds.

GIVE US A CLUE

UK (Thames) Game Show. ITV 1979–91

Presenters: Michael Aspel, Michael Parkinson

Producers: Juliet Grimm, David Clark, Robert Reed, Keith Beckett

Light-hearted celebrity charades game.

Michael Aspel and, from 1984, Michael Parkinson, tried to keep order in this TV version of the ancient parlour game charades. A team of male celebrities (led by Lionel Blair) took on a team of women (captained by Una Stubbs and later Liza Goddard), with each member of the team having to perform a mime in turn, hoping to convey to their colleagues the title of a book, film, TV programme, show, song, etc. To spice things up, a number of risqué titles were dropped in, daring the stars to be a bit cheeky.

GLAISTER, GERARD, DFC (1915–)

Former RAF Squadron Leader and decorated spitfire pilot who became a BBC drama producer. Much of his work has been in a common vein, namely behind the scenes business sagas, as typified by *Oil Strike North*, **The Brothers**, *Buccaneer*, *Howards' Way* and **Trainer**, although probably his greatest achievement was **Colditz**, which he devised with Brian Degas. N.J. Crisp has been another of Glaister's collaborators. Other production credits have included *The Men from Room 13*, **Dr Finlay's Casebook**, *Moonstrike*, *The Revenue Men*, **The Expert**, *Codename*, **Secret Army** and *Kessler*.

GLASER, PAUL MICHAEL (1943–)

Dark-haired American actor and director whose claim to fame has been the role of Detective Dave Starsky in the all-action 1970s cop series **Starsky and Hutch**. Glaser's earliest TV work came in daytime soaps and through guest appearances in shows like **The Waltons**. After hanging up Starsky's chunky cardigans he turned more to directing, although he has cropped up in a number of TV movies, including *The Great Houdinis,* in which he played escapologist Harry Houdini. His wife, Elizabeth, a long-time AIDS sufferer and campaigner, died in 1994.

GLESS, SHARON (1943–)

Blonde American actress, Detective Christine Cagney in **Cagney and Lacey**. Earlier, Gless had broken into television playing secretaries and other secondary roles. She was Holly Barrett in the detective series *Faraday and Company*, nurse Kathleen Faverty in **Marcus Welby, MD**, receptionist Maggie in *Switch* and took minor parts in **McCloud**, *Cool Million* and other shows. When Meg Foster was dropped from *Cagney and Lacey* in 1982, for giving the series a gloss that was too tough and unfeminine, Gless was called up to take her place. She later starred in the legal drama series *The Trials of Rosie O'Neill*.

GLITTERING PRIZES, THE

UK (BBC) Drama. BBC 2 1976

Adam Morris ....Tom Conti

Barbara Morris ....Barbara Kellerman
Lionel Morris ....Leonard Sachs
Joyce Hadleigh/Bradley ....Angela Down
Dan Bradley ....Malcolm Stoddart
Barbara Ransome ....Anna Carteret
Mike Clode......................................Mark Wing-Davey
Anna Cunningham ....Emily Richard
Alan Parks...John Gregg
Bill Bourne ....Clive Merrison
Stephen Taylor ....Eric Porter
Gavin Pope ....Dinsdale Landen

Writer: Frederic Raphael. Producer: Mark Shivas

The changing lives of a group of Cambridge students.

Beginning in 1953, when its protagonists were all Cambridge undergraduates, *The Glittering Prizes* followed a group of young intellectuals through to their middle-age in the 1970s, charting the ups and downs in their varied lives. The central character was Adam Morris, who became a wealthy novelist. Taking the form of six 80-minute plays, the series won much critical acclaim. On a similar theme, author Frederic Raphael followed up with *Oxbridge Blues*, seven plays which were screened in 1984.

GLOVER, BRIAN (1934–)

Yorkshire-born actor, presenter and writer, a one-time professional wrestler. A familiar face on television, Glover has asked the questions on the science show *Don't Ask Me*, played dimwit Heslop in *Porridge*, featured as the frightening Tommy Beamish in *Lost Empires* and carried Peter Davison's bags in *Campion*, as the detective's manservant Magersfontein Lugg. In addition, he starred as Edgar Rowley in the comedy *South of the Border*, appeared as Yorkie in *Minder* and Selwyn Price in *Anna Lee*, and has also been seen in *All Creatures Great and Small*, *Whatever Happened to the Likely Lads?*, *Dixon of Dock Green*, *The Regiment*, *Secret Army*, *Return of the Saint*, *Foxy Lady* and *Bottom*, among many offerings. He is also the voice of the Tetley teafolk in their various commercials.

GMTV

(Good Morning Television) Breakfast television station which – under the consortium name of Sunrise Television – won the early morning ITV franchise from TV-am in the 1991 auctions. Carlton Communications (owner of the franchise for the London region and also the Midlands, via Central) owns 20 per cent of the company, which broadcasts from London's South Bank television centre. The output is a mixture of news, reaction, general magazine items and cartoons. However, its first year on air (beginning 1 January 1993) proved to be rather shaky, with a formal warning given by the ITC for failing to meet the service level promised in its licence application, particularly with regard to current affairs and children's programmes. It did note, though, that the company had already made moves towards addressing this criticism through changes in personnel and the improvement of journalistic elements.

GNOMES OF DULWICH, THE

UK (BBC) Situation Comedy. BBC1 1969

Big ....Terry Scott
Small ....Hugh Lloyd
Old ....John Clive

Creator/Writer: Jimmy Perry. Producer: Graeme Muir

Pearls of wisdom from a trio of garden gnomes.

Big, Small and Old were three stone gnomes in a Dulwich garden who spent their time discussing the state of the human race, prompted by the actions (unseen) of people who passed them by. The gnomes also enjoyed a rivalry with their plastic counterparts in the garden next door.

GOD SLOT

The irreverent term for early Sunday evening when religious programmes have historically been scheduled on British TV. However, the slot has been eroded over the years and ITV has now abandoned it altogether, leaving BBC 1 to uphold the tradition with *Songs of Praise*.

GODDARD, LIZA (1950–)

English actress, fond of plummy, giggly roles. Some of her earliest appearances were alongside *Skippy the Bush Kangaroo*, playing Clancy Merrick. Moving from Australia back to the UK, she was Victoria in *Take Three Girls* (and reprised the role for a 1982 update, *Take Three Women*), Lily Pond/Browne in *Yes, Honestly* and worked with her future husband, Colin Baker, in *The Brothers*. In the 1980s she starred as mistress Nellie Bligh in *Pig in the Middle*, Claire in the advertising sitcom *Watch this Space*, piano teacher Belinda Purcell in *Roll Over Beethoven* and Laurel Manasotti in *That's Love*, as well as being a frequent guest in *Bergerac*, playing diamond thief Philippa Vale. Among her many other credits have been parts in T*he Befrienders*, *Holding On*, *Wodehouse Playhouse*, *Tales of the Unexpected*, *Woof!*, *Doctor Who* and numerous panel games. Her second husband was pop star Alvin Stardust.

GOING FOR A SONG

UK (BBC) Game Show. BBC 1 1965–77

Presenter: Max Robertson

Producers: John Irving, John King, Paul Smith

Subdued quiz in which panellists attempt to guess the value of an antique.

Produced by the BBC in Bristol, *Going for a Song* was the forerunner to *Antiques Roadshow*, but with echoes of the earlier *Animal, Vegetable, Mineral?*. Chairman Max Robertson offered an intriguing piece of antiquity to his distinguished guests (Customers versus Connoisseurs), who worked out what the item was and then estimated its sales value. Points were awarded for the closest guess. Arthur Negus made his name as a regular pundit and the programme was characterized by the twittering of a caged mechanical bird over the opening and closing credits.

GOING STRAIGHT see *Porridge*.

GOLD ROBBERS, THE

UK (LWT) Police Drama. ITV 1969

Detective Chief Supt Cradock ....Peter Vaughan
Detective Sgt Toms ....Artro Morris
Inspector Tompkins ....Michael Wynne

Creators: John Hawkesworth, Glyn Jones.
Producer: John Hawkesworth

An aircraft load of gold bullion is stolen in a breathtaking crime. In charge of the investigation is formidable CID man Cradock.

This 13-part serial, created by John Hawkesworth (*Upstairs, Downstairs*) and Glyn Jones, cast Peter Vaughan in an unusual role. Now famed for his arch-criminal performances (especially 'Genial' Harry Grout in *Porridge*), he found himself on the other side of the law in this earlier outing, with his character totally committed to cracking this dare-devil crime, recovering gold ingots worth £5½ million and, one by one, bringing the perpetrators to book. Not so surprising was George Cole, who appeared as a guest star in one episode, playing a second-rate conman.

GOLDEN GIRLS, THE

US (Witt-Thomas-Harris/Touchstone)
Situation Comedy. Channel 4 1986–93

Dorothy Zbornak ....Beatrice Arthur
Blanche Devereaux ....Rue McClanahan
Rose Nylund ....Betty White
Sophia Petrillo...Estelle Getty
Stanley Zbornak ....Herb Edelman
Miles Webber...Harold Gould

Creator: Susan Harris. Executive Producers:
Paul Junger Witt, Tony Thomas, Marc Sotkin,
Susan Harris

Four mature Florida ladies enjoy their 'golden years' together.

The four sparky 'Golden Girls' were out to prove one thing: not only did life begin at 40, but it got better in the 50s and 60s. The girls shared a roomy bungalow in Miami, owned by Blanche Devereaux, a widowed Southern belle with an enormous appetite for men. Her friends were Dorothy Zbornak, a divorced, level-headed schoolteacher, Rose Nylund, a scatty widow of Scandinavian descent, and Sophia Petrillo, Dorothy's resourceful mother, who had moved in with the others after her Shady Pines retirement home had burned down.

Blanche was the genuine merry widow, openly flirtatious and scandalously brazen, while Dorothy was tall, cynical and a touch domineering. She was occasionally visited by Stan, the hapless husband who had left her after 38 years to live with an air hostess. Naive Rose was prone to misunderstandings and the others dreaded her long-winded and pointless tales about her home town, St Olaf, Minnesota. Sicilian-born Sophia, meanwhile, was dry and forthright. Having suffered a stroke which had damaged the tact cells of her brain, she pulled no punches and everyone received the sharp end of her tongue.

Although the girls lived life to the full, the more worrying side of growing old was never forgotten. Grouped around the kitchen table for midnight ice cream feasts, the foursome openly discussed their feelings and their worries – about men, about their families, about themselves. What came through more than anything was the special relationship they enjoyed, echoed in the theme song, 'Thank You for Being a Friend'.

The Golden Girls came to an end when Dorothy married Blanche's Uncle Lucas (played by Leslie Nielsen) and moved away from Miami. The three others also moved – into a hotel and a spin-off series entitled *The Golden Palace*.

GOLDEN SHOT, THE

UK (ATV) Game Show. ITV 1967–75

Presenters:
Jackie Rae
Bob Monkhouse
Norman Vaughan
Charlie Williams

Producers: Colin Clews, John Pullen, Edward Joffe, Mike Lloyd, Les Cocks, Dicky Leeman

Colourful crossbow shooting for prizes.

In this popular live game show, contestants fired crossbows at cartoon targets in an effort to win cash and other prizes. Hosted initially by Canadian *Spot the Tune* veteran Jackie Rae, *The Golden Shot* was not an immediate hit. In the hands of Rae's successor, Bob Monkhouse, however, it became one of the biggest shows of its day, notching up large audiences for its Sunday teatime timeslot (having transferred from Saturday nights). Monkhouse was himself succeeded by Norman Vaughan and then Charlie Williams, before returning to adminster the last rites to a tired and dying show in 1975.

Based on a successful German concept, the programme consisted of a series of shooting games. Viewers at home, by way of telephone, could direct a blindfolded marksman to fire at the target, using basic directions like 'Up a bit, down a bit, left a bit, fire', etc. Other games involved studio contestants taking over control of the crossbows themselves. They shot at bright, humorous pictures and scored by piercing targets made of apple. The ultimate prize was a treasure chest of gold coins that spilled out on to the studio floor when a slender thread was broken. Celebrities mingled with participants and TV cameras were built into the crossbows to show viewers at home how the contestants were aiming.

Supporting the hosts were the 'Golden Girls', initially Andrea Lloyd, Carol Dilworth and Anita Richardson, but most famously dizzy blonde Anne Aston (whose maths as she added up the target totals always left room for improvement). Aston was later assisted by a guest 'Maid of the Month'. Bernie the Bolt was the silent man who loaded the crossbows, although there were in fact three 'Bernies' employed during the programme's eight-year run (Derek Young, Alan Bailey and, best-remembered, Johnny Baker).

GOOD GUYS, THE

UK (LWT/Haverhall) Comedy Drama. ITV 1992–3

Guy MacFadyean......................................Nigel Havers
Guy Lofthouse ....Keith Barron

Executive Producer: Nick Elliott. Producers: Andrew Montgomery, Michael Whitehall

Two well-meaning, out-of-work characters join forces to help others, but without much success.

When Guy Lofthouse walked out on his marriage and job in Leeds, he found himself in Richmond, Surrey – and somewhat bewildered by life in the south. Meeting his equally unemployed namesake, Guy MacFadyean, the two Guys struck up a friendship and agreed to share a flat. To put some purpose into their empty lives, they set about helping other people, with unpredictable results.

The series was specially created for Nigel Havers and Keith Barron, to enable the two actors to work together. It was made for LWT by Nigel Havers's own production company, Haverhall.

GOOD, JACK (1930–)

TV's Mr Pop Music. Beginning with *Six-Five Special* in 1957, Jack Good revolutionized television coverage of the music scene. At last, here was someone (who had joined the BBC as a trainee only in 1956) actually producing programmes for teenage music fans, even if he cautiously sold it to the stuffy Corporation as a young person's magazine. One of the unusual and pioneering features was use of the audience, not ignoring them but bringing them into proceedings. Controversially sacked a year later, he moved to ABC to produce a rival show, *Oh Boy!*, which ultimately saw the end of the by now staid *Six-Five Special*. In 1959 he created *Boy Meets Girls*, a vehicle for Marty Wilde, and a year later, *Wham!!*. Good was even a hit across the Atlantic, devising *Shindig* and numerous other pop successes. *Oh Boy!* was briefly revived in the late 1970s.

GOOD LIFE, THE

UK (BBC) Situation Comedy. BBC 1 1975–8

Tom Good ....Richard Briers
Barbara Good ....Felicity Kendall
Margo Leadbetter ....Penelope Keith
Jerry Leadbetter ....Paul Eddington

Creators/Writers: John Esmonde, Bob Larbey.
Producer: John Howard Davies

A young couple go self-sufficient in Surbiton.

Tom Good had become tired of the rat race. On his 40th birthday, sick of commuting to his draughtsman's job in the City (where he created cereal gifts for the JJM company), he threw it all in to concentrate on home farming. Ably and inventively assisted by Barbara, his perky wife, the buoyant Tom turned his back garden into an allotment, growing fruit and vegetables and housing chickens, pigs, a cockerel named Lenin and even a goat named Geraldine. For heating and cooking they restored an old cast iron range, and for power they ran a generator in the cellar. Living off the land, and bartering away the surplus with local shopkeepers, the Goods thrived on the joys of self-sufficiency, even if there were moments of deep despair.

It was at times like these that their true blue neighbours, Jerry and Margo, came to the rescue. Although they considered Tom and Barbara to be completely insane, and to have brought 'The Avenue' into disrepute, they remained loyal friends. Even if Margo hated donning wellies to feed the pigs, she still did so and she and Jerry (a former work colleague of Tom's) always took great interest in events next door. In return, the Goods brought a ray of wholesome sunshine into the depressingly snobbish life of their wealthier neighbours.

GOOD MORNING BRITAIN see TV-am.

GOOD MORNING TELEVISION see GMTV.

GOOD OLD DAYS, THE

UK (BBC) Variety. BBC 1 1953–83

Chairmen: Don Gemmell, Leonard Sachs.
Producer: Barney Colehan

The days of the music hall re-created.

Indelibly associated with its loud and wordy compere, Leonard Sachs (who took over from first chairman Don Gemmell), *The Good Old Days* owed just as much to its long-serving producer, Barney Colehan, who was responsible for developing this music hall revival show. Broadcast (somewhat irregularly) from one of the true surviving music halls, the City Varieties in Leeds, the programme lasted over 30 years and provided older viewers with a happy slice of golden age nostalgia. Its guest stars (the likes of Roy Hudd, Danny La Rue, Ray Alan, Ken Dodd, etc.) performed music hall acts in the style of Marie Lloyd and others, and dressed for the part in 1890s costume. So did the studio audience, who donned false sideburns and frilly hats and were encouraged to join in proceedings by singing along or waving a handkerchief. And then there was the polysyllabic Leonard Sachs himself, filled with vociferous verbosity, never using one word when 27 would do, smashing down his gavel and rousing the audience to a rapturous welcome for the most unheard-of performers. The Players' Theatre Company and the Northern Dance Orchestra were the resident supporting artists and each edition ended with the cast and audience joining together in a chorus of 'The Old Bull and Bush'.

GOOD SEX GUIDE, THE

UK (Carlton) Comedy/Information. ITV 1993–4

Presenter: Margi Clarke

Producer: Vicki Barrass

Forthright advice on sex, interspersed with personal views and expert opinions, but with humorous sketches to ease embarrassment.

Margi Clarke's colourful commentary added a down-to-earth, matter-of-factness to the 'awkward' and intimate subjects considered by this late-night programme, which tackled the taboo subject of 'getting the most out of sex'. Among the actors offering light relief through assorted comedy sketches were Tony Robinson, Linda Robson, Pauline Quirke, Stephanie Cole,

Bernard Hill, Roger Lloyd Pack, Julia Hills, Haydn Gwynne and Timothy Spall. Clarke returned with a second series in 1994, with the likes of Leslie Grantham, Nigel Planer and Martin Clunes contributing to the fun.

GOODIES, THE

UK (BBC/LWT) Comedy. BBC 2 1970–80/ITV 1981–82

Graeme	Graeme Garden
Tim	Tim Brooke-Taylor
Bill	Bill Oddie

Creators/Writers: Graeme Garden, Tim Brooke-Taylor, Bill Oddie. Executive Producer: David Bell (LWT). Producers: John Howard Davies, Jim Franklin (BBC), Bob Spiers (LWT)

Zany humour with a trio of do-gooders.

Graeme, Tim and Bill were benefactors to society, available to do anything, anywhere and at any time to help humanity. Taking on the weirdest assignments, they found themselves guarding the Crown Jewels, rescuing London from the advance of a giant kitten, and in other bizarre situations. Sometimes they cooked up their own world improvement schemes and attempted to put them into action. Energetically charging around on a three-seater bicycle (a trandem), the three formed an unlikely team.

Tim was a cowardly patriot, sporting a Union Jack waistcoat, Graeme was a mad scientist type and Bill was an unkempt, hairy cynic. They lived in a typical 1970s flat, dominated by portraits of the Queen (for Tim) and Chairman Mao (for Bill), plus Graeme's cardboard box computer. Their adventures were punctuated with crazy sight gags, slapstick sketches and spoof TV commercials.

There were send-ups galore as the trio took contemporary fads or issues and placed them in different contexts. Examples included episodes entitled *Ecky-Thump* (a North Country spoof on the Kung Fu craze), *Planet of the Rabbits* (a **Doctor Who** parody) and *Bun Fight at the OK Tea Rooms*. Bill Oddie's original music featured prominently and, in one episode, he appeared as pop star Randy Pandy, singing on **Top of the Pops**. The Goodies also had five real life hits in the 1970s (most notably, alas, 'Funky Gibbon' in 1975).

Originally planned as *Super-Chaps Three*, *The Goodies* was one of BBC 2's biggest successes of the 1970s, enjoying repeat showings on BBC 1. However, disillusioned with the Corporation's lack of commitment to the programme, the team moved to LWT for a short run in 1981–2, by which time the concept had dated somewhat.

GOODMAN, JOHN (1952–)

Giant American comic actor, achieving star status as Dan Conner, Roseanne's husband in the successful blue collar sitcom *Roseanne*. Although his film career has really taken off, little else has been seen of him on television, save in a few TV movies.

GOODNIGHT SWEETHEART

UK (Alomo) Situation Comedy. BBC 1 1993–

Gary Sparrow	Nicholas Lyndhurst
Yvonne Sparrow	Michelle Holmes
Phoebe Bamford	Dervla Kirwan
Eric	David Ryall
Ron Wheatcroft	Victor McGuire
PC Reg Deadman	Christopher Ettridge

Creators: Laurence Marks, Maurice Gran.
Executive Producer: Allan McKeown. Producer: John Bartlett

An unhappily married TV engineer wanders through a time warp and picks up a 1940s girlfriend.

London television repair man Gary Sparrow and Yvonne, his personnel officer wife, were going through a sticky patch. She wanted more from life and was heavily involved in her Open University Pyschology degree; he had more interest in simpler matters, like the physical side of their relationship. One day, on his rounds, he wandered down Ducketts Passage, an East End alleyway, found himself lost and popped into The Royal Oak pub for directions. Having been charged tuppence-farthing for his half-pint, he assumed he had discovered a theme pub, but stepping outside again realized that he had actually slipped back in time to 1940. Taking a shine to Phoebe, the landlord's daughter, Gary soon made a habit of popping back to the war years, where the locals (and particularly Phoebe's dad, Eric) distrusted this strange young man with weird ideas who claimed to be a songwriter (his hits included 'Your Song', 'I Can't Get No Satisfaction' and 'I'm Getting Married In The Morning'). Meanwhile Yvonne was increasingly bemused by Gary's new interest in wartime nostalgia. Gary's only confidant was his printer pal Ron but when Gary tried to take him back in time, Ducketts Passage would not oblige. In the second series, shown in 1995, Phoebe's dad had died and she now ran the pub with the help of local bobby PC Deadman (actor Christopher Ettridge was also seen occasionally as Deadman's grandson, a 1990s policeman).

GOODSON, MARK (1915–)

Prolific American inventor of TV quizzes and panel games, usually in conjunction with his partner, Bill Todman. Together they were responsible for the likes of *What's My Line?*, *I've Got a Secret*, *Beat the Clock*, *Call My Bluff*, *The Price Is Right* and *Family Fortunes*. Goodson-Todman Productions was their company, formed after Goodson had worked as a radio announcer and Todman as a scriptwriter. Their ventures into drama productions were not so successful.

GOODYEAR, JULIE (1943–)

Inseparable from bold, brassy Bet Lynch/Gilroy, her character in *Coronation Street*, Julie Goodyear arrived in Weatherfield in 1966, although it wasn't until 1970 that she became a Rover's Return regular. Among her other TV credits have been Granada series like *Pardon the Expression* (the 1966 *Street* spin-off), *A Family at War*, *City '68*, *The War of Darkie Pilbeam*, *The Dustbinmen* and *Nearest and Dearest*.

GORDON, HANNAH (1941–)

Scottish actress seen in both dramatic and comedy roles. Amongst her best remembered performances have been as Suzy Bassett, with John Alderton, in *My Wife Next Door*, as Victoria Jones, Richard Briers's landlady in *Goodbye Mr Kent*, Peter Barkworth's wife (Sylvia Telford) in *Telford's Change* and as Belinda Braithwaite in another banking series, *Joint Account*, with Peter Egan. She played Virginia Hamilton, Lord Bellamy's second wife, in *Upstairs, Downstairs* and her other credits have included parts in *The Rat Catchers*, *Ladykillers*, *Middlemarch*, *Dr Finlay's Casebook*, *Hadleigh*, *The Persuaders!*, *Miss Morrison's Ghosts*, *The Protectors*, *My Family and Other Animals* and some Dickens adaptations. She was also seen with Morecambe and Wise, as one of their harassed guests.

GORDON, NOELE (1923–85)

Crossroads proprietor Meg Richardson/Mortimer, and one-time Queen of the Soaps, Noele Gordon became a household name after a long and varied career on stage and television. She first appeared in a BBC play way back in 1938 and shortly afterwards assisted John Logie Baird by appearing in one of his colour TV experiments. In the 1950s, with a string of stage plays and musicals to her name, Gordon formally studied the new medium of television in the USA and returned to the UK to work for the embryonic ATV as an adviser on women's programmes. This led to on-screen presentation work on programmes such as *Tea with Noele Gordon*, *Fancy That*, *Hi-T!*, some sports shows, the admag *About Homes and Gardens* and eventually, in 1957, the well-remembered *Lunch Box*. In 1964 she was cast as the queen bee of the company's new daily soap opera, and she remained with *Crossroads* until surprisingly axed in 1981. She made just one return visit to the series, on the occasion of her screen daughter, Jill's, marriage to Adam Chance in 1983.

GORING, MARIUS, CBE (1912–)

British character actor with a flair for accents and dialects, remembered by TV buffs as *The Scarlet Pimpernel* in the 1950s and *The Expert* in the 1960s and 1970s. A prolific film performer, Goring's first television appearance came in a Chekhov play in 1938. In 1956 he became TV's master of disguise, Sir Percy Blakeney, alias *The Scarlet Pimpernel*, saver of aristocratic French souls, in a series which he also co-produced. Goring's next starring role came 13 years later and was in quite a different vein. On this occasion he played Midlands pathologist John Hardy in *The Expert*. He resurfaced in 1983 as Dr Emile Englander, one of the Old Men at the Zoo, and among his other credits have been episodes of series as varied as *Edward and Mrs Simpson* (as King George V), *The Fall of Eagles* (as Paul von Hindenburg), *Man in a Suitcase* and *The Wilde Alliance*, plus many single dramas.

GRACE AND FAVOUR see *Are You Being Served?*

GRADE, LORD LEW (LOUIS WINOGRADSKY; 1906–)

Born in Russia, Lew Grade's showbiz career began in the world of dance (he was World Charleston Champion in 1926), but then moved into talent spotting and management. He set up the Lew and Leslie Grade agency with his younger brother and took care of many of the world's finest acts of the 1940s and 1950s. In 1955 he formed a consortium to bid for one of the ITV franchises. The resulting company, Associated Television (ATV), was given the Midlands weekday and the London weekend ITV contracts. Grade and his colleagues also established ITC (Independent Television Corporation) at the same time, with a view to producing films for television. The company was responsible for such dramas as *The Adventures of Robin Hood*, *The Saint*, *Jesus of Nazareth* and the Gerry Anderson puppet series, all aimed purposefully at the American market. Throughout ATV's time on air and ITC's time in production, Grade's influence was enormous and his personality and presence ensured his programmes were never short of publicity. His ventures into the movie business, primarily in the 1970s and 1980s, proved less lucrative. He is the uncle of TV exec-

utive Michael Grade (Leslie's son) and brother of the late Lord Bernard Delfont.

GRADE, MICHAEL (1942–)

Respected British TV executive with experience on both sides of the Atlantic. Grade began as a sports writer before joining his family's theatrical agency and subsequently moving into television. At LWT, he was Head of Light Entertainment and Director of Programmes, and, crossing to the States, spent some time with Embassy Television. He became Controller of BBC 1 in 1984 and later Director of Programmes, and during his four years at the Corporation was given credit for rejuvenating both BBC television networks, with his scheduling expertise widely acclaimed. He repositioned existing shows to their greater benefit (drawing on his intimate knowledge of ITV competition) and was responsible for commissioning and nurturing a host of new ideas. *EastEnders* was a classic case, with Grade firmly committed to its early success. *Edge of Darkness*, *The Late Show*, *Tutti Frutti* and *The Singing Detective* were other notable achievements. Grade's BBC years were not without controversy, however. In 1986 he added to the storm over *The Monocled Mutineer* by passing a press release which wrongly stated that all the facts were authentic, and, a year earlier, he had angered sci-fi fans by postponing a season of *Doctor Who* and cancelling *The Tripods* two-thirds of the way through. Since 1988 he has been chief executive of Channel 4, replacing Jeremy Isaacs. Grade is the son of talent agent the late Leslie Grade and nephew of ITV impresario Lord Lew Grade.

GRAMPIAN TELEVISION

Taking to the air on 30 September 1961, Grampian Television is the independent television contractor for North Scotland (basically from Fife north to Shetland and west to the Hebrides – the largest of all ITV franchise regions). Its main production centre is Aberdeen, but the company also operates smaller studios in Stornoway, Dundee and Inverness. Since 1976 some regional programmes have been made in Gaelic, but, while the company has a good reputation for local news and current affairs, it is not renowned for contributions to the ITV national network.

GRAN, MAURICE

British comedy scriptwriter, in collaboration with partner Laurence Marks. Together Marks and Gran have been responsible for some of the most popular sitcoms and comedy-dramas of the 1980s and 1990s. These have included *Shine On*

Harvey Moon, *Roots*, *Holding the Fort*, *Relative Strangers*, **The New Statesman**, **Roll Over Beethoven**, *Young, Gifted and Broke*, *Snakes and Ladders*, *So You Think You've Got Troubles*, **Birds of a Feather**, **Love Hurts**, **Goodnight Sweetheart**, *Get Back* and *Men of the World*.

GRANADA TELEVISION

A wholly owned subsidiary of the Granada Group, which also has interests in TV rental, cinemas, motorway service stations and the Channel Tunnel, Granada Television was formed in 1955 by Sidney (later Lord) Bernstein and his brother, Cecil, to operate the North of England ITV weekday franchise (ABC were given the weekends). Following the London ITV companies on to the air, its first programmes went out on 3 May 1956. With restructuring and the arrival of Yorkshire Television in 1968, its transmission area was re-centred on the northwest, but for the full seven days a week.

Granada has always occupied a hallowed position amongst ITV companies. One of the big five (along with Carlton, LWT, Central and Yorkshire), it has managed to combine commercial astuteness with a commitment to high-quality programming, an attribute not often recognized in commercial broadcasting. The company has fostered young writers and producers in all areas of programming, from the mass-market appeal of **Coronation Street** to the weaker audience potential of award-winning documentaries like **World in Action** and **Disappearing World**. Granada has also shown itself to be a rival to the BBC in classic drama. **Brideshead Revisited** and **The Jewel in the Crown** were lavish productions in the early 1980s and equal acclaim has since been afforded to productions such as **Prime Suspect** and **Cracker**. However, the company has also been happy to exploit cheap and cheerful, viewer-spinning concepts, including **The Comedians**, **Busman's Holiday**, **Stars in their Eyes**, **You've Been Framed** and **The Krypton Factor**.

In the 1980s Granada opened up its studios to the public, instantly creating one of Britain's major tourist attractions. Viewers can now stroll down Coronation Street, ride a tram along the Baker Street set for **The Adventures of Sherlock Holmes** and take part in a mock debate in an uncannily accurate reproduction of the House of Commons, built for the company's adaptation of Jeffrey Archer's *First Among Equals*.

Despite its impressive record, there were fears that Granada would lose its franchise in the 1991 auctions, when rival company Mersey Television, headed by Phil Redmond, outbid it by several millions. This was one decision which went in favour of quality instead of cash, however, and Granada survived. Since then, Granada – the longest surviving ITV company – has taken overall control of its fellow ITV franchisee, LWT. The company also has shares in BSkyB.

The name Granada was dreamt up by Sidney Bernstein for his theatre business in the 1920s, following a breathtaking visit to the Spanish city of the same name.

GRANDSTAND

UK (BBC) Sport. BBC 1 1958–

Presenters:
Peter Dimmock
David Coleman
Frank Bough
Desmond Lynam
Steve Rider

The BBC's Saturday afternoon sports showcase.

Heading for its 40th birthday, *Grandstand*, the world's longest-running live sports programme, is now a national institution, and Saturday afternoons would not be the same without it. Its format has changed little over the years. Live horse racing has been mixed with boxing, rugby union, rugby league, cricket, motor sports and occasional other events, and all the day's soccer and rugby details have been rounded up to provide a full results service at the end, including reports from the major matches. The final scores, as they happen, have been reported on the Teleprinter and, in latter years, its replacement, the state of the art Videprinter.

Peter Dimmock was the first host but quickly gave way to David Coleman. Frank Bough took over in 1968, but since the 1980s Desmond Lynam and Steve Rider have shared the honours. Other presenters have been drafted in as relief cover over the years, including Harry Carpenter, Harry Gratian, Bob Wilson and, more recently, Helen Rollason (first female presenter), Sue Barker, Ray Stubbs, Dougie Donnelly and Hazel Irvine. The main specialist commentators have been as follows: boxing, Harry Carpenter; rugby union, Cliff Morgan, Bill McLaren and Nigel Starmer-Smith; rugby league, Eddie Waring and Ray French; racing, Peter O'Sullevan, Clive Graham, Julian Wilson, Jimmy Lindley, Richard Pitman and Peter Scudamore; motor sports, Murray Walker; winter sports, Alan Weeks and David Vine; golf, Henry Longhurst and Peter Alliss; swimming, Alan Weekes and Hamilton Bland; cricket, Richie Benaud, Jim Laker, Peter West and Tony Lewis; athletics, Ron Pickering, Stuart Storey, David Coleman and Brendan

Foster. *Football Preview*, the look ahead to the day's soccer, was hosted for many years by Sam Leitch. *Football Focus*, its successor, was fronted by Bob Wilson until his departure to ITV in 1994. The sports results have been read by the famous voices of Len Martin (soccer) and Tim Gudgin (most of the others).

Variations on the *Grandstand* theme have included *Sunday Grandstand* (inaugurated in 1981) and extended versions for the Olympic Games, the World Cup, etc.

GRANGE HILL

UK (BBC) Children's Drama. BBC 1 1978–

Peter 'Tucker' Jenkins	Todd Carty
Mr Tony Mitchell	Michael Percival
Justin Bennett	Robert Morgan
Benny Green	Terry Sue Patt
Trisha Yates	Michelle Herbert
Ann Wilson	Lucinda Duckett
Penny Lewis	Ruth Davies
Judy Preston	Abigail Brown
Alan Hargreaves	George Armstrong
Mr Graham Sutcliffe	James Wynn
Mr Baxter	Michael Cronin
Mr Llewellyn	Sean Arnold
Simon Shaw	Paul Miller
Andrew Stanton	Mark Chapman
Michael Doyle	Vincent Hall
Cathy Hargreaves	Lyndy Brill
Mr Hopwood	Brian Capron
Mrs Bridget McCluskey	Gwyneth Powell
Pogo Patterson	Peter Moran
Michael Green	Mark Bishop
'Gripper' Stebson	Mark Savage
Duane Orpington	Mark Baxter
'Stewpot' Stewart	Mark Burdis
Pamela Cartwright	Rene Alperstein
Annette Firman	Nadia Chambers
Suzanne Ross	Susan Tully
Samuel 'Zammo' McGuire	Lee MacDonald
Roland Browning	Erkan Mustafa
Miss Mooney	Lucinda Gane
Robbie Wright	John Alford
Scruffy McGuffy	Fraser Cains
Mr Bronson	Michael Sheard
Georgina Hayes	Samantha Lewis
Lucinda	Letitia Dean
Danny Kendall	Jonathan Lambeth
Ant Jones	Ricky Simmons
Ziggy Greaves	George Christopher
Mr Mackenzie	Nicholas Donnelly
Mr Griffiths	George A. Cooper
Mr Max Hargreaves	Kevin O'Shea
Mr Geoff Hankin	Lee Cornes
Mr Peter Robson	Stuart Organ
Caroline 'Calley' Donnington	Simone Hyams
Chrissy Mainwaring	Sonya Kearns
Mrs Keele	Jenny Howe
Trevor Cleaver	John Drummond
Mrs Monroe	Anna Quayle
Fiona Wilson	Michelle Gayle
Natasha Stevens	Clare Buckfield
Natalie Stevens	Julie Buckfield
Becky Stevens	Natalie Poyser
Justine Dean	Rachel Victoria Roberts
'Tegs' Ratcliffe	Sean Maguire
Maria	Luisa Bradshaw-White
Jacko Morgan	Jamie Lehane
Robyn	Nina Fry
Miss Jayne Carver	Sally Geoghegan

Creator: Phil Redmond. Executive Producers: Anna Home, Richard Callanan. Producers: Colin Cant, Susi Hush, Kenny McBain, Ben Rea, Ronald Smedley, Albert Barber, Christine Secombe

Realistic tales of life in a London comprehensive school.

In the days when the nearest thing to unruly behaviour on children's television was an elephant wetting itself in the *Blue Peter* studio, it would have been quite unthinkable to have switched on at five o'clock and watched a schoolboy trying to kick his heroin addiction. But times move on and kids' TV certainly caught up with its viewers when the BBC launched *Grange Hill* in 1978.

The brainchild of Liverpudlian writer Phil Redmond (later to take *Brookside* to Channel 4), *Grange Hill* (screened twice a week as a children's soap opera) was school as it really was, with none of the jolly japes and wizard wheezes of Billy Bunter's days. The action took place at Grange Hill Comprehensive and, to make its intended audience feel at home, low, kids'-height camera angles were used. The series showed pupils out of control, insulting teachers, truanting, bullying weaklings, smoking and shop lifting. It covered subjects as intense as child abuse, racism, sex, pregnancy, job hunting and, yes, drugs, and, whilst it received no thanks from Mary Whitehouse, its audience, aged between six and 16, loved it. Critics also failed to note that no one ever benefited from any of the hell-raising. Punishments were suitably doled out and the moral angles were well publicized. The programme's educational value was equally overlooked. In 1986, on the back of pupil Zammo's fight with heroin addiction, the cast released a hit record, 'Just Say No', and the relevant episode of the series was followed by a special factual programme on the subject.

Although lead and supporting characters have come and gone, as pupils have progressed through school (the major players are listed above), the best remembered is Tucker Jenkins (played by future *EastEnder* Todd Carty), who also earned his own spin-off series, *Tucker's Luck*, on leaving school. Carty's *EastEnders* sister, Susan Tully, was another early star, playing Suzanne Ross, and several other members of the prime-time soap cut their TV teeth in the classrooms of *Grange Hill*.

GRANT, ROB

British comedy writer, in collaboration with partner Doug Naylor. Undoubtedly, Grant and Naylor's biggest success has been with the space sitcom *Red Dwarf*, although they have also been major contributors to *Spitting Image*, *Alas Smith and Jones*, *Carrott's Lib* and numerous radio series. Another sitcom product of theirs was *The 10%ers*.

GRANT, RUSSELL (1952–)

Bouncy TV astrologer and contributor to magazine programmes, an early star of the BBC's *Breakfast Time*.

GRANTHAM, LESLIE (1947–)

British actor who shot to fame as *EastEnders'* Dirty Den Watts. During his time in the series, it was revealed that Grantham had spent 11 years in prison for a murder he had committed whilst a soldier in Germany. In confinement he took up acting and, on release, he trained at drama school. His earliest TV roles came with minor parts in *The Jewel in the Crown*, *Doctor Who* and *Bulman*. On leaving *EastEnders*, capitalizing on his new-found status as a TV sex symbol, Grantham moved on to star in *Winners and Losers* (as boxing promoter Eddie Burt), *The Paradise Club* (as nightclub manager Danny Kane) and *99–1* (as undercover cop Mick Raynor).

GRAVES, PETER (PETER AURNESS; 1925–)

Tall American actor, the brother of *Gunsmoke* star James Arness. The brothers' TV breaks came at about the same time. In the mid-1950s, while James was beginning a long career in the guise of Dodge City lawman Matt Dillon, Peter launched into a five-year run as Jim Newton, the father figure in the horsey kids' series *Fury*. In 1960 Graves starred as Chris Cobb, an American stagecoach owner, in the Australian Western *Whiplash*, and, five years later, appeared in the drama series *Court Martial*. Around this time he also appeared in series like *Alfred Hitchcock Presents* and *Route 66*. However, it is as Jim Phelps, team leader of the Impossible Missions Force in *Mission: Impossible* that he is best remembered. It was a role he played for six years. Moving on to TV movies and mini-series, Graves later played Fred 'Palmer' Kirby in the blockbuster *The Winds of War*.

GRAY, DONALD (ELDRED TIDBURY; 1914–78)

Distinguished South African actor and one-time radio and TV announcer who lost an arm in World War II. Despite (or perhaps on account of) this handicap, he achieved international fame in the late 1950s as plummy detective *Mark Saber*. His rich and authoritative vocal tones were later employed by Gerry Anderson for the character of Colonel White, head of Spectrum in *Captain Scarlet and the Mysterons*.

GRAY, LINDA (1942–)

Former model turned actress whose earliest TV credits came in such series as *Marcus Welby, MD* and *McCloud*. From 1978 to 1989 Gray starred as Sue Ellen, JR Ewing's boozy wife in *Dallas*, also trying her hand at directing some episodes. When Ian McShane guest starred in the Texan super soap, Gray repaid the compliment by accepting a part in his somewhat less flashy *Lovejoy* series. She has also been seen in numerous TV movies and a few American programmes that were not screened in the UK, most notably the comedy show *All That Glitters*.

GRAYSON, LARRY (WILLIAM WHITE; 1923–95)

Camp British comedian hailing from the Midlands, once a music-hall drag performer known as Billy Breen. With stories of friends like Everard, Apricot Lil and Slack Alice, Grayson earned himself TV celebrity status in the early 1970s, through one-off guest performances (on shows like *Saturday Variety*) and his own ITV series, *Shut That Door* (named after his catchphrase). A close friend of Noele Gordon, he made a famous cameo appearance in *Crossroads* in 1973, playing a disgruntled motel guest, and returned two years later to act as chauffeur at Noele's TV wedding to John Bentley, when Meg married Hugh Mortimer. However, the highspot of his career came when Bruce Forsyth moved to ITV in 1978 and Grayson was chosen to succeed him as host of the hugely popular *Generation Game*. With Isla St Clair as his partner, Grayson matched Forsyth's success and the series continued for another three years. A tell-the-truth guessing game, *Sweethearts*, in 1987, proved less durable and little was seen of Grayson after. His last TV appearance was in the 1994 Royal Variety Performance.

GREATOREX, WILFRED

British scriptwriter and editor, responsible for creating series like *The Plane Makers* (later *The Power Game*), *Front Page Story* (with Rex Firkin), *Hine*, *The Man from Haven*, *Secret Army* (with Gerald Glaister), *1990* and *Airline*. In 1987 Greatorex tried unsuccessfully to sue advertising agency J. Walter Thompson over the use of

Airline star Roy Marsden in a look-alike TV commercial for the British Airports Authority.

GREEN, HUGHIE (1920–)

Canadian showman, talent spotter and quiz show host, one of ITV's earliest stars. After a career in radio and on stage and screen as a child performer (among his film credits were *Midshipman Easy* and *Tom Brown's Schooldays*), Green spent the war as a pilot in the Canadian airforce, continuing in civil aviation after the hostilities. He also returned to radio, hosting **Opportunity Knocks!** for both the BBC and Radio Luxembourg and then **Double Your Money** for the latter. Both shows transferred to television with the arrival of ITV, *Opportunity Knocks!* running for a marathon 21 years from 1956 (and subsequently revived by Bob Monkhouse in 1987) and *Double Your Money* for 13 years from 1955. In 1971 Green hosted the quiz's natural successor, *The Sky's the Limit*, which was, effectively, *Double Your Money* with air miles. In the early days, Green also compered **Sunday Night at the London Palladium**. His contrived gags and his catchphrase 'I mean that most sincerely, folks' were much mimicked.

GREENE, HUGH CARLETON/SIR HUGH (1910–87)

The brother of novelist Graham Greene and one of the BBC's most famous directors-general. Greene, a former *Daily Telegraph* journalist, was editor of the BBC's German Service during the war and, when hostilities ceased, helped to reorganize broadcasting in Germany. He became the BBC's Director of News and Current Affairs and then was appointed Director-General in 1960, holding the post for over nine years. During this period, a decade of technological advances and social change, Greene was credited with allowing the BBC to move with the times. Under his guidance, the Corporation drifted away from the starchy proprieties of the 1950s and floated into innovative, more permissive waters. The Hugh Greene era was the era of **That Was The Week That Was**, **Steptoe and Son**, **Cathy Come Home** and **Till Death Us Do Part**. It was also the era that prompted Mary Whitehouse's first criticisms of broadcasting standards, although Greene quite happily shrugged off complaints from her fledgling Clean-up TV campaign. However, on one notable occasion, Greene did err on the side of caution, refusing to screen the realistic nuclear war drama **The War Game** in 1966, fearing it would alarm the public (it was eventually shown in 1985). Although, generally, Greene remained steadfast in his protection of the independence of the BBC, his postponement of an episode of *Steptoe and Son* on election night in 1964, allegedly at the request of Harold Wilson, did rather tarnish his reputation with observers. Greene was knighted the same year, but his relationship with the Labour Party later deteriorated. When Wilson appointed Lord Hill, Chairman of the Independent Television Authority, to the position of Chairman of the BBC in 1967, it was seen as a means of keeping Greene in check and a response to some perceived anti-Labour programming controversies. Greene eventually left his post in 1969, but became the first ex-DG to take a seat on the board of Governors, a seat he maintained until 1971.

GREENE, LORNE (1915–87)

Whether as a roving merchant seaman, a reassuring father figure in the Wild West or an intergalactic space commander, Lorne Greene won the respect of more than one generation of TV viewers. Born in Ottawa, Lorne Greene's first field of expertise was radio. Failing to find much acting work, he became an announcer for CBC and during the war established himself as the authoritative 'Voice of Canada'. Moving south to the USA in the 1950s, he began to pick up small TV roles, in programmes like **Alfred Hitchcock Presents**, **Wagon Train** and **Cheyenne**, and then, in 1957, in the UK, won the part of Captain Grant 'Mitch' Mitchell in the adventure series **Sailor of Fortune**. However, it was his next major role which proved definitive. He was cast as Ben Cartwright, patriarch of the Ponderosa in the classic Western **Bonanza**, which ran for 14 years up to 1973. He moved into police work with the short-lived detective drama *Griff* the same year, added his voice to two long-running nature series, *Lorne Greene's Last of the Wild* and *Lorne Greene's New Wilderness*, and in 1978 was launched into outer space to be the Moses-like Commander Adama in the *Star Wars* clone **Battlestar Galactica**. His last starring role was in a fire-fighting caper called Code Red. Among his other credits were TV movies and mini-series such as **Roots** (in which he played slave-owner John Reynolds).

GREENE, RICHARD (1918–85)

British leading man in Hollywood films of the 1930s, who found new fame as the swashbuckling Robin Hood in **The Adventures of Robin Hood**, an early ITV success. The show's 143 episodes proved such a hit that Greene made few TV appearances after, choosing to settle down to a retirement of horse breeding in Ireland.

GREENE, SARAH

Children's TV presenter, a former child actress/model and now the wife of presenter/DJ

Mike Smith. Greene's TV break came with **Blue Peter** in 1980, from which she progressed to *Saturday Superstore, Going Live, Posh Frocks and New Trousers*, the game show *Happy Families,* the Swap Shop *The Exchange* and numerous documentary specials.

GREGSON, JOHN (1919–75)

British actor who, after many film appearances (most notably *Genevieve*), took the role of Commander George Gideon in the police series **Gideon's Way** in 1965. Six years later, he resurfaced in Shirley MacLaine's photojournalist sitcom *Shirley's World,* playing her editor, Dennis Croft, and in 1976 he was Kirby, the risk-taking insurance agent, in Southern's thriller serial *Dangerous Knowledge* a series screened a year after his death.

GRIFFITHS, LEON (1928–92)

British scriptwriter, best remembered as the creator of *Minder.* Griffiths's early TV writing included episodes of **The Four Just Men, Out of the Unknown, Tales of Mystery** and **No Hiding Place** in the 1950s and 1960s. While working on single plays such as the boxing drama *Dinner at the Sporting Club,* in the 1970s he was advised to adapt one of his stories so that it concentrated on just two of its characters, those of a dodgy wheeler-dealer and his jailbird bodyguard. *Minder* was born and with it one of TV's classic creations, Arthur Daley. (Ironically, Daley's fluent Cockney patter was provided by a writer who had been born in Sheffield and brought up in Glasgow.) Griffiths, however, suffered a stroke and the second season had to be written by others, although the Writers' Guild award that the prgramme won was still presented to him personally. Inspired, Griffiths fought his way back to work and resumed his involvement, right up to his death in 1992. His other contributions included the six-part adaptation of *Piece of Cake,* plus scripts for series like **The Racing Game**.

GRIFFITHS, RICHARD (1947–)

Versatile English actor, star of the sitcom *Nobody's Perfect* (as Sam Hooper, alongside Elaine Strich), the bizarre comedy **Whoops! Apocalypse** (as Soviet leader Dubienkin), the thriller **Bird of Prey** (playing snoopy civil servant Henry Jay), the wine comedy *Ffizz* (as Jack Mowbray) and the unsuccessful historical drama **The Cleopatras** (as the grotesque Potbelly). Griffiths has also starred as Trevor Beasley in another comedy, *A Kind of Living,* and played the policeman-chef Henry Crabbe in **Pie in the Sky**. Amongst his many guest appearances have been parts in **Bergerac** and **Minder**.

GRIFFITHS, TREVOR (1935–)

Manchester-born former education officer, one of TV's most political dramatists, espousing left-wing causes, particularly in his notable series **Bill Brand**. His first contribution was *Adam Smith* (written under the pen name of Ben Rae) and among his other offerings have been *Occupations, Comedians, Through the Night, Country, The Last Place on Earth* (the story of Captain Scott) and the skinhead drama *Oi for England.* He has also adapted D.H. Lawrence's *Sons and Lovers* for the small screen.

GRIP

The technician responsible for production hardware like props, camera mountings, dollies and cranes. Where a large crew is involved, the head man is known as the key grip.

GROVE FAMILY, THE

UK (BBC) Drama. BBC 1954–7

Bob Grove	Edward Evans
Gladys Grove	Ruth Dunning
Pat Grove	Sheila Sweet
	Carole Mowlam
Jack Grove	Peter Bryant
Daphne Grove	Margaret Downs
Lenny Grove	Christopher Beeny
Gran	Nancy Roberts

Writers: Michael Pertwee, Roland Pertwee.
Producer: John Warrington

Ups and downs in the life of Britain's first soap family.

The Grove Family was the BBC's first attempt at a grown-up soap, although the Corporation had already produced a children's equivalent in **The Appleyards**. The Groves (named after the BBC's Lime Grove studios) were lower middle-class, just about comfortably off and had come through the postwar shortages like most other 'ordinary' families. This enabled viewers to relate to the characters and made the series very popular.

The family lived in Hendon and consisted of Dad Bob, a jobbing builder, housewife Gladys, elder daughter and assistant librarian Pat, Jack, who was doing National Service and was a bit of a lad, teenage schoolgirl Daphne and cheeky young Lenny (a youthful Christopher Beeny). Completing the household was the hunched, crotchety Gran, a grumble forever on her lips. Cousin Rodney was added for youth interest as the younger Groves grew up.

Drawing heavily on the likes of *Mrs Dale's Diary* and *The Archers* in style, there was very little drama in *The Grove Family.* Reassuringly British (with no intruding US culture), its action focused instead on petty squabbles and occasional domestic strife, but a 'public service' element was also built in. Viewers were made acutely aware of the need to purchase a TV licence, for example, or to protect themselves from burglaries. One story even warned of the dangers of sailing! Scripts were provided by father and son Roland and Michael Pertwee, and, when they asked for a short break after three years' of solid writing, the BBC declined and, much to viewers' dismay, closed down the series altogether.

Little footage of the series is known to exist today, although there was a film spin-off, entitled *It's a Great Day*, in 1955. Also, as part of the BBC's Lime Grove commemorations in 1991, modern-day soap stars stepped in to re-create extracts from original scripts. Mum was played by Sue Johnston, Dad by Leslie Grantham, Gran by Anna Wing, Pat by Sally Ann Matthews, Jack by Nick Berry, Daphne by Kellie Bright and Lenny by Paul Parris.

GROWING PAINS OF ADRIAN MOLE, The see *The Secret Diary of Adrian Mole, Aged 13¾*.

GROWING PAINS OF PC PENROSE, The see *Rosie*.

GRUNDY, REG

Australian head of Grundy International, one of the southern hemisphere's major independent producers of TV programmes, now responsible for international offerings like *Neighbours* and *Going for Gold*.

GS5 see *Ghost Squad*.

GUINNESS, SIR ALEC, CBE (1914–)

Distinguished British film actor whose television work has come late in life. By far his most acclaimed role has been as spycatcher George Smiley in John Le Carré's *Tinker, Tailor, Soldier, Spy* and *Smiley's People*. Among his other credits have been *Caesar and Cleopatra*, *Conversations at Night*, *Gift of Friendship*, *Little Lord Fauntleroy* and *Monsignor Quixote*.

GUN LAW see *Gunsmoke*.

GUNSMOKE/GUN LAW

US (CBS) Western. ITV 1956–

Marshal Matt Dillon	James Arness
Kitty Russell	Amanda Blake
Dr Galen ('Doc') Adams	Milburn Stone
Chester Goode	Dennis Weaver
Quint Asper	Burt Reynolds
Sam	Glenn Strange
Festus Haggen	Ken Curtis
Thad Greenwood	Roger Ewing
Newly O'Brien	Buck Taylor
Mr Jones	Dabbs Greer
Hank	Hank Patterson
Louie Pheeters	James Nusser
Barney	Charles Seel
Howie	Howard Culver
Ed O'Connor	Tom Brown
Percy Crump	John Harper
Ma Smalley	Sarah Selby
Miss Hannah	Fran Ryan

Creators: Norman Macdonnell, John Meston, Charles Marquis Warren. Producers: Norman Macdonnell, Philip Leacock, John Mantley

A strong and virtuous marshal maintains law and order in a Wild West town.

Gunsmoke was a Western with a difference. Before it, viewers had seen the likes of *Hopalong Cassidy* and *The Lone Ranger*, which were essentially kids' fare. Now, for the first time, here was an adult cowboy. It was so well received that it ran for nearly 20 years in the USA and became known to many as the TV Western.

Gunsmoke focused on the fictional figure of Matt Dillon, the strong, no-nonsense marshal of Dodge City in 1870s Kansas. Standing six and a half feet tall, he was a giant physically and inspirationally, a man of great integrity and principle. He was tough but fair, and outlaws quickly realized that they were not welcome on his patch. But Dillon was not flawless. A rather intense and occasionally uncertain man, he was seen to worry and anguish over the right course to take, and he didn't always make the correct decision. However, Dillon knew he could rely on the support of the Dodge City townsfolk. His closest confidants were Doc Adams and Kitty Russell, proprietress of the Longbranch Saloon. Adams was tetchy but kind; Russell was tough, with a soft centre, an early tart with a heart who seemed to have a crush on Dillon, although the relationship was never taken any further. Dillon was also assisted by his deputies, Chester Goode (who brought a touch of comic relief with his limp and his constant coffee-brewing) and, later, Festus Haggen (a drawling hillbilly). Also seen at various times were the rugged half-Indian blacksmith Quint Asper, gunsmith Newly O'Brien and Dillon's friend, Thad Greenwood. Other Dodge City residents included shopkeeper Jones, rancher O'Connor, Percy Crump, the undertaker, a hotel clerk called Howie, Hank, the stable keeper, Ma Smalley, who ran the boarding house, Barney, the telegraph man, and the local drunkard, Louie Pheeters. A year before the series ended, Kitty Russell was replaced in the saloon by a new landlady, Miss Hannah.

Dillon himself did not appear in many later episodes, leaving the stage to the townsfolk and one-off guest stars, although the series always stayed true to its principles of portraying the realistic side of Wild West life. That's what John Wayne had promised when he introduced the very first episode, even though he himself declined the role of the marshal. With William Conrad (who had provided Dillon's voice for years on radio) lacking the looks the part demanded, Wayne recommended the relatively unknown actor James Arness.

When *Gunsmoke* arrived in the UK, as an early ITV import, it was screened under the title of *Gun Law*, although later episodes and re-runs carried the original programme name.

GUTTERIDGE, REG, OBE (1924–)

Long-serving ITV boxing commentator, a one-time amateur champion himself before his career was ended by the loss of a leg during the Normandy campaign. He turned instead to journalism and eventually to boxing writing. Gutteridge has also dabbled in coverage of greyhound racing.

GUYLER, DERYCK (1914–)

Deep-voiced Liverpudlian former radio comedian who moved into television as a foil for Eric Sykes. Playing the part of policeman Corky, Guyler stayed with *Sykes* for many years. He is also remembered as the Desert Rat school caretaker Norman Potter in *Please Sir!* and has been much seen on television playing his specialist musical instrument, the washboard. Amongst his other credits have been supporting roles in the 1950s series *The Charlie Chester Show* and *Emney Enterprises*, and the later sitcoms *Here's Harry*, *Three Live Wires*, *Room at the Bottom* and *Best of Enemies*.

GWYNNE, FRED (1926–93)

Tall (6 ft 5 in) American comic actor, forever remembered as Herman, the lumbering Frankenstein's monster look-alike in *The Munsters*. Previously Gwynne had starred in another successful sitcom, playing inept cop Francis Muldoon in *Car 54, Where Are You?* That role followed appearances in *The Phil Silvers Show* and other series, plus films like *On the Waterfront*. Gwynne also made a living writing and illustrating children's books and was once a copywriter for the J. Walter Thompson advertising agency, a position which gave him financial security while he worked his way into acting in his spare time.

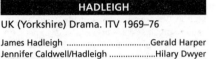

HADLEIGH	

UK (Yorkshire) Drama. ITV 1969–76

James Hadleigh	Gerald Harper
Jennifer Caldwell/Hadleigh	Hilary Dwyer
Charles Caldwell	Gerald James

Executive Producers: Peter Willes, David Cunliffe. Producers: Terence Williams, Jacky Stoller

The life and times of a laid-back Yorkshire squire.

James Hadleigh was the classic smoothie, a refined country gentleman who occasionally had to stoop as low as work to finance his rich tastes. A former civil servant, who had inherited his wealth and his mansion, Melford Park, from his father, Hadleigh still farmed himself out to the Treasury now and again when times grew 'hard' – when his racehorse stable was threatened with closure, for example. At first a most eligible bachelor, the suave, charming Hadleigh finally succumbed to marriage when the attractive (and independently wealthy) Jennifer Caldwell came his way. The series was a spin-off from a series called *Gazette*, the story of a weekly newspaper owned by Hadleigh's father.

HAGMAN, LARRY (1931–)

The son of musical star Mary Martin, Larry Hagman broke into showbiz in the early 1950s, finding work in New York's theatreland. He appeared with his mother in London as an extra in *South Pacific* in 1951 and spent some time in the USAF before working his way into television. His first prominent role was in the US daytime serial *The Edge of Night* in 1961 and then in 1965, Hagman was chosen to play genie master Tony Nelson in the sitcom *I Dream of Jeannie*. The show was a hit and ran for five years and Hagman followed it with film roles and two other US comedies, *The Good Life* and *Here We Go Again*, both of which failed to take off. Then, just when it seemed his career had peaked and was on the slide, up popped the part of TV's all-time Mr Nasty, JR Ewing, in the hugely successful *Dallas*. Hagman soon became vital to the series. He directed as well as starred in it, also becoming joint executive producer, and when JR was shot in 1980 the world stopped to find out who pulled the trigger. The series ran until 1991.

HALE, ALAN, JNR (1918–90)

Cheerful American light and comic actor, best remembered by British TV audiences as *Casey Jones* in the 1950s railroad Western. In the 1960s he was a stalwart of the farce *Gilligan's Island*, playing Jonas Grumby, the skipper of the shipwrecked cruise ship. His dad, whom Alan Jnr resembled physically, was a silent movie star.

HALE, GARETH (1953–)

Former teacher who turned comedian and formed a successful, if at times controversial, double act with another ex-teacher, Norman Pace. After appearances in *The Young Ones*, *Saturday Live* and another comedy show, *The Saturday Gang*, the duo were given their own series by LWT. Never afraid to put pressure on the boundaries of taste, they found themselves at the centre of a storm over a sketch involving a cat and a microwave. Their act also includes an impersonation of a pair of Cockney gangster bodyguards, the two Rons (aka The Management), and a parody of kids' TV (as Billy and Johnny, the patronizing presenters). Hale and Pace also appeared in *Doctor Who* and, in 1994, tried their hand at straight acting in the three-part crime drama *A Pinch of Snuff*.

HALL, ROBIN

Popular Scottish folk singer of the 1950s and 1960s, in partnership with Jimmie MacGregor. Their big break came on the *Tonight* show for which they performed a number every week. After five years, they were given the chance to branch out in *The White Heather Club*, which itself ran for five years. Since their partnership broke up in 1979 Hall has become an occasional folk performer back in Scotland and MacGregor has worked for Radio Scotland and Scottish television.

HALL, WILLIS (1929–)

British scriptwriter, often in collaboration with Keith Waterhouse. Amongst their many credits have been *Budgie*, *Billy Liar*, *Inside George Webley*, *Queenie's Castle*, *The Upper Crusts*, *Our Kid* and *Worzel Gummidge*, plus sketches for *That Was The Week That Was* and *BBC 3*. Hall has also worked solo on the sitcoms *The Fuzz* and *The Bright Side*, written episodes of *Secret Army*, *The Crezz*, *Minder* and other series, and penned notable single dramas like *The Villa Maroc*.

HAMMER HOUSE OF HORROR

UK (ATV/Hammer/Chips/Cinema Arts) Thriller Anthology. ITV 1980

Producer: Roy Skeggs

A collection of suspense tales produced in conjunction with the cinema horror specialists.

The gory one-hour films grouped together as *Hammer House of Horror* featured guest stars like Diana Dors, Denholm Elliott and Hammer favourite Peter Cushing. The 13 stories (under the control of Hammer directors such as Peter Sasdy, Don Sharp and Alan Gibson) revolved around such subjects as voodoo, cannibalism, werewolves, witchcraft and other manifestations of the supernatural.

HAMNER, EARL, JNR (1923–)

American writer whose own life story formed the basis of *The Waltons*, which he created. Hamner acted as narrator on the series and later created and produced the glossy soap *Falcon Crest*, amongst other offerings.

HAMPSHIRE, SUSAN, OBE (1938–)

Demure-looking British actress whose TV debut came as Andromeda in *The Andromeda Breakthrough*, the sequel to the sci-fi classic *A for Andromeda*, thanks to Julie Christie's decision to leave the role. However, for most people their earliest recollection of Hampshire is as the headstrong Fleur in *The Forsyte Saga*. She followed it up with Forsyte look-alikes *The First Churchills* (as Sarah Churchill) and *The Pallisers* (as Lady Glencora Palliser). She has also starred in *The Barchester Chronicles* (as Madeline), *Vanity Fair* (as Becky Sharp) and a musical version of *Dr Jekyll and Mr Hyde*, as well as taking the lead in the Carla Lane sitcom *Leaving* (as Martha Ford) and the Roy Clarke comedy *Don't Tell Father* (as Natasha Bancroft). She also has numerous guest appearances to her name, in programmes as diverse as *The Time Tunnel* and *The Morecambe and Wise Show*. Hampshire has been an active campaigner for sufferers of dyslexia (she is a sufferer herself).

HANCOCK, SHEILA, OBE (1933–)

British comedy actress, the wife of John Thaw. Among her sitcom credits have been *The Rag Trade* (as Carole), *The Bed-Sit Girl* (as Sheila Ross), *Mr Digby Darling* (as devoted secretary Thelma Teesdale), *Now Take My Wife* (as Claire Love) and *Brighton Belles* (as Frances). Hancock has also proved her versatility through serious dramas like 1989's *Jumping the Queue*, in which she played suicidal widow Matilda, in an adaptation of Mary Wesley's book (which Sheila herself sold to the BBC). Other credits have included *Entertaining Mr Sloan*, the 1972 version of Waugh's *Scoop*, *Horizontal Hold*, *The Mating Machine*, *God Our Help*, *Gone to Seed*, *But Seriously – It's Sheila Hancock*, *The Buccaneers* and *Dangerous Lady*.

HANCOCK, TONY (1924–68)

'The lad himself', as he was dubbed, Tony Hancock has been widely acclaimed as one of Britain's funniest ever comedians and a pioneer of TV situation comedy. A member of *Ralph Reader's Gang Show* during the war, Hancock remained on the stage when the hostilities ceased, becoming resident comic at The Windmill and touring other theatres. In 1951 he joined the cast of radio's *Educating Archie* and was such a success that he was given his own show, **Hancock's Half Hour**, in 1954. Two years later the series transferred to television, although not before Hancock had made a couple of sketch series for ITV under the banner of *The Tony Hancock Show*. *Hancock's Half Hour* (finally just known as *Hancock*) ran until 1961, making Hancock the country's number-one comic. He even turned his hand to straight drama, appearing in the 1958 play *The Government Inspector* (part of the Television World Theatre anthology). In 1963 he switched to ITV, leaving behind him his scriptwriters, Ray Galton and Alan Simpson, and with them the peak of his success. His *Hancock* shows for ITV never reached the heights of his BBC work, a career in film fizzled out and Hancock grew more and more depressed. His drink problem was well documented and, always highly self-critical, he took his own life while working on a series for Australian TV in 1968. His last British offering had been *Hancock's* in 1967, in which he played a nightclub owner. Alfred Molina later starred in a *Screen One* production, *Hancock*, which dramatized his tragic last seven years.

HANCOCK'S HALF HOUR

UK (BBC) Situation Comedy. BBC 1956–61

Anthony Aloysius Hancock....................Tony Hancock
Sid ....Sidney James

Creators/Writers: Ray Galton, Alan Simpson.
Producer: Duncan Wood

The highs and lows in the life of a perpetual dreamer.

Hancock's Half Hour, its title announced in breathless, stammering fashion by 'the lad himself', was one of Britain's first major comedy series and remains in the eyes of many a true classic. Beginning on radio in 1954, it quickly transferred to television and introduced to viewers the complex personality of Anthony Aloysius Hancock, inhabitant of 23 Railway Cuttings, East Cheam. The character was a moody, bumptious type, sporting a Homburg hat and a heavy overcoat, a man prone to constant questioning of the whys and wherefores of the world and a gloomy ponderer of his personal circumstances. Life's petty injustices and annoyances were guaranteed

to generate a torrent of observations and criticisms. For instance, what could be worse than reading a thriller novel only to find the last page torn out? Similarly frustrating was the way in which his ambitious plans to improve his station always ended in failure and humiliation, as prophesied by his cynical roommate, played by Sid James.

James, the man who pricked Hancock's bubbles, left the series in 1960 to pursue his own starring roles, and the last season went out simply under the title of *Hancock*, the star having moved to a new address. These episodes included such classics as *The Radio Ham* and *The Blood Donor* (with its oft-quoted exclamation: 'A pint? That's very nearly an armful!').

HANDL, IRENE (1901–87)

Cheerful Cockney character actress, in her latter years well versed in daffy old lady parts. She did not turn to acting until she was 40, but soon secured herself plenty of film, stage and radio work. On television in the 1950s she was seen in variety shows like **Chelsea at Nine** and in the screen version of *Educating Archie* (and previously as Mrs Twistle in *Here's Archie*), as well as with Tony Hancock in **Hancock's Half Hour** and with Charlie Drake in *Laughter In Store* and *Drake's Progress*. However, her biggest TV success was opposite Wilfred Pickles in the OAP sitcom *For the Love of Ada* (as Ada Cresswell from 1970). Among her other major roles were *Barney Is My Darling* (as Ramona Pank), *Mum's Boys* (as Mrs Crystal Pallise), **Maggie and Her** (as Julia McKenzie's nosy neighbour, Mrs Perry), **Metal Mickey** (as the granny) and *Never Say Die* (as Dorothy). Handl also enjoyed scores of guest appearances, ranging from **The Adventures of Robin Hood** and **The Rag Trade** to **Supergran**.

HANLEY, JIMMY (1918–70)

Former child star Jimmy Hanley was a versatile showman, notching up a series of films for Rank in the 1940s and becoming a hit on radio and TV in the 1950s. His most prominent role was as the landlord of *Jim's Inn*, a fictitious pub that he ran with his second wife, Maggie. The series was TV's most popular admag, a vehicle for promoting various goods and services. Customers used to stroll in to discuss their latest bargains at the bar. The series started in 1957, but, in 1963, admags were banned by Parliament and Hanley was out of a job, although he was later seen on the kids' series **Five O'Clock Club**, talking about hobbies. His first wife was actress Dinah Sheridan, with whom he had two children, actress/presenter Jenny and Conservative politician Jeremy.

HANNAY

UK (Thames) Drama. ITV 1988–9

Richard Hannay ....Robert Powell
Count Von Schwabing..........................Gavin Richards

Executive Producer: Lloyd Shirley. Producer: Richard Bates

An Edwardian adventurer confronts agents of Imperial Germany.

Reprising the role he played in the 1978 cinema version of *The Thirty-Nine Steps*, Robert Powell once again stepped into the shoes of Richard Hannay, John Buchan's daring adventurer. On this occasion, timed as 1912, Hannay had returned from 30 years in South Africa to confront the might of Imperial Germany and the attentions of Count Von Schwabing in particular. Various escapades followed for the dashing hero in the tweed suit.

HANRAHAN, BRIAN (1949–)

Distinguished British journalist, who joined BBC TV News as a reporter in 1980. After notable achievements alongside ITN's Michael Nicholson in the Falklands conflict (in one memorable report he declared that, while he couldn't comment on British aircraft losses, he had 'counted them all out and counted them all back in'), Hanrahan became the BBC's Far East Correspondent 1983–6, then Moscow Correspondent 1986–8 and the BBC's Foreign Affairs Diplomatic Correspondent since 1989.

HAPPY DAYS

US (Paramount/Miller-Milkis) Situation Comedy. ITV 1975–

Richie Cunningham.................................Ron Howard
Arthur Fonzarelli ('Fonzie')..................Henry Winkler
Howard Cunningham ....Tom Bosley
Marion Cunningham ....Marion Ross
Joanie Cunningham ....Erin Moran
Warren 'Potsie' Webber ....Anson Williams
Ralph Malph ....Donny Most
Chuck Cunningham ....Gavan O'Herlihy
                                                              Randolph Roberts
Arnold (Matsuo Takahashi) ....Pat Morita
Alfred Delvecchio.....................................Al Molinaro
Charles 'Chachi' Arcola ....Scott Baio
Lori Beth Allen/Cunningham.........Linda Goodfriend
Jenny Piccalo ....Cathy Silvers
Roger Phillips...Ted McGinley
K.C. Cunningham ....Crystal Bernard
Ashley Pfister..Linda Purl
Heather Pfister.............................Heather O'Rourke

Creator: Garry K. Marshall. Executive Producers: Thomas L. Miller, Edward K. Milkis, Garry K. Marshall. Producers: Tony Marshall, Jerry Paris

Nostalgic sitcom based around a middle-class Milwaukee family and their teenage children.

Laced with contemporary pop hits, *Happy Days* followed the Cunningham family throughout the late years of the 1950s and into the 1960s, with particular focus on their teenage son, Richie, and his pals. The Cunninghams lived in Milwaukee, Wisconsin, where chubby, hapless dad Howard owned a hardware store. His red-haired wife, Marion, was a typical housewife of the time, bringing up the children and supporting her husband, but always with a youthful spring in her step. Son Richie was the classic all-American boy, complete with apple-pie looks, and viewers shared his growing pains as he started dating girls and progressed through school. Apart from Richie, there were two other Cunningham kids, Chuck and Joanie. Chuck, however, only appeared in the earliest episodes before moving off to college, to be strangely forgotten by everyone in the cast, including his own mother and father. Joanie, on the other hand, genuinely grew up with the show. At the start, she was just a freckly little kid with only a few lines, but by the end of the run she had developed into one of the star names and even had her own spin-off series, *Joanie Loves Chachi*.

The show was originally intended to focus on Richie and his chum Potsie as they negotiated teenage life in the rock 'n' roll era. While Richie remained central to the show, the rather slow-witted Potsie was gradually pushed into the background, alongside wisecracking red-head Ralph Malph, as an unexpected star was born. That star was Fonzie, the show's leather-jacketed hell-raiser who cruised the streets on a cherished motorcycle. There was always something special about 'The Fonz'. He was cool with a capital C, an expert mechanic with a magic touch and the dream date of every girl in Milwaukee. He moved into the flat above the Cunninghams' garage and, as the series developed, his rough edges became considerably smoother.

Richie, Potsie, Ralph and Fonzie were all regulars at Arnold's, a drive-in diner and soda store run initially by Japanese proprietor Arnold, then by the sad-faced but kind-hearted Al Delvecchio. The boys attended Jefferson High School, before graduating and moving on to the University of Wisconsin in Milwaukee. As they grew older the emphasis switched to kids of Joanie's generation. Richie and Ralph joined the army and were despatched to Greenland (Ron Howard and Donny Most had left the series), while Potsie took a job at the Cunningham hardware store. New faces included Fonzie's cousin, Chachi, who was to become Joanie's boyfriend, and

Roger, Marion's nephew, the school's new basketball coach. Howard's neice, K.C., lived with the family for a while and Joanie's much-talked-about, boy-mad friend, Jenny Piccalo, was eventually seen (played by Cathy Silvers, daughter of comedian Phil Silvers). Other characters introduced over the years included Fonzie's divorcée girlfriend, Ashley Pfister, and her little daughter, Heather. Rock singer Leather Tuscadero, played by Suzi Quatro, was an occasional guest.

Richie eventually married his college sweetheart, Lori Beth (by telephone, with Fonzie acting as proxy groom), and a Richie Junior appeared on the scene. Fonzie joined Al as a partner in Arnold's and even taught at the High School. In the final episode, Joanie and Chachi were married, the whole family (except Chuck) reassembled and Howard thanked viewers for being part of their lives for over ten years.

Apart from *Joanie Loves Chachi*, *Happy Days* led to two other spin-offs, **Laverne and Shirley** and **Mork and Mindy**. The programme was not, as often surmised, based on the film *American Graffiti* (in which Ron Howard had starred) but on an episode of *Love, American Style*, entitled *Love and the Happy Day*, which had featured Howard and Anson Williams as 1950s schoolkids. The original series theme music was Bill Haley's 'Rock Around The Clock', although an original title track soon superseded it, becoming a minor hit itself for a group called Pratt and McLain with Brotherlove.

HAPPY EVER AFTER

UK (BBC) Situation Comedy. BBC 1 1974–8

Terry Fletcher ....Terry Scott
June Fletcher ....June Whitfield
Aunt Lucy ....Beryl Cooke
Susan Fletcher...Lena Clemo
                                                  Pippa Page
Debbie Fletcher ....Caroline Whitaker

Creators: John Chapman, Eric Merriman. Producer: Peter Whitmore

A middle-aged couple are saddled with a geriatric aunt.

Middle-class suburban couple Terry and June Fletcher were just settling down to life on their own after 23 years of marriage. Their two daughters had, at last, fled the nest. Then, out of the blue, June's frail Aunt Lucy arrived. With her squawking pet mynah bird also in attendance, Lucy made sure the Fletchers' burdensome days were not over. The daughters, Susan and Debbie, paid occasional visits to cheer up their patient, resilient mum and blustering, hapless dad.

The series, which was spun-off a 1974 **Comedy Playhouse** pilot, eventually evolved into **Terry**

and June, in which the old bird (and the mynah) had disappeared and the Fletchers were known as the Medfords.

HAPPY FAMILIES

UK (BBC) Situation Comedy. BBC 1 1985

Edith/Joyce/Cassie/Roxanne/Madelaine Fuddle/
....Jennifer Saunders
Guy Fuddle ....Adrian Edmondson
Cook ....Dawn French
Dr De Quincy ....Stephen Fry
Flossie ....Helen Lederer

Writer: Ben Elton. Producer: Paul Jackson

A crazy, crotchety grandmother summons her grandchildren to her deathbed.

Barmy Edith Fuddle, being about to pop her clogs, demanded the presence of her four granddaughters at her bedside. Unfortunately, they were now scattered around the world. To bring them together, their imbecile brother, Guy, was despatched on his travels. Despite constantly losing his way, Guy eventually tracked them all down, one per episode. Cassie was working as a Hollywood soap actress, Madelaine was living with a randy poet in a French artists' commune, Joyce was a novice nun inspired by *The Sound of Music* and Roxanne was in jail.

All the sisters and the grandmother were played by Jennifer Saunders and the series, made by the BBC in Manchester, cleverly varied its camera techniques to reflect the granddaughters' situations. The Hollywood scenes were shot in soap style, arty pastels were used for France, a jolly 1940s style was employed for the convent episode and a hard documentary edge pervaded the prison sequences.

HARBEN, PHILIP (1906–70)

A familiar face on British television from the 1940s through the 1960s, small, bearded Philip Harben was one of the UK's first TV cooks. Presenting in his striped butcher's apron, his major series were *Cookery*, *Cookery Lesson* (a back to basics guide), *Man in the Kitchen* (cookery tips for men), *What's Cooking*, *Headway* (cookery theory) and *The Tools of Cookery*.

HARDING, GILBERT (1907–60)

British TV celebrity of the 1950s, earning a reputation for acute rudeness through appearances on panel games like **What's My Line?** A one-time school master and police officer, Harding had used his skill at languages to enter the BBC's monitoring service. From there, via service overseas, he became host of the radio quizzes *Round Britain Quiz*, **The Brains Trust** and *Twenty*

Questions. Initially earmarked to host *What's My Line?* on alternative weeks, Harding found being a panel member infinitely more suitable and allowed Eamonn Andrews to keep the chairman's job full time. In one famous television moment in 1960, Harding appeared on *Face to Face* only to readily admit that his bad manners and temper were 'quite indefensible'. In the same interview, he broke down when interrogator John Freeman inadvertently touched on the recent death of Harding's mother. Harding died the same year.

HARDY, ROBERT, CBE (1925–)

Powerful British actor whose most prominent TV roles have been as Dudley, Earl of Leicester in *Elizabeth R*, Siegfried Farnon in *All Creatures Great and Small* and the title part in *Winston Churchill – The Wilderness Years*. He also played Alec Stewart in *The Troubleshooters*, Abwehr Sergeant Gratz in Manhunt, Prince Albert in *Edward the Seventh*, Daily Crucible editor Russell Spam (and its proprietor Twiggy Rathbone) in *Hot Metal*, as well as appearing from the early 1960s in many other single dramas and series such as *Mystery and Imagination*, *The Baron*, *Supernatural*, *Upstairs, Downstairs*, *The Duchess of Duke Street*, *The Cleopatras*, *The Far Pavilions*, *Jenny's War*, *The Shooting Party* and *War and Remembrance* (again as Winston Churchill).

HARGREAVES, JACK, OBE (1911–94)

Thoughtful Jack Hargreaves was one of TV's gentler personalities. Whether it was explaining scientific facts to kids on *How!* or delving into the wonders of nature and practising rural crafts on his series *Out of Town*, he was a presenter who moved at his own pace, drawing calmly on his pipe and offering opinions in a relaxed, natural, unhurried way. A former vet's assistant and journalist, his first TV series was *Gone Fishing* for Southern, for whom he was also Deputy Programme Controller in the late 1960s and early 1970s. When Southern lost its franchise in 1981, *Gone Fishing's* successor, *Out of Town*, was cancelled, although Hargreaves did follow it up with a similar effort, *Old Country*, for Channel 4.

HARK AT BARKER

UK (LWT) Situation Comedy. ITV 1969–70

Lord Rustless	Ronnie Barker
Badger	Frank Gatliff
Mildred Bates	Josephine Tewson
Dithers	David Jason
Effie	Moira Foot
Cook	Mary Baxter

Producer: Humphrey Barclay

The misadventures of a lecherous old peer of the realm and his inept staff.

This series, based on Alun Owen's single play *Ah, There You Are*, which was screened as part of *The Ronnie Barker Playhouse* in 1968, featured the lusty, opinionated, cigar-puffing Lord Rustless, as he meandered around his stately home, Chrome Hall. His staff consisted of Badger, the butler, Dithers, the gardener, Mildred, the secretary, Effie, the maid and Cook. Other occasional characters were also played by Ronnie Barker. After two seasons on ITV, Rustless and his employees switched to BBC 2 in 1972 to star in the series *His Lordship Entertains*.

Harlech Television see HTV.

HARPER, GERALD (1931–)

Smooth-talking actor and radio presenter, the epitome of a country gent when portraying *Hadleigh*, a character given his own series after appearances in *Gazette*. Earlier, Harper had been the more flamboyant *Adam Adamant*, a frozen Edwardian adventurer reawakened in the Swinging Sixties. Although a number of smaller TV roles had come his way pre-*Adamant* (in series such as *Skyport*), and Harper had also guested in action series like *The Avengers* and *The Champions*, since *Hadleigh* he has concentrated on radio and stage work.

HARPERS WEST ONE

UK (ATV) Drama. ITV 1961–3

Mike Gilmore	Tristram Jellinek
Edward Cruickshank	Graham Crowden
Harriett Carr	Jan Holden
Oliver Backhouse	Philip Latham
Charlie Pugh	Tenniel Evans
Philip Nash	Bernard Horsfall
Frances Peters	Jayne Muir
Aubrey Harper	Arthur Hewlett
Julie Wheeler	Vivian Pickles

Creators: John Whitney, Geoffrey Belman.
Producers: Hugh Rennie, Rex Firkin, Royston Morley

Behind the scenes at a fictional London department store.

'Shopping with the lid off', as the programme blurb put it, *Harpers West One* focused on events in the lives of the team at Harpers department store in the West End. From customer liaison to personal liaisons, this series looked at all aspects of life in the store, but lasted a mere two seasons. It was co-created by future IBA Director-General John Whitney. *Harpers West One* was also responsible for one of 1961's biggest hit singles, 'Johnny Remember Me' by John Leyton, who turned up in the series playing the character Johnny St Cyr.

HARRIS, ROLF (1930–)

Friendly and excitable bearded Australian TV personality, a musician, a singer, a comedian and a painter rolled into one. Former Junior Backstroke Champion of Australia, Harris arrived in the UK in 1952 to study art, but soon took up showbiz as a career, making his TV debut in *Whirligig*. In 1959 he appeared with Tony Hancock in *Hancock's Half Hour* and in the same year continued in children's TV with *Musical Box,* an animated nursery rhyme show, made with Peter Firmin. During the early 1960s Rolf's regular partner was Coojee Bear, a koala puppet. From 1967 Harris starred in his own Saturday night variety show, inevitably conjuring up a giant painting (using large pots of paint and decorating brushes) to illustrate one of his novel songs. Viewers could also count on odd musical instruments, be they didgeridoos, wobble boards, piano accordians or Stylophones. In the 1980s he hosted *Rolf Harris's Cartoon Time* and among his other credits have been *Rolf's Walkabout, Rolf on Saturday, OK?, Hey Presto, It's Rolf, Rolf's Here! OK?* and *Rolf's Cartoon Club.*

HARRIS, SUSAN

Successful American writer who broke through in the 1970s by creating *Soap*. In the 1980s and 1990s she was responsible for *The Golden Girls, The Golden Palace, Nurses* and *Empty Nest,* all made by Witt-Thomas-Harris, the production company she founded with her husband Paul Junger Witt and another partner, Tony Thomas.

HARRISON, KATHLEEN (1892–)

Veteran British actress, fond of Cockney charlady roles, even though she was born in Lancashire. Her big TV success came in 1966, after a lengthy career in films (most notably in the *Huggett* series), when she was cast as *Mrs Thursday,* a cleaner who inherited a fortune and a controlling interest in a large company. After that, her appearances were confined to guest spots in series like *Danger UXB* and a couple of Dickens adaptations (including the 1978 version of *Our Mutual Friend* as Henrietta Boffin), having turned down the part of *Edna, The Inebriate Woman,* which won Patricia Hayes much acclaim.

HARRY O

US (Warner Brothers) Detective Drama. BBC 1 1974–7

Harry Orwell	David Janssen
Detective Lt Manny Quinlan	Henry Darrow
Lt K.C. Trench	Anthony Zerbe
Sgt Don Roberts	Paul Tulley
Lester Hodges	Les Lannom
Dr Fong	Keye Luke

Creator: Howard Rodman. Executive Producer: Jerry Thorpe. Producers: Robert E. Thompson, Robert Dozier, Buck Houghton, Alex Beaton

A retired cop lives in a beach shack but still works as a private detective.

Former marine Harry Orwell had been pensioned out of the police force after being shot in the back. Despite constant pain from a bullet lodged in his body, he took to working as a private detective, taking on cases that both aroused his interest and supplemented his income. A drop-out among detectives, the grumpy, whisky-swilling Orwell was, all the same, a lot more dependable than his temperamental car, which forced him to make good use of public transport. Based in San Diego, and living in a beach-front cottage, he worked closely with his by-the-book former colleague Lt Manny Quinlan of the local police, but, when Quinlan was killed off, Orwell moved to Santa Monica. Here, life was even less comfortable, as Harry had to deal with the sarcastic Lt Trench. On the plus side, he was able to call on the help of a couple of amateur snoopers, Lester Hodges and Dr Fong.

Actress Farrah Fawcett made her TV debut in this series, appearing as Orwell's next-door neighbour.

HARRY'S GAME

UK (Yorkshire) Thriller. ITV 1982

Captain Harry Brown	Ray Lonnen

Writer: Gerald Seymour. Executive Producer: David Cunliffe. Producer: Keith Richardson

An army captain infiltrates terrorist ranks to track down a killer.

This three-part thriller, screened on consecutive nights, centred on Captain Harry Brown, a specialist called up by the Home Secretary to go undercover in Northern Ireland. His mission: to mingle with the IRA and to hunt down one specific political assassin. The cat-and-mouse action was penned by former ITN reporter Gerald Seymour from his own novel, with the haunting theme song a hit from Clannad in 1982.

HART TO HART

US (Aaron Spelling) Detective Drama. ITV 1980–5

Jonathan Hart	Robert Wagner
Jennifer Hart	Stefanie Powers
Max	Lionel Stander

Creator: Sidney Sheldon. Executive Producers: Aaron Spelling, Leonard Goldberg. Producer: Mart Crowley

A self-made millionaire and his journalist wife spice up their life by chasing crooks.

Jonathan Hart, head of Hart Industries, and his wife, Jennifer (a former world-famous journalist), lived in a mansion in Bel-Air, where they had everything they needed – except excitement. They didn't need to work, so, to add some zest to their sad, pampered lives, they spent most of their time dashing around the world in a private jet, acting as a pair of amateur sleuths. They were supported by Max, their gruff, wrinkled chauffeur, and their dog, Freeway.

The series was created by novelist Sidney Sheldon and borrowed heavily from *The Thin Man* films of the 1930s and 1940s, which starred William Powell and Myrna Loy as Nick and Nora Charles.

HART, TONY (1925–)

Children's TV artist and presenter of *Vision On*, the programme for deaf youngsters. He subsequently gained his own series, *Take Hart* and *Hartbeat*, although some of his early work was as operator of *Quackers* in Ray Alan's *Tich and Quackers*. He also appeared in the long-running series *Whirligig* and *Playbox* and drew the Packi adventures for *Blue Peter* in the late 1950s.

HARTNELL, WILLIAM (1908–75)

Long-serving British character actor, forever remembered as the first *Doctor Who*, playing the role as a mysterious, tetchy, headstrong old man in an Edwardian frock coat. He stayed with the series from its beginnings in 1963 to 1966, when, a combination of dissatisfaction with the series and illness saw him leave. He made one further appearance in the series, in the story called 'The Three Doctors', in which Jon Pertwee's version was given the assistance of his previous incarnations. Previously, Hartnell had starred in *The Army Game*, as the blustery Sgt Major Bullimore, a similar performance to his Sgt Grimshaw in the film *Carry On Sergeant* (just one of over 60 films he made). One of Hartnell's last TV performances was in the anthology series *Crime of Passion*.

HARTY, RUSSELL (1934–88)

Northern presenter and chat show host who worked his way from schoolteaching and producing BBC radio arts programmes to national status through shows such as *Russell Harty Plus* and *Harty*. Along the way, his distinctive 'you are, are you not?' style of questioning was much mimicked. One of his earliest production (and presentation) successes was *Aquarius* in 1969, and Harty continued in front of the cameras for a series of chat shows for LWT (*Eleven Plus*, which became *Russell Harty Plus*). He switched channels in 1980 and gained his own peak-time slot on BBC 2 with the show *Russell Harty*. In one famous instance, model/singer Grace Jones whacked him about the head, believing he was ignoring her. Among his other credits were *Saturday Night People* (with Janet Street Porter and Clive James, for the London ITV region), *All About Books*, **Songs of Praise**, *Harty Goes to Hollywood*, *Russell Harty at the Seaside* and *Favourite Things*. Harty died in 1988 of hepatitis, an illness he picked up while filming a series on the Grand Tour of Europe.

HASS, HANS (1919–) AND LOTTE (1929–)

Austrian husband and wife diving team who pioneered underwater filming for television in the 1950s and 1960s. In 1956 they brought the wonders of the deep to BBC viewers in *Diving to Adventure*, although their longer-running series was *The Undersea World of Adventure*. Their films were dubbed into German, as well as English, to cover both markets. In 1966 Hans presented a different kind of nature programme. Entitled *Man*, it looked at the behaviour of the human race as if observed by outsiders.

HASSELHOFF, DAVID (1952–)

Tall, handsome American actor who shot to fame as co-star (with a car!) of *Knight Rider*, playing do-gooder Michael Knight. After four years behind the wheel of the world's cleverest motor, Hasselhoff moved to the seaside to star in the hugely popular *Baywatch*, as lifeguard Lt Mitch Bucannon. When the network decided to drop the series, Hasselhoff used his own money to produce more episodes under the title of *New Baywatch* and sold them into syndication. His earlier TV career included guest spots in *The Love Boat* and *Police Story*, as well as a seven-year run in a US daytime soap, *The Young and the Restless*.

HAVE GUN WILL TRAVEL

US (CBS) Western. ITV 1959–

Paladin	Richard Boone
Hey Boy	Kam Tong
Hey Girl	Lisa Lu

A mysterious Wild West troubleshooter hires himself out to those seeking justice.

This series centred on the enigmatic Paladin, a cultured, well-educated former West Point student who now lived at the classy Hotel Carlton in San Francisco. A loner, dressed menacingly in black, he appeared cynical and somewhat threatening, but he was also warm and sensitive at the same time, a good man at heart. His work, after all, involved righting wrongs – even if it was for a fee. His love of the good things in life meant that he needed to earn his keep and he operated as a bodyguard, a courier, a private detective, or whatever was asked of him. But, although his gun was for hire, the inscrutable Paladin was a man of principle and was even known to turn on his employers if it appeared that they were the real bad guys. He was a slick operator and far removed from the other, rough and ready ranch-bound TV cowboys of his time.

'Paladin' means 'knightly hero' and is a name given to the knight chess piece, which appeared in white on Paladin's holster and also on his calling card, which bore the words 'Have Gun, Will Travel . . . Wire Paladin, San Francisco'. Any wires received were delivered by Hey Boy, the Chinese hotel hand (who was replaced by Hey Girl for a short period). Duane Eddy had a UK hit with an instrumental version of the theme song, 'The Ballad of Paladin', in 1962.

HAVE I GOT NEWS FOR YOU

UK (Hat Trick) Comedy. BBC 2 1990–

Angus Deayton
Paul Merton
Ian Hislop

Producers: Harry Thompson, Colin Swash

Ultra-topical current affairs satire/quiz.

The television version of Radio 4's *The News Quiz Have I Got News For You* has been a contest between comedian Paul Merton and *Private Eye* editor Ian Hislop, each accompanied by celebrity guests from the worlds of entertainment or politics. The format has relied heavily on the speed of thought and quick wit of its contestants as they have adlibbed answers and jokes to various clips of the week's events. Blacked out words in newspaper headlines, odd ones out and a caption competition have been regular features. Comics such as Alexei Sayle, Tony Hawkes, Vic Reeves and Frank Skinner have been called in as team members, as have writers like Andrew Morton and TV folk like Anne Robinson, Jonathan Ross and Trevor McDonald. Among the political guests have been Neil Kinnock, Cecil Parkinson, Charles Kennedy, Ken Livingstone, Edwina Currie and Sir Rhodes Boyson. When Roy Hattersley failed to show up his place alongside Paul Merton was taken by a tub of lard. Even though scoring has been totally haphazard, it is Hislop's team that has always seemed to lose. Events have been chaired by Angus Deayton, who has contributed as much ribald and risqué humour as the panellists themselves. Thankfully, by pre-recording the show the night before transmission, the libellous bits have been cut out – allegedly.

HAVERS, NIGEL (1949–)

One of TV's aristocratic smoothies, Nigel Havers, son of former Attorney-General Sir Michael Havers, has seldom been short of television work. From early appearances in dramas such as *Upstairs, Downstairs*, *Shabby Tiger* and *Nicholas Nickleby*, Havers moved on to *The Glittering Prizes*, *Pennies from Heaven*, *Nancy Astor* and *Winston Churchill – The Wilderness Years* (as Randolph Churchill). He starred as Paul Craddock in *A Horseman Riding By*, Roy in *Strangers and Brothers* and Dr Tom Latimer in *Don't Wait Up*. He also took the title role (Ralph Gorse) in *The Charmer*, played one of *The Good Guys* (Guy McFadyean) and was Hugh Fleming in *A Perfect Hero*. Among his other credits have been *A Raging Calm*, *An Englishman's Castle*, *Coming Out*, *Unity*, *Goodbye Darling* and *After the Party*.

HAWAII FIVE-O

US (CBS/Leonard Freeman) Police Drama. ITV 1970–

Detective Steve Garrett	Jack Lord
Detective Danny 'Danno' Williams	James MacArthur
Detective Chin Ho Kelly	Kam Fong
Detective Kono Kalakaua	Zulu
Governor Philip Grey	Richard Denning
Wo Fat	Khigh Dhiegh
Detective Ben Kokua	Al Harrington
Che Fong	Harry Endo
Doc Bergman	Al Eben
May	Maggi Parker
Jenny Sherman	Peggy Ryan
Duke Lukela	Herman Wedemeyer
Attorney General John Manicote	Glenn Cannon
James 'Kimo' Carew	William Smith
Lori Wilson	Sharon Farrell
Tom 'Truck' Kealoha	Moe Keale

Creator/Executive Producer: Leonard Freeman. Producers: Bill Finnegan, Bob Sweeney, Philip Leacock, Richard Newton, Douglas Green, B.W. Sandefur

The cases of a special police unit and its tight-lipped, self-righteous leader on the paradise islands of Hawaii.

Five-O was not your normal police force. These guys (a special division of the Hawaiian State Police) worked separately from the Honolulu Police Department, and were directly answerable to the Governor. They operated from the Iolani Palace, the supposed seat of the Hawaiian Government, and their tough, no-nonsense boss was Steve McGarrett.

The blue-suited McGarrett loathed crooks and seemed to have no other passion in life. He was ably supported by his main men, 'Danno'

Williams ('Book 'em Danno' became a catchphrase) and Chin Ho Kelly. Another original colleague, Kono Kalakaua, was written out after a few years, although most of the cast stayed with the show for much of its very long run. When Williams and Kelly eventually left, new officers like Lori Wilson, Truck Kealoha and 'Kimo' Carew were added to see the series through to its close (1980 in its native USA).

Five-O, being independent, was able to avoid the petty bureaucracies of normal police work. Its brief was to keep this tropical paradise clean, to mop up vermin that disrupted the life of Honolulu and the other islands. Consequently, McGarrett and his boys targeted the spivs, the hoodlums and, more purposefully, the organized underworld, especially an elusive oriental villain by the name of Wo Fat.

As well as taking the star role, Jack Lord was also heavily involved behind the scenes of the series. He became an Hawaiian resident and, to many viewers, became synonymous with the islands.

HAWK, JEREMY (CEDRIC LANGE; 1918–)

A former music hall straight man to stars like Arthur Askey, Arthur Haynes and Norman Wisdom, Jeremy Hawk found his niche in the early days of television as a quiz master. As host of **Criss Cross Quiz** and *Junior Criss Cross Quiz* from 1957 to 1962, he was a familiar face in most households. He then presented the improvisation comedy *Impromptu*, but found little TV work later (save a memorable Cadbury's Whole Nut commercial in the 1970s: 'Nuts Who-ole Ha-azelnuts; Cadbury's take 'em and they cover 'em in chocolate') and returned to the stage. Hawk is the father of actress Belinda Lang.

HAWKESWORTH, JOHN (1920–)

British writer/producer, a one-time Rank film scriptwriter, chiefly remembered for period pieces such as **Upstairs, Downstairs** and **The Duchess of Duke Street** (also as creator). In addition, he produced and co-scripted **The Gold Robbers**, created/adapted *The Short Stories of Conan Doyle*, **By the Sword Divided** and **Danger UXB**, also adapted *The Flame Trees of Thika* and worked on episodes of **The Adventures of Sherlock Holmes** and **Crime of Passion**.

HAWKEYE AND THE LAST OF THE MOHICANS

Canada (Normandie) Adventure. ITV 1957–

Nat 'Hawkeye' Cutler ....John Hart
Chingachgook ....Lon Chaney Jnr

Producer: Sigmund Neufeld

Escapades in the American wilderness with a trapper and his Indian comrade.

This drama series, loosely based on the novel by James Fenimore Cooper, featured Nat Cutler, known familiarly as 'Hawkeye', a trapper, fur trader and scout for the US cavalry. His adventures in the northern frontierland, and encounters with the Huron Indians during the 1750s, were shared by his redskin bloodbrother, Chingachgook, the 'Last of the Mohicans'. Star John Hart had previously enjoyed brief TV fame when temporarily taking over the role of the **Lone Ranger** from Clayton Moore.

HAWKINS, PETER (1924–)

British actor best known for voicing children's animated characters. He was the vocal talent behind **The Flowerpot Men**, **The Woodentops**, **Captain Pugwash** and **Tin Tin**. In vision, he appeared in *Whirligig*, amongst other programmes.

HAWTHORNE, NIGEL, CBE (1929–)

British character actor, acclaimed for his tongue-twisting performances as Sir Humphrey Appleby in **Yes Minister** and **Yes Prime Minister**. Hawthorne also played Pierre Curie in *Marie Curie*, Dr Grantly in *The Barchester Chronicles* and the sadistic taxi driver examiner in Jack Rosenthal's play *The Knowledge*. Amongst his other credits have been **Edward and Mrs Simpson**, **Warrior Queen**, *The Hunchback of Notre Dame*, *A Tale of Two Cities*, *The World Cup – A Captain's Tale*, *Jenny's War*, *Mapp and Lucia* and *The Miser*.

HAYES, MELVYN (1935–)

Diminutive English actor. As a teenager he played one of the boys in **Billy Bunter of Greyfriars School** in the 1950s and appeared in **Quatermass II**, plus other dramas. He was the Artful Dodger in the BBC's 1962 adaptation of *Oliver Twist* and, in 1971, he was seen as Albert, the grown-up in **Here Come The Double Deckers**. Hayes was also cast as Gregory in the Jimmy Edwards comedy *Sir Yellow* and played Melvyn Didsbury in the kids' series *Potter's Picture Palace*, as well as providing the voice of Skeleton for the *SuperTed* cartoons. However, by far his most successful role has been as Bombardier 'Gloria' Beaumont, the drag artist in **It Ain't Half Hot Mum**. More recently, he was a judge on satellite TV's talent show *Sky Star Search*. Hayes's second wife was actress Wendy Padbury.

HAYES, PATRICIA (1909–)

London-born actress, generally seen as a foil or support to established comedians like Arthur

Askey, Tony Hancock, Arthur Haynes and Benny Hill. In contrast, her dramatic skills were brought to the fore in the award-winning *Play For Today Edna, The Inebriate Woman*. Hayes has also been seen as neighbour Griselda Wormald in *Hugh and I*, Lillian in *The Trouble with You, Lillian*, Mrs Basket in *Last of the Baskets*, traffic warden Mrs Cantaford in *Spooner's Patch*, mother Alice Tripp in *Marjorie and Men*, Old Pat in *The Lady is a Tramp* and in programmes as varied as *Till Death Us Do Part* (playing the Garnetts' neighbour Min), *The Corn Is Green*, *The Avengers*, *Mr Pye* and *Casualty*.

HAYNES, ARTHUR (1915–66)

One of TV's first star comedians, former radio comic Arthur Haynes specialized in social nuisance characters like a manipulative tramp, the silent Oscar Pennyfeather, and a bemedalled army veteran who was insistent on telling an ungrateful world just what he had done. These appeared in *The Arthur Haynes Show* (written by Johnny Speight and co-starring Nicholas Parsons as his straight man), which was launched in 1956 after Haynes had stolen the spotlight in a series called *Strike a New Note* and had appeared in *The Charlie Chester Show*. He was still starring in his own series when he died suddenly in 1966.

HAZELL

UK (Thames) Detective Drama. ITV 1978–80

James Hazell ....Nicholas Ball
'Choc' Minty ....Roddy McMillan
Cousin Tel ....Desmond McNamara

Creators: Terry Venables, Gordon Williams.
Producers: June Roberts, Tim Aspinall

A crooked London policeman becomes a private eye.

When James Hazell was forced to retire from the police force in his early 30s because of a damaged ankle, he turned to drink and destroyed his marriage. Reformed and dried out, he became a private investigator, helped by his cousin Tel, with his main sparring partner a Scottish CID officer named 'Choc' Minty, who was always threatening to take away Hazell's operating licence.

Even if the series erred on the violent side, Hazell was a fun character, a Jack the Lad with a flair for the telling phrase. A true Cockney, he enjoyed the glamour of his profession and bustled along in life, mixing it with the best, but not always coming out on top. In spoof film noir fashion, Hazell provided a commentary voice-over for each episode. The series was based on books by football manager Terry Venables and Gordon Williams, who also contributed to the TV version.

HEALY, TIM (1952–)

Geordie character actor, familiar from a number of light comedy-dramas. It was as Denis in *Auf Wiedersehen, Pet* that Healy first grabbed the viewers' attention, although he had already appeared in programmes like *Coronation Street*, *Emmerdale Farm*, *Minder*, *The World Cup – A Captain's Tale* and *When the Boat Comes In*. His other credits have included *A Kind of Living*, *A Perfect Spy*, *Cracker* and the kids' show *Tickle on the Tum*. In 1991 he headlined again as ex-patriot Cockney Reg Toomer in *The Boys from the Bush*. In 1994 he was Foxy in the dustbinmen comedy *Common As Muck*.

HEARNE, RICHARD, OBE (1909–79)

Acrobatic Richard Hearne was one of British TV's first clowns, playing the part of a nimble but accident-prone old man in numerous slapstick sketches. The character was Mr Pastry, complete with walrus moustache, long coat tails and gold-rimmed spectacles perched half-way down the nose. Mr Pastry first appeared in one of Hearne's many stage performances and arrived on television in 1946. He went on to star in series such as *Mr Pastry's Progress*, *Leave It to Mr Pastry*, *Ask Mr Pastry* and *Mr Pastry's Pet Shop*, as well as guesting on *Crackerjack* and *Sunday Night at the London Palladium*. Hearne also starred in several films.

HEARTBEAT

UK (Yorkshire) Drama. ITV 1992–

PC Nick Rowan ....Nick Berry
Dr Kate Rowan ....Niamh Cusack
Sgt Oscar Blaketon ....Derek Fowlds
Claude Jeremiah Greengrass ....Bill Maynard
Dr Alex Ferrenby ....Frank Middlemass
PC Alf Ventress ....William Simons
PC Phil Bellamy ....Mark Jordon
George Ward ....Stuart Golland
Gina Ward ....Tricia Penrose

Executive Producer: Keith Richardson.
Producers: Stuart Doughty, Steve Lanning, Keith Richardson

Nostalgic drama about a constable patrolling a Yorkshire moorland beat.

Set in 1964, *Heartbeat* was the story of PC Nick Rowan and his doctor wife, Kate. Having left their London base to return to Kate's home area of the North Yorkshire moors, the Rowans took up residence in the police house in the village of Aidensfield, where Nick became the village bobby. He reported to the grouchy Sgt Blaketon at the Ashfordly police station and his PC colleagues were the skiving, chain-smoking veteran Alf Ventress and the somewhat reckless Phil

Bellamy. Kate became a partner in the Aidensfield general practice headed by old friend Alex Ferrenby, and, following his death in a train accident, she became the village's only doctor. Bain of Rowan's life was the lovable rogue Claude Jeremiah Greengrass, who, with his loyal mutt, Alfred, was usually at the heart of some scam or other. George Ward, assisted by Gina, his trendy Liverpudlian niece, ran The Aidensfield Arms, the local pub.

Heartbeat was based on the *Constable* novels by Nicholas Rhea, the pen name of former Yorkshire policeman Peter Walker. With its liberal use of contemporary pop hits, and careful selection of period furniture and other items, this gentle, nostalgic drama attracted a huge audience. Buddy Holly's 'Heartbeat', sung by Nick Berry, was the programme's theme song.

HECTOR'S HOUSE

France Children's Entertainment. BBC 1 1968–75

Creator: Georges Croses

The domestic adventures of a dog, a cat and a frog.

In this five-minute pre-news filler the Hector in question was a large, sensible-looking dog with floppy ears who shared his home with Zaza, a cat dressed in a red pinafore. Their next-door neighbour (forever nipping over the fence by ladder) was Mrs Kiki, a giggly frog in a gingham overall, who displayed a talent for weather forecasting. The trio enjoyed mild mirth around the house and garden, the two females playing silly jokes on the gullible hound and Hector never failing to gallantly act as a true gentleman, courteously assisting his friends at every turn. His catchphrase was a variation on 'I'm just a big, silly old Hector', adapted according to circumstance into 'big sensible old Hector', 'big sad old Hector', etc. The only other regular was a bird that twittered in a tree at the start and finish of each programme. The series was known in its native France as *La Maison de Tu Tu.*

HEDLEY, JACK (JACK HAWKINS; 1930–)

Solid British character actor whose lead role in the Francis Durbridge thriller *The World of Tim Frazer* in 1960 was not followed up with a starring role until **Colditz** in 1972, in which he played Lt Colonel Preston. However, he did play Corrigan Blake in the 1962 Alun Owen play *You Can't Win 'Em All*, which led to the *Corrigan Blake* series (although John Turner then assumed the title role). Hedley was also seen in **Kate**, as Kate Graham's editor, and in the TV movie version of *Brief Encounter.*

HEINEY, PAUL (1949–)

British TV reporter and presenter, the husband of broadcaster Libby Purves. He first came to light as one of Esther Rantzen's supporting crew on *That's Life* and *The Big Time*, before sharing the limelight with Chris Searle in *In at the Deep End*. He presented *The Travel Show* for BBC 2 and once stepped in as host of *Food and Drink* while Chris Kelly took a season off.

HELEN – A WOMAN OF TODAY

UK (LWT) Drama. ITV 1973

Helen Tulley ....Alison Fiske
Frank Tulley...Martin Shaw
Carole ....Sharon Duce

Producer: Richard Bates

A wife and mother divorces her cheating husband and seeks a new life of her own.

Reflecting the increasingly feminist mood of the time, and for once making the woman in a broken marriage the centre of attention, *Helen – A Woman of Today* related the story of Helen Tulley, a middle-class, thirtysomething mother of two who decided to strive for more from life. It all began with an affair between Frank, her husband, and another woman, Carole. Despite being urged by friends and families to stand by her man, Helen turned instead to study, becoming self-reliant and battling her own way through a cold world. There were 13 episodes.

HENDERSON, DICKIE, OBE (1922–85)

Versatile British entertainer, the son of Dick Henderson, a Yorkshire-born vaudeville comic. Dickie's peak television years were undoubtedly the mid-1950s to the early 1970s. After a decade and a half on the stage, he broke into television alongside Arthur Askey in *Before Your Very Eyes* and went on to compere **Sunday Night at the London Palladium** before being given his own series, *The Dickie Henderson Half-Hour*, in 1958, and then the long-running *The Dickie Henderson Show*. In this song-and-dance sitcom he played himself, with June Laverick cast as his wife. This was followed by another comedy entitled *A Present for Dickie*, in which he found himself entrusted with an Indian elephant. His other notable TV credits were in *I'm Bob, He's Dickie* (with Bob Monkhouse) and *I'm Dickie – That's Showbusiness*.

HENDERSON, DON (1932–)

Softly spoken British actor, the glove-wearing, inhaler-sniffing star of **Bulman** and other series. His character of George Bulman first appeared in

The XYY Man and then in *Strangers*, with his ever-present scarf employed to hide scars left by Henderson's cancer surgery. His weak voice, often put down to a cold in the series, was another by-product of Henderson's illness. Post-Bulman, Henderson moved into *The Paradise Club* (as ex-priest Frank Kane) alongside Leslie Grantham. Among Henderson's many other appearances have been parts in *Poldark*, *Crossroads*, *Dick Turpin*, *New Scotland Yard*, *Dixon of Dock Green*, *Van Der Valk*, *The Onedin Line*, *Warship*, *Doctor Who*, *Knights of God*, *Hot Metal*, *Minder* and *Dead Head*. He is married to actress Shirley Stelfox, with whom he appeared in *Making Out*.

HENDRY, IAN (1931–84)

Determined-looking British actor whose show-business debut was as stooge to Coco the clown. After some notable stage performances, he broke into films in the 1950s, then secured himself some minor roles in such series as *The Invisible Man*, *Probation Officer* and *Emergency – Ward 10*. His first starring part was as Dr Geoffrey Brent in *Police Surgeon*, a series which quickly evolved into *The Avengers*, the character becoming Dr David Keel and linking up with Patrick McNee's John Steed, as a couple of crime fighters. Hendry left *The Avengers* in 1962, to be replaced eventually by Honor Blackman, triggering a major change of direction for the series. He waited four years for his next major role, which arrived in *The Informer*, when he played disbarred barrister Alex Lambert, who worked as a police informer, and was then cast as astronaut Captain Don Quick in the sci-fi fantasy comedy *The Adventures of Don Quick* in 1970. *The Lotus Eaters*, in which he took the part of alcoholic ex-patriot Erik Shepherd, followed in 1972. Amongst Hendy's other credits were guest spots in series like *The Protectors* and *Supernatural*. His most prominent last roles were in *For Maddie with Love*, opposite Nyree Dawn Porter, and a stint in *Brookside* as hard-drinking sailor Davey Jones.

HENRY, LENNY (LENWORTH HENRY; 1958–)

Popular black comedian whose rise to fame was precipitated by a winning performance on *New Faces* in 1975. Majoring initially on gags and impressions, Henry graduated to sitcom in the short-lived *The Fosters* (playing Sonny Foster). Then came *Tiswas* and its late-night offspring, *OTT*, before Henry joined Tracey Ullman and David Copperfield in the sketch show *Three of a Kind*. He appeared on *Saturday Live* and *The Young Ones* and secured his own BBC series, which fluctuated between stand-up comedy, sketches and sitcom, allowing him to develop characters like Algernon the Rasta, Theophilus P. Wildebeeste, Deakus the old Jamaican, Reverend Nat West, PC Ganga and the 'crucial' Brixton pirate radio DJ Delbert Wilkins (who enjoyed a later series all to himself). Henry became a linchpin of the *Comic Relief* appeals and, in recent years, has been seen as the temperamental Gareth Blackstock in *Chef*. He is married to comedian Dawn French and runs the Crucial Films independent production company.

HENSON, JIM (1936–90)

American puppeteer and TV executive, the man responsible for the Muppets (a combination of marionettes and hand puppets). Henson's puppetry was first featured on television in Washington DC through a series called *Sam and Friends*, which ran for six years from 1955. This gave him the exposure to send his creations on to national programmes like *The Tonight Show* and *The Ed Sullivan Show*. In 1969 his Muppet empire really began to move, thanks to a starring role in the new educational kids' series *Sesame Street*. Creatures like Big Bird, Oscar the Grouch and Kermit the Frog helped youngsters worldwide to learn their numbers and letters. However, in order to win his puppets a prime-time slot, Henson was forced to move to the UK, where Lord Grade put up funds for the phenomenally successful *The Muppet Show*. Henson himself voiced some of the characters, including the show's emcee, Kermit. On the back of the Muppets Henson created *Fraggle Rock* and the award-winning *The Storyteller*, starring John Hurt. *Dinosaurs* was his last completed project before he died prematurely in 1990.

HEPTON, BERNARD (1925–)

Serious-looking British character actor whose performance as Archbishop Thomas Cranmer in *The Six Wives of Henry VIII* was followed by a spell in *Colditz* as the kind Nazi Kommandant. He switched sides to play café owner/Résistance fighter Albert Foiret in *Secret Army*, was Pallus in *I, Claudius* and estate agent Donald Stimpson, trying to nail down Nigel Havers, in *The Charmer*. Hepton also took to comedy in *The Squirrels* (as Mr Fletcher) and *Sadie It's Cold Outside* (as Norman Potter). His other credits have included *The Troubleshooters*, *Tinker, Tailor, Soldier, Spy*, *Blood Money*, *Bergerac* and *The Woman in Black*.

HERBS, THE

UK (Filmfair) Children's Entertainment. BBC 1 1968

Narrator: Gordon Rollings

Creator/Writer: Michael Bond. Executive Producer: Graham Clutterbuck

Fragrant happenings in an English country garden, with its herbs as the stars.

Relating the surreal happenings in the garden of Sir Basil and Lady Rosemary, *The Herbs* featured such characters as Constable Knapweed, schoolteacher Mr Onion the Chives (his pupils), Bayleaf the gardener, Aunt Mint, Sage the owl, Tarragon the dragon, Pashana Bedi the snake-charmer and Belladonna. However, the undoubted stars were a manic, tail-chasing dog called Dill and a genial lion, Parsley (later to gain his own spin-off series, *The Adventures of Parsley*). 'Herbidacious' was the magic word which opened the gate to the garden. The action was narrated by Gordon Rollings (Arkwright in the John Smith's beer commercials) and the series aired under the *Watch With Mother* banner.

HERE COME THE DOUBLE DECKERS

UK (Twentieth Century-Fox/Century Films) Children's Entertainment. BBC 1 1971

Scooper	Peter Firth
Billie	Gillian Bailey
Brains	Michael Audreson
Doughnut	Douglas Simmonds
Spring	Brinsley Forde
Sticks	Bruce Clark
Tiger	Debbie Russ
Albert	Melvyn Hayes

Creators: Roy Simpson, Harry Booth. Producer: Roy Simpson

A group of do-gooder kids stumble into musical adventures.

Using a disused double-decker bus housed in a London junk yard as their HQ, the Double Deckers were a bunch of game kids who found themselves wrapped up in a series of zany escapades. Leader of the gang was Scooper (played by Peter Firth, whose career only went up from here) and the other members were the swotty Brains (usually inventing something), the chubby Doughnut, the American Sticks (so-named after his drumming skills), Billie, Spring (future Aswad reggae group-member Brinsley Forde) and tiny Tiger. Albert was their grown-up friend. With its jaunty 'Get on board' theme song, the series, made in the UK, was screened first in the USA before being bought by the BBC.

HERE'S HARRY

UK (BBC) Situation Comedy. BBC 1960–5

Harry Worth	Harry Worth
Mrs Williams	Vi Stevens

Mrs Benson	Doris Gambell
Tommy	Reginald Marsh
Alf	Joe Gladwin

Producers: John Ammonds, John Street

A well-meaning bumbler tackles bureaucracy.

Playing himself, trilby-hatted Harry Worth starred as a clumsy, ineffective, dithering complainer who ended up confusing all around him. Living with his cat, Tiddles, at 52 Acacia Avenue, in the northern town of Woodbridge, Harry made plenty of references to his aunt, Mrs Amelia Prendergast, but she was never seen. However, he did have a housekeeper, Mrs Williams (later replaced by Mrs Benson), and two old friends, Tommy and Alf. Harry moved to London for the last season.

HERE'S LUCY

US (CBS/Lucille Ball) Situation Comedy. BBC 1 1969–71

Lucy Carter	Lucille Ball
Harrison Carter	Gale Gordon
Mary Jane Lewis	Mary Jane Croft
Kim Carter	Lucie Arnaz
Craig Carter	Desi Arnaz, Jnr

Producer: Gary Morton

Lucille Ball's third family sitcom, with the action now set in California.

Here's Lucy was in many ways no more than a name change for **The Lucy Show**, with Lucy still aided in her slapstick routines by Mary Jane Croft, and Gale Gordon still around to provide the foil. However, Lucy had now moved to Los Angeles and her surname had become Carter, although she was still a widow. Her new children, Kim and Craig, were played by her own son and daughter, while Gale Gordon this time played Uncle Harry, Lucy's brother-in-law and owner of the Unique Employment Agency, where she worked as a secretary.

HERGE'S ADVENTURES OF TIN TIN

France (Tele-Hachette) Animation. BBC 1 1962–4

Narrator: Peter Hawkins

Producer (UK): Peggy Miller

A young reporter and his pet dog lurch from scrape to scrape.

Created in 1929 and first seen as a comic strip in the Belgian weekly *Le Petit Vingtième*, Tin Tin was the brainchild of Hergé, alias cartoonist George Rémi. Over the years, the character appeared in over 20 books and made his TV bow in France in 1961 in this series of episodic adventures. Dubbed into English, Tin Tin arrived in the UK a year later and British viewers were treated to the hair-raising (in more ways than one, considering his tufty locks) escapades of the red-headed cub reporter. Loyally at Tin Tin's side was his white fox terrier, Snowy (Milou in the original French), and also lending a hand was the grog-soddened Captain Haddock, the black-bearded skipper of the ship *Karaboudjan*. Other characters seen from time to time were the bowler-hatted Thompson Twins (who gave their name to the 1980s pop group), the deaf and forgetful Professor Calculus and the conspiratorially minded General Alcazar.

With each adventure chopped up into breathless five-minute episodes, complete with cliffhanger endings, Tin Tin was forever immersed in investigations like *The Crab with the Golden Claw*, *Star of Mystery*, *Red Hacham's Treasure*, *Black Island*, *Objective Moon* and *The Calculus Case*. With so many repeat showings over the years, who could now forget the announcer's booming voice heralding another instalment of *Hergé's Adventures of . . . Tin Tin?*

HI-DE-HI!

UK (BBC) Situation Comedy. BBC 1 1981–8

Ted Bovis ....Paul Shane
Gladys Pugh ....Ruth Madoc
Jeffrey Fairbrother ....Simon Cadell
Spike Dixon..Jeffrey Holland
Peggy Ollerenshaw ....Su Pollard
Fred Quilley...Felix Bowness
Mr Partridge ....Leslie Dwyer
Yvonne Stewart-Hargreaves ....Diane Holland
Barry Stewart-Hargreaves ....Barry Howard
Sylvia ....Nikki Kelly
Betty...Rikki Howard
Mary..Penny Irving
Squadron Leader Clive Dempster, DFC ..David Griffin
The Twins ....The Webb Twins
Tracey ....Susan Beagley
April ....Linda Regan
Dawn ....Laura Jackson
Julian Dalrymple-Sykes ....Ben Aris

Creators/Writers: David Croft, Jimmy Perry.
Producers: David Croft, John Kilby, Mike Stephens

Hi-jinx in a British holiday camp at the turn of the 1960s.

Beginning in the summer of 1959, this thinly veiled send-up of Butlins, Pontins and the like focused on events at Maplins holiday camp at Crimpton-on-Sea, progressing season by season into the early 1960s. The pilot programme (screened in 1980) saw the arrival of the members of staff. The new Entertainments Officer was the ineffective Jeffrey Fairbrother, a Cambridge archaeologist who decided to seek pastures new when his wife left him. Also new was young camp comic Spike Dixon, quickly corrupted when taken under the wing of the wily camp host Ted Bovis. Fairbrother's assistant was valleys girl Gladys Pugh who tripled up as sports organizer and Radio Maplin announcer (rousing campers from their slumbers with a lilting 'Morning campers'). Fairbrother instantly warmed her frigid heart, although her smouldering advances were never welcomed. Other members of the entertainments team were bent jockey Fred Quilley, now in charge of the camp horses, grouchy, boozy Punch and Judy man Mr Partridge ('Jolly Uncle Willie' to the kids he hated), snooty, fading ballroom stars Yvonne and Barry Stewart-Hargreaves, and a small group of Yellowcoats, whose job it was to cajole the campers into having fun, whether they liked it or not. Desperate to get in the thick of the action was daffy chalet maid Peggy Ollerenshaw, who longed to abandon her dustpan and brush in favour of a yellow jacket. Always in the background, issuing edicts but never showing his face, was the all-powerful, but illiterate boss man, Joe Maplin. In later series, ex-RAF man Clive Dempster replaced Fairbrother in the entertainments hot seat.

Action centred on the glorious coarseness of everyday holiday camp life. In the daytime, campers gathered around the Olympic-sized swimming pool to witness beauty contests and various slapstick competitions. In the evening they repaired to the Hawaiian Ballroom to be entertained by Ted's vulgar jokes and Spike's silly costumes. Unfortunately for real-life holiday camps, who were trying to live down their primitive past, the series was a huge hit and ran for eight years. Nostalgia was a key to its success, but so was authenticity, with co-writer Jimmy Perry drawing inspiration for the series from his time as a Butlins Red Coat. Perry also composed the theme song, 'Holiday Rock'.

HICKSON, JOAN, OBE (1906–)

Although synonymous today with Agatha Christie's geriatric sleuth **Miss Marple**, Joan Hickson has enjoyed a long and successful film, stage and television career. Indeed, she didn't arrive in St Mary Mead until she was nearly 80 years old. Her earlier TV credits included the roles of the receptionist in the 1950s series *The Royalty*, Mrs Peace, the housekeeper, in **Our Man at St Mark's**, Mrs Morrow in *Good Girl* and Lady Harriet in *Poor Little Rich Girls*, plus a host of appearances in series like **The Invisible Man**, **Nanny** and *Time for Murder*.

HIGH CHAPARRAL, THE

US (NBC/David Dortort) Western. BBC 2
1967–71

Big John Cannon.....................................Leif Erickson
Buck Cannon ....Cameron Mitchell
Billy Blue Cannon ....Mark Slade
Manolito Montoya.............................Henry Darrow
Victoria Cannon......................................Linda Cristal
Don Sebastian Montoya........................Frank Silvera
Sam Butler ....Don Collier
Reno..Ted Markland
Pedro ....Roberto Contreras
Joe ....Robert Hoy
Vasquero ....Rodolfo Acosta
Wind..Rudy Ramos

Creator/Producer: David Dortort

A family struggles to make a living from their ranch.

In **Bonanza** the Cartwrights had their Ponderosa in Nevada. The Cannons in this series lived on The High Chaparral in Arizona Territory, sometime in the 1870s. Head of the family was gritty, hard-working Big John Cannon, assisted in his efforts to establish a cattle ranch by his blond son, Billy Blue, and Buck, John's gruff but fun-loving younger brother. John's first wife was killed by Apaches in the first episode, but he then married Victoria Montoya, daughter of Mexican nobleman Don Sebastian Montoya. When she moved to The High Chaparral so did her brother, Manolito.

Despite constant Indian attacks, wrangles with Mexicans and hassles from rustlers and other outlaws, Big John and his family never flinched from their fight with the land. Reno, Pedro and Joe were their ranch hands, working under the supervision of Sam Butler. When the naive Blue was written out of the series towards its close, he was replaced by Wind, a half-breed who came to live with the Cannons after helping John avert a disaster. The programme's creator, David Dortort, was also the man behind **Bonanza**.

HIGHWAY

UK (Various) Religion. ITV 1983–93

Presenter: Harry Secombe

Executive Producer: Bill Ward

Easy-going Sunday evening hymns and chat from various locations around the British Isles.

Hosted by Harry Secombe from a different venue each week, **Highway** was a roving version of **Stars on Sunday**, produced, in turn, by all the different ITV companies for the network. Harry (later Sir Harry) invited guests to sing religious songs, give

readings or just chat about their lifestyles and spiritual feelings. Secombe himself provided a number of the songs in every programme. For the last series, in 1993, the programme was displaced to early afternoons, as ITV looked for bigger audiences on Sunday teatimes. Secombe returned with a new series, **Sunday Morning with Secombe**, in 1994, in which he chatted to guests at the venue for the week's **Morning Worship**, which then followed.

HIGHWAY PATROL

US (Ziv) Police Drama. ITV 1956–

Chief Dan Mathews ....Broderick Crawford
Narrator ....Art Gilmore

Executive Producer: Vernon E. Clark

No-nonsense crimebusting with an American squad car officer.

There was only one regular in **Highway Patrol** and that was Chief Dan Matthews. Matthews, a chunky, determined, fast-talking police officer with a broken nose, worked for an unnamed force in an unnamed state (the emblems on the patrol cars read simply 'Highway Patrol'). His targets were criminals of all kinds – murderers, bank robbers, smugglers, hijackers and petty thieves – and by posting all-points bulletins, yelling 'Ten-Four' ('Message received and understood') and 'Ten-Twenty' ('Report your position') down his car intercom, the gravel-voiced Matthews always got his man. With nearly all the action taking place out on the road, involving bikes and occasionally helicopters as well as cars, little was seen of Matthews's office base.

Highway Patrol was one of the founding fathers of TV cop shows, even though it came together on a minuscule budget. Over 150 half-hour episodes were made between 1955 and 1959.

HIGHWAY TO HEAVEN

US (NBC) Drama. ITV 1987–

Jonathan Smith ....Michael Landon
Mark Gordon ....Victor French

Creator/Executive Producer: Michael Landon

An angel in training is sent to Earth to help people in trouble.

When Arthur Morton died, he went to Heaven and was groomed as an angel. With his name changed to Jonathan Smith, he was sent back to Earth to gain some experience of helping sad and worried people. He travelled the globe as a wandering labourer, accompanied by one of his first converts, a cynical cop named Mark Gordon. Smith opted for counselling, moral support and leadership by example as means of lightening the loads of others, but he could always call upon his angelic powers, if required. Both lead actors had previously appeared in Michael Landon's earlier success, *Little House on the Prairie*.

HILL, BENNY (ALFRED HAWTHORNE HILL; 1925–92)

Celebrated British funny man whose saucy post-card style of humour made him a favourite around the world. Benny Hill was one British comedy export who even made the Americans laugh and his cheeky grin and feigned air of innocence enabled him to get away with smutty jokes and innuendoes that would have died in the hands of other comics. They certainly wouldn't have been aired in peak hours. The hallmarks of his shows were send-ups of other TV personalities (whether they were Moira Anderson, Fanny Cradock or Jimmy Hill), bawdy songs that exhibited his skill with words (such as his number one-hit, 'Ernie' The Fastest Milkman in the West), and, most provocatively, slapstick chases of scantily clad women. At most times he was ably supported by stooges like Bob Todd, Henry McGee and Jack Wright. Hill's career began in music hall (including a period as a straight man to Reg Varney) and progressed to television via the radio comedy *Educating Archie*. His TV debut came in 1949 and his first series for the BBC was shown in 1955. In 1964 he won plaudits for his portrayal of Bottom in *A Midsummer Night's Dream* and then, in 1969, Hill switched to Thames TV, where he stayed until his show was axed amidst rows over sexism in 1989 (even though he had already toned down the voyeurism and ditched the steamy Hill's Angels dance troupe). Central were prepared to give him another bite of the cherry three years later but Hill died of a heart attack before he could finish the series.

HILL, BERNARD (1944–)

Tall, northern British actor who won acclaim for his portrayal of Yosser 'Gissa Job' Hughes in *Boys from the Blackstuff*. Previously Hill had played Gratus in *I, Claudius*, appeared in *Fox* and was seen in several plays. He later starred as Lech Walesa in Channel 4's *Squaring the Circle*.

HILL, LORD CHARLES (1904–89)

Fondly remembered from the war years as the Radio Doctor, Charles Hill, one-time secretary of the British Medical Association, became Member of Parliament for Luton in 1950, serving in the Ministries of Food, Housing and Local Government, and Welsh Affairs, as well as occupying the positions of Postmaster-General and Chancellor of the Duchy of Lancaster. He left Parliament in 1963 (he was a victim of Macmillan's 'Night of the Long Knives') and took over as Chairman of the Independent Television Authority. At the ITA he insisted that the ITV companies offered more time to ITN (a move that resulted in *News At Ten*) and oversaw the important 1967 franchise reviews. Surprisingly he was transferred virtually overnight to the chairmanship of the BBC in the same year. This appointment was seen as an attempt by Prime Minister Harold Wilson to discipline the BBC's Director-General, Sir Hugh Greene (Greene and Wilson had fallen out). Hill remained with the Corporation until 1972, before becoming Chairman of Abbey National Building Society and Laporte Industries. During his time as BBC Chairman he was criticized for unhinging the delicate relationship between the Director-General and the Chairman, intervening in day-to-day decisions and concentrating greater power in the hands of the Governors.

HILL, JIMMY, OBE (1928–)

British soccer pundit, a former Brentford and Fulham footballer, and later manager of Coventry City, who broke into television with LWT, for which he became Head of Sport and Deputy Controller of Programmes. Via *On the Ball* (part of *World of Sport*) and *The Big Match*, Hill arrived at the BBC, becoming its football expert during the 1970s and 1980s, and hosting *Match of the Day* and other major events. In the mid-1960s Hill was a consultant on the soccer soap *United!*

HILL STREET BLUES

US (MTM) Police Drama. ITV/Channel 4
1981–9

Captain Frank Furillo	Daniel J. Travanti
Sgt Phil Esterhaus	Michael Conrad
Officer Bobby Hill	Michael Warren
Officer Andy Renko	Charles Haid
Joyce Davenport	Veronica Hamel
Detective Mick Belker	Bruce Weitz
Lt Ray Calletano	Rene Enriquez
Detective Johnny 'JD' LaRue	Kiel Martin
Detective Neal Washington	Taurean Blacque
Lt Howard Hunter	James B. Sikking
Sgt/Lt Henry Goldblume	Joe Spano
Officer/Sgt Lucy Bates	Betty Thomas
Grace Gardner	Barbara Babcock
Fay Furillo	Barbara Bosson
Detective/Lt Alf Chesley	Gerry Black
Officer Leo Schnitz	Robert Hirschfeld
Officer Joe Coffey	Ed Marinaro
Chief Fletcher P. Daniels	Jon Cypher
Officer Robin Tataglia/Belker	Lisa Sutton
Assistant DA Irwin Bernstein	George Wyner
Jesus Martinez	Trinidad Silva
Detective Harry Garibaldi	Ken Olin

Detective Patricia 'Patsy' Mayo	Mimi Kuzyk
Mayor Ozzie Cleveland	J.A. Preston
Sgt Stanislaus Jablonski	Robert Prosky
Lt Norman Buntz	Dennis Franz
Celeste Patterson	Judith Hansen
Sidney Thurston ('Sid the Snitch')	Peter Jurasik
Officer Patrick Flaherty	Robert Clohessy
Officer Tina Russo	Megan Gallagher
Officer Raymond	David Selburg

Creators: Steven Bochco, Michael Kozoll. Executive Producer: Steven Bochco. Producers: Gregory Hoblit, David Anspaugh, Anthony Yerkovich

Life with the officers of a busy police station on the seedier side of town.

The Hill Street Station was based in the wrong side of a large, unnamed eastern American city (the exteriors were done in Chicago). Surrounded by the worst elements, drug pushers, prostitutes, racketeers, and more, the policeman's lot at Hill Street was not a happy one. This series revealed how the motley band of law enforcers struggled to cope with daily trauma, and witnessed its effect on their personal lives and working relationships.

In semi-serial form, the programme followed a day's events in Hill Street, from the morning roll call to the last thing at night. The show's own roll call was as follows. Head of the station was Captain Frank Furillo, a patient, quietly spoken, firm commander. Dedicated and responsible, he found himself dealing not only with events on the streets but also with police bureaucracy and turmoil in his personal life. Plagued for alimony by his ex-wife, Fay, he struck up an affair with defence attorney Joyce Davenport which turned into marriage. At work, however, they remained professional adversaries.

Beneath Furillo was Sgt Phil Esterhaus, a fatherly head sergeant who urged his troops to 'Let's be careful out there'. When actor Michael Conrad died three years into the run, Esterhaus was written out (having had a heart attack while making love to widow Grace Gardner). Then there was scruffy undercover detective Mick Belker (known to bite those he arrested), trigger-happy SWAT squad lieutenant Howard Hunter, toothpick-chewing plain-clothesman Neal Washington, his alcoholic partner J.D. LaRue, Detective Alf Chesley and the sensitive community affairs officer, Henry Goldblume. Completing the team were the station's hispanic second-in-command, Ray Callentano, the black/white patrolman team of Bobby Hill and Andy Renko (who were shot in the opening episode), and Lucy Bates, with her partner, Joe Coffey. Leo Schnitz was the desk officer and Fletcher Daniels was the smarmy, ambitious police chief who later ran for mayor.

Added over the years were Robin Tataglia (an officer who married Belker), Detective Harry Garibaldi, Sgt Stan Jablonski (Esterhaus's replacement), Detective Patsy Mayo, Officer Tina Russo, Officer Pat Flaherty, Officer Raymond and the abrasive Lt Norman Buntz, on the face of it a lout, but in fact nobody's fool. The local underworld was also represented, by informer Sid the Snitch and cocky Jesus Martinez, leader of the Diablos gang, as were the city's legal eagles, by prosecutor Irwin Bernstein (as well as Joyce Davenport).

Hill Street Blues was applauded by critics but was not a hit in the ratings. Nevertheless, it won eight Emmys in one season (a record) and attracted a dedicated following. Its success came from its subtle juxtaposition of humour and human drama, and from its realistic characterizations. The storylines were equally true to life. The cops did not always come out on top. Sometimes the cases were never resolved. On other occasions, the cops themselves were seen to be the bad guys. Hand-held, news-style camera work added to the realism. In short, the '*Blues*' changed the face of American cop shows: car chases and shoot-outs were no longer enough after this series. The poignant theme music, by Mike Post, was a UK hit in 1982. Buntz and Sid the Snitch eventually went on to a short-lived spin-off, *Beverly Hills Buntz*.

HINE

UK (ATV) Drama. ITV 1971

Joe Hine	Barrie Ingham
Walpole Gibb	Colin Gordon
Astor Harris	Paul Eddington
Sir Christopher Pendle	Michael Goodliffe

Creator/Producer: Wilfred Greatorex

The tough, grimy world of an international arms dealer.

Joe Hine sold weapons for a living and made enemies along the way. A lone trader, he battled against giant corporations, chancing his arm in a multi-billion pound undercover market in defence equipment. His chief rivals were Walpole Gibb and Astor Harris, men who set out to destroy him. Sick of the hypocritical business, Hine always sought to pull off the last big deal that would allow him to retire in style.

HINES, FRAZER (1944–)

Yorkshire-born actor, best known as *Emmerdale's* Joe Sugden, a role he played off and on for over 20 years. His TV debut came as Jan in *The Silver Sword* and he later travelled with

Doctor Who as Highland warrior Jamie McCrimmon. Among his other credits have been appearances in *Compact*, *Z Cars*, *Coronation Street* and *Duty Free*. His first wife was actress Gemma Craven and his second wife is sportswoman Liz Hobbs.

HIRD, DAME THORA, OBE (1913–)

Respected northern actress, primarily in the comedy vein but just as adept at straight drama, as evidenced by her moving monologue *A Cream Cracker under the Settee* for Alan Bennett's *Talking Heads* series. In the world of sitcoms, Hird will be remembered, to a lesser and greater degree, for her performances as disgrunted housewife Thora Blacklock in *Meet the Wife*, boarding house proprietor Thora Parker in *Ours is a Nice House*, councillor Sarah Danby in *The First Lady*, funeral director Ivy Unsworth in *In Loving Memory*, Salvation Army Captain Emily Ridley in *Hallelujah* and Edie Utterthwaite, the tutting ring leader of the ladies in *Last of the Summer Wine*. Among her many other credits have been the hymn series *Praise Be* (as host), roles in series as varied as *The Adventures of Robin Hood* and *All Creatures Great and Small*, plus single dramas like *A Kind of Loving* in 1962 and *Memento Mori* in 1992.

HIRSCHMAN, HERBERT

Experienced American TV executive, the producer of such series as *Perry Mason*, *The Defenders*, *The Men from Shiloh*, *The Zoo Gang* and *Planet of the Apes*.

HIS LORDSHIP ENTERTAINS see *Hark at Barker*.

HITCH-HIKER'S GUIDE TO THE GALAXY, THE

UK (BBC) Situation Comedy. BBC 2 1981

Arthur Dent ....Simon Jones
Ford Prefect ....David Dixon
The Book (voice only) ....Peter Jones
Zaphod Beeblebrox ....Mark Wing-Davey
Trillian ....Sandra Dickinson
Marvin ....David Learner
Marvin (voice only) ....Stephen Moore

Creator/Writer: Douglas Adams. Producer: Alan J.W. Bell

An inter-galactic guidebook compiler and his human friend flee Earth's destruction and hitch rides across the universe.

Ford Prefect had been a researcher for the electronic *Hitch-Hiker's Guide to the Galaxy*, the ultimate universal reference book. With the book badly needing an update, he had been despatched to Earth to gather information, remaining there for 15 years and making friends with Arthur Dent. One day, learning that the Earth was in imminent danger of demolition to make way for a hyperspace bypass, Prefect revealed that he was not from Guildford after all and urged Dent to escape with him aboard the demolition spacecraft. Unfortunately, the ship was manned by the ugly, sadistic Vogons, a race of green aliens who terrorized others with appalling poetry. Fleeing their clutches, Prefect and Dent joined the Heart of Gold, a spaceship in the hands of two-headed ex-con man and part-time Galactic President, Zaphod Beeblebrox, who was heading for the lost planet of Magrathea. His crew consisted of pilot Trillion (actually a former Earthling named Trisha McMillan) and a manic depressive robot, Marvin the Paranoid Android, who suffered from pains in his diodes.

As the duo thumbed their way around the galaxy, and the bemused Arthur hunted for a good cup of tea, they encountered Slartibartfast (architect of the fjords), the Golgafrinchians (former middle-managers and telephone operatives who had been banned from their planet because of their uselessness) and pan-dimensional beings dressed up as white mice who were desperately seeking the Ultimate Question to Life, the Universe and Everything. They already knew the answer: it was 42. The hitch-hikers also visited the Restaurant at the End of the Universe and were entertained by the talking Dish of the Day and galactic rock star Hotblack Desiato, before ending up on prehistoric Earth, contemplating the events that were to engulf the planet in the eons ahead.

A mixture of fantasy, satire and pun, the series employed some innovative special effects, including the use of video games to stage space battles and mock-computer graphics to show pages from the book. It more than satisfied listeners who had loved the original Radio 4 serial and readers who had enjoyed the two books that followed it. Their fears about its translation into visual humour were, it seems, unfounded.

HITCHCOCK, SIR ALFRED (1899–1980)

Celebrated British film director whose television work, although limited, is listed among TV's all-time classics. In the US-made *Alfred Hitchcock Presents* (later extended into *The Alfred Hitchcock Hour*) he gave viewers an anthology of thrillers, not all directed but at least all overseen by the Master of Suspense himself. He also appeared on screen to top and tail each story, mostly with short quirky or bizarre anecdotes which had little to do with the main feature. In the mid-1980s, after his death, he resurfaced as host of a new run of *Alfred Hitchcock Presents*, his appearances coming courtesy of colorized old footage from the original series.

HOBLEY, MCDONALD (DENNYS JACK VALENTINE MCDONALD-HOBLEY; 1917–87)

One of Britain's earliest on-screen TV announcers, McDonald Hobley, complete with bow tie and dinner jacket, first appeared on the BBC in 1946, sharing announcing shifts with Jasmine Bligh, Sylvia Peters and later Mary Malcolm. During the same period he also presented the magazine programme *Kaleidoscope*, this coming after a pre-war stint in the theatre and radio work in the Far East during the hostilities. After ten years with the BBC, Hobley moved to ABC. Born in the Falkland Islands, one of Hobley's last TV contributions came in a Channel 4 programme about the South Atlantic dependencies.

HODGE, PATRICIA (1946–)

Classy British actress, cast in comedy as well as straight drama roles. Among her TV highlights have been the part of the plummy barrister Phyllida Trant in *Rumpole of the Bailey*, Mary Fisher in *The Life and Loves of a She Devil*, the TV presenter/detective Jemima Shore, in *Jemima Shore Investigates*, and the title role in *The Cloning of Joanna May*. Hodge played Sybilla Howarth in *The Other 'Arf*, starred as Penny Milburn in the sitcom *Holding the Fort* and as Julia Merrygrove in *Rich Tea and Sympathy*. She has also popped up in episodes of *Softly, Softly*, *Edward and Mrs Simpson*, *The Professionals*, *Nanny*, *Robin of Sherwood*, *The Adventures of Sherlock Holmes*, *Inspector Morse* and more, and was seen in the dramas *The Naked Civil Servant* and *The One and Only Phyllis Dixey*, amongst others.

HOGAN, PAUL (1939–)

Australian comedian, a former construction worker who hit the box office big time in the 1980s with the film *Crocodile Dundee*. In-between, *The Paul Hogan Show* was extremely popular Down Under and was imported to the UK by Channel 4. Supported by the likes of Delvene Delaney and John Cornell, Hogan used the 'Benny Hill'-type sketch show to introduce a range of wacky characters like Hoges, a 'no-poofters' man-of-the-world, always dressed in sleeveless shirts, shorts and football socks. It helped put Foster's lager and Vegemite on the map. Hogan married actress Linda Kozlowski in 1990.

HOGAN'S HEROES

US (Bing Crosby) Situation Comedy. ITV 1967–

Colonel Robert Hogan	Bob Crane
Colonel Wilhelm Klink	Werner Klemperer
Sgt Hans Schulz	John Banner
Corporal Louis LeBeau	Robert Clary
Corporal Peter Newkirk	Richard Dawson
Corporal James Kinchloe	Ivan Dixon
Sgt Andrew Carter	Larry Hovis
Helga	Cynthia Lynn
Hilda	Sigrid Valdis

Creators: Bernard Fein, Albert S. Ruddy. Producer: Ed Feldman

Allied soldiers rule the roost at a Nazi PoW camp.

Somewhere in the Nazi empire was Stalag 13, a prisoner-of-war camp nominally commanded by the monocled Colonel Klink and his inept, fat sidekick, Sgt Schultz. In actuality, although their captors didn't realize it, the camp was run by its inmates, and the true supremo was the shrewd, wisecracking American Colonel Robert Hogan. Hogan was ably supported by a troop of versatile Allied soldiers. These were LeBeau, a Frenchman with culinary skills, Newkirk, a brash Cockney, Sgt Carter, the skilful but slow farmboy, and a black electronics genius, Corporal Kinchloe. Between them, the prisoners ran a useful Allied operational base. They supplied intelligence, they assisted refugees and they printed counterfeit money, but, above all, they had a wonderful time. This was more of a hotel than a prison. By lifting the wire fence in garage door style, they could pop out to take the air or seek entertainment in the town. They also had their own sauna in which to sweat off the delights of LeBeau's wonderful Gallic cuisine. Little wonder they never sought to escape.

The series echoed the far more serious Billy Wilder film *Stalag 17*, which was released in 1953, starred William Holden and blended humour with moments of drama and realism.

HOLDING THE FORT

UK (LWT) Situation Comedy. ITV 1980–1

Russell Milburn	Peter Davison
Penny Milburn	Patricia Hodge
Fitz	Matthew Kelly

Creators/Writers: Laurence Marks, Maurice Gran. Producer: Derrick Goodwin

A husband and wife try role reversal.

Young married couple Russell and Penny Milburn had a baby daughter, Emma. However, instead of Russell being the breadwinner, it was

Penny who returned to work, reclaiming her old job with the army. Russell stayed at home, looked after Emma and dabbled with his own brewery, housed in the basement, generally hindered by his pal, Fitz. With Russell and Fitz both ardent pacifists, Penny's source of income was a source of constant friction.

When *Holding the Fort* ended, after three seasons, Fitz was given his own spin-off, *Relative Strangers*, in which he was surprised by John, his 18-year-old son (played by Mark Farmer), a child he had never known about.

HOLIDAY

UK (BBC) Travel. BBC 1 1969–

Presenters:
Cliff Michelmore
Joan Bakewell
Anne Gregg
Frank Bough
John Carter
Desmond Lynam
Eamonn Holmes
Anneka Rice
Jill Dando

Producers: Tom Savage, David Filkin, Jeremy Bennett, Clem Vallence, Colin Strong, Patricia Houlihan

Long-running holiday magazine.

A tourism brochure of the air, *Holiday* is now the oldest travel review programme on British television. Initially its title incorporated the year in question, beginning with *Holiday 69*, but that idea has been dropped in recent seasons. Throughout, its concept has been quite simple: holiday destinations at home and abroad have been featured and appraised in pre-filmed reports, with plaudits given to the best features and less generous comments made about the limitations of each resort. The very first programme included an item on Torremolinos, but some destinations over the years have been attacked as being too fanciful and beyond the limits of the ordinary viewer's pocket. To complement the recorded inserts, *Holiday* has also offered general advice for travellers, publicized last-minute bargains and investigated tourist complaints.

Holiday was once a stalwart of BBC 1's Sunday evening schedules and its Gordon Giltrap theme music, 'Heartsong', led nicely into the God slot during the dark winter months. It has since moved to a peak-time weeknight position. Cliff Michelmore was the chief presenter for 17 years, but his successors have proved less durable, some, like Desmond Lynam and Anneka Rice, lasting only one or two seasons. Anne Gregg spent ten years with the programme, enjoying varying

degrees of prominence, and among the show's many contributing reporters have been Fyfe Robertson, Kieran Prendiville, Sarah Kennedy, Bill Buckley, John Pitman and Kathy Tayler. John Carter was one of the 'experts' in the first series and remained close to the programme for many years. Since 1988 Carter has been involved with Thames TV's rival programme, *Wish You Were Here . . . ?*, which began in 1976. *Wish You Were Here . . . ?* has been introduced chiefly by Judith Chalmers, who was partnered over several series by Chris Kelly.

HOLLAND, JEFFREY (1946–)

British comedian and comic actor, much seen in company with Russ Abbot on his *Madhouse* shows. Holland played up-and-coming camp comedian Spike Dixon in **Hi-De-Hi!** and remained with the Perry/Croft repertory company for its follow-up, **You Rang, M'Lord?**, taking the role of head of the household James Twelvetrees.

HOLLAND, MARY

British actress famed not for a television series but for her role in a long-running commercial. As Katie, Mary was TV's Oxo mum for 18 years from 1958. When the advert was eventually dropped in 1976, Holland was snapped up by Electrolux and later made a commercial for Oxo rivals Bovril.

HOLLYWOOD

UK (Thames) Historical Documentary. ITV 1980

Narrator: James Mason

Writers/Producers: Kevin Brownlow, David Gill

A detailed study of the age of the silent movie.

Subtitled *A Celebration of the American Silent Film* when shown in the USA, *Hollywood* won much acclaim as a well-researched, thoughtful history of the great days of the US film industry. Project masterminds Kevin Brownlow and David Gill took the trouble to explore in depth the background to the world of the silent movie, explaining the context of certain films and, most importantly, screening them in the best possible condition, with appropriate music and at the proper speed. This revealed how these early pieces of cinema were really artistic jewels and not the jumpy, jerky bits of footage most people know them to be. The contributions of the directors, writers, cameramen and performers of the day were also evaluated in this 13-part documentary. Carl Davis supplied the grand theme music.

HOLLYWOOD GREATS, THE

UK (BBC) Documentary. BBC 1 1977–85

Writer/Presenter: Barry Norman

Producer: Margaret Sharp

Warts-and-all documentary portraits of Hollywood's legendary film stars.

Intermittently, over eight years, BBC film critic Barry Norman compiled this collection of biographies of the biggest names in the movie world. Using film clips and interviews to illustrate his points, Norman was not afraid to destroy a few myths in his interpretation of the stars' work and private lives. Among those featured were Judy Garland, Charles Laughton, Ronald Coleman, Joan Crawford, Clark Gable, Errol Flynn, Spencer Tracy, Jean Harlow, Humphrey Bogart, Groucho Marx, Charlie Chaplin, Marilyn Monroe, Edward G. Robinson, John Wayne, Henry Fonda and Steve McQueen. The last contribution was a one-off film on Bing Crosby, shown in January 1985.

HOLM, IAN (IAN HOLM CUTHBERT; 1932–)

Serious-looking British character actor, largely on stage and screen but also prominent on television. The highlight to date has been the part of disgraced spy Bernard Samson in *Game, Set and Match*, which Holm accepted having already supported Alec Guinness in another drama of subterfuge, *Tinker, Tailor, Soldier, Spy*. Holm also starred in *Frankenstein* (one of Thames TV's *Mystery and Imagination* stories), played Paul Presset in the intense drama *We, the Accused* and took the part of Napoleon in *Napoleon and Love*. He appeared as Michael in the trilogy *Conjugal Rites*, assumed the guise of J.M. Barrie in the *Play of the Week* trilogy *The Lost Boys*, played Hercule Poirot in a one-off thriller, *Murder by the Book*, and was seen as Pod in *The Borrowers*, in addition to parts in a host of heavyish dramas and adaptations of classics like *Uncle Vanya* and *The Misanthrope*.

HOLNESS, BOB (1928–)

British radio and television personality, beginning his career with South African radio in 1955. After a number of years with Radio 2, Radio Luxembourg and LBC in London, Holness found himself an unlikely cult figure among teenagers in the 1980s, thanks to his long-running quiz show *Blockbusters*. Among his earlier TV credits were the game shows *Take a Letter* and *Junior Criss Cross Quiz*, and, more seriously, *World in Action* and *What the Papers Say*.

HOLOCAUST

US (NBC/Titus) Drama. BBC 1 1978

Dr Josef Weiss	Fritz Weaver
Berta Weiss	Rosemary Harris
Karl Weiss	James Woods
Inga Helms/Weiss	Meryl Streep
Rudi Weiss	Joseph Bottoms
Anna Weiss	Blanche Baker
Moses Weiss	Sam Wanamaker
Erik Dorf	Michael Moriarty
Marta Dorf	Deborah Norton
Kurt Dorf	Robert Stephens
Reinhard Heydrich	David Warner
Heinrich Himmler	Ian Holm
Adolf Eichmann	Tom Bell

Writer: Gerald Green. Executive Producer: Herb Brodkin. Producer: Robert Berger

Controversial dramatization of the persecution of Jews by the Nazis.

This grim, four-part drama, screened on consecutive nights by the BBC, recounted the atrocities of World War II with particular focus on the plight of European Jews and their persecution and extermination by the Nazis. The Weiss family from Berlin, headed by Dr Josef Weiss, represented the Judaic race and the character of lawyer Erik Dorf was seen as a manifestation of Nazi ambition. Their respective lives were charted from the year 1935 to the end of the hostilities. Despite criticism for turning one of the most horrific periods in history into a semi-soap opera, with sentimental music, pointless dialogue and inevitably subdued horrors, the series became a moving experience for most viewers and won numerous awards.

HOME AND AWAY

Australia (Network 7) Drama. ITV 1989–

Tom Fletcher	Roger Oakley
Pippa Fletcher	Vanessa Downing
	Debra Lawrance
Celia Stewart	Fiona Spence
Alf Stewart	Ray Meagher
Ailsa Hogan/Stewart	Judy Nunn
Donald Fisher	Norman Coburn
Al Simpson	Terence Donovan
Bobby Simpson	Nicolle Dickson
Sophie Simpson	Rebekah Elmaloglou
Viv	Mouche Phillips
Morag Bellingham	Cornelia Frances
Frank Morgan	Alex Papps
Ruth 'Roo' Stewart	Justine Clarke
Steven Matheson	Adam Willits
Matt Wilson	Greg Benson
Lance Smart	Peter Vroom
Sally Keating	Kate Ritchie
Marilyn Chambers	Emily Symons
Emma Jackson	Dannii Minogue
Grant Mitchell	Craig McLachlan
Ben Lucini	Julian McMahon

Carly Morris/Lucini	Sharyn Hodgson
Adam Cameron	Mat Stevenson
Michael Ross	Dennis Coard
Blake	Les Hill
Karen	Belinda Jarrett
Nick Parrish	Bruce Roberts
Simon	Richard Norton
Haydn	Andrew Hill
David Croft	Guy Pearce
Lucinda Croft	Dee Smart
Ryan	Alastair MacDougall
Shane Parrish	Dieter Brummer
Damian Roberts	Matt Doran
Sam Marshall	Ryan Clark
Greg	Ross Newton
Finlay Roberts	Tina Thomsen
Irene Roberts	Lynne McGranger
Luke Cunningham	John Adam
Tug O'Neale	Tristan Bancks
Roxanne Miller	Lisa Lackey
Sarah Taylor	Laura Vazquez
Angel	Melissa George
Jack Wilson	Daniel Amalm
Rob Storey	Matthew Lilley
Shannon Reed	Isla Fisher
Curtis Reed	Shane Ammann
Donna	Nicola Quilter
Selina	Tempany Deckert

Creator/Executive Producer: Alan Bateman

Life with troubled kids in the fictitious Australian resort of Summer Bay.

Home and Away was broadcast by Australia's Seven Network, the station which gave away *Neighbours* in 1985. It was perceived as a rival to that series not only in its native country but also in the UK, where it was purchased by ITV to run head to head with *Neighbours* at lunchtimes and in the early evening.

Set in the coastal town of Summer Bay, near Sydney, *Home and Away* initially focused on foster parents Tom and Pippa Fletcher, who lived in a run-down caravan park. Tom was killed in a car accident early on and his wife, Pippa, has since soldiered on alone (albeit with a different actress in the role). Amongst the most prominent citizens of Summer Bay have been local headmaster Donald Fisher, grocer Alf Stewart, his wife Ailsa, and teacher Grant Mitchell (played by Craig McLachlan, poached from *Neighbours*). The kids were initially headed by Bobby Simpson (one-time co-owner with Ailsa of the local restaurant, The Diner), Carly Morris (later married to former soldier Ben Lucini), orphan Adam Cameron and the studious Steven Matheson, but new generations of youngsters have made their way to Summer Bay over the years, as, melodramatically, the series has mingled tales of romance, death, family secrets and other scandals.

HOME TO ROOST

UK (Yorkshire) Situation Comedy. ITV 1985–90

Henry Willows	John Thaw
Matthew Willows	Reece Dinsdale
Enid Thompson	Elizabeth Bennett
Fiona Fennell	Joan Blackham

Writer: Eric Chappell. Producers: David Reynolds, Vernon Lawrence

A father's life is turned upside down when his grown-up son returns home.

With his parents divorced, Matthew Willows had lived with his mother – until she threw him out. In him she recognized the same stubbornness and other character traits that had led to her separation from his father, Henry, and when Matthew decided to move in with his dad, the sparks began to fly. Henry had long been accustomed to living life at his own pace, in his own grumpy way and only for himself. Now there was a cuckoo in the nest and what's more this cuckoo was a younger version of himself. The result was a series of generation gap conflicts, as father and son did domestic battle. Enid was Henry's housekeeper (actress Elizabeth Bennett reprised the role for the American version, *You Again*, starring Jack Klugman), replaced in later editions by new daily Fiona Fennell. Rebecca Lacey (Hilary in *May to September*) once dropped in as Julie, Matthew's sister.

HONEY LANE see *Market in Honey Lane.*

HONEYCOMBE, GORDON (1936–)

Versatile Gordon Honeycombe is remembered by most viewers as one of ITN's longest serving newscasters, joining the network in 1965. Honeycombe entered broadcasting in radio in Hong Kong and then became a member of the Royal Shakespeare Company. After 12 years at ITN, he left after a dispute over a fire fighters' strike, which he publicly supported, and concentrated instead on his successful writing career. He has had a number of books published and scripted three TV plays. A keen genealogist, he hosted *Family History* for the BBC in 1979 and also acted as narrator on *Arthur C. Clarke's Mysterious World* for YTV. In 1984 he resumed newsreading with TV-am, staying five years before returning to the stage.

HONG KONG BEAT, THE

UK (BBC) Documentary. BBC 1 1978

Producer: John Purdie

A nine-part study of policing in the cramped colony of Hong Kong.

Focusing on the activities of the British Colonial Force as they provided law and order in Hong Kong's busy, lively streets, *The Hong Kong Beat* won much acclaim and also gave rise to its fair share of controversy. It watched as local policemen rounded up the illegal immigrants, drug pushers and other social nuisances which make policing this part of the world so complicated, hazardous and unique. The programme's theme music was a top 30 hit for Richard Denton and Martin Cook in 1978.

HONG KONG PHOOEY

US (Hanna-Barbera) Cartoon. BBC 1 1975

Voices:
Penrod 'Penry' Pooch/Hong Kong Phooey
....Scatman Crothers
Sgt Flint...Joe E. Ross
Rosemary..Kathi Gori
Spot ....Don Messick

Executive Producers: William Hanna, Joseph Barbera. Producer: Iwao Takamoto

The clumsy canine janitor at a police station is actually a superhero trained in the martial arts.

Penrod Pooch (or Penry as he was known to Rosemary, the switchboard operator), worked as the flunky in a big city police station. Unknown to his colleagues, especially the grouchy Sgt Flint, this was no ordinary dog but a crimebuster extraordinaire who operated under the guise of Hong Kong Phooey. Nipping into a hidden room behind the snack machine and leaping into a filing cabinet, Penry donned his oriental superhero costume, before dashing out in the Phooeymobile (garaged in a rubbish bin behind the station) to confront the weirdest criminals in the world. He was accompanied only by Spot, the station's striped cat. Once in action, Phooey demonstrated the martial arts he had learned from a correspondence course, dipping into the *Hong Kong Kung Fu Book of Tricks* to attempt manoeuvres like the slow-motion Hong Kong Phooey Chop (much to the exasperation of his feline companion). Amongst the Mutt of Steel's adversaries were Mr Tornado, the Gum Drop Kid and Professor Presto.

HOPALONG CASSIDY

US (William Boyd) Western. BBC 1955–6

Hopalong Cassidy ....William Boyd
Red Connors ....Edgar Buchanan

Producer: William Boyd

A cowboy samaritan to the rescue on his snow-white charger.

The character of Hopalong Cassidy was created by Clarence E. Mulford around the turn of the century. But it was a different Hopalong from the one the kids knew and loved in the 1950s. Mulford had portrayed Cassidy as a rough, mean vagabond with a bad limp, a man who drank,

swore and smoked. Actor William Boyd turned him into a faultless hero, an idol for the children, immaculately turned out in black to dramatically contrast his silver hair, his silver spurs, his pearl-handled revolvers and his white steed, Topper. No longer troubled by the limp, he lived at the Bar 20 ranch and was accompanied in his adventures by Red Connors. Far from a brawling, tobacco-chewing rough-neck, Cassidy was now a shining paragon of virtue.

William Boyd had already played the role in the cinema, and he picked up the rights to these old B movies when no one else was interested. He and his associate, Toby Anguish, re-edited them and re-packaged them for TV. The first TV Hopalong, therefore, was actually the cinema version revisited. Eventually Boyd produced this new series specifically for television. It became an instant hit with younger viewers and went on to be one of the first great merchandising successes of the small screen.

HOPCRAFT, ARTHUR (1932–)

Sports reporter turned dramatist, whose early TV work still echoed his sporting roots. Among his later works have been the acclaimed 1977 adaptation of *Hard Times* and Le Carré's **Tinker, Tailor, Soldier, Spy**, plus episodes of series like *Nightingale's Boys*.

HOPKINS, SIR ANTHONY (1937–)

Welsh cinema grandee of the 1990s, who, before Hollywood beckoned, focused on television, appearing in work as varied as *War and Peace* (as Pierre), *QB VII* (as Dr Adam Kelno), *The Lindberg Kidnapping Case, Kean* (as Edmund Kean), *Victory at Entebbe, Othello* (as the Moor himself), *A Married Man, The Bunker* (as Hitler), *The Hunchback of Notre Dame* (as Quasimodo), *Hollywood Wives* and *Across the Lake* (as Donald Campbell), most of which were mini-series. Guest appearances in series like **Department S** characterized Hopkins's early career.

HOPKINS, JOHN (1931–)

Acclaimed British writer, the first script editor on **Z Cars**, a series for which he himself penned over 50 episodes. His work on the programme (and an earlier thriller series *A Chance of Thunder* in 1961) led to a couple of notable TV plays, *Fable* (1965) and *Horror of Darkness* (1966), before he contributed a four-part series entitled *Talking to a Stranger* (also in 1966), which depicted the break-up of a family from various viewpoints. It was bestowed with praise and led to a growing involvement in the cinema, although Hopkins continued to script television material, including the hugely expensive *Divorce His, Divorce Hers* for HTV, and *Smiley's People* (with John Le Carré). Other credits have included episodes of *Detective* and two early *Campion* serials, *Dancers In Mourning* (1959) and *Death of a Ghost* (1960).

HORDERN, SIR MICHAEL, CBE (1911–95)

Grand old man of the English stage and screen, whose television work was occasional but notable, if focused at the heavier end of the drama market. His small screen work stretched back to the 1940s (he appeared in a production of *Rebecca* in 1947, for instance) and his major roles were as Willie in *Cakes and Ale*, as Friar Domingo in *Shogun* and as the Reverend Simeon Simcox in *Paradise Postponed*, with other credits including *Edward the Seventh*, *The History Man*, *Ivanhoe*, *Mistress of Suspense*, *Tales of the Unexpected*, *Scoop*, *The Green Man* and a particularly chilling ghost story entitled *Whistle, and I'll Come to You* for *Omnibus*. Hordern also performed Shakespeare for television, including *King Lear*, *Romeo and Juliet* and *The Tempest*. At the other end of the scale, he acted as narrator for *Paddington*, voiced the part of Badger in the 1980s animation of *The Wind in the Willows* and told stories on *Jackanory*.

HORIZON

UK (BBC) Science Documentary. BBC 2 1964–

Award-winning popular science programme.

Beginning monthly but later seen fortnightly, *Horizon* has been a centrepiece of BBC 2's schedules since the channel's inception. Its brief has been science, but the scope has been broad and the treatment flexible. The usual pattern has been to devote a whole programme to one particular issue. Often using remarkable footage, the programme has discussed a topic of general scientific interest, or reviewed the latest scientific advance. On occasions, dramatizations have been used, perhaps to illustrate events in the life of an inventor or chemist.

HORTON, ROBERT (MEAD HOWARD HORTON; 1924–)

Rugged American leading man of the 1950s and 1960s, seen to best effect as trail scout Flint McCullough in *Wagon Train*, following a year in an American soap called *King's Row*. After five years in *Wagon Train*, Horton left the series, allegedly because he was fed up with Westerns. All the same, his next, and to date last, starring role was in another Western, the short-lived *A Man Called Shenandoah* in 1965. Amongst

Horton's other TV credits have been episodes of *Alfred Hitchcock Presents* and another US soap, *As the World Turns*.

HOT METAL

UK (LWT) Situation Comedy. ITV 1986–8

Terence 'Twiggy' Rathbone/Russell Spam	Robert Hardy
Harry Stringer	Geoffrey Palmer
Greg Kettle	Richard Kane
Bill Tytla	John Gordon Sinclair
Max	Geoffrey Hastings
Father Teasdale	John Horsley
Richard Lipton	Richard Wilson

Writers: Andrew Marshall, David Renwick.
Producer: Humphrey Barclay

An ailing tabloid newspaper falls victim to an unscrupulous media baron.

The Daily Crucible, a flabby newspaper at the tabloid end of the market, was being strangled by its competitors and its circulation was plummeting. Its proprietors, Rathouse International, a global media conglomerate headed by the ruthless 'Twiggy' Rathbone, consequently took remedial action, installing a new editor, Rathbone's lookalike, Russell Spam. Spam radically altered the nature of the paper, introducing sex exposés, majoring on political scandals and adding titillation to page three, much to the disgust of managing editor Harry Stringer. But it worked and circulation roared ahead. Stringer (mysteriously lost in a flying incident) was replaced by a new MD, Richard Lipton, in the second and last series.

HOTEL

US (Aaron Spelling) Drama. ITV 1983–

Victoria Cabot	Anne Baxter
Peter McDermott	James Brolin
Christine Francis	Connie Sellecca
Mark Danning	Shea Farrell
Billy Griffin	Nathan Cook
Dave Kendall	Michael Spound
Megan Kendall	Heidi Bohay
Julie Gillette	Shari Belafonte-Harper

Executive Producers: Aaron Spelling, Douglas S. Cramer

The lives and loves of visitors to a swish San Francisco hotel.

From the creators of *The Love Boat*, this series adopted a similar format – introducing guest stars to supply the main action in each episode, with a small supporting permanent cast to provide the background. Events centred around the St Gregory Hotel and the regulars were bearded manager Peter McDermott, his attractive assistant, Christine Francis, Mark Danning, the hotel's PR executive, and Billy Griffin, an ex-con turned security officer. Bette Davis was scheduled to star in the series, playing hotel owner Laura Trent, but, through illness, she only appeared in the first episode. Anne Baxter was brought in to take over in the guise of her sister-in-law, Victoria Cabot. The series was based on the novel by Arthur Hailey.

HOUSE OF CARDS

UK (BBC) Drama. BBC 1 1990

Francis Urquhart ....Ian Richardson
Mattie Storin ....Susannah Harker
Stamper ....Colin Jeavons
Elizabeth Urquhart ....Diane Fletcher
Roger O'Neill ....Miles Anderson
Henry Collingridge ....David Lyon
Anne Collingridge ....Isabelle Amyes
Penny Guy...............................Alphonsia Emmanuel
Lord Billsborough................................Nicholas Selby
Charles Collingridge ....James Villiers
Patrick Woolton ....Malcolm Tierney

Writer: Andrew Davies. Producer: Ken Riddington

A scheming Government whip aims to become Prime Minister – by hook or by crook.

This four-part tale of political intrigue and in-fighting was dramatized by Andrew Davies from the novel by Conservative Party Chief of Staff Michael Dobbs and benefited from being originally screened at the time of Mrs Thatcher's downfall. It went on to become the BBC's best-selling drama of the early 1990s, with sales to some 24 countries.

House of Cards focused on Government Chief Whip Francis Urquhart, a devious man with a desire for power. The story picked up with the demise of a female prime minister and her replacement with a wimpy male successor, giving Urquhart all the motivation he needed to put his Machiavellian plans into action. By the end of the serial Urquhart was comfortably installed in Number Ten. Urquhart's troubles were just beginning, however. In a sequel, *To Play the King* (1993), produced by the same team from another Michael Dobbs novel, Urquhart found himself under pressure from a newly enthroned monarch with liberal tendencies.

HOUSE OF ELIOTT, THE

UK (BBC) Drama. BBC 1 1991–4

Beatrice Eliott ....Stella Gonet
Evangeline Eliott ....Louise Lombard
Lady Lydia Eliott...................................Barbara Jefford
Arthur Eliott...Peter Birch

Jack Maddox ....Aden Gillett
Penelope Maddox ....Francesca Folan
Sebastian Pearce ....Jeremy Brudenell
Piggy Garstone ....Robert Daws
Tilly Watkins/Foss ....Cathy Murphy
Lady Haycock...Jill Melford
Daphne Haycock ....Kelly Hunter
Sir Desmond Gillespie......................David De Keyser
Madge Howell/Althorpe ....Judy Flynn
Betty Butcher ....Diana Rayworth
Agnes Clarke ....Victoria Alcock
Chalmers...Kate Paul
Florence Ranby ....Maggie Ollerenshaw
Ralph Saroyan ....Michael Culver
Lord Alexander Montford ....Rupert Frazer
Lady Elizabeth Montford................Elizabeth Garvie
Alice Burgoyne ....Kate Fahy
Joseph Wint ....Stephen Churchett
Charles Quance...Bill Thomas
Grace Keeble.................................Melanie Ramsey
Larry Cotter ....Ian Redford
Miles Bannister ....Robert Hands
Daniel Page...Richard Lintern
Katya Beletsky ....Caroline Trowbridge
Norman Foss ....Toby Whitehouse

Creators: Jean Marsh, Eileen Atkins. Producer: Jeremy Gwilt

Two impoverished sisters set up their own fashion house in the 1920s.

When their 'respectable' father suddenly died, leaving a host of debts and a mistress to boot, Beatrice (Bea) and Evangeline (Evie) Eliott were shaken out of their somewhat sheltered existence by the need to find their own way in the world. Bea took a job with photographer Jack Maddox, while Evie (12 years her junior) became an apprentice dressmaker. A culmination of their efforts was the setting up of their own London fashion company, The House of Eliott. Their battles to survive in a competitive world and the social prejudices facing independent women at that time provided the focus for later episodes. The personal lives of the girls and their workshop assistants also came to the fore. In the second series, the sisters moved to Paris to compete with international fashion houses. Bea married Jack but, as his career began to take off, cracks developed in their relationship. A third series saw the birth of Bea's baby, Lucy, and Evie's liaison with portrait painter Daniel Page.

Costing some £6 million pounds in its first series alone, *The House of Eliott* was devised by **Upstairs, Downstairs** creators Jean Marsh and Eileen Atkins and bore many of the hallmarks of that popular period drama. Costumes featured in the series were exhibited at the Victoria and Albert Museum in 1992.

HOW!/HOW 2

UK (Southern/TVS/Meridian) Children's Entertainment. ITV 1966–81/1990–

Presenters:
Fred Dinenage (*both*)

Jack Hargreaves
Jon Miller
Bunty James
Marian Davies
Carol Vorderman (*How 2*)
Gareth Jones (*How 2*)

Educational children's series explaining how things happen.

Always popular, *How!* was a series that managed to combine science with humour. Its four studio-bound presenters took turns to explain the scientific reasons why certain things happened. These could be of vital importance or of the most trivial nature. Tricks and experiments involving matchsticks, coins and water were favourite items. The four hosts (palms raised in Red Indian greeting at the beginning and end of each programme) were jokey Fred Dinenage, thoughtful Jack Hargreaves, gadget-minded Jon Miller and Bunty James, who was later replaced by Marian Davies. The series was revived in 1990 under the title of *How 2*. Dinenage returned for the relaunch and was joined by *Countdown* girl Carol Vorderman and kids' TV presenter Gareth 'Gaz Top' Jones.

HOWARD, RON (1954–)

American child actor, today one of Hollywood's most successful directors. Following early appearances in shows like *Dennis the Menace* and *The Twilight Zone*, Ron (or Ronny) Howard's TV career began to move at the age of six when he was cast in the part of Opie Taylor, Andy's son in the extremely popular US sitcom *The Andy Griffith Show*. The series ran from 1960 to 1968 and, in between episodes, Howard took time off to appear in dramas such as *The Fugitive*. In the early 1970s he was a member of *The Smith Family* (Bob Smith), another US comedy, which starred Henry Fonda, before he secured his biggest TV role to date, that of Richie Cunningham in *Happy Days*. Howard had played the role of the fresh-faced 1950s teenager in a pilot episode, seen as part of *Love, American Style*, and he stayed with *Happy Days* for six years, making occasional return appearances later while establishing himself in the movie world.

HOWARD, RONALD (1918–)

A former journalist and the son of Leslie Howard, Ronald Howard was a familiar face in two diverse series, a 1954 version of *Sherlock Holmes* (in the title role) and the action adventure *Cowboy in Africa* (as Wing Commander Howard Hayes) more than a decade later.

HOWARDS' WAY

UK (BBC) Drama. BBC 1 1985–90

Tom Howard ....Maurice Colbourne
Jan Howard ....Jan Harvey
Jack Rolfe....................................Glyn Owen
Avril Rolfe..................................Susan Gilmore
Ken Masters ....Stephen Yardley
Leo Howard ....Edward Highmore
Lynne Howard ....Tracey Childs
Polly Urquhart...........................Patricia Shakesby
Abby Urquhart...........................Cindy Shelley
Gerald Urquhart ....Ivor Danvers
Kate Harvey................................Dulcie Gray
Charles Frere ....Tony Anholt
Bill Sayers..................................Robert Vahey
Sir John Stevens ....Willoughby Grey
Dawn ....Sally Farmiloe
Claude Dupont ....Malcolm Jamieson
Admiral Redfern.........................Michael Denison
Davy ....Kulvinder Ghir
David Lloyd ....Bruce Bould
Orrin Hudson ....Ryan Michael
Sarah Foster ....Sarah-Jane Varley
Mark Foster ....Graham Poutney
Curtis Jaeger..............................Dean Harris
Sir Edward Frere ....Nigel Davenport
Amanda Parker ....Francesca Gonshaw
Anna Lee....................................Sarah Lam
Emma Newsome ....Sian Webber
Richard Spencer ....John Moulder-Brown
Michael Hanley ....Michael Loney
Phil Norton.................................Anthony Head
Richard Shellet ....Oscar Quitak
Vanessa Andenberg ....Lana Morris
Laura Wilde................................Kate O'Mara
James Brooke ....Andrew Bicknell

Creators: Gerard Glaister, Allan Prior. Producer: Gerard Glaister

Glossy soap centring on boats, boardrooms and bedrooms.

Redundant 44-year-old aircraft designer Tom Howard decided to take the plunge and bought into a boat-building business, inspired by the work he had done on his own yacht, *The Flying Fish*. His wife, Jan, having given her life to establishing the family and home, and fearing for the future, was less than impressed with Tom's new venture. Tom's partner in the struggling Mermaid Yard, where they perfected swish boats like the *Barracuda*, was boozy craftsman Jack Rolfe. Rolfe's obsolete business knowledge was supplemented with advice from his shrewd daughter, Avril, soon to be Tom's new lover. In response, Jan became manageress of a fashion house and embarked on affairs with her posing boss Ken Masters and ageing businessman Sir Edward Frere, father of smarmy tycoon Charles Frere. Tom's racing-mad but kind-hearted mother-in-law, Kate Harvey, lent a hand whenever called upon, but the Howards' children, the drop-out student Leo and the spoilt, sailing-mad Lynne, caused more than a few headaches. Lynne married Frenchman Claude Dupont, but he was killed while water skiing. Languid Leo's on/off girlfriend was the prickly Abby Urquhart, whose squabbling parents were also featured.

Howards' Way, set on the River Hamble in fictional Tarrant (real-life Bursledon), was a series about dodgy business deals, gaudy lifestyles, brave men and flashy women. It has been described as the 'first Thatcherite soap' and survived not only the years of boom and bust, but also the tragic death of its main star. When Maurice Colbourne died of a heart attack in 1989, Tom Howard was written out and the rest of the cast bravely soldiered on for one more year. Singer Marti Webb, backed by the Simon May Orchestra, took the programme's theme song, 'Always There', into the Top 20 in 1986.

HOWARTH, JACK, MBE (1896–1984)

Coronation Street's grumpy old Albert Tatlock, a cast original who stayed with the programme until his death in 1984. Previously, Howarth, born into a life of showbiz, had been active on stage and radio, in particular playing Mr Maggs in the radio serial *Mrs Dale's Diary*.

HOWERD, FRANKIE, OBE (FRANCIS HOWARD; 1917–92)

Unique British comedian, known for his 'oohs', 'aahs', 'please yourselves' and stuttering, bumbling delivery (caused by a natural childhood stammer, which he exaggerated for effect). Eventually breaking into showbiz at the end of the war, and making a name for himself on radio shows like *Variety Bandbox*, Howerd was given his first TV show in 1952. It was entitled *The Howerd Crowd* and was followed by numerous variety spots and guest turns over the years. Although his popularity faltered at the turn of the 1960s, and Howerd appeared not to move with the times, he was thrown a lifeline with an appearance on *That Was The Week That Was*, which resulted from a successful appearance in Peter Cook's *Establishment Club*. Howerd never looked back. He went on to star in a London stage version of *A Funny Thing Happened on the Way to the Forum*, which led to a TV lookalike, **Up Pompeii!**, in 1969. In this, as Lurcio the slave, Howerd meandered his way through double entendres and innuendoes (some allegedly too strong for the man himself), trying to deliver a prologue. The series led to a run of film spin-offs, as well as a similar TV outing set in the Middle East, *Whoops Baghdad!*, in 1973. *Further Up Pompeii!* was the name given to a one-off 1975 revival, as well as an unsuccessful LWT special in 1991. In all, Howerd was seldom off TV screens in the 1960s and 1970s, thanks to programmes such as *The Frankie Howerd Show*, *The Howerd Confessions*,

Frankie Howerd Strikes Again, *A Touch of the Casanovas* (the pilot for a never realized series) and *Frankie Howerd on Campus*. His wartime sitcom, *Then Churchill Said to Me*, made in 1982, was not broadcast (because of the Falklands conflict) until UK Gold screened it 11 years later. One of his last series was the kids' comedy *All Change* in 1989, in which he played Uncle Bob.

HOWMAN, KARL

British comic actor, well versed in Jack the Lad-type roles. Howman succeeded Robert Lindsay in the guise of Jakey Smith in the RAF sitcom **Get Some In**, before securing his own series, **Brush Strokes**, playing the gentle womanizer/decorator Jacko. He went on to star with Geraldine McEwan in **Mulberry**. Amongst his other credits have been episodes of **Angels**, **Minder**, **The Sweeney**, **Hazell**, **Fox**, **Shelley**, **The Professionals**, **A Fine Romance**, **Juliet Bravo**, **Dempsey and Makepeace** and **Boon**. He was also in the play **The Flipside of Dominick Hide**.

HR PUFNSTUF

US (Krofft) Children's Comedy. ITV 1970

Jimmy ....Jack Wild
Witchiepoo ....Billie Hayes

Writers: Lennie Weinrib, Howard Morris.
Producers: Sid Krofft, Marty Krofft

A young boy is lured to a magic island by an evil witch.

This lively musical cross between *Robinson Crusoe* and *The Wizard of Oz* told the story of Jimmy, a young lad who owned a talking golden flute named Freddie. To steal the flute, a nasty sorceress by the name of Witchiepoo lured Jimmy to her island home, enticing him into a beautiful boat then leaving him shipwrecked. Thankfully, HR Pufnstuf, the genial dragon mayor of Living Island (as the theme song said: 'He's your friend when things get rough') spotted the boy in distress and sent out his Rescue Racer team to bring him ashore. Thereafter, Jimmy shared the company of Pufnstuf and his comical friends – Judy the Frog, Cling and Clang, Ludicrous Lion and Dr Blinky (a white owl). Also seen were Horsey and Grandfather and Grandmother Clock, and the voices of the Four Winds were heard from time to time. Living with Witchiepoo in her spooky castle were her three sidekicks – a yellow spider named Seymour, a green vulture called Orson and the grey Stupid Bat. She also controlled the Evil Trees and Mushrooms in the Evil Forest as she darted around on her rocket-powered Vroom Broom. With the help of her cronies, and by spying on events around the island through her Image Machine, Witchiepoo scuppered all Jimmy's attempts to return home, but she never gained control of the magic flute.

The programme's non-human characters were represented by colourful, lifelike puppets, with voices supplied by Joan Gerber, Felix Silla and Walker Edmiston, amongst others. Seventeen episodes were made and a feature film version was released in 1970.

HTV (HARLECH TELEVISION)

HTV has been the ITV contractor for Wales and the west of England since 4 March 1968, after winning the franchise from TWW. Initially Harlech Television, the name of the successful bidding consortium, was used on air but was soon shortened to HTV. The company has since retained its franchise on two occasions and offers two separate services for viewers. HTV West (based in Bristol) covers the west of England, with specifically targeted news, sports and features programmes dropped into the general output, while HTV Cymru/Wales (based in Cardiff) does the same for Welsh viewers. The Welsh side of the company also produces Welsh language programmes. These are now screened on S4C, but before the Welsh fourth channel was established in 1982, Welsh programmes replaced certain English-language programmes in the HTV Wales schedules.

HTV West made a name for itself for innovative children's science fiction in the 1970s. Programmes such as *The Georgian House*, *Sky* and *The Children of the Stones* all made it to the national network. It also contributed game shows like *Mr and Mrs*, *Definition*, *Cuckoo in the Nest* and *Three Little Words*. The adventure series *Robin of Sherwood* was another network success.

HUCKLEBERRY HOUND SHOW, THE

US (Hanna-Barbera/Screen Gems) Cartoon.
ITV 1960–4

Voices:
Huckleberry Hound	Daws Butler
Pixie	Don Messick
Dixie	Daws Butler
Mr Jinks	Daws Butler
Yogi Bear	Daws Butler
Boo Boo	Don Messick
Hokey Wolf	Daws Butler
Ding-a-Ling	Doug Young

Creators/Executive Producers: William Hanna, Joseph Barbera

The adventures of an easy-going, never-flustered Southern pooch.

Huckleberry Hound took things as they came. He always saw the good things in life and made

little criticism of the bad – and this despite the cruelest of luck, which invited trees to fall on him and rockets to blow up beneath him. His only response was, 'Man, that was some heavy tree,' or similar remark, probably followed by another cheery refrain of *Clementine*. Painfully slow in thought and speech, this was a dog with all the time in the world and the spirit to give anything a go. The baggy-eyed bloodhound assumed various guises throughout his successful series. He was seen as a French legionnaire, a professor, a fireman and also the dashing Purple Pumpernickel, and became one of the small screen's first cartoon heroes. Sharing his limelight, in their own segments of the show, were *Pixie and Dixie* and *Yogi Bear*. Pixie and Dixie were two Southern mice who tormented Mr Jinks, the cat (who hated 'those meeces to pieces'). Yogi, in conjunction with his sidekick, Boo Boo, was the perennially hungry picnic snatcher of Jellystone National Park who became so popular that he was given his own series. His replacement was the Bilko-like Hokey Wolf, a sharp talking conwolf aided and abetted by the fox Ding-a-Ling.

The Huckleberry Hound Show was the programme that launched former *Tom and Jerry* animators William Hanna and Joseph Barbera into the TV big time. Their first offering had been a cat and dog series called *Ruff and Reddy*, but after Huckleberry Hound they were in a position to produce *The Flintstones*, *The Jetsons*, *Scooby Doo – Where Are You?*, *Wacky Races* and countless other children's favourites.

HUDD, ROY (1936–)

British comedian and entertainer in the music hall tradition, whose TV career kicked off with the sitcom *Tell It to the Marines* but really progressed through regular appearances on *That Was The Week That Was* and *Not So Much a Programme, More a Way of Life*. His own series for the BBC and ITV followed, including *Hudd*, *The Illustrated Weekly Hudd* and *The Roy Hudd Show*, all of which exhibited his versatility and demonstrated his fondness for the music hall greats. These days, whenever a nostalgic programme is on the air, Roy Hudd is never far away. Hudd's dramatic skills were also given the chance to shine when, in 1993, he played Harold Atterbow in Dennis Potter's *Lipstick On Your Collar*. In 1994 he played John Parry in the dustbinmen comedy *Common as Muck*. Hudd has been just as familiar on radio, thanks to his longrunning series *The News Huddlines*.

HUDSON, ROCK (ROY SCHERER; 1925–85)

Hollywood heart-throb of the 1950s and 1960s, whose television work was saved until the end of his career (save for the odd guest appearance on shows like *I Love Lucy* and *Rowan and Martin's Laugh-In*). In 1971 (the same year as he allegedly turned down the Tony Curtis role in *The Persuaders!*), Hudson starred in a TV movie, *Once Upon a Dead Man*, which proved to be the pilot for the Mystery Movie series *McMillan and Wife*, in which he appeared with Susan Saint James. The series ran for six years and, when it ended, Hudson stayed with TV, taking roles in an assortment of mini-series, including *Wheels* (as Adam Trenton) and *The Martian Chronicles* (as Colonel John Wilder). In 1982 he was cast as another detective, Brian Devlin, in a short-lived series entitled *The Devlin Connection* (it was cancelled because Hudson underwent heart surgery), before he resurfaced as Daniel Reece in *Dynasty* in 1984. It proved to be Hudson's last major role before his well-publicized death from an AIDS-related illness a year later.

HUGGINS, ROY (1914–)

Prolific American producer and writer, the creator of series like *Maverick*, *77 Sunset Strip*, *The Fugitive*, *Run for your Life* and *The Rockford Files*. He has also produced *Cheyenne*, *The Virginian*, *Alias Smith and Jones* and *Baretta* among numerous other action series. His own production company was known as Public Arts.

HUGH AND I

UK (BBC) Situation Comedy. BBC 1962–6

Terry Scott	Terry Scott
Hugh Lloyd	Hugh Lloyd
Mrs Scott	Vi Stevens
Mr Crispin	Wallas Eaton
Mrs Crispin	Mollie Sugden
Norma Crispin	Jacquie Wallis
	Jill Curzon
Arthur Wormold	Cyril Smith
	Jack Haig
Griselda Wormold	Patricia Hayes

Creator/Writer: John Chapman. Producer: David Croft

Two friends seek to improve their lot, with disastrous results.

Number 33 Lobelia Avenue, Tooting, was the home of Mrs Scott, her troublesome, unemployed son, Terry, and their lodger, Hugh Lloyd, a worker at a local aircraft factory. Forming a Laurel and Hardy-like double act, the two lads constantly found themselves in hot water, with the bumptious, over-ambitious Terry leading the timid, fretful Hugh astray. Usually 'get rich quick' schemes were to blame. Next to the Scotts, on one side, lived the Crispins, he a loud-mouth, she a snob, and their daughter, Norma, an object of lust for the boys. On the other side were the

Wormolds. Terry and Hugh embarked on more adventurous escapades in the murky world of espionage in their 1968 follow-up series, *Hugh and I Spy*.

HUGHES, GEOFFREY (1944–)

Liverpudlian actor often cast in slobby, layabout roles. For eight years he was kind-hearted bin man Eddie Yeats in *Coronation Street* and more recently he has been seen as Onslow, Hyacinth Bucket's vest-wearing brother-in-law, in *Keeping Up Appearances*. He also played Mr Lithgow in the Channel 4 sitcom *The Bright Side*, Dilk in *Making Out* and has popped up in a range of other series from *Z Cars*, *The Likely Lads*, *You Rang, M'Lord?* and *Curry and Chips* to *The Mind of Mr J.G. Reeder*, *No, Honestly*, *Doctor Who* and *Spender*. He provided the voice for Paul McCartney's character in the cartoon film *Yellow Submarine*.

HUGHES, NERYS (1941–)

Welsh actress most notable on TV as Sandra Hutchinson in *The Liver Birds* (for eight years) and Megan Roberts in *The District Nurse*. She played Maisie, the barmaid, in the comedy drama *The Flying Swan* in 1965, Beth Jenkins in a short-lived YTV sitcom called *Third Time Lucky* in 1982, and has also appeared in *How Green Was My Valley*, presented kids' series like *Play Away*, *Alphabet Zoo* and *Jackanory*, guested in *Doctor Who* and hosted the practical magazine programme *Bazaar*. One of her earliest starring roles was in the 1964 serial *Diary of a Young Man*.

HULL, ROD (1935–)

British entertainer with Australian connections, not least his aggressive, giant Emu puppet. Armed with this uncontrollable beast, Hull was, for a number of years in the 1970s and 1980s, a big name in children's television. He devised and hosted the first *Children's Royal Variety Performance* and starred in *Rod Hull and Emu*, *EBC* (Emu's Broadcasting Company) and *Emu's World*. On one celebrated appearance on *Parkinson*, Emu very clearly ruffled the interviewer's feathers, violently attacking Parky and pushing him on to the floor. Hull has also enjoyed success across the Atlantic.

HUMAN JUNGLE, THE

UK (Independent Artists/ABC) Medical Drama. ITV 1963–5

Dr Roger Corder	Herbert Lom
Dr Jimmy Davis	Michael Johnson
Jennifer Corder	Sally Smith
Nancy Hamilton	Mary Yeomans

Creator: Julian Wintle. Producers: Julian Wintle, Leslie Parkyn

The professional and domestic troubles of a London psychiatrist.

Widower Dr Roger Corder MD, DPM was a specialist on emotional distress and his counselling helped many disturbed patients back to health. He enjoyed a good relationship with his junior colleague, Dr Jimmy Davis, and his supportive secretary, Nancy Hamilton, and stories revolved around the various cases they undertook, with Corder heading out and about to meet his patients in their own surroundings (where he could understand them better). However, the workaholic doctor was less successful in his private life, seldom being able to communicate with his determined teenage daughter, Jennifer.

HUMPHRIES, BARRY (1934–)

Australian entertainer, the creator of larger-than-life housewife megastar Dame Edna Everage and boozy cultural attaché Sir Les Patterson. His series have included *The Dame Edna Experience* and *Dame Edna's Neighbourhood Watch*, and Humphries has also organized *An Audience with Dame Edna*. He was also seen in the single drama *Doctor Fischer of Geneva* and the serial *Selling Hitler* (as Rupert Murdoch).

HUMPHRYS, JOHN (1943–)

Seasoned Welsh journalist, newsreader and presenter, one of the Radio 4 *Today* team since 1987 but still active on television. Humphrys became a BBC foreign correspondent in 1970, working in the USA and South Africa up to 1980. He then took over as diplomatic correspondent before joining the new-look *Nine O'Clock News* team as one of its chief presenters a year later. He stayed with the news until 1986 and still occasionally works as a newsreader on the BBC's main bulletins. Humphrys has also hosted the Sunday political programme *On the Record* and chaired numerous debates and discussion programmes. His brother Bob is a sports presenter with BBC Wales.

HUNNIFORD, GLORIA (1940–)

Northern Ireland-born radio and TV presenter. Hunniford's showbusiness career began in singing (she made her debut at the age of nine), before progressing into radio work in Canada and Northern Ireland, then television (*Good Evening Ulster*). From a base as a Radio 2 presenter (1982–), she moved into UK TV, hosting shows like *Sunday, Sunday*, **Songs of Praise**, *We Love TV*, *Wogan*, **Holiday**, *Gloria*, *Family Affairs* (with her

daughter Caron Keating), *Gloria Live* and **Children In Need**. She was also a regular panellist on *That's Showbusiness*.

HUNT, GARETH (1943–)

London-born actor who came to light as Frederick, the footman, in **Upstairs, Downstairs** and later headlined in *The New Avengers*, playing John Steed's leg man, Mike Gambit. He then turned to comedy and starred in the sitcom *That Beryl Marston*, playing Gerry Bodley, and later *Side By Side*, as plumber Vince Tulley. Hunt has also appeared in **Minder** and **Doctor Who**, plus countless coffee commercials.

HUNTER'S WALK

UK (ATV) Police Drama. ITV 1973–6

Detective Sgt Smith	Ewan Hooper
Sgt Ken Ridgeway	Davyd Harries
PC Fred Pooley	Duncan Preston
DC 'Mickey' Finn	David Simeon
PC Harry Coombes	Charles Rea
Betty Smith	Ruth Madoc

Creator: Ted Willis. Producer: John Cooper

A small police force keeps the peace in a provincial town.

Set in the modest Midlands settlement of Broadstone (actually Rushden, Northants), *Hunter's Walk* focused on the team at the local police station, namely po-faced DS 'Smithy' Smith, 'Mickey' Finn, his junior detective colleague, PCs Pooley and Coombes, and station officer Ken Ridgeway. Faced with routine police investigations, mostly of a domestic nature, they successfully patrolled the streets in steady, **Dixon of Dock Green** fashion (not surprisingly, as this was also created by Lord Ted Willis). Smith's wife was played by future **Hi-De-Hi!** star Ruth Madoc.

HURT, JOHN (1940–)

Award-winning British character actor who, after appearances in series like **Gideon's Way** and *The Sweeney*, shot to fame as Quentin Crisp in Thames TV's **The Naked Civil Servant** in 1975. He followed this with the roles of Caligula in **I, Claudius** and Raskolnikov in *Crime and Punishment* and was **The Storyteller** in Jim Henson's acclaimed children's series.

HYLTON, JACK (1892–1965)

British bandleader who became one of ITV's earliest light entertainment producers, working with Tony Hancock, Alfred Marks, Dickie Henderson, Anne Shelton and others. The early sitcom **Tell It to the Marines** was another success.

IBA see ITC.

I, CLAUDIUS

UK (BBC) Historical Drama. BBC 2 1976

Claudius	Derek Jacobi
Livia	Siân Phillips
Octavian/Augustus	Brian Blessed
Tiberius	George Baker
Caligula	John Hurt
Sejanus	Patrick Stewart
Piso	Stratford Johns
Herod	James Faulkner
Germanicus	David Robb
Agrippa	John Paul
Marcellus	Christopher Guard
Julia	Frances White
Livilla	Patricia Quinn
Agrippina	Fiona Walker
Messalina	Sheila White
Drusilla	Beth Morris
Antonia	Margaret Tyzack
Drusus	Ian Ogilvy
Nero	Christopher Biggins
Castor	Kevin McNally
Macro	John Rhys Davies
Gratus	Bernard Hill
Narcissus	John Cater
Pallus	Bernard Hepton

Writer: Jack Pulman. Producer: Martin Lisemore

The power struggles of Imperial Rome as seen through the eyes of an innocent.

Depicting the debauchery and duplicity of life in ancient Rome, *I, Claudius* was a 12-part dramatization of two novels by Robert Graves: *I, Claudius* and *Claudius the God*. It focused on Emperor Claudius, who related events in his lifetime via flashbacks, taking up the story in the time of the Emperor Augustus (24 BC) when the stammering, limping Claudius was a sickly child. It progressed through the reigns of the despotic Tiberius and the deranged Caligula to reveal how, quite against his desires, Claudius himself became ruler of the empire (and, in effect, the known world). Murder and manoeuvring lay at every turn, interspersed with perverse orgies and gluttonous feasts, with chief of manipulators Claudius's cruel grandmother, the arch-poisoner Livia.

The snake that writhed across the mosaic in the opening titles aptly set the tone for this colourful, often gory series which attracted audiences not normally drawn to historical drama. *I, Claudius* inevitably won much acclaim, not least for the performance of Shakespearean actor Derek Jacobi.

IDENT BOARD

A board displaying details of the programme being recorded. Often incorporating a countdown clock, it is shown to the camera or imposed on the screen at the start of recording to confirm the title, episode, scene, date, etc.

I DIDN'T KNOW YOU CARED

UK (BBC) Situation Comedy. BBC 1 1975–9

Uncle Mort	Robin Bailey
Les Brandon	John Comer
Annie Brandon	Liz Smith
Carter Brandon	Stephen Rea
	Keith Drinkel
Pat Partington/Brandon	Anita Carey
	Liz Goulding
Uncle Staveley	Bert Palmer
	Leslie Sarony
Linda Preston	Deirdre Costello
Mrs Partington	Vanda Godsell
Sid Skelhorn	Ray Dunbobbin
	Bobby Pattinson

Creator/Writer: Peter Tinniswood. Producer: Bernard Thompson

The battle of the sexes in a morose northern household.

The Brandons were a miserable-go-unlucky Yorkshire family living in an industrial town. They consisted of Les and Annie (unhappily married for 25 years), their son, Carter, his wife, Pat, and Annie's mufflered brother, Mort, who 'served all through First World War' and who was forced to move in when his wife, Edna, died. While the women folk harassed and bullied, the men tried desperately to slink away to the pub or Mort's allotment, where he hoisted a Union Jack above his converted railway carriage shed. There Les and Mort aimed to protect young Carter from his socially ambitious new wife over a brew of tea and a hand of dominoes. Carter's response was usually a hesitant 'Aye . . . Well . . . Mmm . . .'. Visits by the terrifying Three Great Aunts From Glossop, much-dreaded works outings and encounters with Unsworth's lively pork pies gave the family plenty to battle over, with only funerals and opposition to 'London beer' likely to bring any harmony. Also seen was senile army veteran Uncle Staveley, who carried the ashes of his 'oppo', Cpl Parkinson, in a box around his neck and whose best conversation was 'I heard that, Pardon?' Linda Preston was the local jezebel who aimed to seduce Carter at every turn.

Creator Peter Tinniswood had earlier introduced the Brandons in a trilogy of novels and Uncle Mort and Carter have also been heard on BBC Radio.

IDIOT BOARD

A cue card, displaying lines or instructions, held next to the camera to help forgetful presenters and actors.

IDLE, ERIC (1943–)

British comedy actor and writer, best known for his work as part of the **Monty Python** team. Previously, Idle had scripted sketches for **The Frost Report** with Tim Brooke-Taylor and other Pythons. He had also written episodes of the Ronnie Corbett comedy **No – That's Me Over Here** and been seen in the children's comedy **Do Not Adjust Your Set**. Post-*Python*, he created and starred in **Rutland Weekend Television** and its spin-off **The Rutles**. Idle also wrote and sang the theme song for **One Foot in the Grave** and was script editor on early episodes of **The Liver Birds**.

I DREAM OF JEANNIE

US (Screen Gems) Situation Comedy.
ITV 1966–

Jeannie...Barbara Eden
Captain/Major Tony Nelson ....Larry Hagman
Captain Roger Healey ....Bill Daily
Dr Alfred Bellows ....Hayden Rorke
General Martin Peterson ....Barton MacLane
Amanda Bellows...............................Emmaline Henry

Creator/Executive Producer: Sidney Sheldon

An astronaut is the master of a beautiful young genie.

When his test mission was aborted, NASA astronaut Tony Nelson parachuted back to Earth and found himself marooned on a desert island. There, he picked up a bottle, uncorked it and let loose a beautiful genie, appropriately named Jeannie, who promised him his every wish. Naturally, the first thing he called for was a rescue helicopter and then returned home to his base at Cocoa Beach, Florida, taking Jeannie along for the ride.

The fun of this series came from the fact that only Tony and his playboy buddy, Roger Healey, knew about Jeannie and only they could see her. NASA's psychiatrist, Alfred Bellows, thought Tony was nuts, of course, and looked for every opportunity to prove it. With Jeannie supposedly being 2000 years old, she had some difficulty interpreting 20th-century expressions and figures of speech, and this led to even more confusion and chaos whenever she stepped in to 'help' her master. She was also in love with Tony, and took every opportunity to spoil his chances with other women. Somewhat ironically, it was Jeannie whose wish finally came true, when she and Tony were married towards the end of the series.

I LOVE LUCY

US (CBS/Desilu) Situation Comedy. ITV 1955–

Lucy Ricardo ....Lucille Ball
Ricky Ricardo ....Desi Arnaz
Ethel Mertz ....Vivian Vance
Fred Mertz.......................................William Frawley
Little Ricky Ricardo ....Richard Keith

Writers: Madelyn Pugh, Bob Carroll. Producer: Jess Oppenheimer

A danceband leader's patience is sorely tried by his scatterbrained wife.

I Love Lucy was a pioneer among TV programmes. It set the pattern for the 'domestic' sitcom, and was the first series to be filmed (before a live audience), rather than transmitted live. This has also contributed to its longevity, since all the original programmes are still available in good condition. It centred on the life of Lucy Ricardo (née MacGillicuddy), a zany, rather immature redhead of Scottish descent, for whom nothing would go right. Her Cuban husband, Ricky, was a danceband leader and Lucy longed to follow him into showbusiness, despite her lack of talent. Failing this, she at least wanted to be more than an ordinary housewife and consequently cooked up endless hare-brained schemes to make money or to improve life around the home, most of them prone to disaster. But, as the programme's title revealed, Ricky really did love Lucy and, although extremely annoyed, he was remarkably forgiving, considering the amount of hassle she caused him.

The Ricardos lived in an apartment on the East Side of Manhattan, where their frumpy landlord and landlady were Fred and Ethel Mertz. Lucy found a willing ally and accomplice in Ethel, who was years younger than her wisecracking, irascible husband, and the two girls often waged a battle of the sexes with the guys. But they were all good friends at heart. In one season, Ricky found fame in Hollywood and the foursome set off on a famous car trek across America; in another, they toured Europe with Ricky's band.

One of the highlights of the series was the birth of Little Ricky in the second season, an event planned to coincide with Lucille Ball's own second pregnancy (the episode was screened the night that Ball's real baby was born). Other developments included Ricky moving on from the Tropicana Club, where he worked, to owning his own nightspot, the Babaloo Club, and then starring in his own TV show.

Lucille and Desi Arnaz were married in real life and owned the programme's production company, Desilu. After their divorce, Lucille developed another two successful comedies in the same vein, **The Lucy Show** and **Here's Lucy,** while Desi went on to produce *The Untouchables*, amongst other programmes. *I Love Lucy* was the first American sitcom to be seen on British television, appearing in ITV's first week on air.

I'M THE LAW

US (Cosman) Police Drama. BBC 1954–5

Lt George Kirby ....George Raft

Executive Producer: Pat Costello. Producer: Jean Yarborough

Very early American cop show set in New York City.

Gangster actor George Raft swapped sides for this half-hour foray into primitive TV policing. Taking on the mantle of Lt George Kirby of the NYPD, Raft's beat was The Big Apple and he patrolled the city streets in search of thugs, murderers and thieves, dishing out knuckle sandwiches and bullets aplenty. Raft also acted as narrator. Lou Costello's brother, Pat, was the show's executive producer, maintaining a very tight budget.

IN AT THE DEEP END

UK (BBC) Documentary. BBC 1 1982; 1984; 1987

Presenters: Chris Serle, Paul Heiney

Executive Producer: Edward Mirzoeff. Producer: Nick Handel

Two reporters take crash courses in other people's professional skills.

That's Life presenters Chris Serle and Paul Heiney alternated as stars of this light-hearted series, which saw them attempting to acquire professional skills and put them to the test – all within a matter of weeks. For instance, Serle was called upon to partner snooker star Steve Davis in a doubles match against Tony Meo and Alex Higgins after receiving coaching from the likes of Ray Reardon, Terry Griffiths and Cliff Thorburn. He also underwent intense training to become a press photographer and then covered a royal assignment for the *Daily Mirror*. Between them Serle and Heiney tried their hand at numerous occupations, including auctioneer, actor, shepherd, opera singer, book-maker and fashion designer.

INCREDIBLE HULK, THE

US (Universal) Science Fiction/Adventure. ITV 1978–82

Dr David Banner ....Bill Bixby
The Incredible Hulk ....Lou Ferrigno
Jack McGee ....Jack Colvin

Executive Producers: Glen A. Larson, Kenneth Johnson. Producers: James D. Parriott, Chuck Bowman

A mild-mannered scientist turns into an angry green monster when provoked.

Scientist David Banner had become a victim of his own experiments on human strength by accidentally exposing himself to a massive dose of gamma rays. The effects of the radiation meant that he turned into a raging green giant whenever he felt angry. Banner could feel the change coming on, but, after the Hulk had indulged in an orgy of violence and then reverted to his true self, Banner could never remember what had happened 'during his absence'.

With the world believing him to be dead, Banner ran from town to town in search of a cure for his weird malady. On his tail was *National Register* reporter Jack McGee, who had guessed Banner's secret and was looking for concrete evidence to back up his suspicions. Inevitably, something always managed to irk the docile Dr Jekyll, releasing the shirt-busting, roaring Mr Hyde figure of the Hulk.

Lou Ferrigno, who played the monster, was a former Mr Universe and the series was based on the early 1960s *Marvel* comic strip by Stan Lee, in which Banner's Christian name was Bruce, not David.

INDEPENDENT TELEVISION COMMISSION see ITC.

INDEPENDENT TELEVISION CORPORATION see ITC.

INDEPENDENT TELEVISION NEWS (ITN)

ITN was established by the 1954 Television Act as a news-gathering organization owned jointly by the various ITV companies. Its first news bulletin was aired on 22 September 1955, when Christopher Chataway read the headlines in a 12-minute programme. Following the introduction of new regulations in the 1990 Broadcasting Act, ITN was re-founded as a profit-making news business with commercial contracts to the ITV companies and other broadcasters. It is now owned by a consortium made up of Carlton Communications, Central Television, the Granada Group, LWT and Reuters (all with 18 per cent holdings), as well as Anglia and Scottish Television (each having 5 per cent). Also in 1990, ITN moved to new purpose-built headquarters in London's Gray's Inn Road.

ITN now provides news 24 hours a day, with the main bulletins being *Lunchtime News* at 12.30

(launched in 1972 under the title *First Report* and now monitoring the day's developing stories, with an emphasis on live interviews), *Early Evening News* at 5.40 (formerly *News At 5.45/5.40*, a 15-minute review of the day's events so far), *Channel 4 News* (the 7 pm in-depth bulletin) and *News At Ten* (the ITN flagship half-hour, airing at 10 pm). The last, introduced in 1967, was Britain's first 30-minute news programme. In addition to these, ITN offers news headlines through the night and a half-hour round-up at 5.30 am known as *Morning News*.

The company also provides news services for other broadcasters. ITN *World News* is a summary of varying length focusing on global affairs. It is seen eight times a day on various international channels, including NBC Super Channel. A bouncy, headline-only format is supplied to Channel 4's *The Big Breakfast* and ITN also compiles radio news bulletins for IRN (Independent Radio News) and Classic FM.

Over and above formal news reports, ITN has also produced a number of feature programmes, which have been broadly news and current affairs based. Between 1957 and 1964, for instance, *Roving Report* was a series of topical documentaries compiled by ITN correspondents around the world. More recently, House to House, fronted by Maya Even on Channel 4, has reported the business of the day from the Houses of Commons and Lords. There have been programmes on royalty, elections, budgets and other state occasions, too. See also News.

INFORMER, THE

UK (Rediffusion) Adventure. ITV 1966–7

Alex Lambert	Ian Hendry
Janet Lambert	Heather Sears
Sylvia Parrish	Jean Marsh
Detective Sgt Piper	Neil Hallett
Cass	Tony Selby

Creators: John Whitney, Geoffrey Bellman. Executive Producer: Stella Richman. Producers: Stella Richman, Peter Collinson, John Whitney

The risky life of a professional informer.

Disgraced and disbarred barrister Alex Lambert had begun to rebuild his life and his shaky marriage. Using the excellent contacts he had made over the years on both sides of the law, he branched out into a new career as a paid informer. Passing on information to Piper, his police contact, Lambert lived off the substantial rewards offered by insurance companies. But secrecy was vital and his life was continually under threat. Not even his wife was party to his true profession and he masqueraded under the guise of a business consultant.

INHERITED AUDIENCE

An audience that a programme gains from the previous show on the same channel, with viewers not bothering to turn over. Planners make use of inherited audiences to give new series a launch pad.

IN LOVING MEMORY

UK (Yorkshire) Situation Comedy. ITV 1979–86

Ivy Unsworth	Thora Hird
Billy Unsworth	Christopher Beeney
Tom Wrigley	Paul Luty
Amy Jenkinson	Avis Bunnage
Ernie Hadfield	Colin Farrell
Mary Braithwaite	Sherrie Hewson

Writer: Dick Sharples. Producer: Ronnie Baxter

A spinster and her hapless nephew run a northern undertaker's.

When Jeremiah Unsworth died in the first episode of this series, he left his unmarried daughter, Ivy, as sole proprietor of his funeral director's business in the Lancashire mill town of Oldshaw. The year was 1929. To help in running the business, Ivy enlisted her gormless nephew, Billy; other local characters, like grave digger Tom Wrigley and bachelor Ernie Hadfield, were also on the scene.

The pilot for this series had been screened some ten years earlier (and indeed topped the ratings). Written by Dick Sharples and produced by Ronnie Baxter, this one-off comedy for Thames cast Edward Chapman and Marjorie Rhodes in the lead roles of Jeremiah and Ivy.

INMAN, JOHN (1935–)

British actor, a stage pantomime dame, known for his camp roles of menswear assistant Mr Humphries in *Are You Being Served?* (through which 'I'm free!' became his catchphrase), rock factory proprietor Neville Sutcliffe in *Odd Man Out* and male secretary Graham Jones in *Take a Letter, Mr Jones*. The character of Mr Humphries resurfaced in the *Are You Being Served?* revival, Grace and Favour, in 1992.

INNES BOOK OF RECORDS, THE

UK (BBC) Comedy/Music. BBC 2 1979–81

Host: Neil Innes

Producer: Ian Keill

Sketches and musical parodies with the former Bonzo Dog man.

In the late 1960s Neil Innes mixed easily with the new breed of alternative comedians, working with the **Monty Python** team and inspiring the wacky pop group The Bonzo Dog Doo Dah Band. In this, his own series, a decade later, he demonstrated his talent for deadpan humour and his flair for uncannily accurate musical send-ups. Anyone who saw *The Rutles* will vouch for this rare ability.

IN SICKNESS AND IN HEALTH see *Till Death Us Do Part.*

INSIDE GEORGE WEBLEY

UK (Yorkshire) Situation Comedy. ITV 1968–70

George Webley ....Roy Kinnear
Rosemary Webley................................Patsy Rowlands

Creators/Writers: Keith Waterhouse, Willis Hall. Producer: Bill Hitchcock

A man's life is dominated by worry.

George Webley was the archetypal worryguts. He fretted over the silliest matters and, in his mind, something was always about to go wrong. Had he left the gas on, for example? His dozy, ever-hungry wife, Rosemary, was far more relaxed.

There was more than an echo of *Inside George Webley* in Paul Smith and Terry Kyan's comedy **Colin's Sandwich**, 20 years later.

INSPECTOR ALLEYN MYSTERIES, THE

UK (BBC) Drama. BBC 1 1993–

Chief Inspector Roderick Alleyn ......Patrick Malahide
Inspector Brad Fox ....William Simons
Agatha Troy ....Belinda Lang

Creator: Ngaio Marsh. Producer: George Gallaccio

A well-bred, academically brilliant detective works for Scotland Yard in the late 1940s.

New Zealand author Dame Ngaio Marsh's toff detective was first brought to television in the 1960s as part of the **Detective** anthology in which he was played by Michael Allinson. Simon Williams donned Alleyn's trilby for a 90-minute special in 1990, but when a series was cast in 1993 it was Patrick Malahide – already familiar as **Minder**'s Sgt Chisholm – who was offered the role. He portrayed Roderick Alleyn as a true gentleman, unfailingly polite but a steely adversary for law breakers. A man with a double first in Classics from Oxford, Alleyn was a policeman almost out of a sense of duty. He moved in aristocratic circles but was never a snob. He was supported in his work by the loyal Inspector Fox and

in his private life by his artistic lady friend Agatha Troy (both William Simons and Belinda Lang had taken the same roles in the 1990 offering).

In the original novels, Alleyn's cases covered the period 1933 to 1980 (two years before his creator's death). For this television rendition, the action was confined to 1948. After a run of five mysteries, Alleyn returned in 1994, not in another series but in the first of a collection of one-off investigations.

INSPECTOR MORSE

UK (Zenith/Central) Police Drama. ITV 1987–93

Chief Inspector Morse ....John Thaw
Detective Sgt Robbie Lewis ....Kevin Whately
Max ....Peter Woodthorpe
Dr Grayling Russell ....Amanda Hillwood
Chief Supt Bell ....Norman Jones
Chief Supt Strange ....James Grout

Executive Producer: Ted Childs. Producers: Kenny McBain, Chris Burt, David Lascelles, Deirdre Keir

The complicated cases of a cerebral Oxford detective.

Chief Inspector Morse (first name always concealed) of the Thames Valley Police was an Oxford graduate and a lover of culture. Poetry, Wagnerian opera and cryptic crosswords were his passions, along with gallons of real ale to oil the cogs of his brilliant detective mind. Somewhat squeamish for a copper, and always with an eye for the ladies (although seldom a success with the opposite sex), Morse cruised the dreaming-spired streets of Oxford in his 1960 Mark 2 red Jaguar, accompanied by his ingenuous sergeant, Lewis, a Geordie making his way up the CID ladder. Unlike the crotchety bachelor Morse, genial Lewis was a family man and the contrast between the two was well contrived. The pair enjoyed a good working relationship, even if Morse was cruelly patronizing at times.

The investigations were unfailingly multi-dimensional and Morse always needed time to collar his man, or woman. His theories regularly went awry, and one murder would turn into two or three before he finally pieced together the solution (often with the help of a chance remark from Lewis), much to the dissatisfaction of his boss, Chief Supt. Strange. Indeed, seldom was there an episode when pathologists Max or Dr Russell did not have to appear more than once.

With each beautifully photographed two-hour episode, there was bags of scope for both character and plot development. Stories initially came from the original novels by Oxford academic

Colin Dexter, who endowed Morse with his own love of classics, culture, crosswords and booze. Indeed, Morse's name was derived from Sir Jeremy Morse, then Chairman of Lloyds Bank and one of Dexter's crossword rivals. Lewis, too, was christened after a crossword setter, although in the books he was Welsh and nearing retirement age. When the novels ran out, Dexter penned a series of new plots for TV, before finally handing over the invention to other writers. His involvement with the series continued, however – as an extra, walking on in every episode, just like Hitchcock before him. The programme's sweeping theme music by Barrington Pheloung was cleverly based on the Morse Code beat for the letters M-O-R-S-E.

INTERFERENCE

Sound or picture distortion caused by external electrical signals.

INTERNATIONAL DETECTIVE

UK (Delfry/ABC) Detective Drama. ITV 1959–61

Ken Franklin ....Arthur Fleming

Producer: Gordon L.T. Scott

The adventures of a calm, systematic detective agency man.

Ken Franklin worked for the William J. Burns International Detective Agency in New York and jetted around the world on various assignments. Given his briefing by W.J. Burns himself (a character never properly seen – just the top of his head or an arm as in the picture), Franklin then used intellect rather than brute force to bring home results. Each episode was entitled 'The . . . Case' (fill in the blank) and was shot in documentary style.

The series was supposedly based on the real files of a William J. Burns agency, although, as the voice-over narrated, '. . . the names of the clients and locations have been changed to protect their privacy'. Star Arthur (Art) Fleming went on to host one of American TV's most popular quiz shows, *Jeopardy*.

INTERPOL CALLING

UK (Rank/Wrather/ATV) Police Drama. ITV 1959–60

Inspector Paul Duval ....Charles Korvin
Inspector Mornay...............................Edwin Richfield

Executive Producer: F. Sherwin Green. Producers: Anthony Perry, Connery Chapell

Cases from the files of the International Criminal Police Organization, Interpol.

Inspectors Duval and Mornay, two detectives operating out of Interpol's Paris headquarters, investigated murders, foiled blackmailers, arrested hijackers, duped drug pushers and apprehended would-be assassins all around the world in this half-hour series. Each episode opened with a speeding car crashing through a checkpoint, setting the pace for the action to follow. Thirty-nine stories were filmed.

IN THE HEAT OF THE NIGHT

US (MGM) Police Drama. ITV 1988–

Chief Bill Gillespie ....Carroll O'Connor
Chief of Detectives Virgil Tibbs ....Howard Rollins
Althea Tibbs...............................Anne-Marie Johnson
Sgt Bubba Skinner ....Alan Autry
Deputy Parker Williams............................David Hart
Deputy Lonnie Jamison.....................Hugh O'Connor
Deputy Willson Sweet ....Geoffrey Thorne
Deputy Junior Abernathy ....Christian Le Blanc

Creator: James Lee Barrett. Executive Producers: Fred Silverman, Juanita Bartlett, David Moessinger, Jeri Taylor, Carroll O'Connor, Hugh Benson, Ed Ledding

TV version of the Oscar-winning film of the same name.

Reprising the roles played by Rod Steiger and Sidney Poitier in the classic movie, Carroll O'Connor, formerly of **All in the Family**, became Police Chief Bill Gillespie and Howard Rollins black cop Virgil Tibbs. Together they aimed to fight crime in the small town of Sparta, Mississippi. Tibbs was a native of the town but had only just returned home, having worked in the high-tech police circles of Philadelphia. He found himself appointed to the role of Chief of Detectives, alongside Gillespie, although the crusty old cop resented the appointment, which had been made by a black mayor seeking black votes. His resentment was not racial (the series had little of the tension of the original film), but centred on his dislike of the modern police methods Tibbs introduced. It was the familiar experience versus youth argument. However, as a team they achieved results and a healthy mutual respect developed between the two men.

Carroll O'Connor was forced to withdraw from a few episodes because of ill health, and his place was taken by Joe Don Baker in the guise of Acting Chief Tom Dugan. Actor Hugh O'Connor, who played Deputy Jamison, was Carroll O'Connor's son

INVADERS, THE

US (Quinn Martin) Science Fiction. ITV 1967–

David Vincent..Roy Thinnes
Edgar Scoville ....Kent Smith
Narrator ....William Conrad

Creator: Larry Cohen. Executive Producer:

Quinn Martin. Producer: Alan A. Armer

An architect tries to alert the world to an alien invasion.

Most people thought David Vincent was paranoid. He believed the world was under threat from a race of aliens whose planet was dying. In the style of Richard Kimble in *The Fugitive*, he moved from town to town attempting to warn the human race, but at the same time keeping himself clear of the Invaders' clutches.

Vincent, an architect, had been driving down a deserted country road and had pulled over to get some sleep. He had been awakened by the arrival of a space ship and the realization that an invasion was taking place. He had run to bring help but the police discovered only a young courting couple who denied everything Vincent had said. It was the first of many brick walls to confront him during the course of the series.

Because the Invaders assumed human form, Vincent had great difficulty persuading people to believe his story. Usually, those in whom he placed his trust turned out themselves to be aliens, as even he had problems spotting them. He soon gathered, though, that they were not complete human clones and that they had some strange defects, most notably a crooked little finger. Another giveaway was the fact that, having no hearts, they had no pulse or emotions.

After many narrow escapes, Vincent managed to convince a small group of citizens that his story was true, and he was thus given seven colleagues (known as 'The Believers') to finance and support his mission to save the planet. The leader of the group was Edgar Scoville, a millionaire electronics executive.

The story never was brought to a climax, but Vincent did have his successes. He thwarted various alien plans and killed a number of Invaders during the course of the series, seeing them glow red and evaporate, leaving behind just a burnt outline on the ground. But the aliens, too, were killers, either using ray guns or a small disc device, which, when applied to the back of the neck, gave the victim heart failure. Only once was the Invaders' true likeness revealed, and even then it was blurred, leaving the viewer truly mystified about these sinister spacemen.

The series was re-run on BBC 2 in 1984 and 1992.

INVISIBLE MAN, THE

UK (Official Films/ITP/ATV) Science Fiction. ITV 1958–9

Dr Peter Brady ....Anonymous
(voice Tim Turner)
Diane Brady ....Lisa Daniely

Sally Brady ....Deborah Watling
Colonel Ward ....Ernest Clarke

Producer: Ralph Smart

An invisible scientist works for the secret service. Dr Peter Brady had become a victim of his own experiments into light refraction and had lost his visibility. Unable to reverse the process and condemned to a life of transparency, he became an intelligence agent and worked for the UK Government in places where more obvious spies literally could not tread. He also helped out friends, the police and other needy persons who learned of his unusual attribute whilst, at the same time, always seeking an antidote for his affliction. Often bandaged up and wearing sunglasses to give him some recognizable form, he was supported by his sister, Diane, and niece, Sally. Colonel Ward was the man at the Ministry. The series was acclaimed for some of its special effects, which included a self-smoking cigarette and self-drinking glass of wine. The man who played Brady was never credited, although the voice turned out to belong to actor Tim Turner.

INVISIBLE MAN, THE

US (Universal) Science Fiction. BBC 1 1975

Dr Daniel Westin...............................David McCallum
Walter Carlson ....Craig Stevens
Dr Kate Westin ....Melinda Fee

Executive Producer: Harve Bennett. Producer: Leslie Stevens

An invisible scientist undertakes covert missions for a West Coast think-tank.

Dr Daniel Westin had perfected the means of making things invisible, but when he heard that the Government wished to use his achievement for military purposes, he destroyed all his equipment, memorized the formula and made himself invisible in order to escape. However, with the reversing procedure ineffective, he was stranded in invisibility.

In an effort to pursue a normal life, Westin had a wig, a realistic face mask and rubber hands created, which he pulled off in times of trouble. So that he could continue his experiments and find a way back to normality, he and his wife, Kate, went to work for the KLAE Corporation (a Californian research unit), occasionally performing undercover missions for his boss, Walter Carlson.

IRD (INTEGRATED RECEIVER/DECODER)

A term for a satellite TV receiver which has a built-in decoder for unscrambling subscription channels.

IRELAND: A TELEVISION HISTORY

UK/Ireland (BBC/RTE) Historical Documentary. BBC 2 1980–1

Presenter/Writer: Robert Kee

Producers: Jeremy Isaacs, Jenny Barraclough

A 13-part account of the development of Ireland. Bravely attempting to portray the history of this country on television for the first time, Robert Kee's Irish documentary began 800 years earlier, at the point where the English first became involved with their island neighbour. It progressed through to the recent troubles and the days of violence, using eye-witness accounts and old film footage to analyse the underlying causes of the unrest. For his efforts, the series won the BAFTA Best Documentary Series award. Kee also supplied an accompanying book.

IRISH RM, THE

UK (Little Bird/Rediffusion/Ulster/RTE/James Mitchell) Drama. Channel 4 1983–5

Sinclair Yeates..Peter Bowles
Philippa Yeates ....Doran Godwin
Flurry Knox ....Bryan Murray
Sally...Lise-Ann McLaughlin
Mrs Knox ....Beryl Reid

An army major resigns his commission to become a Resident Magistrate in colonial Ireland at the turn of the century.

Prim and proper Major Sinclair Yeates had retired to the rural west coast of Ireland in the hope of enjoying peace in his new role of local magistrate, helping to administer British rule. But his hopes of pastoral calm were rudely shattered by parochial disputes, arguments over livestock and sheer, unfathomable blarney, leaving the rather gullible Yeates deep in hot water, especially if his mischievous landlord, Flurry Knox, was involved. The series was based on the 1899 book *Some Experiences of an Irish RM*, by Martin Ross (Edith Somerville) and Violet Florence Martin.

IRON HORSE

US (Screen Gems) Western. BBC 1 1967–8

Ben Calhoun.......................................Dale Robertson
Dave Tarrant...Gary Collins
Barnabas Rogers.....................................Bob Random
Nils Torvald ....Roger Torrey
Julie Parsons...Ellen McRae

Producers: Fred Freiberger, Matthew Rapf

A playboy-gambler becomes a railroad pioneer in the 1880s.

Ben Calhoun had won the Buffalo Pass, Scalplock and Defiance railroad line in a poker game. However, the line was in difficulty, only half-constructed and on the verge of bankruptcy. Undaunted, Ben, together with his pet raccoon, Ulysses, construction engineer Dave, brawny crewman Nils and Barnabas, an orphan clerk, set about reviving the company's fortunes and getting the trains to run on time through the untamed West. Julie Parsons arrived later as proprietor of the Scalplock General Store. (Actress Ellen McRae found greater success after changing her name to Burstyn; she picked up an Oscar for *Alice Doesn't Live Here Anymore* in 1974.)

IRONS, JEREMY (1948–)

British actor, now a Hollywood name but successful on TV first in such series as *Notorious Woman* (as Franz Liszt), *The Pallisers* (as Frank Tregear), *Love for Lydia*, Pinter's adaptation of *Langrishe, Go Down* and *Brideshead Revisited*. In the last, his portrayal of Charles Ryder was widely acclaimed.

IRONSIDE see *A Man Called Ironside*.

ISAACS, JEREMY (1932–)

British producer and TV executive, since 1988 General Director of the Royal Opera House in Covent Garden. Among the highlights of his television days were the acclaimed *The World at War* and Robert Kee's *Ireland: A Television History* (both as producer). He became Programme Controller at Thames and was the first Chief Executive of Channel 4. Isaacs was also seen in front of the cameras in 1989, as the inquisitor in *The Late Show's* revival of *Face To Face*.

IT AIN'T HALF HOT MUM

UK (BBC) Situation Comedy. BBC 1 1974–81

RSM B.L. Williams...............................Windsor Davies
Bombardier 'Gloria' Beaumont ....Melvyn Hayes
Bombardier Solomons ....George Layton
Rangi Ram...Michael Bates
Gunner 'Lofty' Sugden ....Don Estelle
Colonel Reynolds..............................Donald Hewlett
Captain Ashwood ....Michael Knowles
Gunner 'Padoruski' Graham ....John Clegg
Gunner Mackintosh ....Stuart McGugan
Gunner 'Nobby' Clark ....Kenneth MacDonald
Gunner Parkin ....Christopher Mitchell
Gunner 'Nosher' Evans ....Mike Kinsey
Char Wallah Muhammed ....Dino Shafeek
Punkar Wallah..Babar Bhatti

Creators/Writers: Jimmy Perry, David Croft.
Producer: David Croft

Life with an army concert party in the Indian subcontinent.

Set during World War II, *It Ain't Half Hot Mum* focused on the exploits of the Royal Artillery Concert Party as they entertained the active men, and took its name from the content of letters written home by one of its recruits, Gunner Parkin. Joining Parkin in the troupe were Bombardier Solomons (written out after the early episodes), drag artist Bombardier Beaumont (known to all as Gloria), intellectual pianist Gunner Graham, diminutive chief vocalist Gunner 'Lofty' Sugden, Scotsman Gunner Mackintosh, and Gunners Clark and Evans. Their out-of-touch COs were the snooty Colonel Reynolds and his idiotic sidekick Captain Ashwood; but bain of their lives was the Welsh Sgt Major Williams. 'Old Shut Up', as they knew him, considered the concert party to be a bunch of pooftahs (especially Gloria and 'Mr Lah-de-Da Gunner Graham'). He did, however, have more respect for young Parkin, who, in the Sgt Major's eyes, had a fine pair of shoulders and always set a good example to the rest of the unit (Williams thought he was the boy's father). The local wallahs, genuinely considering themselves to be true Brits, provided the racial humour. The late Michael Bates was blacked up as the comical Rangi Ram and, on Bates's death, Dino Shafeek's loyal char wallah gained more prominence, warbling 'Land of Hope and Glory' after each programme's closing credits. The show opened to the troupe's rousing theme song, inviting viewers to 'Meet the gang 'cos the boys are here, the boys to entertain you'.

Windsor Davies and Don Estelle capitalized on their roles for a spin-off single, *Whispering Grass*, which surprisingly topped the UK charts in 1975.

ITC (INDEPENDENT TELEVISION CORPORATION)

ITC was the company founded in 1954 by theatrical businessmen Lew and Leslie Grade, Prince Littler and Val Parnell to bid for one of the first ITV franchises. Initially unsuccessful, ITC turned instead to independent production and distribution, with The Adventures of Robin Hood the first commissioned programme. However, the group were soon asked to join another consortium, which had won a franchise but was having difficulty getting on air. The resulting company became ATV. To avoid conflicts of interest between the broadcasting company and the production company, ATV took over full control of ITC in 1957, making it a wholly-owned subsidiary. ITC went on to specialize in action series like *Danger Man*, *The Saint*, *The Champions*, *Randall and Hopkirk (Deceased)* and *The Prisoner*, as well as most of the Gerry

Anderson puppet series and, in the 1970s, *The Muppet Show*. ITC was sold to Australian businessman Robert Holmes á Court in 1982, who in turn sold it to another Australian, Alan Bond. A management buy-out later conferred control into yet newer hands, and then, in 1995, it was taken over by Polygram.

ITC (INDEPENDENT TELEVISION COMMISSION)

The ITC is the public organization that is responsible for licensing and regulating commercially funded television services in the UK. It replaced both the IBA (Independent Broadcasting Authority) and the Cable Authority on 1 January 1991. It not only grants broadcasting licences to Channel 3 (ITV) companies, Channel 4, cable channels and satellite services but also monitors their progress, ensuring they adhere to the strict standards and guidelines it lays down for programming and advertising. Those failing to do so are liable to penalties. The Chairman, Deputy Chairman and the eight Members of the Commission are all appointed by the Secretary of State for National Heritage and the ITC is funded by licence fees payable by contracting broadcasters.

The ITC's predecessor, the IBA, was responsible for both independent television and independent radio. It had a greater 'hands-on' approach to programme monitoring, with the various contractors needing to agree schedules with the IBA (in accordance with the Broadcasting Act). As a result, the IBA was the legally accountable broadcaster. Under the new system it is the programme company which is legally accountable. The IBA, inaugurated in 1971, was a descendant of the ITA (Independent Television Authority), which was established by Parliament under the Television Act of 1954 and concerned itself solely with the appointment and output of ITV companies in the days before the advent of independent radio.

ITA see ITC.

ITN see Independent Television News.

IT TAKES A THIEF

US (Universal) Spy Drama. ITV

Alexander Mundy	Robert Wagner
Noah Bain	Malachi Throne
Wallie Powers	Edward Binns
Alister Mundy	Fred Astaire

Creator: Collier Young. Producer: Jack Arnold

An expert thief is freed from jail to work for the Government.

Sophisticated, handsome Al Mundy was the perfect cat burglar, yet, somehow, he had been caught and confined in San Jobel prison. Realizing his potential, the US Government offered him a degree of liberty, inviting him to steal for the SIA intelligence agency. Between missions, Mundy was forced to return to custody, but when he was out he certainly made the most of it, travelling all around the world and making contact with hordes of glamorous women, most of whom fell for his style and charm. His father, Alister, another master thief, was introduced later. He had taught his son the tricks of the trade and now found himself joining Alexander on certain missions. Mundy's SIA chief in the early days was Noah Bain. In later episodes (when Mundy was no longer locked up between assignments), Wallie Powers was his agency contact. Running from 1968 to 1970 in its native USA, the programme received only sporadic screenings around the ITV network in the UK.

IT'LL BE ALRIGHT ON THE NIGHT

UK (LWT) Comedy. ITV 1977–

Presenter/Writer: Denis Norden.

Producers: Paul Smith, Paul Lewis

Sporadic collections of out-takes and bloopers from the worlds of film and TV.

When Denis Norden, in an avalanche of puns and corny wisecracks, launched It'll Be Alright on the Night in 1977, he tapped into a new vein of television comedy. Previously, fluffs and foul-ups by professional actors and TV presenters had been discreetly kept away from the viewing public (although, for years, they had been mischievously edited together by TV technicians for private viewing). Now everything came out in the open and the public loved seeing their word-perfect announcers and performers brought crashing down to earth by a Freudian slip of the tongue or the lapse of an imperfect memory. Clips of actors 'corpsing' (creasing up into uncontrollable laughter) were particularly popular. Because such infelicities are everyday occurrences in TV and film production, Norden has been able to gather up the best scraps from the cutting-room floor at least once every couple of years since. The BBC has recently withheld its own out-takes for use in its similar offering, Auntie's Bloomers, hosted by Terry Wogan.

IT'S A KNOCKOUT/JEUX SANS FRONTIERES

UK (BBC) Game Show. BBC 1 1966–82

Presenters:
David Vine
Eddie Waring
Stuart Hall

Producers: Barney Colehan, Cecil Korer, Geoff Wilson

Inter-town silly games contests.

Greasy poles, daft costumes, giant beach balls and impossible obstacle courses were the order of the day in It's a Knockout. Very loosely based on a 1950s series called Top Town, in which amateur entertainers competed for their home town, this series pitched willing and athletic citizens into combat for the right to represent the United Kingdom in the European finals. These finals went out under the title of Jeux Sans Frontières.

Each It's a Knockout contest consisted of a variety of races and battles, in which teams struggled to jump through hoops, climb sticky slopes or splash through water while dressed as outsize cartoon figures. There was usually a theme (often medieval) to link events and a 'joker' could be played to double the points won on any one game. Interspersed throughout was the Mini-Marathon (the Fil Rouge in the Euro-edition), a drawn-out, multi-element game presided over by rugby league's Eddie Waring. Hosting proceedings initially was David Vine, but he gave way to laugh-a-minute Stuart Hall in 1972. Veteran announcer McDonald Hobley and Katie Boyle were also involved in the very early days and Arthur Ellis acted as tournament referee for the duration.

Jeux Sans Frontières began in 1967 and was hosted by a different country each week, but always in the presence of international arbiters Gennaro Olivieri and Guido Pancaldi. After a series of international heats, a grand final was held, featuring the top-scoring team from each country. The UK's first representatives were Bridlington, who took on the rest of the Continent in France.

There were numerous It's a Knockout celebrity specials, the most notable being The Grand Knockout Tournament in 1987, when the four teams competing for charity were captained by HRH The Prince Edward, HRH The Princess Anne, HRH The Duke of York and HRH The Duchess of York. It's a Knockout also transferred to the USA in 1975, where it was renamed Almost Anything Goes. This survived only one year before being superseded by a celebrity series entitled All-Star Anything Goes.

IT'S A SQUARE WORLD

UK (BBC) Comedy. BBC 1960–4

Michael Bentine
Clive Dunn
Frank Thornton
Benny Lee
Len Lowe
Dick Emery

Leon Thau
Ronnie Barker
Louis Mansi
Anthea Wyndham
Janette Rowselle
John Bluthal
Freddie Earlie
Joe Gibbons

Creator: Michael Bentine. Writers: Michael Bentine, John Law. Producers: G.B. Lupino, John Street, Joe McGrath

Madcap, surreal early sketch show.

Collating fictitious reports from the four corners of the world and adding much more besides, *It's a Square World* was a direct ancestor of *Monty Python* and other bizarre comedies. Former Goon Michael Bentine was the brains behind the project and he and an extensive supporting cast starred in a series of zany, visual sketches which pushed back the boundaries of TV comedy. Bentine had a penchant for scale models, using them to weird effect. Boats were a favourite: he caused the Woolwich Ferry to sink in one stunt, and in another famous episode sent a Chinese junk to attack the House of Commons. Bentine also planted a 40-ft whale outside the Natural History Museum, much to the dismay of local drivers, and, on another occasion, sent the BBC Television Centre into space.

A follow-up series, *All Square*, appeared courtesy of ATV in 1966 (for this Bentine located himself in Filthnik, the capital of the fictitious country of Ozonia), and there was a one-off *It's a Square World* revival back on BBC 1 in 1977.

IT'S DARK OUTSIDE

UK (Granada) Police Drama. ITV 1964–5

Detective Inspector Charles Rose ......William Mervyn
Detective Sgt Swift.................................Keith Barron
Anthony Brand ....John Carson
Alice Brand..June Tobin
Detective Sgt Hunter.........................Anthony Ainley
Claire ....Veronica Strong
Fred Blaine..John Stratton
Sebastian..Oliver Reed

Producer: Derek Bennett

The return of the sharp-tongued detective Mr Rose.

It's Dark Outside formed the middle segment of a trilogy of series featuring the acerbic Inspector Rose. He had first appeared in **The Odd Man** six months earlier, as did the character of Detective Sgt Swift, a soft-hearted, pensive copper. Now they were joined by Anthony and Alice Brand, a barrister and his journalist wife, though not for long. By the second season the Brands and Swift were gone, leaving the calm, cold Rose in prime

position, supported by newcomers Detective Sgt Hunter (Anthony Ainley, a future **Doctor Who** Master), his girlfriend, Claire, and her boozy reporter friend, Fred Blaine. A young actor named Oliver Reed appeared in some episodes as Sebastian, the ring-leader of a bunch of tearaways. The programme gained a cult following for its grim, tense, almost film noir atmosphere and also generated a chart-topping single, Jackie Trent's 'Where Are You Now (My Love)'. For more adventures with the refined investigator, see **Mr Rose**.

IT'S GARY SHANDLING'S SHOW

US (Showtime) Situation Comedy. BBC 2 1987–

Gary Shandling ....Gary Shandling
Mrs Ruth Shandling ....Barbara Cason
Nancy Bancroft ....Molly Cheek
Pete Schumaker ....Michael Tucci
Jackie Schumaker ....Bernadette Birkett
Grant Schumaker......................................Scott Nemes
Leonard Smith ....Paul Willson
Phoebe Bass ....Jessica Harper

Creators: Gary Shandling, Alan Zweibel. Executive Producers: Bernie Brillstein, Brad Grey, Gary Shandling

Unusual comedy series in which the star played himself and talked directly to the studio audience. This show was based around the fictitious life of neurotic comic Gary Shandling, with the set modelled around his real-life sitting room. There was a plot (of sorts) in each episode, usually centring on Gary's lack of success with women or other paranoia. He confided in viewers and positively encouraged the studio audience to welcome the guest stars he introduced. Other members of the cast also engaged the audience and the whole show was put together so that it parodied the techniques and conventions of television.

Regular droppers-by to his Sherman Oaks condominium were his mother, his friend Nancy Bancroft and neighbours the Schumakers, whose intelligent young son, Grant, helped Gary with his problems. Nosy Leonard Smith, manager of the building, also appeared. Just before the series ended, Gary married his girlfriend, Phoebe Bass. This break-all-the-rules type of television was not new. The inspiration was very clearly **The Burns and Allen Show** in the 1950s, in which George Burns drew himself aside from the plots to discuss the show with viewers. This technique has become known as 'breaking the fourth wall'.

ITV see Channel 3.

IVANHOE

UK (Sydney Box) Adventure. ITV 1958

Ivanhoe...Roger Moore

Gurth .... Robert Brown
Bart .... John Pike
Prince John .... Andrew Keir
King Richard .... Bruce Seton

Executive Producer: Peter Rogers. Producer: Herbert Smith, Bernard Coote

The chivalrous hero of Sir Walter Scott's novel takes on a 'Robin Hood' mantle.

Ivanhoe returned home after the Crusades to find that good King Richard had been usurped by his wicked brother, Prince John, who was now tyrannizing the people. Having freed Gurth and Bart, two doomed serfs who became his squires, he set about righting wrongs and helping those in distress. This swashbuckling series was Roger Moore's first starring role and he bravely performed his own stunts. Its executive producer, Peter Rogers, went on to develop the *Carry On* series of films.

IVOR THE ENGINE

UK (Smallfilms) Cartoon. ITV 1959–63

Narrators: Oliver Postgate, David Edwards, Anthony Jackson, Olwen Griffiths

Writer: Oliver Postgate. Producer: Oliver Postgate

The homely adventures of a little Welsh steam train.

'In the top left-hand corner of Wales there was a railway called the Merioneth and Llantisily Rail Traction Company Ltd.', so viewers of this animation were told before being introduced to the railway's star employee, Ivor the Engine. Bearing the M&L RTCo. Ltd. livery, the little green puffer was driven by Jones the Steam, who worked in conjunction with colleagues like Owen the Signal and Dai Station, the man who looked after Llaniog Station. Ivor's boiler was fired by Idris, a small dragon with a high-pitched voice, who took up residence when his volcano home was rendered inhabitable. In a series of quaint little adventures, Ivor and Jones chugged around the mountainous landscape of Wales helping out citizens in trouble and longing to sing in the choir, like Ivor's friend Evans the Song.

Ivor the Engine was produced by the Smallfilms partnership of Oliver Postgate and Peter Firmin, with Firmin drawing all the pictures. It was first screened at lunchtime on ITV via Associated-Rediffusion, before transferring to the BBC in 1976. One well-aired story recalls that the directors of A-R deliberately interrupted their board meetings just to watch the five-minute episodes.

JACKANORY

UK (BBC) Children's Entertainment.
BBC 1 1965–

Executive Producers: Anna Home, Angela Beeching. Producers: Joy Whitby, David Coulter, Anna Home, Daphne Jones, David Turnball, Angela Beeching, Christine Secombe, Margie Barbour, Roger Singleton-Turner, Nel Romano

Celebrity storytime for younger viewers.

Jackanory took its name from the nursery rhyme which begins 'I'll tell you a story of Jackanory . . .', and that effectively sums up what the programme has been about, simple story telling. The success and longevity of the programme has stemmed from this most basic of formats, with just a few illustrations and the narrative skills of the guest reader as embellishments.

Characterized in its golden age by twirling kaleidoscope images in its opening and closing credits, *Jackanory* has usually presented just one book a week, its contents abridged to fit over five 15-minute editions with the same reader employed for the duration. The first story to be featured was *Cap of Rushes*, told by Lee Montague. Over the years, more than 700 books have been read, by over 400 storytellers. Bernard Cribbins holds the record for most appearances, followed by the late Kenneth Williams. Many children's favourites have been aired, some more than once, and, in 1979, Tolkien's *The Hobbit* was read to celebrate the programme's 3000th edition. In 1984, HRH The Prince of Wales narrated his own story, *The Old Man of Lochnagar*.

A sister programme of playlets, *Jackanory Playhouse*, was developed in 1972.

JACKSON, GLENDA, MP, CBE (1936–)

Distinguished British film actress and latterly Labour MP for Hampstead and Highgate, whose television highlight was her Emmy-award-winning title role in **Elizabeth R**, though a later appearance as Cleopatra with Morecambe and Wise in a play 'wot Ernie wrote' is ironically just as well remembered by viewers. One of Jackson's last TV performances before taking her seat in the House came in the 1991 John Le Carré drama *A Murder of Quality*.

JACKSON, GORDON, OBE (1923–90)

With his soft Scottish burr and impeccable comportment, Gordon Jackson became one of TV viewers' favourite personalities in the early 1970s in his guise of the reliable butler Hudson in **Upstairs, Downstairs**. His next starring role, however, was in quite a different vein, as George Cowley, the demanding boss of Bodie and Doyle in **The Professionals**. All this came after a lengthy career as a character actor in the British film and theatre industries and television appearances in plays and series like **Dr Finlay's Casebook** and **Mystery and Imagination**. Jackson was one of the hosts of **Stars on Sunday** and also popped up in programmes and TV movies such as *Spectre*, *The Last Giraffe*, **The New Avengers**, *Noble House* (as Supt Armstrong), *My Brother Tom* and *A Town Like Alice* (as Noel Strachan).

JACKSON, KATE (1948–)

American actress, one of the original three **Charlie's Angels**, a role she was awarded after appearing in the supernatural daytime soap *Dark Shadows*, and another US action series, *The Rookies*. Jackson stayed with *Charlie's Angels*, playing the part of team leader Sabrina Duncan, for three years, eventually leaving to concentrate on film work and TV movies. She returned to US prime time TV in 1983, playing secret agent Amanda King in **Scarecrow and Mrs King**, a role which lasted four years. In 1988 she played the lead in the TV series version of the film *Baby Boom*.

JACOBI, SIR DEREK, CBE (1938–)

Distinguished British thespian who won the plaudits of TV viewers with his portrayal of the stammering, bumbling Claudius in **I, Claudius**. Previously, Jacobi had appeared in **The Strauss Family** (as Josef Lanner) and **The Pallisers** (as Lord Fawn), and post-Claudius he starred as spy Kim Burgess in **Philby, Burgess and Maclean**, appeared in *Mr Pye* and, more recently, played the monastic sleuth *Cadfael*. He also contributed to **The BBC Television Shakespeare** (Richard II). In TV movies, Jacobi was seen as Frollo in *The Hunchback of Notre Dame* and Hitler in *Inside the Third Reich*.

JACOBS, DAVID (1926–)

Silken-voiced radio and television personality, one of the original presenters of Top of the Pops when it started in 1964, although Jacobs had already been host of the successful **Juke Box Jury** since 1959. Jacobs also chaired *Tell the Truth* in 1957 and hosted a brief revival of **What's My Line?** in 1973. He has also compèred **Come Dancing** and is the younger brother of drama director John Jacobs.

JACOBS, DAVID

American writer/producer, creator of **Dallas** and its spin-off **Knots Landing**, amongst other prime time TV credits.

JACQUES, HATTIE (JOSEPHINA EDWINA JACQUES; 1924–80)

British character actress and comedienne, mostly seen in matronly roles in the cinema (particularly in *Carry On* films) and as a foil for Eric Sykes on TV. She played Eric's sister in the **Sykes** sitcom for over 20 years from 1960, having previously worked with him on the radio series *Educating Archie*. However, Hattie did once have a series of her own, **Miss Adventure** in 1964, in which she played investigator Stacey Smith, who haplessly stumbled into global escapades. She also starred as Georgina Ruddy in the communal comedy **Our House** in 1960, played Miss Manger in the short-lived sitcom *Charley's Grants* in 1970 and appeared in **Hancock's Half Hour** and as a guest on **That Was The Week That Was** as well as many other shows. She was once married to John Le Mesurier.

JAFFE, SAM (1893–1984)

American actor seen in many series, from **Alfred Hitchcock Presents** to **Alias Smith and Jones** and **Buck Rogers in the 25th Century**, as well as numerous TV movies and mini-series, though he is chiefly remembered as the distinguished Dr Zorba in **Ben Casey**.

JAMES, CLIVE (1939–)

Perceptive, wry Australian journalist, commentator, TV personality, and the TV critic of *The Guardian* in the 1970s. His series *Saturday Night People*, *Clive James on Television*, *The Late Clive James*, *Postcard From . . .* , *Saturday Night Clive* and *The Talk Show with Clive James*, as well as regular New Year's Eve parties, have amply demonstrated his self-effacing wit, droll humour and keenness to poke gentle fun (particularly at foreign television programmes). In addition, James has contributed numerous single features (such as *Clive James and the Calendar Girls*, *Clive James Meets Roman Polanski* and *Clive James Finally Meets Frank Sinatra*) and also presented the film magazine **Cinema** for a while.

JAMES, P.D.

UK (Anglia) Police Drama. ITV 1983–93

Chief Supt/Commander Adam Dalgliesh
....Roy Marsden
John Massingham ....John Vine

Producer: John Rosenberg

The assignments of pensive Scotland Yard detective Adam Dalgliesh.

Unlike Jim Taggart or Inspector Morse, Adam Dalgliesh has never had his name in lights. All his adventures, adaptations of P.D. James's novels, have aired under their individual book titles, but everyone knows he's the star. In fact, he has only had one regular companion, the ambitious copper John Massingham, and that was just for the first three investigations.

A Scotland Yard chief superintendent, Dalgliesh found himself promoted to commander in the story entitled *The Black Tower* and held the rank thereafter. He lived partly in London and partly in Norfolk, where the country lanes were leafy and the seaside towns quiet, but, nevertheless, where murders came thick and fast.

His first TV case, *Death of an Expert Witness*, aired in seven parts in 1983 (predating his fellow cerebral cops Morse, Taggart and Wexford). Then followed *Shroud for a Nightingale*, *Cover Her Face*, *The Black Tower*, *A Taste for Death*, *Devices and Desires* and *Unnatural Causes* in the next ten years, each in serial form (except for the last, a two-hour special) and filled with guest stars like Joss Ackland, Phyllis Calvert, Pauline Collins, Maurice Denham and Susannah York. They also all featured more than one murder for the tall, confident, morally-sound detective to tackle, and, true to the books, the plots were complicated and involved. Furthermore, in the best tradition of TV cops, Dalgliesh was not denied his quirks. Behind his rather formal, stuffy image, he was a competent poet, the son of an Anglican vicar. He was also a widower and lived alone in a converted windmill.

JAMES, SID (1913–76)

South African comic actor, a former professional boxer and a stalwart of the *Carry On* films. On television (and radio) in the 1950s, James was the perfect foil for Tony Hancock in *Hancock's Half Hour*, which led to his own sitcom, *East End – West End*, in 1958. From this base, he went on to star in a succession of comedies. These included *Citizen James* (as champion of the underdog Sid James), *Taxi* (as cabbie Sid Stone), *George and the Dragon* (as chauffeur George Russell), *Two In Clover* (as rat race escapee Sid Turner) and *Bless this House* (as frustrated family man Sid Abbott), all of which gave him ample opportunity to exercise his trademark dirty chuckle. James's earliest contributions came in single dramas in the 1940s.

JAMESON, LOUISE (1951–)

London-born actress with a number of prominent roles to her name. These have included the warrior-turned-companion Leela in *Doctor Who*, Dr Anne Reynolds in *The Omega Factor*, slutty Blanche Simmons in *Tenko* and Susan Young, Jim's girlfriend, in *Bergerac*. Jameson has

also appeared in *Z Cars*, *Emmerdale Farm*, *Casualty*, *The Secret Diary of Adrian Mole Aged 13¾*, *The Gentle Touch*, *Cider With Rosie*, *The Boy Dominic*, *The Bill* and *Rides*, amongst other series.

JANE

UK (BBC) Comedy. BBC 2 1982

Jane...Glynis Barber

Producer: Ian Keill

Ten-minute short based on the wartime cartoon heroine.

Featuring a pre-*Dempsey and Makepeace* Glynis Barber, this inventive filler placed live actors and actresses against cartoon backgrounds to re-create the adventures of the *Daily Mirror*'s forces favourite. Jane, originally drawn by Norman Pett, had a disconcerting habit of losing her outer clothing, which left her struggling through various escapades in nothing but her underwear. The episodes were screened on five consecutive nights and an omnibus edition was shown the following weekend. Two years later, Jane returned in another five episodes entitled *Jane in the Desert*.

JANSSEN, DAVID (DAVID MEYER; 1930–80)

For four years in the 1960s, TV audiences worldwide sweated with David Janssen in his guise of Dr Richard Kimble, aka *The Fugitive*, as his nemesis, Lt Philip Gerard, closed in time and again. It was a role which made Janssen one of TV's biggest stars and followed another lead role as Richard Diamond, Private Detective, between 1957 and 1960. All the same, Janssen had to wait nearly ten years after *The Fugitive* ended for a series to approach the success of his 1960s hit. That was *Harry O*, in which he played wounded private eye Harry Orwell, one of the 1970s quirky investigators. In between had come a largely unnoticed drama, *O'Hara, US Treasury*. Janssen's last dramatic contribution to television was the expensive mini-series *Centennial*, in which he played Paul Garrett. He died of a heart attack just before his 50th birthday.

JARVIS, MARTIN (1941–)

British character actor much seen on TV in series like *Nicholas Nickleby* (title role), *Doctor Who*, *Crime of Passion*, *The Rivals of Sherlock Holmes*, *The Pallisers*, *Within These Walls*, *Juliet Bravo*, *Enemy at the Door*, *Rumpole of the Bailey*, *Murder Most Horrid* and *Inspector Morse*. His major roles have been in *The Forsyte Saga* (as Jon Forsyte) and the sitcom *Rings on their Fingers* (as Oliver Pryde).

He also played Godfrey Ablewhite in the BBC's 1972 adaptation of *The Moonstone* and Uriah Heep in its 1975 version of *David Copperfield*. He is married to actress Rosalind Ayres.

JASON, DAVID (DAVID WHITE; 1940–)

One of British television's biggest stars of the 1980s and 1990s, versatile David Jason came late into the acting world, having first trained as an electrician. He was discovered in a play on Bournemouth pier by producer Humphrey Barclay and his TV break arrived in 1968, in the company of Michael Palin, Terry Jones, Eric Idle and Denise Coffey in the bizarre children's comedy *Do Not Adjust Your Set*. From there he moved into sitcom, with the kids' series *Two Ds and a Dog* (as chauffeur Dingle Bell, again with Denise Coffey) and then with Ronnie Barker in *Hark at Barker*, *His Lordship Entertains* (both as Dithers the gardener) and *Six Dates with Barker*. He appeared in the Doctor series and in his own vehicles, *The Top Secret Life of Edgar Briggs*, playing an inept spy, and *Lucky Feller*, as shy plumber Shorty Mepstead. As the wily old lag Blanco in *Porridge* and the hapless and frustrated shop boy Granville in *Open All Hours*, Jason almost became Ronnie Barker's protégé, but was then given another series of his own, playing Peter Barnes for three years in *A Sharp Intake of Breath*. In 1981 Jason was offered a role which took him to the top of his trade, that of wide boy Del Boy Trotter in *Only Fools and Horses*. After this, Jason never looked back and branched out into straight(er) drama as the porter Skullion in *Porterhouse Blue*, Ted Simcocks in *A Bit of a Do*, chirpy Pop Larkin in *The Darling Buds of May* and the morose copper Jack Frost in *A Touch of Frost*. He also voiced the part of Toad in the 1980s animation of *The Wind in the Willows*, plus the *Dangermouse* and *Count Duckula* cartoon characters.

JASON KING

UK (Scoton/ITC) Detective Drama. ITV 1971–2

Jason King ....Peter Wyngarde
Nicola Harvester ....Ann Sharp
Sir Brian ....Dennis Price
Ryland ....Ronald Lacey

Creators: Dennis Spooner, Monty Berman.
Producer: Monty Berman

Light-hearted *Department S* spin-off featuring novelist Jason King.

Jason King had been the prominent member of the *Department S* team. This was not surprising, given the extravagant lifestyle he enjoyed and the outrageous 1970s fashions he favoured. Now out on his own, he continued writing his 'Mark

Caine' mysteries and indulging in investigations of his own, usually surrounded by beautiful girls. Nicola Harvester was his publisher, and Sir Brian, together with his assistant, Ryland, were civil servants who blackmailed King (over tax evasion) into working for the Government from time to time. His assignments were considerably more down to earth than the baffling *Department S* cases, despite being set in exotic locations.

JAY, SIR ANTONY (1930–)

Former *Tonight* journalist who helped launch *That Was The Week That Was* in 1962. He also served on the Annan Committee which looked into the future of British broadcasting in the 1970s. However, Jay's greatest success came in collaboration with Jonathan Lynn when he created and wrote *Yes, Minister* (and later *Yes, Prime Minister*). The show became a firm favourite with politicians and Jay picked up a knighthood in 1987.

JAY, PETER (1937–)

British journalist, currently the BBC's Economic Editor, regularly seen on news bulletins. From 1972 Jay was the first presenter of *Weekend World*, ITV's Sunday political programme (with John Torode), until leaving in 1977 to take up an appointment as British Ambassador to the USA, bestowed on him by his father-in-law, premier James Callaghan. He returned to television in 1983 as head of TV-am, bringing with him a 'mission to explain', as the new station set out to provide news and information to early morning viewers. However, with audiences and advertising woefully low, Jay was forced to leave after six weeks and with his departure the tone of the programming became less serious.

JAYSTON, MICHAEL (MICHAEL JAMES; 1935–)

British stage and screen actor whose television work has majored on adaptations of classics (such as Edward Rochester in the BBC's 1980 version of *Jane Eyre*), but extends back to dramas like *The Power Game* and *Callan*. He took the part of Charles Rolls in *The Edwardians* episode *Mr Rolls and Mr Royce* (Robert Powell was Royce) and then, in 1975, he starred as *Quiller* in a TV version of the 1966 George Segal spy film *The Quiller Memorandum*. Amongst his later credits have been parts in *Tinker, Tailor, Soldier, Spy* (as Peter Guillam), *A Bit of a Do* (as Neville Badger), *Haggard* (as Sir Joshua), *Doctor Who*, *The Darling Buds of May* and *The Good Guys*.

JEEVES AND WOOSTER

UK (Granada/Picture Partnership) Comedy Drama. ITV 1990–3

Jeeves ....Stephen Fry

Bertie Wooster..Hugh Laurie
Aunt Agatha ....Mary Wimbush
                                    Elizabeth Spriggs
Aunt Dahlia ....Brenda Bruce

Writer: Clive Exton. Executive Producer: Sally Head. Producer: Brian Eastman

An aristocratic air head is bailed out by his savvy butler.

This adaptation of P.G. Wodehouse's tales of upper-class twit Bertie Wooster and his redeeming valet, Jeeves, was tailor-made for the comedy double act of Stephen Fry and Hugh Laurie, who donned period costume for their 1930s roles. As the socializing Wooster stumbled from social disaster to social disaster, sometimes in trepidation of his London aunts Agatha and Dahlia, it was the calm, resourceful Jeeves who rode to the rescue. Later episodes were set in New York.

An earlier (1965–7) BBC version, entitled *The World of Wooster*, starred Ian Carmichael as Wooster and Dennis Price as Jeeves.

JEMIMA SHORE INVESTIGATES

UK (Thames) Detective Drama. ITV 1983

Jemima Shore ....Patricia Hodge

Creator: Antonia Fraser. Producer: Tim Aspinall

A TV reporter discovers blackmail and murder amongst the upper classes.

Jemima Shore was a cat-loving, music-appreciating TV reporter, the writer and presenter of Megalith Television's *Jemima Shore Investigates*. In her spare time, her inquiring mind led her into amateur detective work, prowling around her own high-class social circles and sniffing out crime amidst the aristocracy and the nouveaux riches. The stories were based on the novels by Antonia Fraser.

Shore made her TV bow as early as 1978 when, portrayed by Maria Aitken, she appeared in an *Armchair Thriller* presentation entitled *Quiet as a Nun*.

JENNIE, LADY RANDOLPH CHURCHILL

UK (Thames) Historical Drama. ITV 1974

Jennie Jerome/Lady Randolph Churchill ..Lee Remick
Lord Randolph Churchill ....Ronald Pickup
Duchess of Marlborough ....Rachel Kempson
Duke of Marlborough ....Cyril Luckham
Count Kinsky...Jeremy Brett
George Cornwallis-West ....Christopher Cazenove
Mrs Patrick Campbell ....Siân Phillips
Winston Churchill ....Warren Clarke
Mr Leonard Jerome ....Dan O'Herlihy
Mrs Jerome ....Helen Horton
Aunt Leonie ....Barbara Parkins

Writer: Julian Mitchell. Executive Producer: Stella Richman. Producer: Andrew Brown

The life and career of the mother of Sir Winston Churchill.

This seven-part drama was produced as part of the celebrations to mark the centenary of Churchill's birth and focused on the life of his mother, an American born into a wealthy family. It followed her rise into aristocratic circles after meeting her future husband, Lord Randolph Churchill, at a party off Cowes in 1873. It showed the daring, flirtatious lady campaigning politically on her husband's behalf, giving birth to Winston and progressing her own career by launching a literary magazine. Scripts were vetted by Lady Spencer Churchill, Sir Winston's widow, and filming took place at family homes, including Blenheim Palace. Warren Clarke, playing Winston, was required to age from 16 to 47 during the series.

JESUS OF NAZARETH

UK (ITC/RAI) Drama. ITV 1977

Jesus Christ ....(as a boy) Immad Cohen
                            (as an adult) Robert Powell
Virgin Mary ....Olivia Hussey
Joseph ....Yorgo Voyagis
Mary Magdalene .... Anne Bancroft
Simon .... Peter James Farentino
Judas Iscariot...Ian McShane
John the Baptist.......................................Michael York
Nicodemus...Laurence Olivier
Simeon..Ralph Richardson
Herodias.. Valentina Cortese
Balthazar..James Earl Jones
Melchior ....Donald Pleasence
Gaspar ....Fernando Rey
Joseph of Arimathea ....James Mason
Herod the Great ....Peter Ustinov
Salome..Isabel Mestres
Herod Antipas .... Christopher Plummer
Caiaphas ....Anthony Quinn
Pontius Pilate.. Rod Steiger
Barabbas ....Stacy Keach
The Adulteress................................. Claudia Cardinale
Yehuda ....Cyril Cusack
Amos... Ian Bannen
Elizabeth ....Marina Berti
Anna ....Regina Bianchi
Joel ....Oliver Tobias

Writers: Anthony Burgess, Suso Cecchi d'Amico, Franco Zeffirelli. Executive Producer: Bernard J. Kingham. Producer: Vincenzo Labella

The life of Jesus as seen by Franco Zeffirelli and Lord Lew Grade.

This much publicized epic centred on Jesus as a man, not a myth. By playing down the supernatural, Lew Grade's ITC hoped to present the life of Christ to all religions, and not just to Christians. And, although chock-full of star names, the production was not simply a vehicle for celebrities, with the glitzy sensationalism of early Hollywood versions steadfastly avoided.

The story (in two two-hour episodes) followed Christ from his boyhood (with plenty of footage devoted to his time with Joseph in the carpentry shop), through the inspirational, public part of his life (with the gathering of the disciples and the delivering of the sermons and parables) and on to the crucifixion and resurrection. In line with the Gospels, the miracles were featured but special effects were minimal and it was the words, not the spectacular deeds, of Jesus which became the focus of his greatness.

In conjunction with Italy's RAI network, the film was shot on location in Tunisia and Italy at great expense (9 million) over three years, and the attention to detail in costumes and backdrops was much applauded. The idea for the epic allegedly came from Pope Paul, who had mentioned it to Lew Grade at an audience some years earlier.

JETSONS, THE

US (Hanna-Barbera/Screen Gems) Cartoon. ITV 1963–

Voices:

George Jetson	George O'Hanlon
Jane Jetson	Penny Singleton
Judy Jetson	Janet Waldo
Elroy Jetson	Daws Butler
Astro	Don Messick
Cosmo G. Spacely	Mel Blanc
Rosie	Jean Vander Pyl

Executive Producers: William Hanna, Joseph Barbera

The Flintstones inverted: an animation taking 20th-century lifestyles and applying them to the future, instead of the past.

The Jetsons lived in the 21st century, in the push-button world of Orbit City. Head of the household was 35-year-old George Jetson, who worked at Spacely Space Sprockets, owned by Cosmo Spacely, where the three-hour day was still far too long. With his shopping-mad wife, Jane, and two children, George lived in the Skypad Apartments, which could be conveniently raised above the clouds to avoid bad weather. George also owned a nuclear-powered space car, while Jane had the assistance of a sarcastic robot maid named Rosie to help with the housework. The Jetsons' two children were 15-year-old Judy, a teenybopper, and nine-year-old Elroy, an electronics whizzkid who travelled to school (the Little Dipper School) down a pneumatic tube. The family's Scooby-Doo-like dog was called Astro.

Whereas the Flintstones enjoyed 20th-century comforts à la Stone Age, the Jetsons had high-tech benefits which could only have been imagined when the series was created in the 1960s. Some, such as the video phone, are already now in use, but devices like the 'Foodarackacycle', which provided a selection of meals at the touch of a button, are still a little ahead of us.

The Jetsons' voices sounded familiar: Penny Singleton played Blondie in the 1940s films, Daws Butler was the voice behind Yogi Bear and Don Messick went on to further canine success when voicing Scooby-Doo. Jean Vander Pyl was Wilma Flintstone. New episodes were produced in 1985 and a full-length cinema version was released a few years later.

JEUX SANS FRONTIERES see *It's a Knockout.*

JEWEL IN THE CROWN, THE

UK (Granada) Drama. ITV 1984

Ronald Merrick	Tim Pigott-Smith
Hari Kumar	Art Malik
Daphne Manners	Susan Wooldridge
Sarah Layton	Geraldine James
Susan Layton/Bingham	Wendy Morgan
Sgt Guy Perron	Charles Dance
Lady Manners	Rachel Kempson
Mildred Layton	Judy Parfitt
Count Dimitri Bronowski	Eric Porter
Barbie Batchelor	Peggy Ashcroft
Mabel Layton	Fabia Drake
Lady Chatterjee	Zohra Segal
'Sophie' Dixon	Warren Clarke

Writer: Ken Taylor. Producer: Christopher Morahan

Race and class conflict in wartime India.

Based on *The Raj Quartet*, four books by Paul Scott, *The Jewel in the Crown* (the title of the first book) traced growing unrest in the Indian subcontinent during World War II, by following the lives of certain Britons and locals. At the forefront was sadistic policeman Ronald Merrick, a devious, repressed homosexual bigot who framed Hari Kumar, an Indian reporter, for the rape of Daphne Manners, an ungainly orphan girl who had shunned Merrick's advances. Although the rape outrage happened early on in the story, and Hari and Daphne were soon written out, the incident – and its consequences – came to symbolize the cauldron of race hatred and distrust which was boiling up in India at that time. The plot then switched to the Layton family, ageing missionary Barbie Batchelor and other associates, and the series rolled steadily, dramatically and colourfully on from 1942 to 1947 and the eve of Indian independence, introducing all the while new facets of the cultural problem.

Drawing obvious comparisons with the contemporary feature film *A Passage to India* (which also starred Art Malik and Peggy Ashcroft), *The Jewel in the Crown* was made in both India and the UK, at great expense, but not without a catalogue of production problems, from freak weather conditions in India to a fire at the TV studio in Manchester. Its TV inspiration had been a 1982 Granada play, *Staying On*, featuring Trevor Howard and Celia Johnson.

JEWEL, JIMMY (JAMES MARSH 1909–)

Sheffield-born music hall comedian who successfully took his double act with cousin Ben Warriss into radio and then onto the small screen in the early 1950s. Variety series like *Re-turn It Up* and *The Jewel and Warriss Show*, the sitcoms *Double Cross* and *It's a Living* and appearances on *Sunday Night at the London Palladium* made the duo popular and wealthy, keeping them at the forefront of TV comedy until the 1960s, when their act began to seem rather dated. Jewel left showbusiness but was tempted back by Frank Muir with a part in a BBC play in 1967. This encouraged him to look away from gags and sketches and more seriously at acting roles, and he secured the part of pickle factory owner Eli Pledge, alongside Hylda Baker, in the popular sitcom **Nearest and Dearest** in 1968. He followed up with guest spots in series like **The Avengers** and two further sitcoms, *Thicker than Water* (as father of three daughters Jim Eccles) and **Spring and Autumn** (as pensioner Tommy Butler who befriends a fatherless young lad). Amongst his later credits were **Worzel Gummidge, One Foot in the Grave**, *Look at it This Way*, **Casualty** and the 1981 13-part drama Funny Man, which was based around the life of Jimmy's comedian father (also known as Jimmy Jewel) in the 1920s.

JIM'LL FIX IT

UK (BBC) Children's Entertainment. BBC 1
1975–94

Presenter: Jimmy Savile

Producer: Roger Ordish

Long-running children's programme which made viewers' dreams come true.

A favourite with adults as well as youngsters, *Jim'll Fix It* was a popular segment of Saturday evening viewing for 20 years. Its premise was simple: children (and some adults) wrote in with a special wish and the BBC, fronted by Jimmy Savile from a gadget-loaded armchair, fulfilled the most enterprising requests. The dreams-made-reality varied from meeting favourite pop stars to piloting Concorde and interviewing the Prime Minister. The Osmonds and Pan's People were amongst the first guests. Featured viewers were presented with a 'Jim Fixed It For Me' badge to commemorate the occasion.

JIMMY'S

UK (Yorkshire) Documentary. ITV 1987–

Executive Producer: Chris Bryer. Producers: Richard Handford, Irene Cockcroft

The stresses, the strains, the tears and the smiles at a major general hospital.

This fly-on-the-wall documentary series has lasted longer than most critics would have dared to suggest. Centring on events at St James's Hospital in Leeds (the largest general hospital in Europe), it has witnessed highs and lows in the lives of its numerous patients, doctors and nurses. With its delicate observation of the skill and care of staff, and the heartaches and joys of inmates, *Jimmy's*, originally only a daytime programme, so intrigued viewers that it soon earned itself an evening-time slot. Over the years, the production crew have become almost part of the hospital team. No patient has been obliged to appear and, even if giving initial consent, all have had the right to pull out half-way through filming or to ask for edits to be made.

JIM'S INN see admags.

JOE 90

UK (Century 21/ITC) Children's Science Fiction. ITV 1968–9

Voices:
Joe McClaine/Joe 90 ....Len Jones
Professor Ian McClaine.........................Rupert Davies
Commander Shane Weston.....................David Healy
Sam Loover ....Keith Alexander
Mrs Ada Harris....................................Sylvia Anderson

Creators: Gerry Anderson, Sylvia Anderson. Executive Producer: Reg Hill. Producer: David Lane

The top agent of a global protectorate is a nine-year-old boy brainwashed with expert skills.

Brilliant scientist Professor Ian 'Mac' McClaine had developed a machine which allowed the transfer of people's brain patterns. Known as BIGRAT – Brain Impulse Galvanoscope, Record And Transfer – the equipment was tested and then regularly used on Mac's nine-year-old adopted son, Joe, who became the Most Special Agent for World Intelligence Network (WIN), an agency dedicated to keeping peace around the globe. Furnished with the expert knowledge of an airline pilot, an astronaut, an explosives specialist or even a brain surgeon, Joe McClaine became Joe 90, a special operative whose schoolboy looks enabled him to venture where other agents feared to tread. To activate the new brain patterns and pick up the specialist skills or knowledge he needed, Joe simply donned a pair of scientific glasses, making him look more like the class swot than a secret agent. To help him on his assignments, he was equipped with a special 'school bag', containing a transmitter, a gun and, of course, his magic glasses. Contacts at WIN were its deputy head, Commander Weston, and Weston's assistant, Sam Loover. Mrs Harris was the McClaines' housekeeper.

The programme's opening titles showed BIGRAT at work, with Joe's chair lifted into a metal cage which revolved at high speed. Around him, sophisticated computers whizzed and sparkled as they transferred brain patterns into the boy's mind. *Joe 90* was Gerry Anderson's ninth puppet series, but was considerably less successful than the three which immediately preceded it, *Stingray*, *Thunderbirds* and *Captain Scarlet and the Mysterons*. Amongst the actors lending their vocal cords were *Maigret's* Rupert Davies and Keith Alexander, formerly the voice of the Italian mouse puppet Topo Gigio.

JOHN CRAVEN'S NEWSROUND/ NEWSROUND

UK (BBC) Children's News. BBC 1 1972–

Presenters:
John Craven
Paul McDowell
Roger Finn
Helen Rollason
Juliet Morris
Krishnan Guru-Murthy
Julie Etchingham
Chris Rogers

A bulletin of topical news for juniors.

This innovative series has aimed to make important news stories more accessible to younger viewers. Lasting just five or ten minutes and dropped into the children's schedule four nights a week, *John Craven's Newsround* has presented snippets of real news, explaining the background in fine detail for young minds to grasp. There has always been an emphasis on subjects of youth interest, but the programme has never been patronizing. On some occasions, *Newsround* has even beaten adult news programmes to the punch with breaking stories. The first programme on 12 April 1972 carried details of an earthquake in Iran and the build-up to the launch of Apollo 16. A round-up programme, *Newsround Weekly* (presented by Lucy Mathen), was added in 1977 and *Newsround* (without John Craven) is still running

today, offering four editions a week. The longer *Newsround Extra* (an investigative series introduced in 1975) has been aired on Fridays.

JOHNS, STRATFORD (1925–)

South African actor, best remembered in the guise of Charlie Barlow of *Z Cars*, *Softly, Softly* and *Barlow at Large* fame, following early guest appearances in series like *The Avengers*. Later he was cast as Piso, the head of the guards in *I, Claudius*, union boss-turned-peer Lord Mountainash in Union Castle and the evil killer in Channel 4's *Brond*, amongst many other roles. He also played Barlow in *Jack the Ripper*, a 1973 investigation into the mysterious case of the Victorian murderer, which led to the series *Second Verdict* in 1976, with Barlow and his colleague John Watt (Frank Windsor) taking a look at other unsolved crimes.

JOHNSON, DON (1950–)

Despite appearing in films as early as 1970, Don Johnson failed to make TV inroads (apart from failed pilots, some guest appearances and one role in a version of *From Here to Eternity*) until 1984, when he was cast as Detective James 'Sonny' Crockett in the all-action cop series *Miami Vice*. Running for five years, it made Johnson one of the biggest names of the 1980s, his ultra-casual dress, stubbled chin and permanent scowl engendering a generation of look-alikes. He has twice married actress Melanie Griffith.

JOHNSTON, SUE (1943–)

Northern character actress who gained national prominence through her portrayal of *Brookside* matriarch Sheila Grant. Previously, Sue had played Mrs Chadwick in *Coronation Street* amongst other smaller TV roles. Since leaving Brookside Close, she has been cast as Barbara Grade in *Goodbye Cruel World*, was the mother in a celebratory remake of *The Grove Family* in 1991, took the part of Grace Robbins in the limousine drama *Full Stretch* and starred as rich but frustrated housewife Terese Craven in *Luv*. She has also appeared in *Medics*.

JOKING APART

UK (Pola Jones/Peter Jones/BBC) Situation Comedy. BBC2 1993–

Mark Taylor ....Robert Bathurst
Becky Johnson/Taylor ....Fiona Gillies
Tracy Glazebrook ....Tracie Bennett
Robert Glazebrook ....Paul Raffield
Trevor ....Paul-Mark Elliott

Writer: Steven Moffat. Producer: Andre Ptaszynski

A stand-up comic recalls his failed marriage.

'My wife left me', drily declared comedian and TV scriptwriter Mark Taylor. This preluded a series of flashbacks which recalled his fleeting marriage to Becky Johnson. Having met at a funeral (which Mark had gatecrashed by accident), their romance developed apace, but then fell apart just as quickly, as Mark's stand-up humour took over their relationship. When he cracked one joke too many, Becky left him, tired of being his 'lawfully wedded straight man'. Mark's efforts to win her back from boring estate agent Trevor formed the basis of the rest of the first series and all the second (shown in 1995). Also involved in this farcical comedy of errors were Robert and Tracy, their increasingly bizarre and totally dim friends. Chris Rea's 'Fool If You Think It's Over' (sung by Kenny Craddock) provided the theme music. *Joking Apart* was developed from a one-off *Comic Aside* screened in July 1991.

JONES, CAROLYN (1929–83)

American actress in films since the late 1940s, usually taking offbeat roles. The trend continued in television when, after some early appearances in shows like **Dragnet**, Jones was cast as Morticia Addams, the sultry wife in **The Addams Family**, in 1964. A few years later, she was also seen in **Batman**, playing Marsha, the Queen of Diamonds. Later in her career, Jones focused on daytime soaps, TV movies and mini-series, including **Roots**. At one time, she was the wife of TV executive Aaron Spelling.

JONES, CHUCK (CHARLES M. JONES; 1915–)

American animation producer/director, for 24 years with Warner Brothers, where he created the characters of Roadrunner and Pepe Le Pew amongst others, and contributed to Daffy Duck, Sylvester and Tweety Pie, Porky Pig and Bugs Bunny adventures. He also worked on later **Tom and Jerry** cartoons and became head of children's programmes at the USA's ABC network.

JONES, DAVY (DAVID JONES; 1945–)

Diminutive Manchester-born actor, a would-be jockey but tempted onto the stage instead. One of his first TV breaks came with **Coronation Street**, in which he played Ena Sharples's grandson, Colin Lomax, in 1961. Moving to America, he starred on Broadway as The Artful Dodger in *Oliver*, and took a guest part in **Ben Casey**. However, global fame awaited. In 1966, he successfully auditioned for a role in a new zany comedy about a pop group, becoming the lead singer

of **The Monkees** and embarking on a few years of frenzied touring and filming. Since those days, Jones has only sporadically resurfaced, appearing in TV movies and series such as **Love, American Style** and The Brady Bunch, as well as occasionally piecing together *The Monkees* for nostalgia tours.

JONES, ELWYN (1923–82)

British screenwriter and producer, with contributions to *Jacks and Knaves*, **Z Cars**, *Softly, Softly* and *Jack the Ripper* amongst other scripting credits. He also produced Alun Owen's 1963 sitcom *Corrigan Blake* and created the police series **Parkin's Patch**.

JONES, FREDDIE (1927–)

Versatile British actor, whose television work has varied between the classics, general drama, sitcom and kids' programmes. The highlights have included *Treasure Island*, *Cold Comfort Farm*, *Uncle Vanya*, *Vanity Fair* (as Sir Pitt Crawley), **The Caesars** (Claudius), **Mystery and Imagination** (Sweeney Todd), **The District Nurse** (Dr Emlyn Isaacs), **The Avengers**, *Menace*, **The Return of Sherlock Holmes**, **Inspector Morse**, **Pennies from Heaven**, **In Loving Memory**, *Sob Sisters*, *Mr Wroe's Virgins*, and **The Ghosts of Motley Hall** (as Sir George Uproar).

JONES, GEMMA (1942–)

As the gruff cook and proprietress of The Bentinck Hotel, British actress Gemma Jones found instant fame in **The Duchess of Duke Street** in 1976, but has had few TV roles to talk about since, save the odd guest appearance in series like **Inspector Morse**. Previously, she had played Fleda Vetch in the Henry James drama The Spoils of Poynton (1971) and Princess Victoria in **The Fall of Eagles** (1974).

JONES, GRIFF RHYS (1953–)

Welsh comedian and actor, partner of Mel Smith. A Cambridge Footlights performer (alongside the likes of Rory McGrath and Clive Anderson), Jones was working as a radio producer before he joined Smith, Pamela Stephenson and Rowan Atkinson in **Not The Nine O' Clock News** in 1980, replacing Chris Langham who had left the series after one year. In 1984, Griff and Mel branched out into **Alas Smith and Jones**, their own sketch show, which later became simply Smith and Jones. They also presented The World According to Smith and Jones (voicing over old film clips) for ITV and a series of semi-dramas entitled Smith and Jones in Small Doses for BBC 2. Jones also played Bamber Gascoigne in one memorable episode of **The Young Ones**, and, while always a stalwart of **Comic Relief**, he has turned his hand to straight drama, too, playing Cornelius Carrington in **Porterhouse Blue** and Ian Deasey in **Demob**. With Smith, Jones founded Talkback, the production company responsible for some of their series, plus other comedy hits.

JONES, KEN (1930–)

Liverpudlian comic actor, usually cast in annoying working-class roles. He played prison officer Leslie Mills in **Her Majesty's Pleasure**, Deective. Sgt Arnold Nixon in **The Nesbitts are Coming**, 'Orrible Ives in another prison sitcom **Porridge**, the Archangel Derek in **Dead Ernest**, boxing trainer Dave Locket in **Seconds Out**, park-keeper Tom in **Valentine Park**, Whistle Willy in the kids' comedy **Behind the Bike Sheds** and, more memorably, Rex in **The Squirrels**, Bill Clarkson in **The Wackers** and Clifford Basket in **Last of the Baskets**. Jones has also been seen in **The Liver Birds**, **Boon** and **Hunter's Walk**, amongst numerous series.

JONES, PETER (1920–)

British comedy actor, on television since the 1950s. He is probably best remembered as Mr Fenner, the harassed owner of Fenner's Fashions, in **The Rag Trade** (in 1961 and again in 1977), although he has been widely seen. He was Gerald Garvey in **Beggar My Neighbour**, Roland Digby in **Mr Digby, Darling**, Clive Beauchamp in the airline sitcom **From a Bird's Eye View**, Sidney Pratt in the busking comedy **Kindly Leave the Kerb**, Eddie, the petty crook, in **Mr Big** (also as co-writer), Gerald, the frustrated dad, in the short-lived **I Thought You'd Gone** (again with writing credits), mad Prime Minister Kevin Pork in **Whoops! Apocalypse** and the Voice of The Book in **The Hitch-hiker's Guide to the Galaxy**. Jones also starred in **Oneupmanship** and has a wealth of guest appearances in his portfolio, in series as diverse as **C.A.T.S. Eyes**, **The Goodies**, **The Agatha Christie Hour** and **Rumpole of the Bailey**.

JONES, SHIRLEY (1934–)

American film musical star of the 1950s whose television work was sparse until she was cast as the mom in **The Partridge Family** in 1970, alongside her stepson David Cassidy. Plenty of TV movies followed, as well as her own comedy series in the USA, **Shirley**. She was married to actor Jack Cassidy and is the mother of singer Shaun Cassidy.

JONES, STEVE (1945–)

Bespectacled radio and television presenter, concentrating largely on game shows, notably hosting **The Pyramid Game**, **Jeopardy** and **Search for a Star**. He has also been heard as an announcer and commentator on awards events.

JONNY QUEST,

US (Hanna-Barbera) Cartoon. BBC 1 1965

Voices:
Jonny Quest ....Tim Matthieson
Dr Benton Quest ....John Stephenson
                                                         Don Messick
Roger 'Race' Bannon ....Mike Road
Hadji ....Danny Bravo
Bandit...Don Messick

Writer: Doug Wildey. Executive Producers: William Hanna, Joseph Barbera

Four scientific adventurers travel the world explaining away natural phenomena.

Jonny Quest was the bright 11-year-old son of bearded scientist Dr Benton Quest, leader of a small team of intelligence specialists. With Jonny, an Indian chum named Hadji, their pilot-cum-bodyguard Race Bannon, and miniature bulldog Bandit, Dr Quest whizzed around the globe in a supersonic plane, following up reports of strange happenings and unearthing rare treasures in the style of Indiana Jones. Whether it was the mysterious loss of a ship at sea, the sighting of a mythical creature or another bizarre event, Quest and his crew soon got to the bottom of it, more often than not battling against the clock in the process. They usually concluded their adventures by explaining the scientific reasons for the phenomena encountered.

This sensibly constructed, well-liked, educational cartoon was aired during evening prime time in the USA, just like its Hanna-Barbera predecessors **The Flintstones**, **The Jetsons** and **Top Cat**.

JOSEPH, LESLEY

British actress, most familiar as the man-hungry Dorien Green in **Birds of a Feather**, but with other credits including **Sadie**, **It's Cold Outside**, **Les Girls**, **And Mother Makes Five**, **Minder** and **Horizon**.

JOURNEY TO THE CENTER OF THE EARTH

US (Filmation/Twentieth Century-Fox) Cartoon. BBC 1 1968–9

Voices:
Professor Oliver Lindenbrook ....Ted Knight
Cindy Lindenbrook ....Jane Webb
Alec McEwen.................................Pat Harrington Jnr
Lars..Pat Harrington Jnr
Count Saccnuson ....Ted Knight
Torg ....Pat Harrington Jnr

Executive Producers: Louis Scheimer, Norman Prescott

A party of explorers tries to reach the legendary centre of the Earth.

In an attempt to retrace the steps of explorer Arnie Saccnuson, archaeologist Professor Oliver Lindenbrook gathered together a small team of adventurers, consisting of his niece, Cindy, student Alec McEwen, a guide, Lars, and Gertrude, Cindy's pet duck. Entering a cavern to look for clues, they found themselves trapped when an explosion blocked the entrance. They soon discovered the blast to be the work of the malevolent Count Saccnuson, the last living descendant of the renowned explorer, who, with Torg, his dim henchman, had his own plans for the Earth's core. For the Professor and his team there was no alternative: they just had to follow Arnie's trail (marked 'AS') and hope to find a way back to the surface. As they did so, they were not only hindered by the Count and Torg (who had also been trapped by the bungled explosion), but also encountered a variety of prehistoric monsters, lost civilisations and assorted natural phenomena. The series was very loosely based on Jules Verne's 1865 novel and the 1959 film, starring James Mason.

JOURNEY TO THE UNKNOWN

UK (Hammer/Twentieth Century-Fox) Drama. ITV 1968–9

Producer: Anthony Hinds. Executive Producers: Joan Harrison, Norman Lloyd

An anthology of supernatural suspense tales.

Financed by Twentieth Century-Fox but produced in Britain by Hammer, this anthology of 17 stories embraced both science fiction and psychological horror with its varied tales of murder, twisted minds, sorcery, ESP, medical experimentation and the afterlife. The tone was set by sinister opening titles, which depicted a spooky abandoned fairground. American stars usually took the lead (the likes of Joseph Cotton, Julie Harris, Barbara Bel Geddes, Roddy McDowall and Stefanie Powers were seen), with familiar UK faces in support. Producers Joan Harrison and Norman Lloyd had both worked on *Alfred Hitchcock Presents* and the influence of the Master of Suspense was very apparent. Unfortunately, the progamme did not enjoy a steady run on ITV, appearing first in London and then only sporadically around the network.

JOYCE, YOOTHA (1927–80)

British comic actress, imprinted in viewers' minds as the sex-starved Mildred Roper in *Man about the House* and *George and Mildred*. Joyce came to the role on the back of a run of guest appearances in the 1960s (in programmes like *The Avengers* and in the comedies *Brothers In*

Law and *Corrigan Blake*). She had also starred in the Milo O'Shea sitcom *Me Mammy*, in which she played his willing secretary, Miss Argyll, and *On the Buses*, as Jessie the clippie. She was once married to actor Glynn Edwards.

JUKE BOX JURY

UK (BBC/Noel Gay) Pop Music. BBC 1 1959–67; 1979; BBC 2 1989–90

Presenters: David Jacobs, Noel Edmonds, Jools Holland

Creator: Peter Potter

A celebrity panel reviews new record releases.

Along with *Doctor Who* and *Dixon of Dock Green*, *Juke Box Jury* was one of the stalwarts of Saturday teatime television in the early 1960s. The name of its instrumental theme music, 'Hit and Miss' (a Top 10 entry for the John Barry Seven in 1960), summed up what the programme was all about. Host David Jacobs played a selection of brand new records to a panel of four knowledgeable personalities who then declared whether the records would be 'hits' or 'misses'. While the records played, the cameras focused on the faces of the studio audience, gauging their reaction to the new discs. If the jury's overall conclusion was a 'hit', Jacobs rang a bell; if it was a 'miss' he sounded a klaxon. To add to the excitement, a mystery guest usually lurked in the background, waiting to confront pundits who gave their record the thumbs down.

The very first panel consisted of disc-jockey Pete Murray, singers Alma Cogan and Gary Miller, and 'typical teenager' Susan Stranks (later wife of Robin Ray and presenter of *Magpie*). In December 1963, a massive audience was generated by the fact that The Beatles filled all four pundits' chairs, and, a year later, the jury was temporarily increased to five, to accommodate the Rolling Stones. Although cancelled in 1967 (when the last panel again included Murray and Stranks, as well as Eric Sykes and Lulu), *Juke Box Jury* was briefly revived with Noel Edmonds as chairman in 1979, and once more in 1989, when former *The Tube* presenter Jools Holland became host.

JULIET BRAVO

UK (BBC) Police Drama. BBC 1 1980–5

Inspector Jean Darblay	Stephanie Turner
Tom Darblay	David Hargreaves
Inspector Kate Longton	Anna Carteret
Sgt Joseph Beck	David Ellison
Sgt George Parrish	Noel Collins
PC Roland Bentley	Mark Drewry

Detective Chief Inspector Logan	Tony Caunter
PC Sims	David Gillies
PC Brian Kelleher	C.J. Allen
PC Danny Sparks	Mark Botham
Detective Chief Inspector	Perrin Edward Peel
Detective Sgt Maltby	Sebastian Abineri

Creator: Ian Kennedy Martin. Producers: Terence Williams, Colin Shindler, Jonathan Alwyn, Geraint Morris

Community policing with a female inspector.

Reminiscent of *Z Cars* in its setting, tone and content, *Juliet Bravo* focused on Jean Darblay and Kate Longton, female police inspectors in the small, fictional town of Hartley in Lancashire. Darblay, career copper and housewife, battled against sexism from the start. Her arrival was greeted by distrust and resentment from her fellow officers (especially the obnoxious CID mob), but she rapidly earned respect, enjoying particular support from her solid, dependable sergeants, Joe Beck and George Parrish, as well as her husband, Tom, a social worker. Juliet Bravo was her police call sign. When, after three years, Darblay took promotion and moved on, she was replaced by Kate Longton, who not only took over her patch, but also the headaches which went with it. Cosy and reassuring, with an emphasis on human drama rather than sensational crime, *Juliet Bravo* was written by Ian Kennedy Martin, creator of *The Sweeney*. He brought Stephanie Turner with him (she had played George Carter's wife and, incidentally, was once a WPC in *Z Cars*). The series proved particularly popular with female viewers.

JUNKIN, JOHN (1930–)

British actor, comedy writer and performer, also working as a programme consultant. On screen he has been seen as Wally, Alf Garnett's milkman in *Till Death Us Do Part*, boozy husband Sam Marshall in *Sam and Janet*, Bert Ryding in the Stanley Holloway comedy *Thingumybob*, building foreman Charlie Cattermole in *On the House*, Odius in *Up Pompeii!*, Tim Brooke-Taylor's flatmate, Harold King, in *The Rough with the Smooth* (also as co-writer), Tommy Wallace in *Sharon and Elsie* and, more recently, legal clerk Steven in *Law and Disorder*. Junkin has also revealed his skill at straight drama in the crime thriller *Out* and series like *Penmarric*, *Dick Turpin*, *All for Love* and *All Creatures Great and Small*. Other credits have included *Marty*, *Blott on the Landscape*, *Looking for Clancy* and *Shelley*, while his own comedy series, *Junkin*, ran for four seasons and his radio show *Hello Cheeky* also transferred to TV for a while. Junkin's many writing credits have included *Mr Aitch*, *Langley Bottom* and *Paradise*

Island, plus scripts for many top comedians, including Bob Monkhouse and Mike Yarwood. He also adapted J.B. Morton's *Daily Express* Beachcomber column for Spike Milligan in *The World of Beachcomber* (with Barry Took).

JUST GOOD FRIENDS

UK (BBC) Situation Comedy. BBC 1 1983–6

Vince Pinner	Paul Nicholas
Penny Warrender	Jan Francis
Daphne Warrender	Sylvia Kay
Norman Warrender	John Ringham
Rita Pinner	Ann Lynn
Les Pinner	Shaun Curry
Clifford Pinner	Adam French
Georgina	Charlotte Seely

Creator/Writer: John Sullivan. Producer: Ray Butt

A jilted girl meets up with her former fiancé and they embark on a new on-off romance.

Jack the lad Vincent Pinner had met prim and proper Penny Warrender at a Rolling Stones concert in Hyde Park. Romance had blossomed and they had decided to get married. But, on the day, Vince chickened out. Five years later, he and Penny met by accident in a pub and found themselves drawn into a new love-hate relationship, exasperated by their different class roots and chosen professions. Cheeky, working-class Vince was assistant manager at Eddie Brown's Turf Accountants, while prissy, middle-class Penny worked for the Mathews, Styles and Lieberman advertising agency. Other major characters were Penny's snooty mum, Daphne, her unemployed, hen-pecked dad, Norman, and Vince's gloriously vulgar parents, Rita, a keen rock 'n' roll fan, and Les, a scrap-metal merchant. Also seen was Vince's accident prone younger brother, Cliffy. After numerous false dawns, Vince (now in charge of his dad's business) and Penny (now working in Paris) did indeed manage to tie the knot.

A letter from a girl in the same situation as Penny, published in the problems page of a women's magazine, allegedly inspired John Sullivan to create the series.

JUST JIMMY

UK (ABC) Situation Comedy. ITV 1964–6

Jimmy Clitheroe	Jimmy Clitheroe
Mrs Clitheroe	Mollie Sugden
Danny	Danny Ross

Producer: Ronnie Baxter

The misadventures of an unruly schoolboy.

Translated from BBC Radio, *Just Jimmy* was the television manifestation of *The Clitheroe Kid*, in which 4-ft 3-in Lancastrian comedian Jimmy Clitheroe performed his naughty schoolboy routines. He was supported in this series by Mollie Sugden as his over-the-top mum and Danny Ross as Danny, his older, girls- and motorbikes-mad cousin. Heard of but not seen was Jimmy's pal Billy Jackson.

JUST WILLIAM

UK (LWT) Situation Comedy. ITV 1977–8

William Brown ....Adrian Dannatt
Mr Brown ....Hugh Cross
Mrs Brown ....Diana Fairfax
Ethel Brown ....Stacy Dorning
Robert Brown ....Simon Chandler
Violet Elizabeth Bott ....Bonnie Langford
Mrs Bott ....Diana Dors
Mr Bott ....John Stratton
Douglas ....Tim Rose
Ginger ....Michael McVey
Henry ....Craig McFarlane

Writer: Keith Dewhurst. Executive Producer: Stella Richman. Producer: John Davies

A mischievous schoolboy is a constant handful for his parents.

Richmal Crompton's colourful adventures of trying schoolboy William Brown were first brought to the screen by the BBC in *William* in 1962, with Dennis Waterman and then Dennis Gilmore in the title role. Fifteen years later, William was back with Adrian Dannatt filling Master Brown's shoes.

William was the mischievous type, fond of pranks and tricks and never far from trouble. His band of followers, known as the Outlaws, consisted of Douglas, Ginger and Henry. William had a sister, Ethel, and an older brother, Robert, though his arch-enemy was the dreadful, lisping Violet Elizabeth Bott. She had set her heart on marrying him and promised to scream until she made herself sick whenever she failed to get her way.

Just William made yet another return to the small screen in 1994, when the BBC cast young Oliver Rokison in the lead role.

JUSTICE

UK (Yorkshire) Legal Drama. ITV 1971–4

Harriet Peterson ....Margaret Lockwood
Sir John Gallagher ....Philip Stone
Dr Ian Moody..John Stone
James Eliot ....Anthony Valentine

Creators/Writers: James Mitchell, Edmund Ward Executive Producer: Peter Willes. Producers: James Ormerod, Jacky Stoller

The cases of a junior barrister.

Middle-aged Harriet Peterson was a devoted, dedicated lawyer doing the rounds of the courtrooms of northern England. After the first 13 episodes, and following encouragement from her boss, Sir John Gallagher, she moved to London, where she ultimately discovered a rival in barrister James Eliot, whom she regularly upstaged. With the scripts vetted by a real lawyer, the programme was careful in its detail and depicted the legal system in all its colours. Harriet, for instance, was no Perry Mason and certainly not infallible.

The role provided a triumphant return to the small screen for Margaret Lockwood, who had previously been seen as lawyer Julia Stanford in a one-off play, *Justice is a Woman*, in 1968.

KYTV

UK (BBC) Situation Comedy. BBC 2 1990–3

Mike Channel ....Angus Deayton
Mike Flex ....Geoffrey Perkins
Anna Daptor ....Helen Atkinson Wood
Martin Brown ....Michael Fenton Stevens
Mr Hartford...Philip Pope

Writers: Angus Deayton, Geoffrey Perkins. Producer: Jamie Rix

Mock satellite broadcasting with a fictitious TV station.

KYTV was a spoof on the emerging satellite TV networks, satirizing their programming, poking fun at their technical problems and parodying their broadcasters. The station was named after Sir Kenneth Yellowhammer, its founder and chairman, and the main presenters were Mike Channel, Mike Flex, Anna Daptor and the bumbling Martin Brown. Phil Pope provided the music as well as appearing as continuity announcer. The team sent up every aspect of programming, from travelogues and crime reports to God slots and election coverages. The one-off special, *The Making of David Chizzlenut*, gave viewers the chance to look behind the scenes of a TV classic. KYTV was a follow-up to the same team's Radio 4 series *Radio Active*, in which they mocked the standard of programming at some commericial radio stations.

KALEIDOSCOPE

UK (BBC) Magazine. BBC 1946–53

Host: McDonald Hobley

Producer: John Irwin

Easy-going magazine programme calling on viewer involvement.

This television manifestation of the 1930s radio series *Monday Night at Eight* was comprised of a variety of light-hearted items, from competitions and puzzles to comedy and games. Amongst the features were Word Play (an early version of *Give Us a Clue*), Be Your Own Detective (an observation game), Collectors' Corner (antiques with Iris Brooke), contributions from Memory Man Leslie Welch and Puzzle Corner with Ronnie Waldman (with viewers asked to spot the deliberate mistake). Anyone at home wishing to take part in the 'which year' tune medley competition had to place a copy of the *Radio Times* in their window by noon on broadcast day in order to be spotted and selected. Assisting host McDonald Hobley with events were the likes of Max Kester, Dorothy Ward, Lind Joyce, Garry Miller, John Slater, Diana Decker, Elizabeth Welch and Carole Carr. *Kaleidoscope* was screened once a fortnight.

KARLIN, MIRIAM, OBE (MIRIAM SAMUELS; 1925–)

London-born actress who satirised militant trade unionists in her portrayal of Paddy, the whistle-blowing shop steward in **The Rag Trade**. It was a role she played on two occasions: in the original series in 1961 and in its revival in 1977. Earlier, Karlin had appeared in the 1946 production of *Alice* and then starred with Sid James in his first (post-Hancock) sitcom, *East End – West End*. More recently, she has returned to television in the sitcom **So Haunt Me**, playing Jewish ghost Yetta Feldman, harassing the family who live in her old home.

KARLOFF, BORIS (WILLIAM PRATT; 1887–1969)

Although a master of the horror genre in the cinema, Boris Karloff's major television role was quite different. He played *Colonel March of Scotland Yard* in 1956, head of the Department of Queer Complaints who always wore an eyepatch over his left eye. In a more familiar vein, he also hosted *Out of this World*, an anthology of science fiction stories in the early 1960s, and he continued to make guest appearances, in series like *The Girl from UNCLE* and *Route 66*, until his death in 1969.

KATE

UK (Yorkshire) Drama. ITV 1970–2

Kate Graham	Phyllis Calvert
Donald Killearn	Jack Hedley
Wenda Padbury	Penelope Keith
Miss Wren	Isabel Dean

Producers: Stanley Miller, Peter Mortimer, Pieter Rogers

An agony aunt has problems of her own.

Kate Graham, the widowed mother of a teenage son, worked as the 'Dear Monica' problem page editor for *Heart and Home* magazine. But, as well as dispensing advice to her readers, Kate found herself in demand amongst her colleagues (particularly her editor, Donald Killearn). Furthermore, her own home life in Chelsea was far from settled. Miss Wren was Kate's long-serving secretary.

KAYE, GORDEN (1941–)

British comedy actor, much seen on TV, especially as the reluctant Résistance hero René Artois in *'Allo 'Allo*. Previously, Kaye had popped up in a host of other comedies, including **Till Death Us Do Part, Are You Being Served?, It Ain't Half Hot Mum, The Growing Pains of PC Penrose**, *Oh Happy Band* and **Come Back Mrs Noah** (in which he played the news reporter keeping us up to date on the progress of Mrs Noah's lost spacecraft). He was Ray Benge in the black comedy *Born and Bred*, the neighbour Mr Chatto in *Just Liz* and was also seen in *Last of the Summer Wine* as Maynard Lavery, a TV presenter, and in dramas like **Shoestring, All Creatures Great and Small**, *The Foundation*, *Fame is the Spur* and **Coronation Street** (as Bernard Butler, Elsie Tanner's nephew). In 1987 he narrowly escaped death in the gales which shook southern England, sustaining severe head injuries. He is now fully recovered.

KEACH, STACY (1941–)

American cinema and television actor, known for Shakespearean roles in the 1960s, but famous as the tough detective **Mike Hammer** in the 1980s. Previously, Keach had played Carlson in **Get Smart**, starred in the shortlived detective series *Caribe* and in the Civil War drama *The Blue and the Grey*, as well as playing Barabbas in **Jesus of Nazareth**. He later starred in the mini-series *Mistral's Daughter* and *Hemingway*. Unfortunately, his big-time period in Mickey Spillane's **Mike Hammer** was punctuated by a much-publicized spell in Reading prison for drugs offences.

KEE, ROBERT (1919–)

Distinguished British journalist, a reporter on **Panorama** and **This Week** in the 1950s and 1960s, who joined ITN in the mid-1970s to present the novel lunchtime news bulletin, *First Report*. In 1980 he wrote and presented **Ireland: A Television History** and, in 1983, was a member of TV-am's Famous Five, presenting *Daybreak*, the station's news and information reveille.

KEEL, HOWARD (HAROLD KEEL; 1917–)

American musical star for whom television celebrity arrived late. His earliest TV appearances were as a guest in series like *Here's Lucy* and *The Quest*, but it wasn't until he arrived in *Dallas* in 1981, as silver-haired Clayton Farlow, that Keel became an established TV performer.

KEEN, DIANE (1946–)

Chirpy British actress coming to light as Fliss Hawthorne in *The Cuckoo Waltz* sitcom, though she had already enjoyed credits in *Softly, Softly*, *Crossroads*, *Public Eye*, *The Sweeney*, *Crown Court* and *The Fall of Eagles*, amongst other programmes, including a BBC version of *The Legend of Robin Hood* (as Maid Marian). During and after *The Cuckoo Waltz*, Keen played Empress Chimalma in *The Feathered Serpent,* Laura Dickens in *The Sandbaggers,* Sandy Bennett in another sitcom, *Rings on their Fingers,* Sally Langton in *The Shillingbury Tales* and the title role in the drama *Foxy Lady,* as provincial newspaper editor Daisy Jackson. More recently, she was seen as Jenny Burden in *The Ruth Rendell Mysteries,* novelist housewife Alice Hammond in *You Must Be the Husband* and Connie French in the second series of *September Song.*

KEEP IT IN THE FAMILY

UK (Thames) Situation Comedy. ITV 1980–3

Dudley Rush	Robert Gillespie
Muriel Rush	Pauline Yates
Duncan Thomas	Glyn Houston
Susan Rush	Stacy Dorning
Jacqui Rush	Jenny Quayle
	Sabina Franklyn

Creator: Brian Cooke. Producers: Mark Stuart/Robert Reed

Upstairs-downstairs, generation gap comedy.

This series centred on the Rush family, who lived in Highgate Avenue, Highgate. Nominal head of the household was Dudley, a slightly eccentric, professional cartoonist (drawer of the 'Bionic Bulldog' cartoon). His caricature family consisted of dutiful wife Muriel, and problematic daughters Susan (aged 17) and Jacqui (21), who were constantly tapping him for cash, bringing home unsuitable boyfriends and indulging in reckless pursuits. When the Rushes' old lodger died and his downstairs flat became vacant, the girls took it over, giving themselves more independence and their parents more grey hairs. Duncan was Dudley's Welsh boss, who also moved in with the family, and another regular was the old glove puppet Dudley talked to while drawing.

The series gave rise to an American cover version entitled *Too Close for Comfort*, starring Ted Knight.

KEEPING UP APPEARANCES

UK (BBC) Situation Comedy. BBC 1 1990–

Hyacinth Bucket	Patricia Routledge
Richard Bucket	Clive Swift
Elizabeth	Josephine Tewson
Emmet Hawksworth	David Griffin
Daisy	Judy Cornwell
Onslow	Geoffrey Hughes
Rose	Shirley Stelfox
	Mary Millar
Vicar	Gerald Sim
	Jeremy Gittins
Daddy	George Webb

Creator/Writer: Roy Clarke. Producer: Harold Snoad

A socially climbing housewife lives in fear of letting herself down.

Only one thing mattered to Hyacinth Bucket (pronounced 'bouquet') and that was what other people thought of her. From her suburban base, she moved Heaven and Earth to mix with the right crowd and to ensure that her image remained intact. Sadly, her council-house sisters, the slutty Daisy and the tarty Rose, plus her shirtless brother-in-law, Onslow, ensured it was a battle she was doomed to lose. They looked after Hyacinth's loopy old dad and were always likely to pop round in Onslow's S-reg Cortina (complete with furry dice). Undaunted, Hyacinth badgered her meek, long-suffering husband, Richard, into helping with her candlelight suppers and other socially aspirant schemes and talked up the brilliance of her son, Sheridan (who was away at polytechnic), to all who would listen. She answered the telephone with a ringing 'The Bucket residence: the lady of the house speaking', and hounded Elizabeth, her neighbour, and Elizabeth's divorced brother, Emmet, to the point where they became refugees in their own home. Generally, though, it was Hyacinth's own social gaffes that scuppered her rise to the top.

KEITH, PENELOPE, OBE (1940–)

British comedy actress mostly in plummy, snooty parts. Having appeared in series like *Six Shades of Black*, *Hadleigh*, *Kate* and *The Pallisers* (as Mrs Hittaway), it was as the socially-paranoid Margo Leadbetter, neighbour of the self-sufficient Goods, in *The Good Life*, that Keith found her forté. This led to a series of her own, *To the Manor Born*, in which she played Audrey Fforbes-Hamilton, cruelly ejected from her stately home on the death of her husband. Her later sitcom work has included Moving (as would-be house mover Sarah Gladwyn), Sweet Sixteen (as Helen Walker, a love-struck builder), Executive Stress (as publishing director Caroline Fairchild), No Job for a Lady (as novice Labour MP Jean Price) and Law and Disorder (as barrister Phillippa Troy). Other credits have included The Norman Conquests, Spyder's Web, On Approval and Jackanory. She briefly hosted What's My Line? on the death of Eamonn Andrews.

KELLY, BARBARA (1923–)

Canadian actress and television personality, a familiar face in the 1950s as a panellist on What's My Line? With her husband, the late Bernard Braden, Kelly moved to Britain in 1949 and, together, they made a name for themselves on BBC Radio. Kelly also starred with Braden in the shortlived TV sitcoms The Rolling Stones (as Barbara Stone) and B and B (as herself), as well as making appearances in assorted plays and in programmes like Criss Cross Quiz and Kelly's Eye. She returned to the screen in the 1984 revival of What's My Line? Kelly is the mother of actress Kim Braden.

KELLY, CHRIS (1940–)

British presenter, writer and producer, for many years at Granada, and previously Anglia, working on programmes like World in Action (narrator), Cinema and the children's series Zoo Time, Junior Criss Cross Quiz, Clapperboard and Anything You Can Do. He was Judith Chalmers's partner on Wish You Were Here . . . ? for many years and is currently host of BBC 2's Food and Drink. He is also a published writer, has produced the drama Soldier, Soldier and, in 1989, co-created the security firm drama Saracen with Ted Childs.

KELLY, HENRY (1946–)

Irish journalist turned presenter of game shows, whose major TV break came with Game for a Laugh in 1981. Since then, he has appeared on TV-am and Monkey Business and also hosted the inter-European quiz Going for Gold. Kelly's 'day job' is as a presenter on Classic FM.

KELLY, MATTHEW (1950–)

Tall, bearded British presenter and actor, coming to the fore through Game For A Laugh and subsequently host of Kelly's Eye, You Bet! and Stars in their Eyes. Kelly earlier appeared in the drama Funny Man, the hotel sitcom Room Service (as Dick Sedgwick) and the Peter Davison and Patricia Hodge comedy Holding the Fort, playing the part of Fitz, which was later spun-off into

another series in which he starred, Relative Strangers. Other credits have included The Rather Reassuring Programme, The Critic, Madabout, Quandaries, The Sensible Show and Adventures of a Lifetime.

KELLY, SAM (1943–)

British character actor, usually seen in incompetent or slightly stupid parts, such as the illiterate Warren in Porridge and the inept Captain Hans Geering in 'Allo 'Allo. Amongst his earliest opportunites were episodes of Emergency – Ward 10 and The Liver Birds. He played Norman Elston in the flashback sitcom Now and Then, Les Brooks in the unemployment comedy We'll Think of Something, Grunge in Haggard, Sam the chauffeur in On the Up and he has been seen in more serious roles in Inspector Morse, Boys from the Blackstuff and Christabel. Other credits have included Coronation Street, Thin Air, The Bill, Making Out and Stay Lucky.

KENDAL, FELICITY, CBE (1946–)

Winsome British actress, born into a showbiz family. She proved particularly popular in the 1970s and 1980s, playing whimsical, independent females, beginning with Barbara Good in The Good Life and continuing with Gemma Palmer in Solo and Maxine in The Mistress. Amongst her earliest TV work were episodes of Man in a Suitcase, The Persuaders, Crime Of Passion, Love Story and Edward the Seventh. In 1978, she appeared as Dorothy Wordsworth in Clouds of Glory, Ken Russell's two-part biopic of the Lakeland poets and, more recently, she has been seen in Channel 4's The Camomile Lawn and played Nancy Belasco, an American widow in Cambridge, in the sitcom Honey for Tea.

KENDALL, KENNETH (1924–)

A teacher immediately after the war, Kenneth Kendall joined the BBC in 1948 and became one of the Corporation's first three 'on-screen' newsreaders in 1955. He stayed until 1961, when he left to go freelance and made rare guest appearances in dramas like The Troubleshooters, Doctor Who and Adam Adamant Lives! He returned to the BBC in 1969 and retired 12 years later, after a shake-up of the main news bulletins, soon resurfacing in regional television and as host of Channel 4's popular Treasure Hunt series (working with Anneka Rice).

KENNEDY, SIR LUDOVIC (1919–)

Distinguished British writer, journalist and presenter, one of ITN's first newscasters back in

1956. In 1958 and 1959 Kennedy stood unsuccessfully as Liberal parliamentary candidate for Rochdale (the first occasion being a by-election). In the 1960s he became a reporter on *Panorama* and also worked on *Tonight, 24 Hours, This Week* and *Midweek*. He was the first host of the review programme *Did You See . . . ?* and has also presented *Question Time*. In 1972 he chaired the controversial debate *A Question of Ulster* and, in 1979, he secured a frank interview with Lord Mountbatten only weeks before his untimely death. Kennedy also contributed to the BBC's *Great Railway Journeys of the World* (he did the New York to Los Angeles leg). He married ballerina Moira Shearer in 1950, has written numerous books (including the exposé of the Christie murders, *10 Rillington Place*) and has been a lifelong campaigner against miscarriages of justice and for voluntary euthanasia.

KENNEDY, SARAH (1950–)

Blonde British presenter of *Game For a Laugh, Busman's Holiday, Classmates, Daytime* and various animal series. She was one of the shortlived *Sixty Minutes* team which took over from *Nationwide* and also broadcasts regularly on radio.

KERR, GRAHAM (1934–)

As host of *Entertaining with Kerr: The Galloping Gourmet* in the late 1960s, Canadian Graham Kerr became a housewives' favourite and made swilling wine part of a TV cook's repertoire long before Keith Floyd raised a glass in anger. His 'Galloping Gourmet' nickname came from his mad-dash cooking style and the fact that he tore around the set. Kerr was an international success, but he and his producer wife soon gave it all up and turned to religion, though he did attempt a comeback in 1990.

KEY GRIP see grip.

KICK UP THE EIGHTIES, A

UK (BBC) Comedy. BBC 2 1981–4

Richard Stilgoe
Tracey Ullman
Ron Bain
Miriam Margolyes
Robbie Coltrane
Roger Sloman
Rik Mayall

Producers: Tom Gutteridge, Colin Gilbert

Comedy sketch show introducing a host of new talent.

A product of BBC Scotland's comedy department, which was later to contribute *Naked Video*

amongst other programmes, *A Kick Up the Eighties* featured humorist Richard Stilgoe anchoring a series of offbeat sketches. Tracey Ullman, Robbie Coltrane and Miriam Margolyes all gained valuable early exposure from the series, as did Rik Mayall, billed under his alter-ego of Kevin Turvey, a boring Brummie who delivered a pointless monologue each week.

KILLER see *Taggart*.

KILROY-SILK, ROBERT (1942–)

Former Labour MP who, after the publication of his book, *Hard Labour*, branched out into daytime TV talk shows with *Day By Day*, which was quickly renamed *Kilroy*.

KING, LARRY (1933–)

American journalist and radio and TV presenter, since 1985 host of the influential *Larry King Live* for CNN, which attracts all the top political names and allows viewers telephone access to them.

KINNEAR, ROY (1934–88)

British comedian and actor, originally a member of the *That Was The Week That Was* team and later moving on to star in his own sitcoms, usually portraying breathless, sweaty types. The highlights were *A World of his Own* (as daydreamer Stanley Blake), *Inside George Webley* (as George, a perpetual worrier), *Cowboys* (as building firm manager Joe Jones), *The Clairvoyant* (as title character Arnold Bristow) and *No Appointment Necessary* (as greengrocer/hairdresser Alf Butler). Kinnear also supported hosts of other actors in their series. His credits included *Till Death Us Do Part, The Avengers, The Goodies, The Sweeney, Casualty, Minder* (as Whaley), *George and Mildred* (as George's friend, Jerry) and *The Incredible Mr Tanner* (as Sidney). Kinnear died in 1988 while shooting a 'Musketeers' film in Spain, when his horse slipped and fell, throwing him to the ground.

KINVIG

UK (LWT) Situation Comedy. ITV 1981

Des Kinvig	Tony Haygarth
Netta Kinvig	Patsy Rowlands
Jim Piper	Colin Jeavons
Miss Griffin	Prunella Gee
Mr Horsley	Patrick Newell
Buddo	Simon Williams

Creator/Writer: Nigel Kneale. Producer: Les Chatfield

An electrical repairman is whisked off to Mercury by a sexy spacewoman.

Des Kinvig led a mundane life. Running a back-street electrical repair shop in Bingleton, married to the suffocating Netta and sharing his home with a giant dog named Cuddley, this was one man in urgent need of excitement. It arrived in the form of Miss Griffin, a shapely alien dressed in the slinkiest cat suits and space bikinis, who persuaded Des to join her on trips to Mercury. There, they and the 500-year-old Buddo teamed up against an ant-like race called the Xux, who aimed to take over Earth by giving humans the power to bend cutlery and by flooding the planet with humanoid robots.

Played for laughs, the storyline left viewers wondering whether it had all been a figment of Des's imagination, sparked off by UFO discussions with his anoraky friend, Jim Piper. Creator Nigel Kneale was the writer of *1984* and *Quatermass* in the 1950s.

KLUGMAN, JACK (1922–)

American actor, star of TV's version of *The Odd Couple* (as Oscar Madison) and even better known as the grouchy pathologist *Quincy*. In a long television career, Klugman has appeared in kids' shows, plays and early cult series like *The Twilight Zone*, *Naked City*, *Ben Casey* and *The Defenders*. His first starring role was in a comedy not seen in the UK, *Harris Against the World*. Klugman also played Henry Willows in *You Again?*, a US translation of the John Thaw sitcom *Home to Roost*.

KNEALE, NIGEL (1922–)

Isle of Man-born BBC staff writer and script reader who helped shift the goal posts of TV drama through his adventurous 1953 thriller *The Quatermass Experiment*. A year later, Kneale was responsible for the graphic adaptation of Orwell's *1984*, which caused a storm in Parliament. His next major work was *Quatermass II* in 1955, joined by *Quatermass and the Pit* in 1958. Kneale continued to lean on the boundaries of acceptability with plays like *The Year of the Sex Olympics* (a Theatre 625 presentation, 1968) and *Wine of India* (1970), before leaving the BBC in 1975 to work for ITV. *Beasts*, an anthology of chillers involving animals, was aired in 1976, and *Quatermass* was revived for Euston Films in 1979, before Kneale attempted comedy with the sci-fi sitcom *Kinvig*, in 1981. His most recent works have been *The Woman in Black* and *Stanley and the Women*, with other notable credits over the years including an adaptation of *Wuthering Heights* (1953), *The Creature* (1955), *The Road* (part of the First Night anthology, 1963), *The Crunch* (from Studio '64, 1964), *The Chopper* (for *Out of the Unknown* in 1971) and *The Stone Tape* (1972).

KNIGHT ERRANT

UK (Granada) Adventure. ITV 1959–61

Adam Knight	John Turner
Liz Parrish	Kay Callard
Peter Parker	Richard Carpenter
Tony Hollister	William Fox
Stephen Drummond	Hugh David
Frances Graham	Wendy Williams
Greg Wilson	Stephen Cartwright
Colonel Cope-Addams	Alan Webb

Creator: Philip Mackie. Producers: Warren Jenkins, Kitty Black

A newspaper advertisement leads to a life of adventure for a modern-day crusader.

Adam Knight, a meanderer between jobs, bit the bullet and decided to work for himself, placing a newspaper advert which read: 'Knight Errant '59. Quests undertaken, dragons defeated, damsels rescued. Anything, anywhere, for anyone, so long as it helps. Fees according to means.' The result was a series of interesting and diverse cases, revolving around other people's problems.

Joining Adam in his Knight Errant agency were ex-*Daily Clarion* journalist Liz Parrish and young writer Peter Parker. A later addition to the team was Adam's new business consultant, Tony Hollister, a spirits tycoon. When Adam left for Canada to run his uncle's farm, he was replaced as agency boss by Stephen Drummond, a publisher with little time for his true profession. Drummond's secretary, Frances Graham, also arrived. Peter Parker then returned to his writing and was substituted by Greg Wilson, and a retired army man, Colonel Cope-Addams, added military experience to the set-up.

The first series was entitled *Knight Errant '59*, becoming *Knight Errant '60* when the year changed. After Adam Knight's departure, the programme was renamed *Knight Errant Limited*. Richard Carpenter, who played Peter Parker, switched career himself, from acting to writing, moving on to create series like *Catweazle* and *Dick Turpin*.

KNIGHT RIDER

US (Universal/Glen A. Larson) Science Fiction. ITV 1983–

Michael Knight	David Hasselhoff
Devon Miles	Edward Mulhare
Bonnie Barstow	Patricia McPherson
April Curtis	Rebecca Holden
KITT (voice)	William Daniels
Reginald Cornelius III ('RC3')	Peter Parros

Creator/Producer: Glen A. Larson

An ex-cop rights wrongs with the help of a supercar.

Michael Long, a young police officer, was shot in the face and left for dead. To his rescue came Wilton Knight, a millionaire industrialist (played in the opening episode by Richard Basehart) who himself had little time to live. Long underwent plastic surgery to repair his features and, in respect for his saviour, changed his name to Michael Knight. When the millionaire died, he left his estate to Michael for the benefit of the fight against crime, and Michael accepted the bequest with relish.

As part of the inheritance, Michael took possession of an amazing, computerized black car, known as the Knight Industries Two Thousand, or KITT for short. KITT was not only capable of speeds over 300 mph and equipped with an armoury of lethal weapons, but it also talked, had a moody personality and came whenever Michael needed it. With such a trusty steed, Knight, not surprisingly, often succeeded in his fight for justice.

Knight's helpers were Devon Miles, manager of the dead millionaire's estate, and a mechanic, Bonnie Barstow, who was temporarily replaced by April Curtis and then the laid-back RC3. They operated from a base known as the Foundation for Law and Government in California and followed KITT and Knight in a large support van. KITT, despite its flashy appearance, was no more than a souped-up Pontiac Trans Am.

KNOTS LANDING

US (Lorimar/Roundlay/MF) Drama. BBC 1
1980–1; 1983; 1986–

Gary Ewing	Ted Shackleford
Valene Ewing/Gibson/Waleska	Joan Van Ark
Sid Fairgate	Don Murray
Karen Fairgate/MacKenzie	Michele Lee
Richard Avery	John Pleshette
Laura Avery/Sumner	Constance McCashin
Kenny Ward	James Houghton
Ginger Ward	Kim Lankford
Diana Fairgate	Claudia Lonow
Michael Fairgate	Pat Petersen
Eric Fairgate	Steve Shaw
Jason Avery	Justin Dana
	Danny Gellis
	Danny Ponce
	Matthew Newmark
Abby Cunningham/Ewing/Sumner	Donna Mills
Brian Cunningham	Bobby Jacoby
	Brian Austin Green
Olivia Cunningham/Dyer	Tonya Crowe
Roy Lance	Steven Hirsch
Lilimae Clements	Julie Harris
Amy	Jill Cohen
Joe Cooper	Stephen Macht
M Patrick (Mack) MacKenzie	Kevin Dobson
Ciji Dunne	Lisa Hartman

Chip Roberts	Michael Sabatino
Ben Gibson	Douglas Sheehan
Gregory Sumner	William Devane
Cathy Geary/Rush	Lisa Hartman
Mary-Frances Sumner	Danielle Brisebois
	Stacy Galina
Joshua Rush	Alec Baldwin
Paul Galveston	Howard Duff
Ruth Galveston	Ava Gardner
Peter Hollister	Hunt Block
Linda Martin	Leslie Hope
Jill Bennett	Teri Austin
Paige Matheson	Nicollette Sheridan
Tina	Tina Lifford
Peggy	Victoria Ann-Lewis
Marsha	Marcia Solomon
Anne Winston/Matheson	Michelle Phillips
Jean Hackney	Wendy Fulton
Russell Winston	Harry Townes
Al Baker	Red Buttons
Bobby Gibson	Joseph Cousins
	Christian Cousins
Betsy Gibson	Kathryn and Tiffany Lubran
	Emily Ann Lloyd
Carlos	Carlos Cantu
Jody Campbell	Kristy Swanson
Charles Scott	Michael York
Barbara	Ronne Troup
Ana	Movita Castenada
Johnny Rourke	Peter Reckell
Patricia Williams	Lynne Moody
Frank Williams	Larry Riley
Julie Williams	Kent Masters-King
Harold Dyer	Paul Carafotes
Bob Phillips	Zane Lasky
Mort Tubor	Mark Haining
Danny Waleska	Sam Behrens
Linda Fairgate	Lar Park-Lincoln
Virginia Bullock	Betsy Palmer
Paula Vertosick	Melinda Culea
Ted Melcher	Robert Desiderio
Amanda Michaels	Penny Peyser
Claudia Whittaker	Kathleen Noone
Kate Whittaker	Stacy Galina
Nick Schillace/Dimitri Pappas	Lorenzo Caccialanza
Jason Lochner	Thomas Wilson Brown
Dick Lochner	Guy Boyd
Tom Ryan	Joseph Gian
Steve Brewer	Lance Guest
Charlotte Anderson	Tracy Reed

Creator: David Jacobs. Executive Producers: Lee Rich, Michael Filerman, David Jacobs

Life, love, death and deception in a Californian cul-de-sac.

Having fled the excesses of *Dallas*, Gary Ewing, his family's alcoholic black sheep, arrived in the small town of Knots Landing in California. Remarried to his estranged wife, Val, he settled down in a pleasant cul-de-sac, taking a job at Knots Landing Motors, a classic car dealership owned by one of his neighbours, Sid Fairgate. Sid and his wife, Karen, lived with their three teenage children, Diana, Michael and Eric. Also on the close were scheming, lecherous attorney Richard Avery and Laura, his estate agent wife, as well as recording executive Kenny Ward and his attractive partner, Ginger. Soon to arrive was Sid's divorcée sister, Abby Cunningham. She moved into the cul-de-sac with her two children, Brian and Olivia, and quickly began to undermine her neighbours' relationships, spreading gossip and seducing the menfolk.

So the scene was set, and against this backdrop the usual soap storylines developed, pitting the characters against each other in romance, business and intrigue. Typically, there were murders, scandals, adulterous affairs and bitchy in-fighting, but *Knots Landing* didn't stray too far off what was realistically possible, unlike its glossier contemporaries. Characters came, made a big splash and then disappeared. Gregory Sumner stayed longer than most. He was a dodgy senator with underworld connections who married both Laura (divorced from Richard) and, later, Abby. The Williamses were other new arrivals, a black family hiding out under a witness protection scheme. Gradually, the neighbourhood's younger generation pushed their way to the fore, especially Michael Fairgate, Olivia Cunningham and Paige Matheson, the illegitimate daughter of Karen's new husband, attorney Mack MacKenzie (Sid had been killed when his car drove off a cliff). Gary's brothers from *Dallas* popped into some episodes, and Gary and Val returned the compliment, by occasionally visiting Southfork to see their wayward daughter, Lucy.

Despite winning praise for its 'ordinariness' (well, at least when compared with *Dynasty*), *Knots Landing* didn't really catch on in the UK. The series was dropped by the BBC after just a few years and, when picked up again in 1986, it was only given an afternoon time slot, not the Saturday evening prime time with which it began.

KNOX, BARBARA (1938–)

Northern actress, since 1972 *Coronation Street's* Rita Littlewood/Fairclough/Sullivan. Pre-Weatherfield, Knox (as Barbara Mullaney) had appeared in rep and on radio, as well as in series like *Emergency – Ward 10*, *Mrs Thursday*, *The Dustbinmen*, *Never Mind The Quality, Feel The Width*, *A Family at War* and the pilot play for *Girls about Town*. Mullaney changed her name to Knox on marrying businessman John Knox in the late 1970s.

KOJAK

US (Universal) Police Drama. BBC 1 1974–8

Lt Theo Kojak	Telly Savalas
Captain Frank McNeil	Dan Frazer
Lt Bobby Crocker	Kevin Dobson
Detective Stavros	George Savalas
Detective Rizzo	Vince Conti
Detective Saperstein	Mark Russell
Detective Prince	Borah Silver

Creator: Abby Mann. Executive Producer: Matthew Rapf

Unorthodox police work with a no-nonsense, plain clothes cop in New York City.

Theo Kojak was a distinctive kind of police officer. For starters, he sucked lollipops and wore fancy waistcoats. He called people 'Pussycat' and, even more unusually, when he lifted his trilby, he revealed a magnificent shaven head. Once seen, he was never forgotten.

His policing methods were rather unconventional, too. He worked in the Manhattan South, 13th Precinct of the New York Police Department, where his boss, Frank McNeil, had once been his partner. Kojak's refusal to play the police game by the book meant that promotion had never come his way. Dry and cynical, he was always too ready to bend the rules, which needled his superiors. On the streets, Kojak was supported by another plain clothes cop, Bobby Crocker, though his sharpest banter was reserved for Stavros, the overweight, bushy-haired detective played by Telly Savalas's brother, George (originally credited as 'Demosthenes', his middle name).

Kojak became a cult figure in the UK. Lollipop sales boomed and bald became beautiful. Kids strolled around asking 'Who loves ya, baby?', echoing Kojak's catchphrase. Telly Savalas, although already an established character actor, was propelled to international stardom by the series and even broke into the pop charts, mumbling his way to number one in 1975 with a depressing rendition of David Gates's 'If'. After a couple of sequels in the mid-1980s, the character returned to the screens in a series of TV movies in 1989, by which time he had at last gained promotion to inspector.

KOSSOFF, DAVID (1919–)

Softly-spoken British actor, prominent in the 1950s as hen-pecked Alf Larkin in *The Larkins* and in the 1960s as Marcus Lieberman, boss of the family furniture company, in *A Little Big Business*. Kossoff also took the role of the Sheriff of Nottingham in a 1953 version of *Robin Hood* and appeared in the very first *Armchair Theatre* production, *The Outsider*, in 1956, amongst other plays. Much later, he was seen giving Bible readings on *Stars on Sunday*. He was the father of the late Paul Kossoff, guitarist with the rock band Free.

KRYPTON FACTOR, THE

UK (Granada) Quiz. ITV 1977

Presenters: Gordon Burns, Penny Smith

Creator: Jeremy Fox. Producers: Jeremy Fox, Stephen Leahy, David Jenkins, Geoff Moore, Patricia Pearson, Rod Natkiel, Kieran Roberts, Caroline Gosling

Physical and mental contest to find Britain's 'superperson'.

Taking its name from Superman's home planet, *The Krypton Factor* has aimed to find Britain's brainiest and fittest quiz show contestant. Four contenders have taken part in each heat, progressing to semi-finals and then the Grand Final in which *The Krypton Factor* champion has been declared. They have been subjected to tests of mental agility, intelligence, general knowledge and observation (using film clips and, for many years, an identity parade). An army assault course has been used to assess physical strength and fitness (age and sex handicaps have levelled the playing field), and a flight simulator has been employed to gauge response. Each contestant's final score has been known as his or her Krypton Factor. Gordon Burns has presented the show throughout its long run and was joined by Penny Smith as co-presenter in 1995.

A number of celebrity specials have been produced over the years, as well as a few international challenge editions (the programme was sold to America, amongst other countries). Ross King hosted a short-lived junior version, *Young Krypton*, in 1988.

KUNG FU

US (Warner Brothers) Western. ITV 1973–

Kwai Chang Caine............................David Carradine
Master Po ....Keye Luke
Master Kan ....Philip Ahn
Caine (as a boy) ....Radames Pera

Creator: Ed Spielman. Executive Producer: Jerry Thorpe. Producers: Herman Miller, Alex Beaton

A Chinese half-breed wanders through the Wild West avoiding bounty hunters and looking for his long-lost brother.

A man of few words, the peace-loving Kwai Chang Caine had been born in Imperial China, son of an American sea captain and a local woman. He had grown up in a strict Buddhist temple, becoming a Shaolin priest and benefiting from the wisdom of great sages. There, he had also learnt the martial art of Kung Fu. Having killed a member of the Chinese royal family (in self-defence), he fled to America in the 1870s to seek out his half-brother. However, with a price on his head, he was pursued from town to town by oriental hitmen and other bounty hunters.

The softly-spoken, somewhat spaced-out drifter enjoyed the freedom of his own company and the pleasure of his own thoughts. He found himself helping folk in trouble at every turn, but he was a reluctant hero and always the last to resort to violence, turning the other cheek as much as possible. However, a half-breed stumbling around in the violent Wild West was an easy target for bullies. So, when the situation called for it (every episode), he was forced to draw on his fighting skills. With much of the action filmed in slow motion for effect, Caine effortlessly kicked and chopped down his aggressors, often more than one at a time.

Intercut with flashbacks to his childhood, the programme also showed Caine learning his philosophical approach to life from Master Kan and the blind Master Po, the Buddhist priests who called him 'Grasshopper'. Each episode began by recalling the tortuous initiation ceremony at the temple, Caine lifting a burning hot cauldron with his wrists and so branding them with the mark of the dragon. The series stemmed from the success of the Kung Fu films made by master of the art, Bruce Lee.

KYDD, SAM (1915–82)

British character actor, a supporting player for many big names and a star in his own right on more than one occasion. Probably the highlight of his television career was the 1960s children's series *Orlando*, in which he played former smuggler Orlando O'Connor, a character first seen in the Patrick Allen drama series *Crane*. Amongst his earliest contributions was a 1950 version of *Toad of Toad Hall*. Kydd went on to appear in Harry Worth's first sitcom, *The Trouble with Harry*, play Bosun Croaker Jones in *Mess Mates*, take the part of Smellie in the controversial Johnny Speight comedy *Curry and Chips*, and star as Herbert Quince, valet to Jimmy Edwards in *The Fossett Saga*. He was Sam Weller in *The Pickwick Papers* and one of his last appearances was as Mike Baldwin's father in *Coronation Street*. He was the father of actor Jonathan Kydd.

LADD, CHERYL (CHERYL STOPPEL-MOOR; 1951–)

American leading lady, wife of Alan Ladd's son David. Her first television work involved providing one of the singing voices for the cartoon *Josie and the Pussycats* (under the name Cherie Moore). She later appeared on US TV under her maiden name of Cheryl Stoppelmoor, before, as Cheryl Ladd, she was cast as Kris Munroe, sister of Farrah Fawcett-Major's character, Jill, and her replacement in **Charlie's Angels**. Since the series ended, Ladd has moved into films and TV movies.

LA FRENAIS, IAN (1937–) see Clement, Dick.

LA LAW

US (Twentieth) Legal Drama. ITV 1987–92

Leland McKenzie	Richard Dysart
Douglas Brackman, Jnr.	Alan Rachins
Michael Kuzak	Harry Hamlin
Arnie Becker	Corbin Bernsen
Grace Van Owen	Susan Dey
Ann Kelsey	Jill Eikenberry
Stuart Markowitz	Michael Tucker
Victor Sifuentes	Jimmy Smits
Abby Perkins	Michele Greene
Roxanne Melman	Susan Ruttan
Benny Stulwicz	Larry Drake
Jonathan Rollins	Blair Underwood
Dave Meyer	Dann Florek
Rosalind Shays	Diana Muldaur
Cara Jean (C.J.) Lamb	Amanda Donohoe
Tommy Mullaney	John Spencer
Zoey Clemmons	Cecil Hoffman

Creators: Steven Bochco, Terry Louise Fisher. Executive Producers: David Kelley, Gregory Hoblit

The cases of a prominent Los Angeles law firm.

LA Law has been described as **Hill Street Blues** in a courtroom. Indeed, there were many similarities between the two programmes, not least because *Law*'s co-creator Steven Bochco had also been one of the brains behind the *Blues*. He brought with him much the same format: a large, well-defined cast, interweaving storylines and the ability to mix serious business with the lightest of humour. His collaborator on this series was former **Cagney and Lacey** producer Terry Louise Fisher, herself a former Deputy District Attorney. The law firm in question was that of McKenzie, Brackman, Chaney and Kuzak. McKenzie was the paternal senior partner, Brackman the penny-pinching, balding son of one of the founding partners, and Kuzak the hard-working, compassionate litigation partner. Chaney died at his desk in the opening episode. Working with them were Ann Kelsey (another litigation partner), Stuart Markowitz (the tax partner and Ann's future husband), and the womanizing divorce partner, Arnie Becker. Also in the team were their associ-

ates, the hispanic Victor Sifuentes, new arrival Abby Perkins and Roxanne Melman, Becker's maternal secretary. Grace Van Owen was Kuzak's Deputy DA girlfriend who sometimes had to oppose him in the courtroom. Black lawyer Jonathan Rollins and mentally retarded office boy Benny Stulwicz were added later.

Political and romantic ambitions punctuated the legal activities of the company, with associates vying to become partners and workmates trying to become bedmates. Abby set up on her own but found life hard away from the practice and soon returned. New litigator Roz Shays was brought in and proved too disruptive, before she fell into an empty elevator shaft and was killed, and Grace became a judge, but decided she preferred attorney work and packed it in to join the firm. Later Kuzak left to form his own company, resulting in a name change for the firm to McKenzie, Brackman, Chaney and Becker, and the arrival of three new attorneys. They were freelancer Tommy Mullaney, his former wife, Zoey, and English litigation lawyer C.J. Lamb.

Combining soapy storylines with responsible handling of touchy subjects like AIDS and racial abuse, *LA Law* also proved that TV lawyers were not infallible. Like the cops on Hill Street, the legal eagles in LA were not always successful. In the UK, the series was dropped by ITV in 1992, but further episodes were seen on Sky One.

LAMBERT, VERITY (1935–)

Verity Lambert was one of Britain's earliest female producers. She was the first producer (1963–5) of **Doctor Who** and was fundamental in establishing the series as a popular 'bug-eyed monster' show, instead of the educational series its creator Sydney Newman intended. Lambert was also the first producer of **The Newcomers**, then, in 1966, she co-created and produced **Adam Adamant Lives!** In 1968 she worked on **Detective** and, in 1969, produced *W Somerset Maugham*, a series of stories by the famous author, before moving to LWT, where she was responsible for **Budgie**. Later Head of Drama at Thames and an executive with Euston Films, Lambert nurtured **Minder** from its shaky beginnings into a classic and had other hits with series like **Rock Follies** and **Hazell**, and the trilogy *The Norman Conquests*. She now runs her own independent production company, Cinema Verity, makers of *Coasting*, **Boys from the Bush**, **GBH**, **May to December**, *Sleepers*, *Class Act*, *She's Out* and the ill-fated **Eldorado**.

LAME DUCKS

UK (BBC) Situation Comedy. BBC 2 1984–5

Brian Drake	John Duttine

Tommy	Patric Turner
Angie	Lorraine Chase
Maurice	Tony Millan
Ansell	Brian Murphy
Mrs Drake	Primi Townsend
Mrs Kelly	Cyd Hayman

Creator/Writer: Peter J. Hammond. Producer: John B. Hobbs

A man on the brink of divorce sells his house and moves to the country, taking a motley band of losers with him.

Brian Drake, hit by a lorry and convalescing in hospital, was told by his wife that she wanted a divorce. On release, he sold his house and took off with the proceeds to find a new home in the country. Accompanying him was a reformed arsonist, Tommy, whom he met in hospital, and soon they were joined by the promiscuous Angie and Maurice, a postman who wanted to walk around the world on a 6 ft ball. Completing this collection of lame ducks was Ansell, the incompetent private eye sent by Drake's wife to track him down. They all moved into a cottage in the village of Scar's Edge, where Mrs Kelly was their glamorous but somewhat unpredictable neighbour. For the second series, the setting had changed to a disused railway station at Stutterton Stop.

Lame Ducks was the first venture into comedy by drama writer P.J. Hammond, the creator of *Sapphire and Steel* amongst other programmes.

LAND OF THE GIANTS

US (20th Century-Fox/Irwin Allen) Science Fiction. ITV 1968–

Captain Steve Burton	Gary Conway
Mark Wilson	Don Matheson
Barry Lockridge	Stefan Arngrim
Dan Erikson	Don Marshall
Commander Alexander Fitzhugh	Kurt Kasznar
Valerie Scott	Deanna Lund
Betty Hamilton	Heather Young
Inspector Kobrick	Kevin Hagen

Creator/Executive Producer: Irwin Allen

The crew and passengers of a stricken airliner find themselves stranded on a planet inhabited by giants.

In 1983 a sub-orbital commercial flight from America to London flew through a mysterious cloud and crash-landed on a planet resembling Earth but which was home to people 12 times normal height. The series followed the space castaways' efforts to repair their ship, the *Spindrift*, and return home, while fending off monster insects and animals, or fleeing from the giants, who wanted them for experiments.

The crew were Captain Steve Burton, his co-pilot, Dan Erikson, and stewardess Betty Hamilton. The passengers were engineering executive Mark Wilson, wealthy heiress Valerie Scott, 12-year-old Barry Lockridge and Barry's dog, Chipper. There was one joker in the pack, however, the intriguing, unscrupulous Commander Fitzhugh. Their adversaries in the Land of the Giants were headed by Inspector Kobrick, who worked for the SIB security service.

The series was noted for its elaborate special effects (particularly the use of giant-size props) and was created by Irwin Allen, the inspiration behind *Voyage to the Bottom of the Sea*, *The Time Tunnel* and the similar *Lost in Space*. It was repeated on Channel 4 from 1989.

LANDAU, MARTIN (1928–)

American actor, the husband of Barbara Bain, who starred with him in his two big successes, *Mission: Impossible* (in which he played Rollin Hand) and *Space: 1999* (Commander John Koenig). Previously, Landau had guested on episodes of *The Twilight Zone*, *Bonanza*, *I, Spy* and *The Wild, Wild West*, but has found little work of note in recent years, save the odd TV movie.

LANDEN, DINSDALE (1932–)

British character actor in comedy as well as straight drama. The highlights of his TV career have been the part of Pip in *Great Expectations* and the title roles in *Mickey Dunne* and *Devenish*. He also starred as Barty Wade in *Pig in the Middle* and appeared in *The Mask of Janus*, *The Glittering Prizes* and *Arms and the Man*.

LANDON, MICHAEL (EUGENE OROWITZ; 1936–91)

American actor, writer, director and producer, who entered the business through bit parts in the 1950s, an injury having brought to an end a promising sports career. He starred in the cult movie *I Was a Teenage Werewolf* and took parts in series like *Wanted Dead or Alive* and *Tales of Wells Fargo*, before he was spotted by David Dortort, creator of *Bonanza*, and pitched into the role of Little Joe Cartwright which was to last for 14 years. When Bonanza ended, Landon (who had already gained behind-the-camera experience in the series) created a programme of his own, *Little House on the Prairie*, in which he also starred (as dad Charles Ingalls). When *Little House* finished after eight years, Landon's versatility proved itself yet again as he launched into another of his own productions, **Highway to Heaven**, playing probationary angel Jonathan Smith. The series ended in 1988 and Landon, the producer, followed it with the prime-time series *Father Murphy*, plus a few TV movies. He died in 1991.

LANE, CARLA

Liverpudlian comedy writer whose first major success was **The Liver Birds**, created with her former scripting partner, Myra Taylor. With Taylor, Lane also contributed numerous episodes to **Bless this House** before embarking on a string of hits of her own. These have included *No Strings*, *The Last Song*, **Solo**, **The Mistress**, *Butterflies*, *Leaving*, *I Woke Up One Morning*, **Bread**, *Screaming*, **Luv** and *Searching*. Much of her work has focused on mid-life crises and, in particular, the pressures on a woman, with pathos mixing readily with humour throughout.

LANG, BELINDA (1955–)

Dark-haired British actress, the daughter of former quiz show host Jeremy Hawk. Amongst her more prominent roles have been Kate in **Dear John**, Liza in **Second Thoughts**, Agatha Troy in **The Inspector Alleyn Mysteries** and Bill Porter in **2 Point 4 Children**. Other credits have included *To Serve Them All My Days*, *The Cabbage Patch*, *The Bretts*, *Bust* and **Stay Lucky** (as Lady Karen).

LANGFORD, BONNIE (1964–)

Flame-haired singer, dancer and actress, a former child star seen on **Opportunity Knocks!** (aged six), *Junior Showtime* and as Violet Elizabeth Bott in **Just William**. Later credits have included *The Hot Shoe Show* and **Doctor Who**, in which she played Mel, one of his assistants.

LANGRISHE, CAROLINE (1958–)

British actress probably best known as auctioneer Charlotte Cavendish in **Lovejoy** but with a TV career stretching back to the mid-1970s. She appeared in **The Glittering Prizes**, Anna Karenina and **The Brothers**, as well as playing Jane in the **Play for Today** productions **The Flipside of Dominick Hide** and **Another Flip for Dominick**. She was also Kate in *Pulaski*. **Fortunes of War**, **The Return of Shelley**, *Boon*, **Trainer** and **Cluedo** have been other credits.

LANSBURY, ANGELA, CBE (1925–)

Respected British actress, enjoying a late lease of life as novelist-cum-amateur sleuth Jessica Fletcher in **Murder, She Wrote**. Lansbury's show-business debut came after she was evacuated out of England in 1940. Three years later, she caught the eye in *Gaslight* and embarked on a successful film career. Television work beckoned in the 1950s, with appearances in assorted plays and anthology series, but she soon moved onto the stage instead, notching up hits on Broadway, breaking off in between for more film work. She returned to the small screen in the 1980s, taking parts in some TV movies before being offered her most celebrated role to date, as the perceptive Miss Fletcher, in 1984.

LA PLANTE, LYNDA (LYNDA TITCHMARSH; 1946–)

Liverpudlian actress turned dramatist, making a major impression with her first TV offering, **Widows**. She followed this up with *Widows 2* and then the highly acclaimed **Prime Suspect** series of police dramas. Her other work has included *Framed*, *Civvies* and *Comics*, as well as *She's Out*, the 1995 revival of **Widows**. Also in 1995, La Plante scripted The Governor, the first major series from her own production company, La Plante Productions.

LARAMIE

US (Revue) Western. BBC 1959–64

Slim Sherman	John Smith
Andy Sherman	Bobby Crawford, Jnr
Jess Harper	Robert Fuller
Jonesy	Hoagy Carmichael
Mike Williams	Dennis Holmes
Daisy Cooper	Spring Byington
Gandy	Don Durant
Mort Corey	Stuart Randall

Two friends run a ranch and trading post in the Wild West.

In the 1870s Slim Sherman and his 14-year-old brother, Andy, were orphaned by an outlaw who shot their father on their Wyoming ranch. Rather than leave, they decided to keep up the estate and, with the help of an old friend, Jonesy (played by songwriter Hoagy Carmichael) and Jess Harper, a drifter who put down roots, they set about scratching out a living from the never-too-fruitful property. Andy was eventually written out, and Jonesy left after a year or so, leaving Slim and Jess as partners. As well as raising cattle, they offered a staging post for traffic on the Great Overland Mail Stage Line, which ensured that a host of interesting and troublesome characters passed their way. Later additions to the cast were young Mike Williams, who had been orphaned by Indians, housekeeper Daisy Cooper and ranch hand Gandy. The town sheriff, Mort Corey, was also seen on a regular basis.

LARBEY, BOB see Esmonde, John.

LARGE, EDDIE (EDDIE MCGINNIS; 1942–)

As his stage name suggests, the bigger half of the Manchester comedy duo Little and Large, with Syd Little. Discovered on *Opportunity Knocks!* in 1971, the pair later worked on *Crackerjack*, the impressionists' show *Who Do You Do?* and their own prime time series for Thames (*The Little and Large Telly Show*) and then the BBC (*The Little and Large Show*). They have also been guest stars in numerous variety programmes and game shows.

LARKINS, THE

UK (ATV) Situation Comedy. ITV 1958–60; 1963–4

Alf Larkin	David Kossoff
Ada Larkin	Peggy Mount
Eddie Larkin	Shaun O'Riordan
Joyce Roger	Ruth Trouncer
Jeff Roger	Ronan O'Casey
Sam Prout	George Roderick
Hetty Prout	Barbara Mitchell
Myrtle Prout	Hilary Bamberger
Vicar	Charles Lloyd Pack
Osbert Rigby-Soames	Hugh Paddick
Mrs Gannett	Hazel Coppen

Creator/Writer: Fred Robinson. Producers: Bill Ward, Alan Tarrant

Life with a lively Cockney family.

The Larkins were hen-pecked but shrewd dad Alf, his battleaxe wife, Ada, unemployable son, Eddie, daughter, Joyce, and her American husband, Jeff Roger, an out-of-work writer of cowboy comics. They lived at 66 Sycamore Street, somewhere in the London suburbs and Alf worked in the canteen at a plastics factory. Also seen were snoopy neighbour Hetty Prout, her husband, Sam, and their daughter, Myrtle. Together they found themselves in a variety of farcical situations that proved popular with viewers at the turn of the 1960s (so much so that a spin-off film, *Inn for Trouble*, was released in 1959 and saw the Larkins in charge of a country pub). In the last series, shown three years after the main run, Sycamore Street had been demolished, Alf and Ada (now alone) took over a café and gained a lodger, Osbert Rigby-Soames.

Shaun O'Riordan, who played Eddie Larkin, went on to be one of ATV's major drama and comedy producers, with *George and the Dragon* (again starring Peggy Mount) and *Sapphire and Steel* among his credits.

LARSON, GLEN A.

Highly successful American writer, producer and director, working on such hits as *It Takes a Thief*,

The Virginian, *Alias Smith and Jones*, *McCloud*, *The Six Million Dollar Man*, *Quincy*, *Battlestar Galactica*, *Magnum PI* and *Knight Rider*, many as creator. In the 1950s, he was a member of the Four Preps vocal group, who had three UK hits, most notably 'Big Man'.

LA RUE, DANNY (DANIEL PATRICK CARROLL; 1927–)

Britain's most famous drag artist, Danny La Rue (actually born in Ireland) was almost a regular on *The Good Old Days* and other variety shows in the 1960s and 1970s. His other TV work has been confined to guest appearances and adaptations of his stage shows.

LASSIE

US (Lassie Television) Children's Adventure. ITV 1956–

Jeff Miller	Tommy Rettig
Ellen Miller	Jan Clayton
Gramps Miller	George Cleveland
Sylvester 'Porky' Brockway	Donald Keeler
Matt Brockway	Paul Maxey
Timmy Martin	Jon Provost
Doc Weaver	Arthur Space
Ruth Martin	Cloris Leachman
	June Lockhart
Paul Martin	Jon Shepodd
	Hugh Reilly
Uncle Petrie Martin	George Chandler
Boomer Bates	Todd Ferrell
Cully Wilson	Andy Clyde
Corey Stuart	Robert Bray
Bob Erickson	Jack De Mave
Scott Turner	Jed Allan
Garth Holden	Ron Hayes
Ron Holden	Skip Burton
Mike Holden	Joshua Albee
Dale Mitchell	Larry Wilcox
Keith Holden	Larry Pennell
Lucy Baker	Pamelyn Ferdin
Sue Lambert	Sherry Boucher

Executive Producers: Robert Maxwell, Jack Wrather. Producers: Rudy Abel, Sherman Harris, Bob Golden, William Beaudine Jnr, Bonita Granville Wrather

An intelligent and heroic collie dog saves lives and averts disasters.

In this long-running series, based on the 1943 film *Lassie Come Home*, starring Elizabeth Taylor and Roddy McDowall, the lovable Lassie moved from owner to owner. Initially, she lived with young Jeff Miller and his widowed mother and grandfather on a farm near the town of Calverton. When the Millers moved to the city, Lassie was taken in by the Martin family, who had bought the farm, with Lassie's best friend now Timmy, an adopted orphan. The next home for

Lassie was provided by old-timer Cully Wilson, after the Martins had emigrated to Australia, but he suffered a heart-attack and Lassie's new master became ranger Corey Stuart. After a few years, Corey was hurt in a fire and care of the collie was handed on to two of his colleagues, Scott Turner and Bob Erickson, though Lassie was already beginning to find her own freedom. Eventually, she became a real loner and took to wandering across the USA. At one point, she gave birth to a litter of pups. The last *Lassie* series saw the dog at home with a new family, the Holdens, whose friends were Sue Lambert, a vet, and deaf girl Lucy Baker.

An animated version, *Lassie's Rescue Rangers*, was also produced, before a revival *The New Lassie* appeared in 1989. In this series Lassie lived in California with the McCulloch family, whose Uncle Steve was really young Timmy from the earliest episodes (actor Jon Provost), now grown up and using his real name (Timmy had been a name given to him as an orphan).

Throughout the run, the storylines were always much the same – heartwarming tales of Lassie saving the day, looking after the injured and raising the alarm in times of trouble. Despite her name (and the birth of the pups), Lassie was always played by a male collie. She was created by author Eric Knight.

LAST OF THE BASKETS, THE

UK (Granada) Situation Comedy. ITV 1971–2

Bodkin	Arthur Lowe
Clifford Basket	Ken Jones
Mrs Basket	Patricia Hayes

Creator/Writer: John Stevenson. Producer: Bill Podmore

A factory worker inherits an earldom and all its debts.

When the 12th Earl of Clogborough decided to abdicate after 93 years of holding the title, an heir to the earldom had to be found. It turned out to be Clifford Basket, a boiler tender in a northern factory and an unlikely peer if ever there was. Sadly, what the uncouth Clifford inherited was a run-down mansion and an ever-increasing mound of unpaid bills. At least Bodkin, the Earl's last remaining servant, was still around to guide the unfortunate Basket through his new, demanding lifestyle. The setting was the fictitious Little Clogborough-in-the-Marsh and two series were produced.

LAST OF THE SUMMER WINE

UK (BBC) Situation Comedy. BBC 1 1973–

Norman Clegg	Peter Sallis
Compo Semini	Bill Owen
Blamire	Michael Bates
Foggy Dewhurst	Brian Wilde
Seymour Utterthwaite	Michael Aldridge
Nora Batty	Kathy Staff
Wally Batty	Joe Gladwin
Sid	John Comer
Ivy	Jane Freeman
Wesley Pegden	Gordon Wharmby
Edie Pegden	Thora Hird
Howard	Robert Fyfe
Marina	Jean Fergusson
Pearl	Juliette Kaplan
Glenda	Sarah Thomas
Barry	Mike Grady
Eli	Danny O'Dea
Smiler	Stephen Lewis
Auntie Wainwright	Jean Alexander

Creator/Writer: Roy Clarke. Producers: James Gilbert, Bernard Thompson, Sydney Lotterby, Alan J.W. Bell

Three geriatric delinquents while away their retirement in a series of childish games and pranks.

Last of the Summer Wine has become one of British television's longest running comedies, beginning as a *Comedy Playhouse* presentation in 1973 and then emerging as a series in its own right the same year. Filmed in the Yorkshire village of Holmfirth, it has focused on three mischievous but lovable pensioners who pass their twilight years energetically engaging themselves in assorted romps and antics. The original trio were the seedy, tramp-like Compo Semini, laconic widower (and lifelong Co-op furniture operative) Norman 'Cleggy' Clegg and former Royal Signals sergeant Blamire. When actor Michael Bates was taken ill, Blamire was replaced by another ex-military man, army sign writer Foggy Dewhurst, who, in turn, was substituted for a few years by schoolteacher turned crackpot inventor Seymour Utterthwaite.

As the men have lurched from scrape to scrape, desperately trying to keep them in check have been the disapproving local womenfolk, particularly the redoubtable Nora Batty, the object of Compo's desires in her wrinkled stockings. Also seen in this battle of the sexes have been Wally, Nora's hen-pecked late husband, Seymour's sister, Edie, and her mechanic husband, Wesley, and fiery Pearl and her wimpy husband, Howard (with the brassy Marina as his fancy woman). Howard's Auntie Wainwright, the junk shop owner who never misses a sale, has also been in the action, as have café-proprietor Ivy, and her late husband, Sid. Edie's daughter, Glenda, and her husband, Barry, the short-sighted Eli and the inappropriately-named Smiler (Nora's browbeaten lodger) have also contributed.

In 1988 the series spawned a prequel, which showed the old folk in their formative years. Entitled *First of the Summer Wine*, it featured Peter Sallis as Cleggy's dad, with David Fenwick as the young Norman, Paul Wyett as Compo, Richard Lumsden as Foggy and Paul McLain as Seymour.

LATE, LATE BREAKFAST SHOW, THE

UK (BBC) Entertainment. BBC 1 1982–6

Presenters: Noel Edmonds, Mike Smith

Producer: Michael Hurll

Saturday evening collection of silly stunts, pranks and gags.

A halfway house between **Multi-Coloured Swap Shop** and **Noel's Houseparty**, *The Late, Late Breakfast Show* represented Noel Edmonds's successful transition from children's TV to adult programming. Despite becoming popular for regular features like The Hit Squad (hidden camera jokes staged by former *Candid Camera*man Peter Dulay), bizarre contests like Mr Puniverse and a feature on out-takes entitled The Golden Egg Awards, the series is unfortunately now best-remembered for the death of a member of the public in one of the show's action sequences. In a section entitled Give it a Whirl, a willing viewer was chosen each week to attempt (with prior training) a daredevil stunt for a live outside broadcast hosted by Mike Smith. Sadly, one 'Whirly Wheeler' was killed during practice for a high-rise escapology trick. This led to major ructions within the BBC and the inevitable cancellation of the series after four years on air. The programme's theme music was provided by Gary Kemp of the pop group Spandau Ballet.

LATE NIGHT LINE-UP see *Line-Up*.

LATHAM, PHILIP (1929–)

British actor, familiar in the 1960s and 1970s through his portrayals of Wally Izzard in **Mogul** and **The Troubleshooters** and *Plantagenet Palliser* in **The Pallisers**. Amongst his many other credits have been *The Cedar Tree*, **Maigret**, **Sergeant Cork**, *Justice*, *Love Story*, *Killers*, **Hammer House of Horror**, *Doctor Who*, *No. 10*, **Nanny** and **The Professionals**.

LAUGH TRACK

Also known as canned laughter. Pre-recorded audience laughter that is added to programmes (particularly filmed programmes) to provide atmosphere. Studio-produced shows generally have live audiences which are 'warmed up' before recording starts.

LAURIE, HUGH (1959–)

Eton- and Cambridge-educated actor who rowed in the 1980 Boat Race and starred alongside Emma Thompson, Tony Slattery and others in the 1981 Footlights Revue. It was at Cambridge that Laurie joined forces with Stephen Fry with whom he entered television in the Granada sketch show *Alfresco*. There followed appearances in **The Young Ones**, **Happy Families**, *Saturday Live* and, most prominently, **Blackadder** (as Prince George in **Blackadder the Third** and Lt George in **Blackadder Goes Forth**). The duo also appeared in their own sketch show, *A Bit of Fry and Laurie*, and in Granada's dramatization of **Jeeves and Wooster** (with Laurie finding his niche as the classic upper-class twit Bertie Wooster). Laurie has also successfully undertaken serious parts, as in the drama **All Or Nothing At All**.

LAURIE, JOHN (1897–1980)

As Mr Frazer, the gloomy, penny-pinching undertaker, in **Dad's Army**, John Laurie became a household name, 'We're doomed' becoming his catchphrase. But this rolling-eyed, Scottish actor had already enjoyed decades of showbusiness success by the time the small screen beckoned. Some viewers will recall him in the classic Hitchcock version of *The Thirty-Nine Steps* back in 1935, just one of his dozens of film roles, in addition to extensive stage work. Laurie was also seen on television in the 1930s, though his first major role didn't arrive until 1961, when he played the thriller writer Algernon Blackwood in hosting the anthology series *Tales of Mystery*. In 1966 he was the mad scientist, McTurk, in the kids' adventure series *The Master*, and also appeared in **Dr Finlay's Casebook** in the 1960s, before joining the **Dad's Army** troupe in 1968.

LAVENDER, IAN (1946–)

British actor, usually in comic roles, and easily best remembered for his portrayal of young Frank Pike, the mummy's boy in **Dad's Army**. As Clive Cunliffe, he was stranded in space with Mollie Sugden in the unsuccessful *Come Back Mrs Noah*, played Ginger in *Mr Big*, gormless Ron in the revival of the radio series *The Glums* for Bruce Forsyth's *Big Night* (and later their own short series), and Tom, the dentist, in the sitcom *Have I Got You . . . Where You Want Me?*

LAVERNE AND SHIRLEY

US (Paramount/Miller-Milkis) Situation Comedy. ITV 1977–

Laverne De Fazio	Penny Marshall
Shirley Feeney	Cindy Williams
Carmine Ragusa	Eddie Mekka
Frank De Fazio	Phil Foster
Andrew 'Squiggy' Squigman	David L. Lander

Lenny Kosnowski	Michael McKean
Edna Babish/De Fazio	Betty Garrett
Sonny St Jacques	Ed Marinaro
Rhonda Lee	Leslie Easterbrook

Creator: Garry K. Marshall. Executive Producers: Thomas L. Miller, Edward K. Milkis, Garry K. Marshall. Producers: Lowell Ganz, Tony Marshall, Mark Rothman

Two incident-prone girl flatmates work at a brewery but long for something better.

Laverne De Fazio and Shirley Feeney worked in the bottling section of the Shotz brewery in Milwaukee in the late 1950s. They also roomed together in the basement of a town house. They were ambitious, sought fun and fame, but were always short of cash. Tall Laverne (sporting a large, looping 'L' on her sweater) was rather loud, but very insecure. Petite, dark-haired Shirley was naive and easily taken in. Together they lurched from scrape to scrape.

Their friends featured prominently, particularly the womanizing Carmine, Shirley's on-off boyfriend who liked to be known as 'The Big Ragu' and was always liable to burst into his signature song, 'Rags To Riches'. There were also the well-meaning but very dim brewery truck drivers, Squiggy and Lenny. Laverne's father, Frank, owned the Pizza Bowl, the hangout where the girls bowled and danced. He later married Mrs Babish, Laverne and Shirley's landlady.

Well into its run, *Laverne and Shirley* changed location. It was now the early 1960s and the action had moved to California, where Laverne and Shirley were seeking a career in films. True to form, they ended up working only as shop assistants, in Bardwell's Department Store. All the friends moved with them and a couple of new neighbours, Rhonda, a dancer and model, and Sonny, a stuntman, were introduced. Laverne's father and new stepmother took over a restaurant, Cowboy Bill's. A couple of years later, after a dispute over working hours, actress Cindy Williams asked to be written out and Shirley was married off to army doctor Walter Meany. The show continued for one last season with just Penny Marshall starring and Laverne now working at the Ajax Aerospace Company.

Laverne and Shirley was a very successful spin-off from **Happy Days**, in which the girls had made a couple of fleeting appearances. Penny Marshall was the sister of *Happy Days* creator Gary Marshall and has since made a name for herself as a Hollywood director. 'Making Our Dreams Come True', the theme song performed by Cyndi Grecco, was an American hit single in 1976. The series, originally seen sporadically around the ITV network, has also been re-run on the BBC as a daytime filler.

British leading man in Hollywood, a former child actor and the star of numerous films from the 1930s. His major television role was as Nick Charles in **The Thin Man**, though he also appeared in a US comedy entitled *Dear Phoebe*. He was once married to President John F. Kennedy's sister, Pat.

LAWLEY, SUE (1946–)

Midlands-born journalist and current affairs presenter, originally seen on **Nationwide** and *Tonight*. She has also chaired **Question Time**, the BBC right to reply programme Biteback and other debates, stood in for Terry Wogan on his chat show, read the main BBC news bulletins and presented some interview shows for ITV. She is currently host of the radio series *Desert Island Discs*.

LAWRENCE, JOSIE (WENDY LAWRENCE)

British actress and comedienne, one of the stars of the improvisation series **Whose Line Is It Anyway?** Previously, Lawrence had been seen on *Friday Night Live* (with her Florence from Cradley characterization) and amongst her other appearances have been parts in **Poirot**, Harry Enfield's *Norbert Smith – A Life, The Green Man* (as Lucy) and the kids' comedy *Jackson Pace: The Great Years*. She was Janet Wilkins in the apocalyptic comedy *Not with a Bang*, Lottie in the feature length film *Enchanted April*, Maggie Costello in the cricketing comedy *Outside Edge* and Sophie in *Downwardly Mobile*. She has also starred in her own series, *Josie*.

LAWSON, DENIS (1947–)

Scottish actor seen on TV as DJ Kit Curran in *The Kit Curran Radio Show*, Eddie Cass in the thriller *Dead Head* and Rossi in *The Justice Game*. Other credits include **Bergerac**, *That Uncertain Feeling* and *El C.I.D.*

LAYTON, GEORGE (1943–)

British actor, comedian and writer, his earliest appearances coming as striker Jimmy Stokes in the soccer soap **United!** and as Paul Collier in the various *Doctor* series (some episodes of which he also wrote). Layton was one of the first three presenters of **That's Life** (with Esther Rantzen and Bob Wellings) and played Bombardier Solomons in the earlier seasons of **It Ain't Half Hot Mum**. He was Brian Booth in *My Brother's Keeper* (again also as writer), popped up now and again as Des in **Minder** and the Aussie crook, Ray, in **The Sweeney** and hosted the quiz show *Pass the Buck*. Amongst his other writing credits have been **Don't Wait Up** and *Executive Stress*, and episodes of **On the Buses** and **Robin's Nest**.

LE MESURIER, JOHN (JOHN ELTON HALLILEY; 1912–83)

Elegant British character actor, immortalized as the ineffective Sgt Wilson in Dad's Army but a prominent performer on TV for four decades. He was a regular guest on *Hancock's Half Hour*, appeared as Colonel Maynard in *George and the Dragon*, starred as the hard-up aristocrat Lord Bleasham in *A Class By Himself,* and his performance in the Dennis Potter play *Traitor*, based on the spy Kim Philby, was much acclaimed. Le Mesurier (his stage name was his mother's maiden name) was also seen in such programmes as *The Avengers*, *The Troubleshooters*, *The Goodies*, *Doctor at Large*, *Worzel Gummidge* and *Brideshead Revisited* and his voice was as familiar as his face, thanks to numerous Homepride flour commercials and the children's animation *Bod*, for which he was narrator. His second wife was comedienne Hattie Jacques.

LE VAILLANT, NIGEL

British actor born in Pakistan. Oxford-educated, Le Vaillant has performed Shakespeare on stage and on television is best known as Dr Julian Chapman in *Casualty*, Simon in *Honey for Tea* and Paul Dangerfield in *Dangerfield*. Other credits have included *Brideshead Revisited*, *Jemima Shore Investigates*, *Christabel*, *Call Me Mister*, *Wish Me Luck*, *Poirot*, *Minder*, *Hannay*, *Ladies in Charge* and *Poor Little Rich Girls*.

LEACH, ROSEMARY (1935–)

British actress much seen on television as a supporting player in sitcoms and straight drama, but also with a few notable starring parts to her name. She appeared with Ronnie Corbett in *No – That's Me Over Here*, *Now Look Here . . .* and *The Prince of Denmark*, was Sadie Potter in *Sadie It's Cold Outside*, Queen Victoria in *Disraeli*, Katy Bunting, a late first-time mother, in *Life Begins at Forty*, and swindled widow Joan Plumleigh-Bruce in *The Charmer*. The 1971 version of *Cider with Rosie* gave her another chance to shine and amongst other credits have been parts in *Armchair Theatre* productions and other plays, *The Power Game*, *Rumpole of the Bailey*, *The Jewel in the Crown*, *Jackanory*, *The Roads to Freedom*, *When We Are Married*, *Summer's Lease*, *Titmuss Regained* and a number of TV adaptations of classics.

LEAR, NORMAN (1926–)

Prolific and influential American producer, a former scriptwriter who, in the 1970s, was responsible for introducing a more adult attitude to American situation comedy. The break came with *All in the Family* and its outspoken, bigoted lead character Archie Bunker, based on *Till Death Us Do Part* and Alf Garnett. The series was a huge hit and broke new grounds in exploring what was acceptable in American television. Its spin-offs *Maude* and *The Jeffersons* were just as challenging to the 'honey I'm home' tradition of US comedies, as was *Sanford and Son* (another UK clone, this time of *Steptoe and Son*). Lear was also responsible for the cult comedy *Mary Hartman, Mary Hartman* and became a shrewd media businessman. Much of his early TV (and film) work was in collaboration with Bud Yorkin.

LEARNING CHANNEL, THE (TLC)

Owned by Discovery Communications Inc., the parent company of The Discovery Channel, TLC has broadcast from the Astra 1C satellite since October 1994 and via cable since February 1992. Its seven hours-a-day programming embraces a practical 'hands-on' approach, encouraging adults – this is not a schools channel – to get more out of life by improving their DIY, learning new skills and techniques, and developing new interests and hobbies. Programmes on guitar for beginners, watercolour painting, improving your golf swing, better wall papering and decorating cakes are combined with in-depth documentaries on more serious matters like how to cope with domestic violence, terminal illness or delinquency. The channel slogan is 'From viewing to doing'.

LEIGH, MIKE (1943–)

British writer and director, noted for comedies derived from social observation (particularly of the middle classes) with a strong leaning on his actors' improvisation skills, including those of his wife, Alison Steadman. His most acclaimed works have been *Nuts in May* (1976) and *Abigail's Party* (1977), with other credits including *Hard Labour* (1973), *Kiss of Death* (1977), *Grown-Ups* (1980) and *Home Sweet Home* (1982).

LENNY THE LION SHOW, THE

UK (BBC) Children's Entertainment. BBC 1956–63

Producer: Ronald Eyre, Johnny Downes, Peter Whitmore

Fun, games and pop music with a soppy ventriloquist's lion.

Ventriloquist Terry Hall and his Lenny the Lion puppet were one of the hottest properties in children's television in the late 1950s and early 1960s. Somewhat languid in his appearance, failing to pronounce his 'r's', and prone to burying his maned head in his paw, the wide-eyed Lenny was unusual in being an animal dummy rather than the run-of-the mill talking boy. He was also one of the first dummies to be given arm-movements, which added to his novelty factor. As well as gags, Lenny's programmes (first seen under the *Children's Television* banner), had a strong pop music element. Indeed, his 1962 series was entitled *Pops and Lenny* and listed The Beatles as guests on one occasion.

LENSKA, RULA (1947–)

Tall, flame-haired, British actress of Polish descent who first came to light in *Rock Follies* (playing 'Q' – or Nancy Cunard de Longchamps – of The Little Ladies rock band) and has since been seen in dramas and comedies like *Take a Letter, Mr Jones* (as Mrs Warner, John Inman's boss), Family Pride (as Eva), *Private Schultz*, *Minder*, *Robin of Sherwood*, *Boon*, *An Actor's Life for Me* and *Stay Lucky*. Earlier credits included *Dixon of Dock Green*, *The Brothers*, *Edward the Seventh*, *The Saint* and *Special Branch*. Her second husband is Dennis Waterman.

LEONARD, HERBERT B.

Very successful American producer, responsible initially for children's adventures such as *Circus Boy* and *The Adventures of Rin-Tin-Tin*, before capturing adult audiences with the likes of *Naked City* and *Route 66*.

LETTERMAN, DAVID (1947–)

American comedian and talk show host, a former announcer, weatherman, children's presenter and writer, who, after working with Mary Tyler Moore, eventually broke into the big time courtesy of Johnny Carson's *Tonight* (as a regular guest and stand-in host). This led indirectly to his own series, *Late Night with David Letterman*, in 1982. This cult chat show, famous for its offbeat stunts and camera trickery, has been screened in the UK on Sky One.

LEVIN, BERNARD, CBE (1928–)

Journalist and early TV critic whose television work included writing topical calypsos for *Tonight* and conducting abrasive interviews with people of various professions for *That Was The Week That Was* and its successor *Not So Much a Programme, More a Way of Life*. Never shy of confrontation, Levin was once famously punched off his stool by a member of the studio audience. On another occasion, an interviewee squirted him with a plastic lemon. His later work included *The Levin Interview* and guest spots on panel games like *Face the Music*.

LEVINSON, RICHARD (1934–87)

American executive, a writer and producer, working closely with William Link to create action series like *Columbo*, *Ellery Queen*, *Mannix*, *Banacek*, *Tenafly* and *Murder, She Wrote*, as well as many TV movies. They also contributed episodes to *Alfred Hitchcock Presents*, *The Fugitive*, *Burke's Law* and other dramas.

LEWIS, MARTYN (1945–)

Prominent Welsh newsreader and presenter, formerly with the BBC in Northern Ireland, HTV Wales and ITN but, since 1986, back at the BBC as one of its main frontmen. He has also hosted special reports, *Songs of Praise* and the daytime game show *Today's the Day*.

LEWIS, SHARI (1934–)

American ventriloquist who had her own show on British television in the 1970s, featuring her glove puppets Lamb Chop, Hush Puppy and Charlie Horse.

LIBERACE (WLADZIU VALENTINO LIBERACE; 1919–1987)

Flamboyant American pianist and entertainer whose variety shows were very popular in the 1950s and 1960s. Although he had been classically trained, 'Lee' Liberace forewent all the starchy trappings of a concert pianist and, instead, made brightly sequined costumes, shiny candelabra and a sparkling toothy smile his trademarks. He may have been panned by the critics, but he was loved by his audience and was so unperturbed by all the flak that he coined the memorable phrase 'I cried all the way to the bank'. Fully aware of his outrageous persona, Liberace was happy to camp it up in *Batman*, playing the villain Chandell. His later television work was focused on specials and guest appearances.

LIBRARY FILM

Stock footage used to illustrate a news item or another feature.

LICENCE FEE

The annual fee payable to the Government for the use of radio and television receivers in the UK. This provides the funding for the BBC. The licence (initially wireless only, of course) was introduced at ten shillings in 1922. The fee remained static until 1946, when it was doubled to £1. It has gradually increased over the years and a two-tier licence fee, for monochrome and colour viewing, was instigated in 1967, on the arrival of colour television.

LIFE AND LEGEND OF WYATT EARP, THE

US (Louis F. Edelmann/Wyatt Earp
Enterprises) Western. ITV 1956–

Wyatt Earp	Hugh O'Brian
Bat Masterson	Mason Alan Dinehart III
Ben Thompson	Denver Pyle
Abbie Crandall	Gloria Talbot
Doc Fabrique	Douglas Fowley
Marsh Murdock	Don Haggerty
Jim 'Dog' Kelly	Paul Brinegar
	Ralph Sanford
Doc Holliday	Douglas Fowley
	Myron Healey
Shotgun Gibbs	Morgan Woodward
Morgan Earp	Dirk London
Virgil Earp	John Anderson
Nellie Cashman	Randy Stuart
Old Man Clanton	Trevor Bardette
Sheriff John Behan	Lash La Rue
	Steve Brodie
Doc Goodfellow	Damian O'Flynn

Producer: Robert F. Sisk

**Early western in almost serial form,
depicting the colourful life of the famous
Marshal Wyatt Earp.**

Broadly based on fact, this series followed Wyatt
Earp's career and catalogued his encounters with
the famous outlaws of the Wild West. It began
with the murder of his friend Marshal Whitney,
and Earp agreeing to take on his badge in
Ellsworth, Kansas. The rugged lawman later
moved to Dodge City, where he confronted the
infamous Doc Holliday and was assisted by his
deputy, Bat Masterson. The mayor, Jim 'Dog'
Kelly, was also a friend and Earp's brothers Virgil
and Morgan appeared now and again (but not
Matt Dillon, who, according to **Gunsmoke**, was
also Marshal of Dodge City at that time).

In his last posting, Earp took over as Marshal of
Tombstone, Arizona, meeting some of his most
fearsome adversaries, the Clanton 'Ten Percent
Gang'. With the Tombstone sheriff, Johnny
Behan, in the pocket of Old Man Clanton, Earp
was forced to call up frontiersman Shotgun
Gibbs, a friend from Dodge City, to be his new
deputy. Doc Holliday also showed up, and the
series came to a conclusion with the celebrated
'Gunfight at the OK Corral'. Nellie Cashman,
owner of the Birdcage Saloon, was Earp's romantic attachment. Throughout the series, Earp's
trademark was a pair of 'Buntline Special' pistols
with extended barrels. They allowed him to
shoot his enemies from a long distance – very
useful when dealing with such a bad crowd.

LIFE AND LOVES OF A SHE DEVIL, THE

UK (BBC) Drama. BBC 2 1986

Ruth Patchett	Julie T. Wallace
Bobbo Patchett	Dennis Waterman
Mary Fisher	Patricia Hodge

Writer: Ted Whitehead. Producer: Sally Head

**A spurned wife uses supernatural powers
to wreak revenge on her husband and his
mistress.**

Ruth Patchett was a pathetic specimen.
Hideously ugly and devoid of self-confidence, she
discovered that her businessman husband, Bobbo,
had only married her out of pity and simply used
her to look after the kids and run the home.
When one day he walked out to live with Mary
Fisher, a best-selling authoress, in her luxurious
converted lighthouse, Ruth's hurt and anger
manifested itself supernaturally. Remembering
his parting words in which he dubbed her a 'she
devil', Ruth burned down the family home and
set out on the road of revenge. Using a selection
of disguises and identities to weave her spell,
Ruth manipulated other people into destroying
Bobbo's life and career. Along the way, she struck
a powerful blow for womankind.

The Life and Loves of a She Devil, directed by
Philip Saville and adapted in four parts from Fay
Weldon's novel by Ted Whitehead, gave
unknown actress Julie T. Wallace her big break.
'Uglied' up to fit the bill, Wallace stole the show
but wasn't asked to appear in the 1989 US film
version, *She Devil*, which starred Roseanne Barr.

LIFE AND TIMES OF GRIZZLY ADAMS, THE

US (Sunn Classic) Adventure. ITV 1978–

James Capen 'Grizzly' Adams	Dan Haggerty
Mad Jack	Denver Pyle
Nakuma	Don Shanks
Robbie Cartman	John Bishop

Executive Producer: Charles E. Sellier Jnr.
Producers: Leonard B. Kaufman, Jim Simmons,
Art Stolnitz

**Accused of a crime he did not commit, a
man flees to a satisfying life in the western
American wilderness.**

The Life and Times of Grizzly Adams was based on
the exploits of a real 19th-century refugee who
lived in the Sierra Nevada and struck up a rapport
with animals. In the TV version, Grizzly lived in
a log cabin, at one with nature, wearing only
cloth garments. He fished to eat but never hunted. He was befriended by Mad Jack (also the
show's narrator), an Indian named Nakuma and a
young lad, Robbie Cartman, who lived on a
nearby farm. Adams's constant companion was a
wild bear named Ben which he had rescued from
a ledge while still a cub. Their heartwarming
adventures were built around the call of the wild,
the trials of nature and the disruptive visits of

strangers. The real Adams died in 1860 while touring with P.T. Barnum's circus.

The series, which first aired in the USA in 1977, enjoyed a sporadic screening around the ITV network. The theme song, 'Maybe', was a UK hit for Tom Pace in 1979.

LIFE OF BLISS, A

UK (BBC) Situation Comedy. BBC 1960–1

David Bliss ....George Cole
Zoe Hunter ....Sheila Sweet
Tony Fellows ....Colin Gordon
Anne Fellows ....Isabel Dean

Creator/Writer: Godfrey Harrison. Producers: Graeme Muir, Godfrey Harrison

A shy and confused young bachelor's life is riddled with misunderstanding.

It's hard to imagine George Cole playing a bashful young bachelor prone to verbal gaffes, but that was his role in this long-running radio series which enjoyed some television exposure in 1960 and 1961. As the constantly confused David Bliss, he stumbled from one mishap to another, finding solace in the company of Psyche, his wire-haired fox terrier (barked for by Percy Edwards). Also seen were Bliss's girlfriend, Zoe, and his sister and brother-in-law, Anne and Tony Fellows.

LIFE ON EARTH

UK (BBC/Warner Brothers) Documentary. BBC 2 1979

Host/Writer: David Attenborough

Producers: Christopher Parsons, John Sparks, Richard Brock

Painstaking insight into how life forms developed on our planet.

Reflecting on the geological development of the Earth from the earliest times to the present day, naturalist/broadcaster David Attenborough lucidly explained in this ambitious series how different species of plants and animals came into being and evolved as the planet changed climate. Assisted by spectacular photography (over a million feet of film was shot) and visits to more than 30 countries in three years, Attenborough's colourful history of 3500 million years of nature won acclaim from all quarters, with probably the best remembered scene his frolics with friendly gorillas in a tropical jungle.

Life on Earth was, at the time, the biggest project ever undertaken by the BBC's Natural History Unit in Bristol and prompted three sequels, **The Living Planet** in 1984, **Trials of Life** in 1990 and *The Private Life of Plants* in 1995.

LIFE WITH THE LYONS

UK (BBC/Associated-Rediffusion) Situation Comedy. BBC 1955–6; ITV 1957–60

Ben Lyon ....Ben Lyon
Bebe Daniels Lyon ....Bebe Daniels Lyon
Barbara Lyon ....Barbara Lyon
Richard Lyon ....Richard Lyon
Aggie Macdonald ....Molly Weir
Florrie Wainwright ....Doris Rogers

Producers: Bryan Sears (BBC), Barry Baker (ITV)

At home with an American family in Britain.

The Lyons family of entertainers – dad Ben, his wife, Bebe Daniels, son, Richard and daughter, Barbara – endeared themselves to the British public by staying on in the UK during the war years, instead of fleeing back to their native USA. They remained popular in the 1950s through their BBC radio sitcom in which they played themselves. *Life with the Lyons* then transferred to television, initially on the BBC and then on ITV. Assisting the Lyons was their Scottish housekeeper, Aggie, with Florrie their nosey neighbour. Their dog was called Skeeter. Many of the scripts were penned by Bebe.

LIFE WITHOUT GEORGE

UK (BBC) Situation Comedy. BBC 1 1987–9

Jenny Russell ....Carol Royle
Larry Wade ....Simon Cadell
Amanda ....Rosalind March
Elizabeth Estensen
Ben Morris...Michael Thomas
Sammy..Kenny Ireland
Campbell Morrison
Carol ....Cheryl Maiker
Mr Harold Chambers............................Ronald Fraser
Josie..Selina Cadell

Writers: Penny Croft, Val Hudson. Executive Producer: Robin Nash. Producer: Susan Belbin

Love on the rebound for a dance instructor and an estate agent.

When George Stanton, her live-in lover of five-years' standing, walked out, Jenny Russell, owner of Russell's dance and fitness studio, was distraught. Then a one-night stand with drippy, Marmite-drinking estate agent Larry Wade set her on course for a new on-off love affair. Larry, a partner in Morris, Morris and Wade, was divorced and lived with his dog, Napoleon. Although his intentions towards Jenny were transparent, he was constantly frustrated by her memories of George and this led him to binge on cheese and onion crisps. Jenny's best friend was her neighbour, Amanda, who was having trouble with her womanizing husband, Patrick. They consoled each other. Larry's friend and business partner, Ben, was altogether more ruthless when it came to women and never failed to give Larry worthless advice. Carol was Jenny's receptionist at the studio, where senile Mr Chambers played the piano and country girl Josie was an assistant. The main social rendezvous was the local singles bar, run by gay barman Sammy. The setting was Primrose Hill.

Co-writer Penny Croft also wrote and sang the programme's theme song.

LIFT OFF/LIFT OFF WITH AYSHEA

UK (Granada) Pop Music. ITV 1969–74

Presenters: Ayshea Brough, Graham Bonney, Wally Whyton

Producer: Muriel Young

Pop music magazine for younger viewers.

Airing as part of ITV's children's programming, *Lift Off* was no rival to **Top of the Pops** but was still one of the few outlets for pop on TV in the early 1970s. Although co-hosted initially by Graham Bonney and later by Wally Whyton, the programme's star was actress Ayshea Brough (also seen in **UFO**) and, from 1972, the programme's title was changed to reflect this, becoming *Lift Off with Ayshea*. Ayshea also kept youngsters in touch with the latest pop news via a weekly column in the 'Junior *TV Times*', *Look-In*. As well as highlighting the top bands of the day, *Lift Off* also featured a resident team of dancers. It was produced, like other similar Granada pop shows – *Discothèque*, *Get It Together*, *Shang-A-Lang* and *Arrows* – by former **Five O'Clock Club** hostess Muriel Young.

LIGHT ENTERTAINMENT

The generic term given to programmes like variety shows, quizzes and comedies.

LIKELY LADS, THE/WHATEVER HAPPENED TO THE LIKELY LADS?

UK (BBC) Situation Comedy. BBC 2/BBC 1 1964–6/1973–4

Bob Ferris	Rodney Bewes
Terry Collier	James Bolam
Audrey Collier	Sheila Fearn
Thelma Ferris	Brigit Forsyth

Creators/Writers: Dick Clement, Ian La Frenais. Producers: Dick Clement (*The Likely Lads*), James Gilbert, Bernard Thompson (*Whatever Happened To*)

Life in the 1960s and 1970s with a couple of North-Eastern lads-about-town.

Bob Ferris and Terry Collier were two young pals who worked in a factory making electrical parts. Bob was ingenuous, ambitious and keen to see the good side of people (especially those in authority). Terry was a cynic, proud of his working-class roots and a true Jack-the-lad figure. Theirs was an unusual but solid friendship which saw them tour the pubs of Newcastle in search of beer and birds, chewing the fat over several pints of brown ale and ending up in all manner of scrapes, usually at Terry's instigation and against Bob's better judgement. The series became a surprise hit, even though only screened on BBC 2, but it ended after just two years. Bob, disillusioned with his lot, decided to join the army and Terry resolved to keep him company. But Bob's flat feet kept him in civvy street and he and Terry parted company.

The duo were back together again seven years later, thanks to a remarkably successful revival entitled *Whatever Happened to the Likely Lads?* With the turn of the 1970s, Bob's bourgeois dreams had begun to be realized. Now an executive on the point of marriage to his boss's daughter, Thelma (seen at the end of *The Likely Lads*), he owned his own house and had taken to holidays on the Costa Brava and Saturday nights in the trattoria. Terry, on the other hand, escaping a disastrous marriage in Germany, had not changed, except perhaps to bury himself even further into his proletarian origins and deep-rooted chauvinism. The two met up by chance on a train, inadvertently chatting to each other in the darkness of a tunnel before suddenly realizing who each other was. Their revived friendship was just as loyal, if more strained than before, with Bob and the fierce Thelma cosseting themselves with middle-class comforts and Bob kicking his heels like some latter-day Andy Capp. The lads' altered relationship echoed the social changes that had swept Britain between the 1960s and the 1970s, changes stressed time and again as they reminisced about their heyday and paid dispiriting visits to old stamping grounds that were sadly now unrecognizable or even demolished.

A feature film version was released in 1976.

LIMBO

The use of no scenery in the studio. Plain white/black flooring combines with a plain white/black background to give an infinity effect.

LINDSAY, ROBERT (1949–)

British character actor, usually in comic parts. Lindsay's television break came in 1975 with the sitcom **Get Some In**, in which he played teddy boy Jakey Smith. After sharing the spoils in this National Service comedy, Lindsay was signed up to star in a *Comedy Special* story, playing a Che

Guevara figure on the loose in Tooting. It was called **Citizen Smith** and was so successful it was given its own run. As Wolfie Smith, Lindsay enjoyed four seasons of Marxism in South-West London. He was later cast as boxer Pete Dodds in **Seconds Out**, played wheeler-dealer Mickey Noades in **Give Us a Break** and took the part of Carter in Channel 4's security guard comedy **Nightingales**, as well as topping the bill as rising political star Michael Murray in Alan Bleasdale's acclaimed **GBH**. The Jack Higgins drama **Confessional** was another of his credits and Lindsay has also been seen in numerous Shakespearean roles. In 1994 he starred opposite Alison Steadman in the two-part comedy-drama **The Wimbledon Poisoner**. His first wife was actress Cheryl Hall (also seen in **Citizen Smith**).

LINE-UP/LATE NIGHT LINE-UP

UK (BBC) Arts Magazine. BBC 2 1964–72

Presenters:
Denis Tuohy
John Stone
Michael Dean
Joan Bakewell
Nicholas Tresilian
Sheridan Morley
Tony Bilbow

Late night magazine programme covering most aspects of the arts and popular culture.

Beginning as no more than a ten-minute preamble to the evening's programmes on the fledgling BBC 2, *Line-Up* was soon extended and moved to a new, end of the evening time slot. In doing so, it became a popular arts magazine and a lively talking shop, looking at films, literature and music of all kinds on most nights of the week. Segments of the programme became series in their own right. *Film Night* began as a strand called *The Film World Past and Present*, and the adventurous late 1960s rock show, *Colour Me Pop*, was another *Late Night Line-Up* spin-off. *Disco 2* (a progressive rock show, despite its name) arrived via the same route and eventually led to the durable **Old Grey Whistle Test**.

LINK, WILLIAM (1933–) see Levinson, Richard.

LIP MIKE

A hand-held microphone for use in noisy environments like sports arenas. The mike is pressed against the mouth to eliminate much of the outside sound.

LIPMAN, MAUREEN (1946–)

Versatile British actress, usually in comedy parts. Her earliest credits include roles in *Up the*

Junction, **The Lovers**, *Rooms*, **Crown Court**, **The Sweeney** and the drama *Rogue Male*. After taking the part of Alison Holmes in the shortlived sitcom *A Soft Touch* in 1978, Lipman was given her own series, **Agony**, playing Jane Lucas, an agony aunt. As hard-up landlady Sheila Haddon she starred in **All at No. 20**, but greater praise came with her commercials for British Telecom and her characterization of the classic worry-ridden Jewish mother. Lipman has been seen in numerous plays and her stage tribute to Joyce Grenfell, *Re-Joyce!*, has also reached the small screen. She is married to playwright Jack Rosenthal.

LIPSTICK ON YOUR COLLAR

UK (Whistling Gypsy) Musical Drama.
Channel 4 1993

Pte Francis Francis	Giles Thomas
Pte Mick Hopper	Ewan McGregor
Sylvia Berry	Louise Germaine
Corporal Peter Berry	Douglas Henshall
Colonel Harry Bernwood	Peter Jeffrey
Major Wallace Hedges	Clive Francis
Major Archie Carter	Nicholas Jones
Major Johnnie Church	Nicholas Farrell
Lt. Colonel 'Truck' Trekker	Shane Rimmer
Aunt Vickie	Maggie Stead
Uncle Fred	Bernard Hill
Harold Atterbow	Roy Hudd
Lisa	Kymberley Huffman

Writer: Dennis Potter. Producer: Rosemarie Whitman

The final part of Dennis Potter's semi-autobiographical, musical trilogy which began with Pennies from Heaven and continued with The Singing Detective.

Lipstick on your Collar focused on the social changes sweeping Britain in the 1950s and particularly on the growing awareness amongst young people of their own identities. At the heart of the story was Pte Mick Hopper, a national serviceman working in War Office boredom, having to seek permission to speak and spending his days translating Russian documents as the Cold War gathered momentum. In the background, the Suez Crisis was breaking and the atom bomb proliferating. But the younger generation were now looking to the west and the exciting, glitzy possibilities off-loaded by an influential USA. While his days remained dreary, Hopper broke free in the evenings to play drums in a rock 'n' roll band. A new sexual promiscuity was pervading the country and Hopper fell for the beautiful, dark-haired Lisa, while his Welsh friend, Francis, was dangerously drawn to Sylvia, the blonde bombshell who was badly abused by her bullying husband, Corporal Berry, and agitated by the odious Harold Atterbow.

LISEMORE, MARTIN (1940–77)

British TV executive, the producer of classics like *The Pallisers* and *I, Claudius*, and other adaptations such as *How Green Was My Valley* and *Murder Most English*.

LITTLE BIG BUSINESS, A

UK (Granada) Situation Comedy. ITV 1964–5

Marcus Lieberman	David Kossoff
Simon Lieberman	Francis Matthews
Lazlo	Martin Miller
Charlie	Billy Russell
	Jack Bligh
Naomi Lieberman	Diana Coupland
	Constance Wake
Basil Crane	David Conville
Miss Stevens	Joyce Marlowe

Writer: Jack Pulman. Producer: Peter Eton

Business and family conflicts coincide at a furniture factory.

Marcus Lieberman was the proprietor of a furniture workshop and a stubborn traditionalist at heart. However, when he introduced Simon, his educated and ambitious son, into the business, he was forced to modernize his ways. Such innovation didn't please craftsmen Lazlo and Charlie either. On Simon's side was colleague Basil Crane. This series, with its light Jewish humour, followed a pilot screened in 1963 in which the role of Simon was played by James Maxwell.

LITTLE HOUSE ON THE PRAIRIE/LITTLE HOUSE: A NEW BEGINNING

US (NBC) Drama. BBC 1 1975; ITV 1976–

Charles Ingalls	Michael Landon
Caroline Ingalls	Karen Grassle
Laura Ingalls/Wilder	Melissa Gilbert
Mary Ingalls/Kendall	Melissa Sue Anderson
Carrie Ingalls	Lindsay Greenbush
	Sidney Greenbush
Isaiah Edwards	Victor French
Grace Edwards	Bonnie Bartlett
Nels Oleson	Richard Bull
Harriet Oleson	Katherine MacGregor
Nellie Oleson/Dalton	Alison Arngrim
Willie Oleson	Jonathan Gilbert
Lars Hanson	Karl Swenson
Dr Baker	Kevin Hagen
Reverend Robert Alden	Dabbs Greer
Eva Beadle/Simms	Charlotte Stewart
Ebenezer Sprague	Ted Gehring
Jonathan Garvey	Merlin Olsen
Alice Garvey	Hersha Parady
Andy Garvey	Patrick Laborteaux
Adam Kendall	Linwood Boomer
Albert Ingalls	Matthew Laborteaux
Grace Ingalls	Wendy Turnbeaugh
	Brenda Turnbeaugh
Hester Sue Terhune	Ketty Lester
Almanzo Wilder	Dean Butler
Eliza Jane Wilder	Lucy Lee Flippin
Percival Dalton	Steve Tracy
James Cooper	Jason Bateman
Cassandra Cooper	Missy Francis
Nancy Oleson	Allison Balson
Jenny Wilder (*New Beginning*)	Shannen Doherty
John Carter (*New Beginning*)	Stan Ivar
Sarah Carter (*New Beginning*)	Pamela Roylance
Jeb Carter (*New Beginning*)	Lindsay Kennedy
Jason Carter (*New Beginning*)	David Friedman
Etta Plum (*New Beginning*)	Leslie Landon

Creator: Michael Landon. Executive Producers: Michael Landon, Ed Friendly

A family struggles to make a living on the American plains in the late 19th century.

Here was a western with a difference. Instead of engaging in squabbles with Indians and bandits, the main protagonists of this series enjoyed a peaceful existence, their only fight being with nature in an effort to maintain a comfortable home. *Little House on the Prairie* was based on the autobiographical books by Laura Ingalls Wilder. She appeared as a character in the series, acting as narrator, leading viewers through the changes taking place in the Ingalls household.

The family lived on a smallholding in Walnut Grove, Plum Creek, Minnesota, in the 1870s. Head of the household was Charles Ingalls, hardworking and trustworthy. His wife, Caroline, had born him three children: Laura, her elder sister, Mary, and little Carrie, and the family owned a dog, Jack. In their efforts to scratch out a living, they were supported by their friends, the toughlooking Mr Edwards, Mr Hanson, who owned the mill, and Nels Oleson, the local shopkeeper. Edwards was later replaced by Jonathan Garvey, his wife, Alice, and son, Andy.

Over the years, the Ingalls had their ups and downs, leading to numerous cast changes. They were blessed with a fourth daughter, Grace, but tragedy struck when Mary lost her sight and was forced to attend a special blind school. There she met up with blind tutor Adam Kendall, later to be her husband. As times grew even harder, the Ingalls were forced to sell up and temporarily move to Winoka, Dakota, where they adopted a young orphan, Albert. Mary gave birth to a baby boy who was tragically killed in a fire which also took the life of Alice Garvey.

Laura married Almanzo Wilder, after becoming a teacher, and Nels Oleson's spiteful daughter, Nellie, was also married, to a Jew named Isaac Cohen who hid his religion under the name of Percival Dalton. Adam miraculously regained his sight and headed for New York to work for his father's law company, taking Mary with him. The Ingalls took in two more orphans, Charles and

Caroline Cooper, and another orphan, Nancy, was adopted by Mrs Oleson and proved to be as dislikable as her own daughter, Nellie. Meanwhile, Laura gave birth to a daughter, Rose. In the programme's final season, its star and executive producer, Michael Landon, decided to call it a day, and much rejigging was required before the show could continue. It was renamed *Little House: A New Beginning* and centred on Laura, Almanzo and little Rose. Charles sold the Little House and moved to a job in Burr Oak, Iowa, leaving the homestead to local newspaper proprietors John and Sarah Carter and their two sons.

These heartwarming tales of honest labour and strong family values were similar in flavour to those seen in **The Waltons**, but *Little House* was very much Michael Landon's baby. Not only did he star and produce, he also directed and wrote some of the episodes. The series only lasted one year after his departure. The programme, somewhat unusually, changed channels in the UK, from BBC 1 to ITV, during the course of its initial run. It was re-run on Channel 4 in the early 1990s.

LITTLE, SYD (Cyril Mead; 1942–) see Large, Eddie.

LIVE

A programme transmitted as it takes place; not pre-recorded.

LIVE AID

UK (BBC) Music. BBC 2/BBC 1 1985

Presenters: Janice Long, Richard Skinner, David Hepworth, Andy Batten-Foster, Mike Smith, Mike Ellen, Andy Kershaw, Paul Gambaccini, Steve Blacknell. Producers: John Burrowes, Trevor Dann

Legendary, big-name pop concert in aid of the African famine appeal.

Following the success of Band Aid's chart-topping charity single 'Do They Know It's Christmas?', 'Feed the World' campaigner Bob Geldof conjured up the idea for a globally transmitted live concert. This came to fruition on Saturday 13 July 1985. Beginning at noon (UK time) at Wembley Stadium and continuing through to 4 am from JFK Stadium in Philadelphia, *Live Aid* was simply the biggest rock festival ever to be staged over one day. Satellites beamed pictures from one stadium to the other so that the live audiences could view the staggered events on both sides of the Atlantic. On television, DJs interviewed the stars who urged viewers to ring in with cash pledges. A total of over £60 million was raised as a result. Status

Quo set the ball rolling with a rendition of 'Rocking All Over the World', Phil Collins appeared at both stadia, courtesy of Concorde, and the full list of acts billed to appear was as follows: at Wembley Status Quo, Style Council, Ultravox, Boomtown Rats, Adam Ant, Spandau Ballet, Elvis Costello, Nik Kershaw, Sade, Sting, Phil Collins, Julian Lennon, Howard Jones, Bryan Ferry, Paul Young, Alison Moyet, U2, Dire Straits, Queen, David Bowie, The Who, Elton John, Wham and Paul McCartney. at Philadelphia Bryan Adams, The Beach Boys, Tears For Fears, Simple Minds, The Pretenders, Santana, Pat Metheny, The Thompson Twins, Nile Rodgers, Madonna, Tom Petty, The Cars, Kenny Loggins, Neil Young, Power Station, Eric Clapton, Phil Collins, Robert Plant, Jimmy Page, Paul Martinez, Duran Duran, Patti Labelle, Hall and Oates, The Temptations, Mick Jagger, Tina Turner and Bob Dylan.

LIVER BIRDS, THE

UK (BBC) Situation Comedy. BBC 1 1969–79

Beryl Hennessey	Polly James
Dawn	Pauline Collins
Sandra Hutchinson/Paynton	Nerys Hughes
Carol Boswell	Elizabeth Estensen
Mrs Hutchinson	Mollie Sugden
Mr Hutchinson	Ivan Beavis
Mrs Hennessey	Sheila Fay
Mr Hennessey	Cyril Shaps
Paul	John Nettles
Robert	Jonathan Lynn
Mrs Boswell	Eileen Kennally
	Carmel McSharry
Lucien Boswell	Michael Angelis
Derek	Tom Chadbon
Grandad	Jack Le White
Mr Boswell	Ray Dunbobbin
Father O'Leary	Patrick McAlinney
Derek Paynton	Tom Chadbon

Creators: Carla Lane, Myra Taylor, Lew Schwarz
Producers: Sydney Lotterby, Douglas Argent, Roger Race

The ups and downs in the life of two Liverpudlian flatmates.

Seen by some as a female version of **The Likely Lads**, *The Liver Birds* centred on two perky single girls who shared a bedsit in Huskisson Road, Liverpool, where their life revolved around romance, finance and family troubles. Initially, the two girls were wacky Beryl and prissy Dawn, but that first series (resulting from a 1969 **Comedy Playhouse** pilot) ran to only three episodes. When *The Liver Birds* returned in 1971, Dawn had disappeared and in her place was the naive and ingenuous Sandra. A year later, the girls moved to a more spacious apartment and when Beryl left (to marry Robert, a Londoner played by Jonathan Lynn) at the end of the fourth season, Sandra gained a new flatmate, Carol, whose voice and dress sense both needed volume controls. Also seen over the years were Sandra's boyfriend, Paul (a pre-*Bergerac* John Nettles), her snooty mother and various members of Beryl's and Carol's families. Possibly best remembered was Carol's brother, Lucien, who kept and loved rabbits, but her Catholic mother was another notable creation, as she proved to be a forerunner of *Bread*'s Nellie Boswell (writer Carla Lane even gave her the same surname). Before the series ended, Sandra had married Derek, her vet boss, and Carol had moved in as their lodger.

Although very much associated with Carla Lane, the series was in fact co-created with her former writing partner, Myra Taylor, and Lew Schwarz, and the early episodes were script edited by Eric Idle. From the fourth season, however, Lane was in sole charge. The jaunty theme song, with its 'You dancing? You asking? I'm asking. I'm dancing' tag, was performed by The Scaffold.

Writer: David Butler, John Gorrie. Executive Producer: Tony Wharmby. Producer: Jack Williams

The colourful life of actress Lillie Langtry.

From her birth in the Channel Islands, the life of the beautiful 'Jersey Lily' was always eventful. The highlight was her scandalous relationship with Edward, Prince of Wales, although she was known to have dallied with other royals, while being married to the weak-willed Edward Langtry. In true rags-to-riches style, she rose determinedly from humble beginnings to become one of the most glamorous women of her time (the late 19th century), along the way having the honour of being the first celebrity to promote a commercial product (Pears soap). She became the darling of America and socialized closely with the likes of Oscar Wilde and James Whistler.

For this biopic, actress Francesca Annis reprised the role she had played in ATV's *Edward the Seventh* three years earlier. Over the 13 parts, she was called upon to age from 16 to 70. The series was based on the book *The Prince and the Lily*, by James Brough.

LIVING PLANET, THE

UK (BBC) Documentary. BBC 1 1984

Host: David Attenborough

Executive Producer: Richard Brock. Producer: Ned Kelly

The exhaustive follow up to *Life on Earth*.

Employing the same brilliant photography and imbued with the same infectious enthusiasm as in *Life On Earth*, David Attenborough now turned his attention away from the evolution of plants and animals and fixed his gaze instead on the way lifeforms have learned to live in the modern world. Again, there was no stinting on travel – the team filmed at the edge of volcanic craters, in the baking heat of the Sahara, and in the freezing wastes of the Arctic – to graphically portray just how well flora and fauna have learned to adapt to today's Earth with all its diverse environments. It revealed that nowhere on the planet was devoid of life.

LLOYD, INNES (1925–91)

Innovative British drama producer, for many years with the BBC, working on series like *Doctor Who* (in the Patrick Troughton era) and the anthology *Dead of Night*, as well as many one-off plays. Lloyd also contributed the mini-series *Waugh on Crime*, for the *Thirty-Minute Theatre* collection, and amongst other offerings were *The Snow Goose* (1971), *The Stone Tape*, *Day Out* (both 1972), *Sunset Across the Bay* (1974), *Orde Wingate* (1976), *An Englishman's Castle* (1978), *Speed King* (1979), *Fothergill, Going Gently* (both 1981) and *An Englishman Abroad* (1983).

LLOYD, JEREMY

British comedy actor and scriptwriter, once a cast member of *Rowan and Martin's Laugh-In*. On the writing side, in conjunction with David Croft, Lloyd was responsible for *Are You Being Served?* (and its sequel, *Grace and Favour*), *Come Back Mrs Noah*, *Oh Happy Band!* and *'Allo 'Allo*. Earlier collaboration with Jimmy Grafton resulted in scripts for *The Dickie Henderson Show* and the sitcoms *Vacant Lot* and *Mum's Boys*. Lloyd also co-devised the panel game *Whodunnit?* with Lance Percival.

LLOYD, JOHN (1951–)

Former radio producer responsible for some of the major TV comedies of the 1980s. These included *Not The Nine O'Clock News*, *Spitting Image* and the *Blackadder* series.

LLOYD, KEVIN (1949–)

Best known as *The Bill's* DC 'Tosh' Lines, English character actor Kevin Lloyd has been a familiar face on British television for some 20 years. He was Oscar in *Misfits* and Ricky in *Dear John*. His other credits have included appearances in programmes as varied as *Auf Wiedersehen, Pet*, *By The Sword Divided*, *Z Cars*, *All in Good Faith*, *The Borgias*, *Minder*, *Hazell*, *Andy Capp*, *Dempsey and Makepeace*, *Boon* and *Coronation Street*.

LLOYD, NORMAN (1914–)

American actor and producer, working closely with Alfred Hitchcock on *Alfred Hitchcock Presents* (also as director) in the 1950s. Three decades later, he reappeared in front of the cameras to take the role of Dr Daniel Auschlander in *St Elsewhere*.

LLOYD PACK, ROGER (1944–)

British character and comic actor whose greatest success has come in a supporting role, namely that of the slow-witted Trigger in *Only Fools and Horses*. However, Lloyd Pack (the son of actor Charles Lloyd Pack and father of actress Emily Lloyd) has been much seen on TV. He was David Irving in *Selling Hitler*, Jimmy Ryan in *Moving*, Albert Mason in *Spyder's Web*, Rex Regis in *Health and Efficiency*, and Owen Newitt in *The Vicar of Dibley*, and has also appeared in series like *Stay Lucky*, *Mr Bean*, *Boon*, *Inspector Morse*, *The Krypton Factor* and *The Chief*.

LNB

Low Noise Block down-converter. This attachment to satellite dishes amplifies the signals received and converts them into lower frequency signals before sending them down the cable to the satellite receiver.

LOACH, KEN (1936–)

British drama director, fond of the documentary style and responsible for emotive pieces like *Up the Junction* (1965), *Cathy Come Home* (1966), *In Two Minds* (1967), *The Rank and File* (1971), *The Price of Coal* (1977) and the series *Days of Hope*, amongst other offerings. Earlier he had worked on *Z Cars* and the serial *Diary of a Young Man*.

LOCKHART, JUNE (1925–)

American actress, primarily recalled as the mum, Ruth Martin, in early *Lassie* episodes and as another mother, Maureen Robinson, in *Lost in Space*. She was the daughter of Canadian film star Gene Lockhart.

LOCKWOOD, MARGARET, CBE (MARGARET MARY LOCKWOOD DAY 1916–1990)

British actress for whom television success arrived late. After a long and respectable career in the movies, dating back to the 1930s, Margaret Lockwood only really found her TV niche in 1971, when she donned the wig of barrister Harriet Peterson in *Justice*. Seven years earlier, she had starred in the pub series *The Flying Swan*, playing landlady Mollie Manning, and before that, in 1957, she played a similar role as Mollie Miller, proprietress of the Royalty Hotel in the drama series *The Royalty*. Lockwood also enjoyed numerous other TV drama credits, including *Pygmalion*, as early as 1948.

LOE, JUDY (1947–)

British actress, seen in comedy as well as straight drama roles and also working as a casting advisor on many series. She was Lulli in the children's drama *Ace of Wands*, Celia Kemp in the gameshow sitcom *Good Night and God Bless*, abandoned wife Alison Reynolds in *Missing from Home*, Pam in *Singles* and Elizabeth Stafford in *The Chief*. Amongst her numerous other credits have been *Z Cars*, *Man at the Top*, *Edward the Seventh*, *The Upchat Line*, *Couples*, *Miss Jones and Son*, *Ripping Yarns*, *Heartland*, *When the Boat Comes In*, *Eurocops* and *Yesterday's Dreams*. She was married to the late Richard Beckinsale.

LOGAN'S RUN

US (MGM) Science Fiction. ITV 1978

Logan	Gregory Harrison
Jessica	Heather Menzies
Rem	Donald Moffat
Francis	Randy Powell

Executive Producers: Ivan Goff, Ben Roberts. Producer: Leonard Katzman

In the 24th century, two refugees flee from certain death.

This series, based on the book by William F. Nolan and George Clayton Johnson, and the film starring Michael York, was set in the year 2319 on an Earth devastated by nuclear war. No longer one civilisation, the planet existed only as a series of individual cities, separated by stretches of wilderness. In one such city, the City of Domes, all the citizens had a wonderful lifestyle – they lived only for fun. However, there was one drawback: life was terminated at the age of 30.

Logan, a high-ranking police officer, or a Sandman as they were known, had reached the critical age and was about to undergo the 'Carousel' death ceremony when he decided to make a run for it. He was assisted by Jessica, a young rebel girl, and a humorous android, Rem, whom they met early on their travels. Together, they sought a legendary haven known as Sanctuary, but they were pursued all the way by another Sandman, Logan's former partner, Francis, as they braved the outside world and its hostile inhabitants.

LOLLIPOP LOVES MR MOLE/LOLLIPOP

UK (ATV) Situation Comedy. ITV 1971–2

Maggie Robinson ....Peggy Mount
Reg Robinson ....Hugh Lloyd
Bruce Robinson ....Rex Garner
Violet Robinson ....Pat Coombs

Creator/Writer: Jimmy Perry. Producer: Shaun O'Riordan

A husband and wife's happy little life is disrupted by their close family.

Although she was big, bold and domineering, Maggie Robinson was the perfect partner for her meek and timid husband, Reg. They gave each other the soppy nicknames referred to in the programme's title and their life together in Fulham was a peaceful one. Then, out of the blue, Reg's brother, Bruce, returned from Africa with his wife, Violet, supposedly for a few days' holiday. However, the visitors outstayed their welcome and soon upset Lollipop and Mr Mole's domestic bliss. The second series – with Bruce and Violet still in situ – aired under the truncated title of *Lollipop*.

LONDON WEEKEND TELEVISION see LWT.

LONDON'S BURNING

UK (LWT) Drama. ITV 1988–

Roland 'Vaseline' Cartwright ....Mark Arden
Mike 'Bayleaf' Wilson ....James Hazeldine
Station Officer Sidney Tate ....James Marcus
Sub-Officer John Hallam ....Sean Blowers
Tony Sanders ....Treva Etienne
Malcolm Cross ....Rupert Baker
Bert 'Sicknote' Quigley ....Richard Walsh
Leslie 'Charisma' Appleby....................Gerard Horan
Josie Ingham ....Katharine Rogers
George Green ....Glen Murphy

Colin Parrish...Stephen North
Kate Stevens ....Samantha Beckinsale
Kevin Medhurst ....Ross Boatman
Nick Georgiadis ....Andrew Kazamia
Stuart 'Recall' Mackenzie ....Ben Onwukwe
Clare ....Valerie Holliman
Jean Quigley ....Amanda Dickinson
Kelly...Vanessa Pett
Laura MacKenzie ....Ona McCracken
Maggie ....Shirley Greenwood
Marion Cartwright ....Helen Blizard
Sandra Hallam ....Kim Clifford
Geoff 'Poison' Pearce.........................Michael Garner
Billy Ray ....John Alford

Creator: Jack Rosenthal. Executive Producers: Linda Agran, Nick Elliott, Sarah Wilson. Producers: Paul Knight, Gerry Poulson

High drama with the chirpy crew of a London fire station.

The firefighters of Blue Watch B25, Blackwall made their bow in Jack Rosenthal's 1986 TV film *London's Burning*. It focused on the brave men and women of this undervalued emergency service. Watching them at home and at work, the play introduced such lively characters as Vaseline (a slippery customer), Charisma (who had none) and Sicknote (always ill). The public took to this motley crew of loafers and mickey-takers who selflessly risked life and limb, irrespective of personal problems, and a series was commissioned in 1988. It is still running and has become a stalwart of ITV's autumn Sunday night schedule.

Other members of Blue Watch – a mixture of senior firefighters and rookies – have been Sidney Tate (the father figure), Bayleaf (the mess manager who dreams of opening a restaurant), Josie and Kate (women in a predominantly man's world), Tony, Malcolm, Kevin, George and Colin. Recall (because of his photographic memory), the motorbike-loving Nick, Geoff 'Poison' Pearce and wide boy Billy Ray have been later additions. Incidents have been based on real-life events and have included plane crashes, petrol tanker explosions, tube disasters and hostel fires. The stunts have been spectacular and carefully choreographed. Actor James Hazeldine (Bayleaf) has also directed a number of episodes.

LONE RANGER, THE

US (Apex/Lone Ranger Television) Western. BBC 1956–62

The Lone Ranger..............................Clayton Moore
                                                                    John Hart
Tonto...Jay Silverheels
Dan Reid ....Chuck Courtney
Jim Blaine ....Ralph Littlefield

Creators: George W. Trendle, Fran Striker. Executive Producers: Jack Chertok, Jack Wrather. Producers: Harry Poppe, Sherman Harris

Cult western series, featuring a mysterious masked hero and his Indian companion.

The Lone Ranger's story began when a group of six Texas Rangers was ambushed by a band of outlaws known as the Butch Cavendish Hole in the Wall gang. Only one survived, John Reid, and he was nursued back to health by an Indian, Tonto, whose life Reid had already saved. Swearing to avenge the death of his colleagues, who included his own brother, Reid tracked down the killers. He then began a life as an intriguing Robin Hood character, dedicated to helping those in trouble. He wore a white hat, a black mask to conceal his identity and rode a white stallion named Silver. His loyal companion, Tonto (who rode a horse called Scout), knew him as 'Kemo Sabe', meaning 'trusty scout'.

The Lone Ranger's identity was never revealed, and, as he wandered from town to town routing villains, people were left to wonder 'Who was that masked man?', as he let out a cry of 'Hi-yo Silver' and sped away, refusing payment and gratitude for the help he had provided. The Lone Ranger did have one base which he touched from time to time, the silver mine he had owned with his dead brother. Looked after by old Jim Blaine, this provided him with the wealth to continue his travels and also the silver bullets that he used in his pistol (although the squeaky-clean Lone Ranger never shot to kill; the outlaws usually shot each other or died by accident). Occasionally, Dan Reid, John's nephew, joined the duo, riding a horse called Victor.

The Lone Ranger was played for most of its run by Clayton Moore, though John Hart took over the role for a couple of years. Jay Silverheels, the one and only TV Tonto, was a real Mohawk Indian, who later spoke out against the humbling way Indians had always been portrayed on television. The TV series followed the success of *The Lone Ranger* on American radio in the 1930s. A cartoon version was produced in the 1960s, using the same William Tell Overture by Rossini as its theme music.

LONG JOHN SILVER see *Adventures of Long John Silver, The*.

LONGTHORNE, JOE (1957–)

British singer and impressionist, well known for his take-offs of Shirley Bassey, Johnny Mathis and other vocalists. Longthorne was a regular on the kids' variety series *Junior Showtime* while a teenager in the early 1970s, and then went on to win *New Faces*, before being given his own ITV series in the late 1980s.

LOOK

UK (BBC) Natural History. BBC 1 1955–69

Host: Peter Scott

Producers: Brandon Acton-Bond, Tony Soper, Eileen Molony, Jeffrey Boswell

Innovative British wildlife series.

This pioneering, long-running, in-depth view of the natural world was presented for most of its life by the famous naturalist Peter Scott, founder of the Severn Wildfowl Trust at Slimbridge. Pre-dating Anglia's *Survival* by six years, *Look* was produced by the BBC's wildlife specialists in Bristol and a children's version was also aired. Repeats were at one time shown under the title of *Look Again*. When Scott travelled to Oceania and the Galápagos Islands, the series briefly took the title of *Faraway Look*.

LORD, JACK (JOHN JOSEPH RYAN; 1922–)

American leading man who found his niche (and fortune) as Steve McGarrett, the no-nonsense head of detectives on *Hawaii Five-O*. He played McGarrett for 12 years, making Hawaii his home in the process. An exhibited artist, Lord's other TV work has been confined to guest appearances (usually as baddies) in series like *The Untouchables*, *The FBI*, *Naked City*, *Rawhide*, *Gunsmoke*, *The Fugitive*, *Dr Kildare*, *Bonanza*, *The Man from UNCLE* and *A Man Called Ironside*, as well as the lead role in an early 1960s western series, *Stoney Burke*.

LORD PETER WIMSEY

UK (BBC) Drama. BBC 1 1972–5

Lord Peter Wimsey ....Ian Carmichael
Bunter ....Glyn Houston
Inspector Charles Parker ....Mark Eden

Producer: Richard Beynon, Bill Sellars

Classy crime solving with an elegant aristocrat.

Lord Peter Wimsey was the scourge of all murderers in the 1920s. Created in novels by Dorothy L. Sayers, he came to life in this period TV outing through the monocled impersonation of Ian Carmichael. Wimsey was prim, proper and always a gentleman, and tended to appear a bit of an upper-class twit, but this was a deliberate ploy to fool his adversaries. In truth, he possessed a sharp analytical mind, enhanced by an encyclopedic knowledge of classical music. He loved cricket, enjoyed good conversation and savoured the best food and drink, just part of the bon viveur lifestyle he pursued at his home in Piccadilly.

With never a financial worry, and desperate to restore order to an untidy world, Wimsey was regularly on hand to pick up the pieces of a murder mystery in the most unusual of settings. Invaluable on these occasions was his loyal manservant, Bunter (a former army sergeant colleague), a man who could easily mix with the lower classes and exact information denied to his employer. Police presence was provided by Wimsey's brother-in-law, Inspector Parker (played by future **Coronation Street** villain Mark Eden).

Five of Sayers's novels were dramatized for this TV version: *Clouds of Witness, The Unpleasantness at the Bellona Club, Murder Must Advertise, The Nine Tailors* and *Five Red Herrings*. Three more – *Strong Poison, Have His Carcase* and *Gaudy Night* – were adapted for a series entitled *A Dorothy L. Sayers Mystery*, screened on BBC 2 in 1987, with Edward Petherbridge as Wimsey, Richard Morant as Bunter and David Quiller as Parker. Also featured in this revamp was Harriet Walter as Harriet Vane, Wimsey's crime-writer friend.

LOST IN SPACE

US (Twentieth Century-Fox/Irwin Allen)
Science Fiction. ITV 1965–

Professor John Robinson ....Guy Williams
Maureen Robinson ....June Lockhart
Dr Zachary Smith ....Jonathan Harris
Major Don West ....Mark Goddard
Judy Robinson ....Marta Kristen
Will Robinson ....Billy Mumy
Penny Robinson ....Angela Cartwright
The Robot ....Bob May
The Robot's voice ....Dick Tufeld

Creator/Executive Producer: Irwin Allen.
Producers: Jerry Briskin, William Faralla

A pioneering family finds itself stranded in outer space.

In 1997 an over-populated Earth sent the Space Family Robinson on a five-year mission to a planet in the Alpha Centauri system to plan for colonization. But their spaceship was sabotaged and they became *Lost in Space*. The family consisted of father John Robinson, an astrophysicist, his biochemist wife, Maureen, and children Judy, Will and Penny. Geologist Don West was the pilot of their spaceship, the *Jupiter II*, and a genial, somewhat sarcastic robot provided scientific expertise and controlled the spacecraft. The joker in the pack was Dr Zachary Smith, a foreign agent who had sabotaged the mission by interfering with the robot, but who found himself trapped on board when the ship took off. He was forced to wake the family from their suspended animation to try to rectify the situation.

For most of the first season, the Robinsons survived on a barren planet on which their ship had crash-landed. Stories revolved around their attempts to repair the *Jupiter II* and to find a way home, but each week some strange alien intelligence arrived to throw them into danger. The aliens were always treacherously assisted by the cowardly, workshy Dr Smith, whose sole aim was to find a quick way back to civilization, preferably without the Robinsons. His plans consistently backfired and, just as you thought all was well, the programme ended with another sinister turn of events, a cliffhanger to be resolved next time. In later seasons, the Robinsons did manage to take off, but still Earth eluded them.

At first, *Lost in Space* was quite sensible science fiction, but it became very lighthearted when it was forced into competition with **Batman** on American TV. The plots were somewhat predictable, with the arrogant Dr Smith constantly bringing trouble to the extremely accommodating and surprisingly forgiving family. His closest friend, nine-year-old Will, a wholesome, electronics whiz kid, often ruined Smith's indulgent schemes by staying loyal to his family. Will's blonde sister, Judy, spent much of her time romantically entwined with action man Don West, while his other sister, the dark-haired, 11-year-old Penny, doted over her pet space monkey, which was known as 'The Bloop'.

The character of Dr Smith was only scheduled for six episodes, but actor Jonathan Harris, a late addition to the cast, quickly became the show's star and Smith stayed. Guy Williams had previously starred as the swashbuckling **Zorro**, and Angela Cartwright was one of the Von Trapp children in *The Sound of Music*. Child actor Billy Mumy has more recently been seen (grown up) in another sci-fi series, *Babylon 5*. The robot, which had no name, closely resembled Robbie the robot in the 1956 Walter Pidgeon film *Forbidden Planet*.

LOTTERBY, SYDNEY

Prolific British sitcom producer, working for the BBC on series of varying success, like **The Liver Birds, Me Mammy, Up Pompeii, Sykes, Some Mothers Do 'Ave 'Em, Porridge, Going Straight, Last Of The Summer Wine, Open All Hours, Butterflies, Yes, Minister** (and *Yes, Prime Minister*), *Coming Home, The Last Song, **Ever Decreasing Circles, The Magnificent Evans, Brush Strokes**, Foreign Bodies, **May to December, A Gentleman's Club, As Time Goes By** and, more recently for Central, *Old Boy Network*.

LOTUS EATERS, THE

UK (BBC) Drama. BBC 2 1972–3

Erik Shepherd ....Ian Hendry

Ann Shepherd	Wanda Ventham
Nester Turton	Maurice Denham
Major Edward Woolley	Thorley Walters
Mrs Miriam Woolley	Sylvia Coleridge
Donald Culley	James Kerry
Ruth Stewart	Cyd Hayman
Captain Krasakis	Stefan Gryff
Philip Mervish	Karl Held
Leigh Mervish	Carol Cleveland
Nikos	Antony Stamboulieh
Katerina	Karan David

Creator/Writer: Michael J. Bird. Producer: Anthony Read

Ex-patriot drama set in the sunny climes of Crete.

'To eat the fruit of the lotus is to lose the desire to return home. But everyone who does has a reason.' So read the promotional blurb for this nine-part drama series. Focusing on a little tavern (Shepherd's Bar) in the Cretan resort of Aghios Nicholaos, *The Lotus Eaters* told tales of its proprietors, Erik (an alcoholic) and Ann Shepherd, and the various emigrants who used the bar as a home from home. These included a crusty old major and his wife, scrounging hobo Nestor Turton and squabbling American siblings Philip and Leigh Mervish. Their lives and secrets unfolded as the series progressed. It was revealed for instance that Erik had once been acquitted of the murder of a 15-year-old schoolgirl but was still haunted by the experience.

LOU GRANT

US (MTM) Drama. ITV 1979–

Lou Grant	Edward Asner
Charlie Hume	Mason Adams
Joe Rossi	Robert Walden
Billie Newman/McCovey	Linda Kelsey
Margaret Pynchon	Nancy Marchand
Art Donovan	Jack Bannon
Dennis 'Animal' Price	Daryl Anderson
Adam Wilson	Allen Williams
Carla Mardigian	Rebecca Balding
Reuben Castillo	Emilio Delgado

Executive Producers: Gene Reynolds, James L. Brooks, Allan Burns

Dramas unfold in the newsroom of a Los Angeles daily newspaper.

Lou Grant was a spin-off from the highly successful sitcom *The Mary Tyler Moore Show*, but it was far more serious than its predecessor. Its lead character, Lou Grant, had been News Director at WJM-TV in Minneapolis, in the Mary Tyler Moore series. However, when that show finished, Grant and the other members of the news team were fired. At the age of 50, knowing little else but news, he took a job as City Editor of the *Los Angeles Tribune*, working under Managing Editor

Charlie Hume but often in conflict with the paper's outspoken proprietor, widow Margaret Pynchon.

Colleagues at the newspaper were investigative reporter Joe Rossi, Art Donovan, the Assistant City Editor, and photographer 'Animal'. Also featured was independent young reporter Billie Newman. As a informative, crusading team, they covered all manner of news stories, including sensitive issues such as Vietnamese refugees, child abuse and gun control. It is believed that Ed Asner's outspoken views on such matters may have contributed to the cancellation of the series after five years.

LOVE, AMERICAN STYLE

US (Paramount) Comedy. ITV

Creators: Douglas S. Cramer, Tom Miller. Executive Producers: Arnold Margolin, Jim Parker

An anthology of comedy skits (three or four per show) characterizing love and the American way of life.

There were no regular stars of *Love, American Style*. Guest artistes were called in to perform all the sketches. Each sketch was titled 'Love and . . .' (fill in the blank with the subject matter), and romance of all kinds was featured: amongst old people, amongst young people, extra-marital, intra-marital, and in all sorts of settings. The only familiar faces belonged to a repertory company that performed short comic interludes. One other regular feature was 'Lovemate of the Week' (an attractive bathing beauty).

Guest stars attracted to the series included the likes of Sonny and Cher, Tiny Tim and Burt Reynolds, and one particular episode proved particularly fruitful. *Love and The Happy Day*, starring Ron Howard and Anson Williams, was the pilot for the 1950s nostalgia comedy, **Happy Days**. *Love, American Style* proved to be a useful filler programme for numerous ITV regions. It first aired in the USA in 1969.

LOVE BOAT, THE

US (Aaron Spelling) Comedy. ITV

Captain Merrill Stubing	Gavin MacLeod
Burl 'Gopher' Smith	Fred Grandy
Dr Adam Bricker	Bernie Kopell
Isaac Washington	Ted Lange
Julie McCoy	Lauren Tewes
Vicki Stubing	Jill Whelan
Ashley Covington ('Ace') Evans	Ted McGinley
Judy McCoy	Pat Klous

Executive Producers: Aaron Spelling, Douglas S. Cramer.

Romantic sketches set aboard a luxurious cruise ship.

Three years after *Love, American Style* (in its native USA) came *The Love Boat*, another anthology series centring on romance. The setting this time was the *Pacific Princess* cruise liner, with the storylines provided by each week's passengers. Like its predecessor, *The Love Boat* attracted a wealth of Hollywood talent as guest stars: Jane Wyman, Raymond Burr and Greer Garson, for instance, but it also had a cast of regulars as the ship's crew, and they featured in the various playlets. Headed by Captain Stubing, the staff included the ship's doctor, Adam Bricker, purser Gopher Smith, bartender Isaac Washington, photographer Ace and social director Julie McCoy, later replaced by Judy McCoy. The Captain's 12-year-old daughter, Vicki, was also introduced. The Love Boat Mermaids, a troupe of female singers and dancers, were added to the show later, performing a different musical number each week. Much of the series was filmed on real cruises, with fare-paying passengers performing as extras. The series closed when Captain Stubing married a lady called Emily Heywood, played by Marion Ross of *Happy Days* fame. The theme song, 'The Love Boat', was sung by Jack Jones (Dionne Warwick in the last series).

LOVE, GEOFF (1917–91)

British bandleader, seen in support of many TV stars, particularly Max Bygraves. Amongst his theme tune credits was *Bless This House*. Love also recorded under the pseudonym of Manuel and His Music of the Mountains and was the father of radio personality Adrian Love.

LOVE HURTS

UK (Alomo) Drama. BBC 1 1992–4

Frank Carver	Adam Faith
Tessa Piggott	Zoe Wanamaker
Diane Warburg	Jane Lapotaire
Hugh Marriner	Stephen Moore
Max Taplow	Tony Selby
Mrs Piggott	Hilary Mason
Dr Piggott	Richard Pearson
Bob Pearce	John Flanagan
Jade Carver	Robin Weaver
Malcolm Litoff	Richard Cordery
Grace Taplow	Edna Doré
Simon Friedman	David Horovitch
Anthony Friedman	Ben Fisher
Jonathan Friedman	Laurence Amias
Sandra	Belinda Davison
Alex Friedman	Carl Morris
Marshall Baumblatt	Olivier Pierre
David Ben-Ari	Sasson Gabi
Sam Levison	Rolf Saxon
Mirav Levison	Suzanne Bertish

Creators: Laurence Marks, Maurice Gran.
Producers: Guy Slater, Tara Brem, Irving Teitelbaum

A disillusioned businesswoman and a millionaire plumber try to make a relationship work.

Forty-one and single, Tessa Piggott was a high flyer in the City. But, seeking pastures new, she ditched her boss/lover, moved into her own flat and became a director of the Seed aid agency. At the same time, she met up with rough diamond divorcé Frank Carver, on the face of it a lowly plumber but in fact a millionaire businessman. They, somewhat inconveniently, fell in love, with all its emotional consequences. *Love Hurts* traced the development of Tessa and Frank's relationship, as work pressures and time apart took their toll. They married in the second series, while on business together in Russia, but married life proved just as difficult, as Tessa continued her development work, this time for the Baumblatt Foundation. By the third and final season, she was pregnant, giving birth to baby Alice. Juggling work and parenthood was equally fraught with tension.

LOVE STORY

UK (ATV) Drama Anthology. ITV 1963–74

Single dramas in the romantic vein.

Love Story was the umbrella title for a collection of one-off plays that had romance as their linchpin. It ran steadily for four years initially, but was more sporadic later. Amongst its most prominent contributing writers were Robert Muller, Edna O'Brien, Doris Lessing, Mordecai Richler, Robert Holles, Alfred Shaughnessy, Roman Polanski and the French novelist and screenwriter Marguérite Duras. Judi Dench, Patrick Macnee, Vanessa Redgrave, Jeremy Kemp, Dudley Moore, Julia Foster and Robert Hardy were some of the featured performers.

LOVE THY NEIGHBOUR

UK (Thames) Situation Comedy. ITV 1972–6

Eddie Booth	Jack Smethurst
Joan Booth	Kate Williams
Bill Reynolds	Rudolph Walker
Barbie Reynolds	Nina Baden-Semper
Arthur	Tommy Godfrey
Jacko Jackson	Keith Marsh
Nobby Garside	Paul Luty

Creators/Writers: Harry Driver, Vince Powell.
Producers: Stuart Allen, Ronnie Baxter, Anthony Parker

A bigot's life is turned upside down when a black man moves in next door.

There have been few more controversial sitcoms than *Love Thy Neighbour*. It told the story of white trade unionist Eddie Booth whose new next-door neighbour, Bill Reynolds, was a true blue Tory and, even worse, a black man. It was intended, according to its producers, to take the sting out of racial conflict. Others saw it as a barrage of cheap colour jokes that reinforced racial stereotypes. It is quite true, however, that the bigot always lost out. Eddie was never prepared to give Bill a chance, yet Bill always came up trumps, delighting in humiliating Eddie and always giving as good as he got. For every 'nignog' and 'sambo' hurled across the garden fence, a 'honky' or 'snowflake' was returned with equal force. Meanwhile, to underline the futility of it all, the two wives, Joan and Barbie, became good friends. Arthur, Jacko and Nobby were their pals down the boozer. Remarkably, the series was a huge ratings success and a feature film version was released in 1973.

LOVEJOY

UK (Tamariska/Witzend/McShane) Comedy Drama. BBC 1 1986–94

Lovejoy	Ian McShane
Tinker Deal	Dudley Sutton
Eric Catchpole	Chris Jury
Lady Jane Felsham	Phyllis Logan
Lord Felsham	Pavel Douglas
Charlie Gimbert	Malcolm Tierney
Beth	Diane Parish
Charlotte Cavendish	Caroline Langrishe

Creator: Ian La Frenais. Producers: Richard Everitt, Emma Hayter, Robert Banks Stewart, Jo Wright, Colin Schindler

A shady antiques dealer stumbles into intrigue in the East Anglian countryside.

Dubbed by some 'The Antiques Rogue Show', *Lovejoy* was based on the novels of Jonathan Gash and concerned a slightly dodgy dealer in antiquities. Lovejoy's patch was East Anglia, and, more specifically, rural Essex and Suffolk, which he combed for underpriced treasures to sell on with a nice mark-up. At his side were Tinker, his tweedy, beret-hatted old friend, and young gopher Eric Catchpole. When Eric left to run his uncle's pub he was replaced by Beth, another 'trainee'. Leather-jacketed Lovejoy (who lived in a picturesque country cottage and drove a battered Morris Minor affectionately named Miriam), enjoyed the company of local aristocrat Lady Jane Felsham and, though flirtation was the name of the game, wedding bells never chimed. On Lady Jane's departure, in came university-educated auctioneer Charlotte Cavendish and she almost succeeded in getting the lovable wheeler-dealer to the altar in the very last episode of the series.

Played in humorous-thriller style, *Lovejoy* also employed the television technique known as 'breaking the fourth wall'. As seen earlier in programmes like **The George Burns and Gracie Allen Show** and **It's Gary Shandling's Show**, this called on Lovejoy, in an aside to the camera, to explain events directly to the viewers.

LOVERS, THE

UK (Granada) Situation Comedy. ITV 1970–1

Geoffrey	Richard Beckinsale
Beryl	Paula Wilcox
Beryl's mum	Joan Scott
Roland	Robin Nedwell

Creator: Jack Rosenthal. Writers: Jack Rosenthal, Geoffrey Lancashire. Producers: Jack Rosenthal, Les Chatfield

Two teenagers have different hopes for their relationship.

Geoffrey (or 'Geoffrey Bubbles Bon Bon', as Beryl, his girlfriend, called him) was very concerned with the physical side of their romance, or, more precisely, with the fact that there was no physical side. No matter how hard he tried to consummate their relationship (egged on by his pal, Roland), the scheming Beryl (watched over by her prudish mum) was always too virtuous to give in. 'Percy Filth', as she knew it, was not for her, despite the permissive age in which they lived. Marriage, in her eyes, was a far better objective.

The Lovers proved to be the break that both Paula Wilcox and Richard Beckinsale needed in their fledgling careers. A feature film version followed in 1972.

LOWE, ARTHUR (1915–82)

Fondly remembered British comedy actor, forever the bumptious Captain Mainwaring in **Dad's Army**, but the star of numerous other sitcoms. These included **Potter** (as Redvers Potter), **Bless Me Father** (as Father Duddleswell) and **A.J. Wentworth, BA** (as schoolmaster Wentworth, his last TV role). In the 1960s he was a popular figure as draper Leonard Swindley, the man jilted by Emily Nugent at the altar and the only **Coronation Street** character to be given his own spin-off series (**Pardon the Expression** and *Turn Out the Lights*). Lowe also voiced the *Mr Men* cartoons, appeared in Harold Pinter's first TV play (an **Armchair Theatre** production called *A Night Out*), was steward Sydney Barker in a late 1950s comedy, All Aboard, Dr Maxwell in **Doctor at Large**, Bodkin in **Last of the Baskets**, Micawber in a 1975 BBC version of *David Copperfield* and Louis Pasteur in *Microbes and Men*. Lowe was also seen in the drama *Philby, Burgess and Maclean* and appeared as a guest in *The Avengers*, amongst other series.

LUCY SHOW, THE

US (CBS/Desilu) Situation Comedy. BBC 1962–8

Lucy Carmichael	Lucille Ball
Vivian Bagley	Vivian Vance
Chris Carmichael	Candy Moore
Jerry Carmichael	Jimmy Garrett
Mr Barnsdahl	Charles Lane
Theodore J. Mooney	Gale Gordon
Harry Conners	Dick Martin
Sherman Bagley	Ralph Hart
Harrison Cheever	Roy Roberts
Mary Jane Lewis	Mary Jane Croft

A bored widow seeks a new husband and thinks up hare-brained schemes to improve her life.

In this follow up to *I Love Lucy*, Lucille Ball starred without her husband, Desi Arnaz. Having said that, the format was essentially much the same, with Lucy playing Lucy Carmichael, a scatterbrained widow, living with her two children, Chris and Jerry, in Danfield, Connecticut. She was once again supported by Vivian Vance, this time in the guise of Vivian Bagley, a divorcée friend who, with her son, Sherman, shared a house with the Carmichaels. Lucy's main aspiration was to find herself a new husband, but, as ever, all her best plans crumbled around her. Lucy found a perfect foil for her slapstick antics in her no-nonsense boss Mr Mooney, who succeeded the cantankerous Mr Barnsdahl seen in the earliest episodes. Mooney was President of the Danfield First National Bank and she was his part-time secretary.

After a few seasons, the location of the series was switched to San Francisco, with major cast changes. Lucy still worked for Mr Mooney, who was now Vice-President of the Westland Bank, under boss Harrison Cheever, but her daughter, Chris, was no longer featured. Also gone was Vivian Bagley, to appear only occasionally as a visitor. Lucy's new accomplice was neighbour Mary Jane Lewis.

See also *I Love Lucy* and *Here's Lucy*.

LUMLEY, JOANNA, OBE (1946–)

British actress and former model, typically seen in classy, sophisticated roles, though offering a game alternative as Patsy in the comedy *Absolutely Fabulous*. Lumley's TV career has veered between lead roles and strong supporting parts, with the highlights being the athletic Purdey in *The New Avengers* and the mysterious Sapphire in *Sapphire and Steel*. She was Samantha Ryder-Ross in Jilly Cooper's flatshare sitcom *It's Awfully Bad for Your Eyes, Darling*, played Elaine Perkins, a girlfriend of Ken Barlow, in *Coronation Street*, and starred as Kate Swift in *Class Act*. One of her earliest performances was as a patient in *Emergency – Ward 10* and other credits have included parts in *Steptoe and Son*, *The Protectors*, *Oxbridge Blues*, *The Glory Boys*, *Mistral's Daughter*, *A Perfect Hero* and *Lovejoy*. In 1994 she appeared in the documentary *Girl Friday*, which recounted her nine-day 'survival' challenge on the uninhabited island of Tsarabajina, off the coast of Madagascar.

LUNGHI, CHERIE (1952–)

British actress, as Gabriella Benson the star of the football drama *The Manageress*, but also seen as Dorothy in *The Monocled Mutineer*, Margaret Van de Merwe in *Master of the Game* and also in *Tales of the Unexpected*, *The Praying Mantis*, *Strangers and Brothers*, *Harem* and *The Ruth Rendell Mysteries*, amongst other dramas.

LUV

UK (BBC) Situation Comedy. BBC 1 1993–

Harold Craven	Michael Angelis
Terese Craven	Sue Johnston
Lloyd	Peter Caffrey
Hannah Craven	Sandy Hendrickse
Victor Craven	Russell Boulter
	Stefan Escreet
Darwin Craven	Stephen Lord
Bernie	Jackie Downey
Carro	Debbie Andrews
Eden	Julie Peasgood
Martinique	Jan Ravens
Antonio	Zubin Varla
Tone	Gerard O'Hare
Arthur	Raymond Coulthard
Chezz	Akim Mogaji

Creator/Writer: Carla Lane. Producer: Mike Stephens

A successful Liverpool businessman finds that money can't buy him love or peace at home.

Harold Craven, self-made proprietor of Craven's Ornamental Garden Requisites (mostly plastic flower pots), cared deeply for his wife and children and showered them with gifts. Nevertheless, he found himself head of a family that struggled to express their need for each other. His wife, Terese, was a bored housewife who wanted only one thing – for her husband to say he loved her – and their adopted children brought even more heartache into their stressed lives. Elder son Victor was gay and lived with his boyfriend in an 'out of the way' cottage Harold had bought for them. Daughter Hannah endured a stormy marriage with a dim Italian named Antonio, and whining younger son Darwin still lived at home, dossing his way through life, espousing the animal rights cause and indulging in pseudo-paramilitary manoeuvres to free livestock. Away from the bedlam of home life, Harold relaxed in the company of Lloyd, his perceptive Irish chauffeur, and in the arms of Eden, a beautiful blonde whom he employed as his secretary. Bernie and Carro were the workers who gave Harold a hard time on the factory floor, especially when he insisted on playing them classical music.

In the second series, screened in 1994, Harold abandoned Eden only to find his former mistress bent on revenge, and the factory went through financial difficulties that had repercussions for all the Craven family.

LWT

LWT (formerly London Weekend Television) won the ITV franchise for London weekends in 1967 (under the application name of London Television Consortium), and went on air on 2 August 1968. It retained its franchise in 1980 and again in 1992 and now broadcasts to London from 5.15 pm on Friday to closedown on Sunday, as well as making many programmes for the ITV network at its South Bank studios. Amongst its most notable contributions over the years have been sitcoms like *Doctor in the House* and *On the Buses*, arts programmes like *Aquarius* and *The South Bank Show*, drama such as *Upstairs, Downstairs* and *Bouquet of Barbed Wire*, current affairs series like *Weekend World* and game shows such as *Game for a Laugh* and *Play Your Cards Right*.

LYNAM, DESMOND (1942–)

Laid back Irish-born sports frontman whose charm and style have led him into other presentation work. Beginning his broadcasting career in radio sport, working particularly on boxing commentaries, Lynam's TV break came in the late 1970s with *Nationwide*'s Friday night sports segment and led to *Grandstand*, *Sportsnight*, *Match of the Day* and all major sporting events coverage. He tried one season as presenter of *Holiday* and has also been seen as co-host of *How Do They Do That?*

LYNCH, JOE (1925–)

Irish comedy actor, chiefly recalled as the tailor Patrick Kelly in *Never Mind the Quality, Feel the Width*. He was later seen as Paddy O'Brien in another sitcom, *Rule Britannia*, and was narrator of the children's series *Chorlton and the Wheelies*.

LYNDHURST, NICHOLAS (1961–)

Although widely recognized as plonker Rodney Trotter from the hugely successful *Only Fools and Horses*, Nicholas Lyndhurst's showbiz career began as a child actor. He was seen in numerous kids' dramas, including *The Tomorrow People*, *Heidi* and *Anne of Avonlea* and took the dual lead roles in *The Prince and the Pauper*. He was one of the hosts of the Saturday morning series *Our Show* (along with Susan Tully and others) and played Fletch's son, Raymond, in *Going Straight*, before maturing into adult parts through *Butterflies*, in which he was Ria's son, Adam. Since *Only Fools and Horses* began, Lyndhurst has not looked back and has been a popular choice for sitcom producers. He was Ashley in *The Two of Us*, Peter Chapman in *The Piglet Files* and Gary Sparrow in *Goodnight Sweetheart*. Amongst his other credits have been *Round and Round, Spearhead, Slimming Down* and *To Serve Them All My Days*.

LYNN, JONATHAN (1943–)

British actor, writer and director, a Cambridge Footlights contemporary of Cleese, Chapman, Garden, Brooke-Taylor and Oddie, acclaimed in particular for *Yes, Minister* and *Yes, Prime Minister*, which he scripted in collaboration with Antony Jay. In front of the cameras, he appeared in the sketch show *Twice a Fortnight* and played Danny Hooley in *Doctor in the House*, Beryl's husband (Robert) in *The Liver Birds* and Pete Booth in *My Brother's Keeper* (also as writer). Other acting parts have come in *Barmitzvah Boy, Turnbull's Finest Hour, Outside Edge, The Knowledge* and *Diana*. Amongst Lynn's other writing credits (usually with George Layton) have been episodes of *Doctor at Sea*, *On the Buses* and *My Name is Harry Worth*.

LYTTON'S DIARY

UK (Thames) Drama. ITV 1985–6

Neville Lytton	Peter Bowles
Henry Field	Bernard Lloyd
The Editor	Bernard Archard
Dolly	Holly de Jong

Creators: Peter Bowles, Philip Broadley. Writer: Ray Connolly. Producer: Chris Burt, Derek Bennett

Incidents in the life of a newspaper diarist.

Partly created by its star, Peter Bowles, *Lytton's Diary* began life as part of Thames Television's anthology series *Storyboard* in 1983. Two years later, it became a series. Bowles starred as Neville Lytton, the gossip columnist for *The Daily News*. His investigations into society scandals provided ample titbits for his features and drew him into intrigue. Fourteen episodes were made.

McANALLY, RAY (1926–89)

Irish actor who, after years of supporting roles in the cinema and on TV, became a star late in life. Although he had appeared as gangster Alec Spindoe in *Spindoe* in 1968, it was as Rick, Peter Egan's deceitful dad, in *A Perfect Spy* that he began to steal the show, and he capped that with a BAFTA award-winning performance as left-wing Labour Prime Minister *Harry Perkins* in Channel 4's *A Very British Coup*. Other early appearances had been as a guest in series like *The Avengers* and *Man in a Suitcase*.

McCALLUM, DAVID (1933–)

Blond Scottish actor, busy on both sides of the Atlantic and once a heartthrob as introverted secret agent Illya Kuryakin in *The Man From UNCLE*. UNCLE followed his arrival in the USA in the early 1960s where he enjoyed roles in series like *Perry Mason* and *The Outer Limits*. Later, he was airman Simon Carter in *Colditz*, Dr Daniel Westin aka *The Invisible Man*, Steel in *Sapphire and Steel*, Alan Breck in *Kidnapped*, Diana Rigg's son in *Mother Love* and John Grey in *Trainer*. McCallum has also been in demand for TV movies and guest appearances, and has, at times, turned his hand to directing. His first wife was actress Jill Ireland.

McCASKILL, IAN (1938–)

Quirky Scottish meteorologist, who joined the BBC forecasting team in 1978 and quickly attracted the attentions of impressionists. He worked for a while at Central Television in the early 1980s and has also been seen as a guest on numerous other programmes.

McCLAIN'S LAW

US (MGM) Police Drama. BBC 1 1982

Detective Jim McClain ....James Arness
Detective Harry Gates ....Marshall Colt
Detective Jerry Cross.............................Carl Franklin
Lt Edward DeNisco ....George DiCenzo
Vangie Cruise ....Conchata Ferrell

Creator: Eric Bercovici. Producers: Mark Rafters, Robert H. Justman

A retired detective rejoins the police to hunt for his friend's killer.

Forced to leave the police force in San Pedro, California, some 13 years earlier, because of a leg injury, Jim McClain was dragged back into detective work when his fishing partner was brutally murdered. Convinced that only he was capable of

tracking down the killer, McClain – now aged 52 – persuaded the authorities to take him back into the force, even though detection methods had changed dramatically in his absence. But, with excellent support from colleagues Harry Gates and Jerry Cross, McClain quickly dropped back into the routine. Even though his rough and tumble ways seemed rather archaic at times (and antagonized his boss, Lt DeNisco), he proved reasonably effective. Off-duty, Jim returned to his waterside hang-out, Vangie Cruise's bar.

A welcome change in direction for James Arness, after his 20-odd years in *Gunsmoke*, this series was partly inspired by a 1952 film in which he had starred with John Wayne. Called *Big Jim McLain*, it featured Wayne in the title role as a right-wing special agent rooting out communists in Hawaii.

McCLANAHAN, RUE (1934–)

After plenty of supporting roles, Rue McClanahan was at last able to claim some of the limelight when she was cast as the man-hungry southern belle, Blanche Devereaux, in *The Golden Girls* and *The Golden Palace*. The former brought her back in contact with Bea Arthur, with whom she had appeared in the *All in the Family* offshoot *Maude*. Amongst McClanahan's other credits have been parts in *Lou Grant*, *The Love Boat* and numerous TV movies, as well as the US sitcoms *Apple Pie* and *Mama's Family* (neither screened in the UK).

McCLOUD

US (Universal) Police Drama. ITV 1972–

Sam McCloud ....Dennis Weaver
Peter B. Clifford ....J.D. Cannon
Sgt Joe Broadhurst....................................Terry Carter
Chris Coughlin.......................................Diana Muldaur
Sgt Grover ....Ken Lynch

Creator/Executive Producer: Glen A. Larson

A cowboy becomes a cop in New York City.

Deputy Marshal Sam McCloud had arrived in New York in pursuit of a refugee prisoner. Having caught his man, he decided to stick around for a while and learn the ways of a big city police force, operating in a world far removed from his usual beat of Taos, New Mexico. Riding a horse through the New York traffic and sporting a sheepskin jacket, cowboy boots and a stetson, he joined Manhattan's 27th Precinct, working alongside Sgt Joe Broadhurst. Although McCloud was meant to be the learner, it was Broadhurst who had the greater education, as the determined western lawman dragged him into the thick of the action, shunning the subtler approach to policing usually employed in the city. This did little to endear either of them to their superior, Chief Clifford. But, as our hero would have put it, 'There you go'. Chris Coughlin was McCloud's writer girlfriend.

Based on the Clint Eastwood film *Coogan's Bluff* and derived from a pilot called *Who Killed Miss USA* (aired as *Who Killed Merri-Ann* in the UK), the series was part of ITV's *Mystery Movie* package. A TV movie, *The Return of Sam McCloud*, was made in 1989, with McCloud having become a US senator.

McCLURE, DOUG (1935–95)

American actor, Trampas in *The Virginian* for nine years, but otherwise unfamiliar to British audiences, except for TV movies and mini-series like *Roots* (in which he played Jemmy Brent). In the States, McClure enjoyed several short-run series, but nothing to match *The Virginian*.

MACCORKINDALE, SIMON (1952–)

Successful British actor, now focusing on behind the scenes work. His most notable TV performances have been as Lucius in *I, Claudius*, Joe Kapp in the 1979 revival of *Quatermass*, Jonathan Chase, hero of the sci-fi detective series *Manimal*, and Greg Reardon in *Falcon Crest* (also with directing credits). Other appearances have come in *Just William*, *Jesus of Nazareth*, *Beasts*, *Will Shakespeare*, *The Mannions of America* and *The Dukes of Hazzard*. MacCorkindale is currently married to Susan George (his first wife was Fiona Fullerton) and together they run the Amy International production company.

McCOY, SYLVESTER (1943–)

Scottish actor, dealing in both comic and straight drama roles. Undoubtedly, his most famous character has been *Doctor Who* (the seventh incarnation), which he played from 1987 to 1989. Previously, McCoy had been seen in children's offerings like *Tiswas* and *Dramarama*, sitcoms like *Big Jim* and *The Figaro Club* (as Turps, the painter) and dramas like *The Last Place on Earth* (as Birdie Bowers).

McDONALD, TREVOR, OBE (1939–)

Trinidadian newscaster, the main anchor for *News At Ten*. He joined ITN in 1971 and, after working as a reporter and sports correspondent, became its Diplomatic Correspondent and Diplomatic Editor, also spending seven years with Channel 4 News. McDonald had previously worked in radio and television in the West Indies and for the BBC World and Caribbean Services in London. He has been with *News At Ten* since 1989.

McDOWALL, RODDY (1928–)

British-born actor, formerly a Hollywood child star (particularly remembered with Lassie and Flicka), whose most memorable TV role has been as Galen in *The Planet of the Apes*. His earliest TV credits were in episodes of *Naked City*, *Arrest and Trial*, *Alfred Hitchcock Presents* and *The Invaders*, and he also played The Bookworm in *Batman*. Since *The Planet of the Apes*, McDowall has enjoyed a run of US dramas and TV movies, such as *The Rhinemann Exchange*, *Fantastic Journey* and *Tales of the Gold Monkey*, and guest spots in series like *Wonder Woman*.

McEWAN, GERALDINE (1932–)

English actress much seen on television in roles like Miss Farnaby in *Mulberry*, Anne Dickens in *Tears Before Bedtime*, Mrs Proudie in *The Barchester Chronicles*, Jess's religious fanatic mother in *Oranges are Not the Only Fruit*, Emmeline Lucas (aka Lucia) in *Mapp and Lucia*, the title character in *The Prime of Miss Jean Brodie*, plus many single dramas.

McGANN, JOE (1958–), PAUL (1959–), MARK, STEPHEN (1963–)

Four acting brothers familiar on British TV in the 1980s and 1990s. Joe starred in *Rockliffe's Babies* as PC Gerry O'Dowd and *The Upper Hand* as Charlie Burrows; Mark played Mad Dog in *Scully*, Detective C.J. Brady in *Yellowthread Street* and Halliwell in *The Manageress*; Paul was Mo Morris in *Give Us a Break* and Percy Toplis in *The Monocled Mutineer* and Stephen took the roles of Bob in *Streetwise* and Tex in *Help!* All four have many other credits to their names and appeared together in the 1995 drama series *The Hanging Gale*.

McGEE, HENRY (1929–)

British actor and stooge to leading comics, particularly Benny Hill, Tommy Cooper, Dick Emery and Charlie Drake (as Mr Pugh in *The Worker*). In sitcom, he was Lt Raleigh in *Tell It to the Marines*, appeared with Ronnie Corbett in *No – That's Me Over Here*, and played Dickie Bligh in *Up the Workers* and Dennis in *Let There Be Love*. His other credits have included parts in *The Goodies*, *Rising Damp*, *Sykes* and *Doctor at Large*.

McGOOHAN, PATRICK (1928–)

American-born, British-raised actor whose earliest television credits were in action series like *The*

Adventures of Sir Lancelot and *The Vise*. He became a big name in the 1960s thanks to his starring roles as John Drake in *Danger Man* and Number 6 in his own cult series, *The Prisoner* (he created it and wrote and directed some episodes). At one point, it is claimed, McGoohan was the richest man on TV and allegedly turned down the part of *The Saint*, before it was offered to Roger Moore, because Simon Templar was too promiscuous. In the 1970s he returned to the small screen as medical man Rafferty and in TV movies, but he also worked behind the scenes, directing an episode of *Columbo*, for instance (as well as guest starring in the series).

MACGREGOR, JIMMIE see Hall, Robin.

McINNERNY, TIM (1956–)

British actor whose most prominent roles have been as Lord Percy and, later, Captain Darling in *Blackadder*. However, he has also been seen in dramas as varied as *Edge of Darkness* (as Terry Shields), *The Adventures of Sherlock Holmes*, *Shadow of the Noose* and *A Very British Coup*.

McINTIRE, JOHN (1907–91)

John McIntire's craggy looks were very familiar to viewers in the late 1950s and early 1960s, courtesy of his starring roles in *Naked City* (as Detective Lt Dan Muldoon) and *Wagon Train* (as Christopher Hale, Ward Bond's replacement as trail leader). A few years later, McIntire turned up in another western, *The Virginian*, taking the role of Clay Grainger, new owner of the Shiloh Ranch. With guest appearances in the 1970s in series like *Love, American Style* and *The Love Boat*, plus roles in prime-time American series right up to 1981, McIntire enjoyed a remarkable television career, especially if you consider that he didn't start working in the medium until he was nearly 50, having concentrated earlier on radio acting.

MACKAY, FULTON, OBE (1922–87)

Scottish actor, *Porridge's* by-the-book prison officer Mr Mackay. Previously, he was Willie McGuinness in *Mess Mates*, a regular guest as Jamie in *Dr Finlay's Casebook* and played Detective Supt Inman in *Special Branch*. Amongst his later work were roles in the kids' sci-fi adventure *King of the Castle* (as Hawkspur, a mad scientist), the single dramas *Going Gently* and *A Sense of Freedom*, and a Channel 4 sitcom *Mann's Best Friends* (as lodger Hamish Ordway), as well as the part of the Captain in *Fraggle Rock*. Other appearances over the years were in series such as *The Edwardians*, *The Troubleshooters*, *The Foundation*, *Some Mothers Do 'Ave 'Em*, *Crown Court* and *Going Straight*.

McKENZIE, JULIA (1942–)

British character actress, star of the sitcoms *Maggie and Her* (as Maggie, with Irene Handl), *That Beryl Marston . . .* (as Georgie Bodley, with Gareth Hunt) and *Fresh/French Fields* (as Hester Fields, with Anton Rodgers). She was Mrs Forthby in *Blott on the Landscape* and her singing voice has occasionally been heard in series like *Song By Song*. Amongst her numerous other credits have been appearances in *Adam Bede*, *Absent Friends*, *Fame is the Spur*, *Hôtel du Lac*, *The Two Ronnies* and *The Stanley Baxter Show*, as well as her own programme, *Julia and Company*.

McKENZIE, ROBERT (1917–81)

Enthusiastic Canadian political commentator who brought his 'Swingometer' into BBC election coverages. Though chiefly an academic, his other work included pieces for *Panorama*, *Tonight* and *24 Hours*, as well as a series of his own shortly before he died, *The Pursuit of Power*.

McKERN, LEO (REGINALD MCKERN; 1920–)

Australian actor, identified by most viewers as the irascible legal rogue *Rumpole of the Bailey*. However, McKern's TV appearances have been many. He was one of the actors to play the mysterious Number Two in the cult series *The Prisoner*, popped up in early series like *The Adventures of Robin Hood*, played Zaharov in *Reilly – Ace of Spies*, has numerous guest appearances and TV films to his name and has earned acclaim in single dramas like *The Tea Party*, Jonathan Miller's *Alice In Wonderland*, *The Sun Is God* (playing the artist Turner) and *On the Eve of Publication*. He was a familiar face in the 1980s advertising Lloyds Bank.

MACKIE, PHILIP (1918–85)

British playwright and producer whose long career's highlights (the later ones as writer) were *Maupassant*, *The Victorians*, *Mr Rose*, *The Liars*, *Saki*, *Paris 1900*, *The Caesars*, *Napoleon and Love*, *The Naked Civil Servant*, *Raffles*, *An Englishman's Castle*, *The Organisation*, *Thérèse Raquin*, *Conjugal Rites*, *The Cleopatras* and *Praying Mantis*. A former documentary maker, Mackie joined the BBC as a contract writer in 1954 and later worked for Granada, amongst other companies.

McLACHLAN, CRAIG (1966–)

Australian actor who shot to fame as Henry Ramsey in *Neighbours* before switching soaps and taking on the role of Grant Mitchell in *Home and Away*. He had earlier appeared in *Sons and Daughters*. In 1995 he starred as Ed in the futuristic drama series *Bugs*. McLachlan has had some hit singles in the UK, most notably 'Mona'.

McMANUS, MARK (1940–94)

Scottish actor, a former boxer, whose first major role was as the eponymous lead in the northern mining saga **Sam**, although in his latter years he was known to viewers as the gritty Glasgow detective **Taggart**, making 30 episodes of the series from 1983. McManus was another policeman, Detective Chief Inspector Jack Lambie, in **Strangers** and also appeared in **Colditz**, **The Brothers**, **Crown Court**, *The Foundation*, **Target**, *Union Castle* and other dramas.

McMILLAN AND WIFE

US (Universal) Police Drama. ITV 1972–

Commissioner Stewart McMillan	Rock Hudson
Sally McMillan	Susan Saint James
Sgt/Lt Charles Enright	John Schuck
Mildred	Nancy Walker
Agatha	Martha Raye
Sgt Steve DiMaggio	Richard Gilliland
Maggie	Gloria Stroock

Creator/Executive Producer: Leonard B. Stern.
Producer: Jon Epstein

A San Francisco police chief and his wife stumble across crime at every turn.

Loosely based on *The Thin Man* series of films, *McMillan and Wife* concerned a hapless police commissioner who was continually dragged into detective work by his attractive wife. Stewart and Sally McMillan had a successful marriage, a witty rapport and a nose for crime, which meant that there was no chance of this policeman leaving his work at the office. Whether they were doing the shopping, going to a party or taking a holiday, *something* was bound to arouse their curiosity. Even in bed all they talked about was murder. Little wonder they needed the sharp-tongued Mildred to do their housework.

McMillan and Wife was part of the **Mystery Movie** collection of crime capers and was derived from a pilot movie called *Once Upon a Dead Man*. When, after five years, Susan Saint James and Nancy Walker decided to leave the series, Rock Hudson soldiered on alone, with the title shortened to *McMillan*. Sally was killed off in a plane crash and Stewart was furnished with a new assistant, in the shape of Sgt Steve DiMaggio, who replaced the well-intentioned but slow-witted Sgt Charles Enright, now promoted to lieutenant. Mildred's sister, Agatha, arrived to be his housekeeper, and Maggie was his new secretary. The new format didn't last long, however.

MACMURRAY, FRED (1908–91)

Although primarily a big screen actor, Fred MacMurray was one of America's sitcom greats in the 1950s, thanks to his hit series *My Three Sons*, which was also aired on ITV in the UK. His other television work was concentrated into TV movies.

MACNEE, PATRICK (1922–)

Old Etonian Patrick Macnee will probably only ever be remembered for one television role, that of the debonair, gentleman agent John Steed in *The Avengers* and *The New Avengers*, although he has contributed to numerous TV movies and mini-series since. He played the head of UNCLE in the one-off *Return of the Man from UNCLE* in 1983, was cast in the US series *Empire and Gavilan*, and appeared as a guest in dramas like **Battlestar Galactica**, **Dick Turpin**, **Magnum PI** and **Murder, She Wrote**. A cousin of David Niven, most of Macnee's earliest television work was gained in Canada and the USA (including one role in **Rawhide**), following some stage and film work in Britain before joining the war effort.

McQUEEN, GEOFF (1947–94)

British scriptwriter, a former manager with an electrical company, who broke into television with the snooker room drama **Give Us a Break**. Soon afterwards, McQueen penned a single play for Thames TV's **Storyboard** anthology. Entitled *Woodentop*, it proved to be the pilot for **The Bill**. McQueen's later offerings included the light-hearted dramas **Big Deal** and **Stay Lucky**. His last TV work was *Rules of Engagement* (shown posthumously).

McSHANE, IAN (1942–)

British actor, prominent on both sides of the Atlantic and working in the cinema since the early 1960s. McShane starred as Heathcliff in a 1967 version of *Wuthering Heights*, appeared in the Joe Orton play *Funeral Games* in 1968, played Judas in **Jesus of Nazareth**, Sir Eric Russell in **Roots**, Benjamin Disraeli in *Disraeli* and Bert in *Dirty Money*. His other major credits have been in **Will Shakespeare** and plays and mini-series like *Grand Larceny*, *The Pirate*, *War and Remembrance*, *Bare Essence* and *Evergreen*. Since 1986 he has become familiar as the roguish antiques dealer in **Lovejoy**, a series which he has also co-produced through his own company, McShane Productions. Narration work on **Survival** and guest appearances in series like **Minder**, **Columbo**, **Perry Mason** and **Dallas** (as Don Lockwood) add to his varied portfolio.

MADDEN, CECIL, MBE (1902–87)

Early BBC executive, its first Programme Organizer and a senior producer, responsible in particular for *Picture Page*, beginning in 1936, and Sunday evening drama. After the war, he became Acting Head of Children's Programmes (1950–1) and rose higher up the Corporation's ladder.

MADELEY, RICHARD (1956–)

British presenter, largely associated with daytime television where, with his wife Judy Finnigan, he has presented *This Morning* on ITV. Madeley has also hosted the quiz *Runway*, the panel game *Cluedo* and previously worked as a journalist, reporting for Border, Yorkshire and Granada TV news.

MADIGAN

US (Universal) Police Drama ITV 1973–

Sgt Dan Madigan ....Richard Widmark

Executive Producer: Frank Rosenberg.
Producers: Dean Hargrove, Roland Kibbee

An abrasive New York cop prefers his own company.

Madigan was one of TV's great loners, one of the quirky cops of the 1970s. Living in a spartan one-room flat, he worked for the NYPD during the day, but had little social life at night. Perhaps it was his hard, cool indifference that put people off, with his genuinely soft-centre just too well concealed. At least, having no attachments, he was free to travel, and his work took him a long way from the busy streets of New York City.

After a pilot movie called *Brock's Last Case*, *Madigan* became part of the *Mystery Movie* crime anthology series, showing in feature-length episodes. However, only six were ever made, each known by its setting, for example *The Manhattan Beat*, *The Naples Beat* and *The Lisbon Beat*.

MADOC, PHILIP (1934–)

Welsh actor normally cast in somewhat sombre or menacing roles. He was Magua in the BBC's 1972 version of *Last of the Mohicans*, Detective Chief Supt Tate in *Target*, Lloyd George in *The Life and Times of David Lloyd George* and newspaper baron Fison in *A Very British Coup*. Madoc was also seen in both *Bouquet of Barbed Wire* and its sequel, *Another Bouquet*, the lifeboat drama *Ennal's Point*, *Fortunes of War*, *Singles*, *First Born*, and *Capital City* and has enjoyed guest roles in TV movies and series like *The Avengers*, *Doctor Who*, *The Baron*, *Man in a Suitcase*, *Randall and Hopkirk (Deceased)*, *Department S*, *Manhunt*, *Brookside* and *Dad's Army*, usually playing a villain. He was once married to actress Ruth Madoc.

MADOC, RUTH (1943–)

British actress, popular in the 1980s as *Hi-De-Hi!*'s Welsh camp announcer, Gladys Pugh. Previously, Madoc had appeared in *Hunter's Walk*, as policeman's wife Betty Smith, and in the series *Leave It to Charlie* and *The Life and Times of David Lloyd George* (alongside her first husband, Philip Madoc).

MAGAZINE

A programme made up of assorted features of various lengths and on numerous topics, some inserted on film or video, others presented in the studio.

MAGIC ROUNDABOUT, THE

France Children's Entertainment.
BBC 1 1965–77/Channel 4 1992

Creator: Serge Danot. Narrators/Writers: Eric Thompson, Nigel Planer

A girl and her friends enjoy surreal adventures in a magic garden.

Few series are more fittingly described as 'cult' than *The Magic Roundabout*. Although each episode was just five minutes long and, almost as an afterthought, tagged onto the end of children's hour, this animation became a firm favourite not only with kids but with adult audiences, too. Consequently, there were howls of protest when transmission was switched to an earlier time slot. *The Magic Roundabout* was produced in France by Serge Danot and shown first on French television in 1963. When the series arrived in the UK, the narration was drily and wittily redubbed by Eric (father of Emma) Thompson, who also rewrote the scripts for British consumption. Effectively, the storyline went as follows. Florence would arrive at a carousel owned by the ancient, bewhiskered Mr Rusty, a man whose barrel organ provided the show's theme music. Zebedee, a strange, freckle-faced creature with a waxed moustache and a bedspring for feet, then bounced into the picture and, in a cascade of harp strings, the 'real' nature of life around the roundabout disappeared and all manner of odd things began to happen. New characters drifted into the action, primarily a sleek-haired dog known as Dougal, a quirky snail called Brian and a laid-back rabbit named Dylan. There was also Ermintrude, a flower-chewing cow, the manic cyclist Mr McHenry, a talking train and, occasionally, Florence's friend Paul, plus one or two other chums. When it all got a bit too frenetic, up would bounce Zebedee to declare it was 'Time for bed'.

Children loved the series for its visual humour. Adults enjoyed Thompson's 'in' references to topical issues and personalities of the day. With the arrival of colour television, the surreality of it all became even more apparent, and some viewers began to question just what lay behind the series. Fingers were pointed at the almost hallucinogenic nature of the concept, with The Magic Roundabout itself declared to be an allegory for a 'trip' and Mr Rusty some kind of drug pedlar. It may seem ludicrous but there was plenty of evidence to support this theory. After all, everything was perfectly normal until Florence arrived at the roundabout, Dylan was always spaced out and Dougal's favourite food was sugar cubes (with all their LSD connections)! 'Heavy man', as Dylan would have put it. But even if you dismiss the 'drug culture' theory, The Magic Roundabout will still be fondly remembered by today's parents and grandparents as a cheerful part of everyday life in the 1960s.

A cinema version, Dougal and the Blue Cat, was released in the UK in 1972 and the series was revived by Channel 4 in 1992, with previously unscreened episodes adapted (very much in the Eric Thompson vein) for British audiences by Nigel Planer.

MAGIC WANDS

The flippant term used for programmes that make viewers dreams and wishes come true. One of the first such programmes in the UK was Ask Pickles in the 1950s, but the longest-running example was Jim'll Fix It, which notched up 20 years of giving kids the chance to meet pop stars, drive trains, interview politicians, etc. Some adults' hopes were also fulfilled. Esther Rantzen's The Big Time was another such vehicle, although the most recent offering has been the heavily sentimental Noel's Christmas Presents. Screened on Christmas Day, it has featured Noel Edmonds rewarding brave, sick or deserving folk with their ultimate Christmas gift, usually a visit back to a distant and forgotten homeland or a meeting with a long-lost son or daughter.

MAGICIAN, THE

US (Paramount) Adventure. ITV

Anthony Blake	Bill Bixby
Max Pomeroy	Keene Curtis
Dennis Pomeroy	Todd Crespi
Jerry	Jim Watkins
Dominick	Joseph Sirola

An illusionist uses his talents to assist the cause of justice.

Conjuror Tony Blake had been wrongfully convicted of a crime early in his life. Bitter about the experience, he had left prison vowing to make sure that the same thing couldn't happen to other

innocent people. He aimed to help folk in trouble or under threat, preventing crime wherever he could, making full use of the sleight of hand and other illusionary skills he employed in his stage act. His assistants in his crusade were journalist Max Pomeroy (who gave Blake his leads) and Max's wheelchair-bound son, Dennis. Jerry was the pilot of Blake's private plane, The Spirit. Later, the setting switched to the Magic Castle, a Hollywood nightclub where Blake had a residency.

The series received a sporadic screening around the ITV network, after premièring in its native USA in 1973. Actor Bill Bixby performed many of the illusionist's tricks himself.

MAGILL, RONALD (1920–)

With his mutton chop sideburns, in his guise of Amos Brearly, Ronald Magill was the distinctive landlord of **Emmerdale Farm**'s Woolpack for over 17 years. Previously Magill had focused on stage work, with just a handful of TV appearances to his name. These included episodes of the police series **Special Branch** and Parkin's Patch. He left **Emmerdale** in 1991, but has made return visits to Beckindale.

MAGNIFICENT EVANS, THE

UK (BBC) Situation Comedy. BBC 1 1984

Plantagenet Evans	Ronnie Barker
Rachel	Sharon Morgan
Willie	Dickie Arnold
Bron	Myfanwy Talog
Probert	William Thomas
Home Rule O'Toole	Dyfed Thomas

Creator/Writer: Roy Clarke. Producer: Sydney Lotterby

Shameless philandering with a flamboyant Welsh photographer.

Plantagenet Evans, modestly describing himself as a 'genius, photographer and man of letters', was the most colourful character in a sleepy Welsh town. So colourful in fact that the local chapel folk openly disapproved. Just one of his many scandalous activities was his relationship with Rachel, a local beauty who, as his fiancée and assistant, had her own apartment at his home/studio, much to the concern of her sister, Bron, and Bron's husband, Probert. While modest Rachel played down their affair, Evans himself, dressed in flowing cape and wide-brimmed hat, never shirked attention. As the local franchise holder for Scandinavian log stoves and a part-time antiques dealer, he was also a man of many means, devoted to the cause of making money. Bullying Willie, his loyal but silent sidekick, into doing all the donkey work, he paraded around in his vintage motor, leering at girls, defying the local gossips, plying his artistic trade and disparaging his customers. Also seen from time to time was the town's fervent nationalist, Home Rule O'Toole.

MAGNUM PI

US (Universal/Bellisario/Glen A. Larson)
Detective Drama. ITV 1981–

Thomas Sullivan Magnum	Tom Selleck
Jonathan Quayle Higgins III	John Hillerman
Theodore 'TC' Calvin	Roger E. Mosley
Orville 'Rick' Wright	Larry Manetti
Robin Masters (voice only)	Orson Welles
Mac Reynolds	Jeff MacKay
Lt Maggie Poole	Jean Bruce Scott
Lt Tanaka	Kwan Hi Lim
Agatha Chumley	Gillian Dobb
Francis Hofstetler ('Ice Pick')	Elisha Cook, Jnr
Assistant DA Carol Baldwin	Kathleen Lloyd

Creators: Donald P. Bellisario, Glen A. Larson

A private eye looks after the Hawaiian estate of a mysterious millionaire.

Womanizing Thomas Sullivan Magnum (TS to his friends) was a former naval intelligence officer turned private investigator. He was based on the Hawaiian islands, where his main contract was to protect the estate of writer Robin Masters, who was perpetually away from home and, hence, never seen, only heard. In return, Magnum was provided with luxurious accommodation on the Oahu seafront and the use of his employer's Ferrari. However, all was not plain sailing, thanks to the presence of Jonathan Quayle Higgins III, Masters's crusty English manservant. A former sergeant major, his strict military background jarred with Magnum's easy going approach to life and, while a professional respect developed over the years, there was always much friction between them. Higgins particularly disliked Magnum's abuse of the millionaire's generosity, but he did have the consolation of knowing that his two Doberman pinscher guard dogs, Zeus and Apollo, shared his feelings about the private investigator.

Magnum also took on other assignments, many thrust upon him by Assistant DA Carol Baldwin. For these, he was assisted by two Vietnam veteran colleagues, TC and Rick, but the cases seldom paid their way and Magnum often fouled up. TC ran the Island Hoppers helicopter company, while Rick (real name Orville, which he refused to use) was owner of a bar based on Rick's Café in the film *Casablanca*. He later moved to the exclusive King Kamehameha Beach Club, in joint ownership with Robin Masters. Rick also had some handy connections in the local underworld, such as the dodgy businessman Ice Pick.

With the end of the series in sight, the studio shot a two-hour special in which the hero was killed off and went to Heaven. However, the show continued for one more season and so it had to be explained away as a dream. When the finale did eventually come, Magnum rediscovered his long-lost daughter and rejoined the navy. But a degree of ambiguity veiled the dénouement. Robin Masters, it was suggested, was none other than Higgins himself, but, as this was never properly confirmed, the audience was left in some doubt. *Magnum PI*, mostly billed in the UK simply as *Magnum*, used the same production facilities as *Hawaii Five-O* and the scripts often referred to the Five-O police unit and its leader, Steve McGarrett.

MAGNUSSON, MAGNUS, KBE (MAGNUS SIGURSTEINNSON; 1929–)

Icelandic TV presenter, famous for his 'I've started so I'll finish' role as questionmaster on *Mastermind* since 1972. He is also a keen historian and an expert on Viking matters, resulting in series like *Vikings!*, *Chronicle*, *Unsolved Mysteries*, *BC: The Archeology of the Bible Lands* and *Living Legends*. His earliest TV work was on *Tonight*, after a journalistic career in Scotland, where he was raised. Magnusson has also worked on Icelandic television. He is the father of news presenter Sally Magnusson.

MAGPIE

UK (Thames) Children's Magazine. ITV 1968–80

Presenters:
Susan Stranks
Pete Brady
Tony Bastable
Mick Robertson
Douglas Rae
Jenny Hanley
Tommy Boyd

Executive Producer: Lewis Rudd. Producers: Sue Turner, Tony Bastable, David Hodgson, Randal Beattie, Tim Jones, Leslie Burgess

Lively children's hour magazine.

Transmitted live twice a week from Thames TV's Teddington studios, *Magpie* was conceived as a rival to the BBC's well-established *Blue Peter*. Its trendy trio of presenters, Susan Stranks, Tony Bastable and former Radio 1 DJ Pete Brady, set out to bring kids' TV up to date, with features on pop music (even the theme music was rock-based), fashions and genuinely interesting pastimes. Specialist educational segments like *A Date with Tony* (a regular in-depth look at an historical event) and the *ABC of Space* (with ITN's Peter

Fairley) were introduced and, for humour, the zany Captain Fantastic character (David Jason) from *Do Not Adjust Your Set* was given a five-minute slot. All this might have been viewed as radical, given the wholesome, almost puritan, fare served up by its BBC competitor, but, having said that, the format of the two programmes was remarkably similar and many ideas were shared.

There were plenty of making and cooking projects, animals featured strongly and, each Christmas, *Magpie* annuals accompanied *Blue Peter* books onto the newsagents' shelves. Both programmes offered badges as prizes and both organized yearly appeals. *Magpie*, however, offered ten different badges, awarded for various achievements or contributions, and the *Magpie* appeal was subtly different, too. Instead of calling for used paperback books or milk bottle tops, it asked directly for cash, and the totals raised were indicated by a red line that ran around the entire Thames studio complex. Early efforts were modest in their ambitions and were known as *Magpie Sixpence* appeals, kids being asked to donate a tanner out of their pocket money.

However, *Magpie* and *Blue Peter* seemed to grow further apart over the years. While the BBC show seemed firmly rooted in the 1960s, *Magpie* became more 'with it' by the day and enjoyed a far more relaxed studio atmosphere. Captain Fantastic was quickly dropped and new presenters were gradually drafted in. Mop-haired Mick Robertson, quiet Scotsman Douglas Rae, actress Jenny Hanley and disc jockey Tommy Boyd were later recruits. When *Magpie* ended in 1980, Robertson went on to present a similar, leisure-based series entitled *Freetime*.

The *Magpie* name was derived from the old rhyme which featured in the theme music – 'One for sorrow, Two for joy, Three for a girl and Four for a boy, Five for silver, Six for gold, Seven is a secret never to be told. Eight's a wish and Nine a kiss, Ten is a bird you must not miss'. The programme's fat magpie mascot was known as Murgatroyd.

MAID MARIAN AND HER MERRY MEN

UK (BBC) Children's Comedy. BBC 1 1989–94

Maid Marian	Kate Lonergan
Robin Hood	Wayne Morris
Sheriff of Nottingham	Tony Robinson
Barrington	Danny John-Jules
Rabies	Howard Lew Lewis
Little Ron	Mike Edmonds
King John	Forbes Collins
Gary	Mark Billingham
Graeme	David Lloyd

Creator/Writer: Tony Robinson. Producer: Richard Callanan

Robin Hood with a difference: now Maid Marian is in charge and Robin is a wimp.

This off-beat, award-winning children's comedy, penned by *Blackadder* star Tony Robinson, turned the tales of Sherwood Forest inside out. It cast Robin Hood as an ineffective yuppie figure (known as Robin of Islington) and gave command of the Merry Men to the bold Maid Marian, who egged them on like a school hockey captain. In her ineffective troupe were the midget Little Ron, the Rastafarian Barrington and Rabies. Tony Robinson himself appeared as the Sheriff of Nottingham.

MAIGRET

UK (BBC/Winwell) Police Drama. BBC 1960–3

Chief Inspector Maigret	Rupert Davies
Lucas	Ewen Solon
Madame Maigret	Helen Shingler

Creator: Georges Simenon. Executive Producer: Andrew Osborn

The investigations of the celebrated French detective.

Hero of some 150 stories by Belgian novelist Georges Simenon, and already played in the cinema by Jean Gabin, Maigret, the Paris detective, reached the TV screen in 1960. Produced not by a French company but by the BBC, whom Simenon had approached because of its reputation for drama, this hugely successful series made a star – if a chronically typecast one – out of Rupert Davies.

Maigret was an officer with the Sûreté, the Parisian equivalent of Scotland Yard. Renowned for his pipe, raincoat and trilby trademarks, like Morse and company over 20 years later, he was a thinking man's detective. He solved cases by analysing the characters and personalities of his suspects, and by visiting them at home, where he could learn more about them, rather than calling them into the sterile atmosphere of his office (where a photograph of his beloved Madame Maigret held pride of place on his desk). In his investigations, he was assisted by a young sidekick, Lucas.

Although it failed as a stage play, and despite a disastrous attempt to film the character (Rupert Davies walked off the set), *Maigret* has lingered pleasantly in viewers' minds. Ron Grainer's theme music and the classic opening sequence, showing Maigret striking a match against a wall to light his pipe, are particularly fondly remembered. Davies returned for a one-off 90-minute production, *Maigret At Bay*, in 1969, Richard Harris took over for an HTV film in 1988 and a new TV adaptation, produced by Granada with Michael Gambon in the lead role and Geoffrey Hutchings as Lucas, began in 1992. On this occasion, filming took place in Budapest, rather than Paris (it was cheaper and looked more like 1950s Paris than the real thing).

MAIN CHANCE, THE

UK (Yorkshire) Legal Drama. ITV 1969–75

David Main	John Stride
Julia Main	Kate O'Mara
Sarah Courtenay/Lady Radchester	Anna Palk
Henry Castleton	John Wentworth
Margaret Castleton	Margaret Ashcroft

Creator/Writer: Edmund Ward. Executive Producers: Peter Willes, David Cunliffe, John Frankau, Derek Bennett

A successful young lawyer strives to reach the top.

David Main, in his early 30s, was brash, keen and hungry for success. He shopped around for the best cases, hoping to pocket a share of the profitable legal business, and yet also found himself drawn to the defence of the most humble. His impetuosity led him into precarious situations, but his energy and knowledge of the law carried him through. A stickler for efficiency, Main's high-tech office suite boasted all the latest electrical gadgets. Julia, his wife, appeared only in the first series, but his secretary, Sarah Courtenay, later to become Lady Radchester, stayed with him throughout the show's lengthy run.

MAJORS, LEE (HARVEY LEE YEARY II; 1940–)

American actor Lee Majors has seldom been short of a prime-time TV role since making his TV debut in 1965. After appearances in series like *The Alfred Hitchcock Hour* and *Gunsmoke*, he was cast in the role of Heath Barkley, Barbara Stanwyck's third son in *The Big Valley*. The series ran for four years and, when it ended, Majors quickly moved on to another western, *The Men from Shiloh*. In this revamped version of *The Virginian* he played Roy Tate. A less notable series, *Owen Marshall, Counselor at Law*, followed and then, in 1974, came his biggest role to date, that of bionic man Colonel Steve Austin in *The Six Million Dollar Man*. In 1981 Majors was *The Fall Guy*, stuntman Colt Seavers, in a series that ran for five years and for which Majors also sang the theme song. Then, in 1990, he joined the Vietnam drama series *Tour of Duty*. He has also appeared in numerous TV movies and was once married to actress Farrah Fawcett.

MAKING OUT

UK (BBC) Comedy Drama. BBC 1 1989–91

Queenie	Margi Clarke
Rex	Keith Allen
Carol May	Shirley Stelfox
Stella	Sheila Grier
Pauline	Rachel Davies
Chunky	Brian Hibbard
Norma	Tracie Bennett
Bernie	Alan David
Donna	Heather Tobias
Gordon	Jonathan Barlow
Jill	Melanie Kilburn
Ray	Tim Dantay
Klepto	Moya Brady
Bella	Deborah Norton
Gavin	John Lynch
Simon	Gary Beadle
Frankie	John Forgeham
Mr Beachcroft	Don Henderson
Kip	Tony Haygarth
Colin	David Hargreaves
Sharon	Claire Quigley
Rosie	Jane Hazlegrove
Nicky	William Ash
Avril	Susan Brown

Creator: Franc Roddam. Writer: Debbie Horsfield. Producers: John Chapman, Carol Wilks

Ups and downs in the lives of a group of factory workers.

Set in a converted Manchester mill, home of New Lyne Electronics, *Making Out* revolved around the tumultuous lives of the company's shop-floor workers as they battled against bosses, fought with their men folk and generally tried to make more of their lives. Nominal shop steward was Pauline, but the group's ring leader was the fiery Queenie, whose petty criminal boyfriend, Chunky, was always looking for a quick buck. Carol May was the lady-like granny who chased sexy boss Rex, fellow worker Donna longed for a baby and Klepto was a teenage romantic in conflict with her orthodox Greek family. Then there was Jill, the new girl, who embarked on an affair with Gavin, a Manchester Utd footballer, whilst her husband, Ray, became involved with Rosie, a hairdresser. Amongst the New Lyne bosses were Bernie and Norma. By the time the series ended after three runs, new management had taken over and the company was known as Shangri-La Electronics.

MALAHIDE, PATRICK (1945–)

British actor, now obtaining starring roles after years of notable supporting performances. He was Detective Sgt Chisholm in *Minder*, Raymond/Mark Binney/Finney in *The Singing Detective* and appeared as Arthur Starkey in the kids' fantasy *News at Twelve*, but, in 1988, he was offered the limelight in the sci-fi series *The One Game* and, in 1993, he became Inspector Roderick Alleyn in *The Inspector Alleyn Mysteries*. Other credits have included episodes of *Shoestring*, *Inspector Morse*, *Boon*, *Lovejoy* and *The Ruth Rendell Mysteries*.

MALCOLM, MARY (1918–)

Former radio announcer who became one of the BBC's on-screen continuity announcers after the war. In 1958, she left to go freelance and later worked for German television (making programmes about Britain). Malcolm was the granddaughter of actress Lily Langtry.

MALDEN, KARL (KARL MLADEN SEKULOVICH; 1914–)

American actor of Yugoslav descent whose television career did not take off until the early 1970s, despite having first appeared on the Broadway stage in the 1930s and in the movies in 1940. It was his role as Detective Lt. Mike Stone in a TV movie called *The Streets of San Francisco* which proved the catalyst, with a full-blown series following and running for five years. Malden has since been seen in numerous TV movies, though a second series of his own, entitled *Skag*, proved to be a flop.

MALLENS, THE

UK (Granada) Drama. ITV 1979–80

Thomas Mallen	John Hallam
Donald Radlet	John Duttine
Dick	David Rintoul
Barbara Farrington	Pippa Guard
Constance Farrington/Radlet	Julia Chambers
	June Ritchie
Anna Brigmore	Caroline Blakiston
Barbara Mallen	Juliet Stevenson
Michael Radlet	Gerry Sundquist
Matthew Radlet	Ian Saynor

Writer: Jack Russell. Producer: Roy Roberts

A rogue Victorian squire is the father of numerous bastard children.

Ruthless Thomas Mallen was the lord of High Banks Hall, set amidst the Northumberland Moors. He was a man with a scant regard for women and, having lusted, loved and raped most of his life, was now the father of several illegitimate sons, all easily identified by the trademark Mallen white streak in their hair. As the feuding children began to emerge from the woodwork, so Thomas's troubles increased. He eventually moved in with his nieces Barbara and Constance Farrington and their governess (soon to be his latest lover), Anna Brigmore.

The first seven episodes were based on the lusty novels *The Mallen Litter* and *The Mallen Streak* by Catherine Cookson. These were followed by a second series (entitled *Catherine Cookson's The Mallens*) which focused on Barbara Mallen (the illegitimate daughter of Thomas and Barbara Farrington) and her lover Michael Radlet (the illegitimate son of Constance). These episodes were derived from another Cookson novel, *The Mallen Girl*.

MAN ABOUT THE HOUSE

UK (Thames) Situation Comedy. ITV 1973–6

Robin Tripp	Richard O'Sullivan
Chrissy Plummer	Paula Wilcox
Jo	Sally Thomsett
George Roper	Brian Murphy
Mildred Roper	Yootha Joyce
Larry Simmons	Doug Fisher

Creators/Writers: Johnnie Mortimer and Brian Cooke. Producer: Peter Frazer-Jones

Two girls and a boy share a flat at a time when co-habitation was a novelty.

Needing a third sharer to help pay the rent on their Earl's Court flat, two young, attractive girls, the dark-haired Chrissy and the blonde, toothy Jo, had planned to find another girl. But when Robin Tripp, a catering student, was found sleeping in the bath the morning after a party, they decided to let him move in, especially as he could cook. The new arrangement understandably raised a few eyebrows, particularly with the girls' landlords, George and Mildred Roper, who lived downstairs.

Although there was much mock sexual bravado, this *ménage à trois* was definitely not of the murky kind, despite Robin's attempts to bed the far too sensible Chrissy. The well-signalled humour came from domestic squabbles (like hogging the bathroom), their respective boyfriends/girlfriends, and Robin and Chrissy's attempts to follow Jo's weird logic. There were also nosy interruptions from the Ropers, he a workshy weakling, she a man-devouring social climber with an eye on young Robin.

Two spin-offs followed: *Robin's Nest*, in which Robin opened his own bistro, and *George and Mildred*, following the Ropers' new life on a middle-class housing estate. The series also spawned a feature film of the same title and was translated for American audiences in a less subtle version called *Three's Company*.

MAN ALIVE

UK (BBC) Current Affairs. BBC 2 1965–82

Producer: Michael Latham.

Social pains and pleasures examined through the lives of ordinary people.

This long-running documentary series took an interest in the problems and sometimes happier experiences of ordinary citizens, tackling awkward and difficult subjects in the process. Each film focused on one topic, which could be as varied as agoraphobia and child molesting. Its production team, originally headed by Michael Latham, comprised such notables as Desmond Wilcox, Trevor Philpott, Esther Rantzen, John Pitman and Harold Williamson. Variations on the theme included *The Man Alive Report* in 1976 and *The Man Alive Debate* in 1982.

MAN AT THE TOP

UK (Thames) Drama. ITV 1970–2

Joe Lampton ....Kenneth Haigh
Susan Lampton ....Zena Walker
Margaret Brown ....Avice Landon

Creator: John Braine. Producers: George Markstein, Lloyd Shirley, Jacqueline Davis

An unscrupulous businessman fights to stay ahead of the game.

Picking up the story told in John Braine's novel, *Room at the Top*, and the 1958 Laurence Harvey film of the same name (plus its 1965 sequel, *Life at the Top*), *Man at the Top* concerned Joe Lampton, a pushy, aggressive northerner who had battled his way up the ladder to relative prosperity. Thirteen years on, Lampton now lived in Surrey's stockbroker belt, working as a management consultant. He was determined to stay there and was prepared to pull any stroke to do so. He was also keen on pulling women, as his wife, Susan, was only too aware. In 1973 the series spawned a feature film of its own, also called *Man at the Top* and starring Kenneth Haigh.

MAN CALLED IRONSIDE, A

US (Harbour/Universal) Police Drama. BBC 1 1967–76

Chief Robert T. Ironside.......................Raymond Burr
Detective Sgt Ed Brown........................Don Galloway
Officer Eve Whitfield....................Barbara Anderson
Mark Sanger...Don Mitchell
Officer Fran Belding ....Elizabeth Baur
Commissioner Dennis Randall ....Gene Lyons
Lt Carl Reese ....Johnny Seven
Diana Sanger...Joan Pringle

Creator: Collier Young. Executive Producers: Joel Rogosin, Cy Chermak

A wheelchair-bound cop still gets his man.

Raymond Burr followed up his enormously successful *Perry Mason* role with this series about a top detective who faced early retirement after receiving a crippling injury. Robert T. Ironside had been Chief of Detectives in the San Francisco Police Department, but his career was placed on the line when he was badly injured by a bullet from a would-be assassin. He was expected to quit the force, but, although confined to a wheelchair, he persuaded his superior, Commissioner Randall, to allow him to stay on in a consultative capacity.

So it was that, paralysed from the waist down, the grouchy Ironside was still able to put his 25 years of experience to good use. Living and working from a converted attic above the police department, he travelled to the scenes of crime in a modified police van, assisted and minded by Mark Sanger. Sanger had been a juvenile delinquent, a street rebel, but he mellowed so much during the series that he had even graduated from law school before it ended. Two other colleagues, Sgt Ed Brown and police woman Eve Whitfield, helped put Ironside's ideas into action, with Eve replaced after a few seasons by new policewoman Fran Belding. In America, the show was known simply as *Ironside*. In the UK, some episodes aired under the umbrella title of *The Detectives*.

MAN CALLED SHENANDOAH, A

US (MGM) Western. ITV

Shenandoah...Robert Horton

Creator/Executive Producer: E. Jack Neuman. Producer: Fred Freiberger

A cowboy with amnesia wanders the Wild West looking for his true identity.

Sometime after the American Civil War, a man wounded in a gunfight was found by two buffalo hunters, who took him to the nearest town in the hope of claiming a bounty. As it happened, he was not on the wanted list, but no one actually knew who he was. He recovered but continued to suffer from memory loss. He adopted the name of Shenandoah and set out to find his real self. Drifting from town to town, he searched in vain for clues that would help him to discover his identity. Fortunately, star Robert Horton was no stranger to travelling the prairies, having previously appeared in *Wagon Train*. The series was screened in its native USA from 1965, but was only shown sporadically around the ITV network in the UK.

MAN FROM ATLANTIS

US (Solow) Science Fiction. ITV 1977–8

Mark Harris...Patrick Duffy
Dr Elizabeth Merrill ....Belinda J. Montgomery
C.W. Crawford..Alan Fudge

Mr Schubert ....Victor Buono
Brent ....Robert Lussier

Executive Producer: Herbert F. Solow.
Producer: Herman Miller

An underwater man works for the secret services.

When a half-man, half-fish was washed up on the California shore, it was believed that he was the last survivor of the lost continent of Atlantis. Nursed back to health by naval doctor Elizabeth Merrill, Mark Harris (as she christened him) stayed on to work with her and the Foundation for Oceanic Research in their efforts to learn more about the seas. He was also employed by the US Government to help combat marine crime (and, on occasion, even space aliens).

Mark looked human but benefited from extra sharp senses and superhuman strength. More obviously, his eyes were green and his feet and hands were webbed. These allowed him to swim faster than a dolphin. He also had gill tissue instead of lungs, and this caused major problems as he was forced to return to the sea to 'breathe' every 12 hours. Mark and Elizabeth used a submersible known as the *Cetacean* on their sea patrols and worked for C.W. Crawford, the money-conscious head of the Foundation. Their biggest adversaries were the mad scientist Mr Schubert, and his sidekick, Brent.

MAN FROM INTERPOL, THE

UK (Danziger) Police Drama. ITV 1960

Commander Anthony Smith ....Richard Wyler
Supt Mercer ....John Longden

Producers: Edward J. Danziger, Harry Lee Danziger

The cases of a top Interpol agent.

Anthony Smith was one of Interpol's leading men. His investigations took him all around the world, tracking down international criminals and, occasionally, spies. He specialized in cases where crime crossed national borders, pursuing his targets from country to country. The low-budget productions (still seen occasionally on satellite stations) have gained a reputation for being somewhat unexciting.

MAN FROM UNCLE, THE

US (MGM/Arena) Secret Agent Drama. BBC 1 1965-8

Napoleon Solo ....Robert Vaughn
Illya Kuryakin ....David McCallum
Mr Alexander Waverly ....Leo G. Carroll
Lisa Rogers ....Barbara Moore

Creators: Norman Felton, Sam Rolfe. Executive Producer: Norman Felton

The counter-conspiracy assignments of a secret agent and his partner.

The 'Man from UNCLE' was Napoleon Solo, a suave, relaxed American agent working for an undercover, international, anti-crime organization. UNCLE stood for United Network Command for Law and Enforcement, and head of its agents was elderly Englishman Alexander Waverly. Solo was accompanied on most of his missions by Illya Kuryakin, a sullen blond Russian. Their efforts chiefly centred on foiling the ambitious plans of THRUSH, an eccentric global crime syndicate. Each episode was entitled '*The . . . Affair*' (fill in the blank as appropriate).

UNCLE headquarters was located in Manhattan, with a secret entrance behind the Del Floria tailor's shop. Agents entered the shop and the tailor lifted a clothes press to open a hidden door in a changing cubicle. Once inside, the agents donned special triangular badges to allow them to pass through the corridors of the office. Each agent had his own numbered badge: Solo's was 11, Waverly's 1 and Kuryakin's 2. Solo and Kuryakin never went into action without their collection of electronic gadgetry, including two-way radios concealed in fountain pens. 'Open Channel D' paved the way for a message back to HQ. Yet, for all this technology, the pair constantly required help from ordinary civilians (often a beautiful girl falling for Solo's charms) in achieving their goals. *The Man from UNCLE* came to TV on the back of the James Bond craze. The name Napoleon Solo was actually borrowed from a gangster in *Goldfinger* and producer Norman Felton consulted Bond author Ian Fleming before developing the series. Catching the secret agent wave, *The Man from UNCLE* was, all the same, played with tongues firmly in cheeks (more so even than the Bond originals). However, a couple of years later, following criticism of its spoofiness, the series was firmed up, and a new character, that of Mr Waverly's secretary, Lisa Rogers, was introduced. The show also spawned a spin-off, *The Girl from UNCLE* (with which it alternated weekly in the UK), and a series of eight full-length movies, collated from the TV footage.

The acronym 'UNCLE' was only given its meaning after the series had started, in response to viewers' requests for an explanation of the letters. THRUSH was never spelt out. The Man from UNCLE was re-run on BBC2 from 1993.

MAN IN A SUITCASE

UK (ITC) Detective Drama. ITV 1967-8

McGill..Richard Bradford

Creators: Richard Harris, Dennis Spooner.
Producer: Sidney Cole

A discredited CIA agent turns to detective work.

McGill was a grim, tough man of few words. A former US intelligence agent, he had been wrongly accused of allowing a top scientist to defect to the USSR. Framed and sacrificed in the name of international diplomacy, he had been dismissed from his post, his reputation in tatters. With only a battered suitcase and a gun to his name, he now operated as a private detective and bounty hunter in Britain and on the Continent, never relenting in his search for the evidence which would clear his name.

McGill (whose first name was supposedly John but was never used) charged $500 a day (plus expenses) for his work, although he was sometimes cheated by shady employers. Having a dodgy past himself, and lacking friends in authority, there was very little he could do about it. And that was not the only complication. His former CIA colleagues were always lurking in the background, blackmailing him into doing jobs or threatening to drop him in it at any moment.

MAN IN ROOM 17, THE

UK (Granada) Detective Drama. ITV 1965–6

Oldenshaw ....Richard Vernon
Dimmock ....Michael Aldridge
Imlac Defraits....................................Denholm Elliott
Sir Geoffrey Norton ....Willoughby Goddard

Creator: Robin Chapman. Producer: Richard Everitt

Two top criminologists solve the most baffling crimes without even leaving their room.

Room 17, based near the Houses of Parliament, had been set up by the Government to house the Department of Social Research, a secret unit for investigating the criminal mind. The actual 'Man' was Oldenshaw, a barrister, ex-war correspondent and crime specialist, who recruited as his partner the younger Dimmock, a former student of the Ohio University Institute of Criminology. Together the two men out-thought the most experienced police and counter-intelligence brains in the country. If Scotland Yard or the Government found themselves in need of assistance, they called upon this far-from-dynamic duo whose brain power always delivered the goods. Civil servant Sir Geoffrey Norton was their link with the outside world.

In the second season, Dimmock was replaced by a new specialist, Defraits, but the original pairing

were reunited when a follow-up series, **The Fellows,** came to the screen. To firmly detach the 'Men' and their cerebral work from the nitty gritty of street detection, two film crews with different directors were employed. One handled the scenes inside the Room, the other the rest of the action.

MAN OF THE WORLD

UK (ATV) Adventure. ITV 1962–3

Mike Strait ....Craig Stevens
Maggie ....Tracey Reed
Hank..Graham Stark

Producer: Harry Fine

The adventurous life of a globetrotting photo-journalist.

American Mike Strait enjoyed a glamorous lifestyle. His freelance assignments (mostly for fashion magazines) took him to the four corners of the world. However, instead of merely photographing or reporting his story, Strait unfailingly became involved in the action, finding himself up to his neck in murder, blackmail, espionage and intrigue of all kinds. *Man of the World* gave rise to a spin-off series, **The Sentimental Agent,** drawn from an episode of the same title in which Carlos Thompson played the part of import-export agent Carlos Varela.

MANHUNT

UK (LWT) Drama. ITV 1970

Jimmy Porter ....Alfred Lynch
Vincent ....Peter Barkworth
Nina ....Cyd Hayman
Adelaide ....Maggie Fitzgibbon
Abwehr Sgt Gratz ....Robert Hardy
Lutzig ....Philip Madoc

Creator/Executive Producer: Rex Firkin.
Producer: Andrew Brown

Heroic tales of French Résistance activity during World War II.

Using Beethoven's Fifth symphony as its theme tune (echoing its use as a wartime code by the Allies), *Manhunt* told of the daring exploits of Résistance workers who sought to sabotage German activities and smuggle stranded airmen or vital supplies to Britain from occupied France. The principals were agents Vincent and Nina, plus downed RAF pilot Jimmy. Together, they were on the run from the Nazis, headed by Abwehr Sgt Gratz. Fear, conscience, loyalty and suspicion competed for control of their minds and a tense atmosphere pervaded all 26 episodes.

MANNIX

US (Paramount) Detective Drama. ITV 1971–

Joe Mannix ....Mike Connors

Lou Wickersham	Joseph Campanella
Peggy Fair	Gail Fisher
Lt Adam Tobias	Robert Reed
Lt George Kramer	Larry Linville
Lt Art Malcolm	Ward Wood

Creators: Richard Levinson, William Link.
Executive Producer: Bruce Geller. Producers:
Ivan Goff, Ben Roberts

A private eye prefers fists to computers when trying to get results.

Joe Mannix worked for Lou Wickersham, head of an enterprising, high-tech Los Angeles detective firm known as Intertect. Despite being equipped with the latest crime-prevention technology (including a car computer that transmitted and received photographs and fingerprints of the suspects), Mannix was more at home using the tried and tested combination of his own detective nous and the good, old-fashioned knuckle sandwich.

After leaving Intertect, he became his own boss, setting up a detective agency on the first floor of his apartment block at 17 Paseo Verdes in West LA, and employing widow Peggy Fair as his personal assistant. Her husband (a police officer and a friend of Mannix's) had been killed in action and she turned out to be more than just a secretary herself, lending a hand in investigations and often being held hostage for her pains. Several LA cops also chipped in from time to time, most notably Lieutenants Adam Tobias, Art Malcolm and George Kramer (the last played by Larry Linville, better known as Frank Burns in *M*A*S*H*).

MARCUS WELBY, MD

US (Universal) Medical Drama. ITV 1969–

Dr Marcus Welby	Robert Young
Dr Steven Kiley	James Brolin
Consuelo Lopez	Elena Verdugo
Myra Sherwood	Anne Baxter
Kathleen Faverty	Sharon Gless
Janet Blake/Kiley	Pamela Hensley

Creator/Executive Producer: David Victor

Doctors-and-patients drama, a kind of *Dr Kildare* or *Ben Casey* in reverse.

Thoroughly dedicated, silver-haired GP Marcus Welby ran a practice from his home in Santa Monica, California. After suffering a heart attack, he was forced to take on a younger doctor to help with the workload. That younger man was Steven Kiley, a motorcycling student neurologist. He signed up for a year's experience but never left. Unlike previous medical dramas, in which revered old docs had to keep young hothead physicians in check, this series turned the young-

ster into the level-headed one and made the older man a bit of a maverick. Kind, reassuring Welby employed an unusual technique in dealing with sickness. He believed in treating the whole patient, not just the precise ailment, convinced that psychological and other factors had some bearing in each case. This was all new to the outspoken Kiley, who played it by the book.

Both men led a bachelor existence, though there was a romantic liaison early on for Welby in the form of Myra Sherwood and Kiley eventually married Janet Blake, a PR director at the local Hope Memorial Hospital. Other cast regulars were nurses Consuelo Lopez and Kathleen Faverty (the latter played by Sharon Gless, later famous as Chris Cagney in *Cagney and Lacey*).

MARINE BOY

Japan (Japan Telecartoons/Seven Arts)
Cartoon. BBC 1 1969–70

Voices:

Marine Boy	Corinne Orr
Dr Mariner	Jack Curtis
Bulton	Peter Fernandez
Piper	Jack Grimes
Neptina	Corinne Orr
Cli Cli	Corinne Orr

Producer: Hinoru Adachi

The adventures of a young aquatic hero.

Marine Boy was the son of Dr Mariner, head of Ocean Patrol, an international body dedicated to preserving peace beneath the waves. But Marine Boy was also one of the organization's top agents. Diving into danger, he battled it out with a host of sea foes, including Captain Kidd, Dr Slime and Count Shark, keeping his air supply alive by chewing Oxygum, a revolutionary oxygen-generating bubblegum. This amazing gum had been invented by oceanographer Dr Fumble, who also created Marine Boy's other gadgets, which included an electric boomerang, a bullet-proof wet suit and jet-propelled flying boots. Assisting our hero were Bulton and Piper, his colleagues in the flying submarine known as the P-1, as well as a pet white dolphin called Splasher, a fishy friend called Cli Cli and a mermaid, Neptina (possessor of a magic pearl).

MARK SABER/SABER OF LONDON

UK (Danziger) Detective Drama. ITV
1957–9/1959–61

Mark Saber	Donald Gray
Barny O'Keefe	Michael Balfour
Judy	Teresa Thorne
Stephanie Ames	Diana Decker
Peter Paulson	Neil McCallum
	Gordon Tanner

Bob Page	Robert Arden
Eddie Wells	Jerry Thorne
Ann Summers	Jennifer Jayne
Inspector Brady	Patrick Holt
Inspector Chester/Parker	Colin Tapley

Producers: Edward J. Danziger, Harry Lee Danziger

The cases of a one-armed Scotland Yard detective turned private eye.

Mark Saber has had a chequered TV history. The character first reached the small screen in the USA as a British detective in the New York Police Department (in series entitled *Mystery Theatre* and *Inspector Mark Saber – Homicide Squad*, both with Tom Conway in the title role). However, when he came to Britain in a production called simply *Mark Saber* things had changed considerably. For a start he only had one arm! He now worked as a private detective, supported by sidekick Barny O'Keefe, briefly by a girl named Judy and by his blonde secretary, Stephanie Ames. Two police officers were also prominent, Inspectors Chester and Brady. This series was retitled *The Vise* for US consumption.

To add to the confusion, after a couple of years the concept was reworked yet again, with the title switched to *Saber of London* and our hero now undertaking assignments on the Continent. O'Keefe was replaced by Canadian Pete Paulson, who was in turn replaced by Bob Page and then Eddie Wells, a reformed crook. Ann Summers was introduced as Saber's girlfriend. Inspector Chester was still there, only, for some reason, his name was now Parker.

The programme's star, Donald Gray, was a former BBC announcer who had lost an arm in World War II. He later provided the voice for Colonel White in *Captain Scarlet and the Mysterons*.

MARKET IN HONEY LANE/HONEY LANE

UK (ATV) Drama. ITV 1967–9

Billy Bush	John Bennett
Sam English	Michael Golden
Dave Sampson	Ray Lonnen
Jacko Bennet	Peter Birrel
Jimmy Bentall	Jack Bligh
Polly Jessel	Pat Nye
Danny Jessel	Brian Rawlinson

Creator: Louis Marks. Producer: John Cooper

Events in the lives of London market stall holders.

Set in London's East End, *Market in Honey Lane*, for a while, challenged *Coronation Street*'s supremacy in the ratings. It focused on the vibrant Cockney workers at the fictitious Honey Lane market, with a different character high-lighted in each episode. The protagonists included fruit and veg merchant Billy Bush and the mother and son duo of Polly and Danny Jessel. In September 1968 the title was shortened to *Honey Lane* and transmission was switched to afternoons. The series was cancelled a year later.

The programme was staged and recorded at ATV's Elstree studios. When the BBC took over Elstree, it, too, produced a drama series chiefly centred around London market folk. *EastEnders*, however, has been considerably more resilient than its 1960s predecessor.

MARKS, ALFRED, OBE (1921–)

British comedian and comic actor, big in the 1950s and 1960s through series like *Alfred Marks Time* and **Sunday Night at the London Palladium** (which he compèred). He was Charlie, the fire chief, in the farce **Fire Crackers** in 1964 and starred as Albert Hackett in another sitcom, **Albert and Victoria**, in 1970. Marks has also been a regular on panel games and appeared in the dramas *Paris 1900*, *Funny Man* and *Maybury*.

MARKS, LAURENCE see Gran, Maurice.

MARKS, LOUIS (1928–)

British writer and script editor for both the BBC and ITV companies, working most prominently on science fiction and thriller series like **Doctor Who**, *Dead of Night* and **Doomwatch**, and the soap **Market in Honey Lane** (which he created). He also produced a number of dramas, such as *The Lost Boys*, *Bavarian Night*, *Silas Marner* and the celebrated 1994 version of *Middlemarch*.

MARLOWE – PRIVATE EYE see Philip Marlowe.

MARRIAGE LINES, THE

UK (BBC) Situation Comedy. BBC 1 1963–6

George Starling	Richard Briers
Kate Starling	Prunella Scales
Peter	Ronald Hines
Norah	Christine Finn

Creator/Writer: Richard Waring. Producer: Graeme Muir

The highs and lows of newly-wed life.

Recently married George and Kate Starling lived in a flat in Earl's Court. George worked in the City as a lowly-paid clerk and Kate had been his secretary, but, in keeping with the mood of the times, she now stayed at home. This series focused on their domestic and financial problems, with their compatibility severely tested by endless petty rows that usually saw George heading for the pub. Two neighbours, Peter and Norah, were around for the first season, before they moved away and upmarket, leaving the Starlings depressingly stuck on the first rung of the property ladder. Kate later gave birth to a baby daughter, Helen, which George described as 'The Cuckoo', because her presence added to his domestic duties and interfered with his already restricted social life.

The Marriage Lines was specifically created by writer Richard Waring for the talents of young Richard Briers, who had appeared with him in **Brothers in Law**.

MARSDEN, ROY (1941–)

British actor now known as detective Adam Dalgliesh in P.D. James mysteries like *Death of an Expert Witness*, *Shroud for a Nightingale*, *Cover Her Face* and *The Black Tower*. Previously, Marsden played George Osborne in the BBC's 1972 version of *Vanity Fair*, Neil Burnside in **The Sandbaggers**, Jack Ruskin in **Airline** and Charles Edward Chipping, the eponymous hero of another BBC adaptation, *Goodbye Mr Chips*. He is married to actress Polly Hemingway (an *Airline* co-star).

MARSH, JEAN (1934–)

English actress, best remembered as the dedicated head parlour maid Rose in **Upstairs, Downstairs**, a series which she created with Eileen Atkins in 1971. Twenty years later, Marsh and Atkins also devised **The House of Eliot**. On screen, Marsh has also been seen in the TV version of the film 9 to 5, playing Roz Keith, and in the Sidney Sheldon drama *Master of the Game* (as Mrs Talley), as well as starring as Rosie Tindall in the short-lived sitcom *No Strings*. She was an early guest in **Doctor Who** and appeared in other 1960s series such as *Blackmail* and **The Informer**. Marsh was once married to actor Jon Pertwee.

MARSH, REGINALD (1926–)

Familiar British supporting actor, often in situation comedies as someone's boss. Marsh has appeared in **Coronation Street** (as Dave Smith), **George and Mildred** (as Mildred's brother-in-law, Humphrey) and with Harry Worth in **Here's Harry** and *My Name Is Harry Worth*. Amongst his many other credits have been **Crossroads**, **The Plane Makers**, **The Power Game**, *The Old Campaigner*, *How's Your Father*, *Never Say Die*, **The Ratcatchers**, **Bless This House**, **Terry and June**, **The Good Life**, **Crown Court**, **Whodunnit?**, *Barlow*, **The Sweeney**, *The Handy Gang* and *Help!* He also starred in Joe Orton's play *The Erpingham Camp* and Nigel Kneale's *The Stone Tape*, as well as his own drama *The Man Who Came To Die*.

MARSHALL, ANDREW (1954–)

British comedy writer, often in collaboration with David Renwick. Together they worked on

BBC Radio before moving into television and providing scripts for **Not The Nine O'Clock News** and *Alexei Sayle's Stuff*, as well as creating **Whoops! Apocalypse** and **Hot Metal**. While Renwick has since scored solo with **One Foot in the Grave**, Marshall has developed *Sob Sisters*, **2 Point 4 Children** and *Health and Efficiency*. They joined forces again in 1993 for the Richard Briers comedy, *If You See God Tell Him*.

MARSHALL, GARRY K. (1934–)

American writer, director and producer with a string of TV hits behind him and now active in the cinema. After working as a writer on **The Dick Van Dyke Show** and **The Lucy Show** in the 1960s, Marshall went on to greater things in the 1970s, producing **The Odd Couple** then creating and producing series like **Happy Days** and its spin-offs, **Laverne and Shirley**, **Mork and Mindy** and *Joanie Loves Chachi*. He is the brother of actress/director Penny Marshall, who appeared in **The Odd Couple** and **Laverne and Shirley** (as Laverne), and Marshall has himself been seen in front of the cameras from time to time.

MARTIN, DAVE (1935–) see Baker, Bob.

MARTIN, DICK (1923–)

American comedian, the writing and performing partner of Dan Rowan from 1952. A stand-in spot for Dean Martin in the summer of 1966 proved to be their big break. As a result, they were given their own gag and sketch show, **Laugh-In**, which became a massive international hit. Martin (the dumb one) had earlier been seen in **The Lucy Show**, playing Lucy's friend Harry Conners and, post-*Laugh-In*, he made guest appearances in series like **The Love Boat** as well as involving himself in production. Rowan decided upon retirement when the show ended after five years, but died in 1987.

MARTIN, IAN KENNEDY (1936–)

British screenwriter, usually on crime series, and the creator of **The Sweeney**, **Juliet Bravo**, **The Chinese Detective** and *King and Castle*. Amongst his other writing credits have been episodes of **The Troubleshooters**, *This Man Craig*, *Parkin's Patch*, *Colditz* and **The Onedin Line**. He was also story editor of **Redcap** and is the brother of fellow writer Troy Kennedy Martin.

MARTIN KANE, PRIVATE INVESTIGATOR

UK (Towers of London/ABC) Detective Drama. ITV 1957–8

Martin Kane	William Gargan
Supt Page	Brian Reece

Producer: Harry Alan Towers

An American private eye moves to London.

Martin Kane had been an investigator in New York City. Now taking up residence in England, he brought his transatlantic talents to bear in the capture of British and European criminals, working closely with Supt Page of Scotland Yard. Although this odd combination of wise-cracking gumshoe and tea-drinking English copper rarely strayed outside the office, they still got results.

William Gargan had been the first actor to portray Kane on US television and radio at the turn of the 1950s, and had himself been a private investigator before turning to the stage. He didn't stay with the show for the whole of its US run (three other Martin Kanes – Lloyd Nolan, Lee Tracy and Mark Stevens – were introduced) but, being the original and best, he was brought back for this British version. Ironically, considering the American series had been sponsored by a tobacco company, Gargan later underwent surgery for throat cancer and subsequently dedicated his life to warning others about the dangers of smoking. He died in 1979. The real Martin Kane had not been a detective at all, but was an advertising executive for the J. Walter Thompson agency, producers of the American version.

MARTIN, MILLICENT (1934–)

British singer seen as a guest on various variety shows but chiefly remembered for her contributions (and particularly her topical intros) to *That Was The Week That Was*. She was later given her own variety shows, *Mainly Millicent*, *Millicent* and *The Millicent Martin Show*, and starred as stewardess Millie Grover in the airline sitcom *From A Bird's Eye View*. Her first husband was singer Ronnie Carroll and her second actor Norman Eshley. Martin has since wed a third time.

MARTIN, QUINN (MARTIN COHN; 1922–87)

American producer, initially with Desilu for whom he produced *The Untouchables*. Branching out on his own, Martin founded QM Productions and was responsible for some of the biggest hits of the 1960s and 1970s, including *The Fugitive*, *The FBI*, *The Invaders*, *Cannon*, *The Streets of San Francisco* and *Barnaby Jones*.

MARTIN, TROY KENNEDY (1932–)

British writer, the creator of *Z Cars*, although he left after three months, allegedly concerned at the direction the series was taking. He did, however, return to write the last episode. Amongst his other notable credits have been *Diary of a Young Man* (with John McGrath), *Reilly – Ace of Spies*, the acclaimed *Edge of Darkness*, *The Fourth Floor*, *The Old Men at the Zoo* and episodes of *Out of the Unknown*, *Colditz* and *The Sweeney*. Martin has also worked as a writer in Hollywood. He is the brother of writer Ian Kennedy Martin.

MARY TYLER MOORE SHOW, THE

US (MTM) Situation Comedy. BBC 1 1971–

Mary Richards	Mary Tyler Moore
Lou Grant	Edward Asner
Ted Baxter	Ted Knight
Murray Slaughter	Gavin MacLeod
Rhoda Morgenstern	Valerie Harper
Phyllis Lindstrom	Cloris Leachman
Bess Lindstrom	Lisa Gerritsen
Gordon ('Gordy') Howard	John Amos
Georgette Franklin/Baxter	Georgia Engel
Sue Ann Nivens	Betty White

Creators/Writers/Executive Producers: James L. Brooks, Allan Burns. Producers: Ed Weinberger, Stan Daniels

Life at work and at home with an independent single girl.

This award-winning sitcom was set in the newsroom of a fictitious Minneapolis TV station, WJM-TV, Channel 12, and focused on the working and domestic lives of Mary Richards, the assistant producer of its news programme. Mary, single, friendly, level-headed and very genuine, was also independently minded, a sensible career woman of the 1970s. She arrived at WJM-TV following a break up with her boyfriend. Her boss at the station was Lou Grant, the blustering news producer, with other staff members including the chief newswriter, Murray Slaughter, and Ted Baxter, the dim, conceited anchorman. The newsroom was a real family, even if it was the worst TV news set-up in America.

Mary's best friend was Rhoda Morgenstern, a window dresser by occupation. They had much in common: both were single and in their 30s. Rhoda, however, was in far greater fear of being left on the shelf and was eventually written out into her own series, *Rhoda*, when she moved back to her native New York to find a husband. Another spin-off was *Phyllis*, based around Mary's highly strung, busybodying landlady, Phyllis Lindstrom, who moved to San Francisco with her daughter, Bess, after the death of her never-seen husband, Lars. Later additions to the cast were weatherman Gordy Howard and Sue Ann Nivens, the man-eating hostess of the station's *Happy Homemaker Show*.

When Mary Tyler Moore decided to call it a day, the series was concluded by introducing new management who sacked virtually all the staff.

Only bumbling newsreader Ted kept his job. Lou Grant was another survivor, moving on to Los Angeles and his own drama series, **Lou Grant**. After success in the 1960s as Laura Petrie in **The Dick Van Dyke Show**, Mary Tyler Moore confirmed her star status with this role. Not only that, but the programme established her powerful MTM production company and provided valuable early experience for the creators and performers of many top sitcoms of the 1980s (including producer James L. Brooks, the brains behind **Taxi** and **The Simpsons**).

MASCHWITZ, ERIC, OBE (1901–69)

Versatile British light entertainment producer, with the BBC from 1926 and holding various posts, including Editor of Radio Times, Head of Light Entertainment (1958–61) and Assistant and Adviser to Controller of Television Programmes (1961–3). Maschwitz also worked as a novelist, writing thrillers with Val Gielgud (Sir John's brother) under the pen name of Holt Marvell. He was an accomplished dramatist and, wearing his lyricist's hat, wrote the words to the songs 'These Foolish Things' and 'A Nightingale Sang In Berkeley Square'. Away from the BBC, he worked for MGM in Hollywood, on films like **Goodbye Mr Chips**, before surprisingly returning to the Corporation in 1958 as the new Head of Light Entertainment. Those who thought he was of the wrong generation for the post were quickly proved wrong when he commissioned, amongst other successes, **Juke Box Jury**, **The Black and White Minstrel Show**, **Whack-O!** and **Steptoe and Son**. He left the BBC for Associated-Rediffusion in 1963, where he became producer of special projects and worked on programmes like **Our Man at St Mark's**. His first wife was actress Hermione Gingold.

M★A★S★H

US (20th Century-Fox) Situation Comedy. BBC 2 1973–84

Captain Benjamin Franklin 'Hawkeye' Pierce ....Alan Alda
Captain 'Trapper John' McIntyre ....Wayne Rogers
Major Margaret 'Hot Lips' Houlihan ......Loretta Swit
Major Frank Burns ....Larry Linville
Corporal Walter 'Radar' O'Reilly..........Gary Burghoff
Lt Colonel Henry Blake.................McLean Stevenson
Father Francis Mulcahy ....William Christopher
Corporal Maxwell Klinger ....Jamie Farr
Colonel Sherman T. Potter...................Harry Morgan
Captain B.J. Hunnicut ....Mike Farrell
Major Charles Emerson Winchester III ....David Ogden Stiers
Dr Sidney Freedman ....Alan Arbus
Nurse Kellye Nakahara....................Kellye Nakahara
Igor Straminsky.......................................Jeff Maxwell
Nurse Bigelow ....Enid Kent
Sgt Zale................Johnny Haymer
Sgt Luther Rizzo ....G.W. Bailey
Roy ....Roy Goldman
Soon-Lee ....Rosalind Chao

Creator: Larry Gelbart. Executive Producers: Gene Reynolds, Burt Metcalfe

Life with an anarchic army hospital during the Korean War.

M★A★S★H was based on the film of the same name, starring Donald Sutherland and Eliot Gould. It is rare for a TV spin-off to achieve the success of a mother film, let alone surpass it, but M★A★S★H was an exceptional series, as nearly all TV critics agreed. Many have paid tribute to the writing, acting and production skills that enabled it to extract laughter from the most unlikely scenario of a blood-sodden war.

The series was set in the early 1950s, when the American involvement in Korea resulted in the draft of not only soldiers but also medical men and women, most serving in MASH (Mobile Army Surgical Hospital) units. It followed everyday events in the fictitious 4077th MASH, reflecting and never neglecting the tragedy and futility of war and the seemingly needless loss of life. It was, indeed, an unusual setting for a comedy, but in such numbing circumstances as these, where a sense of humour is vital, it was very apt. Bringing mirth out of madness was Captain Benjamin Franklin Pierce, commonly known as 'Hawkeye'. Drafted from his home town of Crabapple Cove, Maine, where he lived with his father, he was Chief Surgeon and desperately sickened by the pointless bloodshed. Diligent and dedicated to his vocation, he, all the same, had no time for military discipline and refused to doff his cap to the powers that be. Master of the wisecrack and quick retort, Hawkeye could also bring tears to viewers' eyes with his human reflections on the carnage around him.

His roommate, in a tent known as 'The Swamp', was 'Trapper John' McIntyre. Together they alleviated the heaviness of war by playing practical jokes, making advances to the nurses and distilling their own liquor. Butt of their humour was the self-centred, by-the-book jerk, Frank Burns, who tried to pull rank but never succeeded. Someone who had more time for Frank was Chief Nurse Margaret 'Hot Lips' Houlihan, a gutsy blonde with a voice like a foghorn. Despite Frank's well-publicized marriage, the two conducted a covert love affair that was the worst kept secret of the whole war.

In charge of this mayhem was easy-going commanding officer Lt Colonel Henry Blake. His only concern was discipline within the operating theatre and he was admirably supported by his shy company clerk, Walter O'Reilly, nicknamed 'Radar' after his uncanny clairvoyance, especially when choppers bearing wounded soldiers were due to arrive. Cuddly, bespectacled Radar brought out mothering instincts in all the nurses. He slept with a teddy bear and drank only Grape NeHis on his visits to the well-frequented Rosie's Bar. Spiritual comforter to the unit was chaplain Francis Mulcahy, mild-mannered but never afraid to speak his mind.

After the first season, a new arrival added extra colour. He was Corporal Max Klinger, a reluctant soldier of Lebanese extraction from Toledo, Ohio. In an effort to wangle a 'Section Eight' (a discharge for madness) he dressed in women's clothing. M*A*S*H also saw other important cast changes over the years. Colonel Blake was discharged and left for home, only for his plane to be shot down over the Sea of Japan with no survivors. His replacement was the horse-loving, ex-cavalry officer, Colonel Sherman Potter. Potter was a genial commander with plenty of bark, but his bite was reserved, like Blake's, for medical discipline, allowing the madness instigated by Hawkeye and Trapper John to continue – at least until Trapper shipped out. Actor Wayne Rogers left the series to be replaced by Mike Farrell as B.J. Hunnicut, Hawkeye's new accomplice. B.J. (the initials were never explained) was a real family man, shunning all advances and longing to rejoin his wife, Peg, and their little daughter, Erin. Nevertheless, he was as much a joker as Hawkeye, so Frank Burns found no respite here.

Indeed, Frank's days were numbered. The beginning of the end came when Margaret married Lt Colonel Donald Penobscot. Although he was seldom seen and the marriage was short-lived, it brought her involvement with Frank to an end. After the break-up of her marriage, Margaret mellowed somewhat and found herself more in tune with the rest of the camp, but Frank had, by this time, gone AWOL and then been dispatched to another unit, to be replaced by aristocratic Bostonian Major Charles Emerson Winchester III. Pompous Winchester, like Frank, found himself rooming with Hawkeye and B.J. and he was just as easy a victim. He genuinely believed his blue blood placed him in a higher circle than his army colleagues, and he bitterly resented the waste of his enormous medical talents in the 'patch-up' operating theatres of a MASH unit. He did, however, earn a modicum of respect, which sly, sneaky Frank could never have done.

When Radar was allowed home to help his elderly mother run their country smallholding, his place as clerk went to Klinger, who abandoned his female wardrobe and switched back to traditional military attire. In addition to these primary characters, M*A*S*H also saw the comings and goings of many temporary personnel, including psychiatrist Sidney Freedman, who paid occasional visits to check the mental health of both patients and staff.

M*A*S*H was deliberately conceived to shame Americans over their involvement in the Vietnam War, which was still under way when the programme started. But its tactics changed over the years and the last episodes were quite different in style to the first. The blatant anarchy had gone and the show had become less a comedy with dramatic moments and more a drama with comic touches. In its two-hour special finale (which gained America's biggest ever TV audience), Hawkeye harrowingly suffered a nervous breakdown, Winchester was gutted by the senseless killing of the POW musicians he had befriended, and, while everyone else returned home, Klinger, ironically, decided to stay in Korea, having met and married beautiful local girl Soon-Lee. It wasn't quite the end, though. Potter, Mulcahy and Klinger resurfaced in the spin-off series, AfterMASH. There had been an earlier spin-off, too, entitled Trapper John MD, but not featuring Wayne Rogers (it was set 28 years later).

Gary Burghoff was the only leading member of the cast to star in the film version, and Jamie Farr was the only cast member to actually serve in the Korean War. In the pilot for the TV series, the unit chaplain was Father John Mulcahy, played by George Morgan. More notable is the fact that Alan Alda won Emmy awards for his contributions as actor, writer and director in the series – a unique achievement. The concept was based on Richard Hooker's novel, M*A*S*H, which drew on his own experience as a medic in the Korean War. A cover version of the theme tune, 'Suicide Is Painless', was a UK number one hit for a group called The MASH in 1981.

MASSEY, RAYMOND (1896–1983)

Canadian actor remembered by many viewers as the crusty old Dr Leonard Gillespie, mentor of Richard Chamberlain in Dr Kildare. Previously, Massey had enjoyed a film career stretching back to the late 1920s and also starred in an early US anthology series called I Spy (not the Robert Culp/Bill Cosby version). However, after Dr Kildare finished in 1966, not much was seen of him, save the odd TV movie, before he retired.

MASTERMIND

UK (BBC) Quiz. BBC 1 1972–

Presenter: Magnus Magnusson

Creator: Bill Wright. Producers: Bill Wright, Roger Mackay, Peter Massey, David Mitchell

High-brow quiz tournament.

Mastermind has proved to be one of television's most unlikely hits. Initially airing late at night, because schedulers considered it too academic for the viewing masses, it quickly gained a cult following. When it was brought into peak hours as a short-term replacement, it clocked up huge audience figures, so there it has remained.

Each programme (usually staged at a university) has featured four contenders (never 'contestants'), all taking turns to answer questions on a nominated specialist subject and then facing a round of general knowledge posers. The highest scorer (and sometimes the highest scoring loser) has progressed to a semi-final, in which a different specialist subject has had to be chosen. On reaching the four-contender grand final, the participants have been able to revert to their original or second choice topics or opt for a brand new subject. Chosen topics over the years have varied from British Moths, The Works of Dorothy L. Sayers and Old Time Music Hall to Drama in Athens, 500–388 BC, English Cathedrals and Spanish and South American Ethnology. The relentless questioning of host Magnus Magnusson has been likened to interrogation, as, with the lights dimmed, the contender (spot-lit in a lonely black leather chair) has been faced with a barrage of notoriously difficult questions for a keenly timed two minutes.

Mastermind has been responsible for a couple of over-used catchphrases in the English language. 'Pass' (used to skip a question and save time) has become a common reply when someone doesn't know an answer to something, and 'I've started so I'll finish' (Magnus's quip when interrupted by the time-up buzzer) has been open to all sorts of interpretation.

Probably the best-remembered *Mastermind* champions have been taxi driver Fred Housego and train driver Christopher Hughes, but the following have all won the cut-glass *Mastermind* trophy:

1972...Nancy Wilkinson
1973...Patricia Owen
1974..Elizabeth Horrocks
1975...John Hart
1976...Roger Prichard
1977...Sir David Hunt
1978...Rosemary James
1979..Philip Jenkins
1980...Fred Housego
1981...Leslie Grout
1982...No contest
1983...Christopher Hughes
1984..Margaret Harris
1985..Ian Meadows
1986..Jennifer Keaveney
1987...Jeremy Bradbrooke
1988...David Beamish

1989...Mary Elizabeth Raw
1990..David Edwards
1991..Stephen Allen
1992..Steve Williams
1993...Gavin Fuller
1994..Dr George Davidson

MATCH OF THE DAY

UK (BBC) Football. BBC 2/BBC 1 1964–6/1966–

Presenters:
Jimmy Hill
Bob Wilson
Desmond Lynam
Commentators:
Kenneth Wolstenholme
David Coleman
Wally Barnes
John Motson
Barry Davies
Tony Gubba
Alan Parry
Clive Tyldesley

Recorded highlights, and occasional live action, from the day's top football matches.

In these days, when soccer is a prize commodity amongst TV stations, it is hard to believe that regular football coverage did not begin until 1964 and even then was relegated to BBC 2, the minority interest channel. However, once England had won the World Cup in 1966, the mood changed and *Match of the Day* was switched to BBC 1. There it has remained ever since, apart from occasional lapses when the big games have been stolen by ITV or Sky.

The original format involved the playback of highlights of just one of the day's top games. Not to deter spectators, details of the match being covered were not publicized in advance. The first game televised was Liverpool versus Arsenal at 6.30 pm on 22 August 1964 (Liverpool won 3–2, Roger Hunt scored the first *Match of the Day* goal and only 50,000 viewers bothered to tune in). Over the years, a second and then a third match were added, and now all the important goals scored in the Premiership are reviewed as well. During the late 1960s and 1970s, a regional format was pioneered, whereby after the main match, some BBC studios around the country broadcast highlights of local interest.

The programme's chief commentator for many years was Kenneth Wolstenholme, with other contributors including Wally Barnes, David Coleman, Alan Weeks and Idwal Robling (who primarily covered Welsh action). Since 1971 John Motson and Barry Davies have taken charge of matches, supported by the likes of Tony Gubba, Alan Parry, Gerald Sinstadt and Clive Tyldesley.

The programme's presenters have varied, too, the current frontman being Desmond Lynam, and expert analysts have been introduced to highlight the key moments. Jimmy Hill (as well as anchoring the programme for many years) has been one. Others have included Alan Hansen, Trevor Brooking and Gary Lineker.

The title *Match of the Day* has also been used by the BBC for highlights of the Wimbledon tennis championships.

MATT HOUSTON

US (Aaron Spelling/Warner Brothers)
Detective Drama. BBC 1 1983–7

Matlock 'Matt' Houston	Lee Horsley
C.J. Parsons	Pamela Hensley
Bo	Dennis Fimple
Lamar Pettybone	Paul Brinegar
Lt Vince Novelli	John Aprea
Rosa 'Mama' Novelli	Penny Santon
Detective Lt Michael Hoyt	Lincoln Kilpatrick
Chris	Cis Rundle
Roy Houston	Buddy Ebsen

Creator: Lawrence Gordon. Executive Producer: Aaron Spelling. Producer: Michael Fisher

A super-rich playboy tracks criminals in his spare time.

Matt Houston hailed from a wealthy family, a very wealthy family. Having managed their cattle and oil empire in Texas, he moved to California to look after the family's off-shore exploration rigs. However, Matt spent less and less time in the job, once he discovered a new, more exciting hobby: detective work. He proved to be an effective semi-professional sleuth. With the help of his beautiful lawyer friend, C.J., and an amiable Los Angeles cop, Lt Novelli (whose Mama often invited Matt for dinner), Matt revelled in this new adventure. With Bo and Lamar, a couple of squabbling Texan ranch hands, also in tow, Houston Investigations was never going to be a lucrative enterprise, but what did that matter to a loaded young guy like Matt who was surrounded by gorgeous women and all the trappings of a playboy lifestyle, including a luxurious penthouse, his own private helicopter and flashy cars (an Excalibur, a Rolls or a Mercedes)?

In later seasons, the more homely elements (like Mama Novelli's cooking) were abandoned in favour of serious detection, as Matt gave up his oil interests and devoted himself full-time to his hobby. Lt Hoyt was the new, less co-operative police officer on the scene, and Matt's uncle, Roy, also turned up. A retired detective, he joined his nephew back on the streets, linking up with C.J. and the team's state-of-the-art computer (known as Baby), in pursuit of villains.

MATTHEWS, FRANCIS (1930–)

British character actor, star of the late 1960s/early 1970s detective series *Paul Temple* and the voice of Captain Scarlet in *Captain Scarlet and the Mysterons*. He also appeared in the 1960 sitcom *Golden Girl*, was Simon Lieberman with David Kossoff in *A Little Big Business*, Geoffrey Dickens with Geraldine McEwan in *Tears Before Bedtime* and Tom Lawrence with George Cole in *Don't Forget to Write*. Matthews was also featured in the sitcoms *My Man Joe* and *A Roof Over My Head*, starred as Eric the Prologue in Alan Plater's *Trinity Tales* and made guest appearances in *The Avengers*, *The Morecambe and Wise Show* and *Crown Court* amongst other series.

MAUGHAN, SHARON (SHARON MUGHAN)

British actress as well known for her coffee commercials as her acting credits, which have included *By the Sword Divided* (as Anne Lacey/Fletcher), *The Flame Trees of Thika*, *Shabby Tiger*, *Dombey and Son*, *Hannay*, *The Return of the Saint*, *Inspector Morse* and *The Ruth Rendell Mysteries* (billed in some under her real name of Sharon Mughan). She is married to Trevor Eve.

MAVERICK

US (Warner Brothers) Western. ITV 1959–

Bret Maverick	James Garner
Bart Maverick	Jack Kelly
Samantha Crawford	Diane Brewster
Cousin Beauregard Maverick	Roger Moore
Brent Maverick	Robert Colbert

Creator: Roy Huggins. Producers: Roy Huggins/William L. Stewart

Two cowardly brothers are professional poker players in the Wild West.

Maverick was a western with a difference – it was played for laughs. It featured wisecracking Texan Bret Maverick, a full-time card shark who earned a living by preying on losers. It began as a traditional cowboy series but soon turned into a spoof on the Old West, despite the introduction of Bret's more serious younger brother, Bart. (Bart was actually added to ease production problems. With two films crews and two stars alternating as leads, twice as many programmes could be produced.)

The Mavericks were wanderers, stumbling into towns with ridiculous names like Bent Fork and Ten Strike. Unlike other cowboy heroes, these guys were true yellowbellies. When in trouble they followed their Pappy's advice: 'Run!' Both were lazy, untrustworthy and self-centred, yet they often found time to help people in trouble. They generally didn't cheat at cards and in case things turned nasty during a game, they kept a $1000 bill pinned inside their jackets. For a while, Bret had a female rival, attractive swindler Sam Crawford, and the duo spent several episodes trying to out con each other.

Maverick's gentle mockery of the conventional western was highlighted when guest stars like Clint Walker (from **Cheyenne**) and Ty Hardin (from **Bronco**) dropped by. Some episodes were also parodies of **Bonanza** and **Gunsmoke**. Like Clint Walker, James Garner fell out with Warner Brothers and was replaced by Roger Moore as Cousin Beau who, unusually for a Maverick, had won a commendation in the Civil War before moving to England to soak up the culture. A third Maverick brother, Brent, arrived later, but, without Garner, it wasn't long before the series came to an end. A few revivals were attempted in the 1970s and 1980s, none with the success of the original.

MAY TO DECEMBER

UK (Cinema Verity) Situation Comedy. BBC 1 1989–

Alec Callender......................................Anton Rodgers
Zoe Angell/Callender ....Eve Matheson
                                               Lesley Dunlop
Jamie Callender ....Paul Venables
Miles Henty ....Clive Francis
Vera Flood/Tipple ....Frances White
Hilary..Rebecca Lacey
Simone ....Carolyn Pickles
Dot...Kate Williams
Debbie...Chrissie Cotterill
Roy ....Paul Raynor
Rosie MacConnachy ....Ashley Jensen

Creator/Writer: Paul A. Mendelson. Executive Producer: Verity Lambert. Producers: Sydney Lotterby, Sharon Bloom

Generation gap romance between a middle-aged lawyer and a young schoolteacher.

When games mistress Zoe Angell arrived in the Pinner offices of Semple, Callender and Henty to make arrangements for her divorce, little did she know that she would eventually marry Alec Callender, the middle-aged senior partner (and ardent Perry Mason fan) who handled her case. For spritely Zoe and lumbering Alec, it wasn't love at first sight, but seeing each other out of business hours, their relationship began to blossom, much to the surprise of Zoe's greengrocer mum, Dot, and her lonely sister, Debbie. Even more shocked were Alec's prim daughter, Simone, his son, Jamie (who worked with him in the office), and the other members of the office

staff. These were frumpy secretary Miss Flood and over-familiar typist Hilary. While Zoe and Alec moved on to marriage and its inherent difficulties, plus the birth of their daughter, Fleur, so changes took place at the law firm. Jamie was made a partner after the departure of Miles Henty (the company name changed to Semple, Callender and Callender), Miss Flood secured herself a husband, Gerald Tipple, and Hilary, as daffy as ever, eventually made way for an eccentric Scots girl by the name of Rosie MacConnachy.

MAYALL, RIK (1958–)

Anarchic British comedian and comic actor, whose reputation was established by his role as Rick in **The Young Ones** and its echoes in **Filthy, Rich and Catflap** (as Richie Rich) and **Bottom** (as Richie Richard). Earlier, Mayall (once part of an act called 20th-Century Coyote with Adrian Edmondson) had established the character of boring Brummie Kevin Turvey in the sketch series **A Kick Up the Eighties** and also appeared as a member of the *Comic Strip* troupe. He was MP Alan B'Stard in **The New Statesman** and Flashheart in assorted episodes of **Blackadder**. With Adrian Edmondson, he appeared as one of the Dangerous Brothers on *Saturday Live* and amongst his numerous other credits have been *Rik Mayall Presents, Grim Tales, The Lenny Henry Show, Jackanory* and **Happy Families**.

MAYNARD, BILL (WALTER WILLIAMS; 1928–)

Yorkshire-born actor, primarily in comic roles. In the 1970s and early 1980s, he was in much demand as Frank Riley in *The Life of Riley*, Stan the Fryer in **Trinity Tales** and the accident-prone Selwyn Froggitt in **Oh No! It's Selwyn Froggitt** and *Selwyn*. He was the Reverend Alexander Goodwin in the short-lived sitcom *Paradise Island*, Fred Moffat, otherwise known as *The Gaffer*, and played Seth Raven in *Langley Bottom*. More recently, he has been seen as the petty crook Claude Jeremiah Greengrass in **Heartbeat**. Maynard also has plenty of guest appearances to his name, in series as varied as **Up Pompeii!** and **Coronation Street** (as musical agent Micky Malone), and has made his mark in single dramas (particularly *Kisses at Fifty* in 1973).

ME AND MY GIRL

UK (LWT) Situation Comedy. ITV 1984–8

Simon Harrap...................................Richard O'Sullivan
Samantha Harrap ....Joanne Ridley
Nell Cresset...Joan Sanderson
Isobel McCluskey....................................Sandra Clarke

Derek Yates ....Tim Brooke-Taylor
Liz...Joanne Campbell

Creator: John Kane. Writers: John Kane,
Bernard McKenna, Colin Bostock-Smith.
Producer: John Reardon

**A widower struggles to bring up his
teenage daughter.**

Simon Harrap, an executive at the Eyecatchers
advertising agency, found himself alone and in
sole charge of adolescent daughter Samantha
when his wife passed away. To help him cope, his
snooty mother-in-law, Nell Cresset, joined the
household and they also took on a housekeeper,
Isobel. Humour came from Simon's attempts to
set an example, and to keep Samantha on the
straight and narrow (particularly with regard to
homework and boys), while, at the same time,
failing to curb his own recklessness. His friend
and work colleague was Derek Yates and Liz was
his secretary. The theme song was sung by Peter
Skellern.

ME MAMMY

UK (BBC) Situation Comedy. BBC 1 1969–71

Bunjy Kennefick.......................................Milo O'Shea
Mrs Kennefick ....Anna Manahan
Miss Argyll ....Yootha Joyce
Cousin Enda..David Kelly
Father Patrick ....Ray McAnally

Creator/Writer: Hugh Leonard. Producers:
James Gilbert, Sydney Lotterby

**An Irishman's style is cramped by his
clinging mother.**

Forty-year-old Bunjy Kennefick was an Irishman
living and working in London. An executive with
a large West End company, he drove a flash car
and lived in an expensive Regent's Park flat. His
secretary, Miss Argyll, was also his girlfriend.
Unfortunately, his widowed mother had also
crossed the Irish Sea and, being a devout
Catholic, was reluctant to give up her innocent
son to the heady delights of the English capital –
and Miss Argyll in particular. A later addition to
the cast was Bunjy's Cousin Enda, another exile
from the Emerald Isle. The series began life as a
Comedy Playhouse pilot.

MEDICS

UK (Granada) Drama. ITV 1991–

Professor Geoffrey Hoyt ....Tom Baker
Ruth Parry ....Sue Johnston
Dr Robert Nevin ....James Gaddas
Dr Claire Armstrong ....Francesca Ryan
Jess Hardman ....Penny Bunton
Dr Gail Benson ....Emma Cunningham
Dr Alison Makin ....Teddie Thompson

Dr Jay Rhaman....................................Jimmi Harkishin
Toby Maitland-Evans ....Jo Stone-Fewings
Dr Alex Taylor ....Peter Wingfield
                                                        Edward Atterton
Dr Tom Carey ....Hugh Quarshie
Gavin Hall...Ian Redford
Helen Lomax ....Dinah Stabb
Dr Sarah Kemp..................................Patricia Kerrigan
Billy Cheshire.......................................Clarence Smith
Derek Foster ....Nick Dunning

Executive Producer: Sally Head. Producers:
Tony Dennis, Alison Lumb

**The pressures of work on the doctors and
staff at a busy general hospital.**

Described by Tony Dennis, one of the show's
producers, as a programme 'about people doing
an impossible job', *Medics* focused on the staff of
fictitious Henry Park Hospital, examining the
stresses and strains of their intense employment.
At the heart of much of the action were Geoffrey
Hoyt and Ruth Parry. Hoyt was the flamboyant
and eccentric professor of surgery and Parry the
embattled chief executive. Contemporary NHS
politics thrust their way to the top of the agenda
and personal problems, like the death of Hoyt's
wife and his near-fatal car accident, also came to
the fore. Increasing attention was also paid to the
younger members of staff, like student doctor
Alex Taylor, house officer Jess Hardman, new
mother Claire Armstrong and gay doctors Sarah
Kemp and Alison Makin, as the series progressed.

MEET THE WIFE

UK (BBC) Situation Comedy. BBC 1 1964–6

Thora Blacklock ....Thora Hird
Freddie Blacklock ....Freddie Frinton

Creators/Writers: Ronald Wolfe, Ronald
Chesney. Producers: John Paddy Carstairs,
Robin Nash

**A northern couple bicker their way
through married life.**

Thora and Freddie Blacklock were not unhappily
married: they just didn't always see eye to eye.
Thora was bossy and domineering and Freddie
liked to rebel now and again, but whatever
divided them was soon forgotten. It was a marriage much like many others, really, allowing
viewers to feel comfortable with the characters.
Meet the Wife was, consequently, a popular series.
It stemmed from a 1963 *Comedy Playhouse* presentation entitled *The Bed*, in which the
Blacklocks, having just celebrated their silver
wedding anniversary, argued over whether to buy
twin beds to replace their lumpy and uncomfortable matrimonial double.

**MEMOIRS OF SHERLOCK HOLMES,
The** see *Adventures of Sherlock Holmes, The.*

MEN BEHAVING BADLY

UK (Hartswood/Thames) Situation Comedy.
ITV 1992; BBC 1 1994–

Dermot	Harry Enfield
Gary	Martin Clunes
Tony	Neil Morrissey
Deborah	Leslie Ash
Dorothy	Caroline Quentin
Les	Dave Atkins
George	Ian Lindsay
Anthea	Valerie Minifie

Creator/Writer: Simon Nye. Producer: Beryl
Vertue

**Two friends flatshare in typically squalid
bachelor fashion.**

In this series, based on writer Simon Nye's own
novel, Dermot and Gary, a pair of overgrown
adolescents, were the *Men Behaving Badly*. This
involved sharing a flat in South London, neglecting the washing up, using colourful language,
ogling the girl upstairs (Deborah), drooling over
aerobics videos, swilling beer and having limited
success with women. After the first season,
Dermot left to travel the world and was replaced
by the drippy, unemployed Tony, who instantly
fell in love with Deborah. Also seen was Dorothy,
Gary's cynical girlfriend (a nurse), Les, slovenly
landlord of the local boozer (The Crown), and
George and Anthea, Gary's limp colleagues at the
security firm where he worked. Although initially an ITV sitcom, from the third season the programme was screened on BBC 1, at a later transmission time. This allowed the men to behave
just that little bit more badly. Simon Nye, a former bank employee, also created **Frank Stubbs**.

MEN FROM SHILOH, THE see *Virginian,
The.*

MEN INTO SPACE

US (United Artists/CBS) Science Fiction. BBC
1960

Colonel Edward McCauley	William Lundigan
Mary McCauley	Angie Dickinson
	Joyce Taylor
Peter McCauley	Charles Herbert
General Norgath	Tyler McVey

Producer: Lewis Rachmil

The adventures of early space pioneers.

One of TV's first 'space race' series, reaching
American screens less than two years after the first
Sputnik was launched, *Men into Space* centred on
the exploits of brave astronaut Colonel Edward
McCauley, who travelled the solar system, landing on other planets, working at the moon base
and orbiting Earth in a space station. Dramas and
crises revolved around equipment failure or personal problems, rather than alien attacks or visits
from bug-eyed monsters. McCauley's wife, Mary,
and his boss, General Norgath, were also seen
from time to time. Although many of the series'
ideas have yet to come to fruition, this was generally regarded as a sensible, realistic science fiction series and was produced in semi-documentary style in conjunction with the US armed
forces.

MEN'S ROOM, THE

UK (BBC) Drama. BBC 2 1991

Charity Walton	Harriet Walter
Mark Carleton	Bill Nighy
James Walton	Patrick Drury
Jane Carleton	Mel Martin
Sally	Amanda Redman
Margaret	Charlotte Cornwall
Mavis	Cheryl Hall
Pascoe	David Ryall
Tessa Pascoe	Kate Hardie
Swinhoe	Bill Stewart
Steve	James Aubrey
Eric	Ian Redford

Writer: Laura Lamson. Producer: David Snodin

Steamy saga of academic adultery.

Spanning the Thatcher years, *The Men's Room*
was the story of sociologist Charity Walton, a
well-settled mother of four whose life was turned
upside down by an affair with Mark Carleton, the
deceitful, womanizing new head of department at
the university where she worked. Sex and betrayal were the hallmarks of this acclaimed five-part
drama set in London, which also featured
Charity's best friend Sally, a publisher, Margaret,
an outspoken feminist, Swinhoe, a shoplifting
criminologist, and Mavis, a boozy secretary. It
was adapted by Laura Lamson from the novel by
Ann Oakley.

MERCER, DAVID (1928–80)

Prolific British socialist playwright, one of the so-
called 'angry young men' of 1960s drama. Mercer
brought his own political experiences, his criticisms of the failures of the Communist Bloc
regimes and a fascination with psychiatry to his
many television dramas (some seen as *Wednesday
Plays*, but others staged by both the BBC and
ITV companies). He began with a trilogy (now
known as *The Generations*), comprising the plays
Where The Difference Begins (1961), *A Climate of
Fear* (1962) and *The Birth of a Private Man* (1963),
interrupted by *A Suitable Case for Treatment* (1962)
and *The Buried Man* (1963). He later penned
another trilogy made up of *On the Eve of
Publication* (1968), *The Cellar and the Almond Tree*

and *Emma's Time* (both 1970). Amongst other memorable works over the years were *And Did Those Feet?* (1965), *In Two Minds* (1967), *The Parachute* (1968) and *Let's Murder Vivaldi* (1968). His last offering was *Rod of Iron* for Yorkshire TV in 1980.

MERCIER, SHEILA (SHEILA RIX; 1919–)

Yorkshire-born actress, sister of farce star Brian Rix but known to most viewers as *Emmerdale's* Annie Sugden, a role she played for over 20 years. She had previously appeared with her brother in his series *Six of Rix*.

MERIDIAN TELEVISION MERIDIAN

is the ITV franchise holder for the South and South-East of England, winning the contract from TVS in 1991 and taking to the air on 1 January 1993. Meridian operates from three studios, in Southampton, in Newbury and near Maidstone. Its nightly news magazine, *Meridian Tonight* (with three regionalized editions, one from each studio), won the RTS Regional News Magazine Award in its first year on air. The most notable contributions to the ITV network so far have been the dramas *Harnessing Peacocks, Under the Hammer* and *The Ruth Rendell Mysteries*, the comedy *Tracey Ullman: A Class Act* and the travelogue *Coltrane in a Cadillac*. Carlton Communications, the London weekday franchise holder, owns 20 per cent of Meridian and independent producer SelecTV owns 15 per cent, although the largest shareholding (61 per cent) is by the international financial and media group MAI, which also owns Anglia Television.

MERTON, PAUL (PAUL MARTIN)

South London-born comedian, a former civil servant. Merton is best known today as one of the regulars in the topical quiz *Have I Got News For You?*, although he has also been seen on *Whose Line Is It Anyway?* and in two series of his own surreal sketch show for Channel 4. In 1994, he presented a history of the London Palladium for the BBC and a year later hosted *Paul Merton's Life of Comedy*. He is married to actress Caroline Quentin.

MERVYN, WILLIAM (WILLIAM MERVYN PICKWOAD; 1912–76)

British actor whose earliest TV parts (after years on the stage) were as Captain Crocker-Dobson in the naval comedy *The Skylarks* in 1958 and as Sir Hector in *Saki* in 1962. In 1963 he adopted the guise of Chief Inspector Charles Rose in *The Odd Man*, which led to a rather weird spin-off,

It's Dark Outside, in 1964 and finally to the character's own series, *Mr Rose*, in 1967. A year earlier, Mervyn played Sir Gerald in *The Liars* and embarked on a five-year clerical career as the Bishop in *All Gas and Gaiters*. In 1971 he starred as the 43rd Duke of Tottering in the kids' comedy *Tottering Towers*.

MESSICK, DON (1926–)

American cartoon voicer, specializing in canine creations, including *Scooby-Doo*, Muttley in *Wacky Races* and the *Jetsons'* dog Astro. He was also Bamm Bamm in *The Flintstones*, Dr Benton Quest in *Jonny Quest*, Boo Boo in *Yogi Bear*, Snorky in *The Banana Splits*, Aramis in *The Three Musketeers*, Multi Man in *Frankenstein Jr* and *The Impossibles*, Spot the cat in *Hong Kong Phooey*, Pixie in *Pixie and Dixie*, plus Atom Ant, Touché Turtle and many more characters. Messick was originally a ventriloquist, then a radio actor in the 1940s and 1950s.

METAL MICKEY

UK (LWT) Children's Comedy. ITV 1980–3

Father	Michael Stainton
Mother	Georgina Melville
Granny	Irene Handl
Ken	Ashley Knight
Haley	Lucinda Bateson
Janey	Lola Young
Steve	Gary Shail

Writer: Colin Bostock-Smith. Producer: Michael Dolenz

A family's home life is disrupted by a zany robot.

Invented by boy scientist Ken Wilberforce to help out around the home, Metal Mickey brought nothing but chaos to Ken's family. A five-feet tall, magical robot in the R2D2 (*Star Wars*) vein, Mickey spouted the catchphrase 'Boogie boogie' and turned the household upside down with his space-age antics, which included trips to the future, teleportation and conversations with aliens. There were also more mundane happenings, like Mickey trying to become a pop star or Mickey finding himself kidnapped. The show is possibly best remembered, however, for another Mickey – its producer/director was former Monkee, Mickey Dolenz.

MIAMI VICE

US (Universal) Police Drama. BBC 1 1985–90

Detective James 'Sonny' Crockett	Don Johnson
Detective Ricardo Tubbs	Philip Michael Thomas
Lt Martin Castillo	Edward James Olmos
Detective Gina Navarro/Calabrese	Saundra Santiago
Detective Trudy Joplin	Olivia Brown

Detective Stan Switek ....Michael Talbott
Detective Larry Zito ....John Diehl
Izzy Moreno...Martin Ferrero
Caitlin Davies ....Sheena Easton

Creators: Michael Mann, Anthony Yerkovich.
Executive Producer: Michael Mann

Two trendy cops patrol the glitzy but drug-poisoned streets of Miami.

Very much a 1980s programme in its feel, with generous use of contemporary rock music, *Miami Vice* delved behind the cool, pastel shades of this glamorous Florida city and unearthed a seedier side, heavily dependent on the drug culture. Its stars were cops Crockett and Tubbs. Stubble-chinned, heavy-smoking Crockett was an ex-football star, aggressive and straight-talking. He worked under the street name of Sonny Burnett and lived on a houseboat called *St Vitus' Dance*, which he shared with a pet alligator named Elvis. Separated from his wife, Caroline, Crockett now enjoyed the attentions of many of the city's beautiful women, although most of his girlfriends tended to meet a grisly end. Even one he married, rock star Caitlin Davies (played by real-life singer Sheena Easton), bought it.

Dressed in a crumpled light jacket and a T-shirt, Crockett's casual scruffiness contrasted sharply with the silk-shirted, double-breasted, sartorial elegance of his hip partner, Tubbs, a black New York cop, who had come to Miami to flush out the drugs dealer who murdered his brother. Tubbs's undercover identity was Rico Cooper and the duo cruised the tropical streets in Crockett's flash Ferrari Spider, or the Testarossa that replaced it. They were assisted by undercover policewomen Trudi Joplin and Gina Calabrese and detectives Stan Switek and Larry Zito, and their boss was the temperamental Lt Castillo.

Miami Vice was conceived as a sort of MTV cops show, hence the rock video-style photography and the liberal helpings of chart music. The pounding theme tune, by Jan Hammer, became a hit on both sides of the Atlantic in 1985 and numerous guest stars from the rock world dropped in for cameo roles, including Phil Collins, Ted Nugent, James Brown, Glenn Frey and Little Richard. Also featured were celebrities like Bianca Jagger, boxer Roberto Duran and comedian Tommy Chong.

MICHELL, KEITH (1926–)

Australian Shakespearean actor, a former art teacher, whose finest hour came in 1970 as the legendary king in *The Six Wives of Henry VIII*, ageing and fattening up as the series progressed. Michell also starred in the 1972 film version, *Henry VIII and His Six Wives*, and even took up

singing, notching up one minor hit in 1971 'I'll Give You The Earth' and then resurfacing with the novelty single 'Captain Beaky' in 1980. Apart from that, and appearances in a few TV movies, little has been seen of him on television since, although his earliest credits date from 1951 (a production of R.L. Stevenson's *The Black Arrow*) and 1962 (as Heathcliff in *Wuthering Heights*). Michell also played Mark Antony in the 1969 Shakespearean collection *The Spread of the Eagle*.

MICHELMORE, CLIFF, CBE (1919–)

Veteran British presenter, on TV since the 1950s when he fronted *Highlight* and, more notably, *Tonight*, as well as contributing some early sports commentaries. He joined the BBC after working for British Forces radio on *Family Favourites* (through which he met his wife, Jean Metcalfe), and moved into television to write, direct and produce children's programmes like ***All Your Own***. His other notable credits have included ***Panorama***, ***24 Hours***, *Talkback*, *Wheelbase*, *Chance to Meet*, ***Stars on Sunday***, *Home on Sunday*, ***Songs of Praise*** and the charity programme *Lifeline*. He was the first presenter of ***Holiday***, in 1969, worked on the nightly magazine *Day by Day* for Southern Television and hosted the BBC's space and election coverages, as well as the occasional information panel game *So You Think . . . ?* He is the father of TV presenter Guy Michelmore.

MICKEY SPILLANE'S MIKE HAMMER
see Mike Hammer.

MIDNIGHT CALLER

US (December 3rd/Lorimar) Detective Drama.
BBC 1 1989–92

Jack 'Nighthawk' Killian ....Gary Cole
Devon King ....Wendy Kilbourne
Billy Po..Dennis Dun
Lt Carl Zymak ....Arthur Taxier
Deacon Bridges..........................Mykel T. Williamson
Nicky Molloy ....Lisa Eilbacher

Creator: Richard Di Lello. Executive Producer: Robert Singer. Producer: John F. Perry

An ex-cop becomes a radio presenter but can't leave his former life behind.

When Jack Killian accidentally killed his patrol partner while pursuing a crook, his life turned upside down. Although officially cleared of all blame for the death, he decided to quit the force. At a loose end, he accepted the offer of working for beautiful Devon King, as a late-night phone-in host on her radio station, KJCM (98.3 FM) in San Francisco. There (using the nickname of 'Nighthawk') he found himself in contact with all manner of shady people who called him up and left him intriguing cases to solve, which he either passed on to his policeman friend, Carl Zymak, or a newspaper contact, Deacon Bridges, or, more likely, set out to handle himself, often at great personal danger. The phone-in also covered intense moral issues like AIDS and drugs, and Killian proved to be a thoughtful but straight-talking host, if a touch too moody and flip outside the studio. On the other side of the glass was engineer Billy Po. Nicky Molloy later took over as Nighthawk's boss.

MIKE HAMMER

US (Columbia) Detective Drama. ITV 1984–6

Mike Hammer...Stacy Keach
Velda...Lindsay Bloom
Captain Pat Chambers ....Don Stroud
Assistant DA Lawrence Barrington ......Kent Williams
Ozzie the Answer ....Danny Goldman
Jenny ....Lee Benton
The Face..Donna Denton

Executive Producer: Jay Bernstein. Producer: Lew Gallo

Violent, macho and leering private eye series, based on the colourful books by Mickey Spillane.

Spillane's Mike Hammer was a hard New York detective fighting crime in a tough city. His investigations into the underworld, amidst drug pushers, murderers, kidnappers and other such lively characters, were glossily depicted in this series. Assisted by his busty secretary, Velda, the chain-smoking Hammer could also call on the help of his friend Pat, a captain in the New York Police Department. On the streets, he had several contacts, including Ozzie the Answer, and amongst the parade of shapely females on view was Jenny, the bartender at Hammer's regular drinking hole, the Light 'n' Easy bar. Lawrence Barrington, Hammer's legal adversary, was an assistant district attorney who operated by the book and disliked the brawling gumshoe's unorthodox methods. The most intriguing character, however, was a beautiful brunette known as 'The Face'. Hammer caught sight of her in nearly every episode but never managed to meet her. Finally, it was revealed that she was a writer looking to use his exploits as the basis for a series of novels.

When criticism of the show's sexist attitude grew too heavy, the glamorous women were 'toned down', but the violence, if anything, increased, with Hammer's hatred of the criminal fraternity exposed in an orgy of killings and maimings. It says it all that Hammer's best friend was the pistol he called Betsy.

Ironically, filming of the series was interrupted for a year or so because of real-life crime matters,

when actor Stacy Keach spent time in Reading Jail for a drugs offence. Keach was not TV's first Mike Hammer. This honour went to Darren McGavin, star of an American adaptation in the 1950s.

MILES, MICHAEL (1919–71)

New Zealand-born 'quiz inquisitor' of **Take Your Pick**, conducting the quickfire 'yes/no interlude' and asking contestants to 'take the money or open the box' from the very start of ITV broadcasts in 1955. Miles had brought the show over from Radio Luxembourg where it had been a hit for three years. It proved extremely popular on television, too, and ran for 13 years. Undaunted by its cancellation in 1968, Miles returned with a similar format in *Wheel of Fortune* a year later, but died in 1971.

MILLER, DR JONATHAN, CBE (1934–)

Multi-talented British writer, director and producer, who is also a qualified doctor. A product of the Cambridge Footlights troupe that included the likes of David Frost and Peter Cook, Miller arrived in television via the *Beyond the Fringe* revue. Amongst other TV contributions, he edited **Monitor**, produced a version of Plato's *Symposium* and an acclaimed adaptation of *Alice in Wonderland*, worked on **Omnibus**, took charge of the BBC's ambitious Shakespeare project in 1980 and merged his medical and television knowledge in *The Body in Question* in 1978 (as writer and presenter).

MILLIGAN, SPIKE (TERENCE MILLIGAN; 1918–)

Offbeat British comedian, born in India. Through his work with The Goons on radio in the 1950s, Milligan established a reputation for bizarre, quirky humour, which later translated to television in the form of the animated *Telegoons*. He also starred with his fellow Goons in *Idiot Weekly, Price 2d*, **A Show Called Fred** and *Son of Fred* in the 1950s. He guested in **Not Only . . . , But Also . . .** , with Peter Cook and Dudley Moore in the mid-1960s, and then, in 1968, appeared in **The World of Beachcomber**, before launching into his run of innovative **Q** programmes in 1969, beginning with **Q5** and working his way up to Q9. The early episodes pre-dated even **Monty Python** with their free-form sketches, often lacking beginnings and proper endings. Less successful was his interpretation of Pakistani Kevin O'Grady (Paki-Paddy) in Johnny Speight's controversial sitcom **Curry and Chips** (Milligan had previously popped up in Speight's **Till Death Us Do Part**). He wrote the mini-saga *The Phantom Raspberry-Blower of Old London Town* for **The Two Ronnies**, and was a regular on *The*

Marty Feldman Comedy Machine. Amongst Milligan's numerous other contributions have been *Milligan at Large*, *Milligan's Wake*, *Muses with Milligan*, *Oh in Colour*, *The Other Spike*, *The Last Turkey in the Shop Show*, *Milligan for All Seasons* and *There's a Lot of it About*.

MILLS, ANNETTE (1894–55)

The sister of John Mills, Annette Mills was a children's favourite in the 1940s and 1950s when introducing popular puppets like Prudence and Primrose Kitten, Sally the Sealion, Oswald the Ostrich, Louise the Lamb, Monty the Monkey, Mr Peregrine the Penguin and, most famous of all, **Muffin the Mule**. As Muffin danced on top of her piano, Mills sang and played. They first appeared together in 1946, as part of the BBC's *For the Children* series, after Mills had been forced to give up her song and dance career following a couple of bad accidents. She died just eight days after her last appearance with Muffin in 1955.

MILLS, SIR JOHN, CBE (1908–)

Stalwart of the British cinema John Mills has enjoyed relatively few television credits. Most notable have been the offbeat western *Dundee and the Culhane* (as barrister Dundee), the Résistance revival *Zoo Gang* (as Tommy Devon or 'The Elephant'), the 1979 version of **Quatermass** (as Professor John Quatermass), the retirement sitcom *Young at Heart* (as Albert Collyer) and the mini-series **Woman of Substance** (as Henry Rossiter). Mills has also guested on numerous shows, most famously with *Morecambe and Wise*.

MILLS, ROGER

Award-winning British documentary producer and editor, working for the BBC on programmes like *Inside Story*, **Sailor**, **Hong Kong Beat**, *Strangeways*, **Forty Minutes** and Michael Palin's extravagant voyages **Around the World in 80 Days** and *Pole to Pole*.

MILNE, ALASDAIR (1930–)

BBC current affairs producer and director in the 1950s and 1960s, working on programmes like *Highlight*, **Tonight** and **That Was The Week That Was**, who later became the Corporation's Director of Programmes, Managing Director and Director-General (1982–7). Milne was the first Director-General to come from a production background and under his auspices the BBC opened up its breakfast television and daytime television services. His resignation in January 1987, at the behest of the Chairman, led to a period of upheaval and change at the BBC.

MIND OF MR J.G. REEDER, THE

UK (Thames) Detective Drama. ITV 1969–71

J.G. Reeder	Hugh Burden
Sir Jason Toovey	Willoughby Goddard
Mrs Houchin	Mona Bruce
Miss Belman	Gillian Lewis

Executive Producer: Lloyd Shirley. Producers: Kim Mills, Robert Love

In the 1920s a gentle DPP office clerk solves crimes in his own unassuming way.

Mr J.G. Reeder worked for the Department of Public Prosecutions. Although his everyday appearance was quite innocuous (bespectacled, slightly downmarket in dress, and totally unthreatening in manner), he nonetheless possessed a mind capable of cracking the most enigmatic of crimes. As he put it himself, he saw evil in everything, much to the misfortune of crooks up and down the country. Sir Jason Toovey was his department head, and Reeder was assisted first by Mrs Houchin, then by Miss Belman. The series was based on the stories of Edgar Wallace, published in 1925.

MIND YOUR LANGUAGE

UK (LWT) Situation Comedy. ITV 1977–9

Jeremy Brown	Barry Evans
Miss Courtney	Zara Nutley
Danielle Favre	Françoise Pascal
Ali Nadim	Dino Shafeek
Jamila Ranjha	Jamila Massey
Anna Schmidt	Jacki Harding
Juan Cervantes	Ricardo Montez
Giovanni Cupello	George Camiller
Chung Su-Lee	Pik-Sen Lim
Taro Nagazumi	Robert Lee
Maximillian Papandrious	Kevork Malikyan
Ranjeet Singh	Albert Moses
Sid	Tommy Godfrey
Zoltan Szabo	Gabor Vernon
Ingrid Svenson	Anna Bergman
Henshawe	Harry Littlewood
Gladys	Iris Sadler

Creator/Writer: Vince Powell. Producer: Stuart Allen

Mayhem and misunderstanding in an English-for-foreigners class.

English teacher Jeremy Brown bit off more than he could chew when enrolling as instructor of a night-school class for mature foreign students. His multi-national pupils included amorous French girl Danielle Favre, humourless German Anna Schmidt, Italian romeo Giovanni Cupello, and other similarly well-defined racial stereotypes, all of whom had clearly never considered the concept of ethnic tolerance. Misunderstanding and abuse were rife, leading to constant aggression and turning the naive, inoffensive Brown into a quivering, frustrated wreck. Miss Courtney was the dragon-like principal who had the knack of entering the classroom at just the wrong moment, and Sid (later replaced by Henshawe) was the Cockney caretaker.

MINDER

UK (Euston Films/Thames/Central) Comedy Drama. ITV 1979–85; 1988–94

Arthur Daley	George Cole
Terry McCann	Dennis Waterman
Dave	Glynn Edwards
Des	George Layton
Detective Sgt Albert 'Charlie' Chisholm	
	Patrick Malahide
Sgt Rycott	Peter Childs
Maurice	Anthony Valentine
DC Jones	Michael Povey
Ray Daley	Gary Webster
Detective Sgt Morley	Nicholas Day
DC Park	Stephen Tompkinson
Detective Inspector Melsop	Michael Tronghton

Creator: Leon Griffiths. Executive Producers: Verity Lambert, Lloyd Shirley, Johnny Goodman. Producers: Lloyd Shirley, George Taylor, Ian Toynton

The dodgy dealings of one of London's great survivors and his beefy assistant.

Arthur Daley is a name that has become synonymous with shady deals, for this cowardly but lovable rogue specialized in less than reliable, marginally hooky produce dished out at a bargain price. Whether it was mutton-dressed-as-lamb motors from his used car showroom, or crates of appellation uncontrollée from his lock-up, Arthur had the knack of twisting suckers' arms and getting them to buy. Of course, they soon returned the goods, or the law intervened to ensure that Daley's pockets were once again as empty as they started. But this trilby-sporting, cigar-chewing master of cockney slang was never far away from another 'nice little earner'.

Arthur's right hand was Terry McCann, a former professional boxer and occasional jailbird. Now on the straight and narrow (as far as Arthur would allow), McCann – one of life's losers – was easy meat for Daley, who paid him a pittance and promised him the earth. Hired out as a commodity by Arthur to be a bodyguard, bouncer, fetcher or carrier, Terry, nevertheless, was always there to protect his guvnor from someone with a grievance – and such people were not hard to find. The wonderful repartee between Daley and his uncomfortable, generally kind-hearted 'minder' as they worked their way around the fringes of the underworld was even more important than the stories themselves.

Off-duty, the pair could be found in the Winchester Club, run by its genial steward, Dave. This refuge from "Er Indoors' (as Daley referred to his wife) was also the setting for many 'business' meetings. On the side of justice were policemen Chisholm, Rycott and Jones. Just like Wyle E. Coyote and the Road Runner, their sole aim was to catch up with Arthur Daley, the crook with the Teflon finish.

The series was nearly brought to a close on many occasions, as both George Cole and Dennis Waterman contemplated a way out. But when Waterman finally called it a day in 1991, Gary Webster was introduced in the role of Arthur's second cousin's son, Ray, and Daley's schemes and scams continued apace. Pursuit this time came from coppers Morley and Park.

Dennis Waterman also co-wrote (with Gerard Kenny) and performed the theme song, 'I Could Be So Good For You', which he took to number three in the charts in 1980. Cole joined him on a novelty hit, 'What Are We Gonna Get 'Er Indoors' at Christmas 1983, and the partnership was celebrated in a hit for The Firm, 'Arthur Daley ('E's Alright)', in 1982.

MINI-SERIES

A term generally given to glossy dramas (often adaptations of blockbuster novels) spread over a handful of episodes, which are usually scheduled on consecutive nights. The genre was initiated in the 1970s by concepts like *Rich Man, Poor Man* and others in the *Best Sellers* collection.

MINOGUE, KYLIE (1968–)

Australian actress and singer, shooting to fame as Charlene Robinson in *Neighbours* before quitting the series to concentrate on a pop music and film career. Previously Minogue had appeared in series like *The Sullivans* and *The Henderson Kids*. Her sister, Dannii, is also an actress/singer.

MIRREN, HELEN (HELEN MIRONOFF; 1946–)

British film actress who scored some notable TV successes with the *Prime Suspect* mini-series, playing Detective Chief Inspector Jane Tennison. She was Valerie in the 1972 BBC adaptation of Balzac's *Cousin Bette*, has taken roles in numerous classic plays and single dramas like *The Duchess of Malfi* and *The BBC Television Shakespeare* (*As You Like It*), and also appeared in Dennis Potter's acclaimed *Blue Remembered Hills*. *Mrs Reinhard*, *Behind the Scenes*, *Thriller*, *Miss Julie*, *The Serpent Son*, *After the Party*, *Coming Through* and *Jackanory* number amongst her other credits.

MISFIT, THE

UK (ATV) Situation Comedy. ITV 1970–1

Basil 'Badger' Allenby-Johnson ....Ronald Fraser
Ted Allenby-Johnson..............................Simon Ward
Alicia Allenby-Johnson....................Susan Carpenter

Creator/Writer: Roy Clarke. Producer: Dennis Vance

An ex-pat returns from the Far East and finds Britain has changed for the worse.

Fifty-year-old Basil Allenby-Johnson, nicknamed 'Badger' during his many years of rubber planting in Malaya, returned to live with his son, Ted, and daughter-in-law, Alicia, in 1970s London. While in the Orient, the permissive society had by-passed Badger, rendering him shocked and bewildered on arrival back in the old country. The liberal and open-minded attitudes of his hosts were equally baffling. Wherever he went, Badger was the complete *Misfit* of the title. Written by *Last of the Summer Wine* and *Open All Hours* creator Roy Clarke, episodes were one hour in length.

MISS ADVENTURE

UK (ABC) Detective Drama. ITV 1964

Stacey Smith...Hattie Jacques
Henry Stanton ....Jameson Clark

Creators: Peter Yeldham, Marjorie Yeldham. Producer: Ernest Maxin

A female investigator finds herself constantly in hot water.

Lively Stacey Smith worked for the hard-up, London-based Stanton Detective Agency, run by Henry Stanton. Henry sent her off on rather tepid assignments but these always offered more excitement than they promised. For instance, when she boarded a number 22 London bus for her first mission, she somehow ended up in Greece, confronting blackmailers, murderers and jewel thieves. But what she was really looking for was a man. This was an unusual role for distinguished comedy actress Hattie Jacques and one which lasted only 13 episodes and three investigations.

MISS JONES AND SON

UK (Thames) Situation Comedy. ITV 1977–8

Elizabeth Jones.......................................Paula Wilcox
Mrs Jones ....Charlotte Mitchell
                                                              Joan Scott
Mr Jones ....Norman Bird
Geoffrey..Christopher Beeny
Rose Tucker ....Cass Allen
David...David Savile
Penny ....Catherine Kirkwood
Roly Jones...Luke Steensil

Creator/Writer: Richard Waring. Producer: Peter Frazer-Jones

A young, unmarried mum struggles to bring up her baby.

Elizabeth Jones was shocked when her boyfriend left her after a four-year relationship. She was even more surprised to discover she was pregnant. Despite failing to make the appropriate arrangements for claiming benefit, and consequently finding herself short of income, she happily gave birth to a baby son whom she christened Roland Desmond Geoffrey Jones. Her prudish parents were, at first, less than pleased with the situation but soon rallied round to support their daughter, as did her neighbour, Geoffrey, and friend, Rose Tucker. This daring (for the time) comedy focused on Elizabeth's attempts to make ends meet and do the best by her son. In the second series, Geoffrey moved out and a new neighbour, David (a widower), and his daughter, Penny, moved in. David, a writer, and Elizabeth, an illustrator, began to pool their talents and gradually their relationship became less platonic and rather more intimate.

MISS MARPLE

UK (BBC) Detective Drama. BBC 1 1984–92

Miss Jane Marple ....Joan Hickson
Detective Inspector/Chief Inspector Slack
....David Horovitz

Producers: Guy Slater, George Gallaccio

The cases of Agatha Christie's celebrated female sleuth.

In an interpretation far removed from the blustery character portrayed by Margaret Rutherford in 1960s films, Joan Hickson played the role of geriatric detective Miss Marple much closer to the written original, dressed heavily in tweed, with a crocodile skin handbag draped over her arm. Frail, gentle and self-effacing, she relied on a softly spoken investigative technique with a well-chosen query, followed by intense periods of listening. This, combined with a flair for analysing personality traits and an uncanny skill of spotting the out of the ordinary, endowed this elderly, gardening-loving spinster with the talent to suss out even the cleverest murderer. In doing so, she suitably embarrassed the police force in her home of St Mary Mead and other picturesque 1930s villages. In true Christie tradition, the gory side of murder and the cruelty involved was always quickly overlooked, as each case developed into a complex, mind-bending puzzle which only our heroine could solve. The first adaptation to be screened was *The Body in the Library*, with *The Mirror Crack'd from Side to Side* concluding the sporadic, drawn-out series at Christmas 1992, when Joan Hickson retired at the tender age of 86.

MISS WORLD

UK (BBC/Thames) Beauty Contest. BBC/ITV
1951–79/1980–8

Producers: Bryan Cowgill, Humphrey Fisher, Philip Lewis, Michael Begg, Ken Griffin (BBC), Steve Minchin (Thames)

Long-running beauty pageant aiming to discover the world's most attractive girl.

It is hard to believe in these politically correct times that *Miss World* was one of the television highlights of the year in the UK for over three decades. It is even harder to believe perhaps that it is still being screened as an annual TV extravaganza on satellite television. Conceived by Eric and Julia Morley of Mecca in 1951, its unashamed purpose was to choose the most beautiful and charming girl from a collection of national representatives to reign (tiara and all) as *Miss World* for the following 12 months. Vital statistics were quoted, tears were shed, there was much talk of working with children and animals, and the good old British public backed their fancies like horses in the Grand National. There were controversial moments, too. For instance, Helen Morgan (UK), *Miss World* 1974, was forced to resign only days later when newspapers revealed she was actually the mother of a young child. Miss Sweden, Kiki Haakonson, won the first contest and amongst the other well-remembered *Miss World*s were Eva Reuber-Staier (Austria 1969), Marjorie Wallace (USA 1973), Wilnelia Merced (Puerto Rico 1975 – later wife of Bruce Forsyth), Cindy Breakspeare (Jamaica 1976) and Mary Stavin (Sweden 1977). Rosemarie Frankland (1961), Ann Sydney (1964), Lesley Langley (1965) and Sarah-Jane Hutt (1983) were other UK winners.

The venue in the early days was London's Lyceum Ballroom, with music supplied by the Joe Loss Orchestra but, from 1964, the Royal Albert Hall hosted proceedings and the Phil Tate Orchestra provided accompaniment. Amongst the main compères (some for just single years) were David Coleman, Peter West, David Jacobs, Michael Aspel, Simon Dee, Keith Fordyce, Pete Murray, David Vine, Terry Wogan, Ray Moore, Patrick Lichfield, Andy Williams, Paul Burnett, Sacha Distel and Esther Rantzen. When coverage was transferred to ITV via Thames TV from 1980, Judith Chalmers, Peter Marshall, Anne Diamond, Mary Stavin and Alexandra Bastedo were seen in charge at various times.

MISSION: IMPOSSIBLE

US (Paramount) Spy Drama. BBC 1 1970–5

Daniel Briggs	Steven Hill
Jim Phelps	Peter Graves
Cinnamon Carter	Barbara Bain
Rollin Hand	Martin Landau
Barney Collier	Greg Morris
Willie Armitage	Peter Lupus
Voice on the Tape	Bob Johnson
Paris	Leonard Nimoy
Dr Doug Lane	Sam Elliott
Dana Lambert	Lesley Ann Warren
Casey	Lynda Day George
Mimi Davis	Barbara Anderson

Creator/Executive Producer: Bruce Geller

A highly-skilled task force undertakes ridiculously dangerous assignments.

These tales of international intrigue featured the Los Angeles-based IMF (Impossible Missions Force). This was a team of remarkable individuals, each renowned for their distinctive skills, and it was led by Jim Phelps, who took over from Daniel Briggs, the man seen in charge in the very earliest episodes. It was Phelps who collected the team's briefings, which arrived in a parcel containing a self-destructing audio tape. The tape burst into flames five seconds after delivering its message. Along with the tape came a series of photographs to help with the mission, but, beyond these, the team knew they were always on their own. The secret government body issuing the assignment offered no assistance whatsoever and even promised to deny all knowledge of the agents.

Although the tape didn't order the team into action (it always stated 'Your mission, should you choose to accept it . . . '), Phelps always agreed to take on the job. He then devised a complicated plan of attack and chose his task force from a sheaf of possible agents. However, with the exception of occasional guest stars, he always chose the same team. The agents were strong man Willie Armitage, electronics wizard Barney Collier (who created most of their high-tech gadgets), master of disguise Rollin Hand, and fashion model Cinnamon Carter, whose main function was distraction. The last two left after a couple of years and were replaced by Dana Lambert in the glamour role and new disguise expert Paris (played by 'Mr Spock', Leonard Nimoy).

The ultra-cool squad's outrageous missions usually centred on thwarting Communist plots in banana republics and tiny European states, although they did also work against more conventional crime in the United States. By restricting dialogue and characterization to a minimum, and by the use of snappy editing, the producers turned out a series of high-paced, all-action adventures.

Mission: Impossible (mostly billed as *Mission Impossible* – without the colon – in the UK) was revived briefly in 1988 to fill gaps in US TV schedules caused by a Hollywood writers' strike. Filmed in Australia, they again starred Peter Graves as head of a new team of operators, with the self-destructing audio tape now updated to a compact disc.

MRS THURSDAY

UK (ATV) Comedy Drama. ITV 1966–7

Alice Thursday ....Kathleen Harrison
Richard B. Hunter ....Hugh Manning

Creator: Ted Willis. Producer: Jack Williams

A charlady inherits a fortune.

When millionaire tycoon George Dunrich died, he left his estate not to his four grasping ex-wives but to his long-serving and loyal charlady, Alice Thursday. Inheriting his wealth, his multi-national property empire, his Rolls-Royce and his Mayfair mansion, Mrs Thursday moved out of her Mile End home and into the privileged classes. But, until the kind-hearted char learned to distinguish her friends from her enemies, she was chaperoned and protected by the genial Richard Hunter, her aide and business adviser.

Allegedly created by Ted Willis specifically as a vehicle for Kathleen Harrison (cinema's Mrs Huggett), *Mrs Thursday* was a surprise hit, knocking shows like **Coronation Street** off the top of the ratings and giving Harrison a late taste of TV stardom.

MR AND MRS

UK (HTV/Border) Quiz. ITV 1969–88

Presenters: Alan Taylor (HTV), Derek Batey (Border)

Creator: Roy Ward Dickson. Producers: Derek Clark (HTV), Derek Batey, William Cartner (Border)

Married couples win money by answering questions about their partners.

'Which shoe does your husband put on first?' and 'Does your wife carry a handbag – always, sometimes or never?' were typical *Mr and Mrs* questions. This quiz, which had been running in the TWW/HTV area for years before being networked, demanded no more of married couples than to know their partners' little habits and foibles. Three questions were put to the husband and three to the wife. While one was answering questions, the spouse was asked to leave the stu-

dio. He/she was then brought back to put the record straight and give the correct answers themselves. Each right response earned the couple some cash and all six correct answers won the jackpot. There were usually three couples featured on each programme.

The series was produced alternately by HTV and Border (it has been one of the latter company's few contributions to the ITV network). Alan Taylor hosted the HTV programmes and Derek Batey those from Border. A Welsh language version, *Sion a Sian*, was also made. The idea returned to television in the early 1990s when the satellite channel UK Living broadcast *The New Mr and Mrs Show*.

MR BEAN

UK (Thames/Central/Tiger) Comedy. ITV 1990–

Mr Bean ....Rowan Atkinson

Writers: Rowan Atkinson, Richard Curtis, Robin Driscoll. Producers: John Howard Davies, Sue Verne

The virtually silent adventures of a walking disaster zone.

Effectively a vehicle for Rowan Atkinson's mime skills, this near-silent comedy revolved around the accident prone Mr Bean, a gormless, friendless, brainless little chap with a flair for causing havoc. A trip to the sales, a spot of DIY or a day at the seaside, all were likely to bring threats to life and limb to Mr Bean or those around him. Numerous specials were made, as well as regular series.

MR BENN

UK (Zephyr) Children's Entertainment. BBC 1 1971

Narrator: Ray Brooks

Creator/Writer: David McKee

A man discovers magical adventures at the back of a costume shop.

Mr Benn, inhabitant of 52 Festive Road, London, enjoyed escapism. In each episode, he indulged his hobby by walking to a local fancy dress shop, where he was greeted by a shopkeeper who arrived 'as if by magic' and escorted him through to the changing rooms. Donning the outfit of the day, Mr Benn then exited through a special door and into a land of adventure, which was always related to the clothes he was wearing. He was seen as a caveman, a spaceman, a pirate, a cowboy and a hunter, amongst other guises. Inevitably, the courteous and genial Mr Benn was able to provide some valuable assistance to the people he met before the shopkeeper suddenly popped up to lead him back into the changing room. Switching back into his business suit and bowler hat, Mr Benn then strolled off home, taking with him a souvenir of his day's work.

Although the series has been repeated endlessly on the BBC, only 13 episodes of this *Watch With Mother* animation were ever produced.

MR DIGBY, DARLING

UK (Yorkshire) Situation Comedy. ITV
1969–71

Roland Digby	Peter Jones
Thelma Teesdale	Sheila Hancock
Norman Stanhope	Michael Bates
Mr Trumper	Brian Oulton
Olive	Beryl Cooke
Mr Bailey	Peter Stephens
Joyce	Janet Brown

Creators/Writers: Ken Hoare, Mike Sharland.
Producers: Bill Hitchcock, Christopher Hodson

An executive is cosseted by his loyal and devoted secretary.

Thelma Teesdale worked for the Rid-O-Rat pest extermination company as secretary to Mr Roland Digby. From the time he arrived in the morning until he left for home in the evening, Thelma catered for his every need, pulling out all the stops to protect him from the outside world. However, her ambitious plans to secure his advancement were usually ill advised and doomed to failure. Thelma's colleagues included Norman Stanhope.

MR ED

US (Filmways) Situation Comedy. ITV 1962–

Wilbur Post	Alan Young
Carol Post	Connie Hines
Roger Addison	Larry Keating
Kay Addison	Edna Skinner
Gordon Kirkwood	Leon Ames
Winnie Kirkwood	Florence MacMichael
Mr Ed's Voice	Allan 'Rocky' Lane

Creator: Al Simon. Executive Producers: Al Simon, Arthur Lubin. Producer: Herbert W. Browar

A talking horse gives his master headaches.

When architect Wilbur Post decided to give up the city in favour of the countryside around Los Angeles, little did he know what awaited him. With his newlywed wife, Carol, he bought a large country house, and discovered in the barn an eight-year-old palomino, named Mr Ed.

However, this was no ordinary horse: this one could talk and, to prove the point, he introduced every programme with the whinnied words 'Hello, I'm Mr Ed.'

But Mr Ed would only talk to Wilbur, as Wilbur, or 'Buddy Boy' as the horse nicknamed him, was the only human being Ed had found worth talking to. Predictably, this tended to land his master in hot water, particularly when he was overheard talking to the horse. As if that wasn't enough, the cynical and grumpy Mr Ed was also keen on giving Wilbur advice (from the horse's mouth, so to speak), which usually led to even more trouble.

The cast was completed by the Posts' bemused next-door neighbours, Roger and Kay Addison. When actor Larry Keating died, his screen wife, Edna Skinner, continued alone for a while until she was replaced with a new couple, the Kirkwoods. The series was created by Arthur Lubin, who had directed the *Francis* (the talking mule) films, starring Donald O'Connor, in the 1950s.

MR MAGOO

US (UPA) Cartoon. BBC 1962–4

Voices:

Mr Quincy Magoo	Jim Backus
Waldo	Jerry Hausner
	Daws Butler
Millie	Julie Bennett

Executive Producer: Henry G. Saperstein

The misadventures of a short-sighted old codger. Created in the 1940s, myopic Mr Magoo appeared in various TV packages, from half-hour compilations to this series of five-minute shorts. Most of the mirth came from the fact that he couldn't tell a telephone box from a police officer, or an ugly woman from a moose, although with his surly, irascible manner and bulbous nose, he was more than an echo of W.C. Fields. Whereas Fields intensely disliked children, Magoo hated dogs, for instance. (Indeed, it is reputed that Fields used the name Primrose Magoo when checking into hotels.)

Semi-regulars in these short TV animations were Magoo's stupid nephew, Waldo, and Waldo's girl-friend, Millie, although other relatives did appear from time to time. In the longer programmes made later, Magoo sometimes appeared in an historical or literary guise, such as Rip Van Winkle or William Tell. Assorted cinema versions were also produced, beginning in 1949 with *Ragtime Bear*, which saw Magoo in a supporting role.

MR PALFREY OF WESTMINSTER

UK (Thames) Spy Drama. ITV 1984–5

Mr Palfrey	Alec McCowen

The Co-ordinator ....Caroline Blakiston
Blair ....Clive Wood

Executive Producer: Lloyd Shirley. Producer: Michael Chapman

The cases of a master spycatcher.

Mr Palfrey (first name never given) worked for a secret Government department from an office close to the Houses of Parliament. His 'Iron Lady' boss was the similarly unnamed Co-ordinator, and his leg work was done by vicious action man Blair. Through the studious, inquisitorial Mr Palfrey viewers learned much about the mysterious world of counter-espionage. The ten-episode series was spun-off *The Traitor*, a play in Thames TV's **Storyboard** anthology, seen in 1983.

MR ROSE

UK (Granada) Detective Drama. ITV 1967–8

Mr Rose ....William Mervyn
John Halifax ....Donald Webster
Drusilla Lamb ....Gillian Lewis
Jessica Dalton......................................Jennifer Clulow
Robert Trent ....Eric Woolfe

Creator: Philip Mackie. Producers: Philip Mackie, Margaret Morris

A retired police officer can't escape from his previous life.

Chief Inspector Rose, formerly of **The Odd Man** and **It's Dark Outside**, had inherited the wealth of two maiden aunts and taken retirement from the force to concentrate on his cottage garden in Eastbourne and the writing of his memoirs. Having kept copies of all his case files, he had a personal library of crime and the fear that he was about to reveal all brought some of his former adversaries – and colleagues – back into his life. Gratefully picking up the scent and rejecting the boredom of his retirement years, Mr Rose lurched once again from investigation to investigation. Rose's assistants were his manservant, former detective John Halifax, and his attractive secretary, Drusilla Lamb. Drusilla was later replaced by Jessica Dalton, and Robert Trent became Rose's sidekick for the last series.

MR WROE'S VIRGINS

UK (BBC) Drama. BBC 2 1993

John Wroe..Jonathan Pryce
Joanna ....Lia Williams
Leah ....Minnie Driver
Hannah ....Kerry Fox
Martha ....Kathy Burke
Dinah ....Moya Brady
Rachel ....Catherine Kelly
Rebekah...Ruth Kelly
Tobias...Freddie Jones

Moses ....Nicholas Woodeson
Samuel Walker ....Stefan Escreet

Writer: Jane Rogers. Producer: John Chapman

A self-styled prophet of doom demands seven virgins from the local community.

Broadly based on a true-life incident, this drama was set in the mill town of Ashton-under-Lyne, near Manchester. The central figure was John Wroe, founder of a Christian Israelite church in readiness for an impending apocalypse. In 1830 he asked the townsfolk to give him seven virgins for his 'comfort and succour' and the unfolding events were then seen through the eyes of four of the women, one per episode. They were Joanna, a woman of absolute religious conviction and spiritual leader of the commune, whom Wroe chose to father a new messiah; Leah, beautiful, shapely and sexually precocious, who joined Wroe to escape from everyday life, but who found herself rejected by him; Hannah, the educationally liberated, socialist-minded member of the group who was greatly attracted to the grotesque Wroe; and Martha, a devastated, badly beaten mute who had been treated like an animal on her father's farm and whom Wroe transformed through care and attention. The other girls were Dinah, Rachel and Rebekah. The drama was set against the backdrop of great industrial change and religious impropriety, tempered by an epidemic of cholera.

The series was adapted by Jane Rogers from her own novel.

MISTRESS, THE

UK (BBC) Situation Comedy. BBC 2 1985–7

Maxine ....Felicity Kendal
Luke Mansel ....Jack Galloway
                                                      Peter McEnery
Helen Mansel ....Jane Asher
Jenny ....Jenny McCracken
Simon ....Tony Aitken
Jamie ....Paul Copley

Creator/Writer: Carla Lane. Producer: Gareth Gwenlan

The pitfalls of an extra-marital affair.

The Mistress was more a situation tragedy than a situation comedy, dealing, as it did, with the touchy subject of adultery and all its drawbacks and dangers. At the apex of this particular eternal triangle was Maxine, an independent, single-minded woman who lived alone (apart from her pet rabbits) in a comfortable pink flat. Her lover was Luke Mansel, a married businessman, torn between the demanding Maxine and his suspecting wife, Helen. Secret meetings, snatched moments of passion and longed-for dirty weekends were balanced by pangs of guilt and desperate attempts to keep the illicit affair under wraps. Jenny was an old school friend with whom Maxine owned the Flora florist's shop, whilst Simon was Luke's envious work colleague and confidant who suffered chronically from marital boredom.

MITCHELL, DENIS (1912–)

Pioneering British documentary maker, noted for his impressionistic studies of human life, the highlights of his career being *In Prison* (1957), *On Tour* (1958), *Morning in the Streets*, *A Soho Story* (both 1959), *The Wind of Change* (1960), *Chicago – Portrait of a City* (1961), *A Wedding on Saturday* (1964), *Seven Men* (1971), *European Journey* (1972 and 1973) and *Private Lives* (1975). His first contribution (after beginning in BBC radio) was *On the Threshold* in 1955 and he also worked on *This England* and *World in Action*.

MITCHELL, JAMES (1926–)

North-eastern English scriptwriter, the creator of *Callan* and *When the Boat Comes In* and the co-creator of *Justice*, but also contributor to *The Troubleshooters* and *The Avengers*, amongst other series.

MITCHELL, LESLIE (1905–85)

British television's first regular announcer, Leslie Mitchell opened up the BBC service from Alexandra Palace in 1936, welcoming viewers to 'the magic of television'. As a sideline in those early days, he also interviewed guests for *Picture Page*. The Scots-born former actor and radio presenter turned freelance after the war (during which he had worked for British Movietone News), commentating on state and political events for the BBC, but also working for ITV. He was the first presenter of *This Week*, in 1956, briefly Head of Talks at Associated-Rediffusion and, in the 1970s, resurfaced as chairman of the Tyne-Tees nostalgia quiz *Those Wonderful TV Times*.

MITCHELL, WARREN (WARREN MISELL; 1926–)

RADA-trained British character actor, infamous as the bigoted Alf Garnett in *Till Death Us Do Part*. Mitchell's showbusiness career began on the stage and progressed via radio (Radio Luxembourg, plus BBC shows like *Educating Archie*) to television, where some of his first roles were to support Tony Hancock in *Hancock's Half Hour* and Charlie Drake in *Drake's Progress*. He also appeared as Cromwell in the 1955 adaptation of *The Children of the New Forest*. In 1961

Mitchell played Pan Malcov in a short-lived Granada sitcom called *Colonel Trumper's Private War*. More successfully, in 1965, he was cast as the outspoken Alf Ramsey in a *Comedy Playhouse* episode which proved to be the pilot for *Till Death Us Do Part*. Ramsey became Garnett and the series ran from 1966 to 1968 and returned for another three years in 1972. It was briefly revived as *Till Death . . .* by ATV in 1981, and then revamped as *In Sickness and in Health* by the BBC for seven years from 1985. Easily identifiable as Alf, Mitchell's other TV work has been limited, save for performances in classic dramas such as *The Caretaker* and *The Merchant of Venice*, and two further sitcoms – an early sort of *Yes Minister*, *Men of Affairs* (as Sir William), in 1973, and *So You Think You've Got Troubles* (playing Ivan Fox, a Jew in Northern Ireland), in 1991. However, guest appearances in series like *Out of the Unknown*, *The Avengers*, *The Saint* and *The Sweeney* have meant that he has been a regular on our screens for many years.

MIXED BLESSINGS

UK (LWT) Situation Comedy. ITV 1978–80

Thomas Simpson	Christopher Blake
Susan Lambert/Simpson	Muriel Odunton
Aunt Dorothy	Joan Sanderson
Edward Simpson	George Waring
Annie Simpson	Sylvia Kay
William Lambert	Stefan Kalipha
Matilda Lambert	Carmen Munro
Winston Lambert	Gregory Munroe
Mr Huntley	Ernest Clark

Creator/Writer: Sid Green. Producer: Derrick Goodwin

A racially mixed couple struggle to make their marriage acceptable to others.

This adventurous comedy focused on two university graduates, Thomas Simpson and Susan Lambert. It saw them getting engaged, being married and then starting a family, but what made this relationship unusual (for the time) was that Thomas was white and Susan was black. Both sets of parents were convinced the marriage would not work, other relatives disapproved and only Thomas's Aunt Dorothy had confidence in the liaison. Realizing that money was scarce (Susan was a social worker, but Thomas was initially unemployed), she even offered them a home in her basement flat. The programme's theme music was written by actor Peter Davison.

MOGUL see *Troubleshooters, The*.

MOLINA, ALFRED (1953–)

British actor, the husband of Jill Gascoine, with whom he guested in *C.A.T.S. Eyes*. He has also been seen in *Casualty*, played Nigel the wrestler in the shortlived Leonard Rossiter comedy *The Losers* and musician John Ogden in the drama *Virtuoso* and appeared in the TV movies *The Accountant*, *Drowning in the Shallow End* and *Hancock* (as 'the lad himself'). Probably his most prominent role has been as the retired copper Blake in the early series of *El C.I.D.*

MONITOR

A television display showing camera output. Monitors are used by the director to line up and select the next shot and also by presenters to see what is going out while they are on air.

MONITOR

UK (BBC) Arts Magazine. BBC 1 1958–65

Hosts: Huw Wheldon, Jonathan Miller

Producers: Peter Newington, Nancy Thomas, Humphrey Burton

Britain's first successful arts programme.

During its seven-year run, *Monitor* became a Sunday night institution for the learned classes. Screened at around 10 pm, and presented for the most part in relaxed, authoritative fashion by its editor Huw Wheldon, the programme spanned all artistic fields and laid the foundations for later successes like *Omnibus*, *Aquarius* and *The South Bank Show*. *Monitor* also broke new ground by commissioning film profiles of artists from emerging film-makers like Ken Russell and John Schlesinger. These have since become archive classics. Russell, for instance, made biopics of Elgar, Debussy, Rousseau and Bartók, while Schlesinger contributed pieces on Britten and others. Melvyn Bragg co-scripted some of Russell's work.

MONKEES, THE

US (Raybert/Screen Gems) Situation Comedy. BBC 1 1966–8

Davy .... Davy Jones
Micky .... Micky Dolenz
Peter .... Peter Tork
Mike.. Mike Nesmith
Miss Purdy.. Jesslyn Fax
Mr Babbitt... Henry Corden

Creators/Producers: Bert Schneider, Robert Rafelson

Zany humour with a quartet of pop musicians.

In the wake of the success of The Beatles and, particularly, their madcap films *A Hard Day's Night* and *Help!*, a couple of American producers,

Bert Schneider and Robert Rafelson, developed an idea for a TV version and advertised for four young lads to fashion into a pop group. The advert called for 'Four insane boys, aged 17–21'. After auditioning over 400 applicants, they settled on three Americans and one Englishman. Davy Jones was an actor from Manchester who had briefly appeared in *Coronation Street* as Ena Sharples's grandson. He was joined by another actor, Mickey Dolenz, formerly Mickey Braddock of *Circus Boy* fame, and the group was completed by Peter Tork and Michael Nesmith, both of whom did have some musical experience, albeit in the folk medium. Stephen Stills, later of supergroup Crosby, Stills and Nash, was one of the hopefuls turned down for the series.

Musically, their early recordings were made by session musicians, masterminded by producer Don Kirschner, and the series spawned some huge hits on both sides of the Atlantic. 'Last Train To Clarksville', 'I'm A Believer', 'Daydream Believer', 'Pleasant Valley Sunday' and 'A Little Bit Me, A Little Bit You' were the group's biggest successes, and all premièred on the TV show. In the group, the calm, bobble-hatted Nesmith and lank-haired, dozy Tork were the guitarists, the manic Dolenz sang and played the drums, and the hopeless romantic Jones mostly sang but sometimes tapped a tambourine or rattled a maracca.

The series, although borrowing heavily from Dick Lester's Beatles films in concept, was quite original in its own way. This was the first time that comedy had been treated to unusual camera angles (often hand-held), blurred focuses, cranked up or overexposed film and really snappy editing. The plots were less remarkable and featured the band getting into various scrapes and nearly always ending up in some kind of chase sequence.

After the break up of the band and the end of the series, the most musically active was Nesmith, who became a respected performer/producer in the country rock sphere. Dolenz went on to produce and direct the *Metal Mickey* series, Jones also returned to acting, but little was heard of Tork. Jones and Dolenz made a couple of attempts to re-form the band in the 1970s and 1980s, recording and touring again, but with little success.

MONKHOUSE, BOB, OBE (1928–)

Quick-witted British comedian, actor, writer, presenter and quiz show host. Monkhouse's showbiz career began to take off when he sold a joke to Max Miller in 1943, while still a schoolboy. With his partner Denis Goodwin, he took up writing as well as performing and, after working in radio, they broke into television. Their first series, *Fast and Loose*, in 1954, was an instant success and the pair also ventured into game shows, presenting *Bury Your Hatchet*. Monkhouse, heading off solo, compèred **Sunday Night at the London Palladium** and **Candid Camera**. His love of silent films led to his own retrospective, *Mad Movies*, and he also tackled sitcom, playing Bob Mason, a shop assistant turned disc jockey in the very short-lived *The Big Noise*, in 1964. A few years later, Monkhouse replaced Jackie Rae as host of **The Golden Shot** and turned it into a huge Sunday teatime hit. He went on to chair **Celebrity Squares** in 1975, did three years in charge of **Family Fortunes** from 1980, and switched to the BBC to host *Bob's Full House* and the revived talent show **Bob Says Opportunity Knocks** in the middle of the decade. Back on ITV, he was the questionmaster on **The $64,000 Question** and star of the newlywed game show *Bob's Your Uncle*. Amongst his other contributions have been *I'm Bob, He's Dickie* (with Dickie Henderson), a BBC 2 chat show majoring on top comics, the fast-moving joke show *Gagtag*, with Jonathan Ross and Frank Skinner, and the quick recall quiz *Monkhouse's Memory Masters*.

MONOCLED MUTINEER, THE

UK (BBC) Drama. BBC 1 1986

Percy Toplis	Paul McGann
Dorothy	Cherie Lunghi
Charles Strange	Matthew Marsh
Woodhall	Philip McGough
Cruickshank	Nick Reding

Writer: Alan Bleasdale. Producer: Richard Broke

A rebellious private leads a coup on the eve of a World War I battle.

Based on true events recalled in a book by William Allison and John Fairley, *The Monocled Mutineer* was the story of dashing rogue Percy Toplis. The cynical Nottinghamshire miner, a private in the British army, was stationed at the Etaples training camp in France and, on the night before the Battle of Passchendaele in 1917, instigated a mutiny amongst his harshly treated fellow recruits. His partner in the action was Charles Strange, a political idealist. This four-part dramatization by Alan Bleasdale (whose own grandfather had died at Passchendaele) added fiction to the bare facts and depicted how Toplis escaped into the French hills, took to impersonating an army officer and led a group of renegades in the taking of a bridge. He then returned to England and fell in love with Dorothy, a young widow, before being captured in the Lake District and 'executed' for his crimes by MI5 assassin Woodhall.

The series proved to be the most provocative of Bleasdale's works to date and roused the ire of Establishment figures and old soldiers. The suggestion that deserters were executed by their own side (exemplified in the drama by the shooting of an officer named Cruickshank) was heavily condemned. The fact that Michael Grade, the BBC's Director of Programmes, had passed a press release stating that the story was totally factual only made matters worse. According to Grade, the fuss detracted from the quality of the drama itself.

MONTGOMERY, ELIZABETH (1933–95)

Betty Grable insured her legs, so perhaps Elizabeth Montgomery should have sought cover for her nose, for, as winsome witch Samantha Stephens in **Bewitched**, she relied on its twitching to cast her benign spells. Samantha was a role she played for eight years from 1964 and the series was produced by her husband, William Asher. Keeping it in the family, it was her dad, actor Robert Montgomery, who, somewhat reluctantly, gave Elizabeth her TV break, offering her a part in his anthology series *Robert Montgomery Presents* in the early 1950s. She followed this with appearances in dozens of other series but, after leaving *Bewitched*, Montgomery was generally only seen in TV movies.

MONTY PYTHON'S FLYING CIRCUS

UK (BBC) Comedy. BBC 2 1969–74

John Cleese
Michael Palin
Eric Idle
Graham Chapman
Terry Jones
Terry Gilliam
Carol Cleveland

Writers: John Cleese, Michael Palin, Eric Idle, Graham Chapman, Terry Jones, Terry Gilliam. Producers: John Howard Davies, Ian MacNaughton

One of the most innovative comedy programmes ever, combining cerebral wit, visual humour and slapstick in an atmosphere of virtual anarchy.

When it first reached the TV screen in 1969, filling a former religious slot, late on Sunday night, *Monty Python's Flying Circus* understandably met with some bemusement. However, it soon acquired a fervent global following and genuine cult status. Each programme was well endowed with sketches, and held together with animation and one-liner humour, but, essentially, anything went in this manic collage of comedy styles.

The sketches relied heavily on off-beat domestic situations and spoof TV interviews or documentaries, although the series seldom lacked invention. Swaying between incomprehensibility and bad taste, it was a show that shocked and confused, but was always inspired. The Oxbridge background of its writers/performers surfaced in the show's literary and artistic allusions, yet there was always room for juvenile pranks, vulgar asides and general silliness. Amongst the highlights were skits like *The Dead Parrot*, in which John Cleese confronted Michael Palin, a shopkeeper, with the corpse of a bird he had just purchased. Another classic was *The Lumberjack Song*, a rousing Canadian chorus of machismo which unravelled into a celebration of transvestism. There was also *The Argument Clinic*, *Upper Class Twit of the Year*, *The Ministry of Silly Walks*, *Spam* and *Blackmail* (a sadistic game show).

Each of the performers developed his own brand of eccentric. Palin played the downtrodden little man, Eric Idle the nudge-nudge, wink-wink, unsuccessful pervert, Terry Jones the working-class housewife with the piercing voice, Graham Chapman the stuffy, military type and Cleese the tight-lipped TV interviewer, confronted by bizarre interviewees. Wrapped around the sketches were Terry Gilliam's chaotic, surreal cartoons which 'stole' images from classical art. Sometimes they picked up from the punchline of the previous sketch, in the same way that sketches themselves occasionally merged when a character from an earlier skit wandered into the action. Snappily cut together, it was a programme without a beginning and without an end which broke all the rules of television structure. Its opening titles, bouncing along on the music of Sousa's *Liberty Bell*, could appear anywhere in the show, even after the closing credits, and along the way there was plenty of time for developing catchphrases, from Michael Palin's succinct 'It's' to John Cleese's 'And now for something completely different'.

Innovative and inspiring it certainly was, but, if *Monty Python* broke new ground, it could, at the same time, have been seen as the culmination of the unconventional comedy trend that had begun with **That Was The Week That Was**, and developed through **The Frost Report**, **Not Only . . . But Also**, **At Last the 1948 Show** and **Do Not Adjust Your Set**. The Pythons had all learned their craft in such programmes, a craft which was to stand them in good stead in individual projects way after *Monty Python* was laid to rest.

Forty-five programmes were made in total, although John Cleese did not appear in the final season (which went out under the simple title of *Monty Python*). A series of stage shows and feature film was also produced, the earliest films reprising the best of the TV sketches but the later ones taking the Python manic humour to new bounds in mock epics like *Monty Python and the Holy Grail* and the notorious *Life of Brian*.

MOODY, RON (RONALD MOODNICK; 1924–)

British actor whose television work has, by general concensus, not matched his cinema and stage performances. Indeed, his TV outlets have been few. These have entailed a 1961 BBC series entitled *Moody in Storeland*, a show for YTV in 1968 entitled *Moody*, the odd single drama (such as Jack Rosenthal's *Mr Ellis Versus the People* in 1974), TV movies, a couple of kids' series (*Into the Labyrinth*, playing Rothgo, a sorcerer, and *Mike and Angelo*, as Angelo's father), plus a sitcom, **Hart of the Yard** (as Detective Inspector Roger Hart, a London detective working in San Francisco). Moody has, however, guested in numerous other programmes, including **The Avengers**.

MOONLIGHTING

US (Picturemaker) Comedy Drama. BBC 2
1986–9

Maddie Hayes	Cybill Shepherd
David Addison	Bruce Willis
Agnes Dipesto	Allyce Beasley
Herbert Viola	Curtis Armstrong
Virginia Hayes	Eva Marie Saint
Alex Hayes	Robert Webber
MacGilicuddy	Jack Blessing

Creator/Executive Producer: Glenn Gordon Caron. Producer: Jay Daniel

Off-beat sleuthing with a squabbling, but romantically-linked, pair of investigators.

When top fashion model Maddie Hayes was swindled by her financial manager, she found that one of the few investments she still owned was the City of Angels Detective Agency, a private investigation company set up to make a loss to offset against her tax bills. Head of the agency was cocky David Addison, a flippant, streetwise young private eye. Although Maddie intended to sell off the company, Addison ensured she held on to it, renaming the business the Blue Moon Detective Agency, after the Blue Moon shampoo she used to market. With her modelling career now behind her, Maddie decided to take a hand in the running of the business and the aloof, classy blonde and the smirking, stubble-chinned punk became unlikely partners.

From the start, their relationship was electric. They came from widely different backgrounds and they had different ways of working, yet they also had chemistry. Although they sparred and fought their way through investigations, there was always a restrained romance behind their bickering. Maddie toyed with other suitors (even marrying a stranger on a train) and David played the field, but the two eventually caved in and came together. All the same, even while pregnant with his child (later miscarried), the animosity between the partners remained and exploded into violent verbal exchanges (the sharp repartee was the highlight of the programme).

At work, they were successful, taking on a variety of unusual cases and usually gaining positive results, turning the Blue Moon Detective Agency into a viable business at the same time. They were assisted by their scatty receptionist, Agnes Dipesto, who answered the telephone with a little rhyme, and Herbert Viola, the object of Agnes's desires, who joined the team as a clerk but longed to be a detective. His office rival was MacGilicuddy. Maddie's parents, Alex and Virginia, were also seen.

With its witty dialogue style gleaned from the 1940 film *His Girl Friday*, starring Cary Grant and Rosalind Russell, *Moonlighting* was one of those programmes that broke every law of television. Characters spoke to camera, out-takes were shown over the closing credits and actors dropped out of character and addressed the audience as themselves. The surreal air was enhanced with episodes like *Atomic Shakespeare*, based on *The Taming of the Shrew* and written in iambic pentameter, which was performed in period and in costume. However, the programme was plagued with production problems, and re-runs had to be inserted when the latest episodes failed to arrive on time. Stars Shepherd and Willis didn't always see eye to eye and this all contributed to a rather scrappy finish to the series. It faded away rather than going out with a bang. The theme song was a UK hit for Al Jarreau in 1987 and Bruce Willis followed up with hits of his own.

MOORE, BRIAN (1932–)

Experienced British soccer commentator and general sports presenter, whose main credits have been *The Big Match*, **World of Sport** (the *On The Ball* segment), **Who's the Greatest?**, *Midweek Sports Special* and other major occasions. Before joining ITV, Moore worked as a journalist for *The Times* and BBC radio.

MOORE, CLAYTON (1914–)

Television's **Lone Ranger**, Clayton Moore began his movie career in 1938 as a stuntman (he was previously a circus performer). He was offered the part of the masked western hero ten years later and, as soon as the series hit US TV screens, Moore became a huge celebrity. After three years, he fell out of favour with the show's producers over contractual matters and John Hart was brought in as a replacement for 52 episodes, before Moore returned to the role he now felt to be his own. In later years, it took legal action by rights holders to prevent Moore from continuing to wear the *Lone Ranger* garb, without which he refused to be photographed.

MOORE, DUDLEY (1935–)

Oxford-educated classical pianist, jazz performer, actor and comedian, in the early days in collaboration with Peter Cook. Moore, together with Cook, Alan Bennett and Jonathan Miller, was one of the Beyond The Fringe team which proved so successful in Edinburgh and London in 1960-1. TV work soon followed. When the BBC asked him to do a special, he enrolled Cook to compile a couple of sketches. The BBC liked what it saw and gave them their own series *Not Only . . . But Also . . .*, which aired in 1965 and 1966 and then resurfaced in 1970 for one season, as well as a special in 1973. Amongst Moore's other credits were assorted variety shows, an episode of the drama anthology *Love Story* and his own *Not To Mention Dudley Moore*. In the 1970s, however, Moore concentrated mostly on film work, becoming a Hollywood name through his role in *10*. Plenty of other films have followed. Moore's first wife was actress Suzy Kendall, his second, another actress, Tuesday Weld.

MOORE, MARY TYLER (1936–)

American comedy actress and television executive whose *Mary Tyler Moore Show* was one of the USA's biggest successes in the 1970s. A former dancer, her TV break came in unusual circumstances. After a few commercials and small roles, she was cast as Sam, the secretary, in David Janssen's 1959 series, *Richard Diamond, Private Detective*, although the only parts of her that viewers saw were her legs. She quit after three months in favour of appearances in dramas like *Hawaiian Eye*. Two years later, her role as Laura Petrie, the wife in **The Dick Van Dyke Show**, established Moore as a major sitcom star, but her career seemed to be going no further when the series ended in 1966. After a few stage and film disappointments, she was given another chance to shine in her own **Mary Tyler Moore Show** in 1970 and this time didn't let the opportunity pass. It was a ratings hit and its portrayal of an independent, career-minded female (Mary Richards) matched the general mood of the 1970s. Moore and her then husband, Grant Tinkler, founded the production company MTM (Mary Tyler

Moore Enterprises, responsible for such series as *Lou Grant*, *Remington Steele* and *Hill Street Blues*, and later sold to the UK's TVS), but she has enjoyed little screen success of late, with her 1985 and 1988 sitcoms *Mary* and *Annie McGuire* both flopping.

MOORE, PATRICK, CBE (PATRICK CALDWELL-MOORE; 1923–)

Britain's number one stargazer, Patrick Moore has been presenting his monthly series, *The Sky at Night*, since 1957, making it one of the BBC's longest-running programmes. His fascination with astronomy began at an early age and he became a member of the British Astronomical Association when just 11. After working as a navigator in the wartime RAF, Moore was commissioned to write his first books on space and set up his own observatory. All this led to a call from the BBC and eventually *The Sky at Night*. He also hosted the series about eccentrics, *One Pair of Eyes*, in 1969, hosted a kids' astronomy series, *Seeing Stars*, in 1970, and was the resident expert on the BBC's coverage of the lunar missions in the 1960s and 1970s. Moore has recently been seen as *The Gamesmaster* in Channel 4's computer game contest and has been a popular guest in various light entertainment shows – from *Morecambe and Wise* and *Blankety Blank* to *Children in Need* – often exhibiting his prowess on the xylophone.

MOORE, ROGER (1927–)

British leading man who arrived on television in 1958, wearing the chain mail of Sir Walter Scott's *Ivanhoe*, having already made one film in Hollywood and others in England. In 1959, he played Silky Harris in the gold rush caper *The Alaskans* and, a year later, was cast as Cousin Beauregard in *Maverick*. He even introduced *Sunday Night at the London Palladium*. Then, in 1962, came his most celebrated TV characterization, that of Simon Templar, debonair hero of *The Saint*. The series ran for seven years and made Moore – a former film cartoonist and model – an international star. Although he didn't really capitalize on the situation with his next TV outing, *The Persuaders!* (as Lord Brett Sinclair), in 1971, he soon made up for it by making seven films as James Bond. Apart from guest appearances, that put paid to Moore's television career, as he fixed his quizzical gaze (and much mimicked raised eyebrows) firmly on the movie world. Moore's second wife was singer Dorothy Squires.

MORE, KENNETH (1914–82)

British actor, a 1950s cinema favourite who also enjoyed a couple of notable TV roles. These came in 1967, as Jolyon Forsyte in *The Forsyte*

Saga, and seven years later as G.K. Chesterton's cleric-detective, *Father Brown*. More also starred in The White Rabbit, a 1967 dramatization of the heroics of resistance fighter Wing-Commander Yeo-Thomas, and took the part of Peter Ingram in *An Englishman's Castle* in 1978. However, one of his earliest small screen performances came in 1946 as Badger in *Toad of Toad Hall* and he enjoyed numerous other single drama credits, too. More's third wife was actress Angela Douglas.

MORECAMBE, ERIC, OBE (ERIC BARTHOLOMEW; 1926–84)

Possibly Britain's most popular comedian to date, Eric Morecambe took his stage name from his home town. His career began in variety theatres before the war and, when auditioning for a new-talent show in 1941, he met a young entertainer from Leeds by the name of Ernest Wiseman, otherwise known as Ernie Wise. They forged an enterprising double act, but their progress was shattered by war service. However, meeting again by chance in 1947, they were able to resume their joint career. Their first television forays came in the early 1950s in series called *The Youth Parade* and *Variety Parade*. These led, in 1954, to their own disastrous series called Running Wild, which set back their hopes of stardom. Undaunted, the pair continued to improve their act on stage and radio and won a place on the *Royal Variety Performance* in 1960. This resulted in another bite of the TV cherry, when ATV gave them *The Morecambe and Wise Show* in 1961, scripted by Sid Green and Dick Hills. This time they didn't miss their chance and quickly established themselves and the characteristics of their act – Ernie's pomposity, Eric's boyish anarchy, their Abbot and Costello-like exchanges, all underscored by impeccable comic timing. Viewers took to their many sight gags: Eric slipping his glasses askew, for instance, slapping Ernie around the face or pretending to be strangled behind the stage curtain. The public began to refer to Ernie as Little Ern and 'the one with the short, fat, hairy legs'. Unfortunately, their attempts to make it in the movies proved fruitless. Their films The Intelligence Men, That Riviera Touch and The Magnificent Two flopped. In 1968 after Eric had suffered a heart attack, they were tempted over to the BBC where, by common consent, they produced their best work (most scripted by Eddie Braben). A regular feature of their shows was a play 'wot Ernie wrote', which never failed to attract a big-name guest star. Amongst those who giggled their way through proceedings were Glenda Jackson, Diana Rigg, John Mills, Eric Porter, Peter Cushing (to return many times still looking for payment) and

Hannah Gordon. Angela Rippon danced and Shirley Bassey sang in a hobnail boot. The duo were seen in domestic situations (even innocently sharing a double bed). They cruelly disparaged Des O'Connor's singing and were constantly upstaged at the end by the outsize Janet Webb or Arthur Tolcher with his mouth organ. Ernie's alleged hairpiece ('you can't see the join') provided many gags and Eric flicked non-existent pebbles into a paper bag. Most shows closed with a neck-slapping rendition of 'Bring Me Sunshine' (their ITV theme song had been 'Two of a Kind'). *The Morecambe and Wise Christmas Show* became a national institution and, if Eric had put one of his catchphrases, 'What do you think of it so far?', to the nation, he would not have received the usual reply of 'Rubbish!' The partners switched back to ITV in 1978 with less success, while the BBC countered by screening repeats of their best material. However, they soon knew they would have to start treading carefully. Eric's heart problems resurfaced in 1979 and, after surgery, he was forced to take things somewhat easier. The partnership was brought to an end when Eric suffered another, this time fatal, heart attack in 1984. Their last work together was the TV movie *Night Train to Murder*, which was aired in 1985. Ernie has since soldiered on alone, making stage and television appearances and becoming a member of the revived *What's My Line?* panel.

MORGAN, ELAINE (1920–)

Welsh dramatist whose most notable works have included *A Matter of Degree* (1960), *Epitath for A Spy* (1963), *Joey* (1974), *How Green Was My Valley* (1976), *A Pin to See the Peepshow*, an adaptation of Vera Brittain's *Testament of Youth* (1979), *The Life and Times of David Lloyd George* (1981) and episodes of *Dr Finlay's Casebook*, *The Doctors* and *The Onedin Line*.

MORGAN, HARRY (HARRY BRATS-BURG; 1915–)

Veteran American actor with some memorable roles to his name. Morgan arrived in television in the early 1950s, after acting in films (under the name Henry Morgan) since 1942. In the USA, he has notched up no less than a dozen prime-time roles, beginning with the part of Pete Porter in the comedy *December Bride*, which was spun-off into its own series, *Pete and Gladys*. For UK viewers, however, Morgan will be remembered for two roles in particular. In 1967 he joined Jack Webb in a revival of *Dragnet*, becoming Jack's partner Officer Bill Gannon. The role continued for three years. Then, in 1974, he made a one-off guest appearance in *M*A*S*H* and proved such

a hit that he was asked back as the unit's new CO, Colonel Sherman Potter, when McLean Stevenson's Henry Blake left the series. Morgan remained with *M*A*S*H* till its close, eight years later, and his character lived on in the sequel, *After M*A*S*H*. Viewers may also recall him as Doc. Amos B. Coogan in *Hec Ramsey*, Bob Campbell in *Roots: The Next Generations* and a guest star in numerous series, from *Gunsmoke* and *The Wild, Wild West* to *The Partridge Family*.

MORK AND MINDY

US (Miller-Milkis/Henderson/Paramount)
Situation Comedy. ITV 1979–

Mork	Robin Williams
Mindy McConnell	Pam Dawber
Frederick McConnell	Conrad Janis
Cora Hudson	Elizabeth Kerr
Orson (voice only)	Ralph James
Eugene	Jeffrey Jacquet
Exidor	Robert Donner
Franklin Delano Bickley	Tom Poston
Nelson Flavor	Jim Staahl
Remo Da Vinci	Jay Thomas
Jean Da Vinci	Gina Hecht
Glenda Comstock	Crissy Wilzak
Mearth	Jonathan Winters
Miles Sternhagen	Foster Brooks

Creators: Garry K. Marshall, Joe Glauberg, Dale McRaven. Executive Producers: Garry K. Marshall, Tony Marshall. Producers: Bruce Johnson, Dale McRaven

A naive alien arrives on Earth and pals up with a pretty young girl.

Fifteen years after *My Favorite Martian* had created comedy from an alien-human friendship, *Mork and Mindy* came to the TV screen and did the same thing – in subject matter, at least. This time the style was much more frenetic and the alien far less predictable than Uncle Martin in the early series. Mork came from the planet Ork, bleems and bleems away from Earth (as he put it). There, he was considered odd because he had a sense of humour and, when he went too far and poked fun at Orson, their leader, the Orkans sent him to our planet as a punishment, to file reports on the weird lifestyles of Earth's inhabitants. He arrived in a large eggshell-like spacecraft near Boulder, Colorado, and was discovered by Mindy McConnell, an attractive single girl who worked in her dad's music store. She found him intriguing and amusing, was entertained by his child-like ways and touched by his kindness. Consequently, Mork took up residence in Mindy's attic, much to the consternation of her crusty father.

Although he looked human, Mork was prone to talking gibberish and doing wacky things like wearing a suit back to front, sitting on his head or drinking water with his fingers. There were always aspects of Earth life that he could just not comprehend and, at the end of every episode, he reported back his experiences to the unseen Orson, before signing off, twisting his ears and saying 'Nanu Nanu', the Orkan for goodbye.

In later episodes, Mindy's father, Fred, her hip grandmother, Cora Hudson, and Eugene, a black youth who frequented the music store, were written out. Fred later returned and some new characters were introduced when a brother and sister, Remo and Jean Da Vinci, arrived from the Bronx. He worked at the New York Deli and paid for Jean to attend medical school. Also new were Mindy's politically ambitious cousin, Nelson, and Mork's UFO-prophet friend, Exidor, leader of the invisible Friends of Venus clan. Mr Bickley, the crochety neighbour who wrote greeting cards for a living, came into the action a little more, and Mindy took a job in the newsroom of a television station, KTNS, working for boss Mr Sternhagen.

Mork and Mindy's friendship grew deeper and deeper until they eventually married, taking a honeymoon on Ork. Soon after, Mork gave birth by releasing a tiny egg from his navel. The egg grew in size until it burst open to reveal the baby, a fully-grown, middle-aged man. He, in the Orkan tradition, would grow younger, not older, and never want for love and care in his later years. They called the 'baby' Mearth; he called Mork 'Mommy' and Mindy 'Shoe'.

Mork and Mindy was a spin-off from an episode of *Happy Days*, where, in a dream, Mork arrived in Milwaukee and tried to kidnap Richie Cunningham. It made a star out of the relatively unknown Robin Williams, whose unpredictably quirky humour was perfect for the character of Mork. One of his childhood heroes had been comedian Jonathan Winters, and Williams was able to pay his mentor a tribute by helping to cast him as Mearth.

MORLEY, KEN

British actor who became a cult hero with his portrayal of the wobbly-headed, self-important supermarket manager Reg Holdsworth in **Coronation Street** from 1990, but whose TV career has also encompassed programmes like *'Allo 'Allo* (as the German Flockenstuffen), **You Rang, M'Lord?**, **The Fall and Rise of Reginald Perrin**, **Bulman**, *Who Dares Wins*, *All Passion Spent*, *Les Girls*, **Watching** and *The Return of the Antelope*.

MORRIS, COLIN (1916–)

British writer and producer, creator of *Jacks and Knaves*, **The Newcomers** and **The Doctors**.

Amongst his other contributions have been drama-documentaries like *The Wharf Road Mob* (1957), *Who, Me?* (1959) and *Walk with Destiny* (a Winston Churchill biography, 1974), plus episodes of series like **When the Boat Comes In**. He also produced a number of editions of **Z Cars**.

MORRIS, JOHNNY, OBE (1916–)

Fondly remembered for making animals talk, Welsh-born Johnny Morris presented **Animal Magic** for 21 years from 1962. Before moving into television, he had managed a farm in Wiltshire and presented his own local and national radio series, in which he did other people's jobs for a day and travelled around the South-West. On TV, he appeared as *The Hot Chestnut Man*, which made full use of his flair for telling a tale. When **Animal Magic** came along, Morris donned a zoo keeper's uniform and spent many days at Bristol Zoo, adding a whimsical vocal track to the films he made, putting casual quips in the mouths of his animal subjects. It was a trick he used when narrating another children's favourite, the Canadian series **Tales of the Riverbank**. In 1970 Morris took a journey through South America for a series entitled *A Gringo's Holiday*.

MORRIS, JONATHON (JOHN MORRIS; 1960–)

Northern actor whose most prominent role has been as the poetic Adrian Boswell in **Bread** but who has had plenty of other TV credits to his name since the early 1980s, among them *Beau Geste* (as John), *That Beryl Marston . . .* (as Phil), *The Prisoner of Zenda*, *Hell's Bells*, *The Consultant*, **The Agatha Christie Hour** and *The Practice*. For kids, Morris has presented **Jackanory** and chaired the quiz *The Movie Game*.

MORRISSEY, NEIL (1962–)

British actor, usually in comic roles, such as Rocky Cassidy in **Boon** and Tony in **Men Behaving Badly**. Other credits have included the mini-series *Ellis Island*, **Juliet Bravo**, *Fairly Secret Army*, *Roll Over Beethoven*, *C.A.T.S. Eyes*, *Pulaski*, *Gentlemen and Players* and **Comedy Playhouse**.

MORSE, BARRY (1919–)

London-born actor who made his name on the Canadian stage before moving into television. He has enjoyed major roles on both sides of the Atlantic, not least as the relentless Lt Philip Gerard on the trail of David Janssen's Dr Richard

Kimble, *The Fugitive*. The series ran for four years to 1967 and, five years later, Morse took on the role of Mr Parminter in the Gene Barry secret agent caper, *The Adventurer*. He later played Alec Marlowe (The Tiger) in *The Zoo Gang*, Professor Victor Bergman in Gerry Anderson's *Space: 1999*, appeared as Adam Verver in an adaptation of Henry James's *The Golden Bowl* and as Wolf Stoller in *The Winds of War*, Murgatroyd in *A Woman of Substance*, Dr Harley in *Master of the Game* and the US President, former actor Johnny Cyclops, in *Whoops! Apocalypse*.

MORTIMER, BOB (1959–) see Reeves, Vic.

MORTIMER, JOHN, CBE (1923–)

British barrister, writer, dramatist and campaigner for freedom of speech, the creator of *Rumpole of the Bailey*. Amongst his other offerings have been *Will Shakespeare*, *A Voyage Round My Father*, *Paradise Postponed*, *A Summer's Lease*, *Under the Hammer* and the hugely successful adaptation of Evelyn Waugh's *Brideshead Revisited*. Mortimer also contributed to the 1965 satire show *BBC 3*.

MORTIMER, JOHNNIE (1930–)

British comedy scriptwriter, usually in collaboration with Brian Cooke. Together they created series such as *Father, Dear, Father*, *Man about the House*, *George and Mildred*, *Robin's Nest*, *Alcock and Gander*, *Kindly Leave the Kerb*, *Let There Be Love* and *Tom, Dick and Harriet*. The duo also wrote episodes of the sitcoms *Foreign Affairs*, *And Mother Makes Five*, *Full House*, *The Ronnie Barker Playhouse* and *Love Thy Neighbour*. In addition, Mortimer worked on *Never the Twain*, while Cooke contributed to *Close to Home* and *Tripper's/Slinger's Day*.

MOSLEY, BRYAN (1931–)

Yorkshire-born actor, a former stunt-fight choreographer and still a keen fencer who is best known today as Alf Roberts in *Coronation Street*, a part he first played in 1961. Not being a long-term contract-holder, Mosley was forced to leave the series the same year, during an actors' strike, but returned in 1968 and has been in Weatherfield ever since. His other TV work has included *The Villains* episode *Bent*, *Armchair Theatre*, *It's a Square World*, *Z Cars*, *The Plane Makers*, *The Saint*, *The Avengers*, *No Hiding Place*, *A Family at War*, *The Worker*, *Queenie's Castle*, *Doctor Who* and *Crossroads* (as Denis Rutledge).

MOUNT, PEGGY (1918–)

Powerful British character actress, usually seen as a domineering wife or colleague. Her first major TV role set the trend. In *The Larkins*, first seen in 1958, she played Ada, battleaxe wife of David Kossoff's Alf Larkin. In 1961 she was Martha, one of the *Winning Widows*, and, in 1966, she teamed up with Sid James as the appropriately named Gabrielle Dragon in *George and the Dragon*. Somewhat changing track, Mount played widow turned sleuth Virginia Browne in 1969's *John Browne's Body*, but was back on form in 1971, as Maggie, wife of Reg Robinson (Hugh Lloyd) in *Lollipop Loves Mr Mole* (later shortened to *Lollipop* – the series' title came from their affectionate nicknames). From brow-beating men she made the weedy Pat Coombs (also in *Lollipop*) her next target, when playing Flora Petty in *You're Only Young Twice*, but, since that series ended in 1981, Mount has largely been seen in straight roles. She has taken guest spots in dramas like *Inspector Morse*, *Casualty* and *Doctor Who*, although, as if to prove that old habits die hard, she did also appear as Aunt Fanny in the kids' sitcom *All Change* in 1991.

MOWER, PATRICK (1940–)

British actor, a 1970s favourite, following his roles as lecturer Michael West in *Haunted*, agent Cross in *Callan*, Detective Chief Insector. Tom Haggerty in *Special Branch*, Detective Supt Steve Hackett in *Target*, and many panel game appearances (*Whodunnit?*, *What's My Line?*, etc.). In addition to the above, Mower also appeared as reporter John Brownhill in the newspaper drama *Front Page Story* and guested in series like *Dixon of Dock Green*, *The Avengers*, *The Protectors*, *UFO*, *The Sweeney* and *Strangers*.

MTV

MTV, or Music Television, was established as a cable channel in the USA in 1981 by Warner Amex Satellite Entertainment, with the aim of focusing on the rock and pop markets. During its first decade on air, it helped establish the music video as a major source of entertainment for the teens and twenty somethings, and coined a new term, VJ (video jockey), for the presenter linking each item. The first video seen (on 1 August 1981) was 'Video Killed The Radio Star' by Buggles. MTV Europe (launched on 1 August 1987 with the video 'Money For Nothing' by Dire Straits) is now part of a series of global stations comprising also MTV Japan, MTV Brasil, MTV Internacional and MTV Latino. Since February 1989, it has been broadcast free and unencrypted (unscrambled) from the Astra satellites. A sister channel, VH-1, was launched in 1985 to cater specifically for older, thirtysomething music fans. This is also now available via Astra, but is a subscription channel, sold as part of the Sky Multi-Channels package. Amongst MTV's successes have been the cartoon characters *Beavis and Butthead* and the *Unplugged* series, in which rock stars play without electronic amplification. As well as music videos, the station features interviews, concert news and items on film and fashion. The company is currently owned by Viacom, which took control in 1987.

MUFFIN THE MULE

UK (BBC) Children's Entertainment. BBC 1946–55

Host/Creator/Writer: Annette Mills, Jan Bussell
Producers: David Boisseau, Joy Harington, Peter Thompson, Dorothea Brooking, Nan McDonald, John Warrington, Gordon Murray, Peggy Bacon

Song and dance with a puppet mule.

One of the earliest favourites of children's television, the legendary Muffin the Mule made his TV debut in 1946, in a five-minute *For the Children* slot in which he danced atop a grand piano while his co-star, Annette Mills, sang. Muffin and Mills (sister of actor John Mills) were subsequently given their own series and other puppets were introduced, like Oswald the ostrich, Mr Peregrine the penguin, Prudence and Primrose Kitten, Sally the sea-lion, Louise the lamb and Monty the monkey. The strings were pulled by puppeteer Ann Hogarth from behind a screen on top of the piano (Hogarth had bought the piebald mule for just 15s). Muffin's last TV appearance with Annette Mills came in 1955, just days before she died. Muffin then briefly moved to ITV before returning for one last series at the BBC in 1957, accompanied in vision by Jan Bussell.

MUGGERIDGE, MALCOLM (1903–90)

British journalist and commentator, working as an interviewer for *Panorama* in the 1950s and later for Granada. Much of his work involved spiritual matters, initially as a sceptic in many instances, but later as a firm Catholic, gaining the nickname of St Mugg. Muggeridge was never afraid to bring important people, historical and modern, down to earth and his documentaries included *The Thirties*, *Pilgrimage to Lourdes*, *Twilight of Empire* (about India), *Ladies and Gentlemen*, *It is My Pleasure* (reflecting on his own US lecture tour), *A Socialist Childhood* (his own), *Remembering Virginia* (Woolf), *Lord Reith Looks Back*, *A Life of Christ*, *A Quest for Gandhi*,

Something Beautiful for God (about Mother Teresa) and *Tolstoy: Rags to Riches*. He was also seen on *Press Conference*, **The Brains Trust**, *Appointment With . . .* , *Let Me Speak*, **BBC 3**, Jonathan Miller's *Alice in Wonderland* and his own retrospective, *Muggeridge Ancient and Modern*. Outside of broadcasting, Muggeridge had been a teacher in India and Egypt, Moscow correspondent for *The Manchester Guardian*, Deputy Editor of *The Daily Telegraph*, Editor of *Punch* and, at one time, an agent for MI6.

MUIR, FRANK, CBE (1920–)

To many viewers, Frank Muir is best remembered as a team captain on the BBC 2 word game **Call My Bluff**, the one in the bow tie who couldn't sound his 'r's. However, Muir's TV background is far more complex than that. With his writing partner Denis Norden (having already scripted *Take it from Here* and other comedies for radio), Muir penned the Jimmy Edwards series **Whack-O!** and **The Seven Faces of Jim**, Richard Briers's first major outlet, **Brothers in Law**, and the short-lived Bob Monkhouse sitcom *The Big Noise*. He presented a new talent show entitled *New To You* way back in 1946, two decades later guested with Peter Cook and Dudley Moore in **Not Only . . . But Also . . .** , and over the years has brought his wit and wisdom to numerous panel games. With Norden, he wrote and presented the comedy *How to be an Alien*. Behind the scenes, Muir was, at one time, Assistant Head of Comedy at the BBC and, later, Head of Light Entertainment at LWT. In 1992 he presented 13 weeks of *TV Heaven* on Channel 4, reviewing some of the most memorable programmes in the television archives.

MULBERRY

UK (BBC) Situation Comedy. BBC 1 1992–3

Mulberry	Karl Howman
Miss Rose Farnaby	Geraldine McEwan
Bert Finch	Tony Selby
Alice Finch	Lill Roughley
	Mary Healey
The Stranger	John Bennett

Creators/Writers: John Esmonde, Bob Larbey.
Producer: John B. Hobbs

A mysterious manservant enriches the life of a dowdy spinster.

Cantankerous Rose Farnaby lived alone in her musty family home, Farnaby Manor, with only her well-entrenched, conniving servants, Bert and Alice Finch, for company. Then, one day, an enigmatic new figure arrived. Mulberry instantly brightened up the household, sweet-talking the frumpy Miss Farnaby into making more of her life, adding zest to each day and encouraging her to break habits of a lifetime and try her hand at unusual pursuits. He genially ensured that the Finches knew their place and also protected Miss Farnaby from other detractors, like her scheming sisters, Adele and Elizabeth. Where the lovable Mulberry came from no one seemed to know, but his paranormal connections with a figure known only as The Stranger made the mystery even deeper.

MULLARD, ARTHUR (1910–)

Cockney comic actor, popular for his down-to-earth, working-class roles in the 1970s. In particular, he was Wally Briggs in **Romany Jones** and its sequel *Yus My Dear* (both opposite Queenie Watts). Previously, Mullard had guested in **Hancock's Half Hour**, played Arthur Askey's neighbour in a 1961 sitcom, *The Arthur Askey Show*, supported Alfie Bass and Bill Fraser in *Vacant Lot* in 1967 and also appeared in the 1969 kids' comedy *On the Rocks*. At his peak, he was a popular game show panellist, too, on programmes like **Celebrity Squares**.

MULLER, ROBERT (1925–)

British screenwriter, born in Germany and an escapee, with his family, from the Nazis in 1938. Not surprisingly, Nazism has featured prominently in his work, although his later efforts also focused on Gothic horror and history. He wrote pieces for **Armchair Theatre** in the early 1960s, as well as the anthologies **Mystery and Imagination** and **Out of the Unknown**, penned some episodes for **Colditz** in the 1970s and has also worked for German television. Other credits have included *Supernatural* and the plays *Russian Night 1941* and *Secrets*.

MULTI-COLOURED SWAP SHOP

UK (BBC) Children's Entertainment. BBC 1
1976–82

Presenters:
Noel Edmonds
Keith Chegwin
Maggie Philbin
John Craven

Producer: Rosemary Gill

Live, inter-active kids' magazine.

Opening a new front in Saturday morning children's programming, and allowing younger viewers to actually participate in events for once, *Multi-Coloured Swap Shop* was a light-hearted magazine which bound together cartoons, pop music, sport, phone-ins and competitions with a loose 'swapping' theme. Kids were encouraged to ring in with details of toys, books, clothes, etc. (but definitely no pets), they wished to swap, naming the item they were looking for in return. The most interesting exchanges were highlighted in the list of Top Ten Swaps. Celebrity guests were also asked to donate a 'swap' as a competition prize and John Craven organized the 'News Swap', which gave viewers the chance to air their opinions on news items of the day. Maggie Philbin helped out around the studio and Keith Chegwin was out on the road, secretly visiting a different venue each week and calling on locals to turn out in force and bring along their swaps. However, *Multi-Coloured Swap Shop* was very much a vehicle for Noel Edmonds, who relished this early opportunity to show off his live TV skills. (For the record, Edmonds's co-star, the *Swap Shop* dinosaur mascot, was called Posh Paws.)

The series was initially intended as a six-week filler. But it was only after six *years*, when Edmonds decided to move on, that the *Multi-Coloured Swap Shop* came to an end. It was replaced by the similarly styled *Saturday Superstore*. This was hosted by 'General Manager' Mike Read, assisted by Chegwin (still out and about), plus 'Saturday Girl' Sarah Greene. Vicky Licorish and David Icke held court in the 'Coffee Shop' and the 'Music and Sports Departments'.

MULVILLE, JIMMY

Liverpool-born actor, comedian and TV executive, a former Cambridge Footlights performer now working for Hat Trick Productions. He was a member of the **Who Dares Wins** team, co-wrote and appeared as Aulus Paulinus in the Roman spoof *Chelmsford 123*, played Donald Redfern in the sitcom *That's Love* and was Philip in *GBH*. The versatile Mulville has also been programme consultant on **Have I Got News For You**, a writer/producer on **Alas Smith and Jones**, producer of the sitcom *The Big One*, host of *The Brain Game* and contributed reports for *Holiday*.

MUNSTERS, THE

US (Universal) Situation Comedy. BBC 1
1965–7

Herman Munster	Fred Gwynne
Lily Munster	Yvonne De Carlo
Grandpa Munster	Al Lewis
Eddie Munster	Butch Patrick
Marilyn Munster	Beverly Owen
	Pat Priest

Creators: Joe Connelly, Bob Mosher

A ghoulish family scare the living daylights out of their neighbours.

The Munsters hit the TV screen at the same time as **The Addams Family** and there were many similarities between the two series. If anything, *The Munsters* was less subtle than its rival, for while the Addams Family looked more or less normal and just acted odd, the Munsters were real monsters, although of the friendly, kind-hearted type. Nominal head of the household was timid giant Herman, a Frankenstein's monster look-alike, complete with bolted-on head and leaden boots. His wife, Lily, was a vampire who walked around the house in shrouds, wearing a bat necklace. Her father, Grandpa, sometimes known as 'The Count', was an experimental magician who conjured up potions in his cellar laboratory and then struggled to find an antidote. He was known to disappear and hide, or even change into a bat. The Munsters' son was Eddie (actually Edward Wolfgang), a werewolf with a pronounced V-shaped hair cut and pointed ears. He was often seen playing with his wolf man doll. With the family lived Herman's neice, Marilyn, pitied by all for her plainness (in fact, she was an attractive blonde and the only human-looking member of the household).

Stories revolved around the family's contacts with the outside world and the misconception that they were normal and everyone else was strange. Visitors to their rambling Gothic mansion at 1313 Mockingbird Lane, Mockingbird Heights, were at first bemused and then terrified by its contents: heavy cobwebs, suits of armour, secret passages, an electric chair, a coffin telephone booth, and a black cat that roared like a lion. For the Munsters, life was seen in reverse. They talked about noises 'loud enough to wake the living', were worried when the shutters didn't creak at night and adorned the house with weeds instead of flowers. They cruised around town in a souped-up hearse. At night, Lily slept like a corpse, with her arms crossed over her chest, clutching a flower to her bosom. In the day, Herman worked for a funeral home, Gateman, Goodbury & Graves. At all times, Grandpa longed for the Old Country (Transylvania).

Beverly Owen, who played Marilyn, left after the first series and was replaced by Pat Priest. Fred Gwynne, Yvonne De Carlo and Al Lewis reprised their roles in a one-off TV movie entitled *The Munsters' Revenge*, made in 1981, before new actors took over for a limp revival in 1988 called *The Munsters Today*.

MUPPET SHOW, THE

UK (ITC/Henson) Variety. ITV 1976–81

Voices:

Kermit the Frog	Jim Henson
Miss Piggy Lee	Frank Oz
Fozzie Bear	Frank Oz
Zoot	Dave Goelz
Gonzo	Dave Goelz
Statler	Richard Hunt
Waldorf	Jim Henson
Sweetums	Richard Hunt
Sam the Eagle	Frank Oz
The Swedish Chef	Jim Henson
Dr Teeth	Jim Henson
Sgt Floyd Pepper	Jerry Nelson
Rowlf	Jim Henson
Animal	Frank Oz
Captain Link Hogthrob	Jim Henson
Dr Julius Strangepork	Jerry Nelson
Dr Bunsen Honeydew	Dave Goelz
Scooter	Richard Hunt
Beauregard	Dave Goelz
Pops	Jerry Nelson
Lew Zealand	Jerry Nelson
Janice	Richard Hunt
Rizzo the Rat	Steve Whitmire
Robin the Frog	Jerry Nelson

Creators: Jim Henson, Frank Oz. Executive Producer: David Lazer. Producers: Jack Burns, Jim Henson

A wacky troupe of puppet animals tries to stage a variety show.

The Muppets were devised and christened by Jim Henson in America in the 1950s. They were half marionette and half glove puppet, hence their name, and they appeared intermittently on US TV for more than a decade before coming to the fore in the children's educational series *Sesame Street*. The chance of a major show of their own eluded them in America, but Lew Grade put his trust in their abilities and financed the production of *The Muppet Show* in Britain.

The premise of each programme was that the Muppets would organize and perform a variety show, before a live audience. Master of Ceremonies was Kermit the Frog, operated and voiced by Henson himself. He was supported (or hindered) by a large cast of weird animal and humanoid performers and stagehands. Fozzie Bear was a stand-up comedian with the pointed head, small hat and lame jokes. Rowlf was a shaggy dog piano player, and other music came from Dr Teeth and the Electric Mayhem, featuring Animal on drums and laid-back guitarist Floyd. Gonzo was a hook-beaked stuntman and trumpeter whose instrument exploded at the start of each show.

Soon to become co-star with Kermit was blonde Miss Piggy. Her unrequited love for the frog meant she was constantly trying to ensnare him, and anyone who stood in the way of her success felt the power of her left hook. Other notable protagonists were mad scientist Dr Bunsen Honeydew, a crazy Swedish Chef, and a pair of crochety old men, Statler and Waldorf, who heckled the show from their box seats. More barracking came from Sam, the right-wing American eagle. A regular slot in the show was given to the serial *Pigs in Space*, which pitted Captain Link Hogthrob, commander of the starship 'Swinetrek', against the evil Dr Strangepork. A host of famous stars also appeared as the Muppets' guests, Elton John, Peter Sellers, George Burns, Peter Ustinov, Raquel Welch and Rudolf Nureyev, among them, and, apart from the technical mastery of the puppet form, the show's success came from the human nature of its characters, their attempts to succeed and their tendency to fail. The inventiveness of the musical numbers also played a part. Buffalo Springfield's 'For What It's Worth', for instance, was performed with pathos against a field sports backdrop, and the show spawned a couple of chart hits, 'The Muppet Show Music Hall EP' and A.A. Milne's 'Halfway Down the Stairs' (by Kermit's nephew, Robin). The Muppets also made a couple of feature films.

MURDER BAG

UK (Associated-Rediffusion) Police Drama. ITV 1957–9

Detective Supt Tom Lockhart ....Raymond Francis

Creator: Glyn Davies. Producer: Barry Baker. Writers: Barry Baker, Peter Ling

Half-hour detective series that introduced viewers to the snuff-taking Detective Supt Lockhart.

In this early series, Tom Lockhart was assisted in his investigations by different police officers each week, but always present was the 'Murder Bag' of the title. This black briefcase, seen in close-up behind the opening titles, provided Lockhart with the equipment needed to gather forensic evidence. Over 70 items were held in the case, ranging from airtight jars to tweezers, and each week it was called into play in pursuit of yet another murderer. The first 30 episodes did not have separate titles, but case numbers, and were listed as *Murder Bag – Case One*, etc. All subsequent programmes carried titles such as *Lockhart sets a Trap* and *Lockhart Misses a Clue*, and all transmissions were live. From here, the character of Lockhart went on to **Crime Sheet** (where he could investigate more than murder) and then his pièce de résistance, **No Hiding Place**.

MURDER, SHE WROTE

US (Universal) Detective Drama. ITV 1985–

Jessica Fletcher ....Angela Lansbury
Sheriff Amos Tupper ....Tom Bosley
Grady Fletcher ....Michael Horton
Dr Seth Hazlitt ....William Windom
Mayor Sam Booth ....Richard Paul
Sheriff Mort Metzger ....Ron Masak

Creators: Richard Levinson, William Link, Peter S. Fischer. Executive Producer: Peter S. Fischer Producers: Robert F. O'Neill, Robert E. Swanson

A middle-aged novelist solves murder cases in her spare time.

Widow Jessica Beatrice Fletcher lived in Cabot Cove, Maine, and had been a substitute teacher until writing brought her fame and wealth. Her first book, a detective thriller called *The Corpse Danced at Midnight*, was submitted to a publisher by Grady, her accountant nephew, and became a huge success. However, when one of her relatives was suspected of murder, Jessica was able to bring her own detective skills into play. She cleared his name and thus began her investigative career.

Jessica became a sort of American Miss Marple. Travelling the world to promote her books or to visit her many relations, she found herself constantly embroiled in murder mysteries that the local police could not resolve. Piecing together the clues in often very complicated plots, Jessica proved to be a thorough and quick-witted sleuth, bringing many a culprit to book, much to the amazement of the local law enforcers. When not travelling, her acquaintances in Cabot Cove (which itself had more than its fair share of murders) included the local sheriff, Amos Tupper (later replaced by Sheriff Mort Metzger), Mayor Sam Booth and Seth Hazlitt, a doctor with whom she played chess. In later episodes, Jessica moved part-time to New York, living weekdays in a Manhattan apartment while teaching criminology at Manhattan University. On some occasions, Jessica herself did not appear, other than to introduce the week's 'guest sleuth'.

MURDOCH, RUPERT (1931–)

Possibly the world's leading media baron of the late 20th century, Australian-born Rupert Murdoch, the head of the News International empire, has left his mark on the television world as well as in newspapers and publishing. In 1985 he became an American citizen for business reasons and took control of Twentieth Century-Fox and a string of regional TV stations in order to establish a fourth US television network (Fox). Then, in 1989, he pre-empted the launch of British Satellite Broadcasting (BSB), the official UK satellite station, by opening up his own Sky network, which, in 1990, merged with (in many ways absorbed) BSB, becoming British Sky Broadcasting. News International also owns the Asian satellite station, Star TV.

MURPHY, BEN (1941–)

American actor, in television since 1968. His first contributions were guest spots on series like *It Takes a Thief*, *The Virginian* and *The Name of the Game*, and he waited until 1971 to earn a starring role. That came as Thaddeus Jones (aka Kid Curry) in *Alias Smith and Jones*, a bigger hit in the UK than in its native USA, leaving Murphy still looking for a TV breakthrough back home. He followed it with a series of similarly prominent but not overwhelming parts, including the title role in *The Gemini Man* (Sam Casey), a sort of revamped *Invisible Man*. Amongst other dramas, Murphy was also seen in *The Winds of War* (as Warren Henry), and in the series *Griff* and *The Chisholms*.

MURPHY, BRIAN (1933–)

British comic actor chiefly remembered as the hen-pecked, workshy George Roper in *Man about the House* and *George and Mildred*. However, Murphy has also starred in other sitcoms: *The Incredible Mr Tanner* (as busker Ernest Tanner), *L for Lester* (as Lester Small, a hapless driving instructor), and *Lame Ducks* (as Ansell, an inept private eye). In 1995 he was seen as conman George Manners in *Brookside*.

MURRAY, BRIAN (1949–)

Irish actor seen in a variety of series, usually in 'dodgy' roles. The highlights have been *The Irish RM* (as Flurry Knox), *Bread* (as the crooked Shifty), *Perfect Scoundrels* (as con-man Harry Cassidy) and *Brookside* (as the wife-beating Trevor Jordache).

MY FAVORITE MARTIAN

US (Jack Chertok) Situation Comedy. ITV 1963–

Uncle Martin	Ray Walston
Tim O'Hara	Bill Bixby
Lorelei Brown	Pamela Britton
Angela Brown	Ann Marshall
Mr Harry Burns	J. Pat O'Malley
Detective Bill Brennan	Alan Hewitt

Creator: John L. Greene. Producer: Jack Chertok

A journalist befriends a Martian who has crash-landed on Earth.

Los Angeles Sun reporter Tim O'Hara was on the way to an assignment when he discovered a crashed spacecraft and its occupant, a Martian anthropologist who had been studying Earthmen. Seeing the alien was dazed and in need of help, Tim took him home and made him comfortable in his boarding house room, while he worked on the amazing story for his boss, Mr Burns. But, being almost human-like and speaking English, the Martian made a strong impression on Tim, who scrapped the story and decided to keep the alien's identity a secret. He passed him off as his Uncle Martin and found him a room in the house, to give Martin time to repair his ship. No one else knew Martin's secret, though Bill Brennan, a police officer, who arrived in the second series, was always fishing around. He was also Martin's rival for the attentions of their landlady, Mrs Brown. Her teenage daughter, Angela, appeared in the first season.

Preceding *Mork and Mindy* by a decade and a half, *My Favorite Martian* had many similarities. Martin was not as zany as Mork but he did have unusual powers, such as telepathy and the ability to make himself invisible. He could move objects by pointing at them, was a technological genius, could talk to animals and had little retractable antennae on his head.

MY FRIEND FLICKA

US (Twentieth Century-Fox) Children's Adventure. ITV

Ken McLaughlin	Johnny Washbrook
Rob McLaughlin	Gene Evans
Nell McLaughlin	Anita Louise
Gus Broeberg	Frank Ferguson
Hildy Broeberg	Pamela Beaird

Executive Producer: Buddy Adler. Producers: Alan A. Armor, Peter Packer, Sam White, Herman Schlom

A boy's best friend is his horse.

Eleven-year-old Ken McLaughlin lived with his parents, Rob and Nell, ranch hand, Gus, and most importantly his horse, Flicka, on the Goose Bar Ranch near Coulee Springs in turn-of-the-century Montana. In the *Lassie* vein, boy and horse fell into all manner of adventures, although the drama was not always as intense, and much of the action centred on the family's struggles on the northern American frontier. Hildy was Gus's neice.

My Friend Flicka (which was one of the first children's series to be filmed in colour) was based on the book by Mary O'Hara and the 1943 film starring Roddy McDowall. It was shown intermittently around the ITV network after debuting in its native USA in 1956. 'Flicka' is Swedish for 'little girl' and the equine star was a horse called Wahama.

MY GOOD WOMAN

UK (ATV) Situation Comedy. ITV 1972–4

Clive Gibbons	Leslie Crowther

Sylvia Gibbons	Sylvia Sims
Philip Broadmore	Keith Barron
Bob Berris	Glyn Houston
Reverend Martin Hooper	Richard Wilson

Creator/Writer: Ronnie Taylor. Producer: Les Chatfield, William G. Stewart, Ronnie Baxter

A husband suffers because his wife is a compulsive charity worker.

Clive Gibbons was a charity widower. His wife, Sylvia, was so concerned with raising money for good causes and helping out the less fortunate that their life together was rather barren. Despite his efforts to convince her that charity began at home, the hapless Clive was forced to seek solace in the company of his neighbour Philip Broadmore and then, in later episodes, his darts colleague, Bob Berris. Martin Hooper was the vicar benefiting from most of Sylvia's worthy deeds.

MY MOTHER THE CAR

US (United Artists/Cottage Industries/NBC) Situation Comedy. ITV 1965–

Dave Crabtree	Jerry Van Dyke
Abigail Crabtree (voice only)	Ann Sothern
Barbara Crabtree	Maggie Pierce
Cindy Crabtree	Cindy Eilbacher
Randy Crabtree	Randy Whipple
Captain Bernard Mancini	Avery Schreiber

Creators: Allan Burns, Chris Hayward. Producer: Rod Amateau

A man buys a vintage motor car only to find it is his mother reincarnated.

When lawyer Dave Crabtree visited a second-hand car lot in his small Californian town to look for a cheap new car, he found himself inexplicably drawn to a rickety 1928 Porter. He soon discovered why: the car was actually a reincarnation of his late mother. Understandably, he bought the car and restored it, much to the disgust of his wife, Barbara, and two children, Cindy and Randy, who really wanted a station wagon. They couldn't understand why he was so protective about the old boneshaker and why he resisted the villainous attempts by classic car dealer Captain Mancini to take the Porter off his hands. Of course, *they* couldn't hear his mother's voice bellowing out of the car radio, nagging and domineering him just as she had done when she was first alive.

Jerry Van Dyke is Dick Van Dyke's brother but he failed to achieve the same kind of success. *My Mother the Car* was almost universally panned by critics and lasted only one season. For some, it was the worst US sitcom of the 1960s.

MY WIFE NEXT DOOR

UK (BBC) Situation Comedy. BBC 1 1972

George Bassett	John Alderton
Suzy Bassett	Hannah Gordon

Creators: Brian Clemens, Richard Waring. Writer: Richard Waring. Producer: Graeme Muir

A freshly divorced couple live side by side in the country.

When George Bassett was divorced by his wife, Suzy, he decided to make a fresh start. He moved out of London and into the countryside. Unfortunately for George, Suzy had also escaped from the city and they found themselves living as next door neighbours in numbers 1 and 2 Copse Cottages near Stoke Poges. To preserve their independence they drew up an 'Atlantic Charter' of rules and regulations which they attempted to follow on a day-to-day basis, while all the time prying into each other's affairs (domestic and romantic). They were clearly still in love but terrified to admit it, to their mutual cost.

MYSTERY AND IMAGINATION

UK (ABC/Thames) Thriller Anthology. ITV 1966–70

Richard Beckett	David Buck

Creators: Jonathan Alwyn, Terence Feely. Producer: Jonathan Alwyn

Dramatizations of Victorian chillers.

Hosted by David Buck in the guise of Victorian adventurer Richard Beckett (who also appeared in some of the stories), *Mystery and Imagination* presented three series of 19th-century thrillers. These included works by Robert Louis Stevenson and Edgar Allen Poe, as well as lesser known writers, but most were in the spine-tingling Gothic tradition. The classics *Frankenstein* and *Dracula* were both featured, as were *Sweeney Todd*, *The Canterville Ghost* and *The Fall of the House of Usher*.

MYSTERY MOVIE

US (Universal) Mystery. ITV 1972–

Rotating series of TV movies featuring various sleuths and law enforcers.

The *Mystery Movie* umbrella title covered the adventures of **Columbo**, **McCloud**, **McMillan and Wife**, **Madigan**, **Quincy**, **The Snoop Sisters**, **Hec Ramsey**, **Faraday and Company**, **Tenafly**, **Amy Prentiss**, **Cool Million**, **McCoy** and **Banacek**, which aired in sequence on ITV. The most successful concepts (like **Columbo**, **McMillan and**

Wife, *Quincy* and *McCloud*) were later billed simply under their own titles, whereas others (like *McCoy* and *Cool Million*) faded away very quickly. In the USA, the series was broken down into *Sunday Mystery Movie* and *Wednesday Mystery Movie* blocks for airing on NBC.

NAIL, JIMMY (JAMES BRADFORD; 1954–)

Geordie actor, writer, producer and singer, coming to fame as Oz in *Auf Wiedersehen, Pet* and later turning to his own ideas for starring roles. These have come in *Spender*, as the maverick Newcastle copper, and *Crocodile Shoes*, playing singing/songwriting hopeful Jed Shepperd. He now runs his own production company, Big Boy. Nail has also been seen in *Blott on the Landscape*, *Shoot for the Sun*, *Minder* and *Spyship*.

NAKED CITY

US (Shelle/Screen Gems) Police Drama. ITV 1962–

Detective Lt Dan Muldoon.....................John McIntire
Detective Jim Halloran......................James Franciscus
Janet Halloran.......................................Suzanne Storrs
Patrolman/Sgt Frank Arcaro ....Harry Bellaver
Lt Mike Parker ....Horace McMahon
Detective Adam Flint.................................Paul Burke
Libby ....Nancy Malone

Creator: Sterling Silliphant. Executive Producer: Herbert B. Leonard

Grimy, realistic police dramas set in New York City.

'There are eight million stories in the Naked City', revealed the narrator of this programme. Most of them, it seemed, revolved around crime, as the City's police officers (by no means all of them angels) came under the spotlight, combing the seedy streets in search of muggers, murderers and other assorted felons. Veteran cop Dan Muldoon of the 65th Precinct was the programme's first main man but he was killed off early on when his car crashed into a petrol tanker. His younger partner, Jim Halloran, and Jim's wife, Janet, didn't last much longer and were also written out after only one season. Muldoon was replaced by Mike Parker, a tough, determined operator, who was later assisted by Detective Adam Flint and Sgt Frank Arcaro (promoted from his patrolman status in the earlier episodes). Flint's girlfriend, Libby, was also seen. But, in many ways, the real star of the programme was the city itself. The series was filmed entirely on location, with long shots drawing the attention of the viewer away from the personalities and focus-

ing it instead on the bustling metropolis, the hub of all this villainous activity. The jazzy score by Billy May added to the moody atmosphere.

Naked City also specialized in weird episode titles. Examples included *The King of Venus Will Take Care of You*, *Howard Running Bear is a Turtle* and *No Naked Ladies in Front of Giovanni's House*. Guest stars abounded, most just fledgling actors at the time. Dustin Hoffman, Robert Redford, Jon Voight, Gene Hackman, Peter Falk, George Segal and Peter Fonda were the most notable. The story on which *Naked City* was based was written by Broadway columnist Mark Hellinger and an Oscar-winning film version, starring Barry Fitzgerald and Don Taylor, appeared in 1948.

NAKED CIVIL SERVANT, THE

UK (Thames) Drama. ITV 1975

Quentin Crisp...John Hurt

Writer: Philip Mackie. Producer: Barry Hanson

The biography of an outspoken homosexual.

This 90-minute dramatization by Philip Mackie of Quentin Crisp's revealing autobiography was initially turned down by the BBC before being accepted, with caution, by Thames and the IBA. It portrayed events in the life of Crisp, a prominently homosexual government employee and former art school model (hence the title), from the late-1920s to the mid-1970s. John Hurt played the lead with flamboyant effeminism and the work proved influential in opening stubbornly closed eyes to the predicament of gay men in society, thanks to its balanced combination of humour and tenderness. Viewers were shocked; critics doled out awards.

NAKED VIDEO

UK (BBC) Comedy. BBC 2 1986–91

Helen Lederer
Gregor Fisher
Tony Roper
Ron Bain
Andy Gray
Elaine C. Smith
Jonathan Watson
John Sparkes
Louise Beattie

Producers: Colin Gilbert, Philip Differ

Potpourri of comic sketches from North of the Border.

A comedy offering from BBC Scotland, *Naked Video* helped establish the careers of Helen Lederer and Gregor Fisher in particular and also gave the world a handful of well-defined new comic characters. These included Rab C. Nesbitt, the aggressive, Glaswegian street philosopher, and the follicly-challenged Baldy Man (both played by Fisher and later graduating to their own series). Another innovation was Shadwell, the simple-minded Welsh poet, portrayed by John Sparkes. These appeared amidst a collection of running sketches, some of which satirized topical issues. *Naked Video* was derived from a radio programme entitled *Naked Radio*.

NAME THAT TUNE see *Spot the Tune.*

NANCY ASTOR

UK (BBC) Drama. BBC 2 1982

Nancy Langhorne/Astor ....Lisa Harrow
Robert Gould Shaw ....Pierce Brosnan
Waldorf Astor ....James Fox
Chillie Langhorne ....Dan O'Herlihy
Nanaire Langhorne ....Sylvia Syms
Phyllis Brand ....Lise Hilboldt
Lord Revelstoke ....Julian Glover

Writer: Derek Marlowe. Producer: Philip Hinchcliffe

Biography of Britain's first female MP.

In nine episodes, this series traced the ups and downs in the life of Nancy Langhorne, an ambitious Southern belle, the daughter of a tobacco auctioneer from Virginia. It followed her marriage to Robert Gould Shaw, a wealthy Boston playboy, and its subsequent collapse, before charting her romance with a British millionaire politician, Waldorf Astor, proprietor of The *Observer*, whom she went on to marry. When he was elevated to the House of Lords in 1919, Nancy took his place in the House of Commons, thereby carving herself a niche in history as the first woman to take her seat as a Member of Parliament. In the House, her sharp American tongue earned many enemies.

NANNY

UK (BBC) Drama. BBC 1 1981-3

Barbara Gray...Wendy Craig

Creator: Wendy Craig. Writers: Charlotte Bingham, Terence Brady. Producers: Guy Slater, Bernard Krichefski

The life of a children's nurse in the 1930s.

Dreamt up by actress Wendy Craig, who submitted the idea under the pen name of Jonathan Marr, *Nanny* was the story of Barbara Gray, a traditional children's carer, working in the homes of the rich and noble in the 1930s. Her enlightened approach made her a popular and trustworthy choice for wealthy parents. Craig's idea was developed into three series of scripts by the *No, Honestly* husband and wife writing team of Charlotte Bingham and Terence Brady.

NATION, TERRY

Welsh comedy scriptwriter, working in BBC Radio in the 1950s, then on Tony Hancock's ITV series in 1963. Nation then switched more to drama and, in particular, to science fiction, with significant results. Undoubtedly, he will go down in television history as the man who invented the daleks, the pepper pot megalomaniacs from *Doctor Who*, but he also created the 1970s sci-fi classics *Survivors* and *Blake's 7*. In addition, Nation contributed to *No Hiding Place*, *The Baron*, *Department S*, *The Saint*, *The Champions*, *The Avengers*, *The Persuaders!*, *The Protectors*, *Out of the Unknown*, *Out of this World* and other anthologies and dramatized Isaac Asimov's *The Caves of Steel* for BBC 2 in 1964.

NATIONWIDE

UK (BBC) Current Affairs. BBC 1 1969-83

Presenters: Michael Barratt, Bob Wellings, Sue Lawley, Richard Stilgoe, Frank Bough, Dilys Morgan, Brian Widlake, Glyn Worsnip, Valerie Singleton, John Stapleton, Hugh Scully, Sue Cook, Richard Kershaw, Laurie Mayer, Fran Morrison, David Dimbleby

Creator: Derrick Amoore. Producers/Editors: Derrick Amoore, Michael Bunce, Phil Sidey, Ron Neil, Andrew Clayton, Tim Gardam, Paul Corley, Richard Tait, John Gau, Paul Woolwich, Hugh Williams, Roger Bolton

Light-hearted early evening news magazine.

For a decade and a half, *Nationwide* was an integral part of British teatime. Following on from the main early evening news bulletin, Monday to Friday, the 50-minute programme was a mixed bag of newsy items, political discussions, consumer affairs and light entertainment. After the introductory headlines, viewers were sent 'nationwide', i.e. the BBC regions opted out to present their own 20-minute or so local news round-ups (*Points West*, *Look North*, *Wales Today*, etc.). When these programmes finished, they handed back to London and the *Nationwide* studio, although the regions stayed 'live' to feedback reports and local reactions to the day's news, and to allow interviews to take place across the network. Technical problems abounded, with sound or vision going down on a regular basis.

Nationwide seemed to be obsessed with the great British eccentric and always looking for unusual stories about skateboarding ducks or men who claimed they could walk on eggs. Regular features included the programme's Consumer Unit (which developed into a separate series called *Watchdog*) and Price Check, which monitored the cost of living. Richard Stilgoe performed topical songs, Susan Stranks took a stroll down Memory Lane and numerous politicians were put On The Spot. On Fridays, the weekend sporting action was previewed by Desmond Lynam, Peter Walker and other sports presenters in Sportswide and, most Decembers, there was a *Nationwide* Carol Competition.

Michael Barratt, Sue Lawley and Bob Wellings were the mainstays of the programme for many years, with Valerie Singleton and Frank Bough joining from **Blue Peter** and **Grandstand** later. A young John Stapleton and David Dimbleby also acted as anchors. *Nationwide*'s best-remembered reporters included Jack Pizzey, Bernard Falk, Philip Tibenham, Bernard Clarke, Martin Young, and Patti Coldwell, and amongst the frequent contributors from the regional studios were Tom Coyne and Alan Towers (Birmingham), Mike Neville (Newcastle), Bruce Parker (Southampton), Stuart Hall (Manchester), Ian Masters (Norwich) and Hugh Scully (Plymouth). In all, 3131 editions were produced before *Nationwide* gave way to a look-alike programme entitled *Sixty Minutes* in 1984. Hosted by Desmond Wilcox, Sally Magnusson, Nick Ross, Beverly Anderson and Sarah Kennedy, it lasted only one year.

NAYLOR, DOUG see Grant, Rob.

NBC

America's NBC, standing for National Broadcasting Company, was established by RCA to help sell the radio (and later television) equipment it manufactured. Its first radio broadcast came in 1926, with TV following in 1931, and NBC's history remained indelibly linked to the fortunes of RCA for decades. In the 1950s, for instance, the network became the first to broadcast all its programmes in colour, in an effort to boost sales of the newly-developed RCA colour system. Amongst the company's most influential early executives was David Sarnoff, powerful head of RCA for 40 years.

As a network, NBC has nearly always run behind its great rival, CBS, but for many years was comfortably ahead of the third station, ABC, in the ratings. Of the three networks, it is NBC which has probably been the most innovative. It launched the first dual-anchor news programme, for example, and also developed the TV movie concept.

NBC, which was sold to General Electric in 1985, took a majority holding in the European satellite station Super Channel in 1993.

NBC SUPER CHANNEL

Pan-European satellite channel that has had a rather checkered, if reasonably short, history. As

Super Channel, it was established in 1987 by a consortium involving 14 of the 15 ITV franchise holders, plus the Virgin group and Italian interests. The format was general entertainment. However, in 1993, a majority holding in the company was taken up by NBC of America and, in December that year, the programming style changed to target the businessman market. Daytime programmes have since been heavily news- (from ITN and NBC) and finance-oriented, with evenings geared to the businessman 'off-duty', offering documentaries, sports, music and general entertainment programmes like *The Tonight Show with Jay Leno*. Since autumn 1994, the channel has been broadcast unencrypted (free) from Astra's 1D satellite, in addition to its original outlets on Eutelsat II and via cable companies.

NEAREST AND DEAREST

UK (Granada) Situation Comedy. ITV 1968–72

Nellie Pledge	Hylda Baker
Eli Pledge	Jimmy Jewel
Lily	Madge Hindle
Walter	Edward Malin
Stan	Joe Gladwin
Bert	Bert Palmer
	Leslie Sarony
Grenville	Freddie Rayner

Creators: Vince Powell, Harry Driver.
Producers: Peter Eckersley, Bill Podmore

A middle-aged brother and sister grudgingly share control of a northern pickle factory.

Eli and Nellie Pledge, bachelor and spinster, were brought back together on the death of their father, who bequeathed them his Pledge's Pickles business. Bickering and fighting, the pair somehow managed to keep the company afloat, although there was just as much vinegar in their relationship as in the pickle jars. The plots often played second fiddle to the boundless insults they traded, which ranged from 'big girl's blouse' to 'knock-kneed knackered old nosebag'. The show was essentially a vehicle for Hylda Baker's distinctive line in comedy, littered with malapropisms and double entendres. It allowed her a few gems along the way, such as when Nellie remarked that Eli reminded her of that beautiful song from *The Sound of Music*. 'Which one', responded Eli, 'My Favourite Things?'. 'No' came back the put-down, 'Idleswine'.

The Pledges were ably supported in the factory by their down to earth but rather decrepit foreman, Stan, and often had to play host at home to cousin Lily and her silent, quivering husband, Walter, who was plagued with waterworks trouble. The burning question was always 'Has he been?', although we were all assured that 'He knows, you know' (one of Baker's oldest catch-phrases). A cinema version was made in 1972. Hylda Baker moved on to another sitcom in a similar vein. Entitled *Not On Your Nellie*, it saw her cast as Fulham publican Nellie Pickersgill.

NEDWELL, ROBIN (1946–)

British comic actor, popular in the 1970s as the hero of most of the *Doctor* series (Duncan Waring). Nedwell also appeared in *The Lovers*, playing Geoffrey's friend Roland and, when John Alderton left the role of Mike Upchat in *The Upchat Line*, Nedwell stepped in for the sequel, *The Upchat Connection*. He was also pop musician Peter Higgins in *The Shillingbury Tales*, Fiddler in the shortlived comedy *West End Tales* and Harry Lumsdon, *The Climber*, in the 1983 BBC sitcom. Nedwell returned to the small screen in the 1991 Doctors revival, *Doctor at the Top*.

NEGUS, ARTHUR, OBE (1903–85)

Amiable, silver-haired antiques expert prominent in *Going for a Song*, *Antiques Roadshow* and the travelogue *Arthur Negus Enjoys*. His gentle, infor-mative manner encouraged viewers to view their family heirlooms in quite a different light.

NEIGHBOURS

Australia (Grundy) Drama. BBC 1 1986–

Helen Daniels	Anne Haddy
Jim Robinson	Alan Dale
Paul Robinson	Stefan Dennis
Julie Robinson/Martin	Vikki Blanche
	Julie Mullins
Scott Robinson	Darius Perkins
	Jason Donovan
Lucy Robinson	Kylie Flinker
	Sasha Close
	Melissa Bell
Max Ramsay	Francis Bell
Maria Ramsay	Dasha Blahova
Shane Ramsay	Peter O'Brien
Danny Ramsay	David Clencie
Tom Ramsay	Gary Files
Eileen Clarke	Myra De Groot
Des Clarke	Paul Keane
Daphne Lawrence/Clarke	Elaine Smith
Mike Young	Guy Pearce
Dr Clive Gibbons	Geoff Paine
Madge Mitchell/Ramsay/Bishop	Anne Charleston
Charlene Mitchell/Robinson	Kylie Minogue
Henry Mitchell Ramsay	Craig McLachlan
Rosemary Daniels	Joy Chambers
Nell Mangel/Worthington	Vivean Gray
Zoe Davis	Ally Fowler
Jane Harris	Annie Jones
Susan Cole	Gloria Ajenstat
Rob Lewis	Ernie Bourne
Gail Lewis/Robinson	Fiona Corke

Harold Bishop	Ian Smith
Bronwen Davies	Rachel Friend
Sharon Davies	Jessica Muschamp
Nick Page	Mark Stevens
Sally Wells	Rowena Mohr
Todd Landers	Kristian Schmid
Katie Landers	Sally Jensen
Lou Carpenter	Tom Oliver
Josh Anderson	Jeremy Angerson
Melissa Jarrett	Jade Amenta
Joe Mangel	Mark Little
Toby Mangel	Finn Greentree Keene
	Ben Guerens
Kerry Bishop/Mangel	Linda Hartley
Melanie Pearson/Mangel	Lucinda Cowden
Sky Bishop/Mangel	Mirander Fryer
Gemma Ramsay	Beth Buchanan
Hilary Robinson	Anne Scott-Pendlebury
Matthew Williams/Robinson	Ashley Paske
Dr Beverly Marshall	Lisa Armytage
	Shaunna O'Grady
Caroline Alessi	Gillian Blakeney
Christina Alessi/Robinson	Gayle Blakeney
Ryan McLachlan	Richard Norton
Eddie Buckingham	Bob La Castra
Doug Willis	Terence Donovan
Pam Willis	Sue Jones
Adam Willis	Ian Williams
Cody Willis	Amelia Frid
	Peta Brady
Brad Willis	Scott Michaelson
Gaby Willis	Rachel Blakely
Dorothy Burke	Maggie Dence
Glen Donnelly	Richard Huggett
Brenda Riley	Genevieve Lemon
Guy Carpenter	Andrew Williams
Phoebe Bright/Gottlieb	Simone Robertson
Cameron Hudson	Benjamin Mitchell
Beth Brennan	Natalie Imbruglia
Marco Alessi	Felice Arena
Rick Alessi	Dan Falzon
Philip Martin	Ian Rawlings
Hannah Martin	Rebecca Ritters
Debbie Martin	Marnie Reece-Wilmore
Benito Alessi	George Spatels
Cathy Alessi	Elspeth Ballantyne
Stephen Gottlieb	Lochie Daddo
Lauren Carpenter	Sarah Vandenbergh
Michael Martin	Troy Beckwith
Mark Gottlieb	Bruce Samazan
Annalise Hartman	Kimberley Davies
Wayne Duncan	Jonathan Sammy-Lee
Cheryl Stark	Caroline Gillmer
Danni Stark	Eliza Szonert
Brett Stark	Brett Blewitt
Sam Kratz	Richard Grieve
Marlene Kratz	Moya O'Sullivan

Creator/Executive Producer: Reg Watson

Middle-class ups and downs for the residents of a Melbourne cul-de-sac.

From shaky beginnings, *Neighbours* has become one of the success stories of Australian TV. Created by former *Crossroads* producer Reg Watson, it initially aired in 1985 on the country's

Seven Network but dwindling audiences resulted in its cancellation after only six months. The programme's producers Grundy, however, decided to fight on and sold the show to the rival Ten Network. With a complete facelift, including new sets and new, predominantly younger actors (only five remained from the Seven Network episodes), *Neighbours* slowly began to take off. The series arrived in the UK in 1986, as one of the BBC's first daytime offerings. It was originally scheduled at 10 am and 1.30 pm each day but, on the advice of his schoolgirl daughter, BBC 1 Controller Michael Grade moved the 10 am showing to 5.35 pm. There it captured a massive children, housewives and home-from-work audience and never looked back.

Neighbours is set in Ramsay Street, a semi-affluent cul-de-sac in the fictitious Melbourne suburb of Erinsborough. The street took its name from the ancestors of one of its most prominent families, the Ramsays, who dominated the action in the early days along with the Robinsons and the Clarkes. The most noteworthy characters over the years have been widower Jim Robinson, his supportive mother-in-law, Helen Daniels, and his assorted kids, including the pompous Paul and teenager Scott (a role which launched Jason Donovan into celebrity status). The rival Ramsays were at first headed by Max, a plumber, but he quickly gave way to his sister, Madge Mitchell, and her wayward children, former jailbird Henry and car mechanic Charlene (Kylie Minogue's big break). The Clarkes were primarily hapless bank manager Des and his ex-stripper wife, Daphne. These families have been expanded in the course of time to bring in various errant children, ex-wives, forgotten parents, etc., and numerous other residents have come and gone, too. Tittle-tattling Mrs Mangel and her loud son, Joe, the twins Christina and Caroline Alessi, dithery Harold Bishop (Madge's new husband), and the Willis brood are representative of these newcomers.

The concerns of Ramsay Street residents have varied from the life-threatening to the banal, but the sun has always shone and things have generally turned out well. The younger element (the kids of Erinsborough High School), and their middle-aged parents and grandparents have happily shared the limelight, ensuring interest for viewers old and young, and, apart from the school and the close itself, the main focal point has been the Lassiters hotel complex and, in particular, its Waterhole bar and its coffee shop. The programme's theme song was composed by Tony Hatch and Jackie Trent, and sung by Barry Crocker.

NESMITH, MICHAEL (1942–)

American actor and musician, one of The Monkees. When the series ended, Nesmith drifted off into ambitious musical projects with his First National Band, writing the song 'Different Drum' for Linda Ronstadt, plus other tracks, mostly in a country rock vein. He became a pioneer in rock videos which, ironically, brought him back to TV in *Michael Nesmith In Television Parts*, in 1985. Its combination of avant-garde humour and music videos proved familiar to Monkees fans.

NETTLES, JOHN (1948–)

Cornish actor John Nettles's earliest television performances came in series like **A Family at War** (in which he played Ian Mackenzie) and **The Liver Birds** (as Paul, Sandra's boyfriend). Via appearances in series like **The Adventures of Black Beauty** and some single dramas, he arrived in 1981 at his TV *pièce de résistance*, the part of Jim **Bergerac**, the Jersey detective with a drink problem and a gammy leg. It was a role Nettles played for over ten years, making Jersey his home in the process and doing wonders for its tourist trade.

NETWORK

A chain of TV stations linked by cable or satellite in order to broadcast programmes over a larger area. The term is given to the USA's big three stations (NBC, ABC and CBS) which are able to transmit their programmes across the country via the transmitters of their affiliated independent stations. In the UK, a programme transmitted by all the ITV companies (as opposed to only one or two regions) is described as being 'networked'.

NEVER MIND THE QUALITY, FEEL THE WIDTH

UK (ABC/Thames) Situation Comedy. ITV 1967/1968–71

Emmanuel 'Manny' Cohen	John Bluthal
Patrick Kelly	Joe Lynch
Rabbi Levy	Cyril Shaps
Father Ryan	Eamon Kelly

Creators: Vince Powell, Harry Driver.
Producers: Ronnie Baxter, Stuart Allen

Genial ethnic comedy set in an East End tailor's shop.

Manny Cohen and Patrick Kelly were partners in a small tailoring enterprise in the East End of London. Their religious differences provided the chief source of conflict and comedy, as coat-maker Manny, the Jew, always considered Patrick, the trouser-maker, to be a bigoted Catholic.

Similar sentiments flowed in the opposite direction and often the local rabbi and priest needed to intervene. The series stemmed from a one-off *Armchair Theatre* production in 1967, in which Frank Finlay took the part of Patrick Kelly. Thames TV took over production of the series when ABC lost its ITV franchise.

NEVER THE TWAIN

UK (Thames) Situation Comedy. ITV 1981–91

Simon Peel ....Donald Sinden
Oliver Smallbridge ....Windsor Davies
David Peel ....Robin Kermode
Lyn Smallbridge ....Julia Watson
Veronica Barton ....Honor Blackman
Aunt Eleanor..Zara Nutley
Ringo ....Derek Deadman

Creator: Johnnie Mortimer. Writers: Johnnie Mortimer, Vince Powell. Producers: Peter Frazer-Jones, Anthony Parker

Two neighbouring antiques dealers are the best of enemies.

Simon Peel and Oliver Smallbridge were old adversaries. Despite the fact that Simon's son, David, and Oliver's daughter, Lyn, were in love, the squabbling antiques experts could never patch up their quarrel. Not even when David and Lyn were married. Nor when Martin, their mutual grandson, was born. Exacerbating their rivalry was the occasional appearance of Veronica Barton, the lady both men wanted in their lives. When David and Lyn emigrated to Canada, Simon's Aunt Eleanor arrived to keep the two old fools in check.

NEW ADVENTURES OF CHARLIE CHAN, THE

UK (ITC) Detective Drama. ITV 1957–8

Charlie Chan..J. Carrol Naish
Barry Chan ....James Hong
Inspector Duff..Rupert Davies
Inspector Marlowe ....Hugh Williams

Executive Producer: Leon Fromkess. Producers: Sidney Marshall, Rudolph Flothow

Tales of the oriental detective created by Earl Derr Biggers.

Charlie Chan originally found fame in the cinema (played by the likes of Warner Oland, Sydney Toler and Roland Winters), as a smart, proverb-quoting detective from Honolulu who had numerous children. In this series, he had moved to London, but was still supported by his ever-eager 'Number One Son', Barry. As before, the oriental investigator was polite, calm, diligent and very successful.

Earl Derr Biggers's character was allegedly based on Chang Apana, a real Hawaiian police detective. He reappeared in cartoon form in the 1970s, in a series called *The Amazing Chan and the Chan Clan*.

NEW ADVENTURES OF LUCKY JIM, THE

UK (BBC) Situation Comedy. BBC 2 1967; 1982

Jim Dixon ....Keith Barron (1967)
                                    Enn Reitel (1982)

Writers: Dick Clement, Ian La Frenais.
Producers: Duncan Wood (1967), Harold Snoad (1982)

A North Country lad finds it hard to settle in Swinging London.

Based on, and updated from, Kingsley Amis's 1954 novel, *Lucky Jim*, this series related happenings in the life of Jim Dixon, a cautious Yorkshire lad new in London in the permissive 1960s. Not liking what he saw, and finding it hard to fit in, Jim indulged himself in Walter Mitty-like fantasies and private rants about the state of society around him. In 1982 the series was revived under the title of *The Further Adventures of Lucky Jim*. This saw Enn Reitel as Dixon, returning to London after a year in Holland.

NEW ADVENTURES OF WONDERWOMAN, The see *Wonder Woman*.

NEW AVENGERS, THE

UK (Avengers Enterprises/IDTV) Adventure. ITV 1976–7

John Steed ....Patrick McNee
Purdey ....Joanna Lumley
Mike Gambit ....Gareth Hunt

Producers: Albert Fennell, Brian Clemens

The further adventures of John Steed and his daring assistants.

In *The New Avengers*, John Steed was called up once more to thwart extravagant plots by the world's most eccentric saboteurs and assassins. Working undercover for the British Secret Service, as in *The Avengers*, Steed, however, now spent more time on his private stud farm, where he indulged his hobbies of breeding horses and entertaining beautiful women. Ageing a little, but as suave and sophisticated as ever, he was typically supported by a glamorous female, but also, this time, by a tough young male, someone to do the running around.

The newcomers were Purdey and Gambit. Purdey, a former ballerina with a much-copied page boy haircut, was classy, elegant and as hard as nails. Like her predecessors Gale, Peel and

King, she knew how to fight. Her strength was in her kick, and many an assailant felt the power of her long, shapely legs. She was also a good shot and extremely fit. Mike Gambit provided the muscle which Steed now lacked. A former mercenary, he was a weapons specialist and a practitioner of kung fu. Both young colleagues showed Steed the respect he deserved and relied on his wealth of experience and knowledge.

Produced in association with a French TV company and also with some Canadian input, three episodes were filmed in France and four in Canada, with the majority made in the UK.

NEW FACES

UK (ATV/Central) Talent Show. ITV 1973–8/1986–8

Hosts: Derek Hobson, Nicky Martin, Marti Caine

Producers: Les Cocks, Albert Stevenson, Richard Holloway (1986)

Talent show in which hopefuls were openly criticized by a professional panel.

Branded as cruelly frank and downright insensitive, *New Faces* was **Opportunity Knocks!** with bite. It aimed to feature artists who had never appeared on television before and those who dared to participate found their acts subjected to the views of four 'experts'. These included established showbusiness names, record producers, DJs, agents and critics. Amongst regular pundits were Mickie Most, Clifford Davis, Alan A. Freeman, Martin Jackson, Ted Ray, Tony Hatch, Hilary Kingsley, George Elrick, Ed Stewart and bookings agent John Smith. Awarding marks out of ten in four categories, including Star Quality, the panel's forthright comments were known to reduce artists to tears at times. Some were awarded no points at all. Arthur Askey, on the other hand, thought every act was fantastic. Some were, indeed, good enough to make the grade: Lenny Henry, Les Dennis, Jim Davidson, Victoria Wood, Joe Longthorne, Showaddywaddy and Gary Wilmot were the most prominent. *Emmerdale* star Malandra Burrows (using the name of Malandra Newman) appeared as a singer at the age of nine and became the series' youngest winner. Like other heat winners, she progressed to the grand final, where the series winner was decided.

One *New Faces* champion, Marti Caine, went on to host a revival of the series, entitled *New Faces of 86* (then *87* and *88*). Amongst the new celebrity critics was newspaper columnist Nina Myskow. The Johnny Patrick Orchestra provided musical support in the early days, with Harry Rabinowitz's Orchestra taking over in the 1980s.

The show's original 'You're a star' theme song was performed by former Move vocalist Carl Wayne.

NEW SCOTLAND YARD

UK (LWT) Police Drama. ITV 1972–4

Detective Chief Supt John Kingdom	..John Woodvine
Detective Sgt Alan Ward	John Carlisle
Detective Chief Supt Clay	Michael Turner
Detective Sgt Dexter	Clive Francis

Executive Producer: Rex Firkin. Producer: Jack Williams

Two CID officers investigate serious crimes in London.

Kingdom and Ward were two quietly efficient detectives, working from New Scotland Yard. Kingdom was the more thoughtful, Ward the tougher, less approachable partner. Together – and not without friction – they enquired into cases of murder, blackmail, extortion and the new violent crimes of the 1970s. After two years, they were replaced for one more series by the experienced Chief Supt Clay and his junior colleague Detective Sgt Dexter but, throughout, the series avoided the plain 'cops-and-robbers' stereotype of many police series, and depicted police work, more truthfully, as hard and personally distressing. Star Clive Francis was the son of Raymond Francis, *No Hiding Place*'s famous Inspector Lockhart.

NEW STATESMAN, THE

UK (Yorkshire) Situation Comedy. ITV 1987–92

Alan Beresford B'Stard	Rik Mayall
Sarah B'Stard	Marsha Fitzalan
Piers Fletcher-Dervish	Michael Troughton
Crippen	Nick Stringer
Norman Bormann	R.R. Cooper
Beatrice Protheroe	Vivien Heilbron
Kerry Grout	Peter Blake
Sir Stephen Baxter	John Nettleton
Sir Greville	Terence Alexander
Roland Gidleigh-Park	Charles Gray
Mrs Thatcher	Steve Nallon
Neil Kinnock	Johnny More
Sidney Bliss	Peter Sallis

Creators/Writers: Laurence Marks, Maurice Gran. Producers: David Reynolds, Tony Charles, Andrew Benson, Bernard McKenna

The unscrupulous manoeuvrings of an ambitious MP.

Alan B'Stard was the Conservative Member of Parliament for the North Yorkshire constituency of Haltemprice. Styling himself as a country squire, he was not so much a confirmed Thatcherite as a rampant right-winger, a man who had maimed his chief electoral opponent in a car crash to win a 27,000-vote majority and become the youngest MP in the House. Riding roughshod over all who stood in his way (physically as well as metaphorically), sleaze meant nothing to the mean and vicious B'Stard who lined his own pockets, cynically hid behind his parliamentary scapegoat, Piers Fletcher-Dervish, and wriggled his way up the ladder. B'Stard's lesbian wife, Sarah, daughter of the odious Roland Gidleigh-Park, was heiress to a fortune and only stayed with her husband for appearances' sake. Also seen was B'Stard's sex-changing business consultant Norman Bormann (actress Rowena Cooper was billed as R.R. Cooper so as not to give the game away too early). Eventually leaving Parliament, B'Stard found himself imprisoned in a Russian gulag before returning to the political fray as a Euro MP.

Although the series – which used Mussorgsky's 'Pictures At An Exhibition' as its theme music – ended in 1992, a one-off special in which B'Stard was interviewed by Brian Walden was screened on BBC 1 at Christmas 1994.

NEWCOMERS, THE

UK (BBC) Drama. BBC 1 1965–9

Ellis Cooper	Alan Browning
Vivienne Cooper	Maggie Fitzgibbon
Gran Hamilton	Gladys Henson
Philip Cooper	Jeremy Bulloch
Maria Cooper	Judy Geeson
Lance Cooper	Raymond Hunt
Janet Langley	Sandra Payne
Jeff Langley	Michael Collins
Arnold Tripp	Gerald Cross
Bert Harker	Robert Brown
Vera Harker	June Bland
Joyce Harker	Wendy Richard
Jimmy Harker	David Janson
Arthur Huntley	Tony Steedman
Mrs Heenan	Vanda Godsell
Celia Stuart	Beryl Cooke
Charles Turner	Neil Hallett
Andrew Kerr	Robin Bailey
Caroline Kerr	Heather Chasen
Kirsty Kerr	Maggie Don
Margot Kerr	Sally Jane Spencer
Hugh Robertson	Jack Watling
Olivia Robertson	Mary Kenton
Julie Robertson	Deborah Watling
Michael Robertson	Robert Bartlett
Adrian Robertson	Paul Bartlett
Robert Malcolm	Conrad Phillips

Creator: Colin Morris. Producers: Verity Lambert, Morris Barry, Ronald Travers, Bill Sellars

A London family are uneasy about their new life in the country.

The Newcomers, a twice-weekly soap, centred around the Coopers, a London family who moved out of the Smoke, into the sticks and set up home in the fictitious Suffolk village of Angleton (real-life Haverhill). The series' petty dramas revolved around life at work with dad Ellis (a supervisor at Eden Brothers' computer parts factory) and at home, on a new housing estate. Mum Vivienne struggled to cope with their three teenage children (17-year-old Philip, 16-year-old Maria and long-haired, 13-year-old Lance), as well as her glum, live-in mum, as the difficulties of settling into a new neighbourhood became all too evident. Amongst their neighbours was brash, 20-year-old Cockney Joyce Harker, played by a pre-*EastEnders* Wendy Richard. Ellis was written out in 1968, dying of a heart attack, and Vivienne emigrated to New Zealand with new lover Charles Turner. Another family, the Robertsons, subsequently took over the role of 'the newcomers'.

NEWHART, BOB (1929–)

Hit American comedian, master of the monologue and, in particular, the one-sided telephone conversation. His various series ran, off and on, for nearly 30 years in the USA.

NEWMAN, NANETTE (1939–)

British actress and presenter who is probably better known for her detergent commercials these days than her acting credits. Amongst her TV contributions have been the dramas *Stay With Me Till Morning* (as Robin Lendrick) and *Jessie* (title role), and the comedies *Let There Be Love* (as widow Judy Morrison) and *Late Expectations* (as middle-aged mother-to-be Liz Jackson). Newman also appeared in *Prometheus* and *The Endless Game*, and has guested on numerous series, including **The Saint**. She is married to film director Bryan Forbes and is the mother of TV presenter Emma Forbes.

NEWMAN, SYDNEY (1917–)

Canadian drama specialist who joined ABC in 1958 to produce the influential Armchair Theatre series of plays. While there, as Head of Drama, Newman was also co-creator of **The Avengers** (and its forerunner, **Police Surgeon**), as well as the *Target Luna/Pathfinders* sci-fi adventures for kids. Five years later, he was enticed over to the BBC where he became its Head of Drama and gained a reputation as a tough overseer. Amongst the BBC's most notable achievements under his auspices were **Doctor Who** (as creator), **The Wednesday Play** (including classics like *Up the Junction* and **Cathy Come Home**) and **The Forsyte**

Saga. His own productions over the years included Alun Owen's *Lena, O My Lena* (1960), John Wyndham's *Dumb Martian* (1962) and Harold Pinter's *Tea Party* (1965). He subsequently returned to Canada to become Chairman of its National Film Board.

NEWS

Television presentation of the news was initially a voice-only affair. Announcers simply regurgitated radio bulletins. While **BBC Television Newsreel**, which began in 1948, was an advance into moving pictures (if not up to the minute stories), it took until 1954 for the first television news bulletin as we now know it to reach the air. Richard Baker was the first presenter of *BBC Television News*, on 5 July, although, for a further 14 months, no newsreader was seen in vision while delivering the news. It was feared that their facial expressions would detract from their impartiality. Kenneth Kendall became the first newsreader in shot, in September 1955, but, in those days before autocues, he and his colleagues (Baker and Robert Dougall) were forced to read, head down, from a script. The same month, not coincidentally, ITV took to the air, bringing with it the more dynamic forces of ITN (Independent Television News). It was ITN who pioneered the American two-presenter format in the UK when it launched the half-hour *News At Ten* in 1967.

Over the years, technical developments have changed the face of television news presentation. Satellites have provided instant international coverage, computer graphics have added colour and variety to dull items and brightened up studio sets, and Electronic News Gathering (ENG) has enabled reporters and cameramen to send on the spot reports directly back to the studio, with small, lightweight camera equipment allowing access to hitherto impossible situations.

It is believed by many that Angela Rippon was the first national female newsreader, but in fact there were others before her. Barbara Mandell appeared on ITN's lunchtime news as early as 1955 and Nan Winton was seen on the BBC for six months from 1960. Other prominent newsreaders (or newscasters as ITN has traditionally called them) have been Michael Aspel, Corbett Woodall, Bob Langley, John Edmunds, Richard Whitmore, Peter Woods, John Humphrys, John Simpson, Andrew Harvey, Sue Lawley, Jan Leeming, Michael Buerk, Philip Hayton, Nicholas Witchell, Jeremy Paxman, Chris Lowe, Moira Stuart, Jennie Bond, Debbie Thrower, Laurie Mayer, Jill Dando, John Tusa and Edward Stourton (all for the BBC); Christopher Chataway, Robin Day, Ludovic Kennedy, Andrew Gardner, Reginald Bosanquet, Sandy Gall, Gordon Honeycombe, Alastair Burnet, Leonard Parkin, Ivor Mills, Peter Snow, Robert Kee, Trevor McDonald, Rory MacPherson, Michael Nicholson, Alastair Stewart, Selina Scott, Pamela Armstrong, Fiona Armstrong, John Suchet, Carol Barnes, Jon Snow, Sue Carpenter, Dermot Murnaghan, Anne Leuchars and Nicholas Owen (for ITN). Martyn Lewis, Peter Sissons, Anna Ford and Julia Somerville are four newsreaders who have worked for both channels.

NEWS AT TEN see news.

NEWSNIGHT

UK (BBC) Current Affairs. BBC 2 1980–

Presenters:
Peter Snow
Peter Hobday
Charles Wheeler
John Tusa
Donald MacCormick
Gavin Esler
Jeremy Paxman
Sue Cameron
John Simpson
James Cox
Francine Stock
Kirsty Wark

Late night current affairs round up.

Much acclaimed, *Newsnight* (initially four nights a week, later five) has performed the task of reviewing in detail the major news stories of the day, with special emphasis on political and foreign affairs. The original team of presenters was comprised of Peter Snow (still with the programme), Peter Hobday, Charles Wheeler and John Tusa, with news bulletins read by Fran Morrison and sports reports from David Davies. The format was later changed to incorporate just one host/interviewer. Gavin Esler, Jeremy Paxman and Peter Snow have held this position in recent years, relieved occasionally by Sue Cameron, John Simpson, James Cox, Francine Stock and Kirsty Wark.

NEWSROUND see *John Craven's Newsround*.

NICE TIME

UK (Granada) Comedy. ITV 1968–9

Presenters:
Germaine Greer
Jonathan Routh
Kenny Everett

Producers: Mike Murphy, John Birt

Anarchic and bizarre sketch show.

Originally a programme just for the Granada region, *Nice Time* proved so popular that it was extended to the ITV network. It comprised a collection of wacky sketches and inventive stunts, built around viewers' requests for favourite moments from comedy films. However, it is best remembered today for giving young DJ Kenny Everett his TV break, for promoting the then Warwick University lecturer Germaine Greer, and for being produced by future BBC Director-General John Birt.

NICHOLAS, PAUL (1945–)

British singer and actor who used his charm to good effect as Vince Pinner in *Just Good Friends* in 1983. Before that, his biggest role was in a short-lived 1979 BBC sitcom entitled *Two Up, Two Down*, in which he starred with Su Pollard. Nicholas had also guested in numerous series (like *Z Cars* and *Lady Killers*), appeared in assorted films and stage musicals, and notched up a few pop chart hits. He was later seen as the financially embarassed Neil Walsh in *Bust* (1987) and as vet James Shepherd in the comedy *Close to Home* (1989), as well as singing and dancing in variety shows.

NICHOLS, DANDY (DAISY NICHOLS; 1907–86)

British character actress, famous for one role, that of Else, Alf Garnett's much abused wife in *Till Death Us Do Part* and *In Sickness and In Health*. Her one other major part was as Madge in the 1971 sitcom *The Trouble With You, Lillian* (opposite Patricia Hayes), although she also appeared in series like *Emergency – Ward 10*, *Dixon of Dock Green*, *No Hiding Place*, *Mrs Thursday* and *Bergerac*.

NICHOLS, PETER (1927–)

British stage and television dramatist whose earliest TV work dates from the late 1950s. Amongst his most notable offerings (generally in a light, socially observational vein) have been *Promenade* (1959), *The Continuity Man* (1963), *The Hooded Terror* (1963), *The Gorge* (1968), *Hearts and Flowers* (1968), *The Common* (1973), *Forget-Me-Not Lane* (1975) and the *Ben Spray* mini-series of dramas (spread over two decades from 1961). He has also contributed to *Inspector Morse*.

NICHOLLS, SUE (SUSAN HARMAR-NICHOLLS; 1943–)

Known today as Audrey Roberts, Alf's spendthrift wife, in *Coronation Street* (a role she has played since 1979), Sue Nicholls' TV appearances have been many and varied. Some viewers may recall her in *Crossroads*, as waitress Marilyn

Gates, a part which gave her a hit single, 'Where Will You Be?', in 1968. Others may recall her performances as Joan Greengross, Reggie Perrin's devoted secretary, or as Wanda Pickles, Jim Davidson's neighbour in *Up the Elephant and Round the Castle*. Her other credits have included *Not On Your Nellie* (as barmaid Big Brenda), *Rentaghost* (as Nadia Popov), *The Duchess of Duke Street*, *Village Hall*, *Heartland*, *The Professionals*, *Doctor on the Go* and Wodehouse Playhouse. Sue is the daughter of one-time Conservative MP Lord Harmar-Nicholls and lives with former *Coronation Street* bad guy Mark Eden.

NICHOLSON, MICHAEL, OBE (1937–)

Award-winning ITN journalist, with the company since 1963, having previously worked as a political writer with D.C. Thompson. Nicholson has the distinction of covering more wars than any other British TV reporter. These have included the conflicts in Vietnam, Biafra (Eastern Nigeria), the Falklands and in the Gulf. He was ITN's Southern Africa correspondent 1976–81 and presenter of *News At 5.45* for three years from 1982. He is currently the chief foreign affairs correspondent.

NICKELODEON

Children's channel originating on cable TV in the USA in 1979 when it was founded by the Warner Amex company. It was later taken over by Viacom. From the start, the focus of its programming has been on variety for younger viewers, combining cartoons with live programming, youth drama and game shows. Since 1993 it has broadcast to Europe 12 hours a day (7 am–7 pm) from the Astra 1C satellite, as part of the Sky Multi-Channels subscriber package. Nickelodeon is also available via cable companies. In the USA, its daytime service is complemented by Nick At Night, a grown-ups channel which features vintage TV shows.

NIELSENS

The all-important US league table of TV audiences, collated by the AC Nielsen company (using a technical device known as the 'Audimeter' which is attached to television receivers). The term has become synonymous with 'ratings' in America. AC Nielsen was also active in the UK for a while in the 1950s.

NIMMO, DEREK (1933–)

Liverpudlian actor usually seen in rather dithery roles. He has had great success with his clerics Reverend Mervyn Noote in *All Gas and*

Gaiters, Brother/Father Dominic in *Oh Brother* and *Oh Father*, and Dean Selwyn Makepeace in *Hell's Bells*. He also played David in *The Bed-Sit Girl*, Frederick in the comedy *Blandings Castle*, Bingo Little in *The World of Wooster*, David in another sitcom *Sorry I'm Single*, Henry Prendergast in the political comedy *My Honorable Mrs*, Chris Bunting in *Life Begins at Forty* and George Hutchenson in *Third Time Lucky*. More recently, Nimmo also made a well-publicized cameo appearance in *Neighbours*.

NIMOY, LEONARD (1931–)

American actor who will always be *Star Trek's* pointy-eared Vulcan, Mr Spock, even though he has enjoyed plenty of other TV work. Nimoy's TV debut came in the 1950s, with parts in series like *Dragnet* and *Laramie*. More guest appearances came in the 1960s, including in *The Man from UNCLE* and *Get Smart*, before he was cast as Spock, which he followed with the role of Paris, master of disguise, in *Mission: Impossible*. Nimoy has since been seen in TV movies and mini-series (such as *Marco Polo*, as Achmet) and has also worked as a programme narrator.

1984

UK (BBC) Science Fiction. BBC 1954

Winston Smith ....Peter Cushing
O'Brien ....André Morell
Julia ....Yvonne Mitchell
Syme ....Donald Pleasence
Emmanuel Goldstein ....Arnold Diamond
Parsons ....Campbell Gray

Writer: Nigel Kneale. Producer: Rudolph Cartier

Highly controversial adaptation of George Orwell's portentous novel.

Variously criticized and praised by the politicians of the day, this one-off drama shocked the nation. As its title suggested, it focused on life in 1984 (30 years ahead), at a time when a totalitarian regime known as Big Brother was watching over all of Britain. Society was divided into clearly defined groups. First there was the Inner Party, then came the Outer Party. Beyond these 'privileged' citizens were the ordinary masses, the Proles. Language had been eroded away, limiting individual expression by the abolition of words, and videoscreens watched people as they went about their everyday chores, checking for signs of dissent.

At the heart of the action was Winston Smith, a member of the Outer Party who worked as a re-writer of history in the Ministry of Truth. It was his growing rebellion, encouraged by a girlfriend,

Julia, and then viciously curbed by the devious O'Brien in the dreaded Room 101, which exemplified the control of the authorities and the nightmare of life under such a regime. The torture sequence involving live rats is well-remembered.

Transmitted live on a Sunday night, *1984* was repeated – again live – four days later, drawing the biggest audience since the Coronation (largely as a result of the clamour which followed the first showing). The play was written by Nigel Kneale and produced by Rudolph Cartier, two adventurous BBC men who, a year or so earlier, had created the ground-breaking *The Quatermass Experiment*. Kneale revived *1984* in 1965, with David Buck, Jane Merrow and Joseph O'Connor in the lead roles of Smith, Julia and O'Brien, but, unlike its predecessor, it passed virtually unnoticed.

1990

UK (BBC) Drama. BBC 2 1977–8

Jim Kyle ....Edward Woodward
Faceless ....Paul Hardwick
Herbert Skardon ....Robert Lang
Dave Brett ....Tony Doyle
Delly Lomas ....Barbara Kellerman
Dan Mellor ....John Savident
Henry Tasker ....Clifton Jones
Greaves ....George Murcell
Jack Nichols....................................Michael Napier Brown
Kate Smith.......................................Yvonne Mitchell
Lynn Blake ....Lisa Harrow
PCD Inspector Macrae ....David McKail
Tony Doran ....Clive Swift

Creator: Wilfred Greatorex. Producer: Prudence Fitzgerald

An Orwellian vision of the future, in all its depressing glory.

This drama centred on the hypothesis that at the end of the 20th century Britain would be ruthlessly controlled by a government that suppressed all resistance in the name of the common good. Looking just 13 years into the future, *1990* foresaw a Britain where rationing and identity cards were back on the agenda and where *emigration*, not *immigration*, was the problem, as scientists and other dissidents sought to flee the totalitarian state. Overseeing the oppression was a Home Office division known as the Public Control Department (PCD), with the cruel Herbert Skardon at its head, supported by a deputy, Delly Lomas (later replaced by Lynn Blake). Opposing them was resistance leader Jim Kyle, a Home Affairs reporter for one of the three remaining newspapers. With his colleagues, Kyle aimed to smuggle dissidents out of the country and subvert the powers of the PCD by operating an underground press and hindering their every movement.

NIXON, DAVID (1919–78)

Popular British conjuror and game show panellist of the 1950s and 1960s. A former stage partner of Norman Wisdom, Nixon became one of UK TV's earliest celebrities, appearing on the children's show *Sugar and Spice* and using his charm to good effect as a regular panellist on shows like *What's My Line?* and *My Wildest Dream*. In the late 1950s he starred in *It's Magic* and went on to host *Showtime* and *Comedy Bandbox*. In the late 1960s and 1970s, he was given his own shows *Nixon at Nine-Five*, *Now for Nixon*, *The Nixon Line*, *David Nixon*, *Tonight with David Nixon*, *The David Nixon Show* and *David Nixon's Magic Box*, some of which helped introduce an aristocratic foxy puppet by the name of Basil Brush to an enthusiastic audience.

NO HIDING PLACE

UK (Associated-Rediffusion) Police Drama. ITV 1959–67

Detective Chief Supt Tom Lockhart ..Raymond Francis
Detective Sgt Harry Baxter ....Eric Lander
Detective Sgt Russell ....Johnny Briggs
Detective Sgt Perryman.....................Michael McStay
Detective Sgt Gregg ....Sean Caffrey

Producers: Ray Dicks, Richard Matthews, Jonathan Goodman, Peter Willes, Geoffrey Hughes, Ian Fordyce, Michael Currer-Briggs

More adventures with top detective Lockhart.

Detective Chief Supt Lockhart of Scotland Yard, after earlier exploits in the programmes *Murder Bag* and *Crime Sheet*, returned to the screen in this long-running series in which he was assisted by keen, young Detective Sgt Baxter. Baxter's popularity was so great that he was later given his own spin-off series, *Echo Four Two*, before returning to Lockhart's side when that programme failed to take off. When Baxter moved on yet again, replacement sergeants Russell and Perryman were introduced, with Detective Sgt Gregg eventually added as the final partner for this genial, snuff-taking sleuth.

The series was popular with both the public and the police, particularly for its authenticity. Over 230 episodes were produced, many of them transmitted live. When it was taken off in 1965, such was the furore that the producers were forced to extend Lockhart's career by a couple more years. One 1962 episode saw a guest appearance by Patrick Cargill in the guise of *Top Secret*'s Miguel Garetta. Supporting actor Johnny Briggs, of course, has since found fame as *Coronation Street*'s Mike Baldwin, but for the part of Russell, the rather short actor had to wear

built-up shoes. The *No Hiding Place* theme music, performed by Ken Mackintosh and his orchestra, entered the pop charts in 1960.

NO, HONESTLY

UK (LWT) Situation Comedy. ITV 1974–5

Charles 'CD' Danby ....John Alderton
Clara Danby ....Pauline Collins

Writers: Terence Brady, Charlotte Bingham.
Producer: Humphrey Barclay

A couple look affectionately back to the early days of their courtship and marriage.

Clara and CD Danby were a well-matched, romantic couple. She was a children's novelist, the daughter of peer Lord Burrell and author of the 'Ollie the Otter' books. He was a comic actor and together they had become a success. But life hadn't always been so generous. Their early relationship (ten years earlier) had been pitted with minor disasters and these were introduced in flashback form in each episode, after the couple's introductory chat to the camera. Their whimsical approach to life and their fondness for social pranks formed a backdrop to most of the plots, as did Clara's scatty, convoluted logic which bemused and amused her patient, caring husband. The duo then wrapped up each episode with another piece to camera.

This was very much a 'married couples' series, as both the writers, Terence Brady and Charlotte Bingham, and the stars, John Alderton and Pauline Collins, were real-life husbands and wives. With its pieces to camera and Clara's weird logic, it owed more than a little to *The Burns and Allen Show*. When Alderton and Collins called it a day, Donal Donnelly and Liza Goddard were brought in as Matt Browne and Lily Pond, a songwriter and his secretary and the title became 'Yes, Honestly' (it was screened 1976–7). The *No, Honestly* theme song, by Lynsey De Paul, reached the Top Ten in 1974, but 'Yes, Honestly' by Georgie Fame was not a hit.

NO JOB FOR A LADY

UK (Thames) Situation Comedy. ITV 1990–2

Jean Price ....Penelope Keith
Sir Godfrey Eagan................................George Baker
Ken Miller ....Paul Young
Norman..Garfield Morgan
Geoff Price...Mark Kingston
Harry ....Nigel Humphreys
Richard ....Michael Cochrane

Creator/Writer: Alex Shearer. Producer: John Howard Davies

A new, ambitious female MP discovers the House of Commons is a bit of a jungle.

When newly elected Labour MP Jean Price took her seat at Westminster, she quickly learned that its operations were far from straight forward. In dealings with her Tory opposite number, Sir Godfrey Eagan, and her Labour whip, Norman, she soon learned to pick her friends carefully. Principles and practicality, she found, were not always compatible. Advising her was her office share, Scottish MP Ken Miller, while hubby Geoff provided support at home.

NO PLACE LIKE HOME

UK (BBC) Situation Comedy. BBC 1 1983-7

Arthur Crabtree	William Gaunt
Beryl Crabtree	Patricia Garwood
Nigel Crabtree	Martin Clunes
	Andrew Charleson
Paul Crabtree	Stephen Watson
Tracy Crabtree	Dee Sadler
Lorraine Codd	Beverley Adams
Raymond Codd	Daniel Hill
Vera Botting	Marcia Warren
	Ann Penfold
Trevor Botting	Michael Sharvell-Martin
Roger Duff	Roger Martin

Creator/Writer: Jon Watkins. Producer: Robin Nash

A middle-aged couple plan for a quiet life once their children have left home. Sadly, it is not to be.

Arthur and Beryl Crabtree had raised four children and looked forward to the day when their time, once again, would be their own. A second honeymoon was planned as the last of their off-spring finally left home. However, their hopes were soon dashed as one by one the fledglings returned to the nest, disillusioned with life in the outside world. For the children, there simply was no place like home. Eldest of the kids was Lorraine, who had married Raymond Codd, but quickly cast him aside. There were also Nigel, Paul and Tracy (and their assorted boy- and girl-friends), while the Crabtree's domestic bliss was also disturbed by their nosey neighbours, the Bottings, particularly the shrieking, animal-loving Vera. Arthur and Vera's husband, Trevor, often escaped to the greenhouse when things became unbearable, seeking solace in a glass of home-made sherry.

Actress Beverley Adams, who played Lorraine, is the daughter of former *Crackerjack* hostess Jillian Comber.

NO – THAT'S ME OVER HERE

UK (Rediffusion/LWT) Situation Comedy. ITV 1967-8; 1970

Ronnie	Ronnie Corbett
Rosemary	Rosemary Leach
Henry	Henry McGee
Secretary	Jill Mai Meredith

Writers: Graham Chapman, Eric Idle, Barry Cryer. Executive Producer: David Frost. Producers: Bill Hitchcock, Marty Feldman

A middle-class commuter seeks social status.

Life was never straightforward for Ronnie. The little man smartly attired in three-piece suit, bowler hat, brolly and briefcase, aimed high, but somehow always fell well short. This was particularly the case when he strived to outdo his patronizing next door neighbour, Henry, who commuted alongside him to their City offices. Rosemary was Ronnie's long-suffering wife.

Although dropped after one season when Rediffusion lost its ITV franchise, the series was picked up two years later by LWT. Corbett went on to play numerous other 'little man' roles, often accompanied, as here, by Rosemary Leach (see *Now Look Here . . . !*).

NOAKES, JOHN (1934-)

Yorkshire-born actor whose greatest role was as the resident daredevil on *Blue Peter*. Noakes joined the series in 1966, after acting roles in a number of TV series and working on stage as a 'feed' to Cyril Fletcher. He stayed with *Blue Peter* for 12 years, forming part of the series' golden age trio with Valerie Singleton and Peter Purves. Accompanied by his playful collie, Shep ('Get down Shep' became a catchphrase), he even secured his own spin-off series, *Go with Noakes*, in which he continued his hair-raising stunts such as climbing chimneys, leaping out of aircraft and tearing around in racing cars. Later, he worked for YTV and then for TV-am, on their Saturday morning show, but more or less retired to Majorca thereafter. In 1994 he was reunited with Valerie Singleton to present the over-50s afternoon magazine *Next*.

NOBBS, DAVID (1935-)

British novelist and screenwriter, responsible for series like *The Fall and Rise of Reginald Perrin*, *Fairly Secret Army*, *A Bit of a Do* and *The Life and Times of Henry Pratt*. Amongst his other TV work have been scripts for *That Was The Week That Was* and *The Two Ronnies*, and the series *Lance at Large* (for Lance Percival, with Peter Tinniswood), *Shine a Light* (with David McKellar and Peter Vincent), *Keep it in The Family* (with Peter Vincent), *Whoops Baghdad!* (with Sid Colin and David McKellar), *Dogfood Dan and the Carmarthen Cowboy*, *The Glamour Girls*, *The Hello Goodbye Man* and *Rich Tea and Sympathy*.

NODDY

A familiar, contrived shot in news interviews where the interviewer is seen to nod in acknowledgement to the interviewee's answers. These shots are usually recorded at the end of the interview and then dropped in between questions during editing, to smooth over ugly breaks.

NOEL'S HOUSE PARTY

UK (BBC) Entertainment. BBC 1 1991–

Presenter: Noel Edmonds

Executive Producer: Michael Leggo. Producer: Michael Leggo, Jonathan Beazley

Live Saturday evening mélange of gags and silly games.

Following the demise of *The Late, Late Breakfast Show* in 1986, Noel Edmonds returned to Saturday tea-time telly in 1988 with *Noel Edmonds' Saturday Road Show*, in which he pretended to present each programme from a different and exotic location. The emphasis was on silly games, lots of laughs and a few hidden camera tricks. Some elements he then took on to *Noel's House Party*, based at a mock stately home in the fictitious village of Crinkley Bottom. The show has since gone from strength to strength, benefiting from Edmonds's coolness with live television. Amongst the favourite features have been the Gotcha Oscars (in which a celebrity has been conned into making a spoof TV programme), Grab A Grand (celebrities clutching at banknotes in a wind machine to earn money for a lucky viewer), NTV (hidden cameras in people's homes), The Pork Pie (a member of the audience trying to deny a shameful incident in his/her life) and Wait Till I Get You Home (precocious kids telling secrets about their parents). There have also been little quizzes like The Lyric Game, surprise guests and psychedelic drenchings courtesy of the gunge tank. Veteran DJ Tony Blackburn was seen as the butler on many occasions. One newcomer introduced by the show – Mr Blobby, a bloated, pink dummy with yellow-spots – went on to take the country by storm.

NOGGIN THE NOG see *Saga of Noggin the Nog, The.*

NORDEN, DENIS, CBE (1922–)

British comedy writer, the former partner of Frank Muir and with him responsible for such series as *Take It from Here* on radio. For TV, they penned the Jimmy Edwards series *Whack-O!* and *The Seven Faces of Jim*, Richard Briers's *Brothers in Law*, the Bob Monkhouse sitcom *The Big Noise* and their own series *How To Be an Alien*.

He was also seen on the satire show *BBC 3*. In the 1970s Norden was host of the nostalgia game *Looks Familiar* and, since 1977, has presented television out-takes under the title *It'll Be Alright on the Night*, plus assorted other specials involving TV clips. Like his former collaborator Muir, he has also been a familiar face on panel games.

NORMAN, BARRY (1933–)

The son of British film director Leslie Norman, Barry Norman was born into the world of cinema. Since leaving a position with the *Daily Mail*, he has brought his love of the silver screen into TV via programmes such as *The Hollywood Greats* and the long-running *Film* series. He was, for a while in 1982, presenter of *Omnibus* and even hosted the Olympic Games for Channel 4 in 1988. His other series have included *The British Greats*, *The Rank Charm School* and *Barry Norman's Hong Kong*, *Barry Norman On Broadway/In Chicago/In Celebrity City*, plus work on *Late Night Line-Up*. Trivia buffs will know that he once appeared with Morecambe and Wise and that he also directed an episode of *The Saint*.

NORTHERN EXPOSURE

US (Finnegan-Pinchuk/Falahey/Austin Street/Cine-Nevada/Universal) Drama. Channel 4 1992–4

Dr Joel Fleischman	Rob Morrow
Maggie O'Connell	Janine Turner
Maurice Minnifield	Barry Corbin
Chris Stevens	John Corbett
Ed Chigliak	Darren E. Burrows
Holling Vincoeur	John Cullum
Shelly Tambo	Cynthia Geary
Marilyn Whirlwind	Elaine Miles
Ruth-Anne Miller	Peg Phillips

Creators: Joshua Brand, John Falsey. Executive Producers: John Falsey, Andrew Schneider

Events in the off-beat life of an isolated Alaskan town.

Set in the fictional settlement of Cicely, Alaska, miles from civilization, *Northern Exposure* focused on the inter-relationships of its mildly eccentric townsfolk. At the forefront was Jewish New Yorker Joel Fleischman, a newly qualified doctor whose arrival heralded the start of the series. Much against his will, but obliged because the Alaskan state had subsidized his college fees, Fleischman moved to the town to take over the vacant local practice. His escape attempts were always thwarted, but Fleischman's real reason for staying on (though never admitting it) was his love-hate relationship with his landlady, Maggie O'Connell, the air taxi pilot. However, messing with O'Connell was fraught with danger, as her five previous boyfriends had all died in tragic circumstances. Others in the cast were Ed Chigliak, a young Red Indian film buff, and Maurice Minnifield, former NASA astronaut and the town's patriarch. One-time adventurer Holling Vincoeur was proprietor of the local bar/restaurant (The Brick), which he ran with his teenage girlfriend Shelly (whom he had stolen from Maurice), Chris 'In The Morning' Stevens was the town's philosophizing radio DJ and part-time minister, sensible Ruth-Anne ran the all-purpose shop and Marilyn was Fleischman's unflappable, monosyllabic Eskimo assistant. Occasional visitors to town were Adam, a sort of missing link backwoodsman with a talent for cordon blue cookery, his hypochondriac wife, Eve, Bernard, Chris's black half-brother, and Mort, a moose that wandered down the main street during the titles and credits. With its stunning scenery and quirky feel, *Northern Exposure* was often likened to the spooky *Twin Peaks*, but with a much more wholesome atmosphere.

NOT IN FRONT OF THE CHILDREN

UK (BBC) Situation Comedy. BBC 1 1967–70

Jennifer Corner..Wendy Craig
Henry Corner ....Paul Daneman
                                                        Ronald Hines
Trudi Corner ....Roberta Tovey
                                                        Verina Greenlaw
Robin Corner ....Hugo Keith-Johnston
Amanda Corner ....Jill Riddick
Mary ....Charlotte Mitchell

Creator/Writer: Richard Waring. Producer: Graeme Muir

A mother tries to cope with her troublesome family.

Beginning as a 1967 **Comedy Playhouse** presentation called *House in a Tree*, *Not in Front of the Children* was Wendy Craig's first excursion into the daffy, harassed housewife role she was to perfect in later series like **And Mother Makes Three/Five** and **Butterflies**. Here she held together a middle-class household comprising her husband, Henry, and growing children Trudi, Robin and Amanda, trying all the while to moderate between disagreeing parties. The series also ran on BBC radio.

NOT ONLY... BUT ALSO...

UK (BBC) Comedy. BBC 2 1965–6; 1970

Peter Cook
Dudley Moore

Creators: Peter Cook, Dudley Moore.
Producers: Joe McGrath, Dick Clement, James Gilbert

Innovative comedy revue, renowned for its offbeat humour.

Not Only . . . But Also . . . resulted from a one-off show that the BBC commissioned from musician/comedian Dudley Moore. Enlisting the help of his *Beyond the Fringe* partner Peter Cook for a couple of sketches, Moore came up with a formula that worked and the duo were rewarded with this series which initially ran on BBC 2 but was quickly repeated on BBC 1 to much acclaim. Mixing manic comedy with jazzy interludes, each programme began in the most unusual of settings, including, on one occasion, on Tower Bridge and, on another, above a hillside white horse. One regular insert was Poets Cornered, an opportunity for comics like Spike Milligan and Barry Humphries to show off their spontaneous rhyming skills on pain of being dropped into a gunge tank (a whole decade before **Tiswas** popularized this form of punishment). For many viewers, however, the highlights were Cook and Moore's Pete and Dud routines, in which they played two ordinary, but rather dim blokes who discussed issues of the day, cultural matters and flights of fantasy over a sandwich or a pint. Although largely scripted, these sequences were prone to bouts of ad libbing, particularly from Cook. Like Poets Cornered, Pete and Dud found their echo in later comedy work, especially in Mel Smith and Griff Rhys Jones's head-to-head dialogues. Programmes ended with the closing song, 'Goodbye-ee', which, when released as a single, reached number 18 in the 1965 charts.

Although the series ended in 1966 after just two seasons, *Not Only . . . But Also . . .* was revived in 1970 as part of BBC 2's *Show of the Week* showcase, and, in 1971, two programmes recorded in Australia were also screened by the BBC.

NOT THE NINE O'CLOCK NEWS

UK (BBC) Comedy. BBC 2 1979–82

Mel Smith
Griff Rhys Jones
Pamela Stephenson
Rowan Atkinson
Chris Langham

Producers: Sean Hardie, John Lloyd

Topical satire with a new generation of Fringe comedians.

Squared up against BBC 1's main bulletin, as its title suggested, this was BBC 2's spoof of current events, presented from a very familiar newsy studio set. Interspersed with the 'headlines' were topical send ups of anything from the proposed Advanced Passenger Train to **Miss World**, providing the young stars of *Not the Nine O'Clock News* with ample opportunity to show off the talents that were to make them household names in the decade to follow. However, two pilot episodes, shown six months before the series began, featured a totally different cast – Chris Emmett, Christopher Godwin, John Gorman and Jonathan Hyde.

In the first proper series, the limelight shone most brightly on Pamela Stephenson (with her astute Angela Rippon take-offs) and Rowan Atkinson (flexing his facial muscles in portrayals of aliens and other odd-bods), with Mel Smith and the then fourth partner, Chris Langham, lower down the cast list. Langham left for a chequered TV future in writing and stand up comedy, to be replaced by Griff Rhys Jones, who quickly forged a successful liaison with Mel Smith. In the process, the duo introduced some finger puppet sketches that were to develop into the 'head-to-head' gags of later series.

Throughout, the humour ranged from honest, *Two Ronnies*-ish gags to the positively outrageous, particularly in the final series when they really pushed the boat out. Dubbing spoof headlines over existing news footage was one running theme, mocking pop videos was another, and there was also biting satire, wicked parody and skits on other TV programmes like *University Challenge*, *Points of View* and even *Monty Python's Flying Circus*. A selection of books, records and concerts followed to capitalize on the show's enormous success.

NOW LOOK HERE . . .

UK (BBC) Situation Comedy. BBC 1 1971–3

Ronnie	Ronnie Corbett
Mother	Madge Ryan
	Gillian Lind
Laura	Rosemary Leach
Keith	Richard O'Sullivan

Writers: Graham Chapman, Barry Cryer.
Producers: Bill Hitchcock, Douglas Argent

A mummy's boy finds himself at odds with the world.

Seen off to work by his mum each morning, bachelor Ronnie lived in the suburban town of Bramley and worked in an office where he railed against everything in sight (while, at the same time, pretending to be liberal-minded). His chief adversary was his colleague, Keith. In the second and last series, Ronnie finally fled the nest (though not his mother's attentions) by marrying a girl called Laura. The story resumed in a spin-off series called *The Prince of Denmark*, in which he and his new wife ran a pub she had inherited.

NTSC

Standing for National Television System Committee (the body which introduced it as standard), NTSC is the system of television transmission used in the USA. It is based on 525 lines, unlike the British PAL system which operates on 625 lines. NTSC is also standard in Canada and Japan, amongst other countries.

OSS/OFFICE OF STRATEGIC SERVICES

UK (Buckeye/ITC) Spy Drama. ITV 1957–8

Captain Frank Hawthorne	Ron Randell
The Chief	Lionel Murton
Sgt O'Brien	Robert Gallico

Producers: Jules Buck, William Eliscu

World War II espionage tales, based on true events.

OSS stood for Office of Strategic Services, the USA's precursor to the CIA, whose top man was Captain Frank Hawthorne. Against a wartime backdrop, Hawthorne and his colleague, Sgt O'Brien, worked on the Continent to expose foreign spies, rescue stranded personnel and mount sabotage missions, often in conjunction with the French Résistance. The stories were drawn from the files of the real OSS, which had been disbanded after the war, and authenticity was ensured by co-producer William Eliscu who had himself served in the agency. In the UK the series was often billed in full as *Office of Strategic Services*.

OATER

A familiar term for a television western, much in use in the 1960s when series like *Bonanza*, *Rawhide*, *Wagon Train* and *Laramie* were the order of the day. Another nickname is horse opera.

O'BRIEN, RICHARD (1942–)

British actor, writer and presenter with a trademark shaven head. He is probably best known for his work as host of Channel 4's fantasy game show *The Crystal Maze*, though he has also been seen in series like *Robin of Sherwood* (playing the druid Gulnar). O'Brien also wrote the 1977 Premiere film *A Hymn from Jim*. The theatre remains important to him and amongst the plays and musicals he has scripted has been *The Rocky Horror Show*.

O'CONNOR, CARROLL (1922–)

In his guise of bigot Archie Bunker in *All in the Family*, American actor Carroll O'Connor was the USA's Alf Garnett. The role came in O'Connor's middle age, after decades of treading the boards in Europe as well as America. His first TV appearances came in series like *The Rifleman*, *Bonanza*, *Voyage to the Bottom of the Sea* and *I Spy*, playing rather modest roles. But, in 1968, he starred in a risky pilot for *All in the Family*, which became a full series three years later and was a surprise hit. Together with its sequel, *Archie Bunker's Place*, it ran for 12 years in all, topping the ratings on numerous occasions. In contrast, in 1988, O'Connor was cast as Bill Gillespie, Chief of Police, in the TV version of *In the Heat of the Night*. He has also been seen in TV movies.

O'CONNOR, DES (1932–)

British singer, comedian, presenter and talk show host who came to the fore in the 1950s in series like *Spot the Tune*. *The Des O'Connor Show* (for ATV, featuring comic Jack Douglas in support) ran through most of the 1960s (a time when Des was notching up a string of hit singles) and O'Connor's other series for ITV in the 1960s and 1970s included *Des* and *Des O'Connor Entertains*. O'Connor then switched to the BBC for *Des O'Connor Tonight*, a chat/variety show, but that, too, also transferred to ITV. He was once compere of *Sunday Night at the London Palladium* and, in recent years, has hosted a revival of *Take Your Pick* and the talent show *Pot of Gold*. Mercilessly pilloried for his singing by Morecambe and Wise and other comedians, nevertheless O'Connor has remained one of the UK's favourite entertainers.

O'CONNOR, TOM (1939–)

Liverpudlian comic who found his niche as a variety and game show presenter in the 1970s and 1980s. A former teacher, O'Connor broke out of the nightclub circuit and into the big time after winning *Opportunity Knocks!*. He also appeared on *The Comedians* before hosting *Wednesday at Eight* and *London Night Out*. One element of these was the *Name That Tune* quiz which soon became a series in its own right, with O'Connor at the helm. He has also had his own series, *Tom O'Connor*, compered *Night Out at the London Casino* and been seen on numerous panel games, including *Zodiac*, *Password*, *Gambit*, *I've Got a Secret* and *Cross Wits*.

ODD COUPLE, THE

US (Paramount) Situation Comedy. ITV 1971–

Felix Unger ....Tony Randall
Oscar Madison ....Jack Klugman
Murray Greshner ....Al Molinaro
Speed ....Garry Walberg
Vinnie ....Larry Gelman
Roy ....Ryan McDonald
Dr Nancy Cunningham ....Joan Hotchkis
Gloria Unger ....Janis Hansen
Blanche Madison ....Brett Somers
Myrna Turner ....Penny Marshall
Miriam Welby.......................................Elinor Donahue

Executive Producers: Garry K. Marshall, Sheldon Keller. Producer: Tony Marshall

Two incompatible friends share an apartment and get on each other's nerves.

Felix Unger and Oscar Madison had been childhood friends. They were brought together again when both were divorced, and they decided to share Oscar's apartment in Manhattan. The only trouble was that the two were totally incompatible. Felix was a hard-working, cultured photographer, a hypochondriac with an over-the-top need to see everything in its place and lead an organized life. In contrast, Oscar was a slobbish sportswriter for the *New York Herald*. He lived sloppily, ate messily and littered his room with empty beer cans and dirty laundry. Not surprisingly, there was a great deal of friction between the two 'friends'.

Other regulars were Oscar's Thursday night poker partners, Murray the inept cop, Speed the gambler and the gentle Vinnie. Myrna was Oscar's secretary, and Nancy Cunningham was his sporty girlfriend in the early episodes. Felix's girlfriend was Miriam Welby, who lived in the same building, but he was later reunited with his wife, Gloria, and, when he moved out to live with her again, the series ended, leaving Oscar to revel in his regained squalid freedom.

Based on Neil Simon's successful comedy, and the 1968 film starring Jack Lemmon and Walter Matthau, the series also generated a cover version of its own, entitled *The New Odd Couple*, with the same characters now played by black actors. There was also an animated adaptation, featuring a tidy cat and a lazy dog, entitled *The Oddball Couple*.

ODD MAN, THE

UK (Granada) Police Drama. ITV 1962–3

Steve Gardiner ....Edwin Richfield
Chief Inspector Gordon....................Moultrie Kelsall
Chief Inspector Rose ....William Mervyn
Detective Sgt Swift.................................Keith Barron
Judy Gardiner ....Sarah Lawson
South ....Christopher Guinee

Creator: Edward Boyd. Producer: Stuart Latham

Weirdly atmospheric detective series famous for introducing the character of Chief Inspector Rose.

The Odd Man initially centred on five main characters, all involved in or around the murky world of crime. These were Steve Gardiner, a theatrical agent and part-time private eye, his wife, Judy, the grim Chief Inspector Gordon, his amiable colleague, Detective Sgt Swift, and a mysterious, silent villain named South. Although each programme was self-contained, the episodes ran in a serial format, culminating in the murder of Judy by South, and Steve's pursuit of her killer.

Although this series is credited with bringing Inspector Rose (later of *It's Dark Outside* and *Mr Rose*) to our screens, in fact he did not appear until the second season, taking over from Gordon and teaming up with Swift. He was also a rather different character from the one seen later, considerably more unpleasant. Actress Sarah Lawson, although written out in the first season, returned in the third as Judy's twin sister, and the cult series continued its bizarre tales of crime and intrigue.

Creator Edward Boyd specialized in husband and wife sleuths, having written such stories for BBC Radio before moving to television.

ODDIE, BILL (1941–)

Cambridge Footlights graduate, a contemporary of the likes of John Cleese, Graham Chapman, Jonathan Lynn and his own writing partners Tim Brooke-Taylor and Graeme Garden. The Lancashire-born Oddie broke into television through appearances on *BBC 3* and then, more significantly, *At Last the 1948 Show*, *Twice a Fortnight* and *Broaden Your Mind*. He also contributed scripts to *Hark at Barker*, but it was when he joined Brooke-Taylor and Garden in an adventurous new comedy in 1970, that viewers really began to take notice. The series was *The Goodies*, which ran for 12 years and featured Oddie as the hairy, aggressive and cynical member of the trio of do-gooders. He also wrote the music for the show. With Garden, Oddie had already scripted episodes of *Doctor in the House* (he went on to write for some of its sequels, including the 1991 revival *Doctor at the Top*) and when *The Goodies* ended, they penned the short-lived sitcom *Astronauts*. Oddie has since brought his love of bird watching to TV. He also co-wrote and starred in the theatre school comedy *From the Top* (as William Worthington), appeared in the kids' series *The Saturday Banana* and *The Bubblegum Brigade*, and hosted the religious celebration *Festival*. Other credits have included *We Have Ways of Making You Laugh*, *Fax!* and *Titmuss Regained*.

OFFICE OF STRATEGIC SERVICES see *OSS*.

OGILVY, IAN (1943–)

British character actor whose major TV role has been as Simon Templar in *The Return of the Saint* in 1978. Ogilvy was also seen as Rupert in *The Liars*, Laurence in *Upstairs, Downstairs*, Drusus in *I, Claudius* and Richard Maddison in the comedy *Tom, Dick and Harriet*, and featured in dramas like Henry James's *The Spoils of Poynton*, Daniel Defoe's *Moll Flanders*, Tolstoy's *Anna Karenina* and the three-part thriller *Menace Unseen*.

OH BOY!

UK (ABC/ATV) Pop Music. ITV 1958–9; 1979–80

Hosts: Tony Hall, Jimmy Henny

Creator: Jack Good. Producers: Jack Good, Ken O'Neill (1979). Executive Producer: Richard Leyland (1979)

Britain's first real rock 'n' roll programme.

Oh Boy! was created by TV pop pioneer Jack Good after a dispute had led him to pull out of his earlier success, *Six-Five Special*. Whereas the latter had featured magazine items and intrusions of other kinds of music, *Oh Boy!* was pure rock 'n' roll and, as direct competition on Saturday nights, hastened *Six-Five Special*'s demise. It was the programme that made a star out of Cliff Richard, who had been installed by Good as the featured artist, and other regular contributions came from Marty Wilde, the Vernons Girls, the Dallas Boys, organist Cherry Wainer and singer/dancer Kerry Martin. Harry Robinson's band (which provided the music) was re-modelled by Good into Lord Rockingham's XI and went on to have chart hits of its own (most notably 'Hoots Mon' in 1958). All programmes were staged at the Hackney Empire. The programme was briefly revived by ATV in 1979, with Les Gray of Mud, Alvin Stardust, Freddie 'Fingers' Lee, Joe Brown and Shakin' Stevens amongst the regulars.

OH BROTHER!/OH FATHER!

UK (BBC) Situation Comedy. BBC 1 1968–70; 1973

Brother/Father Dominic ....Derek Nimmo
Father Anselm ....Felix Aylmer (*Oh Brother!*)
Master of the Novices ....Colin Gordon (*Oh Brother!*)
Father Harris ....Laurence Naismith (*Oh Father!*)
Mrs Carr............................Pearl Hackney (*Oh Father!*)
Walter ....David Kelly (*Oh Father!*)
Father Matthew...............Derek Francis (*Oh Father!*)

Writers: David Climie, Austin Steele. Producers: Duncan Wood, Harold Snoad, Johnny Downes (*Oh Brother!*), Graeme Muir (*Oh Father!*)

A bumbling novice is accepted into a priory.

Oh Brother! saw the return of Derek Nimmo's plummy, but good-hearted, cleric character first exhibited as Noote in *All Gas and Gaiters*. This time his identity was Brother Dominic, a sincere but hapless novice at Mountacres Priory. Dominic was eventually 'promoted' to Father Dominic for a follow-up series, *Oh Father!*, in which he left the monastery to become curate to Father Harris.

OH NO! IT'S SELWYN FROGGITT/SELWYN

UK (Yorkshire) Situation Comedy. ITV
1976–7/1978

Selwyn Froggitt	Bill Maynard
Mrs Froggitt	Megs Jenkins
Maurice	Robert Keegan
Ray	Ray Mort
Clive	Richard Davies
Jack	Bill Dean
Harry	Harold Goodwin
Vera	Rosemary Martin
	Lynda Baron
Mervyn Price	Bernard Gallagher (*Selwyn*)

Creator/Writer: Alan Plater (not *Selwyn*).
Producer: Ronnie Baxter

The misadventures of an irrepressible but inept handyman.

Bachelor Selwyn Froggitt lived with his long-suffering mum in the fictitious Yorkshire town of Scarsdale. Employed by the local council in its Public Works department, Froggitt fancied himself as a handyman, but his self-confidence was tragically misplaced. Every job he undertook ended in disaster. Froggitt also considered himself a bit of an intellectual, reading the *Times Literary Supplement* for fun, and was secretary of the Scarsdale Workingmen's Club and Institute where he socialized with the likes of Maurice, Clive, Ray and Jack. A thumbs-up cry of 'Magic' and an inane grin became his trademarks.

After three seasons of mayhem in Scarsdale, Froggitt was uprooted for a spin-off series simply called *Selwyn*. This pitched him into the role of Entertainments Officer at the Paradise Valley holiday camp on the Yorkshire coast, where the predictable consequences were witnessed by manager Mervyn Price. Alan Plater created the character of Selwyn Froggitt for a one-off play in 1974 and continued to write most of the scripts for the resultant series.

OLD GREY WHISTLE TEST/WHISTLE TEST

UK (BBC) Rock Music. BBC 2 1971–88

Presenters:
Ian Whitcomb
Richard Williams
Bob Harris
Anne Nightingale
David Hepworth
Mark Ellen
Richard Skinner
Andy Kershaw
Ro Newton

Producer: Michael Appleton

Cult rock music programme.

Taking its name from the old adage that if the grey-haired doorman whistles your tune you've a hit on your hands, *Old Grey Whistle Test* developed out of a progressive rock programme called *Disco 2*, which in turn was a derivative of **Late Night Line-Up**. Unlike **Top of the Pops**, *Whistle Test* did not pander to the pop charts but focused instead on developments in the album and live music worlds. Two bands generally played live in the (unfurnished) studio, with interviews, film inserts and gig news completing the package. Its initial hosts were Ian Whitcomb and Richard Williams, but it was under the guidance of 'Whispering' Bob Harris that the programme's glory years arrived. Harris's laid-back, understated intros and genuine feel for the music added an air of authenticity and authority to proceedings and helped ensure the programme became a must for every self-respecting rock music fan. A succession of other DJs and journalists, beginning with Anne Nightingale, filled the presenter's chair in the 1980s when, for some seasons, the title was officially shortened to *Whistle Test*. The jaunty theme music, played over the 'star-kicker' opening titles was 'Stone Fox Chase', by Area Code 615.

OLIVIER, LORD LAURENCE (1907–89)

Lord Olivier's glorious theatrical and cinematic biography has been well presented in other publications, but his television work, though sparse, was no less well received. His first contribution was a play, *John Gabriel Borkman*, in 1958. Fifteen years later, he was narrator on the award-winning **World at War** and then appeared in **Jesus of Nazareth** as Nicodemus. In the 1980s he starred in a series of dramas, all of which attracted high praise. He was Lord Marchmain in **Brideshead Revisited**, played King Lear for Channel 4 and starred in *A Voyage around My Father* (as Clifford Mortimer) and *The Ebony Tower*. There were also TV movies and mini-series, with his last TV role coming in *Lost Empires*, as fading comedian Harry Burrard. His wives were actresses Jill Esmond, Vivien Leigh and Joan Plowright.

OLLIE BEAK

A children's TV favourite of the 1960s, Ollie Beak was a fluffy, opinionated owl who sported a school cap and spoke with a rich Scouse accent (thanks to his creator, Wally Whyton). He appeared with Whyton and Muriel Young on the likes of *Lucky Dip*, *Tuesday Rendezvous* and *Five O'Clock Club*, fighting for space alongside fellow puppets Pussy Cat Willum and Fred Barker. Beak made a comeback in the early 1980s on the pop show *Get It Together*.

O'MARA, KATE (1939–)

British glamour actress who guest starred in numerous drama series (the likes of *The Avengers*, *The Troubleshooters*, *The Saint*, *Z Cars*, *No Hiding Place*, *Danger Man*, *Market In Honey Lane*, *Court Martial*, *Paul Temple*, *The Champions*, *Department S*, *The Protectors* and *The Main Chance*) while building a career in the British cinema (particularly in Hammer Horror films). In the 1970s and 1980s, however, she gradually made TV her forté with roles like air freight magnate Jane Maxwell in *The Brothers*, Katherine Laker in *Triangle*, The Rani (a renegade Time Lord) in *Doctor Who*, Caress Morell in *Dynasty* and Laura Wilde in *Howards' Way*. O'Mara has also appeared on panel games and with comedians like *The Two Ronnies* and Morecambe and Wise.

OMNIBUS

UK (BBC) Arts. BBC 1 1967–

Long-running BBC arts programme.

The natural successor to *Monitor*, *Omnibus* – with its declared aim of providing 'television to remember' – has proved even more durable than its predecessor. Its creative weekly films and essays have won much acclaim, with amongst the best-recalled Ken Russell's *Dante's Inferno* (about Dante Gabriel Rossetti) in 1967, Tony Palmer's pop music critique *All My Loving* in 1968, and the spooky Jonathan Miller adaptation of M.R. James's *Whistle, and I'll Come To You* in the same year. In 1993, to commemorate the programme's silver jubilee, a series of the best films was repeated on BBC 1. These included works on Kathleen Ferrier, David Bowie, Leonard Bernstein's *West Side Story*, cinematographer Vittorio Storato, The Brothers Grimm and Ken Russell's 1968 profile of Frederick Delius. Henry Livings was the programme's first presenter, though other hosts have included Humphrey Burton, Richard Baker and Barry Norman (who briefly chaired proceedings in the early 1980s).

ON AIR/OFF AIR

Terms denoting when a programme is/is not being transmitted.

ON SAFARI see Denis, Armand and Michaela.

ON THE BRADEN BEAT

UK (ATV) Consumer Affairs. ITV 1962–7

Presenter: Bernard Braden

Producers: Jock Watson, Francis Coleman

Consumer affairs and light entertainment magazine.

On the Braden Beat was ITV's Saturday night answer to *That Was The Week That Was*. However, this programme combined general entertainment and topical humour with consumer investigations and battles against bureaucracy. After five years with ITV, Braden took the show to the BBC, creating *Braden's Week*, in which he was assisted by reporter/researcher Esther Rantzen. Its clear descendent, *That's Life* (without Braden), followed in 1973.

ON THE BUSES

UK (LWT) Situation Comedy. ITV 1969–73

Stan Butler	Reg Varney
Mrs Butler	Cicely Courtneidge
	Doris Hare
Olive	Anna Karen
Arthur	Michael Robbins
Jack	Bob Grant
Inspector Blake	Stephen Lewis

Creators: Ronald Chesney, Ronald Wolfe.
Producers: Stuart Allen, Derrick Goodwin, Bryan Izzard

A bus driver and his conductor lark about on their travels.

Stan Butler was a driver for the London-based Luxton Bus Company, usually working with his conductor mate Jack on the number 11 route to the cemetery gates. Bain of his life was the humourless Inspector Blake, who was always desperate to catch the chirpy pair up to no good. Blakey's catchphrase, 'I 'ate you Butler', was quickly adopted by the viewing public.

Stan lived with his widowed mother, his dowdy sister, Olive, and her gruff, layabout husband, Arthur, but life was brighter at the depot where there were always busty clippies to chase and jokes to play on the much-maligned Blakey. In keeping with the humour of the time, leering and innuendo dominated the series, although there was seldom any serious sexual activity – living with his mum, Stan never had the opportunity, much to his frustration.

Cicely Courtneidge was the first actress to play Stan's mum, although Doris Hare is best remembered in the role, while Stephen Lewis, who played Blakey, took his character into a spin-off series. Entitled *Don't Drink the Water*, and shown in 1974–5, it saw Blakely moving into a retirement home in Spain with his spinster sister (Pat Coombs). After this, Lewis spent some time in the TV wilderness, eventually resurfacing as Smiler, Nora Batty's lodger, in **Last of the Summer Wine**.

Three feature film versions (*On the Buses*, *Mutiny on the Buses* and *Holiday on the Buses*) were released in the 1970s, reflecting the popularity of this cheerfully vulgar comedy, and a US copy, set in New York and entitled *Lotsa Luck*, was also produced.

ON THE MOVE

UK (BBC) Education. BBC 1 1975–6

Alf	Bob Hoskins
Bert	Donald Gee

Writer: Barry Took. Producer: David Hargreaves

Light-hearted attempt to encourage illiterate viewers to learn to read and write.

This series of award-winning, ten-minute programmes, shown on Sunday teatimes, featured Bob Hoskins and Donald Gee as removals men Alf and Bert, who travelled around Britain and remarked on strange words in the English language. The aim was to stimulate people who couldn't read to do something about it. *On the Move* was partly inspired by an Italian series from the 1950s and 1960s, *Non E Mai Troppo Tardi* (*It's Never Too Late*), which tackled that country's chronic illiteracy problem.

ON THE UP

UK (BBC) Situation Comedy. BBC 1 1990–2

Tony Carpenter	Dennis Waterman
Sam	Sam Kelly
Mrs Fiona Wembley	Joan Sims
Ruth Carpenter	Judy Buxton
Maggie	Jenna Russell
Stephanie Carpenter	Vanessa Hadaway
Dawn	Michelle Hatch
Mrs Carpenter	Dora Bryan
	Pauline Letts

Creator/Writer: Bob Larbey. Producer: Gareth Gwenlan

A self-made millionaire has wife and domestic staff troubles.

East Ender Tony Carpenter was somewhat ill at ease with the sumptuous trappings of wealth, even though his own graft had made them possible. Forced to live in a posh Surrey neighbourhood (Esher) by Ruth, his socially superior wife of 16 years standing (who kept walking out on him), he employed a trio of home-based assistants, who also gave him a few headaches (but remained his only true friends). These were Sam, a childhood pal, who had become his butler and chauffeur; widow Mrs Wembley, his tipsy, old-movie-loving housekeeper; and Maggie the Scottish personal assistant who helped with his car hire company (TC Luxury Cars). Tony struggled to justify his extravagant lifestyle, especially to his own mum, an avowed socialist, who did her best to disown him. Adding to the conflict were Stephanie, Tony's problematic, public school-based daughter, and Dawn, the rather dim model Tony dated in later episodes.

Star Dennis Waterman also wrote and sang the programme's closing theme song.

ONE FOOT IN THE GRAVE

UK (BBC) Situation Comedy. BBC 1 1990–

Victor Meldrew	Richard Wilson
Margaret Meldrew	Annette Crosbie
Mrs Jean Warboys	Doreen Mantle
Patrick	Angus Deayton
Pippa	Janine Duvitski
Mr Nick Swainey	Owen Brenman

Creator/Writer: David Renwick. Producer: Susan Belbin

An accident prone pensioner is the world's greatest whinger.

Unceremoniously retiring from his job as a security guard, amateur ventriloquist Victor Meldrew settled down to long days at home, much to the distress of his Scottish wife, Margaret. For Victor was the world's number one complainer. Litter in his front garden was one of his pet hates; the failure of mail order firms to supply the correct goods was another. His curmudgeonly attitude to life was soon recognized by their new neighbours when the Meldrews moved to a modern estate in Bournemouth. On one side lived bus driver Pippa and her cynical, professional husband, Patrick, who, from the strange happenings next door, was firmly convinced that Victor was insane. On the other side lived the very cheerful but very boring Mr Swainey and his invalid mother. The insensitive Mrs Warboys was another close associate (rather too close at times).

Although the series centred on ridiculous misunderstandings and gentle forms of farce, *One Foot in the Grave* also had its surreal elements and more than a touch of pathos. Tender moments intermingled with Victor's yells of outrage ('I don't believe it!') and Margaret's cries of despair. All this made *One Foot in the Grave* the BBC's most popular sitcom in the early 1990s. For Christmas

1993, a feature length special, *One Foot in the Algarve*, was produced. The theme song for the series was co-written and sung by Eric Idle.

ONE MAN AND HIS DOG

UK (BBC) Sheep Dog Trials. BBC 2 1976–

Presenters: Phil Drabble, Robin Page

Producers: Philip S. Gilbert, Ian Smith, Joy Corbett

Shepherds and their faithful hounds round up flocks in a contest for the BBC Television Trophy.

An unlikely hit, *One Man and His Dog* was hosted by flat-capped Phil Drabble for 18 years, before he handed over his crook and wellies to new presenter Robin Page in 1994. Loyal viewers on a Sunday tea time have appreciated the traditional, rural skills of dog handling, epitomized by shepherds who, with just a few whistles, can instruct their charges to herd the most unruly sheep through gates, round posts and into wooden pens. No doubt the beautiful Lake District landscape, with its rolling fields and dry-stone walls, has added to the attraction. Trials experts Eric Halsall, Ray Ollerenshaw and Gus Dermony have also contributed to the series over the years.

ONEDIN LINE, THE

UK (BBC) Drama. BBC 1 1971–80

Captain James Onedin	Peter Gilmore
Robert Onedin	Brian Rawlinson
	James Garbutt
Captain Webster	James Hayter
Elizabeth Onedin/Frazer/Lady Fogarty	Jessica Benton
Anne Onedin	Anne Stallybrass
Captain Baines	Howard Lang
Sarah Onedin	Mary Webster
Callon	Edward Chapman
Emma Callon	Jane Seymour
Albert Frazer	Philip Bond
Daniel Fogarty	Michael Billington
	Tom Adams
Mr Frazer	John Phillips
Charlotte Onedin	Laura Hartong
Letty Gaunt/Onedin	Jill Gascoine
William Frazer	Marc Harrison
Seth Burgess	Michael Walker
Leonora Biddulph	Kate Nelligan
Caroline Maudsley	Caroline Harris
Margarita Juarez/Onedin	Roberta Iger
Dunwoody	John Rapley
Samuel Onedin	Christopher Douglas
Josiah Beaumont	Warren Clarke
Max Van Der Rheede	Frederick Jaeger
Caroline	Jenny Twigge
Tom Arnold	Keith Jayne

Creator: Cyril Abraham. Producers: Peter Graham Scott, Peter Cregeen, Geraint Morris

The saga of a Liverpool shipping line.

James Onedin was the determined, hard-driving master of the *Charlotte Rhodes*, a three-masted schooner, back in the 19th century. In 1860, as a 28-year-old, he had inherited little of his shopkeeper father's estate. Whereas the business went to his elder brother, Robert, and the family cottage to his sister, Elizabeth, all James received was £25, but he set out to make the most of it. With his windfall he purchased the *Charlotte Rhodes* and began to establish his own shipping business. As part of the deal, however, he also agreed to marry Anne (played by Sheila Allen in the pilot), the daughter of the ship's former owner, Captain Webster.

The late 1800s were precarious times and running a merchant ship was not a comfortable business, even with a whiskery old sea dog like Captain Baines (who constantly objected to his master's methods), as first mate. The series followed the boardroom and bedroom exploits of the quick-tempered Onedin, as well as his life on the cruel sea. In the background, adding domestic complications, were his wealthy brother and attractive sister, his troublesome daughter, Charlotte, and his three wives (when Anne died in childbirth, James married Charlotte's governess, Letty Gaunt, who also died, before he wed a Spanish widow, Margarita Juarez).

Running for nine years (and taking the period up to 1886), *The Onedin Line* was derived from a one-off *Drama Playhouse* presentation in 1970 and became a stalwart of BBC 1's Sunday nights. Its evocative theme music came from Khachaturyan's 'Spartacus', intended for a situation far removed from the Dartmouth docksides where this series was filmed.

ONLY FOOLS AND HORSES

UK (BBC) Situation Comedy. BBC 1 1981–

Derek 'Del Boy' Trotter	David Jason
Rodney Trotter	Nicholas Lyndhurst
Grandad Trotter	Lennard Pearce
Uncle Albert Trotter	Buster Merryfield
Raquel	Tessa Peake-Jones
Cassandra Parry/Trotter	Gwyneth Strong
Boycie	John Challis
Marlene	Sue Holderness
Trigger	Roger Lloyd-Pack
Mike Fisher	Kenneth MacDonald
Mickey Pearce	Patrick Murray
Denzil	Paul Barber

Creator/Writer: John Sullivan. Producers: Ray Butt, Gareth Gwenlan

The misadventures of a flashy London spiv and his hapless brother.

Only Fools and Horses was *the* British sitcom of the 1980s. From humble beginnings as a slow-moving idea for a series called *Readies*, it grew into one of the best-loved comedies the BBC has ever produced, ranking alongside **Steptoe and Son**, **Till Death Us Do Part**, **Hancock's Half Hour** and **Fawlty Towers**. Testimony to its popularity is the fact that its Christmas Day specials were the highlight of the BBC's festive season.

Taking its name from the old adage that 'only fools and horses work', the series was constructed around Derek 'Del Boy' Trotter, a market fly-pitcher with an endless supply of dodgy goods fresh off the back of a lorry. Ever the optimist ('this time next year, we'll be millionaires' and 'he who dares, wins' became his catchphrases), Del Boy was the sole provider for his close-knit family, which consisted of his lanky 'plonker' of a brother, Rodney, and his dim old Grandad. Together they shared a council flat (number 368) in the high-rise Nelson Mandela House, Peckham. Swathed in gold, heavily splashed with Brut and puffing a chunky cigar, Del enjoyed the good life, which effectively meant a night down The Nag's Head drinking Drambuie and grapefruit cocktails, followed by a Ruby Murray (a curry). Lovely jubbley, as he would have put it. His choice of women left a lot to be desired, although occasionally he would stumble across a classier girl, which warranted a trip to a Berni Inn.

Rodney, left orphaned when his mother died and his dad cleared off, relied on Del for his well-being, although this effectively scuppered any hopes he harboured of a life of his own. It was Rodney who, despite having two GCEs, was the dogsbody of Trotter's Independent Trading, and the driver of the firm's decrepit, yellow three-wheeled van. Grandad was the silly old sod who ran the home and did the cooking, in between bouts of sulking or simultaneously watching two TV sets. When actor Lennard Pearce died, Grandad also passed away and in his place his equally wily brother, the boys' Uncle Albert, was introduced. An old sea dog with a Capt. Birdseye beard, Albert could instantly break up any party with the ominous words 'During the war . . . '. The Trotters were also well blessed with friends and associates. These included dense road sweeper Trigger (so-named not because he carried a gun but because he looked like a horse), flashy businessman Boycie and his flirty wife, Marlene, Mike, landlord of the pub, and Denzil, a lorry driver. Rodney's pals included the brainless Mickey Pearce.

Writer John Sullivan bravely allowed his characters to mature as the series progressed and moments of pathos were introduced, as when Rodney married yuppie banker Cassandra and Del was left isolated and, for once, alone.

However, Del's momentary introspection soon gave way to love for actress/stripogram girl Raquel, who bore him a son, portentously named Damien, much to Rodney's terror. Although *Only Fools and Horses* has existed only in 'special' form for a number of years, it seems that future series have not been discounted and the Peckham three may be on the loose once again.

ONLY WHEN I LAUGH

UK (Yorkshire) Situation Comedy. ITV 1979–83

Roy Figgis	James Bolam
Archie Glover	Peter Bowles
Norman Binns	Christopher Strauli
Dr Gordon Thorpe	Richard Wilson
Staff Nurse Gupte	Derrick Branche
Matron	Brenda Cowling
Cook	Pamela Cundell

Creator/Writer: Eric Chappell. Producer: Vernon Lawrence

The petty squabbles of a trio of long-term hospital patients.

Bolshy lorry driver Roy Figgis, snooty, upper-class hypochondriac Archie Glover and naive young Norman Binns were the long-stay patients in this hospital comedy. They battled over the best beds, put the wind up new patients, complained about the hospital radio service and wrangled with the medical staff. These included haughty, irascible surgeon Gordon Thorpe and frustrated male nurse Gupte. The ironic 'H.A.P.P.Y.' theme song set the tone.

OPEN ALL HOURS

UK (BBC) Situation Comedy. BBC 2 1976; BBC 1 1981–2; 1985

Arkwright	Ronnie Barker
Granville	David Jason
Nurse Gladys Emmanuel	Lynda Baron
Milkwoman	Barbara Flynn
Mrs Featherstone	Stephanie Cole

Creator/Writer: Roy Clarke. Producer: Sydney Lotterby

Penny pinching with a North Country shopkeeper and his hapless nephew.

Adopting yet another characterization that showed off his comic gifts to great effect, Ronnie Barker, in this series, introduced viewers to Arkwright, the tightest grocer in the North of England. Constantly battling with an entrenched stammer and the advances of 1970s shopkeeping, Arkwright was mean, devious and conniving. He was particularly hard on his young nephew, Granville, the son of Arkwright's sister by an unnamed Hungarian, who had grown up as the grocer's errand boy, shop assistant and general skivvy. But Granville was also a daydreamer and pictured himself in better situations, usually in the arms of some beautiful woman.

Arkwright, too, had romantic aspirations, in his case to fall into the bosom of buxom Gladys Emmanuel, the Morris Minor-driving nurse who lived across the street with her ailing mother. Although she needed to fend off Arkwright's wandering hands and turn a deaf ear to his practised innuendo, she nevertheless harboured a genuine affection for the stingy old grocer.

The days were long in this shop. From well before dawn to well after dusk the lights were on and the door was open. Each programme began with Arkwright setting out his special offers on stalls at the front, winding up with his taking them back in again. In between, confused customers came and went (usually with goods Arkwright had conned them into buying), and Granville had suffered another day of abuse and frustration. But it never prevented him from answering back to his mentor, or smirking whenever Arkwright caught his fingers in the shop's temperamental till.

The characters first appeared in a **Comedy Playhouse** pilot in 1974 but two years passed before a series followed (on BBC 2). This was repeated on BBC 1 in 1979 and new episodes eventually appeared in 1981 and 1982. However, the last series was not transmitted until 1985, four years after David Jason had switched trading places to Peckham market, and taken on the role of Del Boy in **Only Fools and Horses**. An American version of *Open All Hours* was also made, entitled *Open All Night*.

OPENING TITLES

The (often pre-recorded) sequence of film, text and music which identifies a programme, sometimes giving key credits like performers and writers.

OPPORTUNITY KNOCKS!/BOB SAYS 'OPPORTUNITY KNOCKS'

UK (Associated-Rediffusion/ABC/Thames/BBC) Talent Show. ITV 1956–78; BBC 1 1987–90

Hosts: Hughie Green, Bob Monkhouse, Les Dawson

Producers: Peter Dulay, Milo Lewis, Royston Mayoh, Robert Fleming, Keith Beckett, Stewart Morris (*Bob Says*)

Long-running talent show in which viewers at home elected the top act.

Beginning on Radio Luxembourg in the early 1950s, *Opportunity Knocks!* and its ebullient host,

Hughie Green, were brought to television soon after ITV began. There had been talent shows on TV before – *Carroll Levis Discoveries* was one – but none proved to have the stamina of *Opportunity Knocks!*, which not only survived the ITV franchise swap of 1968 but was resurrected by the BBC in 1987, having been cancelled by Thames in 1978.

The format was simple. Green introduced half-a-dozen acts per week ('Friends, we want to hear them', Green declared), each 'sponsored' by a studio guest who offered background information about the performers. At the end of the show, all the acts gave a short reprise of their routine which the studio audience evaluated by applauding. The highest scorers on the 'clapometer' were declared the studio winners, but this counted for nothing. What mattered ('And I mean that most sincerely, folks', Green was known to swear) were the votes of viewers at home, expressed by the mailing in of postcards. At the start of the following week's programme, the winners were announced and were given the chance to repeat their success. A winning contestant could literally return week after week, and, at the end of each series, an all-winners show was put together. Telephone voting replaced postal votes when the BBC revived the show under the title of *Bob Says 'Opportunity Knocks'* (the new host being Bob Monkhouse). Les Dawson, himself probably the programme's greatest find, presented the final season, with the title reverting to *Opportunity Knocks!*.

Other notable performers given their showbusiness break by *Opportunity Knocks!* were Russ Abbot (as part of the Black Abbots group), Freddie Starr, The Bachelors, Frank Carson, Mary Hopkin, Little and Large, Freddie Davies, Peters and Lee, Lena Zavaroni, Ken Goodwin, Pam Ayres, Bonnie Langford, Paul Melba, Tom O'Connor and Paper Lace. But whatever happened to perennial winners like Bobby Crush, Neil Reid, Gerry Monroe, Millican and Nesbitt, Stuart Gillies, Berni Flint and 1960s muscle man Tony Holland? There were hard luck stories, too. Su Pollard was allegedly beaten by a singing dog and a singer called Gerry Dorsey even failed the audition. He changed his name to Englebert Humperdinck and did rather better for himself.

OPT OUT

The term given to the practice by regional TV stations of leaving national output and screening local programmes/inserts instead.

ORANGES ARE NOT THE ONLY FRUIT

UK (BBC) Drama. BBC 2 1990

Jess ....Emily Aston
                                  Charlotte Coleman
Mother ....Geraldine McEwan

Pastor Finch	Kenneth Cranham
May	Elizabeth Spriggs
Mrs Green	Freda Dowie
Elsie	Margery Withers
Miss Jewsbury	Celia Imrie
Cissy	Barbara Hicks
Mrs Arkwright	Pam Ferris
Melanie	Cathryn Bradshaw

Writer: Jeanette Winterson. Producer: Phillippa Giles

A young Lancashire girl rebels against her mother's religious ambitions.

Adapted for television in three parts by Jeanette Winterson, from her own Whitbread Prize-winning novel, *Oranges Are Not the Only Fruit* was the story of Jess, an adopted northern lass who refused to yield to her mum's religious fanaticism. Earmarked as a future missionary, Jess was subjected to oppressive preaching from the bigoted Pastor Finch and made to join in thunderous hymn singing with her mother's geriatric friends. A lesbian encounter with Melanie, a teenage acquaintance, provoked the wrath of the assembled Pentecostals but their primitive efforts to drive the Devil out of the girl backfired and she was lost to them forever.

Despite seeming a risky undertaking by the BBC, as neither the director, Beeban Kidron, nor the producer, Phillippa Giles, had conducted a TV drama before, the serial was widely acclaimed and went on to collect several awards.

ORLANDO

UK (Associated-Rediffusion) Children's Adventure. ITV 1965–8

Orlando O'Connor	Sam Kydd
Steve Morgan	David Munro
Jenny Morgan	Judy Robinson

Producer: Ronald Marriott

Spin-off for children from the adult series *Crane*. Orlando O'Connor had been Crane's right-hand man in the earlier tales of smuggling and petty crime on the North African coast. Now he had returned to Britain and, after failing to establish a boat-building business, had sought out an old Navy friend named Mike. Mike, however, had been killed and Orlando, with the help of Steve and Jenny Morgan, two teenagers who had inherited their uncle's detective agency, set about finding his murderer. This was the first of many adventures for the trio, in which Orlando's life was saved on many an occasion by a magical Arabic charm called a 'Gizzmo', which doubled up as homing device. The action mostly took place around London's docklands.

OSMONDS, THE: ALAN (1949–), WAYNE (1951–), MERRILL (1953–), JAY (1955–), DONNY (1957–), MARIE (1959–) AND JIMMY (1963–)

American singing family, possibly the world's most famous Mormons, who first found TV fame in the 1960s on *The Andy Williams Show*. In the 1970s they were extremely popular, both on television and in the pop charts, with *Donny and Marie* their longest lasting series. They also sang the theme song for the western *The Travels of Jaimie McPheeters*, a series in which they once guested.

OSOBA, TONY

British character actor with some memorable supporting roles behind him. He was the Scottish heavy McLaren in *Porridge*, Detective Sgt Chas Jarvis in *Dempsey and Makepeace*, Freddie in *Making News* and rag trade boss Peter Ingram in *Coronation Street*. Amongst his other credits have been *The Flame Trees of Thika*, *The Professionals*, *Doctor Who*, *Minder*, *The Cleopatras*, *Churchill's People*, *Bergerac*, *The Bill* and *Brookside*.

O'SULLIVAN, PETER, CBE (1918–)

Irish-born horse racing commentator, the voice of the BBC's racing coverage. O'Sullevan has been calling the horses for the Corporation since 1946, when he was racing correspondent for the Press Association. He later wrote for the *Daily Express*, notching up 36 years' service up to 1986.

O'SULLIVAN, RICHARD (1944–)

British actor, once a child performer and seen on TV since the 1950s in series like *Little Lord Fauntleroy*, *All Aboard*, *Dixon of Dock Green* and *The Adventures of Robin Hood* (as Prince Arthur). In the early 1970s he played the sneaky Dr Lawrence Bingham in *Doctor at Large* and its sequel, *Doctor in Charge*, which led to other sitcom roles, most notably that of Robin Tripp in *Man About the House* and *Robin's Nest*. He appeared with Ronnie Corbett in *Now Look Here!* (as Keith), was Richard Gander with Beryl Reid in *Alcock and Gander*, and Howard in *Father, Dear, Father*. Switching briefly to drama, O'Sullivan starred as *Dick Turpin* in the series of the same name in 1979, but he was tempted back to comedy with *Me and My Girl* in 1984, playing widower Simon Harrap. In 1991 he was psychiatrist Adam Charlesworth in *Trouble in Mind*.

OTHER 'ARF, THE

UK (ATV/Central) Situation Comedy. ITV
1980–4

Lorraine Watts	Lorraine Chase
Charles Lattimer	John Standing
Brian Sweeney	Steve Adler
Sybilla Howarth	Patricia Hodge
George Watts	John Cater
Lord Freddy Apthorpe	James Villiers
Bassett	Richard Caldicot
Mrs Lilley	Sheila Keith

Creator/Writer: Terence Howard. Producers:
Tony Charles, Allan McKeown

**A Tory MP has an affair with a Cockney
model.**

The course of love never did run smooth for
upper-class Tory MP Charles Lattimer and the
Cockney model, Lorraine Watts, whom he met in
a restaurant. Sybilla Howarth and Brian Sweeney,
the partners they ditched, remained on the scene
to make life uncomfortable and ultimately Charles
lost his parliamentary seat, forcing him and
Lorraine to open up his home, Dormer House, to
paying guests. Bassett and Mrs Lilley were his
domestic staff, George was Lorraine's dad and Lord
Freddy Apthorpe an aristocratic chum of Charles's.

The Other 'Arf capitalized on model Lorraine
Chase's success as the Cockney girl in adverts for
Campari. When asked by her smoothie suitor
'Were you truly wafted here from Paradise?' she
responded 'No. Luton Airport.' and so launched
her acting career.

OUR HOUSE

UK (ABC) Situation Comedy. ITV 1960–1

Georgina Ruddy	Hattie Jacques
Simon Willow	Charles Hawtrey
Daisy Burke	Joan Sims
Captain Iliffe	Frank Pettingell
Mrs Iliffe	Ina de la Haye
Gordon Brent	Norman Rossington
Herbert Keene	Frederick Peisley
Stephen Hatton	Trader Faulkner
Marcia Hatton	Leigh Madison
William Singer	Bernard Bresslaw
Henrietta	Hylda Baker
Marina	Eugenie Cavanagh

Writers: Norman Hudis, Brad Ashton, Bob
Block. Producer: Ernest Maxin

**Comic capers with the oddball residents of
a large house.**

Carry On Under One Roof may have been a more
appropriate title for this farcical comedy partly
written by *Carry On* scriptwriter Norman Hudis
and starring several of the big screen performers. It
featured a rag bag of nine people who met in an
estate agent's office and, by pooling their funds,
managed to buy a house big enough to accommodate them all. The cohabitors were librarian
Georgina Ruddy, council official Simon Willow,
unemployable Daisy Burke, the artistic, newlywed
Hattons, Yorkshire sea dog Captain Iliffe and his
French violinist wife, bank clerk Herbert Keene
and law student Gordon Brent. When the second
series began, some new house-sharers, including
William Singer, Marina and Henrietta, were added.

After the introductory first episode, which was
billed as *Moving in to Our House*, not all the characters appeared each week.

OUR MAN AT ST MARK'S/OUR MAN FROM ST MARK'S

UK (Associated-Rediffusion) Situation
Comedy. ITV 1963–5/1966

Reverend Andrew Parker	Leslie Phillips
Reverend Stephen Young	Donald Sinden
Mrs Peace	Joan Hickson
Anne Gibson	Anne Lawson
Harry the Yo Yo	Harry Fowler

Creators/Writers: James Kelly, Peter Miller.
Producer: Eric Maschwitz

**Humorous happenings in the daily life of
a country vicar.**

St Mark's, a rural parish centring around the village
of Felgate, was blessed with the Reverend Andrew
Parker as its slightly eccentric vicar. This series
focused on his day-to-day exploits, taking in the
amusing incidents and, occasionally, the sentimental.
He was assisted by his girlfriend, Anne Gibson, and
his housekeeper, Mrs Peace. When St Mark's gained
a new vicar, Stephen Young, a year later, Mrs Peace
remained in situ and a reformed crook by the name
of Harry the Yo Yo (on account of the fact he was
in and out of prison) was employed as sexton/grave
digger. Stephen also brought with him a Scottie dog
named Mr Robertson. The title changed slightly for
the fourth and final season. Becoming *Our Man from
St Mark's*, it saw Stephen promoted to archdeacon
and transferred to a cathedral.

Our Man at St Mark's began a year after a similar
series had aired in the USA. Entitled *Going My
Way*, it starred Gene Kelly and was a small screen
version of the classic 1944 Bing Crosby film.

OUR WORLD

UK (BBC) Entertainment. BBC 1 1967

Presenter: Cliff Michelmore. Producer: Ray
Colley

**Satellite link-up featuring contributions
from TV companies around the world.**

This celebration of satellite technology, sponsored

by the European Broadcasting Union, was broadcast between 8 and 10 pm on the evening of Sunday, 25 June 1967. Hosted by Cliff Michelmore, it employed four satellites and over a million miles of cabling to bring together live pictures from most parts of the globe (the Soviet Union and Poland were notable exceptions, having pulled out because of the Israeli Six-Day War earlier in the month). In all, 18 countries contributed a (non-political) televisual message or other item. The BBC's offering was a live performance of The Beatles singing 'All You Need Is Love'.

OUT

UK (Thames/Euston Films) Drama. ITV 1978

Frank Ross	Tom Bell
Anne Ross	Lynne Farleigh
Evie	Pam Fairbrother
Detective Inspector Bryce	Norman Rodway
Rimmer	Robert Walker
Cimmie	Katharine Schofield
Ralph Veneker	John Junkin
Chris Cottle	Brian Croucher
Vic Lee	Frank Mills
Bernie Machen	Oscar James
Pretty Billy Binns	Peter Blake

Writer: Trevor Preston. Executive Producer: Johnny Goodman. Producer: Barry Hanson

A vicious, bitter criminal is released from jail and looks for revenge.

Tough, intense bank robber Frank Ross, a hardman amongst hardmen, had only one aim in life. Now back on the streets after eight years in prison, he was looking for the person who had shopped him. Nothing got in his way in his quest for the informer and his obsessed meanderings through London's underworld were punctuated by encounters by numerous sad and evil characters. The violence was heavy and the police Ross confronted were as grubby and miserable as the villains they set out to catch. Frank's wife, mentally wrecked by his bleak life of crime, was also seen. A powerful, six-part drama, *Out* won much acclaim.

OUT OF THE UNKNOWN

UK (BBC) Science Fiction. BBC 2 1965–71

Producers: Irene Shubik, Alan Bromly

Well-respected sci-fi anthology series.

Initially taking works by renowned science fiction authors like John Wyndham, Ray Bradbury and Isaac Asimov, this collection of spooky tales proved to be Britain's definitive answer to *The Twilight Zone*. It employed skilled TV writers like Troy Kennedy Martin, Terry Nation and Leon Griffiths as adaptors, and was masterminded by former *Armchair Theatre* story editor Irene

Shubik, who had already attempted a similar concept when working on ABC's *Out of this World*. The tales were not all thrillers, some were satires and comedies, but fantastic space creatures and bug-eyed monsters were steadfastly avoided. The series also attracted some of the best contemporary acting talents – the likes of Marius Goring, George Cole, Warren Mitchell, Donald Houston, David Hemmings and Rachel Roberts – as well as aspiring directors like Ridley Scott, later of *Alien* and *Blade Runner* fame. In 1969, after a two-year gap, the series was revived in colour and the emphasis switched from pure sci-fi to horror and psychological suspense, as new producer Alan Bromly took over the reins.

OUT OF THIS WORLD

UK (ABC) Science Fiction. ITV 1962

Host: Boris Karloff

Producer: Leonard White

An innovative British series of hour-long science fiction plays.

Produced by ABC, already highly successful with its *Armchair Theatre* collection of single dramas, this series was British TV's first attempt at a science fiction anthology. Many of the trends it set, such as using the works of established sci-fi authors, employing first-rate adaptors and leading performers, and varying the style of each play from pure suspense to black comedy, were continued through to its natural successor, the BBC's *Out of the Unknown*. Thirteen episodes were made, and were shown on Saturday nights, with introductions by the softly sinister Boris Karloff.

OUT-TAKES

Material shot but not used in the finished programme, often because of gaffes and blunders. These have proved particularly popular with viewers when grouped in humorous collections like *It'll Be Alright on the Night* and *Auntie's Bloomers*.

OUTER LIMITS, THE

US (Daystar/United Artists) Science Fiction. ITV 1964–

The Control Voice .... Vic Perrin

Creator/Executive Producer: Leslie Stevens. Producers: Joseph Stefano, Ben Brady

Stylish anthology of sci-fi thriller stories.

In the 1950s and 1960s, video static and picture distortion were annoyingly familiar to TV viewers. However, there was always an announcer at hand to confirm that normal programming would resume as soon as possible – unless you happened to be watching *The Outer Limits*. Playing on the poor reliability of TV signals and television equipment, *The Outer Limits* set out to frighten viewers from the start, opening with the loss of the picture and a voice that declared ominously: 'There is nothing wrong with your television set. Do not attempt to adjust the picture. We are controlling transmission. We will control the horizontal. We will control the vertical. For the next hour, sit quietly and we will control all you see and hear. You are about to experience the awe and mystery that reaches from the inner mind to the Outer Limits.'

What followed was one of the 49 sci-fi thrillers that made up *The Outer Limits* anthology. Most concerned Earth invasions by extra-terrestrial life forms and are best remembered for their catalogue of terrifying aliens, which varied from giant insects to intelligent rocks and invisible parasites. But there was much more to *The Outer Limits* than bug-eyed monsters. The camera work applied a stark, film noir veneer to the imaginative stories and, though the monsters took centre stage, it was the humans – or rather human nature – that stole the show, with a moral always drawn from proceedings. Thankfully, the announcer – or Control Voice (the person was never seen) – then restored normality, concluding with the words: 'We now return control of your television set to you, until next week at the same time, when the Control Voice will take you to . . . the Outer Limits.'

The show's first producer, Joseph Stefano, certainly knew how to chill; he had already written the screenplay for Hitchcock's *Psycho*. Being an anthology series, *The Outer Limits* called upon guest artists every week, with stars like Leonard Nimoy, William Shatner, Martin Sheen, Donald Pleasence and David McCallum taking on lead roles. BBC 2 re-ran the entire series in 1980–81. A new version aired on BBC 2 in 1995.

OUTSIDE BROADCAST

Abbreviated to OB, an outside broadcast is a programme or part of a programme that takes place outside the controlled environment of a television studio. An OB at a major sporting event or state occasion, for example, is a complex operation, involving numerous, strategically placed cameras and microphones, all co-ordinated by a director and his/her team working from a mobile control room.

OWEN, ALUN (1926–)

Liverpudlian dramatist, one of British TV's major early playwrights. For *Armchair Theatre* he penned *No Trams to Lime Street* in 1959, quickly followed by *After the Funeral, Lena, O My Lena* (both 1960), *The Rose Affair* (1961), *The Strain* (1963) and *Shelter* (1967), amongst other offerings. *You Can't Win 'Em All* in 1962 led to a six-part series, *Corrigan Blake*, the following year and another play, *Ah – There You Are* (part of *The Ronnie Barker Playhouse* collection), created the character of Lord Rustless and resulted in the series **Hark at Barker** in 1969. The same year, his trilogy comprising *MacNeil, Cornelius* and *Emlyn* (aired under the *Saturday Night Theatre* banner) was aimed at a transatlantic audience, while his later work included *Norma* (1974), *Forget-Me-Not* (1976) and *Kisch, Kisch* (1983). Owen also wrote the screenplay for The Beatles' film *A Hard Day's Night*.

OWEN, BILL, MBE (BILL ROWBOTHAM; 1914–)

Few actors have held down the same television role for over 20 years, but Bill Owen is one of them, thanks to his marathon stint as the seedy Compo in **Last of the Summer Wine**. Owen's TV career, however, stretches way back. In 1951 he played Inspector Lestrade in an ambitious BBC adaptation of the **Sherlock Holmes** mysteries. In 1963, he starred as Fred Cuddell, alongside Sid James, in **Taxi** and, eight years later, played the conniving Sgt Sam Short in *Copper's End*. Amongst his other credits have been **Whatever Happened to the Likely Lads?**, **Tales of the Unexpected**, **Brideshead Revisited** and **Coronation Street**.

OWEN, NICK (1947–)

British journalist and presenter, coming to the fore as host of TV-am's **Good Morning Britain** in 1983, following work as a news and sports frontman for ATV and Central (as well as TV-am). Owen has also hosted the quizzes *Sporting Triangles* and *Hitman*, *Midweek Sports Special* and other sporting events. His breakfast time partnership with Anne Diamond was poached by the BBC for *Good Morning with Anne and Nick* in the early 1990s.

PACE, NORMAN (1953–) see Hale, Gareth.

PADDINGTON

UK (Filmfair) Animation. BBC 1 1976

Narrator: Michael Hordern

Creator/Writer: Michael Bond. Producer: Graham Clutterbuck

The adventures of a somewhat disorientated Peruvian bear in London.

Paddington, the hero of books by Michael Bond since 1958, finally arrived on television in 1976. As a result, a new generation of youngsters were able to appreciate the cuddly bear in the blue duffle coat, floppy hat and wellies who loved marmalade sandwiches and lived with the Brown family. The Browns had found him at Paddington station (hence his name) wearing a tag reading 'Please look after this bear'. Looking after this bear, however, proved increasingly difficult, as the rather bemused but always inquisitive Paddington stumbled from mishap to mishap. Paddington's best friend was antiques dealer Mr Gruber.

These five-minute episodes, shown in the '*Magic Roundabout*' slot' just before the early evening news, featured a model Paddington animated by Ivor Wood against a static drawn background. A more advanced, technically superior, updated *Paddington* was seen in the 1990s, but failed to charm audiences like the original series.

PAGETT, NICOLA (1945–)

British actress, popular on TV in the 1970s in particular, during which time she played Miss Elizabeth in *Upstairs, Downstairs* and took the title role in *Anna Karenina*. In the 1980s she was Adele Fairley in *A Woman of Substance* and Liz Rodenhurst in *A Bit of a Do*. In 1994 she starred with Peter Davison as hairdresser Sonia Drysdale in *Ain't Misbehavin'*. Amongst her other credits have been *The Caesars*, *The Persuaders!*, *Barlow at Large*, *The Sweeney*, *The Rivals of Sherlock Holmes*, *War and Peace*, *French Without Tears*, *Love Story*, *Shadow on the Sun*, *Scoop* and the Dennis Potter play *Visitors*.

PAL

Phase Alternate Line colour television system, developed in Germany and now in use throughout western Europe, except for France, which uses its own SECAM system. PAL, an adaptation of the American NTSC system (using 625 lines in the UK instead of the US 525, and with built-in colour correction), is also the standard in Brazil and China.

PALIN, MICHAEL (1943–)

Sheffield-born actor, comedian, writer and presenter, famously one of the *Monty Python* troupe but with many other strings to his bow. Amongst his first writing credits were sketches for *The Frost Report*, which brought Palin and his writing partner, Terry Jones, in touch with John Cleese, Graham Chapman and Eric Idle. They also scripted for John Bird's comedy, *A Series of Bird's* and *Marty*. In 1967 he appeared in *Twice a Fortnight*, a late-night sketch show, and was then

given the chance to shine in the wacky children's comedy *Do Not Adjust Your Set* (1967–69), working with Idle, Jones, Terry Gilliam, David Jason and Denise Coffey. This led to *The Complete and Utter History of Britain*, a spoof history series he compiled and presented with Jones in 1969. *Monty Python's Flying Circus*, the same year, was a natural progression. Whilst a serving Python, Palin continued to write elsewhere, with one of his regular outlets *The Two Ronnies*, and when the Python team decided to call it a day in 1974, his next TV project was *Ripping Yarns*, a send-up of *Boy's Own* tales, again in collaboration with Terry Jones. In the 1980s Palin drifted away from the small screen and focused more on cinema work. He was tempted back by the chance to emulate Phileas Fogg's attempt to go *Around the World in 80 Days*, for a 1988 BBC documentary series. It proved to be an enormous success and the accompanying book sold over half a million copies – enough to call for a 1991 sequel in which Palin dared to travel from *Pole to Pole*. In between, Palin demonstrated his straight drama skills with an acclaimed performance as schoolteacher Jim Nelson in Alan Bleasdale's *GBH*. Amongst his other credits have been *Great Railway Journeys of the World* (his was London to Kyle of Lochalsh), and the script for the nostalgic TV film *East of Ipswich*. Palin is also a director of Meridian Television, for whom he compiled *Palin's Column*, a documentary series about the Isle of Wight, and starred in *A Class Act* (alongside Tracey Ullman).

PALLISERS, THE

UK (BBC) Drama. BBC 2 1974

Lady Glencora McCluskie/Palliser	Susan Hampshire
Plantagenet Palliser MP	Philip Latham
Duke of Omnium	Ronald Culver
Lord Brentford	Lockwood West
Burgo Fitzgerald	Barry Justice
Phineas Finn	Donal McCann
Countess Midlothian	Fabia Drake
Gerald Maule	Jeremy Clyde
Mrs Hittaway	Penelope Keith
Frank Tregear	Jeremy Irons
Earl of Silverbridge	Anthony Andrews
Lord Fawn	Derek Jacobi
Alice Vavasor	Carole Mortimer
George Vavasor	Gary Watson
Laura Kennedy/Lady Laura Standish	Anna Massey
Lady Dumbello	Rachel Herbert
Marie Goeslar	Barbara Murray
Marchioness of Auld Reeke	Sonia Dresdel
Lizzie Eustace	Sarah Badel
Lady Mabel Grex	Anna Carteret
Reverend Emilius	Anthony Ainley
Barrington Erle	Moray Watson

Writer: Simon Raven. Producer: Martin Lisemore

Six of Anthony Trollope's novels merged into one TV series.

Tracing the rise to power of snooty Plantagenet Palliser, his arranged marriage to the flighty Lady Glencora, and ending with the political emergence of his son, the Earl of Silverbridge, this series followed the ups and downs of the wealthy Palliser family and their associates in Victorian times. This was a family of near-noble birth that strived for power under the Liberal banner, echoing Trollope's own parliamentary yearnings. Dwelling also on personalities, social conflicts and the battle for family supremacy, this dramatization became a reflection of life in Trollope's time. However, made up of 26 episodes, the series was badly disrupted by a BBC labour dispute in July 1974. When filming was finally completed, the Corporation was forced to repeat five earlier episodes to enable viewers to catch up on events. Consequently, although the first part went out in January, the much awaited finale did not arrive until November.

PALMER, GEOFFREY (1927–)

British actor, in a range of supporting and starring roles, usually of a lugubrious nature. In the 1970s, he played Jimmy, Reggie's brother-in-law in **The Fall and Rise of Reginald Perrin**, and Ben, Ria Parkinson's husband in **Butterflies**. Later, Palmer starred as Leo Bannister in Carla Lane's *The Last Song* and loony right-winger Major Harry Truscott in **Fairly Secret Army**. He also appeared as Donald Fairchild with Penelope Keith in *Executive Stress* and as Lionel Hardcastle with Judi Dench in **As Time Goes By**. In addition, Palmer has been seen in **The Avengers**, **Fawlty Towers**, **Doctor Who**, **Bergerac**, **Inspector Morse** and Dennis Potter's *Christabel*, as well as taking the roles of Field Marshall Haig in **Blackadder Goes Forth**, Harry Stringer in **Hot Metal** and the Foreign Secretary in **Whoops! Apocalypse**.

PALMER, TONY (1935–)

British writer, director, rock music critic and documentary maker. His early contributions included the sketch show Twice a Fortnight and teenage pop shows like *How It Is* and *How Late It Is*. These changed the way pop was presented on TV, using music as a background to arts features, politics and other world events. He produced *All My Loving* for **Omnibus** in 1968, which aimed to dispel the myth that rock stars were all delinquents, and has also contributed profiles of Benjamin Britten, Peter Sellers, William Walton, Stravinsky and Richard Burton. Palmer's **All You Need is Love**, a 13-part history of popular music, was screened in 1977.

PAN

The movement of a camera horizontally from left to right or vice-versa, as opposed to tilt which is its up and down manoeuvre.

PANORAMA
UK (BBC) Current Affairs. BBC 1 1953–

Presenters: Patrick Murphy, Max Robertson, Richard Dimbleby, James Mossman, Robin Day, Alastair Burnet, David Dimbleby, Charles Wheeler, Fred Emery, Robert Kee

Editors: Dennis Bardens, Michael Barsley, Rex Moorfoot, Michael Peacock, Paul Fox, David Wheeler, Jeremy Isaacs, John Grist, David J. Webster, Brian Wenham, Frank Smith, Christopher Capron, Roger Bolton, George Carey, Peter Ibbotson, David Dickinson, Tim Gardam, Robert Rowland, Peter Pagnamenta, Mark Thompson, Glenwyn Benson

The world's longest running current affairs programme.

Although noted today for its hard-hitting investigations and reports into matters of political and social concern, *Panorama* began in quite a different vein. It was launched in 1953 as a fortnightly magazine programme, with newspaper journalist Patrick Murphy who quickly made way for Max Robertson as host. Malcolm Muggeridge was the resident interviewer, Denis Mathews was the art critic, Nancy Spain reviewed books and Lionel Hale discussed events in the theatre. After two years, however, *Panorama* was completely revamped to become a 'window on the world'. In came respected commentator Richard Dimbleby and he fronted the programme through its glory days in the late 1950s and early 1960s. Other notable anchormen are listed above. Dimbleby's team included John Freeman (later of **Face to Face**) and Christopher Chataway. Later contributors included Michael Barratt, Trevor Philpott, Michael Charlton and Leonard Parkin.

As well as being noted for its longevity, *Panorama* has also provided some memorable items for the TV archives. In 1961 the Duke of Edinburgh became the first member of the royal family to be interviewed on television when quizzed by Richard Dimbleby. Four years earlier, on 1 April 1957, Dimbleby and his crew sprang a celebrated April Fools' prank on the viewing public, when it presented a documentary on the spaghetti harvest in southern Switzerland.

PARA HANDY – MASTER MARINER
UK (BBC) Comedy Drama. BBC 1959–60

Para Handy McFarlane ....Duncan Macrae

Dan Macphail ....John Grieve
Dougie...Roddy McMillan
Sunny Jim (Davey Green) ....Angus Lennie

Writer: Duncan Ross. Producer: Pharic
MacLaren

**Easy-going tales of a roguish merchant
seaman.**

The *Para Handy* stories written by Neil Munro
(initially under the pen name of Hugh Foulis in
1905 editions of the *Glasgow Evening News*) have
become some of the most televised pieces of literature. This series from the turn of the 1960s
featured Duncan Macrae as Captain Peter 'Para
Handy' McFarlane, the wily skipper of the tiny
Clyde steamer known as *The Vital Spark*, which
plied its trade along the lochs and channels of
western Scotland, delivering goods to isolated
communities. Para Handy was notoriously unreliable and his crew were equally inept.

Under the name of *The Vital Spark*, *Para Handy*
was revived for a *Comedy Playhouse* presentation
in 1965 and a series with the same title followed
a year later. Roddy McMillan took the lead role
in both and John Grieve was once again cast as
Macphail, the chief engineer. Walter Carr took
the part of Dougie the mate and cabin boy/cook
Sunny Jim was played by Alex McAvoy. The
series was revived again in 1974 and then completely recast for a 1994 version, *The Tales of Para
Handy*, starring Gregor Fisher as the boozy old
sea dog. Rikki Fulton was seen as Macphail, Sean
Scanlan as Dougie and Andrew Fairlie as Sunny
Jim. The stories were now set in the 1930s.

PARADISE CLUB, THE

UK (Zenith) Drama. BBC 1 1989–90

Danny Kane.......................................Leslie Grantham
Frank Kane.......................................Don Henderson
Detective Inspector Campbell ....Kitty Aldridge
Carol Kane.......................................Barbara Wilshere
Jonjo O'Brady ....Peter Gowen
Polish Joe ....Leon Herbert
Detective Inspector Sarah Turnbull ......Caroline Bliss
Detective Sgt Nesbit.............................Jack Galloway
Peter Noonan ....Philip Martin Brown

Creator/Writer: Murray Smith. Producer:
Selwyn Roberts

Two dodgy brothers run a seedy dance hall.

Brought together by the death of their mother (a
gangland chief), Danny and Frank Kane found
themselves proprietors of a drinking and dancing
den known as The Paradise Club and deeply
immersed in the activities of the East End underworld. Frank was a disgraced priest whilst Danny
was a yuppie family man living in the Docklands.
Two series were made of their murky adventures.

PARAS, THE

UK (BBC) Documentary. BBC 1 1983

Presenter/Writer: Glyn Worsnip

Executive Producer: David Harrison. Producer:
Bill Jones

**Fly-on-the-wall documentary featuring
recruits to the Parachute Regiment.**

This gruelling, seven-part look at military life
focused on 41 newcomers to 480 Recruit
Platoon of the Parachute Regiment. Recorded
over 22 weeks, it monitored the rookies as they
endured possibly the world's toughest military
training regime to obtain the right to wear the
famous red beret. The series witnessed the initial
41 being reduced in number week by week.

PARDON THE EXPRESSION

UK (Granada) Situation Comedy. ITV 1965–6

Leonard Swindley ....Arthur Lowe
Ernest Parbold ....Paul Dawkins
Miss Sinclair..Joy Stewart
Mrs Edgeley ....Betty Driver
Walter Hunt ....Robert Dorning

Executive Producer: H.V. Kershaw. Producers:
Harry Driver, Derek Granger

**A pompous draper joins a large chain
store and assumes extra responsibility.**

Having the honour of being the only spin-off
series from *Coronation Street*, *Pardon the
Expression* followed the fortunes of Leonard
Swindley, the teetotal, lay preaching, one-time
proprietor of Weatherfield's Gamma Garments
boutique. Mr Swindley was now assistant manager of a branch of the Dobson and Hawks chain
store, a position guaranteed to exaggerate his
pomposity. Ernest Parbold was his buck-passing
boss, Miss Sinclair was the staff manageress and
Mrs Edgeley (played by Betty Driver, the *Street*'s
future Betty Turpin) was in charge of the canteen. When Mr Parbold left after the first series,
Walter Hunt took his place.

Pardon the Expression, taking its name from Mr
Swindley's catchphrase of 'If you'll pardon the
expression', gave birth to a spin-off series of its
own, *Turn Out the Lights*, in which Swindley and
Hunt teamed up as a duo of amateur ghost
hunters. It was screened in 1967, shortly before
Arthur Lowe marched into *Dad's Army* and his
most celebrated role of Captain Mainwaring.

PARKER, FESS (1924–)

American actor, an instant hit as Disney's *Davy
Crockett*. Enjoying his American hero status,
Parker followed up with tales of another pioneer,

Daniel Boone, ten years later, donning a virtually identical buckskin outfit and racoon skin cap in the process.

PARKIN, LEONARD (1929–93)

British reporter and newscaster, with ITN for many years. Initially working as a newspaper journalist in his native Yorkshire, Parkin joined the BBC news team in 1954, later becoming its Canadian and then Washington correspondent. As such, he was the first British reporter to break the news of President Kennedy's assassination. For the BBC, he also worked on *Panorama* and *24 Hours*. In 1967 the year that *News At Ten* was launched, he switched to ITN, for whom he also presented election programmes and later the lunchtime news (*First Report* and *News at One*) and *News at 5.45*, eventually leaving in 1987.

PARKINSON, MICHAEL (1935–)

Undoubtedly king of the chat shows in the 1970s, Yorkshireman Michael Parkinson's career began in newspaper journalism, graduating to work for Granada, where he contributed to local news magazines, *World in Action*, *What the Papers Say* and *Cinema*. He then joined the BBC's *24 Hours* team and produced sports documentaries for LWT, before embarking on his 11-year run as host of *Parkinson*, BBC 1's extremely popular Saturday night chat show in 1971. In 1983, he became one of TV-am's Famous Five, largely working on the weekend output, and later sharing the limelight with his wife, Mary. Parkinson has since chaired the game shows *Give Us a Clue* and *All Star Secrets*, and worked on *The Help Squad*.

PARSONS, NICHOLAS (1928–)

British actor and presenter, first seen on TV in guest roles in series like *The Adventures of Robin Hood* and, more prominently, as stooge to Arthur Haynes, Eric Barker and, later, Benny Hill. At the same time, he was providing the voice for Gerry Anderson's puppet cowboy, Tex Tucker, in *Four Feather Falls*, and pursuing a bright career in British film comedies. In the 1970s, Parsons hosted the remarkably popular quiz show *Sale of the Century*, appeared in the American sitcom *The Ugliest Girl in Town* and, in 1994, chaired a TV version of his successful radio series *Just a Minute*. His has also been a familiar face on panel games and Parsons has never been afraid to mock his own smooth, sugary image with cameo roles in *The Comic Strip Presents*, *The New Statesman* and other comedies, plus the late-night game show *The Alphabet Quiz*.

PARTRIDGE FAMILY, THE

US (Screen Gems) Situation Comedy. BBC 1
1971

Shirley Partridge ....Shirley Jones
Keith Partridge ....David Cassidy
Laurie Partridge ....Susan Dey
Danny Partridge ....Danny Bonaduce
Christopher Partridge....................Jeremy Gelbwaks
....Brian Forster
Tracy Partridge ....Suzanne Crough
Reuben Kinkaid ....Dave Madden

Creator: Bernard Slade. Executive Producer: Bob Claver

Life at home and on the road with a family pop group.

When suburban widow Shirley Partridge casually joined her children's band as a singer, little did she know that a career as a pop star beckoned. Putting together a song called 'I Think I Love You' in the family's garage-cum-rehearsal room, the group sold the track to a record company. It became a hit and turned the family into top performers. Climbing aboard a painted up old school bus, Shirley and her kids then headed off on tour across America from their home in San Pueblo, California. Apart from Mom, the family consisted of 16-year-old Keith, 15-year-old Laurie, freckly Danny, aged ten (who organized the band), Chris, aged seven, and five-year-old Tracy. Their agent (who disliked children) was Reuben Kinkaid. The family had a dog called Simone.

Like The Monkees before them, The Partridge Family grew into a real-life pop group and had hits on both sides of the Atlantic. However, they never claimed to perform on the actual recordings, apart from vocals by Shirley Jones and David Cassidy. Their biggest hits in Britain were cover versions of 1960s classics like ''Breaking Up Is Hard To Do', 'Looking Through the Eyes of Love' and 'Walking In The Rain'. David Cassidy quickly outgrew the series, branching out on his own and becoming one of the 1970s' first teenage idols. Shirley Jones was his real life stepmother. *The Partridge Family* was inspired by the experiences of the Cowsills, a Rhode Island family of a mom and her kids who had American hits in the 1960s.

PASTRY, MR see Hearne, Richard.

PATHFINDERS

UK (ABC) Children's Science Fiction. ITV
1960–1

Professor Wedgwood ....Peter Williams
Conway Henderson ....Gerald Flood
Geoffrey Wedgwood ....Stewart Guidotti

Valerie Wedgwood	Gillian Ferguson
Jimmy Wedgwood	Richard Dean
Professor Mary Meadows	Pamela Barney
Harcourt Brown	George Coulouris
Margaret Henderson	Hester Cameron
Ian Murray	Hugh Evans
Captain Wilson	Graydon Gould

Creators: Malcolm Hulke, Eric Paice. Producer: Sydney Newman

Escapades in outer space with the pioneering Wedgwood family.

Following on from an adventure in six parts, which went out under the programme title *Target Luna*, this series featured three more adventures for this early space family: *Pathfinders in Space*, *Pathfinders to Mars* and *Pathfinders to Venus* were all broadcast as part of ITV's Sunday *Family Hour*.

In *Target Luna* (incidentally with a completely different cast), Professor Wedgwood had successfully managed to send his son, Jimmy, and pet hamster, Hamlet, into lunar orbit and back. In the first of the *Pathfinders* stories, the scientist and his family went a step further and actually landed on the moon. Despite being stranded on the surface and facing alien threats, they eventually escaped back home. In the second story the destination was Mars. Again fraught with danger, and despite unexpected outside interference, the expedition was once more a success. The third tale picked up from the return journey to Earth and involved the rescue of a rival astronaut from the planet Venus under the gaze of menacing pterodactyls and an erupting volcano. As well as members of the Wedgwood family, the adventures involved several other transient characters, in particular science reporter Conway Henderson and Professor Meadows, the leading female authority on space.

Pathfinders was produced by future **Doctor Who** creator Sydney Newman, and partly devised by Malcolm Hulke, writer of *Doctor Who* and **Crossroads** stories amongst other TV work. Although somewhat crude, the series was itself a pathfinder for children's science fiction television.

PAUL TEMPLE

UK (BBC/Taurus) Detective Drama. BBC 1
1969–71

Paul Temple	Francis Matthews
Steve Temple	Ros Drinkwater

Creator: Francis Durbridge. Producers: Alan Bromly, Peter Bryant, Derrick Sherwin

A writer of detective novels is also a part-time private eye.

Paul Temple, aged 35, impeccably bred, suave, cool and sophisticated, was also amazingly wealthy. Living in a swish Chelsea apartment with his wife, Steve, he needed to write only one book a year to maintain his extravagant lifestyle. Consequently, the couple spent the rest of their time touring Britain and Europe, using Paul's finely-honed analytical mind to root out international criminals. Temple drove a Rolls Royce Silver Shadow Coupé and thoroughly enjoyed his opulent existence, but he abhorred violence of all kinds.

The character of Paul Temple was created by writer Francis Durbridge back in the 1930s, and the inspiration is said to have been a fellow passenger on a train, who looked like a private detective. By 1938 Paul Temple had appeared on BBC Radio, conceived as a Canadian-born, Rugby School- and Oxford-educated son of an army officer. With some three dozen novels to his name, Temple had turned to amateur detection, helping out Scotland Yard with some of their more baffling crimes, and had met up with Steve Trent, a Fleet Street journalist whom he went on to marry. Six actors played the role on radio but some critics have suggested that the TV version (one of the BBC's first colour productions) was tailor-made for the urbane Francis Matthews.

PAXMAN, JEREMY (1950–)

Yorkshire-born journalist and presenter, frontman of **Newsnight** and previously a reporter in Northern Ireland. Amongst his other credits have been **Panorama**, **Tonight**, **Breakfast Time**, *The Six O'Clock News* and regional programmes. Paxman took over from Ludovic Kennedy as chairman of the review programme **Did You See . . . ?** and has since been questionmaster in the revival of **University Challenge**.

PAY PER VIEW

A system devised to allow viewers to watch certain additional programmes (films, sporting events, etc.) on the payment of an on-the-spot fee. Whereas the primitive concept looked at coins and slots as a method of payment, today's sophisticated technology uses telephones, credit cards and invoices. It has already been employed by cable channels in the USA.

PEACOCK, MICHAEL (1929–)

British news and current affairs producer (**Panorama**, etc.) who joined the BBC as a trainee in 1952 was given the responsibility of launching BBC 2 in 1964. He later became Controller of BBC 1 and then briefly worked for LWT. After some time as an independent producer and consultant, Peacock joined Warner Brothers for a few years in the 1970s.

PEAK PRACTICE

UK (Central) Drama. ITV 1993–

Dr Jack Kerruish	Kevin Whately
Dr Beth Glover	Amanda Burton
Dr Will Preston	Simon Shepherd
Sarah Preston	Jacqueline Leonard
Dr Daniel Acres	Tom Beard
Dr John Reginald	Andrew Ray
Kim Beardsmore	Esther Coles
Ellie Ndebala	Sharon Hinds
Isabel de Gines	Sylvia Syms
James White	Richard Platt
Chloe White	Hazel Ellerby
Sandy	Melanie Thaw
Trevor Sharpe	Shaun Prendergast
Alice North	Margery Mason
Francine Sinclair	Veronica Quilligan
Andrew Attwood	Gary Mavers

Creator: Lucy Gannon. Producers: Tony Virgo, Michele Buck

Fresh from working in deepest Africa, an ambitious doctor becomes a partner in a Derbyshire general practice.

Dr Jack Kerruish was disillusioned with city life and city medicine. Having enjoyed a fulfilling three years establishing a medical centre in Africa, he returned to London in search of a new career direction. He wanted to join a country practice and was eventually accepted into a somewhat wobbly partnership in the Peak District village of Cardale. His colleagues were Beth Glover and Will Preston, two local doctors who had decided to keep their independence and fight on in their dilapidated surgery when threatened by competition from a new, flashy health centre. Kerruish's financial input was important, but he also brought new technology and dynamism to the practice. However, Kerruish soon found that, if the city had its problems, so did the country, as he came face to face with the everyday hardships of rural life and the emotional problems of the local community. There was also the practice to re-establish, the bank to stave off, and the rival health centre to keep an eye on.

Kerruish was very much his own man. Sometimes selfish and insensitive, he found himself often at odds with his partners, even though he became romantically linked with Beth and, by the end of the second series, seen in 1994, they had been married. In the third series, a year later, Kerruish's wanderlust had returned and he set out once more on an assignment in Africa. At the time of writing, plans were being laid for a fourth series, but without its stars Kevin Whately and Amanda Burton, who had decided to leave.

PEAK TIME/PRIME TIME

The hours when TV audiences are at their greatest, and so the time of day of particular importance to advertisers. Known generally as peak time in the UK, the hours are 7.00–10.30 pm. Prime time in the USA covers 7.30–11 pm.

PEARSON, NEIL

British actor, best-known as hot-headed CIB detective Tony Clark in **Between the Lines** and newsroom romeo Dave Charnley in **Drop the Dead Donkey**. Other credits have included *Chelmsford 123*, *That's Love*, *Les Girls*, *This is David Lander* and the single drama *Oi For England*.

PEASGOOD, JULIE

Blonde British actress with a host of drama and sitcom credits to her name. Amongst the most notable parts have been Fran in **Brookside**, Roxy in **September Song**, Eden in **Luv** and Anne in **First Born**. Others have included *Survivors*, *Seven Faces of Woman*, *Clayhanger*, **Lord Peter Wimsey**, **Boon**, **Taggart**, **Brush Strokes**, **2 Point 4 Children**, *Van der Valk*, *The 10%ers*, **Spender**, *Chandler & Co.* and **Perfect Scoundrels**. She has been TV critic for *Good Morning With Anne and Nick* and has been heard on countless television commercials.

PEBBLE MILL AT ONE/PEBBLE MILL

UK (BBC) Magazine. BBC 1 1972–86; 1991–

Presenters:
Bob Langley
Tom Coyne
Marian Foster
David Seymour
Donny MacLeod
Jan Leeming
Bob Hall
Tony Francis
Philip Tibenham
Jonathan Fulford
Marjorie Lofthouse
David Freeman
Paul Gambaccini
Anna Ford
Paul Coia
Josephine Buchan
Magnus Magnusson

Producers: Roy Ronnie, Roger Ecclestone, Roger Laughton, Malcolm Nisbet, Jim Dumighan, Peter Hercombe

Light-hearted early afternoon magazine.

This frivolous lunchtime filler was the BBC's response to ITV's new afternoon series like **Crown Court** and **Emmerdale Farm**. Broadcast live from the foyer of Pebble Mill, the BBC's Birmingham TV centre, it featured music, celebrity interviews, fashion items, gardening with Peter Seabrook, and cookery with Michael Smith and Glyn Christian. The title was shortened to *Pebble Mill* in later years and a few spin-off programmes were created. *Saturday Night at the Mill* ran from 1976, Norman Vaughan hosted *Pebble Mill Showcase* in 1978 and *Pebble Mill on Sunday* appeared in 1979. Although cancelled in 1986 to make way for the *One O'Clock News* and programmes like *Neighbours*, the series has since been revived as part of the BBC's daytime package. Hosted by Judi Spiers, Alan Titchmarsh, Gloria Hunniford and Ross King, it is now more of a chat show and comes from a studio rather than the entrance hall.

PENHALIGON, SUSAN (1950–)

British actress born in the Philippines who has enjoyed a number of prominent roles on television. Most notably, she was Prue Sorenson in Andrea Newman's *Bouquet of Barbed Wire* in 1976 and in 1987 starred in Fay Weldon's *Heart of the Country*. She was Helen, Judi Dench's sister in *A Fine Romance*, guested in *Public Eye*, *Upstairs*, *Downstairs*, *Country Matters*, *Remington Steele* and *Bergerac*, and has also appeared in single dramas like Jack Rosenthal's *Polly Put the Kettle On* and the BBC's 1977 adaptation of *Count Dracula*. More recently, Penhaligon has been seen as Julia Charlesworth, Richard O'Sullivan's wife in *Trouble in Mind*.

PENNIES FROM HEAVEN

UK (BBC) Drama. BBC 1 1978

Arthur Parker...Bob Hoskins
Eileen...Cheryl Campbell
Joan Parker..Gemma Craven
The Accordian Man ....Kenneth Colley
Tom ....Hywel Bennett
The Headmaster ....Freddie Jones
The Inspector ....Dave King

Writer: Dennis Potter. Producer: Kenith Trodd.

An unhappily married sheet music salesman finds life is not as kind as his songs make out.

Arthur Parker, an itinerant song-plugger and music salesman, really loved his music. Given the chance he would drift away from his fractious marriage and into the fantasy world of song lyrics. A meeting with a young teacher named Eileen led him to be unfaithful to his wife, Joan, but the consequences of his actions came home to haunt him in a nightmare of abortion and prostitution set against the backdrop of the 1930s Depression.

What was innovative about *Pennies from Heaven* was the use of contemporary 1930s tunes to underpin the plot, their banal words given new meaning when contrasted with the various goings-on. As in Hollywood pictures, the actors suddenly broke into song and dance, but this time merely mimed to the original recordings. Sometimes, men mimed to women's voices and vice-versa. It was a technique which Dennis Potter re-employed in *The Singing Detective* eight years later and again in the third part of his musical trilogy, *Lipstick on your Collar*, in 1993. A film version of *Pennies from Heaven*, also scripted by Potter and starring Steve Martin and Bernadette Peters, was made in 1981.

PENTELOW, ARTHUR (1924–91)

Northern actor known to viewers as *Emmerdale's* Henry Wilks for 19 years, having previously been seen in the football soap *United!* (as the supporters' club chairman Dan Davis) and plenty of other series, including *Emergency – Ward 10*, *Z Cars*, *The Troubleshooters*, *Armchair Theatre*, *Hadleigh*, *Budgie* and *Coronation Street* (as park-keeper George Greenwood).

PEPPARD, GEORGE (1928–)

American actor, popular in the cinema in the 1960s, after making his TV debut a decade earlier, in series like *Alfred Hitchcock Presents*. In the 1970s Peppard returned to the small screen, taking the role of *Mystery Movie* detective *Banacek*. Two years into the series, he moved onto another prime-time drama, *Doctors' Hospital*, but left a year later. He then played Blake Carrington in the pilot for *Dynasty*, but was not given the series role and, just when it seemed that his career was petering out, up popped the character of cigar-chomping *A-Team* leader Colonel John 'Hannibal' Smith, which made him a great favourite with youngsters all over the world. The series ran for four years from 1983. Peppard has also been seen in numerous TV movies.

PERFECT SCOUNDRELS

UK (TVS) Comedy Drama. ITV 1990–2

Guy Buchanan ....Peter Bowles
Harry Cassidy ....Bryan Murray

Creators: Peter Bowles, Bryan Murray.
Executive Producer: Graham Benson.
Producers: Tim Aspinall, Terence Williams, Tony Virgo

Two sophisticated conmen team up to swindle shadier members of society.

Meeting at the funeral of a master conman, suave Guy Buchanan and rough diamond Harry Cassidy were coaxed into joining forces to avenge the death of their old ally. Executing an elaborate sting on the alleged murderer, the two lovable rogues discovered themselves swindled when the 'dead' man took care of the proceeds. However, realizing how well they performed in tandem, Guy and Harry made their double act permanent, despite personal differences which threatened their partnership. For instance, Harry, an Irish parrot fancier, lacked vital discipline, which angered the smooth-talking Guy, and an element of mutual distrust pervaded their business dealings. They worked as latter-day Robin Hoods, for the most part only picking on those who ripped off others. The third and final season, though, showed the perfect scoundrels in a new light, as they occasionally targeted less deserving victims.

Actors Peter Bowles and Bryan Murray, who had worked together in *The Irish RM*, devised this series as a vehicle for their own talents.

PERRIE, LYNNE (JEAN DUDLEY; 1931–)

Pint-sized, Yorkshire-born actress and cabaret performer, Perrie played Ivy Tilsley/Brennan in *Coronation Street* from 1979 until written out in 1994. Previously, Perrie (sister of comic/actor Duggie Brown) had been seen in series like *Queenie's Castle* (as Mrs Petty), *Crown Court* and *Follyfoot*, as well as in a number of single dramas, such as *Leeds United* and Slattery's *Mounted Foot*.

PERRY, JIMMY (1923–)

OBE British actor and comedy scriptwriter, usually in collaboration with David Croft, with whom he created the doyen of British sitcoms, *Dad's Army* (based on his own misadventures as a youth in the Home Guard). With Croft, Perry went on to script other comedy favourites like *It Ain't Half Hot Mum* (echoing his time as a Royal Artillery concert party manager), *Hi-De-Hi!* (Perry was a Butlins redcoat) and *You Rang, M'Lord?* Perry also penned *The Gnomes of Dulwich*, *Lollipop Loves Mr Mole*, *Room Service* and, with Robin Carr, wrote the shopkeeping sitcom *High St Blues*.

PERRY MASON

US (Paisano) Legal Drama. BBC 1 1961–7
New series in 1990s

Perry Mason	Raymond Burr
Della Street	Barbara Hale
Paul Drake	William Hopper
Hamilton Burger	William Talman
Lt Arthur Tragg	Ray Collins
Lt Anderson	Wesley Lau
Lt Steve Drumm	Richard Anderson

Creator: Erle Stanley Gardner. Executive Producers: Gail Patrick Jackson, Arthur Marks. Producers: Ben Brady, Art Seid, Sam White

The cases of an almost invincible Los Angeles defence barrister.

Created by writer-lawyer Erle Stanley Gardner in 1933, defence attorney Perry Mason was remarkable. His brilliant analytical mind, his vast experience in the legal field, and his finely-honed powers of advocacy enabled him to succeed in even the most hopeless cases. With any other barrister, dozens of defendants would have gone straight to the electric chair. With Perry Mason, not only were they acquitted but the real culprits were unearthed. Admirably supported by his loyal and efficient secretary, Della Street, and his hardworking case investigator, Paul Drake, Mason was virtually unbeatable. It's true that he did, in fact, lose three cases, but all had mitigating circumstances, such as the defendant who refused to give evidence to clear her name.

Mason's technique was based on methodical, painstaking collation of all the evidence, relying heavily on Drake's ability to dig up some new facts. Very often the vital clues did not arrive until the last minute, with Drake charging into the courtroom to pass the information to his burly boss. It was then that Mason's verbal skills were put to the test, to extract a confession from one of the witnesses, or even one of the spectators. All this was particularly frustrating for prosecuting attorney Hamilton Burger, Mason's chief adversary, and the testifying police officer, Lt Tragg (later replaced by Lt Drumm). And just in case the audience had not been able to keep up with events, Perry, Paul and Della gathered together in the finale to talk through and explain each case.

In the very last episode, *The Case of the Final Fade-Out*, creator Erle Stanley Gardner guest-starred as the judge. However, the series was revived in 1973 under the title of *The New Perry Mason*, with Monte Markham in the lead role. It bombed, but Raymond Burr picked up the reins again for a 1985 TV movie that saw Della accused of murder and Perry leaving his new-found place on the judges' panel to defend her. An intermittent run of feature-length episodes followed, in which Mason was assisted by Della and Paul Drake Jnr, son of the original investigator (actor William Hopper had died and Barbara Hale's real-life son, William Katt, was drafted in to do the running around). Drake was later replaced by Ken Malansky, played by William R. Moses. William Talman, who had played Ham Burger, had also died and Mason now encountered a new opponent in Michael Reston, played by *M*A*S*H*'s Major Winchester, David Ogden Stiers.

PERSUADERS!, THE

UK (Tribune/ITC) Adventure. ITV 1971–2

Danny Wilde ....Tony Curtis
Lord Brett Sinclair ....Roger Moore
Judge Fulton ....Laurence Naismith

Creator/Producer: Robert S. Baker

Two playboys tackle corruption amongst the jet-set.

Danny Wilde was a rough diamond, a fun-loving American from the streets of Brooklyn. But he was also rich. Through skilful buying and selling of oil stocks, he had made himself into a multi-millionaire. In contrast, Lord Brett Sinclair had found things rather easy. Born into the English aristocracy and heir to a fortune, he had never needed to work. Together, they comprised an unlikely team of investigators, tracking down villains in the glamour spots of the world.

Their liaison stemmed from a party on the French Riviera, at which they had both been guests. There they were coerced by a retired judge named Fulton into joining his fight for justice. He wanted them to use their spare time and many millions to help him catch those criminals who fell through the usual legal nets, realizing they could work in places where conventional detectives could not go. Wilde and Sinclair took up the challenge as a bit of a lark, enjoying visiting Europe's highspots, wining and dining in all the best places and meeting scores of beautiful women along the way. As they came from totally different backgrounds and upbringings, the rapport between the two stars was one of the keystones of the programme.

Glossy and expensively-produced, *The Persuaders!* was deliberately aimed at the American market. Sadly, it failed to take off in the States and didn't last long in Britain as a result. The theme music, by John Barry, was a Top 20 hit in the UK in 1971.

PERTWEE, BILL (1926–)

British actor, usually in comic roles and best remembered as the obnoxious ARP Warden Hodges in *Dad's Army*. He has also been seen in other Jimmy Perry and David Croft productions, including *You Rang, M'Lord*, as the scrounging policeman PC Wilson. He had earlier played another policeman, in the Sid James/Victor Spinetti sitcom *Two in Clover* and amongst his other credits are parts in the comedies *Sykes*, *Billy Liar*, *Chance in a Million* and *Tom, Dick and Harriet*. Bill is the cousin of Jon Pertwee.

PERTWEE, JON (JOHN PERTWEE; 1919–)

British actor, much heard in BBC radio comedy in the postwar years and also making a few inroads into the cinema. However, it was television that gave Pertwee his finest hours. In 1970 he took over one of the classic roles on UK TV, namely that of *Doctor Who*, succeeding Patrick Troughton. It was a role he played for four years. Pertwee was largely responsible himself for his next major series. He recalled Barbara Euphan Todd's *Worzel Gummidge* books and sold the concept of a series to Southern Television, securing himself the role of the famous talking scarecrow in the process. When Southern lost its ITV franchise, production stopped, but Pertwee proceeded to make further episodes in New Zealand, entitled *Worzel Gummidge Down Under*. His other credits have been as varied as the panel game *Whodunnit?* (as host), *Six-Five Special*, *Jackanory*, *The Avengers*, *The Goodies* and a 1946 version of *Toad of Toad Hall*, in which he played the Judge. He is the cousin of actor Bill Pertwee, brother of playwright Michael Pertwee and father of actor Sean Pertwee. Jon's first wife was *Upstairs, Downstairs* star Jean Marsh.

PETERS, SYLVIA

British television personality of the 1940s and 1950s, working as one of the BBC's on-screen continuity announcers (in rota with Mary Malcolm and McDonald Hobley). She joined the Corporation in 1947, making use of her talents as a former dancer to also introduce *Television Dancing Club* with Victor Sylvester and *Come Dancing* in its formative years. For children's television she read the *Bengo* stories. Peters eventually left the BBC to freelance for commercial television.

PETROCELLI

US (Paramount) Legal Drama. BBC 1 1978–9

Tony Petrocelli.......................................Barry Newman
Maggie Petrocelli.................................Susan Howard
Pete Ritter ....Albert Salmi
Lt John Ponce.................................David Huddleston

Creators: Sidney J. Furie, Harold Buchman, E. Jack Neuman. Executive Producers: Thomas L. Miller, Edward J. Milkis

A Harvard-educated lawyer of Italian descent opens a legal practice for ranchers.

Tony Petrocelli and his wife, Maggie, had given up their lucrative city life and moved west into the fictitious town of San Remo, setting up home in a camper-van. Having hired ranch hand Pete Ritter as an investigator, Petrocelli opened up a legal practice, providing help for the local cattle-farmers. Unfortunately, his sophisticated eastern methods were not always appreciated and many clients could not afford to pay him at the end of the day. As a result, the Petrocellis were not the richest attorney family in America. Lt Ponce was Tony's friend, despite being the police officer who worked against him on many cases.

Based on the 1970 film, *The Lawyer*, in which Barry Newman played the part of Petrocelli, the series was innovative in using flashback sequences to show how crimes had occurred from the viewpoints of various characters. It was filmed in Tucson, Arizona.

PETTIFER, JULIAN (1935–)

British journalist and presenter working for programmes like *Tonight*, *Panorama* and *24 Hours* after appearing on Southern Television. As well as award-winning reports from the Vietnam War and a raft of documentaries and various nature programmes, Pettifer has also hosted *Biteback* (the BBC viewers' response programme) and the quiz *Busman's Holiday* and contributed to *Assignment*.

PEYTON PLACE

US (Twentieth Century-Fox) Drama. ITV 1965–

Constance Mackenzie/Carson	Dorothy Malone
	Lola Albright
Allison Mackenzie	Mia Farrow
Dr Michael Rossi	Ed Nelson
Leslie Harrington	Paul Langton
Rodney Harrington	Ryan O'Neal
Norman Harrington	Christopher Connelly
Matthew Swain	Warner Anderson
Betty Anderson/Harrington/Cord/Harrington	
	Barbara Parkins
Julie Anderson	Kasey Rogers
George Anderson	Henry Beckman
Dr Robert Morton	Kent Smith
Steven Cord	James Douglas
Hannah Cord	Ruth Warrick
Elliott Carson	Tim O'Connor
Eli Carson	Frank Ferguson
Nurse Choate	Erin O'Brien-Moore
Dr Clair Morton	Mariette Hartley
Dr Vincent Markham	Leslie Nielsen
Rita Jacks/Harrington	Patricia Morrow
Ada Jacks	Evelyn Scott
Mrs Dowell	Heather Angel
Stella Chernak	Lee Grant
Gus Chernak	Bruce Gordon
Dr Russ Gehring	David Canary
DA John Fowler	John Kerr
Marian Fowler	Joan Blackman
Martin Peyton	George Macready
	Wilfred Hyde-White
Sandy Webber	Lana Wood
Chris Webber	Gary Haynes
Lee Webber	Stephen Oliver
Rachael Welles	Leigh Taylor-Young
Jack Chandler	John Kellogg
Adrienne Van Leyden	Gena Rowlands
Eddie Jacks	Dan Duryea

Carolyn Russell	Elizabeth 'Tippy' Walker
Fred Russell	Joe Maross
Marsha Russell	Barbara Rush
Reverend Tom Winter	Bob Hogan
Susan Winter	Diana Hyland
Dr Harry Miles	Percy Rodriguez
Alma Miles	Ruby Dee
Lew Miles	Glynn Turman
Jill Smith/Rossi	Joyce Jillson

Creator/Producer: Paul Monash

The inhabitants of a small New England town have many dark secrets to hide.

Based on the novel by Grace Metalious, which had already been adapted for two feature films, *Peyton Place* found its way to the small screen courtesy of the success of *Coronation Street* in the UK. Realizing that a TV soap opera could be sustained in prime time on a twice-a-week basis, and was not just worthy of daytime filler status, producer Paul Monash took up Metalious's tale of sexual intrigue and closet skeletons to develop this hugely successful series. It turned out to be the programme which made stars of Ryan O'Neal and Mia Farrow, and was the first American soap to be sold to Britain.

The setting for the series was the small, fictitious town of Peyton Place in New England. The central characters were bookstore-keeper Constance MacKenzie and her illegitimate daughter, Allison, who was romantically involved with Rodney Harrington, the son of wealthy mill manager Leslie Harrington. There was also handsome, young GP Mike Rossi (Constance's heartthrob), Betty Anderson (Rodney's wife on two occasions, who, in-between, married drunken lawyer Stephen Cord), and Elliot Carson (Allison's secret father who spent 18 years in prison and who later ran the town newspaper). Throughout the show's run, well over a hundred actors and actresses were introduced, and the storyline wandered from trivial family scandals and illicit romances right through to sensational murders and nail-biting court cases.

The most significant event in the show's early years was the disappearance of Allison MacKenzie. When Mia Farrow left the series, her character was written out, lost on a foggy night. Other notable storylines saw Rodney acquitted of murder, the marriage of Norman Harrington (Rodney's younger brother) to Rita Jacks, daughter of barkeeper Ada Jacks, and the death and funeral of the town's father figure, Rodney's mill-owning grandfather, Martin Peyton. When the series ended, Mike Rossi was in the dock, on trial for murder, and Rodney was confined to a wheelchair.

Viewers of re-runs may be confused by seeing Lola Allbright as Constance MacKenzie in some early episodes. She temporarily replaced Dorothy Malone who was seriously ill. Wilfred Hyde-White did the same for George Macready, the actor who played Martin Peyton. *Return to Peyton Place*, a daytime sequel employing different actors, reached US screens in 1971, and several members of the original cast resurfaced in a couple of TV movies, *Murder in Peyton Place* (1977) and *Peyton Place: The Next Generation* (1985).

PHIL SILVERS SHOW, THE

US (CBS) Situation Comedy. BBC 1957–60

M/Sgt Ernest T. Bilko	Phil Silvers
Cpl Rocco Barbella	Harvey Lembeck
Cpl Henshaw	Allan Melvin
Colonel John Hall	Paul Ford
Pte Duane Doberman	Maurice Gosfield
Pte Sam Fender	Herbie Faye
Sgt Rupert Ritzik	Joe E. Ross
Pte Dino Paparelli	Billy Sands
Pte Zimmerman	Mickey Freeman
Mrs Nell Hall	Hope Sansberry
Sgt Grover	Jimmy Little
Sgt Joan Hogan	Elisabeth Fraser

Creator/Writer: Nat Hiken

A sharp-witted, scheming sergeant is head of a US Army platoon.

Master Sgt Ernie Bilko was an inmate of the fictitious Fort Baxter army camp, near Roseville, Kansas (and later at Camp Freemont, California), although inmate is probably not the right word. Nominal head of the base was Colonel John Hall, but it was Bilko who pulled all the strings, certainly as far as his own comfortable lifestyle was concerned. Not many army sergeants could sleep in late, come and go as they pleased, avoid physical labour or drive around in their CO's car. But not every sergeant was Sgt Bilko.

This balding, bespectacled motor pool NCO was the master of the money-making scam. He'd bet on anything, from drill competitions to shooting practices. If a good singer turned up in his platoon, he'd use him to win a choir contest or secretly tape his voice to sell to a record company. He had an eagle eye for losers and set out to take them to the cleaners. However, his best-laid plans often backfired, mostly because, behind his brash exterior, Bilko was too kind-hearted and couldn't go through with the kill.

Assisting Bilko with his schemes were his corporals, Barbella and Henshaw, and his inept company of enlisted men, most notably the fat, dozy Doberman (regularly employed as a fall guy) and the pessimistic Pte Fender. Although loyal to Bilko, the platoon was also wary of its sergeant, knowing his conniving ways, but, in fairness, Bilko was always very protective of his boys. One of his easier preys was the superstitious Mess Sgt Ritzik, another compulsive gambler.

The series comprised a run of poker games, betting coups and other outrageous money-making ventures, all doomed to failure. But the highlight was quick-thinking, smooth-talking Bilko himself, who could extricate himself from the tightest of corners with a phoney smile, a sackful of charm and a few empty promises. Joan Hogan provided Bilko's romantic interest, although he was not averse to flattering Mrs Hall, the Colonel's wife, if it opened a few doors.

Originally titled *You'll Never Get Rich* when first screened in America, *The Phil Silvers Show* has also been billed as *Sgt Bilko*. It has enjoyed re-run after re-run all over the world and helped establish many careers, especially amongst its writers, who included creator Nat Hiken and future playwright Neil Simon. The show also gave opportunities to up and coming young actors like Dick Van Dyke and Alan Alda (the casting director for the series was ex-World Boxing Champion Rocky Graziano, whose real name, incidentally, was Rocco Barbella, the same as one of Bilko's corporals). Maurice Gosfield, who played Doberman, later provided the voice for Benny the Ball in the Bilko cartoon spoof *Boss/Top Cat*.

Four years after the series ended, Phil Silvers resurfaced in the role of Harry Grafton, a devious factory foreman in *The New Phil Silvers Show*, but the programme only lasted one season.

PHILBIN, MAGGIE (1955–)

Manchester-born presenter, coming to light on *Multi-Coloured Swap Shop*, on which she appeared with Keith Chegwin, whom she later married. Philbin later added a scientific dimension to her work, presenting *Tomorrow's World*, *Hospital Watch* and *Bodymatters Roadshow*.

PHILIP MARLOWE

US (ABC) Detective Drama. BBC 1960

Philip Marlowe	Philip Carey

Raymond Chandler's famous detective given a rather smoother edge.

This TV portrayal of Chandler's celebrated gumshoe transformed Marlowe from a rough diamond into a softer, more gentlemanly type. His name and his devoutly independent status were the only echoes of the hard-bitten character made famous by Humphrey Bogart. A truer interpretation followed in 1984, in *Marlowe – Private Eye*, a five-episode LWT series starring Powers Boothe. Six more episodes, again featuring Boothe, were made in Canada in 1986.

PHILLIPS, CONRAD (CONRAD PHILIP HAVORD; 1925–)

One of British TV's first action heroes, Conrad Phillips played the title role in *The Adventures of William Tell* in 1958. Previously, apart from small parts in series like *The Count of Monte Cristo* and *The New Adventures of Charlie Chan*, Phillips had worked in the theatre and it was to the stage that he returned for most of the 1960s. He resurfaced to play Robert Malcolm in *The Newcomers* and, in the 1970s and 1980s, was a guest on numerous series, from *Sutherland's Law*, *Cribb*, *The Adventures of Sherlock Holmes* and *Howards' Way* to *Fawlty Towers*, *Never the Twain*, *The Gaffer* and *Sorry!* He appeared in the 1973 drama *The Man Who Was Hunting Himself*, played NY Estates's MD Christopher Meadows in *Emmerdale Farm* and was also seen in children's dramas like *Into the Labyrinth*, mini-series like *The Master of Ballantrae* and TV movies such as *Arch of Triumph*. He was back in William Tell country in the late 1980s for a French-American version entitled *Crossbow*, in which he played Tell's mentor, Stefan.

PHILLIPS, SIÂN (1934–)

Welsh actress, winning much acclaim for her portrayal of the manipulative Livia in *I, Claudius*. She also played Clemmie in *Winston Churchill – The Wilderness Years*, George Smiley's wife Ann in *Tinker, Tailor, Soldier, Spy* and *Smiley's People*, and appeared in the dramas *Siwan* (in the title role), *How Green Was My Valley* (as Beth Morgan), *Shoulder To Shoulder* (as Emmeline Pankhurst), *Jennie, Lady Randolph Churchill* (as Mrs Patrick Campbell), *Warrior Queen* (as Boudicca) and *Crime and Punishment* (as Katerina Ivanova). Amongst her other offerings have been *The Quiet Man*, *Heartbreak House*, *Off to Philadelphia in the Morning* and *Vanity Fair*, plus guest spots on the likes of *Jackanory* and *Perfect Scoundrels*. Her first husband was actor Peter O'Toole.

PHILPOTT, TREVOR

British reporter, once with *Tonight*, *Panorama* and *Man Alive*, but given his own series of documentaries, including *The Philpott File* (from 1969).

PHOENIX, PATRICIA (PATRICIA PILKINGTON; 1923–86)

As *Coronation Street's* brassy Elsie Tanner, Irish-born, Manchester-raised Pat Phoenix became one of TV's favourite scarlet women. She joined the series at its outset in 1960, having worked her

way through the theatre and performed as a youngster on radio's *Children's Hour*. She had even written scripts for Harry Worth and Terry Hall and Lenny the Lion. Phoenix played the fiery Elsie for 24 years (apart from a few years away in the 1970s) and, when she left the *Street* in 1984, she remained on our screens in the sitcom *Constant Hot Water* (playing Phyllis Nugent, a seaside landlady) and as an agony aunt for TV-am. Her last TV role was in the *Unnatural Causes* anthology series, in which she played a bedridden actress. Phoenix was at one time married to her screen partner Alan Browning, but they had separated before he died. Shortly before she herself died, of lung cancer in 1986, she wed her companion and old friend, actor Tony Booth.

PICKERING, RON (1930–91)

London-born athletics coach who became a highly respected BBC sports commentator. Pickering's break came when he discovered young Welsh long-jumper Lynn Davies, whom he coached to a gold medal at the Tokyo Olympics in 1964. He joined the BBC for coverage of the 1968 Olympics and never looked back, becoming the Corporation's main athletics pundit and covering other events such as basketball. Pickering was also seen as host of *The Superstars* and *We Are the Champions*.

PICKLES, WILFRED, OBE (1904–78)

British actor and presenter whose Yorkshire accent caused some consternation when he began reading the news on national radio in the 1940s. Pickles was also popular a decade later, when he hosted (together with his wife, Mabel) *Ask Pickles* for the BBC. A sort of heavily sentimental *Jim'll Fix It* or *Surprise, Surprise* of its day, it specialized in reuniting members of families. Pickles also took to acting, gaining guest spots in series like *Dr Finlay's Casebook* before securing a starring role in *For the Love of Ada*, which began in 1970. As gravedigger Walter Bingley, he courted Irene Handl's Ada Cresswell in a gentle comedy about a senior citizen's romance. Pickles later also hosted *Stars on Sunday* for a while.

PICTURE BOOK

UK (BBC) Children's Entertainment. BBC 1955–63

Presenters: Patricia Driscoll, Vera McKechnie

Writer: Maria Bird. Producers: Freda Lingstrom, David Boisseau

Early toddlers' magazine programme.

The Monday segment of the *Watch With Mother* strand belonged to *Picture Book* from 1955 to the mid-1960s (including re-runs). Hosted initially by Patricia Driscoll, with stories read by Charles E. Stidwill, the programme was taken over by Vera McKechnie when Driscoll left to star as Maid Marian in *The Adventures of Robin Hood*. *Picture Book* was more of a magazine programme than an early *Jackanory*, with Driscoll and McKechnie turning the pages to introduce various items. One page showed how to make something – paper lanterns, for instance. Another introduced the puppet adventures of Bizzy Lizzy, a wispy-haired little girl with a magic wishing flower on her dress. Bizzy Lizzy was allowed four wishes by touching the flower, but if she wished a fifth time all her wishes flew away. She later starred in a series of her own. *Picture Book* also had a page for animals, and more puppets, the Jolly Jack Tars, filled another. These sailors in their berets and hooped shirts drifted across the ocean to strange lands like Bottle Island, sometimes in search of the 'Talking Horse'. The principals were the Captain (complete with bushy moustache), Mr Mate, Jonathan the deck hand and Ticky the monkey. Before the last page was turned and it was time to 'put the *Picture Book* away' for another day, Sausage, the programme's marionette dachshund, was also usually seen.

PICTURE PAGE

UK (BBC) Magazine. BBC 1936–9; 1946–52

Presenters: Joan Miller, Joan Gilbert, Mary Malcolm

Creator/Editor: Cecil Madden. Producers: George More O'Ferrall, Royston Morley, Harold Clayton, John Irwin, Stephen McCormack, Michael Mills

Early magazine programme curiously based around a telephone switchboard.

Canadian actress Joan Miller was the presenter of *Picture Page* and for this role she took the part of a telephone operator. In very contrived fashion, she called up the guests who had been booked to appear and patched them into vision. As 'The Switchboard Girl', Miller became one of TV's earliest personalities, predating even the official opening of the BBC television service (*Picture Page* began life as an experimental test programme before 'real' programming began). Miller was assisted in proceedings by Leslie Mitchell, who took care of the interviews, and also seen were Jasmine Bligh and John Snagge. About 20 items were packed into each hour-long edition and two programmes a week were transmitted. Amongst the guests persuaded to appear were Danny Kaye, Maurice Chevalier, Will Hay, Sabu, Dinah Sheridan and Sophie Tucker. When the television service was revived after the war, *Picture Page* came back, too, with Joan Gilbert taking over as presenter.

PIE IN THE SKY

UK (Witzend) Drama. BBC 1 1994–

Henry Crabbe ....Richard Griffiths
Margaret Crabbe ....Maggie Steed
Assistant Chief Constable Freddy Fisher
....Malcolm Sinclair
WPC/Sgt Sophia Cambridge.................Bella Enahoro
Steve Turner ....Joe Duttine
Linda ....Alison McKenna
John...Ashley Russell
Henderson...Nick Raggett
Nicola...Samantha Janus

Creator: Andrew Payne. Producers: Jacky Stoller, David Wimbury

A detective turned restauranteur is called back into action against his will.

After 25 years in the police force, podgy Detective Inspector Henry Crabbe decided to retire from Barstock CID and pursue a new career based on his hobby, gastronomy (and in particular traditional British cooking). Unfortunately, his accountant wife was not so keen, nor was Freddy Fisher, the Assistant Chief Constable who valued Crabbe's investigative skills. Despite opening his own restaurant, named Pie In The Sky, in the fictitious town of Middleton, Henry was not allowed to take full retirement. A little, unfortunate incident in his last case was used by Fisher to blackmail Crabbe into staying on part-time, resulting in the rotund chef being constantly dragged away from his kitchen and once again into police matters.

At his restaurant, Crabbe was a perfectionist, carefully choosing his vegetables from Henderson, a small local grower who also worked as washer-up. In addition, Crabbe kept his own chickens, whose nerves he soothed with extracts from Elgar. Steve Turner, an ex-con, was taken on as co-chef and Linda (later replaced by Nicola) and John waited at tables. WPC Cambridge was usually the bringer of bad tidings from the local nick.

The series was created by Andrew Payne specifically for star Richard Griffiths, and Griffiths was closely involved in the development of the programme and its characters. With a recipe or cooking tip included in every episode, *Pie In The Sky* proved popular with foodies as well as crime fans.

PIG IN THE MIDDLE

UK (LWT) Situation Comedy. ITV 1980–3

Nellie Bligh...Liza Goddard
Bartholomew 'Barty' Wade ....Dinsdale Landen
Terence Brady
Susan Wade ....Joanna Van Gyseghem

Creators/Writers: Charlotte Bingham, Terence Brady. Producer: Les Chatfield

A middle-aged man drifts between his wife and his mistress.

Barty and Susan Wade were a middle-class couple living in East Sheen. Sadly, Barty's life was not his own and he was constantly nagged by his fussy wife for over-eating and watching too much television. At one of Susan's many parties, Barty met up with fun-loving Nellie Bligh and, taking her as his 'other woman', was able to indulge himself in many of the happy pursuits Susan had banned – such as picnics in the country. However, despite Nellie's advances, Barty remained celibate. Even when he eventually walked out on his wife, it was only to move in next door to Nellie. When Dinsdale Landen left the series, the programme's co-writer, Terence Brady, stepped into the lead role.

PIGOTT-SMITH, TIM (1946–)

British actor, an award-winner for his portrayal of bigot Ronald Merrick in *The Jewel in the Crown*. He also starred in *Fame is the Spur*, was Brendan Bracken in *Winston Churchill – The Wilderness Years*, Hardy in *I Remember Nelson* and Chief Constable John Stafford in *The Chief*. Other appearances have come in classic plays (including Shakespeare) and in dramas like *Wings*, *The Glittering Prizes*, *North and South*, *The Hunchback of Notre Dame*, *The Lost Boys*, *The Secret Case of Sherlock Holmes*, the *Horizon* special, *Life Story*, and, like many other actors, *Doctor Who*.

PILGER, JOHN (1939–)

Award-winning Australian journalist working in the UK and specializing in hard-hitting investigations. From a background on *World in Action*, Pilger has gone on to expose the atrocities of Cambodia in *Year Zero – The Silent Death of Cambodia* and *Cambodia – Year One* (a follow-up), the treatment of Vietnam War veterans back home in the USA and to compile reports on hidden matters in Nicaragua, Japan and other countries. In 1974 he was given his own series, *Pilger*.

PILOT

A trial programme for a possible series. A pilot is used to see if the idea works, to iron out any previously unforeseen problems and, if aired, to gauge public response. Sometimes the pilot is then used as the first episode of the series, or repeated as a prologue to the series. Pilots are also sometimes aired as part of an anthology, with *Comedy Playhouse* a classic example. This series of pilots has resulted, over the years, in sitcoms like *Steptoe and Son*, *Till Death Us Do Part*, *The Liver Birds* and *Citizen Smith*. In the 1970s the trend in the USA was to produce feature length TV movies as pilots. Consequently, *The Marcus Nelson Murders* served as the pilot for *Kojak*, *Smile Jenny You're Dead* for *Harry O*, etc.

PINK PANTHER SHOW, THE

US (DePatie-Freleng) Cartoon. BBC 1 1970–

Voice:
The Inspector.................................Pat Harrington Jnr

Executive Producers: David DePatie, Friz Freleng

The animated misadventures of a hapless pink cat.

The Pink Panther was originally created for the Blake Edwards film of the same name, starring Peter Sellers as the bungling Inspector Henri Clouseau on the trail of a stolen gem stone called The Pink Panther. The cartoon cat only appeared in the titles sequence, and then only for a few seconds. However, the exposure was enough to earn some cinema releases of his own, before this TV version began in America in 1969.

The series initially contained some puppet sketches and was hosted by comedian Lenny Schultz. More familiar to UK viewers, however, were the 100 per cent cartoon packages which followed, with the series' name changing a number of times as its animated components alternated. The classic combination comprised two Panther cartoons sandwiching the latest case of The Inspector, an inept Clouseau clone. Other notable partners for The Panther were the Ant and the Aardvaark, and Crazylegs Crane. Yet there was only one star, The Pink Panther himself – 'the one and only, truly original panther, Pink Panther, from head to toe'.

Plodding around on his hind legs, the flat-footed pink cat with a long, looping tail was a compulsive do-gooder, a character whose best-laid plans were guaranteed to go awry. Stoically accepting every disaster Nature hurled his way (apart from an occasional gnashing of the teeth or the raising of an eyebrow), the stone-faced, silent feline was completely resigned to the catastrophes in his life. He was so accident prone that on a bright, sunny day, a single cloud was known to hover over his head, spouting rain. All this as Henry Mancini's 'durrum, durrum' theme music wafted along in the background.

The opening and closing sequences were familiar, too, showing The Panther being ushered in and out of a flashy (real-life) sports car, parked outside the show's theatre. Although it earned some lengthy runs in the BBC's Saturday tea time slot, the show was also well employed as a filler programme, plugging gaps when sporting events overran, or another series finished early. In addition, the programme generated an enormous amount of cheap merchandising, ranging from pencil cases to sickly pink chocolate bars.

PINKY AND PERKY

UK (BBC/Thames) Children's Entertainment. BBC/ITV 1957–68/1968–71

Creators: Jan Dalibor, Vlasta Dalibor. Producers: Trevor Hill, Stan Parkinson

Pop music and fun with two puppet piglets.

Created by Czech immigrants Jan and Vlasta Dalibor, Pinky and Perky were Britain's favourite string puppets in the late 1950s and early 1960s. The twin pigs were identical in all respects, except that Pinky wore red and Perky wore blue (not much use on black and white TV), and that Perky usually donned a hat in front of the cameras. Their repertoire consisted of high pitched (fast-forwarded tape) jokes and songs, including versions of contemporary pop hits. Their theme song was 'We Belong Together'. The piglets ran their own fictitious television station, PPC TV, which employed some of their animal friends, the likes of Horace Hare, Ambrose Cat, Conchita the cow, Morton Frog, Basil Bloodhound, Bertie Bonkers the baby elephant, Vera Vixen and a pop group called The Beakles. The various human straightmen keeping them company (at different times) were John Slater, Roger Moffat, Jimmy Thompson, Bryan Burdon and Fred Emney. The prancing porkers were also seen in various other series, such as *Pinky and Perky's Pop Parade* and *Pinky and Perky's Island*, but, after 11 years at the BBC, Pinky and Perky defected to the other side, making programmes for Thames until 1971.

PINTER, HAROLD, CBE (1930–)

British dramatist, widely applauded for his dialogues but criticized by some for the obscure nature of his plays. He was initially commissioned for stage and radio, but came to the fore via **Armchair Theatre** in 1960 with his first television play, *A Night Out*. After further dramas for ITV – *Night School* (also 1960), *The Collection* (1961) and, more controversially, *The Lover* (1963) – Pinter switched to the BBC. He wrote *Tea Party* for a pan-European anthology series entitled *The Largest Theatre in the World* in 1965, which he followed with *The Basement*, a visually adventurous offering for BBC 2's *Theatre 625* in 1967. Although Pinter then branched out into cinema work, he returned to the small screen in 1973 with a contribution to a series of short plays aired

under the title of *Monologue* and, three years later, his drama *The Collection* was screened in the prestigious anthology *Laurence Olivier Presents The Best Of . . .* , with Olivier himself among the cast. Pinter's adaptation of Aidan Higgins's *Langrishe, Go Down* was shown as a *Play of the Week* in 1978 and *The Hothouse* followed in 1982 with, at the end of the decade, *The Heat of the Day*, adapted from Elizabeth Bowen's novel. Pinter's first wife Vivien Merchant starred in some of his earliest works and Pinter himself occasionally appeared, too, under the stage name of David Baron. He was also seen in the 1964 adaptation of Sartre's *In Camera* and in the 1976 drama *Rogue Male*. After his first marriage ended, Pinter married novelist/historian Lady Antonia Fraser.

PLANE MAKERS, THE/POWER GAME, THE

UK (ATV) Drama. 1963–5/1965–9

John Wilder	Patrick Wymark
Pamela Wilder	Barbara Murray
	Ann Firbank
Don Henderson	Jack Watling
Arthur Sugden	Reginald Marsh
Caswell Bligh	Clifford Evans
Kenneth Bligh	Peter Barkworth

Creator: Wilfred Greatorex. Producers: Rex Firkin, David Reid

Friction between unions and bosses at an aircraft factory.

The Plane Makers was set in the hangers and workshops of the fictitious Scott Furlong aircraft factory and focused on industrial strife and management quandries. The company's managing director was John Wilder, a man everyone loved to hate. Wilder was to take on even greater prominence when the series was renamed *The Power Game* after two years. With the action transferred off the shop floor and into the boardroom, more attention was given to Wilder's wheelings and dealings. After the failure of a vertical take off aircraft project, the bullying businessman left Scott Furlong, took a seat on the board of a bank and picked up a knighthood. He began scheming in pastures new and discovered a rival in the shape of tycoon Caswell Bligh. When the final series was shown in 1969, three years after the previous run, Sir John was ensconced in diplomatic circles as a member of the Foreign Office, burrowing away for Britain around the world. The series ended with the sudden death of its star, Patrick Wymark.

PLANER, NIGEL (1955–)

British actor and writer, usually in comedy roles. His break came with *The Comic Strip* (which he helped to found with Peter Richardson, his

414

partner in an act called The Outer Limits) and he subsequently appeared in the troupe's run of Channel 4 films. Around the same time, he was writing for *Not The Nine O'Clock News* and playing Lou Lewis in *Shine on Harvey Moon*. Then came *The Young Ones*, in which he created the role of the hippy Neil, which won him and his co-stars a cult following. Planer followed this with a more conventional sitcom in *Roll Over Beethoven* (as rock 'n' roll star Nigel Cochrane), but returned to anarchy as Filthy in *Filthy, Rich and Catflap*. He tried light drama in *King and Castle* (as debt collector David Castle) and heavier matters in Dennis Potter's *Blackeyes*. Planer was also seen in *Blackadder*, played a pregnant man in the drama *Frankenstein's Baby* and offered viewers acting advice in *Nicholas Craig – The Naked Actor* and its various sequels. In 1992 he took over from the late Eric Thompson as writer and narrator of *The Magic Roundabout* and a year later starred as hapless French teacher Laurence Didcott in *Bonjour La Classe*.

PLANET OF THE APES, THE

US (Twentieth Century-Fox) Science Fiction. ITV 1974–5

Galen	Roddy McDowall
Alan Virdon	Ron Harper
Pete Burke	James Naughton
Urko	Mark Lenard
Zaius	Booth Colman

Executive Producer: Herbert Hirschman.
Producer: Stan Hough

Two astronauts crash-land on a planet ruled by apes, where man is the subservient race.

In 1980 three American astronauts had been approaching the Alpha Centauri system when they ran into radioactive turbulence. Activating an automatic homing device, they were sent spinning back to Earth, but through a time warp that dumped them 2000 years into the future. One of the crew, Jonesy, died on impact but there were two survivors, Alan Virdon and Pete Burke. They discovered an Earth with a remarkably different social structure from the planet they had left. In the year 3085, man was no longer in control. A holocaust had come and gone, during which the monkey race had taken over the planet. Orang-utans were the ruling species, gorillas were the violent law enforcers and chimpanzees the more gentle intellectuals. The apes talked, wore clothes, rode horses and toted guns. Humans were simply slaves and menial workers.

Virdon and Burke began a life on the run, steering clear of gorilla guerillas and seeking a way of returning to their own time. Only an inquisitive,

peace-loving chimpanzee named Galen afforded them any assistance as they hid from angry Urko, the gorilla chief of security. Zaius was the more rational orang-utan councillor who tried to keep Urko in check. However, the series ended without conclusion after only 14 episodes. It had not been a success in the USA.

The programme was based on the successful film series that began with *Planet of the Apes* and ended with *Battle for the Planet of the Apes*, in which Roddy McDowall played various lead ape roles similar to Galen. The original idea came from Pierre Boulle's book *The Monkey Planet*.

PLATER, ALAN (1935–)

North-eastern writer with many credits. Plater has contributed to series like *Z Cars*, *Softly, Softly*, *Crane*, *Cribb*, *Flambards*, *The Adventures of Sherlock Holmes*, *Maigret* and *Miss Marple*, as well as presenting his own original series like *The First Lady*, *Oh No! It's Selwyn Froggitt*, *Trinity Tales* and *Middlemen*, plus *The Beiderbecke Affair* and its two sequels, *The Beiderbecke Tapes* and *The Beiderbecke Connection*. He has also penned original plays like *Ted's Cathedral*, *To See How Far It Is* (a trilogy for Theatre 625), *Close the Coalhouse Door*, *Seventeen Per Cent Said Push Off* and *The Land of Green Ginger*, the Premiere film *Give Us A Kiss, Christabel*, and adapted other works for the small screen, like A.J. Cronin's *The Stars Look Down*, Trollope's *The Barchester Chronicles*, Olivia Manning's *Fortunes of War*, L.P. Hartley's *Feet Foremost*, J.B. Priestley's *The Good Companions* and Chris Mullin's *A Very British Coup*. Other notable scripts have included *A Day in Summer*, *Misterioso*, *The Referees* and *Orwell On Jura*.

PLAY AWAY

UK (BBC) Children's Entertainment. BBC 2 1971–84

Presenters: Brian Cant, Derek Griffiths, Chloe Ashcroft, Lionel Morton, Toni Arthur, Julie Stevens, Carol Chell, Dave Wood, Tony Robinson, Anita Dobson, Floella Benjamin, Alex Norton, Delia Morgan

Producers: Cynthia Felgate, Ann Reay, John Smith, Anne Gobey, Jeremy Swan

Entertainment and education for younger children.

A natural progression from *Play School*, *Play Away* was a Saturday afternoon programme aimed at children up to the age of seven. Accordingly, it featured somewhat less infantile games and songs than seen in its well-established sister programme and also threw in a few jokes. The series did, however, share many of the same presenters, although some new faces were also introduced (including Tony Robinson and a young Jeremy Irons). A studio audience added to the fun. Music was provided by pianist Jonathan Cohen and the Play Away Band, and the theme song was written by Lionel Morton.

PLAY FOR TODAY

UK (BBC) Drama Anthology. BBC 1 1970–84

Influential collection of single dramas.

Play for Today was effectively **The Wednesday Play** under a different name (the transmission day having moved to Thursday) and what the latter had contributed to 1960s TV drama, the former emulated in the 1970s and early 1980s. The *Play for Today* collection featured tragedies, comedies and fantasies, with, amongst its most celebrated offerings, Jim Allen's *The Rank and File*, Jeremy Sandford's *Edna, The Inebriate Woman* (both 1971), Hugh Whitemore's *84 Charing Cross Road* (1975), Mike Leigh's *Nuts in May* (1976) and *Abigail's Party* (1977), Jack Rosenthal's *Bar Mitzvah Boy* (1976), Dennis Potter's *Blue Remembered Hills* (1979) and Jeremy Paul and Alan Gibson's *The Flipside of Dominick Hide* and *Another Flip for Dominick* (1980 and 1982). The series also introduced **Rumpole of the Bailey** in 1975 and won notoriety for two plays that were initially banned: Dennis Potter's *Brimstone and Treacle* (1976, eventually screened in 1987) and Roy Minton's *Scum* (1977, screened in 1991).

PLAY OF THE MONTH

UK (BBC) Drama Anthology. BBC 1 1965–79; 1982–3

Sunday night collection of old and new plays.

Airing originally once a month, as its title suggests, but then more sporadically, this anthology of single dramas won much acclaim for its treatment of established works and also for its new commissions. Noted offerings included John Osborne's *Luther* in 1965, Rudolph Cartier and Reed de Rouen's *Lee Oswald – Assassin* in 1966, Arthur Miller's *Death of a Salesman* also in 1966, David Mercer's *The Parachute* in 1968, and adaptations of E.M. Forster's *A Passage to India* in 1965 and *A Room with a View* in 1973, by Santha Rama Rau and Pauline Macauley, respectively.

PLAY SCHOOL

UK (BBC) Children. BBC 2 1964–88

Presenters: Patrick Abernethy, Bruce Allen, Mike Amatt, Nigel Anthony, Stan Arnold, Toni Arthur, Chloe Ashcroft, Johnny Ball, Janine Barry, Ben Bazell, Floella Benjamin, Stuart Bradley, Christopher Bramwell, Brian Cant, Stephen Cartwright, Carol Chell, Gordon Clyde, John Colclough, Miranda Connell, Kate Copstick, Hilary Crane, Brian Croucher, Paul Danquah, Simon Davies, Ray C. Davis, Jonathan Dennis, Susan Denny, Marian Diamond, Diane Dorgan, Heather Emmanuel, Sheelagh Gilbey, Jon Glover, John Golder, Gordon Griffin, Derek Griffiths, Elvi Hale, Jane Hardy, David Hargreaves, Fred Harris, Maggie Henderson, Terence Holland, Wayne Jackman, Emrys James, Brian Jameson, Colin Jeavons, Dawn Keeler, Judy Kenny, Robert Kitson, Robin Kingsland, Kerry Jewell, Lloyd Johnson, Jona Jones, Rick Jones, Marla Landi, Ian Laughlan, Phyllida Law, Carole Leader, Sarah Long, Bridget McCann, Stuart McGugan, Michael Mann, Nigel Makin, Nick Mercer, Dibbs Mather, Elizabeth Millbank, Mary Miller, Delia Morgan, Ann Morrish, Lionel Morton, Susan Mosco, Carmen Munroe, Libby Murray, Jennifer Naden, Lesley Nightingale, Janet Palmer, Angela Piper, Valerie Pitts, Karen Platt, Peter Reeves, Gordon Rollings, Beryl Roques, Sheila Rushkin, Dev Sagoo, Michael Scholes, Andrew Secombe, Shireen Shah, Johnny Silvo, Lucie Skeaping, Evelyn Skinner, Jon Skolmen, Don Spencer, Julie Stevens, Virginia Stride, Ben Thomas, Eric Thompson, Christopher Tranchell, Valerie Turnbull, Miguel Villa, Carole Ward, Liz Watts, John White, Mela White, Wally Whyton, Rod Wilmott, Heather Williams, Barry Wilsher, Fraser Wilson, Rosalind Wilson, Lesley Woods, Sam Wyse, Lola Young

Creator: Joy Whitby. Producers: Joy Whitby, Cynthia Felgate, Molly Cox, Ann Reay, Peter Ridsdale Scott, Anne Gobey, Michael Grafton-Robinson, Michael Cole, Peter Wiltshire, Christine Secombe, Judy Whitfield, Albert Barber, Nick Wilson, John M.A. Lane, Sue Peto, Christine Hewitt, Penny Lloyd, Greg Childs, Roy Milani, Martin Fisher

Fun and games for the pre-school age.

'Here is a house. Here is a door. Windows: one, two, three, four. Ready to knock? Turn the lock. It's *Play School.*' These were the words that introduced the under-fives to *Play School*, the first programme seen on BBC 2. It wasn't meant to be the first, but a celebration outside broadcast from Paris the night before had been wiped out by a power cut and the honour of opening up Britain's third TV channel fell to the first programme in the next day's schedule (*Play School* went out at 11 am).

A mixture of songs, mimes and stories, *Play School* provided a daily dose of mild education and entertainment for the youngest viewers for 24 years. In its hey-day, there were two presenters per programme (one male, one female), aided by William Blezard on piano, and each pair worked for a whole week before giving way to two of their colleagues. They were ably assisted by the *Play School* toys: two bears, Little Ted and Big Ted; two dolls, the staid Hamble (retired and replaced in 1986 by Poppy, a black doll) and raggy Jemima; and the villain of the piece, Humpty, a stuffed egg with arms, legs and a face. Dressed up and bounced on many a knee, these toys became known to every child in the land. The show also had a rocking horse, Dapple, and real animals. Katoo, the cockatoo, was the best known, alongside rabbits George and Peter, a guinea pig called Elizabeth, Henry and Henrietta mice and two goldfish, Bit and Bot.

The programme opened with a study of the calendar, with the day, month and date carefully spelled out, and each day had a theme. Monday was Useful Box Day, Tuesday was Dressing Up Day, Wednesday was Pets Day, Thursday was Ideas Day and Friday, Science Day. A central feature was the glance at the clock and a chance to tell the time, using the 'big hand, little hand' system, followed by a look at the models at the base of the clock that set the scene for the daily story (sometimes told by a guest reader: the first tale was *Little Red Hen*, read by Athene Seyler). After all this came the dilemma of which window to look through – the arched, the square or the round – before a film about some outside activity or workplace. All these features were held together by a series of songs, dances, mimes and games of pretend, led by presenters who tended to overuse the prompt: 'Can you do that?'. Songs about catching fishes alive and wibbly, wobbly walks were used over and over again, and some renditions were more tuneful than others.

The programme brought to light many notable performers whose talents were only hinted at by their monosyllabic duties here. The first show's presenters were Virginia Stride and Gordon Rollings (later Arkwright in the John Smith's beer commercials), and amongst other fondly remembered hosts were the whimsical Brian Cant, mime specialist Derek Griffiths, ex-Four Pennies vocalist Lionel Morton, quirky Johnny Ball and dreadlocked Floella Benjamin. Emma Thompson's parents, Phyllida Law and Eric (*Magic Roundabout*) Thompson, were also prominent in the show's early days, as was musician Rick Jones, subsequently presenter of *Fingerbobs*.

PLAY YOUR CARDS RIGHT

UK (LWT/Talbot) Game Show. ITV 1980–7; 1994–

Presenter : Bruce Forsyth

Creator: Chester Feldman. Producers: David Bell, Alasdair Macmillan, Paul Lewis (1994)

Game show involving some general knowledge and a lot of luck with cards.

A 'higher or lower' card game, *Play Your Cards Right* combined knowledge of public opinion with a little gambling technique. Contestant couples guessed how many people out of a survey sample of 100 believed this or that. The first couple's guess was used as a marker by the second couple, who then simply stated 'higher' or 'lower'. The winners took control of the card game and progressed along a board turning over playing cards, guessing whether the next card would be higher or lower than the one before. A wrong answer gave control to their opponents. For contestants successfully negotiating the final card round, and amassing enough points by gambling along the way, the prize was a new car. Enthusiastically hosted as ever by Bruce Forsyth, the series generated a host of new Brucie catchphrases, most notably 'You get nothing for a pair – not in this game', 'What do points make? Prizes!' and 'It could still be a big night, if you play your cards right'.

Under the name of *Bruce Forsyth's Play Your Cards Right*, the show returned to the screen in 1994, after an absence of seven years. The concept was derived from the US game show *Card Sharks*.

PLEASE SIR!

UK (LWT) Situation Comedy. ITV 1968–71

Bernard Hedges	John Alderton
Norman Potter	Deryck Guyler
Miss Doris Ewell	Joan Sanderson
Mr Cromwell	Noel Howlett
Mr Price	Richard Davies
Mr 'Smithy' Smith	Erik Chitty
Eric Duffy	Peter Cleall
Frankie Abbott	David Barry
Dennis Dunstable	Peter Denyer
Maureen Bullock	Liz Gebhardt
Sharon Eversleigh	Penny Spencer
	Carol Hawkins
Peter Craven	Malcolm McFee
Penny Wheeler/Hedges	Jill Kerman

Creators/Writers: John Esmonde, Bob Larbey.
Producers: Mark Stuart, Phil Casson

A hesitant, naive teacher's first job is in a rough inner-city school.

Recent graduate Bernard Hedges secured his first appointment as English and History teacher at Fenn Street Secondary Modern, under the auspices of headmaster Mr Cromwell. From the start, his unruly class, 5C, went out of their way to make life difficult for him, but they soon came to respect the bashful yet dedicated master, whom they nicknamed 'Privet'.

Behind the desks the youths included loudmouth Frankie Abbot, who acted hard but always ran to his mother, slow-witted Dennis, who came from a deprived home, brash class leader Eric Duffy, flirtatious Penny, and Maureen, the evangelical Christian who had a crush on her teacher. The staff were just as unhelpful. Apart from the incompetent headmaster, there was the thick-skinned, Welsh maths and science teacher Pricey, the formidable deputy head, Doris Ewell, dithery old Smithy, and a former Desert Rat, caretaker Norman Potter, who was terrified of the kids but enjoyed great influence with the headmaster. After a couple of years, Hedges acquired a girl-friend, Penny Wheeler, who went on to become his wife.

Please Sir! was inspired by the 1967 film *To Sir, with Love*. Its own feature film was released in 1971 and a spin-off, *The Fenn Street Gang*, followed on TV, tracing the lives of the teenagers after leaving school. *Please Sir!* continued simultaneously for one more year, but the new kids and teachers introduced failed to catch on. The American version was *Welcome Back Kotter*, featuring a young John Travolta amongst the pupils.

PLEASENCE, DONALD (1919–95)

British character actor, a specialist in macabre and sinister roles. In addition to his long film career, Pleasence was seen in numerous TV dramas, including Dennis Potter's *Blade on the Feather*, Joe Orton's *The Good and Faithful Servant*, the tabloid satire *Scoop* and Gerald Savory's adaptation of *Double Indemnity*. He was Syme in the classic Nigel Kneale version of *1984*, Prince John in *The Adventures of Robin Hood*, Melchior in *Jesus of Nazareth*, Reverend Septimus Harding in *The Barchester Chronicles* and also starred in *The Rivals of Sherlock Holmes*, in which he played Carnacki, the ghost hunter. He made a number of mini-series and TV movies and was seen as a guest in *The Outer Limits*, *Dick Turpin* and *Columbo*. Occasionally, he appeared with his actress daughter, Angela Pleasence.

PLOWRIGHT, DAVID (1930–)

Distinguished British TV executive, closely associated with Granada Television, which he joined in 1957 having previously been a newspaper journalist. With Granada, he worked on regional news magazines before moving up to edit *World in Action*. In 1968 he was made the station's Programme Controller, in 1975, its Managing Director and, in 1987, Chairman of the company. He has also been an important figure in the ITV network and was once Chairman of the Independent Television Companies Association and a director of ITN. In his time at Granada, Plowright – brother of actress Joan Plowright – was widely respected and involved himself

closely in programming matters. He even produced episodes of *Coronation Street*. However, in 1992, to the dismay of many of his colleagues, he left in controversial circumstances, reputedly concerned at the company's lack of commitment to, and investment in, quality programming.

POGLES' WOOD

UK (Smallfilms) Children's Entertainment. BBC 1 1966–7

Voices: Oliver Postgate, Olwen Griffiths, Steve Woodman

Creator/Writer/Producer: Oliver Postgate

The fairy tale adventures of a woodland family.

Originally entitled *The Pogles*, *Pogles' Wood* focused on the day-to-day happenings in the yokel life of the industrious Mr Pogle, his domesticated wife, their son Pippin and pet squirrel Tog, all of whom lived in a tree in the heart of the forest. Their magic bean plant was also closely monitored. However the witch who added a touch of menace in *The Pogles* had long since departed by the time *Pogles' Wood* began. Film footage of the countryside was cut into each episode and the wonders of nature were admired. This *Watch With Mother* contribution, with puppets by Peter Firmin, proved so popular that it gave birth to a children's comic, *Pippin*.

POINTS OF VIEW

UK (BBC) Viewer Response. BBC 1 1961–71; 1979–

Presenters:
Robert Robinson
Kenneth Robinson
Barry Took
Anne Robinson

Fast-moving viewer response programme.

This spritely little offering was originally conceived as a five-minute filler for dropping in before the news, but has become one of the BBC's longest running programmes. It has consisted chiefly of viewers' moans and groans about the Corporation's output, though not all feedback has been negative. Extracts from letters have been read out on air by announcers and, strangely, most contributions seem to have begun with the words 'Why, oh why, oh why?'. Critics have knocked the programme for offering only token criticism of the BBC and for being of little constructive benefit. The presenters' cheery put-downs have perhaps fostered this idea.

Robert Robinson was the original host, followed by Kenneth Robinson. Barry Took picked up the reins in the late 1970s and Anne Robinson has been in the hot seat most recently. Having the name Robinson obviously helps if you want to host *Points of View* (Tony Robinson was also once a stand-in). From 1963 Robert Robinson presented a children's version, *Junior Points of View*, a job he then relinquished to Sarah Ward.

POIROT

UK (LWT/Carnival) Detective Drama. ITV 1989–

Hercule Poirot	David Suchet
Captain Arthur Hastings	Hugh Fraser
Inspector/Chief Inspector Japp	Philip Jackson
Miss Lemon	Pauline Moran

Executive Producers: Nick Elliott, Linda Agran. Producer: Brian Eastman

The cases of the famous Belgian detective.

Along with beer, chocolates and Tin Tin, Hercule Poirot is one of Belgium's greatest exports, even if he was only a figment of Agatha Christie's fertile imagination. Having already been characterized by the likes of Albert Finney and Peter Ustinov on film, Poirot came to TV in the capable hands of British actor David Suchet, brother of ITN newscaster John. It pitched him into the art deco London of the 1930s, giving him a small flat in the luxurious Whitehaven Mansions and allowing crime to follow him wherever he went.

Joining the fastidious sleuth with the curly moustache, fancy cane and 'little grey cells' was his loyal companion, Captain Hastings, a sporty, well-heeled ladies' man who drove a green Lagonda. Also on the scene was the inept Inspector Japp, a Scotland Yard officer who never failed to point the finger at the wrong suspect. Putting matters right, Poirot, with his obtuse continental accent and lop-sided, oval head, calmly gathered together all the likely candidates and, after a meticulous explanation of the facts, quietly and efficiently nailed the guilty party.

POLDARK

UK (London Films/BBC) Drama. BBC 1 1975–7

Ross Poldark	Robin Ellis
Demelza	Angharad Rees
Elizabeth	Jill Townsend
George Warleggan	Ralph Bates
Francis Poldark	Clive Francis
Charles Poldark	Frank Middlemass
Caroline	Judy Geeson
Reverend Ossie Whitworth	Christopher Biggins
Verity	Norma Streader
Judd	Paul Curran

Producers: Anthony Coburn, Richard Beynon, Morris Barry

An 18th-century Cornish squire fights to keep his estate in order and his emotions in check.

Returning home from doing battle with the Americans in their War of Independence, dashing Cornish squire Ross Poldark discovered his late father's estate in ruin, the tin mines up for sale and the love of his life, Elizabeth, betrothed to his cousin Francis. Determined to rectify matters, Ross set about tackling the local powers that be, especially the evil George Warleggan. He aimed to re-establish the Poldark name and bring justice to his workers and other oppressed Cornish folk. He even took on the invading French. However, one battle he struggled to win was with his heart over the fair Elizabeth, even after she was married to Francis and he to Demelza, the fiery, nit-ridden, urchin servant girl he had made pregnant.

Winston Graham's novels were adapted by the BBC into 29 serial episodes and, thanks in no small part to the good looks of its leading man, *Poldark* was one of the most popular dramas of its time.

POLE TO POLE see *Around the World in 80 Days.*

POLICE

UK (BBC) Documentary. BBC 1 1982

Editor: John Shearer

Out and about with the officers of the Thames Valley Police.

This warts-and-all documentary series focused on E Division of the Thames Valley Police as they patrolled the streets of Reading and its environs over a nine-month period. Amongst various incidents, it showed the force organizing a stake out for a planned robbery and, at the other extreme, saw officers accused of beating up a drunk. One detective broke down in tears after being demoted, but the most controversial of the 11 episodes dealt with a rape case in which police treatment of the victim brought howls of protest. The series was directed by Roger Graef and Charles Stewart.

POLICE FIVE

UK (ATV/LWT) Factual. ITV 1962–90

Presenter: Shaw Taylor

Short filler programme in which police request help in solving crimes.

With questions like 'Were *you* in the neighbourhood', host Shaw Taylor appealed for viewers' assistance in tracking down criminals and preventing future incidents. Produced in conjunction with New Scotland Yard, this series focused on crimes in the capital, although regional equivalents were also shown in other ITV areas. Taylor's parting advice was 'Keep 'em peeled'. LWT also produced *Junior Police Five* in the 1970s.

POLICE SQUAD!

US (Zucker/Zucker/Abrahams/Paramount) Situation Comedy. ITV 1983

Sgt/Lt Frank Drebin	Leslie Nielsen
Captain Ed Hocken	Alan North
Ted Olson	Ed Williams
Johnny the Snitch	William Duell
Norberg	Peter Lupus
Al	John Wardell

Creators: Jerry Zucker, David Zucker, Jim Abrahams. Producer: Bob Weiss

Ridiculous satire on all established cop shows.

Police Squad!, from the team that produced the cinema hit *Airplane*, was a zany, over the top collection of word plays and sight gags that parodied every cliché and action sequence of 'serious' police programmes. Its star, Leslie Nielsen, played the stone-faced Frank Drebin, whose rank varied from lieutenant down to sergeant. Gathered around him were his boss, Captain Hocken, lecherous lab technician Ted Olson, officer Norberg, and Johnny the Snitch, a shoeshine boy with all the latest words on the street (in fact he could answer questions on anything, as long as someone was paying). There was also Al, an officer so tall his face never fitted on the screen. Old TV gimmicks were ripe for the picking: the narrator read out a different episode title to that shown on the screen, 'Tonight's Guest Star' was instantly murdered and forgotten for the rest of the show, and the programme ended with the classic freeze-frame finish seen in many early series, only this time it was the actors themselves who did the freezing, struggling to hold their poses as the credits rolled by.

Only six episodes of *Police Squad!* were made, however, and its ratings were low, probably because the programme demanded so much attention from viewers with its many puns and background jokes. All the same, the series did spawn a couple of successful feature films, *The Naked Gun: From the Files of Police Squad!* and *The Naked Gun 2½: The Smell of Fear*, not to mention a collection of Red Rock cider advertisements.

POLICE SURGEON

UK (ABC) Police Drama. ITV 1960

Dr Geoffrey Brent	Ian Hendry
Inspector Landon	John Warwick
Amanda Gibbs	Ingrid Hafner

Producers: Julian Bond, Leonard White

A police doctor gets too involved in his cases.

Geoffrey Brent was a doctor with the Bayswater police who had the knack of solving cases which baffled his detective colleagues. The programme was seen by many as the basis for *The Avengers*, as Ian Hendry soon went on to fill the similar role of Dr David Keel in the first episodes of that long-running series. This British-made *Police Surgeon* should not be confused with the Canadian series of the same name, starring Sam Groom.

POLICE WOMAN

US (David Gerber/Columbia) Police Drama. ITV 1975–9

Sgt Suzanne 'Pepper' Anderson	Angie Dickinson
Lt Bill Crowley	Earl Holliman
Detective Joe Styles	Ed Bernard
Detective Pete Royster	Charles Dierkop
Cheryl	Nichole Kallis
Lt Paul Marsh	Val Bisoglio

Creator: Robert Collins. Executive Producer: David Gerber. Producer: Douglas Benton

A glamorous police woman works undercover for the Los Angeles Police Department.

Blonde divorcée Pepper Anderson worked for the criminal conspiracy bureau of the LAPD, as part of the vice squad, taking on unusual undercover roles. Posing as prostitutes, strippers, gangsters' molls and other ladies of the underworld, she infiltrated the seamier side of LA society, backed up by her colleagues Joe Styles and Pete Royster. The drama came from the highly risky (and risqué) situations in which she was placed. The squad chief, and Pepper's best friend, was Lt Bill Crowley. In the earliest episodes, Pepper's autistic sister, Cheryl, a student at a special school, was occasionally seen.

Police Woman was a spin-off from an American anthology series called *Police Story*, in which Angie Dickinson once appeared as an officer named Lisa Beaumont.

POLLARD, SU (1949–)

British actress, comedian and singer, specializing in daffy females. It was as Peggy, the ambitious chalet maid, in *Hi-De-Hi!* that she made her name, having earlier appeared on *Opportunity Knocks!* and with Paul Nicholas in a short-lived sitcom entitled *Two Up, Two Down*. She played Peggy for eight years and followed it with virtually the same role in *You Rang, M'Lord*, this time in the guise of parlour maid Ivy Teasdale. Pollard also sang the theme song ('Starting Together') for the fly-on-the-wall documentary series, *The Marriage*, and other credits have included *The Comedians*, *Summer Royal* and *Get Set for Summer*.

PORRIDGE

UK (BBC) Situation Comedy. BBC 1 1974–7

Norman Fletcher ....Ronnie Barker
Lennie Godber ....Richard Beckinsale
Mr Mackay..Fulton Mackay
Mr Barrowclough ....Brian Wilde
Ingrid Fletcher...Patricia Brake
Harry Grout ....Peter Vaughan
Lukewarm ....Christopher Biggins
McLaren ....Tony Osoba
Warren ....Sam Kelly
Mr Venables................................Michael Barrington
Blanco ....David Jason
Harris..Ronald Lacey
Heslop ....Brian Glover
Ives...Ken Jones
Judge Rawley ....Maurice Denham
Jarris..David Daker

Writers: Dick Clement, Ian La Frenais.
Producer: Sydney Lotterby

Fun behind bars with a wise old lag and his ingenuous young cellmate.

Norman Stanley Fletcher was an habitual criminal who accepted imprisonment as an occupational hazard, according to his trial judge. So it was that this Muswell Hill wide boy with a heart of gold was sentenced to a five-year term in HMP Slade, an isolated prison in deepest Cumbria. Much against his wishes, he was forced to share a cell with young Lennie Godber, a first-time offender from Birmingham. Fletch became a father-like figure to the amiable Godber, helping him to weather his first period of confinement, showing him the tricks of survival and leading him through the vagaries of prison etiquette.

Fletcher's considerable experience in incarceration brought him respect from most of the criminals around him, the likes of 'Bunny' Warren, illiterate and easily-led; decrepit Blanco; 'Black Jock' McLaren, the Glaswegian heavy, and Lukewarm, the gay cook. But there were also less agreeable inmates like 'Orrible' Ives, the slimy Harris and 'genial' Harry Grout, the wing's Mr Big, who ran all the rackets and enjoyed life's little luxuries in his own, comfortably appointed private room. On the other side of the fence was Mr Mackay, the chief warder. Despairing of the ineffective governor, Mr Venables, he longed to regiment the prisoners and rule the prison with an iron jackboot. But, like his easily-conned, hen-pecked assistant, Mr Barrowclough, he was never a match for our hero.

Laced together with Fletcher's sparkling wit and skilful repartee, *Porridge* extolled the ironies and paradoxes of prison life, never glorifying life inside but cleverly commenting on the difficulties and pressures endured by convicted criminals. The series – which grew out of a play called *Prisoner and Escort*, seen as part of the *Seven of One* Ronnie Barker anthology in 1973 – became a firm favourite in jails all across Britain. However, a short-lived TV sequel, *Going Straight* (featuring Fletcher's life back on the outside), failed to reach the heights of the original. A cinema version of *Porridge* was released in 1979.

PORTER, ERIC (1928–95)

British stage actor who won acclaim for his TV portrayal of Soames in *The Forsyte Saga*. He was later seen in dramas like *Churchill and the Generals* (as Sir Alan Brooke), *Anna Karenina* (as Alexei Karenin), *Winston Churchill – The Wilderness Years* (as Neville Chamberlain), *Oliver Twist* (as Fagin), *The Adventures of Sherlock Holmes* (as Moriarty) and *The Jewel in the Crown* (as Count Dimitri Bronowski). His television appearances dated back to the 1950s.

PORTER, NYREE DAWN, OBE (1940–)

New Zealand-born actress seen on British TV in single dramas and series like *The Forsyte Saga* (as Irene), *The Liars* (Hermione), *Never a Cross Word* (Deirdre Baldock) and *The Protectors* (the Contessa di Contini). Lesser roles have come in *Doctor in Charge* and *Anne of Green Gables*, amongst other programmes.

PORTERHOUSE BLUE

UK (Picture Partnership) Comedy. Channel 4 1987

Skullion...David Jason
Sir Godber Evans ....Ian Richardson
The Dean...Paul Rogers
Senior Tutor ....John Woodnutt
The Bursar ....Harold Innocent
The Prelector..Ian Wallace
Cornelius Carrington.........................Griff Rhys Jones
Lionel Zipser..John Sessions
Professor Siblington ....Willoughby Goddard
Sir Cathcart ....Charles Gray
Mrs Biggs...Paula Jacobs
Lady Mary...Barbara Jefford

Writer: Malcolm Bradbury. Producer: Brian Eastman

A new principal attempts to drag an ancient college into the modern world and finds his efforts resisted.

Porterhouse, the most archaic of Cambridge colleges, found itself in the hands of a new Master,

Sir Godber Evans. Evans wanted to abandon many college traditions and bring procedures up to date, but was resisted chiefly by the old head porter, Skullion, who was summarily sacked after 45 years' service. This four-part adaptation of Tom Sharpe's black comedy depicted the ensuing developments, including a famous scene where thousands of condoms were released up the college chimneys, floated around the elegant spires and settled in the college grounds.

POST-PRODUCTION

The work done on a programme after the recording has finished. This principally involves editing and sound dubbing.

POSTMAN PAT

UK (BBC/Woodlands Animation) Animation. BBC 1 1981; 1991–92; 1995

Narrator: Ken Barrie

Creator/Writer: John Cunliffe. Producer: Ivor Wood

The daily rounds of a rural postman.

Accompanied by Jess, his black and white cat, Postman Pat did the rounds of the countryside around Greendale (based on the Lake District), providing assistance above and beyond the call of duty to the local residents, who included postmistress Mrs Goggins. Pat's red post van bore the registration number PAT 1. Although only 13 episodes were originally produced, they were firm favourites with toddlers for years. Bryan Daly provided the music and narrator Ken Barrie's rendition of the catchy theme song entered the UK charts no less than three times between 1982 and 1983, but on no occasion climbing higher than number 44. However, when the song was played as a joke on Terry Wogan's radio show, it brought the programme to the attention of a wider audience and sparked a merchandising boom on which the real-life Post Office capitalized with glee.

POT BLACK

UK (BBC) Snooker. BBC 2 1969–86; 1991–

Creator/Commentator: Ted Lowe. Presenters: Keith Macklin, Alan Weeks, David Icke, Eamonn Holmes, David Vine

Producers: Philip Lewis, Reg Perrin, David Kenning, John G. Smith

Innovative TV snooker championship.

An ideal exhibition vehicle for colour television, *Pot Black*, a popular, one-frame, annual snooker tournament, was devised by 'whispering' commentator Ted Lowe. The series, unexpectedly, ran and ran, but was eventually overshadowed by the extensive televising of 'real' snooker. As such, it became a victim of its own success and was taken off in 1986. *Junior Pot Black* was produced instead. The *Pot Black* returned, hosted by Eamonn Holmes, in 1991. A year later it was revamped as *Pot Black Timeframe*, and saw players having to pocket the balls in a set time. The original format was revived a year later, with David Vine as emcee. The theme tune was entitled 'Ivory Rag'.

POTTER

UK (BBC) Situation Comedy. BBC 1 1979–80; 1983

Redvers Potter	Arthur Lowe
	Robin Bailey
Aileen Potter	Noel Dyson
The Vicar	John Barron
'Tolly' Tolliver	John Warner
Diana	Honor Shepherd
Harry Tooms	Harry H. Corbett
Jane	Brenda Cowling

Creator/Writer: Roy Clarke. Producers: Peter Whitmore, Bernard Thompson

A cantankerous former businessman can't help interfering in other people's affairs.

Redvers Potter, former MD of Pottermints ('the hotter mints'), a firm founded by his grandfather, was in need of new horizons after selling his share in the company. He took up jogging, nosed his way into other people's business and struck up friendships with Tolly, his antiques dealer neighbour, and the local vicar, who seemed as out of touch with reality as the bumbling Potter himself. Potter's independent wife, Aileen (though she preferred to be called Madge) took regular rollockings from her pedantic husband but remained defiant, while the Vicar's largely silent wife, Jane, was no more than an unpaid housekeeper. Also seen was a sad local villain, Harry Tooms, who tried to reinvent his life in the company of the curmudgeonly old buffers.

The title role unfortunately had to be recast when Arthur Lowe died between series. Into the breach stepped Robin Bailey.

POTTER, DENNIS (1935–94)

Controversial but innovative British playwright, responsible for some of the most acclaimed dramas seen on television, but also for some of the most criticized. Much of Potter's writing had autobiographical undertones, echoing a childhood in the Forest of Dean and a life dogged by illness (psoriatic arthropathy, later exemplified in *The Singing Detective*). The susceptibility of youth, patriotism, the power of religion and nostalgia of all kinds (particularly musical) pervaded his bold screenplays and he seldom shunned multi-layered storylines and frank sexual content. An Oxford graduate, Potter once stood as Labour parliamentary candidate, wrote for *That Was The Week That Was* and worked on the *Daily Herald* in the early 1960s as a reporter and TV critic. In fact, his understanding of television matters was exhibited in his own screenwriting, as he sought to move the barriers of TV convention. His first offering was a *Wednesday Play*, *The Confidence Course*, in 1965. The same year he contributed *Alice, Vote, Vote, Vote For Nigel Barton* and its prequel, *Stand Up, Nigel Barton*. His *Son of Man* (1969), in which he humanised Christ, brought howls of disapproval from the Establishment and, in a way, his *Casanova* (1971), with its nudity, was not unexpected by those who raised the clamour. *Brimstone and Treacle*, made in 1976, was deemed to be too upsetting with its rape of a handicapped girl and was not screened until 1987, but Potter won new fans with his *Pennies from Heaven* in 1978. *Blue Remembered Hills* (1979) famously put actors like Colin Welland, Michael Elphick and Helen Mirren into children's clothing, but it is *The Singing Detective*, shown in 1986, which many consider to be his most fitting memorial. Later efforts such as *Blackeyes* (1989) and *Lipstick on Your Collar* (1993) were not as well received, although still attracted their share of protest. Amongst Potter's many other works were *Emergency Ward 9* (1966), *Message for Posterity* (1967), *A Beast with Two Backs* (1968), *Angels are So Few* (1970), *Traitor* (1971), *Double Dare* (1976), *The Mayor of Casterbridge* (adaptation 1978), *Rain on the Roof, Cream in My Coffee, Blade on the Feather* (all 1980), F. Scott Fitzgeralds's *Tender is the Night* (1985), *Visitors* (1987) and *Christabel* (1988). Potter's last dramas, *Karaoke* and *Cold Lazarus*, chiselled out under great strain in his dying days, were to be screened, according to the author's wishes, consecutively on BBC 1 and Channel 4 in autumn 1995. To the end he expressed his love of television and his sadness at increased commercialization which, he felt, was ruining the medium.

POWELL, ROBERT (1944–)

British actor whose first major TV role was as Toby Wren in *Doomwatch* in 1970. He soon followed it with the lead in Thomas Hardy's *Jude the Obscure*, but it wasn't until he played Christ in the blockbuster *Jesus of Nazareth* in 1977 that Powell became a major star. His other credits have included *Pygmalion*, *The Edwardian's* episode *Mr Rolls and Mr Royce* (as Royce), *The Four Feathers*, *Looking for Clancy*, *The First Circle* and *Merlin of the Crystal Cave*. He was Dr Henry Fynn in the

mini-series *Shaka Zulu* and was cast as John Buchan's hero *Hannay*, having already taken the role in a film version of *The Thirty-Nine Steps*. In the early 1990s Powell was seen in company with Jasper Carrott, playing inept copper Dave Briggs in *Canned Carrott* and its spin-off *The Detectives*. His wife Barbara 'Babs' Lord is a former Pan's People dancer.

POWELL, VINCE

Prolific British scriptwriter, for many years in collaboration with his former comedy partner Harry Driver. Together, they penned mostly sitcom material, but enjoyed excursions into drama through episodes of *Coronation Street* and *Adam Adamant Lives!* Their biggest successes came with *Bless this House*, *Never Mind the Quality, Feel the Width*, *Two in Clover*, *Nearest and Dearest*, *Spring and Autumn*, *Love Thy Neighbour*, *Mike and Bernie* and *For the Love of Ada*, all of which they created and wrote. Other credits included scripts for *Here's Harry* (Worth) and *Pardon the Expression*. Since Driver's death in 1973, Powell has devised and written *The Wackers*, *Rule Britannia*, *My Son Reuben*, *Mind Your Language*, *Odd Man Out*, *Young at Heart*, *Father Charlie*, *Bottle Boys* and contributed episodes of *Paradise Island*, *A Sharp Intake of Breath*, *Never the Twain*, *Slinger's Day* and *Full House*, amongst other series.

POWER GAME, The see *Plane Makers, The.*

POWERS, STEFANIE (STEFANIA FEDERKIEWICZ; 1942–)

American actress who shot to international stardom as April Dancer, *The Girl from UNCLE*, in 1966, after just a few small roles in series like *Bonanza*. The fame didn't last, however, when the series was cancelled after just one year, and Powers was forced to climb her way back to the top in the theatre and through guest spots in programmes like *Love, American Style* and *Marcus Welby, MD*. It worked and, though one prime-time drama, *The Feather and Father Gang*, was not a huge success, Powers did find her métier as millionairess adventurer Jennifer Hart in *Hart To Hart*. She has also been seen in numerous mini-series and TV movies, notably *Mistral's Daughter* and *Washington: Behind Closed Doors*.

PRAED, MICHAEL (1960–)

British actor seen on TV in series like *The Professionals* and *The Gentle Touch* before hitting the big time as *Robin of Sherwood*, which in turn led to his being cast (after a stint on the Broadway stage) as Prince Michael of Moldavia in *Dynasty*. In 1995 Praed was seen as Marty James in the legal drama series *Crown Prosecutor*.

PREQUEL

Follow-up to a drama in which the action pre-dates that in the original programme, often introducing younger versions or ancestors of the original's main characters. Examples have included *First of the Summer Wine* and *Dallas: The Early Years*.

PRESENTATION CONTROLLER

The technician who presses the buttons to send programmes, trailers and commercials to air.

PRESS GANG

UK (Richmond Films/Central) Children's Adventure. ITV 1989–93

Lynda Day	Julia Sawalha
Spike Thomson	Dexter Fletcher
Kenny Phillips	Lee Ross
Sarah Jackson	Kelda Holmes
Matt Kerr	Clive Ward
Danny McColl	Charlie Creed-Miles
Tiddler	Joanna Dukes
Billy Homer	Andy Crowe
Julie Craig	Lucy Benjamin
Frazz Davis	Mmoloki Chrystie
Sam Black	Gabrielle Anwar
Colin Mathews	Paul Reynolds
Jennie Eliot	Sadie Frost

Creator: Bill Moffat. Writer: Steven Moffat. Producer: Sandra C. Hastie

The trials and tribulations of running a school newspaper.

In this acclaimed children's drama, the GCSE pupils of Norbridge High ran a youth newspaper called the *Junior Gazette*, an offshoot of the local press. Its hard-nosed editor was Lynda Day. American Spike Thomson was the number-one reporter, genial Kenny Phillips the deputy editor, and slippery Colin Mathews the advertising manager. Adopting a far more adult approach than previous efforts in the same vein (*Adventure Weekly*, *A Bunch of Fives*, etc.), *Press Gang* drew comparisons with **Hill Street Blues**, **Lou Grant** and other thoughtful US dramas, thanks to its realism and its level-headed treatment of touchy subjects like child abuse, drugs and even local politics and corruption. Serious press issues like censorship, morality and privacy were also prominent. The series also explored relationships between its protagonists, particularly the Lynda and Spike will-they, won't-they tease, and allowed its characters to mature season by season. Filmed cinematically, it also dabbled in dream sequences, flashbacks, fantasies and, on one occa-

sion, a **Moonlighting**-esque parody of the film *It's a Wonderful Life*. Both its stars, Julia Sawalha and Dexter Fletcher, have moved on to bigger things, while former teacher Steven Moffat, who made his TV writing debut with *Press Gang*, later scripted the sitcom **Joking Apart**.

PRICE IS RIGHT, THE

UK (Central/Talbot) Game Show. ITV 1984–8

Presenter: Leslie Crowther

Producer: William G. Stewart

Manic game show in which contestants win prizes by knowing the price of goods in the shops.

'Come on down' was the gimmicky catchphrase employed by Leslie Crowther when hosting this all-action game show. Selecting contestants at random from a hyped-up studio audience, Crowther urged the chosen ones to join him in a series of games that shared one theme – guessing the value of household items. The contestants with the closest guesses picked up the prizes. Before arriving in the UK, *The Price is Right* had been one of America's most popular game shows, first airing in 1956.

PRIME SUSPECT

UK (Granada) Police Drama. ITV 1991–5

Detective Chief Inspector/Supt Jane Tennison	Helen Mirren (*1*, *2*, *3* and series)
Detective Sgt Bill Otley	Tom Bell (*1* and *3*)
Detective Chief Supt Mike Kernan	John Benfield (*1*, *2* and series)
George Marlow	John Bowe (*1*)
	Tim Woodward (series)
Moyra Henson	Zoe Wanamaker (*1*)
Detective Inspector Muddiman	Jack Ellis (*1*, *2* and series)
Detective Inspector Burkin	Craig Fairbrass (*1* and *2*)
Detective Inspector Richard Haskons	Richard Hawley (*1*, *2*, *3* and series)
Detective Chief Inspector John Shefford	John Forgeham (*1*)
Peter Rawlins	Tom Wilkinson (*1*)
Detective Sgt Oswalde	Colin Salmon (*2*)
DC Lillie	Philip Wright (*2* and *3*)
DC Jones	Ian Fitzgibbon (*2*)
Detective Supt Rosper	Andrew Tiernan (*2*)
Vera Reynolds	Peter Capaldi (*3*)
Jimmy Jackson	David Thewlis (*3*)
Commander Chiswick	Terrence Hardiman (*3*)
Inspector Larry Hall	Mark Strong (*3*)
WPC Norma Hastings	Karen Tomlin (*3*)
Supt Halliday	Struan Rodger (*3*)
WPC Kathy Bibby	Liza Sadovy (*3*)
Detective Inspector Dalton	Andrew Woodall (*3*)
Detective Inspector Ray Hebdon	Mark Drewry (*3*)

Creator: Lynda La Plante. Writers: Lynda La Plante (*1* and *3*), Allan Cubitt (*2*), Paul Billing (series), Eric Deacon (series), Guy Hibbert (series). Producers: Don Leaver (*1*), Paul Marcus (*2, 3* and series), Brian Park (series)

An ambitious woman detective fights sexism within the force.

Jane Tennison was a single-minded, career policewoman whose progress through the ranks had been impeded by male prejudice, until, that was, she won the battle to take charge of an intriguing murder case. At long last her abilities were given the chance to shine through, though there was still plenty of resentment from colleagues like Sgt Bill Otley. Such was the success of the two-part drama that *Prime Suspect 2* followed a year later. A second sequel, *Prime Suspect 3*, shown in 1993, saw Tennison moving from her base at Southampton Row to Soho's vice squad. A subsequent series of three single dramas was screened in 1995.

Taking the role of this hard-nosed copper signalled a major change in career direction for former Shakespearean actress Helen Mirren. Her new severe hair cut and sober suits were a world away from the roles she once enjoyed on stage. But Mirren had little difficulty in convincing viewers and went on to collect the BAFTA Best Actress award for three consecutive years. It was not enough for Hollywood, however, and when Universal bought the film rights to *Prime Suspect*, she was not considered for the lead role.

PRIME TIME see peak time.

PRINGLE, BRYAN (1935–)

British character actor, a familiar face in situation comedies. He was Cheese and Egg in *The Dustbinmen* and Sgt Flagg in *The Growing Pains of PC Penrose*. He has also been seen in *Room Service*, *Auf Wiedersehen, Pet*, *The Good Companions*, *Love Story*, *The Management*, *Paradise Postponed*, *Blind Justice*, *Once Upon a Time in the North*, *King and Castle*, *Flying Lady*, *Inspector Morse*, *All Creatures Great and Small*, *After Henry*, *Prime Suspect*, *Perfect Scoundrels*, *Rumpole of the Bailey*, *Boon* and plenty more series.

PRISONER, THE

UK (Everyman/ATV) Adventure. ITV 1967–8

The Prisoner (Number 6) ....Patrick McGoohan
The Butler ....Angelo Muscat

Creator/Executive Producer: Patrick McGoohan. Producer: David Tomblin

A secret agent is held captive in a mysterious Italianate village.

In the opening titles of *The Prisoner*, a sports car was seen to race through the streets of London beneath a thundery sky. An unnamed British intelligence agent stepped out and burst into a Whitehall office, abruptly handing in his resignation. Returning home to pack a suitcase, he was overcome by a puff of gas, waking up in a quaint, turreted village, surrounded by mountains and sea. As each episode then made clear, the agent was trapped. There was no escape from the village and he was constantly pumped for information, mostly about his sudden resignation. He had even lost his identity and was now known simply as Number 6, though he continued to claim 'I am not a number. I am a free man.'

And that, on the face of it, was all *The Prisoner* was about: a man held against his will, subjected to interrogation and attempting to escape. But there was far more to this series and so many questions were left unanswered. Who were his captors? Why were they holding him? Indeed, who was our hero? And would he ever be able to get away? All viewers knew was that head of the village was Number 1, and he was never seen, leaving his chief operative, Number 2, to deal with Number 6. But even Number 2 changed from episode to episode and the only face Number 6 could always recognize was that of the silent, dwarf butler.

Number 6 was not the only captive, but he was the only one who still had the will to break out. The others had already been brainwashed, going through the motions of their everyday life, playing human chess on the giant board in the village square, saying 'Be seeing you' and staggering on with their purposeless existence. And who were they anyway? In contrast, Number 6's mind was firmly set on escape, slipping away from the village's penny farthing bicycles, its golf-cart taxis, piped blazers, closed circuit security cameras and the floating, bouncing, white balloon-like guard known as Rover. Inevitably, his plans were foiled. Enigmatic to the end, *The Prisoner* concluded with a story that saw Number 6 being invited to take over the community and at last revealing the face of Number 1 – it was his own. A missile was launched to destroy the village, and Number 6 fled with the butler and two other inmates. As he raced through London in his sports car, with the skies once again thundery, a certain familiarity shone through. With the doors of his house slamming closed behind him, could it have been that the nightmare really was over, or had it just begun again?

Many conclusions have been drawn from this classic series. Was the village a sort of retirement home for burned out secret agents, or was it some kind of enemy intelligence centre? Or could it have been that The Prisoner was really only trapped in his own mind, a victim of a severe nervous breakdown, a theory supported by the circular pattern of events, including the conclusion, and the revelation of Number 1's face as his own. Certainly there were statements about democracy, personal freedom and social engineering in there, but the surreal nature of the series made it difficult for anyone to pin it all down.

The star of the series, Patrick McGoohan, was also the creator and driving force. Many fans believed *The Prisoner* to be a sequel to his previous success, **Danger Man**, although this was never stated. Instead, McGoohan has subsequently agreed that the programme was an allegorical conundrum. Not for nothing was his independent production company called Everyman, in direct reference to medieval morality plays.

Actors who played Number 2 included Leo McKern, Anton Rodgers, Peter Wyngarde and Patrick Cargill. The village used for filming was Portmeirion in North Wales, created as an Italian fantasy by architect Sir Clough Williams-Ellis.

PRISONER: CELL BLOCK H

Australia (Grundy) Drama. ITV 1979–

Lynn Warner	Kerry Armstrong
Bea Smith	Val Lehman
Vera Bennett	Fiona Spence
Freida 'Franky' Doyle	Carol Burns
Karen Travers	Peita Tommano
Jeannie 'Mum' Brooks	Mary Ward
Erica Davidson	Patsy King
Meg Morris/Jackson	Elspeth Ballantyne
Jim Fletcher	Gerard Maguire
Pat O'Connell	Monica Maughan
Dr Greg Miller	Barry Quin
Doreen Anderson	Collette Mann
Marilyn Anne Mason	Margaret Laurence
Elizabeth Birdsworth	Sheila Florance
Bill Jackson	Don Baker
Chrissie Latham	Amanda Muggleton
Anne Yates	Kristy Child
Noelene Burke	Jude Kuring
Barbara Davidson	Sally Cahill
Rita Connors	Glenda Linscott
Pixie Mason	Judy McBurney
Joan Ferguson	Maggie Kirkpatrick
Anne Reynolds	Gerda Nicholson
Jean Vernon	Christine Amor
Eddie Cook	Richard Moir
Steve Wilson	Jim Smillie
Jock Stewart	Tommy Dysart
Bill Jackson	Don Barker
Steve Faulkner	Wayne Jarratt

Creator/Executive Producer: Reg Watson.
Producers: Phil East, Marie Trevor, Ian Bradley, John McRae, Sue Masters

Low-budget, far from glitzy soap set in an Australian women's jail.

The Wentworth Detention Centre housed some of Melbourne's toughest female criminals and, through a series of rather far-fetched plots, examined the inter-relationships of the prisoners, their warders, and fringe characters such as partners on the outside, prison doctors and other officials. The series dealt openly with issues such as lesbianism and wanton assault (by both prisoners and guards) and in its own melodramatic way stripped the front off hard-bitten inmates to reveal personal tragedies that had led them to a life of crime. It showed how some matured to successfully rehabilitate themselves on their release, although it also made it clear that, for others, prison life was the only option.

Principal characters early on were Governor Erica Davidson, her deputy Jim Fletcher, brutal warder Vera Bennett and the more sympathetic guard, Meg Jackson (married to prison psychologist Bill Jackson). Ring-leader of the prisoners was Bea Smith (doing time for the murder of her husband), and other protagonists were the lesbian biker and armed-robber Franky Doyle, Karen Travers, a deeply religious ex-schoolteacher (also convicted of the murder of her husband), and dumb blonde Lynn Warner, the nanny who always denied murdering a child in her care. Thumb-sucking Doreen Anderson was the easily-led unmarried mother-turned-forger, Marilyn Mason was a prostitute and the prison nympho, 'Mum' Brooks the gentle, well-respected gardening lover (yet another imprisoned for killing her husband), and Lizzie Birdsworth the alcoholic, chain-smoking mass-murderer who was hell-bent on escape. Greg Miller was the prison doctor.

The show, originally entitled simply *Prisoner*, was renamed *Prisoner: Cell Block H* to avoid confusion with Patrick McGoohan's cult series of the 1960s in the UK and USA. Its creator, Reg Watson (a former **Crossroads** producer), and one of its producers, Marie Trevor, later moved on to the rather more successful **Neighbours**.

PRIVATE INVESTIGATOR

UK (BBC) Detective Drama. BBC 1958–9

John Unthank	Campbell Singer
Bill Jessel	Douglas Muir
James Wilson	Allan McClelland
Peter Clarke	Ian White
Mrs Layton	Ursula Camm

Creator/Producer: Arthur Swinson

The cases of an unspectacular private eye.

Keeping himself to himself, with a view to avoiding attention and preserving his cover, Scottish private investigator John Unthank was rolled out by the BBC for two pieces of detective work, spread over nine weeks. The first concerned

French currency fraud, the second a job for the National Canine Defence League on the Mediterranean. His restrained approach was an ocean apart from that of the wisecracking American sleuths of his era.

PRIVATE SCHULZ

UK (BBC) Comedy Drama. BBC 2 1981

Private Schulz...Michael Elphick
Major Neuheim ....Ian Richardson
Bertha Freyer ....Billie Whitelaw
Solly..Cyril Shaps
Professor Bodelschwingh ....David Swift

Writer: Jack Pulman. Producer: Philip Hinchcliffe

A German fraudster reluctantly works for SS Counter Espionage.

This series centred around the real-life, wartime attempt by the Nazis to flood Britain with forged £5 notes, with the aim of destroying the economy. Placed in charge of the adventurous scheme (by the mad Major Neuheim) was the stoic Private Schulz, a cowardly, small-time wheeler-dealer who had spent time in Spandau jail for fraud, before being mistakenly drafted into the SS. Schulz consequently weaved his way from scam to scam under the cover of war. Also seen was the Dietrich-esque Bertha Freyer.

PROBATION OFFICER

UK (ATV) Drama. ITV 1959–62

Philip Main...John Paul
Jim Blake...David Davies
Iris Cope ....Honor Blackman
Margaret Weston ....Jessica Spencer
Stephen Ryder ....Bernard Brown

Creator: Julian Bond. Producers: Antony Kearey, Rex Firkin

Drama in the lives of a team of probation officers.

Charged with the welfare of delinquents, criminals and other social unfortunates, members of the probation service constantly find themselves dragged into the affairs of others. This series depicted – in semi-documentary style – some of the typical problems faced by a team from inner London, and originally featured Philip Main, Jim Blake and Iris Cope as its main protagonists. Numerous other characters were introduced during the programme's three-year run and the cast lists changed frequently.

PRODUCER

The executive in charge of a programme, taking the original idea and drawing together the resources to make it happen. These resources include the budget and the crew, from the director and camera team to the performers. Sometimes, particularly in non-drama programming, the producer may provide more 'hands-on' creative input. Otherwise, he or she delegates this to the director, but still assumes overall responsibility for the finished project.

PRODUCTION ASSISTANT

The production assistant or PA is the producer and director's right-hand person. PAs work on a programme right from its earliest days, helping in the planning and staging, and continue their involvement through to the eventual recording or live transmission.

PROFESSIONALS, THE

UK (Avengers Mark 1/LWT) Spy Drama. ITV 1977–83

George Cowley ....Gordon Jackson
William Bodie ....Lewis Collins
Ray Doyle ....Martin Shaw
Murphy ....Steve Alder

Creator: Brian Clemens. Executive Producers: Albert Fennell, Brian Clemens. Producers: Sidney Hayers, Raymond Menmuir

The violent activities of a secret crime-busting unit.

'The Professionals' were the men and women of CI5 (Criminal Intelligence 5), a covert agency set up by the Government to specialize in criminal intelligence in the way that MI5 centred on military intelligence. The aim was to pre-empt trouble and so to nip crime in the bud. Head of the section was no-nonsense, ex-MI5 man George Cowley. He assembled around him a team of the toughest operatives, none more resilient and respected than Bodie, a former SAS and Parachute Regiment hero who exuded confidence. Bodie's partner was Doyle, an ex-copper with a much-derided curly perm. Fresh from an East End CID division, he was calm on the outside but harboured a rage within which threatened to burst out at any second. The pair were affectionately known as 'The Bisto Kids' to Cowley, who they knew as 'The Cow'.

The programme was created by Brian Clemens, the brains behind some of **The Avengers'** best adventures, although this all-action, macho series did not share the light-hearted, tongue-in-cheek, quirky qualities of his earlier work. It was parodied by The Comic Strip in their one-off satire, The Bullshitters.

PROMPTER see Autocue.

PROPERTIES OR PROPS

Studio or set furnishings/decorations intended to provide realism or convey a certain atmosphere.

PROTECTORS, THE

UK (ABC) Adventure. ITV 1964

Ian Souter	Andrew Faulds
Robert Shoesmith	Michael Atkinson
Heather Keys	Ann Morrish

Producer: Michael Chapman

Three professional troubleshooters nip crime in the bud.

'We sell security. Object: To prevent crime.' This was the motto of The Protectors, a trio of crime specialists working from a swish London office. The three were former insurance claims inspector Ian Souter, ex-policeman Robert Shoesmith and their girl Friday, Heather Keys. Operating in the twilight zone between the underworld and the security services, this determined trio acted to prevent crimes from taking place. The bearded, relaxed Souter, a Scotsman, was intelligent, experienced and decisive, Shoesmith had an understanding of the criminal mind which bordered on admiration, and Keys had an expert's eye for art forgeries. After placing an advertisement in newspapers, encouraging potential clients to 'Call Welbeck 3269', they found themselves protecting people in fear of an imminent crime, or those who had already fallen victim. They called themselves SIS, standing for Specialists In Security, and their assignments led them into murder, espionage and other forms of intrigue.

Two of the stars headed off in rather different career directions when this short-lived series came to an end. Andrew Faulds became a Member of Parliament and Ann Morrish went on to present **Play School**, amongst other television roles.

PROTECTORS, THE

UK (Group Three/ITC) Adventure. ITV 1972–4

Harry Rule	Robert Vaughn
Contessa di Contini	Nyree Dawn Porter
Paul Buchet	Tony Anholt
Suki	Yasuko Nagazami
Chino	Anthony Chinn

Producers: Gerry Anderson, Reg Hill

Three top investigators join forces to save the world from international crime.

The Protectors were Harry Rule, the Contessa di Contini and Paul Buchet. Together they blazed around Europe's top resorts, darting from flashy cars into private jets and meeting crime head on.

They tackled spies, drug pushers, smugglers, thieves and murderers. Rule was their leader, an ultra-cool American working from a high-tech office in London. He lived in a Tudor country mansion with an Irish wolfhound named Gus and was looked after by his au pair, Suki (a martial arts expert). The Contessa di Contini was Lady Caroline Ogilvy, an elegant English widow whose late Italian husband had left her a villa in Rome. Her speciality was art and antiques fraud, and she was chauffeured around by a karate chopping driver named Chino. Baby-faced Paul Buchet was an amorous Frenchman who operated out of a Paris apartment. Their glossy, rather violent adventures were produced by puppet master Gerry Anderson. Tony Christie belted out the closing theme song, 'Avenues and Alleyways', a UK chart hit in 1973.

PUBLIC EYE

UK (ABC/Thames) Detective Drama. ITV 1965–75

Frank Marker	Alfred Burke
Mrs Helen Mortimer	Pauline Delany
Detective Inspector Firbank	Ray Smith
Ron Gash	Peter Childs

Creators: Roger Marshall, Anthony Marriott. Executive Producers: Lloyd Shirley, Robert Love Producers: Don Leaver, John Bryce, Richard Bates, Michael Chapman, Kim Mills, Robert Love

The poorly-paid investigations of a grimy private detective.

Frank Marker was an unambitious detective, a sad character who dipped in and out of the murky underworld pond. He worked for next to nothing, sometimes not even getting paid for his troubles, but his satisfaction came from a job well done and the escapism it provided from his own drab world. He operated out of seedy, backstreet offices, firstly in London, then Birmingham and, finally, Brighton. He was a one-man band whose professional trust was often abused. On one occasion, he went to jail for handling stolen jewellery, even though he was only acting as a go-between for the insurers and the thieves.

Marker was joined later in the series by Mrs Mortimer, his landlady, as well as Inspector Firbank, a copper whose feathers Marker repeatedly ruffled. Ron Gash was a fellow detective who wanted Marker to join him in a partnership. The first three seasons (with quirkily-named episode titles like They Go Off in the End, Like Fruit and I Went to Borrow a Pencil, and Look What I Found) were produced by ABC TV, but when it lost its ITV franchise, production was taken over by its successor, Thames Television.

PULMAN, JACK (1925–80)

British writer first on TV in the 1950s with his own dramas but later better known for his adaptations. The highlights were *I, Claudius*, *War and Peace* and *Crime and Punishment*. Of his own creations, *Private Schulz* and the David Kossoff sitcom *A Little Big Business* were among the most notable, as well as the plays *A Book with Chapters In It*, *Nearer to Heaven* and *You Can't Have Everything*.

PURSUERS, THE

UK (Crestview/ABC) Police Drama. ITV
1961–2

Detective Inspector John Bollinger ....Louis Hayward
Detective Sgt Steve Wall ....Gaylord Cavallaro

Executive Producer: Donald Hyde

The cases of two Scotland Yard detectives and a loyal Alsatian police dog.

Middle-aged Detective Inspector John Bollinger patrolled the streets of London, assisted by Detective Sgt Wall and, usually, a large, black German Shepherd dog named Ivan. Its human star, the South African Louis Hayward, arrived on television having been a Hollywood actor since the 1930s. Thirty-nine episodes were made of this half-hourly series.

PUSSY CAT WILLUM

Famous TV puppet cat of the 1950s and early 1960s, partnered on screen by former skiffler Wally Whyton and Muriel Young. His obnoxiously smug attitude strangely gained him many admirers when he appeared in children's programmes like *Small Time*.

PYKE, DR MAGNUS, OBE (1908–92)

British scientist turned TV presenter in the 1970s, thanks to the YTV series *Don't Ask Me* and *Don't Just Sit There*, on which he was the resident pundit. His natural enthusiasm, fast talking and flailing arms made him an instant celebrity.

QED

UK (BBC) Documentary. BBC 1 1982–

Editors: David Filkin, Simon Campbell-Jones, Susan Spindler

Wide-ranging documentary series with a scientific bent.

Spontaneous combustion, overcoming drug addiction, the intense training of children to be sporting superstars, the effect of smoking on the human body and the chemistry of sexual attraction have all been typical subjects aired in this ambitious series of sometimes light-hearted science documentaries. Various producers have contributed programmes.

QUANTUM LEAP

US (Bellisarius) Science Fiction. BBC 2
1990–94

Dr Sam Beckett ....Scott Bakula
Al Calavicci ....Dean Stockwell

Creator/Producer: Donald Bellisario

A scientist is stranded in the past.

Scientist Sam Beckett was heavily involved in a secret time travel project known as Quantum Leap. One day, turning himself into a human guinea pig, he used the machine to go spinning back in time. But there he became stranded, thrown forwards and backwards to different eras within a period of 30 years of his own birth (1953). In each episode, he found himself trapped in the body of another person, which could have been male or female. One week he was a trapeze artist who had to prevent his sister suffering a tragic fall, another week a high school quarter back trying to stop two team mates from throwing an important game. While he was allowed to meddle with time in such minor instances, Sam was prohibited from altering anything major, such as Kennedy's assassination. In his temporary persona, though he looked the part to all concerned, to viewers he still appeared as the same old Sam.

While waiting to be returned to his own time, Sam's only hope was to fulfil his temporary roles as flawlessly as possible, trying not to arouse suspicions and aiming to win the day for the person concerned. To this end, he was aided by the hologramatic image of a colleague, a cigar-chewing admiral called Al. Al (seen only by Sam) brought news of the efforts to return Sam home, as well as assorted tit-bits about the people and the times in which he had been stranded, using a hand-held terminal linked to a computer named Ziggy. But Al's information was always incomplete, with the key details left out until the last possible moment. Having averted disaster, or at least having carried off his historical impersonation without too much distress, Sam, with a tremulous 'Oh boy!', was whisked away into another time zone and another body. Unfortunately, the final episode did not make happy viewing for fans of Sam Beckett. He learned that there was simply no way back to the present day. This was one hero who wasn't coming home.

QUATERMASS

UK (BBC/Thames/Euston Films) Science
Fiction. BBC 1953; 1955; 1958–9; ITV 1979

The Quatermass Experiment (BBC 1953)
Professor Bernard Quatermass..............Reginald Tate
Judith Carroon ....Isabel Dean
Victor Carroon ....Duncan Lamont
John Paterson ....Hugh Kelly
James Fullalove ....Paul Whitsun-Jones
Dr Gordon Briscoe..John Glen
Chief Inspector Lomax ....Ian Colin
Detective Sgt Best ....Frank Hawkins

Quatermass II (BBC 1955)
Professor Bernard Quatermass...........John Robinson
Paula Quatermass....................................Monica Grey
Dr Leo Pugh ....Hugh Griffiths
Captain John Dillon...................................John Stone
Vincent Broadhead...............................Rupert Davies

Quatermass and the Pit (BBC 1958–9)
Professor Bernard Quatermass ....André Morell
Barbara Judd ....Christine Finn
Dr Matthew Roney.......................................Cec Linder
Sladden ....Richard Shaw
Col Breen ....Anthony Bushell
Captain Potter...John Stratton
James Fullalove ....Brian Worth

Quatermass (ITV 1979)
Professor Bernard Quatermass....................John Mills
Joe Kapp ....Simon MacCorkindale
Clare Kapp ....Barbara Kellerman
Kickalong ....Ralph Arliss
Caraway ....Paul Rosebury
Bee ....Jane Bertish
Hettie...Rebecca Saire
Marshall..Tony Sibbald
Sal ....Toyah Wilcox

Writer: Nigel Kneale. Producers: Rudolph
Cartier (BBC), Ted Childs (Thames). Executive
Producer: Verity Lambert (Thames)

**The alien-thwarting adventures of
Professor Bernard Quatermass, grandfather of all TV science fiction heroes.**

The name 'Quatermass' has become synonymous
with early TV sci-fi, yet relatively few viewers
would have seen the original ground-breaking
series. Transmitted live in 1953, when homes
with TVs were few and repeats impossible, it
nonetheless managed to set the trend for TV hor-
ror-fantasy, leading to three follow-ups, the last
26 years later. The brains behind the project was
Nigel Kneale, a BBC staff writer given the
chance to branch out with his own ideas. What
he foresaw in *The Quatermass Experiment* was a
new kind of TV thriller, adventurous in both its
subject matter and presentation. It concerned
astronaut Victor Carroon who returned to Earth
contaminated by an alien life form. As the alien
vegetable gradually took over Carroon's body and
threatened to reproduce in vast quantities, to

devastating effect, it was left to level-headed space
scientist Professor Quatermass to track him
down. Cornering Carroon at Westminster
Abbey, Quatermass appealed to what remained of
his human nature, urging Carroon to destroy
himself and save the planet.

When Quatermass resurfaced two years later,
production techniques had advanced somewhat
and this time the Professor was called upon to
protect Earth from aliens who had infiltrated
people's minds and bodies. The invaders had been
using a synthetic food factory as a secret acclimatization centre. Identifying the alien base as being
an asteroid on the other side of the planet,
Quatermass and his colleague, Dr Pugh, set off in
the Professor's own latest space rocket to destroy
it. The original Quatermass, Reginald Tate, died
just weeks before this second series, leaving John
Robinson to take over the character.

The third element in the saga, *Quatermass and the
Pit*, was the most sophisticated of the BBC versions, concentrating on the idea that Martians
had arrived on Earth millions of years earlier and
imparted certain attributes to man's ancestors, a
process that explained away phenomena like
ghosts, demons and ESP. This came to light as the
last traces of blitzed London were being redevel-
oped and a five million-year-old skull was discovered next to an alien rocket in a deep pit. The
Professor (now played by André Morell), aided by
palaeontologist Matthew Roney, was brought in
to restore order.

No more was heard of Quatermass until Thames
and Euston Films picked up the reins in 1979. In
a story Kneale had first penned around ten years
earlier, John Mills became the fourth actor to play
the scientist who returned to London from a
Scottish retirement to look for his missing granddaughter, Hettie. Once again aliens were at the
heart of the problem, bringing chaos to society
and harvesting and taking away hordes of young
people (hippies known as 'Planet People') at
places as diverse as Wembley Stadium and ancient
stone circles. Teaming up with Joe Kapp, a young
Jewish astronomer, Quatermass not only foiled
the aliens but retrieved Hettie along the way.

The first three *Quatermass* stories were also filmed
by Hammer and released on the cinema circuit,
two with Brian Donlevy in the title role. The
films were given new titles for American audiences: *The Creeping Unknown*, *Enemy from Space*
and *Five Million Years to Earth* (starring Andrew
Keir), respectively.

QUAYLE, SIR ANTHONY, CBE (1913–89)

Anthony Quayle's finest hours definitely came on
the stage and in the cinema, but he made his con-

tribution to television's archives as well. He starred as criminologist Adam Strange in the 1968 series *The Strange Report*, acted as narrator for the award-winning *Six Wives of Henry VIII* (amongst other series) and appeared in numerous TV movies, plays and mini-series, including *QB VII* (as Tom Bannister), *Moses the Lawgiver* (as Aaron), *Masada* (as Rubrius Gallus), *The Last Days of Pompeii* and *The BBC Television Shakespeare* (*Henry IV* parts I and II).

QUEENIE'S CASTLE

UK (Yorkshire) Situation Comedy. ITV 1970–2

Queenie Shepherd......................................Diana Dors
Raymond Shepherd ....Freddie Fletcher
Douglas Shepherd ....Barrie Rutter
Bunny Shepherd ....Brian Marshall
Jack..Tony Caunter
Mrs Petty ....Lynne Perrie

Creators: Keith Waterhouse, Willis Hall.
Producers: Graham Evans, Ian Davidson

A Yorkshire matriarch runs her family with a rod of iron.

Queenie Shepherd was the undoubted head of the impoverished Shepherd clan. Dominating her motley trio of sons (Raymond, Douglas and Bunny), she lived in the Buckingham flats, a Yorkshire housing development. Also part of the household was Queenie's brother-in-law, Jack, and poking her nose in – and risking Queenie's ready wrath – was their neighbour Mrs Petty (a pre-*Coronation Street* Lynne Perrie). Another *Street* star, Bryan Mosley, was seen as their landlord.

QUEST, THE

US (Columbia) Western. BBC 1 1976–7

Morgan Beaudine ....Kurt Russell
Quentin Beaudine ....Tim Matheson

Creator: Tracy Keenan Wynn. Executive Producer: David Gerber. Producers: Mark Rodgers, James H. Brown

In the Wild West of the 1880s, two brothers set out to find their long-lost sister.

Morgan Beaudine and his sister, Patricia, had been taken captive when children by Cheyenne Indians, but they had become separated. Morgan had been raised by the Indians and given the name of 'Two Persons', and, although he had now returned to white society, he still trusted Indians more than his own kind. He also dressed like a redskin and spoke their language – a useful asset in the Wild West. His brother, Quentin, had enjoyed a quite different upbringing, living with an aunt and being educated in San Francisco. He

planned to be a doctor, but first things first. Their sister was still missing, so the brothers hit the road in an attempt to track her down and reunite the family. Their 'Quest' proved long and largely fruitless.

QUESTION OF SPORT, A

UK (BBC) Quiz. BBC 1 1970–

Presenters: David Vine, David Coleman

Producers: Nick Hunter, Mike Adley

Light-hearted quiz featuring sporting personalities.

Hosted initially by David Vine, but in the hands of David Coleman since 1979, *A Question of Sport* has achieved an audience appeal that reaches beyond the realms of traditional sports fans. The relaxed, jokey atmosphere and flippant banter have made the series into a popular light entertainment show, with high viewing figures to boot. Two teams of three sporting celebrities (each containing a resident captain) work their way through several rounds of sporting teasers, answering questions on their own individual events as well as general sporting matters. Favourite rounds have included the picture board (identifying the personality from an obscure picture), what happened next? (guessing the sequence of events after the film has stopped), the mystery personality (revealed only in short glimpses through unusual camera angles) and the 60-second rapid fire section (worth up to nine points).

A Question of Sport team captains have included Cliff Morgan, Henry Cooper, Gareth Edwards, Emlyn Hughes, Willie Carson, Bill Beaumont and Ian Botham. In 1987 the programme achieved a rare coup, when HRH The Princess Anne was recruited onto Emlyn Hughes's team to celebrate the 200th edition.

QUESTION TIME

UK (BBC) Debate. BBC 1 1979–

Chairmen:
Robin Day
Peter Sissons
David Dimbleby

Studio–audience-led political debate.

Question Time has been based on a simple formula: take three politicians of different persuasions, plus one 'neutral' – often an industrialist or academic – and throw them to the lions (in the form of a studio audience of mixed political views). Without pre-knowledge, the panellists have to answer tricky, topical questions put to them by the gathered masses. Keeping order, and helping to put the panellists on the spot, was initially Robin Day, whose inimitably gruff style helped establish the series. When he retired in 1989, his seat was taken, amidst much publicity, by then Channel 4 newscaster Peter Sissons. Sissons has subsequently handed over control to David Dimbleby. Over the years, several fill-in hosts have also been employed to cover for sickness. These have included Sue Lawley and Ludovic Kennedy. The idea for *Question Time* was based on Radio 4's *Any Questions*.

QUILLEY, DENIS (1927–)

British actor seen in a variety of series from the kids' sci-fi thriller *Timeslip* (as Commander Traynor) to the sitcom *Rich Tea and Sympathy* (as biscuit magnate George Rudge). He played Richard Shelton in a 1951 version of R.L. Stevenson's *The Black Arrow*, Gladstone in *No. 10*, Quadratus in the mini-series *Masada*, Peter in another mini-series, *AD*, and amongst his other credits have been *Dixon of Dock Green*, *Clayhanger*, *The Bretts*, *After the War* and *Family Album*, plus single dramas.

QUINCY

US (Universal/Glen A Larson) Detective Drama. ITV 1977–85

Quincy ME	Jack Klugman
Lt Frank Monahan	Garry Walberg
Sam Fujiyama	Robert Ito
Danny Tovo	Val Bisoglio
Lee Potter	Lynette Mettey
Dr Robert J. Asten	John S. Ragin
Sgt Brill	Joseph Roman
Eddie	Ed Garrett
Marc	Marc Scott Taylor
Diane	Diane Markoff
Dr Emily Hanover	Anita Gillette

Creators: Glen A. Larson, Lou Shaw. Executive Producer: Glen A. Larson. Producers: Lou Shaw, Peter Thompson, Robert F. O'Neill, Michael Star

An inquisitive pathologist keeps unearthing new clues and frustrating the local police.

Widower Quincy worked for the Los Angeles County Coroner's Office as a medical examiner. A man of principle, he had abandoned a lucrative medical practice in order to take on this demanding job, but he was born to it. The quick once-over of the corpse was not for Quincy. He went into every detail and, just when the cops thought they had a 'natural causes' case on their hands, the pushy pathologist unearthed something more suspicious. Indeed, so pushy was Quincy, that the police could hardly ignore him. But, just in case

they did, much to the consternation of his boss, Dr Asten, Quincy often turned detective himself and went out looking for clues, assisted by his young colleague, Sam Fujiyama.

In his private life, Quincy had a girlfriend, Lee Potter, though such was his dedication to his job, their romance never quite took off. He therefore lived alone, on a boat moored near a bar called Danny's Place, where he spent whatever free time he had. Lee soon left the scene, but Quincy later met psychiatrist Emily Hanover, whom he subsequently married. Quincy's christian name was never given, though a once-seen business card did give his initial as R.

The series (known in the USA as *Quincy, ME*) began life as a part of the *Mystery Movie* anthology, but proved so popular in the USA that it was given its own regular slot.

QUIRKE, PAULINE (1959–)

A teenage performer in the 1970s, Pauline Quirke has now developed into an adult star, thanks largely to roles in *Angels* (as Vicki Smith), *Shine on Harvey Moon* (Veronica) and *Birds of a Feather* (Sharon Theodopolopoudos). She appeared in *Dixon of Dock Green* aged ten, and worked in all manner of kids' shows for Thames, including *You Must Be Joking* and her own series, *Pauline's Quirkes* and *Pauline's People*. She has also been seen in *The Duchess of Duke Street*, *Crown Court*, *Lovely Couple*, *Girls on Top*, *Rockliffe's Babies* and *Casualty*.

QUIZ BALL

UK (BBC) Quiz. BBC 1 1966–72

Presenters: David Vine, Barry Davies, Stuart Hall

Producers: Bill Wright, Mary Evans

Light-hearted soccer quiz involving football league teams.

Quiz Ball was a game show in the *A Question of Sport* vein, but with its sporting content confined to association football. In each match, two league soccer teams competed for the right to advance through the knock-out tournament. Arsenal played Nottingham Forest in the very first programme. Teams were comprised of players, management and celebrity supporters and they answered questions of varying degrees of difficulty to progress along an electronic scoreboard (designed like a football pitch) towards goal. A hard question was the equivalent of a 'long ball', catapulting the team into their opponents' penalty box if answered correctly, whereas easier questions could be pieced together like a passing game for a slower approach. The team with the most goals won the match. There was even an international element to the tournament, with special Home International matches taking place between England, Wales, Scotland and Northern Ireland. David Vine was the first chairman and question-master, followed by Barry Davies and finally Stuart Hall.

R3

UK (BBC) Science Fiction. BBC 1 1964–5

Sir Michael Gerrard ....John Robinson
Miss Brooks ....Brenda Saunders
Dr George Fratton..............................Moultrie Kelsall
Dr May Howard ....Elizabeth Sellars
Dr Peter Travers ....Richard Wordsworth
Dr Jack Morton ....Simon Lack
Betty Mason...Janet Kelly
Pomeroy ....Edwin Richfield
Tom Collis ....Derek Benfield
Porter..Maxwell Foster
Phillip Boult ....Michael Hawkins
Dr Richard Franklin....................................Oliver Reed

Creator: N.J. Crisp. Producers: Andrew Osborn, John Robins

Drama centring on the private and professional lives of a team of scientists.

Focusing on the staff of R3 (short for Research Centre No. 3, a division of the Ministry of Research), this series examined how scientists cope with the responsibilities and demands of their jobs, and how these affect their domestic lives. Effectively, it took eggheads and boffins and gave them a human dimension. Sir Michael Gerrard (played by former Professor Quatermass, John Robinson) was director of the unit, supported by his number two, Dr George Fratton. Beneath him worked a team of dedicated scientists, struggling to cope with the morality of certain experiments and the social consequences of new discoveries. In the second season, the focus moved to the department's trouble-shooting agency, known as Consultancy Service, a specialist team geared up to solving problems beyond normal human knowledge. It was led by Phillip Boult, aided by a young Oliver Reed in the role of genial Dr Richard Franklin.

RAB C. NESBITT

UK (BBC) Situation Comedy. BBC 2 1990–

Rab C. Nesbitt ....Gregor Fisher
Mary Nesbitt..Elaine C Smith
Gash Nesbitt ....Andrew Fairlie
Burney Nesbitt ....Eric Cullen
Jamesie Cotter..Tony Roper

Creator/Writer: Ian Pattison. Producer: Colin Gilbert

The downs and downs of tenement life with a Glasgow street philosopher.

Sporting a string vest and a grubby headband, and brandishing a rolled-up newspaper, Rab C. Nesbitt made his name in the *Naked Video* sketch show, taking the Establishment to task in an opinionated drunken stupor. Following a New Year's special in 1989 (*Rab C. Nesbitt's Seasonal Greet*), this series was launched and showed the aggressive waster at home and at play, battling with his wife, Mary, and obnoxious kids, Gash and Burney, squabbling with his drinking chums (including his best mate Jamesie) and bamboozling the forces of law and order with unfathomable Scottish gibberish.

RACING GAME, THE

UK (Yorkshire) Detective Drama. ITV 1979–80

Sid Halley ....Mike Gwilym
Chico Barnes ....Mick Ford

Executive Producer: David Cunliffe. Producer: Jacky Stoller

A disabled jockey turns to private detective work.

Horse racing has never fared well in TV drama. Like the much criticized *Trainer* a decade later, this attempt to bring the colour of the sport of kings into viewers' living rooms was doomed to failure. Based on the hugely successful novels by former Royal jockey Dick Francis, this six-part series focused on one Sid Halley, a jump jockey who had suffered a bad riding accident and lost a hand. Denied a return to his true vocation, Halley did the next best thing – he hovered around the fringes of racing society, setting himself up as a private investigator and mingling with some of the murkier characters in the racing world. Despite successes against dopers and nobblers, betting coup merchants and horsenappers, he and his assistant, Chico Barnes, failed to win over viewers and a second series didn't come under starter's orders.

RAFFLES

UK (Yorkshire) Crime Drama. ITV 1977

L.J. Raffles.......................................Anthony Valentine
Bunny Manders...........................Christopher Strauli
Inspector Mackenzie ....Victor Carin

Writer: Philip Mackie. Executive Producer: David Cunliffe. Producer: Jacky Stoller

Audacious robberies performed with aplomb by a turn-of-the-century gentleman thief.

A first-class cricketer, man about town and a general good egg, Raffles had but one excitement in life – the buzz that came from pulling off risky thefts from his upper-class associates, often under the noses of the authorities. Part of the pleasure lay in seeing his police adversary, Inspector Mackenzie, humiliated time and again. From his first daring theft of a £10,000 diamond necklace at a stately home, Raffles was loyally supported by Bunny Manders, his former public school fag and the only man in the world who knew of his old friend's escapades. Manders was a reliable colleague and constantly reminded Raffles of his gentleman's code.

The series was based on the original stories of E.W. Hornung, with the pilot episode, *Raffles – The Amateur Cracksman*, screened as a one-off in 1975. In this pilot, Mackenzie was played by James Maxwell. Christopher Hodson produced.

RAG, TAG AND BOBTAIL

UK (BBC) Children's Entertainment. BBC 1953–5; 1958

Narrators: Charles E. Stidwill, David Enders, James Urquhart

Writer: Louise Cochrane. Producers: Freda Lingstrom, David Boisseau

The hedgerow adventures of a trio of country animals.

Rag, Tag and Bobtail was the Thursday segment of the **Watch with Mother** strand and featured the little escapades of glove puppets Rag (a hedgehog), Tag (a mouse) and Bobtail (a clover-chewing buck rabbit). The puppets were created and controlled by Sam and Elizabeth Williams and 26 episodes were made. Episodes one and two were never screened but the remaining 24 were repeated endlessly until the programme was replaced in 1965.

RAG TRADE, THE

UK (BBC/LWT) Situation Comedy. BBC 1961–3; ITV 1977–8

BBC:

Mr Fenner	Peter Jones
Reg	Reg Varney
Paddy	Miriam Karlin
Carole	Sheila Hancock
Little Lil	Esma Cannon
Judy	Barbara Windsor
Shirley	Wanda Ventham
Janet	Amanda Reiss
Sandra	Sheena Marshe
Betty	Patricia Denys
Myrtle	Claire Davenport
Olive	Stella Tanner
Gloria	Carmel Cryan

LWT:

Mr Fenner	Peter Jones
Paddy	Miriam Karlin
Tony	Christopher Beeny
Olive	Anna Karen
Kathy	Diane Langton
Lyn	Gillian Taylforth
Jo-jo	Lucita Lijertwood
Mabel	Deddie Davies

Creators/Writers: Ronald Chesney, Ronald Wolfe. Producers: Dennis Main Wilson (BBC), Bryan Izzard, William G. Stewart (LWT)

Union strife at a clothing factory.

Set in the East End dressmaking workshop of Fenner Fashions, *The Rag Trade* focused on the him-and-us relationship between the unscrupulous, scheming boss Mr Fenner and his workshy employees, with militant Paddy, the shop steward, always ready to blow her whistle and order 'Everybody out!'. Carole was the shop treasurer, with Little Lil the buttonholer and tea maker. Other girls came and went during the series' two-year run but always stuck in the middle was Reg, the factory foreman.

A huge hit in the early 1960s, *The Rag Trade* was revived with less success in 1977. Only Peter Jones and Miriam Karlin survived from the original cast, and newcomers like Christopher Beeny (as foreman Tony) and Anna Karen (reprising her **On the Buses** role of Olive) were added to the roll call of workers.

RAINBOW

UK (Thames/HTV/Tetra Films) Children's Entertainment. ITV 1971–92; 1994

Presenters: David Cook, Geoffrey Hayes

Executive Producers: Charles Warren, Alan Horrox. Producers: Pamela Lansdale, Vic Hughes, Charles Warren, Lesley Burgess, Sheila Kinany, Paul Cole

Education and entertainment for the pre-school age.

Although effectively ITV's answer to **Play School**, *Rainbow* was more a British **Sesame Street**. It was hosted originally by David Cook but more famously by former **Z Cars** actor Geoffrey Hayes (from 1973). Judi Dench was occasionally seen as a storyteller in the early days, and Stephanie Beacham filled the same role later, but better remembered are the *Rainbow* puppet characters. Taught and instructed as if they were kids (indeed they acted as surrogate children to convey the educational angle), the first puppets were Moony, a sad-looking mauve creature, and his antithesis, Sunshine, a livelier, yellow one. For many years, however, the puppet cast was comprised of Zippy, an oval headed, wide-eyed creation with a painful-looking zip for a mouth, George, a pink hippopotamus, and Bungle, a good-natured bear originally played by actor John Leeson. Music was provided by the trio of Rod (Burton), Jane (Tucker) and Matthew (Corbett of Sooty fame), with Freddy (Marks) later taking the place of Matthew. Roger Walker was also once a member of the musical team. The singers were later given their own spin-off series, appropriately entitled *Rod, Jane and Freddy*. The programme ended its long lunchtime run when Thames TV lost its franchise, although it later returned minus Geoffrey and with a new female puppet called Cleo in an afternoon slot.

RANDALL AND HOPKIRK (DECEASED)

UK (ITC) Detective Drama. ITV 1969–70

Jeff Randall..Mike Pratt
Marty Hopkirk ....Kenneth Cope
Jean Hopkirk..Annette Andre
Inspector Large ....Ivor Dean

Creator: Dennis Spooner. Producer: Monty Berman

Unorthodox investigations by a private eye and his partner, a ghost.

Jeff Randall and Marty Hopkirk were partners in a private detection agency, or rather, they had been, until Marty was murdered in a hit-and-run incident. Returning as a ghost, he helped Jeff bring his killers to book, but, from that time onward, Marty was obliged to remain on Earth (for 100 years), having broken a rule of the afterlife by staying down here after daybreak. As the old rhyme went:

Afore the sun shall rise anew
Each ghost unto his grave must go.
Cursed be the ghost who dares to stay
And face the awful light of day.
He shall not to the grave return
Until a hundred years be gone.

Being a ghost, Marty was visible to only one person, Jeff. Not even his bemused widow, Jean, who was Jeff's secretary, knew of his presence. But this rendered him remarkably useful in the detection game, as a valuable source of information, despite the fact that he could not get physically involved. Sadly, he was also rather unreliable and very frustrating: many a time Jeff was left waiting for his white-suited, deceased partner to show up with a vital clue, or to warn him of impending danger. Inspector Large was the programme's token grumpy copper.

The series, played with a generous slice of humour, was shown in the USA under the title *My Partner the Ghost* but was not a great success across the Atlantic. BBC 2 re-ran the series in 1994.

RANDALL, JOAN AND LESLIE

One of TV's first husband and wife couples, the Randalls starred in their own mid-1950s sitcom, appropriately titled *Joan and Leslie* but later changed to *The Randall Touch*. Previously, Leslie had appeared in a short variety programme entitled *Leslie Randall Entertains*, from which Joan and Leslie evolved. They later appeared as investigators Jane and Dogobert Brown in the *Detective* anthology and advertised Fairy Snow for nine years before splitting up. Leslie headed off for TV work in the USA and Australia, but returned in the 1970s to write plays and work in radio. Joan was sometimes billed under her maiden name of Joan Reynolds.

RANGE RIDER, THE

US (Flying A) Western. BBC 1955–

The Range Rider....................................Jock Mahoney
Dick West ....Dick Jones

Executive Producer: Armand Schaefer. Producer: Louis Gray

A mysterious do-gooder and his friend roam the West, helping folk in trouble.

This early western featured the exploits of the honest, principled and tough Range Rider and his boyish sidekick, Dick West. Together they drifted across the Wild West of the 1860s, putting outlaws in their places, rescuing helpless civilians and assisting the forces of law and order in their own unconventional way. They must have been the two most athletic cowboys around, for rarely did they spurn the chance to leap from their horses, rope in the criminals and perform whatever heroic feat was required. This was largely because the two stars were fit and brawny themselves and were willing to do their own stuntwork (actor Jock Mahoney later went on to play Tarzan).

Dressed in a fringed buckskin shirt and a white stetson, The Range Rider wore no boots, only Indian moccasins. His horse was called Rawhide. Dick, sporting a dark, military-style shirt and a black hat, rode a steed called Lucky. The theme song for the show was 'Home On The Range'.

RANTZEN, ESTHER (1940–)

Doyenne of TV consumerists, Esther Rantzen began her career in radio production, arriving in television as a production assistant on *Man Alive* and a researcher/reporter on *Braden's Week*. When the series ended, she produced and presented her own series which looked at the quirks of everyday life and stood up for the embattled consumer. Entitled *That's Life*, it ran for 21 years from 1973, making Rantzen a household name. It also gave her the opportunity to expand into other programmes. These included *The Big Time*, *Hearts of Gold* and *Children in Need* (associated with her main charity concern, Childline). She is married to TV presenter and producer Desmond Wilcox. Since the end of *That's Life*, she has presented a BBC 2 twice-weekly topical discussion show called *Esther*.

RAPHAEL, FREDERIC (1931–)

British screenwriter, author of *The Glittering Prizes* and its sequel, *Oxbridge Blues*. His other credits have included *Rogue Male* (1976), *The Serpent Son*, *School Play* (both 1979), *After the War* (1989) and the 1978 Premiere film *Something's Wrong* (also as director).

RAT CATCHERS, THE

UK (Associated-Rediffusion) Spy Drama. ITV 1966–7

Peregrine Smith	Gerald Flood
Brigadier Davidson	Philip Stone
Richard Hurst	Glyn Owen

Producer: Cyril Coke

The assignments of a top secret counter-espionage team.

The Rat Catchers were based in Whitehall but officially had no name or number; their existence was denied by the highest authorities and they worked in the greatest secrecy. Their role was to defend the country from foreign threats, and obey orders without question. As a result, they lived and operated in a violent, hazardous world. The three members of the team were wealthy playboy Peregrine Smith, cold, analytical Brigadier Davidson (the brains of the team), and newcomer Richard Hurst, a former Scotland Yard superintendent. It was with Hurst's arrival that viewers first learned about the squad, and his uncertain start revealed just how unsavoury this profession could be. Indeed, it was a far cry from the glitzy world of James Bond, their cinema contemporary.

RATINGS

The audience figures enjoyed by television programmes, arranged in order of popularity. These are of particular value to advertisers but are also a useful pointer for programme makers when gauging the success of their projects. The statistics are compiled using various means, from simple consumer surveys and viewer diaries to electronic attachments to television receivers. Numerous companies have collated the information in the UK over the years. The American giant, AC Nielsen, was active in the 1950s, but also involved have been Gallup, Pulse, TAM (Television Audience Measurement) and AGB (Audits of Great Britain), the last producing figures for the Joint Industry Committee for Television Audience Research (JICTAR), a committee representing the interests of ITV companies and their advertisers. In 1981, at the behest of the 1977 Annan Committee's review of broadcasting in the UK, the separate BBC and JICTAR ratings systems were amalgamated into the Broadcasters' Audience Research Board (BARB). The collation method in use today is complex and involves drawing data by meter from sample households that are selected to provide a cross-section of ages, sex and economic and social status.

RAVEN, SIMON (1927–)

British novelist and screenwriter, initially scripting his own plays like *Royal Foundation*, *The Scapegoat*, *The Move Up Country* and *Soirée at Bossom's Hotel* in the 1960s, before turning to adaptations like *The Pallisers* and series dramas such as *Edward and Mrs Simpson* in the 1970s.

RAWHIDE

US (CBS) Western. ITV 1959–

Gil Favor	Eric Fleming
Rowdy Yates	Clint Eastwood
Wishbone	Paul Brinegar
Pete Nolan	Sheb Wooley
Jim Quince	Steve Raines
Joe Scarlett	Rocky Shahan
Harkness 'Mushy' Mushgrove	James Murdock
Hey Soos Patines	Robert Cabal
Clay Forrester	Charles Gray
Jed Colby	John Ireland
Ian Cabot	David Watson

Creator/Producer: Charles Marquis Warren

The adventures of a cattle-driving team as they cross the Wild West.

Chiefly remembered for being the show that gave Clint Eastwood his first taste of stardom, *Rawhide* was a western for men by men, a kind of *Wagon Train* with cows and precious few women. It revolved around a team of cattle drovers, trying to lead a herd from San Antonio, Texas up to Sedalia, Missouri, sometime in the 1860s, well before the railroad arrived to allieviate this chore. Gil Favor was the head of the team, with Eastwood's Rowdy Yates the second in command, later to assume control when Favor was written out. Also in the troop were trail scout Pete Nolan, cook Wishbone, Mushy, the drover, and a Mexican, Hey Soos (Jesus). Their men-against-the-elements voyage was constantly interrupted by encounters with intriguing strangers, so much so that when the series ended seven years later, they still hadn't reached the end of the trail.

The 'Keep them doggies rollin'' theme song was a UK hit for Frankie Laine in 1959. Sheb Wooley, who played Pete Nolan, was also a comedian-cum-country singer and had already broken into the UK Top 20 in 1958 with 'The Purple People Eater' (a number one in the USA).

RAY, ROBIN (ROBIN OLDEN)

British actor/presenter, largely interested in the arts and, in particular, music and the cinema. Amongst his credits has been *Film Buff of the Year* (as questionmaster), *Call My Bluff* (as first chairman) and *Face the Music* (as panellist). The son of comedian Ted Ray, Robin is the brother of actor Andrew Ray and is married to former *Magpie* presenter Susan Stranks.

RAY, TED (CHARLES OLDEN; 1905–77)

Music hall comedian/violinist who came to television following success with *Ray's a Laugh* on the radio. His *Ted Ray Show* was popular in the 1950s and he also compèred *Spot the Tune* on some occasions. In the 1970s, he was back on the small screen as a regular panellist on the gag show *Jokers Wild* and the talent show *New Faces*. He was the father of actors Andrew and Robin Ray.

RAYNER, CLAIRE (1931–)

One of Britain's leading agony aunts, former nurse Claire Rayner is a familiar face on UK TV. She has answered problems and preferred advice on TV-am and in her own series *Claire Rayner's Casebook*, as well as appearing as a guest on many magazine programmes. She is also a published novelist.

READY, STEADY, GO!

UK (Associated-Rediffusion) Pop Music. ITV 1963–6

Hosts:
Keith Fordyce
David Gell
Michael Aldred
Cathy McGowan

Producer: Frances Hitching. Executive Producer: Elkan Allan

Influential British pop music show, a focal point of the beat boom.

'The Weekend Starts Here' was the slogan of this lively pop showcase that opened up each week to the sound of Manfred Mann's '5-4-3-2-1', and later the same band's 'Hubble Bubble Toil and Trouble'. Airing early on a Friday evening, the weekend really did begin here for many teenagers, particularly those outside of London, for whom this was one of the few opportunities to savour the heady years of British beat. The kids took their lead from *RSG!* in dance, in fashion and, of course, in musical taste.

Technically advanced for its era, particularly in the innovative camera work, *RSG!* enjoyed the patronage of nearly all the leading acts, who seldom missed the chance to appear. But it also bravely introduced lesser-known artists, including obscure bands from across the Atlantic. Far more lively than the rather static 'Top of the Pops', *RSG!* boasted a tiny studio, crammed full of excited youths enjoying a club-like atmosphere, nudging and pressing against the featured artists as they bopped to the music. Gary Glitter, years before stardom of his own, worked as one of the all-important crowd controllers.

The hosts (at various times) were Keith Fordyce, David Gell, Michael Aldred and Cathy McGowan, a young discovery who quickly mastered the art of presenting TV pop. She had answered an advertisement calling for a 'typical teenager' to act as an advisor on the show, but was soon pushed in front of the cameras. Her success lay in the fact that she was one of the fans; the viewers could identify with her as she fluffed her lines, grinned at inappropriate moments and panicked during interviews with celebrities. She was one of the teenagers, not a long-in-the-tooth broadcaster, and she soon became a style leader herself. When the programme switched to a larger studio and bands were obliged to perform live instead of miming, McGowan was kept on as solo presenter.

The series drew to a close just as the beat boom came to an end. The fact that it was axed at the height of its popularity has clearly helped maintain its respected status as a TV pop classic. Compilations were shown on Channel 4 in the 1980s, courtesy of drummer-turned-entrepreneur Dave Clark, who now owns the rights to the tapes.

REAL LIVES

UK (BBC) Documentary. BBC 1 1984–5

Executive Producers: Peter Pagnamenta, Edward Mirzoeff

A series of close inspections of how people live today.

This documentary series looked at the lives of people from all parts of society, examining what made them tick. Amongst those featured were a defecting Russian violinist, drug pushers, Los Angeles street gang members, finalists in a 'True Romances' contest and a British army unit going back to Northern Ireland as civilians. One programme due for transmission in the second series caused a major stir. Entitled *At the Edge of the Union*, it focused on two individuals at opposite extremes in the Northern Irish troubles. The two were Gregory Campbell and Martin McGuinness. The fact that McGuinness was said to have been an IRA supporter enraged the Government which felt that terrorists should not have been given the oxygen of publicity. Home Secretary Leon Britton intervened (without seeing the programme) and called for it to be withdrawn. This led to a dispute between the BBC's Board of Governors, who agreed with his sentiments, and the BBC Management, who wanted it to be screened. The programme was not transmitted and, in protest at what they viewed as interference in the BBC's independence, journalists from both BBC and ITN staged a one-day strike. With some changes, the programme was finally shown in October 1985, two months late.

RECORD BREAKERS

UK (BBC) Children's Entertainment. BBC 1 1972–

Presenters:
Roy Castle
Ross McWhirter
Norris McWhirter
Dilys Morgan
Fiona Kennedy
Julian Farino
Cheryl Baker
Ron Reagan Jnr
Kriss Akabusi
Mark Curry

Producers: Alan Russell, Eric Rowan, Greg Childs

The tallest, the shortest, the latest and the greatest: TV's answer to the *Guinness Book of Records*.

Record Breakers is one programme which is unlikely to run out of ideas. After all, there is always someone about to break a new record, however brave or daft it may be. For over 20 years, this series has been featuring some of the world's wackiest record-setters and even claiming a few firsts of its own, by arranging record-breaking attempts in the studio (over 300). Its host, until his untimely death in 1994, was Roy Castle, a man who was a record breaker on many occasions in his own right. In the very first programme he created the world's biggest one-man band, with over 40 instruments at his disposal. He also set records for the world's fastest tap-dance

(24 beats a second) and for wing-walking across the Channel, not to mention riding on top of a 39-man motorcycle pyramid and leaping from the top of the Blackpool Tower. For such achievements, as he sang in the theme song, 'You need dedication'. The *Guinness Book of Records* founders, Norris and the late Ross McWhirter, assisted Roy in the early days and Norris has continued to make appearances from time to time. For one season, Ron Reagan Jnr (son of the former US President) reporting from America, was a co-host, but Cheryl Baker was Castle's partner for most of his latter years and has remained in charge alongside ex-athlete Kriss Akabusi with former **Blue Peter** man Mark Curry recently joining as roving reporter.

REDCAP

UK (ABC) Police Drama. ITV 1964–6

Sgt John Mann .... John Thaw

Creator: Jack Bell. Producer: John Bryce

Investigations into crime in the armed forces, conducted by a tough, no-nonsense military policeman.

John Mann was a sergeant in the Special Investigation Branch of the Royal Military Police – the 'Redcaps' – and a thorough one at that. His forceful, demanding investigations rooted out army crooks all over the world, from Malaya and Borneo to Aden and Cyprus, and, although he reserved a softer side of his character for those in genuine distress, his fuse was short and regularly lit. The series provided good training for John Thaw, with John Mann's bluster carried through to Jack Regan in **The Sweeney** and his sullen solitude resurfacing in **Inspector Morse**.

RED DWARF

UK (Paul Jackson/Grant Naylor/BBC) Situation Comedy. BBC 2 1988–89; 1991–

Arnold J. Rimmer, BSc, SSC	Chris Barrie
Dave Lister	Craig Charles
Cat	Danny John-Jules
Holly	Norman Lovett
	Hattie Hayridge
Kryten	David Ross
	Robert Llewellyn

Creators/Writers: Rob Grant, Doug Naylor. Executive Producer: Paul Jackson. Producers: Ed Bye, Hilary Bevan Jones

Space age sitcom featuring the last survivor on a spaceship and his annoying non-human companions.

When Technician Third-Class Dave Lister was sentenced to a period in suspended animation (or 'stasis'), sometime in the 24th century, for smuggling a cat aboard his spaceship, little did he know that he would wake up three million years later and be the sole survivor of a radiation leak. Resigned to roaming the cosmos in the five-mile long, three-mile wide mining ship *Red Dwarf*, Lister discovered that all 168 other crew members had died and his only companions were Holly, the ship's computer, Cat, a hybrid lifeform evolved from his pet cat, and a hologram of his obnoxious former roommate and supervisor, Arnold J. (Judas) Rimmer.

While the deadpan Holly (seen only as a face on a TV screen) was a bit of a practical joker (for a computer), the overzealous Rimmer was devoid of humour and the exact opposite of Lister in every way. Their incompatibility – in *Steptoe and Son* fashion – was central to the series. Desperately ambitious, Rimmer, sadly, was also a coward and unfailingly inept (it had been his error that led to the fatal radiation leak). Being a hologram, he couldn't touch anything and relied on Holly for his existence and well-being. Lister, on the other hand, whiled away his time eating junk food, watching videos, slagging off 'smegging' Rimmer and lounging on his bunk, perhaps dreaming of Christine Kochanski, another dead crewmate (played in flashbacks by one-time Altered Images singer Clare Grogan). However, it was Cat who proved to be the most intriguing character. Portrayed as a narcissistic, black dude in snappy dress, Cat looked human (except for his fangs and six nipples), but possessed feline instincts. Lining his stomach and looking good were paramount. He toyed with a roast chicken as a cat would a bird, took 'cat-naps', licked his laundry clean and sprayed perfume from an aerosol to mark out his territory.

In later seasons, a new Holly was introduced, with comedian Hattie Hayridge replacing Norman Lovett as the dry, lugubrious computer, and an android, Kryten, was added to the cast. Discovered working as a manservant to three human girls (who had long-since perished), the angular robot temporarily joined *Red Dwarf* in the second series. But, with a new actor in the role, he took up permanent residence the following year. The only other regular characters were a couple of silent robot helpers called scutters and a few talking appliances, like an outspoken toaster.

Red Dwarf, though slow to pick up audiences, rapidly gained cult status and enhanced the reputations of Liverpudlian poet/comedian Craig Charles and impressionist/comedian Chris Barrie. Its creators, Rob Grant and Doug Naylor, had previously worked with Barrie on *Spitting Image*.

REDIFFUSION see Associated-Rediffusion.

REDMOND, PHIL (1949–)

Liverpudlian comedy writer whose early efforts included episodes of *Doctor at Sea*, *Doctor in Charge* and *The Squirrels*. In 1976 he changed direction and took an idea for a realistic school-days programme to the BBC. The idea was commissioned and *Grange Hill* was born. Redmond followed this up with *Going Out*, a programme about struggling school-leavers, for Southern Television and then began work on a major project for the BBC. Provisionally entitled *County Hall*, it aimed to dramatize the workings of a major local authority. Somewhat disillusioned, Redmond moved into the independent sector. He set up Mersey Television and sold an idea for a vibrant, down-to-earth soap opera to Channel 4. As *Brookside*, it aired on the station's first night and has proved to be one of its major successes, despite a rather shaky start when there was much criticism of its strong language. Amongst Redmond's other work has been the police series *Waterfront Beat*. Mersey Television, meanwhile, unsuccessfully challenged Granada for the ITV North-West England franchise in 1991.

REDMOND, SIOBHAN

Scottish actress, best-known for her role as Detective Sgt Maureen Connell in the police series *Between the Lines*. Earlier, Redmond had appeared with Stephen Fry, Hugh Laurie, Emma Thompson, Ben Elton and Robbie Coltrane in the Granada comedy *Alfresco*, before joining Don Henderson in *Bulman*, playing his sidekick Lucy McGinty. Redmond was also seen in *The Advocates*, *The Bill* and, more recently, in the comedy *The High Life* (as air stewardess Shona Spurtle).

REES, ROGER (1944–)

Welsh actor who has enjoyed TV work on both sides of the Atlantic, most notably as Malcolm in *Singles* and millionaire Robin Colcord in *Cheers*. He was also the lead in the RSC's screen version of *The Life and Adventures of Nicholas Nickleby*, appeared with Laurence Olivier in *The Ebony Tower* and has other credits like *Bouquet of Barbed Wire*, *Under Western Eyes*, *Saigon – Year of the Cat*, *Imaginary Friends* and *The Voysey Inheritance*, plus *TV Shakespeare*.

REEVES, GEORGE (GEORGE BREWER; 1914–59)

TV's first Superman, George Reeves at one time looked to have a promising film career ahead of him. He appeared in *Gone with the Wind* in 1939, but then things gradually headed downhill.

Turning to television, he landed the role which was, at last, to make him a household name, that of the 'Man of Steel' in **The Adventures of Superman**, which began in the USA in 1951. He played Superman for six years, suffering cruelly from typecasting when it ended. Two years later, he was found shot dead, but the official suicide verdict has been challenged by those close to him

REEVES, VIC (JIM MOIR: 1959–)

North-eastern comedian, partner of Bob Mortimer. Both failed punk rockers, Reeves was managing an alternative comedy venue in London where Mortimer, a solicitor, was a regular heckler. Joining forces, they developed the *Vic Reeves Big Night Out* act which toured universities and secured its own slot on Channel 4 in 1990. There it gained a cult following for its absurd humour, catchphrases like 'You wouldn't let it lie' and novel characters like The Man With The Stick, The Ponderers, Les and Wavy Davy. Subsequently, the duo moved to the BBC with a similarly off-beat show entitled *The Smell of Reeves and Mortimer* and new characters such as The Bra Men. Reeves has also had a number one hit with a cover of Tommy Roe's 'Dizzy'.

REGIMENT, THE

UK (BBC) Drama

Lt Richard Gaunt ....Christopher Cazenove
RSM William Bright ....Michael Brennan
Colonel Frederick Gaunt ....Richard Hurndall
Lt Colonel Gaunt-Seymour ....Richard Wordsworth
Lt James Willoughby...............................John Hallam
Hon. Alice Gaunt...............................Wendy Williams
Charlotte Gaunt....................................Wendy Allnutt

Creators: Robin Chapman, Jack Gerson, Nick McCarty. Producers: Anthony Coburn, Terence Dudley

The fortunes of an army regiment as seen through the eyes of two families.

Beginning as a single play (part of the **Drama Playhouse** collection in 1970), *The Regiment* focused on the years 1895–1904 and the events that unfolded around the Cotswold Regiment. With the Boer War and then the days of the Raj in India as backdrops, the series particularly looked at members of two families, the Gaunts and the Brights, and their varied positions in the greater scheme of things.

REID, BERYL, OBE (1920–)

British actress/comedienne who has enjoyed her own series (*The Beryl Reid Show* and *Beryl Reid*), plus a host of guest parts. Amongst her earliest roles was as Arethusa Wilderspin in a sitcom

called *The Most Likely Girl* in 1957. She then starred with Jimmy Edwards in the comedy *Bold as Brass*, played Rene Jelliot and Marigold Alcock in the sitcoms *Wink to Me Only* and *Alcock and Gander*, took the part of Mrs Knox in **The Irish RM** and appeared as Grandma in **The Secret Diary of Adrian Mole, Aged 13¾** and its sequel, **The Growing Pains of Adrian Mole**. Her cameo role as Connie Sachs in *Tinker, Tailor, Soldier, Spy* won her a BAFTA award and she went on to act in the follow-up, *Smiley's People*. Reid has also been seen in *A-Z*, **The Good Old Days**, **Minder**, **Doctor Who**, **The Beiderbecke Tapes**, **Cracker** and *A Perfect Spy*, amongst numerous other series in the last four decades.

REID, MIKE (1940–)

Cockney comedian and actor, coming to the fore in **The Comedians** with his 'Terr-i-fic' catchphrase and aggressive style of joke telling. He moved into children's TV to 'manage' the hectic game show *Runaround* and later played Arthur Mullard's brother, Benny Briggs, in **Yus My Dear**, as well as appearing in the drama **Big Deal**. More recently he has been better known as Frank Butcher in **EastEnders**, a role that he played for six years from 1988. Reid has also hosted his own variety series, *Mike Reid's Mates and Music*.

REILLY – ACE OF SPIES

UK (Euston Films/Thames) Spy Drama. ITV 1983

Sidney Reilly ....Sam Neill
Fothergill ....Peter Egan
Bruce Lockhart..Ian Charleston
Cummings..Norman Rodway
Dzerzhinsky ....Tom Bell
Stalin..David Burke
Lenin..Kenneth Cranham
Basil Zaharov ....Leo McKern
Margaret Thomas/Reilly ....Jeananne Crowley
Inspector Tsientsin ....David Suchet
Baldwin ....Donald Morley
Count Massino ....John Castle

Writer: Ian Kennedy Martin. Executive Producer: Verity Lambert. Producer: Chris Burt

Dramatization of the life of one of Britain's first secret agents.

In early Revolutionary Russia, Sidney Reilly, born in Odessa and raised by an aristocratic Russian family, operated as a British agent, aiming to topple the Bolshevik regime and install a new British-approved government with himself at its head. His attempt failed, however, and Reilly was executed at the hands of the Supreme Soviet Revolutionary Tribunal.

This lavish 12-part drama was based on the biography of the real Reilly by Robin Bruce

Lockhart. Although the character was artistically spiced up for TV, Reilly was himself a colourful and intriguing personality: suave, cool and daring, with a keen eye for the ladies.

REITH, LORD JOHN (1889–1971)

Lord Reith was effectively the BBC's founding father. Born in Scotland, Reith had served in World War I and had managed a large engineering works in Coatbridge before being appointed to the job of General Manager of the newly inaugurated British Broadcasting Company in 1922. (While this may seem a surprising background, it has to be considered that there were few people at the time with experience of broadcasting in any form.) In 1927 he became what was by then the British Broadcasting Corporation's first Director-General and was knighted the same year. He left the Corporation in 1938 to become Chairman of Imperial Airways and later a Government minister during the war, having set the course of public service broadcasting the BBC was to successfully follow for decades. Reith's view of broadcasting was as more than mere entertainment for the masses. He insisted that the new media of radio and television also contributed to the intellectual and moral fabric of society – the mission was to inform and educate as well as to entertain. He was made a baron in 1940 and, in his honour, the BBC founded the prestigious annual Reith Lectures in 1948.

RELATIVE STRANGERS see *Holding the Fort.*

REMINGTON STEELE

US (MTM) Detective Drama. BBC 1/Channel 4
1983–4/1986–7

Remington Steele ....Pierce Brosnan
Laura Holt ....Stephanie Zimbalist
Murphy Michaels ....James Read
Bernice Foxe ....Janet De May
Mildred Krebs ....Doris Roberts

Creators: Michael Gleason, Robert Butler.
Executive Producers: Michael Gleason, Gareth Davies. Producers: Glenn Gordon Caron, Lee Zlotoff

An ambitious blonde opens a detective agency, names it after a man and then finds someone to play the part.

When Laura Holt set up the Laura Holt Investigations detective agency, she found that work was hard to come by. The problem was that no-one seemed to trust a female detective. So, she created an imaginary male boss for herself, renaming the company Remington Steele Investigations. At last the business began to pay.

Although it was easy at first to make excuses for her absent chief, Laura soon realized that there would have to be a real Remington Steele to keep the customers happy. As chance would have it, a suitable candidate conveniently turned up on her doorstep. He was actually a con man, trying to get his hands on some jewels Laura was protecting. But the couple hit it off from the start. He was suave, handsome and just the job, so they agreed that he should become Remington Steele and he joined the agency as a partner.

Nothing much was ever revealed about this dark, handsome stranger of Irish descent, least of all his real name. There were occasional hints about his murky past but he developed into a more than useful detective and the business boomed. His encyclopedic knowledge of classic Hollywood movies proved particularly handy, enabling him to solve cases by recreating memorable scenes from films like *The Third Man*, *Casablanca* and *Key Largo*. He and Laura flirted with each other, though it took some time for the full-blown affair to take off and even then it was not properly consummated until the final season. The romantic tension between the duo helped give the show some buzz and their sparkling repartee introduced a comic dimension to the plot, but it was never of the same level witnessed later in **Moonlighting** (created by one of *Remington Steele's* producers, Glenn Gordon Caron).

Also seen were Murphy Michaels, Laura's first partner who left to form his own agency, and secretary Bernice Foxe, who was replaced by former tax inspector Mildred Krebs. All the episodes had titles containing 'Steele' puns, such as *Steele Crazy After All These Years*, *Thou Shalt Not Steele* and *You're Steele the One for Me*.

Stephanie Zimbalist was the daughter of **The FBI** and **77 Sunset Strip** star Efrem Zimbalist Jnr, who guest-starred in one episode. Although Pierce Brosnan became a Hollywood name as a result of this series, he also found it to be an impediment to future success. It was an open secret that his name had been pencilled in as the next James Bond when Roger Moore retired, but, because of his contractual commitments to *Remington Steele*, the part was given to Timothy Dalton. When Dalton eventually quit the Bond role in 1994, Brosnan was free and promptly signed up as 007.

RENALDO, DUNCAN (RENALDO DUNCAN; 1904–80)

American character actor, busy in the 1930s and 1940s in a variety of film roles, including that of **The Cisco Kid**, a part that he brought to television in 1950, running for six years. As the western rogue with the heart of gold, he became one of TV's earliest stars. Renaldo was also associate producer on the series.

RENWICK, DAVID

British comedy writer, often in partnership with Andrew Marshall. Together they penned scripts for BBC Radio before moving into television and writing sketches for *Not The Nine O'Clock News* and *Alexei Sayle's Stuff*, as well as creating *Whoops! Apocalypse*, *Hot Metal* and the 1993 Richard Briers comedy, *If You See God Tell Him*. Renwick, without Marshall, also provided gags for *Mike Yarwood In Persons* earlier in his career, although his greatest success has undoubtedly come through his enormously popular sitcom *One Foot in the Grave*.

REPEAT

The second or subsequent showing of a TV programme, usually to fill gaps in the schedule, to cover holiday periods (when low audiences do not merit new productions) or, occasionally and increasingly, because the quality of the original warrants another screening. The new interest in classic television has made repeats (once the bane of viewers' lives, or at least claimed to be) a growing segment of the TV market. In the USA, repeats are known as reruns and have always enjoyed a regular place in the schedules. With new programmes generally aired in the States between September and May, reruns have traditionally come into their own from June to August. Furthermore, once a national network has exhausted its contract for running and rerunning a series, its producers have often sold it into syndication, giving independent stations across the country the chance to buy old episodes of popular series for screening locally. That is why viewers can always find episodes of classics from the 1950s onwards doing the rounds of the USA's smaller TV stations.

RE-RUN see repeat.

RESEARCHER

A member of the production team whose job is to look into possible issues and subjects for programming, to brief presenters on background information, to investigate locations prior to shooting and to contact and vet potential contributors, be they experts, interviewees or game show contestants.

RETURN OF SHELLEY, The see *Shelley*.

RETURN OF SHERLOCK HOLMES, The see *Adventures of Sherlock Holmes, The*.

RETURN OF THE SAINT, THE
UK (ITC) Adventure. ITV 1978–9

Simon Templar ....Ian Ogilvy

Executive Producer: Robert S. Baker. Producer: Anthony Spinner

A revival of the charming 1960s international adventurer.

Nine years after Roger Moore hung up Simon Templar's halo, lookalike Ian Ogilvy tried it on for size. Similar in many ways, although critically less well received, this regeneration of Leslie Charteris's dashing, confident hero once again saw our hero whizzing around the globe, relaxing in the company of beautiful women and escaping from many life-threatening situations – all against a backdrop of international intrigue.

REYNOLDS, BURT (1936–)

American actor who served his apprenticeship in television before becoming a Hollywood superstar. His breaks came in the 1950s, primarily in a series called *Riverboat,* in which he shared the lead for one season. There followed guest spots in programmes like *Alfred Hitchcock Presents*, *Route 66* and *The Twilight Zone* before Reynolds joined the cast of *Gunsmoke*, playing the half-breed blacksmith Quint Asper. He left after three years to star in his own vehicle, *Hawk*, a police series about an Indian detective in New York. In 1970 he was cast as *Dan August*, another cop, this time in California, and, returning to the small screen, he was retired lawman, B.L. Stryker, in a *Mystery Movie* series in 1989. A year later Reynolds starred as football coach Wood Newton in the rustic sitcom *Evening Shade*. Reynolds also has some production credits to his name and was married to *Laugh-In* girl Judy Carne for three years in the 1960s.

REYNOLDS, DEBBIE (MARY FRANCES REYNOLDS; 1932–)

Popular American actress and singer, star of the sitcom *The Debbie Reynolds Show* in the late 1960s (playing scatterbrained housewife Debbie Thompson). She has previously been married to American singer Eddie Fisher and is the mother of actress Carrie Fisher.

RHODA
US (MTM) Situation Comedy. BBC 2 1974–81

Rhoda Morgenstern/Gerard	Valerie Harper
Brenda Morgenstern	Julie Kavner
Joe Gerard	David Groh
Ida Morgenstern	Nancy Walker
Martin Morgenstern	Harold J. Gould

Carlton the Doorman (voice only)	Lorenzo Music
Donny Gerard	Todd Turquand
Myrna Morgenstein	Barbara Sharma
Gary Levy	Ron Silver
Sally Gallagher	Anne Meara
Johnny Venture	Michael Delano
Jack Doyle	Ken McMillan
Ramon Diaz, Jnr	Rafael Campos

Creators: James L. Brooks, Allan Burns.
Executive Producers: James L. Brooks, Allan
Burns, Charlotte Brown. Producers: David
Davis, Lorenzo Music

**Life with a single Jewish girl in New York
City.**

A spin-off from *The Mary Tyler Moore Show*,
Rhoda followed the fortunes of Mary's best
friend, Rhoda Morgenstern. In the original
series, Rhoda had been insecure, overweight and
man-hungry; back in her native New York in this
follow-up, she had regained some self-confidence, lost some weight and generally had a more
positive outlook on life. She now lived with her
podgy bank clerk sister, Brenda, after failing to
settle down with her parents, Martin and Ida.
Brenda, like Rhoda, was on the lookout for a
husband, but Rhoda found hers first, in the shape
of Joe Gerard, divorced father of ten-year-old
Donny and owner of the New York Wrecking
Company.

Rhoda and Joe took an apartment in Brenda's
block, where Carlton was the doom-laden doorman viewers never saw. But Joe went out to work
and Rhoda was stuck at home, frustrated and
bored. Not surprisingly the marriage was
doomed to failure, especially after Rhoda formed
her own window dressing business with a bashful
old schoolfriend, Myrna Morgenstein. Joe and
Rhoda divorced and she returned to the singles
bars, accompanied by Brenda and some new
acquaintances, air hostess Sally Gallagher and
boutique-owner Gary Levy. Also seen was
Rhoda's on-off boyfriend, a Vegas lounge singer
named Johnny Venture. In the final series, Rhoda
went to work with Jack Doyle and Ramon Diaz
at the struggling Doyle Costume Company. By
now, the singles habit had spread: even her parents had now split up.

Rhoda, like *The Mary Tyler Moore Show*, was
very much a 1970s series. It was also richly ethnic, applauded for its abundant Jewishness
(despite the fact that neither Valerie Harper nor
Nancy Walker, who played Rhoda's mother,
were Jewish themselves).

RICE, ANNEKA (ANNIE RICE; 1958-)

British presenter, born in Wales but initially
working on radio and TV in Hong Kong. Her

UK break came with Channel 4's adventurous
game show *Treasure Hunt* in 1983, in which she
did much leaping from helicopters and running
about looking for clues. In recent years, she has
become known for *Challenge Anneka*, a charity-
oriented programme involving unlikely feats like
publishing a book or building an orphanage in a
matter of days. Rice also worked on TV-am's
Good Morning Britain, contributed to *Wish You
Were Here . . . ?* and presented one season of
Holiday. She has hosted the exotic game show
Passport and been seen on various panel games
and special reports.

RICH, LEE

Former advertising executive who founded
Lorimar Productions (with Merv Adelson) in
1968. The company achieved several prime-time
hits, including *The Waltons*, *Dallas*, *Knots
Landing*, *Falcon Crest* and *Flamingo Road*,
before it was eventually taken over by Warner
Brothers. Rich moved on to MGM/United
Artists (as Chairman and Chief Executive) but left
in 1990 to go back into independent production.

RICHARD THE LIONHEART

UK (Danziger) Adventure. ITV 1962–3

King Richard	Dermot Walsh
Prince John	Trader Faulkner
Lady Berengaria	Sheila Whittington
Blondel	Iain Gregory
Sir Gilbert	Robin Hunter
Sir Geoffrey	Alan Hatwood
King Philip of France	Trader Faulkner
Leopold of France	Francis de Wolfe
Hugo	Glyn Owen
Marta	Anne Lawson

Producers: Edward J. Danziger, Harry Lee
Danziger

**King Richard returns from the Crusades
to stop Prince John stealing the English
throne.**

Prince Richard was away with his army when
news reached him of the death of his father, King
Henry. Worse still, his younger brother, John, had
designs on the throne that was legally Richard's,
and so Lionheart returned home to put an end to
the plot. It was not to be a quick affair, however,
as John and his knaves proved elusive and determined, resulting in a series of swashbuckling
adventures in which Richard's life was always in
danger. His other enemies included Leopold and
Philip of France, as well as the Saracen Saladin,
and some of the action took place back in the
Holy Land.

RICHARD, WENDY (1946-)

British actress, in TV since the early 1960s. Her
major roles have been as blouse-busting Miss

Brahms in *Are You Being Served?* and, in total contrast, dowdy Pauline Fowler in *EastEnders*. However, she also played supermarket manageress Joyce Harker in *The Newcomers*, appeared with Dora Bryan in *Both Ends Meet* and Hylda Baker in *Not On Your Nellie*, and was Doreen, one of the *On the Buses* clippies, and Pearl, the housekeeper, in the kids' series *Hogg's Back*. Amongst her many other credits have been parts in *Harpers West One*, *Dixon of Dock Green*, *Z Cars*, *Danger Man*, *No Hiding Place*, *Please Sir!* and *Dad's Army*. In 1992 she resurrected Miss Brahms in *Grace and Favour*. At the start of her career, she was the girl on the Mike Sarne chart-topper 'Come Outside' (1962).

RICHARDS, STAN (STAN RICHARDSON; 1930–)

Yorkshire-born actor, a former musical-comedy entertainer on the nothern clubs circuit, seen in programmes like *Coronation Street*, *Crown Court*, *The Cuckoo Waltz*, *The Price of Coal*, *All Creatures Great and Small*, *Last of the Summer Wine* and various plays before taking the role of poacher/gamekeeper Seth Armstrong in *Emmerdale Farm* in 1977.

RICHARDSON, IAN (1934–)

Scottish actor whose portrayal of the devious Francis Urquhart in Michael Dobbs's *House of Cards* and *To Play the King* was highly acclaimed. In a long and varied TV career, Richardson has also played Bill Haydon in *Tinker, Tailor, Soldier, Spy*, Major Neuheim in *Private Schulz*, Ramsey MacDonald in *No. 10*, (Uncle) Frederick Fairlie in *The Woman in White*, Nehru in *Lord Mountbatten: The Last Viceroy*, Michael Spearpoint in Channel 4's *The Gravy Train* and *The Gravy Train Goes East*, Anthony Blunt in the 1987 play about the British traitor and Sir Godber Evans in *Porterhouse Blue*. He has also been seen in programmes as varied as *Horizon*, *Sorry!*, *Mistral's Daughter*, *A Voyage Round My Father*, *Churchill's Generals*, *The Master of Ballantrae*, *Charlie Muffin* and *Star Quality*, as well as Shakespearean offerings.

RICHARDSON, MIRANDA (1958–)

Versatile British actress seen in dramas like *After Pilkington*, *Performance*, *Redemption*, *The Storyteller*, *Snapshots* and *A Woman of Substance* but best remembered for her naughty schoolgirl interpretation of Queen Elizabeth I in *Blackadder II*. She was also seen in *Blackadder the Third* (as highwaywoman Amy Hardwood) and *Blackadder Goes Forth* (as Nurse Mary).

RICH MAN, POOR MAN

US (Universal) Drama. ITV 1976

Rudy Jordache	Peter Strauss
Tom Jordache	Nick Nolte
Julie Prescott/Abbott/Jordache	Susan Blakely
Axel Jordache	Edward Asner
Mary Jordache	Dorothy McGuire
Willie Abbott	Bill Bixby
Duncan Calderwood	Ray Milland
Teddy Boylan	Robert Reed
Virginia Calderwood	Kim Darby
Teresa Sanjoro	Talia Shire
Bill Denton	Lawrence Pressman
Kate Jordache	Kay Lenz
Asher Berg	Craig Stevens
Joey Quales	George Maharis
Linda Quales	Lynda Day George
Marsh Goodwin	Van Johnson
Irene Goodwin	Dorothy Malone
Arthur Falconetti	William Smith
Clothilde	Fionnula Flanagan

Writer: Dean Reisner. Executive Producer: Harve Bennett. Producer: Jon Epstein

Two brothers grow up in very different ways and achieve contrasting success and happiness.

Rich Man, Poor Man was one of *the* television events of the 1970s. With a cast list littered with big names, this adaptation of Irwin Shaw's mammoth 1970 novel of the same name can be viewed today as the original blockbuster mini-series. It captivated world audiences and led to a boom in dramatizations of popular novels, which were screened under the *Best Sellers* umbrella title (usually on consecutive nights). These included Taylor Caldwell's *Captains and Kings*, Robert Ludlum's *The Rhinemann Exchange*, Arthur Hailey's *Wheels*, John Jakes's *The Bastard* and Harold Robbins's *79 Park Avenue*.

Rich Man, Poor Man was the story of the Jordache brothers, sons of an impoverished immigrant family, and followed their lives and relationships from 1945 through to the mid 1960s. The intelligent one, Rudy, broke free from his deprived roots to become a successful businessman and politician. The brawny one, Tom, meandered from scrape to scrape, taking up boxing for a while, dabbling in crime and always likely to meet an unhappy end. The boys' parents were Axel and Mary Jordache, and Julie Prescott was the girl both brothers loved.

Two sequels followed. *Rich Man, Poor Man – Book II*, picking up the story in 1965, focused on the now Senator Rudy Jordache, his fight against corporate greed and the family feuds that still engulfed him. A new generation of rich and poor men were seen in the form of his surrogate kids, Wesley Jordache (Tom's son) and Billy Abbott (son of Julie). *Beggarman, Thief*, set in the late 1960s, switched attention to the boys' sister, Gretchen, a film-maker who had previously not been seen.

RIDLEY, ARNOLD, OBE (1896–1984)

British actor and writer, fondly remembered as the incontinent old Private Godfrey in *Dad's Army*, a role he assumed at the tender age of 72. Previously, he had played a vicar in *Crossroads*. By far his greatest achievement, however, was his penning, in 1925, of the famous stage play *The Ghost Train* (televised as early as 1937), amongst other theatre scripts.

RIFF RAFF ELEMENT, THE

UK (BBC) Drama. BBC 1 1993–4

Joanna Tundish	Celia Imrie
Petula Belcher	Mossie Smith
Roger Tundish	Ronald Pickup
Carmen	Jayne Ashbourne
Declan	Cal Macaninch
Acky Belcher	Trevor Peacock
Granny Grogan	Brenda Bruce
Boyd Tundish	Nicholas Farrell
Mortimer Tundish	Richard Hope
Phoenix	Pippa Guard
Nathan Tundish	Ashley Wright
Dearbhla	Kate Binchy
Alister	Greg Wise
Vincent	George Costigan
Oliver Tundish	Stewart Pile
Nelson	Dicken Ashworth
Maggie Belcher	Susan Brown
Father Casper	Lionel Guyett

Creator/Writer: Debbie Horsfield. Producer: Liz Trubridge

Families from different class backgrounds share a stately home.

Roger Tundish, recently recalled ambassador to San Andres, upset his family on arrival home at Tundish Hall in Lancashire. With the house falling into disrepair and finances tight, he was forced to advertise for new tenants for one wing. 'The riff-raff element need not apply', he stated. However, that was precisely what he got when his daughter-in-law, Joanna, employed Petula Belcher as resident cook, and the rest of the common-as-muck Belcher family took up residence. Not just class friction but adultery, pregnancy and crime, including murder, ensued. Much acclaimed, a second series of this light drama followed in 1994.

RIFLEMAN, THE

US (Four Star/Sussex) Western. ITV

Lucas McCain	Chuck Connors
Mark McCain	Johnny Crawford
Marshal Micah Torrance	Paul Fix
Milly Scott	Joan Taylor
Lou Mallory	Patricia Blair
Sweeney	Bill Quinn
Eddie Holstead	John Harmon
Hattie Denton	Hope Summers

Producers: Arthur Gardner, Arnold Laven, Jules Levy

A Wild West rancher helps keep order with the aid of a specially adapted gun.

Dour, level-headed Lucas McCain had arrived in New Mexico after the death of his wife. He had purchased the Dunlap Ranch, four miles south of North Fork, and was now struggling to make it pay. At the same time, he was trying to raise his 12-year-old son, Mark, teaching him lessons in life and showing him right from wrong. But Lucas also had a third job to do. Whenever outlaws arrived in town, or there was a threat to law and order, he was always called upon to save the day, bailing out the town's helpless marshal, Micah Torrance. He did have some assistance, however, in the form of his converted .44 Winchester rifle that allowed rapid fire. It gave Lucas a distinct advantage over his adversaries.

Like most cowboys, Lucas was provided with a little romantic interest, first with shopkeeper Milly Scott, and then with Lou Mallory, ambitious proprietress of the Mallory House Hotel. Other townsfolk included Eddie Holstead, owner of the Madera House Hotel, shopkeeper Hattie Denton and Sweeney, bartender at the Last Chance Saloon. All in all though, this was a rather heavy, sombre half-hour western, screened between 1958 and 1963 in the USA and then sporadically around the ITV network in the UK.

RIGG, DAME DIANA (1938–)

British actress leaping to fame as the karate-chopping Emma Peel in *The Avengers* in 1965, having already made appearances in programmes like *Armchair Theatre*. She played Mrs Peel for three years and later credits have included her own sitcom, entitled *Diana* and *Made in America*, in which she played divorcée and fashion co-ordinator Diana Smythe, plus *The Diana Rigg Show*, *Bleak House* (as Lady Dedlock) and the Andrew Davies thriller *Mother Love*.

RIN TIN TIN see *Adventures of Rin Tin Tin, The*.

RINGS ON THEIR FINGERS

UK (BBC) Situation Comedy. BBC 1 1978–80

Oliver Pryde	Martin Jarvis
Sandy Bennett/Pryde	Diane Keen

Victor ....Tim Barrett
Mr Gordon Bennett................................John Harvey
Mrs Bennett...Barbara Lott
Mr Pryde..Keith Marsh

Creator/Writer: Richard Waring. Producer: Harold Snoad

Shall-we, shan't-we marriage dilemmas for a young couple.

Oliver Pryde had been happy sharing six years of his life and his West Acton flat with his winsome girlfriend Sandy Bennett, but he still valued his independence. Sandy, on the other hand, was desperately keen on marriage. With the occasional interference of relatives and workmates, the two ditherers attempted to find a way forward, with wedding bells, unfortunately for Oliver, the ultimate answer. Subsequent episodes centred on their marital strife and preparations for the birth of their first child. With its traditionalist hubby at work, little lady at home stance, feminists loathed it.

RIPCORD

US (United Artists) Adventure. BBC 1 1964–5

Ted McKeever..Larry Pennell
Jim Buckley ....Ken Curtis
Chuck Lambert ....Paul Comi
Charlie Kern ....Shug Fisher

Producers: Maurice Unger, Leon Benson

The all-action adventures of a pair of crime-fighting skydivers.

Ted McKeever and Jim Buckley, proprietors of Ripcord Inc., were parachuting teachers who doubled up as crimebusters. Although they often hired themselves out for dangerous rescue and recovery work, they were more usually found apprehending criminals, dropping from the skies like avenging angels. Sometimes their battles took place in mid-air. They were supported in their work by their pilot, Chuck Lambert, later replaced by Charlie Kern.

RIPPING YARNS

UK (BBC) Comedy. BBC 2 1977–9

Michael Palin
Terry Jones

Writers: Michael Palin, Terry Jones. Producer: Alan J.W. Bell

Over-the-top Boys' Own adventures satirized.

Tongue-in-cheek escapism lay at the heart of this series of playlets that parodied classic schoolboy literature. Heroic tales of crossing the Andes by frog, escaping from Stalag Luft 112B and more

were delivered po-faced by Michael Palin and Terry Jones from their own screenplays which celebrated every exaggeration and cliché of the Victorian and Edwardian originals. Ridiculous in the true **Monty Python** way, the lead characters bounded with youthful exuberance and naivety, with their creators taking an almost cruel pleasure in sending up this uniquely British form of fiction. Two series were produced, two years apart, following a one-off comedy, *Tomkinson's Schooldays*, in 1976.

RIPPON, ANGELA (1944–)

British presenter, a former newspaper journalist, generally considered to have been the UK's first female newsreader, although this honour actually belongs to Barbara Mandell who read the ITN news way back in 1955. Rippon arrived on national TV in 1973 via news magazines in the South-West. Working initially as a reporter, she went on to front *News Review* and then *The Nine O'Clock News*. On the 1978 *Morecambe and Wise Christmas Show*, she revealed new talents, pushing aside the news desk and kicking her way through 'Let's Face The Music and Dance'. Not surprisingly, she was later recruited to present **Come Dancing**. In 1983 she became one of TV-am's Famous Five presenters, although her time at the station was, as for the others, somewhat brief. She has never been short of radio or television work, however, and has also presented **The Eurovision Song Contest**, **Antiques Roadshow**, *Masterteam*, **What's My Line?** and **Top Gear** amongst many other programmes, and has read the news occasionally on **The Big Breakfast**.

RISING DAMP

UK (Yorkshire) Situation Comedy. ITV 1974–8

Rupert Rigsby ....Leonard Rossiter
Ruth Jones ....Frances de la Tour
Alan Moore ....Richard Beckinsale
Philip Smith......................................Don Warrington
Brenda ....Gay Rose
Spooner ....Derek Newark

Creator/Writer: Eric Chappell. Producer: Vernon Lawrence

The inhabitants of a seedy boarding house suffer the intrusions of its even seedier owner.

Rupert Rigsby, grubby, lecherous, ignorant, nosey and tight-fisted (and those were just his good points) was the owner of a horribly run-down northern boarding house that was home to an odd mix of lodgers. Rigsby lived on the ground floor with his cat Vienna. Upstairs, long-haired Alan, a medical student, shared one room with Philip, the son of an African tribal chief, and another room was taken by frustrated spinster Miss Jones, a university administrator. Although liberally treated to decrepit furnishings and the eponymous rising damp, the one thing Rigsby's paying guests did not receive was privacy. Given the opportunity to catch his lodgers 'at it', the snooping Rigsby would barge in. Whatever secrets lay in their personal lives, Rigsby prised them out into the open. However great their hopes and dreams, Rigsby would sneer and jeer at them. His own ambition, though, was to share a night of torrid passion with Miss Jones, but, like his other plans, it was never realized. Brenda and Spooner were two of Rigsby's later lodgers.

The series sprang from a one-off play entitled *The Banana Box* (in which the landlord was called Rooksby) and gave Leonard Rossiter the first chance to show off his acclaimed comic timing. Indeed, most of the series' humour came from his sharp, glib delivery. A film version was released in 1980.

RIVALS OF SHERLOCK HOLMES, THE

UK (Thames) Detective Drama. ITV 1971–3

Dr Thorndyke..John Neville
                                                              Barrie Ingham
Horace Dorrington ....Peter Vaughan
Jonathan Pride.......................................Ronald Hines
Arthur Hewitt...................................Peter Barkworth
Professor Van Dusen ....Douglas Wilmer
Max Carrados ....Robert Stephens
Simon Carne ....Roy Dotrice
Carnacki...Donald Pleasence
Dixon Druce...John Fraser
Lady Molly ....Elvi Hale
Romany Pringle ....Donald Sinden
Bernard Sutton ....Robert Lang
Polly Burton...Judy Geeson
Inspector Lipinzki ....Barry Keegan
Laxworthy ....Bernard Hepton
Monsieur Valmont ....Charles Gray
Lt Holst ....John Thaw
Dabogert Trostler....................................Ronald Lewis
William Drew ....Derek Jacobi
Mr Horrocks...Ronald Fraser
Hagar ....Sara Kestelman

Executive Producers: Lloyd Shirley, Kim Mills. Producers: Robert Love, Jonathan Alwyn, Reginald Collin

Series of literary adaptations which revealed that Sherlock Holmes was not the only great detective of Victorian times.

The self-contained episodes of this period anthology featured investigations from the case-books of different literary sleuths. One or two cropped up more than once. Authors whose work was featured included Arthur Morrison (Horace Dorrington, Arthur Hewitt and Jonathan Pride), R. Austin Freeman (Dr

Thorndyke), Baroness Orczy (Polly Burton) and Jacques Futrelle (Professor Van Dusen). Notable performances came from John Thaw as Danish detective Lt Holst, Robert Stephens as blind detective Max Carrados, Donald Pleasence as Carnacki, a ghost hunter, and Sara Kestelman as Hagar, a gypsy detective. The series was based on a literary collection put together by one-time BBC Director-General Sir Hugh Greene.

RIVER, THE

UK (BBC) Situation Comedy. BBC 1 1988

Davey Jackson ....David Essex
Sarah McDonald.....................................Katy Murphy
Aunt Betty ....Vilma Hollingbery
Tom Pike ....Shaun Scott
Colonel Danvers ....David Ryall

Creator/Writer: Michael Aitkens. Producer: Susan Belbin

An ex-con lock keeper and a young Scots girl fall in love on the riverbank.

Set in the fictitious rustic settlement of Chumley-on-the-Water, *The River* focused on London-born lock keeper Davey Jackson, revealing how his idyllic existence was thrown into turmoil by the arrival of a wayward Scots girl. Sarah McDonald, a refugee from society, was forced to call on Davey's help when the propeller on her narrowboat was damaged in an accident. While the relevant repairs were made, Davey took the aggressive Sarah into his cottage and a romance slowly developed, despite the best efforts of Davey's grumpy Aunt Betty (an active Marxist). It was subsequently revealed that Davey had retired to this rural backwater after serving six months in prison for allegedly forging banknotes. Tom Pike was Davey's assistant lock keeper and Colonel Danvers the local nob and snob. Some of the action took place in the local boozer, The Ferret, presided over by an unconscious landlord, Jim.

Star David Essex also wrote and performed the programme's theme song.

RIVIERA POLICE

UK (Associated-Rediffusion) Police Drama. ITV 1965

Inspector Legrand ....Brian Spink
Lt Colonel Constant Sorel ....Frank Lieberman
Supt Adam Hunter ....Geoffrey Frederick
Supt Bernie Johnson ....Noel Trevarthen

Producer: Jordan Lawrence

Crime fighting on the Côte d'Azur.

Legrand, Sorel, Hunter and Johnson were four determined police officers plying their trade against such glamorous backdrops as the Cannes

Film Festival, the Monaco Grand Prix and the Nice Flower Festival. They usually worked separately (except for the opening episode) to put the block on killers, thieves and other exponents of crime in the South of France. However, despite its sun, sea, sand and scantily-clad beauties, the series never took a hold, not even when following *Coronation Street* in the transmission schedules.

RIX, SIR BRIAN (1924–)

Britain's number one farceur, largely in the theatre but on many occasions seen to lose his trousers on TV, too. Rix has also had his own series, *Dial Rix* and *Six of Rix*, and presented a programme for handicapped viewers, *Let's Go*. He starred with Warren Mitchell in an early form of *Yes Minister*, entitled *Men of Affairs* (playing MP Barry Ovis) in 1973, and played James, opposite Lynda Baron, in the house-buying comedy *A Roof Over My Head* in 1977. Rix is the brother of *Emmerdale's* Sheila Mercier.

ROACHE, WILLIAM (1932–)

Coronation Street's Ken Barlow, William Roache has been with the series since its inception back in 1960, making him the longest surviving cast member. His previous TV experience was confined to small parts in Granada series like *Skyport* and *Knight Errant* and a single drama, *Marking Time*, and, since being in the *Street*, he has had little opportunity to work elsewhere on television. He is the father of actor Linus Roache (who once played Ken's son, Peter).

ROBBINS, MICHAEL (1930–92)

Former straight man to comics like Dick Emery and Tommy Cooper, British actor Michael Robbins hit the big time when he was cast as Arthur, Reg Varney's layabout brother-in-law, in the hit sitcom *On the Buses* in 1969. His previous TV work had largely consisted of plays and guest spots in series like *Callan*, but thereafter Robbins was known as a solid comedy actor. Amongst his later credits were *How's Your Father* (as Eddie Cropper), *Fairly Secret Army* (as Sgt Major Throttle), *The New Statesman* and the dramas *Legacy of Murder* and *Adam Bede*.

ROBERTSON, DALE (1923–)

One of TV's western heroes, rugged Dale Robertson was the star of *Tales of Wells Fargo* (as Jim Hardie) and *Iron Horse* (as Ben Calhoun). He also hosted the long-running anthology series *Death Valley Days* in the late 1960s and early 1970s and resurfaced in 1981 as Walter Lankershim in *Dynasty*. A 1987 adventure series, *J.J. Starbuck*, proved short-lived.

ROBERTSON, FYFE (1902–87)

Much-mimicked, distinctive Scottish roving reporter, a former newspaper journalist who was seen on *Tonight* and *24 Hours* in the 1950s and 1960s but remained on TV up to the turn of the 1980s. Some of his last contributions were nostalgic documentaries broadcast under the title of *Robbie* in the 1970s.

ROBIN HOOD see *Adventures of Robin Hood, The*.

ROBIN OF SHERWOOD

UK (HTV/Goldcrest) Adventure. ITV 1984–6

Robin of Loxley	Michael Praed
Robert of Huntingdon	Jason Connery
Little John	Clive Mantle
Will Scarlet	Ray Winstone
Maid Marion	Judi Trott
Much	Peter Llewellyn-Williams
Friar Tuck	Phil Rose
Nasir	Mark Ryan
Sheriff of Nottingham	Nickolas Grace
Guy of Gisburne	Robert Addie
Abbot Hugo	Philip Jackson
Herne the Hunter	John Abineri
Edward of Wickham	Jeremy Bulloch
Lord Owen	Oliver Cotton
Sir Richard of Leafad	George Baker
Gulnar	Richard O'Brien
Baron Simon de Belleme	Anthony Valentine

Creator: Richard Carpenter. Executive Producer: Patrick Dromgoole. Producers: Paul Knight, Esta Charkham

The Robin Hood legend, boosted with a dose of magic.

In this imaginative version of the famous 12th-century legend, Robin Hood (Robin of Loxley) was said to have possessed deep spiritual powers which assisted him in his fight with the Sheriff of Nottingham. His adventures began when his home at Loxley Mill was destroyed by Norman soldiers. Swearing revenge, Robin encountered the mystical Herne the Hunter, who appeared to him in the form of a man with a stag's head. He endowed Robin with Albion, one of the Seven Swords of Wayland, and Robin then assumed the mantle of the Hooded Man, legendary saviour of the oppressed Saxon folk ('Robin in the Hood' becoming 'Robin Hood'). Maid Marion (Lady Marion of Leaford), Little John, Will Scarlet, Friar Tuck and all the familiar names joined Robin in his struggle, as the episodes combined various facets of the Robin Hood legend with the zest of pagan sorcery. The cast was predominantly young and the action suitably brisk as they fought to free the people of England.

After two seasons, Michael Praed left for the USA, Broadway and eventually *Dynasty*, and was replaced by Sean Connery's son, Jason. The storyline had it that Robin of Loxley was killed in an ambush but his revolutionary spirit was assumed by a new Hooded Man, the blond-haired Robert of Huntingdon, a lad of noble birth who, like his predecessor, had been inspired by Herne the Hunter.

ROBIN'S NEST

UK (Thames) Situation Comedy. ITV 1977–81

Robin Tripp ....Richard O'Sullivan
Victoria Nicholls ....Tessa Wyatt
James Nicholls ....Tony Britton
Albert Riddle ....David Kelly
Marion Nicholls ....Honor Blackman
                                                                Barbara Murray
Gertrude ....Peggy Aitchison

Creators: Johnnie Mortimer, Brian Cooke.
Producer: Peter Frazer-Jones

A recent catering graduate opens his own bistro with the help of his girlfriend.

Fresh from the successful **Man about the House**, Robin Tripp had now left his two female flat-mates and teamed up with his live-in lover, air hostess Vicky Nicholls. They lived above their own Fulham restaurant – Robin's Nest – where they were not-so-ably assisted by their one-armed washer-up, Albert Riddle, an Irish ex-con with an endless line in blarney. The fly in the ointment was Vicky's disapproving dad, James Nicholls, a far from sleeping partner in the busi-ness, although her divorced mother, Marion, was far more sympathetic about her daughter's co-habitation with a long-haired cook. Tensions were eventually eased with a marriage and, even-tually, the birth of twins. Also seen in later episodes was restaurant help Gertrude.

ROBINSON, ANNE (1944–)

Red-haired, Liverpudlian presenter, a national newspaper journalist who was given her televi-sion break on **Breakfast Time** as TV critic and then hosted **Points of View**. Since then, Robinson had also presented the consumer affairs programme **Watchdog**.

ROBINSON, ROBERT (1927–)

British journalist and presenter, a specialist in panel games, thanks to long spells as chairman of **Call My Bluff** and **Ask the Family**. Robinson also hosted **Points of View** and The Book Programme, and worked on Picture Parade and **All Our Yesterdays**. Occasionally, he has presented his own travelogues. As interviewer on **BBC 3** in 1965, it was Robinson who faced Kenneth Tynan when he famously became the first person to use the 'F' word on British TV.

ROBINSON, TONY (1946–)

British comedian, actor and writer, chiefly remembered for his portrayal of Baldrick, the most menial of manservants, in the various **Blackadder** manifestations. Robinson was also a member of the **Who Dares Wins** team (in which he bravely appeared naked on more than one occasion), a guest presenter of **Points of View** and host of the cartoon series Stay Tooned. He wrote and appeared in the kids' comedy Maid Marian and Her Merry Men (playing the Sheriff of Nottingham), was the headmaster in Teenage Health Freak and the storyteller in Blood and Honey. On Sunday mornings, Robinson hosted the biblical series The Good Book Guide. He has also been seen in programmes as diverse as **Play Away**, **The Good Sex Guide**, **The Young Ones** and **Bergerac**, and made one of the BBC's Great Journeys in 1994.

ROBSON, LINDA (1958–)

Cockney actress, a former child performer. Although she is well known today as Tracey Stubbs in **Birds of a Feather** (alongside her life-long friend Pauline Quirke), Robson's TV career stretches back to the 1970s. As a 12-year-old, she appeared in Jackanory Playhouse and went on to pop up in numerous Thames TV series, includ-ing Pauline's Quirkes, as well as the teenage drama Going Out (as Gerry) for Southern. Moving into adult TV, Robson was seen in **Within these Walls**, **Cribb**, **Agony**, **The Other 'Arf**, **L for Lester**, **Harry's Game**, Up the Elephant and Round the Castle, **The Bill**, **South of the Border** and plen-ty of other dramas, including **Shine On Harvey Moon**, in which she played Harvey's daughter, Maggie.

ROCK FOLLIES

UK (Thames) Drama. ITV 1976–77

Anna Wynd...................................Charlotte Cornwell
Devonia 'Dee' Rhoades ....Julie Covington
Nancy 'Q' Cunard de Longchamps ....Rula Lenska
Derek Huggin ....Emlyn Price
Harry Moon ....Derek Thompson
Kitty Schreiber ....Beth Porter
Rox ....Sue Jones-Davies

Writer: Howard Schuman. Executive Producer: Verity Lambert. Producer: Andrew Brown

Life on the road with an ambitious female rock group.

The Little Ladies were a struggling girl rock band, lurching from gig to gig, striving to rise out of the sordid lower reaches of the rock music business. This series followed their ups and downs (mostly downs), as they fought to avoid exploitation – often sexual – and establish themselves as genuine musicians. Derek Huggin was their less than helpful manager.

Busby Berkeley-inspired fantasy sequences added extra colour to this six-part drama. The music was original and penned by Roxy Music guitarist Andy Mackay, leading to a soundtrack album and a hit single, 'OK?', which also featured Sue Jones-Davies whose character, Rox, joined the band in the second series. Also new was pushy American agent Beth Porter. This second series was entitled *Rock Follies of '77*.

UK (BBC) Documentary. BBC 1 1985–

Producers: Ann Freer, Sue Mallinson (1994)

Historical review of events year by year played over a soundtrack of contemporary pop hits.

Beginning in 1956, at the birth of the age of rock 'n' roll, this innovative series used old newsreel and TV clips to illustrate world events year by year. To add to the period feel, rock and pop records of the day provided the soundtrack. Each track was carefully selected to ensure that its lyrics tied in with the theme of the archive footage and some concert performances were also relived. The years up to 1979 were reviewed over successive series and the programme returned in 1994 to update coverage to the end of the 1980s.

ROCKFORD FILES, THE

US (Universal/Cherokee/Public Arts) Detective Drama. BBC 1 1975–82

Jim Rockford ....James Garner
Joseph 'Rocky' Rockford ....Noah Beery, Jnr
Detective Sgt Dennis Becker ....Joe Santos
Beth Davenport ....Gretchen Corbett
Evelyn 'Angel' Martin ....Stuart Margolin
John Cooper ....Bo Hopkins
Lt Alex Diehl ....Tom Atkins
Lt Doug Chapman ....James Luisi
Gandolph Fitch ....Isaac Hayes
Lance White ....Tom Selleck

Creators: Roy Huggins, Stephen J. Cannell. Executive Producers: Stephen J. Cannell, Meta Rosenberg. Producers: Roy Huggins, Charles Johnson, David Chase

An ex-con turns private investigator, taking on cases of rough justice.

Jim Rockford had been imprisoned in San Quentin for five years, for a robbery he did not commit, and, when new evidence exonerated and freed him, he devoted his life to investigating other dodgy cases on which the police had closed

their books. He formed the Rockford Private Detective Agency, of which he was the sole employee. Having been a jailbird himself, he could call upon his crooked connections to gather vital information (especially his weasely ex-cellmate, Angel Martin). But, because he was treading on their toes and undermining their work, he was not popular with the local cops.

Jim's chief rival (but also a good friend) was Detective Sgt Dennis Becker. John Cooper was his legal ally (albeit disbarred), and Rocky, his retired truck driver father, also lent a hand, though he was always trying to talk his son into finding a real job. Jim's one-time girlfriend, Beth Davenport, proved useful, too. She was the attorney who bailed him out whenever he found himself behind bars again.

Rockford lived on a Los Angeles beach in a scruffy caravan and, unlike TV's more sophisticated private eyes, he didn't have a fancy office or a sexy secretary. All he had was a crummy answerphone, which switched itself on at the start of each episode. Rockford charged $200 a day for his work (plus expenses), but often ended up unpaid and usually much the worse for wear. He hated violence and seldom carried a gun, so he was always looking nervously over his shoulder, relying on his wry sense of humour to carry him through the murky business of private detection. But he knew how to play dirty, too, and, if the end justified the means, he was not adverse to donning a disguise, slipping a few bribes or playing the conman.

In the final series, Jim gained another rival, in the form of private eye Lance White, who irked Jim by solving cases with the minimum of effort and, usually, a huge slice of luck. Played by Tom Selleck, it presaged his star role as *Magnum*.

ROCKLIFFE'S BABIES/ ROCKLIFFE'S FOLLY

UK (BBC) Police Drama. BBC 1 1987–88/1988

Detective Sgt Alan Rockliffe (*Babies/Folly*)..Ian Hogg
PC David Adams (*Babies*) ....Bill Champion
PC Keith Chitty (*Babies*)..........................John Blakey
PC Steve Hood (*Babies*)............................Brett Fancy
PC Gerry O'Dowd (*Babies*) ....Joe McGann
PC Paul Georgiou (*Babies*) ....Martyn Ellis
WPC Karen Walsh (*Babies*) ....Susanna Shelling
WPC Janice Hargreaves (*Babies*)
....Alphonsia Emmanuel
Detective Inspector Charlie Flight (*Babies*)
....Edward Wilson
Detective Supt Munro (*Babies*)............Malcolm Terris
Chief Supt Barry Wyatt (*Babies*) ....Brian Croucher
Detective Inspector Derek Hoskins (*Folly*)
....James Aubrey
Inspector Leslie Yaxley (*Folly*) ....Ian Brimble
DC Paul Whitmore (*Folly*)......................Aaron Harris

WPC Sgt Rachel Osborne (*Folly*) ......Carole Nimmons
PC Guy Overton (*Folly*)....................Craig Nightingale
WPC Hester Goswell (*Folly*)............ Elizabeth Morton
PC Alfred Duggan (*Folly*) ....John Hartley

Creator: Richard O'Keefe. Producers: Leonard Lewis (*Babies*), Ron Craddock (*Folly*)

An experienced police sergeant takes a team of rookie detectives under his wing.

Rockliffe's Babies followed the progress of seven young police officers as they trained to become detectives. It showed them venturing into some of London's seediest areas as part of the Met.'s Victor Tango division, coming to terms with the stresses and strains of the job and coping with their demanding, and less than perfect, supervisor, Detective Sgt Alan Rockliffe. His 'babies' consisted of two WPCs, Hargreaves and Walsh, plus five male officers, Adams, Chitty, Hood, O'Dowd and Georgiou, men and women of diverse backgrounds now forced to work together.

After two successful seasons, Rockliffe was given his own spin-off series, *Rockliffe's Folly*, in which he moved out of the capital and took up a new appointment in Wessex, believing it to be a softer option. He soon discovered that hard crime still existed, even in this rural backwater.

RODDENBERRY, GENE (EUGENE RODDENBERRY; 1921–91)

American TV executive, one-time writer for series like **Highway Patrol**, **Naked City**, **Dr Kildare** and particularly **Have Gun, Will Travel**, but whose claim to fame was always **Star Trek**, which he created and produced. Roddenberry was also responsible for **Star Trek: The Next Generation**. He was married to actress Majel Barrett, who played Nurse Christine Chapel in **Star Trek**.

RODGERS, ANTON (1933–)

British actor seen on television since the late 1950s, although his major roles have been in recent years, primarily as William Fields in **Fresh/French Fields** and as Alec Callender in **May to December**. Rodgers played Lt Gilmore in *The Skylarks*, a 1958 comedy, was one of the actors to appear as *Number Two* in **The Prisoner**, took the part of Stanley Featherstonehaugh Ukridge in the P.G. Wodehouse series *Ukridge*, and was policeman David Gradley in the short-lived psychic series *Zodiac*. He played Edward Langtry in **Lillie**, appeared in Roy Clarke's *Pictures*, was Detective Inspector Purbright in *Murder Most English* and starred in Frederic Raphael's ten-part drama *After the War*, as well as guesting in various action series, such as **The Protectors** and **Randall and Hopkirk**

(Deceased). Other credits have included *The Organisation*, **Rumpole of the Bailey**, plus assorted single dramas.

ROGERS, ROY (LEONARD SLYE; 1912–)

The King of the Cowboys, Roy Rogers began his career in country and western music. He performed for a while under the name of Dick Weston, before legally changing his name to Roy Rogers in 1942. In the late 1930s Rogers was groomed as a Hollywood cowboy, taught to ride and pitched into a series of westerns, beginning with *Under Western Skies* in 1938. He became one of kids' TV's first favourites when he drifted onto the small screen, usually accompanied by his wife Dale Evans (the 'Queen of the West') and his trusty steed, Trigger. Some of Rogers's old movies were also edited down for TV consumption.

ROGERS, TED (1935–)

Twinkly-eyed, fast-talking British comic whose finest hour arrived with the game show *3–2–1* on which he was the finger-twiddling host for nine series. Previously, Rogers had been seen in numerous variety shows, from the *Billy Cotton Band Show* to **Sunday Night at the London Palladium**.

ROLL OVER BEETHOVEN

UK (Central) Situation Comedy. ITV 1985

Belinda Purcell ....Liza Goddard
Nigel Cochrane ....Nigel Planer
Oliver Purcell ....Richard Vernon
Marvin ....Emlyn Price
Lem ....Desmond McNamara

Creators/Writers: Laurence Marks, Maurice Gran. Producers: Tony Charles, Allan McKeown

A famous rock star and a demure music teacher fall in love.

Crusty retired headmaster Oliver Purcell was not amused to hear that legendary rock star Nigel Cochrane had decided to give up touring and was intending to move into his staid, peaceful village. He was even more disturbed when his own daughter, Belinda, began to give Nigel piano lessons, and when they fell in love, he very nearly needed oxygen. It was an unlikely romance. Belinda, usually the dutiful, demure daughter, hardly seemed the type to turn a rock legend's head, but turn it she did, and when Nigel decided to go back on the road, Belinda supported him by writing songs with his pals Marvin and Lem. Eventually, she cut her own album and dad, despite his bluster, was really quite pleased.

ROMANY JONES

UK (LWT) Situation Comedy. ITV 1973–4

Bert Jones ....James Beck
Betty Jones..Jo Rowbottom
Wally Briggs ....Arthur Mullard
Lily Briggs ....Queenie Watts
Jeremy Crichton-Jones ....Jonathan Cecil
Susan Crichton-Jones ....Gay Soper

Producer: Stuart Allen

Neighbour vs. neighbour on a run down campsite.

Workshy Bert Jones lived with his wife, Betty, in a battered, leaky, ant-ridden caravan on a grotty campsite. Their nearest neighbours were bluff Cockneys Wally and Lily Briggs and, needless to say, they didn't always see eye to eye. Beginning as a one-off play in 1972, the series had just completed one successful run when actor James Beck died. Recasting was necessary and snooty Jeremy and Susan Crichton-Jones were introduced as Wally and Lily's new neighbours. In 1976, the Briggses were given their own spin-off show, *Yus My Dear*, in which Wally took a job as a bricklayer and they were transferred to the comfort of a council house. Wally's sponging brother, Benny (played by Mike Reid), was thrown in for company.

ROOBARB AND CUSTARD

UK (Bob Godfrey) Children's Entertainment. BBC 1 1974

Narrator: Richard Briers

Creator/Writer: Grange Calveley. Producer: Bob Godfrey

Cat and dog one-upmanship.

Drawn in dazzling colours and in a distinctive, half-finished, wobbly style (making a virtue out of a low budget), *Roobarb and Custard* concerned the daily battles of an ambitious green dog (Roobarb) and a cynical pink cat (Custard). Producer Bob Godfrey likened the relationship to the one shared by Tony Hancock and Sid James. Events took place in a back garden, with a fenceful of smirking birds taking sides with the winner. Quirkily narrated by Richard Briers and filled with adult wit, it became a favourite with all ages, although it was aimed squarely at the children's market.

ROOTS

US (ABC/David L. Wolper) Drama. BBC 1 1977

Kunta Kinte ....LeVar Burton
Toby (Kunta Kinte) ....John Amos
Binta ....Cicely Tyson
Omoro ....Thalmus Rasulala
Nyo Boto ....Maya Angelou
Kadi Touray ....OJ Simpson
The Wrestler ....Ji-Tu Cumbuka
Kintango ....Moses Gunn
Fiddler...Louis Gossett Jnr
Gardner ....William Watson
Kizzy ....Leslie Uggams
Captain Thomas Davies ....Edward Asner
Third Mate Slater ....Ralph Waite
John Reynolds ....Lorne Greene
Mrs Reynolds ....Lynda Day George
Dr William Reynolds ....Robert Reed
Carrington ....Paul Shenar
Tom Moore ....Chuck Connors
Ordell ....John Schuck
Mingo ....Scatman Crothers
Stephen Bennett............................George Hamilton
Evan Brent ....Lloyd Bridges
Tom Harvey ....Georg Stanford Brown
Irene Harvey ....Lynne Moody
Sam Bennett ....Richard Roundtree
Ames ....Vic Morrow
The Drummer ....Raymond St Jacques
Missy Anne ....Sandy Duncan
Squire James....................................MacDonald Carey
Chicken George Moore ....Ben Vereen
Mrs Moore ....Carolyn Jones
Sir Eric Russell ....Ian McShane
Sister Sara ....Lillian Randolph
Jemmy Brent ....Doug McClure
Justin..Burl Ives
Lewis ....Hilly Hicks

Writers: William Blinn, Ernest Kinoy, James Lee, Max Cohen. Executive Producer: David L. Wolper. Producer: Stan Margulies

The saga of a black American family, from its roots in slavery to the Civil War.

If *Rich Man, Poor Man* was the mini-series that launched the idea of dramatizing popular novels with a star-studded cast, *Roots* was the serial which ensured the concept stayed well and truly afloat. This 12-hour drama was an enormous success, telling the story of various generations of a black American family, picking up the action around 1750 with the birth of a boy to a Gambian tribe. At the age of 17, the boy, Kunta Kinte, was kidnapped by white slave traders and taken to America. Adopting the new name of Toby, he was set to work on the southern plantations, but remained doggedly independent, even losing a foot in an attempt to escape. The series then followed the misfortunes of Kunta Kinte and his clan over a hundred-year period. It saw his daughter, Kizzy, raped by her owner and giving birth to a son later known as Chicken George (because of his prowess with fighting birds), who spent some time in slavery in England. George's son, Tom, fought in the American Civil War and with his family looked forward to the emancipation of slaves that followed it. But, as they embarked on a move to Tennessee and the dream of a better life, they discovered that their new 'freedom', with its grim poverty, poor education and feeble rights, was not the true liberty they had envisaged.

That wasn't the end of the *Roots* saga, however. In 1979, a sequel, entitled *Roots: The Next Generations* (featuring top actors like Henry Fonda, Marlon Brando and Richard Thomas), picked up the story in the 1880s and ran through to the late 1960s. It saw Tom, his daughter and then his granddaughter begin to make inroads in society. At the end of the family line came Alex (played by James Earl Jones), a noted writer who was sufficiently intrigued by his family history that he returned to Africa to learn how his great-great-great-great grandfather, Kunta Kinte, had been so cruelly robbed of his freedom.

Roots and *Roots: The Next Generations* were adapted from the book by Alex Haley – the Alex of its storyline. The success of the original series (over half the population of America watched the final episode) can be put down partly to its all-star cast, and partly to the fact that the USA was swept with blizzards on the eight consecutive nights on which the series was shown. Some critics have claimed that white Americans gave the series their time in repentance for the sins of their ancestors. Others have simply suggested that sensationalism was the reason for its success, questioning the accuracy of the facts and describing the series as a glossy combination of 'shackles, whips and lust'.

ROSE, MONICA

Chirpy Cockney teenager who sprang to fame as a contestant on *Double Your Money* in 1963. Her personality impressed presenter Hughie Green so much that he made her the permanent hostess. She continued to partner Green on the follow-up quiz *The Sky's the Limit* in 1971.

ROSEANNE

US (Carsey-Werner/Full Moon & High Tide)
Situation Comedy. Channel 4 1989–

Roseanne Conner	Roseanne (Barr/Arnold)
Dan Conner	John Goodman
Jackie Harris	Laurie Metcalf
Rebecca 'Becky' Conner/Healey	Lecy Goranson
	Sarah Chalke
Darlene Conner	Sara Gilbert
David Jacob 'DJ' Conner	Michael Fishman
Crystal Anderson/Conner	Natalie West
Booker Brooks	George Clooney
Ed Conner	Ned Beatty
Mark Healey	Glenn Quinn
Bonnie	Bonnie Sheridan
Leon Carp	Martin Mull
Bev Harris	Estelle Parsons
Arnie Merchant	Tom Arnold
Nancy	Sara Bernhard
Nana Mary	Shelley Winters
David Healey	Johnny Galecki
Fred	Michael O'Keefe

Creator: Matt Williams. Executive Producers: Marcy Carsey, Tom Werner, Roseanne Barr/Arnold, Tom Arnold. Producers: Matt Williams, Jeff Harris

Down-to-earth comedy of life in Middle America.

Roseanne and Dan Conner, two heavyweight wisecrackers, lived in the lacklustre town of Lanford, Illinois. Dan worked as a dry-waller in the building industry where work was patchy; Roseanne flitted from job to job, abusing her employers and dreaming of the day when the bills stopped arriving. But there was not much chance of that with three demanding kids to support. Eldest was Becky, a typically precocious teenager, anxious to grow up and dismissive of her parents' efforts to keep the family afloat. Next was sports-mad tomboy Darlene, comfortable with her plainness, acerbic in her wit and always her dad's best buddy. Runt of the litter was DJ, a slightly off-beat juvenile, the jewel of his parents' eyes and the bane of his sisters' lives.

Hovering around the comfortable but functional home was Roseanne's unmarried sister, Jackie Harris. Moping between jobs (she was once a cop and then a truck driver) and boyfriends, she was Roseanne's confidante and disrupter of Dan's mealtimes. On the fringes was Rosie's half-baked friend Crystal, who later married Dan's absent father, Ed, and an assortment of work colleagues and bosses from Roseanne's times as plastic factory worker, sweeper-up at a beauty salon and coffee shop waitress in a shopping mall. The Conners also tried their hand at running a motorbike repair shop and, when that failed, Roseanne joined Jackie, their grating mum, Bev, and bisexual friend Nancy in opening The Lunch Box, a loose meat diner.

The novel thing about *Roseanne* was the sheer ordinariness of its lead characters. Here was a family that ate convenience foods, watched TV all day and lived on the telephone. They worked hard yet got nowhere, but the family unit remained whole, even if it did stretch at the seams from time to time, especially when Becky ran off and married her punk boyfriend, Mark, and Darlene also left home for art college and secretly moved in with Mark's brother, David. An enlightened approach to parenthood and an irrepressible sense of humour made the family work, even in the most difficult of times.

ROSENTHAL, JACK (1931–)

Award-winning British screenwriter, creator of the comedy series *The Dustbinmen*, *The Lovers*,

Sadie It's Cold Outside and *Moving Story* and writer of many single dramas notable for their wry humour and clever social observation. Amongst the highlights have been *Pie in the Sky*, *Green Rub* (both 1963), *There's A Hole In Your Dustbin, Delilah* (1968, which proved to be the pilot for *The Dustbinmen*), *Another Sunday and Sweet FA* (1972), *Polly Put the Kettle On, Mr Ellis Versus The People* and *There'll Almost Always Be an England* (all 1974, the last two from the *Village Hall* anthology), *The Evacuees* (1975), *Ready When You Are, Mr McGill, Bar Mitzvah Boy* (both 1976), *Spend, Spend, Spend* (1977), *Spaghetti Two-Step, The Knowledge* (1979), *P'tang Yang Kipperbang* (1982), *Mrs Capper's Birthday* (1985), *Fools on the Hill* (1986), *And a Nightingale Sang* (1989) and **London's Burning** (1986, which, again, led to a fully-fledged series, but with no Rosenthal involvement). Rosenthal also wrote for Maureen Lipman's *About Face* series (she is his wife). His earliest TV work was on **Coronation Street** (some 200 episodes, plus some as producer), **The Odd Man** (with his one-time partner Harry Driver), **That Was The Week That Was**, *The Villains*, **Pardon the Expression**, **Mrs Thursday** and **Comedy Playhouse**.

ROSENTHAL, JIM (1947–)

British sports frontman, formerly in newspapers and then with BBC Radio. For ITV Sport, he has presented coverage of athletics, soccer, boxing and other major events.

ROSIE/THE GROWING PAINS OF PC PENROSE

UK (BBC) Situation Comedy. BBC 1 1975–81

PC Michael 'Rosie' Penrose ....Paul Greenwood
Sgt Flagg ....Bryan Pringle (*Growing Pains*)
PC Wilmot ....Tony Haygarth
Gillian Chislehurst ....Frankie Jordan
Millie Penrose ....Avril Elgar
                                                        Patricia Kneale
Uncle Norman ....Alan Surtees
Auntie Ida ....Lorraine Peters
Bill Chislehurst.......................................Don McKillop
Glenda Chislehurst ....Maggie Jones
Chief Inspector Dunwoody ....Paul Luty
Sgt West ....Barry Hart
WPC Brenda Whatmough........Penny Leatherbarrow
Merv ....Robert Gillespie
                                                              John Cater

Creator/Writer: Roy Clarke. Producers: Douglas Argent, Bernard Thompson

The misadventures of a hapless young constable and his associates.

Viewers were introduced to young PC Penrose, or 'Rosie' as he was familiarly known, in the series *The Growing Pains of PC Penrose*. A friend-ly but exceptionally naive copper, he was based at a Yorkshire police station, where he was cruelly bullied by his superior, the formidable Sgt Flagg. However, when the series' title was shortened to *Rosie*, he was given a compassionate move back to his home town of Ravens Bay, to be near his 'invalid' mother, Millie. He now found himself living with his flighty mum at his Auntie Ida's house, where his Uncle Norman spent most of his time in the garden (whether he liked it or not). At work, Rosie was paired with PC Wilmot, a more experienced, but also more reck-less bobby whom Rosie often had to bail out of trouble and protect from the clutches of WPC Whatmough. Chief Inspector Dunwoody was their no-nonsense boss and Merv their short-sighted, inept supergrass. Rosie also had a girl-friend, the demanding, clinging Gillian, whose factory-owning dad had little time for her PC boyfriend.

This gentle comedy was written by Roy Clarke (who used to be a policeman himself) and intro-duced up-and-coming actor Paul Greenwood. Greenwood returned to police ranks a decade later, but this time much further up the ladder, when he took the part of *Spender*'s by-the-book boss, Supt Yelland. Greenwood also co-wrote and sang the theme song for *Rosie*.

ROSS, JOE E. (1905–82)

American comic actor, seen as Sgt Rupert Ritzik in **The Phil Silvers Show** and later a star in his own right, playing the podgy Officer Gunther Toody in *Car 54, Where Are You?* A later series, *It's About Time* (in which he played a caveman), was less successful and he soon turned to anima-tion voicing as a new career path (amongst others, he was the voice of Sgt Flint in **Hong Kong Phooey**).

ROSS, JONATHAN (1960–)

Former TV researcher (on programmes like Channel 4's *Soul Train*) who became an instant hit in the mid-1980s when he hosted his own chat show, *The Last Resort*. His snappy suits and dis-tinctive speech impediment (a soft 'R'), quickly ensured celebrity status. He has since hosted *One Hour with Jonathan Ross*, a tea time chat show for Channel 4 (*Tonight With Jonathan Ross*), *The Saturday Zoo* and sat in on *Wogan*. Ross's other credits have included *The Incredibly Strange Film Show*, *Gagtag*, *Americana* (a documentary series about American lifestyles), *Fascinating Facts!* and numerous award ceremonies as emcee. He runs his own (Channel X) production company. His brother Paul is also a presenter.

ROSS, NICK (1947–)

British current affairs anchorman, initially working for the BBC in Northern Ireland. He was
once presenter of **Breakfast Time** and the
Nationwide successor **Sixty Minutes**, but is best
known for being at the helm of **Crimewatch UK**
since 1984. Ross has also hosted its associated
programmes **Crimewatch Files** and **Crimestoppers**,
plus **Watchdog**, **On the Record** and **Did You
See ... ?**, as well as presenting and directing **Out
of Court** and contributing to series like **Man Alive**
and **Horizon**.

ROSSINGTON, JANE (1943–)

Blonde British actress, Jill Richardson/
Harvey/Chance in **Crossroads** throughout the
series' entire run. Indeed, it was Jane who uttered
the first words on the programme: 'Crossroads
Motel, can I help you?'. Her other TV credits
have been few, notably the part of nurse Kate
Ford in **Emergency – Ward 10** before **Crossroads**,
and an episode of **Dramarama** since.

ROSSITER, LEONARD (1926–84)

Much acclaimed British actor, a viewers'
favourite as the seedy landlord Rigsby in **Rising
Damp**. He proved just as popular when suffering
a mid-life crisis as the lead in **The Fall and Rise
of Reginald Perrin**. Rossiter did not turn professional until his late 20s and his flair for comedy
was even slower to raise its head. When he first
arrived on the small screen in the 1960s, after
notable stage performances, he was primarily a
straight actor. One of his early roles was that of
Detective Inspector Bamber in **Z Cars**, although
he also appeared in the satire show **BBC 3**.
Amongst his other credits were the controversial
Nigel Kneale play **The Year of the Sex Olympics**,
the HTV movie **Thick as Thieves**, the Andrew
Davies drama **Fearless Frank** and the Roy Clarke
Comedy Playhouse presentation **Pygmalion Smith**.
He also guested in series like **The Avengers** and
Steptoe and Son and was regularly seen spilling
Cinzano over Joan Collins in commercials.
Rossiter's final sitcoms were **The Losers** (as
wrestling manager Sydney Foskett) and **Tripper's
Day** (as supermarket manager Norman Tripper).
Screened posthumously, his portrayal of King
John in a **BBC Shakespeare** offering was a last
reminder of his versatility. Both his wives were
also in the acting business: Josephine Tewson and
Gillian Raine.

ROTHWELL, ALAN (1937–)

Northern actor on television for over 30 years.
Undoubtedly, his best remembered part was that
of the ill-fated David Barlow (Ken's brother) in
Coronation Street, which he played for eight years
up to 1968. Taking time out from the **Street**,
Rothwell was also seen in the South American
spy caper **Top Secret** (as Mike) and he later moved
into children's entertainment as producer, writer
and presenter of **Picture Box**. He has been seen in
Z Cars, **Crown Court**, **All Creatures Great and
Small** and **Children's Ward**, amongst other series,
and also played junkie Nicholas Black in
Brookside for a while in the 1980s.

ROUTH, JONATHAN

The Jeremy Beadle of the early 1960s, Jonathan
Routh was **Candid Camera**'s chief prankster –
until he became too easily recognized. He also
presented the innovative **Nice Time** with Kenny
Everett and Germaine Greer in 1968.

ROUTLEDGE, PATRICIA, OBE (1929–)

British actress much seen in supporting roles until
blooming as Hyacinth Bucket (pronounced
'Bouquet') in Roy Clarke's **Keeping Up
Appearances**. Other appearances of note have
come in 1964's **Victoria Regina** (as Queen
Victoria), the BBC's 1975 version of **David
Copperfield** (as Mrs Micawber), the short-lived
comedy **Marjorie and Men** (as divorcée Marjorie
Belton) and in Alan Bennett's **Talking Heads**.
Routledge has also been seen in **Z Cars**, **Sense
and Sensibility**, **Nicholas Nickelby**, **Steptoe and Son**,
The Cost of Loving, **A Visit from Miss Protheroe**, **The
Two Ronnies**, **Crown Court**, **Tales of the
Unexpected**, **First and Last** and **Victoria Wood – As
Seen on TV**, plus many other dramas.

ROVING REPORT

UK (ITN) Documentary. ITV 1957–64

Creator/Editor: Geoffrey Cox. Reporters:
Robin Day, George Ffitch, Tim Brinton, John
Hartley, Reginald Bosanquet, Huw Thomas,
Lynne Reid Banks, Ian Trethowan, Neville
Barker, Elizabeth Kenrick, John Whale

Producers: Michael Barsley, Robert Verrall

**Series of short documentaries looking at
people and places in the news around the
world.**

Roving Report was ITN's first and more-or-less
only programme that was not exclusively news-
based. It consisted of a collection of documentary
films of about 20 minutes in length, compiled by
ITN reporters as they travelled the world. The
films were often by-products of a news-seeking
expedition but, nevertheless, had their own distinct character and aimed to paint a picture of the

people of a foreign city or country at that time in the news, reflecting their views, thoughts, ways of life, etc. The first programme was recorded atop the Empire State Building. Robin Day was the chief reporter in the early days.

ROWAN, DAN (1922–87) see Martin, Dick.

ROWAN AND MARTIN'S LAUGH-IN

US (Romart) Comedy. BBC 2 1968–71

Dan Rowan
Dick Martin
Gary Owens
Ruth Buzzi
Judy Carne
Goldie Hawn
Arte Johnson
Henry Gibson
Eileen Brennan
Jo Anne Worley
Roddy-Maude Roxby
Larry Hovis
Pigmeat Markham
Charlie Brill
Dick Whittington
Chelsea Brown
Mitzi McCall
Alan Sues
Dave Madden
Jeremy Lloyd
Teresa Graves
Pamela Rodgers
Byron Gilliam
Lily Tomlin
Ann Elder
Dennis Allen
Johnny Brown
Barbara Sharma
Nancy Phillips
Harvey Jason

Executive Producers: George Schlatter, Ed Friendly

Hugely popular and influential, fast-moving gag show.

Hosts of *Laugh-In* were Dan Rowan, a smooth straightman, and his grinning fool of a partner, Dick Martin, but they were more than backed up by a large cast of zany comedians who worked around them. The show itself was a cross between slapstick and satire, a sort of Keystone Cops meet *That Was The Week That Was*, all fused together on bright sets by 1960s TV technology. There were gags galore, not all of them terribly funny, but the weight of numbers meant that the audience just had to find something amusing.

Catchphrases became *Laugh-In*'s speciality. From Dan and Dick's 'You bet your sweet bippy' and 'Look that up in your Funk and Wagnalls', to 'Sock it to me', a cue for Judy Carne to get a thorough soaking. Even Richard Nixon dropped in to say it. Popular features and sketches included 'Letters to *Laugh-In*', the 'Flying Fickle Finger of Fate' (a mock talent show award), and the non-stop joke wall that wound up each programme, with cast members flinging open doors to belt out one-liners. All this came after Rowan and Martin had parodied the old Burns and Allen ending ('Say goodnight, Dick.', 'Goodnight Dick').

Also memorable were the man riding a toddler's tricycle; Henry Gibson, the flower-power poet; and Ruth Buzzi as Gladys, the vicious lady on the park bench thrashing Arte Johnson's Tyrone, a dirty old man, with her umbrella. Johnson also popped up from behind a pot plant, as a German soldier muttering 'Very interesting, but stupid', Lily Tomlin appeared as Ernestine, the sarcastic telephone operator, and Alan Sues played a gormless sports presenter. Then there was Gary Owens, hand cupped over his ear, bellowing into the microphone to welcome viewers to 'Beautiful Downtown Burbank', Pigmeat Markham, whose 'Here Comes The Judge' was a UK chart hit in 1968, and Goldie Hawn establishing herself as a dumb, giggly blonde.

The jokes were topical, sometimes controversial and generally very silly, but they were held together by slick editing, cameo appearances from guest stars and the hectic pace of the show. *Laugh-In* was the world's favourite comedy programme for two or three years. When it ended, Buzzi and Owens were the only cast members (apart from the hosts) still with it. The show was revived in 1979 but its time had long passed and this version is only notable for the fact that Robin Williams was one of the supporting performers.

ROWLANDS, PATSY (1934–)

British actress, often seen as a dowdy wife, but enjoying a long and varied TV career to date. Amongst her wife roles have been Rosemary in *Inside George Webley*, Betty in *Bless this House* and Netta in *Kinvig*. In contrast she was Sally Army Sister Alice Meredith in *Hallelujah* and also appeared as police officers in the kids' series *Follow that Dog* and the sitcom *The Nesbitts Are Coming*. Rowlands took the roles of Miss Twitty in another children's series *Tottering Towers*, Susan in *The Squirrels* and Flossie Nightingale, an actor, in *Rep*. To add to the variety, she has also been seen in dramas like *Public Eye*, *Juliet Bravo*, *Père Goriot*, *Kate*, *The History of Mr Polly* and *Crimestrike*, as well as comedies like *Robin's Nest*, *In Loving Memory*, *Carry On Laughing* and *George and Mildred*.

ROY ROGERS SHOW, THE

US (Roy Rogers) Western. ITV 1955–7

Roy Rogers
Dale Evans
Pat Brady

Executive Producers: Art Rush, Mike North. Producers: Jack C. Lacey, Bob Henry, Leslie H. Martinson

Clean cut, modern-day western with the 'King of the Cowboys' and his wife, Dale Evans, 'Queen of the West'.

Living on the Double R Bar Ranch, in Paradise Valley, near Mineral City, singing cowboy Roy Rogers was an important force in the maintenance of law and order in the neighbourhood. He also owned a diner, the Eureka Café, which was run by Dale Evans, and he was assisted by an incompetent sidekick, Pat Brady, cook at the diner and driver of an unreliable jeep known as Nellybelle. Roy, of course, rode Trigger, alongside Dale on Buttermilk. Bullet the Alsatian dog trotted along in tow and the Sons of the Pioneers vocal group helped Roy with the musical content.

ROYAL CANADIAN MOUNTED POLICE

Canada/UK (CBC/Crawley Films/BBC) Police Drama. BBC 1960–61

Cpl Jacques Gagnier ....Gilles Pelletier
Constable Scott ....John Perkins
Constable Bill Mitchell ....Don Francks

Producers: George Gorman, Harry Horner, Bernard Girard

Stirring adventures of the RCMP.

As if to prove that a Mountie always got his man, this joint Canadian/UK production brought us heroic tales from the frozen north. It centred on the town of Shamattawa and its Royal Canadian Mounted Police headquarters, following the local officers in their efforts to enforce law and order.

ROYAL VARIETY PERFORMANCE

UK (ATV/BBC) Variety. ITV/BBC 1 1960–

Annual charity concert in the presence of Her Majesty The Queen or other members of the royal family.

A prestigious showbusiness extravaganza, the Royal Variety Performance was instituted in 1912 and became a yearly event in 1921. It was first televised for ITV in 1960 by Lew Grade's ATV, which covered proceedings again the following year. Since 1962, however, the BBC has enjoyed the right to stage the show on alternate years. Amongst the stars of the first televised show (held at the Victoria Palace theatre) were Norman Wisdom, Harry Worth, Benny Hill, Frankie Howerd, Cliff Richard and The Shadows, Max Bygraves, Russ Conway, Liberace and Nat 'King' Cole. In 1963, The Beatles took the Prince of Wales Theatre by storm and, in 1980, on the occasion of her 80th birthday, the Queen Mother

revelled in the tribute to music hall days paid by Chesney Allen, Arthur Askey, Charlie Chester, Billy Dainty, Charlie Drake, Arthur English, Cyril Fletcher, Stanley Holloway, Roy Hudd, Richard Murdoch, Sandy Powell, Tommy Trinder and Ben Warriss. Bernard Delfont staged each show from 1961 to 1978.

ROYLE, CAROL (1954–)

British actress probably best recalled as Jenny in *Life Without George*, which she quickly followed with the role of Jessica in Dennis Potter's controversial *Blackeyes*. Royle also starred in *Girl Talk*, *Ladies in Charge* (as Diana Granville) and in Alan Plater's version of L.P. Hartley's vampire story, *Feet Foremost* (part of the *Shades of Darkness* anthology), and amongst her other credits have been parts in series like *Blake's 7*, *The Racing Game*, *The Cedar Tree*, *The Professionals*, *Heartland*, *Bergerac*, *The Outsider* and *Oxbridge Blues*. She is the daughter of actor Derek Royle and sister of actress Amanda Royle.

RUMPOLE OF THE BAILEY

UK (Thames) Legal Drama. ITV 1978–80; 1983; 1987–8; 1991–2

Horace Rumpole ....Leo McKern
Claude Erskine-Brown ....Julian Curry
Phyllida Trant/Erskine-Brown ....Patricia Hodge
Guthrie Featherstone...............................Peter Bowles
George Frobisher..................................Moray Watson
Uncle Tom ....Richard Murdoch
Hilda Rumpole ....Peggy Thorpe Bates
                                      Marion Mathie
Henry ....Jonathan Coy
Justice Bullingham...Bill Fraser
Diane ....Maureen Derbyshire
Fiona Allways ....Rosalyn Landor
Marigold Featherstone ....Joanna Van Gyseghem
Samuel Ballard QC...................................Peter Blythe
Liz Probert ....Samantha Bond
                                        Abigail McKern
Nick Rumpole ....David Yelland
Judge Graves ....Robin Bailey

Creator/Writer: John Mortimer. Executive Producer: Lloyd Shirley. Producers: Irene Shubik, Jacqueline Davis

The cases of a gruff, old barrister with a zest for justice.

Colourful, middle-aged Horace Rumpole differed from his legal colleagues in his distinct lack of ambition and his genuine interest in clients. Indeed, when the series started, he was expected to take up the position of Head of Chambers at his father-in-law's law firm, but declined it because of his love of courtroom drama. His brusque, down-to-earth manner ruffled many a rival's feathers, and he revelled in a joyful lack of respect for authority (he called judges 'Old Darling').

Rumpole only took defence cases and his clients came mostly (though not uniquely) from the lower classes. He proved a saviour on most occasions, craftily turning trials in the favour of his clients. Out of the courtroom, he enjoyed smoking cigars, quoting the *Oxford Book of English Verse*, drinking the Pomeroy's Wine Bar claret (Château Fleet Street, as he knew it) and disappointing his wife, Hilda, 'She who must be obeyed'. He was retired to Florida after a couple of seasons, but returned in a two-hour special at Christmas 1980. Further series followed intermittently. Amongst his more refined legal contemporaries were Samuel Ballard (his Head of Chambers), Erskine-Brown and his future wife, the snobbish Phyllida Trant. The part of junior barrister Liz Probert was eventually filled by Leo McKern's own daughter, Abigail.

The series was written by real-life barrister John Mortimer and the character first appeared in a BBC 1 **Play for Today** in 1975. When the Corporation declined to take up the option of a series, Mortimer and his producer Irene Shubik transferred the irascible old brief to Thames Television.

RUSHTON, WILLIAM (1937–)

British satirist and cartoonist, coming to the fore on **That Was The Week That Was** and its follow-up **Not So Much a Programme, More a Way of Life**. He went on to host *The New Stars and Garters* with Jill Browne, to guest in **Not Only ... But Also ...** and to play Plautus in **Up Pompeii!**, before being given his own series *Rushton's Illustrated*. He has also been seen in programmes like *Up Sunday*, *Don't Just Sit There* and *Dawson and Friends*, and has been a popular guest on panel games. Rushton was one of the founders of *Private Eye* magazine.

RUSSELL, KEN (1927–)

British director responsible for some outrageous movie moments but more restrained, if just as adventurous, in his television work. Russell began by contributing material for series like **Monitor** and **Omnibus** and has given the TV archives some notable documentary-drama portraits of composers like Bartok, Elgar, Wagner, Delius and Debussy, plus other artistic personalities like Isadora Duncan (*Isadora*, 1966), Dante Gabriel Rossetti (*Dante's Inferno*, 1967) and Wordsworth and Coleridge (*Clouds of Glory*, 1978).

RUTH RENDELL MYSTERIES, THE

UK (TVS) Police Drama. ITV 1987–92

Detective Chief Insp. Reg Wexford ......George Baker

Detective Inspector Mike Burden	
....	Christopher Ravenscroft
Dora Wexford	Louise Ramsay
Jean Burden	Ann Penfold
Jenny Ireland/Burden	Diane Keen
Detective Sgt Martin	Ken Kitson
Dr Crocker..	John Burgess
Sgt Barry Vine	Sean Pertwee

Executive Producer: Graham Benson.
Producers: John Davies, Neil Zeiger

The investigations of a slow-speaking, but sharp-thinking country policeman.

Reg Wexford was one of the great thinking coppers of the 1980s. Like Dalgliesh, Taggart and Morse, he eschewed the hard-hitting, screaming tyres-kind of police work much enjoyed by 1970s detectives, in favour of the painstaking, analytical, working-on-a-hunch sort of investigation. Created by novelist Ruth Rendell while on holiday in Ireland (hence the name Wexford, apparently), the Detective Chief Inspector took his first name from Ruth's uncle, Reg, although most of his character traits allegedly came from her father, a softly-spoken but firm teacher.

Rendell's novels had a sort of serial structure, with the private lives of the characters and assorted sub-plots developing from book to book. By adapting the novels out of sequence (beginning with *Wolf to the Slaughter*), this continuity was marred to some degree, but the southern 'soapiness' of the books still came through. The tales were set in the fictitious Hampshire town of Kingsmarkham (Romsey was used for filming purposes), a sleepy backwater which, like Morse's Oxford and Bergerac's Jersey, quickly witnessed more than its fair share of murders. Out and about on investigations, the fatherly Wexford was assisted by the aptly-named Detective Inspector Mike Burden, a gloomy man with no smile and little to smile about (his wife had died of cancer). Even when he remarried, Burden remained rather morose. At home, Wexford's understanding wife, Jean, proved to be a rock of support and a source of great encouragement. Their grown-up daughters were also seen from time to time.

Like all good TV cops, the affable, well-heeled Wexford had his share of gimmicks, particularly a rich, Hampshire burr when he spoke, an enjoyment of good cooking and an evidently well-educated manner, manifested in his fondness for quoting Shakespeare. And like all good TV cops, he always got his man. Sometimes it took two or three episodes, but his tortoise-like approach ensured the right result eventually. By the time the series ended in 1992 (partly due to TVS losing its franchise), all 13 existing Ruth Rendell novels had been covered, plus a few of her short stories and a handful of new scripts (including some from star George Baker). *The Ruth Rendell Mysteries* title has since been revived by Meridian, although these intermittent thrillers have not featured Inspector Wexford.

RUTLAND WEEKEND TELEVISION

UK (BBC) Situation Comedy. BBC 2 1975–76

Eric Idle
David Battley
Neil Innes
Henry Woolf
Terence Bayler
Gwen Taylor

Creator/Writer: Eric Idle. Producer: Ian Keill

Ambitious programming from Britain's smallest television network.

Based in Rutland, England's one-time smallest county, this spoof series was the brainchild of **Monty Python** star Eric Idle, who cast himself as the programme controller of Rutland Weekend Television. RWT, for short, presented a variety of programme parodies, some, like *The History of the Entire World*, described as 'mini-spectaculars'. Neil Innes provided the musical content which reached its zenith in the one-off, 1978 documentary sequel, *The Rutles*. Telling the story of the world's greatest pop band, known individually as Dirk, Ron, Stig and Barry, but collectively as The Rutles, it intercut spoof interviews with celebrities like Mick Jagger with scenes from the life of the so-called Pre-fab Four. The musical numbers included all-time classics like 'All You Need Is Lunch', 'WC Fields Forever', 'Cheese and Onion' and 'A Hard Day's Rut', and an accompanying album (with uncannily Beatle-like vocals and soundtracks) was released. An EP, headed by the track 'I Must Be In Love', made the lower reaches of the UK charts.

RUTLES, The see *Rutland Weekend Television.*

S4C

(Sianel Pedwar Cymru) The Welsh fourth channel, S4C was established by the Broadcasting Act 1980 and provides 30 hours a week of Welsh language programming, ten hours of which are supplied free of charge by the BBC in accordance with its obligations under the Broadcasting Act 1990. The remainder of the Welsh programmes are commissioned by S4C from HTV and other independent producers. Before S4C went on air on 1 November 1982 (a day earlier than Channel 4), BBC Wales and HTV Cymru/Wales mixed Welsh language programmes with their English

language output. Now they only carry programmes in English. The English language part of S4C's schedule is made up of programmes also seen on Channel 4 (over 80 per cent of Channel 4's output), although these are usually rescheduled to give Welsh programmes prominence during peak hours. This practice has not been over-popular with viewers in predominantly English-speaking parts of the Principality.

S4C's Welsh output takes in light entertainment, drama, news, current affairs, sports and children's programmes. Amongst the most popular has been BBC Wales's *Pobol y Cwm*, a daily soap opera which, uniquely, is rehearsed, recorded and transmitted all on the same day. A subtitled version has also been seen on BBC 2 in the rest of the UK, under the translated title of *People of the Valley*. The channel has also made a name for itself in the field of animation, commissioning some very successful cartoons from independent producers like Siriol and Bumper Films. These have included *Super Ted*, *Wil Cwac Cwac* and *Fireman Sam*. S4C is funded by a grant from the Treasury and its own advertising sales. It is accountable to a public body known as The Welsh Fourth Channel Authority, whose members are appointed by the Secretary of State for National Heritage. The channel's full name, Sianel Pedwar Cymru, means Channel Four Wales.

SABER OF LONDON see *Mark Saber.*

SACHS, ANDREW (1930–)

German-born actor whose finest hour came with *Fawlty Towers*, in which he played the hapless and hopeless Spanish waiter, Manuel. On the back of his success in the series, Sachs has been given the lead role in a few other sitcoms, all of which, sadly, have proved rather short-lived. Primarily, these have been *Dead Ernest* (as the late Ernest Springer), *There Comes A Time* (as Tony James, who didn't have long to live) and *Every Silver Lining* (as café-owner Nat Silver). Sachs, the father of radio and TV presenter John Sachs, has, however, been seen – or heard as narrator – in plenty of other programmes, from dramas like *The History of Mr Polly*, *The Tempest*, **Bergerac**, *James and the Giant Peach* and **Crown Court** to series as varied as **The World About Us**, **Points of View** (as guest presenter), *Supersense*, **Rising Damp** and the language lessons *When In Spain*. He also presented a programme about his birthplace, *Berliners*.

SACHS, LEONARD (1909–90)

South African actor who found greater fame as the supereloquent, gavel-smashing chairman of **The Good Old Days**, a position he held from

1953 until the series ended in 1983. Amongst his acting credits were parts in Nigel Kneale's *1984*, *The Adventures of Robin Hood*, *Crown Court*, *A Family At War*, *The Man from Haven*, *The Glittering Prizes*, *Elizabeth R* (as the Count de Feria) and *Coronation Street* (as Sir Julius Berlin). His last TV play was entitled *Lost for Words* and recorded shortly before he died.

SAGA OF NOGGIN THE NOG, THE

UK (Smallfilms) Children's Entertainment. BBC1 1959–65

Narrators: Oliver Postgate, Ronnie Stevens.

Creator: Peter Firmin. Producer: Oliver Postgate

The magical adventures of a norse king.

Using ten-minute episodes in serial form, this characterful animation told the story of Noggin, Prince (later King) of the Nogs, who sailed to the Land of the Midnight Sun to fetch Nooka, Eskimo Princess of the Nooks, to be his queen. His guide on his voyage was Graculus, a great, green talking bird raised from an egg by Nooka, who subsequently became the Royal Bird. Various other adventures befell the brave Noggin, including an encounter with the Ice Dragon and an attempt by his wicked uncle, Nogbad the Bad, to seize his throne. Other characters like Noggin's son Prince Knut, the mighty Thor Nogson and inventor Olaf the Lofty were also seen.

Noggin the Nog was the second offering (after *Ivor the Engine*) from the Smallfirms duo of writer/narrator Oliver Postgate and illustrator Peter Firmin. Vernon Elliott wrote the music. In 1982 two colour stories appeared – a re-make of *Noggin and the Ice Dragon* and a new story, *Noggin and the Pie*.

SAILOR

UK (BBC) Documentary. BBC 1 1976

Producer: John Purdie

A frank account of life with the crew of HMS *Ark Royal*.

This 11-part documentary series provided an insight into events in port and at sea with the 2500 men who crewed the aircraft carrier *Ark Royal*. A camera team lived aboard for ten weeks, capturing the high spots and the low. It saw drunken sailors in disgrace after unruly nights on the town and relived dramas like the winching of a seaman off a submarine for urgent medical treatment. The sailors' antics and their language were both colourful, but viewers, generally, loved it. The theme song, 'Sailing' by Rod Stewart, became a Top three hit for a second time, on the back of the series.

SAILOR OF FORTUNE

UK (ATV/Michael Sadler) Adventure. ITV 1955–6

Grant Mitchell ....Lorne Greene
Sean ....Jack MacGowan
Seamus...Rupert Davies
Johnny ....Paul Carpenter

Writer: Lindsay Galloway. Producer: Michael Sadler

An honest sea captain finds himself embroiled in other people's murky operations.

American Grant 'Mitch' Mitchell was the skipper of the freighter *The Shipwreck*. He travelled the world trying to make a living shipping cargo, although intrigue followed him wherever he roamed. There was always someone who needed his help and his ports of call were exotic, even though filming never ventured beyond the bounds of Elstree Studios. All the same, the series provided a springboard for both Lorne Greene and Rupert Davies.

SAINT, THE

UK (ATV/New World/Bamore/ITC) Adventure. ITV 1962–9

Simon Templar ....Roger Moore
Inspector Claude Eustace Teal ....Ivor Dean

Creator: Leslie Charteris. Producers: Robert S Baker, Monty Norman

A self-supporting amateur sleuth foils crime around the world.

The Saint was Simon Templar (ST being his initials), an independently wealthy adventurer who travelled the globe stumbling into intrigue. Using a business card depicting a matchstick man with a halo, and driving a yellow two-seater Volvo P1800 with the number plate ST1, Templar mingled with the élite and discovered crime at every turn. His devilishly good looks, the twinkle in his eye and his suave manner helped him appear cool in virtually every circumstance, whether it was rescuing blackmail victims or disrupting elaborate robberies. The unruffled, totally self-assured Templar was an unqualified success, and a wow with the women who included 1960s beauties like Samantha Eggar, Dawn Addams, Julie Christie and Gabrielle Drake. Templar's friendly adversary was the peppermint-sucking Inspector Claude Teal, sarcastically described by The Saint as 'Scotland Yard's finest'. He had been played by three other actors (Campbell Singer, Wensley Pithey and Norman Pitt) before Ivor Dean was confirmed in the role.

The Saint was created by writer Leslie Charteris in 1928 and had already been a hit on radio and in the cinema (most notably starring George Sanders) before the TV series began. Moore, of course, later took his adventurer character into James Bond films, with Ian Ogilvy filling his shoes for a 1970s revival, *The Return of the Saint*. Simon Dutton was cast in a 1989 version, but only a couple of episodes made it to the screen.

ST ELSEWHERE

US (MTM) Medical Drama. Channel 4 1983–9

Dr Donald Westphall	Ed Flanders
Dr Mark Craig	William Daniels
Dr Victor Ehrlich	Ed Begley, Jnr
Dr Jack Morrison	David Morse
Dr Ben Samuels	David Birney
Dr Annie Cavanero	Cynthia Sikes
Dr Wayne Fiscus	Howie Mandel
Dr Cathy Martin	Barbara Whinnery
Dr Peter White	Terence Knox
Nurse Helen Rosenthal	Christina Pickles
Dr Daniel Auschlander	Norman Lloyd
Dr Hugh Beale	GW Bailey
Dr Philip Chandler	Denzel Washington
Dr V.J. Kochar	Kavi Raz
Dr Wendy Armstrong	Kim Miyori
Nurse Shirley Daniels	Ellen Bry
Luther Hawkins	Eric Laneuville
Dr Bob Caldwell	Mark Harmon
Dr Michael Ridley	Paul Sand
Joan Halloran	Nancy Stafford
Mrs Ellen Craig	Bonnie Bartlett
Dr Elliot Axelrod	Stephen Furst
Nurse Lucy Papandrao	Jennifer Savidge
Dr Jackie Wade	Sagan Lewis
Warren Coolidge	Byron Stewart
Dr Emily Humes	Judith Hansen
Nurse Peggy Shotwell	Saundra Sharp
Dr Alan Poe	Brian Tochi
Mrs Hufnagel	Florence Halop
Dr Roxanne Turner	Alfre Woodard
Ken Valere	George Deloy
Terri Valere	Deborah May
Dr Seth Griffin	Bruce Greenwood
Dr Carol Novino	Cindy Pickett
Dr Paulette Kiem	France Nuyen
Dr John Gideon	Ronny Cox

Creators: Joshua Brand, John Falsey. Executive Producer: Bruce Paltrow

Life, death and humanity at a Boston teaching hospital.

St Elegius was a decaying old hospital in one of Boston's roughest suburbs. Run by the city, it was used as a dumping ground for patients by the more elitist medical centres, hence its nickname of St Elsewhere. In **Hill Street Blues** fashion (the show was by the same production company), *St Elsewhere* took viewers on a journey through hospital life, but shunned all the old medical drama stereotypes. Here the medics were fallible, the patients were nervous and the interactions believable. There were no miracle cures and the seediness of the environment was always apparent.

Realism was a keystone of *St Elsewhere*, with echoes of **Hill Street Blues** in its pace, style and camera work. But it was also an adventurous show, taking chances with scripts and characters, leaving the viewer wondering what the producers would try next. It became a programme for baby-boomers, chock-full of references to pop culture, such as tannoy messages for doctors from other TV shows, throw-away allusions to pop songs or gentle parodies of films such as *The Towering Inferno*, all played with a straight face and no explanation. In the final episode, the dénouement of **The Fugitive** was restaged, as, off-camera, a one-armed man climbed an amusement park water tower.

Chief of staff at the hospital was Daniel Westphall, the widower father of a teenage girl and an autistic son. His heart surgeon was the insensitive Mark Craig, whose loyal junior was Victor Ehrlich. Wayne Fiscus was the emergency specialist, Ben Samuels a randy surgeon and Daniel Auschlander, the hospital's administrator, was a liver expert who, ironically, was suffering from liver cancer. Other members of the team included dedicated but trouble-torn Jack Morrison, psychiatrist Hugh Beale, Annie Cavanero, who tended to get over-involved with her patients, anaesthetist V.J. Kochar, obese Elliot Axelrod, black Philip Chandler and much-married nurse Helen Rosenthal. More tragically, there were also Peter White, who raped pathologist Cathy Martin only to be shot by nurse Shirley Daniels, Wendy Armstrong, who committed suicide, and Bob Caldwell, a promiscuous surgeon who contracted HIV. When the hospital was taken over by a private health care company, the Ecumena Hospitals Corporation, the dirty word 'profit' began to make its presence felt and, as financial pressures grew, the new Chief of Services, Dr John Gideon forced a showdown with Westphall, who 'mooned' at him and resigned.

Like **Hill Street Blues**, *St Elsewhere* easily won over the critics but failed to gain a big audience. Somehow, though, it clung on for six years, before, in its last episode, the producers wound up the series with a cute little twist. The hospital was seen in miniature, as a model inside a snow globe, held intently by Westphall's autistic son. In the room, Westphall and another cast member were talking, but, it appeared, they were no longer doctors. As his father took the globe away from the child, viewers were led to believe that *St Elsewhere* had been just a figment of the boy's imagination.

SAINT JAMES, SUSAN (SUSAN MILLER; 1946–)

American former model who has had three big hit series to her name, principally *McMillan and Wife* (as the 'Wife', Sally McMillan) in the 1970s. Her first starring role was in a collection of movies entitled *The Name of the Game* in 1968, which followed useful guest appearances in series like *It Takes a Thief* and *A Man Called Ironside*. In the 1980s, Saint James was seen in *Kate and Allie*, playing Kate McArdle. She has also starred in numerous TV movies.

SALE OF THE CENTURY

UK (Anglia) Quiz. ITV 1971–83

Presenter: Nicholas Parsons

Producers: Peter Joy, Bill Perry

Quiz in which contestants answer questions, win money and spend it on bargain prizes.

'The Quiz of the Week', as it was billed in the opening announcement, *Sale of the Century* was a remarkably popular quiz game that allowed contestants to use the cash they won to buy prizes at bargain prices. Three contestants took part, answering general knowledge questions on the buzzer. These began at £1 in value, progressing to £3 and then £5. As they began to accumulate cash, the questions were interrupted by bargain offers, tempting contestants to spend some of their winnings on such things as a set of garden furniture for £15. At the end of the game, the person with the most money left could try for the Sale of the Century (a choice of super-bargains) by answering additional questions. Nicholas Parsons was the questionmaster, John Benson acted as announcer and assorted male and female models adorned the prizes.

SALLIS, PETER (1921–)

Peter Sallis has been *Last of the Summer Wine*'s Norman Clegg for over 20 years, although the English actor has been a familiar sight on British TV screens for many years. He also appeared in *First of the Summer Wine*, playing Cleggy's father, and was the caretaker, Mr Gudgin, in the children's comedy *The Ghosts of Motley Hall*, insurance company manager Arthur Simister in the sitcom *Leave It to Charlie* and Sidney Bliss in *The New Statesman*. Sallis guested with Patrick Troughton in *Doctor Who* and his other credits – varying between serious and humorous work – have included *Softly, Softly*, *Barlow*, *The Diary of Samuel Pepys*, *Public Eye*, *Spyder's Web*, *The Moonstone*, *The Pallisers*, *Raffles*, *Tales of the Unexpected*, *Yanks Go Home*, *Ladykillers*, *The Rivals of Sherlock Holmes*, *Strangers and Brothers* and *The Bretts*. He also provided the voice for Rat in the 1980s animation *The Wind in the Willows* and the voices for *The Wrong Trousers*.

SAM

UK (Granada) Drama. ITV 1973–5

Sam Wilson	Kevin Moreton
	Mark McManus
Jack Barraclough	Michael Goodliffe
Polly Barraclough	Maggie Jones
George Barraclough	Ray Smith
Ethel Barraclough	Alethea Charlton
Toby Wilson	Frank Mills
May Dakin	Mona Bruce
Alan Dakin	John Price
Sarah Corby/Wilson	Jennifer Hilary

Creator/Writer: John Finch. Producer: Michael Cox

A young lad grows up in a poor mining town in the Pennines.

Ten-year-old Sam Wilson arrived in the Yorkshire town of Skellerton with his mother, following the death of his dad. There his life revolved around his grandparents, Toby Wilson and Jack and Polly Barraclough, and also close at hand were his uncle and aunt, George and Ethel Barraclough. Glumly reflecting the hardship of the 1930s and 1940s, the series saw Sam turn into a man (boy actor Kevin Moreton gave way to future **Taggart** Mark McManus). As he grew older, he rebelled against the mining mentality that had forced him down the pits at the age of 14. Over three series, viewers witnessed Sam venture out to sea and return to work in an engineering factory. He married Sarah Corby and settled in the town of Golwick, but, all the while, his poverty-ridden past remained in his mind and the welfare of his family continued to haunt him.

SANDBAGGERS, THE

UK (Yorkshire) Spy Drama. ITV 1978–80

Neil Burnside	Roy Marsden
	Richard Vernon
	Dennis Burgess
Willie Caine	Ray Lonnen
Sir Geoffrey Wellingham	Alan MacNaughton
Laura Dickens	Diane Keen
Jeff Ross	Bob Sherman
Karen Milner	Jana Sheldon
Matthew Peele	Jerome Willis
Mike Wallace	Michael Cashman
Diane Lawler	Elizabeth Bennett

Creator: Ian Mackintosh. Executive Producer: David Cunliffe. Producer: Michael Ferguson

The assignments of a top secret British security unit.

'The Sandbaggers' was the colloquial title given to the Special Intelligence Force, or SIF, a government-funded counter-espionage squad. Head of the team was tough, determined Neil Burnside. On receiving his team's missions from their boss, C, it was Burnside's decision which of the Sandbaggers to send into action, knowing full well that his colleagues would be risking life and limb in the service of their country. Accordingly, he gave his men and women every assistance he could, but remained assured in the knowledge that if they had to die, then the result would be worth it. That was the pressurized world of the Sandbaggers, depicted in a heavier, less glitzy and gimmicky style than other secret agent programmes.

SANDERSON, JOAN (1912–92)

British actress, famous for her female dragon roles on television. Sanderson made her name for such characterizations in *Please Sir!* as the redoubtable Doris Ewell, having already appeared in *All Gas and Gaiters* after years on the stage and some TV plays. Later, she took the part of Eleanor, Prunella Scales's mother in *After Henry* (on both radio and television) and Richard O'Sullivan's mother-in-law, Nell Cresset, in the long-running *Me and My Girl*. She also played Mrs Richards, a deaf, never satisfied guest in one memorable episode of *Fawlty Towers*. In contrast to her battleaxe roles, Sanderson was the benign Aunt Dorothy in the mixed-race comedy *Mixed Blessings* and her other credits included *Upstairs, Downstairs*, *Ripping Yarns*, *Rising Damp*, *The Ghosts of Motley Hall*, *Full House* and Michael Palin's TV movie *East of Ipswich*. Her last series, screened shortly after her death in 1992, was *Land of Hope and Gloria*, in which she played Nanny Princeton who tried to protect a stately home from its pushy new American publicist (Sheila Ferguson).

SANDFORD, JEREMY

Former journalist with an interest in social campaigning, Jeremy Sandford was a new name to British TV drama when he scripted the provocative and disturbing *Cathy Come Home* in 1966. He followed it up five years later with the award-winning *Edna, The Inebriate Woman*.

SAPPHIRE AND STEEL

UK (ATV) Science Fiction. ITV 1979–82

Sapphire...Joanna Lumley
Steel...David McCallum
Silver..David Collings

Creator/Writer: P.J. Hammond. Executive Producer: David Reid. Producer: Shaun O'Riordan

Time-travelling troubleshooters foil agents of chaos and destruction.

In this imaginative series, time was perceived as a tunnel, with different time zones spread along its length. Outside lay dark forces of chaos and destruction which took advantage of any weakness in the tunnel's fabric to enter and wreak havoc. Whenever this happened, Sapphire and Steel were sent to investigate.

Little was revealed about the two protagonists. From the programme's introduction viewers learned that: 'All irregularities will be handled by the forces controlling each dimension. Transuranic heavy elements may not be used where there is life. Medium atomic weights are available: Gold, Lead, Copper, Jet, Diamond, Radium, Sapphire, Silver and Steel. Sapphire and Steel have been assigned.' So, it appeared, Sapphire and Steel were elements sent from above, although their forms were human.

Stunning Sapphire, true to her name, wore bright blue; blond-haired Steel, cold and humourless, dressed in grey. They each had special powers. Sapphire could see through time, gauge the history of an object just by holding it and even turn the clock back for a while. The analytical Steel enjoyed phenomenal strength; he could resist the flow of time and reduce his body temperature to below zero. But sometimes these superhuman attributes were not enough and the pair needed assistance. Usually it came from another element, Silver, but Lead also joined the fray on one occasion.

The nightmarish storylines centred on the pursuit of disruptive forces. In their first outing, Sapphire and Steel were called in to arrest a time warp after the reading of historic nursery rhymes had brought Roundhead soldiers to the 20th century. In another, a haunted railway station was drawn back into the era of World War I. The dark forces were seldom seen, except as faceless beings or globes of light. The longer they were allowed to remain in a dimension of time, the stronger they became, and they tested the dynamic duo to the extreme.

SARNOFF, DAVID (1891–1971)

Russian-born American broadcasting pioneer, a former wireless operator who, allegedly, was the first to receive the distress call from the sinking *Titanic* in 1912. Working initially for Marconi, he was employed by RCA when it took over his former company. He eventually rose to President of the company and created the NBC radio and TV networks as a market for selling RCA receivers. Sarnoff was also one of the earliest proponents of public service broadcasting.

SATELLITE

An orbiting space station used for relaying television signals around the world. The satellite works, in its simplest form, by acting as a reflector. Signals can be sent to a satellite and bounced off it like a mirror to another location around the globe that would otherwise (because of the curvature of the planet) be out of direct transmission contact (such as across the Atlantic). Modern satellites, however, actually take the signals on board, amplify them and retransmit them, carrying news reports, live and recorded programming and other items around the world in a fraction of a second. The receiving station, or household, captures the signal in a dish, which varies in size depending on its location. Nearly all satellites are of the synchronous or geostationary type, that is they maintain a fixed position above the equator by orbiting at exactly the same speed as the Earth revolves. By so doing, synchronous satellites allow themselves to be used at all times, whereas unfixed satellites in random orbit can only be called into use at certain times of the day. The most famous of satellites have been Telstar, launched in 1962 (in random orbit, but still able to provide the first transatlantic pictures) and Early Bird, otherwise known as Intelsat I, launched in 1965. The Sky satellite network uses the various Astra satellites, beaming signals up from the UK and bouncing them back over most of Europe.

The term satellite also refers to a small TV station that operates by simply retransmitting the output of a larger station (with perhaps a few local interest programmes added in for community value).

SATURDAY SUPERSTORE see *Multi-Coloured Swap Shop.*

SAUNDERS, JENNIFER (1958–)

British comedienne, actress and writer, usually seen with Dawn French, her partner since their days with *The Comic Strip* and before. Appearing in all *The Strip's* Channel 4 films, Saunders went on to star in the Ben Elton sitcom *Happy Families*, playing various members of the Fuddle family, and also appeared as the boring Jennifer in *Girls On Top*, a sitcom she co-wrote with French and Ruby Wax. The BBC 2 sketch show *French and Saunders* was launched in 1987 and one of its items proved to be the 'pilot' for Saunders's hugely successful series *Absolutely Fabulous*, in which she starred as the boozy, drug-obsessed, fashion promoter Edina Monsoon. Saunders has also been seen in *The Young Ones*, on *Comic Relief* and *Saturday Live* and in *The Storyteller*. She is married to comedian Adrian Edmondson.

SAVALAS, TELLY (ARISTOTLE SAVALAS; 1924–94)

Powerful American actor of Greek descent. Noted for his trademark shaven head, he became one of the 1970s' biggest stars in his guise of New York cop Lt Theo *Kojak*. Savalas actually took to acting fairly late in life. A war veteran with a Purple Heart, he was Director of News and Special Events for ABC before taking his first on-screen role in 1959. Through guest spots on series like *Naked City*, *The Untouchables*, *The Fugitive* and *Burke's Law*, he worked his way into the cinema, where he was usually cast as a bad guy. Allegedly, it was for the part of Pontius Pilate in *The Greatest Story Ever Told* that he first shaved his head. His first major TV role was in a series called *Acapulco* in 1961, but it didn't last and he waited until *Kojak* in 1973 for a taste of small screen stardom. His later work concentrated on mini-series and TV movies.

SAVILE, SIR JIMMY, OBE (1926–)

Yorkshire-born disc jockey and TV presenter, a relentless worker for charitable causes. Savile's working career began as coal miner, before he branched out into nightclub management. Ever the extrovert, he began broadcasting for Radio Luxembourg and arrived on television as the very first presenter of *Top of the Pops*, in 1964. He joined Radio 1 in 1968 and continued to expand his TV work. He hosted *Clunk Click* (based on his car seatbelt campaigns) and this led to the magic wand series *Jim'll Fix It* in 1975. Jim fixed it, in all, for nearly 20 years. In addition, Savile has even hosted *Songs of Praise*. His trademark bleached hair, tracksuit, yodel and giant cigar have made him an easy prey for impressionists.

SAVILLE, PHILIP (1930–)

British director, responsible for many acclaimed dramas. These have included *Armchair Theatre* presentations such as Harold Pinter's *A Night Out* (1960), episodes of *Out of the Unknown*, plus *Hamlet At Elsinore* (an ambitious 1964 outside broadcast from Denmark), Sartre's *In Camera* (also 1964), Alan Sharp's *The Long Distance Piano Player* (1970), *Gangsters*, the 1976 *Play For Today* which became a series, and the 1977 version of *Count Dracula*. Saville also directed the series *Boys from the Blackstuff* and *The Life and Loves of a She Devil.*

SAWALHA, JULIA

British actress coming to the fore in the kids' drama series *Press Gang* (as junior newspaper editor Lynda Day) and then *Absolutely Fabulous* (as Edina's daughter Saffron). Sawalha has been in demand for numerous other dramas, too, including *Inspector Morse*, *El C.I.D.*, *Casualty*, *Second Thoughts* (as Hannah) and *Martin Chuzzlewit* (as Mercy Pecksniff).

SAYLE, ALEXEI (1952–)

Liverpudlian comedian, actor and writer, distinctive in his tight suit and skinhead haircut, whose aggressive, no-nonsense style established him at the forefront of the new stand-up comics of the 1980s. At one time the compere of the Comedy Store and Comic Strip clubs, Sayle moved into television with other members of *The Comic Strip*, appearing in their sequence of Channel 4 films and also taking part in the ill-fated late night *Tiswas* spin-off, *OTT*. He was cast as Jerzy Balowski, *The Young Ones'* Russian landlord (and the rest of his family), and played another Russian, Commissar Solzhenitsyn, in *Whoops! Apocalypse*. He has since had his own sketch series, *Alexei Sayle's Stuff*, and has also been seen as Milcic in *The Gravy Train*, as a futuristic DJ in *Doctor Who* and as forger Conny Kujau in the drama *Selling Hitler*, amongst numerous other programmes.

SCALES, PRUNELLA (PRUNELLA ILLINGWORTH; 1932–)

British actress seen mostly in sitcom roles, starting with *Marriage Lines* in 1963 as Kate Starling alongside Richard Briers. Scales also appeared with Ronnie Barker in *Seven of One* but, undoubtedly, the highlight to date has been as the grating Sybil Fawlty in *Fawlty Towers* in the late 1970s. She followed *Fawlty Towers* with the role of Dolly in Mr Big and a couple of star vehicles of her own, *Mapp and Lucia* (as Elizabeth Mapp, with Geraldine McEwan) and *After Henry* (as widow Sarah, on both radio and TV). Early in her career she played bus conductress Eileen Hughes in *Coronation Street* and other credits have come in *Bergerac*, *Target*, *Never the Twain*, *Jackanory*, Alan Bennett's play *Doris and Doreen*, and as the Queen in the TV film *A Question of Attribution*. In 1995 she starred as Mrs Tilston in the Carla Lane sitcom *Searching*.

SCARLET PIMPERNEL, THE

UK (Towers of London/ITP) Adventure. ITV 1955–6

Sir Percy Blakeney/The Scarlet Pimpernel
....Marius Goring
Chauvelin ....Stanley Van Beers
Sir Andrew Ffoulkes ....Patrick Troughton
Lord Richard Hastings ....Anthony Newlands
The Countess ....Lucie Mannteim
Prince Regent ....Alexander Gauge

Producers: Dennis Vance, David Macdonald, Marius Goring

The daring escapades of a mysterious hero operating in Georgian England and Revolutionary France.

Although ruthlessly persecuted by the cruel Chauvelin and his followers, the aristocrats of France knew they had an ally to count on – the elusive and intriguing Scarlet Pimpernel, alias English nobleman Sir Percy Blakeney. In contrast to his dashing alter ego, Blakeney was weak and foppish, always cleverly deflecting suspicion of his true identity. He was also a master of disguise, and elaborate costume and make-up changes contrived to preserve our hero from a violent death at the guillotine. The series was based on the book by Baroness Orczy.

SCHOFIELD, PHILLIP (1962–)

British presenter who gained his first broadcasting experience while living with his family in New Zealand. Moving back to the UK, Schofield won the job of presenting Children's BBC, which led to the Saturday morning magazines *Saturday Superstore* and *Going Live!*. He proved such a hit with younger viewers that he was cast as Joseph in the stage musical *Joseph and the Amazing Technicolor Dreamcoat*. He then presented *Television's Greatest Hits* for the BBC before being lured over to ITV to present live series like *Talking Telephone Numbers* and *Schofield's Quest*.

SCOOBY DOO, WHERE ARE YOU?

US (Hanna-Barbera) Cartoon. BBC 1 1970–2

Voices:
Scooby Doo ....Don Messick
Shaggy..Casey Kasem
Freddy..Frank Welker
Daphne Blake ....Heather North
Velma ....Nicole Jaffe

Creators: Ken Spears, Joe Ruby. Executive Producers: William Hanna, Joseph Barbera. Producer: Iwao Takamoto

The misadventures of a cowardly canine and his teenage pals.

Although his coat was brown with black spots, Great Dane Scooby-Doo had a broad yellow streak right down his back. Far from protecting his human companions, it was Scooby who dashed for cover in times of trouble (leaving his friends to call after him and giving rise to the series title). Scooby's colleagues were Shaggy, a bumbling youth who bribed the ever-ravenous pooch with Scooby Snacks, Velma, the bespectacled brains of the unit, Daphne, who was always the first to find trouble, and level-headed Freddy, the nominal leader of the group. Together they travelled in a transit van known as The Mystery Machine and no matter where the gang arrived, problems were only around the corner. Usually, the mysteries involved criminals who dressed up as ghosts in order to commit heinous crimes, but, one way or another the gallant amateur detectives always put an end to their activities (with precious little help from Scooby and Shaggy). In later seasons, Scooby was joined by a pup nephew, Scrappy-Doo, and the lovable hound was also seen in *Laff-a-Lympics* amongst other animations. Producers Hanna-Barbera obviously liked the concept because they soon issued another dog and teen detective cartoon, entitled *Goober and Tthe Ghost Chasers*.

SCOTLAND YARD see *Case Histories of Scotland Yard*.

SCOTT, BROUGH (1942–)

British National Hunt jockey turned journalist and TV presenter. Brough Scott has worked for ITV and Channel 4 racing since the 1970s, hosting all the major meetings. He has also been seen in other sports coverage.

SCOTT, JACK (1923–)

British meteorologist who became one of TV's best-known faces through 42 years' service as a weatherman with the Met. Office, appearing on BBC TV (1969–83) and Thames Television (1983–88). On retiring from forecasting, Scott hosted the Channel 4 senior citizens' magazine, *Years Ahead*.

SCOTT, MIKE (1932–)

British TV executive and presenter, mostly with Granada Television. Scott joined Granada as a floor manager, eventually becoming a director. Behind or in front of the camera he has worked on local news programmes, **World in Action**, **Cinema** and, when daytime TV arrived, *The Time, The Place*. He was Programme Controller at Granada from 1979 to 1987.

SCOTT, TERRY (1927–94)

British comic actor, the archetypal hapless husband in cosy, domestic sitcoms. Scott starred alongside Norman Vaughan in *Scott Free* in 1957, but the most famous of his early screen partners was Hugh Lloyd, with whom he appeared in 1962 in **Hugh and I**, and, later, *Hugh and I Spy*. They were also seen together in **The Gnomes of Dulwich**. In 1969, in the series *Scott On ...* , he was teamed for the first time with June Whitfield, who was to be his screen wife for many years.

Together, they endured suburban silliness as the Fletchers in **Happy Ever After** and the Medfords in **Terry and June**. Scott was also familiar in the 1970s as the schoolboy in the *Curly Wurly* commercials and was cast in an early version of **Sorry!**, *Son of the Bride*, as Mollie Sugden's mummy's boy, in 1973. In the 1980s he provided the voice for the character of Penfold in the **Dangermouse** cartoons.

SCOTTISH TELEVISION (STV)

The ITV contractor for Central Scotland, on air continuously since 31 August 1957. It has survived all the franchise reorganizations, despite concerns about its local programming in the mid-1960s. The main broadcasting centre is in Glasgow, with a smaller production base in Edinburgh. Amongst the company's contributions to the ITV network have been the drama series **Take the High Road** and **Taggart**, and the quiz show **Wheel of Fortune**. Some local programmes have been produced in Gaelic.

SCRAMBLING see encryption.

SCREEN TEST

UK (BBC) Children's Quiz. BBC 1 1970–84

Presenters: Michael Rodd, Brian Trueman, Mark Curry

Producers: John Buttery, David Brown, Tony Harrison

Observation quiz for kids based on film clips.

The contestants on *Screen Test* viewed a series of clips from popular films and were then tested on their observation skills. Interviews and features on the movie world also formed part of this long-running programme, which was hosted for many years by Michael Rodd.

SCRIPT EDITOR

Usually employed on a long-running series, the script editor is responsible for ensuring that scripts supplied by a team of writers conform to the style of the series as a whole, taking into account character continuity, plot developments, etc.

SEA HUNT

US (Ziv/United Artists) Adventure. ITV 1958–

Mike Nelson ....Lloyd Bridges

Producer: Ivan Tors

Excitement with an underwater adventurer-for-hire.

This action series featured former navy diver Mike Nelson, a freelance agent who offered his underwater skills to anyone who wished to employ him. Working from his boat, *The Argonaut*, and travelling the globe, Nelson took on jobs for salvage companies, insurance firms, film-makers and especially the US Government, swimming into all manner of tight scrapes and always coming up with the goods. Lloyd Bridges was the only regular, though his two young (at the time) sons, Beau and Jeff, also made guest appearances. The real star, however, was the sea itself, with all its underwater glory. The series was briefly revived with little success in 1987, when TV's Tarzan, Ron Ely, donned Nelson's mask and flippers.

SEAGROVE, JENNY (1958–)

Malaysian-born actress who made her TV name with the lead role (Emma Harte) in the mini-series *A Woman of Substance* in 1985. Earlier, Seagrove had played Laura in Wilkie Collins's *The Woman in White* and Diana Gaylorde-Sutton in Andrew Davies's adaptation of R.F. Delderfield's *Diana*. She was also seen in the 1987 *Sherlock Holmes* special, *The Sign of Four*, and has many other TV movies and dramas to her name, including *In Like Flynn*.

SECAM

Séquential Couleur á Mémoire, the system of television transmission developed in and used by France. It operates off 625 lines like the British PAL system, but the two are incompatible. Those countries with a French colonial interest (in Africa and the Middle East, for instance), have also adopted the SECAM system, as have the Eastern European countries (although their SECAM is modified).

SECOMBE, SIR HARRY, CBE (1921–)

Welsh comedian, singer and presenter, coming to the fore as one of The Goons on BBC Radio. The most popular of his series have been *The Harry Secombe Show* (on both ITV and BBC), *Secombe and Friends* and *Secombe with Music*, all of them variety shows, although for most of the 1980s and early 1990s, he was strongly associated with the religious travelogue *Highway*, which followed many appearances on *Stars on Sunday* in the 1970s.

SECOND THOUGHTS

UK (LWT) Situation Comedy. ITV 1991–3

Bill Macgregor ....James Bolam
Faith Grayshot ....Lynda Bellingham
Joe...Mark Denham
Hannah...Julia Sawalha
Liza ....Belinda Lang
Richard ....Geoffrey Whitehead

Creators/Writers: Jan Etherington, Gavin Petrie. Producers: David Askey, Robin Carr

Two divorcées begin a relationship, despite the attentions of teenage children and a former wife.

Bill Macgregor was the art editor of a style magazine who began a relationship with divorcée Faith Grayshot. However, the odds were stacked against them, thanks to the interference and the personal problems of Faith's teenage kids, Joe and Hannah, and the devious doings of Bill's promiscuous ex-wife, Liza, who happened to work in the same office as him. Suspicion and distrust ruled.

The series, which began on BBC Radio in 1988 and ran simultaneously on television for a while, was based on the real-life romance of its creators, *TV Times* journalists Jan Etherington and Gavin Petrie, both of whom had been divorced before beginning a new life together.

SECOND VERDICT

UK (BBC) Drama. BBC 1 1976

Detective Chief Supt Charlie Barlow..Stratford Johns
Detective Chief Inspector John Watt ..Frank Windsor

Producer: Leonard Lewis

Two fictional detectives examine real-life murder mysteries.

Charlie Barlow and John Watt, the *Z Cars* and *Softly, Softly* heavyweights, were the stars of this enigmatic series. Having joined forces to re-examine the Jack the Ripper story in 1973, the duo were paired up again to look at six more true crime mysteries of the past. These included *Who Killed the Princes in the Tower?*, *Lizzie Borden* and *The Lindbergh Kidnapping*.

SECONDS OUT

UK (BBC) Situation Comedy. BBC 1 1981–2

Pete Dodds ....Robert Lindsay
Tom Sprake ....Lee Montague
Dave Locket..Ken Jones
Hazel..Leslie Ash

Writer: Bill MacIlwraith. Producer: Ray Butt

A talented amateur boxer turns professional with a wily manager.

Pete Dodds, an amateur boxer with plenty of potential but also a tendency to clown about, turned professional and was taken under the wing of successful manager Tom Sprake. To keep him in line, Sprake paired Dodds with irritating little trainer Dave Locket, relying on the pair's incompatibility to keep Dodds focused on the job. With Locket to nark him at every turn, Dodds began to climb towards the top. First he claimed the British middleweight title and then fought for the European crown. Hazel was Pete's girlfriend.

SECRET ARMY

UK (BBC/BRT) Drama. BBC 1 1977–9

Lisa Colbert	Jan Francis
Albert Foiret	Bernard Hepton
Flt Lt John Curtis	Christopher Neame
Sturmbahnführer Ludwig Kessler	Clifford Rose
Monique Duchamps	Angela Richards
Natalie	Juliet Hammond-Hill
Brandt	Michael Culver
Max Brocard	Stephen Yardley
Alain	Ron Pember
Dr Pascal Keldermans	Valentine Dyall
François	Nigel Williams
Madelaine Duclos	Hazel McBride
Reinhardt	Terrence Hardiman
Paul Vercors	Ralph Bates
Captain Durnford	Stephen Chase
Bradley	Paul Shelley
Louise	Maris Charles
Rennert	Robin Langford
Andrée Foiret	Eileen Page
Gaston	James Bree
Jacques	Timothy Moran

Producer: Gerard Glaister

The daring exploits of the Belgian Resistance.

This series centred on the activities of Lifeline, an underground Résistance movement in Belgium during World War II. This extremely courageous secret army specialized in smuggling trapped Allied servicemen back to Britain, via a number of escape routes and safe houses. Head of the organization was Lisa Colbert, codenamed Yvette, a young teacher who became a Résistance worker after the killing of her parents. She was assisted chiefly by Albert Foiret, proprietor of Le Candide, a Brussels restaurant which operated as the movement's base. Ironically, it was also a hostelry favoured by German officers, which added to the danger. The other key functionaries were Foiret's mistress, Monique, Natalie, RAF liaison John Curtis and, later, forger Max Brocard. Chief amongst the Nazis were local head Brandt, his much firmer replacement, Reinhardt, and the cruel Kessler, the local Gestapo leader. Madelaine Duclos was his lover. By the end of the series the war had ended and Kessler had assumed a new identity to escape trial. He was to resurface as a German businessman (using the alias Manfred Dorf) in a spin-off

series, *Kessler*, in 1981, in which his wartime secrets began to be exposed.

Secret Army was probably the most unlikely of TV series to earn itself a parody. But it did just that when *'Allo 'Allo* came along in 1984. Although the setting had been transposed to France, all the other distinctive elements were present, from the long-suffering restaurateur, to the Résistance operatives and the pompous Nazis. If anything, the series has been overshadowed by this spoof successor.

SECRET DIARY OF ADRIAN MOLE, AGED 13¾, THE/GROWING PAINS OF ADRIAN MOLE, THE

UK (Thames) Situation Comedy. ITV 1985/1987

Adrian Mole	Gian Sammarco
Pauline Mole	Julie Walters
	Lulu (*Growing Pains*)
George Mole	Stephen Moore
Grandma Mole	Beryl Reid
Bert Baxter	Bill Fraser
Pandora	Lindsey Stagg
Queenie	Doris Hare
Nigel	Steven Mackintosh
Mr Lucas	Paul Greenwood

Creator/Writer: Sue Townsend. Executive Producer: Lloyd Shirley. Producer: Peter Sasdy

A teenage boy chronicles his troubles in his diary as his family self-destructs.

This series, adapted by Sue Townsend from her own best-selling novel, *The Secret Diary of Adrian Mole, Aged 13¾* was set in the Midlands and focused on the adolescent woes which befell young, bespectacled Adrian. In addition to the usual teenage travails of school, spots, girls and peer pressure, Adrian also found himself in the midst of family turmoil. His mum, Pauline, and dad, George, had gone their separate ways and now only traded insults. Also involved was his Grandma and an elderly character he befriended, Bert Baxter, while Pandora was the girl Adrian had set his heart on. When the second series began, using the new name of *The Growing Pains of Adrian Mole*, and with Adrian aged 16, his (now pregnant) mum was played by pop singer Lulu.

SECRET SERVICE, THE

UK (Century 21/ITC) Children's Science Fiction. ITV 1969

Father Stanley Unwin	Stanley Unwin
Matthew Harding (the gardener: voice only)	
	Keith Alexander
Matthew Harding (the agent: voice only)	Gary Files
Mrs Appleby (voice only)	Sylvia Anderson
The Bishop (voice only)	Jeremy Wilkin

Creators: Gerry Anderson, Sylvia Anderson. Executive Producer: Reg Hill. Producer: David Lane

Short-lived Gerry Anderson combination of live action and puppetry.

Fifty-seven-year-old parish priest Father Unwin was no ordinary country parson. In fact, he was an undercover agent for BISHOP (British Intelligence Secret Headquarters, Operation Priest) who possessed a special device ('The Minimiser') for reducing people and objects to one third of their normal size. This device was found in a book lent to Unwin by one of his late parishioners and was put to good use on behalf of the security services. Usually, it was the priest's bumpkin gardener, Matthew, who was shrunk, in order to take on dangerous missions on behalf of the country. When minimised, the priest carried Matthew around in a briefcase. Unwin, who drove a vintage Model T Ford named Gabriel, also had a radio built into his mock deaf aid, through which he was given assignments by his commander, 'The Bishop'. It was also used for contacting other BISHOP agents. Mrs Appleby was Unwin's blissfully ignorant housekeeper.

The series provided a stepping stone between the Supermarionation adventures of **Stingray**, **Thunderbirds** et al and Gerry Anderson's move into live action with **UFO**. But it failed to attract a network audience (being screened only in the Midlands, the South and the North-West) and was limited to just 13 episodes. Double-speaking comedian Stanley Unwin played the priest in long-shots, with a puppet clone used for close ups. His gobbledygook was a feature of the series, which he described as: 'Parochial guile and crafty for the deep joy of the Secret Serve'.

SECRET SOCIETY

UK (BBC) Current Affairs. BBC 2 1987

Presenter/Writer: Duncan Campbell

Producer: Brian Barr

Highly controversial series about covert British agencies and operations.

Although six episodes of this investigative series were planned, only four made it to the screen on time. One was eventually shown a year late, and the other was assigned to the dustbin. This curtailment was a result of political sensitivity, particularly over an episode revealing plans for a secret British spy satellite known as Zircon. On 31 January 1987, the BBC offices in Glasgow were raided by Special Branch officers and over 30 boxes of tapes and material relating to the programme were confiscated. The BBC Chairman, Marmaduke Hussey, made a strong protest to the Government and there was uproar in the House of Commons. *The Zircon Affair* finally aired as a 75-minute special, introduced by Ludovic Kennedy, in 1988, but another edition, entitled *Cabinet* and alleging election dirty tricks was never broadcast, being deemed too out of date by the time the initial fuss had died down. The four episodes which were screened concerned DHSS computer databanks, emergency laws in times of national crisis, the influence of the Association of Chief Police Officers on Government policy, and the UK's radar defence network.

SELBY, TONY (1938–)

English actor, usually in comic roles. Probably his most memorable creation was the loud-mouthed Corporal Marsh in **Get Some In**, although he has been seen in numerous other sitcoms. He played Les Robinson in the lighthouse comedy *Shine a Light*, Norman Lugg in the Dick Emery comedy-thriller series *Jack of Diamonds* and the scheming handyman Bert Finch in **Mulberry**. Selby's earliest TV work came in single dramas like Harold Pinter's *A Night Out* and Nell Dunn's *Up the Junction*. He has also been seen in series like *Tom Grattan's War*, **Department S**, **The Informer**, **C.A.T.S. Eyes**, **Minder**, **Doctor Who**, **The Sweeney**, **Bergerac**, **Casualty** and **Lovejoy**, and played Sam in the children's adventure series **Ace of Wands**.

SELLECK, TOM (1945–)

Tall, moustached American actor whose ability to combine macho action with a one-of-the-lads type of humour made him one of TV's hottest names in the 1980s, largely thanks to an eight-year stint as **Magnum, PI**. Earlier, Selleck had made occasional visits to **The Rockford Files** to play the annoyingly perfect detective Lance White, although his TV career dates back to the early 1970s and he gained his first small screen experiences in soap opera (*The Young and the Restless*), TV movies and series like **Charlie's Angels**. His movie career began at about the same time. In 1989 Selleck was executive producer on the Burt Reynolds detective series *B.L. Stryker*.

SELLERS, PETER, CBE (1925–80)

Although he became a major movie celebrity in the 1960s and 1970s, Peter Sellers sadly left little in the TV archives. After graduating from radio work with his fellow Goons, he was seen in the 1950s comedies *Idiot Weekly*, *Price 2d*, **A Show Called Fred**, *Son of Fred* and *Yes, It's the Cathode-Ray Tube Show*, but, after that, sightings were restricted to occasional variety and chat shows, plus guest spots on series like **Not Only ... , But**

Also ... and *The Muppet Show*. He was also seen in Jonathan Miller's version of *Alice in Wonderland* and, over the years, heard on commercials for Kennomeat and PG Tips. Sellers was married to actresses Britt Ekland and Lynne Frederick.

SELWYN see *Oh No! It's Selwyn Froggitt*.

SENSE OF GUILT, A

UK (BBC) Drama. BBC 1 1990

Felix Cramer	Trevor Eve
Sally Hinde	Rudi Davies
Helen Irving	Lisa Harrow
Richard Murray	Jim Carter
Inge Murray	Malgoscha Gebel
Elizabeth Cramer	Morag Hood
Carey Hinde	Philip McGough
Marsha Hinde	Kate Duchene
Karl Murray	David Chittenden
Peter Murray	Charlie Condou
Jamal Khan	Kulvinder Ghir

Writer: Andrea Newman. Producer: Simon Passmore

Steamy saga of passion and betrayal.

A Sense of Guilt was a drama which set the TV review columns buzzing. 'With more pairing than Noah's Ark', as *Radio Times* put it, this seven-part serial by Andrea (*Bouquet of Barbed Wire*) Newman primarily focused on selfish, philandering writer Felix Cramer. Returning to London after years overseas, Felix seduced the step-daughter of his best friend, making her pregnant and destroying the lives of those around him. However, there were many other covert and illicit goings-on, too, enough to attract audiences of around nine million viewers.

SENTIMENTAL AGENT, THE

UK (ATV) Adventure. ITV 1963

Carlos Varela	Carlos Thompson
Suzy Carter	Clemence Bettany
Chin	Burt Kwouk
Bill Randall	John Turner

Producer: Harry Fine

The adventures of an import-export agent.

Smartly dressed and always charming, Carlos Varela ran an international trading company in London, but was usually seen jetting around the globe on the trail of some criminal. His outer appearance was tough but it concealed a generous heart, which often led him into trouble (hence the title). His two main accomplices were secretary Suzy Carter and valet Chin. The character had originally appeared in an episode of *Man of the World*.

SEPTEMBER SONG

UK (Granada) Drama. ITV 1993–

Ted Fenwick	Russ Abbot
Billy Balsam	Michael Williams
Cilla	Susan Brown
Arnie	Michael Angelis
Roxy/Jenny	Julie Peasgood
Sarah Fenwick	Barbara Ewing
Katherine Hillyard	Diana Quick
Connie French	Diane Keen
Yannis Alexiou	George Savides
Philip Hathaway	Pip Miller
Vicky	Rebecca Callard
Cyril Wendage	Frank Windsor
Mrs Trigger	Jan Waters
Tom Walker	Matt Patresi

Writer: Ken Blakeson. Producers: Gareth Morgan, Brian Park

Two unlikely friends seek adventure in Blackpool, with mixed results.

Ted Fenwick and Billy Balsam had known each other for years. Ted, a gentle, sensitive schoolteacher, eased the strains of caring for his sick wife with a nightly drink at the pub where Billy worked as barman. Billy, a chain-smoking, former stand-up comic, then decided to go back on the stage, finding himself a compère's job at a Blackpool strip club, The Magic Cat. When his wife died, Ted agreed to spend the summer sharing Billy's camper van at the seaside. Their fortunes were mixed: Billy met exotic dancer Cilla, was spotted by a talent scout and offered the job he'd always dreamed of, as a TV audience warmup man. Ted fell in love with a stripper named Roxy, but the feelings were not reciprocated and Billy's indiscretions about Ted's previous love life led to a bitter argument. But when Billy suffered a life-threatening heart attack, it was Ted who returned to keep him out of trouble and ensure his recovery.

In a second series, screened in 1994, Ted took Billy on a Greek island cruise for recuperation. Ted met up with an old flame, Katherine Hillyard, while Billy once again turned to the bottle. For the third series, in 1995, the action switched to Cromer, where Billy found work as a pier comic and Ted tried to come to terms with his uneasy relationship with Katherine.

The series was originally written for Radio 4 in 1991 and some material for the script was provided by the late Tom Mennard, formerly Sam Tindall in *Coronation Street* (the original story was based on Mennard's experiences as a stand-up comic). When it transferred to television, it provided Russ Abbot with his first serious acting role.

SEQUEL

A programme following on from another, taking members of the established cast into new situations.

SGT BILKO see *Phil Silvers Show, The.*

SERGEANT CORK

UK (ATV) Police Drama. ITV 1963–6

Sgt Cork	John Barrie
Bob Marriott	William Gaunt
Detective Joseph Bird	Arnold Diamond
Supt Billy Nelson	John Richmond
Supt Rodway	Charles Morgan

Creator: Ted Willis. Producer: Jack Williams

The cases of a detective years ahead of his time in Victorian London.

Bachelor policeman Sgt Cork worked for the fledgling CID at Scotland Yard. He was a man of vision who deplored bureaucracy and believed in the value of scientific evidence in tracking down criminals. His ideas were pooh-poohed by many of his contemporaries, including his obstructive superior, Detective Joseph Bird. However, he did have Supt Nelson on his side, as well as his supportive, bright, young colleague, Bob Marriott, and, when Bird was removed, another ally was found in Supt Rodway. The series, characterized by its dark, cobbled streets, swirling cloaks, top hats, and horse-drawn hansom cabs, found an echo in *Cribb* in the early 1980s.

SERIAL

Drama broken into a number of episodes with a continuous storyline.

SERIES

A collection of programmes featuring the same cast and situation but with storylines generally confined to one episode, rather than continuing from episode to episode.

SERLE, CHRIS (1943–)

British actor turned presenter, thanks to a spell as one of Esther Rantzen's assistants on *That's Life*. With Paul Heiney, Serle later shared the limelight in the spin-off series *In at the Deep End* and has also been seen in *Sixty Minutes*, *People*, *Medical Express*, educational programmes like *Shoot the Video* and the TV archive series *Windmill*.

SERLING, ROD (1924–75)

Anyone who has seen the cult series *The Twilight Zone* will have soon realized that it was Rod Serling's series. The American writer not only scripted most of the episodes, but created it, produced it and top and tailed each episode with explanatory dialogue. He began writing in the late 1940s and, in 1956, he joined the staff of CBS's anthology series *Playhouse 90*. His second script for the series, *Requiem for a Heavyweight*, remains one of the most acclaimed in TV history and won Serling an Emmy. *The Twilight Zone*, his own idea, ran for six years from 1959 and, when it ended, Serling went on to write for numerous other series. He also contributed some notable film screenplays, including *Planet of the Apes*. One of his last TV projects was another suspense anthology, *Night Gallery*, in the early 1970s.

SERPICO

US (Emmet G Lavery/Paramount) Police Drama. BBC 1 1977

Frank Serpico	David Birney
Lt Tom Sullivan	Tom Atkins

Executive Producer: Emmet G. Lavery.
Producers: Don Ingalls, Barry Oringer

An undercover cop combats subversion inside and outside the force.

This short-lived series was based on the 1973 film of the same name starring Al Pacino, which, in turn, was derived from the true-life story of a New York cop, as written up by Peter Maas. Frank Serpico worked in New York's 22nd Precinct where his target was corruption. Ethically unassailable himself, his job was to root out officers on the take and lift the lid on bent officials. Not surprisingly, he made himself many enemies along the way. His investigations took him into the world of organized crime, sniffing around drug dealers, smugglers and racketeers. When he went undercover, fellow cop Tom Sullivan was his police liaison. The real Frank Serpico was forced to retire from duty after being shot in the face.

SESAME STREET

US (Children's Television Workshop) Children's Education. ITV/Channel 4 1971– ; 1987–

Bob	Bob McGrath
Gordon	Matt Robinson
	Roscoe Orman
Mr Hooper	Will Lee
Susan	Loretta Long
David	Northern J. Galloway
Luis	Emilio Delgado
Maria	Sonia Manzano
Linda	Linda Bove
Gina	Alison Bartlett
Lillian	Lillias White
Uncle Wally	Bill McCutcheon
Mr Handford	David Langston Smyrl

Gabriela ....Gabriela Rose Reagan
Miles ....Miles Orman
Kermit ....Jim Henson
Big Bird ....Frank Oz
　　　　　　　　　　　　　　　　Carroll Spinney
Cookie Monster...Frank Oz
Oscar the Grouch ....Frank Oz
　　　　　　　　　　　　　　　　Carroll Spinney
The Count von Count ....Jerry Nelson
Miss Piggy ....Frank Oz
Bert ....Jim Henson
Ernie..Frank Oz

Creator: Joan Ganz Cooney. Executive Producers: David D. Connell, Jon Stone, Al Hyslop. Producers: Samuel Y. Gibbon Jnr, Bob Cuniff, Dulcy Singer, Al Hyslop, Michael Cozell

Innovative educational programme for pre-school children.

Acclaimed by some and slated by others, *Sesame Street* was created to address the dearth of pre-school education in the USA. Funded by the non-profit-making Children's Television Workshop, it has introduced kids to numbers, letters and social skills, using a fast-paced, *Rowan and Martin*-type, all-action approach to cater for short attention spans. Heavy repetition of the main points (which have been packaged up like TV commercials) has been another key feature.

The setting has been a fake city backstreet (Sesame Street), where the residents have provided a degree of continuity. These have included Gordon and Susan, a young black couple, and Bob, their white neighbour. The sweet shop was run by Mr Hooper in the early days and Luis and Maria were amongst later additions to the crew. A row of rubbish bins has lined one side of the road and in one of these has lived a creature called Oscar the Grouch. Oscar was just one of Jim Henson's many Muppet characters which gained important early exposure in the series. Another was Big Bird, a dim, giant canary. Each programme has contained animated inserts, filmed items, sketches, songs and games, and has been 'sponsored' by a number or a letter of the alphabet: 'Today's programme is brought to you by the letter 'T'.

Over the years, the scope of *Sesame Street* has been broadened to include other aims, such as teaching cultural diversity, reasoning, women's roles, problem solving, health and ecology, and the pace has slowed slightly, to take account of criticism for being overstimulating. The programme was originally aimed at the deprived kids of the inner cities but found favour instead with most of America and then earned enormous sales all around the world. In the UK, *Sesame Street* was originally screened on ITV, but its most recent airings have been on weekday lunchtimes on Channel 4.

SESSIONS, JOHN (JOHN MARSHALL; 1953–)

Scottish-born actor/comedian, a specialist in improvization, as evidenced by his many appearances on *Whose Line Is It Anyway?* Sessions has also been seen in programmes as varied as *Tall Tales*, *Educating Marmalade*, **The New Statesman**, *Porterhouse Blue*, **Girls on Top**, *Life with Eliza*, *Tender is the Night*, **Happy Families**, **Boon** and *Laugh, I Nearly Paid My Licence Fee*, and provided some of the voices for **Spitting Image**. He also played Boswell in *Tour of the Western Isles*.

SET

The scenic construction on which a programme is presented or a drama performed.

SEVEN FACES OF JIM, THE

UK (BBC) Situation Comedy. BBC 1961

Jimmy Edwards

Writers: Frank Muir, Denis Norden. Producer: James Gilbert

Anthology comedy series: a Jimmy Edwards showcase.

With the title of each episode beginning *The Face of . . .* , this series covered the subjects of Devotion, Genius, Power, Dedication, Duty, Guilt and Enthusiasm, all in sitcom fashion, allowing the series' star, Jimmy Edwards, to show off a range of new comic creations. A second series, entitled *Six More Faces of Jim*, ran in 1962. This time the topics were Fatherhood, Renunciation, Wisdom, Perseverance, Loyalty and Tradition. This latter series saw the television première of radio's comic family The Glums (of *Take It from Here* fame), with Edwards as Mr Glum, Ronnie Barker playing Ron and June Whitfield as Eth.

77 SUNSET STRIP

US (Warner Brothers) Detective Drama. ITV 1959–

Stuart Bailey ....Efrem Zimbalist, Jnr
Jeff Spencer ....Roger Smith
Gerald Lloyd ('Kookie') Kookson III ....Edd Byrnes
Roscoe...Louis Quinn
Suzanne Fabray ....Jacqueline Beer
Lt Gilmore..Byron Keith
Rex Randolph ....Richard Long
J.R. Hale ....Robert Logan
Hannah ....Joan Staley

Creator: Roy Huggins. Executive Producers: Bill Orr, Jack Webb. Producers: Roy Huggins, Howie Horowitz, William Conrad

A private detective partnership takes on challenges around the world from its Hollywood offices.

77 Sunset Strip, in the nightclub area of Hollywood, was the base for Stu Bailey and Jeff Spencer, college graduates who had turned to private eye work after experience in undercover government agencies. Bailey was a language expert, Spencer had a degree in law and both were skilled in judo. However, from the outset, their exploits were overshadowed by their association with Kookie, a cool, ambitious youth who ran the parking lot at the neighbouring Dino's (Dean Martin's) restaurant. His obsessive hair combing and novel turns of phrase became his trademarks, although British audiences were bemused by such jive talk as 'making the long green' (earning money), 'piling up the Zs' (sleeping) and 'a dark seven' (a bad week).

Kookie soon became the star of the show, upstaging the two leads, and actor Edd Byrnes sought better terms. When he walked out after failing to agree a contract, he was temporarily replaced as parking lot attendant by Troy Donohue. Byrnes soon settled his differences, however, and Kookie returned as a fully-fledged part of the detective team, which had briefly taken on another partner, Rex Randolph. Suzanne Fabray was their French receptionist and Roscoe, a racetrack tout from New York, their informant. J.R. Hale was Kookie's new parking lot replacement and he, like Kookie, had his quirks, one of which was talking in abbreviations.

The final series of the programme featured only Stu Bailey, as a globetrotting private eye. His offices were no longer on Sunset Strip and he had a new secretary, Hannah. This restructuring was the idea of new executive producer Jack Webb, of **Dragnet** fame. William Conrad, the future Frank Cannon, was also one of the show's producers.

Edd Byrnes confirmed his teen idol status by making the charts on both sides of the Atlantic in 1960 with a song called 'Kookie Kookie (Lend Me Your Comb)', which he recorded for the series with Connie Stevens. Better remembered is the programme's finger-snapping theme tune.

SEXTON BLAKE

UK (Rediffusion/Thames) Children's Detective Drama. ITV 1967–71

Sexton Blake	Laurence Payne
Edward Clark ('Tinker')	Roger Foss
Mrs Bardell	Dorothea Phillips
Inspector Cutts	Ernest Clark
Inspector Van Steen	Leonard Sachs
Inspector 'Taff' Evans	Meredith Edwards
Inspector Cardish	Eric Lander
Inspector Davies	Charles Morgan

Producer: Ronald Marriott

Whodunnits for kids, featuring a 1920s detective.

Sexton Blake was the great detective of the Roaring Twenties. Like his illustrious predecessor, Sherlock Holmes, he lived in London's Baker Street, had a housekeeper (Mrs Bardell) and enjoyed the company of an assistant, Tinker. However, for Holmes's pipe, substitute a cigar. Solving crimes off their own bat, or called in by various Scotland Yard inspectors to succeed where they had failed, Blake, Tinker and his bloodhound, Pedro, cruised the streets of the capital in a white Rolls Royce nicknamed 'The Grey Panther'.

The character was created back in the 19th century by Harry Blyth and first appeared in a boys' weekly called *The Halfpenny Marvel*. Blake also featured in several movie versions over the years and resurfaced on TV in 1978 in a BBC serial entitled *Sexton Blake and the Demon God* (with Jeremy Clyde as Blake and Philip Davis as Tinker). This earlier series was initially produced by Rediffusion but Thames took over production after the 1968 franchise changes.

SEYMOUR, JANE (JOYCE FRANKENBERG; 1951–)

British actress, a former dancer who has made her name in the cinema, but has also been seen in various television offerings, usually glossy TV movies and mini-series. Before moving to Hollywood, Seymour was seen in British series like *The Strauss Family*, **The Onedin Line** (as Emma Callon), *The Hanged Man*, *The Pathfinders*, *Here Come the Double Deckers* and *Our Mutual Friend* (as Bella Wilfer). In the USA, she has starred in *Captains and Kings*, *East of Eden*, *Jack the Ripper*, *War and Remembrance* and *The Woman He Loved* (as Mrs Wallis Simpson), amongst many dramas. Most recently, Seymour has portrayed Doctor Quinn, Medicine Woman.

SHADOW SQUAD

UK (Associated-Rediffusion/Granada)
Detective Drama. ITV 1957–9

Vic Steele	Rex Garner
Don Carter	Peter Williams
Ginger Smart	George Moon
Mrs Moggs	Kathleen Boutall

Producer: Barry Baker

Two private eyes solve cases with a little help from their charlady.

Detective Vic Steele had resigned from the Flying Squad, tired of the rules and regulations which hampered his work. Sprung from the bureaucratic straightjacket, he set up his own agency, assisted by Londoner Ginger Smart, and named it Shadow Squad. Often calling on the help of their cleaner, Mrs Moggs, the pair investigated all manner of intriguing crimes. After 26 episodes, Steele was mysteriously written out and the agency was handed over to another ex-cop, Don Carter (Steele was sent off on a mission to Australia, never to return). Production, at the same time, switched from Associated-Rediffusion to Granada.

It was the Carter/Smart combination which made this twice-weekly show a success, although a spin-off entitled *Skyport*, featuring Ginger as an airport security man, failed to 'take off' and lasted only one year. The final *Shadow Squad* episode was set in a TV studio, which was revealed to be Granada's own in a *Moonlighting*-style dénouement. As it ended, the two detectives shook hands and walked off the set for good.

SHAFT

US (MGM) Detective Drama. ITV 1974–6

John Shaft ....Richard Roundtree
Lt Al Rossi...Ed Barth

Executive Producer: Allan Balter. Producer: William Read Woodfield

The adventures of a smooth, streetwise private eye.

Sharp-talking, straight-shooting John Shaft was based in New York, although his assignments did not confine him to that city. Calm, efficient and ruthless, this slick, trendy, black detective helped clients in all kinds of difficulty, right across America. Lt Al Rossi was his tame police contact. The series was inspired by the popular *Shaft* film trilogy, which also starred Richard Roundtree and used the same funky theme music by Isaac Hayes. However, with the sex and violence toned down for TV viewing, this television version lacked the edge of the cinema releases.

SHANE, PAUL (1940–)

Yorkshire-born comedian and actor, a miner and a comic on the northern clubs' circuit before turning professional. It was as holiday camp host Ted Bovis in *Hi-De-Hi!* that he became noticed, playing the role for eight years. As shifty butler Alf Stokes in *You Rang, M'Lord*, two years later, he more or less reprised the role but then went on to star as unscrupulous theatrical agent Harry James in the comedy *Very Big Very Soon*. Amongst Shane's early guest appearances was a spot in *Coronation Street* as postal worker Frank Draper. He was also seen in *Turtle's Progress* and *Muck and Brass*.

SHARON AND ELSIE

UK (BBC) Situation Comedy. BBC 1 1984–5

Elsie Beecroft ....Brigit Forsyth
Sharon Wilkes.....................................Janette Beverley
Stanley ....John Landry
Roland Beecroft ....Bruce Montague
Ivy...Maggie Jones
Elvis Wilkes..Lee Daley
Ike Hepworth ....Gordon Rollings
Tommy Wallace ....John Junkin

Writer: Arline Whittaker. Producer: Roger Race

Two female workmates don't see eye to eye.

In this generation gap comedy, early middle-aged Elsie Beecroft worked as a supervisor in the greetings cards and calendars printing firm of James Blake and Son, based in Manchester. When Sharon Wilkes, a punk school-leaver, was taken on as secretary to the company boss, Elsie did not approve. With the slightly snooty Elsie always ready to act above her station, the scene was set for some healthy workplace conflict. However, this quickly dissolved into friendship and the two girls joined forces in a long-running battle for employee rights. They even socialized outside work hours.

SHATNER, WILLIAM (1931–)

Canadian actor with a number of television roles to his name since the mid-1950s but who will always be remembered as Captain James T. Kirk, the he-man skipper of the USS *Enterprise* in *Star Trek*. Before *Star Trek* began its three-year voyage on America's screens in 1966, Shatner had been seen in numerous drama anthologies, some westerns and the odd cop series like *Naked City*. He starred in the pilot of *The Defenders* and episodes of *The Twilight Zone* and *The Outer Limits*, and allegedly turned down the role of *Dr Kildare*. Shatner did, however, take a leading part in a legal drama series, *For the People*, in 1965. Because it was cancelled after only three months, he found himself available to take on *Star Trek* a year later (Jeffrey Hunter, who had appeared in the series' pilot, was not free). In the 1970s Shatner was a familiar guest in series like *A Man Called Ironside* and *Hawaii Five-O*, and also took a role in another ill-fated series, this time a western called *The Barbary Coast*. In 1982 he donned the policeman's uniform of Sgt *T.J. Hooker*. The series ran for five years and earned Shatner a new generation of fans. In 1989 he began narrating the series *Rescue 911*, which reconstructed real-life dramas.

SHAUGHNESSY, ALFRED (1915–)

British writer, the script editor of *Upstairs, Downstairs*. Shaughnessy's own aristocratic upbringing was given much of the credit for the historical accuracy in this series. His other major contributions have been the similarly genteel afternoon drama *The Cedar Tree*, episodes of *The Adventures of Sherlock Holmes* and the pilot for *Ladies in Charge*. One of his earliest offerings was a musical biography of music hall star Marie Lloyd, *Our Marie* (written with Christopher Barry), which was broadcast in 1953.

SHAW, MARTIN (1945–)

Versatile British actor seen in series like *Coronation Street* (as hippie Robert Croft), *Doctor in the House* (as Huw Evans) and *Helen – a Woman of Today* (as Helen's husband, Frank Tulley), before achieving lead status in *The Professionals* in the role of CI5 agent Ray Doyle. He later played Robert Falcon Scott in *The Last Place on Earth*, starred in the dramas *The Most Dangerous Man in the World* (about the assassination attempt on the Pope in 1981) and *Cream in My Coffee*, and made a light-hearted guest appearance in *Robin of Sherwood*. Other credits have included parts in *Villains*, *Sutherland's Law*, *Beasts*, *Z Cars*, *The Duchess of Duke Street*, *The New Avengers* and Shakespearean plays. He was also seen as Chief Constable Alan Cade in *The Chief*.

SHELLEY/THE RETURN OF SHELLEY

UK (Thames) Situation Comedy. ITV 1979–82; 1988–92

James Shelley	Hywel Bennett
Frances Smith	Belinda Sinclair
Mrs Edna Hawkins	Josephine Hewson
Gordon Smith	Frederick Jaeger
Forsyth	Kenneth Cope
Isobel Shelley	Sylvia Kay
Paul	Warren Clarke
Alice	Rowena Cooper
Desmond	Garfield Morgan
Carol	Caroline Langrishe
Graham	Andrew Castell
Phil	Stephen Hoye
Ted Bishop	David Ryall

Creator: Peter Tilbury. Producer: Anthony Parker

A university graduate shirks work, battles bureaucracy and bemoans the upheavals of life.

James Shelley, a geography graduate who looked down on those less well-educated than himself, wanted more from life, but not if he had to work for it. Living on social security, the 28-year-old shared a flat with his girlfriend, Fran, in Pangloss Road, North London, from where he conducted a permanent war with the taxman and other establishment figures, as well as Fran's dad,

Gordon. Mrs Hawkins was his landlady. Over subsequent series, Shelley did find sporadic work, once as a copywriter and on another occasion with the Foreign Office, but his inability and unwillingness to hold down a job led Fran (now his wife and mother of his daughter, Emma) to kick him out. Shelley moved into his friend Paul's flat and continuously wrangled with Desmond, the building's porter, before deciding to leave for the USA and the Middle East to teach English. Six years later, in 1988, he re-emerged with the same chip on his shoulder and petulant pout on his lips in *The Return of Shelley*. Carol and Graham were his hosts on his comeback, and this time he railed against yuppies and the Americanization of British society. Later episodes reverted to the original title and saw the Hancockian hero lodging with Ted Bishop and then moving in with a community of old folk.

SHERLOCK HOLMES

UK (BBC) Detective Drama. BBC 1 1965

Sherlock Holmes	Douglas Wilmer
Dr Watson	Nigel Stock
Inspector Lestrade	Peter Madden
Mrs Hudson	Mary Holder
Mycroft Holmes	Derek Francis

Producer: David Goddard

The BBC's second attempt at televising The Greatest Detective.

Having put together an unlikely team of actors for a 1951 version of six Conan Doyle stories, the BBC tried again 14 years later. In the earlier series, Holmes had been played by Alan Wheatley (the future Sheriff of Nottingham in *The Adventures of Robin Hood*), assisted by a pre-*No Hiding Place* Raymond Francis as Watson and a young Compo, Bill Owen, as Inspector Lestrade. On this occasion, Douglas Wilmer was handed Holmes's pipe and magnifying glass, and was aided, or rather hindered, by an inept Dr Watson played by Nigel Stock. The characters had originally been seen in a one-off story, *The Speckled Band*, under the *Detective* season in 1964 with Wilmer and Stock. Twelve stories were covered. Stock reprised his role three years later, when Peter Cushing replaced Wilmer as lead in *The Cases of Sherlock Holmes*. See also *The Adventures of Sherlock Holmes*.

SHERRIN, NED (1931–)

Although associated with the Radio 4 series *Loose Ends* these days, Ned Sherrin was one of the BBC's current affairs team that brought *Tonight* to the screens in the 1950s. He also devised, produced and directed the ground-breaking *That Was The Week That Was* in 1962, as well as its less successful offsprings, ***Not So Much a Programme, More a Way of Life*** and ***BBC 3***.

SHE'S OUT see *Widows*.

SHILLINGBURY TALES

UK (ATV) Comedy Drama. ITV 1981

Peter Higgins	Robin Nedwell
Sally Higgins	Diane Keen
Major Langton	Lionel Jeffries
Cuffy	Bernard Cribbins
Jake	Jack Douglas
Harvey	Joe Black
Reverend Norris	Nigel Lambert
Mrs Simpkins	Diana King
Mandy	Linda Hayden

Creator/Writer: Francis Essex. Producer: Greg Smith

Affairs in the life of a picturesque English village.

The Shillingbury Tales, set in the fictitious village of Shillingbury, was developed by Francis Essex from his own one-off play, *The Shillingbury Blowers*, screened in 1980. In the single drama, the 'Blowers' were members of an inept local brass band which was kicked into life by pop musician Peter Higgins. However, when the series began, other village events came under the microscope. Peter had married Sally Langton, daughter of the local aristocrat, Major Langton, and had settled into the village. Also in the action was Cuffy the tinker, a scruffy, mischievous tramp who lived in a run-down caravan. He was given his own spin-off series in 1983, with many of the Shillingbury villagers making up the supporting cast.

SHINE ON HARVEY MOON

UK (Central/Witzend/Meridian) Comedy Drama. ITV 1982–5; 1995–

Harvey Moon	Kenneth Cranham
	Nicky Henson
Rita Moon	Maggie Steed
Maggie Moon	Linda Robson
Stanley Moon	Lee Whitlock
Lou Lewis	Nigel Planer
Nan	Elizabeth Spriggs
Veronica	Pauline Quirke
Harriet Wright	Fiona Victory
Eric Gottlieb	Leonard Fenton
Freida	Suzanne Bertish

Creators/Writers: Laurence Marks, Maurice Gran. Producers: Tony Charles, Allan McKeown

Postwar trouble and strife for a former serviceman and his family.

Returning home to Hackney from wartime service in India as a corporal (stores clerk) in the RAF, former professional footballer Harvey Moon discovered his home destroyed and his family life in tatters. His flighty wife, Rita, had run off with other men, his 17-year-old daughter, Maggie, was seeing his old pal, Lou Lewis, and his mother, Nan, remained as redoubtable as ever. Add to this the problems of rationing, postwar shortages and the constraints of living in a prefab (later demolished by an unexploded bomb), and Harvey's lot was not a happy one. However, he set about making a new life for himself, becoming a Labour councillor, dating Harriet Wright, his worldly son Stanley's headmistress, and taking up residence with Eric Gottlieb and his sister, Freida. Eventually, he and Rita were, somewhat precariously, reunited.

Beginning with six half-hour episodes, *Shine on Harvey Moon*, a nostalgic comedy drama, was later extended into 60-minute instalments and ran for three years, covering the period 1945–8. In 1995 the programme was exhumed, with Nicky Henson replacing Kenneth Cranham in the lead. The story was taken up in 1953, Coronation year, with immigrants flooding into Britain looking for work and Maggie set to marry Lou (now 'One Lung Lou', having lost the other). In-between, creators Laurence Marks and Maurice Gran had returned to the 1940s with another offering, ***Goodnight Sweetheart***.

SHIVAS, MARK (1938–)

Successful British executive, one-time film critic and host of ***Cinema*** but far better remembered for his work as producer on dramas like ***The Six Wives of Henry VIII***, ***Casanova***, ***The Glittering Prizes***, *Rogue Male*, *The History Man*, ***Telford's Change***, *The Three Hostages*, *On Giant's Shoulders*, ***The Borgias***, ***Winston Churchill – The Wilderness Years***, *The Price* and ***The Storyteller***.

SHOESTRING

UK (BBC) Detective Drama. BBC 1 1979–80

Eddie Shoestring	Trevor Eve
Erica Bayliss	Doran Godwin
Don Satchley	Michael Medwin
Sonia	Liz Crowther

Creator/Producer: Robert Banks Stewart

Private detective work with a local radio presenter.

Eddie Shoestring was a radio presenter – but he was also a detective. Working for West Country-based Radio West, Shoestring used his airtime as a springboard for detective work, asking listeners to ring in with investigations he could pursue and information he could use. Usually, the cases were run-of-the-mill affairs, all set in the Bristol area, but, occasionally, something juicier turned up to spur the 'private ear' into action. When the crime had been solved, the outcome was related on air, with names changed to protect the innocent.

Shoestring had not always been a broadcaster. He had been egged into the job by the station receptionist, Sonia (played by Leslie Crowther's daughter), after helping the station out on an early investigation. Before that he had been a computer expert but had suffered a nervous breakdown and had spent some time in a mental institution. He now lodged with lawyer Erica Bayliss, an occasional girlfriend who joined in some of the sleuthing. Don Satchley was Eddie's station manager.

Although scruffily dressed and prone to drinking sprees, Shoestring was not to be underestimated. He was multi-talented. Not only was he a keen sketch artist (sketching was his therapy) and a good mimic, but he enjoyed an excellent, sensitive rapport with his listening public. However, when times were bad, he retreated to his run-down houseboat for moments of reflection. The boat was almost as decrepit as his car, a beaten-up Ford Cortina estate.

After just two, highly successful seasons, Trevor Eve decided to move back into the theatre. It left *Shoestring*'s creator, Robert Banks-Stewart, with plenty of unused ideas, so he developed a new series about another rehabilitating detective, this time based in Jersey (see **Bergerac**). *Shoestring*'s presence was not quite eradicated, however, as the name Radio West was bought up by the real-life independent radio station set up to serve the Bristol area.

SHOGUN

US (Paramount) Drama. BBC 1 1982

John Blackthorne	Richard Chamberlain
Lord Toranaga	Toshiro Mifune
Lady Toda Buntaro-Mariko	Yoko Shimada
Lord Ishido	Nobuo Kaneko
Vasco Rodriguez	John Rhys-Davies
Friar Domingo	Michael Hordern
Father Alvito	Damien Thomas
Omi	Yuki Meguro
Yabu	Frankie Sabai
Dell' Aqua	Alan Badel

Writer/Producer: Eric Bercovici. Executive Producer: James Clavell

A 17th-century adventurer is captured by the Japanese and adapts to their culture.

Based on the real-life story of Elizabethan seaman Will Adams, *Shogun* told of John Blackthorne, the English pilot of a Dutch vessel that was wrecked on the Japanese coast in the early 1600s. Taken under the wing of the powerful Toranaga, one of the feudal state's great war lords, Blackthorne adopted the name of Anjin-san and quickly acclimatized to the Japanese way of living. The series watched Blackthorne embark on a steamy affair with Lady Mariko (a married noblewoman interpreter), confront western emissaries (traders and Jesuit preachers) and take part in the many bloody conflicts which characterized Japanese life. His quest: to become the first western-born Shogun (a supreme Samurai warrior).

This easy-paced, six-part series was adapted from James Clavell's epic novel of the same name, with Clavell working on the project as executive producer. It was filmed on location in Japan, with much of the dialogue in Japanese.

SHOOTING SCRIPT

A version of a programme script which details all the camera shots required.

SHOW CALLED FRED, A

UK (Associated-Rediffusion) Comedy. ITV 1956

Peter Sellers
Spike Milligan
Valentine Dyall
Graham Stark
Kenneth Connor
Patti Lewis
Max Geldray

Writers: Spike Milligan, John Antrobus, Maurice Wiltshire, Dave Freeman

Off-beat comedy sketch show.

Written by Spike Milligan and others, and also featuring fellow Goon Peter Sellers, assorted comics and Canadian singer Patti Lewis, *A Show Called Fred* was one of TV's first surreal comedies. It followed hot on the heels of another Peter Sellers offering, *Idiot Weekly, Price 2d* (also 1956), in which he played the editor of a Victorian newspaper. A sequel, *Son of Fred*, performed by the same team but with Johnny Vyvyan and Cuthbert Harding added to their number, was screened in the same year. *The Best of Fred* was a 1963 compilation of both series. Future Beatles film director Dick Lester directed proceedings.

SHUBIK, IRENE (1935–)

British drama producer. Previously an historian, Shubik's first job in television was as story editor to the influential Sydney Newman on programmes like **Armchair Theatre** and **Out of this World** at ABC. Moving into production, she switched with Newman to the BBC in 1963 and worked largely on *The Wednesday Play* and *Play for Today*, although she was also responsible for the *Out of the Unknown* science-fiction anthology and the Georges Simenon collection *Thirteen Against Fate*. She left the BBC in the mid-1970s, when its drama department declined to pursue a series of *Rumpole of the Bailey*, after John Mortimer's one-off play had proved a hit. She took the idea to Thames instead. Later, Shubik was the driving force behind Granada's televising of Paul Scott's *Raj Quartet* as *The Jewel in the Crown* (having produced the single drama *Staying On*, based on Scott's novel), although she was not involved in the production herself. Amongst her many credits have been *Last Train through Harecastle Tunnel* (1969), *Hearts and Flowers* (1970) and *Wessex Tales* and *The General's Day* (both 1973).

SIANEL PEDWAR CYMRU see S4C.

SILVERA, CARMEN

Comedy actress born in Canada, primarily recalled as the tuneless Madame Edith in *'Allo 'Allo*. In the early 1960s, she played Camilla Hope in the magazine soap *Compact,* and was also seen in one episode of *Dad's Army*, as Captain Mainwaring's fancy woman. Other credits have included *Sergeant Cork*, *Z Cars*, *Beggar My Neighbour*, *New Scotland Yard*, *Doctor Who*, *Within These Walls*, *Lillie*, *Whoops! Apocalypse*, *Tales of the Unexpected* and *The Gentle Touch*.

SILVERS, PHIL (PHILIP SILVER-SMITH; 1912–85)

New York-born former burlesque comedian, one of TV's early greats. Despite having an up and down stage and movie career, and failing to make the grade as a variety compère on *The Arrow Show* in 1948, his later portrayal of the wonderfully devious Sgt Bilko in *You'll Never Get Rich* was so commanding that the programme's title was changed to *The Phil Silvers Show*. Four years into its run (when it was at its peak in 1959), the show was cancelled so that the studio could cash in on syndicated re-runs. An attempt to revive the premise as *The New Phil Silvers Show* in 1963 (in which he played factory foreman Harry Grafton) flopped and his TV career never recovered. He was given a semi-regular role (Shifty Shafer) in *The Beverly Hillbillies* in 1969, but otherwise his later appearances were either variety specials or guest spots in series like *Gilligan's Island* and *The Love Boat*. His daughter, Cathy, played flirt Jenny Piccalo in *Happy Days* and Silvers once dropped into the series as her screen dad.

SIMPSON, ALAN (1929–) see Galton, Ray.

SIMPSON, BILL (1931–86)

One time Scottish Television announcer Bill Simpson is clearly imprinted in most viewers' minds as the headstrong young Dr John Finlay in *Dr Finlay's Casebook*, the BBC series which ran for nine years from 1962. His later TV work was sparse, the highlight being roles in *Scotch on the Rocks* and *Kidnapped*, but with guest spots in *When the Boat Comes In* and *The McKinnons*, too.

SIMPSON, JOHN, CBE (JOHN FIDLER-SIMPSON; 1944–)

Distinguished British journalist who joined the BBC as a news reporter in 1970. He became its Dublin correspondent two years later, before moving to Brussels in 1975 to cover the increasingly important Common Market business. Simpson was the Corporation's Southern Africa correspondent from 1977 and then took over as diplomatic correspondent in 1978 before holding the position of political editor from 1980 to 1981. Also in the early 1980s, he presented *The Nine O'Clock News* with John Humphrys. From 1982, he was the BBC's diplomatic editor, switching, in 1988, to foreign affairs editor.

SIMS, JOAN (1930–)

British comedy actress often seen on the small screen, as well as in films. Sims has sometimes taken the part of a doddery old lady (in *Till Death Us Do Part*, for example), but now fills middle-aged roles (such as housekeeper Mrs Wembley in *On the Up*). In a long and varied career, she was a guest in *The Adventures of Robin Hood* in the 1950s, Daisy Burke in *Our House* in 1960, Janet with John Junkin in *Sam and Janet* in 1966, and has also enjoyed major roles in the comedies *Lord Tramp*, *Born and Bred*, *Cockles* and *Farrington of the FO*. Other credits have included *Carry On Christmas*, *Sykes*, *Only Fools and Horses*, *The Dick Emery Show*, *Ladykillers* (as Amelia Elizabeth Dyer), *Poor Little Rich Girls*, *Worzel Gummidge*, *Crown Court*, *As Time Goes By* and the kids' series *Tickle on the Tum* and *Jackanory Playhouse*.

SIMULCAST

A simultaneous broadcast of a programme by a television station and a radio station, usually in order to obtain better sound quality from the radio's FM frequency. Simulcasts have been used for opera, rock concerts, stereo and quadrophonic experiments and other major events. *Top of the Pops* was simulcast on BBC 1 and Radio 1 for a few years.

SINDEN, DONALD, CBE (1923–)

Resonant-voiced actor, generally cast in upright, snooty, typically English parts. On stage since the mid-1930s and in films since the 1950s, Sinden's first TV starring role came in 1964, in the comedy *Our Man at St Mark's*, as Reverend Stephen Young, having already appeared occasionally in the sitcom *A Life of Bliss*. Twelve years later he played butler Robert Hiller in *Two's Company* and followed this sitcom with another, *Never the Twain*, in which he played antiques dealer Simon Peel. Sinden has also been seen in *The Organisation* and in numerous single dramas and classic plays, as well as guesting in series like *The Prisoner* and with Morecambe and Wise. In 1979, in complete contrast, he presented a series of documentaries, *Discovering English Churches*. He is the father of actors Jeremy and Marc Sinden.

SINGING DETECTIVE, THE

UK (BBC) Drama. BBC 1 1986

Philip E. Marlow ....Michael Gambon
Nurse Mills/Carlotta...........................Joanne Whalley
Mark Binney/Mark Finney/Raymond Binney
....Patrick Malahide
Mrs Beth Marlow/Lili ....Alison Steadman
Philip Marlow (aged ten) ....Lyndon Davies
Mr Marlow ....Jim Carter
Nicola Marlow...Janet Suzman
Dr Gibbon ....Bill Paterson
Schoolteacher/Scarecrow ....Janet Henfrey
Mark Binney (aged ten) ....William Speakman

Writer: Dennis Potter. Producers: Kenith Trodd, John Harris

A hospitalized thriller writer hallucinates into paranoia.

Trying to explain *The Singing Detective* in just a few words is a difficult task. For a start, one wouldn't call it a detective series, although there were elements of that genre involved. There was also a romance angle, and, as in writer Dennis Potter's earlier offering, *Pennies from Heaven*, music held the plot together. Essentially, this six-part drama was the story of a suffering man, Philip Marlow, who descended into paranoia as his debilitating skin diseases worsened, leading him to conjure up images of the people around him as alien to his well-being. It meandered through time back to the 1930s, it looked at the patient as a young boy, examining his formative years, and it infiltrated the pages of fiction, as people became characters from one of his own books, *The Singing Detective*. It confused reality and fantasy, and offered a weird psychoanalytical insight into the lead character.

Claustrophobically confined to hospital (the Sherpa Tensing ward), tortured by unbearable psoriasis, the grouchy Marlow found his temperature sweeping up and down, causing his mind to wander. Believing his wife, Nicola, was conspiring with a lover, Mark Finney, to sell his book's film rights, he drifted back to his Forest of Dean childhood to recall a devious classmate called Mark Binney (or was it Finney?). He remembered seeing his mother make love in the woods to her fancy man, Raymond Binney, a Mark Finney look-alike, and longed for the days when he climbed high trees and was master of all he surveyed. At other times, he swooned off into the pages of his own novel, picturing himself as the eponymous hero, attempting to solve the mystery of a girl dredged from the Thames, trailed all the while by two shadowy figures, in a nostalgic echo of Chandler's Philip Marlowe tales. Back in reality, the sick author fought desperate verbal battles against a doctor whose opinion he derided, and was then required to restrain his sexuality as the beautiful Nurse Mills worked soothing ointment into his suffering, flaking body.

Brilliant to some, outrageous to many and confusing to most (at least until all the pieces fell into place), *The Singing Detective* was in part an autobiographical tale. Potter himself suffered badly from psoriasis, and had grown up in the Forest of Dean. The evocative 1930s/1940s tunes like 'Cruising Down The River' and 'Dem Bones' were also clearly from Potter's younger days. When all the fuss had subsided, the general reaction was that this was an all-time classic TV drama, skilfully crafted, magnificently produced and highly entertaining. It was shown again shortly after Potter's premature death in 1994.

SINGLES

UK (Yorkshire) Situation Comedy. ITV 1988–91

Malcolm Price ....Roger Rees
Pamela ....Judy Loe
Clive Bates ....Eamon Boland
Jackie Phillips...Susie Blake
Dennis Duval ....Simon Cadell
Di...Gina Maher

Creators/Writers: Eric Chappell, Jean Warr. Producers: Vernon Lawrence, Nic Phillips, Graham Wetherell

Four lonely hearts meet in a singles' bar and embark on a series of duplicitous relationships.

Pamela, married for 20 years but now separated, and her recently divorced friend, Jackie, attended a singles' bar as a step towards finding a new relationship. There they met up with bachelor market trader Malcolm and hospital porter Clive, whose wife had left him with three children to raise. Malcolm's claim to be 'big in imports' and

Clive's fake profession of 'doctor' were exposed by Di, the club's Liverpudlian barmaid, but the girls and guys struck up a friendship all the same and it lasted, through peaks and troughs, for two series. Malcolm and Pamela paired up, as did Clive and Jackie. For the third and final series, Malcolm was replaced by failed thespian Dennis Duval (actor Roger Rees had moved on to play Robin Colcord in *Cheers*).

SINGLETON, VALERIE, OBE (1937–)

Actress turned TV presenter whose first television appearances were in ITV admags. She moved to the BBC as an announcer in 1962 and the same year joined *Blue Peter*. With Christopher Trace she inaugurated the series' golden age, which continued through her partnership with John Noakes and Peter Purves.

Singleton famously joined Princess Anne on the 1971 *Blue Peter Royal Safari To Kenya*, but left *Blue Peter* a year later (her replacement was Lesley Judd), to work on *Nationwide* (initially on its Consumer Unit), *Tonight*, *The Money Programme* and BBC Radio. She continued to make occasional visits to the *Blue Peter* studio throughout the 1970s and was sent on Blue Peter Special Assignments. Singleton also presented the series *Val Meets the VIPs*, in which she interviewed celebrities. She returned to the screen in 1993, as host of *Travel UK*, and, the next year, shared the limelight once again with John Noakes in the over-50s afternoon magazine programme, *Next*.

SIR FRANCIS DRAKE

UK (ABC/ATV) Adventure. ITV 1961–2

Sir Francis Drake	Terence Morgan
Queen Elizabeth	Jean Kent
Trevelyan	Patrick McLoughlin
John Drake	Michael Crawford
Mendoza	Roger Delgado
Walsingham	Richard Warner
Don Pedro	Alex Scott

Producer: Anthony Bushell

Swashbuckling, maritime adventures with the sailor hero of Queen Elizabeth I.

Sir Francis Drake was Admiral of The Queen's Navy and, from his flagship, *The Golden Hind*, patrolled the oceans for Britain. His travels took him across the Atlantic and into conflict with our continental near-neighbours, although whenever trouble threatened, Drake would always win through, often showing off his fencing skills in the process. Although accurate in period detail, the programme's storylines were largely fictitious. The production was especially notable, in hindsight, for its cast, which included in particular a young Michael Crawford, as well as Roger Delgado (the original Master in *Doctor Who*). Guest stars were noteworthy, too, and included David McCallum, Nanette Newman and Warren Mitchell.

SIR LANCELOT see *Adventures of Sir Lancelot, The*.

SISSONS, PETER (1942–)

Senior BBC newsreader who joined ITN in 1964 as a trainee. Working his way up the network's ladder, he became foreign correspondent, industrial editor and presenter of the lunchtime bulletin *News at One* and *Channel 4 News*. He moved to the BBC in 1989 as Robin Day's successor in the chair of *Question Time* (he stayed four years) and also to present the Corporation's main bulletins.

SITCOM

Situation comedy, a humorous, episodic series of programmes in which a well-defined cast of characters, confined in one location or set of circumstances, respond predictably to new events.

TV's first comedy offerings were carry-overs from radio or the music hall, but it soon carved its own niche in the world of humour by developing the situation comedy, a type of comedy that made a virtue out of the constraints of early television production. In those primitive days, camera manoeuvrability was limited and dramas and comedies were generally played out entirely within the four walls of a studio set. Consequently, with the situation static, humour had to come from strong characterization.

Most sitcoms have centred around the family. Right from the earliest successes of *The George Burns and Gracie Allen Show* and *I Love Lucy* to today's *Roseanne* and *2 Point 4 Children*, the family unit has been the cradle of the action. This is not so surprising as the family comprises a set number of inter-dependent characters, living in the same location and forced to react with each other to changing events. The workplace has been another popular venue, as typified by programmes like *Taxi* and *On the Buses*. However, provided the circumstances are well defined and the characterization is suitably strong, virtually any setting can be used. For *The Phil Silvers Show* it was a US Army base; for *Cheers* a Boston bar. As if to prove the point, the most successful of sitcoms have had the most unlikely of settings – *M*A*S*H*'s Mobile Army Surgical Hospital in the Korean War, and the Résistance bar in occupied France in *'Allo 'Allo*, for instance.

Whereas American sitcoms employ teams of ever-changing writers, most of Britain's memorable sitcoms have come from a small corps of authors, the likes of Ray Galton and Alan Simpson, Johnny Speight, John Esmonde and Bob Larbey, Dick Clement and Ian La Frenais, Jimmy Perry and David Croft, Vince Powell and Harry Driver, Ronald Chesney and Ronald Wolfe, Johnnie Mortimer and Brian Cooke, Maurice Gran and Lawrence Marks, Roy Clarke, Eric Chappell, John Sullivan, Carla Lane, George Layton, David Nobbs, David Renwick and Andrew Marshall. Many of their works began as pilots in the *Comedy Playhouse* anthology.

SITTING PRETTY

UK (BBC) Situation Comedy. BBC 1 1992–

Annie Briggs ....Diane Bull
Tiffany..Alison Lomas
Sylvie ....Heather Tobias
Kitty ....Vilma Hollingbery
George ....John Cater

Creator/Writer: John Sullivan. Producer: Susan Belbin

A 1960s jet-setter, impoverished by her late husband, is driven back to her lowly roots.

Annie Briggs had seen better days. A 1960s good-time girl, once known as 'the Jackie Onassis of Bethnal Green', she had rubbed shoulders with the big names, drifted from party to party and travelled the world on the arms of rich playboys. However, when her husband, Boris, died suddenly, he left her penniless and staring the realities of the 1990s in the face. Her lovely home, her cars and even her dog were repossessed and she was forced to move into her last piece of property, the pokey flat she had given to her daughter, Tiffany. Tiffany, or 'Dumpling' as her mum called her, was a trainee nurse. She had seldom seen her mother while growing up, having been packed off to boarding school while Annie toured the world. Now, claustrophobically trapped within the same four walls, she saw too much of her (and heard too many of Annie's Shirley Bassey tapes). Soon the flat, too, was taken away and Annie and Tiffany moved in with Annie's mum, Kitty, hypochondriac dad, George, and twin sister, Sylvie, at Sunnyside Farm, a small chicken ranch in the country. Frumpy Sylvie, an ex-hippy with a grown-up air steward son named Lonestar (whose dad she reckoned was Bob Marley), particularly resented her sister's presence, or rather the fact that she never lifted a finger around the home, unless it was to paint the nail. 'Phenomenal', as Annie would have put it.

SITUATION COMEDY see sitcom.

SIX ENGLISH TOWNS

UK (BBC) Documentary. BBC 2 1978

Presenter/Writer: Alec Clifton-Taylor

Producer: Denis Moriarty

An enthusiastic analysis of building styles around England.

Alec Clifton-Taylor, a keen admirer of architecture, took viewers on a ramble through six of the country's most interesting towns in this series for BBC 2. Paying particular attention to houses and terraces, and making clear his views on modern developments, Clifton-Taylor took in visits to Chichester, Richmond (Yorkshire), Tewkesbury, Stamford, Totnes and Ludlow. The series proved so popular that *Six More English Towns* followed in 1981. These were Warwick, Berwick upon Tweed, Saffron Walden, Lewes, Bradford on Avon and Beverley. *Another Six English Towns* – Cirencester, Whitby, Bury St Edmunds, Devizes, Sandwich and Durham – rounded off the trilogy in 1984.

SIX-FIVE SPECIAL

UK (BBC) Youth Magazine. BBC 1957–8

Presenters: Peter Murray, Josephine Douglas, Freddie Mills, Jim Dale

Producers: Jack Good, Josephine Douglas, Dennis Main Wilson

Pioneering youth music programme.

With its 'Over the points, over the points' theme song (by Johnny Johnson), the *Six-Five Special* rolled into town in February 1957, initially scheduled for a six-week run. Instead it ran for nearly two years. Conceived by the BBC as a means of capturing the youth market, and filling the Saturday 6–7 pm vacancy created by scrapping the Toddlers' Truce, it proved to be a major step forward for pop music on TV.

Co-producers Jack Good and Jo Douglas were charged by the BBC with the development of the series, being two of the younger members of staff. Good was undoubtedly the prime mover and pushed the Corporation's conservative instincts to the limit. He wanted spontaneity, movement and energy; the BBC wanted something rather more sedate. Good dragged the clapping and jiving studio audience into shot and whipped up a degree of excitement; the BBC countered by balancing rock 'n' roll with skiffle, jazz and even classical music, and filling out the show with wholesome magazine items (comedy, sport, general interest, etc.). Such restrictions proved too much for Good and he left for ITV where he was given the freedom he needed to produce a real rock 'n' roll show, *Oh Boy!* When this was pitched opposite *Six-Five Special* in the schedules, the latter's days were numbered. It eventually gave way to a replacement pop show called *Dig This!*

Hosting *Six-Five Special* in its first year were Pete Murray, Jo Douglas and boxer-turned-TV presenter Freddie Mills. Jim Dale took over in the post-Good days. The resident band were Don Lang and His Frantic Five and, amongst the guest performers were the likes of Tommy Steele and the Steelmen, Adam Faith (making his TV debut) and, to illustrate the wide range of musical styles covered, Lonnie Donegan, Laurie London, Johnny Dankworth and Shirley Bassey. *Six-Five Special*'s early popularity resulted in a spin-off film (of the same name) and two stage shows. A New Year's Eve special, appropriately titled *The Twelve-Five Special* and presented from London Airport, was seen in 1957.

SIX MILLION DOLLAR MAN, THE

US (Universal/Harve Bennett) Science Fiction. ITV 1974–

Colonel Steve Austin	Lee Majors
Oscar Goldman	Richard Anderson
Dr Rudy Wells	Alan Oppenheimer
	Martin E. Brooks
Peggy Callahan	Jennifer Darling
Jaime Sommers	Lyndsay Wagner
Andy Sheffield	Vincent Van Patten

Creator: Henri Simoun. Executive Producer: Glen A. Larson, Harve Bennett, Allan Balter. Producers: Michael Gleason, Lee Sigel, Joe L. Cramer, Fred Freiberger, Richard Irving

An astronaut, rebuilt after an horrendous accident, uses his superhuman powers to work for an intelligence service.

Steve Austin was a NASA astronaut whose lunar landing vehicle crashed on a test flight. The authorities decided to rebuild him at a cost of $6 million, using nuclear-powered technology devised by boffin Dr Rudy Wells. Austin was given a replacement right arm, which endowed him with tremendous strength, two new legs, which allowed him to run at up to 60 mph, and a left eye with a built-in telescope. He became a cyborg: part-man, part-machine, a superman who was still vulnerable in usual human ways.

The new 'bionic' man put his amazing abilities to work on behalf of the Office of Scientific Information (OSI), an international secret agency run by the US Government, where his boss was Oscar Goldman. Austin was joined in his adventures by his girlfriend, tennis star Jaime Sommers. She, too, had been rebuilt, following a sky-diving accident. Her first appearance was short-lived, as her body rejected the implants, and she was believed to have died. But doctors and technicians resurrected her from a coma to take part in further bionic adventures alongside Austin, before she was given her own series, *The Bionic Woman*. There was also a bionic boy (teenage athlete Andy Sheffield), a bionic dog and even a $7 million man, a racing driver named Barney Miller, rebuilt as Austin's back up. However, he blew a fuse and Austin had to destroy him.

Also seen in the series was secretary Peggy Callahan, and the brains behind the bionics, Dr Wells (who must have had surgery himself, because he was played by two different actors). The series was based on a handful of TV movies that had been spun off the book *Cyborg* by Martin Caidin.

SIX WIVES OF HENRY VIII, THE

UK (BBC) Historical Drama. BBC 2 1970

Henry VIII	Keith Michell
Catherine of Aragon	Annette Crosbie
Anne Boleyn	Dorothy Tutin
Jane Seymour	Anne Stallybrass
Anne of Cleves	Elvi Hale
Catherine Howard	Angela Pleasence
Catherine Parr	Rosalie Crutchley
Duke of Norfolk	Patrick Troughton
Thomas Cromwell	Wolfe Morris
Archbishop Cranmer	Bernard Hepton
Lady Rochford	Sheila Burrell
Sir Thomas Seymour	John Ronane
Narrator	Anthony Quayle

Creator: Maurice Cowan. Producers: Ronald Travers, Mark Shivas, Roderick Graham

The life and loves of King Henry VIII.

This award-winning, six-part costume drama told the story of England's celebrated monarch through his relationships with his six wives, one per episode. It saw Henry growing in age (and size) from a slim 17-year-old to an obese 56-year-old at the time of his death. It also helped erode the cinematic Charles Laughton 'glutton' stereotype, introducing further dimensions to the man's character.

As a lead figure, Henry VIII provided much scope for the writers. Although 400 years old, his story made good 1970s TV drama, rich in sex and violence. Here was a man who married six different women, chiefly to give himself an heir, beheaded two, divorced two and saw one die shortly after childbirth. Then there were the whispered conspiracies, the treacherous double-dealing, the bloody murders and the major religious wrangles which were prevalent in those troubled times. It made a star out of a former artist, the Australian Keith Michell, and was reworked with different actresses for a film version, *Henry VIII and His Six Wives* in 1972. Originally screened on BBC 2, the series nevertheless drew huge audiences.

64,000 QUESTION, The see *Double Your Money.*

$64,000 QUESTION, The see *Double Your Money.*

SIXTY MINUTES see *Nationwide.*

SKIPPY, THE BUSH KANGAROO

Australia (Norfolk International) Children's Adventure. ITV 1967–9

Matt Hammond	Ed Devereaux
Sonny Hammond	Garry Parkhurst
Mark Hammond	Ken James
Jerry King	Tony Bonner
Clarissa 'Clancy' Merrick	Liza Goddard
Dr Anna Steiner	Elke Neidhardt
Dr Alexander Stark	Frank Thring

Writers: Ross Napier, Ed Devereaux. Executive Producers: John McCallum, Bud Austin. Producers: Lee Robinson, Dennis Hill

Heart-warming tales of a boy and his pet kangaroo.

Set in Australia's Waratah National Park, *Skippy, The Bush Kangaroo*, with its catchy sing-along theme song, related the adventures of Sonny Hammond, son of Chief Ranger Matt Hammond and younger brother of Ranger Mark Hammond, and blonde teenager Clancy Merrick (a young Liza Goddard). But the real star of the show was Sonny's intuitive pet kangaroo, Skippy. Once injured and near to death, Skippy was nursed back to health by Sonny and remained ever loyal thereafter, to the point where the bounding marsupial would even warn his master of impending danger with a distinctive 'tut tut'. Also seen were local pilot Jerry King and hordes of colourful Australian mammals. In 1993 the BBC showed *The New Adventures of Skippy.*

SKY see BSkyB.

SKY AT NIGHT, THE

UK (BBC) Astronomy. BBC 1 1957–

Presenter: Patrick Moore

Producers: Paul Johnstone, Patricia Owtram, Patricia Wood, Pieter Morpurgo

Small screen astronomy.

Hosted for its entire run of nearly 40 years by Patrick Moore, *The Sky at Night* – the world's longest running science programme – has charted events in the space world on a monthly basis. Its first programme went out six months before *Sputnik I*, the first man-made satellite, was launched and so it can justifiably claim to have been ahead of the space race. As well as monitoring the progress of various probes and rockets, the fast-talking, ultra-enthusiastic Moore has also guided viewers on an exploration of the heavens, pointing out unusual phenomena and revealing the location of the various constellations. The dramatic theme music has been 'At The Castle Gate', from *Pelleus and Mélisande*, by Sibelius. A children's version of the programme, under the title of *Seeing Stars*, was screened in 1970.

SKYPORT see *Shadow Squad.*

SKY'S THE LIMIT, The see *Double Your Money.*

SLATER, JOHN (1916–75)

British character actor, in TV plays during the 1940s but more familiar in series like *Z Cars* (as Detective Sgt Tom Stone). He was also a regular partner of the puppet pigs *Pinky and Perky*, and, for a number of years, was seen promoting Special K cereal (a not unfamiliar activity to Slater who had hosted the *Slater's Bazaar* admag in the late 1950s).

SLATTERY, TONY (1959–)

British comedian, actor and presenter, ubiquitous on TV in the early 1990s. Slattery made his name in the improvization show *Whose Line Is It Anyway?*, having already appeared in the late-night comedy *Saturday Stayback*, and went on to star in the sitcoms *That's Love* (as Tristan Beasley) and *Just a Gigolo* (as Nick Brim). He co-wrote the kids' series *Behind the Bike Sheds*, hosted the film magazine *Saturday Night at the Movies*, shared the limelight with Mike McShane in *S&M* and took over from Stephen Fry in the investigative reporter spoof *This is David Lander* (it was renamed *This Is David Harper* to accommodate the change). He has also presented *Trivial Pursuit* for the satellite Family Channel and other credits have included *Boon* and *Drowning in the Shallow End.*

SLINGER'S DAY see *Tripper's Day.*

SMART, RALPH (1908–)

British producer/writer/director, working largely for ITC on various action romps. He is chiefly remembered for creating and producing *The Invisible Man* and *Danger Man*, but also contributed in various ways to *The Adventures of Robin Hood*, *The Buccaneers*, *The Adventures of Sir Lancelot*, *The Champions*, *The Protectors* and *Randall and Hopkirk (Deceased)*.

SMITH AND JONES see *Alas Smith and Jones*.

SMITH, DELIA, OBE

The modern-day queen of TV cooks, thanks to her 30-part *Delia Smith's Cookery Course* in the 1970s. Smith entered television after preparing food for cookery photographs and then writing a column for the *Evening Standard*. Her first programme for the BBC came in 1973. Other contributions have included *One is Fun*, *Delia Smith's Christmas* and *Delia Smith's Summer Collection*. The books that have accompanied her series have sold in vast numbers.

SMITH, JACLYN (1947–)

American actress who played agent Kelly Garrett throughout *Charlie's Angels'* five-year run (even though her partners came and went). Previously, Smith had been seen in US TV commercials and as a guest in series as varied as *McCloud* and *The Partridge Family*. She later took to TV movies, playing amongst other characters Jackie Kennedy in *Jacqueline Bouvier Kennedy* in 1981 and *Mystery Movie* detective Christine Cromwell in the series of the same name in 1989.

SMITH, JULIA

British drama producer and director, chiefly associated with *EastEnders*, which she co-created with Tony Holland. Smith had previously produced *Angels* and *The District Nurse* (also as creator) and had contributed to BBC programmes from the 1960s, including *Doctor Who*, *Jury Room*, *Dr Finlay's Casebook*, *The Newcomers*, *The Railway Children* and *Z Cars*. A much-vaunted later soap, *Eldorado*, failed to attract a large enough audience and lasted only one year.

SMITH, LIZ

English character and comedy actress, arriving on television in the 1970s after bringing up her two children. She has appeared in many single dramas and series, with perhaps the best-remembered roles being Mrs Brandon in *I Didn't Know You Cared* and Bette in *2 Point 4 Children*. Other credits have included *Bootsie and Snudge*, *The Sweeney*, *No, Honestly*, *Crown Court*, *Now and Then*, *The Life and Loves of a She Devil*, *Cluedo*, *King and Castle*, *Bust*, *The Bill*, *Valentine Park*, *Lovejoy*, *El C.I.D.*, *Making Out*, *The Young Indiana Jones Chronicles* and *Bottom*.

SMITH, MEL (1952–)

British comedian, actor and director, first coming to prominence as a member of the *Not The Nine O'Clock News* team in 1979. With his partner, Griff Rhys Jones, Oxford graduate Smith became one of the in comics of the 1980s, starring in *Alas Smith and Jones*, *Smith and Jones in Small Doses*, *The World According to Smith and Jones*, and, more simply, *Smith and Jones*. Together, they founded the Talkback independent production company. Smith was also seen as ruthless property developer Tom Craig in the drama *Muck and Brass* and worryguts Colin Watkins in *Colin's Sandwich*, and guested in *The Young Ones* and *Minder*. In 1994 he starred in the comedy drama *Milner*.

SMITH, MIKE (1955–)

Blond-haired British presenter, a former Capital Radio and Radio 1 disc jockey who left radio to pursue a TV career. His credits have included *Breakfast Time*, *The Late, Late Breakfast Show* (with Noel Edmonds) and *Trick or Treat* (with Julian Clary). Smith has also hosted *Top of the Pops* and the celebrity quiz *That's Showbusiness*. He once sat in for Terry Wogan on his thrice-weekly chat show and has often been called up to present special programmes on motor fairs, charity events, medical matters, etc. He is married to presenter Sarah Greene, with whom he fronted *The Exchange* in 1995.

SMITH, MURRAY (1940–)

Former paratrooper turned scriptwriter and novelist. Amongst Smith's major TV successes have been episodes of *Minder*, *The Sweeney* and *Hammer House of Horror*. Smith was the major writer on *Strangers* and *Bulman*, then moved on to create *The Paradise Club*. He also adapted the novelist's work for *Frederick Forsyth Presents*.

SMITH, RAY (1936–91)

Welsh actor much seen on TV from the 1960s. Coming from mining stock himself, it seemed appropriate that he appeared in the drama serial *Sam* (as collier George Barrowclough) and played punchdrunk boxer Dai Bando in the BBC's 1976 adaptation of *How Green Was My Valley*. As Detective Inspector Firbank, Smith was partner to Frank Marker in *Public Eye*, and he was also seen as Albert Mundy in *We'll Meet Again*, although, it is as the bawling boss of *Dempsey and Makepeace*, Chief Supt Gordon Spikings, that he will be best remembered. His last screen appearance came in BBC 2's version of *The Old Devils*. Smith's career also took in series like *Z Cars*,

A Family at War, *Callan*, *Gideon's Way* and such dramas as *Rogue Male*, *The Sailor's Return* and *Masada*.

SNOW, JON (JONATHAN SNOW; 1947–)

Award-winning English newscaster, a former IRN/LBC radio news reporter who joined ITN in 1976. He became its Washington correspondent in 1983 and was later its diplomatic correspondent before taking over as anchor for *Channel 4 News* on the departure of Peter Sissons in 1989. He is the cousin of fellow journalist Peter Snow.

SNOW, PETER (1938–)

British current affairs presenter, working primarily on *Newsnight* and the BBC's election coverages (complete with modern 'swingometer'). Snow was formerly a reporter and newscaster for ITN, which he joined in 1962. He is the cousin of newscaster Jon Snow.

SO HAUNT ME

UK (Cinema Verity) Situation Comedy. BBC 1
1992–4

Yetta Feldman	Miriam Karlin
Sally Rokeby	Tessa Peake-Jones
Pete Rokeby	George Costigan
Tammy Rokeby	Laura Simmons
	Laura Howard
David Rokeby	Jeremy Green
Mr Bloom	David Graham
Carole Dawlish	Julia Deakin

Creator/Writer: Paul A. Mendelson. Producers: Caroline Gold, Sharon Bloom

A family discover their new home is haunted by a Jewish ghost.

When Pete Rokeby threw in his job as an advertising executive to concentrate on full-time writing, he and his family aimed to keep their overheads low by moving house, from an upmarket neighbourhood to a dowdy street. Their new home, they quickly discovered, was prone to icy blasts, bumps in the night and, strangely, a lingering smell of chicken soup – all down to the ghost of one-time resident Yetta Feldman. Following her death (choking on a chicken bone), Yetta's spirit had driven away everyone who had taken over her home, but the Rokebys proved to be different. Gradually making herself visible to them one by one, Yetta became a nagging grandmother to kids Tammy and David, and an annoying cuckoo to Pete and his beleaguered wife, Sally. All the same, the family sort of adopted the old lady and helped find her long-lost daughter ('Carole, with an E'). Yetta's Jewish mothering

instincts were brought to the fore again later, when Sally gave birth to a new baby. Also seen was Mr Bloom, the Rokebys' melancholy neighbour.

Creator Paul A. Mendelson drew partly on autobiographical experiences when working on this comedy. He, too, was once in advertising and left to pursue a writing career. With hits like *May to December* and *So Haunt Me*, he was clearly more successful than Pete Rokeby.

SOAP

US (Witt-Thomas-Harris) Situation Comedy.
ITV 1978–

Jessica Tate	Katherine Helmond
Chester Tate	Robert Mandan
Corrine Tate	Diana Canova
Eunice Tate	Jennifer Salt
Billy Tate	Jimmy Baio
Benson Dubois	Robert Guillaume
Grandpa Tate ('The Major')	Arthur Peterson
Mary Dallas Campbell	Cathryn Damon
Burt Campbell	Richard Mulligan
Jodie Dallas	Billy Crystal
Danny Dallas	Ted Wass
The Godfather	Richard Libertini
Claire	Kathryn Reynolds
Peter Campbell	Robert Urich
Chuck Campbell	Jay Johnson
Dennis Phillips	Bob Seagren
Father Timothy Flotsky	Sal Viscuso
Carol David	Rebecca Balding
Elaine Lefkowitz	Dinah Manoff
Dutch	Donnelly Rhodes
Sally	Caroline McWilliams
Detective Donahue	John Byner
Polly Dawson	Lynne Moody
Saunders	Roscoe Lee Browne
Carlos 'El Puerco' Valdez	Gregory Sierra
Announcer	Rod Roddy

Creator/Writer/Producer: Susan Harris.
Executive Producers: Tony Thomas, Paul Junger Witt

Parody of US daytime soap opera, featuring two related families.

The Campbells and the Tates lived in the town of Dunn's River, Connecticut. Jessica Tate and Mary Campbell were sisters, but, otherwise, the families had little in common, for the Tates were wealthy and lived in a mansion, and the Campbells were working class, and lived on the other side of town. Their day-to-day lives were depicted in serial form, just like an American soap opera, but the events were always hugely exaggerated.

These families certainly had their problems. Each member had a hang up of some kind. Jessica was married to Chester Tate, a wealthy, but untrustworthy stockbroker, and they had three troublesome children. Corrine was their more flirtatious daughter, Eunice was involved with a married Senator, and then there was their 14-year-old adolescent brat, Billy. The household was completed by Jessica's father, the Major, whose mind was still in World War II. They were all looked after by an obnoxious black manservant, Benson, who refused to cook anything he disliked himself. When he left to star in his own spin-off series, *Benson*, he was replaced by a new butler, Saunders.

Mary lived with her impotent second husband, Burt, who had inadvertently killed her first spouse. A nervous wreck, he struggled to control his wayward stepsons, Jodie, a transvestite, and delinquent Danny, who found himself involved in organized crime. Burt also had two sons from his previous marriage, Chuck, who thought his ventriloquist dummy, Bob, was real, and Peter, an amorous tennis coach who was murdered in the shower.

Even before it reached the screens, *Soap* invited a torrent of criticism by pre-publicizing its open treatment of taboo issues, especially extra-marital sex, homosexuality, racism, religion and terminal illness. But, when the producers promised to tone things down a little, and the first episodes were actually seen in all their overplayed glory, criticism subsided. All the same, *Soap's* storylines still meandered between such risqué topics as divorce, voyeurism, irresponsible affairs, illegitimate children and cold-blooded murders. It also touched on cloning, abduction by aliens, and even the seduction of a priest and the exorcism of a baby.

SOAP OPERA

The tag given to open-ended, long-running, mostly domestic dramas involving a stable cast of characters, usually of middle- or working-class background. Each episode generally involves a number of continuous storylines at various stages of development.

The term derives from 1930s American radio when soap and detergent companies used to sponsor the 15-minute radio series which ran daily to fill the daytime schedules. In these dramas, everyday problems assumed crisis proportions and dialogue easily outstripped action. With the arrival of television as a mass medium in the 1950s, the format transferred to the screen, although programmes now ran for 30 minutes. The soap manufacturers remained heavily involved. One company, Procter and Gamble, even set up a TV studio to produce their own.

Britain's first attempt at TV soap opera was **The Grove Family**, on BBC in 1954. Of course, the detergent makers had no involvement and, unlike many of their successors, the Groves didn't last long – a mere three years. With the birth of commercial television in 1955, Britain was treated to its first daily soap, *Sixpenny Corner*, the everyday story of a garage, run by Bill and Sally Norton (Howard Pays and Patricia Dainton) in a new town called Springwood. **Emergency – Ward 10** added a medical dimension in 1957 but it wasn't until 1960 that the soap concept really took off in the UK, with the arrival of **Coronation Street**. Even then, the *Street*, like *The Grove Family* and *Ward 10* screened only twice a week, was not a soap in the truest sense. Nearer was **Crossroads**, transmitted five days a week from 1964, until the IBA eventually cut it back to three.

The mundane nature of the soap opera has been pushed aside since the late 1970s. The arrival of **Dallas**, **Dynasty** and other glitzy offerings, shot like small feature films, gave rise to the 'supersoap', where the action took place on quite another plane from the down-to-earth world of the original soaps. British versions have also changed their spots. **Brookside** and **EastEnders** have introduced a new and vigorous reality, and issues like abortion, rape, drug abuse and gruesome murder now pervade many such series. Exceptions are the tame melodramas from Australia (such as **Neighbours** and **Home and Away**), that have filled UK screens in the afternoons and, of course, **Coronation Street**, which remains a fine heir to the soap legacy. When you consider how the nation was gripped by *Coronation Street's* Mike–Deirdre–Ken affair in 1983, you can appreciate just why the men from the detergent companies were happy to give their name to this form of popular drama.

SOFTLY, SOFTLY/SOFTLY, SOFTLY TASK FORCE

UK (BBC) Police Drama. BBC 1 1966–76

Detective Chief Supt Charlie Barlow..Stratford Johns
Detective Chief Inspector John Watt ..Frank Windsor
Detective Chief Inspector Harry Hawkins
....Norman Bowler
PC Henry Snow ....Terence Rigby
Inspector Gwyn Lewis ....Garfield Morgan
Mr Blackitt..Robert Keegan
DC Stone ....Alexis Kanner
DC Box...Dan Meaden
Detective Inspector Sgt Evans
....David Lloyd Meredith
Assistant Chief Constable Gilbert............John Barron
P/W Detective Sgt Allin ....Peggy Sinclair
Chief Constable Calderwood ....John Welsh
Detective Inspector Cook ....Philip Black
Chief Constable Cullen ....Walter Gotell

Creator: Elwyn Jones. Producers: David E. Rose, Leonard Lewis, Geraint Morris

The further cases of detectives Barlow and Watt.

One of the most successful spin-offs ever, *Softly, Softly* ran for ten years in parallel with **Z Cars**, its mother series. It took up the story of the 'nice and nasty' double act of Barlow and Watt, after they left Newtown and headed south to the fictional region of Wyvern (somewhere near Bristol). Promoted to the ranks of detective chief superintendent and detective chief inspector, respectively, one of the first people they encountered was their retired former desk sergeant, Blackitt, and his dog, Pandy. Among their new colleagues were the jovial Welshman Sgt Evans, miserable dog-handler PC Henry Snow (and his most famous charge, Inky) and a local detective inspector, Harry Hawkins. The show's title was derived from the adage 'Softly, softly, catchee monkey'.

In 1969 *Softly, Softly* became the more cumbersome *Softly, Softly – Task Force* and saw Barlow and Watt working for Thamesford Constabulary's CID Task Force. In 1969 Barlow went his own way, branching out into **Barlow at Large** and **Barlow**. He was reunited with Watt, however, for a novel reinvestigation of the Jack the Ripper case in 1973 and a subsequent series, **Second Verdict** in 1976, which looked at other such mysteries.

SOLDIER, SOLDIER

UK (Central) Drama. ITV 1991–

Major Tom Cadman	David Haig
Laura Cadman	Cathryn Harrison
Lance Cpl/Cpl/Sgt Paddy Garvey	Jerome Flynn
Cpl Nancy Thorpe/Garvey RMP	Holly Aird
CSM Chick Henwood	Sean Baker
Colour Sgt Ian Anderson	Robert Glenister
Cpl/Sgt Tony Wilton	Gary Love
Lt Nick Pasco	Peter Wingfield
Fusilier/Lance Cpl Dave Tucker	Robson Green
Lt Colonel Dan Fortune	Miles Anderson
Carol Anderson	Melanie Kilburn
Juliet Grant	Susan Franklyn
Joy Wilton	Annabelle Apsion
Donna Tucker	Rosie Rowell
2nd Lt/Lt/Captain Kate Butler	Lesley Vickerage
Major Bob Cochrane	Simon Donald
Fusilier 'Midnight' Rawlins	Mo Sesay
Fusilier Jimmy Monroe	Ian Dunn
Rachel Elliot/Fortune	Lesley Manville
Padre Simon Armstrong	Richard Hampton
2nd Lt Alex Pereira	Angus MacFadyen
Lt Colonel Mark Osbourne	Patrick Drury
Captain/Major Kieran Voce	Dorian Healy
CSM Michael Stubbs	Rob Spendlove
Marsha Stubbs	Denise Welch
Fusilier Luke Roberts	Akim Mogaji
Bernie Roberts	Rakie Ayola
Lt Colonel Nicolas Hammond	Robert Gwilym
Major Tim Radley	Adrian Rawlins
Lt Colonel Ian Jennings	John Bowe
Isabelle Jennings	Gabrielle Reidy
Fusilier Eddie Nelson	Paterson Joseph
Major James McCudden	John McGlynn
Lt Jeremy Forsythe	Ben Nealon
Fusilier Joe Farrell	David Groves

Creator: Lucy Gannon. Producers: Chris Kelly, Christopher Neame, Ann Tricklebank

The rigours of life in today's army.

Soldier, Soldier focused on the men and women of the King's Fusiliers Infantry Regiment as they toured the world on active and inactive duty. The first episode saw them return to their Midlands base from a six-month tour of duty in Northern Ireland. Later series followed them to Hong Kong, New Zealand, Germany, Bosnia, Cyprus and back to the UK, where they were stationed on guard duty at the royal palaces. As well as the tough routine of army life, the series examined the camaraderie of the force and witnessed the stresses and strains such an existence placed on the personal lives of soldiers and their families. New additions to the battalion arrived every series, as some members left or were tragically killed. Those that remained from the early days – the likes of Paddy Garvey, Dave Tucker and Tony Wilton – attempted to make their way up the ladder of promotion with varying degrees of success.

SOLO

UK (BBC) Situation Comedy. BBC 1 1981–2

Gemma Palmer	Felicity Kendal
Danny	Stephen Moore
Mrs Palmer	Elspet Gray
Gloria	Susan Bishop
Sebastian	Michael Howe

Creator/Writer: Carla Lane. Producer: Gareth Gwenlan

A 30-year-old woman kicks out her boyfriend, chucks in her job and goes it alone.

Discovering that her live-in boyfriend, Danny, had been having an affair with her best friend, Gloria, Gemma Palmer decided to reassert her independence. She turfed Danny out of her flat and her life, broke off relations with Gloria and, for good measure, resigned from her job. Going solo was not without its problems, however, but thankfully Gemma's supportive mum was usually at hand in times of crisis. In the second series, Danny had left the scene for good and Gemma had gained a new platonic friend, Sebastian.

SOME MOTHERS DO 'AVE 'EM

UK (BBC) Situation Comedy. BBC 1 1973–5; 1978

Frank Spencer	Michael Crawford
Betty Spencer	Michele Dotrice
Mr Lewis	Glynn Edwards

Writer: Raymond Allen. Producer: Michael Mills, Sydney Lotterby

A kind-hearted, but naive, simpleton courts disaster at every turn.

Frank Spencer was an accident awaiting to happen. Sporting a knitted tank top, unfashionable long mac and a beret, wherever he went he brought chaos and confusion. DIY jobs resulted in the systematic destruction of his house while, at work (whenever he found any), machinery exploded and his bosses despaired. And yet poor Frank, with his infantile voice, unfortunate turn of phrase, expressive shoulder twitches and hurt looks, always tried hard and meant well. He was gravely offended by criticism and deeply shocked at everything untoward. At his side through thick and thin were his over-loyal wife, Betty, and baby daughter, Jessica. Mr Lewis, the irascible neighbour seen in the last series, was just one of Frank's many adversaries.

Some Mothers Do 'Ave 'Em made a star out of Michael Crawford, but the actor worked hard for his success. His characterization was so precise that it kept impressionists in gags for years after. He also chipped in with occasional ad libs, plotted the stories for some episodes and even performed many of his own stunts that included driving a car halfway over a cliff, and narrowly escaping a collapsing chimney stack.

SOMERVILLE, JULIA (1947–)

British journalist and news presenter who joined the BBC as a sub-editor in 1973 and went on to become labour affairs correspondent and then to anchor *The Nine O'Clock News*. She was poached by ITN in 1987, for whom she has been one of the mainstays of *News at Ten* and other bulletins. Somerville has also hosted the current affairs series *3D*. She underwent a successful operation for a brain tumour in the early 1990s.

SONGS OF PRAISE

UK (BBC) Religion. BBC 1 1961–

Television's longest running religious programme.

A well-rehearsed combination of hymns, prayers, blessings and inspirational interviews, *Songs of Praise* has been an integral part of Sunday evenings for some 35 years. A different venue has hosted proceedings each week and efforts have been made to reflect all denominations and all parts of the UK (and sometimes overseas). However, cynics have pointed out that featured churches have been artificially filled for recordings, with many infrequent congregationists drawn in by the presence of cameras. The first transmission came from Tabernacle Baptist Chapel in Cardiff.

The programme's presenters have been many and diverse. They have included in recent years Cliff Michelmore, Pam Rhodes, Debbie Thrower, Roger Royle, Sally Magnusson, Gloria Hunniford, Alan Titchmarsh and Hugh Scully, with Cliff Richard, Russell Harty, Jimmy Savile and even Eddie Waring listed amongst one-time hosts.

SOOTY see Corbett, Harry.

SORRY!

UK (BBC) Situation Comedy. BBC 1 1981–8

Timothy Lumsden	Ronnie Corbett
Mrs Phyllis Lumsden	Barbara Lott
Mr Sidney Lumsden	William Moore
Muriel	Marguerite Hardiman
Kevin	Derek Fuke
Frank	Roy Holder
Freddie	Sheila Fearn
Chris	Chris Breeze
Jennifer	Wendy Allnutt

Writers: Ian Davidson, Peter Vincent. Producer: David Askey

A 40-year-old librarian can't break free from his over-powering mother.

Short, bespectacled, moped-riding bachelor Timothy Lumsden lived at home in Oxfordshire with his domineering, blue-rinsed mother and his hen-pecked, timid father (if his father hadn't been banished to the shed). Although his sister, Muriel, had married and moved away, Timothy had never had the courage to do so, largely because his mother refused to let him, not believing he had grown up. She still cajoled him with kiddy talk, and threatened him with all manner of kiddy treats and punishments. As a result, Timothy was bashful, rather apologetic (hence the programme title) and always a little uncertain in the company of females. He enjoyed a few pints down the pub with his friend Frank, and was well placed in the library where he worked, but, whenever the prospect of his leaving the nest materialized, his mother always put her foot down and ensured he remained firmly tied to her apron strings.

Timothy certainly did not live at home for the comforts: Mrs Lumsden's cooking was something to avoid, with everything from starters to desserts likely to be curried. Nor was privacy a possibility. Yet it was soon clear that Timothy was as wary of leaving home as his mother was determined to keep him there. And it was this stop-go dash for independence which ran at the heart of the series. *Sorry!* was not entirely dissimilar to an earlier Ronnie Corbett vehicle, *Now Look Here* . . . .

SOUL, DAVID (DAVID SOLBERG; 1943–)

Blond American actor/singer, once billed as the Mystery Singer on *The Merv Griffin Show* in the USA, for which he donned a hood. Moving into acting, Soul secured guest parts in various series (including *Star Trek*) and minor roles in US shows like *Here Come the Brides* and *Owen Marshall, Counselor At Law*, before getting his big break with the all-action police series **Starsky and Hutch** in 1975. As Detective Ken 'Hutch' Hutchinson, Soul became an international star, and this led to another foray into the music world, resulting in two number-one hits in the UK ('Don't Give Up On Us' and 'Silver Lady'). He co-hosted the early magazine show *Six Fifty-Five Special* (with Sally James) in 1982 and played Rick Blaine in a TV remake of *Casablanca* a year later. He has since taken roles in the series *The Yellow Rose* and *Unsub*, and has been seen in many TV movies.

SOUTH BANK SHOW, THE

UK (LWT) Arts. ITV 1978–

Presenter/Editor: Melvyn Bragg

Executive Producer: Nick Elliott. Producer: Nigel Wattis

Acclaimed Sunday night arts programme.

The successor to *Aquarius*, The South Bank Show picked up where the former left off, thoughtfully and unhurriedly covering all corners of the arts world, from the classical elements through to pop culture. Conducted throughout by Melvyn Bragg, the programme has combined in-depth interviews with studio performances and film profiles, to great effect. Its theme music has been Julian Lloyd-Webber's *Variations*.

The 1991 series, for instance, included features on personalities as varied as **Monty Python** animator Terry Gillian, Austrian cellist Heinrich Schiff, Irish poet Seamus Heaney, British playwright John Osbourne and Forces' sweetheart Vera Lynn.

SOUTH RIDING

UK (Yorkshire) Drama. ITV 1974

Sarah Burton	Dorothy Tutin
Robert Carne	Nigel Davenport
Mrs Beddows	Hermione Baddeley

Writer: Stan Barstow. Producer: James Ormerod

A schoolteacher finds the going tough in the poverty-stricken 1930s.

This 13-part adaptation of Winifred Holtby's novel was set in 1932, in the fictitious South Riding of Yorkshire. It told of a progressive schoolmistress, Sarah Burton (head of Kipling Girls High School) who found her plans for her pupils hindered by injustices in society. Also prominent were Alderman Mrs Beddows and Councillor Robert Carne. The series was repeated on Channel 4 in 1987.

SOUTHERN TELEVISION

Southern was the ITV contractor for the South of England from 30 August 1958 until 31 December 1981, when its franchise was taken over by TVS. There was, however, considerable surprise, if not shock and fury, at the decision of the IBA to terminate Southern's licence, as the company had a good record in local programming and was also a more than useful contributor to the ITV network. Its national offerings included drama series like **Winston Churchill – The Wilderness Years** and the quiz show *Wheel of Fortune*, but it was through children's programmes that Southern gained particular respect. *Freewheelers*, *Bright's Boffins*, *The Saturday Banana*, *Runaround*, **How!**, *Little Big Time* and **Worzel Gummidge** were just some of the company's many contributions to children's viewing. In addition to its programming record, Southern had never been formally criticised by the IBA, except for some concern over the make up of the company (62.5 per cent was jointly owned by Associated Newspapers Group and DC Thomson), and its perceived weak coverage of certain parts of Kent. Southern believed the latter wasn't entirely their problem as the IBA had ordered key transmitters to broadcast London signals instead of Southern's. It was interesting to note that when the new franchise was awarded to TVS, the official name of the transmission area was changed from South of England to South and South-East of England (thereby, perhaps, upholding Southern's argument).

SPACE

US (Dick Berg/Stonehenge/Paramount) Science Fiction. ITV 1987

Norman Grant	James Garner
Elinor Grant	Susan Anspach
John Pope	Harry Hamlin
Penny Hardesty/Pope	Blair Brown
Stanley Mott	Bruce Dern
Rachel Mott	Melinda Dillon
Martin Scorcella/Leopold Strabismus	David Dukes
Dieter Kolff	Michael York
Liesl Kolff	Barbara Sukowa
Randy Claggett	Beau Bridges
Debbie Dee Claggett	Stephanie Faracy
Senator Glancey	Martin Balsam
Finnerty	James Sutorius
Tucker Thomas	G.D. Spradlin
Cindy Rhee	Maggie Han

Funkhauser	Wolf Kahler
Marcia Grant	Jennifer Runyon
Skip Morgan	David Spielberg
Paul Stidham	Ralph Bellamy

Writers: Dick Berg, Stirling Silliphant.
Executive Producer: Dick Berg. Producer:
Martin Manulis

Dramatization of the race into space.

This 13-hour mini-series told the story of
America's space programme, using the lives of fictional characters to reveal the real stresses and
strains brought about by the space effort. Picking
up from the end of World War II, it focused on
the battle between the Americans and the
Russians for Nazi Germany's top rocket specialists. It continued through US political wrangles in
the 1950s to the foundation of NASA and its subsequent space race successes, including the spectacular trips to the moon. Its lead characters were
naval hero-turned-senator Norman Grant, his
alcoholic wife, Elinor, her devious lover Leopold
Strabismus (a TV evangelist whose real name was
Martin Scorcella), and Penny Pope, Norman's
mistress who was an ambitious lawyer with the
Senate Space Committee. Also prominent were
muck-raking reporter Cindy Rhee, German
rocket scientist Dieter Kolff and dedicated astrophysicist Stanley Mott, with former Korean War
pilots John Pope (Penny's husband) and Randy
Claggett taking the honours as the astronauts on
the lunar project. The series was based on James
A. Michener's novel of the same title and cost a
staggering £35 million to make. Sadly, its audience figures never justified this expense.

SPACE: 1999

UK (ITC/RAI/Gerry Anderson/Group Three)
Science Fiction. ITV 1975–7

Commander John Koenig	Martin Landau
Dr Helena Russell	Barbara Bain
Professor Victor Bergman	Barry Morse
Captain Alan Carter	Nick Tate
First Officer Tony Verdeschi	Tony Anholt
Maya	Catherine Schell
Sandra Benes	Zienia Merton
Yasko	Yasuko Nagazumi
Paul Morrow	Prentis Hancock
David Kane	Clifton Jones
Dr Bob Mathias	Anton Phillips
Moonbase computer (voice only)	Barbara Kelly

Creators: Gerry Anderson, Sylvia Anderson.
Executive Producer: Gerry Anderson.
Producers: Sylvia Anderson, Fred Freiberger

**A nuclear waste dump on the moon
explodes and the inhabitants of a moonbase are hurled out into space.**

Space: 1999 was conceived as a kind of British
Star Trek by puppet experts Gerry and Sylvia

Anderson. It focused on the adventures of the
crew of Moonbase Alpha (or Alphans, as they
became known) who found themselves stranded
in space. On September 9, 1999, a nuclear waste
depository on the dark side of the moon
exploded and jettisoned the moon, its space
research station and all 311 inhabitants out,
through a black hole, into deepest space. As they
whizzed through the galaxies, desperately trying
to find a new home before their supplies ran
out, the reluctant travellers encountered all
manner of *Star Trek*-like aliens. One such alien,
Maya, who possessed the ability to turn herself
into plants or animals and who was the last survivor of the planet Psychon, joined the crew and
became the girlfriend of Tony Verdeschi, the
first officer.

Stars of the show were ex-*Mission Impossible*
heroes, husband and wife Martin Landau and
Barbara Bain. Here, Landau played the grim
moonbase commander who had just taken up his
post when the explosion took place. Bain was the
chief physician. Other prominent characters were
the chief pilot, Alan Carter, and Professor Victor
Bergman, the brains behind the moonbase (written out after the first series).

Space: 1999 was made in association with Italy's
RAI organization and was widely acclaimed for
its advanced special effects, masterminded by
expert Brian Johnson. Years of detailed model-
making had taught the Andersons how to stage
quite spectacular space scenes, but other aspects
of the production were roundly criticized, from
the wooden acting to the somewhat far-fetched
concept. Not even the arrival of former *Star Trek*
producer Fred Freiberger managed to save the
day and the series ended without a proper conclusion.

SPACE PATROL

UK (National Interest/Wonderama) Children's
Science Fiction. ITV 1963–4

Voices:

Captain Larry Dart	Dick Vosburgh
Husky	Ronnie Stevens
Slim	Ronnie Stevens
Colonel Raeburn	Murray Kash
Professor Haggerty	Ronnie Stevens
Marla	Libby Morris
Cassiopea	Libby Morris
Gabblerdictum	Libby Morris

Creator/Writer: Roberta Leigh. Producers:
Roberta Leigh, Arthur Povis

**A tri-planetary space force protects the
solar system.**

In the year 2100, Space Patrol was the active unit
of the United Galactic Organization, a peace-

keeping body formed by the natives of Earth, Mars and Venus. This series featured the exploits of its lead ship, *Galasphere 347*, and its crew of Earthman Captain Larry Dart, the Martian Husky and the Venusian Slim. Back at base, Colonel Raeburn gave the orders, assisted by his Venusian secretary, Marla. Professor Haggerty was the unit's somewhat erratic scientific genius, and Cassiopea his daughter. Also seen was the Gabblerdictum, a kind of Martian parrot.

Space Patrol reached the screen just as Gerry Anderson's futuristic adventures were beginning to take off, with **Supercar** and **Fireball XL5** already on the air. It was scripted by Anderson's former colleague, Roberta Leigh.

SPALL, TIMOTHY (1957–)

London-born actor who is still remembered as boring Barry in *Auf Wiedersehen, Pet* from the early 1980s, even though he has taken numerous straight drama roles since and starred in other comedies. In 1993 he donned the mantle of would-be wide boy Frank Stubbs in *Frank Stubbs Promotes* and, the next year, was both slovenly Kevin Costello in *Outside Edge* and anarchic Phil Bachelor in *Nice Day at the Office*. Spall's other credits have included works as diverse as *The Cherry Orchard*, *Great Writers*, **Boon**, *Performance* and *Murder Most Horrid*.

SPARKLIES

Black and white specks which appear on satellite pictures in times of bad weather or other interference, or when the signal is weak.

SPECIAL

An individual, usually celebratory (for holidays, etc.), episode of a long-running series, or a one-off variety show.

SPECIAL BRANCH

UK (Thames/Euston Films) Police Drama. ITV 1969–74

Detective Inspector Jordan	Derren Nesbitt
Supt Eden	Wensley Pithey
Detective Supt Inman	Fulton Mackay
Detective Chief Inspector Alan Craven	
	George Sewell
Detective Chief Inspector Tom Haggerty	
	Patrick Mower
Detective Sgt North	Roger Rowland
Commander Nicols	Richard Butler
Commander Fletcher	Frederick Jaeger
Strand	Paul Eddington

Executive Producers: Lloyd Shirley, George Taylor. Producers: Reginald Collins, Robert Love, Geoffrey Gilbert, Ted Childs

The investigations of an élite division of Scotland Yard.

Although this series is best remembered for the exploits of snappily-dressed detectives Craven and Haggerty, they were latecomers to *Special Branch*. For the first two seasons, the featured officers were Inspector Jordan and his superior, Supt Eden (later substituted by Supt Inman). Alongside Craven and Haggerty, Detective Sgt North and Commander Nicols were also added, though they were soon replaced by Commander Fletcher and a snooty civil servant named Strand. The thrust of *Special Branch* investigations was international crime and espionage. The team were assigned to high-pressure, undercover operations which involved plugging gaps in security, preventing murders and foiling attempts at sabotage. It was the first series to show a British copper in trendy clothing (Jordan) and is also notable for being the first programme made by Thames TV's offshoot, Euston Films, which took over production after the first two seasons had gone out on videotape.

SPEED, DORIS, MBE (1899–1994)

As snooty Annie Walker, landlady of the Rovers Return, Doris Speed elevated herself above other residents of **Coronation Street** for 23 years. Born into a showbiz family, Speed had worked part-time on stage, radio and early television (series like *Shadow Squad* and *Skyport*), before she became Annie at the age of 61. It was a role that *Street* creator Tony Warren had written specifically for her but she had to be persuaded to accept it and, in doing so, she took retirement from an office job at Guinness in Manchester (she was with the brewery for 41 years). Speed left the series in 1983, shortly after the tabloid press had revealed her true age to be 84, much to the surprise even of her bosses at Granada.

SPEIGHT, JOHNNY (1921–)

Controversial British comedy scriptwriter, the creator of *Till Death Us Do Part*'s legendary Alf Garnett in 1965. By putting bigoted statements and bad language in the mouth of his number-one character, Speight attracted the full wrath of Mary Whitehouse and assorted Establishment figures. Others, however, recognized that such frankness exposed prejudices in society and applauded the writer. But worse was to come for Speight when he penned the sitcom *Curry and Chips* for LWT in 1969. Starring Eric Sykes and a blacked up Spike Milligan, it was seen as a racist joke too far and did not survive longer than one season. Speight, a former milkman who also wrote for *The Arthur Haynes Show* and *Sykes*, as well as various radio comedies, introduced Alf (then known as Alf Ramsey) in a 1965 *Comedy Playhouse* presentation. *Till Death Us Do Part* began a year later, running, off and on, for nine years. The format was sold to the USA and screened as *All in the Family*, with Archie Bunker as the lead character. Speight has since resurrected Garnett on more than one occasion, including in *In Sickness and in Health* in 1985. Amongst his other offerings have been *Them* (a comedy about tramps, starring Cyril Cusack, in 1972), its female counterpart *The Lady is a Tramp* 12 years later (featuring Patricia Hayes and Pat Coombs as bag ladies), *Spooner's Patch* (with Ray Galton) in 1979 and *The Nineteenth Hole* (with Eric Sykes again) in 1989. Speight also contributed to Marty Feldman's 1974 comedy series, *Marty Back Together Again*.

SPELLING, AARON (1928–)

American TV executive, specializing in glossy, glitzy dramas. A former actor and writer (on series like *Wagon Train*), Spelling's early successes as a producer included *Burke's Law*. He then joined with fellow executive Leonard Goldberg to produce series like *Starsky and Hutch*, *The Love Boat*, *Charlie's Angels*, *Fantasy Island* and *Hart to Hart*. His next partner was Douglas S. Cramer, with whom he collaborated on popular series such as *Dynasty* (and its less successful spin-off *The Colbys*), *Hotel* and *Beverly Hills 90210*. With Cramer, he established Aaron Spelling Productions, later renamed Spelling Entertainment Inc.

SPENDER

UK (BBC) Police Drama. BBC 1 1991–3

Spender	Jimmy Nail
Stick	Sammy Johnson
Supt Yelland	Paul Greenwood
Detective Sgt Dan Boyd	Berwick Kaler
Frances	Denise Welch
Keith Moreland	Tony McAnaney
Laura	Dawn Winlow
Kate	Lynn Harrison
Detective Chief Supt Gillespie	Peter Guinness

Creators: Jimmy Nail, Ian La Frenais. Producers: Martin McKeand, Paul Raphael

A maverick Geordie cop is seconded back to his home city to work undercover.

Detective Sgt Spender, a plain-clothed cop with unorthodox methods, worked for the Metropolitan Police. However, his superiors were increasingly frustrated by his approach to the job and, when a partner was badly injured, they transferred Spender back to his home patch of Newcastle-upon-Tyne, after 15 years away.

Although it was only intended as a one-off assignment, Spender soon found himself permanently back on the Tyne, snooping around where the local cops – being too well known – could not tread. He was perfect for the job: his dishevelled looks and rough diamond appearance, with tousled hair, pierced ear and chiselled face, hardly marked him out as a policeman, and his thick Geordie accent firmly established him as a local.

Despite his years away, Spender could still count on a few useful contacts, most notably Stick, a convicted building society robber, whom he dragged into investigations and tapped for the word on the streets. Detective Sgt Dan Boyd, a ring-rusty desk clerk, was assigned as Spender's police liaison and they occasionally met up at the music shop owned by crippled rock guitarist Keith Moreland. Not being the shy type, Spender always found his way into the thick of the action, usually ending up on the wrong end of a bust up. But his individual approach generally brought results (after a set-back or two along the way), satisfying his no-nonsense boss, Supt Yelland (Detective Chief Supt Gillespie from the second series).

There were other sides to Spender's personality, too. Beneath his gritty, determined façade, he possessed a heart of gold. He remained on good terms with his ex-wife, Frances, who still lived in the city, and his two young daughters, Laura and Kate, brought out an even softer part of his nature. But Spender was committed to his job, and, even when Frances was killed in the third series and Spender was given permanent custody of his children, he found it hard to balance his responsibilities.

Spender was a series with character. Newcastle's distinctive accents and familiar streets and bridges offered an intriguing backdrop, and a driving rock soundtrack helped keep up momentum. Jimmy Nail not only starred in the programme, but he also co-created it with Ian La Frenais and provided scripts for a number of episodes.

SPENSER: FOR HIRE

US (John Wilder/Warner Brothers) Detective Drama. BBC 1 1989–93

Spenser	Robert Urich
Hawk	Avery Brooks
Susan Silverman	Barbara Stock
Assistant DA Rita Fiori	Carolyn McCormick
Lt Martin Quirk	Richard Jaeckel
Sgt Frank Belson	Ron McLarty

Executive Producer: John Wilder. Producers: Dick Gallegly, Robert Hamilton

A cultured private eye stalks the streets of Boston.

Spenser (first name not given) was a rarity amongst private detectives. This ex-cop was a man of principle who knew and enjoyed literature, his trademark being quotes from Wordsworth and other classic writers. He was also a former boxer, and a gourmet cook to boot. He cruised the streets of Boston in a vintage Mustang car, assisted in his work, by Hawk, a bald, Magnum-toting, black street-informer who was later given his own spin-off series (*A Man Called Hawk*). Guidance counsellor Susan Silverman was Spenser's girlfriend in early and later episodes, with Assistant DA Rita Fiori keeping our hero on his toes in the interim. Lt Quirk was the local police contact and Belson was his wisecracking colleague from the homicide department. The series was based on the books by Robert B. Parker.

SPITTING IMAGE

UK (Central) Comedy. ITV 1984–

Voices:
Chris Barrie
Enn Reitel
Steve Nallon
Jan Ravens
Harry Enfield
Pamela Stephenson
Jon Glover
Jessica Martin
Rory Bremner
Hugh Dennis
Kate Robbins
John Sessions

Creators: Michael Lambie-Martin, Peter Fluck, Roger Law. Producers: Jon Blair, John Lloyd, Geoffrey Perkins, David Tyler, Bill Dare, Giles Pilbrow

Cruel satire from latex puppets.

With respect for no-one, be they the royal family, Mother Teresa or even Margaret Thatcher, the *Spitting Image* team have been pulling the rug from under prominent personalities for over ten years. Using rubber puppets beautifully crafted by Peter Fluck and Roger Law, and some of the country's leading impressionists and comedians for voices, the series has slaughtered holy cows while poking fun at politicians, entertainers, sportsmen and other world figures. The wit has been topical and direct, if at times patchy, initially drawing controversy but later earning a degree of respect or at least resignation. Some celebrities have even declared themselves honoured to have their caricature captured in latex. Amongst the most memorable depictions have been Kenneth Baker as a slug, Norman Tebbit as a skinhead, the Pope as a swinging dude and Gerald Kaufman as Hannibal Lecter.

Developed by Fluck and Law from an idea by LWT graphics artist Michael Lambie-Martin, the series' early writers included the likes of Ian Hislop, Rob Grant and Doug Naylor. But, as well as humour, there has been pathos, too, particularly in some of the musical numbers – the reworking of the Police song 'Every Breath You Take' as 'Every Bomb You Make', for instance. At the other end of the scale, though, was 'The Chicken Song', a chart-topping 1986 spin-off that ridiculed the Benidorm brigade and their summer disco songs.

SPONSORSHIP

Although common in the USA in the 1950s, sponsorship is new to British television. In America, sponsors virtually owned the programmes, paying for production and the cost of the airtime, gaining editorial control and reaping the benefits of the exposure their products gained. The system went out of favour in the 1960s, when production expenses increased and sponsors were forced to share costs with other advertisers. A form of sponsorship has arrived in the UK since 1991 (having been banned previously), with newspapers attaching their names to game shows and other companies happy to be seen 'in association with' sports coverage or travel programmes. Unlike in the USA, the sponsor is allowed no editorial influence, nor can its products be prominently displayed in the programme. Indeed, so-called 'product placement' is prohibited in any programme, sponsored or not. News and current affairs programmes are debarred from taking sponsorship.

SPOONER, DENNIS (1932–86)

British writer who scripted parts of Tony Hancock's unsuccessful ITV series, *Hancock*, before finding his niche in the world of science fiction and adventure dramas. Spooner has contributed episodes to **Doctor Who**, **No Hiding Place**, **Fireball XL5**, **Stingray**, **Thunderbirds**, **The Avengers**, **The Baron**, **The Protectors**, **UFO**, **Doomwatch**, **Hammer House of Horror**, **Bergerac** and **The Professionals**. However, he has particularly endeared himself to cult TV fans by creating or co-creating **Man in a Suitcase**, **The Champions**, **Department S** and **Randall and Hopkirk (Deceased)**.

SPOONER'S PATCH

UK (ATV) Situation Comedy. ITV 1979–82

Inspector Spooner	Ronald Fraser
	Donald Churchill
DC Bulsover	Peter Cleall
PC Killick	John Lyons
PC Goatman	Norman Rossington

Kelly ....Dermot Kelly
Mrs Cantaford...........................Patricia Hayes
Jimmy the Con ....Harry Fowler

Creators/Writers: Johnny Speight, Ray Galton.
Producer: William G. Stewart

The day-to-day events in a hopelessly inept police station.

Inspector Spooner, head of the small, suburban Woodley police station, craved a quiet, comfortable life. Sadly, rather than heading out onto the golf course each day, he found himself called down from his upstairs flat to clear up the mess his corrupt and incompetent juniors had created. DC Bulsover, for instance, was one officer to keep in check, a CID officer who thought he was Starsky or Hutch, and drove around in a flashy red and white motor. There were also the bigoted PC Goatman and the sarcastic PC Killick to watch over, although some of Spooner's biggest problems came from the quick-tempered traffic warden, Mrs Cantaford. To add to the confusion, Kelly, an Irish grass, plagued the station with his presence, before he was replaced by another informer, Jimmy the Con.

No less than three actors played the title role in this relatively short-lived series. Ian Bannen starred in the pilot episode, followed in the series proper by Ronald Fraser and then Donald Churchill. Although it combined the writing talents of Johnny Speight (*Till Death Us Do Part*) and Ray Galton (*Hancock's Half Hour* and *Steptoe and Son*), the series proved a disappointment to most viewers.

SPORTS REVIEW OF THE YEAR

UK (BBC) Sport. BBC 1 1954–

Annual sports showcase with awards for the best achievers.

Sports Review of the Year was launched way back in 1954 and has become one of the BBC's major annual events. Transmitted live early in December, with a tense, nervous atmosphere, it has focused on the sporting year just passed, replaying the key action and interviewing the winners and losers. In a light-hearted diversion, good 'sports' like Frank Bruno have tried their hands at silly stunts, such as fairground shooting stalls, taking hockey penalties, performing snooker tricks, changing the tyres on a Formula One racing car and pitting their wits against electronic games. The *Sports Personality of the Year* award has provided the climax to the evening (a full list of winners is given below), with other presentations made to *Overseas Personality of the Year* and the best team. Cool-headed hosts Desmond Lynam and Steve Ryder have held the show

together in recent years, succeeding the likes of Peter Dimmock, David Coleman, Harry Carpenter and Frank Bough.

Sports Personality of the Year winners:

1954 Chris Chataway	1974 Brendan Foster
1955 Gordon Pirie	1975 David Steele
1956 Jim Laker	1976 John Curry
1957 Dai Rees	1977 Virginia Wade
1958 Ian Black	1978 Steve Ovett
1959 John Surtees	1979 Sebastian Coe
1960 David Broome	1980 Robin Cousins
1961 Stirling Moss	1981 Ian Botham
1962 Anita	1982 Daley Thompson
Lonsbrough	1983 Steve Cram
1963 Dorothy Hyman	1984 Torvill and Dean
1964 Mary Rand	1985 Barry McGuigan
1965 Tommy Simpson	1986 Nigel Mansell
1966 Bobby Moore	1987 Fatima
1967 Henry Cooper	Whitbread
1968 David Hemery	1988 Steve Davis
1969 Ann Jones	1989 Nick Faldo
1970 Henry Cooper	1990 Paul Gascoigne
1971 HRH The	1991 Liz McColgan
Princess Anne	1992 Nigel Mansell
1972 Mary Peters	1993 Linford Christie
1973 Jackie Stewart	1994 Damon Hill

SPORTSVIEW

UK (BBC) Sport. BBC 1954–68

Presenters: Peter Dimmock, Brian Johnston, Frank Bough

Editors: Paul Fox, Ronnie Noble, Cliff Morgan, Alan Hart.

Early midweek sports round-up.

Replaced after 14 years on air by *Sportsnight with Coleman* in 1968, *Sportsview* was the BBC's first major sports showcase, predating *Grandstand* by four years. Peter Dimmock was the programme's first host, introducing such sporting milestones as Roger Bannister's four-minute mile on 6 May 1954. *Sportsview* was also adventurous technically. It was the first BBC programme to use a teleprompter and amongst its other innovations was the placing of cameras inside racing cars. A younger viewers' version, *Junior Sportsview*, with hosts including Peter Dimmock, Billy Wright and Kenneth Wolstenholme ran between 1956 and 1962, and the annual *Sports Review of the Year* was another by-product.

SPOT THE TUNE

UK (Granada) Quiz. ITV 1956–62

Presenters: Ken Platt, Ted Ray, Jackie Rae, Pete Murray

Producers: Wilfred Fielding, Johnny Hamp

Musical quiz game.

In this self-explanatory quiz, contestants were asked to spot the tune given only a few bars to work on. There was a jackpot (increasing by £100 a week), to be won by those with an ear for music. Singer Marion Ryan (mother of 1960s pop stars Paul and Barry Ryan) helped pose the questions, accompanied by the Peter Knight Orchestra.

The format was revived in the 1970s as *Name That Tune*, a segment of the variety show *Wednesday at Eight* and subsequently a programme in its own right. Tom O'Connor and, later, Lionel Blair hosted proceedings, Maggie Moone was the resident songstress and the Alan Braden band struck up the tunes.

UK (Thames) Situation Comedy. ITV 1973–7

Tommy Butler	Jimmy Jewel
Charlie Harris	Charlie Hawkins
Vera Reid	June Barry
Brian Reid	Larry Martyn
Betty Harris	Jo Warne

Creators/Writers: Vince Powell, Harry Driver.
Producers: Ronnie Baxter, Mike Vardy,
Anthony Parker

A lonely old man finds company with a 12-year-old lad.

It seemed life was over for 70-year-old former railway worker Tommy Butler when his home was demolished and he was forced to live with his daughter and son-in-law, Vera and Brian Reid, in a high-rise flat. It was clear that he wasn't really wanted in their home and, to be fair, the cantankerous old moaner made little effort to fit in. His only friend was Nelson, a stuffed green parrot. However, Tommy found a new soul mate in the form of Charlie Harris, a cheeky, somewhat wayward young Cockney lad who was neglected by his hard-up, divorced mother, Betty. Tommy and Charlie became firm friends and shared many an outing. Their mutual interest in football and railways bound them together and Charlie loved Tommy's far-fetched tales of the past.

This gentle comedy, with moments of sentimentality, followed on from a one-off 1972 play in which Tommy's daughter and son-in-law were Betty and Joe Dickinson (played by Gaye Brown and Larry Martyn).

UK (ATV) Spy Drama. ITV 1972

Charlotte 'Lottie' Dean	Patricia Cutts
Clive Hawksworth	Anthony Ainley
Wallis Ackroyd	Veronica Carlson
Albert Mason	Roger Lloyd Pack

Creator: Richard Harris. Producer: Dennis Vance

International intrigue with three agents of a secret governmental unit.

The 'Web' of this programme's title was a top-secret, undercover, anti-espionage organization, and 'Spyder' referred to any of its agents. There were three prominent activists: Lottie Dean, Clive Hawksworth and Wallis Ackroyd. Individually or collectively, they investigated bizarre and complicated cases of infiltration and international deception. Albert Mason, Lottie's butler was also seen. This light-hearted thriller, filled with red herrings, was created by Richard Harris and mostly penned by comedy writer Roy Clarke (later responsible for *Last of the Summer Wine*, *Open All Hours*, etc.).

UK (ATV) Situation Comedy. ITV 1975–7

Mr Fletcher	Bernard Hepton
Rex	Ken Jones
Susan	Patsy Rowlands
Harry	Alan David
Burke	Ellis Jones
Carol	Karin MacCarthy

Creator: Eric Chappell. Producer: Shaun O'Riordan

Petty squabbles with the staff of a TV rental company.

Beginning as a one-off play in 1974, this comedy focused on life in the offices of International Rentals, a television hire firm. Head of the accounts staff was Mr Fletcher and bickering beneath him were his hapless minions Rex, Susan, Harry, Burke and Carol (played by Susan Tracy in the pilot). Joining creator Eric Chappell in scripting the series were writers like Kenneth Cope (of *Randall and Hopkirk* fame) and *Brookside*'s Phil Redmond. Chappell revamped the idea for the 1991 sitcom, *Fiddlers Three*, which starred Peter Davison and Paula Wilcox.

Northern actress, most familiar as the redoubtable Nora Batty in *Last of the Summer Wine*, a role she has played for some 20 years. However, Staff has also been seen in both *Coronation Street* (as corner shop proprietress Vera Hopkins) and *Crossroads* (as Doris Luke), as well as a third soap, *Emmerdale Farm* (as Winnie Purvis). She was Mrs Blewett, one of Arkwright's customers, in *Open All Hours* and later played interfering grandmother Molly Bickerstaff in the comedy *No Frills*. Her other credits have included *Hadleigh*, *Sez Les* and *The Benny Hill Show*.

STANWYCK, BARBARA (RUBY STEVENS; 1907–90)

After a long and successful career in Hollywood, spanning nearly 40 years, Barbara Stanwyck at last ensured herself television posterity in 1965 when she was cast as Victoria Barkley, the matriarch of the Barkley family, in the western **The Big Valley**. Her earlier excursions into TV had comprised guest spots in series like **The Untouchables**, **Rawhide** and **Wagon Train**, in addition to her own short-lived anthology series, **The Barbara Stanwyck Show**. The Big Valley ran in the USA until 1969 and, after making a few TV movies, Stanwyck officially retired from the business in 1973. She was tempted back to the small screen on two occasions, however. In 1983 she played Mary Carson in **The Thorn Birds** and, in 1985, was Constance Colby in **The Colbys**. Her second husband was actor Robert Taylor.

STAR MAIDENS

UK/W Germany (Portman) Science Fiction.
ITV 1976

Fulvia ....Judy Geeson
The President ....Dawn Addams
Adam ....Pierre Brice
Shem ....Gareth Thomas
Octavia ....Christine Kruger
Rudi ....Christian Quadflieg
Liz ....Lisa Harrow
Professor Evans..Derek Farr

Creators: Graf Von Hardenberg, Graefin Von Hardenberg. Producer: James Gatward

Two male refugees from a female-dominated planet escape to Earth.

Adam and Shem were male slaves on Mendusa, a planet ruled exclusively by women. There, men were no more than the subservient race, confined to a life of drudgery while their women folk lived in luxury. Making a break for it, the two men stole a spaceship and fled to Earth, pursued by Adam's mistress, Supreme Councillor Fulvia, and her assistant, Octavia. Their arrival was monitored by Earth scientist Professor Evans, whose young colleagues, Rudi and Liz, were then taken hostage and whisked off into space when Fulvia failed to corner her escapees. With two Mendusans on Earth and two humans on Mendusa, the series followed the battle against the 'Star Maidens' on both worlds.

Thirteen episodes of Star Maidens were produced as a joint venture between British and West German companies, although the series (played mainly for laughs) was never successful in the UK, enjoying only sporadic screenings around the ITV network. A planned second series was quickly shelved.

STAR TREK

US (Norway/Paramount) Science Fiction.
BBC 1 1969–71

Captain James T. Kirk ....William Shatner
Mr Spock...Leonard Nimoy
Dr Leonard McCoy ....DeForest Kelley
Mr Sulu ....George Takei
Lt Uhura ....Nichelle Nichols
Engineer Montgomery Scott ....James Doohan
Nurse Christine Chapel ....Majel Barrett
Ensign Pavel Chekov ....Walter Koenig
Yeoman Janice Rand ....Grace Lee Whitney

Creator/Executive Producer: Gene Roddenberry. Producers: Gene L. Coon, John Meredyth Lucas, Fred Freiberger

The voyages of the starship _Enterprise_.

In the 23rd century, Earth had become a member of the United Federation of Planets, a galactic union that ran a joint defence organization, Starfleet. Its starships plied the cosmos, hoping to bring peace to other civilizations, or to at least discover more about alien life forms. The USS Enterprise was one of those ships and Star Trek followed its adventures on a five-year mission to 'boldly go when no man has gone before'.

The Enterprise was a massive exploration-cum-messenger craft which cruised at 'warp' speeds, all of which were faster than light. Protected by high-tech deflector shields and phasers, it whisked its crew of 428 from galaxy to galaxy and from life-threatening adventure to life-threatening adventure. The spaceship never landed: the crew were simply 'beamed down' onto the surface of a planet, to tackle new adversaries (with the minimum of special effects).

Commander of the ship was 34-year-old Captain James Tiberius Kirk, an American from Iowa. His Chief Navigator was the Japanese Mr Sulu, assisted by the Russian Chekov (added in the second season to provide international balance). Lt Uhura, the communications officer, was a sultry African, and Chief Engineer was Montgomery 'Scotty' Scott. However, the key members of Kirk's team were always his first officer, Mr Spock, and the ship's doctor, 'Bones' McCoy. McCoy, an expert in space psychology from Georgia, USA, always considered himself to be a simple 'country' doctor. He was an emotional chap, quite unlike his perennial sparring partner, Spock, who, being half-Vulcan, was devoid of human instincts. Green-blooded and pointy-eared, Spock was only interested in what was logical, his mind working through the facts like a computer. Kirk proved to be a mixture of the two, an often impetuous man with strong powers of leadership, a (sometimes) athletic frame and a firm belief in humanity as a force for overcoming evil. Consequently, *Star Trek* stories (beginning and ending with Kirk's entry into the Captain's Log) usually had a moral theme, with the crew facing up to alien civilizations which echoed the cruelest regimes our own world has seen, such as the ancient Romans and the Nazis. Social issues of the day, such as civil rights and the Vietnamese war, were also reflected. The *Enterprise* had two main enemies, the militaristic Romulans and the greasy, barbarous Klingons, although all kinds of weird and wonderful foes were likely to turn up. *Star Trek* was devised by Gene Roddenberry, previously scriptwriter on **Have Gun, Will Travel**, and he perceived the programme as a sort of **Wagon Train** in space. It was not an instant hit, in fact it flopped in the USA. In the UK, it was eventually picked up by the BBC and only screened after the entire run had ended in America. However, reruns have ensured that the programme has gained a cult following, manifested in a legion of international fans known as 'Trekkies', for whom part of the attraction are the show's many clichés and sayings. A UK chart-topper from 1987, 'Star Trekkin'' by a group called The Firm, parodied its classic lines like 'Klingons on the starboard bow', 'It's life Jim, but not as we know it' and 'It's worse than that, he's dead Jim'.

Star Trek's pilot episode, *The Cage*, starred Jeffrey Hunter as Christopher Pike, the first captain of the *Enterprise*, but it has been rarely seen, with some of its footage reworked into a later episode called *The Menagerie*. Only Leonard Nimoy and Majel Barrett from the main cast appeared in the pilot. A series of seven feature-length movies was made years after filming of the TV show finished in 1969, and a cartoon version was also issued. **Star Trek: The Next Generation** (see below) picked up the story again in 1989 and another spin-off, *Deep Space Nine*, has also now been produced.

STAR TREK: THE NEXT GENERATION

US (Paramount) Science Fiction. BBC 2 1990–

Captain Jean-Luc Picard	Patrick Stewart
Commander William Riker	Jonathan Frakes
Lt Geordi La Forge	LeVar Burton
Lt Worf	Michael Dorn
Lt Tasha Yar	Denise Crosby
Dr Beverly Crusher	Gates McFadden
Counsellor Deanna Troi	Marina Sirtis
Lt Commander Data	Brent Spiner
Wesley Crusher	Wil Wheaton
Dr Katherine Pulaski	Diana Muldaur
Guinan	Whoopi Goldberg
Ensign Ro Laren	Michelle Forbes
Transporter Chief Miles O'Brien	Colm Meaney

Executive Producer: Gene Roddenberry

The voyages of the starship *Enterprise*, resurrected.

In this series, which began 18 years after production of the original **Star Trek** ceased, time had moved on to the 24th century, 78 years after Kirk and Co.'s exploits. This *Enterprise* was new: a vessel eight times as spacious as the original ship, with over 2000 crew members (including children), and much advanced technology.

The ship's commander was the fatherly Jean-Luc Picard, not as emotional or impetuous as his predecessor, Kirk, and less inclined to soil his hands. He delegated off-ship missions to his 'Number 1', the good-looking, bearded Riker. Also on the bridge was Lt Geordi La Forge, a blind black helmsman who could see through a pair of scientific sunglasses. He later became Chief Engineer. Deanna Troi, Riker's ex, was a half-Betazoid who worked as an advisor, warning of impending danger by reading people's emotions. Data, a pale-faced encyclopedic android who longed to be human, and Lt Tasha Yar, the security chief who was killed by an alien, also appeared. Lt Worf was a Klingon, from the race that was once Starfleet's enemy, and the ship's medical officer was Dr Beverly Crusher, later temporarily replaced by Dr Kate Pulaski. Crusher's kid-genius son, Wesley, was also on board, and comedienne Whoopi Goldberg dropped in from time to time, playing the part of Guinan, bartender in the ship's Ten Forward lounge.

Storylines, as in the original series, generally offered a moral – Gene Roddenberry was back in charge – and the show was warmly received by 'Trekkies'. But *Star Trek: The Next Generation* was slow to come to the UK. It first turned up in video shops, before being bought by Sky. BBC 2 secured the rights for terrestrial transmission, but episodes were screened some time after premiering on satellite.

STARR, FREDDIE (1944–)

Unpredictable British comedian and impressionist with a cheeky grin, coming to the fore on **Opportunity Knocks!** and establishing himself on **Who Do You Do?** Starr's career has experienced several ups and downs, the ups including several series of his own, such as *The Freddie Starr Experience* and *The Freddie Starr Showcase* (a talent show). In 1980 he shared the limelight with Russ Abbot in *Variety Madhouse*, which, when Starr left, was renamed *Russ Abbot's Madhouse*. Starr has also been a popular variety show and panel game guest.

STARS AND GARTERS

UK (Associated-Rediffusion) Variety.
ITV 1963–6

Hosts: Ray Martine, Jill Browne, Willie Rushton

Producers: Daphne Shadwell, John P. Hamilton, Rollo Gamble, Elkan Allan

Traditional pub entertainment presented from a fake hostelry.

A cross between the earlier *Café Continental* and the later *Wheeltappers' and Shunters' Social Club*, Stars and Garters was a variety show dressed up as pub entertainment. Host Ray Martine and his pet mynah bird invited viewers to share in the pubby atmosphere and watch top acts, supported by resident performers like Kathy Kirby, Tommy Bruce, Clinton Ford, Kim Cordell, Vince Hill, Debbie Lee, Al Saxon, Queenie Watts and Julie Rayne. The Alan Braden and Peter Knight orchestras provided musical accompaniment. Martine was later replaced as host by *Emergency – Ward 10* star Jill Browne, who compèred events with Willie Rushton. The title became *The New Stars and Garters* at the same time.

STARS IN THEIR EYES

UK (Granada) Entertainment. ITV 1990–

Presenters: Leslie Crowther, Matthew Kelly

Executive Producer: Dianne Nelmes. Producer: Jane Macnaught

Viewers impersonate their favourite singing stars.

A cross between a talent show and a vehicle for impressionists, *Stars in their Eyes* has offered members of the public the chance to emulate their favourite musical performers. Togged up in appropriate gear by the wardrobe department and given the looks of their idols by make up, the contestants have then performed with the Ray Monk Orchestra to prove that they can sound like the real thing, too. A grand final (usually live) has been held at the end of each series. Leslie Crowther was the original host but, incapacitated by his car accident, his place as compère has since been taken by Matthew Kelly.

STARS ON SUNDAY

UK (Yorkshire) Religion.
ITV 1969–79

Presenter/Executive Producer: Jess Yates

Cosy, Sunday evening celebrity showcase with a religious slant.

Stars on Sunday, ITV's answer to *Songs of Praise*, specialized in attracting top showbusiness names into the studio to sing hymns or give Biblical readings. Masterminded and presented by Jess 'The Bishop' Yates (father of Paula), its mixture of big stars and spiritual comforts made it extremely popular, and viewers' requests flooded in. Amongst the international celebrities to contribute were Bing Crosby, Princess Grace of Monaco, Johnny Mathis, Raymond Burr and Howard Keel, while heading the home-grown talent were The Beverley Sisters, James Mason, Harry Secombe, Gracie Fields, John Gielgud, John Mills and Anna Neagle. The Archbishops of Canterbury and York also made appearances, as did Prime Minister Edward Heath. The resident singing troupe were The Poole Family, fronted by little Glyn Poole, and, as well as traditional hymns, moral modern pieces were also featured.

In 1974 the programme was rocked by the 'actress and the bishop' scandal, when Yates's relationship with Anita Kay, a showgirl over 30 years his junior, was splashed over the tabloids. Yates was forced to leave the series and his career never recovered. His immediate, short-term replacement as host was Anthony Valentine but numerous personalities picked up the reins for the show's last five years on air. These included Moira Anderson, Wilfred Pickles, Robert Dougall, Cliff Michelmore and Gordon Jackson.

STARSKY AND HUTCH

US (Spelling-Goldberg) Police Drama.
BBC 1 1976–81

Detective Dave Starsky ....Paul Michael Glaser
Detective Ken ('Hutch') Hutchinson ....David Soul
Captain Harold Dobey ....Bernie Hamilton
Huggy Bear ....Antonio Fargas

Creator: William Blinn. Executive Producers: Aaron Spelling, Leonard Goldberg. Producer: Joseph T. Naar

Two buddy-buddy undercover cops patrol the seedier areas of LA.

Dave Starsky and Ken 'Hutch' Hutchinson were cops. More than that they were pals and it showed in their work. Hutch was blond, Starsky was dark-haired, and their lifestyles contrasted just as sharply. Starsky enjoyed junkfood and streetlife, Hutch preferred health foods and the quiet life. But the main thing was that they knew they could depend on each other and this ran right to the heart of their working relationship.

Stationed in one of LA's seamiest districts, the casually-dressed duo concentrated only on the most serious crimes, hustling drug pushers, pimps and other society dregs, and apprehending muggers, rapists and racketeers. Screaming around the streets in Starsky's souped up, red Ford Torino with a loud white strip along its side, they were hardly inconspicuous for undercover policemen. What's more, if they could enter a car through a window rather than the door, then they would, probably leaping onto the bonnet first. Yet they still got results, usually bending the rules along the way but ultimately keeping their fiery boss, Captain Dobey (played by Richard Ward in the pilot), happy. Huggy Bear was their hip street contact.

The show became less aggressive over the years, in response to anti-violence campaigns in the States, but the programme always enjoyed greater success in Britain, where the two principals were big stars. Paul Michael Glaser's chunky cardigans became fashion items and David Soul was able to reprise his recording career, notching up a string of middle of the road hits, including a couple of number ones, 'Don't Give Up On Us' and 'Silver Lady'.

STAY LUCKY

UK (Yorkshire) Drama. ITV 1989–93

Thomas Gynn	Dennis Waterman
Sally Hardcastle	Jan Francis
Kevin	Chris Jury
Lively	Niall Toibin
Pippa	Emma Wray
Samantha Mansfield	Susan George
Franklyn Bysouth	Ian McNeice
Isabel	Rula Lenska
Jo	Leslie Ash

Creator: Geoff McQueen. Executive Producer: Vernon Lawrence. Producers: David Reynolds, Andrew Benson, Matthew Bird

A Cockney wide boy meanders between jobs, follows his heart and finds unlikely girlfriends.

On the run from the London underworld, Thomas Gynn met up with recently widowed, northern businesswoman Sally Hardcastle at an A1 service station and, more by chance than design, the two reluctantly ended up sharing a houseboat. At one point, Thomas – ducking and diving – drove minicabs in Newcastle, while the headstrong Sally ran her narrowboat charter company in Yorkshire. By the third season, Thomas had spent time behind bars and Sally had long left the scene. Thomas then saved the life of Samantha Mansfield, administrator of the Yorkshire Industrial Museum, who gave him a job and more besides, before he enjoyed a fling in Eastern Europe with Isabel, a British trade official in Hungary. Finally, Jo, a dancer, became the new girl his life. Pippa and Lively, two old friends, were usually on the scene and Franklyn Bysouth was Thomas's one-time cellmate. Now a dodgy businessman, he took Thomas under his wing and offered him work.

STEADMAN, ALISON (1946–)

British actress, the wife of playwright Mike Leigh in some of whose works (*Nuts In May* and *Abigail's Party*) she has also been seen. Steadman's

TV career opened in the early 1970s. She was WPC Bayliss in *Z Cars* and took the part of Bernadette Clarkson in *The Wackers*. In the 1980s she played Mrs Marlow and Lili in *The Singing Detective* and, in the 1990s, she was Edda Goering in *Selling Hitler*. Steadman was also cast as Lauren Patterson in the comedy *Gone to the Dogs* and continued to appear in its 'sequel', *Gone to Seed*, although the characters were different (she now played Hilda Plant). All her TV series work has been underpinned by many roles in single dramas like *Through the Night*, *P'tang Yang Kipperbang*, *The Muscle Market* and *The Caucasian Chalk Circle*. In 1994 she starred opposite Robert Lindsay in the two-part comedy-drama *The Wimbledon Poisoner*.

STEPHENSON, PAMELA (1951–)

Actress and comedienne born in New Zealand, a member of the *Not The Nine O'Clock News* team from 1979. Her other credits have included appearances in *Within These Walls*, *Space: 1999*, *Target*, *The New Avengers*, *The Professionals*, *Hazell* (alongside her first husband, Nicholas Ball), *Funny Man*, *Lost Empires*, *Move Over Darling* and the American series *Saturday Night Live*. She has also provided voices for *Spitting Image*. Her second husband is comedian Billy Connolly.

STEPTOE AND SON

UK (BBC) Situation Comedy.
BBC 1 1962–5; 1970–4

Albert Steptoe	Wilfrid Brambell
Harold Steptoe	Harry H. Corbett

Creators/Writers: Ray Galton, Alan Simpson. Producers: Duncan Wood, John Howard Davies, David Croft, Graeme Muir, Douglas Argent

A pretentious bachelor can't escape his grubby, old father and the rag and bone business they share.

There are few shows in the history of television which have reaped such wide appreciation as *Steptoe and Son*, Ray Galton and Alan Simpson's saga of a socially-aspirant son and the dirty old dad who kept him anchored to the mire of a scrapyard. Harold Steptoe, in his late 30s, dreamed of a life away from the squalid, junk-filled house he shared with his father at 24 Old Drum Lane, Shepherd's Bush. He longed to progress his cultural interests and to embark on some romantic journey, but was always hauled back to sub-working-class grime by his disgusting, emaciated old man. His plans for soirées in gentrified circles usually collapsed into nights at The Skinner's Arms or argumentative evenings in front of the box, thanks to the efforts of his seedy father. Albert Steptoe was vulgarity personified, a man who washed his socks only when taking a bath. He cooked and generally ran the house, while Harold did the rounds with Hercules (later Delilah) the carthorse, but Albert's idea of culinary finesse was edging a pie with his false teeth. Albert's greatest skill lay in scuppering his son's dreams of a better life. Whenever Harold made a dash for freedom, the clinging, devious old man always stood in the way, using emotional blackmail to deny his son independence.

The gloriously coarse series – which was as much a tragedy as it was a comedy – ran in two bites, in the early 1960s (it first aired in 1962 as a *Comedy Playhouse* episode called *The Offer*) and then sporadically in the early 1970s (the first new season was billed as *The Return of Steptoe and Son*). A radio series was also produced and the show spawned a US cover version, *Sanford and Son,* as well as two far less successful feature films, *Steptoe and Son* and *Steptoe and Son Ride Again.*

Amongst the classic episodes were 'A Star is Born' (in which Harold set his sights on the world of amateur dramatics, only to be upstaged by his dad), 'Divided We Stand' (the two fell out so badly that they physically split the house in two), 'And So To Bed' (Harold purchased a trendy water bed, with predictable consequences) and 'The Desperate Hours' (the Steptoes are held hostage in their own home by an escaped convict played by Leonard Rossiter).

STEVENS, CRAIG (GAIL SHEKLES; 1918–)

American actor popular at the turn of the 1960s, thanks to his portrayal of suave detective Peter Gunn and his role as photo journalist Mike Strait in *Man of the World*. A third series, *Mr Broadway*, proved less successful. In later years, he played David McCallum's boss, Walter Carlson, in *The Invisible Man*, Asher Berg in *Rich Man, Poor Man* and, for a while, Craig Stewart in *Dallas*.

STEWART, ALASTAIR (1952–)

British journalist, presenter and newscaster. Stewart's initial TV work was for Southern Television in the late 1970s, before he joined ITN as its industrial correspondent in 1980. He was later Washington correspondent and anchor on various news bulletins, including *News at Ten*, *News at 5.40* and *Channel 4 News*. He also worked on ITN specials, like election coverages, but left to launch *London Tonight*, Carlton TV's new regional news programme in 1993. Later he hosted Radio Five Live's Sunday morning political programme and since 1994 has presented *The Sunday Programme* for GMTV.

STEWART, WILLIAM G. (1935–)

British comedy producer/director and latterly quiz show host. Stewart made his name in the late 1960s and early 1970s through comedies like *Mrs Thursday* (as director), *Father, Dear, Father, Bless This House, My Good Woman, And Mother Makes Five, Down the Gate, The Many Wives of Patrick, Paradise Island, My Name is Harry Worth, Spooner's Patch* and *The Rag Trade*. In the 1980s he worked on the short-lived Alf Garnett revival *Till Death . . .* and also produced the Channel 4 comedies *The Lady is a Tramp, The Nineteenth Hole* and *The Bright Side*, as well as the ITV game show *The Price is Right*. Since 1987; he has both produced and presented (very dryly) the daily quiz show *Fifteen to One* for Regent Television, Channel 4.

STICK MIKE

The hand-held microphone much used by news reporters and variety show compères.

STILGOE, RICHARD (1943–)

British humorist, musician and presenter. Cambridge Footlights graduate Stilgoe was a familiar face in the 1970s, writing topical ditties for *That's Life* and *Nationwide*. He was the front man on the sketch series *A Kick Up the Eighties* and appeared in *And Now the Good News*. Stilgoe has also been involved in the theatre. Amongst his successes have been the musicals *Starlight Express* and *Phantom of the Opera*, for which he penned lyrics.

STINGRAY

UK (AP Films/ATV/ITC) Children's Science Fiction. ITV 1964–5

Voices:
Captain Troy Tempest	Don Mason
George 'Phones' Sheridan	Robert Easton
Atlanta Shore	Lois Maxwell
Commander Sam Shore	Ray Barrett
Titan	Ray Barrett
Sub Lt Fisher	Ray Barrett
X20	Robert Easton

Creators: Gerry Anderson, Sylvia Anderson.
Producer: Gerry Anderson

The crew of a supersub save the world.

Stingray was the number-one craft of WASP, the World Aquanaut Security Patrol, which operated out of the city of Marineville, in the year 2000. With peace now established on land, the Earth's population had begun to harvest the minerals and other riches of the sea, which is where they encountered new enemies. WASP was the Earth's response to the dangers of the ocean.

Head of WASP was Commander Shore, a man crippled in a sea battle and now confined to a hoverchair. His assistant was Sub Lt Fisher, and Shore's daughter, Atlanta, also lived and worked in Marineville. Most of the action centred on the daring crew of Stingray itself, and in particular its fearless commander, Captain Troy Tempest. Voted 'Aquanaut of the Year', Tempest was the hero of the series, although he did have a juvenile tendency to sulk. His patrol partners were the amiable Phones (real name George Sheridan), who operated the craft's hydrophone sonar system, and Marina, a beautiful mute girl from the shell-like, undersea world of Pacifica, where she grew up as the daughter of Emperor Aphony. Tempest had saved her life and now she was in love with him. Back at Marineville, Marina owned a pet seal, Oink, and vied with Atlanta for Troy's attentions.

The arch-enemy of WASP was Titan, ruler of Titanica, who was assisted by his inept land-based agent, X20. Titan was also the power behind the evil Aquaphibians who menaced the ocean in mechanical Terror Fish, firing missiles from the large, gaping fish mouths. Stingray, a high-tech, blue and yellow supersub (with a number 3 on its tailfins), fired back Sting Missiles. Atomic-powered, the supersub could also leap from the waves like a salmon and dive deeper and travel faster than any other submarine.

Stingray was Gerry Anderson's third venture into Supermarionation. It was also the first British TV programme to be filmed in colour, even though it could only be shown in black and white on its initial run in the UK. Tension, for viewers, began to mount from Commander Shore's opening words at the start of each episode: 'Stand by for action. Anything can happen in the next half-hour!', but the closing theme song, 'Aquamarina', sung by Garry Miller, provided a soothing finish.

STOCK, NIGEL (1919–86)

One-time child performer who grew into one of Britain's most prolific character actors. His film career began in the 1930s and he was also an early arrival on television. In 1947, he appeared in the Borstal play *Boys In Brown* and the farce *The Happiest Days of your Life*, and he continued to pop up in dramas for the next 30-odd years. In the 1960s, he guested on **The Troubleshooters** and **The Prisoner** and, in 1965, took on the mantle of Dr Watson for the BBC's **Sherlock Holmes** (alongside Douglas Wilmer), a role he reprised three years later in *The Cases of Sherlock Holmes* (with Peter Cushing). Soon after, he joined **The Doctors** and then graduated to the title role of Dr Thomas Owen in *Owen, MD*. In the 1970, he

was Hoof Commissaris Samson in **Van Der Valk** and appeared in series like **Colditz** and **Tinker, Tailor, Soldier, Spy**. In 1981 he was cast as Wally James in **Triangle**. Other appearances included parts in *And No Birds Sing*, *Churchill's People*, *A Tale of Two Cities*, **Yes Minister** and *The Pickwick Papers*.

STOPPARD, MIRIAM (1937–)

British TV pop doctor who came to the fore in the 1970s as host and expert on YTV's science series **Don't Ask Me**, *Don't Just Sit There* and **Where There's Life**. Other credits have included *The Health Show* and *People Today*.

STOPPARD, TOM, CBE (THOMAS STRAUSLER; 1937–)

Czech-born British playwright, a former freelance journalist who has mostly contributed to stage, radio and films, specializing in complex and intellectual productions. His *Professional Foul* (a 1977 *Play of the Week*) was an award-winner. Amongst his other television offerings have been *Every Good Boy Deserves Favour* (1979) and an adaptation of *Three Men in a Boat* (1975).

STORYBOARD

UK (Thames) Drama Anthology. ITV 1983–9

Intermittent series of drama pilots.

Much in the style of **Comedy Playhouse**, *Storyboard* was Thames TV's experimental drama anthology, giving airtime to assorted pilot episodes in the hope that some would turn into fully-fledged series. Some, indeed, did. These were **The Bill** (derived from the 1983 *Storyboard* episode entitled *Woodentop*), **Lytton's Diary**, **Mr Palfrey of Westminster** (from a pilot called *The Traitor*), **King and Castle** and *Ladies in Charge*.

STORYTELLER, THE

UK (TVS/Jim Henson) Children's Entertainment. Channel 4 1988

The Storyteller ....John Hurt

Classic European folk tales brought to life with imaginative and colourful special effects.

Using all the invention of Jim Henson's Creature Shop, *The Storyteller* was TVS's award-winning rendition of the great European fairy tales. The Hobbit-like Storyteller related each tale in dramatic fashion at the side of his hearth, with his easily-startled dog at his feet. Skilful animation by the Muppet team and complex special effects ensured the series captured the imagination.

STRACHAN, MICHAELA (1966–)

Popular British children's presenter, seen first on TV-am hosting *Wide Awake Club*. Her other kids' series have included *Owl TV, But Can You Do It On TV?* and *The Really Wild Show*, and she was also seen with Pete Waterman in the late-night music show *The Hit Man and Her*.

STRANGE REPORT, THE

UK (Arena/ITC) Detective Drama. ITV 1968–9

Adam Strange...................................Anthony Quayle
Hamlyn Gynt ....Kaz Garas
Evelyn McLean ....Anneke Wills
Chief Supt Cavanagh.................................Gerald Sim
Professor Marks...............................Charles Lloyd Pack

Creator/Executive Producer: Norman Felton.
Producer: Robert Berger

The adventures of a retired criminologist and his young assistants.

Adam Strange was a renowned expert on the criminal mind, a former Home Office criminologist. Although retired, he was called back into action whenever the authorities were baffled by a case, or needed help in sensitive areas. The investigations were complex and the crimes intricate, but Strange always had the answers, combining his vast experience with the latest techniques in a forensic laboratory at his Paddington flat. Assisted by a young American museum researcher, Ham Gynt, and a model and artist neighbour, Evelyn McLean, Strange, rather unusually, raced to the scenes of crime in an unlicensed black taxicab. Each episode was given a 'report' number: 'Report 4407: HEART – No Choice for the Donor', for instance, concerned an investigation into plans to use a live donor for a heart transplant, and 'Report: 3906: COVERGIRLS – Last Year's Model' revolved around a mystery in the fashion world.

STRANGE WORLD OF GURNEY SLADE, THE

UK (ATV) Situation Comedy. ITV 1960

Gurney Slade ....Anthony Newley

Creator: Anthony Newley. Writers: Sid Green, Dick Hills. Producer: Alan Tarrant

A young man wanders through life in a state of fantasy.

In this bizarre, whimsical but short-lived series (only six episodes were made), the title character of Gurney Slade lived in a world of his own imagination. Talking to trees and animals, fantasizing about women, conjuring up unusual characters and bringing static beings to life, this young Londoner meandered his way through a number of weird situations.

Anthony Newley, the programme's creator and star, allegedly plucked the character's name from that of a West Country village and, in devising this series, he developed a concept which was simply too far ahead of its time. Audiences in 1960 were used to comfortable domestic comedies and that's what *The Strange World of Gurney Slade* appeared to be, when it began by focusing on a family squabbling at home.

But when Gurney suddenly stood up and walked off the set and into his own surreal world, he failed to take the bemused audience with him and the programme quickly came to an end.

STRANGERS

UK (Granada) Police Drama. ITV 1978–82

Detective Sgt George Bulman ....Don Henderson
DC Derek Willis....................................Dennis Blanch
Detective Sgt David Singer ....John Ronane
Detective Chief Supt Jack Lambie......Mark McManus
WDC Linda Doran ....Frances Tomelty
WDC Vanessa Bennett ....Fiona Mollison
Detective Chief Inspector Rainbow
....David Hargreaves
Inspector Pushkin ....George Pravda
William Dugdale ....Thorley Walters

Producer: Richard Everitt

Scotland Yard detectives infiltrate crime rings in the North-West.

Notable for the return of the glove-wearing, inhaler-sniffing, Shakespeare-quoting Sgt Bulman, first seen in *The XYY Man*, *Strangers* once again teamed the quirky detective with DC Derek Willis. This time they found themselves based in Manchester, joined by WDC Linda Doran, an expert in self-defence who was later replaced by WDC Vanessa Bennett, a driving specialist. They operated as Unit C23, literally 'strangers' in a neighbourhood where local police officers would have been too well-known. Assisted by Detective Sgt Singer, who provided local knowledge, they took their assignments from the somewhat ineffective Detective Chief Inspector Rainbow.

After two seasons, the format was changed. The team moved back to London but expected to be given missions anywhere in the country. They became the 'Inner City Squad', under the command of Detective Chief Supt Lambie, a tough, no-nonsense officer played by Mark McManus in a rehearsal for *Taggart*. Bulman was also introduced to William Dugdale, a university lecturer who had secret service connections and who was to assist him even more in the follow-up series, *Bulman*. Willis was promoted to detective sergeant, and Bulman himself became a detective chief inspector in the penultimate season. The series ended with Bulman planning to marry Lambie's ex-wife. However, by the time *Bulman* reached the screen, the engagement had clearly fallen through.

STRAUSS FAMILY, THE

UK (ATV) Historical Drama. ITV 1972

Johann Strauss	Eric Woolfe
Johann Strauss Jnr	Stuart Wilson
Anna Strauss	Anne Stallybrass
Adele	Lynn Farleigh
Emilie Trampusch	Barbara Ferris
Josef Lanner	Derek Jacobi
Eduard	Tony Anholt

Writers: David Butler, Anthony Skene, David Reid. Executive Producer: Cecil Clarke. Producer: David Reid

The life and times of Austria's famous musical family.

Spanning most of the 19th-century and tracing 75 years of musical creativity from father and son Johann Strauss, Snr and Jnr, this biopic wafted along to the strains of authentic Viennese waltzes, sweepingly performed by the London Symphony Orchestra. But, beyond the music, the duo's lives and loves were also depicted. The series was made as part of ATV's historical drama spree in the mid-1970s.

STRAUSS, PETER (1942–)

Largely seen in TV movies and blockbuster mini-series, American actor Peter Strauss made his TV name in the two *Rich Man, Poor Man* serials, playing Rudy Jordache. He was also Eleazar ben Yair in *Masada*, Dick Diver in *Tender is the Night* and Abel Rosnovski in *Kane and Abel*, as well as starring as Peter Gunn in a 1989 TV movie revival of the 1950s detective.

STREET-PORTER, JANET (JANET BULL; 1946–)

British presenter and TV executive with a pronounced down-to-earth London accent. Janet Street-Porter came to the fore as a presenter for LWT, hosting, amongst other programmes, *Saturday Night People* with Clive James and Russell Harty. At the turn of the 1980s, she switched to behind the scenes work and then joined Channel 4, where she developed teenage output through *Network 7*. In 1988 she moved to the BBC to take up the post of Head of Youth Programming, which resulted in the *DEF II* programme strand and the commissioning of series like *Rough Guide To ...* and *Rapido*. She was later the BBC's Head of Independent Entertainment Productions, bringing in series like *Ps and Qs* and

How Do They Do That? In 1994 she joined Ffyona Campbell on the last leg of her round the world charity walk, recording the highlights for a six-part BBC 2 documentary, *The Longest Walk*. The same year, Street-Porter left the BBC to work in cable television.

STREETS OF SAN FRANCISCO, THE

US (Quinn Martin) Police Drama. ITV 1973–

Detective Lt Mike Stone	Karl Malden
Inspector Steve Keller	Michael Douglas
Inspector Dan Robbins	Richard Hatch
Lt Lessing	Lee Harris
Sgt Sekulovich	Art Passarella
Officer Haseejian	Vic Tayback

Executive Producer: Quinn Martin. Producers: William R. Yates, John Wilder, Cliff Gould

A veteran police officer and his young assistant tackle crime in the Bay Area of San Francisco.

Detective Lt Mike Stone was a widower with 23 years' experience in the force. He now worked for the Bureau of Inspectors Division of the San Francisco Police Department, where he was paired with 28-year-old Inspector Steve Keller, a college graduate. Stone's tried and tested techniques were occasionally questioned by Keller whose ideas were more modern, but they struck up an effective, wise old head/eager young enthusiast partnership. When Keller left to take up teaching, he was replaced by another young cop, the athletic Dan Robbins, for the programme's last season (1976–7 in the USA).

For realism, some of the filming actually took place in the offices of the San Francisco Police Department and the city's hilly streets were put to good use for the many car chases. The inspiration and the characters were drawn from Carolyn Weston's novel, *Poor, Poor Ophelia*.

STRIDE, JOHN (1936–)

British character actor, star of *The Main Chance* (as solicitor David Main) and *The Wilde Alliance* (as fiction writer/detective Rupert Wilde). He also played Lloyd George in *Number Ten* and was seen in *Diamonds* (as Frank Coleman), the BBC Television Shakespeare production of *Henry VIII* and the dramatization of *The Trial of Klaus Barbie*. Other credits have included *Love Story*, *Lytton's Diary*, *The Old Devils* and Agatha Christie's Poirot.

STRIKE IT LUCKY

UK (Thames/Central) Quiz. ITV 1986–

Presenter: Michael Barrymore

Executive Producer: Robert Louis. Producer: Maurice Leonard

Easy-going game show involving quiz questions and a bank of illuminated TV screens.

A game of general knowledge and chance, *Strike It Lucky* has been a very effective vehicle for the talents of Michael Barrymore. His ease with the general public has been highlighted in his dealings with (and gentle mockery of) the three pairs of contestants, and his manic, physical style of comedy has been accommodated by a large, sprawling set.

The six contestants have been divided up into question answerers and 'screen strikers'. By choosing to give two, three or four correct answers to questions in a given category (with a list of possible responses shown on a screen to help them), a contestant has allowed his or her partner to advance the equivalent number of steps along a wide, raised stage. Each step has housed a TV screen which, when 'struck' has revealed a prize or a 'hot spot'. Contestants have been able to stick with the prize or advance further along the stage. A hot spot has cancelled all the prizes won in that turn and attention has then switched to the next pair of contestants.

The first contestants to cross the stage have been offered a jackpot question, which has taken them to the grand finale if answered correctly. For this finale the two contestants have progressed along the stage together, striking screens, occasionally answering questions and hoping to avoid a set number of hot spots which would end their bid for the top prize of several thousand pounds in cash.

STRIPPING

A scheduling term meaning the transmission of the same programme on the same channel at the same time, five or more consecutive nights a week (as *Neighbours* has been in the UK, for instance).

STRITCH, ELAINE (1926–)

American actress with a number of comedies and quizzes behind her in her native USA, as well as stage and film credits, but primarily known to UK viewers as writer Dorothy McNab, alongside Donald Sinden, in the culture clash sitcom *Two's Company*. She has also been seen in the UK in the comedies *My Sister Eileen* (as Ruth Sherwood) in 1964 and *Nobody's Perfect* (as Bill Hooper) in 1980, plus series as diverse as *Tales of the Unexpected* and *The Cosby Show*.

STUBBS, UNA (1937–)

British dancer and actress, first appearing in series like *Cool for Cats* and *Not Only . . . , But Also . . . .* In 1966 she began a nine-year (on and off) run as Alf Garnett's daughter, Rita, in *Till Death Us Do Part*, reprising the role occasionally in the follow-up series, *In Sickness and in Health*, in the 1980s. Stubbs was one of the team captains in the charades game *Give Us a Clue* and played Aunt Sally in *Worzel Gummidge* and *Worzel Gummidge Down Under*. She took the role of Mrs Plugg in the 1989 comedy *Morris Minor's Marvellous Motors* and was also seen in *Fawlty Towers* and *Happy Families*.

SUBTITLE

Text superimposed on the screen (usually at the bottom) to provide a translation of foreign dialogue or to allow viewers with hearing difficulties to follow the action.

STV See Scottish Television.

SUCHET, DAVID (1946–)

Much appreciated British actor, the brother of ITN newscaster John Suchet. David is undoubtedly best known for his work as Agatha Christie's *Poirot*, although he has enjoyed many prominent roles. He played Blott in *Blott on the Landscape*, was Edward Teller in *Oppenheimer*, Inspector Tsientsin in *Reilly – Ace of Spies*, Sigmund Freud in *Freud* and the title role in Shakespeare's *Timon of Athens*. Amongst his other credits have been parts in dramas like *Oxbridge Blues*, *Ulysses*, *King and Castle*, *Nobody Here But Us Chickens* and *Time to Die*.

SUCHET, JOHN (1944–)

British journalist and newscaster, once with Reuters and the BBC but, since 1972, on ITN's staff. As well as working as ITN's Washington correspondent in the early 1980s, Suchet has fronted most of the main news bulletins, including *News at Ten*, *News at 5.40* and the lunchtime programmes. His brother is actor David Suchet.

SUGDEN, MOLLIE (1922–)

British character actress, the first choice of many producers when casting domineering or interfering, over-the-top mother figures. She played Mrs Clitheroe (Jimmy's mum) in *Just Jimmy*, Mrs Hutchinson (Sandra's mum) in *The Liver Birds*, Mrs Waring (Duncan's mum) in *Doctor in Charge*, Suzy's mum in *My Wife Next Door*, Terry Scott's mum in *Son of the Bride* and Ida Willis (Robert Price's natural mum) in the adoption comedy

That's My Boy. She was also Mrs Crispin in *Hugh and I*, Flavia in *Up Pompeii!*, Mrs Noah in *Come Back Mrs Noah*, Nora Powers in *My Husband and I* (opposite her real-life husband, William Moore) and Nellie Harvey, landlady of The Laughing Donkey, in *Coronation Street*. Undoubtedly, her most popular character, however, has been Mrs Slocombe in *Are You Being Served?* and *Grace and Favour*. She has also been seen in other comedies like *Please Sir!* and *For the Love of Ada*, and panel games like *Whodunnit?*

SULLAVAN BROTHERS, THE

UK (ATV) Drama. ITV 1964–5

Paul Sullavan	Anthony Bate
John Sullavan	Tenniel Evans
Beth Sullavan	Mary Kenton
Robert Sullavan QC	Hugh Manning
Patrick Sullavan	David Sumner

Creator: Ted Willis. Producer: Jack Williams

Legal eagling with a family law team.

The Sullavan Brothers were three solicitors and a barrister who worked in tandem for the benefit of their distressed clients. The barrister was Robert, a big, bulldozing type who took on the most serious cases. The team administrator was Paul, a logical, level-headed thinker, John was the blind, cultured idealist, and youngest brother Patrick was a handsome, vintage car aficionado who did most of the leg work. Also involved was John's wife, Beth.

SULLIVAN, ED (1901–74)

The most famous of all variety show hosts, Ed Sullivan's background was in newspaper journalism. It was as a Broadway columnist that he was introduced to the major showbusiness names of the 1930s, leading to his own immersion in radio and film work as an impresario and compère. When TV began to take off, Sullivan was quickly in the action, pioneering the variety show format with *The Toast of the Town* (soon renamed *The Ed Sullivan Show*) from 1948. In this legendary Sunday night American programme, Sullivan introduced to viewers many budding or emerging stars, and gave countless others their TV debut. They ranged from Dean Martin and Jerry Lewis (in the very first show) to Elvis Presley and The Beatles. The series ran until 1971. Never known for his ease in front of the camera, nevertheless Sullivan, nicknamed 'The Great Stone Face', was one of TV's early giants.

SULLIVAN, JOHN (1946–)

London-born comedy writer, a former scene shifter at the BBC who knew he could write better scripts than the ones he was servicing. He talked producer Dennis Main Wilson into looking at his idea for a comedy based around a South London Marxist revolutionary, and **Citizen Smith** was born, initially as an episode of *Comedy Special*. Sullivan's next creation has been widely acclaimed as his greatest to date, namely **Only Fools and Horses**, although he has also delighted viewers with **Just Good Friends**, **Dear John** and **Sitting Pretty**. His London roots tend to show through in all his work.

SULLIVANS, THE

Australia (Crawford) Drama. ITV 1977–82

David Sullivan	Paul Cronin
Grace Sullivan	Lorraine Bayly
John Sullivan	Andrew McFarlane
Tom Sullivan	Steven Tandy
Terry Sullivan	Richard Morgan
Kitty Sullivan	Susan Hannaford
Harry Sullivan	Michael Caton
Geoff Sullivan	Jamie Higgins
Jim Sullivan	Andy Anderson
Maggie Baker	Vikki Hammond
Anna Kaufman	Ingrid Mason
Lotte Kaufman	Marcella Burgoyne
Hans Kaufman	Leon Lissek
Jack Fletcher	Reg Gorman
Magpie Haddern	Gary Sweet

An Australian family struggles to come to terms with World War II.

Beginning in 1939, *The Sullivans* told the continuing story of the Melbourne-based Sullivan family, headed by engineering foreman dad Dave and devout Catholic mum Grace. They had four children: John was a medical student but also a pacifist and he joined the army very reluctantly; his brother, Tom, was also recruited, while third son Terry was still only a freckle-faced youth when the hostilities began. The family's daughter was 13-year-old Kitty (played by 24-year-old actress Susan Hannaford). Anna Kaufmann was John's girlfriend, a beautiful girl who suffered cruel abuse as anti-semitism spread around the world.

Inspired by Granada's *A Family At War*, *The Sullivans* followed the family through thick and thin as the war took a grip on the Antipodes. Scenes of desert and jungle conflicts were combined with everyday domestic ups and downs, but many of the most poignant moments came after the war had ended. Terry's demise into petty crime was disturbing enough but more shocking still was Kitty's suicide following a visit to the devastation of Hiroshima with her photographer husband.

The Sullivans was a popular lunchtime offering in the UK, beginning just a year after its Australian première and conceived by ITV as a ready replacement for **Emmerdale Farm**, which had been promoted to peak hours. In its native country, the series paved the way for later international hits like **Prisoner: Cell Block H, Neighbours** and **Home and Away**, with many of *The Sullivans'* performers popping up in new guises in Wentworth, Erinsborough and Summer Bay.

SUNDAY NIGHT AT THE LONDON PALLADIUM

UK (ATV) Variety. ITV 1955–67; 1973–4

Comperes:
Tommy Trinder
Hughie Green
Alfred Marks
Robert Morley
Arthur Haynes
Dickie Henderson
Bruce Forsyth
Don Arrol
Dave Allen
Norman Vaughan
Jimmy Tarbuck
Des O'Connor
Roger Moore
Jim Dale (1973)

Creator: Val Parnell. Producers: Albert Locke, Francis Essex, Jon Scoffield, Colin Clews

Weekly showcase of international stars, at the world's number-one variety theatre.

Sunday Night at the London Palladium was a British institution in the 1950s and 1960s. It was the show that everyone talked about the next day at work and brought the world's most celebrated stars, plus the best of home-grown talent, into the living room of the ordinary citizen. The first ever show featured Gracie Fields and Guy Mitchell, and other stars appearing during its initial 12-year run included Judy Garland, Bob Hope, Johnny Ray, Liberace, Petula Clark, The Beatles and The Rolling Stones. The cheeky Italian mouse puppet, Topo Gigio, was a regular visitor. The programme's first host was music hall comedian Tommy Trinder, who set the tone with his sharp adlibs and fast-talking style. Others are listed above, with, apart from Trinder, the main presenters being Norman Vaughan, Jimmy Tarbuck and Bruce Forsyth. Forsyth, like Trinder before him, was the perfect compère for the show's games interlude, *Beat the Clock*, which was based on the American quiz show of the same name and involved couples performing silly tricks or stunts within a set time period. Bruce kept order by yelling 'I'm in charge' and prizes were awarded to successful participants. **The Generation Game** was a logical progression for Forsyth.

The format of *Sunday Night at the London Palladium* seldom wavered. Lasting an hour, it began with the high-kicking Tiller Girls and then a welcome from the compère. He introduced a couple of lesser acts, before launching into *Beat the Clock*. The second half of the show was devoted to the big name of the week and the programme was rounded off with the entire cast waving goodbye from the famous revolving stage. Although cancelled in 1967, *Sunday Night at the London Palladium* was briefly revived in 1973, with Jim Dale as host. Its heyday had long gone, however, and it only survived one year.

SUPERCAR

UK (AP Films/ATV/ITC) Children's Science Fiction. ITV 1961–2

Voices:
Mike Mercury ....Graydon Gould
Professor Popkiss ....George Murcell
                                                                         Cyril Shaps
Jimmy Gibson ....Sylvia Anderson
Dr Beaker ....David Graham
Mitch..David Graham
Masterspy ....George Murcell
                                                                         Cyril Shaps
Zarin ....David Graham

Creators: Gerry Anderson, Reg Hill. Writers: Martin Woodhouse, Hugh Woodhouse, Gerry Anderson, Sylvia Anderson. Producer: Gerry Anderson

Adventures with the crew of an amazing land, sea and air vehicle.

Gerry Anderson's first science fiction series was based around a unique vehicle – a car, a plane and a submarine all rolled into one. Test pilot of Supercar was racing driver-cum-airman–cum-deep sea diver Mike Mercury, who was joined on his missions by Professor Popkiss and the stammering Dr Beaker, co-inventors of the car. Also aboard were freckly ten-year-old Jimmy Gibson (one of two brothers Mike and Supercar had rescued at sea), and Mitch, Jimmy's talking monkey. The Supercar team were based at a secret laboratory in an American desert but their travels saw them helping people and averting disasters all over the world. Their day to day enemies were the Sidney Greenstreet/Peter Lorre-type partnership of Masterspy and his sidekick, Zarin, who aimed to steal Supercar and use it for their evil ends. Of course, they never succeeded.

Somewhat primitive by the standards of his later efforts, *Supercar* nevertheless was a breakthrough for Gerry Anderson, taking his puppet expertise to new levels and cementing his new partnership with Lew Grade's ITC production and distribution company. It was also the series that coined the phrase 'Supermarionation', to express the elaborate style of puppetry involved.

SUPER CHANNEL see NBC Super Channel.

SUPERGRAN

UK (Tyne-Tees) Children's Comedy.
ITV 1985–7

Granny Smith ('Supergran')......................Gudrun Ure
Scunner Campbell ....Iain Cuthbertson
Inventor Black...Bill Shine
Inspector Higgins ....Robert Austin
The Muscles..Alan Snell
                                    Brian Lewis
Eddison ....Holly English
PC Leekie ....Terry Joyce
Tub ....Lee Marshall
Willard..Ian Towell

Writer: Jenny McDade. Producers: Keith
Richardson, Graham C. Williams

**An old lady becomes a superheroine and
uses her powers to help others.**

Struck by a beam from a magic ray machine,
gentle old Granny Smith found herself accidentally endowed with superhuman powers.
Adopting the guise of Supergran, she set out to
defend the good folk of Chisleton against baddies
like Scunner Campbell. Also in the action was
Inventor Black, the man whose magic ray had
transformed the old lady. Supergran was based on
the books by Forrest Wilson. Billy Connolly co-
wrote the programme's theme music.

SUPERMAN

US (Lippert/National Periodical Publications)
Science Fiction. ITV 1956–7

Superman/Clark Kent ....George Reeves
Lois Lane ....Phyllis Coates
                                     Noel Neill
Jimmy Olsen ....Jack Larson
Perry White ....John Hamilton
Inspector William Henderson ....Robert Shayne

Producers: Robert Maxwell, Bernard Luber,
Whitney Ellsworth

**TV's first rendition of the comic strip
saga.**

Created by Jerome Siegel and Joe Shuster in
1938, Superman was a refugee from the planet
Krypton who lived on Earth and was endowed
with superhuman powers. Under his alter-ego of
Clark Kent, he lived in Metropolis and worked as
a reporter for *The Daily Planet*, an ideal position
for hearing about crime as it happened. Stripping
off his spectacles and donning his tights and cape,
Superman raced to the rescue of helpless civilians,
who often turned out to be his friends and colleagues. Demonstrating his superhuman strength
by smashing down walls and bending iron bars,
he was hailed as 'faster than a speeding bullet',
once spectators had worked out that it was not a
bird or a plane that had just flown past, but
Superman himself. Those friends and colleagues
included top reporter Lois Lane (in love with
Superman, but disparaging of Clark Kent) and
hapless trainee newshound Jimmy Olsen. His
boss was pipe-smoking editor Perry White, who
was often heard to exclaim 'Great Caesar's ghost',
whenever anything startling happened, which
was pretty often.

George Reeves, who had played Brent Tarleton
in *Gone with the Wind*, suffered chronically from
typecasting after this role, to the point where he
was unable to work and eventually took his own
life. Co-star Noel Neill reappeared briefly in the
1970s film version, this time as Superman's
mother. Superman returned to the TV screens in
1994, in *The New Adventures of Superman*, with
Dean Cain as the 'Man of Steel' and Teri Hatcher
as Lois Lane.

SUPERSTARS, THE

UK (BBC) Sport. BBC 1 1975–82; 1985

Presenters: David Vine, Ron Pickering

Producers: Ian Smith, Peter Hylton Cleaver

**International sportsmen tackle
representatives from other sports in a
contest of fitness and skill.**

Beginning as a domestic UK event (initially entitled *Sporting Superstars*), but later going
international, *The Superstars* was an innovative
test of power, fitness, skill and adaptability. It
aimed to discover which sports provided the
best all-round athletes and competitors by pitting top names against each other in a series of
contests. These ranged from gym tests (push
ups, squat thrusts, etc.), to disciplines like football control, rifle shooting, distance running,
sprinting, cycling, basketball, archery,
weightlifting, swimming and rowing.
Competitors were not allowed to compete in
their own sports or in sports akin to their own.
The series made household names of lesser
known sportsmen like judo star Brian Jacks and
rugby league's Keith Fielding. A spin-off series,
The Superteams, matched team competitors
from various sports.

SURGICAL SPIRIT

UK (Granada) Situation Comedy. ITV 1989–

Dr Sheila Sabatini ....Nichola McAuliffe
Dr Jonathan Haslam ....Duncan Preston
Joyce Watson ....Marji Campi
George Hope-Wynne............................David Conville
Neil Copeland ....Emlyn Price
Simon Field ....Lyndam Gregory

Giles Peake ....Simon Harrison
Sister Cheryl Patching.....................Suzette Llewellyn
Dr Michael Sampson ....Beresford Le Roy
Daniel Sabatini ....Andrew Groves

Creator: Peter Learmouth. Executive Producers: David Liddiment, Al Mitchell. Producer: Humphrey Barclay

A senior surgeon's tongue is as sharp as her scalpel.

Sheila Sabatini was a hard working surgeon at the Gillies Hospital. She was also hot tempered, opinionated and sharp-tongued, but this didn't prevent her anaesthetist colleague, Jonathan Haslem, from beginning a relationship with her (once her divorce had come through). Their on-off affair ran for six seasons amidst weekly hospital crises and against a backdrop of open conflict in the operating theatre. Involved in matchmaking was the hospital's gossipy administrator Joyce Watson, and her efforts paid off when the two were wed in 1994. Also seen were fellow surgeon Neil Copeland, houseman Giles Peake, sister Cheryl Patching, her live-in boyfriend Dr Michael Sampson, George Hope-Wynne, a consultant surgeon with more interest in private medicine, and Sheila's teenage (later medical student) son, Daniel. A seventh series was screened in 1995.

UK (LWT) Entertainment. ITV 1984–

Presenters:
Cilla Black
Christopher Biggins
Bob Carolgees
Gordon Burns

Producers: Bob Merrilees, Brian Wesley, Linda Beadle, Colman Hutchinson

Magic wand show in which members of the public are given heart-warming surprises.

Surprise, Surprise was created as a showcase for Cilla Black and was her first TV series for over eight years. It initially paired her with Christopher Biggins, but he was dropped after the first series, to be replaced in 1986 by Bob Carolgees. The aim of the show has been to make dreams come true in *Jim'll Fix It* fashion for various members of the general public, acting on advice from relatives and friends. One segment entitled *Searchline*, hosted for five years by Gordon Burns, hoped to re-establish contact between broken families and long-lost friends. In true Cilla tradition there have been a 'lorra lorra laffs', but plenty of tears, too.

UK (Anglia) Natural History. ITV 1961–

Creator: Aubrey Buxton
Producers: Aubrey Buxton, Colin Willock, Caroline Brett

Long-running, highly successful wildlife series.

Undoubtedly Anglia Television's greatest product, *Survival* has been seen in more countries (112) around the world than any other British programme (in some cases under the title of *The World of Survival*). Beginning in 1961 with a short series of films about London wildlife (with production assistance from Associated-Rediffusion), *Survival* has since expanded to cover nature stories all over the globe. Creator Aubrey Buxton was associated with the programme for many years and introduced some of the early episodes. Colin Willock has also been a major influence. The painstakingly-made, half-hour films (occasionally an hour in length, when they have been billed as *Survival Special*) have been narrated by the likes of David Niven, Peter Scott, Kenneth More, John Hedges, Brian Blessed, Duncan Carse, Ian Holm and Robert Hardy. Programmes have focused on the threat to wildlife, the environment and native peoples. Some of the best remembered have been *Tarantula!*, *The Painter and The Fighter* (African tribes people) and *Highgrove – Nature's Kingdom* (animal life on the Prince of Wales's estate). John Forsythe has introduced the series for American viewers. Over 750 programmes have now been produced and *Survival* has picked up some 130 international awards.

UK (BBC) Science Fiction. BBC 1 1975–7

Abby Grant ....Carolyn Seymour
Greg Preston..Ian McCulloch
Jenny Richards ....Lucy Fleming
Charles Vaughan ....Denis Lill
Dave Long...Brian Peck
Tom Price...Talfryn Thomas
John ....Stephen Dudley
Lizzie ....Tanya Ronder
Vic Thatcher...Terry Scully
Paul Pitman ....Christopher Tranchell
Alan ....Stephen Tate
Mrs Emma Cohen.........................Hana-Maria Pravda
Seth ....Dan Meaden
Charmian Wentworth ....Eileen Helsby
Agnes ....Anna Pitt
                                                              Sally Osborn
Arthur Russell.......................................Michael Gover
Pet Simpson ....Lorna Lewis
Ruth Anderson ....Celia Gregory
Hubert ....John Abineri
Jack ....Gordon Salkild
Dave ....Peter Duncan

Creator: Terry Nation. Producer: Terence Dudley

The survivors of a killer plague struggle to rebuild civilization and establish a future for the world.

Imagine a world that suddenly grinds to a halt. A world where 95 per cent of the population is wiped out in just a few weeks by a rogue virus and where the remaining 5 per cent have to battle to stay alive. Imagine a world where, for all the modern technology around him, man is forced to fall back on primitive skills to feed himself and to establish a pattern of law and order. This was the imagination of Terry Nation, the creator of the Daleks and the inspiration behind *Survivors*.

As graphically depicted in the programme's opening titles, the world had been gripped by a deadly virus, accidentally released when a scientist in the Far East smashed a test-tube. Inadvertently spread by jet-setting businessmen, the virus had quickly reached Britain, where *Survivors* took up the story. It centred on a motley band of individuals, people who had either been immune to the plague or who had somehow recovered from it. At the forefront was suburban housewife Abby Grant, who watched her husband die in the first episode but who still hoped to find her lost son, Peter. Young secretary Jenny Richards, architect Charles Vaughan and the group's leader-elect, engineer Greg Preston, were also prominent. The first episodes revealed how they found each other as they wandered around derelict towns and villages, seeking food, shelter and, above all, other people. After that, attention turned to their efforts to re-establish civilization and to harness whatever specialist talents remained in the survivors around them – the likes of doctors, electricians and teachers. Along the way, they encountered unpleasant characters, such as cowardly Welsh labourer Tom Price, and other communities which expressed their own perverse forms of law, order and justice.

Getting all the survivors to work in harmony proved impossible. Suspicion was rife and greed and power were two elements they found hard to subdue. Effectively, the Dark Ages had returned. The desperate need to reclaim society and to re-invent the skills needed to replenish supplies of food, medicine, transport, power and other essentials formed the backbone of the series, which, after three seasons, ended on a more optimistic note than it had begun. Common sense and human spirit were beginning to shine through and, although the going remained tough, there was, at least, some kind of future beckoning.

Survivors has become cult science fiction viewing, enjoying repeat performances on satellite TV.

There has, however, been one notable criticism voiced, namely that all the goodies were middle-class and that working-class survivors were portrayed as violent, devious or, at the very least, uncouth.

SUTHERLAND'S LAW

UK (BBC) Legal Drama. BBC 1 1973–6

John Sutherland.................................Iain Cuthbertson
Alex Duthie...Gareth Thomas
Christine Russell ....Maev Alexander
Sgt McKechnie.......................................Don McKillop
Dr Judith Roberto Sutherland ....Edith MacArthur
Gail Munro ....Harriet Buchan
Chief Inspector Menzies ....Victor Carin
David Drummond ....Martin Cochrane
Helen Matheson ....Virginia Stark
Kate Cameron .... Sarah Collier

Creator: Lindsay Galloway. Producers: Neil McCallum, Frank Cox

The cases of a procurator fiscal in a Scottish fishing town.

John Sutherland held the post of procurator fiscal, a legal position somewhere between an investigative prosecuting lawyer, an American district attorney and a coroner. Under Scottish law, the police do not prosecute criminals themselves, they have to go to the procurator fiscal for action. So it was that Iain Cuthbertson, fresh from playing the rogue Charlie Endell in *Budgie*, became a reformed character and as Sutherland began to act on behalf of the people against the criminal fraternity. He was supported at various times by Alec Duthie, Christine Russell, Gail Munro, David Drummond and Helen Matheson. The beautiful West Coast views were a bonus. The series stemmed from a 1972 *Drama Playhouse* presentation.

SUTTON, SHAUN OBE (1919–)

British writer, producer and director, working mostly on children's dramas (such as *Billy Bunter of Greyfriars School*, *Bonehead* and *The Silver Sword*) before becoming the BBC's Head of Drama 1969–81. Amongst his other work was direction on *The Troubleshooters*, *Z Cars*, *Kipling* and *Detective*. He later produced some of the *BBC Television Shakespeare* presentations.

SWEENEY, THE

UK (Euston Films/Thames) Police Drama. ITV 1975–8

Detective Inspector Jack Regan ....John Thaw
Detective Sgt George Carter..........Dennis Waterman
Chief Inspector Frank Haskins..........Garfield Morgan

Creator: Ian Kennedy Martin. Executive Producers: Lloyd Shirley, George Taylor, Ted Childs

Rough, tough and violent crime busting with a no-nonsense pair of Flying Squad detectives.

Taking its name from the Cockney rhyming slang for Flying Squad ('Sweeney Todd'), this was one of television's most physical cop shows. It featured the investigations of door-smashing, crook-thumping, heavy-drinking Detective Inspector Jack Regan and his junior partner, Detective Sgt George Carter. Hard, and sometimes unquestioning, Regan had little time for rules and regulations. In his leather jacket and 70s-style kipper ties, he was also a bit of a lad, found off-duty in the boozer, chatting to the local villains, or in bed with yet another woman (he was, not surprisingly, estranged from his wife). Carter was his loyal number two, learning the trade from his mentor, and picking up the bad habits along with the good. Like his boss, he, too, was pretty useful with his fists. Supervising the operations, often in desperation at the tactics involved, was Chief Inspector Haskins.

The series began seven months after a pilot episode, *Regan*, part of the *Armchair Cinema* anthology, was screened in 1974, and it ended in 1978, when Regan was banged up for allegedly taking bribes. No charges were brought, but Regan had had enough and decided to call it a day. Through *The Sweeney*, the public was introduced to a new kind of policeman, one the authorities tried to deny existed but one which certain real-life lawmen privately acknowledged to be alive and kicking, especially kicking. Indeed, Jack Quarrie, a former Flying Squad officer, was the programme's technical advisor. But, for all its bad language and excessive violence, the series also had its humorous side, highlighted in the Regan-Carter cockney repartee and an episode which featured Morecambe and Wise as guest stars. Two feature films were also made.

SWIFT, CLIVE (1936–)

Familiar British character actor, seen in numerous supporting roles, most recently as the hen-pecked Richard Bucket in *Keeping Up Appearances*. He was Detective Inspector Waugh in *Waugh on Crime*, six 1970 *Thirty-Minute Theatre* productions, and was Mr Nesbitt in the sitcom *The Nesbitts are Coming*. Amongst his many other credits have been parts in *Compact, Clayhanger, The Brothers, Love Story, The Liver Birds, South Riding, Tales of the Unexpected, Winston Churchill – The Wilderness Years, Beasts, The Gentle Touch, Shelley, Doctor Who, Minder, A Very Peculiar Practice, Inspector Morse*, various adaptations of the classics and more.

SWIT, LORETTA (1937–)

Blonde American actress of Polish descent, *M*A*S*H*'s Margaret 'Hotlips' Hoolihan, but also Christine Cagney in the pilot movie for *Cagney and Lacey* (although not the series). She has since been seen in numerous other TV movies, with her earliest appearances coming in series like *Gunsmoke*, *Hawaii Five-O* and *Mannix*.

SWORD OF FREEDOM

UK (Sapphire/ITC) Adventure. ITV 1959–61

Marco del Monte	Edmund Purdom
Angelica	Adrienne Corri
Sandro	Rowland Bartrop
Duke de Medici	Martin Benson
Francesca	Monica Stevenson
Machiavelli	Kenneth Hyde

Executive Producer: Hannah Weinstein.
Producer: Sidney Cole

Robin Hood in an Italian Renaissance setting.

Marco del Monte was a 15th-century Florentine painter, much sickened by the excesses of the city-state's ruling family, the Medicis. Supported by Angelica, his former pick-pocket model, and his broad-shouldered friend, Sandro, he constantly took on the might of the authorities, displaying a flair for swordsmanship as well as art, as he rode to the rescue of many an oppressed compatriot. In his sights were the Duke de Medici and his cruel sister, Francesca.

SYKES

UK (BBC) Situation Comedy. BBC 1 1960–5; 1971–9

Eric	Eric Sykes
Hattie	Hattie Jacques
Mr Brown	Richard Wattis
Corky	Deryck Guyler

Writers: Johnny Speight, Eric Sykes. Producers: Dennis Main Wilson, Sydney Lotterby, Philip Barker, Roger Race

A hapless brother and sister share a suburban home.

Life at 24 Sebastopol Terrace was seldom simple. Home to bachelor brother Eric and spinster sister Hattie, it played host to assorted domestic crises. With Eric constantly trying to better himself, misunderstandings were rife and often involved Eric and Hattie's snooty, interfering neighbour, Mr Brown, or Corky, the pompous neighbourhood bobby.

Initially, this long-running series went out under the title of *Sykes and . . .* , with the object, implement or creature that was about to cause chaos inserted into the title. Examples included *Sykes and a Telephone* and *Sykes and a Plank*. Some early episodes were scripted by Johnny Speight, but the lion's share of programmes were penned by Eric Sykes himself.

SYKES, ERIC, OBE (1923–)

British comedian and writer, who broke into radio after the war, penning scripts for *Educating Archie* and other series. He also wrote for television: *The Howerd Crowd* for Frankie Howerd in 1952 and Tony Hancock's first TV sketches, screened as *The Tony Hancock Show* by ITV in 1956. *The Goonish Idiot Weekly, Price 2d* was another of his early outlets and he was also involved in the film world by the time his long-running sitcom, *Sykes*, began in 1960. Apart from a seven-year hiatus in the middle, the series ran until 1979, just before his screen sister Hattie Jacques died. Originally, the *Sykes* scripts were written by Johnny Speight, but Eric soon took control himself, although his relationship with Speight was to resume in 1969, when Sykes played the liberal factory foreman in the controversial *Curry and Chips*. He and Speight teamed up again in 1989 for another sitcom, *The Nineteenth Hole*. Sykes has also been known for his visual humour, exemplified in *Mr H Is Late* and his 1967 silent film short *The Plank,* which was remade for television in 1979. He also directed the TV film *If You Go Down to the Woods Today* in 1981 and other credits in his long career have included *Sykes Versus ITV* (a mock court case), *Sykes and a Big Big Show*, *It's Your Move* (as writer and director) and guest spots on *Not Only . . . , But Also . . . .*

SYLVANIA WATERS

Australia Documentary. BBC 1 1993

Producer: Paul Watson

Warts and all, 12-part documentary about the daily life of a typical Australian family.

In the fly-on-the-wall tradition of his earlier programme *The Family*, producer Paul Watson captured the domestic ups and downs of the Baker-Donaher family in one of Sydney's well-off suburbs. Heads of the family were rich divorcees Noeline Baker and Laurie Donaher, proud of the hard-working way in which they had built up their wealth and determined to enjoy it to the full. Inter-family squabbles added spice to the story, with running arguments between Noeline and her elder son, Paul, the unfolding drama of his wife, Dione's, pregnancy and the teenage trials of younger son, Michael, who narrated the programme.

These real-life *Neighbours* caused a storm in their native Australia when they were criticised for their brash, bigotted behaviour and their heavy drinking/smoking lifestyle.

SYNDICATION

An American term for the sale of programmes to independent stations (rather than the national networks) for screening locally. Old, repeat episodes of prime-time series are syndicated, as are new series which the major networks decline to take up. Some programmes are made specifically for syndication (low-budget features, game shows, etc.) and occasionally a major series begins or only airs in syndication (*Star Trek: The Next Generation* is one example). Many British series have only been seen in the USA in syndication.

TAGGART

UK (Scottish) Police Drama. ITV 1983–

Detective Chief Inspector Jim Taggart	Mark McManus
Detective Sgt Peter Livingstone	Neil Duncan
Supt McVitie	Iain Anders
Supt Murray	Tony Watson
Detective Sgt/Detective Inspector Mike Jardine	James Macpherson
Jean Taggart	Harriet Buchan
Alison Taggart	Geraldine Alexander
Dr Andrews	Robert Robertson
WDC/W Detective Sgt Jackie Reid	Blythe Duff
DC Stuart Fraser	Colin McGredie

Creator: Glenn Chandler. Producer: Robert Love

Gruesome murder investigations with a gritty Glaswegian detective.

Jim Taggart worked for the Glasgow CID. Covering the Northern Division, he was hard-nosed, firm and dedicated, yet was saddened by his job to the point of cynicism. His wife, Jean, had been wheelchair-bound for over 20 years (since the birth of their daughter, Alison), and she was largely resigned to her husband's devotion to work, not that he had a lot to say when he did eventually return home. Working with the down-to-earth Taggart was the university-educated Detective Sgt Peter Livingstone, a man from quite different social roots. Livingstone was later replaced by Mike Jardine, a keen, young tee-totaller (much to Taggart's disgust) who worked his way up from detective constable under his mentor's tutelage. Their assignments involved the grisliest, most distressing and baffling murders, all set against the distinctive backdrop of Glasgow city, with a touch of wry Scottish humour to sugar the pill.

Combining one-off stories with short serials, in a somewhat intermittent fashion, *Taggart* began with a thriller entitled *Killer* in 1983 and seemed likely to end with the premature death of its star Mark McManus in 1994. However, Taggart continued into 1995, with Jardine and Detective Sgt Jackie Reid moving into centre stage.

TAKE A LETTER

UK (Granada) Game Show. ITV 1962–4

Presenter: Bob Holness

Producers: John Hamp, Max Morgan-Witts

Crossword-based, family puzzle game.

By solving clues and choosing letters to complete mystery words, the contestants in this popular programme attempted to win small cash prizes. The amount won depended on the number of letters selected before the correct answer was given. Future *Blockbusters* host Bob Holness took charge of proceedings.

TAKE THE HIGH ROAD/HIGH ROAD

UK (Scottish) Drama. ITV 1980–

Elizabeth Cunningham	Edith Macarthur
Fiona Cunningham/Ryder	Caroline Ashley
Isabel Blair/Morgan	Eileen McCallum
Brian Blair	Kenneth Watson
Jimmy Blair	Jimmy Chisholm
Alice McEwan/Taylor	Muriel Romanes
Dougal Lachlan	Alec Monteath
Gladys Lachlan	Ginni Barlow
Grace Lachlan	Marjorie Thomson
Donald Lachlan	Steven Brown
Alan McIntyre	Martin Cochrane
Davie Sneddon	Derek Lord
Mrs Mary Mack	Gwyneth Guthrie
Lorna Seton	Joan Alcorn
Obadiah Arthur Murdoch	Robert Trotter
Alex Geddes	James Cosmo
Inverdarroch	John Stahl
Bob Taylor	Iain Agnew
Fergus Jamieson	Frank Wylie
Ken Calder	Bill Henderson
Dr Sandy Wallace	Michael Elder
Archie Menzies	Paul Kermack
Max Langemann	Frederick Jaeger
Jane Steedman	Ingrid Hafner
Sheila Lamont/Ramsey	Lesley Fitz-Simons
Sir John Ross-Gifford	Michael Browning
Lady Margaret Ross-Gifford	Jan Waters
Eric Ross-Gifford	Richard Greenwood
Joanna Simpson/Ross-Gifford	Tamara Kennedy
Emma Aitken	Amanda Whitehead
Greg Ryder	Alan Hunter
Sam Hagen	Briony McRoberts
Jockie McDonald	Jackie Farrell
Sadie McDonald	Doreen Cameron
Trish McDonald	Natalie Robb
Gary McDonald	Joseph McFadden
Carol McKay/Wilson	Teri Lally
Lynne McNeil	Gillian McNeill
Ian McPherson	John Young
Effie MacInnes	Mary Riggans
Jennifer Goudie	Victoria Burton
Paul Martin	Peter Bruce
Alun Morgan	Mike Hayward
Menna Morgan	Marion Jones
Nick Stapleton	Stephen Hogan
Sgt Murray	James McDonald
Reverend Michael Ross	Gordon MacArthur
Morag Stewart	Jeannie Fisher
Tee Jay Wilson	Andrew Gillan
Miss Symonds	Harriet Buchan
Eddie Ramsey	Robin Cameron
George Carradine	Leon Sinden
Sarah Gilchrist	Shonagh Price
Callum Gilchrist	Jim Webster
Judith Crombie	Anne Marie Timoney
PC Douglas Kirk	Graeme Robertson
Phineas ('Fin') North	William Tapley

Creator: Don Houghton. Producers: Clarke Tait, Frank Cox, John G. Temple

Life in a rural Scottish community.

A sort of *Emmerdale Farm* north of the Border, *Take the High Road* has been the long-running saga of the good folk of Glendarroch and the next-door parish of Auchtarne. The main characters have included local gossip Mrs Mack, shopkeepers Isabel and Brian Blair, their heart-throb son, Jimmy, and unscrupulous land-manager Davie Sneddon. Others to feature have been the hypocritical Mr Murdoch, postman Fergus Jamieson, farmer Inverdarroch, old-fashioned Dr Wallace, minister Mr McPherson, *Auchtarne Herald* reporter Sheila Ramsey and Ardvain crofter Dougal Lachlan, but the series has also focused on the Lairds of Glendarroch House, to whose estate the village belongs. When the first Lady Laird, Elizabeth Cunningham, was dramatically killed in a car accident in 1987, and her daughter, Fiona, also left the house (she later married ruthless businessman Greg Ryder), Glendarroch gained new Lairds in the shape of Sir John and Lady Margaret Ross-Gifford. Being English, they were looked upon with distrust. Action has taken place in such settings as Blair's Store and the Ardnacraig Hotel, the latter run by the Ross-Giffords' son, Eric, and his wife, Joanna. The real-life village used for filming has been Luss on Loch Lomond.

Despite enjoying large audiences in its native Scotland, *Take the High Road* has only gained an afternoon time slot elsewhere in the UK. Nevertheless, it has become a firm favourite with housewives and has been sold to numerous other countries. The title was shortened to *High Road* in 1995.

TAKE THREE GIRLS

UK (BBC) Comedy Drama. BBC 1 1969–71

Kate	Susan Jameson

Avril	Angela Down
Victoria	Liza Goddard
Mr Edgecombe	David Langton
Jenny	Carolyn Seymour
Lulie	Barra Grant

Creator: Gerald Savory. Producer: Michael Hayes

Ups and downs in the lives of three girl flatsharers.

The three girls in question were the cello-playing deb Victoria (one of life's losers), failed actress Kate (a struggling single parent) and Cockney art student Avril. Together they shared a flat in London SW3 and with it their experiences of life as single women in the capital. Four of the 50-minute episodes were devoted to each girl's story. Also seen was Victoria's mean dad, Mr Edgecombe. When the second series began, only Victoria remained of the original trio, Kate having been married off and Avril leaving to work in Paris. Victoria was joined by new flatmates Jenny, a journalist, and Lulie, an American psychology graduate. A four-part reunion special, entitled *Take Three Women* and featuring Victoria, Kate and Avril, was screened in 1982. Thirteen years on from the earliest episodes, it saw Victoria widowed and raising her young daughter alone, Kate living with the teacher of her 13-year-old son and Avril proprietess of an art gallery. Music for early and later episodes was performed by folk, jazz and blues band Pentangle.

TAKE YOUR PICK

UK (Associated-Rediffusion/Arlington/-Thames) Quiz. ITV 1955–68; 1992–

Hosts: Michael Miles, Des O'Connor (1992).
Announcer: Bob Danvers-Walker

Popular quiz game played for laughs.

Hosted by New Zealander Michael Miles, billed as 'your quiz inquisitor', *Take Your Pick* took its place in the very first ITV schedules and stayed there (alongside its great rival, **Double Your Money**) for 13 years. Like *Double Your Money*, it graduated to television from Radio Luxembourg, where it had been a hit for three years. *Take Your Pick* involved contestants answering three general knowledge questions successfully to pick up a key to a numbered box. Each box contained details of a prize, although three of the prizes were worthless – a prune or a clothes peg, for example. Before the box was opened, Miles attempted to buy the key from the contestant, offering him or her ever-increasing sums of money. 'Take the money or open the box?', he asked, at the same time encouraging the audience to yell their advice. While some heads were turned by the prospect of cash in hand, others risked all on the turn of the key. To add to the excitement, there

was also the mysterious Box 13, the contents of which were unknown even to Miles, and the additional prospect of winning the Treasure Chest of Money or Tonight's Star Prize. The booming voice of Bob Danvers-Walker announced the prizes and Harold Smart gave a quick burst on the organ to add to the thrill.

To reach the questions stage, contestants – plucked from the studio audience just minutes before the show began – had to survive a gruelling ordeal in which Miles asked them questions about their life, work, hobbies, family, etc. Without hesitation, and without nodding or shaking their heads, participants had to respond avoiding the use of the words 'yes' and 'no'. Those that lasted longest progressed to the general knowledge phase. The 'Yes/No Interlude', as it became known, was patrolled by Alec Dane, who banged a gong whenever the forbidden words were uttered.

A year after *Take Your Pick* ended, Michael Miles resurfaced with a similar concept entitled *Wheel of Fortune*. Not to be confused with the later American import (hosted in the UK by Nicky Campbell; see separate entry), this *Wheel of Fortune* offered star and booby prizes just like *Take Your Pick*, only this time they were determined by the spin of a large wheel. Danvers-Walker and Smart were again in support. *Take Your Pick* itself was revived with some success in 1992. Des O'Connor took over from the late Miles and Jodie Wilson acted as his assistant and gongmistress, before she gave way in 1994 to the Australian twins Gayle and Gillian Blakeney, once of *Neighbours* fame.

TALES FROM EUROPE

Various (including BBC) Children's Drama Anthology. BBC 1 1964–9

Producer (UK): Peggy Miller

Anthology of Euro-fairy tales with an English commentary.

Effectively a pooling of material, *Tales from Europe* was the umbrella title given to a collection of children's drama serials (mostly fairy stories) produced by television companies all across the Continent. Each was shown in its native language, with an English narrative dubbed on top. Probably the best-remembered offering was a 1958 East German film called *The Singing Ringing Tree*, starring Christel Bodelstein as a beautiful but bad-tempered princess who wanted a magic tree for a wedding gift. Charles-Hans Vogt played the prince who tried to find her one and Antony Bilbow gave the English narrative.

TALES OF MYSTERY

UK (Associated-Rediffusion) Suspense Anthology. ITV 1961–3

Algernon Blackwood ....John Laurie

Executive Producer: John Frankau. Producer: Peter Graham Scott

Suspense anthology centring on the supernatural.

John Laurie, the rolling-eyed, spooky undertaker from **Dad's Army**, was the host of this series of half-hour thrillers. He took on the guise of writer Algernon Blackwood, the author of many of the bizarre tales that were adapted for the programme. Laurie generally introduced ghost stories, but the base was extended in the second and third seasons to include other supernatural yarns with a twist in the tail. Plenty of established British actors filled the lead roles, including Harry H. Corbett, Patrick Cargill, Peter Barkworth, Francesca Annis and Dinsdale Landen.

TALES OF PARA HANDY, The see *Para Handy – Master Mariner.*

TALES OF THE RIVERBANK

Canada (Dave Ellison/Ray Billings) Children's Entertainment. BBC 1960–4

Narrator (UK): Johnny Morris

Creators/Writers/Producers: Dave Ellison, Paul Sutherland. Producer (UK): Peggy Miller

Messing about on the water with a cute little hamster and his big friend, a white rat.

Tales of the Riverbank – screened by the BBC as part of the **Watch With Mother** lunch-time strand from 1963, but before that at around 5 pm – concerned the everyday affairs of busy Hammy Hamster, his friend Roderick the Rat and their wildlife associates, like GP the guinea pig. The animals were real, with words put into their mouths by the whimsical Johnny Morris. Their homes were furnished as human homes and they enjoyed all human comforts, including musical instruments, cars, aeroplanes and even a little boat in which to travel up and down the river. Produced in Canada, the series was filmed at high speed, so that the rodents' movements appeared slower and more deliberate in playback. And, because hamsters lose their looks after about nine months, dozens of look-alikes were called up to play Hammy over the years. The series was repeated on BBC1 until 1971 and also aired under the title of *Hammy Hamster's Adventures on the Riverbank* on ITV in the 1970s. A sequel, entitled *Further Tales of the Riverbank*, was also seen on Channel 4 in the 1990s.

TALES OF THE UNEXPECTED

UK (Anglia) Suspense Anthology. ITV 1979–88

Executive Producer: John Woolf. Producer: John Rosenberg

A collection of tales with a twist.

Originally introduced by Roald Dahl, whose short stories formed the core of this anthology, *Tales of the Unexpected (Roald Dahl's Tales of the Unexpected* for the first series) offered a weekly carousel ride of suspense and black humour, with always a neat, unsuspected quirky ending. Sinister fairground music played over the opening titles, which featured the slinky silhouette of a siren female dancer.

Some of Dahl's stories had already been treated to TV interpretation by **Alfred Hitchcock Presents**, but these mystery tales forwent Hitchcock's sardonic, oddball introductions, concentrating instead on a simple moral warning from the author. Even these were phased out when other writers were brought in. With a different cast for every episode, guest stars abounded, ranging from John Gielgud, Telly Savalas and Joan Collins to Joseph Cotton, Brian Blessed and Wendy Hiller. The series was a great export success for Anglia.

TALES OF WELLS FARGO see *Wells Fargo.*

TALK SHOW

Although the term talk show can apply to all kinds of interview programmes, it is more precisely connected with American audience participation shows like *Donahue* and *The Oprah Winfrey Show*, where selected members of the studio audience reveal their emotional hang ups and particular points of pique. Because of their low production costs, talk shows are popular choices for daytime programming. The term can also apply to celebrity interviews in the *Parkinson* and *Wogan* vein, although these are generally known as chat shows in the UK.

TARBUCK, JIMMY (1940–)

Liverpudlian comic turned TV quizmaster. A former Butlin's red coat, Tarbuck arrived on our screens in 1963 on programmes like *Comedy Bandbox* and, more notably, **Sunday Night at the London Palladium**, on which he proved to be an overnight success. He was so popular, in fact, that he made a number of quick return visits and, just two years later, took over as the show's compère. In tandem with the Merseybeat boom, he swiftly grew into one of the biggest names of the 1960s and 1970s, a familiar face on various star-studded shows and launching numerous series of his own.

These included *It's Tarbuck*, *Tarbuck at The Prince of Wales*, *The Jimmy Tarbuck Show*, *Tarbuck's Back* and *Tarbuck's Luck*, a sort of sitcom with guests. He later tried his hand at quizzes and chat shows. He hosted the gambling quiz *Winner Takes All* for many years and later presented *Tarby's Frame Game*. In 1984 he was in the chair for *Tarby and Friends*, although he has not forgotten his variety roots, emceeing events *Live from Her Majesty's* and *Live from the Palladium* in the 1980s. Actress Liza Tarbuck is one of his two daughters.

TARGET

UK (BBC) Police Drama. BBC 1 1977–8

Detective Supt Steve Hackett	Patrick Mower
Detective Sgt Louise Colbert	Vivien Heilbron
Detective Chief Supt Tate	Philip Madoc
Detective Sgt Frank Bonney	Brendan Price
DC Dukes	Carl Rigg

Producer: Philip Hinchcliffe

The rough, tough tactics of a regional police force.

In *Target*, viewers were, for once, treated to a police series based outside the big cities. But this was no village bobby fantasy. Instead, it surveyed the hard-hitting tactics of a Hampshire crime squad, working in and around an unidentified major port. Seventies trendy Patrick Mower was the actor charged with bringing the series some sex appeal as it was pitched into rivalry with ITV's *The Sweeney* to see which cops could punch the hardest. *Target* probably won fists up, but was criticized for its excessive violence and for its lack of humour, which, for many, was *The Sweeney*'s saving grace. A second series followed, but with the action toned down somewhat, though its main man, Steve Hackett, was just as unscrupulous as ever.

TARGET LUNA see *Pathfinders*.

TARMEY, WILLIAM (WILLIAM PIDDINGTON; 1941–)

Mancunian actor, a former builder and shop-keeper who entered showbusiness as a part-time singer, gradually picking up 'extra' work on a number of TV series. He appeared in dramas like *Crown Court*, *Strangers* and *The Ghosts of Motley Hall* before, in 1979, he was given the chance to appear as Jack Duckworth in *Coronation Street* and since becoming a regular cast member in 1983 has never looked back.

TARRANT, CHRIS (1946–)

British presenter, a former teacher who broke into television with ATV in Birmingham. As host

and producer of the anarchic *Tiswas*, he brought a new strain of children's television to the UK, making the show a cult favourite with adults, too. His attempt at a proper grown-up, late night version, *OTT* (Over The Top), failed miserably, however, and was replaced by another Tarrant offering, *Saturday Stayback*, after one series. Tarrant then headed into radio, taking over as breakfast presenter on London's Capital Radio, while making a name for himself in the advert voice-over world and contributing to LWT's *The Six O'Clock Show*. He succeeded Clive James and Keith Floyd in the chair of what became *Tarrant on TV*, and has since hosted numerous game shows, including *Everybody's Equal*, *Lose a Million*, *The Main Event* and *Pop Quiz*.

TARZAN

US (Banner) Adventure. ITV 1967–

Tarzan	Ron Ely
Jai	Manuel Padilla, Jnr
Jason Flood	Alan Caillou
Rao	Rockne Tarkington
Tall Boy	Stewart Raffill

More adventures with the apeman created by Edgar Rice Burroughs.

In this television version, Tarzan (the Earl of Greystoke) returned from civilization to live once again amongst his animal friends. This time, there was no Jane and no pidgin English, but at least the Tarzan yodel was authentic – they used the Johnny Weissmuller original. Now Tarzan was accompanied by a chimpanzee called Cheetah and Jai, a young native orphan he had befriended. Tracking down illegal hunters and other *persona non grata*, the Lord of the Jungle became a kind of game keeper and animal doctor. Also seen were Jai's tutor, Jason Flood, Rao, the local vet, and Rao's assistant, Tall Boy. The show was shot in Mexico and Brazil.

TAXI

UK (BBC) Comedy Drama. BBC 1963–4

Sid Stone	Sid James
Fred Cuddell	Bill Owen
Terry Mills	Ray Brooks
Madeleine	Vanda Godsell
Sandra	Diane Aubrey
Bert Stoker	Toke Townley
Dolly Stoker	Clare Kelly
Jean Stoker	Janet Kelly

Creator: Ted Willis. Writers: Ted Willis, Harry Driver, Jack Rosenthal. Producers: Michael Mills, Harry Carlisle, Douglas Moodie

A London taxi driver involves himself with other people's problems.

Driver Sid Stone owned his own cab and plied his trade on the streets of London. Unfortunately,

Sid also had a flair for interfering in other people's business, be they his fare-paying customers, his partner, Fred Cuddell, or his young colleague, Terry Mills. The three drivers shared rooms in a converted house and, in the second season, the upstairs neighbours, Bert and Dolly Stoker (with daughter Jean), were introduced. By that time, however, Fred had left the scene. Sid's girlfriends were Madeleine (in the first series) and Sandra (thereafter).

TAXI

US (Paramount/John Charles Walters)
Situation Comedy. BBC 1 1980-5

Alex Reiger	Judd Hirsch
Bobby Wheeler	Jeff Conaway
Louie De Palma	Danny De Vito
Elaine Nardo	Marilu Henner
Tony Banta	Tony Danza
Latka Gravas	Andy Kaufman
John Burns	Randall Carver
'Reverend' Jim 'Iggie' Ignatowski	Christopher Lloyd
Simka Dahblitz Gravas	Carol Kane
Jeff Bennett	J. Alan Thomas
Zina Sherman	Rhea Perlman

Creators/Writers/Executive Producers: James L. Brooks, Stan Daniels, Ed Weinberger, David Davis. Producers: Glen Charles, Les Charles

The sad, frustrated lives of a team of New York cabbies.

If you can't do the job you want, you can always drive a taxi until a suitable position becomes available. It'll only be for a while. Well, that was what the drivers at the Sunshine Cab Company believed. Here was a bunch of rainbow chasers, dreamers hoping that the right door would open so they could leave the grubby garage and move on to their chosen career. Sadly, you knew that they were likely to be driving taxis for the rest of their lives.

Amongst the crew was Tony Banta, a boxer who lost every fight, Bobby Wheeler, a failed actor, and Elaine Nardo, a single mother who longed to run an art gallery. More intriguing were Latka Gravas, the immigrant garage mechanic who could hardly speak English, and the wacky Reverend Jim, a burned out hippy who lived in a condemned flat and was oblivious to the world around him. While they planned their perfect futures they were hustled and hassled by the firm's lecherous dispatcher, the vicious, pint-sized Louie De Palma who barked out instructions from his 'cage'. He charged the cabbies for phone messages, spied on Elaine as she changed clothes and generally became their common enemy. Only one cabby was happy with his lot. That was kind, thoughtful Alex Reiger, a man with limited horizons. He was number one driver, a father figure and the best friend of all his colleagues.

Other characters who appeared were naive, romantic student John Burns (a driver for one season), and Simka, a scatter-brained compatriot of Latka's who went on to become his wife. Also seen was Rhea Perlman as Louie's girlfriend, Zina, a vending machine stocker. She and Danny De Vito were actually married during a *Taxi* lunchbreak and when the show's producers moved on to create **Cheers**, they took Perlman with them. De Vito and Christopher Lloyd soon became major Hollywood names, starring in films like *Romancing the Stone* and *Back to the Future* respectively, but Andy Kaufman, who played the zany Latka, tragically died of cancer in 1984.

TAYLOR, GWEN (GWEN ALLSOP; 1939-)

British actress seen mostly in comedy or light drama roles on television. Most prominent have been the parts of Amy Pearce in **Duty Free**, Rita Simcocks in **A Bit of a Do**, Liz in *Sob Sisters*, Celia Forrest in *The Sharp End*, Annie in *Screaming* and Gen in *Conjugal Rites*. Earlier credits included **Rutland Weekend Television** and numerous single dramas, including Alan Plater's Play For Today, *The Land of Green Ginger*.

TAYLOR, KEN (1922-)

British writer responsible for dramas like *The China Doll* (1960), *Into the Dark*, *The Tin Whistle Man* (both 1962), *The Devil and John Brown* (1964) and a trilogy beginning with *The Seekers* (also 1964). He also adapted H.G. Wells's *Days to Come* in 1966 and was later co-writer of **The Borgias**. Somewhat more successfully, Taylor wrote the screenplay for **The Jewel in the Crown** and he has contributed to popular series like **Miss Marple**.

TAYLOR, SHAW (1924-)

British presenter, most familiar urging viewers to 'keep 'em peeled' as host of **Police Five** (from 1962). Previously, Shaw had been quizmaster on the show **Dotto** and was later seen in ITV's motoring magazine *Drive-In*.

TBS

(Turner Broadcasting System) TBS, founded by Ted Turner, is the parent company of CNN, CNN International, TNT and Cartoon Network. Once a family business known as the Turner Advertising Company and specializing in billboard hoardings, the company changed its name when Turner bought into the world of television. In total, it operates 12 news and entertainment networks around the world. Part of the company's considerable assets is the 3300-title film library of the old MGM studios, which has been used to good effect in programming the TNT channel.

TCC see Children's Channel, The.

TELECINE

A machine which allows films and film inserts to be shown on television by converting them into electronic signals. In news programmes, filmed reports converted by telecine have now been replaced by videotape and VCRs.

TELEGOONS, THE

UK (BBC/Grosvenor Films) Comedy. BBC 1963–4

Writers: Spike Milligan, Eric Sykes, Larry Stephens. Producer: Tony Young

Animated, visual version of classic radio scripts from *The Goon Show*.

Although some new material was specially recorded, this puppet series essentially made use of archive radio programmes for its soundtrack. As in the radio days, *The Telegoons* were voiced by Peter Sellers, Harry Secombe and Spike Milligan, taking the parts of the characters Neddy Seagoon, Major Denis Bloodnok, Bluebottle, Eccles, Henry Crun, Moriarty, Minnie Bannister, Brigadier Grytpype-Thynne and others.

TELEPLAY

An old fashioned word (used in the 1950s and 1960s) for the script of a fictional drama programme, equivalent to screenplay in the cinema.

TELERECORDING

A primitive means of recording TV pictures onto film, used in the days before video tape as a way of preserving live broadcasts. Effectively, the TV screen was filmed and a telecine machine was used for playback. The system was known as kinescope in the USA.

TELETEXT

A TV screen-based data system that conveys information about news, sports, weather, recipes, travel, etc. It also offers subtitles for hearing impaired viewers on certain programmes. The viewer with a special Teletext TV set can call up the information at the press of a button. For the technically minded, the information is carried in the blanking interval of the TV waveform. The BBC's text service is known as Ceefax. ITV's service, having previously been known as Oracle, has been operated by Teletext Ltd since 1993. Teletext Ltd also provides Channel 4's service, 4-Tel.

TELETHON

The name given to a television broadcast marathon (lasting an entire evening or longer), specifically designed to draw attention to one or more causes and usually tied in with a charity appeal. The name was appropriated by ITV for their regular appeals in the late 1980s, although the best-known annual telethon is the BBC's **Children In Need**. Others have included **Comic Relief**.

TELEVISION

UK (Granada) Documentary. ITV 1984

Narrator: Ian Holm

Producer: Leslie Woodhead

The history of television, by television.

Tracing the development of the 20th-century's major communications medium, right from the pioneering days of Logie Baird and others (although not in a strict chronological order), this 13-part documentary squared up to the difficult task of evaluating the impact and style of television. Old footage, interviews, discussions, reconstructions and plenty of illustrative clips and flashbacks helped the producers to reflect on television's treatment of news, politics, drama, comedy, commercials, etc. Filming took place right across the globe, showing East Berliners watching West German TV, extracts from a Samurai drama in Japan, an outside broadcast in Indonesia and the transmission of Soviet news simultaneously in places as far apart as Tashkent and Siberia. An edited version was prepared for transmission in the USA, taking out certain British examples and adding in American substitutes.

TELEVISION DANCING CLUB

UK (BBC) Entertainment. BBC 1948–64

Producer: Richard Afton

Long-running dance showcase.

Pre-dating its sister programme, **Come Dancing**, by two years, *Television Dancing Club* was largely devoted to the dance music of Victor Sylvester and his Ballroom Orchestra. Sylvester also offered dance instruction and was assisted by hostesses Patti Morgan and Sylvia Peters. For the last season, 1963–4, the title was shortened to *Dancing Club*.

TELEVISION SOUTH see TVS.

TELEVISION SOUTH WEST see TSW.

TELEVISION TOP OF THE FORM

UK (BBC) Quiz. BBC 1 1962–75

Presenters:
Geoffrey Wheeler
David Dimbleby

Paddy Feeny
John Edmunds
John Dunn

Producers: Innes Lloyd, Bill Wright, Mary Evans

General knowledge tournament for grammar school kids.

Launched on radio in 1948 and emulated on television from 1962, *Top of the Form* was a contest for well-behaved high school children. Schools were invited to put forward a team of four pupils, of varying ages, to compete in a national tournament to find who really was 'Top of the Form'. In the early days, two questionmasters were employed, one in the assembly hall of one school and the other similarly housed at another. Geoffrey Wheeler and David Dimbleby were the first to fill these roles and Boswell Taylor was the programme's chief question setter. In 1967 a special *Transworld Top of the Form* was seen. Linking teams in the UK and Australia, it was chaired by Aussie anchorman Bill Salmon.

TELEVISION WALES AND WEST see TWW.

TELFORD'S CHANGE

UK (BBC) Drama. BBC 1 1979

Mark Telford .... Peter Barkworth
Sylvia Telford .... Hannah Gordon
Tim Hart .... Keith Barron
Maddox .... Colin Douglas
Helen Santon .... Zena Walker

Writer: Brian Clark. Producer: Mark Shivas

A successful banker opts for the quiet life and, in so doing, puts his marriage on the line.

High-flying, middle-aged bank official Mark Telford had reached a crossroads in life. Should he continue in the fast lane or was it time to take things a little more easily? He opted for the latter, accepting an appointment as the manager of a branch in the provinces. His wife, Sylvia, however, refused to be dragged away from London where she was carving out a career in show-business. The result was a ten-episode soapy drama that focused on the intriguing clients of the country bank and the various twists and turns of the Telfords' marriage, which was threatened by the intrusion of Sylvia's friend Tim Hart.

TELL IT TO THE MARINES

UK (Associated-Rediffusion) Situation Comedy. ITV 1959–60

Leading Seaman White .... Alan White
Cpl Surtees .... Ronald Hines
Lt Raleigh .... Henry McGee
Petty Officer Woodward .... John Bascombe
Whittle.. Ian Whittaker
Kilmartin Dalrymple .... Ian MacNaughton
Commander Walters .... Ian Colin
Major Howard .... Jack Allen

Creator: Ted Willis. Writers: Eric Paice, Malcolm Hulke. Producer: Milo Lewis

The Navy and the Marines share a traditional rivalry.

Exploiting the long-standing tensions between the men of the Royal Navy and those of the Royal Marines, *Tell It to the Marines* featured petty squabbles, minor battles and endless joking between the two forces. Principal amongst the protagonists were Leading Seaman White and Marine Cpl Surtees, with superior officers like Lt Raleigh and Major Howard also in the fray.

TELLY ADDICTS

UK (BBC) Quiz. BBC 1 1985–

Presenter: Noel Edmonds

Producers: Juliet May, John King, Richard L. Lewis

Teams of contestants test their knowledge of television.

In this light-hearted quiz, two teams of four have competed to show off their knowledge of television history. For the first nine years, the teams were made up of family members only, but, in 1994, the rules were relaxed to allow friends, workmates, etc. to make up the numbers. (Also in 1994, *The Archers* actor Charles Collingwood was recruited to fool around while reading out the scores.) At the end of a knockout tournament the *Telly Addicts* Champions have been found. The first winning team was the Payne family from Swindon, but in that inaugural series the rules were different. Instead of progressing through a knockout, the winning family stayed on to meet new challengers week after week. In 1995 the series celebrated its tenth anniversary with *Champion Telly Addicts*, an additional tournament designed to find the best of the best.

The origins of *Telly Addicts* lay in a series entitled *Telly Quiz*, presented by Jerry Stevens, which was seen on BBC 1 between Christmas Eve 1984 and 2 January 1985. In *Telly Quiz*, celebrities took on viewers, as they did in an early rival to *Telly Addicts*, ITV's *We Love TV*, which was hosted by Gloria Hunniford.

TEMPO

UK (ABC) Arts. ITV 1961–7

Presenters: Lord Harewood, Leonard Maguire

Creator: Kenneth Tynan. Editors: Kenneth Tynan, Peter Luke, Clive Goodwin

Fortnightly arts magazine.

Conceived as a response to the BBC's successful *Monitor* programme, *Tempo* was a 50-minute (later 25-minute) arts indulgence hosted first by Lord Harewood, then by Leonard Maguire and others. As well as the classic arts of painting, sculpture, ballet and music, *Tempo* also reviewed film, literature and drama, with the aim of allowing a mass audience to appreciate the artistic world without the intrusion of academic opinion.

TENKO

UK (BBC) Drama. BBC 1 1981–4

Rose Millar	Stephanie Beacham
Marion Jefferson	Ann Bell
Sylvia Ashburton	Renee Asherson
Major Yamauchi	Bert Kwouk
Dr Beatrice Mason	Stephanie Cole
Kate Norris	Claire Oberman
Minah	Pauline Peters
Vicky Armstrong	Wendy Williams
Sally Markham	Joanna Hole
Nellie Keene	Jeananne Crowley
Gerda	Maya Woolfe
Mrs Domenica Van Meyer	Elizabeth Chambers
Christina Campbell	Emily Bolton
Blanche Simmons	Louise Jameson
Dorothy Bennett	Veronica Roberts
Joss Holbrook	Jean Anderson
Debbie Bowen	Karin Foley
Verna Johnson	Rosemary Martin
Maggie Thorpe	Elizabeth Mickery
Alice Courtenay	Cindy Shelley
Edna	Edna Doré
Colonel Clifford Jefferson	Jonathan Newth
Bernard Webster	Edmund Pegge
Cpl Jackson	Colin Dunn
Major Sims	David Gooderson
Sister Ulrica	Patricia Lawrence
Miss Hassan	Josephine Welcome
Johnny Saunders	Gregory de Polnay
Harry Milne	Andrew Sharp
Father Lim	Ric Young
Tom Redburn	Daniel Hill
Jack Armstrong	Ivor Danvers
Simon Treves	Jeffrey Hardy
Dolah	Ronald Eng
Shinya	Takashi Kawahara
Kasaki	Takahiro Oba
Yukio	Peter Silverleaf
Sato	Eiji Kusuhara
Joan	Dawn Keeler
Timmy	Nigel Harman

Creator: Lavinia Warner. Writers: Jill Hyem, Anne Valery, Paul Wheeler. Producers: Ken Riddington, Vere Lorrimer

The hardships of female prisoner of war camps in 1940s Malaya.

Following the invasion of Singapore by Japan in 1942, the expatriot women of Britain and Holland were torn from their menfolk and imprisoned in makeshift holding camps. *Tenko* – meaning 'roll call' in Japanese – told the story of one such group of women, trapped in filthy conditions, abused, beaten and degraded, thousands of miles from home and out of reach of assistance. Their appalling living conditions, their relationships with their captors, and the relationships between the women themselves (where race and class became prominent issues) were documented in this hugely popular programme which ran for three seasons.

Appointed head of the women was Marion Jefferson, the wife of a colonel and the obvious choice as leader. Around her were gathered the likes of rape victim Rose Millar, Beatrice Mason, a formidable doctor, nurses Kate Norris and Nellie Keene, ageing academic Joss Holbrook, Dorothy Bennett who, having lost both her husband and her child, turned to prostitution with the guards, tarty Cockney Blanche Simmons and the ladylike Verna Johnson. The formidable Sister Ulrica was head of the Dutch section, which also featured the nauseatingly selfish Mrs Van Meyer. The cruelty of their captors was too underplayed, according to some viewers, but, nevertheless, the prisoners were subjected to enormous humiliation, torturous working conditions, malnutrition, disease, long marches to new camps and insufferable indignity beneath a baking Asian sun.

The first series depicted how the women struggled to adjust to captivity and how the hope of release lingered long in their minds. By the second season, that hope had largely disappeared, replaced by a determination to survive, as their personal values changed dramatically. The last series concerned the end of the war and the efforts of the survivors to come to terms with life back in society, coping with estranged husbands and shattered lifestyles. A one-off reunion episode, played as a murder mystery and set in 1950, was produced in 1985.

The series was created by Lavinia Warner, who had researched the history of Japanese POW camps for a *This Is Your Life* programme on Margo Turner, a nursing corps officer who had once been held captive. Warner developed the idea into an *Omnibus* documentary before dramatizing the harrowing events in *Tenko*.

TERRAHAWKS

UK (Anderson Burr/LWT) Children's Science Fiction. ITV 1983–6

Voices:

Zelda	Denise Bryer

Sgt Major Zero ....Windsor Davies
Captain Mary Falconer ....Denise Bryer
Dr Tiger Ninestein...............................Jeremy Hitcher
Lt Hiro ....Jeremy Hitcher
Lt Hawkeye ....Jeremy Hitcher
Captain Kate Kestrel ....Anne Ridler
Yung-Star ....Ben Stevens
Cy-Star...Anne Ridler
Hudson ....Ben Stevens
Space Sgt 101 ....Ben Stevens

Creator: Gerry Anderson. Writer: Tony
Barwick. Producers: Gerry Anderson,
Christopher Burr

**A defence force protects the Earth from
an ugly alien witch queen.**

There were no strings attached in *Terrahawks*. In
Gerry Anderson's major contribution to 1980s
television, his 'Supermarionation' progressed into
'Supermacromation', an advanced form of glove
puppetry. However, following the tried and
tested Anderson formula, the heroes were unsur-
prisingly familiar. They were the Terrahawks, an
elite squad of dare-devils who risked life and limb
to save the Earth from alien invasion in the year
2020.

Headed by Dr Tiger Ninestein, the ninth clone
of an Austrian-American scientist, Gerhard Stein,
the Terrahawks consisted of ace pilot Mary
Falconer, Hawkeye, an American athlete with
computer-aided vision, Lt Hiro, the team's computer boffin, and pop singer-turned-pilot, Kate
Kestrel. From Hawknest, a secret South
American base, they faced the cunning might of
the cackling, prune-faced android, Zelda, and her
equally hideous allies from the planet Guk. These
included her useless son, Yung-Star, and her
spiteful twin sister, Cy-Star. With the use of
cube-shaped robots, and other agents like Yuri,
the space bear, and MOID (Master of Infinite
Disguise), Zelda aimed to take over the planet.
The Terrahawks, in their spaceship known as
Hawkwing, covered her every move, assisted by
round robots called Zeroids. These were controlled when on Earth by Sgt Major Zero and
when in space by Space Sgt 101, pilot of the
Zeroid spacecraft, Spacehawk. Also on display
was Hudson, a Rolls-Royce with a mind of its
own, a clear throwback to Anderson's
Thunderbirds days.

TERRY AND JUNE

UK (BBC) Situation Comedy. BBC 1 1979–87

Terry Medford ....Terry Scott
June Medford ....June Whitfield
Sir Dennis Hodge ....Reginald Marsh
Miss Fennel ....Joanna Henderson
Rosemary Frankall ....Beattie
Malcolm..Tim Barrett
John Quayle

Creator: John Kane. Producers: Peter
Whitmore, Robin Nash

**Mishaps and misunderstandings in the life
of a typical suburban couple.**

Terry and June Medford were an ordinary
middle-class couple whiling away their middle
age in suburban Purley – except that Terry was
bumptious, ham-fisted, over-ambitious and help-
lessly accident prone, and June was the archetypal long-suffering wife who had to pick up the
pieces. Terry commuted into the city where he
worked for Sir Dennis Hodge, a man likely to call
at the Medfords' home just at the wrong
moment, usually with farcical consequences.

Safe, silly and unspectacular, *Terry and June* was
effectively a reworking of an early Scott/
Whitfield sitcom, **Happy Ever After**, but without
the old lady, the mynah bird or occasional visits
from grown-up children seen in the earlier
outing.

TERRY-THOMAS (THOMAS TERRY HOAR STEVENS; 1911–90)

Although largely known for his film work, gap-
toothed, plummy comedian Terry-Thomas was
one of TV's earliest stars, appearing on the BBC
from the 1940s in programmes like *To Town With
Terry*, *How Do You View?* and *Strictly Terry-
Thomas*. He later headed for the USA where his
'frightfully-Englishness' led to more TV success
(including guest appearances in series like **Burke's
Law**), but he found his better days behind him
when he returned to the BBC in 1968 for a
short-lived comedy entitled *The Old Campaigner*,
in which he played travelling salesman Jimmy
Franklin-Jones. He was a second cousin of
Richard Briers.

TEST CARD

A card marked with colours, shades, patterns and
lines of various sizes and thicknesses, used by
engineers to calibrate cameras and monitors for
best performance. The test card was a familiar
sight until daytime television arrived in the
1980s, with TV installers using it to set up and
adjust receivers. The BBC colour test card featured a schoolgirl, a blackboard and some toys.
The girl's name was Carol Hersey and she consequently holds the record for being the most-seen
person on British television.

THAMES TELEVISION

Formed by the merger of two ITV contractors
(ABC and Associated-Rediffusion), at the instigation of the ITA, Thames took over the London
weekday franchise on 29 July 1968. Its franchise

was retained during the 1980 reviews but was surprisingly taken away from the company in the 1991 auctions, when Thames was outbid by Carlton Communications. This decision, amongst others, seriously brought into question the logic of the new auction system, whereby the franchise was awarded to the highest bidder, providing the ITC was satisfied that business plans were viable and commitments to programme quality would be met. It effectively ignored Thames's remarkable programming record which had brought many notable contributions to the ITV network. Amongst the company's biggest hits were *The Sweeney*, *Minder*, *This Is Your Life*, *Man about the House*, *The World at War*, *Rock Follies*, *Bless this House*, *This Week*, *The Wind in the Willows*, *The Bill* and *Wish You Were Here . . . ?*

Thames has since concentrated on programme production and also helped establish the satellite channel UK Gold, which broadcasts archive Thames material alongside old BBC favourites. A consortium headed by Thames was the sole bidder for the proposed Channel 5 project, when it was first touted, but, with doubts about the viability of the new network and the company's business plan, the licence was not awarded by the ITC.

THANK YOUR LUCKY STARS

UK (ABC) Pop Music. ITV 1961–6

Presenters: Keith Fordyce, Brian Matthew, Jim Dale

Producers: Philip Jones, Helen Standage, Keith Beckett, Milo Lewis

Successful Saturday evening pop show.

Planned as ITV's answer to *Juke Box Jury*, *Thank Your Lucky Stars* presented the pop sensations of the day miming to their latest tracks. Keith Fordyce and, later, Brian Matthew were the frontmen. Also seen was Don Moss. The segment known as Spin A Disc (a shamelessly direct copy of *Juke Box Jury*) called on a panel of celebrities and local teenagers to give their views on record releases and it was in this part of the programme that 16-year-old office clerk Janice Nicholls was discovered in 1962. Her broad Black Country accent, displayed when she declared 'Oi'll give it foive', made her an instant favourite and ensured she became a programme regular. *Thank Your Lucky Stars* also gave The Beatles their first national television exposure, in February 1963. Jim Dale took over as presenter in 1965, but the programme was cancelled a year later, just as the British beat boom was coming to a close.

THAT WAS THE WEEK THAT WAS

UK (BBC) Comedy. BBC 1962–3

David Frost
Millicent Martin

Lance Percival
Bernard Levin
William Rushton
Roy Kinnear
John Wells
Timothy Birdsall
Kenneth Cope
David Kernan
John Bird
Al Mancini
Roy Hudd
Eleanor Bron

Producer: Ned Sherrin.

Hard-hitting, revolutionary satire, week by week, *That Was The Week That Was* broke new ground for television. Airing on a Saturday night, it was a product of the BBC's current affairs department rather than its light entertainment crew, a fact reflected in its commitment to topicality and its biting tone. The programme looked at the major events of the previous week, ridiculed them, drew comment and exposed ironies. At the helm was a young David Frost, who became host after both Brian Redhead and John Bird had declined the position. Frost's team included the likes of Willie Rushton, Roy Kinnear, Lance Percival, Bernard Levin and Millicent Martin, whose opening song recalled the week's news in its lyrics. The remainder of the programme was given over to sketches, interviews and guest spots, with scripts written by the likes of Kenneth Tynan, Dennis Potter and Keith Waterhouse. For the first time, sacred cows like racism, royalty, politics and religion were slaughtered in a humorous fashion, prompting much criticism from the Establishment. Individuals were also singled out for treatment. The then Home Secretary Henry Brooke came in for some noticeable flak, for instance, as did record producer Norrie Paramour. Bernard Levin upset many viewers with his forthright opinions (to the point where one night a member of the studio audience pushed him off his stool). In addition, the programme adopted a technically *laissez faire* approach which allowed cameras to wander into shot and the studio audience to be seen, something which had seldom been experienced before on prim and proper British television.

The format and title also transferred to the USA, again with Frost in the chair. His Stateside collaborators included Alan Alda and Tom Bosley, but the show didn't really click. Back in the UK, *TW3* (as it became known) was taken off before the election year of 1964 (in case it influenced voters) and was succeeded by two short-lived sequels, *Not So Much a Programme, More a Way of Life* and *BBC 3*.

THAT'S LIFE

UK (BBC) Consumer Affairs. BBC 1 1973–94

Presenters: Esther Rantzen, George Layton, Bob

Wellings, Kieran Prendiville, Glyn Worsnip, Cyril Fletcher, Paul Heiney, Chris Serle, Bill Buckley, Doc Cox, Gavin Campbell, Michael Groth, Joanna Munro, John Gould, Maev Alexander, Adrian Mills, Grant Baynham, Mollie Sugden, Howard Leader, Simon Fanshawe, Scott Sherrin, Kevin Devine

Creator: John Lloyd. Producers/Editors: Esther Rantzen, Henry Murray, Peter Chafer, Michael Bunce, Ron Neil, Gordon Watts, John Morrell, Bryher Scudamore, Shawn Woodward, John Getgood

Consumer/light entertainment magazine filled with silly stunts, painful puns and invaluable investigations.

Originally planned for just a six-week run, *That's Life* continued instead for 21 years. The series was conceived as a follow-up to the Saturday night offering **Braden's Week**, in which Bernard Braden and a team of reporters made people laugh and fought consumers' battles. One of those reporters was Esther Rantzen and, installed in the new *That's Life* format, she quickly made the series her own.

Rantzen was assisted by an ever-changing team of mostly male reporters, with George Layton and Bob Wellings her first co-stars. Cyril Fletcher joined in 1974 to recite his odd odes and to pick out funny misprints from newspapers (a job later done by Mollie Sugden and Doc Cox amongst others), and Richard Stilgoe, the Fivepenny Piece and Victoria Wood were recruited to provide witty songs. A weekly vox pop saw Esther out on the streets of London, challenging punters to sample strange items of food or drink. Invariably, she bumped into Annie, an elderly lady who became a stalwart of the programme.

That's Life also offered plenty of daft stories about talented pets and quirky pastimes, but its real merit was as a consumers' champion. It presented a 'Heap of the Week' award for shoddily-made goods, dished out 'Jobsworth' and plain English accolades for excessive bureaucracy and tackled conmen on their doorsteps. More importantly still, the programme also campaigned heavily for the protection of children, a crusade which resulted in the establishment of the Childline charity.

In 1984 a story which moved every viewer concerned two-year-old Ben Hardwicke, a toddler suffering from an incurable liver disease. Ben sadly died, but not before the case for child organ transplants had been thoroughly aired. As part of the campaign, Marti Webb released a version of Michael Jackson's 'Ben', which reached the Top Five in 1985.

That's Life, with its careful balance of the silly and the serious, its brassy theme music and topical closing cartoons (drawn by Rod Jordan), became an intrinsic part of Saturday, and later Sunday, evenings for many viewers.

THAT'S MY BOY

UK (Yorkshire) Situation Comedy. ITV 1981–6

Ida Willis	Mollie Sugden
Dr Robert Price	Christopher Blake
Angie Price	Jennifer Lonsdale
Mrs Price	Clare Richards
Wilfred Willis	Harold Goodwin
Miss Parfitt	Deddie Davies

Writer: Pam Valentine, Michael Ashton. Producer: Graeme Muir

A housekeeper discovers her employer is really her son.

After endlessly pestering a domestic employment agency, fearsome Ida Willis was finally installed in the position of housekeeper to young Dr Robert Price and his model wife, Angie. Gradually realizing that Robert was the son she gave away for adoption at birth, Ida became increasingly possessive of him, much to the despair of his adoptive mother. The young doctor was left to dither between the two. The family (and housekeeper) later moved to Yorkshire, where Ida gained a friend, Miss Parfitt, and also had her brother, Wilfred, to keep her occupied.

THAW, JOHN CBE (1942–)

Characters as well-defined as **Inspector Morse**, **The Sweeney**'s Jack Regan and **Home to Roost**'s Henry Willows testify to the versatility of award-winning British actor John Thaw. Thaw's first starring role was in **Redcap** in 1965, playing military policeman John Mann. Apart from the series listed above, he has also been seen as Stan, a crook, in the comedy *Thick as Thieves*. He was Francis Drake in a 1980 TV movie, *Drake's Venture*, Bomber Harris in the controversial dramatization of wartime RAF activity, Stanley Duke in *Stanley and the Women*, Peter Mayle in *A Year in Provence*, James Kavanagh in *Kavanagh QC* and Labour Party leader George Jones in the *Screen Two* presentation *The Absence of War*. Guest appearances in programmes like *Z Cars*, *The Avengers*, *The Morecambe and Wise Show* and *The Onedin Line* have added to his credits. Thaw is married to actress Sheila Hancock.

THICK AS THIEVES

UK (LWT) Situation Comedy. ITV 1974

George Dobbs	Bob Hoskins
Stan	John Thaw
Annie	Pat Ashton
Tommy Hollister	Trevor Peacock
Daphne	Nell Curran

Creators/Writers: Dick Clement, Ian La Frenais. Producer: Derrick Goodwin

Two crooks share one house and one woman.

When petty criminal George 'Dobbsie' Dobbs was released from prison after three years, he returned home to Fulham to discover his best pal, Stan, shacked up with his missus, Annie. Rather than punching each other's lights out, they reluctantly agreed to share the house, with predictable consequences, especially when on the run jailbird Tommy Hollister also moved in. Daphne was Annie's friend and much needed confidante.

Only eight episodes were produced, although creators Dick Clement and Ian La Frenais had made plans to develop the series, sending its two main protagonists back inside. Instead, largely because actor John Thaw had been signed up for *The Sweeney*, they returned to the BBC for whom they developed their Ronnie Barker pilot *Prisoner and Escort* into another old lag comedy – *Porridge*.

THIN MAN, THE

US (MGM) Detective Drama. BBC 1957–8

Nick Charles ....Peter Lawford
Nora Charles...Phyllis Kirk
Lt Ralph Raines ....Stafford Repp
Lt Steve King...Tol Avery

A husband, a wife and their dog are a team of amateur detectives.

The first thing to forget about this series is the Thin Man. There wasn't one. That character had appeared in the film from which the series was derived, and in which our heroes, Nick and Nora Charles, made their debut. Played by William Powell and Myrna Loy, this pair of amateur sleuths appeared in five more cinema features before arriving on TV in the hands of Peter Lawford and Phyllis Kirk.

Nick had been a private eye with the Trans-American Detective Agency, but now, fabulously rich, he and his new wife, Nora, had retired to a swanky apartment on New York's Park Avenue and settled into a world of good living. However, Nick found old habits die hard, and he soon returned to the detective game, this time with his devoted wife at his side. The couple's wire-haired fox terrier, Asta, also played a part, sniffing out clues like a bloodhound. What the plots lacked in depth, was compensated for by the sparkling husband and wife repartee.

These characters, created by novelist Dashiell Hammett, have proved highly influential. If you ever wondered where the likes of *Hart to Hart*, *McMillan and Wife* and *The Wilde Alliance* found their inspiration, look no further.

THIRD MAN, THE

UK/US (BBC/National Telefilm/British Lion) Drama. BBC 1959–64

Harry Lime ....Michael Rennie
Bradford Webster ....Jonathan Harris
Arthur Shillings.....................................Rupert Davies

Executive Producer: Vernon Burns. Producer: Felix Jackson

The further adventures of Graham Greene's treacherous Viennese double-dealer.

In a move away from the famous cinema version starring Orson Wells, the TV *Third Man* cast Michael Rennie as Harry Lime, a charming amateur sleuth – quite unlike the film character – officially running an import-export agency but travelling the world to pin down crooks and help people in trouble at the same time. Specializing in works of art, the suave, sophisticated Lime's companies included Harry Lime Ltd, in London, and its equivalent, Harry Lime Inc., in New York. In his work he was assisted by his treasurer-cum-manservant, Bradford Webster (played by a pre-*Lost in Space* Jonathan Harris), and on his investigations he enjoyed a close liaison with Scotland Yard's Arthur Shillings (Rupert Davies in training for his future role as *Maigret*). A joint UK/US production, filming took place in both Shepperton Studios and Hollywood.

THIRTYSOMETHING

US (MGM/United Artists) Drama. Channel 4 1989–92

Michael Steadman...Ken Olin
Hope Murdoch Steadman ....Mel Harris
Elliot Weston ....Timothy Busfield
Nancy Weston ....Patricia Wettig
Melissa Steadman.............................Melanie Mayron
Ellyn Warren ....Polly Draper
Professor Gary Shepherd ....Peter Horton
Janey Steadman ....Brittany and Lacey Craven
Ethan Weston ....Luke Rossi
Brittany Weston ....Jordana 'Bink' Shapiro
Miles Drentell ....David Clennon
Susannah Hart/Shepherd ....Patricia Kalember
Steve Woodman ....Terry Kinney
Jeffrey Milgrom ....Richard Gilliland
Lee Owens..Corey Parker
Billy Sidel..Erich Anderson

Creators: Ed Zwick, Marshall Herskovitz. Producers: Ed Zwick, Marshall Herskovitz, Paul Haggis

Light-hearted drama series centring on a group of upwardly mobile friends in Philadelphia.

Against a background of disappearing youth and unfulfilled careers, *thirtysomething* introduced viewers to seven professional people in their thirties, children of the baby-boomer generation, now adults in a yuppie world. There were two couples and three singles, and the programme traced their lives, their loves, their fears and their ambitions.

Michael and Elliot were colleagues at an advertising agency who branched out into their own business. Hope and Nancy were their respective wives. Hope was a Princeton graduate and writer who put her own career on hold in order to raise little Janey (and later Leo); Nancy was a 1960s flower child with artistic pretensions, who looked after her and Elliot's school-age children, Ethan and Brittany. The three other protagonists were Gary Shepherd, a long-haired college classics lecturer, Melissa Steadman, Michael's photographer cousin, and Ellyn Warren (Hope's best friend), an administrator at the City Hall. Both Melissa and Ellyn drifted in and out of affairs, before Ellyn eventually married an old flame, Billy Sidel.

The series focused on each of the characters as they reached the crossroads and crises that affect everyone's lives, like the death of a parent (Michael's father), marital problems (Nancy and Elliot went through a messy separation) and personal illness (Nancy was diagnosed as having ovarian cancer). Career matters were always under discussion, particularly when Michael and Elliot's business collapsed and they were forced to work for the devious Miles Drentell. Romance was never far away, as when Gary married Susannah Hart and they had baby Emma. Nor was death. Gary was then killed in a car accident. It was not surprising to discover that most of the programme's audience were in their 30s themselves. Viewers clearly identified with the series, sharing the characters' childhood memories and facing up to the same challenges of maturity.

THIS IS YOUR LIFE

UK (BBC/Thames) Entertainment.
BBC 1955–64; ITV 1969–94; BBC 1 1994–

Presenters: Eamonn Andrews, Michael Aspel

Creator: Ralph Edwards. Producers: T. Leslie Jackson, Vere Lorrimer, Robert Tyrrel, Malcolm Morris, Jack Crawshaw

The lifestory of an unsuspecting celebrity retold with the help of surprise guests.

Taking people unawares, surrounding them with friends and family, and reliving the major moments in their life is what this programme has been all about. *This is Your Life* began on American TV in 1952, with Ralph Edwards, its creator, also acting as host. In the UK it has meandered between channels, beginning first on

the BBC in 1955 and running for nine years. After a five-year hiatus, Thames picked up the format for ITV and the company continued to produce the show when it returned to the BBC in 1994. Over the years, it has consistently topped the ratings.

The same formula has been followed from the start. The unsuspecting victim has been cornered by the presenter (usually in disguise) at a public event or at a contrived meeting, informed 'This is Your Life' and then whisked away to a nearby TV studio, where close family and friends have welcomed the feted one. Other guests have been introduced as the host has worked his way chronologically through the person's life, reading from a large red book. Mystery voices hidden behind closed doors have given way to forgotten faces and warm embraces. Amusing anecdotes have been told and glowing tributes have been paid. The final guest has usually been someone special: a child from the other side of the world, an inspirational teacher from the distant past, a person who has saved the celebrity's life, or vice-versa. Buckets of tears have been shed.

The very first victim was Eamonn Andrews, who was already signed up to be the programme's regular host. Ralph Edwards had flown over from the USA to conduct the inaugural programme but, after the *Daily Sketch* had spoiled the launch by revealing that the subject was going to be Stanley Matthews, a new victim had to be found. Andrews expected boxer Freddie Mills to be the target. Instead, it was Andrews himself. When Thames revived the series, its first victim was Des O'Connor. Some celebrities refused outright to appear. Soccer star Danny Blanchflower was one; novelist Richard Gordon (of *Doctor in the House* fame) was another. To avoid such embarrassments, the programme is now pre-recorded.

Not all those featured have been famous. One or two guests per series have come from the ranks of anonymous worthies – brave airmen, industrious charity workers, selfless foster parents, etc. Probably the highest profile victim was Lord Mountbatten, the subject of a *This is Your Life* special in the Jubilee Year of 1977.

When Eamonn Andrews died in 1987, Michael Aspel picked up the big red book. The one used on screen only contains the programme script, but a real biographical scrapbook is later presented as a memento to the featured guest. Regular consultants to the series have been Roy Bottomley and Tom Brennand.

THIS WEEK

UK (Associated-Rediffusion/Thames) Current Affairs. ITV 1956–78; 1986–92

Presenters: Rene Cutforth, Leslie Mitchell, Michael

Westmore, Ludovic Kennedy, Daniel Farson, Brian Connell, Alastair Burnet, Jonathan Dimbleby

Editors/Producers: Caryl Doncaster, Peter Hunt, Cyril Bennett, Peter Morley, Jeremy Isaacs, Cliff Morgan, Phillip Whitehead, David Elstein

Award-winning weekly current affairs reports.

ITV's answer to *Panorama*, *This Week* began life as a simple topical news magazine with the slogan 'A window on the world behind the headlines'. In the mid-1960s, *This Week* changed to adopt the single investigation format it employed until its demise in 1992. Among its celebrated crew were reporters like Desmond Wilcox, James Cameron, Robert Kee, Llew Gardner and, later, Jonathan Dimbleby. For some reason, the programme was renamed *TV Eye* in 1978 (when one of its reporters was the temporarily unseated Labour MP Bryan Gould), but the original title was restored in 1986. *This Week's* stirring theme music was an excerpt from Sibelius's *Karelia Suite*.

THOMAS, ANTONY (1940–)

British documentary film-maker, known for his passionate involvement in his work. His prize-winning trilogy *The South African Experience* aired in 1977, although infinitely more controversial was his *Death of a Princess* in 1980, a dramatized account of the execution of an Islamic princess who had adopted some western ideas and so questioned the values of Islam. It led to an international row and the disruption of diplomatic relations between Britain and Saudi Arabia. Other contributions have included *Where Harry Stood*, *The Japanese Experience* (both 1974), *The Arab Experience* (1975), *The Good, The Bad and The Indifferent* (1976) and *The Most Dangerous Man in the World* (1982).

THOMAS, GARETH

Welsh Shakespearean actor who has enjoyed a number of popular roles on television. Probably his most prominent was as the rebel leader Roj Blake in *Blake's 7*, even though he was only a member of the cast for the first two seasons. He was also DC Ron Radley in *Parkin's Patch*, Dr Philip Denny in *The Citadel*, Reverend Mr Gruffydd in *How Green Was My Valley*, Major General Horton in *By the Sword Divided*, scientist Adam Brake in *Children of the Stones*, Owen in *The Knights of God*, refugee Shem in *Star Maidens*, and Morgan in *Morgan's Boy*. Thomas has also appeared in *Shades of Darkness*, *Hammer House of Horror* and numerous single dramas.

THOMAS THE TANK ENGINE AND FRIENDS

UK (Clearwater/Britt Allcroft/Central) Animation. ITV 1984–6; 1992

Narrators: Ringo Starr, Michael Angelis (1992)

Writers: Britt Allcroft, David Mitton. Executive Producer: Britt Allcroft. Producers: Britt Allcroft, David Mitton, Robert Cardona

The adventures of a steam railway engine and his fellow vehicles.

Narrated initially by Beatle Ringo Starr and then in the same dry, Liverpudlian manner by Michael Angelis, *Thomas the Tank Engine and Friends* was the television incarnation of Reverend Wilbert Awdry's children's stories from the 1940s. Star of the show was Thomas, the blue tank engine bearing the number 1. Unlike most children's characters, Thomas was not always a goodie, and was prone to bouts of moodiness, depicted in his expressionful face and rolling eyes (painted on the front). All the same, he became a hero for toddlers and a massive merchandizing business took off as a result.

Joining Thomas in his scrapes on the island of Sodor were old Edward, the blue number 2 engine, Henry (green, number 3), Gordon (blue, number 4), James the mixed traffic engine (red, number 5), Percy the saddle tank (green, number 6), Toby the tram engine (brown, number 7), Montague, a Great Western engine familiarly known as 'Duck' because he waddled (green, number 8), the twin black engines Donald (number 9) and Douglas (number 10), and Oliver (green, number 11). Thomas's carriages were Annie and Clarabel, and also seen were Daisy the diesel rail car, Diesel, a diesel engine, and Henrietta, another carriage. All operated under instructions from the Fat Controller, who, like the drivers, firemen and other human characters, was simply seen as a static figurine. Thomas's other acquaintances were Terence the tractor, Harold the helicopter and Bertie the bus.

Thomas the Tank Engine and Friends, made using models, was one of the few British animations to be sold to the USA.

THOMPSON, EMMA (1959–)

Versatile British actress and all-purpose entertainer, the daughter of Eric 'voice of *The Magic Roundabout*' Thompson and former *Play School* presenter Phyllida Law. Now an international film name, Emma, a Cambridge Footlights graduate, has also been acclaimed for her television work, which began with a comedy series entitled

Alfresco for Granada (alongside such budding stars as Robbie Coltrane, Ben Elton, Stephen Fry, Hugh Laurie and Siobhan Redmond). She joined Coltrane again in the musical drama *Tutti Frutti* (as Suzi Kettles) and in *Fortunes of War* she played opposite her husband, Kenneth Branagh, when taking the role of Harriet Pringle. Unfortunately, her adventurous sketch series, *Thompson*, a showcase for her multi-talents, was not so universally well received. She has also been seen in *The Winslow Boy* and *Knuckle*, guested in *The Young Ones* and *Cheers*, and appeared with Jasper Carrott in *Carrott's Lib*.

THORN BIRDS, THE

US (ABC) Drama. BBC 1 1984

Father Ralph de Bricassart ....Richard Chamberlain
Meggie Cleary ....Sydney Penny
                                                            Rachel Ward
Mary Carson ....Barbara Stanwyck
Fiona 'Fee' Cleary ....Jean Simmons
Archbishop Contini-Verchese ..Christopher Plummer
Luke O'Neill ....Bryan Brown
Paddy Cleary..Richard Kiley
Rainer Hartheim ....Ken Howard
Justine ....Mare Winningham
Luddie Mueller ....Earl Holliman
Anne Mueller ....Piper Laurie
Dane..Philip Anglim

Writer: Carmen Culver. Producers: David L. Wolper, Stan Margulies

Forbidden love in the Australian outback.

The Thorn Birds was the story of ambitious and handsome Catholic priest Ralph de Bricassart who found himself dragged off the straight and narrow by Meggie Cleary, the beautiful daughter of an Australian sheepfarmer, a girl he had known from an early age (Sydney Penny played Meggie as a child). Set between the years 1920 and 1962, the five-part serial chronicled the consequences of their illicit love affair – for the priest's conscience and his clerical career, and for Meggie, who gave birth to a son, Dane, who followed his father into the church. Hovering in the background was Meggie's matriarchal grandmother, Mary Carson, who herself had designs on the heart-throb churchman. *The Thorn Birds* was adapted by Carmen Culver from Colleen McCullough's steamy novel.

THORNE, ANGELA (1939–)

British actress, typically seen in upper-class parts as characterized by her roles in *To the Manor Born* (Marjory Frobisher), *Three Up, Two Down* (Daphne Trenchard) and *Farrington of the F.O.* (Harriet Emily Farrington). Thorne has also played serious drama, with credits including *The Canterville Ghost*, *Haunted* and *The Good Guys*.

THORNTON, FRANK (FRANK THORNTON BALL; 1921–)

Staunch British comedy support, coming into his own in the guise of Captain Peacock in *Are You Being Served?* and *Grace and Favour*. Otherwise, Thornton has been seen as a straight man to many comics, including Tony Hancock (in *Hancock's Half Hour*), Michael Bentine (in *It's a Square World*) and Spike Milligan (in *The World of Beachcomber*). Thornton was also Commander Fairweather of *HMS Paradise* in the 1964 sitcom of the same name.

THORP, RICHARD (1932–)

Emmerdale's publican Alan Turner has, in fact, enjoyed a long career on TV. British actor Richard Thorp first appeared on our screens back in the 1950s, when he played heart-throb Dr John Rennie in *Emergency – Ward 10*, also starring in its spin-off, *Call Oxbridge 2000*. He was later seen in series like *Honey Lane*, *A Family at War*, *Public Eye*, *The Cedar Tree*, *Strangers* and *To the Manor Born* and with comedians Harry Worth and Benny Hill before he joined *Emmerdale Farm* as 'Fatty' Turner, then boss of NY Estates, in 1982.

THREE OF A KIND

UK (BBC) Comedy. BBC 1 1981–3

Tracey Ullman
Lenny Henry
David Copperfield

Producer: Paul Jackson

Comedy sketch show featuring three promising performers.

As a showcase for emerging talent, *Three of a Kind* certainly delivered the goods. Lenny Henry had already been seen on *New Faces*, *The Fosters* and *Tiswas*, and Tracey Ullman had appeared in West End musicals. They were drawn into a team with fellow comic David Copperfield (not to be confused with the American illusionist) by producer Paul Jackson and presented two series of sketches and monologues which were well received. Everyone knows what happened to Henry and Ullman, but the fate of David Copperfield remains a mystery to many viewers (he retired to the world of cabaret).

Three of a Kind was also the title of another vehicle for up and coming talents which was screened in 1967. The three in question then were Lulu (not that she was *that* new), Mike Yarwood and Ray Fell (the David Copperfield of the trio, who went on to appear on the Las Vegas cabaret circuit).

3–2–1

UK (Yorkshire) Game Show. ITV 1978–87

Presenter: Ted Rogers

Executive Producer: Alan Tarrant. Producers: Derek Burrell-Davis, Mike Goddard, Ian Bolt, Terry Henebery, Graham Wetherell

Game show in which contestants decipher clues to win prizes.

3–2–1 was based on the Spanish quiz *Uno, Dos, Tres* and focused on three married couples as they battled for the right to win valuable prizes. The first segment of the game was a quiz, after which one couple was eliminated. The rest of the show was devoted to a series of playlets, songs and sketches featuring a repertory company of comics and surprise celebrity guests. Chris Emmet was one of the resident comedians and the Brian Rogers' Connection were the supporting dance troupe. The sketches all followed a theme: Aesop's Fables, the circus, etc., and, following each skit, one of the guests read out a related riddle which referred to a prize. When the two remaining couples had been whittled down to one by an elimination question, the final couple then had to decide which of the cryptic clues to discard in the search for the best prize (usually a car). One prize they all wanted to avoid was the new metal rubbish bin, representing the show's robotic mascot, Dusty Bin. Compère Ted Rogers fast-talked his way through each show, twirling his fingers in a *3–2–1* salute. He was supported by a team of hostesses known as The Gentle Secs.

THREE UP, TWO DOWN

UK (BBC) Situation Comedy. BBC 1 1985–9

Sam Tyler	Michael Elphick
Daphne Trenchard	Angela Thorne
Nick Tyler	Ray Burdis
Angie Tyler	Lysette Anthony
Major Giles Bradshaw	Neil Stacy
Wilf	John Grillo

Creator/Writer: Richard Ommanney.
Producers: David Askey, John B. Hobbs

A stuck-up widow and a down-to-earth widower share a flat and a grandchild, but have little else in common.

With a new son (Joe) to look after and finances stretched, photographer Nick Tyler and his model wife, Angie, decided to install one of the child's grandparents in their basement flat, as a live-in baby sitter. This meant that either Nick's working-class dad, Sam, or Angie's well-bred mum, Daphne, would take up residence, but, because of a mix-up, both were invited and both accepted. Reluctantly agreeing to share the flat, in order to be near their grandchild, Cockney Sam and Cheltenham-raised Daphne became the worst of enemies, despite Sam's obviously warm feelings towards his cold, snooty flatmate. His easy-going, earthy manner frustrated her and his taxidermy hobby only made matters worse, filling the flat with stuffed penguins and other dead creatures. However, after a disastrous fling with conman Giles Bradshaw, Daphne finally realized that the kind-hearted Sam was really the man for her, despite their many differences, and the two embarked on a rather more harmonious co-existence. Also seen was the theatrically-minded Wilf, the zoo-keeper who provided animals for Sam to stuff.

THRELFALL, DAVID (1953–)

Northern Shakespearean actor who took the part of Leslie Titmuss MP in John Mortimer's *Paradise Postponed* and *Titmuss Regained*. He was also seen in the RSC's *The Life and Adventures of Nicholas Nickleby* (as Smike), played Prince Charles in BSkyB's *Diana: Her True Story* and turned to comedy for the sitcoms *Nightingales* (as security guard Bell) and *Men of the World* (as travel agent Lenny Smart). In addition, Threlfall appeared with Sheila Hancock in *Jumping the Queue*, and other credits have included *Scum, The Gathering Seed, A Murder of Quality* and *Clothes in the Wardrobe*.

THRILLER

UK (ATV) Suspense Anthology. ITV 1973–6

Creator: Brian Clemens

Series of feature-length film thrillers.

Created and largely written by Brian Clemens, *Thriller* offered a collection of twist-in-the-tail stories designed to keep the audience on the edge of their seats. The best-remembered contributions included *A Coffin for the Bride* (starring Helen Mirren), *Only a Scream Away* (Hayley Mills), *Nurse Will Make It Better* (Diana Dors), *The Crazy Kill* (Denholm Elliott) and *Who Killed Lamb?* (Stanley Baker).

THROUGH THE KEYHOLE

UK (Yorkshire) Game Show. ITV 1987–

Presenters: David Frost, Loyd Grossman

Executive Producer: Kevin Sim. Producers: Ian Bolt, Chantal Rutherford Browne

Who lives where game show featuring celebrity panellists.

In this easy-going, family panel game, Loyd Grossman has led a camera team through the various rooms of a celebrity's house, pointing out features of decor, their style of living and evidence of hobbies and professions. Three famous guests have then had to guess to whom the house belongs, taking note of extra clues from host David Frost. The householder has subsequently strolled on to confront the panellists.

THROWER, DEBBIE (1957–)

British presenter and newsreader, born in Kenya. After working in newspapers and radio, Thrower joined BBC South as a reporter on the news magazine *South Today*, before going national and reading the main BBC news bulletins. At this time, she was also seen in programmes like *Out of Court*, *Lifeline*, action reports like *Hospital Watch* and as host of *Songs of Praise*. Returning to regional broadcasting, she took over as presenter of TVS's *Coast to Coast*, which evolved into *Meridian Tonight* (she fronts the Southampton-based edition) when the franchise changes took effect.

THROWER, PERCY, MBE (1913–88)

The doyen of television gardeners, Percy Thrower was host of *Gardening Club* for 12 years from 1955. He continued at the forefront of its successor, *Gardeners' World* (filmed in his own home), when it began in 1968. As well as having green fingers, Thrower proved to be a popular TV personality, popping up in numerous other programmes, including *Blue Peter* (1974–88) where he designed their famous Italian sunken garden in 1978.

THUNDERBIRDS

UK (AP Films/ATV/ITC) Children's Science Fiction. ITV 1965–6

Voices:
Jeff Tracy	Peter Dyneley
Scott Tracy	Shane Rimmer
Virgil Tracy	David Holliday
	Jeremy Wilkin
Alan Tracy	Matt Zimmerman
Gordon Tracy	David Graham
John Tracy	Ray Barrett
Lady Penelope Creighton-Ward	Sylvia Anderson
Brains	David Graham
Parker	David Graham
The Hood	Ray Barrett
Tin-Tin	Christine Finn
Kyrano	David Graham
Grandma	Christine Finn

Creators: Gerry Anderson, Sylvia Anderson.
Producers: Gerry Anderson, Reg Hill

A 21st-century family runs a global rescue service, using advanced aircraft and technology.

In the year 2063 International Rescue (IR) had been established by retired astronaut Jeff Tracy in a mountain refuge on his isolated Pacific island. Utilizing futuristic aircraft devised by Brains, a stammering, bespectacled genius, he sent into action a squad of brave, humanitarian rescuers – all his own sons, named after the first five Americans in space and dedicated to averting disasters.

The stars of the show were the Thunderbirds themselves, wonderfully high-tech vehicles capable of incredible speeds and amazing manoeuvres. Thunderbird 1 (with Scott, Jeff's eldest son and second-in-command, at the helm) was a combination of reconnaissance jet and rocket. Thunderbird 2 (piloted by the softly-spoken, piano-playing Virgil) was the fleet's freighter, carrying machinery like the burrowing tool, The Mole, and the team's submarine, Thunderbird 4, in a series of six pods which could be inserted into its belly. Thunderbird 4, when called into use, was controlled by aquanaut Gordon Tracy, an enthusiastic, practical joker who was always keen for action. Their blond-haired, impetuous brother, Alan, piloted the rocket Thunderbird 3, taking it into orbit to join the team's space station, Thunderbird 5, manned by the fifth son, John, the loner of the family. John and Alan sometimes switched jobs.

The Thunderbirds could be called out at any time. Usually, the siren was sounded by Thunderbird 5, picking up distress messages from all around the globe. Thunderbird 1 was the first on the scene, making full use of its 7000 mph velocity, allowing Scott to liaise with base and advise the slower Thunderbird 2, following in its wake. The elaborate take-off procedures from Tracy Island were a highlight of the show. Swivelling walls and sinking sofas conveyed the pilots out of the luxurious Tracy home to the hangars beneath, with shutes and slides positioning them perfectly in their crafts, before swimming pools retracted and palm trees fell back to reveal hidden launch pads. Once in action, the boys reported back via a video intercom, which superimposed their faces onto wall portraits. All messages were punctuated with the acknowledgement 'F.A.B.'.

However, the whole International Rescue set-up was a mystery to the rest of the world, and the identity of the Thunderbird pilots shrouded in secrecy. The only parties in the know were the Tracys themselves, their island staff and a special London agent and her butler. The staff were Kyrano, Jeff's oriental manservant, and his daughter, Tin-Tin (an electronics expert and Alan's romantic interest). The London agent was Lady Penelope Creighton-Ward, a true aristocrat with a cool, calm approach to dealing with thugs. She travelled in a souped-up, well-armed, pink Rolls

Royce (registration FAB 1; FAB 2 was her luxury yacht), which was driven by her shifty-looking, safe-cracking butler, Parker, a Cockney best remembered for his loyal 'Yes M'Lady'. Hounding the rescuers was the evil, bald-headed Hood. He was Kyrano's half-brother and lived in a temple in a Thai jungle, but he was also a master of disguise and travelled the world trying to ensnare the Tracy brothers and their fabulous machines. He also had power over Kyrano, his eyes lighting up whenever he cast his 'hoodoo' spell.

The series has been widely acknowledged as Gerry Anderson's masterpiece. Filmed in hour-long episodes to corner the prime-time market, the format provided plenty of scope for character development and tension building. By this stage, the Supermarionation production technique had almost reached perfection. The puppets' eye and lip movements were synchronized with the dialogue and their control wires were so thin (one 5000th of an inch) that they were barely noticeable. With its stirring theme music by Barry Gray, sophisticated special effects and multitude of explosions, *Thunderbirds* captured an adult, as well as a children's, audience. A bandwagon rolled out in *Thunderbird* merchandise and two feature films were also produced, *Thunderbirds Are Go* and *Thunderbird Six*. The series was repeated to much acclaim on BBC 2 in 1991.

TILBURY, PETER (1945–)

British writer and actor, the creator of *Shelley* and *Chef!* His other writing credits have included episodes of *Birds of a Feather*, the play *Sprout* and the sitcoms *Sorry, I'm a Stranger Here Myself* (with David Firth) and *It Takes a Worried Man* (in which he also starred as Philip Roath). In addition, his acting career has taken in series like *Dixon of Dock Green*, *The Expert*, *C.A.T.S. Eyes*, *Fortunes of War*, *Casualty* and *The Bill*.

TILL DEATH US DO PART

UK (BBC) Situation Comedy. BBC 1 1966–8; 1972–5

Alf Garnett	Warren Mitchell
Else Garnett	Dandy Nichols
Rita	Una Stubbs
Mike	Anthony Booth
Bert	Alfie Bass
Min	Patricia Hayes

Creator/Writer: Johnny Speight. Producers: Dennis Main Wilson, Brian Winston, David Croft

A bigoted East End docker shares his home with his dim wife, his liberal daughter and her left-wing husband.

Alf Garnett remains one of TV's most memorable creations. He has been loved and he has been hated, but he is unlikely to be forgotten. The man who brought racist views and foul language into British living rooms is a hard act to follow. Although today's 'alternative' comedians aim to shock, their impact has been negligible in comparison with TV's first controversial loudmouth.

The Garnetts lived in London's decaying East End, long before the Isle of Dogs was transformed into a yuppie paradise. Their little docker's terraced house was home to four adults: Alf, his wife, Else, daughter, Rita, and son-in-law, Mike. Such close habitation induced claustrophobia and an endless amount of personal friction. On one side, there was Alf, a bald, bespectacled bigot, patriotically standing up for The Queen and cheerfully pushing the blame for the country's ills on to 'Darling Harold' Wilson and immigrants. Mind you, if he had succeeded in shipping out the immigrants and dislodging the Labour Party from government, he still wouldn't have been happy with Edward Heath in charge – he was a grammar school boy, not a traditional Tory like Winston Churchill. On the other side was Mike, a long-haired, unemployed, Liverpudlian socialist, 'Shirley Temple' or 'randy Scouse git', as he became known. In between were the phlegmatic Else and the giggly Rita, both talking more sense in the few words they uttered than either of their verbose husbands.

Alf's rantings were heavily criticized by the church, Mary Whitehouse and politicians, but his character had other sides to it, too. He was incredibly selfish, and extremely mean to his long-suffering wife. Yet Else took it all in her rather sluggish stride, shrugging off insults like 'silly old moo' and conjuring up sharp retorts to put Alf firmly in his place. Whenever that happened, he donned his West Ham scarf and skulked off to the pub. When Dandy Nichols briefly left the series in the 1970s (Else went to visit her sister in Australia), Alf's invective was directed against his neighbours, Bert and Min.

Till Death Us Do Part began as an episode of *Comedy Playhouse* in 1965. In this pilot, Warren Mitchell played Alf Ramsey (as in the football manager), with Gretchen Franklin (Ethel in *EastEnders*) as his maligned wife. The series proper ran from 1966 to 1968 and was exhumed for a new run in 1972. A short-lived 1981 version, *Till Death...* (produced by ATV), was followed by a new BBC revival in 1985. This time the title had been changed to *In Sickness and In Health*, ironically appropriate considering the obvious illness of Dandy Nichols. The Garnetts had been rehoused in a new development, without Rita or Mike, with the antagonizer's role filled by a gay, black home-help, provocatively named Winston. This series continued even after Nichols's death in 1986, but, by this time, the political climate had changed. Even though Alf could slate the incumbent Tory government for being a bunch of spivs ruled over by a grocer's daughter, the bite had disappeared and the series was far less successful. Johnny Speight's monstrous creation had had his day. An American version of *Till Death Us Do Part*, *All in the Family*, was just as big and controversial.

TILT

The pivoting of a camera vertically up and down, as opposed to a pan, which involves horizontal movement from left to right or vice-versa.

TIME TUNNEL, THE

US (Twentieth Century-Fox/Irwin Allen)
Science Fiction. BBC 1 1968

Dr Tony Newman	James Darren
Dr Doug Phillips	Robert Colbert
Dr Ann MacGregor	Lee Meriwether
Lt General Heywood Kirk	Whit Bissel
Dr Raymond Swain	John Zaremba

Creator/Executive Producer: Irwin Allen

Two scientists are trapped in a man-made 'time tunnel' and are thrown into assorted historical adventures.

Tony Newman and Doug Phillips were working on a top secret project to build a machine which could transport people backwards or forwards in time. When a penny-pinching goverment official arrived at their research centre, hidden beneath the Arizona desert, to demand evidence of progress, Tony was forced to enter the 'time tunnel' to prove it worked. However, as he knew, the machine was not yet perfected and his risk backfired, leaving him swirling in the mists of time. He eventually materialized on the deck of the *Titanic* on the day before it sank. Seeing him trapped, Doug volunteered to rescue him. Despite their best efforts to convince the ship's captain of the impending doom, he, of course, took no notice and the pair had to be whisked away from the disaster just as it happened.

This set the pattern for other adventures. The team back at base (Drs Swain and MacGregor), whilst not being able to retrieve the scientists, could, however, move them in and out of situations and occasionally caught glimpses of their lost colleagues. Tumbling through time, the travellers fell into adventure after adventure, always arriving at a key point in history – the Alamo before its capitulation, Krakatoa on the point of eruption, Pearl Harbor in advance of the Japanese attack. They also witnessed the French Revolution, the siege of Troy and the Battle of Gettysburg. Ample use was made of old cinema footage to keep expenditure within the show's very limited budget.

TIMESLIP

UK (ATV) Children's Science Fiction. ITV
1970–1

Liz Skinner	Cheryl Burfield
Simon Randall	Spencer Banks
Frank Skinner	Derek Benfield
Jean Skinner	Iris Russell
Commander Traynor	Denis Quilley
Frank	John Aikin
Devereaux	John Barron
Beth Skinner	Mary Preston
2957	David Graham

Creators: Ruth Boswell, James Boswell. Writers: Bruce Stewart, Victor Pemberton. Producer: John Cooper

Two teenagers move backwards and forwards in time through an invisible time barrier.

On holiday in the Midlands village of St Oswald with her parents, Liz Skinner and her friend Simon Randall were intrigued by the disappearance of a young girl at the site of an old wartime weapons base. Also interested was the mysterious Commander Traynor, once Liz's dad's CO when the base was active. The teenagers discovered an invisible fence and felt their way along it until they came to a hole. Squeezing through, they found themselves back in 1940 and embarked upon an adventure in which they helped a young Mr Skinner to dismantle a secret laser before it was stolen by the Germans. The job done, Liz and Simon returned through the time barrier to find themselves not in their original 1970 but in 1990, at an Antarctic research station called the Ice Box. Experiments were being performed there on human beings, using a longevity drug known as HA57. They met up with Beth, an unpleasant older version of Liz, and also discovered her parents, with her father entombed in ice, the victim of a botched experiment. Leading the project was base director Morgan C. Devereaux, who, it transpired, was actually a clone. The kids escaped back to their own time, only to be persuaded to return to the future once more by an anxious Commander Traynor.

On this occasion, they arrived again in 1990, but in a tropical, baking hot Britain, the result of a failed experiment in climate control. They encountered a friendly Beth and also an older Simon, known simply by the number 2957, who was in charge of a team of clones. But that was not the last of their adventures, and they discovered that Commander Traynor was not all he seemed when they took another trip through the barrier and surfaced in 1965.

The first episode of this imaginative science fiction series was introduced by ITN's science correspondent Peter Fairley, who was called up to explain to the young audience the general concept of time travel. The fact that such a prologue was necessary indicated how complex the subsequent episodes were, as they followed the two friends backwards and forwards through time, discovering the unavoidable interdependence of the past and the future, and of actions and consequences.

Timeslip's four adventures (*The Wrong End of Time*, *The Time of the Ice Box*, *The Year of the Burn-Up* and *The Day of the Clone*) ran back to back, as one 26-week series. It is fondly remembered by science-fiction fans and was co-created by ITV sci-fi specialist Ruth Boswell, later producer of *The Tomorrow People*.

TIMOTHY, CHRISTOPHER (1940–)

Welsh-born actor whose role as vet James Herriot in *All Creatures Great and Small* has dominated his TV career. However, Timothy has also been seen in series like *Some Mothers Do 'Ave 'Em*, *Kate* and *Jackanory Playhouse*, plus single dramas and Shakespearean classics.

TIN TIN see *Hergé's Adventures of Tin Tin*.

TINGWELL, CHARLES (1923–)

Australian actor, a heart-throb in the 1950s thanks to his portrayal of surgeon Alan Dawson in *Emergency – Ward 10*. His later UK TV work was limited, although he did provide the voice for Dr Fawn in *Captain Scarlet and The Mysterons*. Back home Down Under, Tingwell starred as Inspector Lawson in the long-running police series *Homicide* from the mid-1960s. He was recently seen as a guest 'doctor' in *Home and Away*.

TINKER, TAILOR, SOLDIER, SPY

UK (BBC) Spy Drama. BBC 2 1979

George Smiley	Alec Guinness
Toby Esterhase	Bernard Hepton
Roy Bland	Terence Rigby
Percy Alleline	Michael Aldridge
Bill Haydon	Ian Richardson
Peter Guillam	Michael Jayston
Lacon	Anthony Bate
Ricki Tarr	Hywel Bennett
Connie Sachs	Beryl Reid
Control	Alexander Knox
Mendel	George Sewell
Jim Prideaux	Ian Bannen
Ann Smiley	Sîan Phillips
Spikely	Daniel Beecher

Writer: Arthur Hopcraft. Producer: Jonathan Powell

A British spy catcher is brought out of retirement to lead the hunt for a mole.

World-weary British intelligence agent George Smiley suddenly found himself dragged back into the field of international espionage when his old boss, Control, needed his help in tracking down a mysterious double agent. Back at the 'Circus' – as the intelligence agency was known – Smiley discovered that most of Control's top men were under suspicion, each being targeted for investigation under codenames like 'Tinker', 'Tailor', 'Soldier' and 'Poor Man'. Despite struggling with the humiliation of his wife's adultery, Smiley diligently set about his task and painstakingly uncovered vital clues which put him on the road to unmasking the mole.

Based on John Le Carré's novel of the same name, *Tinker, Tailor, Soldier, Spy* was dramatized by Arthur Hopcraft in seven episodes and won enormous acclaim. It wasn't the end of Smiley's intelligence career, however. Three years later he resurfaced (again played by Alec Guinness) in another of Le Carré's offerings, *Smiley's People*. The character reappeared once more in a 1991 two-hour Thames production called *A Murder of Quality*, in which he was played by Denholm Elliott.

TISWAS

UK (ATV/Central) Children's Entertainment. ITV 1974–82

Presenters: Chris Tarrant, John Asher, Trevor East, Sally James, Lenny Henry, John Gorman, Clive Webb, Sylvester McCoy, Frank Carson, Bob Carolgees, Gordon Astley, Fogwell Flax, Emil Wolk, Den Hegarty, David Rappaport

Producers: Peter Harris, Glyn Edwards, Chris Tarrant

Anarchic Saturday morning live entertainment.

Tiswas was the series which tore up the rule books of kids' TV. In contrast with *Multi-Coloured Swap Shop*, its BBC Saturday morning rival, *Tiswas* ditched goody-goody, wholesome fare in favour of raucous, get-stuck-in slapstick. Custard pies and buckets of water reigned supreme. Silly sketches featured the likes of Lenny Henry and Frank Carson, plus Bob Carolgees and his punk dog, Spit. Former Scaffold member John Gorman played the appropriately named Smello, but who was the Phantom Flan Flinger, who terrorized the studio audience with his foaming pies? Anchors Trevor East, and particularly Chris Tarrant and Sally James, made no attempt to restrain the erupting chaos as they struggled to introduce cartoons, interview pop stars and take competition calls on the Wellyphone (made of old gum boots).

Tiswas began as a regional show in the Midlands in 1974 and took several years to gain full network coverage. ITV companies then opted out of various segments of the show in order to drop in their own cartoons and adventure series. Apart from its sheer anarchy, what made *Tiswas* such a cult series was the fact that adults loved it, too, and there were plenty of dubious, 'grown-up' gags thrown in for them to enjoy. There was even a waiting list of 'mature' viewers demanding to be trapped in 'The Cage' and subjected to regular dousings. This adult following eventually led to a late-night spin-off entitled *OTT* (*Over the Top*) in 1982, hosted by most of the *Tiswas* crew, with the addition of Helen Atkinson-Wood and Alexei Sayle. Sadly, crudeness took over and the series was quickly cancelled. *Tiswas*, too, suffered, largely from the loss of Chris Tarrant, and it soon followed *OTT* into the TV archives.

Tiswas (the name was said to be an acronym for Today Is Saturday, Watch and Smile) also generated a hit single when Tarrant, James, Carolgees and Gorman joined forces as The Four Bucketeers to enter the 1980 Top 30 with The Bucket of Water Song.

TITCHMARSH, ALAN (1949–)

Yorkshire-born, Kew-trained gardening expert turned television presenter. In addition to green-fingered programming, Titchmarsh has also become associated with **Songs of Praise**, **Pebble Mill** and other daytime programmes. Other credits have included **Nationwide**, **Breakfast Time** and *Titchmarsh's Travels*.

TITLES see closing titles and opening titles.

T.J. HOOKER

US (Spelling-Goldberg/Columbia) Police Drama. ITV 1983–

Sgt T.J. Hooker ....William Shatner
Officer Vince Romano ....Adrian Zmed
Captain Dennis Sheridan ....Richard Herd
Fran Hooker ....Lee Bryant
Vicki Taylor ....April Clough
Officer Stacy Sheridan.....................Heather Locklear
Officer Jim Corrigan ....James Darren

Creator: Rick Husky. Executive Producers: Aaron Spelling, Leonard Goldberg. Producer: Jeffrey Hayes

An experienced police officer teaches rookies rights and wrongs.

Honest and decent, plain-clothes detective T.J. Hooker had grown tired of investigations and longed to return to the beat. Reverting to his former role of sergeant, he was assigned to the Academy Precinct of the L.C.P.D. where his keen, young partner was Vince Romano. While performing his duties in an exemplary fashion, Hooker became a role model for trainee officers, educating them in the moral dimensions of policing, as well as the strategic and physical aspects. He had seen one of his partners killed in action and over the years had had plenty of time to contemplate the good and bad sides of law enforcement.

Hooker was divorced, but still friendly with his ex-wife, Fran, a nurse. His police family included rookies Vicki Taylor and Stacy Sheridan, the latter the daughter of his hard-nosed boss, Captain Dennis Sheridan. She was later promoted to patrol officer and teamed up with veteran Jim Corrigan. Cameo appearances from stars like the Beach Boys and Leonard Nimoy were common. The 'L.C.' of L.C.P.D. was never explained, nor were Hooker's initials, T.J.

TLC see The Learning Channel.

TNT

(Turner Network Television) Entertainment channel launched on cable in the USA by Turner Broadcasting in 1988, majoring on old movies and sports. It transferred to Europe in September 1993, sharing a channel with its sister broadcaster, Cartoon Network, on the Astra 1C satellite. Broadcasting from 8 pm to 6 am, it omits the sport for its European viewers, but screens classic American movies from the Turner (former MGM) library. Soundtracks are available in seven languages. Like Cartoon Network and Turner's other Astra channel, CNN, the signal is unscrambled and free to owners of satellite receivers.

TO THE MANOR BORN

UK (BBC) Situation Comedy. BBC 1 1979–81

Audrey Fforbes-Hamilton ....Penelope Keith
Richard De Vere ....Peter Bowles
Marjory Frobisher ....Angela Thorne
Brabinger ....John Rudling
Mrs Polouvicka.....................................Daphne Heard
Rector ....Gerald Sim
Big Lemington ....Anthony Sharp
Ned ....Michael Bilton
Mrs Patterson................................Daphne Oxenford

Creator: Peter Spence. Producer: Gareth Gwenlan

A widow is forced to sell her stately home and move into more limited surroundings.

When Audrey Fforbes-Hamilton's husband died, he left her his stately pile, Grantleigh Manor, but also a mound of death duties to pay. Not being able to keep up the estate, Audrey was forced to sell the property to supermarket tycoon Richard De Vere. She being strictly old money, and he being nouveau riche, she was desperate to keep an eye on his activities, to make sure he did not destroy the character of the estate. By moving into one of the manor's lodges with her ageing butler, Brabinger, and with the use of a pair of binoculars, she was, at least, able to monitor proceedings. But not even that was enough. Distrusting the new Lord of the Manor, resenting his position and also fancying him quite a bit, Audrey was always meddling in De Vere's affairs. She guided him in the etiquette of lordship and ensured – as far as she could – that Grantleigh was still run on traditional lines. Audrey's old school chum, Marjory Frobisher, dropped in regularly to keep her friend in her place, while Richard's Czech mother, Mrs Polouvicka, acted as a matchmaker for her son and Audrey, whom she considered perfect for each other. Her efforts bore fruit at the end of the series when the two were married – and Audrey was at last back in charge at the manor. The series was filmed at Cricket St Thomas in Somerset.

TODD, BOB (1921–92)

One of the UK's leading comic supports, Bob Todd played straight man to numerous comedians, including Dick Emery, Michael Bentine, Des O'Connor and, particularly, Benny Hill. Todd arrived in showbusiness late, having served in the RAF and worked as a cattle farmer. He talked himself into a part in the Sid James sitcom *Citizen James* in 1963 and, in addition to a marathon stint in *The Benny Hill Show*, later worked on series like *Marty, Mike and Bernie's* (Winters) *Show, Hancock's, The Best Things in Life, Doctor at Sea, Funny Man, Q9* and his own comedy, *In for a Penny* (in which he starred as Dan, a lavatory supervisor). He was similarly well-known for commercials, once advertising stock cubes with a cry of 'It's beef!'.

TODDLERS' TRUCE

The one-hour gap in transmission, between 6 and 7 pm, designed to allow mums to put children to bed (after children's programmes had finished) and to allow older children to get on with their homework. The Truce was respected by both BBC and ITV until February 1957. Commercial considerations then gained the

upper hand. ITV filled the gap with action series like *The Adventures of Robin Hood*, while the BBC went for the news/current affairs audience with *Tonight* on weeknights and the youth market on Saturday with *Six-Five Special*.

TODMAN, BILL see Goodson, Mark.

TOM AND JERRY

US (MGM) Animation. BBC 1 1967–

Creators: William Hanna, Joseph Barbera.
Producer: Fred Quimby

A cat and a mouse are the worst of enemies, with violent consequences.

Tom and Jerry have been playing cat and mouse since 1940, when these short theatrical cartoons were first screened. On television, they have become two of the most popular and enduring characters, with the BBC happily dropping in the five-minute episodes whenever programmes have run short or technical problems have delayed regular transmissions.

Each cartoon has adopted the same format, effectively an extremely violent, breathtaking chase around a house, a garden, a ship, etc., with the cat (Tom) desperately trying to get even with the wily mouse (Jerry). Much flattening of faces, crumbling of teeth and crushing of tails has been witnessed, but viewers have also noticed various differences in animation styles from film to film. The first (and generally regarded as the best) selection came from the years up to 1958, when the characters' creators Bill Hanna and Joe Barbera were still employed on the project at MGM. The studio then decided to drop out of animation and Hanna and Barbera went their own successful way, developing the likes of *Huckleberry Hound, The Flintstones* and *Scooby Doo*. MGM commissioned 13 more *Tom and Jerry*s from the Prague studio of Gene Deitch in 1961 and then 34 more films were made by cult animator Chuck Jones with Les Goldman between 1963 and 1967. Further episodes were made as part of a longer children's cartoon compilation in 1975, but received little acclaim.

TOMORROW PEOPLE, THE

UK (Thames) Children's Science Fiction. ITV 1973–9

John	Nicholas Young
Stephen	Peter Vaughan-Clarke
Carol	Sammie Winmill
Kenny	Steve Salmon
Tim (voice only)	Philip Gilbert
Jedekiah	Frances de Wolff
	Roger Bixley
Professor Cawston	Brian Stanion

Elizabeth	Elizabeth Adare
Tyso	Dean Lawrence
Mike Bell	Mike Holloway
Hsui Tai	Misako Koba
Andrew Forbes	Nigel Rhodes

Creator: Roger Price. Producers: Ruth Boswell, Roger Price, Vic Hughes

A team of telepathic teenagers use their powers to save the Earth.

The Tomorrow People were homosuperions: the first exponents of the next stage in man's development after homosapiens (or 'saps', as they became known). They were teenagers endowed with powers of telepathy, telekinesis and ESP, and became Earth's first 'ambassadors' to the Galactic Empire. By employing their advanced minds, they were able to thwart malevolent aliens and protect the Earth from invasion and interference. The first Tomorrow Person to become aware of his special powers and to come to terms with them was John, a lean, dark-haired, level-headed lad who was able to counsel and help other youngsters enduring this painful transition, known as 'breaking out'. The next two were Carol and Kenny, who left after the first series to work on the Galactic Trig (a Galactic Empire space complex), but new Tomorrow People broke out on a regular basis and took their places in the cast. They were Stephen (in the programme's first episode), Elizabeth, Tyso, Mike, Hsui Tai (played by Mike Holloway, the drummer in the teenage band Flintlock), and Andrew. They travelled by 'jaunting', a process of teleportation in which mind power alone took them from place to place and they even went back in time and into space to confront villains like the bearded Jedekiah, an evil alien robot. In and out of their secret hideout ('The Lab'), somewhere off the London Underground, they were assisted and guided by a deep-voiced, paternal computer called Tim.

The Tomorrow People was touted as an ITV rival to **Doctor Who**, filling the kids' fantasy slot vacated by **Ace of Wands**. At first, it was intriguing and adventurous, but after a few seasons the plots thinned and the special effects became very weak. Its creator, Roger Price, pursued the idea yet again in a new version beginning in 1992, which cast **Neighbours** star Kristian Schmid as a Tomorrow Person.

TOMORROW'S WORLD

UK (BBC) Science. BBC 1 1965–

Presenters: Raymond Baxter, James Burke, William Woollard, Michael Rodd, Judith Hann, Anna Ford, Kieran Prenderville, Maggie Philbin, Su Ingle, Peter Macann, Howard Stableford, Kate Bellingham, Carmen Pryce, John Diamond, Carol Vorderman

Producers/Editors: Glyn Jones, Max Morgan-Witts, Michael Latham, Peter Bruce, Lawrence Wade, Dick Gilling, Michael Blakstad, David Filkin, Richard Reisz, Dana Purvis, Edward Briffa

A weekly look at new inventions and discoveries.

Initially titled *Tomorrow's World . . . in the Making Today*, this long-running, popular science programme has looked at the very latest innovations and discoveries for over 30 years, explaining how they work and describing how the new technology could be of use to mankind in major or minor ways. Studio experiments and dry runs have illustrated proceedings.

For years, *Tomorrow's World*'s chief presenter was Raymond Baxter, supported by the likes of James Burke, William Woollard and Michael Rodd, although the number of participants has increased significantly in the last decade. An occasional inventors' insert has been compiled by Bob Symes. Transmitted live for most of its existence (with hazardous consequences when experiments backfired), it has been pre-taped in recent years, too, allowing its reporters like Shahnaz Pakravan, Monty Don, Vivienne Parry and Rebecca Stephens to travel the world in search of innovations.

TONIGHT

UK (BBC) Current Affairs. BBC 1957–65

Presenter: Cliff Michelmore

Producers/Editors: Donald Baverstock, Alasdair Milne, Antony Jay, Peter Batty, Gordon Watkins, Derrick Amoore

Easy-going but influential nightly news magazine.

Conceived as a means of filling the Toddler's Truce (see separate entry) on weeknights, *Tonight* offered a review of the major events of the day, mixed with songs, unusual items and bits of humour. Presented by the unflappable Cliff Michelmore (whose closing remarks were 'The next *Tonight* will be tomorrow night'), *Tonight* numbered amongst its reporters Alan Whicker, Derek Hart, Fyfe Robertson, Geoffrey Johnson Smith, Trevor Philpott, Polly Elwes, Julian Pettifer, Macdonald Hastings, Kenneth Allsop, Brian Redhead and Magnus Magnusson. Cy Grant performed topical calypsos and Robin Hall and Jimmie Macgegor were the resident folk singers who rounded off each show.

When *Tonight* ended in 1965, many of its crew were shunted off into its late-night replacement, **24 Hours**. Of its producers, Alasdair Milne went on to become BBC Director-General and Antony Jay later co-wrote the hugely successful comedy **Yes Minister**. *Tonight*, as a title, was revived in 1975, with presenters Sue Lawley, Donald MacCormick, Denis Tuohy and John Timpson hosting a show (again late in the evening) which was altogether less frivolous than the original early evening show. It ran for four years on BBC 1.

TOOK, BARRY (1928–)

British comedy writer and performer, discovered on a Carroll Levis talent show in 1952. As well as performing stand up routines, Took then went on to write for radio and television, scripting for series like *Colonel Trumper's Private War* and, with his partner Marty Feldman, **The Army Game**, **Bootsie and Snudge**, *The Walrus and The Carpenter*, *Barney is My Darling*, *Scott On . . .* , *Marty* and *Marty Back Together Again*. Took also wrote and produced Kenneth Horne's *Horne a Plenty* and, with John Junkin, he adapted *The World of Beachcomber* for Spike Milligan from J.B. Morton's *Daily Express* column. As a consultant to the BBC comedy department in the late 1960s, he was instrumental in seeing that **Monty Python's Flying Circus** reached the screen and also helped **The Goodies** get off the ground. His later writing work has included the sitcom *A Roof Over My Head*, the drama *Scoop* (adapted from the Evelyn Waugh novel) and the illiteracy campaign series **On the Move**. Took also brought his wry humour to bear from the chair of **Points of View** for many years, and amongst his other credits has been the television magazine *TV Weekly*, for which he has presented a nostalgia spot, *TV Replay*.

TOP CAT see *Boss Cat*.

TOP GEAR

UK (BBC) Motoring Magazine. BBC 2 1978–

Presenters: Angela Rippon, Barrie Gill, Noel Edmonds, William Woollard, Sue Baker, Jeremy Clarkson, Quentin Willson, Tiff Needell, Chris Goffey, Tony Mason, Janet Trewin, Michele Newman

Executive Producer: Dennis Adams. Producers: Derek Smith, Jon Bentley, Ken Pollock

Long-running motoring magazine.

Road testing new models, highlighting innovations and generally keeping the motorist well-informed, *Top Gear* was itself given a test drive in the BBC Midlands area in 1977 before being launched as a networked series a year later. Its first hosts were Angela Rippon and Barrie Gill. Noel Edmonds was behind the wheel for a while, but Jeremy Clarkson has been in pole position most recently, assisted by reporters like Tiff Needell, Tony Mason and Janet Trewin.

TOP OF THE FORM see *Television Top of the Form*.

TOP OF THE POPS

UK (BBC) Pop Music. BBC 1 1964–

Producers: Johnnie Stewart, Colin Charmey, Stanley Dorfman, Mel Cornish, Robin Nash, Brian Whitehouse, David G. Hillier, Stanley Appel, Michael Hurll, Paul Ciani, Ric Blaxill

The UK's premier chart music show.

With the immortal words 'It's Number One, it's Top of the Pops', Britain's top pop programme made its bow on New Year's Day 1964 and quickly became the most influential music programme on air. From the start, record companies clamoured for their artists to appear, recognizing the boost the programme gave to new releases and to fledgling or fading careers. It remains just as important to the trade today.

The programme has unashamedly been based around the Top 30/Top 40 singles' chart and albums have never had much of a look in. To emphasize this, each programme has given a run-down of the latest chart positions and ended with the number one song. Other contributions have come from chart (or soon to be chart) artists, most appearing in the studio. For many years, when important artists were not available, the resident *Top of the Pops* dancers performed to the records. Pan's People (Babs, Ruth, Dee Dee, Louise, Andrea, plus choreographer Flick Colby, and later Cherry and Sue) enjoyed this privilege for nine years up to 1976. Ruby Flipper, Legs and Co. and finally Zoo replaced them, but dance troupes were abandoned in 1983, in favour of pop videos.

The very first presenter was Jimmy Savile, who hosted the show from its original home in a converted Manchester church. On that landmark programme were stars like The Rolling Stones, The Dave Clark Five, The Swinging Blue Jeans, Dusty Springfield and The Hollies. Savile and three other DJ colleagues, Pete Murray, David Jacobs and Alan Freeman, took turns to host the show during its formative years. Other radio personalities (mostly drawn from Radio 1) have dominated the programme since those days. These have included Tony Blackburn, Noel Edmonds, Dave Lee Travis, Ed Stewart, David 'Kid' Jensen, John Peel, David Hamilton, Peter Powell, Simon Bates, Tommy Vance, Mike Read, Andy Peebles, Gary Davies, Richard Skinner, Mike Smith, Steve Wright, Janice Long, Bruno Brookes, Simon Mayo, Mark Goodier, Nicky Campbell and Jakki Brambles. In October 1991 the 'personality DJ' was abandoned in favour of lesser known, younger hosts like Tony Dortie and

Mark Franklin. At the same time *Top of the Pops* inherited a new home at BBC Elstree and began to focus more on live bands, for the first time wavering from its chart-only format. Since then, other celebrities, including pop stars like Gary Glitter and comedians like Jack Dee, have shared the compèring.

Before miming to records was officially outlawed by the Musicians' Union in 1966, records were visibly placed on a turntable and guests simply mouthed the words. Denise Sampey spun the discs in the earliest programmes, but model Samantha Juste took over and is the girl everyone remembers at Jimmy Savile's side, even though she hardly ever spoke. When the mime ban came into force, artists had to pre-record their contributions or perform live. Accompaniment usually came from Johnny Pearson and his *Top of the Pops* Orchestra, with the Ladybirds providing backing vocals.

Top of the Pops has always had distinctive theme music, although this has been changed on numerous occasions. During the 1970s CCS's version of Led Zeppelin's 'Whole Lotta Love' was used. This was replaced by 'Yellow Pearl' by Phil Lynott in 1981 and there have since been other theme tracks.

TOP SECRET

UK (Associated-Rediffusion) Spy Drama. ITV 1961–2

Peter Dallas ....William Franklyn
Miguel Garetta ....Patrick Cargill
Mike ....Alan Rothwell

Producer: Jordan Lawrence

The all-action adventures of a pair of secret agents in South America.

Peter Dallas was a tough, but likeable British intelligence agent based in Argentina. Given a year's secondment, he found himself working for local businessman Miguel Garetta (who also had secret service connections) in a fight against crime and subversion. Delving into matters which the everyday law enforcers could not touch, Dallas worked undercover to undermine crooks and spies throughout South America and was joined on his assignments by Mike, Garetta's young nephew.

The show made a star out of William Franklyn (later the Schweppes 'Shh! You know who!' man), while Patrick Cargill moved on from this tough man role to specialize in farces and sitcoms like *Father, Dear, Father*. Alan Rothwell is better remembered as David Barlow in *Coronation Street*. The show's theme tune, 'Sucu Sucu' by Laurie Johnson, was a hit in 1961 for several artists.

TOP SECRET LIFE OF EDGAR BRIGGS, THE

UK (LWT) Situation Comedy. ITV 1974

Edgar Briggs ....David Jason
The Commander ....Noel Coleman
Buxton ....Michael Stainton
Jennifer Briggs ....Barbara Angell
Spencer ....Mark Eden
Cathy ....Elizabeth Counsull

Creators: Bernard McKenna, Richard Laing.
Producer: Humphrey Barclay

Counter-espionage capers with a bumbling British secret agent.

Edgar Briggs worked for SIS, the Secret Intelligence Service, and was strangely successful at his job, considering that he was probably the most incapable agent British security ever employed. A paperwork error had resulted in his transfer to the position of personal assistant to The Commander of SIS and meant that the hapless Briggs was involved in the most hush-hush undercover operations. Inevitably, he fouled up the best-laid plans – by shredding vital documents, inadvertently announcing secret tactics over a tannoy system or handing over his holiday snaps instead of an important film. But, amazingly, Briggs had the knack of bringing matters to a satisfactory conclusion. This early starring role for David Jason lasted only 13 episodes.

TORCHY

UK (Pelham Films/AP Films/ABP) Children's Entertainment. ITV 1960

Voices: Olwyn Griffiths, Kenneth Connor, Jill Raymond, Patricia Somerset

Creator/Writer/Producer: Roberta Leigh

A battery-powered doll has fun at a toys' refuge in space.

Torchy, the battery boy, lived in Topsy Turvy Land, a haven in space where abused and neglected toys savoured their freedom, and walked and talked like humans. The land (where the only rain was orange juice) was ruled by King Dithers from his Orange Peel Palace and had its mixture of good and bad toys. These ranged from the pirate doll, Pongo, to Pom Pom the poodle, Sparky the baby dragon, Squish the space boy, Pilliwig the clown and Flopsy the rag doll, most living in the settlement of Fruitown (all the houses being made of fruit, with Torchy's a pineapple). Torchy, boarding his giant rocket, was also able to travel back to Earth, where he assisted his friend, dear old Mr Bumbledrop, and ran into old adversaries like Bossy Boots, a domineering little girl, and Bogey, a particularly naughty boy. Only Torchy and Pom Pom were able to visit Earth, because they were *moving* toys; the others would have reverted to their static former selves. But even Torchy had his problems. Occasionally, he hit trouble when his battery failed and the magic beam from the lamp on his hat grew dim. Future puppetmaster Gerry Anderson directed some of the episodes.

TORS, IVAN (1916–83)

Hungarian writer who moved to the USA and became a successful producer of wildlife adventures series, most notably *Sea Hunt*, *Flipper*, *Daktari* and *Gentle Ben*, through his own Ivan Tors Productions. Amongst his other credits were action series like *Ripcord*.

TOUCH OF FROST, A

UK (Yorkshire/Excelsior) Drama. ITV 1992–

Detective Inspector William Edward 'Jack' Frost
....David Jason
Supt Mullett ....Bruce Alexander
Detective Chief Inspector Allen................Neil Phillips
DC Clive Barnard ....Matt Bardock
Shirley Fisher.......................................Lindy Whiteford

Executive Producers: Vernon Lawrence, Richard Bates, Philip Burley. Producer: Don Leaver

The investigations of a lonely and rather disorganized detective.

Representing a change of career direction for comic star David Jason, the 'serious' role of DI Jack Frost of the Denton police revealed new talents in Britain's top sitcom actor. Frost, a moustached, greying little copper was a terrier-like investigator. Despite being almost shambolically disorganized and having a grudge against authority, he proved himself to be perceptive and thorough. The fact that his wife was terminally ill (she died in the first episode) was not allowed to interfere with his work, but his irritability when trying to give up smoking did shine through. Viewers instantly took to the sandwich-munching, George Cross-winning policeman who had once been shot on duty, and three series of two-hour films have been produced to date. Frost was the creation of novelist R.D. Wingfield.

TRAINER

UK (BBC) Drama. BBC 1 1991–2

Mike Hardy ....Mark Greenstreet
Rachel Ware..Susannah York
John Grey ....David McCallum
James Brant ....Nigel Davenport
Hugo Latimer ....Patrick Ryecart
Joe Hogan ....Des McAleer
David Ware ....Marcus D'Amico
Kath Brant...Sarah Atkinson
Frances Ross ....Nicola King
Jack Ross ....Ken Farrington
Nick Peters ....Floyd Bevan
Mo Ratcliffe ....Audrey Jenkinson
Alex Farrell..Claire Oberman
Robert Firman ....John Bowe
Sue Lawrence ....Melanie Thaw

Creator/Producer: Gerald Glaister

A young trainer tries to succeed in the competitive world of horse racing.

Mike Hardy was the lead character in this horse saga set amongst the padded anoraks and green wellies of the Sport of Kings. Given the chance to set up as a trainer in his own right, Hardy secured the backing of grouchy businessman James Brant who sent his best horses to Hardy's Arkenfield Stables. Also on Hardy's side was wealthy widow and stud owner Rachel Ware, local gambler John Grey and head lad Joe Hogan. However, Hardy also had his enemies, including his former boss, rival trainer Hugo Latimer, and he also battled with a drink problem. After an only moderately successful first season, *Trainer* rode on to a second year, which saw James Brant disappear and Hardy fall in love with Alex Farrell, the girl sent to administer Brant's estate.

Trainer was filmed on the Berkshire downs and on racecourses up and down the country. The village pub, The Dog & Gun was actually The Crown & Horns at East Ilsley, just north of Newbury. The theme song, co-written by disc jockey Mike Read, was performed by Cliff Richard.

TRAINING DOGS THE WOODHOUSE WAY

UK (BBC) Information. BBC 2 1980

Host: Barbara Woodhouse

Producer: Peter Riding

Education for dog-owners.

What was intended as a straightforward course for would-be dog handlers turned into a cult TV hit, thanks to the eccentricities of its bossy, senior citizen host. Barbara Woodhouse, aged 70, and a former horse trainer, had developed her own forceful techniques for teaching dogs obedience. Her snapped commands and shrill requests soon made her a household name, with her personality and character enhanced by a staid, woolly-kilt-and-sensible-shoes appearance. Her techniques received much criticism at the time and have continued to do so since her death in 1988, although it was always the nervous owners who looked terrified, not the hounds.

TRANSPONDER

The satellite component that collects signals beamed up from the ground, amplifies them and sends them back to dish receivers. On the Astra satellites, most channels are allocated one transponder, although some share, transmitting only for a set number of hours each day.

TRAVANTI, DANIEL J. (1940–)

American actor who, after some 20 years of playing bit parts in series like *Route 66*, **The Man from UNCLE**, *Perry Mason*, **The Defenders**, *Lost in Space*, *Gunsmoke*, *Kojak* and *Hart to Hart*, suddenly found fame as Captain Frank Furillo in **Hill Street Blues** in 1981. Consequently, Travanti can now command better roles, such as in the 1989 BBC political drama *Fellow Traveller*. He has also been seen in numerous TV movies.

TRAVELLING MAN

UK (Granada) Drama. ITV 1984–5

Lomax..Leigh Lawson
Robinson ....Terry Taplin

Creator: Roger Marshall. Executive Producer: Richard Everitt. Producer: Brian Armstrong

A former drug squad officer, freed from prison, sets out to find his son and to track down the man who framed him.

The life of Detective Inspector Lomax of the Metropolitan Police Drugs Squad had suddenly fallen apart. Framed for the theft of £100,000 after a drugs seizure went awry, he spent two years behind bars for a crime he did not commit. On his release, he found that his wife, Jan, had left him and Steve, his drop-out son, was hiding away on Britain's canal network. To add to his worries, the police had placed him under surveillance (in case the money turned up), and the underworld were also on his tail. Almost as threatening was Robinson, an investigative reporter in pursuit of a story.

Stepping aboard his own narrow boat, named *Harmony*, Lomax made off along the waterways and mixed with canal folk, hunting for the man who set him up and hoping to trace his missing son. The result was a sort of **The Fugitive** for the 1980s.

TREACHER, BILL (1937–)

British actor best-known as Arthur Fowler in *EastEnders*, a role he has played since the series' inception in 1985. Earlier credits included **Z Cars**, **Bless this House**, **Grange Hill**, *Angels*, **The Professionals**, **The Agatha Christie Hour**, *Maggie and Her* and *Sweet Sixteen*. Radio fans will remember his voice as that of Sidney, the milkman, in *Mrs Dale's Diary*.

TREASURE HUNT

UK (Chatsworth) Game Show. Channel 4
1982–9

Presenters: Kenneth Kendall, Anneka Rice, Wincey Willis, Annabel Croft

Creator: Ann Meo. Producers: Malcolm Heyworth, Peter Holmans

Helicopter-oriented adventure game.

In this all-action game show, two studio-bound contestants yelled directions to a 'runner' who darted around the countryside in a helicopter looking for clues. Each treasure hunt took place within a 50-mile radius of its starting point and, by using maps and solving five riddles discovered on the way, the contestants aimed to claim the treasure (£1000) within the 45-minute time limit. Kenneth Kendall tried to keep calm in the studio along with Wincey Willis, while Anneka Rice (and, in 1989, ex-tennis star Annabel Croft) acted as runner, supported by an athletic roving camera team. Croft also appeared in the similarly styled *Interceptor* (1989–90) in which contestants attempted to avoid enemy agents.

TRETHOWAN, SIR IAN (1922–90)

British political journalist (*Daily Sketch*) who joined ITN in 1958, working as newscaster, diplomatic editor and political editor. He switched to the BBC in 1963, to contribute to **Panorama** and *Gallery*, then, between 1970 and 1975 was Managing Director of BBC Radio, on one occasion famously sacking Kenny Everett for making a joke about the wife of a politician. He became Managing Editor of BBC Television in 1976 and the BBC's Director-General in 1977, holding the position for five years. He was later Chairman of Thames Television. Trethowan was knighted in 1980.

TREVOR, WILLIAM, CBE (1928–)

British dramatist, known for his sensitive treatment of old folk and women. Amongst his offerings have been *The Baby Sitter* (1965), *The Mark Two Wife* (1969), *The General's Day* (1972), *O Fat White Woman* (1978), *Eleanor, Secret Orchid* (both 1980), *Mrs Ackland's Ghost, Matilda's England* (the latter a trilogy; both 1981), *Autumn Sunshine* and *Ballroom of Romance* (both 1982).

TRIALS OF LIFE, THE

UK (BBC) Natural History. BBC 1 1990

Presenter/Writer: David Attenborough

Executive Producer: Peter Jones. Producer: Keenan Smart

The survival of the fittest in the animal world.

Produced by the BBC's Natural History Unit, *The Trials of Life* formed the third part of David Attenborough's epic wildlife documentary series, which had begun with **Life on Earth** and continued with **The Living Planet**. In this 12-part voyeuristic examination of animal behaviour, Attenborough turned his attention to the struggle for survival of the planet's many species, from birth to death, via feeding, reproduction, etc. The colourful and detailed footage was painstakingly shot over a three-year period, by over 30 cameramen. Attenborough's next project was *The Private Life of Plants*, shown in 1995.

TRIANGLE

UK (BBC) Drama. BBC 1 1981–3

Katherine Laker	Kate O'Mara
John Anderson	Michael Craig
Matt Taylor	Larry Lamb
Tom Kelly	Scott Fredericks
Wally James	Nigel Stock
Nick Stevens	Tony Anbolt
Marion Terson	Diana Coupland
George Larsen	Dennis Burgess
Christine Harris	Sandra Payne
Dougie Evans	Christopher Saul
Charles Woodhouse	Paul Jerricho
Jo Bailey	Elizabeth Larner
Peter Nuttall	Jonathan Owen
Tony Grant	Philip Hatton
Judith Harper	Joan Greenwood
Mrs Landers	Dawn Addams
Sarah Hallam	Penelope Horner
Penny Warrender	Sandra Dickinson
Kevin Warrender	Peter Arne
David West	George Baker
Arthur Parker	Douglas Sheldon
Sandy McCormick	Helena Breck
Joe Francis	David Arlen

Creator/Producer: Bill Sellars

Drama with the passengers and crew of a North Sea ferry.

Triangle is one of those programmes its producers and participants probably want to forget, given the amount of flak fired in its direction. Indeed, the twice-weekly series only lasted three seasons, the last without its star (Kate O'Mara) who had already quit. The premise was fairly simple. Action took place aboard a ferry making the triangular journey of Felixstowe–Gothenburg –Rotterdam–Felixstowe. Initial intrigue followed the appointment of a new chief purser, Katherine Laker, who turned out to be the daughter of a Triangle Lines bigwig. Subsequently, there was much vying for position and numerous skulking visits to strange cabins in the dead of night.

Bravely experimenting with new lightweight equipment and actually filming aboard a moving ship (the *Tor Scandinavia*), the team, unfortunately, encountered all manner of unforeseen problems. Most daytime cabin shots had to be taken with the curtains drawn to avoid glare, and the movement of the North Sea upset the crew and performers alike. Worse still, there was little viewer interest. The bleak and icy waters of northern Europe just didn't have the appeal of the warm, azure Caribbean lagoons that made **The Love Boat** such a success.

TRINDER, TOMMY, CBE (1909–89)

Chirpy Cockney comedian who arrived on television after years of musical hall and film work. In 1955 he was the first compère of **Sunday Night at the London Palladium**, which benefited from his quick thinking and skill with the ad lib. 'You lucky people' became his catchphrase.

TRINITY TALES

UK (BBC) Drama. BBC 2 1975

Eric the Prologue	Francis Matthews
Stan the Fryer	Bill Maynard
Dave the Joiner	Paul Copley
Judy the Judy	Susan Littler
Nick the Driver	Colin Farrell
Smith the Man of Law	John Stratton
Alice the Wife of Batley	Gaye Brown

Creator/Writer: Alan Plater. Producer: David Rose

A group of rugby fans tell tall stories on the way to a cup final.

Writer Alan Plater took Chaucer's *Canterbury Tales* and placed them in a contemporary setting for this innovative six-part series. It concerned a minibus of Wakefield Trinity fans making their way down to Wembley for the Rugby League Challenge Cup Final. To while away the miles, they each told a story (all of which were somewhat far-fetched, with slapstick elements). The six episodes were subtitled *The Driver's Tale*, *The Fryer's Tale*, *The Judy's Tale*, *The Joiner's Tale*, *The Wife of Batley's Tale* and *The Man of Law's Tale*.

TRIPODS, THE

UK (BBC) Children's Science Fiction. BBC 1 1984–5

Will Parker	John Shackley
Henry Parker	Jim Baker
Beanpole (Jean-Paul)	Ceri Seel
Duc de Sarlat	Robin Langford
Count	Jeremy Young
Countess	Pamela Salem
Eloise	Charlotte Long
Ozymandias	Roderick Horn

Vichot	Stephen Marlowe
Mme Vichot	Anni Lee Taylor
Fritz	Robin Hayter
Krull	Jeffrey Perry
Ulf	Richard Beale
Master 468	John Woodvine
Boll	Edward Highmore
Borman	James Coyle
Coggy	Christopher Guard
Ali Pasha	Bruce Purchase
Speyer	Alfred Hoffman
Jeanne	Elizabeth McKechnie

Writers: Alick Rowe, Christopher Penford.
Producer: Richard Bates

Three youths flee tyrannical alien machines in a medieval world of the future.

Based on three novels by John Christopher, *The Tripods* was an adventurous exercise in science fiction by the BBC. Sadly, the ratings and expenses did not balance out and the series was cancelled two-thirds of the way through, leaving viewers stranded in mid-story.

The tale concerned a trio of youths living in the year 2089 at a time when the Earth had been ruled by ruthless, three-legged alien machines known as the Tripods for over 100 years. A medieval society had been restored to the planet, with all children 'capped' at the age of 16 to ensure complete subservience. Two English teenagers about to be processed (which involved attaching a metal plate to their heads) decided to make a break for it in an attempt to reach the White Mountains of Switzerland, where the Free Men allegedly lived. The two were cousins Will and Henry Parker. Making it as far as France, they were joined by a local youth, Beanpole, and together they lurched from danger to danger, progressing south to the safe lands.

Series two picked up in the year 2090 as the three boys and their Free Men hosts plotted to overthrow the Tripods and free the human race. A newcomer, Fritz, replaced Henry and the trio headed for the Tripod Annual Games in the guise of competitors, in an attempt to infiltrate the Tripods' City of Gold. They encountered the Masters, the monsters from the planet Trion which had devised the machines, and learned of their sinister plans for the Earth. And that was where the BBC left it – with the Tripods still in control and the boys back on the run. Twenty-five episodes were made in total, although sci-fi fans were left crying out for a few more to set the story straight. Those keen enough will have turned to the original novels: *The White Mountains*, *The City of Gold and Lead*, and *The Pool of Fire*.

TRIPPER'S DAY/SLINGER'S DAY

UK (Thames) Situation Comedy. ITV
1984/1986–7

Tripper's Day:

Norman Tripper	Leonard Rossiter
Hilda Rimmer	Pat Ashton
Alf Battle	Gordon Gostelow
Mr Christian	Paul Clarkson
Hardie	Philip Bird
Laurel	David John
Higgins	Andrew Paul
Sylvia	Liz Crowther
Marlene	Charon Bourke
Dottie	Vicky Licorish

Slinger's Day:

Cecil Slinger	Bruce Forsyth
Mr Christian	Paul Clarkson
Hardie	Philip Bird
Fred	David Kelly
Colin	Charlie Hawkins
Shirley	Jacqueline De Peza
Miss Foster	Suzanne Church

Creator: Brian Cooke. Writers: Brian Cooke (*Tripper's/Slinger's Day*), Vince Powell (*Slinger's Day*). Producers: Anthony Parker (*Tripper's Day*), Mark Stuart (*Slinger's Day*)

Days in the life of a harrassed supermarket manager.

Years before *Coronation Street* introduced Reg Holdsworth as TV's supermarket supremo, this comedy series pitched Leonard Rossiter into the role of Norman Tripper, manager of the Supafare Supermarket. As Tripper, Rossiter marshalled his staff like a US police chief, reflecting his fascination with American cop series. He also embarked on an affair with canteen manageress Hilda Rimmer. It proved to be Rossiter's last TV offering and, following his untimely death, the programme was retitled and recast. It became *Slinger's Day*, with Bruce Forsyth enrolled as Supafare's new manager, Cecil Slinger, but with only two members of Tripper's supporting staff maintained, namely Mr Christian and Hardie. New members of Slinger's team were Fred, Colin, Shirley and Miss Foster.

TRODD, KENITH

Acclaimed British producer, closely associated with playwright Dennis Potter, working on *Double Dare*, *Brimstone and Treacle* (both 1976), **Pennies from Heaven** (1978), *Blue Remembered Hills* (1979), *Blade on the Feather*, *Rain in the Roof*, *Cream in my Coffee* (all 1980), **The Singing Detective** (1986) and *Christabel* (1988). Trodd, a campaigner for filmed, rather than videotaped, drama, has also been responsible for Julia Jones's *Faith and Henry* (1969), Leon Griffiths's *Dinner at the Sporting Club* (1978), Derek Mahon's *Shadows* on our Skin (1980) and Jim Allen's *Caught on a Train* (1980) and *A United Kingdom* (1981), amongst other plays.

TROUBLESHOOTERS, THE/MOGUL

UK (BBC) Drama. BBC 1 1965–72

Brian Stead	Geoffrey Keen
Willy Izzard	Philip Latham
Peter Thornton	Ray Barrett
Alec Stewart	Robert Hardy
Robert Driscoll	Barry Foster
Derek Prentice	Ronald Hines
Steve Thornton	Justine Lord
Jane Webb	Phillippa Gail
Roz Steward	Deborah Stanford
Mike S. Zabo	David Baron
Eileen O'Rourke	Isobel Black
Charles Grandmercy	Edward de Souza
James Langely	John Carson
Britte Langely	Anna Matisse
Letz Perez	Barbara Shelley

Creator: John Elliot. Producers: Peter Graham Scott, Anthony Read

Power struggles and other excitement in the oil industry.

Mogul International was a major oil production company, headed by managing director Brian Stead and his financial controller Willy Izzard. In the first series, which was simply entitled *Mogul*, much of the action took place at executive level but, as attention shifted to the younger and more dynamic members of staff, the title was changed to *The Troubleshooters* and the drama moved out of the office and onto the rigs scattered around the world. The key, globetrotting 'troubleshooters' were Peter Thornton and Alec Stewart.

The 'soapy', boardroom and bedroom elements apart, the series was much respected in the real oil world for its attention to detail and accuracy in technical matters. Issues covered in the storylines, such as explosions, earthquakes, company take overs and the discovery of new oil fields, uncannily foretold real events and this no doubt contributed to its seven-year residence on UK screens. The Mogul company was allegedly based on BP.

TROUGHTON, PATRICK (1920–87)

British Shakespearean actor who first worked on television as early as 1948. He appeared in *Toad of Toad Hall* in 1950, starred in a 1953 BBC version of *Robin Hood*, played Sir Andrew Ffoulkes in *The Scarlet Pimpernel* in 1955 and was Captain Luke Settle in the 1960 Civil War drama *The Splendid Spur*. Troughton also took the small role of George Barton in *Coronation Street*, but it was as the second *Doctor Who* (1966–9) that he became a household name. Later, he played the

Duke of Norfolk in *The Six Wives of Henry VIII*, Nasca in *The Feathered Serpent*, journalist J.P. Schofield in the comedy *Foxy Lady* and Perce (Nicholas Lyndhurst's granddad) in *The Two of Us*. Seldom away from the small screen, Troughton was also seen in many other productions, including *The Invisible Man*, *Man of The World*, *A Family at War*, *Special Branch*, *The Protectors*, *The Sweeney*, *The Saint*, *The Goodies*, *Doomwatch*, *Dr Finlay's Casebook*, *Colditz*, *Churchill's People*, *Minder*, *Z Cars*, *Survivors*, *The Box of Delights*, *Inspector Morse*, *All Creatures Great and Small* and assorted single dramas. One of his last roles was as the rebel Arthur in *Knights of God* in 1987. He was the father of actors David and Michael Troughton.

TRUMPTON see *Camberwick Green*.

TSW

(Television South West) The ITV contractor for South-West England from 12 August 1981 to 31 December 1992, TSW succeeded Westward Television onto the air. This was one of the more predictable changes of the 1980 franchise round, as Westward had suffered badly from boardroom turmoil in the run up to the reallocations. TSW broadcast from a Plymouth base, but made little contribution to the ITV network during its 11-year franchise tenure, the most prominent being editions of *Highway* and *About Britain*, plus the canine quiz *That's My Dog*. In applying for the continuation of its licence in the 1991 franchise auctions, the company was deemed to have 'overbid' by the ITC, which then appointed Westcountry Television as the new contractor for the South-West region.

TTT see Tyne Tees Television.

TUBE, THE

UK (Tyne Tees) Rock Magazine. Channel 4 1982–7

Presenters: Jools Holland, Paula Yates, Leslie Ash, Muriel Gray, Gary James

Producers: Malcolm Gerrie, Paul Corley

Influential 1980s rock magazine.

The *Ready, Steady, Go!* of the 1980s, *The Tube* was presented live on a Friday tea time from the studios of Tyne Tees in Newcastle. Live bands, star interviews, reviews and reports were combined to produce an up-to-the-minute look at the rock music scene and the programme became a launching pad for many of the decade's most prominent names, including Frankie Goes To Hollywood, Paul Young, U2 and The Eurythmics. Established stars like Elton John,

David Bowie and Tina Turner also made appearances. Model and pop columnist Paula Yates was accompanied as host by former Squeeze keyboards man Jools Holland and their flippant and controversial presentational style (Holland was once suspended for using a four-letter word in a programme trailer), combined with numerous technical fluffs, contrasted sharply with the slick patter of the fab DJs and the glossier presentation of *Top of the Pops*. Muriel Gray, Gary James and, briefly, Leslie Ash also hosted proceedings.

TUGBOAT ANNIE see *Adventures of Tugboat Annie, The*.

TULLY, SUSAN (1967–)

London-born actress, on TV since her teens hosting Saturday morning series like *Our Show* and *The Saturday Banana*. She took the role of Suzanne Ross in **Grange Hill** and then joined **EastEnders** at its inception in 1985, playing Michelle Fowler.

TURNER BROADCASTING SYSTEM see TBS.

TURNER NETWORK TELEVISION see TNT.

TURNER, TED (1938–)

Flamboyant and ambitious American TV executive, head of Turner Broadcasting System (TBS) and one of the most influential TV magnates of the 1980s. Turner sold off his family's advertising business in the early 1970s, purchasing instead a small Atlanta television station, which he renamed WTBS. In 1976, by beaming its signal off a satellite to cable systems in other parts of the USA, Turner created one of the first 'superstations'. In 1980 he defied the advice of experts and set up a 24-hour cable news station. That was CNN, now globally relayed by satellite and one of the world's most watched channels, its reputation enhanced by coverage of the Gulf War (1991). TBS has also launched the TNT channel (Turner Network Television), which screens old movies from the MGM/United Artists archives (also in Turner's ownership). Turner is married to actress Jane Fonda.

TUTTI FRUTTI

UK (BBC) Comedy Drama. BBC 1 1987

Danny McGlone	Robbie Coltrane
Suzie Kettles	Emma Thompson
Eddie Clockerty	Richard Wilson
Vincent Diver	Maurice Roeves
Bomba MacAteer	Stuart McGugan
Fud O'Donnell	Jake D'Arcy
Dennis Sproul	Ron Donachie

Creator/Writer: John Byrne. Producer: Andy Park

On the road with a Scottish rock 'n' roll band.

Returning home from New York for the funeral of his brother, Big Jazza ('The Beast of Rock'), who had been killed in a car crash, failed artist Danny McGlone stumbled into singer Suzie Kettles, an old flame. Donning drainpipes and crepe soles, he found himself enrolled alongside her into his late brother's rock 'n' roll band, The Majestics, billed as 'Scotland's Kings of Rock'. The Majestics comprised guitarist Vincent Diver, bass player Fud O'Donnell and drummer Bomba MacAteer and were shakily managed by Eddie Clockerty. As they set out on tour to celebrate 25 years in the business, their roadie was Dennis Sproul. The six-episode series followed the band as they travelled from gig to gig, and watched the developing relationship between the slobbish Danny and the hard-nosed Suzie.

TV-AM

TV-am won the franchise for the ITV breakfast slot in 1980 and went on air with its *Good Morning Britain* programme on 1 February 1983. This followed early difficulties that delayed the launch and allowed the BBC to get ahead of the game by presenting its own **Breakfast Time** on 17 January the same year. TV-am's teething troubles were not over, however.

The company ambitiously took to the air with a self-declared 'mission to explain'. Its 'Famous Five' presenters were all big names: Robert Kee (who hosted the earliest segment of the day, known as Daybreak), Angela Rippon, David Frost, Michael Parkinson and Anna Ford. Peter Jay was the company's chief executive. However, its formal, somewhat highbrow approach soon lost favour with viewers who preferred the BBC's warmer, more casual style. As audiences shrank, changes needed to be made. Jay left after only six weeks. Rippon and Ford quickly followed, sacked by station boss Timothy Aitken, to make room for fresher presenters like Anne Diamond and Nick Owen. Greg Dyke was brought in to mastermind a revival and instigated a more lightweight style of programming. The station's fortunes were improved yet further when a glove puppet named Roland Rat was introduced during school holidays. The streetwise rodent quickly built up a cult following and eventually transferred to his own series on BBC 1. A weekend segment for kids, Wide Awake Club, hosted by Timmy Mallett, was also added. When Greg Dyke left to become programme controller at TVS, he was succeeded by Bruce Gyngell who ran the station for the rest of its time on air. On the studio couch new hosts Lorraine Kelly and Mike Morris took over from Diamond and Owen. By the time of the 1991 franchise renewals, TV-am was in good shape financially and enjoyed a sizeable audience. David Frost's and, later, Maya Even's Sunday programme was an important part of the political week. This was not enough, however, and, when the company was outbid by Sunrise Television (later renamed GMTV), the ITC awarded the franchise to their rivals, to the fury of all at TV-am. Even former premier Margaret Thatcher, whose Government had introduced the auction system, was contrite. She wrote to Gyngell apologising for TV-am's downfall. TV-am's last day on air was 31 December 1992.

TV EYE see *This Week.*

TVS (TELEVISION SOUTH)

TVS was the company that controversially 'stole' the South and South-East of England ITV franchise from the well-established Southern Television during the 1980 licensing round. Making an application for the contract under the consortium name of South and South-East Communications, the company's strongest cards were its original personnel, which included notable broadcasting executives like Michael Blakstad (formerly of the BBC and Yorkshire Television) and Anna Home (from BBC children's programmes). Awarded the licence, it adopted the broadcasting name of TVS, bought the old Southern studios in Southampton and went on air on 1 January 1982. The company proceeded to open up new studios in Maidstone and split its regional news coverage into southern and south-eastern sectors. It made programmes like *C.A.T.S. Eyes*, *Davro's Sketch Pad*, *Fraggle Rock*, *The Storyteller* and *Catchphrase* for the ITV network and expanded internationally, ambitiously taking over the MTM Entertainment company (producers of *Hill Street Blues* and *Lou Grant* amongst other shows) in 1988, a move which unfortunately caused TVS some financial distress. When re-applying for its licence in 1991, TVS was deemed to have 'overbid' by the ITC and lost its franchise to Meridian Television broadcasting finally on 31 December 1992. The TVS company and its Maidstone studios were subsequently bought by The Family Channel.

TW3 see *That Was The Week That Was.*

24 HOURS

UK (BBC) Current Affairs. BBC 1 1965–72

Presenters: Cliff Michelmore, Kenneth Allsop, Ian Trethowan, Michael Barrett, Robert McKenzie, David Dimbleby, Ludovic Kennedy

Producers/Editors: Derrick Amoore, Anthony Whitby, Anthony Smith, Peter Pagnamenta, Tony Summers, John Dekker, Gordon Watts, David Harrison, Michael Bukht, Michael Townson

Late-night current affairs series.

The replacement for *Tonight*, 24 Hours reviewed the day's news events from a late-night (10.30 pm) standpoint, rather than a teatime position. It inherited many members of the *Tonight* crew, including anchorman Cliff Michelmore, and ran for seven years, before giving way to *Midweek* in 1972. Amongst the reporting team were the likes of Michael Parkinson, Robin Day, David Lomax, Julian Pettifer, Fyfe Robertson, Leonard Parkin and Philip Tibenham.

Its most controversial moment came in 1971 with a film entitled *Yesterday's Men*. Referring to a slogan used by the Labour Party about the Conservatives in the previous year's general election, it featured an interview with ex-Prime Minister Harold Wilson in which reporter David Dimbleby quizzed him about the profits he received from his published memoirs. This angered Wilson and a cut was made, but the whole style of the film, with its satirical Gerald Scarfe cartoons and songs by The Scaffold, still caused a furore when broadcast. Matters were complicated by the following evening's 24 Hours film about the Conservatives, a much kinder documentary entitled *Mr Heath's Quiet Revolution*. The BBC Programmes Complaints Commission was established as a consequence of this particular dispute.

TWILIGHT ZONE, THE

US (Cayuga) Science Fiction. ITV 1963–

Host/Narrator: Rod Serling

Creator/Writer/Executive Producer: Rod Serling. Producers: Buck Houghton, Herbert Hirschman, Bert Granet, William Froug

Cult anthology of science-fiction thrillers.

The Twilight Zone was a labour of love for one man, Rod Serling. An Emmy-winning TV playwright, Serling not only created and produced the series, he also wrote most of the episodes and appeared on screen as host and narrator. He developed a simple format of half-hour playlets (some one-hour episodes were also produced), which succinctly told a story with a curious, often shocking, twist in the tail. The storylines effectively merged illusion and reality, introduced intriguing concepts and ideas, and conveyed a moral message. Some episodes were subtle human parables, others were downright spooky. The black and white footage added a sinister tone but special effects were virtually non-existent.

One classic episode concerned a bank clerk who loved to read. Sneaking away into a vault one lunchtime to delve into his book, he emerged to find that a nuclear disaster had destroyed all life on Earth. He was the only survivor. At last he could read to his heart's content. Then he dropped and broke his glasses. Another episode told of an alien who arrived on Earth to offer help. It accidentally left behind a book called *To Serve Man*. By following the alien's advice, Earth was ridden of hunger and war, and humans began to pay visits to the alien's home planet. Then a translator finished decoding the book, to find it was actually a cookery manual. And then there was the episode starring Agnes Moorehead as a woman whose home was invaded by miniature alien spacemen. Once she had fought them off, it was revealed that the spacemen were actually NASA astronauts who had landed on a planet of giants. It was she who had been the alien.

The series played host to a horde of guest stars, ranging from William Shatner, Charles Bronson and Burt Reynolds to Mickey Rooney, Roddy McDowell and Robert Redford. Airing between 1959 and 1965 in its native USA, *The Twilight Zone* received only sporadic screenings in the UK. ITV first transmitted some episodes, but further runs (including previously unseen episodes) came on BBC 2 and Channel 4 in the 1980s.

The concept was picked up again for a 1983 cinema film *Twilight Zone the Movie*, in which four directors (Steven Spielberg, John Landis, Joe Dante and George Miller) reworked three original TV scripts, plus one unused story by Serling. A second television version came along in 1985. Filmed in colour, in an hour-long format, featuring two or three stories per episode, it met with little success. There was no Rod Serling this time.

TWIN PEAKS

US (Lynch/Frost/Spelling Entertainment/ABC)
Drama. BBC 2 1990–1

Agent Dale Cooper	Kyle MacLachlan
Sheriff Harry S. Truman	Michael Ontkean
Leland Palmer	Ray Wise
Sarah Palmer	Grace Zabriskie
Laura Palmer/Madeleine Ferguson	Sheryl Lee
Jocelyn 'Josie' Packard	Joan Chen
Catherine Martell	Piper Laurie
Pete Martell	Jack Nance
Major Garland Briggs	Don Davis
Bobby Briggs	Dana Ashbrook
Benjamin Horne	Richard Beymer
Audrey Horne	Sherilyn Fenn
Jerry Horne	David Patrick Kelly
Shelly Johnson	Mädchen Amick
Leo Johnson	Eric Da Re
Dr William Hayward	Warren Frost
Donna Hayward	Lara Flynn Boyle
Eileen Hayward	Mary Jo Deschanel
Big Ed Hurley	Everett McGill
Nadine Hurley	Wendy Robie
James Hurley	James Marshall
Hank Jennings	Chris Mulkey
Norma Jennings	Peggy Lipton
Lucy Moran	Kimmy Robertson
Dr Lawrence Jacoby	Russ Tamblyn
Deputy Andy Brennan	Harry Goaz
Deputy Tommy 'The Hawk' Hill	Michael Horse
Mike Nelson	Gary Hershberger
Richard Tremayne	Ian Buchanan
Margaret, the log lady	Catherine E. Coulson
Windom Earle	Kenneth Welsh
Annie Blackburne	Heather Graham

Creators/Executive Producers: David Lynch, Mark Frost

Surreal mystery-cum-soap opera set in the Pacific North-West of America.

Twin Peaks exemplified the power of hype. This bizarre series arrived with such a fanfare that the TV public around the world simply couldn't ignore it. Early episodes in the USA topped 35 million viewers and, despite its relegation to BBC 2, it attracted an extremely healthy audience in the UK. However, for all the promotion and the merchandising which followed, the series failed to hang on to its viewers and it ended with a whimper rather than a bang.

At least partly responsible for its decline was its incredibly weird plot, which meandered in and out of minor tales without getting to the bottom of the main question: 'Who killed Laura Palmer?'. That was the mystery that FBI agent Dale Cooper was hoping to resolve when he arrived in the sleepy lumber town of Twin Peaks, in pine-covered Washington State. Laura, a 17-year-old homecoming queen, had been fished out of the lake, her body naked and draped in a plastic sheet. Through his investigations, Cooper was to uncover more and more about Laura's shady lifestyle, and about the dark secrets, skull-duggery and sexual intrigue which went to make the town of Twin Peaks the Peyton Place of the 1990s.

Cooper's detection methods were strange to say the least. For a start, most of his leads came from ESP or from dreams involving midgets. His findings were then dictated to his unseen assistant, Diane, via a microcassette recorder, between mouthfuls of his favourite cherry pie and 'damn fine coffee'. Of little help were the local sheriff, Harry S. Truman, a man of few words, and his tearful deputy, Andy Brennan. But, little by little, Cooper uncovered the truth about this spooky, misty backwater. Illicit love triangles were unearthed, nasty plots to take over the town's Packard Sawmill were exposed, and some of the strangest people kept cropping up – like a dwarf who talked backwards, like the Log Lady, who nursed a piece of timber in her arms, and like Audrey Horne, the teenage seductress who tied knots in cherry stalks with her tongue. Yet, although the finger of suspicion pointed at most of the eccentric townsfolk, the identity of Laura's killer remained obscure. Eventually, to most viewers' relief, it was revealed to be Laura's own father, Leland, but only because he had become possessed by the so-called Killer BOB. Even then Cooper did not take the hint. He stayed in Twin Peaks, investigating other murders, and the arty quirkiness of the series continued into a second season.

Criticized as being the proverbial triumph of style over substance, *Twin Peaks* was, at least initially, powerful viewing. A creation of cult film director David Lynch (of *Eraserhead*, *The Elephant Man* and *Blue Velvet* fame), and **Hill Street Blues** writer Mark Frost, its haunting, sinister atmosphere was skilfully manufactured. The dreamy, oddball feel and cinematic look were later echoed in the more successful **Northern Exposure** and the weird *Eerie, Indiana*. The haunting theme music was by Angelo Badalamenti and location shooting took place in the once-peaceful, one-horse town of Snoqualmie Falls, Washington, a community now beseiged by devoted fans.

TWIZZLE see *Adventures of Twizzle, The.*

TWO IN CLOVER

UK (Thames) Situation Comedy. ITV 1969–70

Sid Turner ....Sid James
Vic Evans ....Victor Spinetti

Creators/Writers: Vince Powell, Harry Driver. Producer: Alan Tarrant

Two City clerks move to the country and find it less appealing than they imagined.

Londoner Sid Turner and Welshman Vic Evans were clerks in a City insurance office and thoroughly fed up with their lot. Throwing in their jobs, they purchased Clover Farm, a smallholding in the country. However, with problematic livestock to look after, and the insular locals difficult to agree with, they soon realized that country life was not as calm and trouble free as they had first thought. Their rustic dream became more of a nightmare.

TWO OF US, THE

UK (LWT) Situation Comedy. ITV 1986–90

Ashley ....Nicholas Lyndhurst
Elaine ....Janet Dibley
Perce ....Patrick Troughton
Tenniel Evans

Mr Jennings...Paul McDowell
Mrs Jennings ....Jennifer Piercey

Creator/Writer: Alex Shearer. Producers: Marcus Plantin, Robin Carr

Two young people live together despite having different outlooks on life.

Computer programmer Ashley and his girlfriend, Elaine, didn't always see eye to eye. In fact, they usually talked at cross purposes. Nevertheless, they were happy to share a flat and a relationship of sorts. Ashley was keen on marriage; Elaine was not, but they did eventually tie the knot and settled down to a life of marital ups and downs. Ashley's parents and his granddad, Perce, were also seen.

2 POINT 4 CHILDREN

UK (BBC) Situation Comedy. BBC 1 1991–

Bill Porter ....Belinda Lang
Ben Porter ....Gary Olsen
Rona ....Julia Hills
Jenny Porter ....Clare Woodgate
Clare Buckfield
David Porter ....John Pickard
Christine ....Kim Benson
Bette ....Liz Smith

Creator/Writer: Andrew Marshall. Producer: Richard Boden

A working mum struggles to balance professional and domestic responsibilities.

Centring around the Porter family of Chiswick, *2 Point 4 Children* viewed (sometimes surreally) the life of a working mum, her easy-going husband and their two troublesome teenagers as they sought to make ends meet. Head of the household was Bill Porter, first seen working in Hanson's bakery with her man-hungry friend and neighbour, Rona. They later moved to an airline meals factory before setting up their own catering company, working from home. Bill's husband, Ben, was a central heating engineer who employed the rebellious Christine as his assistant. The Porters' two children were stroppy, boy-crazed Jenny and adolescent David, who was usually to be found dabbling in murky pursuits. An occasional visitor, much to everyone's dread, was Bill's mum, Bette.

Beginning very much as a UK version of **Roseanne**, *2 Point 4 Children* quickly found its own direction. With fantasy sequences becoming more and more the norm, it also gained in popularity and secured itself a run of Christmas specials, in addition to its regular series.

TWO RONNIES, THE

UK (BBC) Comedy. BBC 1/BBC 2 1971–86

Ronnie Barker
Ronnie Corbett

Executive Producers: James Gilbert, Michael Hurll. Producers: Terry Hughes, Peter Whitmore, Brian Penders, Paul Jackson, Marcus Plantin, Michael Hurll

Gags and sketches from a long-standing comedy partnership.

Messers Barker and Corbett, the big and the small of TV comedy, had first worked together in the mid-1960s when contributing to various David Frost programmes. Although they each enjoyed individual opportunities to shine (such as **Sorry!** for Corbett and **Porridge** for Barker), their joint efforts are equally well remembered.

The Two Ronnies ran for 15 years from 1971 and was hugely successful. Most programmes were shown on BBC 1, but some aired under the *Show of the Week* banner on BBC 2. Calling upon a host of talented scriptwriters (including the likes of David Nobbs, David Renwick and assorted *Pythons* – as well as Gerald Wiley, a pseudonym used by Barker himself), each show followed a simple format, opening and closing with mock news items. In-between, 'in a packed programme', viewers were treated to cocktail party sketches, a boistrous costume musical, a meandering Corbett monologue delivered from a big chair and doses of Barker's astounding pronunciation power, with a decent helping of gentle smut thrown in for good measure. There were also spoof serials like *The Phantom Raspberry Blower of Old London Town* (written by Spike Milligan), *The Worm That Turned* and the cases of private investigators Charley Farley and Piggy Malone. Regular musical guests broke up the humour. These included middle-of-the-road performers such as Barbara Dickson, Elaine Paige and the Nolan sisters. Finally, it was 'Goodnight from me, and goodnight from him'.

TWO'S COMPANY

UK (LWT) Situation Comedy. ITV 1975–9

Dorothy McNab ....Elaine Stritch
Robert Hiller ....Donald Sinden

Creator: Bill MacIlwraith. Producers: Stuart Allen, Humphrey Barclay

Friction between a brash American author and her staid British butler.

American thriller writer Dorothy McNab had taken up residence in London, employing traditional butler Robert Hiller to manage her household. As depicted by the bald eagle and proud lion in the programme's titles, this was no happy arrangement. For a start, Dorothy was one of the worst type of Americans, loud and rather uncouth, a cheroot smoker with a pushy attitude to life. Hiller was very much of the old school, a

champion of etiquette and decorum with impeccable manners. Their love-hate relationship provided the humour. An American version, *The Two of Us*, starring Peter Cook and Mimi Kennedy, followed in 1981.

TWW (TELEVISION WALES AND WEST)

TWW was the original ITV contractor for South Wales and the West of England, taking to the air on 14 January 1958 from studios in Cardiff and Bristol. Coverage of the northern and western parts of the Principality did not fall into its initial remit but was instead looked after by Wales West and North (WWN), which began broadcasting in 1962. However, when WWN folded a year later, TWW was allowed to absorb its territory. TWW's contributions to the national ITV network were few (most notable, probably, was *Land of Song*), but it did have the added obligation of producing a number of programmes in the Welsh language. TWW lost its franchise to Harlech Television in the 1967 reshuffle, eventually leaving the airwaves on 3 March 1968.

TYNAN, KENNETH (1927–80)

British critic, infamous for being the first person to use the 'F' word on British television. The controversial utterance came not as a piece of thoughtless abuse but as part of a debate about theatre censorship taking place on the satirical programme **BBC 3** in 1965. Robert Robinson was the interviewer at the time. This has tended to overshadow Tynan's other television achievements, which included editing ITV's answer to **Monitor**, *Tempo*, and taking part in the 1950s quiz **The $64,000 Question**, in which he answered questions on jazz. He also made some programmes about method acting and contributed to the documentary series *One Pair of Eyes*.

TYNE TEES TELEVISION (TTT)

Tyne Tees Television took to the air on 15 January 1959, to serve the far North-East of England from its Newcastle upon Tyne studios. Its successful consortium included film producer Sidney Box and *News Chronicle* impresarios George and Alfred Black.

Having one of the smallest ITV regions, the company's ambitions were always modest in the early days. However, horizons were raised in 1974, when its programmes were broadcast for the first time to most of North Yorkshire, following a transmitter swap with Yorkshire Television, which was instigated by the IBA. At the same time, in order to stabilize finances and maximize advertising potential, Tyne Tees and Yorkshire set up a joint holding company known as Trident Television. (The third 'prong' of Trident was intended to be Anglia 'Television, which had also exchanged transmitters with Yorkshire, but the IBA ruled out Anglia's involvement.) Trident was eventually disbanded on the instructions of the IBA when it reappointed both Tyne Tees and Yorkshire to their franchises in 1980. However, following successful bids by the two companies in the 1991 auctions, they have again merged under the Trident name.

Amongst Tyne Tees best-remembered programmes have been daytime variety and game shows like *Those Wonderful TV Times*, the current affairs series *Face the Press*, the children's drama **Supergran**, the drama-documentary *Operation Julie*, and the pop shows *The Geordie Scene*, *Razzamatazz* and, for Channel 4, **The Tube**.

TYZACK, MARGARET (1931–)

British character actress, seen in a number of prominent roles in classic serials. She was Winifred Forsyte in **The Forsyte Saga**, Bette Fischer in *Cousin Bette*, Princess Anne in **The First Churchills**, Antonia in **I, Claudius** and also appeared in the 1979 revival of **Quatermass**.

UFO

UK (ATV/Century 21/ITC) Science Fiction. ITV 1970–3

Commander Edward Straker	Ed Bishop
Colonel Alec Freeman	George Sewell
Captain Peter Karlin	Peter Gordeno
Lt Gay Ellis	Gabrielle Drake
Colonel Paul Foster	Michael Billington
General Henderson	Grant Taylor
Colonel Virginia Lake	Wanda Ventham
Dr Jackson	Vladek Sheybal
Joan Harrington	Antonia Ellis
Nina Barry	Dolores Mantez
Lt Mark Bradley	Harry Baird
Captain Lew Waterman	Gary Myers
Lieutenant Ford	Keith Alexander
Skydiver navigator	Jeremy Wilkin

Creators: Gerry Anderson, Sylvia Anderson. Executive Producer: Gerry Anderson. Producer: Reg Hill

A secret defence agency protects Earth from space invaders.

UFO was puppet-specialists Gerry and Sylvia Anderson's first full attempt at real-life action, and in this series Earth was pitted against a mysterious alien force, sometime in the 1980s. Arriving in weird, pyramid-shaped spacecraft, the intruders were seldom seen. Viewers did learn,

however, that they had green skin and breathed not air but liquid, and that they were a sterile race, having lost the power of reproduction. The only way for them to survive was by kidnapping humans and stealing their organs for transplantation.

The general public was not alerted to the threat, for fear of causing widespread panic. Instead, a secret global defence unit was formed to anticipate UFO attacks and thwart any landings. SHADO (Supreme Headquarters, Alien Defence Organisation), whose command centre, Control, was housed deep beneath the Harlington-Straker film studios on the outskirts of London, was spearheaded by abrasive USAF officer Ed Straker, working under the cover of a film producer. Straker was assisted by the amiable Colonel Freeman, the moody Captain Karlin (who had lost his sister to the intruders), dare-devil test pilot Colonel Paul Foster and Lt Gay Ellis, the shapely commander of the organization's futuristic Moonbase, the first line of defence (where, for some reason, all operatives wore white cat suits, string vests and purple wigs).

SHADO was well prepared for a UFO attack. Its Interceptor spacecraft, crewed by females and launched from the moon, were first into action, when alerted by the SID (Space Intruder Detector), a reconnaissance satellite. If this line was breached, Skydivers were called into play. These nuclear submarines were capable of underwater and aerial combat. If all else failed, and land defence was required, SHADO air-dropped its SHADO-mobile supertanks into the fray.

UFO was clearly more adult-oriented than the Andersons' Supermarionation series. The characters had fuller profiles, the plots had darker tones and the uniforms (being filled with real people not woodentops) were certainly more provocative. One or two episodes touched on murky subjects such as hallucination, drugs and sex, and contrived to give the series a falsely risqué reputation. As a result, it was denied a network screening on ITV and floated between Saturday mornings and late nights around the country. It seems schedulers could not make up their minds whether this was kids' or adults' fare.

UK GOLD

Nostalgia channel with the slogan 'Prime time all the time' which broadcasts 19 hours a day from the Astra 1B satellite, as part of Sky's Multi-Channels package. A sister channel to UK Living, UK Gold's brief is to transmit archive material from the BBC and Thames Television, plus some programmes from overseas. Comedy features prominently, as do classic drama, old soaps, pop concerts and films. Consequently, past favourites like **Bless this House**, **Colditz**, **The Two Ronnies**, **Doctor Who**, **Minder**, **When the Boat Comes In**, **Tenko** and **Citizen Smith** have shared transmission hours with early episodes of **EastEnders**, **Dallas** and **Neighbours**. Some programmes have been screened more than once a day. The channel's holding company, UK Gold Broadcasting Ltd, is jointly owned by BBC Enterprises (20 per cent), Thames Television (15 per cent), Cox Cable Communications (38 per cent) and Flextech (27 per cent). The station went on air in 1992.

UK LIVING

Sister channel to UK Gold, UK Living, using the slogan 'You can't help getting involved', is dedicated to women's interests. As a result, programming has majored on cookery (repeats of Keith Floyd, Delia Smith, etc.), fashion, agony aunts, romance, gardening, health and female-oriented game shows. It has broadcast *The Best of Anne and Nick* at weekends, plus its own daily magazine (*Living Magazine*), hosted by Jane Irving – just one programme out of 18 hours or so freshly made each week for the channel. Any imports shown have also had a female bias and have included the American series **Cagney and Lacey**, *Kate and Allie* and **Charlie's Angels**. Feature films have usually been of the emotional type. In 1995 UK Living began re-runs of early **Brookside** episodes.

ULLMAN, TRACEY (1959–)

British actress, comedienne and singer, a hit on both sides of the Atlantic. Ullman first came to light in 1981 on **Three of a Kind**, in which she shared the honours with Lenny Henry and David Copperfield. She also appeared in **A Kick Up the Eighties** and then joined Dawn French, Jennifer Saunders and Ruby Wax as one of the **Girls on Top** (Candice) in 1985. After heading off to Hollywood, Ullman was given her own sketch programme, *The Tracey Ullman Show*, in 1987, which ran for three years, was a ratings success and won her an Emmy. It also helped launch the cartoon series *The Simpsons*, but did not take off when screened in the UK, being deemed 'too American'. Back home, Ullman appeared in *A Class Act* in 1993 for the new ITV company Meridian, of which her producer husband, Allan McKeown, is a director. She has also made some TV specials.

ULSTER TELEVISION (UTV)

Ulster Television, or UTV as it is now known, has provided the Independent Television service for Northern Ireland since 31 October 1959. Always having to tread a fine line politically, because of the region's sensitivities, Ulster has had one of the more difficult tasks in the ITV network. Nevertheless, it has survived every franchise shake-up. Notable contributions to ITV's national output have been few, however.

UNITED!

UK (BBC) Drama. BBC 1 1965–7

Gerry Barford	David Lodge
Jack Birkett	Bryan Marshall
Jimmy Stokes	George Layton
Kenny Craig	Stephen Yardley
Horace Martin	Harold Goodwin
Ted Dawson	Robin Wentworth
Frank Sibley	Arnold Peters
Mary Barford	Ursula O'Leary
Kevin Barford	Peter Craze
Dan Davis	Arthur Pentelow
Mick Dougall	Robert Cross
Curly Parker	Ben Howard
Jean Jones	Mitzi Rogers
Danny South	Mark Kingston
Dave Rockway	Christopher Coll
Bryn Morrison	Derek Sherwin
Mark Wilson	Ronald Allen
Dick Mitchell	Tony Counter
Chris Wood	Mike Redfern

Creator: Brian Hayles. Producers: Bernard Hepton, Anthony Cornish, David Conroy, John McRae

Life in and around a struggling soccer club.

As one strand of the BBC's autumn 1965 soap offensive (the other strand was **The Newcomers**), *United!* was another attempt by the Corporation to break the popular drama stranglehold held by **Coronation Street**. Airing on Monday and Wednesday evenings, it focused on the struggling Second Division team of Brentwich United, just as the new manager, Londoner Gerry Barford, was drafted in to keep the club afloat. Sadly, his best efforts failed to boost the team's affairs and, by 1966, another new boss, Mark Wilson, had succeeded him.

Most prominent amongst the team members were goalkeeper Kenny Craig and strikers Jimmy Stokes and Jack Birkett (the team captain). Club trainer was Horace Martin, Ted Dawson was the chairman and the secretary was Frank Sibly. Don Davis was chairman of the supporters' club. Boardroom battles, personal problems and domestic friction combined with the soccer stories throughout and also seen were Barford's wife, Mary, and their soccer-mad, 18-year-old son, Kevin. Jimmy Hill acted as technical advisor and match action was filmed at Stoke City's Victoria Ground. These efforts were all in vain, however, and *United!* left the screen in 1967, 18 years before the BBC did finally achieve its soap breakthrough with *EastEnders*.

UNIVERSITY CHALLENGE

UK (Granada) Quiz. ITV 1962–87; BBC 2 1994–

Presenters: Bamber Gascoigne, Jeremy Paxman (1994)

Creator: Don Reid. Producers: Barrie Heads, Patricia Owtram, Douglas Terry, Peter Mullings, Kieran Roberts (1994)

Long-running intellectual quiz for teams of university students.

A decade before **Mastermind** made its debut, Granada's *University Challenge* had already cornered the market in high-brow trivia, becoming, like *Mastermind*, an unexpected success. No one could have anticipated that a programme which posed questions about nuclear physics or Renaissance artists would run for 25 years.

Scholarly question-master Bamber Gascoigne took delight in taxing Britain's brightest young brains and added a touch of personality to what was otherwise a drably presented programme. Two four-person teams from competing universities or colleges did battle for a half-hour in a bland, ugly set, with a split screen employed to impose one team above the other. A round of questions opened with a 'starter for ten' (which became a catchphrase), and continued with three bonus questions. There were no holds barred and topics ranged from the sublime to the ridiculous, from Rachmaninov's piano concertos to First Division goalkeepers. The winning team stayed on to face a new challenge the following week, hoping to achieve three consecutive wins and win a place in the end of the series knock-out. The first contest took place between the universities of Reading and Leeds. In 1994 the programme was exhumed by Granada, who sold it to the BBC. Jeremy Paxman was installed as host and a somewhat jazzier set was employed. A straight knock-out tournament replaced the original 'challenge' format.

University Challenge was closely modelled on the US series *College Bowl*, and champion teams from both sides of the Atlantic occasionally faced-off in a special match. A number of notable personalities appeared as contestants in their youthful days, including writer Clive James, comedian Stephen Fry and Conservative politicians Malcolm Rifkind and David Mellor.

UNTOUCHABLES, THE

US (Desilu/Langford) Police Drama. ITV 1966–

Eliot Ness...Robert Stack
Agent Martin Flaherty ....Jerry Paris
Agent William Youngfellow.............Abel Fernandez
Agent Enrico Rossi ....Nick Georgiade
Agent Cam Allison...........................Anthony George
Agent Lee Hobson ....Paul Picerni
Agent Jack Rossman ....Steve London
Frank ('The Enforcer') Nitti ....Bruce Gordon
Al Capone ....Neville Brand
'Mad Dog' Coll ....Clu Gallagher
Narrator...Walter Winchell

Executive Producers: Jerry Thorpe, Leonard Freeman, Quinn Martin. Producers: Howard Hoffman, Alan A. Armer, Alvin Cooperman, Lloyd Richards, Charles Russell, Fred Freiberger

A US treasury official and his incorruptible men home in on gangsters in Prohibition Chicago.

Based on the life of the real Eliot Ness, who brought Al Capone to book in 1931 (for non-payment of taxes), *The Untouchables* told the story of an honest, upright and dedicated Treasury man as he sought to rid Chicago of organized crime. The dour, tight-lipped Ness and his whiter-than-white colleagues earned themselves the nickname 'The Untouchables' from the fact that they couldn't be bribed or influenced in any way.

The capture of Capone had been portrayed in a two-part TV special starring Robert Stack as Eliot Ness, which was screened in the USA as part of the *Desilu Playhouse* anthology. It proved so successful that this series ensued, although fact quickly gave way to fiction as it took hold. Although it showed the agents rounding up the likes of Frank Nitti (Capone's right-hand man), Ma Barker, Bugs Moran, Dutch Schultz, Walter Legenza and 'Mad Dog' Coll, the real Ness had had nothing to do with these events. Criticism also came from Italianate Americans who complained how their names were being dragged through the mud in every episode. In response, the producers added a disclaimer to the end of the show, admitting that much of the action was fictional, and also cut down the number of Italian criminals.

The Untouchables was a notable violent programme, filmed in stark, realistic black and white, with plenty of gunfire to keep its large audience enthralled. It aired in its native USA from 1959 to 1963. ITV companies in the UK were slower to bite. Kevin Costner took over the Ness role for a 1987 cinema version, directed by Brian De Palma.

UP POMPEII!

UK (BBC) Situation Comedy. BBC 1 1970

Lurcio ....Frankie Howerd
Ludicrus Sextus ....Max Adrian
　　　　　　　　　　　　　　　　　　　　　Wallas Eaton

Erotica ....Georgina Moon
Ammonia..Elizabeth Larner
Nausius ....Kerry Gardner
Senna...Jeanne Mockford
Plautus ....Walter Horsbrugh
                                                                    William Rushton
Ambrosia ....Lynda Baron
Flavia ....Mollie Sugden
Odius...John Junkin
Prodigus...David Kernan

Creator: Talbot Rothwell. Writers: Talbot
Rothwell, Sid Collin. Producers: Michael Mills,
David Croft, Sydney Lotterby

**Innuendo and double entendre in old
Pompeii.**

The centre of attention in this Roman farce was
Lurcio, the weatherbeaten slave of randy senator
Ludicrus Sextus. Constantly diverted from his
attempts to deliver '*The Prologue*' to the viewing
audience, Lurcio was obliged to act as a go-
between for Ludicrus and the rest of his household and their friends as they all sought to bed
one another. Lurcio kept viewers informed about
the goings on through asides to the camera.
Ammonia was Ludicrus's wanton wife, Erotica
the appropriately named daughter and Nausius
the wimpy son. Other characters floated in and
out of the action, not least batty old Senna, the
soothsayer who foolishly predicted the destruction of the town.

Based on Frankie Howerd's stage success in the
musical *A Funny Thing Happened on the Way to the
Forum*, *Up Pompeii!* also spawned a feature film,
leading to various other '*Up*' films for Howerd. It
gained a TV sequel in 1973, *Whoops Baghdad!*,
with the action transferred to the Middle East and
Howerd adopting the guise of servant Ali Oopla.
In addition, two revival specials have been seen,
both called *Further Up Pompeii!*, one in 1975 and
the other (for ITV) in 1991. The programme's
heavy innuendo (daring for the time) was
allegedly at times a touch too strong even for
Frankie Howerd himself.

UPPER HAND, THE

UK (Central) Situation Comedy. ITV 1990–5

Charlie Burrows...Joe McGann
Caroline Wheatley ....Diana Weston
Laura West ....Honor Blackman
Joanna Burrows...Kellie Bright
Tom Wheatley ....William Puttock
Michael Wheatley ....Nicky Henson

Executive Producer: Paul Spencer. Producer:
Christopher Walker

**A former footballer becomes housekeeper
to a female advertising executive.**

Injured soccer star Charlie Burrows needed a
new vocation. A widower, he also needed a good

environment in which to bring up his teenage
daughter, Joanna. So, he applied for and was
taken on as live-in housekeeper to Henley-based
business executive Caroline Wheatley, mother of
young Tom and separated wife of Michael, a
wildlife film-maker. Caroline's man-hungry
mother, Laura West, her assistant at the Blake and
Hunter advertising agency, was also on the scene.
Problems with the kids, as well as more mundane
domestic matters, drew Charlie and Caroline into
conflict, but, at the same time, helped foster their
growing romance. After four seasons of amiable
squabbling, love finally won through and Charlie
and Caroline were engaged to be married. A
one-off, hour-long special in 1995 saw the
dithering duo finally make it to the altar.

The Upper Hand, which enjoyed six long runs on
ITV, was based on the US sitcom *Who's the Boss*,
but shared the same theme music as another
American series, **Knots Landing**.

UPSTAIRS, DOWNSTAIRS

UK (LWT/Sagitta) Drama. ITV 1971–5

Mr Angus Hudson ....Gordon Jackson
Mrs Kate Bridges ....Angela Baddeley
Rose ....Jean Marsh
Lord Richard Bellamy ....David Langton
Lady Marjorie Bellamy.........................Rachel Gurney
Captain James Bellamy ....Simon Williams
Elizabeth Bellamy/Kirbridge ....Nicola Pagett
Georgina Worsley ....Lesley-Anne Down
Daisy...Jacqueline Tong
Edward..Christopher Beeny
Sarah..Pauline Collins
Emily ....Evin Crowley
Alfred ....George Innes
Roberts ....Patsy Smart
Pearce ....Brian Osborne
Laurence Kirbridge ....Ian Ogilvy
Hazel Forrest/Bellamy.....................Meg Wynn Owen
Ruby ....Jenny Tomasin
Thomas Watkins....................................John Alderton
Virginia Hamilton/Bellamy ....Hannah Gordon
Frederick ....Gareth Hunt
Alice ....Anne Yarker
William ....Jonathan Seely
Lily ....Karen Dotrice
Sir Geoffrey Dillon ....Raymond Huntley
Lady Prudence Fairfax...........................Joan Benham
Marquis of Stockbridge.................Anthony Andrews

Creators: Jean Marsh, Eileen Atkins. Executive
Producer: Rex Firkin. Producer: John
Hawkesworth

**Events in the lives of a turn-of-the-century
London family and their loyal servants.**

Much-praised, fondly remembered and hugely
successful, *Upstairs, Downstairs* focused on life at
165 Eaton Place, London, home of MP David
Bellamy, his lady wife, Marjorie, and their two

children, James and Elizabeth. The family was rich, but not extravagantly so, with most of their wealth inherited on Lady Bellamy's side (she was the daughter of a prime minister). So David's career was vital to the upkeep of the family's home and its standing in society, something which the indiscretions of his wayward children continually placed in jeopardy.

But, as the title suggested, the 'Upstairs' goings-on were only half the story, with the 'Downstairs' world of the Bellamys' domestic staff equally as prominent. Head of the servants was Mr Hudson, the highly responsible, softly-spoken but firm Scottish butler, a man who knew his place and made sure other staff members knew theirs. A father figure to the servants, he masterminded the team effort which kept the house afloat, ably assisted by Mrs Bridges, the gruff, plump cook, and Rose, the level-headed chief housemaid. Beneath them worked the younger staff – chubby, daydreaming parlour maid Sarah, maturing footman Edward, loyal housemaid Daisy (later Edward's wife), pathetic maid Ruby, and, in later episodes, new footmen Thomas and Frederick.

The series began in 1903, shortly after the death of Queen Victoria, and ran through until 1930. Along the way, in cosy, soap opera fashion, it depicted the household's struggles to win through in times of adversity, whether social (such as a visit by the King for dinner) or real (when Rose's fiancé was tragically killed in the Great War). It reflected all the early fads and fashions of the 20th century, from the Suffragette movement to the jazz age, writing historical events into the plot. The General Strike was one example and the loss of Lady Marjorie on the *Titanic* another. Lord Bellamy remarried (to Scottish widow Virginia Hamilton), his ward Georgina moved in to replace the petulant Elizabeth, and other characters came and went, both above and below stairs, before disaster struck at the end of the series. The family's wealth was lost in the 1929 Wall Street Crash, James committed suicide and Eaton Place had to be sold. The last scene showed Rose closing the door on 30 years of her life, surrounded by moving echoes of the past.

Upstairs, Downstairs – widely acclaimed for its historical accuracy and shrewd social comment – was the brainchild of Jean Marsh and fellow actress Eileen Atkins (who had created the role of Sarah for herself but found herself committed to stage work when the programme began). They repeated the exercise in devising *The House of Eliott* in the 1990s. Despite the first six episodes being made in black and white, *Upstairs, Downstairs* enjoyed sales all across the world and led to a spin-off series, *Thomas and Sarah*, which followed the two young servants as they took up a new appointment in the country. An American version, *Beacon Hill*, set in 1920s Boston, was also attempted but didn't succeed.

UTV see Ulster Television.

V

US (Daniel H. Blatt and Robert Singer/ Warner Brothers) Science Fiction. ITV 1984–

Mike Donovan	Marc Singer
Dr Julie Parrish	Faye Grant
Diana	Jane Badler
Nathan Bates	Lane Smith
Robin Maxwell	Blair Tefkin
Elizabeth	Jenny Beck
	Jennifer Cooke
Ham Tyler	Michael Ironside
Willie	Robert Englund
Elias	Michael Wright
Kyle Bates	Jeff Yagher
Lydia	June Chadwick
Sean Donovan	Nicky Katt
Mr Chiang	Aki Aleong
Charles	Duncan Regehr
Martin/Philip	Frank Ashmore
Lt James	Judson Scott
Howard K. Smith	Himself

Creator: Kenneth Johnson. Executive Producers: Daniel H. Blatt, Robert Singer

Earth is taken over by Nazi lizards from outer space.

V began as two successful mini-series (*V* and *V: The Final Battle*) and then expanded into a weekly run, which was never as popular. The 'V' in the title actually stood for 'Visitors' and 'Victory', with the storyline revolving around an alien invasion of Earth and the underground resistance to it. The Visitors came from somewhere near the star Sirius, arriving in Los Angeles in the late 20th century in massive spacecraft, ranging in size from three- to five-miles wide. They ostensibly came in peace, offering advice and technical help to the Earth's population in return for some vital minerals. However, once the human race had been wooed, the Visitors began to take over the planet, using subtle coercion and clever propaganda.

If this sounds familiar, it was because *V* was modelled on the rise of Fascism in Germany before World War II. But in case the metaphor passed some viewers by, there were some even more obvious references. The aliens dressed in uniforms with swastika-type motifs. They formed an elite squad of stormtroopers, like the SS, and rounded up all opposition, confining subversives

in concentration camps. But, like the Nazis, they also met resistance.

Working against them was TV journalist Mike Donovan, who had penetrated an alien spaceship and discovered their true intentions. He learned that the Visitors were not humanoids at all but forked-tongued, giant, rodent-eating reptiles whose scaly skin was revealed whenever their flesh was torn. They had come to steal Earth's water and, more menacingly, to take back frozen humans as food. Pursued by the aliens, Mike teamed up with scientist Julie Parrish (a concentration camp escapee), mercenary Ham Tyler, a friendly alien named Willie (played by the film world's future Freddie Kruger, Robert Englund) and young Robin Maxwell, who had been seduced by a Visitor and given birth to a hybrid child, Elizabeth. They hid out in the Club Creole and adopted the 'V for Victory' sign as their emblem. Thankfully, by the end of the mini-series, they had seen off the oppressors with the aid of a specially produced bacterial red dust.

When the weekly series began, the Visitors soon regained the upper hand. Diana, their evil, duplicitous leader, was back in control, thanks to chemical magnate Nathan Bates (whose Scientific Frontiers Corporation had manufactured the lethal red dust), who sprang her from a Nuremburg-style trial. The underground still battled valiantly and the half-alien Elizabeth rapidly developed into a teenager with special mental powers. When the climax came, Diana and her cronies were thwarted by a mutual desire for peace between the two races.

V is well-remembered for one classic scene in which Jane Badler, as Diana, swallowed a mouse. It was actually done using chocolate mice, a mechanical jaw for close ups and a false expandable throat, which showed the mouse slipping down, but it looked very realistic and upset the squeamish.

VCR see videotape.

VH-1 see MTV.

VHS

Video cassette format established by JVC in Japan in 1976 and now the standard for domestic users. It was initially challenged in the market place by Sony's Betamax system, launched a year earlier, which some claimed provided a better image. However, although both systems use ½ inchwide tape inside the cassette, the VHS tape recorded and played back longer and gradually saw off its rival. VHS stands for Video Home System.

VTR see videotape.

VALENTINE, ANTHONY (1939–)

British character actor, often cast in sinister, sneery roles. Amongst these have been the parts of Toby Meres in *Callan* and Major Mohn in *Colditz*. As a teenager in the early 1950s Valentine was one of the actors to play Harry Wharton in *Billy Bunter of Greyfriars School*. He also appeared in *Whirligig* and the 1955 adaptation of *Children of the New Forest* and went on, in the 1960s, to pop up in *Dr Finlay's Casebook*, playing Bruce Cameron. Valentine was TV's *Raffles* in the 1970s and had prominent roles in *Justice* and the thriller series *Codename*. As Maurice, he was an occasional visitor to *Minder* and as Simon De Belleme, he was a mystic sorcerer in *Robin of Sherwood*. He has been seen in numerous single dramas and his guest parts have included series like *Department S*, *The Avengers*, *Space: 1999*, *Hammer House of Horror*, *Tales of the Unexpected*, *Bergerac*, *The Casebook of Sherlock Holmes*, *Lovejoy* and *Body and Soul*, and, in complete contrast, he also once hosted *Stars On Sunday*.

VAN DER VALK

UK (Thames/Euston Films/Elmgate) Police Drama. ITV 1972–3; 1977; 1991–2

Piet Van der Valk	Barry Foster
Arlette Van der Valk	Susan Travers
	Joanna Dunham
	Meg Davies
Kroon	Michael Latimer
Samson	Nigel Stock
	Ronald Hines
Wim Van der Valk	Richard Huw

Creator: Nicholas Freeling. Executive Producers: Lloyd Shirley, George Taylor, Brian Walcroft. Producers: Michael Chapman, Robert Love, Geoffrey Gilbert, Chris Burt

The investigations of a Dutch detective.

Set against the cosmopolitan backdrop of Amsterdam, with its reputation for drugs and prostitution, this series explored the world of local CID officer Van der Valk. The blond, curly-haired, impulsive detective scoured the canals and polders of the Dutch city in his search for common criminals and those involved in more subversive activity.

After an initial two-year run, the series was brought back in 1977 by Euston Films, with Joanna Dunham now in the part of Arlette, Van der Valk's wife. It was revived yet again in 1991, cashing in on the Morse, Dalgliesh, Taggart and Wexford success stories. This time yet another actress, Meg Davies, came in to play Arlette and

Van der Valk now also had a policeman son, Wim. The role of his boss, Samson, was taken by Ronald Hines on this occasion. In this two-hour series, Van der Valk, greying and still rather uncharismatic, had been promoted to Commissaris.

The character of Van der Valk was created by author Nicholas Freeling in 1962. The programme's catchy theme music, 'Eye Level' by the Simon Park Orchestra, surprisingly topped the British singles chart in 1973.

VAN DYKE, DICK (1925–)

American entertainer whose showbusiness ambitions seemed limited when he worked as an announcer for southern TV stations, having already failed to make the grade in a mime act. But, moving to New York, he filled in for Andy Williams and other stars, guested in *The Phil Silvers Show* and quickly became one of the latest names on Broadway, before launching his own sitcom, *The Dick Van Dyke Show*, in 1961. The series, in which he played writer Rob Petrie, brought him international fame and a host of Emmy awards. It ran for five years. Van Dyke then looked for greater achievements in the movies, but his material, by common consent, was not the best and he returned to television. His later series (such as *The New Dick Van Dyke Show*, with Dick as talk-show host Dick Preston) did not prove particularly successful, however, and he has largely been seen in specials and TV movies in recent years.

VARNEY, REG (1922–)

London-born comic actor, initially working as a teenage singer and ragtime pianist in workingmen's clubs. He moved on to the music halls and, after the war, teamed up with Benny Hill, who acted as Reg's stooge. It wasn't until the turn of the 1960s that Varney began to make television inroads. He was cast as Reg, the foreman, in the very popular sitcom *The Rag Trade* and followed it up with a children's series *The Valiant Varneys*. He also starred in *Beggar My Neighbour* in 1967, playing Harry Butt, before, in 1969, *On the Buses* arrived. Hugely successful, it ran for four years and even had three film spin-offs. It was very much Varney's series, and his clippie-chasing Stan Butler character was always at the centre of the action. When *On the Buses* ended, Varney starred in yet another sitcom, but *Down the Gate*, featuring Reg as fishmarket porter Reg Furnell, proved to be short-lived. Working on stage elsewhere in the world, and convalescing after heart problems, UK viewers have seen little of Reg Varney in recent years.

VAUGHAN, NORMAN (1927–)

Liverpudlian entertainer who made his name as compère of *Sunday Night at the London Palladium*, taking over from Bruce Forsyth in 1962. Vaughan, then a comparative unknown, had previously worked as a compère on stage shows and had first been seen on TV in 1954, but by the time his three-year spell at the Palladium ended, he was one of Britain's brightest stars. Along the way, he conjured up the thumbs-up, thumbs-down catchphrases of 'Swinging' and 'Dodgy'. Another catchphrase was 'Roses grow on you', taken from his commercials for chocolates. In 1972, he took over from Bob Monkhouse as host of the popular game show *The Golden Shot*, but stayed with the programme for only one year. He hadn't finished with game shows, however, as he went on to co-devise *Bullseye* for Central Television. Working more on stage as an actor, Vaughan's TV appearances have largely been on panel games and variety shows in the last couple of decades, although he did also compère *Pebble Mill Showcase* in 1978.

VAUGHAN, PETER (PETER OHM; 1924–)

Silver-haired British actor, familiar in sinister and menacing roles. One of his best-remembered creations was that of pampered prison baron 'Genial' Harry Grout in *Porridge*, which he followed with another sitcom success as Charlie Johnson, Wolfie Smith's prospective father-in-law and class enemy in *Citizen Smith*. However, Vaughan's TV career stretches back to the 1950s. One of his first starring roles was in the 1960 newspaper drama *Deadline Midnight* and he went on to play Bill Sykes in a 1962 adaptation of *Oliver Twist* and Long John Silver in a 1968 version of *Treasure Island*. He took the lead in 1969's *The Gold Robbers* (Detective Chief Supt Cradock) and starred as Billy Fox in the 1980 series *Fox*. Vaughan has also been seen in many other productions, including mini-series and more adaptations of the classics. In 1995 he played Frank Ashworth in *The Choir*. Both his wives have been actresses: Billie Whitelaw and Lillias Walker.

VAUGHN, ROBERT (1932–)

One of TV's international stars of the 1960s, Robert Vaughn was Napoleon Solo, *The Man from UNCLE*, from 1964 to 1968. His undercover days were not over, however, and he returned to our screens as Harry Rule in *The Protectors* in 1972. His first appearances came in the 1950s, when he took minor roles in series like *Dragnet*, and his first prime-time lead arrived in 1963 in a US drama called *The Lieutenant*. For most of the 1970s, Vaughn was cast in TV movies and glossy mini-series, and continued to be active in the cinema (he had been one of *The Magnificent Seven* back in 1960, amongst other credits). He played Chief of Staff Frank Flaherty in *Washington: Behind Closed Doors* in 1978 and resurfaced in 1986 to take the role of General Hunt Stockwell in *The A-Team*.

VERNON, RICHARD (1925–)

Distinguished English actor, often cast in upright, slightly aristocratic roles. One of his best remembered was as Oldenshaw, *The Man in Room 17* (or at least one of them) in the series of the same name and its sequel, *The Fellows*, both in the mid-1960s. Vernon also starred in *The Duchess of Duke Street* (as Major Smith-Barton), *Edward the Seventh* (as Lord Salisbury), *The Sandbaggers* (as 'C'), *A Gentlemen's Club* (as George), *L for Lester* (as bank manager Mr Davies), *Roll Over Beethoven* (as Oliver, Liza Goddard's crusty old dad), *Something in Disguise* (as Herbert Browne-Lacey) and, more recently, *Class Act* (as Sir Horace Mainwaring, Joanna Lumley's frail father). Other credits have included *Playhouse: Mystery and Imagination*, *Legacy of Murder*, *Return of the Antelope*, *Paradise Postponed* and numerous single dramas, including *Suez 1956*.

VERY PECULIAR PRACTICE, A

UK (BBC) Comedy Drama. BBC 2 1986–8

Dr Stephen Daker	Peter Davison
Dr Bob Buzzard	David Troughton
Dr Jock McCannon	Graham Crowden
Dr Rose Marie	Barbara Flynn
Lyn Turtle	Amanda Hillwood
Chen Sung Yau	Takashi Kawahara
Maureen Cahagan	Lindy Whiteford
Mrs Carmen Kramer	Gillian Rainer
Ernest Hemmingway	John Bird
Dorothy Hampton	Frances White
Dr Grete Grotowska	Joanna Kanska
Jack B. Daniels	Michael J. Shannon
Julie Daniels	Toria Fuller
Sammy Limb	Dominic Arnold
Professor George Bunn	James Grout
Nuns	Sonia Hart
	Elaine Turrell

Creator/Writer: Andrew Davies. Producer: Ken Riddington

Surreal tales of life at an ailing university medical practice.

Keen, idealist, rather neurotic young doctor Stephen Daker had a rude awakening on his arrival at Lowlands University. Accepting a position in the medical centre, in the hope of starting a new life after a messy marital break up in Walsall, he discovered anarchy and moral decline all around him and chiefly amongst his professional colleagues.

His genial but boozy boss, Jock McCannon, had hopelessly lost control of the practice and spent most of his time dictating his forthcoming book, *The Sick University*. This left room for the cynical and amoral Bob Buzzard to introduce dubious, money-making schemes and for the devious arch-feminist Dr Rose Marie (who believed that illness was something men inflicted on women) to scheme against the male species. Daker at least found humanity in the form of chirpy police student Lyn Turtle, and his Burmese mathematician flatmate, Chen Sung Yau.

In the second series, when Lyn had departed, the prickly Pole Grete Grotowska, an art historian, became Daker's new girlfriend. At this time, sinister forces were on the move at Lowlands. An unscrupulous new American vice-chancellor (Jack B. Daniels) had been appointed and right-wing market forces were taking over. Throughout both series, two mysterious, silent nuns flitted around the campus, rumaging in waste bins, doing quirky things and generally becoming the programme's trademark. Elkie Brooks sang the theme song, which was written by Dave Greenslade.

In 1992 Andrew Davies followed up *A Very Peculiar Practice* with a *Screen One* presentation entitled *A Very Polish Practice*. Set in Warsaw, amidst decaying Communism and advancing capitalism, it featured Stephen, Grete (now his wife) and Bob Buzzard, who was in town on a business trip and hoping, as ever, to make a fast buck.

VICTORY AT SEA

US (NBC/Project 20) Documentary. BBC 1952–3

Narrator: Leonard Graves

Producer: Henry Saloman

American history of World War II sea battles.

Introduced for British audiences by Michael Lewis, Professor of History at the Royal Naval College in Greenwich, this ground-breaking documentary examined the maritime context of the war effort. Using combat footage (from both sides of the conflict), in 26 parts it discussed key events like the bombing of Pearl Harbor. The production team worked closely with the US Navy, and Richard Rodgers provided a rousing musical score. The series' award-winning status ensured plenty of reruns in the early 1950s.

VIDEO WALL

A bank of television monitors each showing different images or each contributing one part to a larger image.

VIDEOTAPE

Video Tape Recording or VTR – a means of translating television signals on to magnetic tape, for future playback – was first pioneered in the early 1950s but the technology was primitive and the resolution poor. It wasn't until the Ampex Corporation launched a completely new system in 1956 that the industry began to take it seriously. Colour versions arrived two years later and the Ampex system remained in international use until the late 1970s, by which time simpler, cheaper and better quality reel-to-reel systems had been introduced. Professionally, 2 inch and 1 inch Quad tape systems have been in use, though ¾-inch U-matic, ½-inchVHS and Betamax, and ¼-inch Quatercam have also been employed (the smaller tapes mostly by amateurs). Cassette-based systems (Video Cassette Recorders, or VCRs) are now commonplace and have provided more flexibility in news gathering. They have also enabled domestic viewers to enjoy record and playback facilities, of course. Sony's Video 8 (8-mm tape) and its high resolution sister, Hi-8, are popular with camcorder users.

VINE, DAVID (1936–)

British sports frontman, a newspaper journalist who entered television with Westward TV but joined the BBC in 1966. He has largely focused on skiing (as host of Ski Sunday), show jumping and snooker, but has been involved with most sports and most BBC sports programmes. He was the first question master on *A Question of Sport*, introduced *The Superstars* and also presented *It's a Knockout* and *Jeux Sans Frontiers* with Eddie Waring.

VIRGIN OF THE SECRET SERVICE

UK (ATV) Spy Drama. ITV 1968

Captain Robert Virgin ....Clinton Greyn
Mrs Virginia Cortez............................Veronica Strong
Doublett ....John Cater
Karl Von Brauner...............................Alexander Dore
Klaus Striebeck ....Peter Swannick
Colonel Shaw-Camberley.....................Noel Coleman

Creator: Ted Willis. Producer: Josephine Douglas

The dangerous assignments of a patriotic British agent in the early 1900s.

Intrepid Captain Robert Virgin more than worked for the British secret service; he lived and breathed to defend British honour at a time when the Empire was beginning to crumble. From the North-West Frontier of India to all parts of the Middle and Far East, Virgin fought for his country, obeying the orders of his superior, Colonel

Shaw-Camberley, protecting his emancipated lady assistant, Mrs Cortez, and physically fending off his ruthless adversaries, Karl Von Brauner and Klaus Striebeck. Doublett was his loyal batman.

VIRGINIAN, THE/MEN FROM SHILOH, THE

US (Universal) Western. BBC 1 1964–73

The Virginian ....James Drury
Judge Henry Garth ....Lee J. Cobb
Trampas ....Doug McClure
Steve Hill ....Gary Clarke
Molly Wood...Pippa Scott
Betsy Garth..Roberta Shore
Randy Garth ....Randy Boone
Sheriff Brannon ....Harlan Wade
Deputy Emmett Ryker ....Clu Gulager
Belden ....LQ Jones
Jennifer..Diane Roter
Starr..John Dehner
John Grainger ....Charles Bickford
Stacy Grainger ....Don Quine
Elizabeth Grainger.......................................Sara Lane
Sheriff Abbott ....Ross Elliott
Clay Grainger ....John McIntire
Holly Grainger ....Jeanette Nolan
David Sutton ....David Hartman
Jim Horn ....Tim Matheson
Colonel Alan MacKenzie ....Stewart Granger
Roy Tate ....Lee Majors
Parker ....John McLiam

Executive Producer: Norman MacDonnell. Producers: Howard Christie, Paul Freeman, Jim McAdams

An eastern ranch foreman brings new methods to a western cattle farm.

This cowboy series was set on the Shiloh Ranch in Medicine Bow, Wyoming Territory. At the thick of the action was the ranch foreman, known only as 'The Virginian'. Little else was ever revealed about this mystery man of few words, but stern, level-headed and embued with a strong sense of justice, he was a respected figurehead for the local community. His presence at Shiloh reflected how eastern influence and modern thinking spread across America in the 1880s, eroding primitive western ways.

The ranch was owned initially by Judge Garth, then by brothers John and Clay Grainger, and finally by Englishman Colonel McKenzie (by which time the era had moved on to the 1890s and the programmed retitled *The Men From Shiloh*). On the range Trampas was The Virginian's impulsive young friend, one of a supporting cast of family members, ranch hands and assorted lawmen. Many top stars were introduced in one-off supporting roles – Bette Davis, Ryan O'Neal, George C. Scott, Charles Bronson, Telly Savalas and Lee Marvin, to name but a handful –

and, as in **Wagon Train**, stories tended to focus on these visitors, rather than on the rather aloof members of the regular cast.

The Virginian was TV's first feature-length western series, presenting virtually a movie a week. It was loosely based on the turn-of-the-century book of the same name by Owen Wister, which had also been covered three times for the cinema, most notably starring Gary Cooper in 1929.

VISION MIXER

The name given to the equipment that enables its operator (also known as a vision mixer) to select, mix, cut and fade different camera shots (or introduce visual effects) during recording or transmission on the instructions of the director.

VISION ON

UK (BBC) Children's Entertainment.
BBC 1964–76

Presenters: Pat Keysell, Tony Hart, Larry Parker, Ben Benison, Wilf Lunn, Sylvester McCoy, David Cleveland

Producers: Ursula Eason, Leonard Chase, Patrick Dowling

Juvenile entertainment accessible to youngsters with hearing impediments.

Vision On was the more politically correct follow-up to a programme baldly entitled *For Deaf Children,* which had begun in 1952. Aiming to cater for children with hearing difficulties as well as those with adequate hearing, *Vision On* was, as its name suggested, a visual extravaganza. Arty features by Tony Hart, a former graphic artist, dominated the show and one regular feature was 'The Gallery', displaying drawings sent in by young viewers. There were also crazy inventions to look at, lots of sight gags and sketches, plus the misadventures of pipe-cleaner men Phil O'Pat and Pat O'Phil. Co-host Pat Keysell signed for those who could not hear and, in the first series, there was also an emphasis on lip reading. From the second series, however, words became increasingly irrelevant, and the programme had little verbal content beyond a courteous hello and goodbye each week. However, lively music and weird and wonderful sounds remained important to the make up as the producers recognized that deaf people could pick up vibrations and appreciate the feel of the programme in this way.

When *Vision On* ended in 1976, it was succeeded by a more obvious art programme, again hosted by Tony Hart and entitled *Take Hart*. It was in *Take Hart* that the popular plasticine creature named Morph (created by future Oscar-winner Nick Parks) made his debut.

VITAL SPARK, The see *Para Handy – Master Mariner.*

VOLUME

The intensity of sound reproduction and the control on the receiver to adjust this.

VORDERMAN, CAROL (1960–)

Brainy British presenter, coming to the fore as a number-crunching hostess on **Countdown** in 1982 but since seen on a variety of science-based or educational programmes, including **How 2**, *Notes and Queries with Clive Anderson* and *Tomorrow's World.*

VOX POP

The views of people in the street when stopped by a reporter, which are then edited into a sequence for use in current affairs or magazine programmes.

VOYAGE TO THE BOTTOM OF THE SEA

US (Twentieth Century-Fox/Irwin Allen)
Science Fiction. ITV 1964–

Admiral Harriman Nelson	Richard Basehart
Commander/Captain Lee Crane	David Hedison
Lt Commander Chip Morton	Robert Dowdell
CPO Curley Jones	Henry Kulky
CPO Francis Sharkey	Terry Becker
Stu Riley	Allan Hunt
Kowalsky	Del Monroe
Crewman Sparks	Arch Whiting
Crewman Patterson	Paul Trinka
Doctor	Richard Bull

Creator/Executive Producer: Irwin Allen

The crew of a super-submarine take on threats to the world.

The *Seaview* was the world's most advanced nuclear submarine, created by its commander, Retired Admiral Harriman Nelson and housed in a pen 200-ft down at his Nelson Institute of Marine Research, at Santa Barbara, California. Six hundred feet long, the supersub could dive deeper (4450 ft) and travel faster (70 knots) than any of its rivals, and was equipped with all the latest devices, including atomic torpedoes. It carried a separate mini-sub, a diving bell, a snowcat and an innovative 'flying fish', a small vessel capable of both water and air travel.

The action was set 13 years in the future and, although their role was meant to be research, Nelson and his crew were constantly called upon to maintain peace below the waves, by thwarting aggressors, whether human, fish or alien. After a reasonably serious beginning, the storylines soon plummeted to ridiculous depths. One of the most memorable villains was Professor Multiple, played by Vincent Price, who tried to take over the *Seaview* using life-like puppets. In addition, the ship confronted all manner of outrageous monsters from the deep. There were werewolves, enemy orchids, giant jellyfish, supersquids, even Nazis. One adventure took place inside a whale.

Valiantly assisting Nelson in his protection of our planet were the youngest submarine captain ever, Captain Lee Crane, and fellow officers Chip Morton, Francis Sharkey and Curley Jones. The show was created by low-budget sci-fi specialist Irwin Allen (*Lost in Space*, *Land of the Giants*, etc.), and was spun off his 1961 cinema version starring Walter Pidgeon. Much of the film footage was re-used in the TV series, and the sub itself was also a relic of the movie.

WKRP IN CINCINNATI

US (MTM) Situation Comedy. ITV 1981–

Andy Travis ....Gary Sandy
Arthur Carlson ('Big Guy') ....Gordon Jump
Jennifer Marlowe ....Loni Anderson
Les Nessman.................................Richard Sanders
Herb Tarlek ....Frank Bonner
Gordon Sims (Venus Flytrap) ....Tim Reid
Bailey Quarters ....Jan Smithers
Johnny Caravella (Dr Johnny Fever)
....Howard Hesseman
Lillian 'Mama' Carlson ....Carol Bruce

Creator: Hugh Wilson

A dying radio station is kicked into life when a new programme director takes over.

WKRP, one of Cincinnati's 18 radio stations, was losing money hand over fist. Its drab playlist only attracted a drab, ageing audience and drab advertising sponsors. But all that changed when new programme controller Andy Travis arrived. He encouraged the station's elderly owner, Mama Carlson, to take a chance, switch to rock and put some life back in the programming. Her son, Arthur, the incompetent station manager (commonly known as 'Big Guy') was not so keen, but Mrs Carlson bought the idea and the ratings began to take off. All the same, it was obvious that this radio station would never be a huge success.

The WKRP team consisted of Les Nessman, a bumptious news, weather and farming reporter, Baily Quarters, Andy's young assistant who became a journalist, and the station's top two DJs, Dr Johnny Fever (real name Johnny Caravella), the laid back, jive-talking morning presenter, and Venus Flytrap (Gordon Sims), a cool, black night-time jock. Holding the station together was busty, blonde, secretary Jennifer Marlowe, constantly pursued by obnoxious ad salesman Herb Tarlek.

Nine years after the series ended, a new version was produced for syndication in the USA. Only three members of the original cast were recalled: Arthur Carlson, Herb Tarlek and Les Nessman.

WWN see Wales West and North.

WACKY RACES

US (Hanna-Barbera/Heatter-Quigley) Cartoon. BBC 1 1969–70

Voices:
Dick Dastardly ....Paul Winchell
Muttley ....Don Messick
Peter Perfect ....Daws Butler
Penelope Pitstop.....................................Janet Waldo
Luke and Blubber Bear ....John Stephenson
Rufus Ruffcut ....Daws Butler
Rock and Gravel Slag...............................Daws Butler
Professor Pat Pending............................Don Messick
The General ....John Stephenson
Clyde ....Paul Winchell
Sergeant ....Daws Butler
Private Pinkley..Paul Winchell
Red Max ....Daws Butler
The Ant Hill Mob..Mel Blanc
Big Gruesome...Daws Butler
Little Gruesome.......................................Don Messick
Sawtooth ....Don Messick
Ring-a-Ding Convert-a-Car ....Don Messick
Narrator ....Dave Willock

Creators/Executive Producers: William Hanna, Joseph Barbera

Animated series of hair-raising contests between eccentric drivers and their weird vehicles.

Based loosely on the film *The Great Race*, *Wacky Races* drew together America's finest drivers, each behind the wheel of the strangest speed machines. In each episode, the 11 daredevil teams lined up for a cross-country race, eager to claim the title of 'The World's Wackiest Racer'. In car no. 1, the Boulder Mobile, were the cavemen Slag brothers, Rock and Gravel, and they were joined on the starting grid by the Gruesome Twosome in the Creepy Coupé (no. 2), inventor Professor Pat Pending in his Ring-a-Ding Convert-a-Car (3), the Red Max in the Crimson Haybailer (4), girl racer Penelope Pitstop in the Compact Pussycat (5), the General, Sgt and Private Pinkley in the Army Surplus Special (6), gangster Clyde and The Ant Hill Mob in the Bulletproof Bomb (7), Luke and Blubber Bear in the Arkansas Chugabug (8), the all-American Peter Perfect in his Turbo Terrific (9), and Rufus Ruffcut and Sawtooth in the Buzz Wagon (10). Villain of the piece was the appropriately named

Dick Dastardly in the Mean Machine (00), whose sole aim was to win at all costs, especially if it meant cheating. Thankfully, usually through the ineptitude of his sniggering dog sidekick, Muttley, Dastardly's attempts to impede his rivals always backfired.

The series, one of the most popular cartoons to come out of the prolific Hanna-Barbera studio, gave birth to two spin-offs, *The Perils of Penelope Pitstop* and *Dastardly and Muttley in their Flying Machines,* a clone of *Those Magnificent Men in their Flying Machines,* in which they tried to 'Stop the Pigeon', but never did. 'Drat and triple drat' as Dastardly would have put it.

WAGNER, LYNDSAY (1949–)

TV's **Bionic Woman** (Jaime Sommers), Lyndsey Wagner's road to television fame began with modelling and rock singing in the 1960s. Turning to acting, she appeared as a guest in shows like **The Rockford Files** and **Marcus Welby, MD,** but her break came with an episode of **The Six Million Dollar Man,** in which she played his ill-fated girlfriend. Despite the fact that she died in the episode, the producers liked her so much they spun her off into her own bionic series which ran for two years from 1976 and won her an Emmy. Her later work has involved a US prime-time police drama, *Jessie,* plus plenty of TV movies and mini-series, such as *Scruples.*

WAGNER, ROBERT (1930–)

American actor who first came to light in the cinema in the 1950s. A decade later, movie work not proving so fruitful, Wagner moved into television, starring in the adventure series **It Takes a Thief,** playing Alexander Mundy. He crossed the Atlantic to take the part of Flt Lt Phil Carrington in **Colditz** but then returned to Hollywood to star in *Switch.* In 1979 he began possibly his most successful role, that of millionaire adventurer Jonathan Hart in **Hart to Hart,** which ran for five years. His most recent major series was the drama series *Lime Street* (1985), which only ran to five episodes as a result of the death of one of his co-stars, Samantha Smith (the schoolgirl who had gained global fame by writing to Soviet leader Yuri Andropov to ask for peace). Wagner has largely been seen in TV movies and glossy dramas since. His wife – on two occasions – was the late Natalie Wood.

WAGON TRAIN

US (Revue/Universal) Western. ITV 1958–62/ BBC 1962–3

Major Seth Adams	Ward Bond
Flint McCullough	Robert Horton
Charlie Wooster	Frank McGrath
Bill Hawks	Terry Wilson
Christopher Hale	John McIntire
Duke Shannon	Scott Miller
Cooper Smith	Robert Fuller
Barnaby West	Michael Burns

Producer: Howard Christie

The adventures of a wagon train as it crosses the West in the 1880s.

This wagon train, although studio-bound in reality, supposedly ran from St Joseph ('St Joe') in Missouri to California, echoing the hazardous journey across the plains and the Rocky mountains endured by many 19th-century settlers. The train's leader was middle-aged father figure Major Seth Adams, replaced by Chris Hale when actor Ward Bond died in 1960. Ensuring that Indians did not impede progress was frontier scout Flint McCullough, later replaced by Duke Shannon and Cooper Smith. Other regulars were lead wagon driver Bill Hawks and cook Charlie Wooster. A 13-year-old orphan, Barnaby West, found wandering the trail alone, also joined the train.

In many ways, the regular cast merely provided the backdrop. For while they sometimes had their own tale to tell, most of the action was introduced by travellers who came and went, briefly joining the train and then heading off again. They brought with them hopes, experiences, but usually trouble, ensuring a different story every week. Many episodes were simply known as *The . . . . . Story,* with the name of the guest character filling the gap. John Wayne, James Coburn, Ernest Borgnine, Shelley Winters, Jane Wyman, Lee Van Cleef, Lou Costello, Bette Davis, Mickey Rooney and Ronald Reagan were all among the big names taking on these roles. *Wagon Train* also tried its hand at the classics, with a couple of episodes devoted to what were effectively revamps of *Great Expectations* and *Pride and Prejudice.* The series was based on the 1950 John Ford movie, *Wagonmaster,* in which Ward Bond had appeared, although not in the same role.

Wagon Train was one of those oddity programmes which switched channels in the UK (from ITV to BBC) during its first showing. Most episodes were an hour long, but some feature-length films were also made. Actor Robert Horton left the show in 1962, allegedly fed up of westerns. However, his next starring role came in another oater, **A Man Called Shenandoah** and co-star John McIntire also held on to his spurs, moving on next to **The Virginian.**

WAITING FOR GOD

UK (BBC) Situation Comedy. BBC 1 1990–

Diana Trent	Stephanie Cole

Tom Ballard	Graham Crowden
Harvey Bains	Daniel Hill
Jane Edwards	Janine Duvitski
Geoffrey Ballard	Andrew Tourell
Marion Ballard	Sandy Payne
Jenny	Dawn Hope
Basil Makepeace	Michael Bilton
Davey	Ross Thompson
Jamie Edwards	Paddy Ward
Reverend Dennis Sparrow	Tim Preece

Creator/Writer: Michael Aitkens. Producer: Gareth Gwenlan

Two stroppy inmates keep the staff of an old folks' home on their toes.

Tom Ballard and Diana Trent were neighbours at the Bayview Retirement Home in Bournemouth. Tom, a former accountant, had been dumped in the home by his thoughtless son, Geoffrey, and grasping daughter-in-law, Marion, in the series' first episode, but remained philosophical about it all. His natural cheer, his eccentric sense of humour and his flair for adventure remained undiminished. He paired up, to form a formidable, subversive geriatric duo, with the next-door resident, retired photo-journalist Diana Trent, for whom 'trout' would have been a more appropriate surname. Domineering and dismissive, the acid-tongued Diana had largely given up on enjoyment before Tom arrived, but now they led the home's cynical manager, Harvey Bains, and his fawning, drippy assistant, Jane Edwards, a merry dance. They scuppered all Harvey's cost-cutting measures with threats of bad publicity and goaded their fellow residents into demanding more from life. When finances became tight, Diana was forced to move in with Tom, but she fought tooth and nail against marriage. Also seen were Jenny, the good-natured waitress, OAP colleagues like Basil, Davey and Jamie, and, later, spaced out vicar Dennis Sparrow.

WALDEN, BRIAN (1932–)

MP turned political interviewer Brian Walden took over as host of LWT's *Weekend World* in 1977 from Peter Jay. He himself relinquished the hot seat to another ex-politician Matthew Parris nine years later but, when the programme ended in 1988, he returned to interrogate parliamentarians in *The Walden Interview* (later retitled simply *Walden*). His soft 'R's and his relentless pursuit of his interviewee have made him a favourite with mimickers. Prior to TV, he had been Labour MP for Birmingham All Saints and Birmingham Ladywood from 1964 to 1977.

WALES WEST AND NORTH (WWN)

The short-lived ITV contractor for West and North Wales (TWW held South Wales), which came on air on 14 September 1962, but went out of business, because of low advertising revenue, on 26 January 1964. To date, WWN has been the only ITV franchise holder to go broke. Appreciating that the transmission area was too small to support an independent station, the ITA amalgamated it into the South Wales and West of England ITV region, allowing TWW to expand its coverage across the whole of the Principality.

WALKER, CLINT (NORMAN EUGENE WALKER; 1927–)

Giant American actor who became an overnight success in 1955 when cast as the mysterious wanderer *Cheyenne*. His subsequent contractual wrangles with Warner Brothers have been well documented and resulted in his walking out for a while (Ty Hardin was introduced as Bronco Layne to fill the gap in production). Walker eventually returned to *Cheyenne* but still longed to leave the series on a permanent basis. When his contract ended in 1962, he spent most of his time away from showbusiness, just making a handful of cameo appearances. When he did try to return in the 1970s, it was not with a great deal of success. His TV movies were not particularly well received and a new prime-time drama, *Kodiak*, didn't make the grade.

WALKER, ROY (1940–)

Northern Irish entertainer, first seen on *New Faces* in 1977 and then as one of *The Comedians*, before hosting the guessing game *Catchphrase*. He has also had his own series, *Licensed for Singing and Dancing*, and compèred *Summertime Special*. His son Mark is a TV presenter, too.

WALL, MAX (MAXWELL LORIMER; 1908–90)

British comedian, famed for his silly walks, pained expressions and ridiculous black tights and big boots. After years on the stage and in radio, Wall was given his own television show in the 1950s and continued to make guest appearances on variety shows in the following decades. He played Tommy Tonsley in the 1978 sitcom *Born and Bred* and also made cameo appearances in *Coronation Street* (as Harry Payne, a friend of Elsie Tanner), *Emmerdale Farm* (as Arthur Braithwaite), *Crossroads* (as Walter Soper, a cousin of Arthur Brownlow), *Minder* (as Ernie Dodds, a jailbird) and the kids' series *Danger – Marmalade at Work* (as a judge).

WALTER, HARRIET (1950–)

British Shakespearean actress seen in such series as *A Dorothy L. Sayers Mystery* (as Lord Peter Wimsey's companion Harriet Vane) and the Channel 4 kidnap thriller *The Price*, plus the play *Amy*, in which she starred as aviator Amy Johnson. More prominently, Walter also played Charity Walton in the steamy, academic serial *The Men's Room*.

WALTERS, JULIE (1950–)

Acclaimed British actress, known for her versatility. She appeared with Victoria Wood in the Granada series *Wood and Walters*, and the two have worked together many times, in plays like *Talent*, the series *Victoria Wood – As Seen on TV* (she played the inept charlady Mrs Overall in the *Crossroads* spoof *Acorn Antiques*) and *Victoria Wood*, and TV films like *Pat and Margaret*. Walters appeared in *Boys from the Blackstuff*, played Pauline Mole (Adrian's young mum) in *The Secret Diary of Adrian Mole, Aged 13¾* and Mrs Murray (Robert Lindsay's pensioner mum) in *GBH*. She also delivered one of Alan Bennett's monologues in the *Talking Heads* series and starred in her own series, *Julie Walters and Friends*.

WALTON, KENT (1925–)

Canadian sports commentator, for years ITV's voice of wrestling on Saturday afternoons. In the late 1950s, however, Walton worked in a quite different field, that of pop music, as host of the teenage music show *Cool for Cats* and DJ with Radio Luxembourg.

WALTONS, THE

US (Lorimar) Drama. BBC 2 1974–82

John Walton	Ralph Waite
Olivia Walton	Michael Learned
Zeb (Grandpa) Walton	Will Geer
Esther (Grandma) Walton	Ellen Corby
John Boy Walton	Richard Thomas
	Robert Wightman
Mary Ellen Walton/Willard	Judy Norton-Taylor
Jason Walton	Jon Walmsley
Erin Walton	Mary Elizabeth McDonough
James Robert 'Jim-Bob' Walton	David W. Harper
Ben Walton	Eric Scott
Elizabeth Walton	Kami Cotler
Ike Godsey	Joe Conley
Corabeth Godsey	Ronnie Claire Edwards
Aimee Godsey	Rachel Longaker
Sheriff Ep Bridges	John Crawford
Mamie Baldwin	Helen Kleeb
Emily Baldwin	Mary Jackson
Verdie Foster	Lynn Hamilton
Reverend Matthew Fordwick	John Ritter
Emily Hunter/Fordwick	Mariclare Costello
Yancy Tucker	Robert Donner
Flossie Brimmer	Nora Marlowe
Maude Gormsley	Merie Earle
Dr Curtis Willard	Tom Bower
Reverend Hank Buchanan	Peter Fox
J.D. Pickett	Lewis Arquette
John Curtis Willard	Marshall and Michael Reed
Cindy Brunson/Walton	Leslie Winston
Rose Burton	Peggy Rea
Serena Burton	Martha Nix
Jeffrey Burton	Keith Mitchell
Toni Hazleton	Lisa Harrison
Arlington Wescott Jones ('Jonesy')	Richard Gilliland
Narrator	Earl Hamner, Jnr

Executive Producers: Lee Rich, Earl Hamner Jnr

Sentimental tales of a Virginian family during the Depression and World War II.

The Walton family lived in the town of Walton's Mountain, in the Blue Ridge Mountains of Jefferson County, Virginia. Mom and Dad were Olivia and John, she a caring, devoted mother, he a solid father figure and part-owner of the family's sawmill, with Grandpa Walton.

The Waltons had seven children, plus a dog named Reckless. The eldest was John-Boy, a fresh-faced youth with writing ambitions. He majored in English at Boatwright University, started a local newspaper, *The Blue Ridge Chronicle*, had a novel published which took him to New York, then worked as a war correspondent during the hostilities. The next in line was Mary Ellen, who became a nurse, married Dr Curtis Willard, gave birth to little John Curtis and then saw her husband die at Pearl Harbor (or so it was thought). When he resurfaced in Florida, he decided not to return to Virginia, leaving Mary Ellen with the new man in her life, fellow pre-med student Jonesy. The Waltons' other sons were Jim-Bob, Jason and Ben, and the two youngest daughters were Elizabeth and Erin. They didn't play such prominent roles but were always on hand to help out during family crises, of which there were plenty.

Grandma was taken ill, then Grandpa died (actor Will Geer passed away between seasons). Olivia suffered an attack of tuberculosis and was sent away to recuperate in a sanitarium, with her place as housekeeper given to her cousin, Rose. Then the war arrived and saw the boys taken off with the armed forces, leaving the sawmill short-staffed and forced into temporary closure. Meanwhile, the other townsfolk also had their ups and downs. Most prominent were storekeeper Ike Godsey and his prim wife, Corabeth, the vicar Reverend Fordwick, who married schoolteacher Emily Hunter, and two fading spinster sisters, Mamie and Emily Baldwin.

The Waltons shunned sex and violence for human tragedy and family drama. It showed the children growing up and getting married, followed by domestic upheaval after domestic upheaval and portrayed a good-natured family struggling to survive in one of America's poorest areas at a time of great deprivation. All stories were told through the moist eyes of John Boy.

The series was created by Earl Hamner Jnr, who also acted as narrator. The stories were based on his own life, which had first been portrayed in a 1963 Henry Fonda film, *Spencer's Mountain*. *The Waltons* (which began as a TV movie called *The Homecoming*). It was so squeaky-clean and wholesome that it attracted much parody, particularly for its closing sequence when the family, tucked up in bed, all called 'Goodnight' to each other as the household lights were dimmed one by one. After the series ended, three TV movie specials were produced to update events in Walton's Mountain.

WANAMAKER, ZOE (1949–)

American-born actress, the daughter of US actor and director Sam Wanamaker. She has been seen in *Edge of Darkness*, *Inspector Morse*, *Paradise Postponed*, *Prime Suspect* and other dramas. However, it has been as Tessa Piggott alongside Adam Faith in *Love Hurts* that she has become well-known.

WAR GAME, THE

UK (BBC) Drama. BBC 1 1985

Writer/Producer: Peter Watkins

Graphic portrayal of nuclear destruction.

One of the BBC's most controversial projects, *The War Game* depicted in harrowing images the aftermath of an imaginary nuclear attack on the UK. Initially showing civilians preparing for the onslaught, the 50-minute film then revealed in stark black and white footage the horrors of the resulting chaos.

The War Game was made in drama-documentary style as a film for *Monitor* in 1965 and producer Peter Watkins employed mostly non-professional actors to add to the realism. However, the overall effect was so startling and distressing that Director-General Sir Hugh Greene banned its transmission, fearing it would alarm or confuse the old and fretful in society. Although it was released for cinema showings, it was not televized until 20 years later, when it was screened as part of the BBC's 40th-anniversary commemoration of the bombing of Hiroshima.

WAR IN THE AIR

UK (BBC) Documentary. BBC 1954–5

Narrator: Robert Harris

Writer/Producer: John Elliot

Analysis of the role of aircraft in combat.

With Sir Philip Joubert as series adviser, *War in the Air* was a 15-part retrospective on the role

played by air power before, during and immediately after World War II. The half-hour programmes were made in collaboration with the Air Ministry. Sir Arthur Bliss composed the theme music, which was performed by the London Symphony Orchestra under Muir Mathieson.

WARING, EDDIE, MBE (1910–86)

For many years, Eddie Waring was the voice of rugby league on the BBC and his excitable commentaries were as much a part of the entertainment as the match itself. His northern accent, novel approach and well-oiled catchphrases like 'early bath' and 'up and under' readily exposed him to the impressionists of the day. Waring gave his first TV commentary in 1946, having previously managed both Dewsbury and Leeds rugby league clubs. Additionally, he was one of the presenters of *It's a Knockout* and *Jeux Sans Frontières* (usually taking charge of the Mini-Marathon). Always game for a laugh, Eddie was also seen as a guest in *The Goodies* and *The Morecambe and Wise Show*. At one time, in complete contrast, he hosted *Songs of Praise*, too. He retired in 1981.

WARING, RICHARD (1925–94)

British comedy writer majoring on domestic sitcoms. Amongst his contributions were *Marriage Lines*, *The World of Wooster*, *Not in Front of the Children*, *Bachelor Father*, *And Mother Makes Three/Five*, *My Wife Next Door*, *My Honourable Mrs*, *Miss Jones and Son* and *Rings on their Fingers*. Waring provided some early 1960s scripts for Charlie Drake, wrote episodes of *Dixon of Dock Green* and was seen as an actor, too. He played Henry Blagrove alongside Richard Briers in the 1962 comedy *Brothers in Law*.

WARNER, JACK, OBE (HORACE JOHN WATERS; 1895–1981)

As the totally reliable copper George Dixon in *Dixon of Dock Green*, Jack Warner became a national institution. Born in London's East End, Warner, the brother of radio and stage entertainers Elsie and Doris Waters (otherwise known as Gert and Daisy), followed his sisters into showbusiness. He also won fame on radio, 'Mind my bike' becoming his catchphrase on Garrison Theatre during the war, and he also played Joe Huggett, head of the Huggett family in a series of films and radio programmes. In 1949 Warner played PC Dixon in the film *The Blue Lamp* and was shockingly shot dead. However, the character struck a chord with cinema audiences and prolific writer Ted Willis was encouraged by the BBC to furnish Dixon with his own TV series. *Dixon of Dock Green* started in 1955 and ran for 21 years. Apart from occasional variety appearances, and the linkman's role on the BBC's *Christmas Night with the Stars* package, it was Warner's only major TV role. He was 80 when it ended.

WARSHIP

UK (BBC) Drama. BBC 1 1973-7

Commander Nialls...............................Donald Burton
Lt Commander Beaumont.......................David Savile
Lt Commander Kiley ....John Lee
Lt Palfrey ....Michael Cochrane
Lt Last ....Norman Eshley
Lt Parry ....Richard Warwick
Master at Arms Heron........................Don Henderson
Commander Murton ....Malcolm Terris
Lt Boswall ....Christopher Coll
Lt Peek ....Andrew Burt
Lt Leading Regulator Fuller ....James Cosmo
Commander Glenn ....Bryan Marshall
Captain Holt ....Derek Godfrey
Lt Commander Napier ....Robert Morris

Creators: Ian Mackintosh, Anthony Coburn
Producers: Anthony Coburn, Joe Waters

Drama on the high seas with a Royal Navy frigate.

Routine and not so routine manoeuvres gave rise to the action in this durable military soap opera. Amidst much naval banter and a plethora of stiff upper lips, the crew of HMS *Hero*, a Royal Navy frigate (number F42), stuck loyally to its chores, which involved anything from NATO exercises to Cold War face-offs, policing fishing wars or picking up defecting spies. Most of the attention focused on the commissioned ranks. The BBC worked closely with the Navy on the series and the military collaboration even extended to the supply of a real warship for filming.

WASHINGTON: BEHIND CLOSED DOORS

US (Paramount) Drama. BBC 1 1977-8

President Richard Monckton...............Jason Robards
William Martin ....Cliff Robertson
Linda Martin...Lois Nettleton
Sally Whalen ....Stefanie Powers
Frank Flaherty......................................Robert Vaughn
Esker Anderson ....Andy Griffith
Bob Bailey ....Barry Nelson
Myron Dunn ....John Houseman
Carl Tessler...Harold Gould
Adam Gardiner ....Tony Bill
Hank Ferris ....Nicholas Pryor
Lars Haglund ....Skip Homeier

Creator: David W. Rintels. Executive Producer: Stan Kallis. Producer: Norman Powell

Fictional tale of intrigue in 1970s American politics.

Based on the novel *The Company* by John Ehrlichman, a former aide to President Nixon, this six-part mini-series was essentially Watergate with the names changed. It didn't take viewers long to realize that President Richard Monckton was meant to be Nixon, or that his predecessor Esker Anderson was Lyndon Johnson. Robert Vaughn played Monckton's devious right-hand man, Frank Flaherty, as the White House manoeuvred to avoid being implicated in a political scandal.

WATCH WITH MOTHER

UK (BBC) Children's Entertainment. BBC 1953-80

Programmes for pre-school age children.

Watch with Mother was an umbrella title for various offerings from the BBC's children's department. In the immediate postwar years, its predecessor had been *For the Children* (with *Muffin the Mule*, et al), but, in 1953, the title was changed to complement the radio series *Listen with Mother* and new component programmes were introduced. Originally, *Watch with Mother* aired at around 3.45 in the afternoon, Tuesday-Thursday, as part of the *Children's Television* sequence, but more familiar is the 1.30 pm slot it occupied for most of its 27 years on air.

Running from Monday to Friday, the classic *Watch With Mother* line up consisted of *Picture Book* on Mondays, *Andy Pandy* on Tuesdays, *The Flowerpot Men* on Wednesdays, *Rag, Tag and Bobtail* on Thursdays and *The Woodentops* on Fridays. Later additions in the 1960s were *Tales of the Riverbank*, *Camberwick Green*, *Pogles' Wood*, *Joe Trumpton*, *The Herbs*, *Bizzy Lizzy* (first seen in *Picture Book*), *Chigley*, *Mary, Mungo and Midge*; other favourites in the 1970s were *Mr Benn*, *Bagpuss*, *Fingerbobs*, *Barnaby* and *The Mister Men*. In 1980 the formula was maintained but, with occupational and viewing habits changing, the name *Watch with Mother* was discarded in favour of the less politically troublesome *See-Saw*.

WATCHDOG

UK (BBC) Consumer Affairs. BBC 1 1985-

Presenters:
Nick Ross
Lynn Faulds Wood
John Stapleton
Anne Robinson
Alice Beer

Editors: Lino Ferrari, Sarah Caplin.

Effective consumer affairs programme.

Launched as a programme in its own right, having been a segment of the defunct *Nationwide* and its equally defunct successor, *Sixty Minutes*, *Watchdog* was initially presented by Nick Ross with Lynn Faulds Wood. Faulds Wood was later joined as co-host by her husband, John Stapleton. Anne Robinson took over in 1993, assisted by Alice Beer, Chris Choi, Simon Walton and other reporters. The aim of the series has been to expose conmen, lift the lid on shoddy workmanship and give the real facts about consumer goods. Viewers have been invited to write and ring in with their personal experiences. In 1995 Judith Hann and Alice Beer presented *Watchdog Healthcheck*, which focused on medical matters.

WATCHING

UK (Granada) Situation Comedy. ITV 1987–93

Malcolm Stoneway	Paul Bown
Brenda Wilson	Emma Wray
Mrs Stoneway	Patsy Byrne
Mrs Joyce Wilson	Noreen Kershaw
Pamela Lynch	Liza Tarbuck
David Lynch	John Bowler
Lucinda	Elizabeth Morton
Harold	Al T. Kossy
Cedric	Bill Moores

Creator/Writer: Jim Hitchmough. Executive Producer: David Liddiment. Producer: Les Chatfield

A couple enjoy bird watching but struggle to keep their relationship on the rails.

Set in Merseyside, *Watching* took its name from the bird watching hobby enjoyed by its male lead, Malcolm Stoneway, and his girlfriend, Brenda Wilson. Unfortunately, their relationship was seldom stable and there was much to-ing and fro-ing across the Mersey to their respective mothers' homes as one tiff led to another. When this happened, they spent more time watching each other than watching birds. Brenda's sister, Pam, generally had an easier time of it, marrying David Lynch and starting a family, but neither the Wilsons nor the Stoneways seemed content with their lot and there was a compatibility problem between the two clans. Brenda's mum was slightly batty and Malcolm's rather snooty. During one period of 'divorce', Malcolm married a girl called Lucinda, but the marriage broke down and he and Brenda were soon watching each other again.

WATER MARGIN, THE

Japan (NTV) Drama. BBC 2 1976–8

Lin Chung	Atsuo Nakamura
Kao Chia	Kei Sato
Wu Sung	Hajine Hana
Hu San-niang	Sanae Tschida
Hsiao Lan	Yoshiyo Matuso

Writer: David Weir

Flailing swords and mystic magic in medieval China.

Adapted by David Weir from translations of the original Japanese script, *The Water Margin* told of 108 chivalrous knights aroused from their graves to combat tyranny and corruption in the Orient, from their base in the water margins of Lian Shan Po. The hero was Lin Chung, with Hsiao his wife. This Japanese treatment of the 14th-century Chinese classic by Lo Kuan-Chung proved surprisingly popular. Amongst those voicing the English version were Bert Kwouk and Miriam Margolyes. In 1979 Weir adapted another Japanese/Chinese serial, Wu Ch'eng-en's *Monkey*, which starred Masaaki Sakai as a Buddhist pilgrim.

WATERHOUSE, KEITH CBE (1929–)

British newspaper journalist, novelist and TV scriptwriter. His series have generally involved humour or light drama and most have been in conjunction with Willis Hall. These have included **Inside George Webley**, **Queenie's Castle**, **Budgie**, **Billy Liar** (from Waterhouse's 1959 novel), *The Upper Crusts*, *Our Kid* and **Worzel Gummidge**. Alone, Waterhouse has also written *West End Tales*, *Andy Capp*, *The Happy Apple*, **Charters and Caldicot**, *The Upchat Line*, *The Upchat Connection* and the TV film *Charlie Muffin*. In addition, Waterhouse and Hall supplied sketches for the satire shows **That Was The Week That Was** and **BBC 3**, and contributed to anthologies like *The Sunday Play* and *Studio '64* in the early 1960s.

WATERMAN, DENNIS (1948–)

British leading man, a one-time schoolboy actor, on TV since the late 1950s. In the 1970s he became familiar in action roles like **The Sweeney**'s George Carter and **Minder**'s Terry McCann, but, more recently, has played comedy, as millionaire East Ender Tony Carpenter in **On the Up**, for instance, and wide boy Thomas Gynn in **Stay Lucky**. Waterman's TV career began with plays like *Member of the Wedding* (1959) and *All Summer Long* (1960), and the title role in *William* (as in **Just William**) in 1962. He appeared as Judy Carne's brother, Neville Finch, in the transatlantic sitcom *Fair Exchange* the same year and subsequently guested in series like **Journey to the Unknown** and **Man about the House**. He played King Harold in *Churchill's People* and was seen in Alan Plater's Premiere film *Give Us a Kiss, Christabel*. He himself was instrumental in bringing the story of a Durham miners' football team's victory in the first ever 'World Cup' to our screens in the drama *The World Cup – A Captain's Tale* (as co-producer and star) in 1982 and was later seen as Bobbo in Fay Weldon's serial *The Life and Loves of a She Devil*. His third wife is actress Rula Lenska.

WATKINS, PETER (1936–)

Pioneering British film-maker who employed documentary newsreel techniques and non-professional actors in his dramatic reconstructions. His *Culloden* in 1964 surprised viewers with its graphic depiction of the last battle to be fought on British soil, but more controversy followed *The War Game*, a year later. This account of the aftermath of a nuclear attack was, in fact, banned from transmission by the then BBC Director-General Sir Hugh Greene. It was eventually shown in 1985 as part of a season of programmes marking the 40th anniversary of the dropping of the atomic bomb on Hiroshima. Watkins later worked in Scandinavia, his Edvard Munch biopic being screened in the UK in 1976.

WATLING, JACK (1923–)

British actor familiar in the 1960s as Don Henderson in *The Plane Makers* and *The Power Game*. He also guested in *Doctor Who*, *No Hiding Place*, *Dixon of Dock Green*, *Hancock's Half Hour*, *Boyd QC* and other popular series, and was a late arrival in *The Newcomers*. Watling, the father of actress Deborah Watling, and the step-father of actress Dilys Watling, continued to work in television throughout the 1970s and 1980s. In 1972, he played Doc Saxon in the wartime RAF series *The Pathfinders*. In 1977 he appeared with Hugh Lloyd in *Lord Tramp* and in 1981 he starred as Dr Carmichael in the sitcom *Doctor's Daughters*. Later, he was occasionally seen as Frank Blakemore in *Bergerac*.

WAX, RUBY (1953–)

American comedienne and actress, the intrusive host of *Don't Miss Wax*, *Wax on Wheels*, *East Meets Wax* and *The Full Wax*. In 1985 she co-wrote and co-starred in *Girls on Top* (as Shelley). She has also been script editor on *Absolutely Fabulous*.

WEATHER

The world's first television weather forecast was broadcast by the BBC on 20 November 1936 at 4.01pm and lasted six minutes. An anonymous hand sketched in the isobars on a weather chart, while an off-screen voice provided the forecast over a bed of light music – all somewhat different to today's world of computer graphics and personality weather presenters. The first on-screen meteorology men appeared in Canada and the USA, quickly bringing a showbiz element to proceedings in an attempt to keep viewers switched on. In the UK no weather man was seen until 1954, when George Cowling gave the first in-view summary for the BBC on 11 January. Cowling, like his successors, was a Meteorological Office employee, not a BBC man. The first weather woman was Barbara Edwards, who made her bow in 1974. Amongst other notable weather folk (on the BBC) have been Bert Foord, Graham Parker, Jack Scott, Keith Best, Michael Fish, Ian McCaskill, Jim Bacon, John Kettley, Bernard Davey, Suzanne Charlton, Peter Cockroft, Rob McElwee, Penny Tranter, Richard Edgar, Helen Young and Francis Wilson (who worked on *Breakfast Time* forecasts). Bill Giles took over as head of the BBC's team in 1983, a move that coincided with the introduction of flashy computer imagery and a new emphasis on the personalities of the presenters. ITV began its own national weather forecasts in 1989, with Alex Hill, Siân Lloyd, Trish Williamson and Martyn Davies the most prominent forecasters. In the USA, The Weather Channel is a 24-hour cable service which reports on national and local conditions.

WEAVER, DENNIS (1924–)

American actor who has been seldom short of work since making his TV debut in the 1950s, in series like *Dragnet*. Weaver went on to take the role of Matt Dillon's deputy, Chester Goode, in *Gunsmoke* and stayed with the series for nine years until 1964. He left to star in his own vehicle, *Kentucky Jones*, but it failed to take and, instead, Weaver headed into children's adventures as the dependable family man Tom Wedloe in *Gentle Ben*. Two years later, he found himself another durable role when he was cast as *McCloud*, the backwaters sheriff who brought his southern ways to New York City. When it ended in 1977, Weaver was still in demand and he has since taken parts in a host of prime-time US series and dramas which have not, however, transferred to the UK. He has also been seen in numerous TV movies.

WEBB, JACK (1920–82)

One of American TV's golden greats, former radio announcer Jack Webb made his mark as the glamourless, 'just the facts' policeman Joe Friday in the long-running crime series *Dragnet*. It was, in effect, Jack Webb's show. It was he who created it for US radio in 1949, bringing a new realism into police series and using genuine police files as sources for his stories. Webb had previously played other cops on radio, but none with the down-to-earth character of Friday, and none with the same success. When it transferred to TV in 1952, Webb was also its producer. The series ran for seven years and was revived for another three years in 1967, again with Webb in front of and behind the camera. He did very little acting otherwise, but his Mark VII production company did turn out a number of US series, including *The DA*, *Pete Kelly's Blues*, *Adam 12* and *Hec Ramsey*. He also produced the final season of **77 Sunset Strip** and was head of Warner TV for a while. Webb was once married to actress-singer Julie London.

WEDNESDAY PLAY, THE

UK (BBC) Drama Anthology. BBC 1 1964–70

Adventurous and influential vehicle for 1960s dramatic talent.

Quickly gaining a reputation for breaking new ground in television drama, *The Wednesday Play* was a showcase for emerging playwrights. Taking its cue from ABC's **Armchair Theatre** and the angry young men of the late 1950s, its gritty, social commentaries also furnished it with a left-of-centre image. The first *Wednesday Play* was Nikolai Leskov's *A Crack in the Ice*, dramatized by Ronald Eyre, and amongst other notable offerings were Sartre's *In Camera*, adapted by Phillip Saville (1964), David Mercer's *And Did Those Feet?*, Dennis Potter's *Vote, Vote, Vote for Nigel Barton* and *Stand Up, Nigel Barton*, Nell Dunn's *Up the Junction* (all 1965) and Jim Allen's *The Lump* (1967). Probably the most controversial and important play was Jeremy Sandford's study of a homeless family in **Cathy Come Home** (1966).

In addition to the writers listed, others like Peter Nichols, James Hanley, James O'Connor, Nigel Kneale and Michael Frayn also contributed memorable material, and production and direction was skilfully handled by the likes of Rudolph Cartier, Don Taylor, Tony Garnett, Ken Loach, Gilchrist Calder, Kenith Trodd, James MacTaggart, Waris Hussein, Jack Gold, Alan Bridges, Roger Smith, Irene Shubik and Charles Jarrott.

With a change of transmission day and the start of a new decade, *The Wednesday Play* eventually gave way to **Play for Today**.

WEEKEND WORLD

UK (LWT) Current Affairs. ITV 1972–88

Presenters: Peter Jay, John Torode, Mary Holland, Brian Walden, Matthew Parris

Producers: John Birt, Barry Cox

Influential Sunday lunchtime political programme.

Weekend World was the programme that introduced politics to Sunday lunchtimes. Launched as a means of filling the gap between news bulletins and current affairs series like **This Week** and **World in Action**, the series brought leading politicians and industrialists into the studio and quizzed them over the state of the nation, economic plans, foreign policies, etc. Major events in the week ahead were flagged up. John Torode and Mary Holland shared the presentation with Peter Jay in the early days, although Jay soon became sole frontman. When he left to take up an appointment as British Ambassador to the USA in 1977, he was replaced by former Labour MP Brian Walden. Ex-Tory MP Matthew Parris was in charge for the final two years from 1986. The programme's powerful theme music was 'Nantucket Sleighride' by American rock band Mountain.

WEEKS, ALAN (1923–)

Veteran BBC sports commentator (since 1951), specializing in ice events these days but also heard over football matches, swimming, gymnastics and on other major occasions. He also fronted the **Pot Black** series. Prior to working in television (and sometimes during), Weeks publicized ice shows and the Brighton Tigers Ice Hockey Club.

WEINSTEIN, HANNAH (HANNAH DORNER; 1911–84)

American independent film-maker of the 1950s, formerly a *New York Herald Tribune* journalist and a publicist. Her interest in film began in the early 1950s and led to her joining forces with ATV to produce action series like **The Adventures of Robin Hood**, **Sword of Freedom** and **The Buccaneers**. She also produced **Colonel March of Scotland Yard** and **The Four Just Men**. Weinstein then returned to the USA, where she spoke out against racial discrimination in the film industry.

WELDON, FAY (1933–)

British novelist and playwright noted for her feminist stance and her portrayal of women who dare to break free from men's shadows. Amongst her TV offerings have been the plays *The Fat Woman's Tale*, *A Catching Complaint* (both 1966), *Poor Cherry* (1967), *Splinter of Ice* (1972) and *Life for Christine* (1980). She also contributed to episodes of **The Doctors**, **Upstairs, Downstairs** (including the pilot) and the anthology series **Menace**, and, in 1980, she adapted Jane Austen's *Pride and Prejudice*. Her novel **The Life and Loves of a She Devil** was dramatized to great acclaim by the BBC in 1986 and a year later *Heart of the Country* was also well received. In 1991 ITV produced her *The Cloning of Joanna May* and *Growing Rich*.

WE'LL MEET AGAIN

UK (LWT) Drama. ITV 1982

Helen Dereham	Susannah York
Major Jim Kiley	Michael J. Shannon
Albert Mundy	Ray Smith
Vera Mundy	June Barry
Ronald Dereham	Ronald Hines
Patricia Dereham	Lise-Ann McLaughlin
Jack Blair	Patrick O'Connell
Colonel Rufus Krasnowici	Ed Devereaux
M/Sgt Joe 'Mac' McGraw	Christopher Malcolm
M/Sgt Chuck Ericson	Joris Stuyck

Creator: David Butler. Writers: David Butler, David Crane, John Gorrie. Producer: Tony Wharmby

An Englishwoman falls for an American major during the wartime 'invasion' of Britain by the USA.

'Over paid, over sexed and over here' was the familiar description applied to US military personnel stationed in the UK during World War II, and this 13-part drama set out to prove its validity. Based around the sleepy Suffolk market town of Market Wetherby, *We'll Meet Again* focused on the impact made on its residents by the arrival of 2000 men from the US Eighth Air Force 525th Bomb Group. At the forefront of the action was Helen, wife of the paraplegic Ronald Dereham, who found herself drawn to the charms of suave Yank Jim Kiley.

To keep within the show's modest budget, only one B-52 bomber was seen, with the rest of the action involving models or stock footage.

WELLAND, COLIN (COLIN WILLIAMS; 1934–)

Northern actor and writer. In front of the camera his most familiar performances have been in *Z Cars* (as PC David Graham), *Cowboys* (as Geyser) and Dennis Potter's *Blue Remembered Hills*. As a writer, he has contributed plays like *Bangelstein's Boys* (1969), *Say Goodnight to Your Grandma*, *Roll On Four O'Clock* (both 1970), *Kisses at Fifty* (1973), *Jack Point, Leeds United* (both 1974) and *Your Man from the Six Counties* (1976). He also wrote *The Wild West Show*. Greater acclaim has come for his cinema screenplays (including an Oscar for *Chariots of Fire*).

WELLS FARGO

US (Overland/Juggernaut/Universal) Western. BBC 1957–64

Jim Hardie	Dale Robertson
Beau McCloud	Jack Ging
Jeb Gaine	William Demarest
Ovie	Virginia Christine
Mary Gee	Mary Jane Saunders
Tina	Lory Patrick

Producers: Earle Lyon (Overland), Nat Holt (Juggernaut)

The adventures of a stagecoach company troubleshooter in the Gold Rush days.

In the 1860s Jim Hardie was a roaming agent for the passenger and shipping company of Wells Fargo, Incorporated, based in the Californian town of Gloribee. His duties extended from ironing out problems with employees to preventing the hijacking of coaches and the theft of the gold bullion they carried. The series, initially half-hour in length, was expanded to full-hour episodes in 1961, when it switched production companies from Overland to Juggernaut. At the same time, Hardie settled down a little, bought the Haymaker Farm ranch on the outskirts of San Francisco and was given a cast of co-stars. These were his ranch supervisor, Jeb Gaine, his young assistant, Beau McCloud, and a widowed neighbour, Ovie (who fancied Jeb), plus her two daughters, Mary Gee and Tina. Despite these distractions, Hardie still fulfilled his duties for the company in exemplary fashion.

Properly titled *Tales of Wells Fargo*, the series was known only as *Wells Fargo* in the UK.

WEST, TIMOTHY, CBE (1934–)

British actor, often seen in distinguished, hard-nosed or blustery roles, with probably his best-remembered portrayal that of *Edward the Seventh*. That apart, West has taken major parts in very many series. They include *Big Breadwinner Hog* (as Lennox), *Churchill and the Generals* (as Winston Churchill), *The Monocled Mutineer* (the General), *A Very Peculiar Practice* (the aptly named Dr Furie), *Crime and Punishment* (Inspector Porfiry), *Brass* (Bradley Hardacre), *The Good Dr Bodkin Adams* (Adams) and *Masada* (Vespasian). Among other important credits have been *Hine*, *Cottage to Let*, *Hard Times*, *The BBC Television Shakespeare's Henry VIII* (and other TV classics), *Harry's Kingdom*, *Shadow on the Sun* and *Blore MP*. He is married to actress Prunella Scales, with whom he once guested in *After Henry*, and is father of actor Sam West.

WESTCOUNTRY

The ITV franchise holder for the South-West of England, Westcountry first went on air on 1 January 1993, having outbid the existing service provider, TSW. A judicial review followed the ITC's move to award the contract to

Westcountry, but the decision was upheld. From the start, Westcountry went for an entirely new approach to regional programming, bringing in the latest technology and a host of new faces. This initially alienated some viewers but gradually audiences settled down. Its main studios are in Plymouth, but there are seven smaller studios across the region which between them provide some 11 hours a week of local programming. There has been little contribution to the national network to date.

WESTWARD

Serving South-West England, Westward took to the air on 29 April 1961 and remained the ITV contractor for the region until 11 August 1981. The company became indelibly linked to its outspoken executive chairman, Peter Cadbury, who campaigned vehemently for the South-West ITV region to be enlarged up as far as Bristol (the part of the West Country controlled by TWW and later HTV West). Cadbury also found himself involved in internal disputes, and a major boardroom tussle in 1980 helped seal Westward's fate as the franchise reappraisals loomed large. Even though programme standards were deemed to be good and there was local satisfaction with the service provided, the licence was awarded instead to TSW, which then purchased Westward's Plymouth studios. For many years, Westward was administratively joined to Channel Television, in an effort to maximize advertising potential for the two stations and keep down office costs. Westward produced few national programmes of note.

WHACK-O!

UK (BBC) Situation Comedy. BBC 1956–60; 1971–2

Professor James Edwards....................Jimmy Edwards
Mr Oliver Pettigrew ....Arthur Howard
                                            Julian Orchard (1971)
Mr F.D. Price Whittaker ....Kenneth Cope
Mr S.A. Smallpiece ....Norman Bird
Mr Lumley ....John Stirling
Mr R.P. Trench ....Peter Glaze
Mr Halliforth ....Edwin Apps
                                            Peter Greene (1971)
Parker ....David Langford
Mr Forbes ....Keith Smith
Mr Proctor ....Brian Rawlinson
Mr Dinwiddie ....Gordon Phillott
                                            Harold Bennett (1971)
Mr Cope-Willoughby ....Frank Raymond
Matron ....Barbara Archer
                                            Elizabeth Fraser
                                            Charlotte Mitchell
Taplow ....Gary Warren (1971)
Potter ....Greg Smith (1971)

Creators/Writers: Denis Norden, Frank Muir.
Producers: Douglas Moodie, Eric Fawcett, Douglas Argent (1971)

A public school is tyrannized by its bumptious, cane-swishing headmaster.

Professor James Edwards, MA was the principal of Chislebury School, an educational establishment that he ruled with an iron cane. While the schoolboys were always easy targets for the bullying, manipulative headmaster, so, too, were his staff and in particular his weedy right-hand man, Mr Pettigrew (played by Leslie Howard's brother, Arthur). Other members of staff came and went during the programme's four-year run.

Whack-O! was briefly revived in 1971, with Julian Orchard in the role of Pettigrew and the indomitable Jimmy Edwards again donning the boozy principal's cap and gown.

WHAT THE PAPERS SAY

UK (Granada) Current Affairs. ITV 1956–82; Channel 4 1982–9; BBC 2 1990–

Presenters: Kingsley Martin, Brian Inglis, Stuart Hall

Weekly review of newspaper headlines.

What the Papers Say is one of those programmes that has done the rounds of the channels, and yet has been produced by the same company, Granada, since its inception in 1956. The first hosts were *New Statesman* editor Kingsley Martin and *The Spectator*'s assistant editor, Brian Inglis, who alternated appearances. Inglis eventually became sole host. Under the temporary title of *The Papers*, in 1969, Stuart Hall inherited the presenter's chair, and various other personalities and Fleet Street scribes have filled that seat since. The role of them all has been to consider the week's newspaper coverage, to discuss the headlines, to analyse the treatment of big issues and to follow lines of opinion and bias, often with a light and very humorous touch. Each edition has lasted 15 minutes.

WHATELY, KEVIN (1951–)

North-Eastern actor who came to the fore as Neville in *Auf Wiedersehen, Pet* in 1983, but won even more acclaim for his subsequent performance as *Inspector Morse*'s genial sidekick, Detective Sgt Lewis. Whately has also starred in the medical drama series *Peak Practice*, playing Dr Jack Kerruish. One of his earliest TV appearances was as a miner in *When the Boat Comes In*.

WHATEVER HAPPENED TO THE LIKELY LADS? see *Likely Lads, The.*

WHAT'S MY LINE?

UK (BBC/Thames) Panel Game. BBC 1 1951–63; BBC 2 1973–4; ITV 1984–90

Hosts: Eamonn Andrews, David Jacobs, Penelope Keith, Angela Rippon

Creators: Mark Goodson, Bill Todman. Producers: T. Leslie Jackson, Dicky Leeman, Harry Carlisle, John Warrington, Richard Evans, Ernest Maxin (1973), Maurice Leonard (1984)

A celebrity panel tries to guess contestants' occupations.

What's My Line? was one of the biggest successes in television history. Not only did it enjoy three runs on British television but it was also a hit in its native USA, where it eventually ran for 25 years. And yet the formula was remarkably simple. Contestants 'signed in', gave a brief mime to illustrate the work they did (or part of it), and four celebrity panellists then tried to guess the profession, by asking the contestant questions which illicited no more than a yes or no answer. If the occupation was not discovered by the time ten 'nos' had been received, the contestant was declared the winner and took away a certificate to prove it. The host acted as adjudicator to ensure that fair questions were asked and that contestants always told the truth.

The first UK host was Eamonn Andrews and he chaired the quiz until its cancellation in 1963 (except for a short period when Australian Ron Randall took over in 1954 and a few other occasions when Gilbert Harding, Jerry Desmonde and Elizabeth Allen took charge of events). David Jacobs was frontman for the short-lived 1970s version and Andrews returned for an ITV revival in 1984. On Andrews's death in 1987, Penelope Keith and then, more permanently, Angela Rippon were drafted into the presenter's chair. Panellists varied, but the classic 1950s line-up was Barbara Kelly, David Nixon, Lady Isobel Barnett and the notoriously grouchy Gilbert Harding. Under the guidance of David Jacobs, the panel consisted of Lady Barnett, Kenneth Williams, William Franklyn and one other. Barbara Kelly returned in 1984, accompanied mostly by Jilly Cooper and George Gale.

In 1994 *What's My Line?* was revived yet again, this time as a regional programme (not fully networked) by Meridian Television. Emma Forbes was installed as presenter and Roy Hudd, Kate Robbins and June Whitfield were the regular panellists.

WHEATLEY, ALAN (1907–91)

Respected British actor, a former radio announcer who turned to stage and screen acting in the 1930s and was much seen on TV in the 1950s. It was as the dastardly Sheriff of Nottingham, Richard Greene's adversary in *The Adventures of Robin Hood*, that he is best remembered, although he was an early TV *Sherlock Holmes* in a BBC series way back in 1951. He also appeared in two versions of the thriller play *Rope* (1950 and 1953).

WHEEL OF FORTUNE

UK (Scottish) Quiz. ITV 1988–

Presenter: Nicky Campbell

Executive Producer: Sandy Ross. Producers: Stephen Leahy, Anne Mason

Colourful game show broadly based on Hangman.

Derived from the phenomenally popular American show of the same name, *Wheel of Fortune* gave Scottish Television its first big success in the world of networked game shows. Hosted by Radio 1 disc jockey Nicky Campbell, the programme has invited three contestants to answer general knowledge questions, spin a large wheel marked with variously numbered segments and guess the missing letters of a mystery phrase. Whatever number has been indicated by the pointer when the wheel stops has been translated into points in the player's bank. Contestants correctly identifying the phrase have picked up an extra prize and the highest overall scorer has attempted one more phrase in the grand finale, in the hope of collecting even bigger rewards – a car or a large cash sum. Angela Ekaette was the hostess/letter-turner in the early programmes, with Carol Smillie making the job her own later.

Wheel of Fortune was also the name of a successor programme to *Take Your Pick*, offering star and booby prizes on the turn of a wheel and hosted by Michael Miles.

WHEELER, SIR MORTIMER (1890–1976)

Distinguished British archaeologist, discoverer and recoverer of many important sites, who became an unlikely television personality in the 1950s, thanks to his appearances on the erudite panel game *Animal, Vegetable, Mineral?*

WHEELTAPPERS' AND SHUNTERS' SOCIAL CLUB

UK (Granada) Variety. ITV 1974–6

Presenters: Bernard Manning, Colin Crompton

Creator/Producer: John Hamp

Variety show with a northern clubland atmosphere.

Presented from the fictitious Wheeltappers' and Shunters' Social Club, this series offered a collection of decent acts from the northern clubs scene plus some international names, all performing in the smoky, noisy atmosphere of a mock-up club concert hall. Earthy comedian Bernard Manning was compère, competing for attention with bell-ringing 'concert chairman' Colin Crompton, who was forever interrupting to announce that the meat pies had arrived or that the bingo would start in half an hour.

WHELDON, SIR HUW, OBE (1916–86)

Once described as 'the best Director-General the BBC never had', Welshman Huw Wheldon joined the Corporation in 1952 as its publicity officer. He then became a senior producer, working on programmes such as *Press Conference* and *Men in Battle*. Wheldon also appeared in front of the camera, conducting interviews for *Panorama* and hosting kids' shows such as *All Your Own*. More famously, he became editor and presenter of the arts magazine *Monitor*. Wheldon was subsequently promoted to the positions of Head of Documentary and Music Programmes (1963–5) and Controller of Programmes (1965–8). In 1968 he took over as Managing Director of Television, becoming Deputy Director-General in 1976. On leaving the boardroom, Wheldon returned to presenting, with the series *Royal Heritage* (timed to coincide with the Queen's Jubilee in 1977). From 1979 until shortly before his death in 1986, Sir Huw was President of the Royal Television Society.

WHEN THE BOAT COMES IN

UK (BBC) Drama. BBC 1 1976–7; 1981

Jack Ford	James Bolam
Jessie Seaton	Susan Jameson
Bella Seaton	Jean Heywood
Bill Seaton	James Garbutt
Tom Seaton	John Nightingale
Billy Seaton	Edward Wilson
Dolly	Madelaine Newton
Matt Headley	Malcolm Terris
Lady Caroline	Isla Blair
	Lois Baxter
Arthur Ashton	Geoffrey Rose
Duke of Bedlington	William Fox
'Geordie' Watson	Ian Cullen
Roddy	Martin Duncan
Channing	Christopher Benjamin
Sarah	Rosalyn Bailey
Sir Horatio Manners	Basil Henson

Creator: James Mitchell. Producers: Leonard Lewis, Andrew Osborn, David Maloney

Lives and loves in the depressed North-East.

Centring on one Jack Ford, a shipyard fitter who dabbled in unionism and politics, before working

his way up the capitalist ladder, *When the Boat Comes In* depicted the hard days of the 1920s in the cobbled streets of Galashield (based on South Shields, where author James Mitchell's dad had once been mayor). Ford was a Jack the lad-type figure, a rough diamond with a good heart who was closely allied to the Seaton family, especially attractive daughter Jessie, a schoolteacher. Her brother, Tom, was Jack's miner friend and her younger brother, Billy, became a doctor and brought free medicine to the local people. Dolly was another of Ford's girlfriends and Ashton the po-faced teacher Jessie eventually married.

Using Ford, man of the people, as guide, and beginning with his return from the Great War to a land rife with injustice, Mitchell effectively portrayed the deep, grim poverty of this proud industrial region and the earthy but noble character of its people. After three series, the programme ended with Jack heading for a new life in the USA, only to return four years later on the run from the FBI. This last season, set in the 1930s, saw our hero involved in the Jarrow marches and also taking part in the Spanish conflict.

Familiar through its jaunty 'thou shalt catch a bloater' theme song (written by David Fanshawe and sung by Alex Glasgow), *When the Boat Comes In* introduced viewers to the peculiarities of the lilting Geordie dialect, and has since been fondly remembered as a poignant piece of social history.

WHERE THERE'S LIFE

UK (Yorkshire) Medical. ITV 1981–9

Presenters: Miriam Stoppard, Rob Buckman

Executive Producer: Duncan Dallas. Producers: John Fanshawe, David Taylor, Ian McFarlane, Derek Goodall, Irene Garrow, Anne Pivcevic, David Poyser, Paul Bader

Discussion programme about medical matters.

Hosted by doctors Miriam Stoppard and Rob Buckman, the long-running *Where There's Life* talked to ordinary people about the medical traumas in their life and instigated debate about healthy lifestyles. It also considered new ideas and developments in the world of medicine.

WHICKER, ALAN (1925–)

Britain's most travelled TV reporter, Alan Whicker, was born in Egypt. After entering journalism, he became a war correspondent and then joined the influential current affairs series *Tonight* when it began in 1957. His dry, distinctive delivery and his ability to play the ordinary Brit abroad led to his own series for the BBC, *Whicker's World*, in 1959. Initially, a compilation of his *Tonight* reports, it soon broadened into new assignments, many under individual series titles, like *Whicker Down Under* in 1961. In 1968 he defected to the newly-formed Yorkshire Television, where he continued to notch up air mile after air mile in the pursuit of oddities overseas and insights into other people's lifestyles. He later returned to the BBC and, in the 1980s, presented *Living With Uncle Sam* and *Living With Waltzing Matilda*, series about British ex-patriots in the USA and Australia. He then turned down the chance to emulate Phileas Fogg and go *Around the World in 80 Days* (Michael Palin stepped in and reaped the rewards), preferring instead to take things rather more easily in *Around Whicker's World: The Ultimate Package*, in which he shadowed a wealthy tour party as they made their champagne circumnavigation. Amongst his other offerings have been *Whicker on Top of The World* (1962), *Whicker Down Mexico Way* (1963), *Whicker's New World*, *Whicker In Europe* (both 1969), *Whicker's Walkabout* (1970), *The World of Whicker* (1971), *Whicker's Orient*, *Whicker Within a Woman's World* (both 1972), *Whicker's South Seas*, *Whicker Way Out West* (both 1973), *Around Whicker's World in 25 Years* (1982) and *Whicker's World: A Taste of Spain* (1992). He also gained unexpected access to Haiti dictator Papa Doc Duvalier for a famous 1969 documentary, *Papa Doc – The Black Sheep*. Always an easy option for impressionists, the bespectacled Whicker was once famously parodied by *Monty Python* in a sketch called 'Whicker Island'.

WHIPLASH

UK (ATV) Western. ITV 1960–1

Christopher Cobb	Peter Graves
Dan	Anthony Wickert

A western set not on the plains of America but in the Australian bush.

Chris Cobb was an American who had arrived in Australia in the 1850s to establish Cobb & Co., the country's first stagecoach line. Even though he was based Down Under, and not in the Wild West, he faced the usual collection of cowboy outlaws, his only concession to local culture being the use of boomerangs and bullwhips to tame his opponents. Thirty-four episodes were made, but star Peter Graves made more of an impression when he later appeared as Jim Phelps in *Mission: Impossible*.

WHIRLYBIRDS

US (CBS/Desilu) Adventure. BBC 1958–62

Chuck Martin	Ken Tobey
Pete 'PT' Moore	Craig Hill
Janet Culver	Sandra Spence
Helen Carter	Nancy Hale

Producer: N. Gayle Gitterman

Two helicopter pilots find adventure.

Chuck Martin and PT Moore were two young pilots who founded their own helicopter charter company, Whirlybird Service, based in Longwood Field, California. Everyday proved to be an adventure, as the young daredevils flew their aircraft into tense and dangerous situations. With stunts aplenty, this was an all-action series that appealed to younger viewers. It was produced by Lucille Ball and Desi Arnaz's Desilu company.

WHISTLE TEST see *Old Grey Whistle Test*.

WHITE, BETTY (1924–)

Cheerful American comic actress, a US hit as early as 1953 with her first sitcom, *Life with Elizabeth*, and successful throughout that decade in quizzes, variety shows and the comedy *Date with the Angels*. However, it wasn't until the 1970s that she began to attract the attention of viewers elsewhere in the world, having fallen out of the mainstream in the 1960s. As man-hungry Sue Ann Nivens in **The Mary Tyler Moore Show** her prime time career took off again and she followed it with game show appearances and her own comedy *The Betty White Show*, in which she played Joyce Whitman. For most people, however, White is the naive, dim-witted but caring Rose Nylund from **The Golden Girls** and *The Golden Palace*, a role she picked up in 1985, when in her sixties.

WHITE, CAROL (CAROLE WHITE; 1942–91)

British actress, a child film star in the 1950s, on TV in the mid-1960s and then quickly moving on to Hollywood. White's forte was the ingenue, the girl who was easily led, attracted by bright lights and ending up in trouble, as she exemplified in the powerful dramas *Up the Junction* and **Cathy Come Home**.

WHITE, FRANCES (1938–)

British character actress, seen in many and varied parts on TV since the 1970s. She was Andrea Warner in *A Raging Calm*, Julia in *I, Claudius*, Linda Clark in *A Little Bit of Wisdom*, secretary Dorothy Hampton in **A Very Peculiar Practice** and Kate Hamilton in **Crossroads**. White has been best known in the 1990s as Miss Flood in the comedy **May to December**.

WHITE HEATHER CLUB, THE

UK (BBC) Variety. BBC 1 1958–68

Presenters: Robert Wilson, Andy Stewart, Robin Hall, Jimmie Macgregor

Producer: Iain MacFadyan

Singing and dancing Scottish style.

An extension of the traditional Hogmanay parties, *The White Heather Club* was an excuse for Scottish performers to don their best kilts and jig around to the best folk songs and ballads North of the Border. Featuring stars like Moira Anderson, Duncan Macrae, Roddy McMillan, The Joe Gordon Folk Four, James Urquhart, Jimmy Logan, dancers Isobel James and Dixie Ingram and band leaders Jimmy Shand and Ian Powrie, the series, produced by the BBC from its Springfield Road studio in Glasgow, ran and ran – for 285 editions. Tenor Robert Wilson was the first host, giving way after six programmes to Andy Stewart and the *Tonight* pairing of Robin Hall and Jimmie Macgregor.

WHITE HUNTER

UK (ITP) Adventure. ITV 1958–60

John Hunter ....Rhodes Reason

Producer: Norman Williams

Adventures in the African jungle with the appropriately named John Hunter, guide and game-handler. The series was based on the true-life tales of John A. Hunter, supposedly 'the surest and fastest shot in Africa', and author of the books *African Safari* and *Hunter's Tracks*. *White Hunter* was filmed in East Africa and made full use of the abundant wildlife. Thirty-nine episodes were made.

WHITEHOUSE, MARY, CBE (1910–)

Former schoolteacher who turned moral crusader when establishing her Clean-Up TV campaign in 1964 and formalizing it as The National Viewers' and Listeners' Association a year later. *Till Death Us Do Part* (not surprisingly) was one programme to raise her blood pressure and she was particularly critical of the works of Dennis Potter. The regime of Sir Hugh Greene, the BBC's Director-General in the permissive 1960s, was blamed for contributing to moral decay. She had nothing to do with the 1990s comedy sketch show *The Mary Whitehouse Experience*!

WHITELAW, BILLIE, CBE (1932–)

British actress who arrived on TV in the 1950s, appearing as a guest in series like *The Adventures of Robin Hood* and playing Mary, the daughter of *Dixon of Dock Green*, soon to be married to his young colleague Andy Crawford. She left *Dixon* after just one year but, in 1958, was given her own sitcom, *Time Out for Peggy*, in which she played Peggy Spencer, the hapless proprietress of a run-down boarding house. She was Josephine in Thames TV's 1974 series *Napoleon and Love*, and, in 1981, she turned to comedy again, taking the role of Bertha Freyer in *Private Schulz*. Amongst her many notable performances in single dramas have been Alun Owen's *Armchair Theatre* offerings *No Trams to Lime Street* (1959) and *Lena, O My Lena* (1960), the *Supernatural* presentations *Countess Ilona* and *The Werewolf Reunion* (1977), the mini-series *Jamaica Inn* (1983), *The Dressmaker* (1988) and *A Murder of Quality* (1991). More recently, Whitelaw has been seen in *The Cloning of Joanna May* and *Firm Friends*.

WHITFIELD, JUNE, OBE (1925–)

Solid British comedy support, the archetypal suburban sitcom wife thanks to her long partnership with the late Terry Scott in the series *Happy Ever After* (as June Fletcher) and *Terry and June* (as June Medford). Whitfield had previously appeared with Scott in *Scott On . . . .* After success on radio in *Take It from Here* (as Eth in The Glums) and other series, June's first TV appearances came in the 1950s, in shows like *Idiot Weekly, Price 2d* and *Hancock's Half Hour* (she was the nurse in the famous Blood Donor episode). She appeared again with Hancock in 1967, playing Esmeralda Stavely-Smythe, a waitress in *Hancock's*, his last TV series. Whitfield was seen in the 1961 comedy *The Arthur Askey Show*, supported Stanley Baxter in *Baxter on Travel* in 1964, and was Rose Garvey, one of the wives, in *Beggar My Neighbour* in 1967. She starred as Mabel Pollard, Harry H. Corbett's perennial fiancée, in the sitcom *The Best Things in Life* in 1969 and the same year was cast as Millie Goswick, a music hall singer, in *The Fossett Saga*. More recently, she has gamely turned her hand to 'newer' comedy, guesting with Julian Clary in *Terry and Julian* and playing the part of Jennifer Saunders's mum in *Absolutely Fabulous*.

WHITNEY, JOHN (1930–)

British TV executive, a former writer and producer who scripted for 1950s and 1960s series like *The Verdict Is Yours*, *Harpers West One*, *The Hidden Truth* and *The Informer*, in collaboration with Geoffrey Belman (the last three also as creators). He was script editor on *The Plane Makers* and later became Head of LWT, before advancing to the position of Director-General of the IBA in 1982.

WHO DARES WINS

UK (Holmes) Comedy. Channel 4 1984–8

Rory McGrath
Philip Pope
Jimmy Mulville
Julia Hills
Tony Robinson

Comedy sketch show featuring an up and coming team of writers/comedians.

In the view of most critics, the often satirical but not necessarily topical *Who Dares Wins* succeeded where similar 'alternative' sketch shows failed, because it was genuinely funny. It was also innovative. Amongst the best-remembered items was a series on pandas plotting to escape from a zoo. Julia Hills played a tense, accident-prone TV interviewer and Tony Robinson spent two programmes totally naked.

WHO DO YOU DO?

UK (LWT) Comedy. ITV 1972–6

Freddie Starr
Peter Goodwright
Faith Brown
Janet Brown
Margo Henderson
Roger Kitter
Barry Cryer
Johnny More
Jerry Stevens
Len Lowe
Dailey and Wayne
Paul Melba
Little and Large
Aiden J. Harvey

Creator/Producer: Jon Scoffield

Comedy sketches featuring top impressionists.

Although leaning heavily on the talents of Freddie Starr and Peter Goodwright, *Who Do You Do?* also featured most of the other leading impressionists of the day in a series of gags and skits. Tightly editing together its various components, the programme offered a gag a second in the style of *The Comedians*. The series was renamed *New Who Do You Do?* in 1975 and *Now Who Do You Do?* in 1976 (when the cast incorporated new faces like Michael Barrymore, Les Dennis and Dustin Gee).

WHO-DUN-IT

UK (ATV) Mystery Anthology. ITV 1969

Inspector Jeremy Moon ....Gary Raymond

Creator: Lewis Greifer. Producer: Jack Williams

Series of single plays with a murder theme, offering viewers the chance to spot the culprit.

Hosted by and starring fictional detective Inspector Jeremy Moon, this 13-episode series of Agatha Christie-type murder mysteries was set in the 1930s. Each week, after the discovery of a body – on one occasion that of a Hollywood film star on a transatlantic liner – the Inspector would begin his investigations, pausing at the end of the second act to invite the viewing public to hazard a guess as to *Who-Dun-It*, before finally revealing all.

WHODUNNIT?

UK (Thames) Panel Game. ITV 1972–8

Hosts: Edward Woodward, Jon Pertwee

Creators/Writers: Jeremy Lloyd, Lance Percival. Producers: Malcolm Morris, Robert Reed, Dennis Kirkland, Anthony Parker, Leon Thau

Celebrity panellists attempt to spot the culprit in a series of half-hour mysteries.

Hosted initially by Edward Woodward and then by Jon Pertwee, this light-hearted panel game offered celebrity guests the chance to find the killer in a mystery playlet. After seeing the action on tape, each celebrity was allowed to request a short action replay of a telling moment and then to question all the characters involved. Finally, they were called upon to name the guilty party who would, in a great show of bravado, stand up to take the rap. The performers changed from week to week, but a handful of panellists became regulars, most notably Patrick Mower and Anouska Hempel. Created by comedians Jeremy Lloyd and Lance Percival, the formula was rehashed for *Cluedo* in the 1990s.

WHOOPS! APOCALYPSE

UK (LWT) Comedy . ITV 1982

Johnny Cyclops...Barry Morse
Premier Dubienkin ....Richard Griffiths
The Deacon ....John Barron
Commissar Solzhenitsyn ....Alexei Sayle
Kevin Pork ....Peter Jones
Foreign Secretary ....Geoffrey Palmer
Chancellor of the Exchequer ....Richard Davies
Shah Mashiq Rassim.........................Bruce Montague
Lacrobat ....John Cleese
Jay Garrick ....Ed Bishop
Abdab ....David Kelly

Creators/Writers: Andrew Marshall, David Renwick. Producer: Humphrey Barclay

A world dominated by crackpot politicians rushes towards World War III.

In this irreverent comedy, attempts to restore Shah Mashiq Rassim to the throne of Iran by the use of the nuclear Quark bomb proved disastrous when events went haywire and Israel was blown up. This action sent the world spinning towards

Armageddon, with the balance of power fought over by US President Johnny Cyclops (a lobotomized former actor from Omaha) and Soviet Premier Dubienkin. In the middle was idiotic British Prime Minister Kevin Pork. The Deacon was the USA's crazed security adviser and also in the fray was international terrorist Lacrobat.

WHOOPS BAGHDAD! see *Up Pompeii!*

WHOSE LINE IS IT ANYWAY?

UK (Hat Trick) Comedy. Channel 4 1988–

Presenter: Clive Anderson

Creators: Dan Patterson, Mark Leveson.
Producer: Dan Patterson

Celebrity improvisation game show.

Transferring to television from Radio 4, *Whose Line Is It Anyway?* has brought the drama school discipline of improv – improvisation – into the world of mainstream comedy. Each programme has featured four adlibbing comedians working singly, in pairs or all together, to execute a series of parlour games. Host Clive Anderson has asked the studio audience for suggestions for some games, others have been pre-determined, but all have demanded instant response and imagination from the assembled performers. Favourite guests have included Tony Slattery, John Sessions, Josie Lawrence, Greg Proops, Paul Merton, Sandi Toksvig, Mike McShane and Ryan Stiles. Music has been supplied by Richard Vranch at the piano. Editions have also been made in the USA for airing on both sides of the Atlantic.

A similar concept, entitled *Impromptu*, was shown on BBC 2 in 1964. Produced by David Croft, it called on a resident team of performers (Victor Spinetti, Lance Percival, Anne Cunningham, Peter Reeves and Betty Impey) to act out a whole programme, working from basic instructions given to them on cards by Jeremy Hawk.

WHYTON, WALLY (1929–)

Former skiffle musician Wally Whyton was one of ITV's favourite children's entertainers from the late 1950s through to the 1970s. He began his showbiz career with The Vipers group (who notched up three hits in 1957) and found his way into television by sitting in for Rolf Harris on one show. Whyton was soon in demand for series like *Small Time*, *Musical Box*, *The Three Scampis* and *Five O'Clock Club*, where he worked with Muriel Young, Bert Weedon and puppets like Pussy Cat Willum, Ollie Beak, Fred Barker, Joe Crow and Spike McPike. He was later seen as co-host of Ayshea Brough's pop show, *Lift Off With Ayshea* (produced by his former colleague Muriel Young), and has enjoyed plenty of radio work, too.

WIDOWS

UK (Thames/Euston Films) Crime Drama. ITV 1983–5

Dolly Rawlins	Ann Mitchell
Linda Perelli	Maureen O'Farrell
Shirley Miller	Fiona Hendley
Bella O'Reilly	Eva Mottley
	Debby Bishop
Detective Inspector Resnick	David Calder
Harry Rawlins	Maurice O'Connell
Audrey Withey	Kate Williams
DC Andrews	Peter Machon
Kathleen Resnick	Thelma Whiteley
Trudie	Catherine Neilson

Creator/Writer: Lynda La Plante. Executive Producers: Verity Lambert, Linda Agran, Johnny Goodman. Producers: Linda Agran, Irving Teitelbaum

Four inexperienced female crooks pull off a daring armed robbery.

When arch-villain Harry Rawlins was killed in an attempted hold up, his wife, Dolly, inherited his well-laid plans for future robberies. One involved attacking a security van in a subway and Dolly fancied her chances of pulling it off. She assembled around her three other widows: attractive, blonde Shirley Miller and dark-haired Linda Perelli (whose husbands were killed along with Harry), plus black stripper Bella O'Reilly, whose husband had died of a drugs overdose. Together they planned the raid meticulously, but with the Fisher brothers (Harry's old adversaries) lurking around, and Detective Inspector Resnick deeply suspicious, keeping their secret was not easy. Yet all went swimmingly and the four girls flew off to Rio with suitcases full of cash.

It was in the sequel two years later that their troubles began. Their tongues became loose and their behaviour invited comment. Most alarming was the fact that Harry was not dead, but had faked his death to live with another woman and was now out to regain the money which was rightly his. In this second series, Bella was played by Debby Bishop, following the death of Eva Mottley.

The story was picked up yet again in 1995 in a second sequel entitled *She's Out*. This saw Dolly Rawlins released from an eight-year jail term and surrounded by a new troupe of female felons, as well as numerous other unsavoury characters, all after her stashed away loot.

WILCOX, DESMOND (1931–)

Award-winning British documentary maker and current affairs reporter, married to Esther Rantzen, with whom he worked when co-editor

of the long-running *Man Alive* series and editor of *Braden's Week*. In the early 1960s Wilcox was a reporter with *This Week* and he returned in front of the cameras in 1983, as anchor on the short-lived successor to *Nationwide*, *Sixty Minutes*. The same year, he began writing, presenting and producing *The Visit*, a series which accompanied people undertaking dramatic, life-changing journeys. The highlight was the story of *The Boy David*, a young Peruvian Indian receiving facial plastic surgery in the UK. Wilcox employed the same documentary techniques when following the wedding plans of a young couple from Cardiff in another 1980s series, *The Marriage*.

WILCOX, PAULA (1949–)

British comedy actress, starring as Beryl in *The Lovers*, after appearances in series like *The Dustbinmen* and *Coronation Steet* (as Ray Langton's sister, Janice). Around the same time, she popped up in another comedy, *On the House*, but enjoyed far more success as Chrissy in *Man about the House*. When this series ended, Wilcox was cast in her own sitcom, the daring (for the time) single parent comedy *Miss Jones and Son* (as Elizabeth Jones). After a few quiet years, Wilcox resurfaced in the 1985 Channel 4 comedy *The Bright Side*, playing prison widow Cynthia Bright, and, in 1991, she took the role of Roz Fiddler in Peter Davison's sitcom *Fiddlers Three*. Wilcox was one of the team captains on the game show *Crazy Comparisons* and other credits over the years have included guest spots in *The Liver Birds*, *Hadleigh*, *Kate* and *Boon*.

WILDE ALLIANCE, THE

UK (Yorkshire) Detective Drama. ITV 1978

Rupert Wilde ....John Stride
Amy Wilde..Julia Foster
Christopher Bridgewater ....John Lee
Bailey ....Patrick Newell

Executive Producer: David Cunliffe. Producer: Ian Mackintosh

A thriller writer and his wife become involved in real-life intrigue.

Rupert Wilde was a successful author of detective novels and lived with his attractive wife, Amy, in a luxurious country mansion in Yorkshire. However, for the Wildes, life imitated art, and the lively couple themselves became sleuths as they stumbled into a series of investigations, any of which could have come from Rupert's books. Rupert's agent, Christopher Bridgewater was also dragged into the action. This was a short-lived British attempt at a *McMillan and Wife/Hart to Hart/The Thin Man*-type series. Just 13 episodes were made.

WILDE, BRIAN

British comedy actor, best known for his roles as starchy Foggy Dewhurst in *Last of the Summer Wine* and prison warder Mr Barrowclough in *Porridge*. Earlier, Wilde had appeared in the dramas *The Men in Room 13* and *A Man Called Harry Brent*, the sitcoms *For the Love of Mike* and *Room at the Bottom*, and also played Bloody Delilah in *The Dustbinmen*. Other credits have included the parts of radio station boss Roland Simpson in *The Kit Curran Radio Show* and Major Wyatt in *Wyatt's Watchdogs*.

WILL SHAKESPEARE

UK (ATV) Drama. ITV 1978

Will Shakespeare ....Tim Curry
Christopher Marlowe ....Ian McShane
Edward Alleyn ....André Morell
Earl of Southampton ....Nicholas Clay
Hamnet Sadler ....John McEnery
Sir Thomas Walsingham ....Simon MacCorkindale
Anne Hathaway ....Meg Wyn Owen
Ingram Frizer ....Simon Rouse

Writer: John Mortimer. Producer: Peter Wood

The life of the Bard of Avon.

With historical facts rather thin on the ground, writer John Mortimer added more than a touch of fiction to his dramatization of the life and times of William Shakespeare. This bustling six-part series followed young Will as he broke through into theatrical circles and gradually established himself as the finest playwright of his generation. Viewers were treated to a new 'human' angle on the bard, with Tim Curry portraying him as a bawdy and romantic type, hovering around the Globe Theatre and mingling in the court of Queen Elizabeth.

WILLIAM TELL see *Adventures of William Tell, The*.

WILLIAMS, ANDY (1930–)

Easy-going American singer, once a member of the Williams Brothers singing group, who hosted his own variety series in the USA through most of the 1960s and 1970s. The show was carried by the BBC in the UK and, amongst other things, introduced viewers to the Osmond Brothers.

WILLIAMS, DORIAN OBE (1914–85)

BBC equestrian events commentator from 1951, retiring in the early 1980s. Williams, an acknowledged horse expert, also wrote numerous books on equine matters.

WILLIAMS, KENNETH (1926–88)

British comedian and comedy actor, well-known from *Carry On* films and various radio series but also familiar on television, his catalogue of funny voices and shocked faces and his skill as a raconteur making him popular on chat shows and panel games. He supported Tony Hancock in the early days of *Hancock's Half Hour* and also provided the voices for the *Willo The Wisp* cartoon series and many commercials. One of his last contributions was the voice of the computer (SID) in the kids' comedy *Galloping Galaxies* in 1985.

WILLIAMS, MICHAEL (1935–)

Versatile British actor, at home with both dramatic and comedy roles. In the former vein, he played The Duke of Alençon in *Elizabeth R*, Philip Hart in *A Raging Calm*, Alan Crowe in *The Hanged Man*, William Essex in *My Son, My Son*, Uncle Davey in *Love in a Cold Climate* and Billy Balsam in *September Song*. Comedy-wise, Williams was Mike in *A Fine Romance* (with his real-life wife Judi Dench), N.V. Standish in *Double First* and Barry in *Conjugal Rites*. He has many other credits, too, including *TV Shakespeare*.

WILLIAMS, ROBIN (1952–)

Energetic, quickfire, quirky American comedian, who shot to fame in the 1970s when he was spotted playing LA nightclubs. A master of improvisation and ad lib, he was given a role in the short-lived revival of *Laugh-In* and contributed to *The Richard Pryor Show*, but a bigger break came with a guest appearance in the sitcom *Happy Days*. Cast as zany alien, Mork from Ork, he proved such a hit that his own series, *Mork and Mindy*, was soon on the screens, running for three years. That took Williams into the cinema and he has since become one of Hollywood's biggest names.

WILLIAMS, SIMON (1946–)

Smooth British actor, winning fans with his portrayal of Captain James Bellamy in *Upstairs, Downstairs* and later seen in the comedies *Agony* (as Laurence Lucas), *Kinvig* (as Buddo) and *Don't Wait Up* (as Dr Charles Cartwright). He also played Simon Company in the musical drama *Company and Co.*, and, more recently, was cast as barrister Gerald Triggs in the sitcom *Law and Disorder*. He has been a team captain on *Crazy Comparisons* and also featured in series like *The Regiment*, *Wodehouse Playhouse*, *Strangers* and *Bergerac*.

WILLIS, BRUCE (1959–)

American actor born in Germany who shot to fame as the jive-talking, ultra casual detective David Addison in *Moonlighting* in 1985, having previously acted on stage and made a few TV appearances in shows like *Hart to Hart* and *Miami Vice*. He quickly turned his attention to the movie world and also notched up a few hit singles. He is married to actress Demi Moore.

WILLIS, LORD TED (1918–92)

One of TV's most prolific writers and programme creators, Ted Willis pioneered working-class, 'kitchen sink' dramas and social realism with his scriptwriting of the 1950s. Amongst his brainchildren – revealing a flair for both comedy and straight pieces – were *Dixon of Dock Green* (1955), *Tell It to the Marines* (1959), *Sergeant Cork*, *Taxi* (both 1963), *The Four Seasons of Rosie Carr*, *The Sullavan Brothers* (both 1964), *Mrs Thursday* (1966), *Virgin of the Secret Service* (1968), *Coppers End* (1971) and *Hunter's Walk* (1973). In all, he created 41 television series. In addition, his single dramas included *Woman in a Dressing Gown* in 1956, the 1959 *Armchair Theatre* presentation *Hot Summer Night* and an adaptation of Richard Gordon's *Doctor in the House* in 1960. He was made a peer in 1963.

WILSON, DENNIS MAIN

Long-serving British light entertainment producer and occasional director, initially working in radio but associated with numerous TV sitcoms, such as *The Two Charleys*, *Sykes*, *The Rag Trade*, *Till Death Us Do Part*, *Scott On . . .* , *Them*, *Well Anyway*, *Citizen Smith*, *Mr Big* (director/producer), *Time of my Life*, *L for Lester*, *Roger Doesn't Live Here Anymore* and *The Lady is a Tramp* (director). Other comedies have included *Lance at Large* (for Lance Percival), *A Series of Bird's* (for John Bird), *Marty* and *Marty Back Together Again* (both for Marty Feldman).

WILSON, DONALD (1910–)

British screenwriter, script editor and producer, largely on BBC historical dramas (he was one of the Corporation's early contract writers). Amongst his writing credits have been *The Six Proud Walkers* (1954 and again in 1962), *The Royalty* (1958, with Michael Voysey), *No Wreath for the General* (1960), *Hornblower* (1963), *The Flying Swan* (1965), *The First Churchills* (1969, as writer, director and producer), *Anna Karenina* (1977, as writer and producer) and, most celebrated of all, *The Forsyte Saga* (1967, as producer and co-writer).

WILSON, FRANCIS (1949–)

Scottish weather presenter, known for his relaxed, easy-going style which initially won him fans

while working on Thames News. From 1978–82 Wilson then moved to the BBC's *Breakfast Time* and *Breakfast News* before defecting to Sky in 1992.

WILSON, RICHARD, OBE (1936–)

Award-winning Scottish actor and director, a former scientist who, after years of supporting others, playing vicars, doctors and barristers, found his niche as the grumpy Victor Meldrew in *One Foot in the Grave*. Otherwise, Wilson has played Rev. Martin Hooper in *My Good Woman*, Jeremy Parsons QC in *Crown Court*, Dr Gordon Thorpe in *Only When I Laugh*, the TV chaplain in *Room at the Bottom*, newspaper managing editor Richard Lipton in *Hot Metal*, Eddie Clockerty, the manager of the Majestics, in *Tutti Frutti*, pier-lover Richard Talbot in *High and Dry*, Reverend Green in *Cluedo* and Ben Glazier in *Under The Hammer* (also as director). In addition, he has been seen in *A Sharp Intake of Breath*, *Dr Finlay's Casebook*, *Inspector Morse*, *Whoops! Apocalypse* and many other series and single dramas.

WILTON, PENELOPE (1946–)

British actress, probably best recalled as Ann, the long-suffering wife of the pedantic Martin Brice in *Ever Decreasing Circles*. However, Wilton was also a member of the cast of *The Norman Conquests* and played Beatrice in Carla Lane's *Screaming*. She also appeared in *The Monocled Mutineer* and has taken roles in dramas like *King Lear*, *The Widowing of Mrs Holroyd* and *The Sullen Sisters*.

WIND IN THE WILLOWS, THE

UK (Thames) Animation. ITV 1984–8

Voices:
Mole	Richard Pearson
Rat	Peter Sallis
Toad	David Jason
Badger	Michael Hordern

Producers: Mark Hall, Brian Cosgrove

Rural roving in Edwardian England with a motley band of creatures.

Following the success the previous year of a 90-minute, animated musical adaptation of Kenneth Grahame's 1908 classic novel, Thames launched this series of additional rodent tales. Peter Sallis took over the role of Rat from Ian Carmichael, but otherwise the principal voicers remained in place. The success of the series lay chiefly in the quality of the animation, with each model reputedly costing around £5000 to build.

WINDS OF WAR, THE

US (ABC) Drama. ITV 1983

Commander Victor 'Pug' Henry	Robert Mitchum
Natalie Jastrow	Ali MacGraw
Byron Henry	Jan-Michael Vincent
Warren Henry	Ben Murphy
Madeline Henry	Lisa Eilbacher
Rhoda Henry	Polly Bergen
Berel Jastrow	Topol
Aaron Jastrow	John Houseman
Palmer 'Fred' Kirby	Peter Graves
Pamela Tudsbury	Victoria Tennant
Alistair Tudsbury	Michael Logan
Leslie Slote	David Dukes
President Franklin D. Roosevelt	Ralph Bellamy
Winston Churchill	Howard Lang
Adolf Hitler	Gunter Meisner
Brigadier General Armin Von Roon	Jeremy Kemp
Narrator	William Woodson

Writer: Herman Wouk. Producer: Dan Curtis

The globe-trotting escapades of an American military attaché in the early years of World War II.

Beginning with the German advance into Poland in 1939 and continuing through to the Japanese attack on Pearl Harbor in 1941, this mammoth drama was the story of one man's war. It focused on 'Pug' Henry, an American naval officer who was sent around the world meeting the likes of Churchill and Hitler but who found personal problems along the way. These came from his unfaithful wife, Rhoda, pilot son Warren, artistic son Byron and student daughter Madeline, as well as an English rose named Pam, with whom he embarked on an affair, and an eccentric Jewish girl, Natalie, who found herself in Poland as the Germans invaded and who became Byron's lover. *The Winds of War*, adapted in eight parts from his own novel by Herman Wouk, cost £26 million to make and was heralded with a loud fanfare of publicity. However, viewers and critics were less than impressed on the whole. A sequel, *War and Remembrance*, which dramatized the remainder of Wouk's book and covered the final years of the war, was screened in 1989.

WINDSOR, FRANK (1927–)

Frank Windsor, for most viewers, is John Watt, star of *Z Cars* and *Softly, Softly*. However, before arriving in Newtown, the Midlands-born actor had been seen in the Shakespearean anthology *An Age of Kings* and as scientist Dennis Bridger in the sci-fi classic *A for Andromeda*. Amongst his later credits has been the role of Harry Bradley in the Rolls Royce drama *Flying Lady*, plus *Crown Court*, *Whodunnit?*, *Kidnapped*, *Into the Labyrinth* and *Boon*, as well as a 1973 attempt to discover the truth behind *Jack the Ripper* (again in the guise of John Watt) and a follow-up series looking at other unsolved crimes, *Second Verdict*.

WINFREY, OPRAH (1954–)

American Oprah Winfrey was the first black woman to host a major US daytime talk show (*The Oprah Winfrey Show*, 1986) and proved so successful that she quickly became the richest woman on TV (according to *TV Guide*, the US listings magazine). Her career began as a teenager in Nashville where she worked as a newsreader. Moving to Baltimore and then Chicago, she transferred into talk shows, rapidly outgunning her daytime rivals and soon being syndicated nationwide. Her shows (screened initially on Channel 4 in the UK) are highly emotionally charged and sometimes have a strong personal involvement from Oprah, such as her admission of childhood abuse and her well-publicized weight-watching regime. She now owns her own production company, Harpo Productions.

WINGS

UK (BBC) Drama. BBC 1 1977–8

Sgt/2nd Lt Alan Farmer ....Tim Woodward
Captain Triggers....................................Nicholas Jones
Lt Charles Gaylion ....Michael Cochrane
Lt Richard Bravington ....David Troughton
Lt Michael Starling ....Michael Jayes
Sgt Mills..Roger Elliott
Harry Farmer ....John Hallam
Molly Farmer ....Anne Kristen
Lorna Collins ....Sarah Porter

Creator: Barry Thomas. Producer: Peter Cregeen

Stirring action in the skies during World War I.

Over two series, *Wings* focused on the daring pilots of the Royal Flying Corps, the pioneers of air combat during the Great War. Tackling the Hun in their sheepskin jackets, leather hats and goggles were French-based aviators Farmer, Triggers, Gaylion, Bravington and others. Farmer was initially the odd man out, being a poorly educated blacksmith who taught himself to fly and subsequently gained promotion from NCO ranks to join the snooty commissioned men. The series took as its inspiration events in the lives of real RFC airmen and made good use of numerous re-created old flying machines. Alexander Faris composed the sweeping period theme music.

WINKLER, HENRY (1945–)

American actor, producer and director, whose creation of Fonzie, the superhuman biker with the heart of gold, turned the sitcom *Happy Days* from a ratings also-ran into America's number-one show. Winkler was with the series for its entire run (1974–84), becoming a US institution in the process. When it ended, he moved behind the scenes, creating (with John Rich) *MacGyver* and producing other projects. He has also been seen in a few TV movies.

WINNER TAKES ALL

UK (Yorkshire) Quiz. ITV 1975–87

Presenters: Jimmy Tarbuck, Geoffrey Wheeler

Creator: Geoffrey Wheeler. Producers: Guy Caplan, Lawrie Higgins, Ian Bolt, Don Clayton, Terry Henebery, Graham Wetherell

Long-running quiz in which contestants gambled on the answers to questions.

Jimmy Tarbuck welcomed the guests and the unseen Geoffrey Wheeler asked the questions in this popular general knowledge quiz show. The four contestants competed in a little knock-out tournament to find one winner who would 'take all', namely a big cash prize, at the end of each programme. The winner then stayed on the following week, risking a proportion of his winnings in the pursuit of more money.

Five questions were offered, one at a time, together with six possible answers. Each answer was accompanied by appropriate odds, ranging from even money, through 2–1, 3–1, 4–1 and 5–1 to the rank outsider at 10–1. The contestants had to select an answer and back it with a proportion of their points bank, losing the gambled points if the answer was wrong, but reaping the rewards if they gambled correctly. The contestant with the most points was the winner. In the final round, pounds replaced points, but only the winner could take away his final total. When Jimmy Tarbuck left the series in 1987 to present a new game show, *Tarby's Frame Game*, Geoffrey Wheeler (who was also the devisor of the series) was brought into vision as joint host and question master.

WINSTON CHURCHILL – THE WILDERNESS YEARS

UK (Southern) Historical Drama. ITV 1981

Winston Churchill ....Robert Hardy
Clementine ....Siân Phillips
Stanley Baldwin ....Peter Barkworth
Neville Chamberlain ....Eric Porter
Samuel Hoare ....Edward Woodward
Bernard Baruch ....Sam Wanamaker
Brenden Bracken ....Tim Pigott-Smith

Creators: Martin Gilbert, Richard Broke. Executive Producer: Mark Shivas. Producer: Richard Broke

Dramatization of Churchill's period of political 'exile'.

After a meteoric rise to prominence in the early decades of the century, Churchill's political career ground dramatically to a halt during the 1930s. A change in leadership at the Conservative Party and momentous movements on the world stage left the always outspoken Churchill sitting in the shadows, his voice singing out of tune with many of his own political colour. This drama looked back at those 'wilderness years', viewing how the great man bided his time, speaking out in vain on issues such as the rise of fascism and self-government for India, offering support for Edward VIII in the Abdication Crisis and waiting for that moment when the country would again call upon his services. The eight-part series was one of Southern Television's last productions.

WINTERS, MIKE (MICHAEL WEINSTEIN; 1930–) AND BERNIE (BERNIE WEINSTEIN; 1932–91)

British comedy double act of the 1950s, 1960s and 1970s, real life brothers who originally worked together as part of a music and impressions band. After gaining radio experience, they were given the comedy residency on **Six-Five Special** in 1957 and, after a few ups and downs, were hosts of *Big Night Out* and *Blackpool Night Out* in the 1960s. They also starred in *Mike and Bernie's Show*, *Mike and Bernie's Scene* and the sitcom *Mike and Bernie*. Their act was essentially traditional music hall crosstalk, with Mike the straightman and Bernie the idiot. However, differences came to the fore and the brothers split up in 1978. Mike became a businessman in Florida, while Bernie teamed up Schnorbitz, his St Bernard dog, starred in his own series, *Bernie*, and hosted game shows like *Whose Baby?* He also perfected an impersonation of Bud Flanagan and performed it on stage and TV, with Leslie Crowther as his partner Chesney Allen.

WIPE

A visual effect in which one camera shot displaces another on the screen, 'wiping' across from side to side, top to bottom or even breaking through in contrived patterns. The facility was much employed in 1970s pop music programmes.

WISDOM, NORMAN, OBE (1915–)

Acknowledged as one of Britain's great screen clowns, diminutive Norman Wisdom has made his mark in the story of television, too, even though his TV work generally fitted in and around his film career. On the back of a stage partnership with David Nixon, Wisdom was given his first TV series, *Wit and Wisdom*, in 1948, followed in 1953 by *It's Wisdom* and, in 1956, by *The Norman Wisdom Show*. In 1960, on one famous TV occasion, he was the lone star of *Sunday Night at the London Palladium*, taking over the whole show, papering the set and eventually being chased off by compère Bruce Forsyth. With his best cinema days behind him, he turned to sitcom in 1970 with *Norman*, a series about a taxman-turned-musician, and followed it with *Nobody is Norman Wisdom*, as Nobody, a daydreamer. His next series, *A Little Bit of Wisdom*, ran for three years, with various situations and characters. In contrast, his performance as a man dying of cancer in the 1981 drama *Going Gently* won much acclaim and, enjoying his switch to straight acting, he was later seen as a guest in **Bergerac**. Other guest appearances have included a part in **Last of the Summer Wine**.

WISE, ERNIE, OBE (Ernest Wiseman; 1925–) see Morecambe, Eric.

WISE, HERBERT (1924–)

British director responsible for **I, Claudius** and *The Norman Conquests*, plus episodes of such series as *The Victorians*, **Z Cars**, *Six Shades of Black*, **Upstairs, Downstairs**, **The Six Wives of Henry VIII**, **Elizabeth R**, **The BBC Television Shakespeare**, **Rumpole of the Bailey**, **Inspector Morse**, **The Ruth Rendell Mysteries** and the PD James Adam Dalgliesh story *Death of an Expert Witness*. Single dramas include Reginald Rose's *The Cruel Day* (part of *Drama '61*), Stewart Love's *The Big Donkey* (1963), *Walk With Destiny* (1974) and Nigel Kneale's *The Woman in Black* (1989).

WISH ME LUCK

UK (LWT) Drama. ITV 1988–90

Liz Grainger	Kate Buffery
Mathilde 'Matty' Firman	Suzanna Hamilton
Colonel James Cadogan	Julian Glover
Kit Vanston	Michael J. Jackson
Faith Ashley	Jane Asher
Vivien Ashton	Lynn Farleigh
Emily/Adele	Jane Snowden
Lewis Antoine	Jeremy Nicholas
Virginia/Dominique	Catherine Scholl

Creators: Jill Hyem, Lavinia Warner. Executive Producer: Nick Elliott. Producers: Colin Shindler, Lavinia Warner, Michael Chaplin

The escapades of the brave men and women who infiltrated German-occupied France.

Like the similarly-styled **Manhunt** and **Secret Army**, *Wish Me Luck* was set in World War II and focused on the daring young people who risked life and limb to spy on the enemy and sabotage the Nazi advance. Two women in particular were highlighted: well-bred blonde Liz Grainger and young Cockney Matty Firman, both agents of the Special Operations Executive. Colonel James Cadogan was the boss of their spy network in France, assisted by Faith Ashley. Agents Vivien and Emily joined the team in the second series.

WISH YOU WERE HERE . . . ? see *Holiday*.

WITCHELL, NICHOLAS (1953–)

Red-haired BBC newsreader, a former Northern Ireland reporter and foreign correspondent (Beirut and the Falklands) who joined the Corporation as a trainee in 1976. He has fronted all the main bulletins, and contributed to *Panorama*, but has concentrated more on *Breakfast News* in recent years, as well as hosting a Sunday morning political programme for Radio 5 Live.

WITHERS, GOOGIE (GEORGETTE WITHERS; 1917–)

British leading lady of stage and screen who starred on TV late in life when taking the role of Governor Faye Boswell in the women's prison drama *Within These Walls* in 1973. Her earliest TV appearances had come in the 1950s, in single dramas, and, since leaving *Within These Walls*, she has been seen in a handful of TV movies, such as *Hotel du Lac* and *Northanger Abbey*.

WITHIN THESE WALLS

UK (LWT) Drama. ITV 1974–8

Faye Boswell	Googie Withers
Charles Radley	Jerome Willis
Chief Officer Mrs Armitage	Mona Bruce
Dr Mayes	Denys Hawthorne
Miss Clarke	Beth Harris
Helen Forrester	Katharine Blake
Susan Marshall	Sarah Lawson

Executive Producer: Rex Firkin. Producer: Jack Williamson

Drama centring on the governor of a women's prison.

Set in HMP Stone Park, *Within These Walls* focused on its newly installed governor, Faye Boswell, as she set out to liberalize the firmly run institution. She quickly realized that all would not be plain sailing and met resentment not only from the inmates but from the staff, too. The impact on her personal life was also scrutinized. Boswell lasted three years before making way for a new governor, Helen Forrester, who was in turn succeeded by Susan Marshall in 1978. The series was the inspiration for the Australian soap *Prisoner: Cell Block H*, which proved much more durable.

WITT, PAUL JUNGER

American producer, working on series like *The Partridge Family* in the early 1970s, before producing the comedies *Soap* and *Benson* (both written by his wife, Susan Harris) in partnership with Tony Thomas. Joining forces in Witt-Thomas-Harris Productions, they have since handled all Harris's other hits, including *The Golden Girls*, *The Golden Palace, Empty Nest* and *Nurses*. Witt and Thomas have also produced *Beauty and the Beast* and *Blossom*.

WODEHOUSE PLAYHOUSE

UK (BBC) Comedy. BBC 1 1975–8

John Alderton
Pauline Collins

Writer: David Climie. Producers: David Askey, Michael Mills, Gareth Gwenlan

Anthology of P.G. Wodehouse comedies.

Adapted by David Climie from the short stories of P.G. Wodehouse, this collection of 1920s high society farces starred the husband and wife pairing of John Alderton and Pauline Collins in a variety of different roles. Three series were made.

WOGAN, TERRY (1938–)

Irish presenter and chat show host. A one-time bank clerk, then a presenter with RTE in Dublin, Wogan joined the BBC in the 1960s and was one of Radio 1's original team of presenters in 1967. His Radio 2 breakfast show in the 1970s and early 1980s gained a cult following and established his distinctively witty, self-effacing presentational style. Items like 'Fighting the Flab' and 'Wogan's Winner' characterized the show and his constant digs at *Dallas* ensured the soap became a hit in the UK. Although he had already hosted a chat show for ATV, *Lunchtime with Wogan* in 1972, it wasn't until 1979, when he began five years at the helm of the panel game *Blankety Blank*, that his TV career began to take off. In 1980, he turned his hand to chat shows with *What's On Wogan*, a live Saturday tea-time programme. Two years later, it metamorphized into *Wogan* and was transmitted late on a Saturday night, before being promoted in 1985 to an early evening, thrice-weekly live event. Terry quickly became *the* TV personality of the 1980s and was seldom off British screens. Since *Wogan* ended to make way for the ill-fated *Eldorado* in 1992, he has returned to radio and his old Radio 2 slot in the morning, saving room all the same for another music and chat show, *Wogan's Friday Night*, on BBC 1. He has been co-host (mostly with Sue Cook) of the annual charity telethon *Children in Need* since 1980, and can be heard every year disparaging the entries on the

Eurovision Song Contest. Amongst his other TV credits have been *Come Dancing*, *Miss World*, *You Must Be Joking*, *Do The Right Thing* and the occasional bloopers programme *Auntie's Bloomers*.

WOLFE, RONALD see Chesney, Ronald.

WOLSTENHOLME, KENNETH, DFC (1920–)

British soccer commentator, a contributor to *Sports Special* in the 1950s and the voice of football with the BBC in the 1960s, thanks to his work on *Match of the Day*. It was Wolstenholme who uttered the famous words 'They think it's all over. It is now.' at the end of the 1966 World Cup final. He left the BBC in 1971, to make way for a new generation of commentators, after 23 years with the Corporation, but continued to cover soccer for Tyne Tees before retiring. He has since made numerous guest appearances and has become somewhat of a cult figure. Prior to entering broadcasting, Wolstenholme had been a bomber pilot in the war and was awarded the DFC.

WOMAN OF SUBSTANCE, A

UK (Portman Artemis) Drama. Channel 4
1985

Emma Harte	Jenny Seagrove
	Deborah Kerr
Henry Rossiter	John Mills
Laura Spencer	Diane Baker
Bruce McGill	George Baker
Olivia	Gayle Hunnicutt
Adele Fairley	Nicola Pagett
Paula	Miranda Richardson
Paul McGill	Barry Bostwick
Shane O'Neill	Liam Neeson
Murgatroyd	Barry Morse

Writer: Lee Langley. Producer: Diane Baker

An ambitious servant girl drives her way to the top.

Told in flashback and beginning in 1905, *A Woman of Substance* was the rags to riches story of Emma Harte, a Yorkshire lass from the servile classes who made her way up through society. Her ambitions took her out of the scullery and into the world of business. She moved to the USA and became one of the world's wealthiest women, owning a major chain of department stores. Jenny Seagrove played Emma up to the age of 49, with Deborah Kerr taking over for the heroine's later years. Adapted by Lee Langley from Barbara Taylor Bradford's romantic novel, this mini-series was shown on three consecutive nights on Channel 4 in 1985. A year later, a sequel made in America and entitled *Hold That Dream*, once again saw Seagrove and Kerr in the role of Harte.

WOMBLES, THE

UK (Filmfair) Children's Entertainment. BBC 1
1973

Narrator: Bernard Cribbins

Creator/Writer: Elizabeth Beresford

A small colony of cuddly conservationists keeps Wimbledon Common free of litter.

'Underground, overground, wombling free', the long-nosed, furry Wombles of Wimbledon Common were Britain's foremost ecologists in the 1970s. 'Making good use of the things they found, things that the everyday folk left behind', the incredibly devious Wombles turned trash into useful items – useful to a Womble at least. Their burrow was wallpapered in discarded news print and there was always some new contraption being conjured up. Headed by Great Uncle Bulgaria, the Wombles were Tomsk, Orinoco, Tobermory, Wellington, Bungo and their French housemaid, Mme Cholet.

Based on the stories by Elisabeth Beresford, the five-minute Wombles tales, animated by Ivor Wood, were whimsically narrated by Bernard Cribbins. Mike Batt performed the theme music which became a hit in 1974 and led to a spate of other Wombling pop pieces. A feature film, *Wombling Free*, was released in 1977, and the busy little creatures were resurrected by ITV in the late 1980s.

WONDER WOMAN

US (Warner Brothers) Science Fiction. BBC 1
1978–80

Diana Prince/Wonder Woman	Lynda Carter
Steve Trevor	Lyle Waggoner
Joe Atkinson	Normann Burton
Voice of IRA	Tom Kratochzil

Executive Producer: Douglas S. Cramer.
Producer: Bruce Lansbury

A superwoman uses her powers to fight subversion.

Wonder Woman, a creation of cartoonist Charles Moulton, actually appeared in two different settings on TV in the 1970s. Firstly, in a series entitled *The New, Original Wonder Woman*, she lived in the 1940s. She was discovered amongst a race of Amazon women on Paradise Island, an uncharted piece of land somewhere in the Caribbean, by a crash-landed US major, Steve Trevor. The women, refugees from ancient Greece and Rome, had lived on the island since about 200 BC, having stumbled across a magical material called Feminum, which, when moulded into bracelets or belts, gave them superhuman powers.

The future Wonder Woman was Princess Diana, daughter of Hippolyte, the Queen of the Amazons. Nursing the wounded soldier back to health, she fell in love and returned with him to civilization. There, she assumed the identity of Diana Prince and became his secretary in the War Department. However, whenever trouble beckoned, she took on the mantle of Wonder Woman, performing a quick change of clothes by spinning herself around and donning a patriotic red, white and blue costume, complete with Feminum belt to give her strength and Feminum bracelets to deflect bullets. The magical lasso she carried forced her enemies (mostly Nazis) to tell the truth.

This series was not shown in the UK. We did catch up with her, however, in the second series, *The New Adventures of Wonder Woman*, in which the setting was 1970s America. Diana had once again returned from Paradise Island, showing no sign of ageing, to take up a post as an agent for the Inter-Agency Defense Command (IADC). Her boss was Joe Atkinson and her close colleague was the son of her former friend, Steve Trevor, conveniently the double of his father. For the IADC, Diana fought against crazed scientists, saboteurs, terrorists and aliens, and, like all the agents, was assisted by a talking Internal Retrieval Associative computer (IRA). Only IRA knew Diana's alter-ego.

The statuesque Lynda Carter was perfectly built to fill this Amazonian role – she had been Miss America in 1973. All the same, a 1974 pilot film cast Cathy Lee Crosby in the title role.

WONDER YEARS, THE

US (Black/Marlens) Situation Comedy.
Channel 4 1989–93

Kevin Arnold	Fred Savage
Kevin (adult: voice only)	Daniel Stern
Jack Arnold	Dan Lauria
Norma Arnold	Alley Mills
Wayne Arnold	Jason Hervey
Karen Arnold	Olivia d'Abo
Paul Pfeiffer	Josh Saviano
Gwendolyn 'Winnie' Cooper	Danica McKellar
Coach Ed Cutlip	Robert Picardo

Creators/Writers/Producers: Neal Marlens, Carol Black. Executive Producer: Bob Brush

Light-hearted, nostalgic tales of growing up in suburban America in the late 1960s.

The Wonder Years focused on young Kevin Arnold, a 12-year-old (at the programme's beginning), just starting out at the Robert F. Kennedy Junior High School in 1968 and desperate to make the right impression with his peers, especially the girls. The adult Kevin (never seen) acted as narrator, telling viewers just what his younger self had been thinking at that time. The result was a whimsical, poignant observation of adolescent woes in an era of social change.

Kevin was the youngest child of a typical suburban family. His mom and dad were 1940s teenagers turned parents and householders, overtaken somewhat by time and finding it difficult to relate to their children (especially after a hard day's work). Wayne, Kevin's obnoxious brother, teased him mercilessly, while his sister, Karen, was into every peace and protest movement of the day. Kevin's best friend was Paul, a gangly, nerdy type with glasses and a brace, and Winnie Cooper was the girl next door that Kevin had his eye on. Old newsreel clips added period atmosphere, as did music of the time (the show's theme was 'With a Little Help from My Friends'), but this was a programme whose success came from the strength of its characterization and its scripts, not cheap nostalgic in-fills.

WOOD, DUNCAN

BBC comedy producer of the 1950s, 1960s and early 1970s, working with Benny Hill and also responsible for such classic sitcoms as *Hancock's Half Hour* and *Steptoe and Son*, *Citizen James*, *The Bed-Sit Girl*, *Oh Brother!*, *The Further Adventures of Lucky Jim*, *The World of Beachcomber* and *Now, Take My Wife . . .* were other notable production credits. Wood also directed a farewell performance of *Beyond the Fringe* in 1964. He moved to Yorkshire Television in the 1970s as Head of Light Entertainment where he commissioned series like *Rising Damp*, *Oh No! It's Selwyn Froggitt* and *3–2–1*.

WOOD, VICTORIA (1953–)

Northern comedienne, musician and lyricist, coming to light in the *New Faces* talent show in 1975 (in which she was beaten by Marti Caine). A year later, she secured herself fortnightly work writing topical songs for *That's Life* and by the end of the decade was moving into her own comic plays like *Talent*, *Nearly a Happy Ending* and *Happy Since I Met You*, usually with her regular partner Julie Walters. Together they hosted a show for Granada entitled *Wood and Walters*, before Victoria switched to the BBC and began a run of successful comedies, amongst them *Victoria Wood – As Seen on TV* (a sketch and monologue show with a repertory cast of Walters, Celia Imrie, Patricia Routledge, Duncan Preston and Susie Blake, and featuring the *Crossroads* spoof, *Acorn Antiques*), *Victoria Wood Now* and *Victoria Wood*. For LWT, she treated a celebrity gathering to *An Audience with Victoria Wood*. In 1994 she starred again with Julie Walters in the comedy *Pat and Margaret.* She is married to entertainer Geoffrey Durham (aka The Great Soprendo).

WOODENTOPS, THE

UK (BBC) Children's Entertainment.
BBC 1955–8

Voices: Peter Hawkins, Eileen Brown, Josephina Ray

Creators: Freda Lingstrom, Maria Bird.
Producer: Freda Lingstrom. Writer: Maria Bird

Idyllic life down on the farm with an industrious puppet family.

Friday's *Watch With Mother* offering was brought to the screen by the same team responsible for Tuesday's (*Andy Pandy*) and Wednesday's (*The Flowerpot Men*). The Woodentops were Daddy Woodentop (seldom seen with a shirt on his back), Mummy Woodentop (so busy in the kitchen that she needed daily help from Mrs Scrubbitt), high-pitched twins Jenny and Willy Woodentop, and, completing the family, Baby Woodentop, still in his mother's arms. Also seen was Sam, the man who helped Daddy Woodentop in the garden, as well as Buttercup the cow and a rascally hound by the appropriate name of Spotty Dog, in fact 'the biggest spotty dog you ever did see'. With action thin on the ground, the best toddlers could hope for was Jenny or Willy getting into a scrape and being late for dinner, or Spotty taking the odd liberty with his caring owners. All ended well, however, and the whole cast waved goodbye over the closing credits. Once again Audrey Atterbury and Molly Gibson pulled the strings, and what strings they were.

WOODHOUSE, BARBARA (1910–88)

Irish-born doctor's wife and farmer, who took to training horses and specifically dogs, becoming an unlikely TV celebrity in the process. Barbara Woodhouse, the bossy granny in a Scottish kilt and sensible shoes, pioneered 'quick training' methods for dogs, barking shrill orders and yanking them into submission with her much-criticized choke chains. But she was equally as tough on inept owners, who soon felt the sharp end of her tongue if they failed to bring their pets into line. After years of supplying star animals for films, TV series and commercials, Barbara's heyday arrived in 1980 when she hosted an educational series entitled *Training Dogs The Woodhouse Way*, which was considered to be light entertainment of the first order by many viewers. She later took her message around the country in The Woodhouse Roadshow and also hosted *The Woodhouse World of Animals, Barbara Woodhouse's Problem Dogs* and other canine and equine programmes.

WOODWARD, EDWARD, OBE (1931–)

British actor fond of tough, determined roles like that of secret agent *Callan* and avenging angel Robert McCall in *The Equalizer*. Amongst his other credits have been the anthology series *Detective* (as Edgar Allen Poe's Auguste Dupin), *1990* (as journalist Jim Kyle), *Winston Churchill – The Wilderness Years* (as Sir Samuel Hoare), *Common as Muck* (as Nev) and an American crime series *Over My Dead Body* (as Maxwell Becket, a Scotland Yard detective who retired to San Francisco to write mystery novels). He also appeared in the 1967 adaptation of Evelyn Waugh's *Sword of Honour* and the three-part 1978 drama *The Bass Player and the Blonde*, and has plenty of other single plays in his portfolio. His earliest guest appearances came in 1960s series like *Mogul, The Saint* and *Mystery and Imagination*. Woodward, the father of actor Tim Woodward and husband of actress Michele Dotrice, also hosted the 1970s panel game *Whodunnit?* and was occasionally heard singing on TV in 1970s variety shows.

WORKER, THE

UK (ATV) Situation Comedy. ITV 1965–6; 1969–70

Charlie ....Charlie Drake
Mr Whittaker.......................................Percy Herbert
Mr Pugh ....Henry McGee

Writers: Charlie Drake, Lew Schwarz.
Producers: Alan Tarrant, Shaun O'Riordan

An unemployable nuisance is the scourge of the local labour exchange.

Although he was known as the Worker, Charlie didn't – work, that is, at least not for more than one day at a time, such was his inability to hold down a job. Apparently, he had fouled up 980 jobs in 20 years. As a result, the irrepressible, ginger-haired imp banged on the counter of the Weybridge labour exchange every other morning, much to the frustration of the clerks, first Mr Whittaker then, more famously, Mr Pugh (or Mr Peooow, as our hero dubbed him). Such antagonism unfailingly ended with Pugh grabbing Charlie by the throat and winching him off the ground. After a gap of three years, the series was brought back in 1969, and it was briefly revived once more in 1978 as part of *Bruce Forsyth's Big Night*, with Drake and McGee again doing battle in the job centre.

WORKING TITLE

The provisional title of a programme, used during preparations and planning but which may be changed before the programme reaches the air.

WORLD ABOUT US, THE

UK (BBC) Natural History. BBC 2 1967–86

Long-running series featuring the wonders of nature and assorted global explorations.

Initially making use of amateur footage, but soon becoming fully professional in its contributions, *The World About Us* ran for nearly 20 years. It was commissioned by David Attenborough (then head of BBC 2) to illustrate the scope of colour television (which had just been introduced), the glorious hues of the natural world providing the perfect subject matter. Major geographical expeditions were also featured (one went up the Orinoco and Amazon by hovercraft), and Jacques Cousteau's undersea explorations also formed part of the package.

WORLD AT WAR, THE

UK (Thames) Historical Documentary. ITV 1973–4

Narrator: Laurence Olivier

Producer: Jeremy Isaacs

Eye-opening account of World War II.

Thoroughly researched (with historical accuracy monitored by Noble Frankland), *The World at War* looked at the 1939–45 conflict in 26 episodes. From the rise to power of Hitler to the bombing of Hiroshima, all the dramas and horrors of the war were documented using old film footage (some newly unearthed) and harrowing eye-witness accounts. The accompanying book sold half-a-million copies and the series won awards all around the world. It was repeated on BBC 2 in 1994.

WORLD IN ACTION

UK (Granada) Current Affairs. ITV 1963–

Creator: Tim Hewat

Producers: Tim Hewat, David Plowright, Leslie Woodhead, Jeremy Wallington, Gus McDonald, Denis Mitchell, Michael Apted, Mike Wooller, John Birt, Ray Fitzwalter, Alex Valentine, Brian Lapping.

Long-running, award-winning current affairs series.

Launched with the intention of providing 'not simply the news but the full background story', *World In Action* has become one of the world's most acclaimed public affairs series. From the first edition, when it focused on the nuclear arms race, the series has never been afraid to confront authority. Its hard-hitting, in-depth investigations have caused embarrassment to many politicians and industrialists, exposing scandals and unearthing hidden facts. Programmes have generally been half-hour in length and aired on Monday evenings.

WORLD OF SPORT

UK (Various) Sport. ITV 1965–85

Presenters: Eamonn Andrews, Richard Davies

Four-and-a-half hour Saturday sports marathon.

ITV's answer to *Grandstand*, *World of Sport* tried somewhat unsuccessfully to compete with its BBC rival for 20 years, before finally throwing in the towel. Although, as an overall package, it was never on terms with *Grandstand* (largely because the BBC controlled all the major events), *World Of Sport* did enjoy a sizeable following for its minority sports, particularly horse racing and wrestling.

World of Sport was a team effort involving most ITV companies, with studio facilities and programme production provided by LWT in later years. Its first host was Eamonn Andrews, supported by a team of Fleet Street sub-editors who clattered around in the background, thrusting latest scores and other news items into his hand as he talked to camera. Richard 'Dickie' Davies took over in 1968 and remained in charge until the programme was cancelled in 1985. Fred Dinenage was Davies's relief presenter.

For many years the running order featured football to start, followed by horse racing and the likes of snooker, darts and motor sports, with wrestling taking over the second half of the programme and leading into the results service at about 4.45 pm. Some events were screened under the umbrella subtitle of *International Sports Special*, which embraced anything from show jumping and water skiing to Australian rules football and arm wrestling. In the early days, Fred Trueman and Ian Wooldridge were specialist contributors to the programme and Peter Lorenzo previewed the day's soccer. When the football slot was retitled *On the Ball*, Brian Moore and Jimmy Hill were drafted in as hosts. Ian St John and Jimmy Greaves were the last football pundits and when *World of Sport* was cancelled their slot survived as a programme in its own right, entitled *Saint and Greavsie*.

World of Sport was the pioneer of multi-course racing coverage, as an all-action alternative to one-card racing. Its *ITV Seven* (an accumulator based on the winners of all seven featured races) became a popular bet. Trilby-hatted John Rickman took charge of racing affairs for many years, and also seen were John Oaksey, Ken

Butler, Brough Scott and Derek Thompson, with commentaries by Tony Cooke, John Penney, Raleigh Gilbert and Graham Goode and results from John Tyrrel. Wrestling was in the capable hands of former disc-jockey Kent Walton and other commentators included Tony Green for darts, John Pulman for snooker, Adrian Metcalfe for athletics and Reg Gutteridge for boxing.

WORTH, HARRY (HARRY ILLINGSWORTH; 1920–89)

Yorkshire-born comedian and comic actor, most-ly seen as a genial, bungling interferer who ended up confusing all and sundry. Breaking into show-biz as a ventriloquist, Worth, a former miner, abandoned his dummies on the advice of Stan Laurel and became a stand-up comic. In 1959, he began his first TV series, the sitcom *The Trouble With Harry*, and, a year later, starred in *Here's Harry*, in which he introduced his trademark shop window routine, using his reflection to make it look like he was waving all four limbs at once. *Here's Harry* ran for five years and was fol-lowed during the 1960s and 1970s by *Harry Worth*, *Thirty Minutes' Worth*, *My Name Is Harry Worth* (titled after his catchphrase), *How's Your Father* (as Harry Matthews, an out-of-touch wid-owed father of two teenagers) and *Oh Happy Band!* (playing himself as a brass band conductor). He was also seen as William Boot in the BBC's 1972 serialization of Evelyn Waugh's newspaper spoof *Scoop*.

WORZEL GUMMIDGE

UK (Southern) Children's Adventure. ITV
1979–81

Worzel Gummidge	Jon Pertwee
Aunt Sally	Una Stubbs
The Crowman	Geoffrey Bayldon
John Peters	Jeremy Austin
Sue Peters	Charlotte Coleman
Mr Peters	Mike Berry
Mrs Braithwaite	Megs Jenkins
Mr Braithwaite	Norman Bird
Dolly Clothes-Peg	Lorraine Chase
Mrs Bloomsbury-Barton	Joan Sims
Colonel Bloodstock	Thorley Walters
Mr Shepherd	Michael Ripper

Writers: Keith Waterhouse, Willis Hall.
Executive Producer: Lewis Rudd. Producer:
James Hill

The adventures of a living scarecrow.

Worzel Gummidge, a warty scarecrow with a turnip head, straggly straw hair and a unique line in yokelese, was the friend of young John and Sue Peters. They had just moved to the country when they stumbled across this mischievous character in Ten Acre field of Scatterbrook Farm and he trans-formed their life with his clumsy antics and good-natured humour. Wherever Worzel went, disaster followed. His girlfriend was Aunt Sally, a skittle doll, although he also fell for Saucy Nancy, a ship's figurehead, and flirted with a tailor's dummy called Dolly Clothes-Peg. The Crowman was Worzel's creator and could fashion new heads for him to change his character, if required.

The series, written by Keith Waterhouse and Willis Hall, was based on the books of Barbara Euphan Todd and was largely the idea of star Jon Pertwee. In marked contrast to his role as *Doctor Who*, this part gave him the chance to show off his comedy skills, which had been honed on BBC Radio for so many years. When Southern Television lost its ITV franchise, production was halted, until the idea was picked up by a New Zealand company in 1987, with Worzel taking up residence in the Antipodes in a series called *Worzel Gummidge Down Under*. Jon Pertwee also had a minor chart hit with 'Worzel's Song' in 1980.

TV's first Worzel Gummidge was Frank Atkinson, who played the part in the 1953 series *Worzel Gummidge Turns Detective*.

WRATHER, JACK (1918–84)

Texan oil and TV executive who purchased the rights to *Lassie* and *The Lone Ranger* and reaped the benefits of his foresight when both proved to be perennial and global hits. His company, Wrather TV Productions, produced both series, plus other juvenile action series like *Sergeant Preston of the Yukon*. He was also prominent in television sales and syndication, forming with Lew Grade the American wing of ITC, ITC Inc., to distribute Wrather and ITC programmes in the USA, although he was later bought out by Grade. He was married to actress Bonita Granville.

WYATT EARP see *Life and Legend of Wyatt Earp, The*.

WYMAN, JANE (SARAH JANE FAULKS; 1914–)

Oscar-winning American actress who has enjoyed two bites of the TV cherry. In the 1950s, on the back of her Hollywood success, Wyman was called up by US TV to host two series of drama anthologies. In the 1960s and 1970s, her small screen appearances were relatively few, but she bounced back in 1981 when cast as Angela Channing, matriarch of the vineyards in *Falcon Crest*. She played the part for nine years and has also been seen in numerous TV movies. Wyman was married to Ronald Reagan from 1940 to 1948.

WYMARK, PATRICK (PATRICK CHEESEMAN; 1926–70)

Popular British actor of the 1960s. Formerly a Shakespearean stage performer, Wymark shot to fame as John Wilder, the ruthless managing director in **The Plane Makers** and its sequel, **The Power Game**. Sadly, he had little time to capitalize on his success, dying suddenly at the age of 44, not long after the last series of *The Power Game* ended.

WYNDHAM-GOLDIE, GRACE, OBE (1900–86)

Influential BBC current affairs producer of the 1950s. Moving into television from radio, she became Assistant Head of Talks in 1954 and, from this position, was responsible for shaking up and revamping **Panorama** in 1955 and launching **Tonight** two years later. In 1962 Wyndham-Goldie was promoted to Head of Talks and Current Affairs. She retired in 1965.

WYNGARDE, PETER (CYRIL LOUIS GOLDBERT; 1928–)

French-born actor whose earliest television appearances came in 1950s plays like *Rope* and *A Tale of two Cities*. In subsequent years, he starred in episodes of the anthology series *On Trial* and **Out of this World**, before becoming a familiar guest face in ITC action series like **The Baron**, **The Avengers**, **The Prisoner** and **The Champions**. In 1969 he was cast in his most famous role, that of flamboyant novelist/secret agent Jason King in **Department S** and, although only one of a trio of agents, he proved so popular that he was brought back in his own spin-off, entitled simply **Jason King**, in 1971. His TV work has been thin since, but he has been spotted in **Doctor Who**, **Bulman** and **The Two Ronnies**.

XYY MAN, THE

UK (Granada) Spy Drama. ITV 1976–7

William 'Spider' Scott	Stephen Yardley
Maggie Parsons	Vivienne McKee
Detective Sgt George Bulman	Don Henderson
DC Derek Willis	Dennis Blanch
Fairfax	Mark Dignam
Laidlaw	William Squire

Producer: Richard Everitt

A genetically odd catburglar is recruited by British intelligence.

Spider Scott was different. In his cell structure he had a spare chromosome, an extra 'Y' chromo-

some which made him noticeably tall and instilled in him the urge to steal. He had become a practised catburglar, one of the best, but had retired – until the mysterious Fairfax of the British secret service enticed him to commit a break-in at a foreign embassy. After the embassy affair and its drawn-out consequences, Spider found it difficult to go straight again, especially when Fairfax reappeared, asking him to spring a criminal from jail. On his trail at all times were Detective Sgt Bulman and DC Willis of Scotland Yard (and later of **Strangers**). This early incarnation of Bulman was quite unlike the quirky later model. Here he was far from sympathetic, and was rough and unstinting in his pursuit of the elusive Spider.

The series was based on the book by Scottish author Kenneth Royce and began with a three-part mini-drama in 1976.

YTV see Yorkshire Television.

YARDLEY, STEPHEN (1942–)

Tall British actor, now popular for the man you love-to-hate-type of role, thanks to his portrayal of slimy Ken Masters in **Howards' Way**. Previously, Yardley's most prominent credit had been as Spider Scott, the burglar with the genetic defect, in **The XYY Man**, although his TV appearances began in the 1960s in series like **Dr Finlay's Casebook**, **United!** (he was Kenny Craig, Brentwich United's goalkeeper) and **Z Cars** (as PC Alec May). Yardley was also in the cast of the BBC's 1981 version of *The Day of the Triffids* and has been seen in series like **Secret Army**, **Widows**, **Remington Steele** and **Coronation Street**.

YARWOOD, MIKE, OBE (1941–)

Britain's number-one impressionist of the late 1960s and the 1970s, Mike Yarwood's career really took off on a 1964 edition of **Sunday Night at the London Palladium**, when his impersonation of premier Harold Wilson, amongst others, put him on the map. Yarwood soon grew into one of TV's top attractions, hosting his own series and many Christmas Day extravaganzas. Wilson remained probably his greatest success, although he also won applause for his general attention to detail (particularly for his victims' mannerisms) and for his mimicry of the likes of Brian Clough, Eddie Waring, Alf Garnett, Robin Day and Ted Heath. With such a political bias to his act, the arrival of the inimitable Mrs Thatcher at Number 10 contributed to his demise and his career sadly veered off course in the 1980s. At a time when comedy was demanding a harder edge, Yarwood quickly lost ground to Rory Bremner and a new breed of satirists. His cause was not helped by a run of personal problems and a few mini-comebacks have since failed to bring him back into the limelight. Yarwood's major series over the years have been *Three of a Kind* (with Lulu and Ray Fell), *Will the Real Mike Yarwood Stand Up*, *Look – Mike Yarwood* and *Mike Yarwood in Persons*.

YATES, JESS (JESSE YATES; 1918–93)

British TV presenter and producer, generally associated with the long-running **Stars on Sunday** showcase, through which he earned the nickname 'The Bishop'. However, Yates, a former cinema organist, worked in television from the early 1950s, climbing his way up from designer to writer, producer and director. Series like *The Good Old Days*, *Top Town* and *Come Dancing* gave him a grounding in light entertainment that he was to exploit when, after some years away from the business, he returned to TV with the fledgling Yorkshire Television in 1968. Under his auspices as Head of Children's Programmes, such series as *Junior Showtime*, *The Flaxton Boys*, *The Boy Dominic*, *Origami* and the educational *How We Used To Live* reached the screen, before Yates turned his attention to religious programming with *Choirs on Sunday* and eventually **Stars on Sunday**. He was unceremoniously dropped from the show in the mid-1970s after disclosures about his private life and he never returned to television in a big way afterwards. Yates was the father of model/presenter Paula Yates.

YEAR IN PROVENCE, A

UK (BBC) Comedy/Drama. BBC 1 1993

Peter Mayle ....John Thaw
Annie Mayle..Lindsay Duncan
Colombani....................................Jean-Pierre Delage
Amedee Clement.....................................Jo Doumerg
Antoine Riviere.................................Marcel Champel
Marcel ....Bernard Spiegel
Madame Hermonville........................Annie Sinigalia
Huguette Clement............................Francine Olivier

Writer: Michael Sadler. Producer: Ken Riddington

Twelve-part dramatization of Peter Mayle's best-seller about life in the South of France.

Peter and Annie Mayle, an advertising executive and an accountant, bravely abandoned their rat race jobs to move to their farmhouse home in the Luberon, where, they hoped, a relaxing new world awaited them. However, things did not quite work out as planned. For while the views were beautiful and the food glorious, the local

French neighbours and workers proved totally unpredictable and petty disasters lurked around every corner – not to mention the constant threat of British visitors. Mayle's attempts to settle into writing a novel proved fruitless and a far better book eventually emerged from the frustrating and complicated situations which unfolded as they tried to set up their new home.

Although much promoted by the BBC and supported by a serialized feature on *Peter Mayle's Provence* in *The Radio Times*, *A Year in Provence* was considered by most critics to be one of the flops of 1993.

YES, HONESTLY see *No, Honestly*.

YES, MINISTER/YES PRIME MINISTER

UK (BBC) Situation Comedy. BBC 2
1980–2/1986–8

Right Honourable James Hacker MP ..Paul Eddington
Sir Humphrey Appleby ....Nigel Hawthorne
Bernard Woolley ....Derek Fowlds
Anne Hacker ....Diana Hoddinott
Sir Arnold Robinson ....John Nettleton

Creators/Writers: Antony Jay, Jonathan Lynn. Producers: Stuart Allen, Sydney Lotterby, Peter Whitmore

An ambitious government minister is put firmly in his place by his chief civil servant.

Yes, Minister followed the political career of one Jim Hacker, initially an MP for an unnamed party, but later divulged to be a Tory. It opened with Hacker – a man with Churchillian delusions – taking up his first ministerial position (Administrative Affairs) and teaming up with Permanent Under-Secretary Sir Humphrey Appleby. Filled with bright ideas for cleaning up his department, Hacker began to set the wheels in motion, only to find himself stonewalled by the career civil servant, who was intent on keeping the power out of politicians' hands and firmly in the control of the permanent staff. And it was these concepts of idealism against political reality, and perceived power against real power, which underpinned the entire series, with Hacker flying ambitious kites and Sir Humphrey cheerfully shooting them down.

While the persuasive Sir Humphrey bamboozled Hacker with his tongue-twisting, jargon-loaded, over-stretched explanations, Hacker's genial Private Secretary Bernard Woolley hovered nervously in the middle, gently offering opinions on the implications and complications of this or that decision (especially if they affected Hacker's political future). But Hacker must have heeded their advice pretty well in the first three series, for a 'Major' career move quickly followed. When the incumbent prime minister resigned, three candidates stood for the top job – two extremists and the rather mundane Hacker. By stealing the middle ground, Hacker (somewhat by default) found himself installed in Downing Street for the final two seasons, which went out under the title of *Yes, Prime Minister*.

The series was much acclaimed by real politicians, who enjoyed the show's cynical dismissal of Whitehall intrigue and its insight into the machinations of government. Harold Wilson's former secretary, Lady Falkender, acted as a consultant on the first two series, and the political accuracy of the programme was seldom questioned. Even Margaret Thatcher dubbed it her favourite (before dubbing writer Antony Jay a knight in the Honours' List). Jay and Jonathan Lynn (a former *Doctor in the House* star) had conceived the idea while working for John Cleese's training video company in the mid-1970s, but, though the pilot script was bought by the BBC in 1977, production did not begin until after the 1979 general election.

YESTERDAY'S MEN see *24 Hours*.

YOGI BEAR

US (Hanna-Barbera) Cartoon. ITV 1960–4

Voices:
Yogi Bear	Daws Butler
Boo Boo	Don Messick
Ranger John Smith	Don Messick
Cindy Bear	Julie Bennett
Snagglepuss	Daws Butler
Yakky Doodle	Jimmy Weldon
Chopper	Vance Colvig

Creators/Executive Producers: William Hanna, Joseph Barbera

A hungry bear preys on picnickers in a national park.

Holidaying families were never safe when Yogi was around, for the crafty bear with the healthy appetite was always likely to talk them out of their lunch. Dressed in a tie and a pork pie hat, Yogi, with his bear cub sidekick, Boo Boo, prowled the expanses of Jellystone National Park, skilfully avoiding the attentions of Ranger John Smith. After all, as Yogi himself declared, he was 'smarter than the average bear'. Also seen at times was Yogi's Southern sweetheart, Cindy Bear, prone to cries of 'Ah do declare'.

Yogi Bear (named after New York Yankees pitcher Yogi Berra) first appeared in *The Huckleberry Hound Show*, although quickly outgrew his second fiddle status. Awarded his own series, Yogi was himself then supported by other cartoons. These featured the theatrical lion, Snagglepuss (fond of thespian exclamations like 'Heavens to Murgatroyd'), and a talkative duck, Yakky Doodle, who was closely guarded by his pal, Chopper the Bulldog. In the 1970s, in later series, Yogi moved out of Jellystone and into more adventurous situations, taking on environmental crusades and even risking space travel.

YORKIN, BUD (ALAN YORKIN; 1926–)

American TV executive in partnership with Norman Lear when creating such 1970s series as *All in the Family*, its spin-offs *Maude and the Jeffersons*, and *Sanford and Son*. Together they founded Tandem Productions. Earlier, Yorkin had produced variety shows, before working with Lear in the cinema in the 1960s.

YORKSHIRE TELEVISION (YTV)

Yorkshire Television has been the ITV contractor for the region east of the Pennines since 1968, when previous encumbent Granada was obliged by the ITA to refocus its coverage on the North-West. A consortium known as Telefusion Yorkshire Ltd won the franchise in 1967 and on 29 July a year later, Yorkshire Television (its chosen broadcasting name) went on air, hastily constructing purpose-designed studios in Leeds. Former BBC producer Donald Baverstock was its first programme controller and he was succeeded in 1973 by another BBC executive, Paul Fox. Alan Whicker was another board member and major shareholder.

Yorkshire's initial 'trading' area was not just the county of Yorkshire, but also parts of Derbyshire and Nottinghamshire. However, changes were made in the early 1970s, when the company lost most of North Yorkshire to Tyne Tees (thanks to an IBA transmitter swap) and then gained Lincolnshire and Humberside from Anglia (another transmitter reallocation). To stabilize the three companies (Yorkshire, Tyne Tees and Anglia) and to maximize advertising revenue, a new holding company, known as Trident Television, was proposed. However, the IBA declined to allow Anglia to join and Trident was formed out of Yorkshire and Tyne Tees only. When, in 1980, both companies' franchises were renewed, the IBA insisted on them leaving Trident and becoming independent once more. The Trident partnership was resumed after the 1991 franchise auctions, which were again successful for both companies.

From the start, Yorkshire has been charged with the role of a network provider, that is being one of the big five companies which supply the bulk of ITV's national programmes. Its successes have been many, including *Whicker's World*, **The Sky's the Limit**, *Emmerdale Farm*, *Where There's Life*, *Winner Takes All*, *Hadleigh*, **The Main Chance**, *Rising Damp*, **The Beiderbecke Affair**, *Duty Free*, *3–2–1*, *Follyfoot*, *A Bit of a Do* and **The Darling Buds of May**.

YOU BET!

UK (LWT) Game Show. ITV 1988–

Presenters: Bruce Forsyth, Matthew Kelly

Executive Producer: Marcus Plantin. Producers: Richard Hearsey, Alasdair Macmillan, Linda Beadle

Light-hearted panel game in which celebrities and the studio audience bet on the skills of a guest enthusiast.

Hosted originally by Bruce Forsyth, and by Matthew Kelly since 1991, *You Bet!* has been a showcase for the skills and talents of its many guests, who have attempted to perform odd feats related to their hobbies or professions within a given time. Could three divers put up a tent underwater, for example? How much would politician Roy Hattersley know about his favourite programme, **Coronation Street**? Each guest has been sponsored by one of the celebrity panellists and, if the guest has failed in his task, the celebrity has been forced to accept a forfeit. The studio audience, meanwhile, has gambled on whether the guest will make the grade, and all profits have been directed to charity. The series was originally based on a Dutch format.

YOU RANG, M'LORD?

UK (BBC) Situation Comedy. BBC 1 1990–3

Alf Stokes	Paul Shane
Ivy Teesdale	Su Pollard
James Twelvetrees	Jeffrey Holland
Mrs Lipton	Brenda Cowling
Lord George Meldrum	Donald Hewlett
Honourable Teddy Meldrum	Michael Knowles
Poppy Meldrum	Susie Brann
Cissy Meldrum	Catherine Rabett
Lady Lavender Meldrum	Mavis Pugh
Henry	Perry Benson
Mabel	Barbara New
PC Wilson	Bill Pertwee
Sir Ralph Shawcross	John Horsley
Lady Agatha Shawcross	Angela Scoular

Creators/Writers: Jimmy Perry, David Croft. Producer: David Croft

Life up and down stairs in an eccentric 1920s household.

An hour-long pilot, screened in 1988, set the scene for this *Upstairs, Downstairs* send up which had more than an echo of other Perry/Croft sitcoms, especially **Hi-De-Hi!** It began in 1918, in the trenches of World War I and with the discovery of the body of an army officer by two foot soldiers. One of the soldiers, Alf Stokes, looted the officer's possessions, as the other, James Twelvetrees, vainly argued against the theft. However, discovering that the officer was not in fact dead, the two men carried him to safety. He turned out to be Captain Edward Meldrum, known to others as 'the Honourable Teddy', and in return for their life-saving efforts, he promised the men a favour.

Back in civvy street, nine years later, Twelvetrees had cashed in his favour and had been taken on as head of the household at the Meldrum residence, which was presided over by the well-meaning Lord Meldrum. When their butler died, the bad penny Stokes arrived and, much to Twelvetrees's disgust, talked his way into the job. He brought with him as parlour maid his daughter, Ivy, but kept their relationship secret (she used her mother's maiden name). Like all the parlour maids employed before her, Ivy, despite her plain looks, was relentlessly pursued by the randy Teddy, a true upper-class twit, while his flighty sister, Poppy, took a similar shine to Twelvetrees. The other Meldrum family members included the gay Cissy, who dressed like a man, and the bedridden, food-throwing Lady Lavender, the Lord's batty mother. Family friends were Sir Ralph and Lady Agatha Shawcross, Lady Agatha also being Lord Meldrum's secret lover.

The serving staff comprised cook Mrs Lipton, boot boy Perry (regular recipient of clipped ears) and lowest of the low scullery maid Mabel. A regular visitor to the kitchen was the scrounging local bobby, PC Wilson, a devotee of Mrs Lipton's culinary skills. While the upright Twelvetrees conducted his affairs in the most honest and decent fashion, the sly Stokes worked on plans to swindle his betters and line his own pockets. And so the series continued for three years, finally ending when the Meldrum family fell on desperate times and were forced to give up their home and staff.

The programme's theme song was sung by Bob Monkhouse and Paul Shane.

YOUENS, BERNARD (BERNARD POPLEY; 1914–84)

Remembered as one of TV's most lovable characters, the boozy, workshy Stan Ogden in **Coronation Street**, Bernard Youens was, in real life, a totally different person from the slob he played on screen. And far from only being able to garble 'A pint and a pie, missus', Youens was an eloquent, well-spoken performer. Indeed, after years in rep, he arrived in television by taking a continuity announcer's job at Granada, where he worked with the late Ray Moore. His first TV acting parts were also with Granada, in series like **Shadow Squad** and **Knight Errant**, although he turned down the chance to audition for **Coronation Street** when it began in 1960. However, four years later, he worked his way in as Stan Ogden and stayed with the series (through considerable restricting illness in later years) until his death in 1984.

YOU'LL NEVER GET RICH see *Phil Silvers Show, The.*

YOUNG, ALAN (ANGUS YOUNG; 1919–)

British-born actor/comedian, raised in Canada, who became a reasonable success in the USA. By far his most memorable role was as Wilbur Post, straight man to **Mr Ed**, the talking horse in the early 1960s, although, by that time, Young had already picked up an Emmy and headlined in his own variety series, *The Alan Young Show*, and the USA's *Saturday Night Revue*. In 1957 he was seen on this side of the Atlantic in Granada's variety series **Chelsea at Nine**.

YOUNG, MURIEL (1928–)

British presenter, one of Associated-Rediffusion's earliest continuity announcers. However, it was as a star of kids' TV in the late 1950s and early 1960s, in series like *Small Time, Tuesday Rendezvous* and **Five O'Clock Club**, that she became known to viewers nationwide, working with performers like Howard Williams, Wally Whyton and Bert Weedon, plus puppets Ollie Beak, Fred Barker, Pussy Cat Willum and others. In the late 1960s she moved north to Granada to become Head of Children's Programmes. There, as producer, she established such favourites as **Clapperboard, Lift Off With Ayshea**, *Get It Together* and other pop shows for the Bay City Rollers (*Shang-a-Lang*), Marc Bolan (*Marc*) and *The Arrows*. In 1982 Young worked on *Ladybirds*, two series about female singers, for Mike Mansfield's independent production company and Channel 4. She retired from television in 1986.

YOUNG ONES, THE

UK (BBC) Situation Comedy. BBC 2 1982–4

Rick	Rik Mayall
Neil	Nigel Planer
Vyvyan	Adrian Edmondson
Mike	Christopher Ryan
Jerzy Balowski (and his family)	Alexei Sayle

Writers: Ben Elton, Rik Mayall, Lise Mayer.
Producer: Paul Jackson

Four anarchic students share a decrepit house.

The Young Ones were Rick, Neil, Vyvyan and Mike. Sneering Rick was the Cliff Richard fan who owned a pet hamster known as SPG (Special Patrol Group), long-haired Neil was the melancholic, vegetarian hippy and the stud-headed Vyvyan was gormlessly aggressive. Diminutive Mike was the most 'normal' of the bunch, although his wide boy tendencies and moments of paranoia marked him out, too, from the rest of the public. In an atmosphere of absolute squalor (even the stale food began to move), the four led a life of mindless violence and brainless conversation, rebelling against the world outside. The storylines were vague and the comedy was heavily slapstick, usually involving the destruction of the house or of each other, but there were moments of surreal humour, too: talking bannisters, new lands appearing outside the front door, etc. The boys' Russian landlord, Jerzy Balowski, (or other members of his family, all played by Alexei Sayle) was given his own five-minute slot in the programme in which he demonstrated his encyclopedic knowledge of Merseybeat and his ability to rant.

Viewers tuned in to *The Young Ones* to be shocked. The younger generations loved it and felt the series was right on their wavelength. More 'mature' critics were appalled at the wanton violence, infantile jokes and total disrespect for society, but many of these, too, were won over as the series progressed. It was a series that certainly shook up television comedy and heralded the age of the 'alternative' comedian. Indeed, *The Young Ones* has continued well beyond its 12 episodes, with Mayall and Edmondson's later offerings **Filthy, Rich and Catflap** and **Bottom** essentially extensions of the series. Nigel Planer, in the guise of Neil, also had a spin-off hit single in 1984, with a cover of Traffic's 'Hole In My Shoe'.

YOUNG, ROBERT (1907–)

American movie actor of the 1930s who never really found his niche until television arrived. There his homely, kindly features were put to good use in an award-winning domestic sitcom, *Father Knows Best* (as dad Jim Anderson), that ran for six years (having already been a hit on radio). Unusually, it also enjoyed prime-time repeat showings until 1963, although the 1960s were generally leaner years for Young, and another comedy, *Window on Main Street*, didn't take. However, in 1968, his first TV movie, **Marcus Welby, MD**, sparked another long-running series, in which Young played a gentle, understanding family practitioner. It ended in 1976 and Young has done little television since, save the odd commercial, occasional TV movie and a couple of *Father Knows Best* reunions.

YOUR LIFE IN THEIR HANDS

UK (BBC) Documentary. BBC 1958–64;
BBC 2 1980–6; 1991

Producers: Bill Duncalf, Peter Bruce, Humphrey Fisher (1958), John Mansfield, Fiona Holmes (1980), Stephen Rose (1991)

The wonders of surgery explored in close detail.

This innovative series was conceived with a tri-partite purpose in mind: to investigate new medical techniques, to applaud the medical profession and to provide 'reassurance' for citizens at home. However, with its blood and guts visuals, *Your Life in their Hands* excited some viewers and alarmed others.

The pre-recorded programmes interviewed sick patients, watched their admission to hospital, heard the prognosis of the experts and learned of the action intended by the surgeon. Overhead mirrors, microscopes and numerous cameras were then used to capture events in the operating theatre, before the patient's recovery was monitored in the weeks and months that followed. Never before on British television had gallstones been removed. Open heart surgery was even more dramatic and caesarean birth was just as graphically demonstrated. Predictably, there was an outcry from the Establishment. The British Medical Association criticized it for frightening, rather than reassuring, viewers and there were reports of sick people prefering suicide to treatment, having seen the programme. Other doctors warmly applauded the programme's frankness and its educational value.

When the series was revived in 1980, operations were shown for the first time in full, gory colour and were definitely not for the squeamish. For this series, surgeon Robert Winston acted as the informative narrator. Five more editions were screened in 1991.

YOU'VE BEEN FRAMED

UK (Granada) Comedy. ITV 1990–

Presenter: Jeremy Beadle

Producers: Jane Macnaught, Kieran Roberts, Mark Gorton

Selections of home video howlers.

You've Been Framed has ridden the wave of interest in home video bloopers that has swept around the world since the introduction of the cam-

corder. Emulating similar programmes in the USA, Japan and elsewhere, it has gathered together some of the most amusing clips of video footage, most of which have shown people falling over, children unwittingly misbehaving or pets displaying unusual talents. A contest for the best British clip was incorporated into early programmes but was later abandoned. The BBC attempted to cash in with its own version, *Caught in the Act*, hosted by Shane Richie, but it failed to take off.

YUS MY DEAR see *Romany Jones*.

Z CARS

UK (BBC) Police Drama. BBC 1 1962–65;
1967–78

Detective Chief Inspector Charlie Barlow	Stratford Johns
Detective Sgt John Watt	Frank Windsor
PC William 'Fancy' Smith	Brian Blessed
PC John 'Jock' Weir	Joseph Brady
PC Herbert 'Bert' Lynch	James Ellis
Detective Inspector/Supt Dunn	Dudley Foster
PC Bob Steele	Jeremy Kemp
PC Ian Sweet	Terence Edmond
Sgt Twentyman	Leonard Williams
Sgt Blackitt	Robert Keegan
PC David Graham	Colin Welland
Detective Supt Miller	Leslie Sands
Detective Inspector Bamber	Leonard Rossiter
Detective Inspector Sam Hudson	John Barrie
Detective Sgt Tom Stone	John Slater
PC Owen Culshaw	David Daker
PC Alec May	Stephen Yardley
PC Bill Newcombe	Bernard Holley
Detective Inspector Brogan	George Sewell
Detective Inspector Todd	Joss Ackland
Detective Inspector Alan Witty	John Woodvine
PC Mick Quilley	Douglas Fielding
Detective Inspector Goss	Derek Waring
DC Joe Skinner	Ian Cullen
Detective Sgt Hagger	John Collin
WPC Jill Howarth	Stephanie Turner
DC Scatliff	Geoffrey Hayes
PC Render	Alan O'Keefe
WPC Bayliss	Alison Steadman
Detective Inspector Moffat	Ray Lonnen

Creator: Troy Kennedy Martin. Producers: David E. Rose, Colin Morris, Ronald Travers, Richard Beynon, Ron Craddock, Roderick Graham

Long-running and influential police drama series, highlighting the work of patrol car policemen.

In 1962 the *Dixon of Dock Green*-type of police series was already looking dated. The cosy life of a community copper had been lost forever, certainly in the big cities at least, and it was time for television to reflect this change. However, it wasn't until writer Troy Kennedy Martin was confined to bed with mumps, and to pass the time tuned into the police wavelengths, that such a change became a possibility. Martin instantly recognized that what he was hearing was a world away from George Dixon's weekly homilies and decided to work his findings into an idea for a new programme. The result was Z Cars, a police series that aimed to portray the *real* relationship between the police and the community.

Filled with northern grit and heavily influenced by contemporary 'kitchen sink' dramas, Z Cars was set on Merseyside, at a time when the Liverpool docklands were undergoing radical social change. Traditional streets, now designated slums, were making way for high-rise blocks of concrete flats, functional but soulless living spaces that rapidly turned into fertile breeding grounds for unrest. The pace of life was quickening and crime was responding in its own unpleasant fashion. To combat this crime wave, police were taken off the beat and placed in patrol cars, with the aim of providing a swifter response. Z Cars depicted the efforts of one such patrol team as it roamed the streets of both the old district of Seaport and the modern development of Newtown.

The very first episode revealed how the death of a police officer had led to the formation of the team. Detective Inspector Barlow and Detective Sgt Watt were invited to select their new elite squad, and it introduced viewers to the four patrolmen who were chosen. In the first patrol car, Z Victor 1, were burly northerner 'Fancy' Smith and rugby-playing Scot Jock Weir. In Z Victor 2 were Irishman Herbert Smith and red-headed Bob Steele. Both cars were Ford Zephyrs, initially Mark 4s, later Mark 6s. Supervising events back at the station was old-fashioned copper Sgt Twentyman, replaced after a year by the sour-faced Sgt Blackitt, when actor Leonard Williams suddenly died.

However, Z Cars didn't just focus on the new type of crime in the early 1960s, or the police response to it, but, for the first time on British television, it actually dared to suggest that policemen were not as wholesome as they ought to be. Troy Kennedy Martin had wanted the crooks to win through now and again, to show that police were not infallible, but this was too much to ask of a staid BBC. However, he did get away with showing policemen as real human beings, with complicated home lives and vices of their own. Martin and his colleagues painted them as gamblers, drinkers and, most controversially of all, wife beaters (an early episode showed Bert Lynch only gently admonishing Bob Steele for giving his wife, Janey, a black eye in a domestic dispute). Real-life police withdrew their co-operation in response to such excesses.

Another innovation was the Stratford Johns portrayal of Charlie Barlow as a nasty superior officer, not adverse to dishing out aggression. Johns was tired of seeing bumbling, ineffective TV detectives. What he wanted was a police officer who actually made the running, was hard on his subordinates and was not afraid to pound suspects into submission. Together with the gentler John Watt, he offered the classic combination of the nice and the nasty, and such was their success they headed off to the Regional Crime Squad after three years and a series of their own, *Softly, Softly*.

Watt and Barlow's departure was intended to be the finale for Z Cars, but it returned to the screens in 1967, installing John Barrie and John Slater as Detective Inspector Hudson and Detective Sgt Stone, as their replacements. New Panda cars roared into action and some fresh constables were added to the team, although continuity was maintained through Weir and Lynch (a man who was to rise steadily through the ranks). The format switched from 50-minute episodes to two 25-minute programmes a week, and continued in this vein until 1971, when the longer forms were re-introduced.

Other notable characters to come and go over the years were young PC Ian Sweet, who was tragically drowned in an heroic rescue attempt, PC David Graham, Lynch's second partner (an early break for actor/writer Colin Welland), the sarcastic Inspector Dunn, Geordie heart-throb PC Joe Skinner, his partner, PC Mick Quilley, and Leonard Rossiter, playing it straight as Chief Inspector Bamber. Indeed, future stars fared rather well, either as guests or regulars. They included John Thaw, Judi Dench, Stephanie Turner (*Juliet Bravo*), Kenneth Cope, Alison Steadman, David Daker, Stephen Yardley, George Sewell, Joss Ackland, Patrick Troughton, Geoffrey Hayes (*Rainbow*) and Ralph Bates, whose character pulled a gun on Joe Skinner and shot him dead.

Like **Dixon of Dock Green** before it, Z Cars found itself left behind by other cop shows in the 1970s. Not only were the likes of **Kojak** and **Starsky and Hutch** screaming onto British TV screens, but there was also our own **The Sweeney** to contend with. Still Z Cars rolled on, probably showing a more realistic image of 1970s policing than its contemporaries, until the end finally arrived in 1978.

Originally transmitted live, making use of crude techniques like back projection for car scenes, *Z Cars* looks very dated today. However, the quality of writing, from the likes of Martin, Alan Plater, Elwyn Jones and John Hopkins, is still apparent in the few surviving episodes from those early days. The last episode, penned by Martin, brought the newly promoted Detective Chief Superintendent Inspector Watt back to Newtown and featured cameo appearances from Joseph Brady, Brian Blessed, Jeremy Kemp and Colin Welland. Over the previous 16 years, the programme's unforgettable theme tune (based on the folk song 'Johnny Todd') had become synonymous with TV policing.

ZEE TV

Formerly TV Asia, this subscriber channel began broadcasting for limited hours (6 am to 4 pm) in July 1992 on cable and from the Astra 1B and 1C satellites. It switched to the Astra 1D satellite in January 1995 and extended its hours, becoming Zee TV on 1 March 1995, following a merger of its parent company, Asia TV Ltd, with the Essel Group (Zee Telefilms Ltd) of India. Its target audience is European viewers with links to the Indian subcontinent and it offers a mix of films, light entertainment, magazines, soap opera, news and documentaries.

ZERO ONE

UK (BBC/MGM) Adventure. BBC 1 1962–5

Alan Garnett	Nigel Patrick
Maya	Katya Douglas
Jim Delaney	Bill Smith

Producer: Lawrence P. Bachmann

The cases of an airline detective.

Zero One was the call sign of International Air Security, an organization dedicated to the safety of air travel all around the world. Its London agent was Alan Garnett and he was called up to combat hijackers, prevent disasters and generally preserve peace in the air and at airports. Jim Delaney was his assistant and Maya his secretary.

ZIMBALIST, EFREM, JNR (1918–)

American actor, the son of classical music entertainers Efrem Zimbalist and Alma Gluck. Zimbalist Jnr enjoyed two major starring roles between the late 1950s and mid-1970s. He was Ivy League-educated detective Stu Bailey in *77 Sunset Strip* for six years from 1958 and then quickly donned the mantle of Inspector Lew Erskine of *The FBI*, to ensure he remained on US TV screens until 1974. He has since appeared in *Hotel* (as Charles Cabot), TV movies and

mini-series, as well as a revival of *Zorro* (as Don Alejandro). Amongst his numerous guest appearances over the years have been spots in *The Phil Silvers Show*, *Maverick* (as Dandy Jim Buckley) and *Remington Steele* (alongside his daughter, Stephanie Zimbalist).

ZOO GANG, THE

UK (ATV/ITC) Adventure. ITV 1974

Tommy Devon	John Mills
Stephen Halliday	Brian Keith
Alec Marlowe	Barry Morse
Manouche Roget	Lilli Palmer
Lt Georges Roget	Michael Petrovitch
Jill Burton	Seretta Wilson

Creator: Paul Gallico. Producer: Herbert Hirschman

Four French Résistance fighters reunite to maintain law and order on the Riviera.

Nearly 30 years after disbanding at the end of the war, the so-called Zoo Gang found themselves back in business. Each member of this crack Résistance unit possessed individual skills and operated under animal codenames. Team organizer was Tommy Devon, or Elephant, as he was known. When an old Nazi adversary walked into his jewellery shop on the French Riviera, he called up surviving members of the squad to bring the war criminal to book. His colleagues were Stephen Halliday (a New York businessman and electronics expert, codenamed Fox), Canadian Alec Marlowe (Tiger, a mechanical genius), and Madame Manouche Roget (Leopard, the widow of another team member, Claude Roget – or Wolf – who had died at the hands of the Gestapo). Manouche ran a bar in Nice and was skilled in explosives. Her son, Georges, a French policeman, was also seen. Having nailed the Nazi, the four stayed together to bring justice to the Côte d'Azur in Robin Hood fashion for five more episodes. The theme music was provided by Paul and Linda McCartney.

ZOO QUEST

UK (BBC) Natural History. BBC 1954–61

Producers: David Attenborough, Paul Johnstone

Global expeditions in search of rare wildlife.

Zoo Quest, a collaboration between the BBC Talks Department and London Zoo, recorded zoological searches for rare animals in the far corners of the world such as the hunt for paradise birds in Madagascar. The aim was to bring examples back for exhibition and protection at the Zoo. Individual series' titles reflected the nature of the expedition. They included *Zoo Quest to Guiana*, *Zoo Quest for a Dragon* (the komodo dragon) and *Zoo Quest in Paraguay*.

ZOO TIME

UK (Granada) Natural History. ITV 1956–68

Presenters: Desmond Morris, Harry Watt, Chris Kelly

Producers: Milton Shulman, Derek Twist, David Warwick, Peter Mullings

Studies of animal behaviour at London Zoo.

Initially introduced by animal watcher Desmond Morris, and aimed at the younger viewer, *Zoo Time* focused on the inmates of London Zoo and examined their innate behaviourial instincts. Harry Watt became host in 1960 and Chris Kelly took over in 1967, by which time the action had switched to Chester Zoo. Spin-off programmes like *A to Zoo*, *Breakthrough* and *Animal Story* were produced contemporaneously.

ZORRO

US (Walt Disney) Western. ITV 1958–

Don Diego de la Vega ('Zorro')	Guy Williams
Don Alejandro de la Vega	George J. Lewis
Bernardo	Gene Sheldon
Captain Monastario	Britt Lomond
Sgt Garcia	Henry Calvin
Corporal Reyes	Don Diamond
Nacho Torres	Jan Arvan
Elena Torres	Eugenia Paul
Magistrate Galindo	Vinton Hayworth
Anna Maria Verdugo	Jolene Brand
Senor Gregorio Verdugo	Eduard Franz

Executive Producer: Walt Disney. Producer: William H. Anderson

A mysterious masked cavalier continually thwarts the local tyrant.

In 1820 Don Diego de la Vega had been summoned home from Spain to southern California by his father, Don Alejandro, to assist in the overthrow of the new local tyrant. Merciless Captain Monastario had taken control of the local Fortress de Los Angeles and all the nobles of the area felt under threat. Much was expected of the well-educated Don Diego. Sadly, it seemed that their hopes were to be dashed, as the young nobleman turned out to be something of a fop. But, under the secret disguise of Zorro, a swashbuckling masked swordsman, he made sure that the cruel Captain and his cronies – the stupid, slobbish Sgt Garcia and Corporal Reyes – were put firmly in their place.

Everyone knew when Zorro had visited – he carved a distinctive 'Z' with the point of his sword – but only one man knew his true identity, his dumb servant, Bernardo, who also pretended to be deaf in order to spy for his master. Don Diego's two trusty steeds were the black Tornado (for use as himself) and the white Phantom (ridden by Zorro). Anna Maria Verdugo was Don Diego's romantic interest.

Zorro, meaning 'fox' in Spanish, was created by author Johnston McCulley in 1919. He had already been played in the cinema by the likes of Douglas Fairbanks and Tyrone Power before Guy Williams took on the role. Williams himself is possibly better remembered as Professor John Robinson in **Lost in Space**.

ZWORYKIN, VLADIMIR K. (1889–1982)

Russian-born American engineer, one of the pioneers of television. In the 1920s he produced an all-electronic television system that quickly found favour over Baird's electromechanical units. It was based on his development of the iconoscope (the cathode ray tube used in cameras) and the kinescope (the tube in the receiver).